Microsoft Office Projects for Windows 95

Philip A. Koneman
William J. Belisle
Gary R. Brent
James A. Folts
Marianne B. Fox
Lawrence C. Metzelaar
Paul B. Thurrott

The Benjamin/Cummings Publishing Company, Inc.
Menlo Park, California • Reading, Massachusetts
New York • Don Mills, Ontario • Harlow, U.K. • Amsterdam
Bonn • Paris • Milan • Madrid • Sydney • Singapore • Tokyo
Seoul • Taipei • Mexico City • San Juan, Puerto Rico

Senior Editor: *Maureen A. Allaire*
Project Editor: *Nancy E. Davis, Kathy G. Yankton*
Developmental Editors: *Rebecca Johnson, Shelly Langman, Evelyn Spire*
Contributing Editor: *Pauline Johnson*
Executive Editor (B&E, CIS, MIS): *Michael Payne*
Project Manager: *Adam Ray*
Associate Production Editor: *Jennifer Englander*
Marketing Manager: *Melissa Baumwald*
Custom Publishing Operations Manager: *Michael Smith*
Senior Manufacturing Coordinator: *Janet Weaver*
Composition and Film Buyer: *Vivian McDougal*
Copy Editors: *Robert Fiske, Vocabula; Barbara Conway*
Technical Editors: *Lynda Fox Fields, Brian and Dawn Remmel*
Proofreaders: *Holly McLean Aldis, Roseann Viano*
Indexer: *Mark Kmetzko*
Text Design: *Mark Ong, Side-by-Side Studios*
Cover Design: *Annabelle Ison*
Cover Art: ©*Steven Guarnaccia/The Image Bank*

The Benjamin/Cummings Publishing Company, Inc.
2725 Sand Hill Road
Menlo Park, CA 94025
http://www.aw.com/bc/is

ISBN 0-8053-2757-6 bundled version
ISBN 0-8053-2749-5 stand alone version
1 2 3 4 5 6 7 8 9 10—DOW—00 99 98 97 9

Contents

PART I: WINDOWS 95

Project 2: File Management with My Computer and Explorer 64

Part II: Microsoft Word 7

Overview 89

Project 1: Creating a Document 99

Project 2: Editing a Document 120

PROJECT 4: USING FORMULAS IN A WORKSHEET 310

PROJECT 5: VISUALIZING INFORMATION WITH CHARTS 349

Part IV: Integrated Project 1

Integrated Project : Embedding an Excel Worksheet in a Word Document 381

Part V: Microsoft Access 7

Overview 407

Project 1: Previewing the Power of Access 424

Project 2: Designing and Creating a Database 446

Part VII: Microsoft PowerPoint 7

Overview 589

Project 1: Creating a Presentation 607

Project 2: Polishing a Presentation 632

Project 3: Working with Text Objects 654

Preface

Welcome to *Microsoft Office Projects for Windows 95*. We invite you to explore how you can take advantage of the newest Windows 95 features of the popular Microsoft Office suite using this completely up-to-date text. With the "documentcentric approach," Microsoft Office for Windows 95 allows you to focus on your work, not the software. Using the project-based approach of *Microsoft Office Projects for Windows 95* you will learn how to use Office applications as powerful productivity tools at work, home, or school. When you have completed the step-by-step projects in this text you will be equipped to tackle any project using Microsoft Office for Windows 95 with confidence and proficiency.

WHAT'S NEW

Microsoft Office for Windows 95 is more than just an upgrade from the previous version, because it takes advantage of the new Windows 95 operating system. Using *Microsoft Office Projects for Windows 95,* you will learn how to increase your productivity by fully utilizing all the new features of Office 95:

Easier to Use

In addition to learning the individual Office applications, you will learn how to organize your documents in an electronic resource called **Microsoft Binder.** Just like a three-ring binder, this tool allows you to collect, print, and distribute collections of documents from each of the Office applications. **Microsoft Shortcut Bar** allows you to easily launch applications and switch among applications that are currently running.

Access to the Internet

Office for Windows 95 helps you navigate the **Internet** more quickly and easily with a host of new communications capabilities, including integrated e-mail and group scheduling, workgroup capabilities, and on-line communications.

Easier to Collaborate

Microsoft Schedule+, a powerful personal time and project management tool, can be used individually or in a workgroup setting to manage your daily schedule, personal contacts, and to-do lists. **Microsoft Exchange** allows you to send and receive electronic mail and fax documents if your computer is equipped with a modem.

Automatic and Simple

IntelliSense technology "senses" your intent and then "intelligently" delivers the desired result. Routine tasks such as spell checking are automatic; more complex tasks are made simple. With these enhancements you can concentrate on what's important—creating your document.

Multitasking

With full 32-bit performance, Office for Windows 95 applications take advantage of enhanced system resources and multitasking capabilities of Windows 95. You can now conduct file searches, on-line communications and other common tasks while editing a document.

The Project Approach

The structure of *Microsoft Office Projects for Windows 95* is simple—it teaches you beginning and more advanced skills for each of the four Office applications (Word, Excel, Access, and PowerPoint®)—and then takes your skill further by introducing you to the exciting possibilities of document creation using the data sharing capabilities available with OLE (Object Linking and Embedding). All of this is done within the context of realistic scenarios that reflect settings and situations you are familiar with in your personal life, at school, and in your career. These real-world themes ensure that you will understand the relevance of the material and be able to apply the skills you learn in the text outside the classroom.

Introduction to Windows 95

This Introduction familiarizes you with Microsoft Windows 95 before you launch into Microsoft Office. Learn the basics of this newly redesigned operating system, such as starting and logging on to Windows, manipulating windows and their controls, using Windows Help, and shutting down Windows. You also learn the basics of file management using **My Computer,** how to get started with Windows 95 using the **Taskbar** and **Start button,** launch application programs, and switch between programs using the Taskbar.

Hands-On and Problem-Solving

Each of the four Office applications is covered in depth in four to five projects that teach both beginning and advanced skills. Hands-on exercises put you to work using the applications almost immediately. These projects help you master key concepts and problem-solving techniques you will need to use the Office suite to its fullest potential in and outside the classroom.

Documentcentric

One of the great strengths of the Microsoft Office suite is the ability to integrate four individual software applications. Office for Windows 95 takes this even further with its documentcentric approach to building multiapplication files. *Microsoft Office Projects for Windows 95* provides three projects to help you understand and use the powerful integration capabilities found in Microsoft Office. These integrated projects build on the skills learned in the individual application projects and teach how to use and integrate the components of the Microsoft Office suite.

The Internet

Get "wired" with our all new "Introduction to the Internet and the World Wide Web." This extensive project helps you gain a greater understanding of this valuable and rapidly expanding area of computing. You learn what e-mail is, how to use and send e-mail, and how to access FTP and World Wide Web sites.

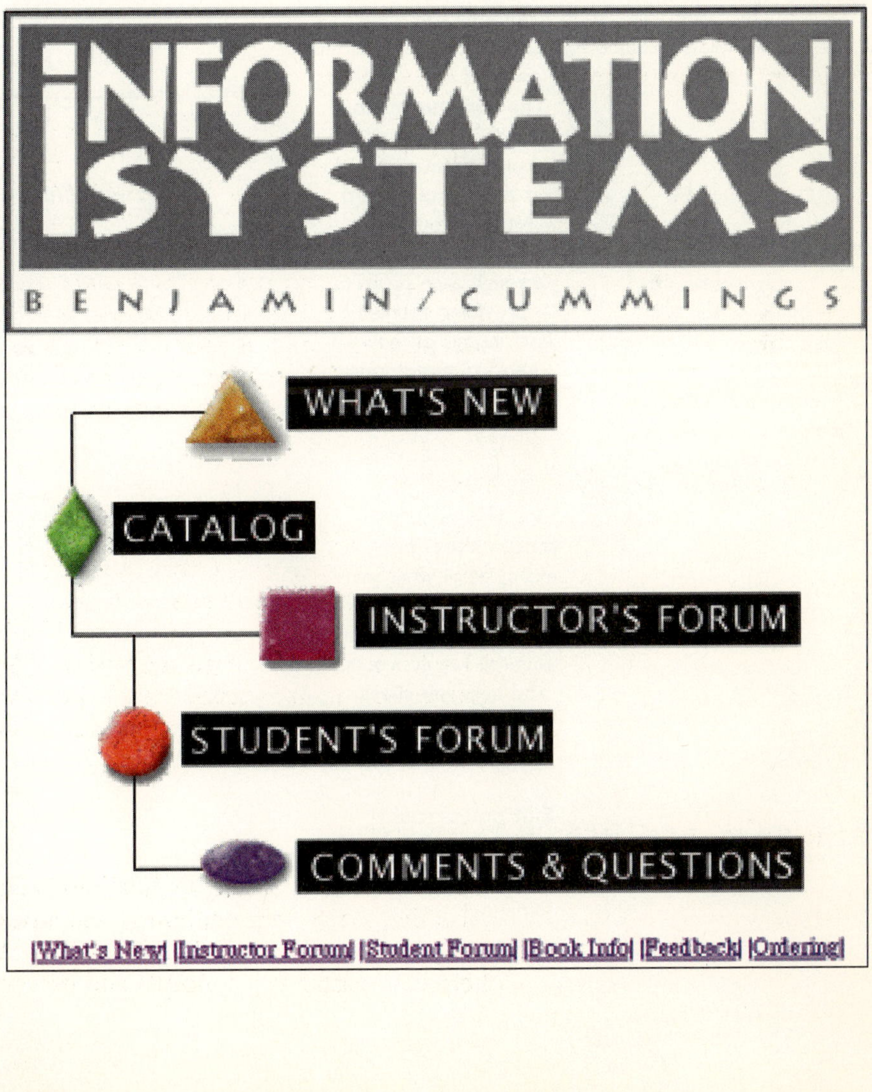

PROJECT 2: BUILDING A LARGER WORKSHEET

OBJECTIVES

After completing this project, you will be able to:

- Move a cell
- Check the spelling of worksheet data
- Use preselected ranges for data entry
- Copy the contents of a cell
- Use relative cell references in formulas
- Use the @SUM @function and the Sum SmartIcon

CASE STUDY: SALES OF AUDIO RECORDINGS

From 1975 to 1990, the popularity of the kinds of media used for recorded music shifted dramatically. These changes are illustrated in Figure 2.1.

	A	B	C	D	E	F	G
1	Shipments of Audio Recordings						
2	(in millions of dollars)						
3		1975	1980	1985	1990		
4	Phonograph Records						
5	LP Albums	1485	2290.3	1280.5	86.5		
6	Singles	211.5	269.3	281	94.4		
7	Total Records	?	?	?	?		
8	Tapes						
9	8-tracks	583	526.4	25.3	0		
10	Cassettes	98.8	776.4	2411.5	3472.4		
11	Total Tapes	?	?	?	?		
12	Compact Discs						
13	Regular CDs	0	0	389.5	3451.6		
14	CD Singles	0	0	0	6		
15	Total CDs	?	?	?	?		
16	Grand Total	?	?	?	?		
17							

Figure 2.1

Designing the Solution

In this project, you will build a 1-2-3 worksheet that will calculate the totals indicated by the question marks in Figure 2.1. You will create formulas to calculate totals for each year in each media category (records, tapes, and CDs) and grand totals (the totals of records, tapes, and CDs combined). You will then format the worksheet so the information is optimally readable.

Each project begins with **Learning Objectives** that describe the skills and commands you will master.

Projects revolve around **Case Studies**, which provide real-world scenarios so you can learn an application in a broader context.

Designing the Solution introduces you to important problem-solving techniques. You will see how to analyze the case study and design a solution before you sit down at the computer.

Each topic begins with a brief explanation of concepts you will learn and the operations you will perform.

The **computer icon** provides a cue that you should begin working at the computer and **Numbered steps** guide you step-by-step through each project, providing detailed instructions on how to perform operations.

Visual cues such as **screen shots** provide examples of what you will see on your own computer screen, reinforce key concepts, and help you check your work.

Exit points identify good places in each project to take a break.

IN-10
INTRODUCTION TO WINDOWS

USING THE CONTROL MENU

When you select the Control menu box in the upper-left corner of a window, the Control menu drops down. If you are using a keyboard, the ***Control menu*** enables you to control window operations, such as moving, sizing, and closing windows. Mouse users perform these operations by clicking, double-clicking, or dragging windows. You can use the Control menu to close any window, including the Program Manager window. By closing the Program Manager window, you will exit Windows, in addition to closing the Program Manager.

To close the active window:

1 Mouse: Click the Control menu box.
or Keys: Press ALT and then press SPACE

Be sure to click the Control menu box only once. Your screen should look like the one in Figure 9.

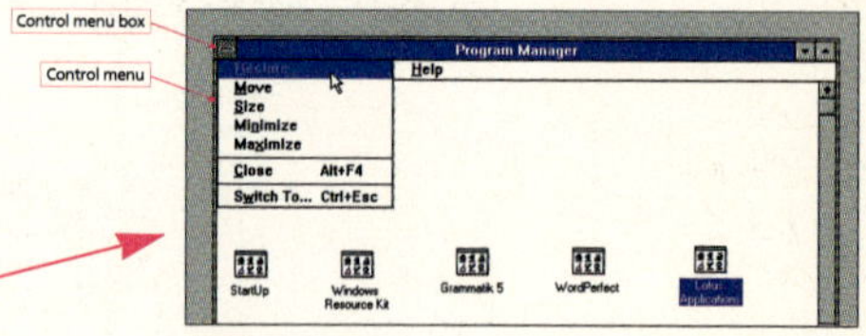

Figure 9

2 Choose Close.

Notice that you get a dialog box to exit Windows.

3 Select Cancel.

Most dialog boxes contain a Cancel button than enables you to cancel a command.

EXIT **If necessary, you can save you file, exit Windows and continue this project later.**

MOVING A WINDOW

Occasionally one window will hide another. A window can be moved by dragging its title bar or by using the Control menu.

Key Terms are boldfaced and italicized and appear throughout each project.

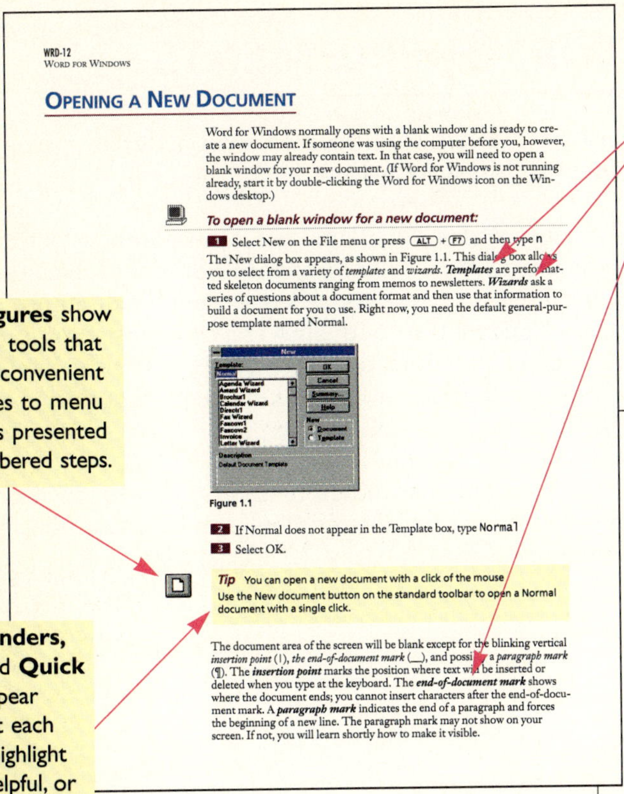
WRD-12
WORD FOR WINDOWS

OPENING A NEW DOCUMENT

Word for Windows normally opens with a blank window and is ready to create a new document. If someone was using the computer before you, however, the window may already contain text. In that case, you will need to open a blank window for your new document. (If Word for Windows is not running already, start it by double-clicking the Word for Windows icon on the Windows desktop.)

To open a blank window for a new document:

1 Select New on the File menu or press ALT + F7 and then type n

The New dialog box appears, as shown in Figure 1.1. This dialog box allows you to select from a variety of *templates* and *wizards*. ***Templates*** are preformatted skeleton documents ranging from memos to newsletters. ***Wizards*** ask a series of questions about a document format and then use that information to build a document for you to use. Right now, you need the default general-purpose template named Normal.

Figure 1.1

2 If Normal does not appear in the Template box, type Normal

3 Select OK.

Tip You can open a new document with a click of the mouse
Use the New document button on the standard toolbar to open a Normal document with a single click.

The document area of the screen will be blank except for the blinking vertical *insertion point* (|), *the end-of-document mark* (_), and possibly a *paragraph mark* (¶). The ***insertion point*** marks the position where text will be inserted or deleted when you type at the keyboard. The ***end-of-document mark*** shows where the document ends; you cannot insert characters after the end-of-document mark. A ***paragraph mark*** indicates the end of a paragraph and forces the beginning of a new line. The paragraph mark may not show on your screen. If not, you will learn shortly how to make it visible.

Margin figures show on-screen tools that are often convenient alternatives to menu commands presented in the numbered steps.

ips, Reminders,
utions, and **Quick Fixes** appear throughout each
roject to highlight
nportant, helpful, or
ertinent information
out each application.

Study Questions (Multiple Choice, Short Answer, and For Discussion) may be used as self-tests or homework assignments.

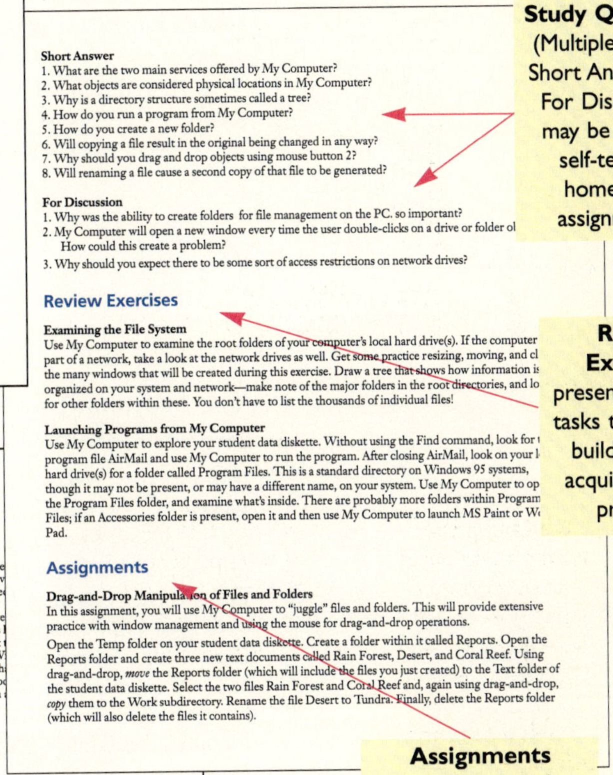
Short Answer
1. What are the two main services offered by My Computer?
2. What objects are considered physical locations in My Computer?
3. Why is a directory structure sometimes called a tree?
4. How do you run a program from My Computer?
5. How do you create a new folder?
6. Will copying a file result in the original being changed in any way?
7. Why should you drag and drop objects using mouse button 2?
8. Will renaming a file cause a second copy of that file to be generated?

For Discussion
1. Why was the ability to create folders for file management on the PC. so important?
2. My Computer will open a new window every time the user double-clicks on a drive or folder ol
How could this create a problem?
3. Why should you expect there to be some sort of access restrictions on network drives?

Review Exercises

Examining the File System
Use My Computer to examine the root folders of your computer's local hard drive(s). If the computer part of a network, take a look at the network drives as well. Get some practice resizing, moving, and cl the many windows that will be created during this exercise. Draw a tree that shows how information is organized on your system and network—make note of the major folders in the root directories, and lo for other folders within these. You don't have to list the thousands of individual files!

Launching Programs from My Computer
Use My Computer to explore your student data diskette. Without using the Find command, look for t program file AirMail and use My Computer to run the program. After closing AirMail, look on your l hard drive(s) for a folder called Program Files. This is a standard directory on Windows 95 systems, though it may not be present, or may have a different name, on your system. Use My Computer to op the Program Files folder, and examine what's inside. There are probably more folders within Program Files; if an Accessories folder is present, open it and then use My Computer to launch MS Paint or W Pad.

Assignments

Drag-and-Drop Manipulation of Files and Folders
In this assignment, you will use My Computer to "juggle" files and folders. This will provide extensive practice with window management and using the mouse for drag-and-drop operations.

Open the Temp folder on your student data diskette. Create a folder within it called Reports. Open the Reports folder and create three new text documents called Rain Forest, Desert, and Coral Reef. Using drag-and-drop, *move* the Reports folder (which will include the files you just created) to the Text folder of the student data diskette. Select the two files Rain Forest and Coral Reef and, again using drag-and-drop, *copy* them to the Work subdirectory. Rename the file Desert to Tundra. Finally, delete the Reports folder (which will also delete the files it contains).

Review Exercises present hands-on tasks to help you build on skills acquired in the projects.

Assignments require critical thinking and encourage synthesis and integration of project skills.

Each project ends with **The Next Step** which discusses the concepts from the project and proposes other uses and applications for the skills you have learned, a **Summary,** and a list of **Key Terms and Operations.**

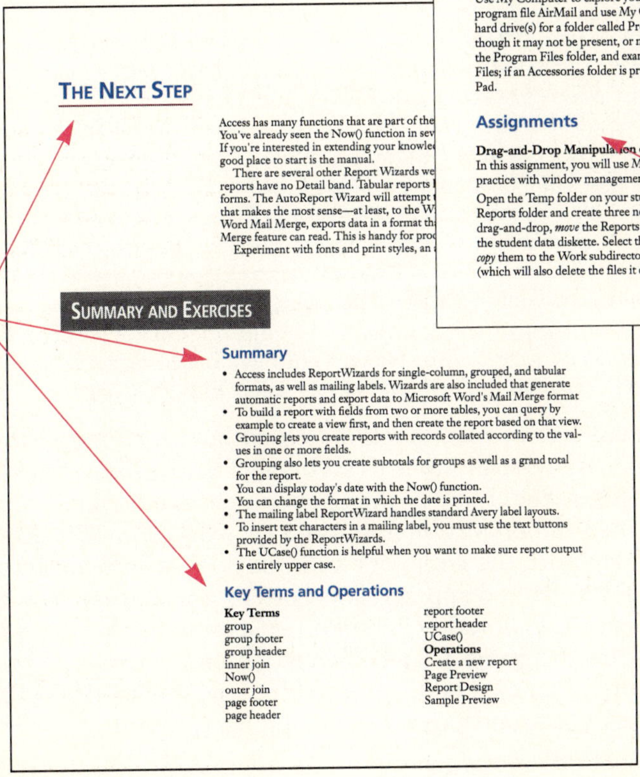
THE NEXT STEP

Access has many functions that are part of the
You've already seen the Now() function in sev
If you're interested in extending your knowle
good place to start is the manual.
There are several other Report Wizards we
reports have no Detail band. Tabular reports
forms. The AutoReport Wizard will attempt
that makes the most sense—at least, to the W
Word Mail Merge, exports data in a format th
Merge feature can read. This is handy for pro
Experiment with fonts and print styles, an

SUMMARY AND EXERCISES

Summary

- Access includes ReportWizards for single-column, grouped, and tabular formats, as well as mailing labels. Wizards are also included that generate automatic reports and export data to Microsoft Word's Mail Merge format
- To build a report with fields from two or more tables, you can query by example to create a view first, and then create the report based on that view.
- Grouping lets you create reports with records collated according to the values in one or more fields.
- Grouping also lets you create subtotals for groups as well as a grand total for the report.
- You can display today's date with the Now() function.
- You can change the format in which the date is printed.
- The mailing label ReportWizard handles standard Avery label layouts.
- To insert text characters in a mailing label, you must use the text buttons provided by the ReportWizards.
- The UCase() function is helpful when you want to make sure report output is entirely upper case.

Key Terms and Operations

Key Terms
group
group footer
group header
inner join
Now()
outer join
page footer
page header
report footer
report header
UCase()
Operations
Create a new report
Page Preview
Report Design
Sample Preview

A Note to the Instructor: Supplements

You get extra support for this text from supplemental materials including the Instructor's Manual and Instructor Data Disk.

The Instructor's Manual includes Test Bank and Transparency Masters for each project in the student text, as well as Expanded Student Objectives, Answers to Study Questions, and Additional Assessment Techniques. The Test Bank contains two separate tests with answers, and consists of multiple choice, true/false, and fill-in questions referenced to pages in the student's text. Transparency Masters illustrate over one hundred key concepts and screen captures from the text.

The Instructor's Data Disk contains student data files, answers to selected Review Exercises, answers to selected Assignments, and the test files from the Instructor's Manual in ASCII format.

Acknowledgements

The Benjamin/Cummings Publishing Company would like to thank our reviewers for their valuable contributions:

Joseph Aieta, *Babson College;* Bob Barber, *Lane Community College;* Jacquelyn Crowe, *Spokane Community College;* Ralph Duffy, *North Seattle Community College;* Dan Flynn, *Shoreline Community College;* Jonathan Frank, *Suffolk University;* Patrick Gilbert, *University of Hawaii;* Maureen Greenbaum, *Union County College;* Sunil Hazari, *East Carolina University;* William Hightower, *Elon College;* Seth Hock, *Columbus State Community College;* Cynthia Kachik, *Santa Fe Community College;* Ron Leake, *Johnson County Community College;* Randy Marak, *Hill College;* Gail Miles, *Lenoir-Rhyne College;* Carolyn Monroe, *Baylor University;* John Passafiume, *Clemson University;* Louis Pryor, *Garland County Community College;* Tonia Queen, *Brevard Community College;* Michael Reilly, *University of Denver;* Dick Ricketts, *Lane Community College;* Cynthia Thompson, *Carl Sandburg College;* JoAnn Weatherwax, *Saddleback College;* David Whitney, *San Francisco State University;* James Wood, *Tri-County Technical College;* Allen Zilbert, *Long Island University*

I would like to first thank my co-authors for their shared vision and significant contributions to sections of this project. On behalf of all the authors, I would like to thank our respective families for their continued patience and understanding while we worked on this project. Without their support, the completion of this book would not be possible. Finally, my gratitude and appreciation goes to my colleagues in the School of Business at Colorado Christian University for their support during my work on this project. Gary Ewen, Connie Harris, Kevin Miller, Thom Scheffel, Nancy Todd, John White, and Vickey Wood are dedicated professionals, and I cannot envision working with a more supportive and lively group!

Philip Koneman
Colorado Christian University

Introduction to Microsoft Office for Windows 95

Objectives

After completing this introduction, you should be able to:

- Describe the new features of Microsoft Office for Windows 95
- Launch Office 95
- Use the Shortcut Bar to launch applications
- Customize the Shortcut Bar
- Create Schedule+ file and add an appointment to it
- Create a binder and add documents to it
- Get online Help
- Exit Office 95

Microsoft Office for Windows 95 represents a significant step forward in software development. Designed to take advantage of the features of the new Windows 95 operating system, Microsoft Office for Windows 95 contains significant enhancements that extend the usability of Microsoft Office and Microsoft Office Professional 4.3 for Windows 3.1.

Office 95 is an integrated ***software suite,*** combining powerful applications for word processing, spreadsheet, database management, and presentations. In addition to providing you with these powerful stand-alone tools, Office 95 emphasizes the ***integration*** of both data and applications for the completion of entire projects, not just individual documents. Whether you are an experienced Microsoft Office user or a beginning computer user, *Microsoft Office Projects for Windows 95's* project-oriented approach provides you with the right tools at the right time for completing both simple and complex tasks.

Microsoft Office for Windows 95 is available in two versions: Standard and Professional. The Standard version includes Word, a powerful tool for word processing; Excel, a tool for performing calculations and manipulating numeric data; and PowerPoint, which allows you to create stunning presentations using the computer. The Professional version includes all the tools available in the Standard version plus Access, a powerful relational database management system. Both versions include Schedule+, a personal time and project management tool that can be used in conjunction with other users if you are running Office 95 on a computer network. In addition, both versions allow you to use Exchange to send and receive electronic mail and fax documents, if your computer is equipped with a modem.

If you have used previous versions of Microsoft Office, this Introduction will familiarize you with the new features of Office 95. If you have never used Microsoft Office before, you will learn how to launch the individual Office applications. You will also learn how to organize your documents in an electronic resource, the Binder.

New Features of Office 95

Microsoft Office for Windows 95 differs from previous versions of Office by providing greater functionality without significantly changing the user interface. This means that if you have used Office before, you will be able to take advantage of the benefits Office 95 has to offer without learning a new set of commands and procedures. If Office 95 is the first Office suite you have had, you'll find that the consistent interface shared among all Office 95 applications makes learning how to use the suite easy. Once you learn the location and function of the various menu items and buttons in one application, you will know how to complete the most common tasks in the others.

Office 95 is more than just an upgrade from previous versions of Microsoft Office. Office 95 takes advantage of Windows 95, an entirely new ***operating system.*** Office 95 contains the following features not available in previous versions of the software:

- *True 32-bit performance.* Office 95 applications for full 32-bit applications that take advantage of the greater system resources and multitasking capabilities of Windows 95. For example, you may conduct file searches, online communications, or other common tasks while editing a document.
- *IntelliSense technology.* IntelliSense technology senses user intent and then intelligently delivers the desired result. Routine tasks are made automatic, and more complex tasks are made simple. The new Auto features

automate many tasks, such as Spell-It in Microsoft Word, which spell-checks your document as you type. Other new Auto features include AutoComplete in Microsoft Excel, AutoClipArt in PowerPoint, and Filter by Selection in Microsoft Access. Enhanced wizards walk you through the completion of complex tasks. For example, the Answer Wizard immediately provides solutions and suggestions to a wide range of questions you might have about using Office 95.

- *Sharing information among applications.* Sharing information among applications has been made even easier with features such as WriteUp from PowerPoint to Word, Convert to Microsoft Access in Microsoft Excel, the Binder, and the new Shortcut Bar. These enhancements to the Microsoft Office suite of applications simplify working with individual applications and sharing data among applications. For example, using the metaphor of a three-ring binder, the Binder allows you to collect, print, and distribute collections of documents from each Office application. The Shortcut Bar allows you to launch applications easily and switch quickly among applications that are currently running.

STARTING MICROSOFT OFFICE 95

How you start Office 95 depends on how your computer or network is configured. If Windows 95 is configured to load Office 95 automatically at startup, your screen will look similar to Figure I.1 once Windows 95 is finished loading.

Figure I.1

If your computer or network is not configured to load Office 95 automatically, you can easily start Office 95 in one of two ways. You can use the Start button to launch the application by opening a series of menus that disappear once the task is completed. If you want the Windows 95 interface to behave like Windows 3.1, you can use the Start button to open a series of windows that remain visible until they are closed or minimized on the desktop.

To launch Office 95 using a series of menus:

1 Start Windows 95 if necessary.

2 Click the Start button using the left mouse button.

3 Move the mouse pointer over the Programs menu item.

4 Move the mouse pointer over the Microsoft Office 95 menu item. Your screen should look like Figure I.2.

5 Choose the Microsoft Office Shortcut Bar menu item.

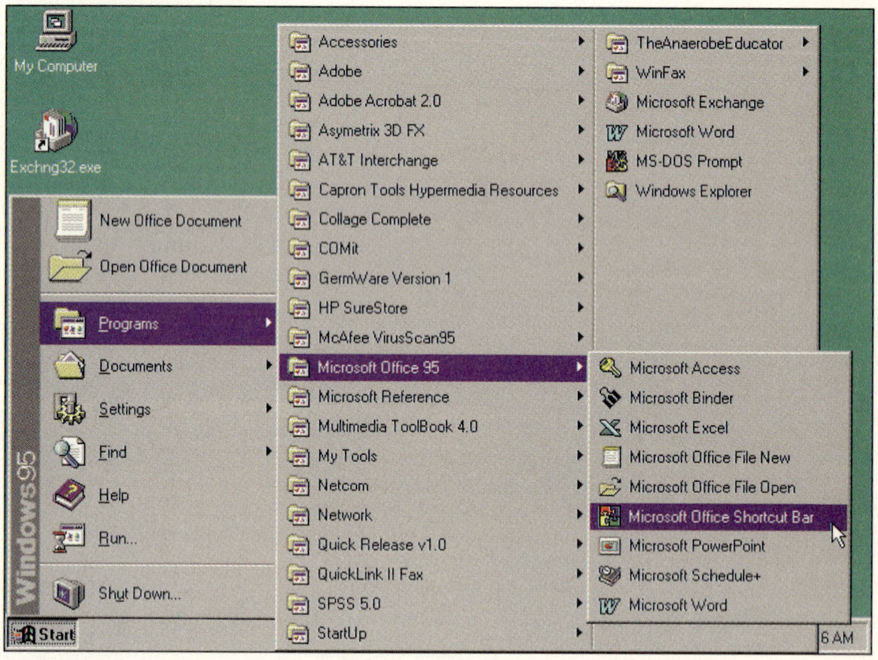

Figure I.2

To launch Office 95 by opening a series of windows:

1 Start Windows 95 if necessary.

2 Click the Start button using the right mouse button.

3 Select Open to open the Start window.

4 Select Programs to open the Programs window.

5 Select Microsoft Office 95 to see the Microsoft Office program icons. Your screen should look like Figure I.3.

6 Select the Microsoft Office Shortcut Bar icon.

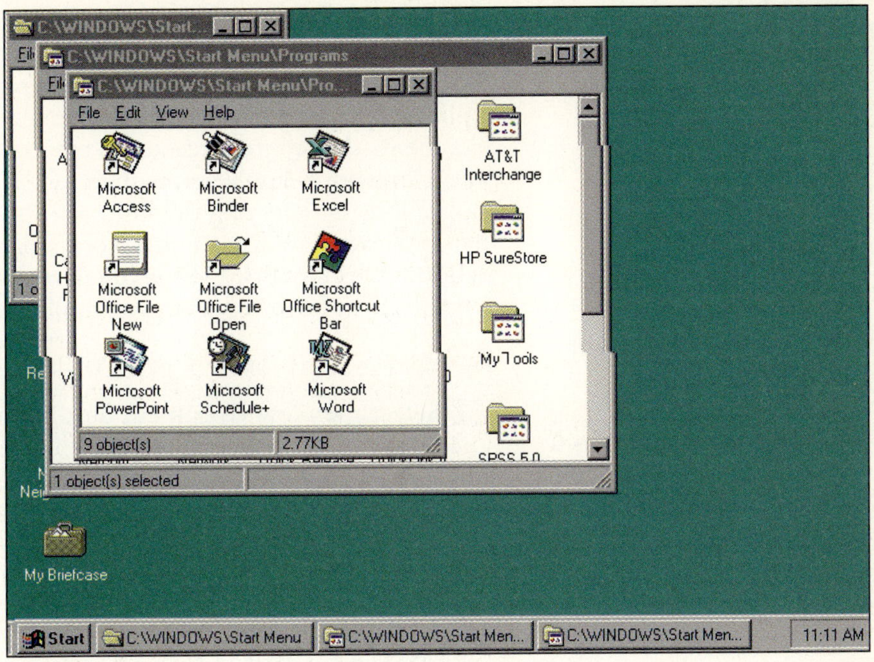

Figure I.3

Reminder Any Windows 3.1 user who needs help in learning how to navigate within Windows 95 should use the right mouse button to select the Start button. You can then open the Program menu and associated submenus as individual windows, which mimics the way you use Windows 3.1.

Using the Shortcut Bar

Regardless of how you start Office 95, the Shortcut Bar will appear in the upper-right corner of the Office 95 opening screen. The Shortcut Bar accomplishes what the name implies: It provides multiple ways of simplifying common tasks. The term ***shortcut*** in Windows 95 refers to an icon that points to an object, which can be an application program, a folder, or an individual document. The Shortcut Bar consists of buttons, represented by icons, that contain shortcuts. You can use the tools on the Shortcut Bar to create new documents, open existing documents, add entries to a Schedule+ file, or access the Office 95 online Help system. Although the arrangement of buttons on your computer or network may differ, a typical configuration of the buttons is shown in Figure I.4.

Figure I.4

Launching Applications Using the Shortcut Bar

Office 95 is *document-centric,* not *application-centric.* Although individual applications are used to create documents, the emphasis is on creating documents that contain resources created in a variety of applications, not on the individual applications themselves. Thus, you launch individual applications by selecting the button for starting a new document within that application. You can also work with other applications to create additional documents. This is called ***multitasking.*** In the following steps you will learn how to launch two applications and create two documents.

To start a new Word document:

1 Select the New Document button on the Shortcut Bar. The dialog box shown in Figure I.5 appears.

2 Select the General tab, if it is not already selected.

3 Select the Blank Document icon to launch Microsoft Word.

4 Select the New Document button again.

5 With the General tab active, double-click the Blank Workbook icon to launch Microsoft Excel.

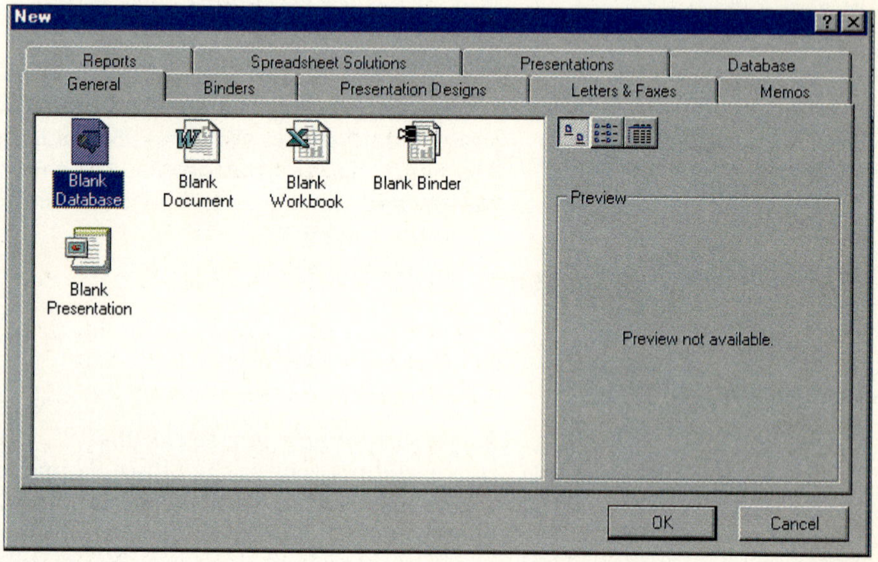

Figure I.5

Using the Taskbar to Switch Between Open Applications

The open applications should be displayed in the Taskbar, as shown in Figure I.6. The dark outline on the top and left edge of the Excel button indicates that Excel is currently the ***active*** application: Excel was the last application you launched in the previous steps. In the following steps you will move between open applications by clicking the desired application button on the Taskbar.

Figure I.6

To make Word the active application and close it, then close Excel:

1 Select the Word button on the Taskbar.

2 Select the Close button to exit Word.
You have not entered data into Word, so you are not prompted to save your work before exiting. Notice that Excel is again the active application.

3 Select the Close button again to exit Excel.
Your screen should once again look like Figure I.3.

> ***Tip*** You can also choose Exit from the File menu to close an active application.

CUSTOMIZING THE SHORTCUT BAR

You can customize the Shortcut Bar to assist you in managing your document and software resources. You can customize three aspects of the Shortcut Bar: how it appears, where it appears, and what it contains. You can make changes to the Shortcut Bar easily using the right mouse feature of Office 95.

Changing the Appearance of the Shortcut Bar

You can customize the Shortcut Bar by changing its colors and the size of its icons using the View folder in the Customize dialog box. You will now make the icons on the Shortcut Bar larger.

To change the size of the Shortcut Bar icons:

1 Place the mouse pointer inside the gray portion of the Shortcut Bar icon and press the right mouse button.
The pull-down menu shown in Figure I.7 appears.

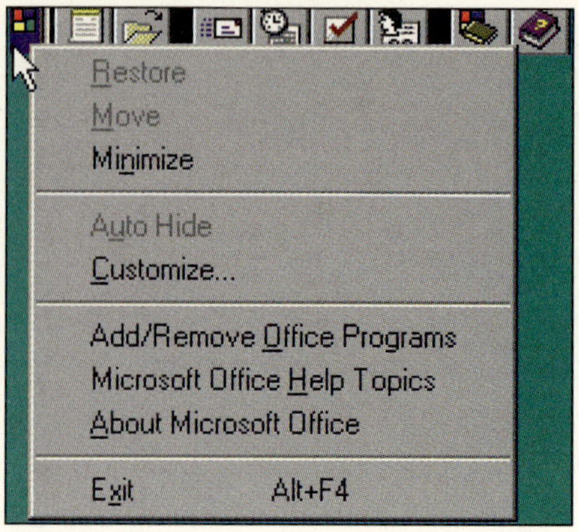

Figure I.7

2 Choose the Customize menu item.

3 Select the Buttons tab. The dialog box will now look like Figure I.8.

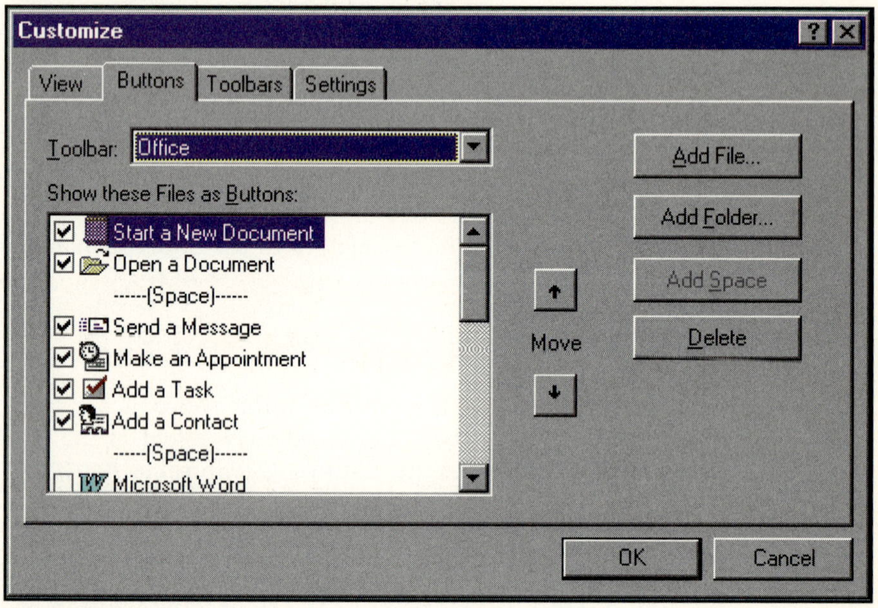

Figure I.8

4 Select Large Buttons under Options, and then select OK. The Shortcut Bar should now look like Figure I.9.

Figure I.9

5 Repeat steps 1 through 4, except this time deselect the Large Buttons option to change the Shortcut Bar icons back to the smaller size.

Changing the Location and Orientation of the Shortcut Bar

You can further customize the Shortcut Bar by changing its location and orientation. By default, the Shortcut Bar is anchored to the title bar at the top of the screen and displayed horizontally. In the following steps you will "tear off" the Shortcut Bar and move it to a new location. You will then change its orientation from horizontal to vertical.

To change the location and orientation of the Shortcut Bar:

1 Move the mouse pointer inside any portion of the Shortcut Bar not occupied by a button.

2 While holding down the left mouse button, drag the Shortcut Bar down from the title bar.

3 Release the left mouse button. The Shortcut Bar now looks similar to Figure I.10.

Figure I.10

To change the Shortcut Bar to a vertical orientation:

1 Move the mouse pointer to the lower border of the Shortcut Bar until it turns into an arrow icon.

2 Hold the left mouse button, and drag the Shortcut Bar down.

3 Release the left mouse button.
The Shortcut Bar now looks similar to Figure I.11.

Figure I.11

4 Reattach the Shortcut Bar to the title bar by dragging any portion of the bar back to the title bar.

Adding Icons to the Shortcut Bar and Changing the Order of Icons

You can also customize the Shortcut Bar by adding and removing icons, or by changing the order in which the buttons appear. Additional icons that provide shortcuts to applications, folders, or individual documents can easily be added to the Shortcut Bar.

To add the Word, Excel, PowerPoint, and Access icons to the Shortcut Bar:

1 Use the right mouse button to display the Customize dialog box.

2 Select the Buttons tab.

3 Scroll the list of available buttons so that the Word, Excel, PowerPoint, and Access buttons are visible.
The dialog box now looks like Figure I.12.

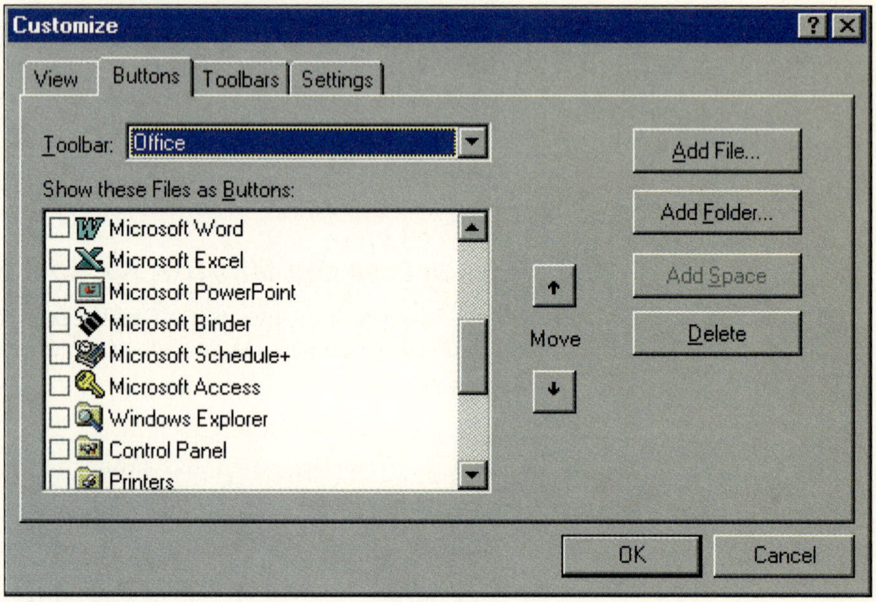

Figure I.12

4 Select the Word, Excel, PowerPoint, and Access items in the Buttons dialog box.
These items now have checkmarks next to them.

5 Select OK.
The Shortcut Bar now looks like Figure I.13.

Figure I.13

To change the location of Access and Word icons:

1 Use the right mouse button to display the Customize dialog box, and then select the Buttons tab.

2 Select the Microsoft Access icon in the list using the left mouse button. The Buttons tab dialog box now looks like Figure I.14.

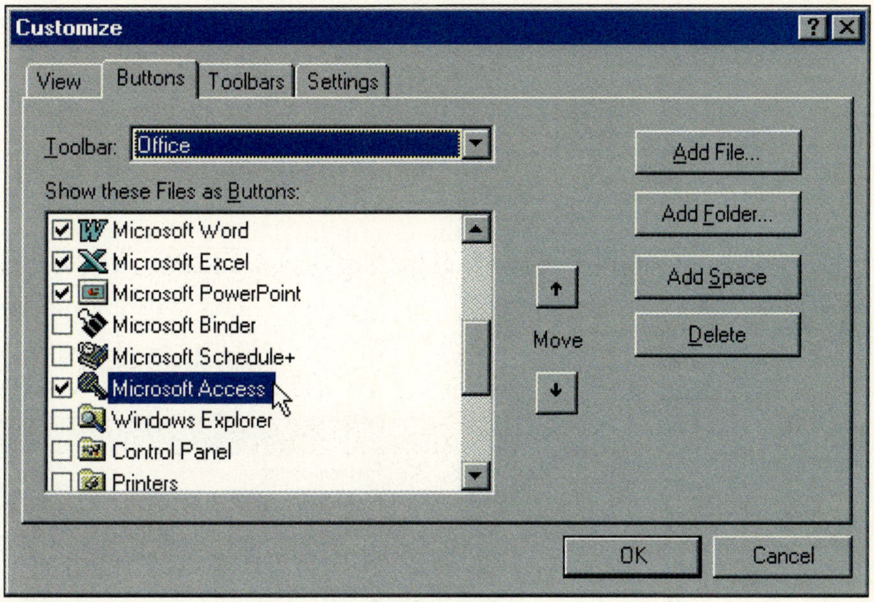

Figure I.14

3 Click the Move up arrow button five times.

4 Select the Microsoft Word icon in the list, and click the Move down arrow three times.

5 Select the Binder icon, and then select the Add Space button.

6 Select OK.

The Shortcut Bar icons for Access, Excel, PowerPoint, and Word now look like those in Figure I.15.

Figure I.15

EXIT If necessary, you can exit Office 95 now and continue this Introduction later.

Using Schedule+

As you worked with the Shortcut Bar, you may have noticed several icons between the New Document and Help icons. These icons are used to add data to Schedule+, a new addition to the Office suite of applications. Schedule+ is a powerful application that you can use individually or in a workgroup setting to manage daily schedules, personal contacts, and to-do task lists.

Using the Shortcut Bar buttons that launch Schedule+, you can easily send electronic mail, schedule appointments, add tasks to a list, or add a new contact to your address database. In the following steps you will create a Schedule+ file and add an appointment to it.

To create a Schedule+ file:

1 Launch Office 95, if necessary.

2 Click the Make an Appointment button on the Shortcut Bar.

3 Depending on how your computer or network is configured, you may see the Group Enabling dialog box shown in Figure I.16. If this appears, select the No, work alone option, and then select OK.

4 The Schedule+ Logon dialog appears, prompting you for a Schedule+ logon name.

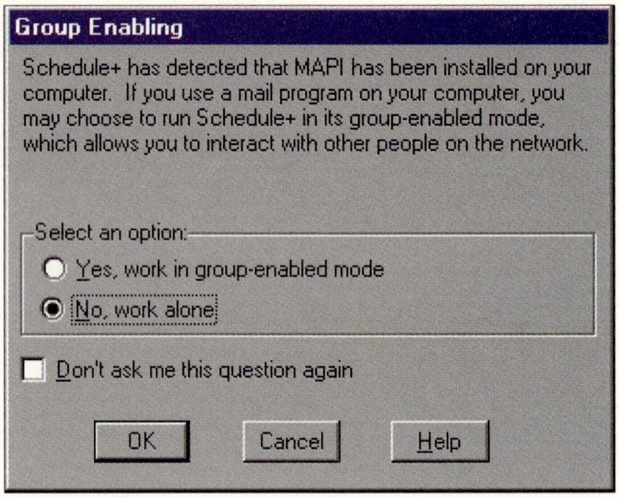

Figure I.16

Type your name in the User name box, as shown in Figure I.17.

5 If you have never used Schedule+ before, the Microsoft Schedule+ dialog box will appear.

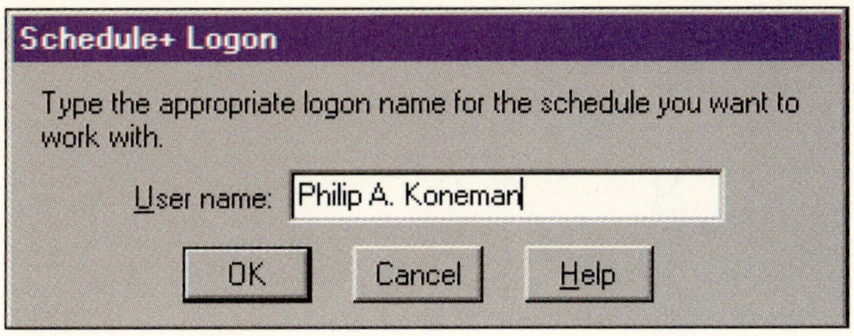

Figure I.17

Select the option to create a new schedule file, as shown in Figure I.18.

6 You are prompted for a file name for your new schedule file.

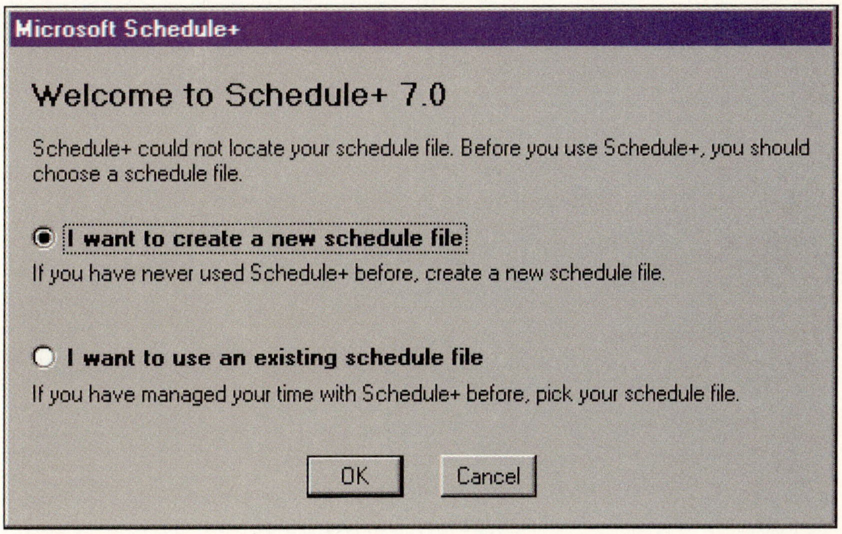

Figure I.18

Select the default location, and enter `Personal` as a file name, as shown in Figure I.19.

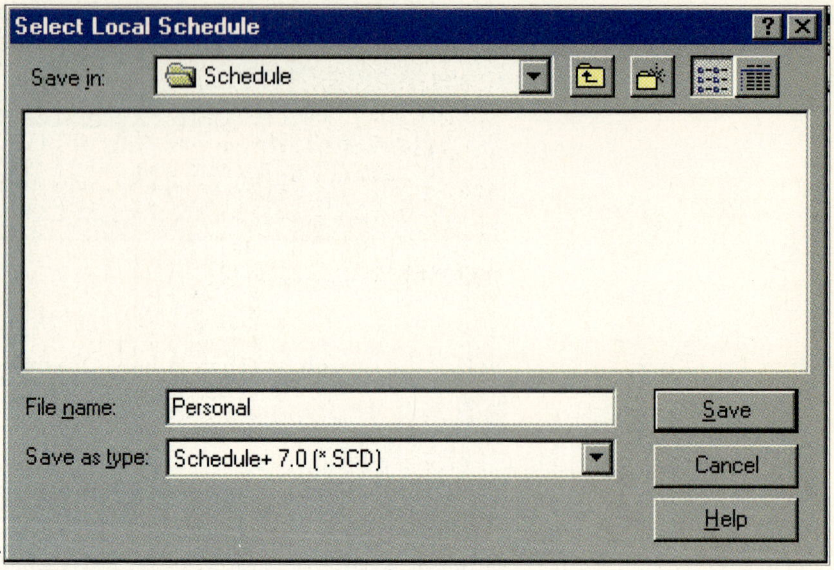

Figure I.19

You have created a schedule file, and the Appointment dialog box is visible on the screen.

To add an appointment to your schedule file:

1 Select the General tab if it is not already active in the Appointment dialog box.

2 Click the up-arrow icon to the right of the Start time until the time displayed is 9:00 AM.

3 Click the up-arrow icon to the right of the End time until the time displayed is 9:30 AM.

4 Click the down-arrow icon to the right of the Start date box. When the calendar appears, click the right arrow, select October 1996, and click the 15th day, as shown in Figure I.20.

5 Repeat step 4 to set October 15, 1996, as the End date.

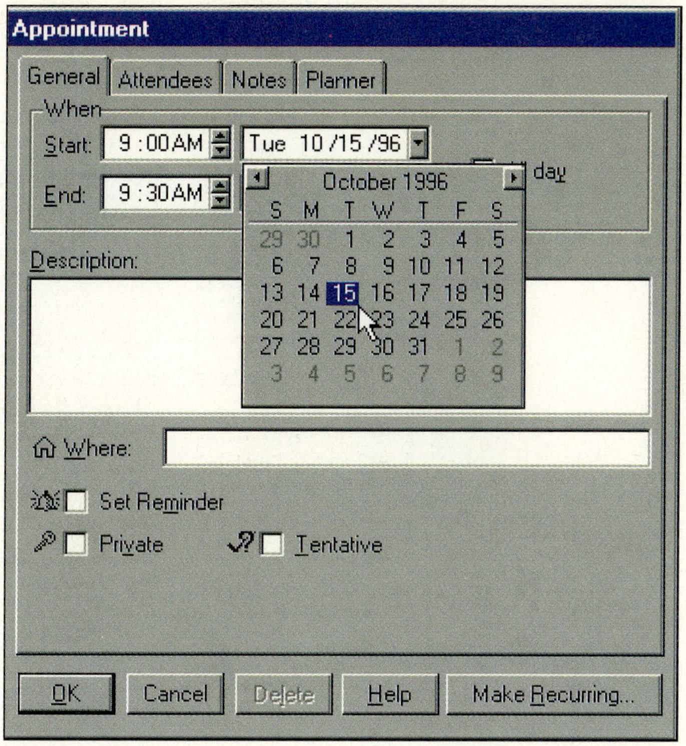

Figure I.20

6 Type **`Pick up bulk coffee bean order`** in the Description box. The screen now looks like Figure I.21.

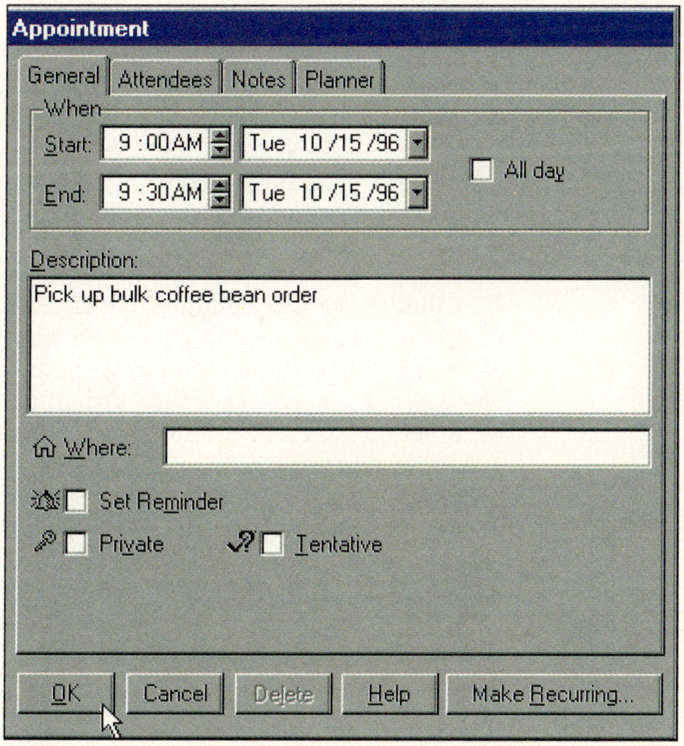

Figure I.21

7 Select OK.

Your appointment will be added to your personal schedule file for Tuesday, October 15, 1996, as shown in Figure I.22.

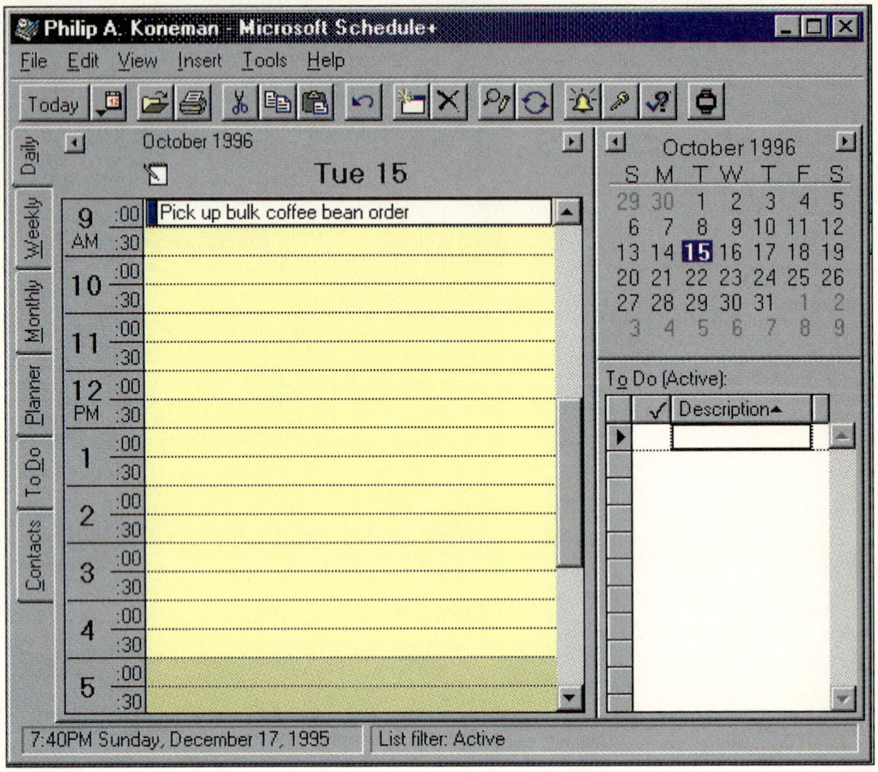

Figure I.22

Schedule+ has many features that allow you to customize your personal schedule, which you are encouraged to explore on your own.

Using the Binder

The Binder is a new addition to Office 95. In the same way that a three-ring binder keeps related papers together, an Office ***binder*** will keep electronic files created with different applications together in one visual workspace for easy access and editing. For example, if you have a Word document, an Excel worksheet, and a series of PowerPoint slides that make up a report, you can place each file in a binder and work with them together or individually. You can check the spelling, apply a consistent style, add page numbers, and print the documents contained in a binder. You can also work on the documents individually. In the following steps you will add a new Word document and Excel worksheet to a binder.

To create an Office binder:

1 Click the Start a New Document button on the Shortcut Bar. If the Shortcut Bar is not visible, use the Windows 95 Start button to launch Office 95.

The New dialog box appears as shown in Figure I.23.

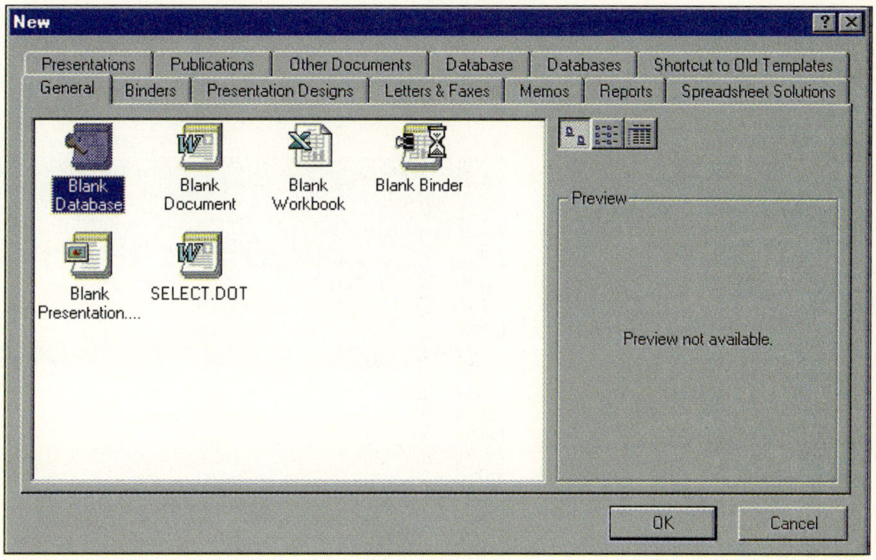

Figure I.23

2 Select the Blank Binder icon, and then select OK.
The screen contains a new binder with the default name Binder1, as shown in Figure I.24.

A binder has three primary parts: a menu bar containing three menus, a left pane for document icons, and a right pane for the associated documents. In the following steps you will use the menu bar to add two new documents to Binder1 and notice what happens to both panes.

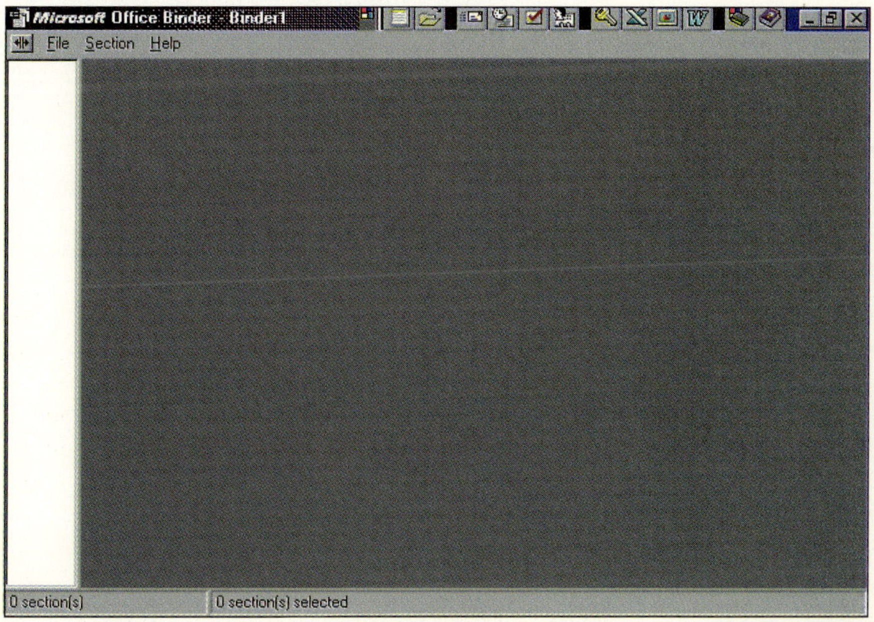

Figure I.24

To add two new documents to Binder1:

1 Choose Section from the menu bar, and then choose Add. The Add Section dialog box appears as shown in Figure I.25.

2 Select Microsoft Word Document, and then select OK.

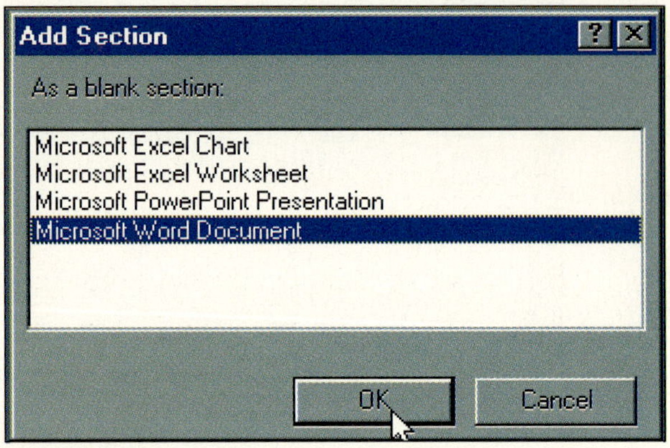

Figure I.25

A Word document icon is added to the left pane, and a blank Word document appears in the right pane, as shown in Figure I.26.

> ***Tip*** Notice that the Binder menu bar has changed: It will always contain the menu items for the current file's application.

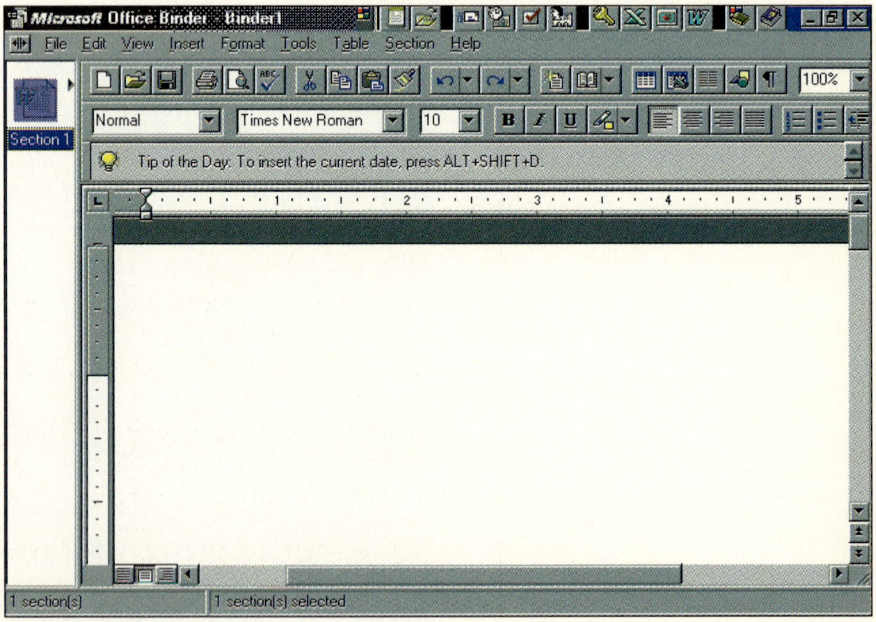

Figure I.26

3 Repeat steps 1 and 2 to add a new Excel document to Binder1. Note that the position of the Section menu item has changed.

One of the advantages of a binder is that it allows you to switch quickly among applications. In addition, a binder behaves like any other window in the Windows 95 environment: It can be minimized, maximized, or resized. Since you last added a new Excel worksheet to your binder, it should be the active application.

To minimize and restore a binder and make a different binder document active:

1 Click the Minimize button in the upper-right corner of the active binder window.
An icon representing Binder1 appears on the Taskbar.

2 Click the Binder1 icon to restore the binder to its previous size.

3 Click the Word icon in the left pane of Binder1.
The Word document becomes the active document, as shown in Figure I.27.

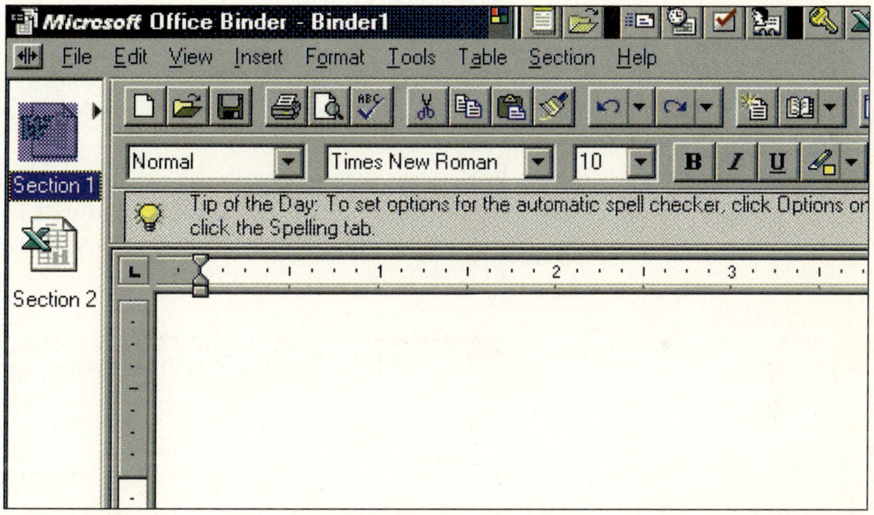

Figure I.27

You will know the Word document is active because the Word icon named Section1 appears in a blue color in the left pane of the binder, and the menu items, Standard toolbar, and document window contain objects specific to Word.

You save a binder like any other Office document: you can select either the Save or Save As menu options, or you can click the Save or Save As buttons on the Standard toolbar.

To save and close the current binder:

1 Choose the Save Binder option from the File menu.
Since you have not previously saved Binder1, the Save Binder As dialog box shown in Figure I.28 appears.

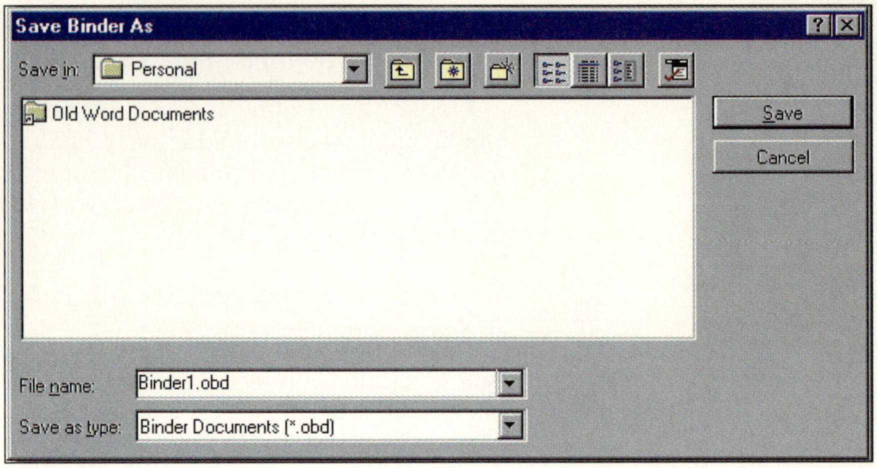

Figure I.28

2 Select the Save button to accept the default filename Binder1. The name in the binder's title bar changes to indicate that the binder is now saved to disk.

> ***Tip*** Notice the .obd extension included in the binder's filename. You can quickly identify an Office binder by this extension.

3 Choose Close from the File menu to close the current binder. Microsoft Office binders simplify many document formatting and management tasks. You will work more with binders in each of the integrated projects later in this book.

EXIT

If necessary, you can exit Office 95 now and continue this Introduction later.

Getting Online Help

As with previous versions of Microsoft Office, online help is available from the Help menu or Help buttons appearing in various dialog boxes and toolbars. A new feature of the Help system in Office 95 is the Answer Wizard. The Answer Wizard gives you the ability to ask a question regarding a task, and depending on the complexity of the task, the wizard will either display the steps necessary to complete the task or prompt you to complete each step required to solve the task.

Using the Answer Wizard to get help:

1 Launch Office 95 if necessary.

2 Select the Answer Wizard button on the Shortcut Bar. The Answer Wizard dialog box shown in Figure I.29 appears.

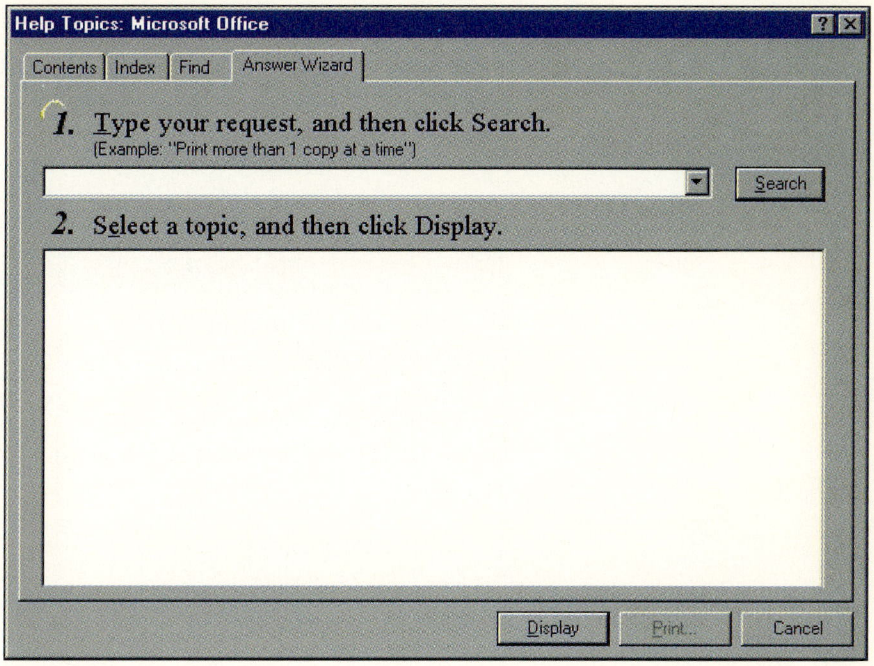

Figure I.29

> ***Tip*** You can use the Contents and Index tabs in the Answer Wizard dialog box to search for and locate specific help topics quickly.

3 Type **`Open a file`** in the text entry box, and then click the Search button.

4 Highlight the fourth Help topic as shown in Figure I.30.

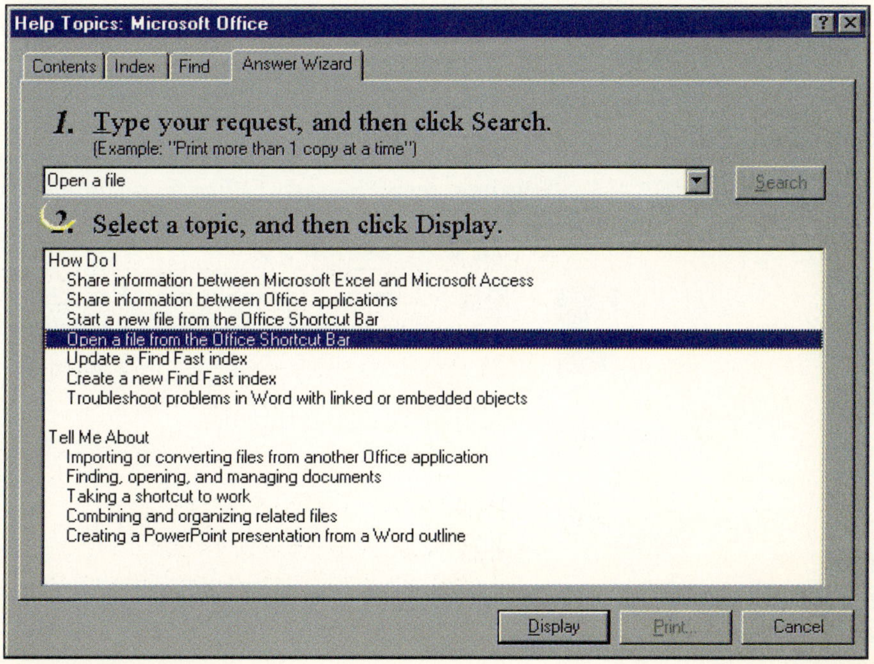

Figure I.30

5 Click the Display button.
The Help topic shown in Figure I.31 appears.

6 When you finish reading about this topic, select the topic's Close button to close the Help topic dialog box.

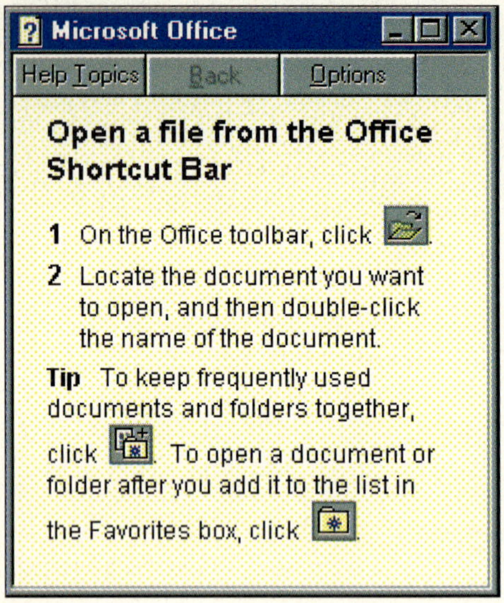

Figure I.31

Exiting Office 95

To exit most Microsoft software programs, you have to choose Exit from the File menu or the close button in the application window. As you work with individual programs such as Word and Excel, you must exit them before opening another package or exiting Windows.

Office 95 is different. Whenever the Shortcut Bar is visible on the screen, Office 95 is running, even if you are working in another software program that is not part of Office 95.

You can exit Office 95 by selecting Exit from the Shortcut Bar. Office 95 will close down, and the Shortcut Bar will no longer be displayed on the screen. To start Office 95 again, you will select the Start button.

To exit Office 95:

1 Select the Office Shortcut Bar icon bar with the right mouse button.
The menu shown in Figure I.32 will appear.

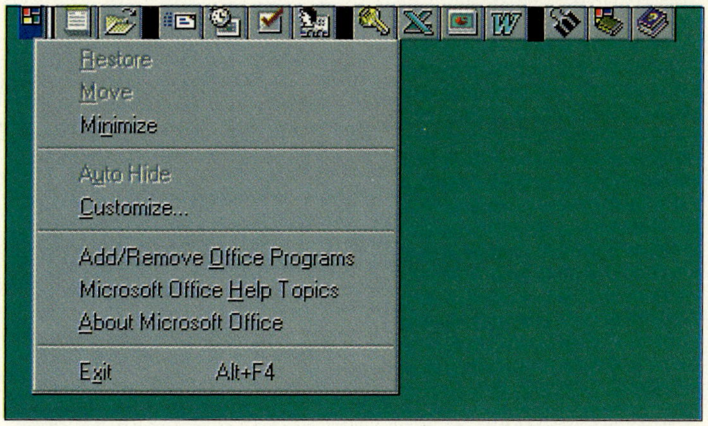

Figure I.32

2 Select Exit from the menu.

The Next Step

What applications do you use frequently? What Windows accessories do you like to have available to you quickly? Think carefully about how you work, and then use the Shortcut Bar to customize your desktop and keep documents together in a binder. The more efficient your workspace, the more energy you have to create your files. As the old saying goes, "work smarter, not harder." In the projects that follow we will assist you in making Office 95 work for you.

Office 95 includes some additional programs, or tools, that you can use in every Office application: WordArt, the Equation Editor, the ClipArt Gallery, and Microsoft Graph are just a few. You'll learn more about these tools as you work through the projects in this book.

Summary and Exercises

Summary

- Microsoft Office for Windows 95 is an integrated software package that incorporates new features such as true 32-bit performance, IntelliSense technology, and new ways to share information easily among applications.
- Office includes the applications Word, Excel, Schedule+, and PowerPoint. The Professional version also includes Access.
- Multiple Office applications can be open concurrently, and related documents can be stored in an electronic binder.
- Information can be shared among all Office applications.
- The Shortcut Bar controls access to individual applications and provides ways to accomplish common tasks.
- The Shortcut Bar can be customized to display any and all of the Office 95 products, as well as other Microsoft programs and accessories.

- By default the Shortcut Bar is attached to the Office 95 title bar, and the icons are displayed horizontally.
- The Shortcut Bar can be moved anywhere on the screen and can have a vertical orientation. Its icons can be displayed in any order.
- Microsoft Office normally remains open while you work in Windows 95, but it can be exited and started again.

Key Terms and Operations

Key Terms
active
binder
integration
multitasking
operating system
shortcut
software suite

Operations
Add a task to your personal schedule using Schedule+
Create an Office binder
Customize the Shortcut Bar
Launch Microsoft Office using the Windows 95 Start button
Order the Shortcut Bar
Switch between Word and Excel using a binder

Study Questions

Multiple Choice

1. Office 95 is
   a. available only to businesses for office use.
   b. a word processing package.
   c. an accounting program.
   d. a software suite.

2. An integrated software suite
   a. is a group of networked software programs.
   b. has products that can be used together to share information.
   c. is a program that can be used in multiple languages at the same time, such as French and German.
   d. must be bought from the same store.

3. The only real limitation(s) to using Office 95:
   a. is when the software suite is loaded on a stand-alone PC and not on a network.
   b. is the availability of the software on the network and the number of users.
   c. are found in the hardware capacities of the computer being used.
   d. are the security levels granted to non-network users.

4. An Office binder is
   a. a piece of paper granting you a single-user license for Office 95.
   b. a notebook used to organize the printed documentation accompanying Office 95.
   c. an electronic resource used to store related Word, Excel, Access, and PowerPoint documents.
   d. not available on a stand-alone computer but only in a networked environment.

5. The Shortcut Bar
   a. can be modified to display all or some of the Office 95 products.
   b. is always visible when Windows 95 is running.
   c. cannot display Windows accessories or programs.
   d. closes when one of the Office 95 products is started.

Short Answer

1. What products make up the Standard version of the Office 95 suite?
2. What products make up the Professional version of Office 95?
3. How do you customize the Shortcut Bar?
4. What software programs can be added to the Shortcut Bar?
5. How is an Office binder created?

For Discussion

1. What are some advantages to using a software suite?
2. Discuss some reasons why you would share information between different applications.
3. Describe how a binder will assist you in organizing your work.
4. What are you looking forward to the most about learning how to use the Office 95 products?

PART I

Windows 95

Overview

Objectives

After completing this Overview, you should be able to:

- Start Windows
- Locate and identify the various components of the Windows desktop
- Manipulate objects with a mouse
- Use windows and controls
- Use Windows Help
- Shut down and log off Windows

The history of computing, though rich in folklore and technical milestones, is still fairly brief. It was not so long ago that interacting with a computer required flipping banks of switches or feeding stacks of punched cards into a hopper to run a program. Today, modern ***operating systems*** provide an interface between the user and the computer that is far more enjoyable and productive.

The primary purpose of an operating system is to shield the user from the complexities of the underlying hardware. It is a testament to the power of software that computers are now far more complicated yet also far easier to use than in the early days of computing. An operating system is itself a program that provides an environment within which other programs, called ***application programs,*** can run. Application programs use a wide variety of features that are built in the operating system to provide a consistent interface to the user. The part of the operating system that you see and interact with, called a ***graphical user interface (GUI),*** is similar on all modern operating systems, allowing the use of a pointing device called a mouse as well as the standard keyboard. GUIs also support the concept of ***windows,*** or overlapping rectangular areas on-screen, each of which can contain its own program, or ***process.*** These programs run independently of each other and allow the user to be more productive.

Windows 95 is the culmination of years of GUI work on the part of Microsoft and features a powerful, advanced user interface, or ***shell.*** The shell allows you to explore the Windows 95 "world" visually in a variety of ways. Windows 95 is highly customizable, meaning that users can configure their systems easily. Windows 95 also runs the most popular software available: software designed for Windows 3.1, the predecessor to Windows 95. In addition to this legacy software, it runs the latest 32-bit software designed specifically for Windows 95. The 32-bit software is faster and more powerful than the 16-bit software required for previous versions of Windows.

Windows 95 is an exciting operating system that bridges the past with today's technical advances. To users of earlier operating systems, Windows 95 is a thrill to work with, full of features that were previously unavailable anywhere.

A Note to the Student

This module assumes that

- Microsoft Windows 95 is installed on the computer you will be using as you work through the projects
- You know your user name and password, if required
- A blank, formatted diskette will be placed in drive A: (your 3½ inch disk drive).

STARTING WINDOWS

When you turn on the computer, Windows will be loaded into memory. This is known as booting, or starting, Windows. After some introductory screens, the Windows desktop will appear.

To start Windows:

1 Turn on the computer system.
The message *Starting Windows 95* appears. Then the Windows "splash" screen will appear.

2 If a window appears asking you to type a user name and password, you should do so now.

USING THE DESKTOP

The Windows desktop provides the backdrop for each session you spend with Windows. Microsoft designed the Windows desktop to be a friendly place but it may not seem so at first glance. Don't despair; there is plenty to do and see on the desktop, and soon you will be launching and using application programs. Figure 0.1 shows a typical view of the Windows desktop at startup.

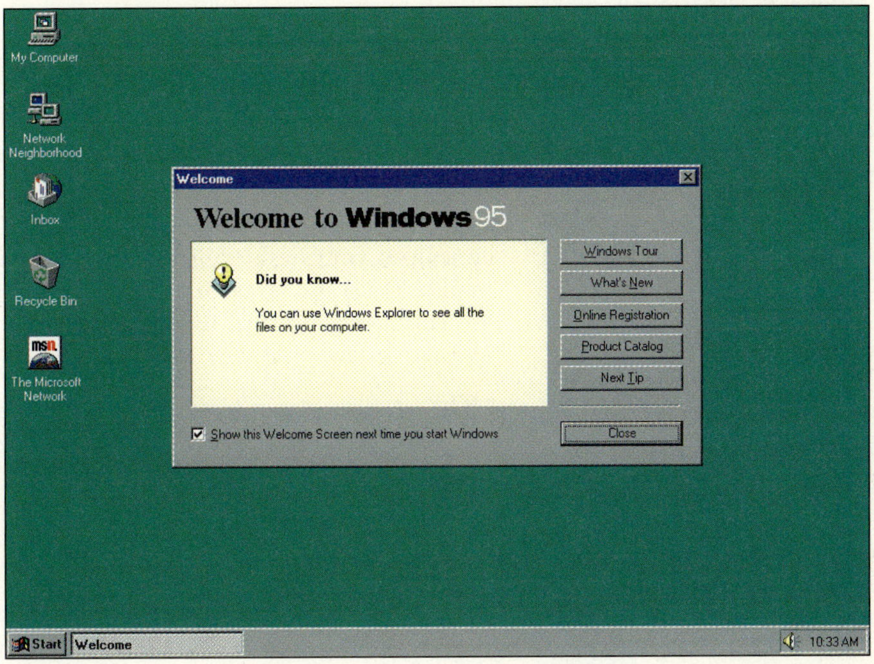

Figure 0.1

Caution The Windows desktop on your screen may be different in some ways from the figures in this module. Because Windows is highly customizable, different sites may have changed the system colors, icons, font styles, and other attributes. This module uses the standard setup for all of its figures.

Desktop Objects

All the parts of the desktop you see are called ***objects.*** This generic term refers to any of the "things" that are on the desktop. Windows uses what is called a noun-verb paradigm, where each object is a noun, and any action you can do with an object is a verb. The Windows desktop will include several objects called *icons,* which usually consist of My Computer, Network Neighborhood, Inbox, and Recycle Bin. An ***icon*** is a graphical representation of an object, and as with any object, you can perform unique actions with it.

While you will be learning more about each of these objects in upcoming projects, a quick look at the items that make up the Windows desktop will provide a brief overview.

My Computer

The My Computer icon is like a doorway into the file system of the computer. My Computer offers the user a straightforward way to browse, or maneuver, through the computer's resources. These resources can include floppy, hard, and CD-ROM drives, and system configuration options.

Network Neighborhood

Network Neighborhood is similar to My Computer, allowing you to browse through network resources such as computers and shared printers. Systems that are not connected to a network may not have this icon.

Inbox

Inbox is the icon for Microsoft's powerful Exchange program and may not appear on your desktop. Exchange is used to send and receive electronic mail (e-mail) and faxes. Sites that have installed Microsoft Plus! for Windows 95 will have additional features built into Exchange.

> ***Tip*** A figure next to text or a numbered step, shown above, represents the button or icon you will use. This type of margin figure appears frequently throughout the module.

Recycle Bin

People familiar with the Macintosh computer will immediately recognize that the Windows Recycle Bin is very similar to the Macintosh Trashcan. It provides a place to store deleted files that can later be permanently removed or recovered.

Taskbar

The Taskbar, shown in Figure 0.2, is the gray area that runs along the bottom of the Windows desktop. By default, the Taskbar always remains visible, and it gives the user an easy way to switch between running programs. The Taskbar has a section at the far right called the status area, or the tray notification area, which displays a clock and, depending on how Windows is configured, miniature icons representing utility programs that are always in memory. In Figure 0.2 the status area has two small utilities installed: a volume control for the sound card, and an audio CD player utility program.

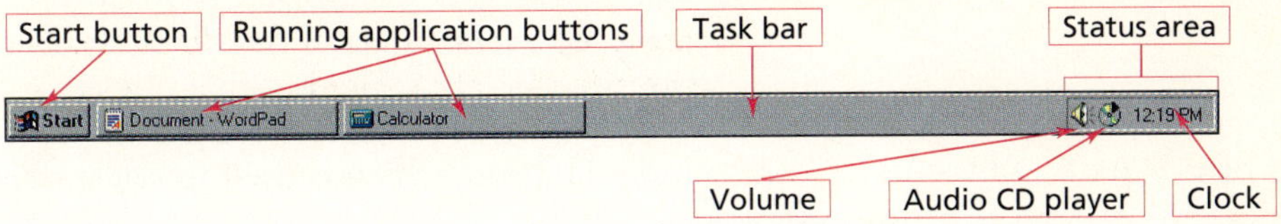

Figure 0.2

The Taskbar also contains the Start button.

Start Button

Located at the far left end of the Taskbar, the Start button provides one-click access to a cascading menu of programs, documents, settings, and other objects. The Start button is designed to provide a direct way for the user to access application programs.

Using the Mouse

While it is possible to use Windows without a mouse, doing so is painful at best. A mouse, popularized by the Macintosh computer in the mid-1980s, has become standard equipment on all personal computers and is required to navigate Windows effectively. If you have not had any experience with a mouse, you may find it awkward at first, but using it will soon become second nature.

Moving the Mouse

A mouse is used to move around a small pointer, usually shaped like an arrow, on the screen. The mouse rolls along on a flat surface on a small rubber ball located on its underside. Rolling the ball along the table will cause the pointer on-screen to move—this is how you control the mouse. You should practice moving the mouse now if you are unfamiliar with it.

To move the mouse:

1 Grasp the mouse in your hand.
Your index finger should rest lightly on the leftmost button, and your middle finger should rest on the right button.

2 Move the mouse in a circular motion.
Observe the pointer on-screen as you move the mouse. Try to keep the mouse moving in small, tight circles.

Using the Mouse Buttons

Most PC-compatible mice have two buttons, located at the top of the mouse, that are used to select, or ***click,*** objects. To click an object, you position the pointer over the object and then press and immediately release the mouse button. The ***left mouse button*** is the primary button. Unless a right click is specified, always click with the left button. Clicking an object with the left mouse button selects that object. In Windows, when you click an object with the ***right mouse button*** (right click) you will see on-screen a ***pop-up menu,*** a small free-floating window containing properties and options that are related to that object.

It is time to practice using the mouse buttons. First you will try the left mouse button, which is used to select objects.

To click with the left mouse button:

1 Move the mouse pointer to the icon for My Computer, as shown in Figure 0.3.

Figure 0.3

2 Press and immediately release the left mouse button with your index finger to click the My Computer icon.
The My Computer icon is selected. You can tell that it is selected because its color will change to a blue hue, as shown in Figure 0.4.

Figure 0.4

Tip To deselect an object, just click anywhere else on the screen. You will normally want to click somewhere in a blank area of the desktop. If the My Computer icon is selected and you click the Network Neighborhood icon, then the Network Neighborhood icon becomes selected and the My Computer icon is deselected.

3 Practice clicking other icons on the Windows desktop, getting a feel for moving the pointer and for selecting objects with the mouse. When you are done, click the left mouse button anywhere over a blank spot on the desktop to deselect any objects.

Typically, you use the right mouse button to view a pop-up menu for the currently selected object. This menu, sometimes called a context menu, is a small window that lists the various options available for that object. The menu that appears will be slightly different for each object, because each object will have different commands, attributes, and possible actions. The pop-up menu appears next to the current pointer location. A disk drive object, for example, would have options for formatting, disk copying, and other disk-related functions. Almost every object in Windows responds like this to a right-click, including the desktop.

To click with the right mouse button:

1 If My Computer is still selected, click anywhere over a blank spot on the desktop with the left mouse button to deselect My Computer.

2 Click the desktop with the right mouse button.
A pop-up menu appears.

3 Click the My Computer icon with the right mouse button.
The pop-up menu that appears is slightly different than the one that appears when the desktop is clicked with the right mouse button.

Double-Clicking with the Mouse

Although single-clicking the mouse buttons is fairly common, the most common mouse action is ***double-clicking,*** pressing the mouse button twice quickly and then releasing it. Double-clicking is done only with the left mouse button, and it is usually done to open an object. Opening can be different things to different objects. For an application program, opening means launching, or starting, that program. Opening a drive object will actually open a window displaying the contents of the drive.

To double-click:

1 Position the mouse over a blank area of the desktop.

2 Quickly press the mouse button twice in succession to double-click the desktop.
Nothing will actually happen. The desktop is an object that cannot be opened by double-clicking. Most of the time, you will double-click icons.

3 Position the mouse pointer over the My Computer icon and double-click.
Your screen should resemble Figure 0.5.

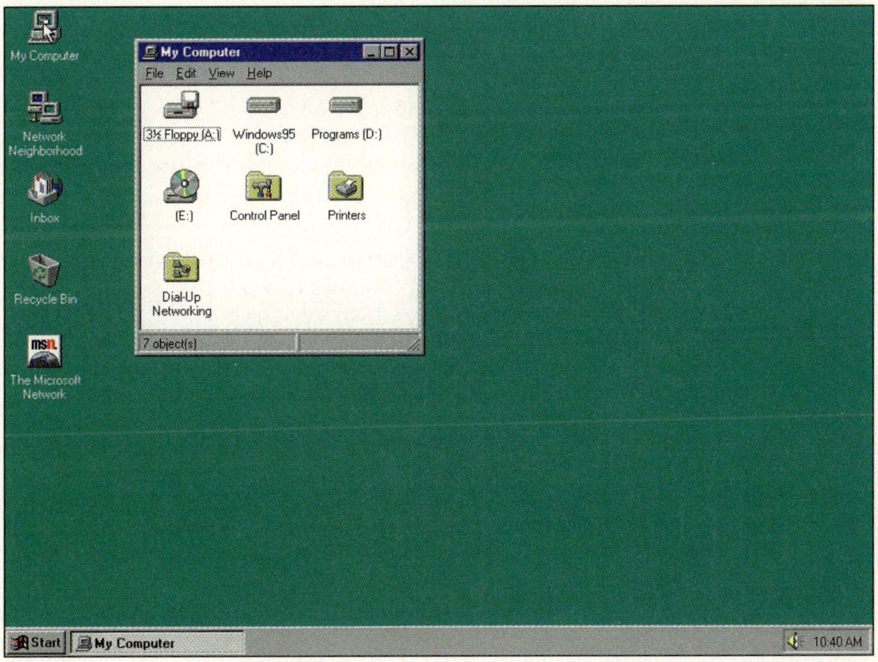

Figure 0.5

Caution Because of the customization options available in Windows, it is possible that your screen does not resemble Figure 0.5. To make your screen more closely follow the standard appearance used in the figures in this module, right-click a blank area in the My Computer window, choose View, and then Large Icons. Also, your My Computer window may show a toolbar of icons under the menu bar that is not seen in the figures. If you would like to turn this off, choose Toolbar from the View menu.

Reminder The distinction between the different mouse clicks is important. A single-click with the left mouse button will *select* an object, a single-click with the right mouse button will *display* a pop-up menu, and a double-click (which is always done with the left mouse button) will *open* an object.

Exiting Windows

Windows requires that you properly shut down the system when you are done using it for the day. Do not turn the PC's power off while Windows is running! This could damage Windows, cause a loss of data, or at the very least leave seemingly random temporary files on the computer's hard drive. Windows is a fairly complex system and needs to do some housecleaning before it shuts down.

Caution Do not turn off the computer while Windows is running!

Shutting down, or exiting Windows, is straightforward and requires only that you select the Shut Down option from the Start menu. Please note that the following steps will ultimately result in the machine being turned off. In a computer lab environment, it may be preferable to perform a different shut-down procedure.

To exit Windows:

1. Click the Start button on the Taskbar.
The Start menu appears.
2. Select the option titled Shut Down by clicking it with the left mouse button.
The Shut Down Windows dialog box appears, offering you several options.
3. Select *Shut down the computer?*, and then click the Yes button.
Windows is performing its shut-down tasks.
4. Windows will inform you when it is safe to turn off the computer.

Using Windows

One of the major advantages of a graphical user interface is the use of overlapping windows. A window is just a rectangular area of the screen, like a box, that contains a running program or other information.

Window Components

Most windows consist of the same primary components. A component is nothing more than a piece or element of an object. The initial My Computer window, shown in Figure 0.6, contains many common window components (remember that the contents of the window may be slightly different on your computer).

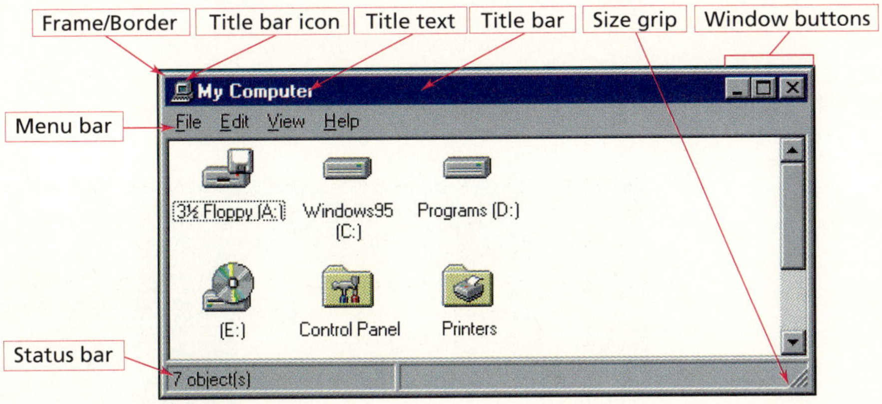

Figure 0.6

Window Frame

Each window has a ***frame,*** or border, that defines the outer edges of that window, as shown in Figure 0.6. In the My Computer window, for example, the window is sizable, meaning that users can resize the window as they see fit. One visual clue that the window is sizable is that it contains a ***size grip*** in the lower-right corner. The size grip is a special handle designed to make resizing (by *dragging*) more obvious to the user.

The action of holding down a mouse button while an object is selected is called ***dragging.*** Like most of the concepts in this Overview, dragging objects with the mouse is a basic Windows skill.

To resize a window:

1 Make sure Windows is running, then open a My Computer window by double clicking the My Computer icon.

2 Position the pointer over the My Computer size grip, as shown in Figure 0.7.
The pointer changes to a diagonal double arrow, indicating that the window can now be resized.

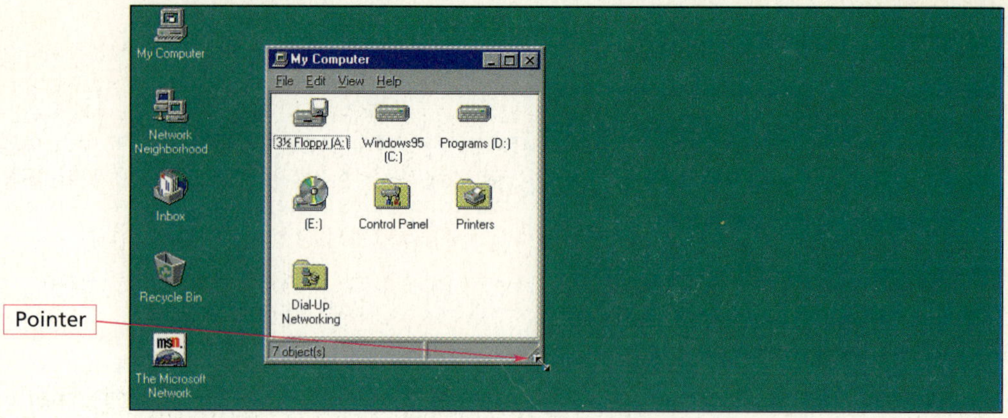

Figure 0.7

3 Drag the size grip by pressing the mouse button and holding it down as you move the pointer diagonally back and forth. A shadow outline of the My Computer window moves with the pointer, as shown in Figure 0.8.

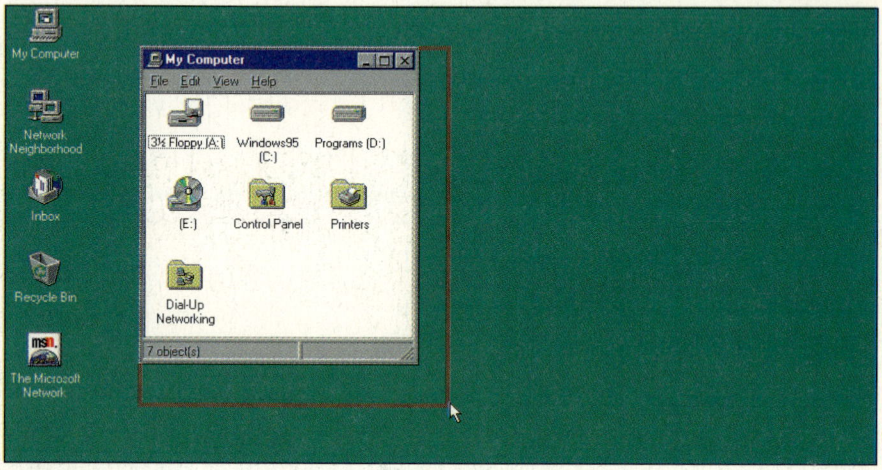

Figure 0.8

The outline shows where the window borders will be when you release the mouse button.

4 Release the mouse button.
The My Computer window is resized.

You may want to experiment with the size grip, sizing the window differently each time and seeing the effect it has.

Title Bar

The title bar is the colored bar along the top edge of a window. It contains a caption, called the ***title text,*** that identifies the window. The title text will duplicate the name of the icon you clicked to open the window. The title bar houses the title bar icons and serves as the primary place for grabbing the window so that it can be dragged (moved) to a new location.

You drag the window by positioning the mouse pointer on the title bar, holding down the left mouse button, and moving the mouse. This dragging action is similar to what you did to resize a window, except that in this case you are dragging the title bar instead of the size grip. You should become comfortable moving windows around with the mouse.

To drag a window with the title bar:

1 Position the mouse pointer over the title bar of the My Computer window, as shown in Figure 0.9.

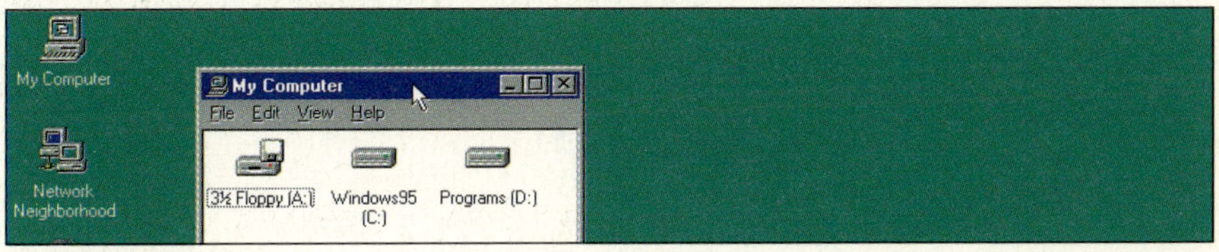

Figure 0.9

2 Drag the My Computer window by pressing and holding down the left mouse button and then moving the mouse in a circular pattern. Again, a shadow outline of the window moves with the mouse pointer, as shown in Figure 0.10.

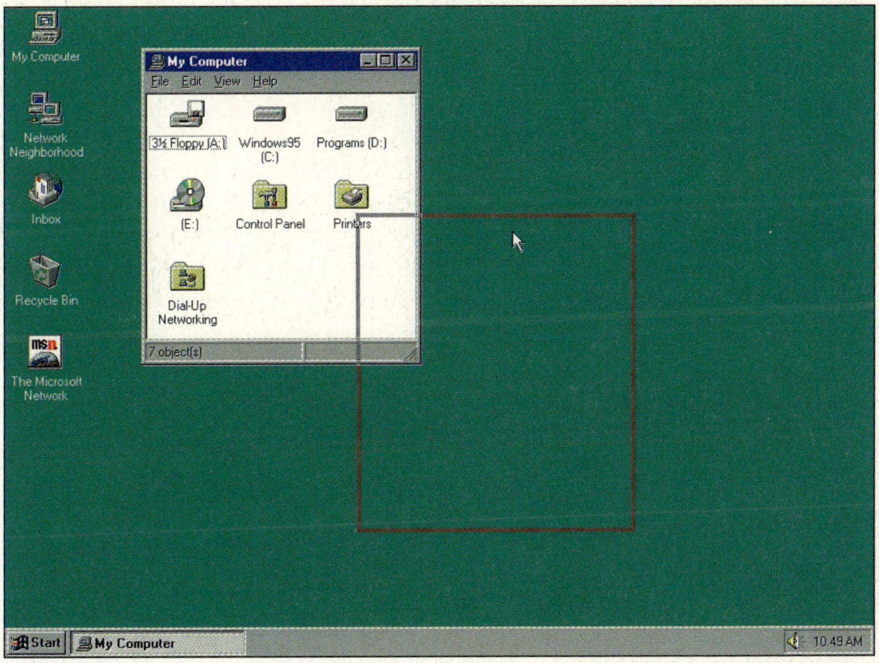

Figure 0.10

3 Release the mouse button.
The window is repositioned wherever you release the button.

Window Buttons

Window buttons perform specific window commands when you select them. These commands are Close, Minimize, Maximize, and Restore. The My Computer window, by default, will display the Minimize, Maximize, and Close window buttons, as shown in Figure 0.11. The Restore window button is available after you maximize a window; it replaces the Maximize button.

Figure 0.11

The Close window button performs the most obvious action. Clicking the Close window button with the mouse closes the window.

To close a window:

1 Position the pointer over the Close window button on the My Computer window.

2 Click the Close window button.
The window is closed.

The Minimize, Maximize, and Restore window buttons are closely related and are used to change the state of the window you are manipulating. You will recall that it is possible to size the window to your heart's content, in small increments, with the size grip and the borders of a sizable window. The Minimize, Maximize, and Restore window buttons allow you to quickly size a window to preset dimensions.

The Minimize button makes the window disappear from the screen, although the window will retain its Taskbar button. A minimized window has *not* been closed; it is just hidden from view. This can be useful when there are many windows on the screen, and you want to clean things up a bit but keep the various windows readily available. When a window is minimized, you can restore it to its former size and position by selecting its Taskbar button.

To minimize a window:

1 Double-click the My Computer icon to open the My Computer window.

2 Click the Minimize window button.
The window disappears but its Taskbar button remains, as shown in Figure 0.12.

Figure 0.12

3 Click the My Computer Taskbar button to restore the window.

The Maximize window button expands the window to occupy the whole screen (less the space occupied by the Taskbar). When a window is maximized, the Maximize window button is replaced by the Restore window button. Clicking the Restore button will return the window to the size and location it was before it was maximized.

To maximize and restore a window:

1 Click the Maximize window button.
The My Computer now appears maximized. The Maximize window button has been replaced by a Restore window button.

2 Click the Restore window button to restore the My Computer window to its original size and location.

Menu Bar

Many windows will have a ***menu bar*** located directly under the title bar. Menu bars contain ***menu titles,*** which can be selected to access ***pull-down menus.*** These menus contain ***menu items,*** which represent commands that you can select to perform various actions. The My Computer window, shown in Figure 0.13, has a somewhat typical menu bar.

Figure 0.13

When you select a menu title, that menu is displayed and the menu title is highlighted. The menus in Windows will remain open until you select something else.

To select menus in a window:

1 If the My Computer window is not already open, open it now by double-clicking the My Computer icon.

2 Move the mouse pointer to the File menu title, and select the File menu title by clicking it.
The File menu appears as shown in Figure 0.14.

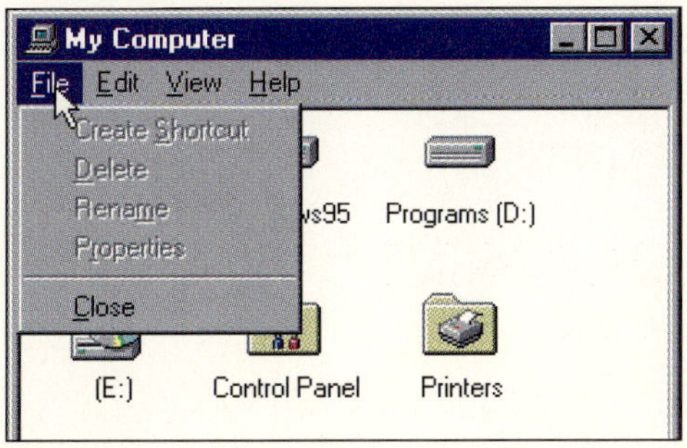

Figure 0.14

3 Release the mouse button, making sure that you do not press any other buttons.
Notice that the menu stays open.

4 Move the pointer slowly over the Edit, View, and Help menu titles, watching as each corresponding menu opens as the pointer moves from menu title to menu title.

5 Move the mouse in a circular motion around the screen.
The menu remains open unless you click something else on the Windows desktop.

6 Move the pointer over the File menu title again.
The File menu opens.

7 Move the pointer slowly down and up the menu, noticing that each menu option is highlighted as you pass the pointer over it.

8 Finally, move the pointer over the Close menu option in the File menu.
The Close option is highlighted, as shown in Figure 0.15.

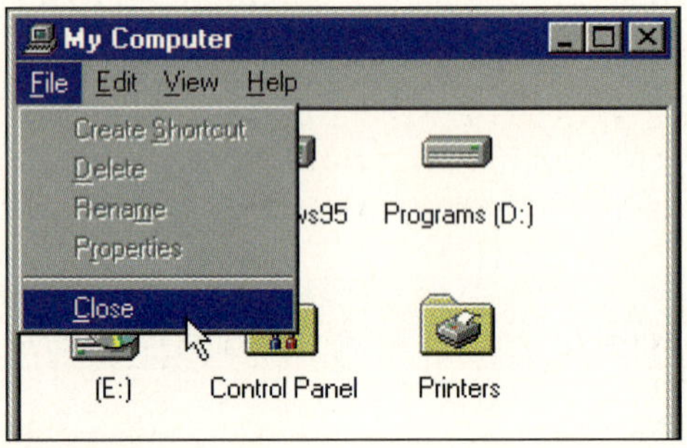

Figure 0.15

9 Select the Close menu option by clicking the left mouse button.
The My Computer window is closed.

Status bar

A ***status bar*** appears at the bottom of a window, although one is not found in each window. It is used to display important information about the window or program. The status bar in the My Computer window, for example, will display the number of objects found in that window, as shown in Figure 0.16.

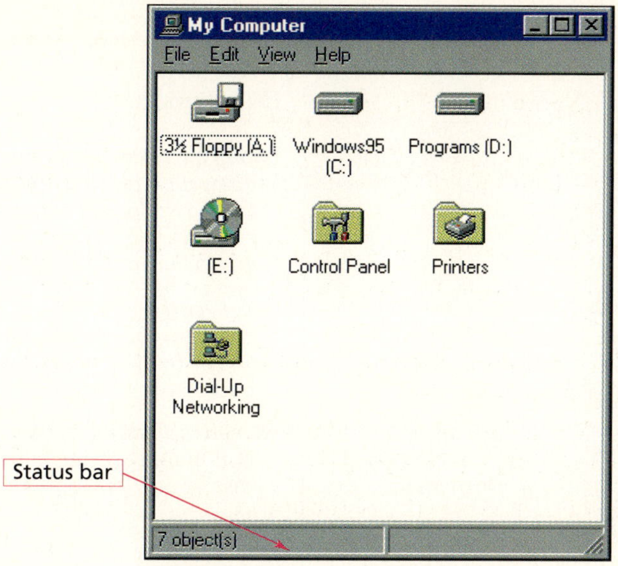

Figure 0.16

When you select an object in the My Computer window, the status bar will change to display information about the currently selected object. For example, if a hard drive is selected, then the status bar displays information about that drive's free space and capacity.

EXIT If necessary, you can exit Windows 95 now and continue this Overview later.

Using Controls

Controls are the means by which you interact with windows. They are graphic objects such as buttons, scroll bars, and text boxes that allow you to perform actions, issue commands, and display information. Generally, each control's appearance is also designed to suggest its use; arrows and buttons are clicked, text boxes invite you to provide input or use the information they display, check boxes toggle functions on and off.

Table 0.1 summarizes the major controls.

Tip Most controls can be disabled; that is, though you might be able to see them on-screen, they cannot be selected or used with the mouse.

Table 0.1

Example [Image]	Name	Description
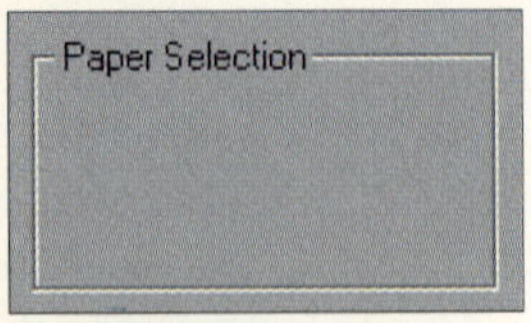	Group box, also called frame	***Group boxes*** are used extensively as containers to organize other controls. You can read group box titles to help identify the purpose of a group of controls. Normally, you do not manipulate a group box itself but rather the controls it contains.
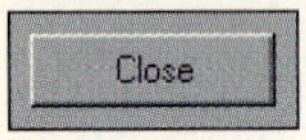	Command button, also called push button	When clicked, a ***command button*** performs some action (usually immediately). Typical command buttons are Open, Close, Cancel, and OK.
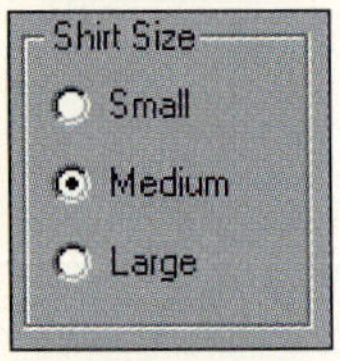	Option button, also called radio button	An ***option button*** can be on or off. In a group of option buttons, the buttons are *mutually exclusive;* that is, only one option can be on at a time.
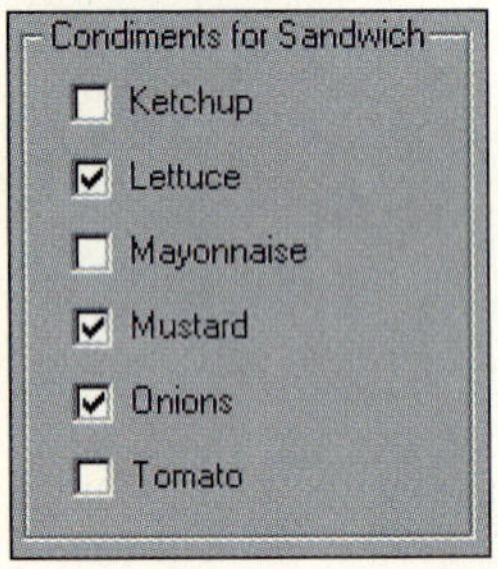	Check box	A ***check box*** can be either on (checked) or off (unchecked). In a group of check boxes, each box can be set independently of the others; that is, any combination of on and off is possible in the group.
 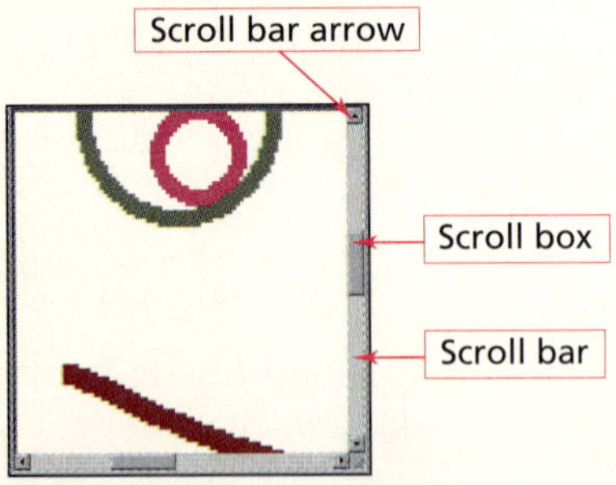	Scroll bar/Scroll box	A ***scroll bar*** is used to change your view of a document (text, image, list, chart, and so on) that is larger than can be seen in the viewing window. The size of the ***scroll box*** is proportional to the amount of the total image you can see. The larger the scroll box, the more of the complete image is visible. The position of the scroll box indicates the position of the viewing window in relation to the edges of the complete document. The ***scroll bar arrow,*** located at the ends of both scroll bars, moves the window in the smallest increment.
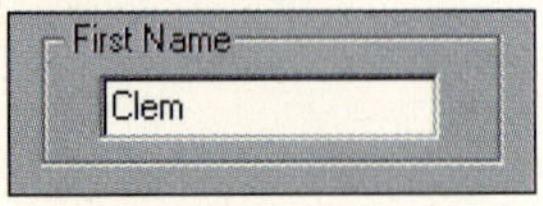	Text box, also called Edit box	***Text boxes*** allow you to type in text of your choice. You can also select and edit text already in a text box.

Example [Image]	Name	Description
	List box	A ***list box*** displays a list of items; you can use the mouse to select one (or sometimes several) of the items. If the list is long, scroll bars are included to allow you to move through the list.
	Combo box	A ***combo box*** combines a text box with a list box. If you don't find what you are looking for in the list, you can type it in at the top of the combo box.
	Spin box, also called spinner	Clicking the arrows to the right of a ***spin box*** causes the value in the box to change (up or down).
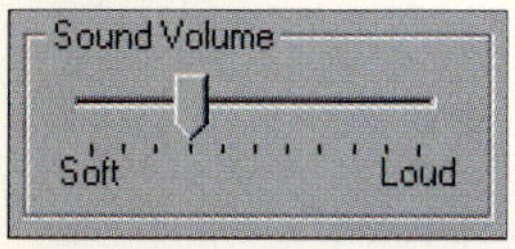	Slider, also called trackbar	***Sliders*** are used to adjust the magnitude of certain settings whose numerical description may not be as easily understood.
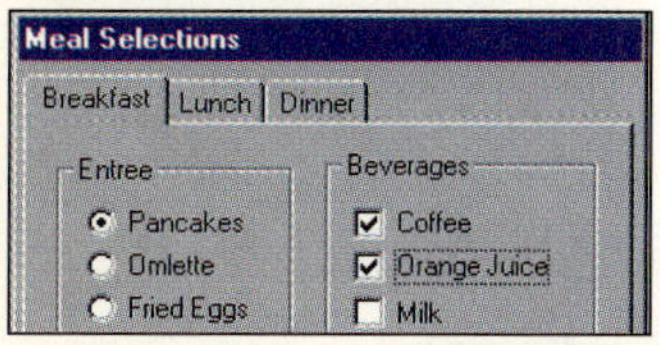	Tab, or tabbed Dialog box, also called notebook tab control or property sheet	***Tabs*** are used to organize different "pages" or panels of controls. Clicking on a tab brings its page into view, where you can then manipulate its controls. Tabs make it possible for menus to be shallower (have a shorter series of choices).

GETTING HELP IN WINDOWS

Windows has an array of tools that provide you various levels of help. One of the biggest complaints with previous versions of Windows was the Help system. If you are making the transition from Windows 3.x, you will be happy to see that the amount and quality of help that now exists has increased dramatically. If you are new to Windows, you will probably wonder what people were talking about when they said that computers were unfriendly!

Context-Sensitive Help

Windows provides context-sensitive help for almost every object on the screen. This help takes several forms, but you are already familiar with the biggest one: the pop-up menu. When you right click an object, a context-sensitive pop-up menu appears.

Reminder If you are ever unsure about exactly what you can do with any object, just right click it.

Tooltips

Tooltips, another form of contextual help, are small pop-up windows that appear over a control when the mouse pointer alights over the control for a short period of time. The pop-up window will display a brief text message that describes the control. Typically, tooltips are displayed over controls that have graphic, rather than textual, labels.

The Help Topics Dialog Box

Windows offers extensive help and reference information, right on the computer. The Help system offers excellent search features, and contents and indexing capabilities. Best of all, the same Help interface is used in every Windows program, not just for Windows itself. Once you have learned how to use Help, you do not need to learn a new Help system for every application program too.

The Help system is accessed through the Help Topics dialog box. This can be quickly accessed from the Start button, located in the lower-left corner of the screen.

To open the Help Topics dialog box:

1 Click the Start button.
The Start menu appears.

2 Choose the Help menu item on the Start menu.
The Help Topics dialog box opens as shown in Figure 0.17.

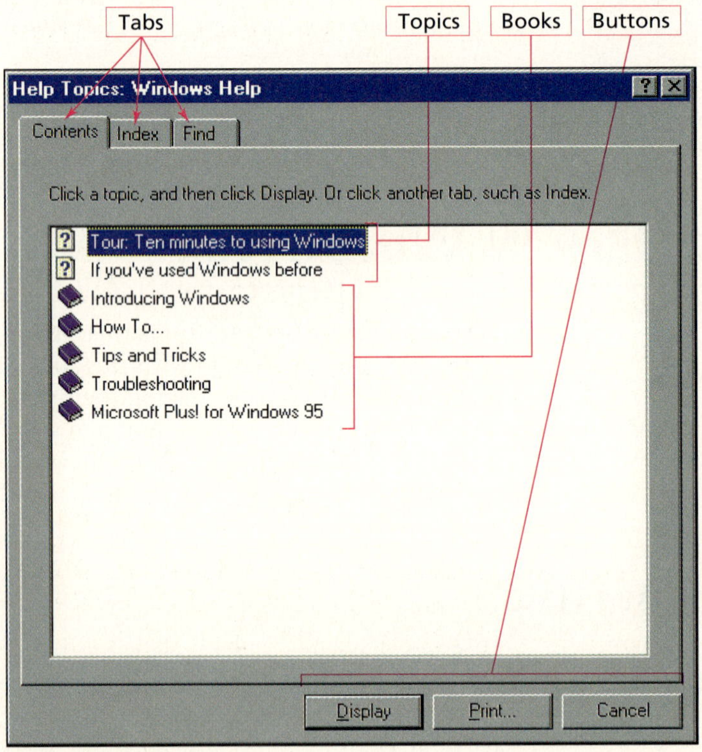

Figure 0.17

The Help Topics dialog box has three tabs, or pages. Like tabs in a notebook, these can be selected, which takes you to the next tab or "turns" the page.

Contents Page

The Contents page, which appears in the front by default, displays a list of *books* and *topics,* organized by category. ***Topics*** are informational files that you can open and read, and ***books,*** like their real-world counterparts, can be opened revealing a list of topics. To view a topic, you can double-click on the topic or its icon, which resembles a little piece of paper with a question mark on it. To open a book, you double-click the book title or its icon.

> ***Tip*** Like most actions in Windows, there is an alternative way to open the books and topics in Help. You can also click a book or topic with the left mouse button and then click the Display button, found at the bottom of the dialog box.

You will now take a look at one of the topics. Since you are new to Windows, you may want to find out something about it. The Introducing Windows book looks like it may hold some relevant information.

To explore the Contents page of Windows Help:

1 Double-click the book labeled *Introducing Windows.*
A new list of books appears.

2 Double-click the book labeled *Getting Your Work Done.*
This displays a list of topics.

3 Double-click the topic labeled *The basics.*
This window offers you the chance to find out about various Windows basics, most of which you learned about in this Overview. You may want to read up on some concepts here or just look around.

4 Move the pointer slowly over the label *Moving windows.*

> ***Tip*** If your Help topics does not include this one, choose another that interests you.

The pointer changes from a small arrow to a little hand that points to the gray box as you pass over it. This is a visual clue that the item you are pointing at is a link and can be accessed with a single click. When you select this item, you will jump to a new page in Help. This type of interface is called hypermedia, and is also the interface for the Internet's most popular service, the World Wide Web.

5 Select *Moving windows.*
The right side of the window displays a small video player that plays a short animation describing how to move windows.

6 Click the Video Play button, located near the bottom of the window. The button resembles the Play button on a CD player or VCR. Now you can watch a short video. A lot of the topics in this section contain short videos like this that describe how to move, scroll, and close windows. Check them out if you are interested.

7 Close the Help window by clicking the Close button, located at the upper right corner of the window.

Index Page

The Index page of the Help Topics dialog box is a list of topics sorted by keyword, much like the index in a book. There is a place to enter a keyword, or you can select a keyword from the list.

Find Page

The third page in the Help Topics dialog box, Find, provides you with full text-search capability. This means that Find will search the Help files for *any* word, using a database that contains *every* relevant word that exists in those Help files (it does not search for words like *the* and *that,* however). Obviously, this is a powerful feature. If you cannot find the help you need in the Contents or Index pages, then the Find page is the place to look.

Find is a little more complex than Contents or Index. Basically, you will enter the word that you are looking for. Help will search its database, looking for words in the database that match the word you entered. It will display a list of these words, which you can choose from. Based on the word (or words) you choose, Find will display a list of Help pages that contain those words.

The Next Step

This has been a whirlwind introduction to Windows 95. Make sure you re-read any sections that seem unclear to you or access the Windows Help system if you feel that you need more assistance. Project 1 will acquaint you with the various components of the Taskbar and Start menu, explain how to launch application programs, and show you how easy it is to run more than one program at a time.

This concludes the Overview. You can take a break and exit now, or go on to work the Study Questions.

SUMMARY AND EXERCISES

Summary

- Windows 95 is a modern operating system that employs the desktop metaphor and a graphical user interface.
- Overlapping rectangular areas called windows are used to contain separate programs.
- Everything in Windows is an object.
- The mouse is the primary navigational tool for use with Windows.
- Context-sensitive pop-up menus abound in Windows, offering options and properties for the currently selected object.
- Windows can run more than one application program at any given time.
- Windows provides extensive on-line help.
- Windows must be shut down properly before you turn off the computer.

Key Terms and Operations

Key Terms
application program
book
check box
click
combo box
command button
double-click
drag
drop-down menu
frame
graphical user interface (GUI)
group box
icon
left mouse button
list box
menu bar
menu item
menu title
object
operating system
option button
pop-up menu
process
right mouse button
scroll bar
scroll bar arrow
scroll box
shell
size grip
slider
spin box
status bar
tab
text box
title text
tooltips
topic
window

Operations
Click the mouse buttons
Close a window
Display a pop-up menu
Double-click
Get help
Maximize windows
Minimize windows
Move the mouse
Move windows
Restore windows
Select a menu item
Shut down Windows
Size Windows
Start Windows
Use a menu
Use controls

Study Questions

Multiple Choice

1. What does GUI stand for?
   a. general underlying integrator
   b. guaranteed user input
   c. graphics uniform interpreter
   d. graphical user interface
   e. grammatical universal interface

2. Which scroll bar component moves the window in the smallest increment?
   a. scroll bar shaft
   b. thumb
   c. scroll bar arrow
   d. scroll box
   e. None of the above.

3. To open a pop-up menu
   a. click the object with the left mouse button.
   b. click the object with the right mouse button.
   c. double-click the object with the left mouse button.
   d. double-click the object with the right mouse button.
   e. click the pop-up menu toolbar button while the object is selected.

4. Everything in a Window is a(n):
   a. icon.
   b. program.
   c. data fork.
   d. object.
   e. process.

5. When shutting off your computer for the day, which option should you select from the Shut Down Windows dialog box?
   a. Shut down the computer?
   b. Restart the computer?
   c. Restart the computer in MS-DOS mode?
   d. Close all programs and log on as a different user?
   e. None of the above.

Short Answer

1. Windows facilitates multiple programs being run simultaneously, which is called __________.
2. The __________ is used to resize the window.
3. Name the three components of a scroll bar.
4. Name the three tabs of the help window.
5. Name the four types of window buttons.

For Discussion

1. What is the difference between an operating system and an application program?
2. Why do you think a GUI environment like Windows 95 makes running more than one program at a time easier?
3. Describe why the mouse is so important in Windows.

PROJECT 1: GETTING STARTED WITH WINDOWS

Objectives

After completing this project, you should be able to:

- Maneuver through the Start menu
- Use the Start button and Start menu to launch application programs
- Use documents
- Run more than one program at a time
- Switch between windows using the Taskbar

USING THE START BUTTON

In the "good old days" of DOS, users were confronted with an unfriendly C:\> prompt when the system finished loading. Earlier versions of Windows improved the situation somewhat, providing a more pleasing graphical screen, with windows and icons. Unfortunately, Program Manager, the old Windows shell, was not friendly enough: New users were often unsure where they should begin, confronted with an interface that seemed to offer no help. The Start button in Windows 95 remedies this situation, providing an obvious place to begin your exploration of Windows.

Opening the Start Menu

To start Windows and open the Start menu:

1 If you have not already done so, turn on the computer system.
Windows will load.

2 If necessary, log on to Windows using your user name and password.

3 Close any open windows.

4 Click the Start button.
The Start menu opens as shown in Figure 1.1.

Figure 1.1

Touring the Start Menu

The Start menu is called a ***cascading menu*** because its submenus cascade, or flow off of, the main menu. The Start menu has several hierarchies of menus, logically categorized. The menu items on the main Start Menu are Programs, Documents, Settings, Find, Help, Run, and Shut Down. To the right of some items on the Start menu are right arrows. These arrows indicate that submenus open when you select those items. Now you will take a look at the Start menu and its major features.

The Programs Menu Item

The Programs menu item cascades to reveal a menu of application and accessory programs. Programs is at the top of the main Start menu for a reason: When running Windows, you are doing so to use application programs like Word and Excel. The Programs menu contains both *program items* and *program group items.* The ***program items,*** which may include the MS-DOS prompt and Explorer as well as other application programs installed on your system, are denoted by miniature application program icons. The programs are executable, meaning that selecting the icons will cause that program to run. ***Program group items,*** like Accessories, are system tools that are indicated on the Programs menu by a special program group icon. When you select this icon, further menus are revealed. For example, when you select the ***Accessories*** program group icon, you will see a menu of the small programs that are included with Windows. These programs include a paint program, a calculator, a word processor, and others.

To display submenus on the Start menu:

1 Move the pointer over the Programs menu item, being careful not to press a mouse button.
After a brief pause, a new menu opens as shown in Figure 1.2.

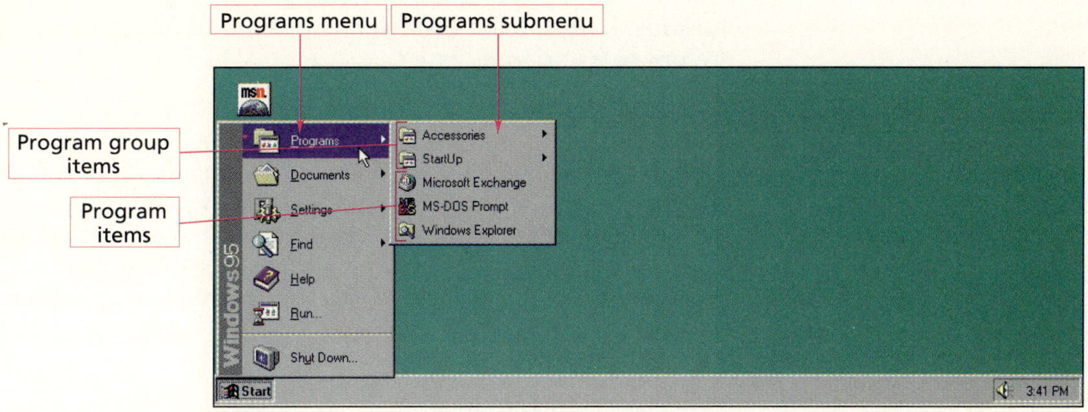

Figure 1.2

2 Move the pointer over the Accessories program group. The Accessories menu cascades open as shown in Figure 1.3.

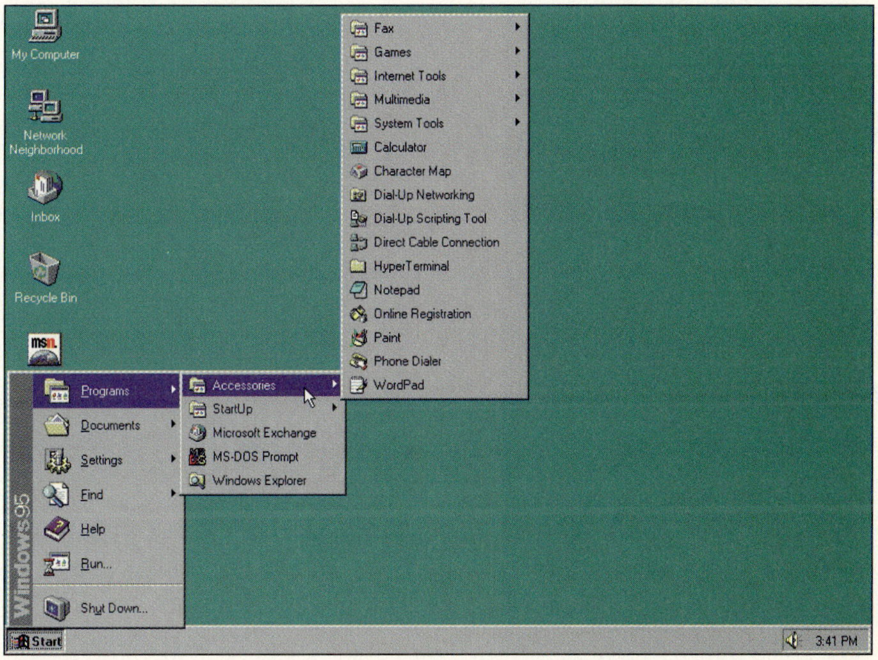

Figure 1.3

Reminder The program and program group items on your screen may be slightly different than the ones shown in the figure. Each site will have different software installations, and the Start menu will accordingly be different to reflect what software is available.

You can close each succeeding cascading menu by selecting items on previous menus. To close all menus but the main Start menu, move the pointer over to one of the items on the main Start menu that does not cascade, such as Find or Help. The menu should collapse, or close, and return to its original state.

The Documents Menu Item

The Documents menu displays a list of the last 15 documents you accessed. If, for example, you write a letter in a word processing document, save it, and then close the word processor, that letter will appear as an item in the Documents menu. This provides you with a quick way to return to the documents you have been working on recently.

The Settings Menu Item

The *Settings* menu items allow you to change the Windows configuration options, configure the Start menu, and set up your printer.

The Find Menu Item

Windows offers a powerful search utility program called Find, which can be accessed most easily from the Find menu item. You can use Find to find files or folders on your computer, find computers on a network, or find files or folders on other computers on a network.

The Help Menu Item

Help is easily accessible through the Start menu. Refer to the Overview if you need a refresher on using Help.

The Run Menu Item

The Run menu item allows you to run a Windows or DOS program quickly by typing its name and pressing ENTER Typically, it is used to execute infrequently accessed programs that are not represented in the Start menu.

The Shut Down Menu Item

As described in the Overview, the Shut Down menu item brings up a dialog box with various Windows shut-down and restart options.

EXIT If necessary, you can exit Windows 95 now and continue this project later.

Working with Application Programs

Windows is pretty interesting in and of itself, but the big question is "What can you do with it?" Operating systems exist to provide an environment for application programs to run in. There are more application programs available for Windows than for any other operating system, and Windows 95 can also run programs written for MS-DOS and older versions of Windows.

You have looked at the Start menu but have not used it for its primary purpose: starting application programs. If you want to write a letter, for example, you will need to start a word processor. You have also looked quickly at the powerful Find utility, but what happens when you find the file you were looking for? Why were you looking for that file in the first place? Most likely, you wanted to open it. If it is a bitmap graphic file, then you probably want to open it into a paint program so you can edit or print it out.

Launching Programs

Programs can be ***launched,*** or started (sometimes referred to as executed or run) in many ways. Here, we will discuss the most direct way: through the Start menu. The Start menu is, as you recall, a doorway to the application programs that exist on your computer. Cascading menus lead you through program groups that contain program items. The program items on the Start menu are shortcuts, or links, to programs that exist somewhere on the hard drive of the computer. Using the Start menu does not require you to understand where these programs reside, although you will be learning about that in upcoming projects. All you need to do is find the program item you want, select it to launch the program, and then use the program.

To launch a program from the Start menu:

1. Restart Windows, if necessary.
2. Open the Start menu.
3. Move the pointer to the Programs program group item.
The Programs submenu cascades open.
4. Move the pointer to the Accessories program group item.
The Accessories submenu cascades open.
5. Move the pointer to the Paint menu item, as shown in Figure 1.4.

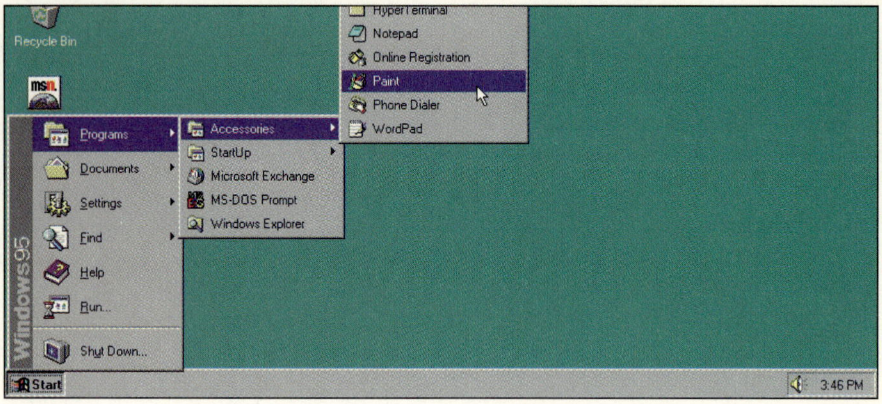

Figure 1.4

6 Select the Paint program item to launch the Paint program. The screen should now resemble Figure 1.5. If the Paint window appears maximized, you can click the Restore window button to make it a smaller window.

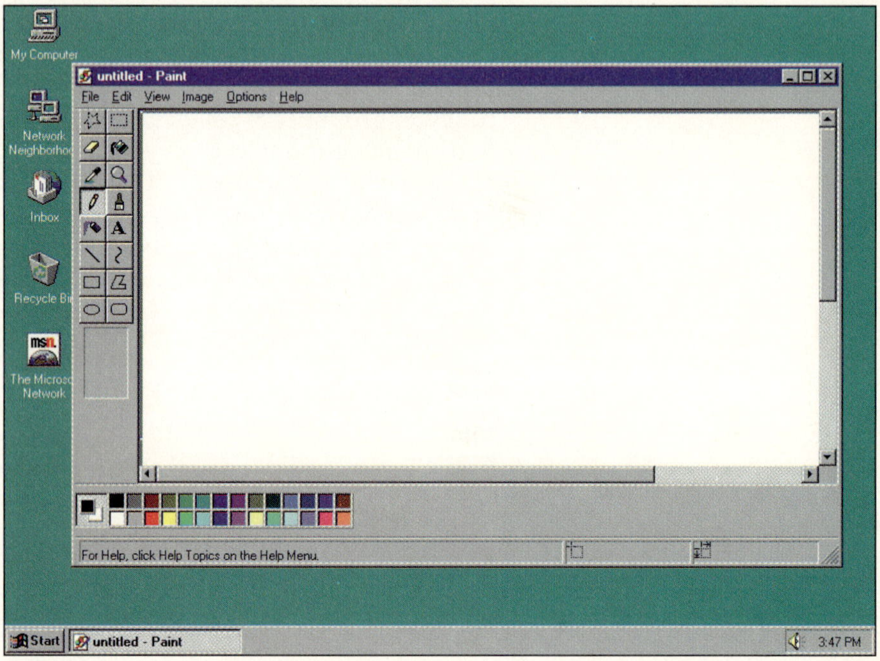

Figure 1.5

Paint, like most Windows applications, runs in a resizable window. It has an application icon, a title bar, and window buttons. It also has a ***toolbox,*** running along the left side of the window, as well as a color palette. A toolbox is a collection of icons that gives you quick access to commonly needed tools similar to the toolbars that many application programs use.

Any time a window is opened, a corresponding button is placed on the Taskbar. Opening Paint places a button on the Taskbar that has a title identical to the title on the Paint window, in this case *untitled—Paint.*

Using Documents

Application programs are the tools that you use to create *documents.* A ***document*** is any kind of data file—a letter, image, or other file that is created by an application program. Paint has loaded with the caption *untitled-Paint* in the title bar. There is no document name in the title yet because the document that is loaded into Paint right now is blank, or empty. Most application programs will start with an empty document. This allows you to get to work right away, without having to create the empty document first.

There are several operations involving documents. You can choose, for example, to save the current document or open a previously saved document. For now, you will open a Paint document, which is known as a *bitmap* file.

To open a bitmap file:

1 Select File from the menu bar.

2 Select the Open menu option, as shown in Figure 1.6.
The Open dialog box appears showing the folders and bitmap files in the Windows folder.

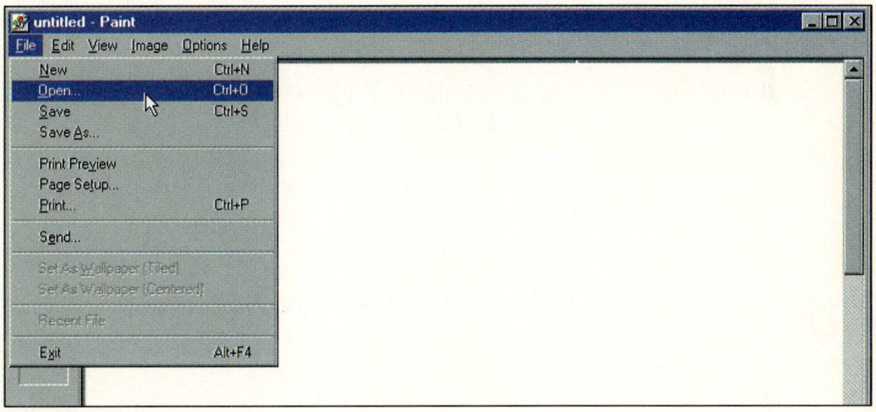

Figure 1.6

The screen will now resemble Figure 1.7.

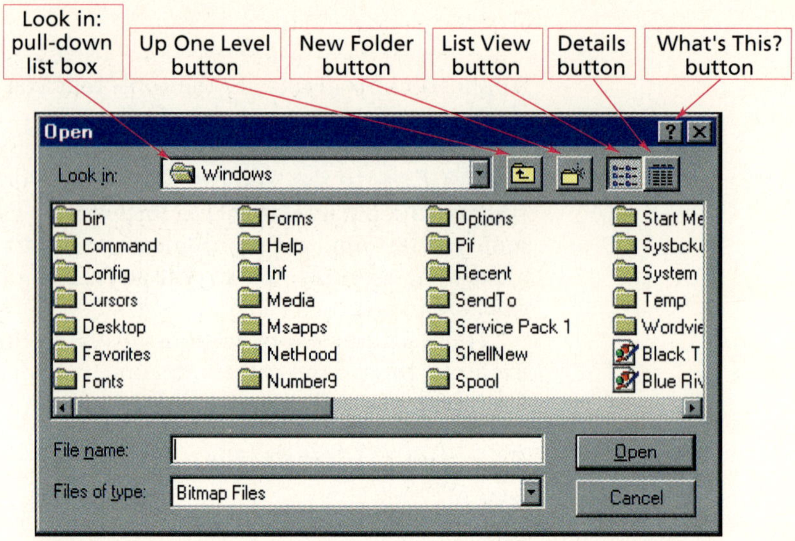

Figure 1.7

3 Select one of the bitmap files and then click the Open button. The bitmap file is now loaded into Paint.

You may want to play around with Paint for a few minutes—it is a fun program. It allows you to create 256-color graphical images and has a surprisingly broad range of tools, given the fact that it comes free with Windows. When you are done painting, you will take a look at how application programs in Windows can coexist with each other. Make sure you leave Paint running, though; you will be using it in the next section.

Multitasking with Windows

The ability of an operating system to run more than one program at a time is called ***multitasking.*** Windows supports multitasking handily—you can have dozens of programs running in Windows with little loss in speed, especially if your computer has a lot of memory. The usefulness of multitasking is something that is hard to understand until you have experienced it. You may think that you would never want to run more than one program at a time, but once you start using this feature, you will find it hard to believe that there was a time when such a thing was impossible. Like most features in Windows, multitasking is handled in a straightforward way. You will now launch a second program to demonstrate some simple multitasking techniques.

To launch another application program:

1 Make sure that Paint is still running.
If it isn't, follow the steps in the previous section to launch Paint again.

2 Open the Start menu, select the Programs group item, and then select Accessories.

3 Select WordPad.
WordPad is a word processor that is provided free with Windows. After a brief pause while the program loads, the WordPad window appears as shown in Figure 1.8.

Figure 1.8

When two or more windows are open, you can choose which window is the current, or selected, window by selecting the title bar of the program you wish to bring to the foreground.

> ***Tip*** You could actually select any area of a program's window to bring it to the foreground. It is safest to select the title bar, however, because you could cause an unintended action to occur if you select an area of the window that contains controls or data.

To switch between running programs:

1 Use the mouse skills you developed in the Overview to resize and drag the Paint and WordPad windows as necessary so the screen resembles Figure 1.9. Make sure that WordPad is in the foreground by selecting its title bar.

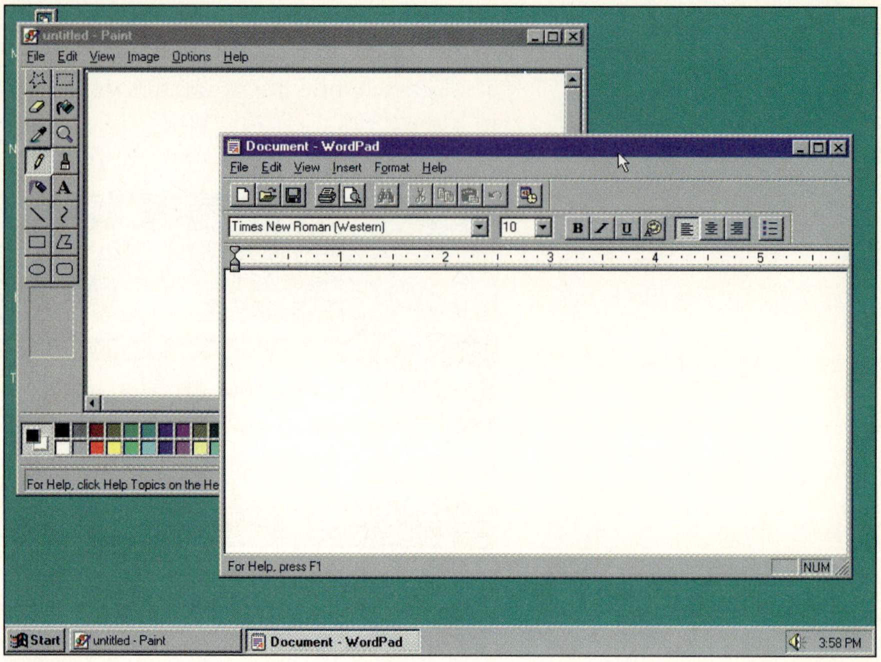

Figure 1.9

2 Select the Paint title bar.
The WordPad title bar becomes gray, indicating that it is no longer the current window. Paint's title bar, meanwhile, becomes blue, and the entire Paint window springs to the foreground and overlaps WordPad. This effect is shown in Figure 1.10.

Figure 1.10

3 Select the WordPad title bar to bring it to the front again.

Reminder This module uses the default Windows screen colors. If your setup has been modified, the colors may be different.

Using the Taskbar to Switch Between Programs

The method of selecting each program's title bar works fine if you can get at the title bars, but what happens when a window is maximized and you want to reach another window that is completely hidden beneath the maximized window? An inelegant solution would be to minimize the maximized application and then restore it when you were done with the other window. While this would work, there is a better way. You will recall that the Taskbar displays a button for each window that is open. This includes windows that are open but minimized. Selecting a window's Taskbar button will bring that window to the front and make it the currently selected window.

To use the Taskbar to switch between programs:

1 Click the Maximize window button to maximize the WordPad window. Now the Paint window is hidden, although Paint is still running.

2 Click Paint's Taskbar button, as shown in Figure 1.11.

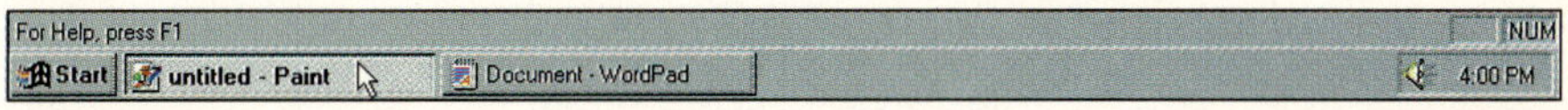

Figure 1.11

Paint now jumps to the front.

3 Click WordPad's Taskbar button.
WordPad, once again, is the current window.

4 Close the WordPad and Paint windows and any other windows that may still be open.

You will find the Taskbar very convenient as you use Windows. Many application programs are run maximized, and the Taskbar gives you an easy way to switch from window to window, similar to the way that a channel-changer on a television set can switch from one TV station to another. You know that a television program on one channel is still being shown even if you are watching something else. You can verify this by changing channels if you wish. The Taskbar accesses running programs in a similar manner.

The Next Step

Windows is a powerful operating system that can exist on a stand-alone computer or on a network. It supports a variety of controls that make interacting with the operating system easy, and it lets you run multiple programs at the same time. This multitasking is made easier with the Taskbar, which allows you to switch among all running programs. In the next project you will begin your exploration of file management. Managing files is important on any computer, and My Computer offers a simple yet powerful interface for this task.

This concludes Project 1. You can either shut down Windows now or go on to work the Study Questions, Review Exercises, and Assignments.

Summary and Exercises

Summary

- The Start menu is a logical place to start exploring Windows. You open the Start menu by double-clicking the Start button, located in the lower-left corner of the screen.
- The Start menu is a cascading menu featuring quick links to application programs and system tools.
- Find is a powerful utility program that can locate files and folders on the computer's drives.
- Documents are data files created by application programs.
- Windows can multitask, or run more than one program at a time.
- You can switch between running programs with the Taskbar.

Key Terms and Operations

Key Terms
accessories
cascading menu
document
file extension
launch
multitasking
program items
program group items
toolbox

Operations
Find files
Launch application programs with the Start menu
Multitasking with the Taskbar
Navigate the Start menu
Open a document file
Run more than one program at a time

Study Questions

Multiple Choice

1. Most application programs load with
   a. the last document opened.
   b. an empty document.
   c. a blank screen.
   d. a pretitled document.
   e. a graphic.
2. How do you get from one window to a hidden window?
   a. Minimize the window in the foreground.
   b. Reopen the application from Programs.
   c. Use the Find menu.
   d. Use the button on the taskbar.
   e. None of the above.
3. Multitasking means
   a. connecting two or more computers in parallel.
   b. connecting two or more computers in serial.
   c. connecting two or more computers to a single printer.
   d. connecting two or more printers to a single computer.
   e. running two or more programs on the same computer simultaneously.

4. *Launching* a program means to
   a. copy the program to a hard disk
   b. load a program into main memory and execute (run) it.
   c. save a data file from an application to any type of disk storage.
   d. install a program to a hard disk.
   e. exit (close) a program window.
5. What file type is commonly used to identify Windows graphics?
   a. ISO
   b. bitmap (BMP)
   c. ANSI
   d. color map
   e. palette file (WPF)

Short Answer

1. What items will you find on the Start menu?
2. How do you collapse a menu?
3. __________ are data files created by application programs.
4. How do you switch between running programs?
5. Running more than one program at a time is called __________.

For Discussion

1. What is the most direct way to launch a program? What is one way to open a document? Why are they different?
2. Why is multitasking such an important feature of Windows?

Review Exercise

Using the Start Menu

Different corporate and educational sites running Windows 95 will have varying contents for the Start menu. You should acquaint yourself with what is available on the system you use.

Begin by clicking on the Start menu and noting each of the options that initially appear. Then proceed to examine any menu items that have submenus. Get a sense of how things are organized on your particular system—what the major branches and subbranches of the Start menu contain. Practice "backing out" of submenus with the mouse. For the Programs submenu, write down a list of the items available (including the submenus within Programs).

Assignment

Multitasking and Window Manipulation

Use the Start menu to launch the following three accessory programs: Calculator, Paint, and WordPad. Maximize each program's window. Practice using the Taskbar buttons to switch among the three programs. Finally, practice resizing, moving, and minimizing each program's window. When you are finished, close each of the programs.

Project 2: File Management with My Computer and Explorer

Objectives

After completing this project, you should be able to:

- Use My Computer and Explorer to browse through the resources on your computer
- Recognize and use folders and files
- Create, copy, move, rename, and delete files
- Use Cut, Copy, and Paste with files

Managing Files with My Computer

The hard drive on the computer you are using is filled with thousands of ***files.*** Don't worry, that's not a bad thing—the files on the computer make up the Windows operating system, the application programs you use, and the documents you create. A file is nothing more than a collection of ***bytes,*** small units of information storage that are magnetically smeared across the surface of a disk or etched with a laser onto the underside of a CD-ROM.

Windows offers several methods of dealing with files. In this project you will be exploring the simplest file-management tool: My Computer. You will recall that the My Computer object, an icon sitting on the Windows desktop, is intended to be the obvious place to go when you want to look at the files and resources on your computer.

My Computer is a browser and file manager. This means that it is used to examine and manipulate the files that exist on your computer's disk drives. It also supplies a front end, or interface, to various system resources like configuration options, printers, and Dial-Up Networking.

Tip Dial-Up Networking is not installed on every Windows system.

Taking a Closer Look at My Computer

It's time to take a closer look at the My Computer window and examine its various components. This section focuses on the objects that are specific to My Computer.

To open the My Computer window:

1 Start Windows if you have have not already done so, and log on to the network if required.

2 Insert a blank formatted diskette in drive A: if you have not already done so.

3 Double-click My Computer.
The My Computer window opens as shown in Figure 2.1

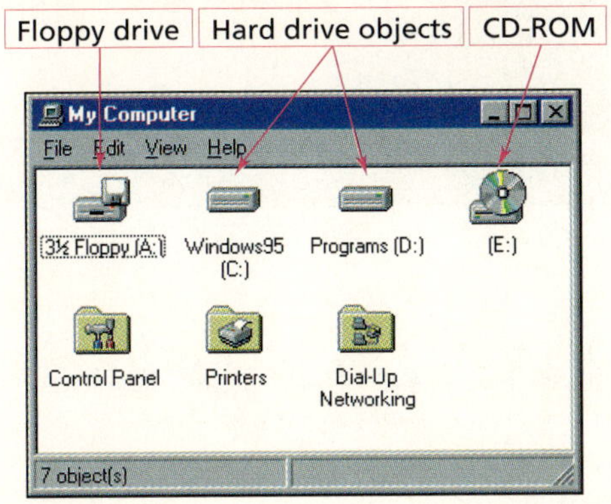

Figure 2.1

Reminder The My Computer window on your system may differ slightly, depending on the hardware and software that is installed. Some computers will have two or more floppy drives, or only one hard drive. Some may not have a CD-ROM drive. You may also not see a Dial-Up Networking folder. Don't worry, the basics will be the same.

The My Computer window consists of various objects that represent physical and logical locations in your computer. Physical locations include all types of drives: floppy, hard, CD-ROM, and others. The logical locations are represented by icons that look similar to file folders. These special folders represent system resources, such as printers and system configuration tools.

The File System

The computer's file system consists of at least one hard drive, usually C:, and at least one floppy drive, usually A:. The C: drive is the boot, or start-up, drive, and it is from here that the system will load when you start the computer. Back when DOS was king, you would be confronted with a C:\> prompt when the system finished booting and would then have to type obtuse commands to navigate through the file system. Today, Windows boots to a graphical interface, and to navigate through the file system, all you need is a mouse. For starters you will take a look at the file system on the C: drive.

To look at the file system on drive C:

1 Double-click the C: drive icon.
A new window opens as shown in Figure 2.2

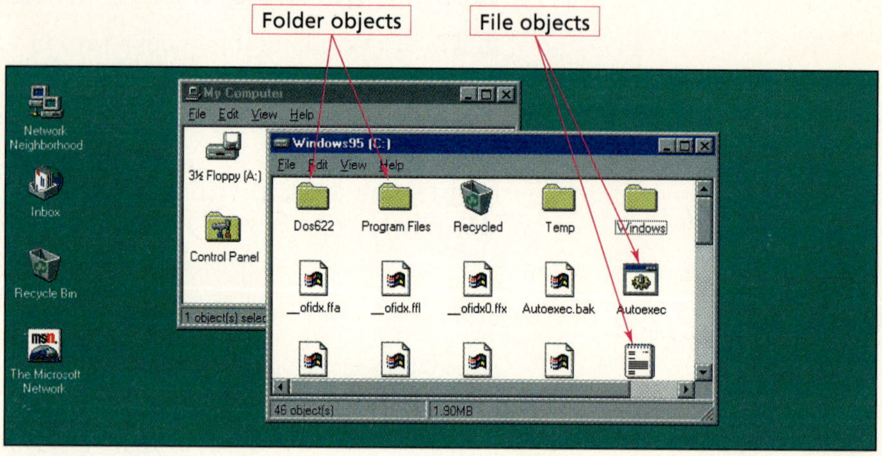

Figure 2.2

The new window displays the contents of drive C:.

Files and Folders

The C: drive contains files and *folders.* ***Folders*** are objects that contain files and possibly other folders. When the IBM PC first came out, there was no way to store files in folders; files on any given disk (usually a low-capacity floppy disk) all had to be in the single root directory of the disk. As advancements in storage capacity and the proliferation of files made this method unreasonable, the ability was added to allow folders, or directories as they were then called, to exist on a disk. This made it possible to arrange files logically on a disk so you could, for example, have separate directories for your DOS files, word processing program files, and data files. Today, computer file systems are made up of many nested folder levels, with folders inside of folders inside of folders.

You may have heard the term ***tree*** used to describe a directory structure. In many ways a directory structure *is* like a tree, but the tree is upside down. As shown in Figure 2.3, a simple directory structure would have the ***root,*** or ***parent,*** folder at the top. The root can have files in it (like startup files that need to be there when the system boots), and folders, like Windows and Temp. These folders can then have files and other folders inside of them (and they do—the Windows directory contains hundreds of files in dozens of directories!).

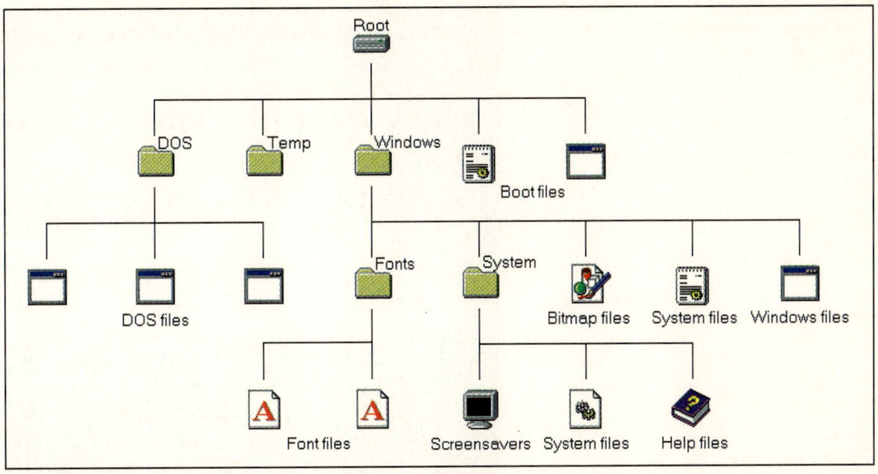

Figure 2.3

Opening Folders

Every time you open a drive object in My Computer, a new window opens, displaying the name of the drive in its title bar to let you know what you are looking at. You are also confronted with a list of folders and files that are contained within that drive. Opening a folder will likewise display the contents of that folder.

To open a folder in My Computer:

1 If it is not already open, double-click the drive C: icon in My Computer.

2 Double-click the folder called Windows.
A new window opens as shown in Figure 2.4.

> ***Tip*** *Windows* is the default name for the directory where the Windows files are stored. It is possible, however, for this directory to have another name, like Win or Win95.

Notice that folders are displayed first, in alphabetical order. Then files are displayed, also alphabetically. Notice also that a Taskbar button is created for every window you open from My Computer, allowing you to easily navigate among these windows. Figure 2.4 shows the three Taskbar buttons and windows that you should see.

Figure 2.4

Running Programs from My Computer

You can also execute programs from My Computer by double-clicking that program or its icon. You will try this out with a program called Notepad, which is a simple text editor that comes with Windows.

To run a program from My Computer:

1 Use the scroll bars to scroll through the Windows folder until you find the Notepad program icon.

2 Double-click the Notepad icon.
The Notepad program opens. As you would expect, a new Taskbar button for Notepad is created as well.

3 Click the Close button to close Notepad.
Alternatively, you could choose Exit from the File menu.

Navigating Through Multiple Windows

Now you have got a number of windows open, and the screen is starting to get a bit cluttered. My Computer is consistent in the way that *something* happens every time you double-click an object. If you double-click a program file, that file executes. If the file is a document, then that document is loaded into an application program that is able to display it. If a folder is double-clicked, a new window opens.

This type of reaction from the system is great because it gives you feedback on your actions. The problem is, how do you deal with all those windows on the screen if you have been opening folder after folder? It is possible to have dozens of open windows on the screen.

Unfortunately, there is no easy answer. Some people like the way My Computer does things. Others, especially those who enjoyed using the File

Manager in Windows 3.1, will probably like using Explorer more than My Computer. Explorer performs the same functions as My Computer using a slightly different interface. The differences between Explorer and My Computer are described later in this project.

EXIT If necessary, you can exit Windows 95 now and continue this project later.

Manipulating Files and Folders

Browsing through the file system, opening and closing files, is all very nice, but you need to have a reason for doing so. The types of operations that you can do with files and folders is extensive, but the most common are creating, copying, moving, renaming, and deleting.

Creating Files

You can create document files in Windows with application programs, but you can also create certain types of files without opening an application at all. The types of files you can create this way are determined by the software installed on your computer. With only Windows installed, you should be able to create, at the very least, text files, bitmap files, and WAV (music and sound) files. Now you will create an empty text file on your diskette.

To create a blank text file:

1 Reopen Windows if necessary.

2 Insert a work diskette if necessary, and bring the My Computer window to the foreground.

3 Double-click the drive A: icon.
A window opens, displaying the folders and files on the diskette.

> ***Tip*** If the diskette in drive A: is not formatted (prepared for use), Windows will allow you to format it now. Go ahead and do so, and then continue with these steps.

4 Right-click an empty spot in the A: window.
A pop-up menu for drive A: appears as shown in Figure 2.5.

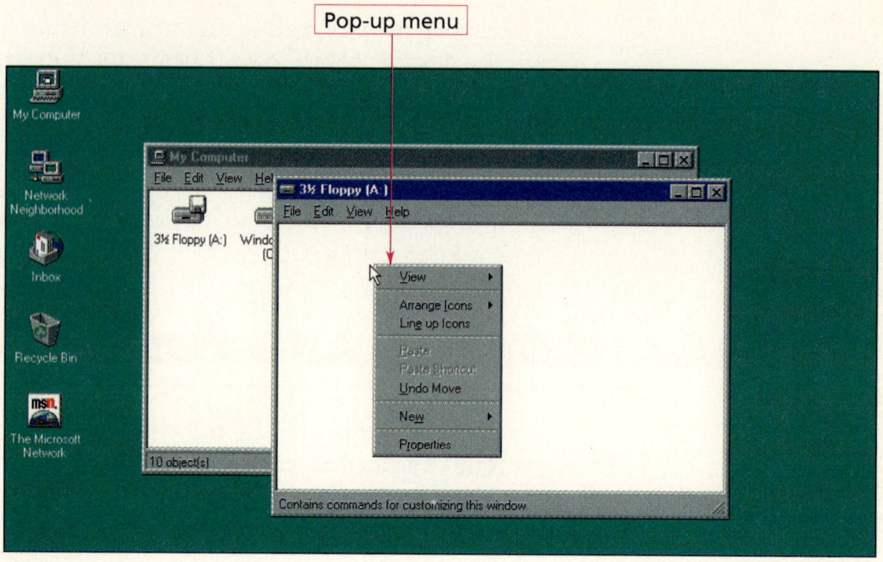

Figure 2.5

5 Select the New menu item.
A submenu cascades open. (You could also just move the pointer over the New menu item and wait a moment. The submenu will appear after a brief pause.)

6 Select Text Document.

7 A new text file appears in the drive A: window, with the highlighted title New Text Document, as shown in Figure 2.6.

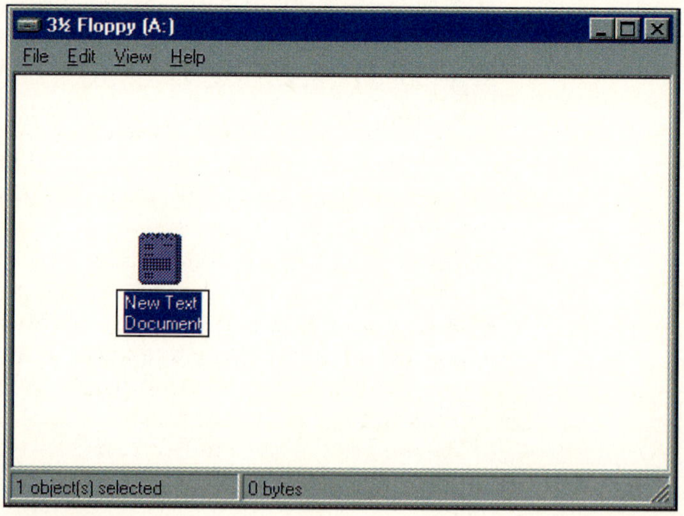

Figure 2.6

When a title is highlighted, you can change the title by simply typing a new one.

8 Type `My first text file` and press ENTER
The name of the file you have created is *My first text file*. The file itself is empty, meaning that it contains no text.

You have created a new text file without having to open Notepad or some other text editor. To launch Notepad, you could now double-click on this file.

Creating Folders

You can create new folders in a similar manner. In fact, you will find that the creation of folders is a far more common occurrence than creating blank document files.

To create a new folder:

1 As before, select a blank area of the drive A: window and right-click.
A pop-up menu opens.

2 Select New and then Folder.
A new folder appears, with the highlighted caption *New Folder*.

3 Type `My first folder` and press (ENTER) to name the new folder.
As you can see, folder creation is a relatively simple procedure.

> ***Reminder*** Folders are not files, they are containers that can hold files and other folders. Think of a folder as being equivalent to a desk drawer or actual file folder: they are all used to store documents.

Copying Files and Folders

You have created a new folder and a new file. Now what? You can *copy* your text file into the new folder. ***Copying*** a file means that you are creating a duplicate of that file in another location. The end result is that you will have two identical files with the same name in different places. When you back up a hard drive, for example, you are making a copy of the files on that hard drive and placing them in another place where, you hope, they will be safe.

The copy operations for files and folders are virtually identical. Remember that copying a folder will copy *all* of that folder's contents. This means that copying a folder full of other folders and files will make a duplicate copy of all of those items as well.

One way of copying a file entails performing an operation called ***drag and drop,*** which is one of the most common Windows operations. When using drag and drop, you select an object with the mouse and move, or drag, it across the desktop to its new location, which could be on another drive or another computer completely if you are on a network.

Objects have default operations when dragged and dropped using the left mouse button. It is better to use the right button, however, which displays a pop-up menu for each drag and drop, giving options for operations.

> ***Caution*** It is not a good idea to rely on default drag and drop operations. If you are unsure what the drag and drop is going to do, use the right mouse button. That way you cannot accidentally move a file, effectively deleting it from its original location.

To copy a file using My Computer:

1 Right-click the icon for the new text document, *My first text file,* but **do not** let go of the mouse button.
When done properly, no pop-up menu appears.

2 Drag the file icon to the icon for the new folder, *My first folder,* while holding down the right mouse button.

3 When you have reached the folder, release the mouse button.
A pop-menu appears as shown in Figure 2.7.

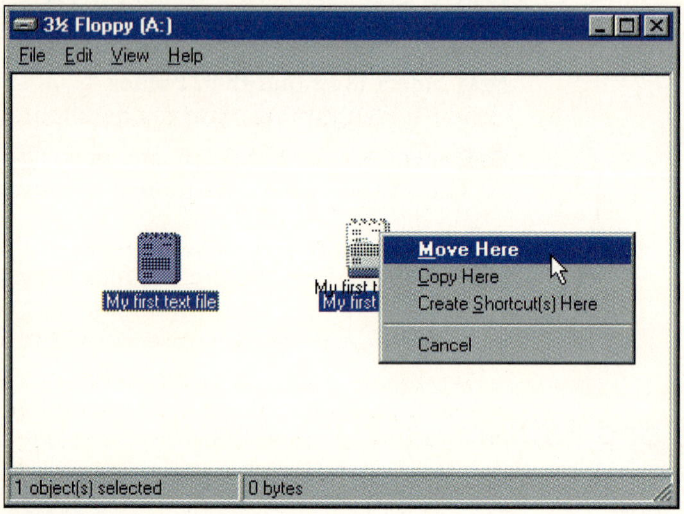

Figure 2.7

4 Select Copy Here.
The disk drive grinds away for a second, and then the window returns to the way it was before you copied the file. Notice that the original text file you created is still sitting there, as before.

5 Open the folder labeled *My first folder.*
A new window opens and displays the duplicate copy of the text file that you made, as shown in Figure 2.8.

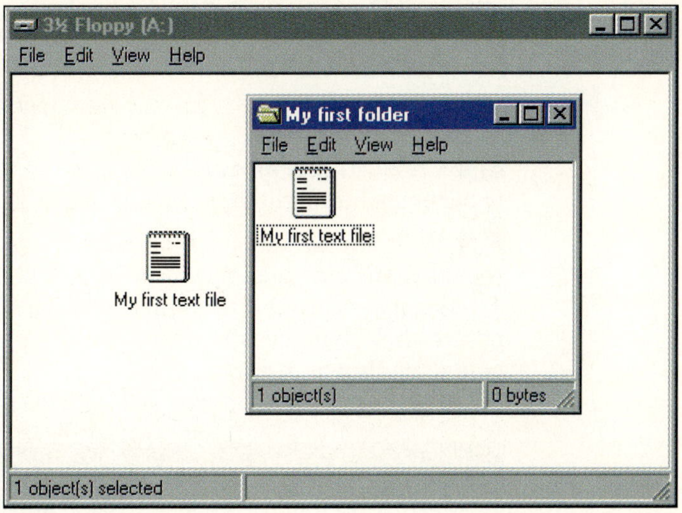

Figure 2.8

6 Close the *My first folder* window.

Moving Files and Folders

What if you want to "pick up" a file and *move* it to a new location (and not just create a duplicate)? In other words, you want to move the file from one place to another. This action is called, appropriately enough, ***move.*** The move operation is also very similar for files and folders. Remember that moving a folder moves all of its contents as well.

As you did with copying, you will move a file by performing a drag and drop operation with the right mouse button. The only real difference between copy and move is that you will choose the Move option when the drag is complete. You will begin by creating a new file to move.

To move a file:

1 Right-click a blank area in the drive A: window.
A pop-up menu appears.

2 Select New and Bitmap Image.

3 Name the new image *My first bitmap.*

4 Right-click *My first bitmap,* drag it to *My first folder,* and then release the mouse button.
A pop-up menu appears.

5 Select Move Here.
Your file disappears.

6 Open *My first folder* to see that your *My first bitmap* file has indeed been moved.

Renaming Files and Folders

When you create a new file or folder, you are given the chance to name it when it is created. You may want to rename the file later, though. This is easily accomplished using the ***rename*** operation, and the action is exactly the same for both files and folders. In this example, you will rename the new bitmap file you just created and moved.

To rename a file:

1 Click *My first bitmap.*
It becomes highlighted, showing that it is selected.

2 Wait a moment and then click it again, making sure that you select the label and not the icon.
A box appears around the object's label, and the label is highlighted. The pointer has changed into an insertion point, meaning that text can be edited, as shown in Figure 2.9.

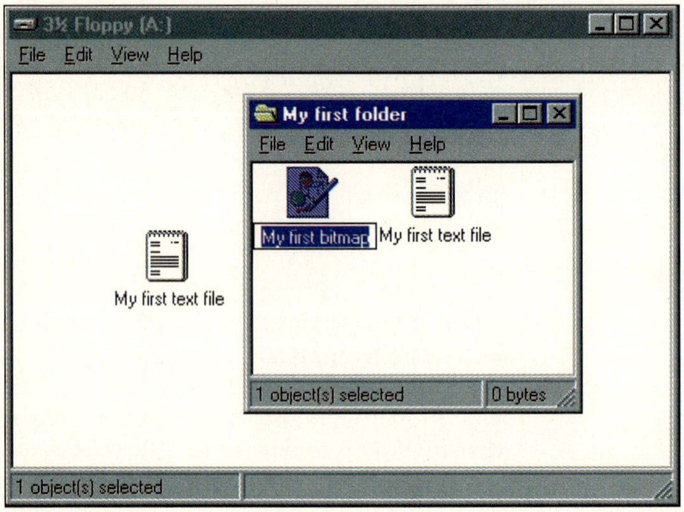

Figure 2.9

3 Type **`I renamed this bitmap!`** as the new title, and then press ENTER
The bitmap has been renamed. That's all there is to it.

> ***Tip*** If you select the title too quickly, the system will read your two clicks as a double-click and will open the file you are trying to rename. In the case of your bitmap file, Windows will launch Paint. If this happens, close Paint and try again—this time making sure to time your clicks a little farther apart.

Deleting Files and Folders

There comes a time for every file or folder when it has outlived its usefulness. The demonstration files and folder you have been working with were fun for a while, but their services are no longer required. You will now delete them. Deleting a file sounds rather ominous, but in fact deleted files and folders can be recovered later under certain conditions.

When you delete Windows files, they are placed in a special folder called the Recycle Bin. The Recycle Bin is represented on the Windows desktop by the Recycle Bin icon. It works like a real recycle bin: When you delete a file or folder, it is placed in the Recycle Bin (which is really just a folder) so you can reuse it later. To physically remove the file from the hard drive forever, you must empty the Recycle Bin.

You will now delete the newly created text document and folder (which has two files in it). You could delete them separately, but Windows supports a handy extended-selection feature that will allow you to delete both objects at once.

To delete files and folders with My Computer:

1 If it is still open, close the window *My first folder*.
The drive A: window remains open and is in the foreground.

2 Drag the pointer across the window, creating a rectangular region that covers the *My first folder* and *My first text file* objects, as shown in Figure 2.10.

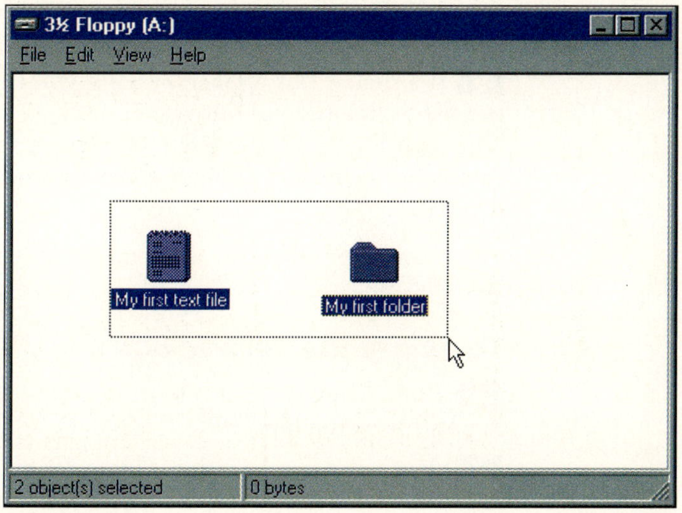

Figure 2.10

Make sure you do not select any other objects.

> ***Tip*** You can also select multiple objects with CTRL To do this, select the first object normally. Then hold down CTRL and select each additional object.

3 Release the mouse button and position the mouse pointer over either of the selected icons.

4 Holding the mouse button down, drag the two files to the Recycle Bin icon on the desktop, as shown in Figure 2.11.

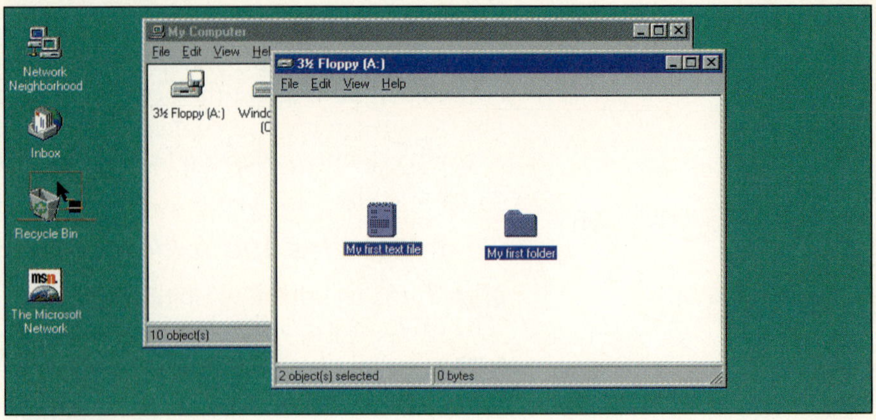

Figure 2.11

5 Release the mouse button.

6 If a dialog box appears, asking you if you are sure you want to delete the files, click the yes button.
The icon for the Recycle Bin changes from an empty looking bin to one that is full of papers. This is a visual indication that the files have been deleted.

To remove these files from the hard drive for good, you must empty the Recycle Bin.

To empty the Recycle Bin:

1 Right-click the Recycle Bin object.
A pop-up menu appears.

2 Select the option titled *Empty Recycle Bin.*
A dialog box will appear, asking you if you are sure that you want to delete the files. You are.

3 Click the Yes button.
The files are now removed for good.

4 While you are cleaning up, close any other windows that may be open, using the skills you have developed thus far.

Using Cut, Copy, and Paste with Files

As you become more acquainted with various application programs, you will find that you frequently use the operations Cut, Copy, and Paste. These operations are similar to the Move, Copy, and Delete operations you looked at earlier. In the past Cut, Copy, and Paste were used in application programs like word processors to manipulate text. Today they are integrated right into Windows and are used to manipulate files and folders as well. You can access Cut, Copy, and Paste most easily by right-clicking the object you want to manipulate and then selecting the appropriate options in the resulting pop-up menu.

> ***Tip*** You can also access the Cut, Copy, and Paste operations from the Edit menu of almost any window.

Cut and Paste

The Cut operation is used in conjunction with Paste to move a file or folder. You will recall that moving a file or folder means that you delete it from its original location and transfer it to a new location. It is analogous to grabbing any object you may find around the house and putting it someplace else. The object still exists, but it is in a different place.

Reminder Multiple selections are possible as well when performing Cut and Paste, or Copy and Paste, operations. You can select more than one file and/or folder and perform these same operations.

To Cut and Paste a file from My Computer:

1 Double-click the My Computer icon.
The My Computer window opens.

2 Double-click the A: drive.
A new window opens.

3 Create a new text file called CutNPaste using the skills you developed in the previous section.

4 Right-click CutNPaste and select the Cut option from the pop-up menu that appears.
The CutNPaste file icon dims somewhat, indicating that it is ready to be moved.

5 Create a new folder named Temp and double-click on it to open the folder.
A window opens, displaying Temp folder.

6 Right-click a blank area of the Temp window.
A pop-up window appears.

7 Select Paste.
The CutNPaste file is moved into the Temp folder.

8 Close the Temp window.
You can no longer see the CutNPaste file in the window that displays the contents of the Text folder, because it is now in the Temp folder.

9 Close the drive A: and My Computer windows.

Copy and Paste

Copy and Paste are used together when you want to make a duplicate of a file or folder, but want to leave the original where it was. The operations are the same as those used in the Cut and Paste example above, with the only difference being that you select Copy instead of Cut.

As you can see, there are a wealth of file-browsing and management options in Windows. For users in a network environment, the same concept of browsing extends to the network as well.

Using Windows Explorer

My Computer provides a basic way to browse the file system and perform file management. Advanced users appreciate a more streamlined interface than My Computer, though, and some people may not like the way My Computer opens a new window every time they double-click a folder or drive object. Windows addresses these issues with an advanced browser and file manager called Windows Explorer, or simply Explorer. Explorer is everything that My Computer is and more, and it offers an advanced interface with which to navigate through the resources on the computer.

The Explorer program allows you to perform any file-management duties, run programs, and open documents, all from a single dual-paned window. This window, shown in Figure 2.12, is split in half vertically. The left half, or ***All Folders pane,*** displays drive and folder icon objects and the right pane, called the ***Contents pane,*** shows the files and folders in the current drive or folder. Opening a folder or drive in Explorer will *not* cause a new window to open, although it will cause the view in the Contents pane to change.

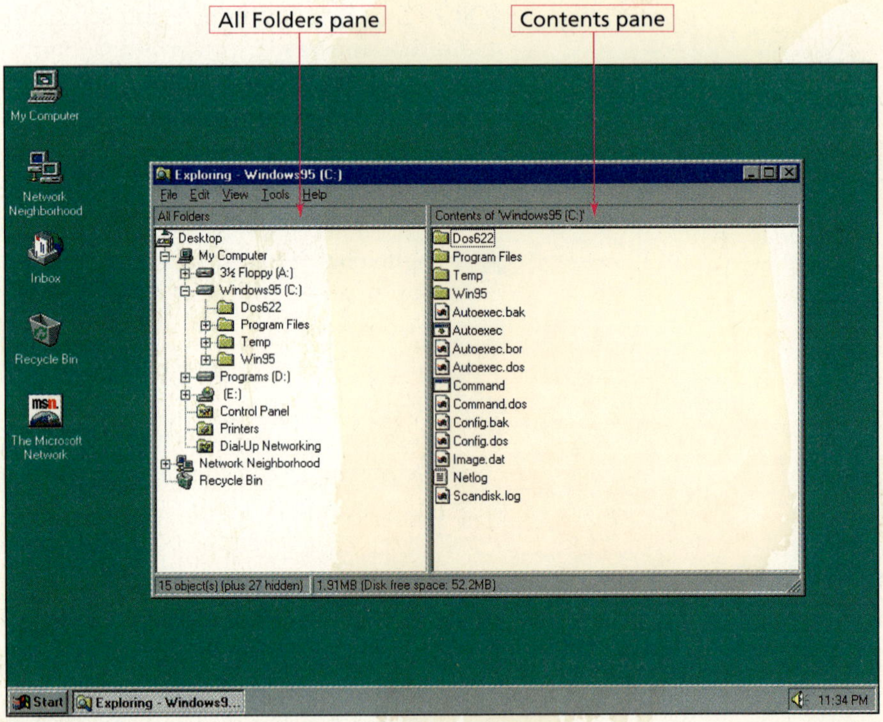

Figure 2.12

Launching Windows Explorer

Explorer, like many programs in Windows, can be launched in several ways. By default, Explorer appears in the Programs group of the Start menu.

To launch Explorer:

1 Click the Start button.
The Start menu appears.

2 Move the pointer over the Programs item.
A submenu opens, as shown in Figure 2.13.

3 Click the Windows Explorer item to launch Explorer.

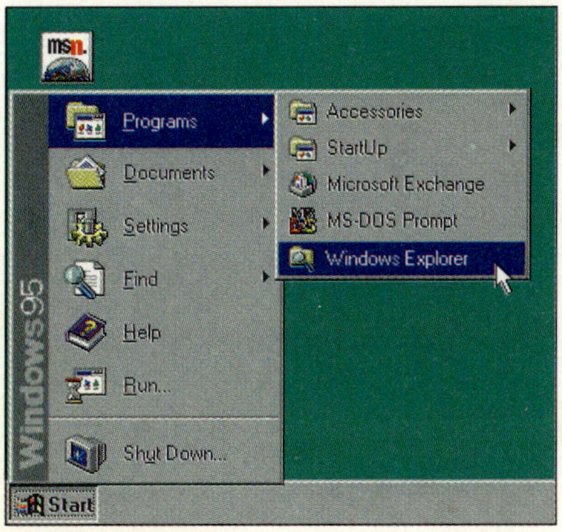

Figure 2.13

Navigating with a Dual-pane Window

The All Folders pane, also known as the Tree pane, is a collapsing "tree" view of the entire system. Each branch on this tree can be expanded and collapsed as you desire, making the view of the file system very adjustable. By default, the Explorer will display its view of your system from the desktop on down, through each of the drives and the resources that make up your computer. This tree view resembles an outline: The indenting style emphasizes the hierarchical nature of the data you are viewing. A file system is inherently hierarchical, with folders inside of folders, and the outline-style tree view offers a logical way to view this data.

Notice the lines and the boxes with plus and minus signs in them in the All Folders pane. The lines indicate the hierarchical relationship between objects. An Expand button (a small box with a plus sign in it) indicates that the object it is next to can be expanded to show more detail. You will see this button next to drive and folder objects. If a drive or folder object is already expanded, the button will change to a Collapse button (a small box with a minus sign in it), indicating that the object can be "closed" to hide the details of its contents. The Expand and Collapse buttons are shown in Figure 2.14.

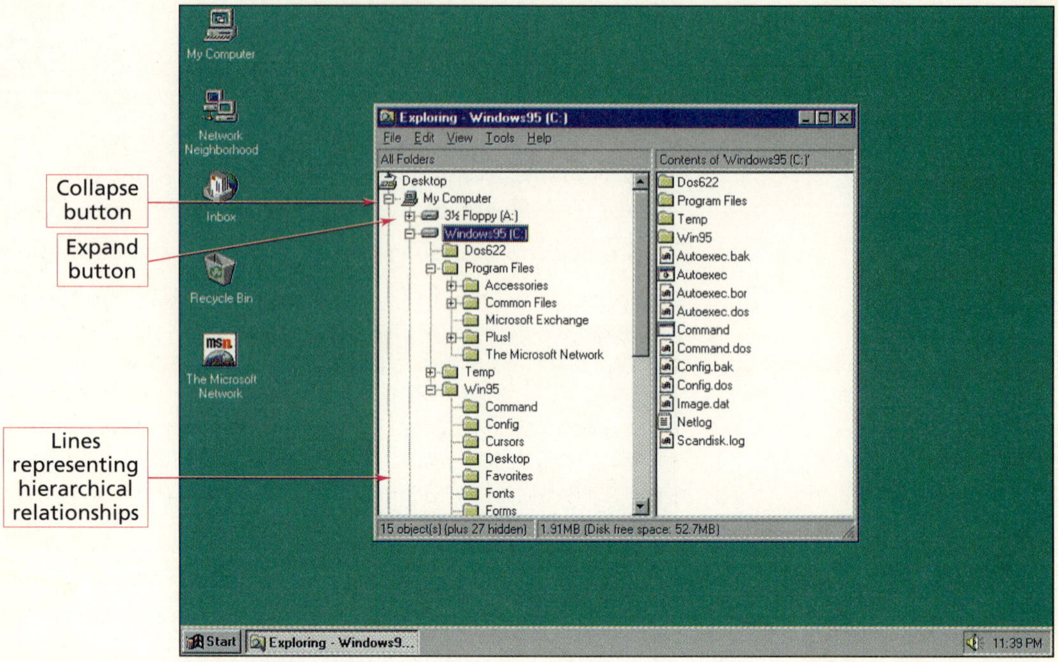

Figure 2.14

Expand and Collapse Buttons

You can use the Expand and Collapse buttons to change the view on the All Folders pane of the Explorer window. The view in the Contents pane will not be affected.

Clicking an Expand or Collapse button affects only the branch that you are working with and will not change the properties of other levels in the tree. Likewise, expanding and collapsing will not change the view in the Contents pane.

Opening a Drive or Folder

The Contents pane can only show one folder's worth of data at a time, so using the Expand and Collapse buttons allows you to navigate to the exact place you would like to view without having to display each subsequent branch in the Contents pane. At some point, though, you will want to see the details in the Contents pane; you can do this by clicking the icon in the All Folders pane that represents the object whose contents you would like to view.

Drives and folders can be opened by clicking their icons in the All Folders pane or by double-clicking them in the Contents pane.

To display the contents of a drive or folder in the Contents pane, you can single-click that object's icon in the All Folders pane or double-click the icon if it is in the Contents pane.

CHANGING VIEW STYLES FOR FOLDER CONTENTS

You can easily change the way items are arranged in the Explorer window. By default, Explorer uses ***List view,*** which automatically sorts the files and folders by type and then alphabetically within each type group. Folders are displayed first and then the files.

There are three other view types, *Large Icons, Small Icons,* and *Details.* ***Large Icons view,*** which is the default view in My Computer, displays the objects as icons. ***Small Icons view*** displays the objects as smaller icons—the same icons that you would see in a window's title bar, in fact. *Large Icons* and *Small Icons* views sort the files alphabetically without regard to type. Folders, as always, are displayed before files. The fourth style, ***Details view,*** adds information about each object's type and the date it was last modified. Details view allows you to sort the objects in various ways as well.

The View menu has items for each of the view styles, and these can be chosen to determine your view preference. The current view style will be marked with a bullet. Alternatively, you can select the view style using the view buttons in the toolbar, located under the menu in the Explorer window. The view buttons are shown in Figure 2.15.

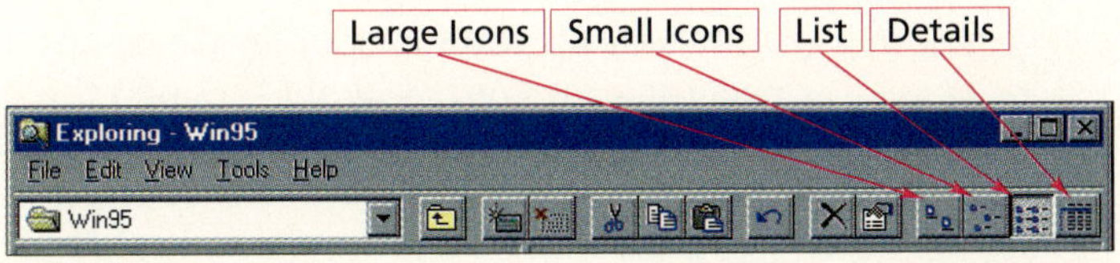

Figure 2.15

Tip If the toolbar is not visible, you can activate it by choosing Toolbar from the View menu.

Tip The View style options discussed in this project are also available in My Computer.

USING THE EXPLORER TOOLBAR

The Explorer toolbar, shown in Figure 2.16, offers one-click access to many of Explorer's options. Earlier you looked at the view style buttons. Clicking a button on a toolbar is faster than searching for that option in a menu. You will now take a look at the other buttons and the Go to a Different Folder drop-down list box on the Explorer toolbar.

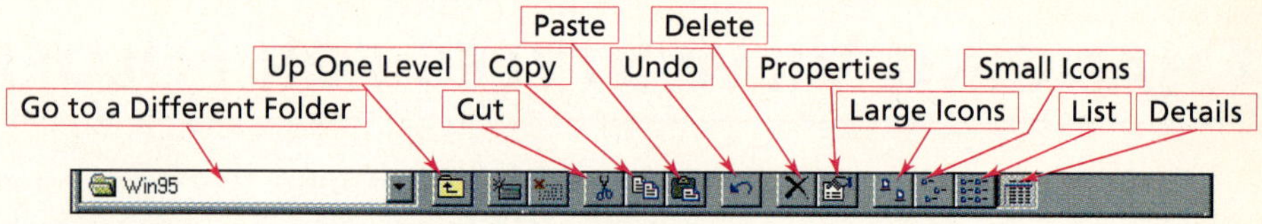

Figure 2.16

Tip If you have trouble remembering which button is which, the Explorer toolbar items have tooltips that will remind you.

Toolbar Items

The Explorer toolbar is a logically arranged collection of buttons, and one drop-down list box situated at the left end of the toolbar. In this section you will explore the various components of the toolbar.

Go to a Different Folder List Box

The leftmost item in the Explorer toolbar is the Go to a Different Folder drop-down list box. This item allows you to choose the resource you want to explore. Resources include the desktop, disk drives, system configuration options, networking resources if present, the Recycle Bin, and other items, depending on your system. To open the drop-down list box, you can click anywhere within its frame or directly on the down arrow located on the right side of the list box.

You may wonder why such a list box exists, when all of the information that it displays is available in the All Folders pane. There are several reasons, but the most important is this: Selecting resources from the drop-down list box will not affect the hierarchical structure of the tree view in the All Folders pane. Jumping from resource to resource with the list box allows you to change the Contents pane without affecting the All Folders pane. This will become important when you begin using Explorer for file management and want to retain the tree view but need to navigate to a different drive.

The Up One Level Button

As you know, Windows organizes objects in a hierarchical structure. It will often be preferable, as you navigate from folder to folder, to return to a folder you have been to previously. In the following steps you will look at the Up One Level button, which allows you to change the focus of the Contents pane to the folder directly above the one you are in currently.

Network Drive Buttons

There are two network buttons in Explorer, Map Network Drive and Disconnect Network Drive. They are used for advanced networking functions and will not be discussed in this module.

Cut, Copy, and Paste Buttons

The Cut, Copy, and Paste buttons on the toolbar work like their menu counterparts: First you select an object that you would like to move (cut) or copy, and then you click the Cut or Copy button. Next you navigate to the location you would like to place the file, display that location in the Contents pane, and click the Paste button.

The Undo Button

The Undo button is used to reverse the last operation you performed in Explorer. This will work for operations like Cut and Paste, Copy and Paste, and Delete. In the previous section you copied a file into the Temp folder on the student data diskette. If you had done this action in error, you could reverse it by pressing Undo.

The Delete Button

The Delete button, located just to the right of Undo, is used to remove objects in Explorer. It works as you would expect: You select the object or objects you want to delete and press the button.

Large Icons, Small Icons, List, and Detail Buttons

The view buttons were discussed in an earlier section of this project. If you need to review their use, you may reread it now.

The Next Step

My Computer and Explorer offer similar ways to browse through the resources on your computer where files, folders, and other resources are all readily accessible. They are also file managers and offer a wealth of file-management operations, such as Create, Copy, Move (Cut), Rename, and Delete. You can run programs from My Computer and Explorer, and double-clicking a document icon will cause the application program that created that document to load.

This concludes Project 2. You can either shut down Windows now or go on to work the Study Questions, Review Exercise, and Assignments.

Summary and Exercises

Summary

- My Computer and Explorer are resource browsers and file managers.
- A computer's file system will generally consist of at least one floppy drive and one hard drive.
- These drives can contain files and folders. Folders are objects that can contain other files and folders.
- Programs can be run from within My Computer or Explorer by double-clicking the program name or its associated icon.
- Opening a document in My Computer or Explorer will cause the application program that created that document to run, with that document loaded.

- There are several common file and folder operations, including Create, Copy, Move (or Cut), Rename, and Delete.
- Copying and Moving files can involve the common drag and drop operation.

Key Terms and Operations

Key Terms
all folders pane
byte
contents pane
copy
details view
drag and drop
file
folder
large icons view
list view
move
parent
rename
root
small icons view
tree

Operations
Browse through a file system
Change view styles
Collapse & expand the tree
Copy files and folders
Create files and folders
Delete files and folders
Drag objects
Go up one level
Manage files
Move files and folders
Navigate with multiple windows
Open documents with My Computer
Open folders
Rename files and folders
Run programs with My Computer
Use copy and paste with files and folders
Use cut and paste with files and folders

Study Questions

Multiple Choice

1. My Computer and Explorer windows contain all of the following except
   a. hard drive icon(s).
   b. floppy drive icons(s).
   c. a printer folder.
   d. a formatting folder.
   e. folders for system resources.
2. When the computer starts, which drive is normally the boot, or start-up, drive?
   a. B
   b. A
   c. C
   d. the CD-ROM drive
   e. none of the above
3. Folders can contain
   a. files only.
   b. Program Manager groups only.
   c. any object.
   d. files and other folders.
   e. other folders only.

4. What happens if you open a document in My Computer or Explorer?
   a. The document is executed.
   b. A pop-up menu appears.
   c. The document is placed in the Recycle Bin.
   d. Documents cannot be opened in My Computer.
   e. The document is opened using a program that can manipulate it.

5. Which operation would you use if you wanted to make a duplicate of a file, but leave the original where it was?
   a. Cut
   b. Copy
   c. Paste
   d. Move
   e. Create

Short Answer

1. What objects are considered physical locations in My Computer or Explorer?
2. Why is a directory structure sometimes called a tree?
3. How do you run a program from My Computer?
4. How do you create a new folder?
5. Will copying a file result in the original being changed in any way?
6. Why should you drag and drop objects using the right mouse button?
7. Will renaming a file generate a second copy of that file?
8. What file operation would you use to erase a file?
9. Cut and Paste is the same as what other operation?
10. What two operations could be used to make a duplicate of a file or folder?

For Discussion

1. The ability to create folders revolutionized file management on the PC. Why was this so important?
2. My Computer will open a new window every time the user double-clicks a drive or folder icon. How could this create a problem?
3. Describe what happens when you open a folder using Explorer. How is it different from opening a folder using My Computer?

Review Exercise

Examining the File System

Use My Computer to examine the root folders of your computer's local hard drive(s). If the computer is part of a network, take a look at the network drives as well. Get some practice resizing, moving, and closing the many windows that will be created during this exercise. Draw a tree that shows how information is organized on your system and network; make note of the major folders in the root directories, and look for other folders within these. You do not have to list the thousands of individual files!

Assignments

Dragging and Dropping Files and Folders

In this assignment you will use My Computer to "juggle" files and folders. This will provide extensive practice with window management and using the mouse for drag and drop operations.

On a blank disk, create two folders called Reports and Text. In the Text folder, create another folder called Work. Open the Reports folder, and create three new text documents called Rain Forest, Desert, and Coral Reef. Using drag and drop, move the Reports folder (which will include the files you just created) to the Text folder of the diskette. Select the two files Rain Forest and Coral Reef and, again using drag and drop, copy them to the Work folder. Rename the file Desert to Tundra. Finally, delete the Reports folder (which will also delete the files it contains).

Using Cut-and-Paste

This assignment resembles the preceding one, but you will use cut and paste operations. Using Explorer, create folders called Work and Text if they do not already exist.

Open the Work folder. Create a folder within it called Accounts. Open the Accounts folder, and create three new text documents called Payroll, Receivables, and Payables. Using cut and paste, move the Accounts folder (which will include the files you just created) to the Text folder of the diskette. Select the file Payroll and, again using cut and paste, copy it to the Work folder. Rename the Receivables file to Income Statement. Finally, delete the Accounts folder (which will in turn delete the files it contains).

PART II

Microsoft Word 7

Overview

Objectives

After completing this overview, you should be able to:

- Start the Word for Windows program
- Customize the Word for Windows screen
- Get help
- Exit Word for Windows

People have been processing words for centuries using chisels, quills, pens, and pencils. In the mid-1800s, the first typewriters added mechanical precision and speeded matters up somewhat, but they were still clumsy and relatively inefficient. Revision and editing required cutting and pasting, and ultimately retyping. It was not uncommon for a letter or manuscript to be retyped several times before it was complete. If the manuscript was for publication, it would then need to be completely retyped by a typographer to put it into publishable form.

The first real word processor was the IBM Magnetic Tape/Selectric typewriter, introduced in 1964. It recorded the typist's keystrokes on a magnetic tape and allowed the tape to be revised and then played back on an electric typewriter directly from the tape. It was awkward and slow by today's standards, but it reduced the amount of retyping needed to produce finished documents. Today, ***word processing*** involves the use of a computer to write, edit, format, store, and print documents.

Using a Word Processor

Not only have modern word processors eliminated cutting, pasting, and retyping, but they also have combined writing, revising, editing, and often the publication process itself into one integrated system. With your word processor, you can pull together elements from many sources, such as charts, graphs, photographs, or drawings, as well as words. You can format your documents as only commercial typesetters could a decade ago—using different typefaces and sizes, using columns and borders, or including graphics with your words. Word processing will make your written communication easier and probably more effective and more attractive.

Most people who use personal computers use them for word processing. Many use them for nothing else. Word processors vastly simplify the creation and development of documents. Text that is typed on the computer keyboard is stored on a magnetic disk. The text can be called back up on the computer screen and revised and saved repeatedly. At any time in the preparation process, the text can be printed out.

Modern word processors offer a variety of tools to assist in the document preparation process. Today's full-fledged word processors do much more than manipulate words. They are an integral part of the desktop publishing process, allowing you to combine words, pictures, charts, equations—even sound and movies—in your documents. They allow extensive formatting choices and can print on anything from a simple dot-matrix printer to a complex typesetting machine. Or they can prepare documents that will never be printed on paper, but instead appear solely in electronic form as e-mail or as a page on the World Wide Web.

Using Word for Windows

Word processing programs vary widely in their capabilities and ease of use. Microsoft Word for Windows 95 is an industrial-strength word processor, as capable of producing the Great American Novel or a complex technical manual as it is preparing a one-page memo or the envelope to put that memo in. Word for Windows 95 probably contains more features and capabilities than you'll ever need. Despite its power, however, you should find it relatively easy to learn and use for basic writing needs. As your needs as a writer grow, those advanced features will be there for you to use, but they won't be in the way in the meantime.

Word for Windows 95 can make your writing easier and more polished. Correcting and editing your writing with a word processor allows your ideas to flow onto paper more easily. Then you can use a variety of features to revise and develop your document. You can easily insert, delete, and correct words. You can move, copy, and delete blocks of text. Word for Windows can consult its electronic dictionary on the fly to check the spelling of each word as you type. You can use the electronic thesaurus to find alternative word choices while you're writing or revising. You can use a grammar checker that looks for common style and usage problems. Word for Windows 95 will even correct keyboarding errors as you type. For example, if you accidentally type *adn*, it will automatically substitute *and.*

Sophisticated formatting capabilities allow you to create professional-quality documents that look as though they came from a printshop rather than out of a printer. Word for Windows 95 is a ***WYSIWYG*** word processor, which means what you see is what you get. Because what you see on the screen is what you will get from your printer, you can see how formatting changes will affect your final document. With a click of the mouse, you can create numbered lists, bulleted lists, or indentations. With another click, you can create a table and then format it to present data you either type in or import from spreadsheets or databases. Click again for the Word for Windows integrated drawing program. For a term paper or lab report, you can add headers and footers, footnotes, or a table of contents. You can add columns and pictures to the format for your organization's newsletter. Word for Windows also contains a variety of templates and automatic formatting features to help you give your documents a polished, professional look.

Word for Windows 95 is a powerful writing, editing, and publishing tool. You'll find your investment in learning how to use it rewarded in added ease and flexibility in writing, in the creative options it lends to your written communication, and in the polish it allows you to give your written presentation.

Starting Word for Windows 95

In this module, you will create, edit, save, and print several documents. Work all numbered steps in order so that your document content and screen displays will coincide with those described. Your screen display may differ slightly, depending on your system configuration. You can interrupt your work at the end of any series of numbered steps and exit Word for Windows. If you wish to retrieve the document later and continue where you stopped, be sure to save your document ***(file)*** before exiting. You can print your document at any point.

To start Word for Windows 95:

1 Make sure that Windows 95 is running on your computer.

2 Click the Start button in the bottom-left corner of your monitor screen.

3 Launch Word from the Start menu.

You may need to navigate through the Programs and Microsoft Office options to access Microsoft Word, depending on the way your system and desktop are organized. Check with your instructor or lab assistant if you need help with this step.

The Word for Windows 95 screen will appear on the monitor, as shown in Figure 0.1.

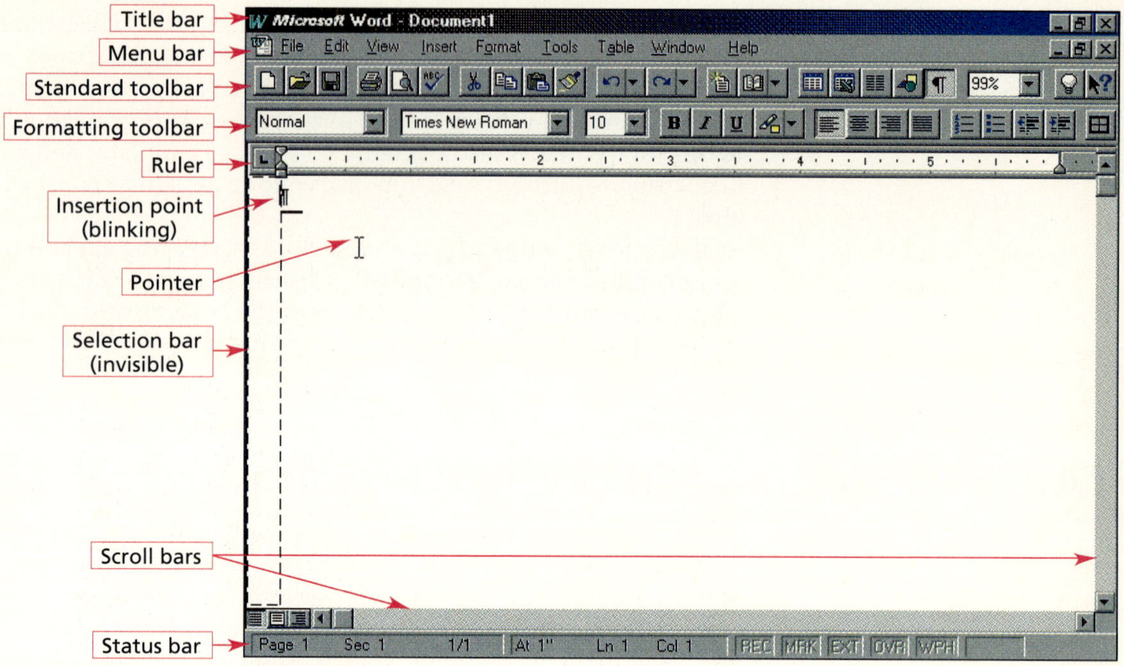

Figure 0.1

The Word for Windows Screen

The Word for Windows screen is organized into several areas that allow you not only to view your document, but also to manipulate it in a variety of ways.

Title bar: contains the title of the application (Microsoft Word) and the name of the document file you're working on (probably Document1 if you haven't named the file yet).

Menu bar: gives you access to word processing commands.

Standard toolbar: contains buttons that allow you to perform many word processing tasks with one click of the mouse.

Formatting toolbar: contains information, lists, and buttons related to formatting your document.

Ruler: displays and allows you to control margins, indents, tab settings, and so on.

Scroll bars: are used to move around in your document; the horizontal scroll bar also includes buttons to display your document in different ways.

Status bar: gives basic information about your document or about word processing modes.

Selection bar: is an invisible area at the left edge of the screen used to select part of your document with a mouse.

You can customize the Word for Windows screen to suit your preferences and working habits. The Standard toolbar, Formatting toolbar, and ruler can all be individually turned on or off. You can also add other specialized toolbars. You can even display your document full screen, with no menus, rulers, or toolbars showing.

To turn the Standard toolbar off and on:

1 Choose Toolbars from the View menu.
The dialog box shown in Figure 0.2 will appear on the screen.

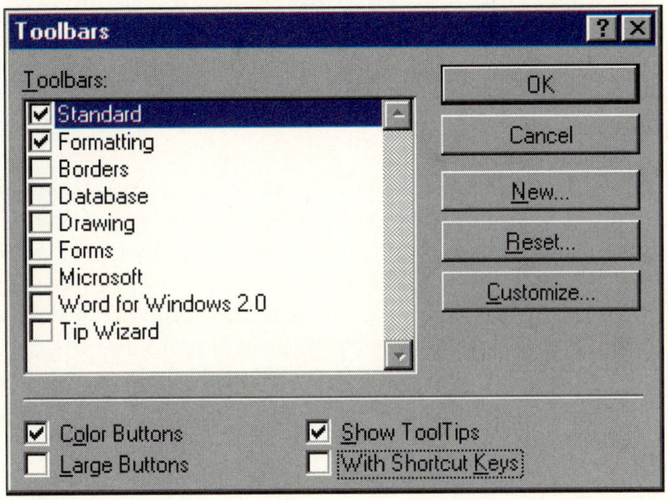

Figure 0.2

2 Click Standard to clear the check box.

3 Select OK.
Note that the Standard toolbar disappears. You can turn it back on by reversing the procedure. This time you will use the right mouse button, used in a number of different contexts, to pop up a shortcut menu.

4 Position the mouse pointer anywhere on the Formatting toolbar, and click the *right* mouse button to produce the pop-up menu shown in Figure 0.3.

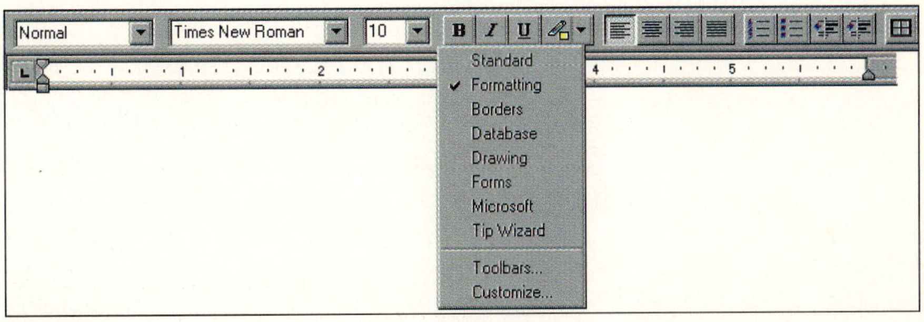

Figure 0.3

5 Select Standard from the pop-up menu to turn the toolbar back on.
You use the View menu to turn the ruler on and off. When the ruler is visible, a check mark appears beside it on the menu list.

To turn the ruler off and on:

1 Select Ruler from the View menu to turn it off.

2 Select Ruler from the View menu a second time to turn it back on.
If you want to see your text alone, with no menus or toolbars showing, you can switch to full-screen view.

To change to full-screen view:

1 Choose Full Screen from the View menu.
When you want the menus and toolbars back, you can drop out of full-screen view easily.

2 Press ESC or click the center of the Full Screen button, located near the bottom of the screen, to exit full-screen view.

Getting Online Help

Word for Windows offers several types of online Help. You can point at icons using the mouse pointer, and Word will tell you what the icons are used for. You can use a similar help feature to find out how to fill in dialog boxes. Word even includes a comprehensive online manual, with a table of contents and an index, and also allows you to type in questions in your own words to find out how to use various Word features.

The simplest of Word's help tools are ToolTips, which will help you identify the icons on toolbars until you learn the ones you use the most.

To use ToolTips:

1 Turn on the Standard toolbar if it is not already visible.

2 Position the mouse pointer over the third icon from the left edge of the toolbar, and let it rest there for a few seconds.
Notice that a small box appears, identifying the icon as the Save button. Notice also that the status bar, at the bottom of the screen, explains what the button is used for in more detail.

3 Point at other icons on any of the toolbars to see what they do.
ToolTips give you only limited information about icons. To find out about other Word features, you can use the Help button, at the right edge of the Standard toolbar. For instance, you can use the Help button to find out a little more about the Save icon or to find out about the Save As option on the File menu.

To use the Help button:

1 Click the Help button at the right edge of the Standard toolbar.

Notice that the mouse pointer changes shape to include a question mark. When you click icons or menu options while the mouse pointer has this help shape, Word will give you information rather than activating the icon or option.

2 Click the Save icon to open a Help box that explains what the icon does.

3 Click anywhere on the screen to close the Help box.

4 Click the Help button again to get the question-mark mouse cursor shape.

5 Select Save As from the File menu to find out what the Save As command does.

6 Click anywhere on the screen to close the Help box.

To find out even more information about Word features, you can consult the online manual contained in the Help Topics dialog box. You can access this information using its table of contents, its index, its database (find), or the Answer Wizard, where you type in questions in your own words.

To get help about naming documents when you save them:

1 Select Microsoft Word Help Topics from the Help menu.
The Help Topics dialog box will appear on your screen, as shown in Figure 0.4.

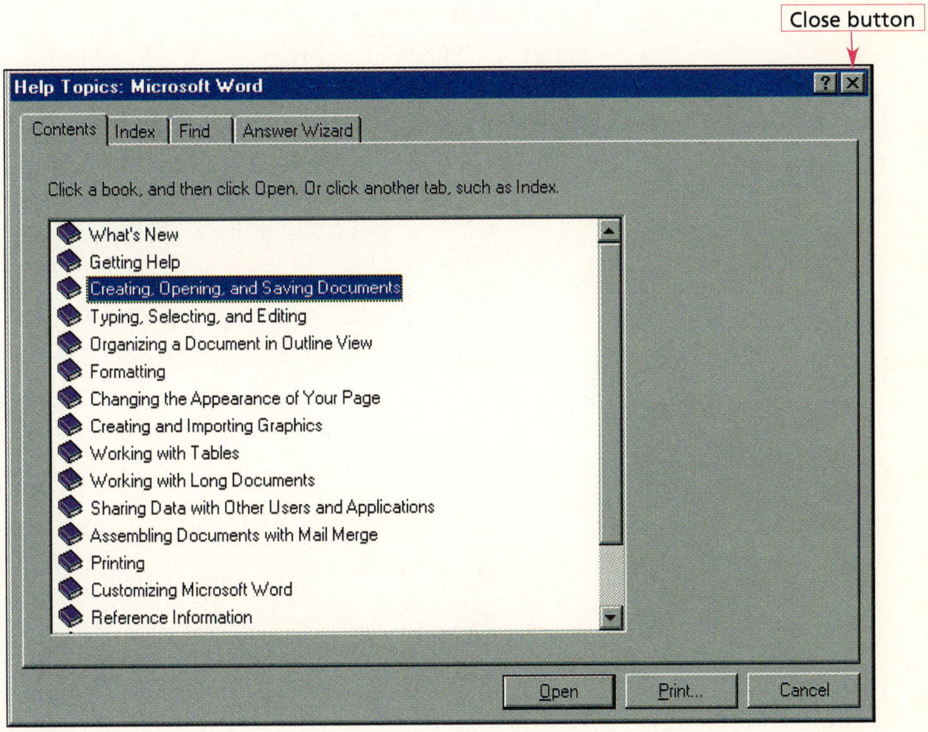

Figure 0.4

2 Click the Contents tab if it isn't already on top.

3 Click the Creating, Opening, and Saving Documents book, then click the Open button.

4 Double-click the Saving and Closing Documents book.

5 Double-click the Naming documents topic.

6 Close the Help box by pressing ESC or clicking the close button in the upper-right-hand corner of the Help box.

To get help about saving documents using the help index:

1 Select Microsoft Word Help Topics from the Help menu.

2 Click the Index tab.

3 Type **save** to locate topics about saving.

4 Double-click the "open document(s)" subtopic (located under the saving documents topic).

5. Scroll down the Help box until you see a list of topics under the heading "What do you want to do?"
Notice that the mouse pointer changes shape from an I-beam to a hand when you position it over the list of topics. The pointed hand indicates a link to further information about a related topic. If you click a link, you'll get more information about the topic it points to.

6. Click the topic "Save a new, unnamed document" to get step-by-step information about saving a new document.
7. Close the Help box.

Word can also give you a hand in filling out dialog boxes by displaying ScreenTips.

To use Screen Tips to get help in using the Answer Wizard:

1. Select Answer Wizard from the Help menu.
2. Click the small question-mark icon in the upper-right corner of the help window.
3. Click the Type your request text box near the top of the help window.
4. Click again to close the explanation box.

If you're not sure where to look for help in the index or contents, the most flexible help tactic is to use the Answer Wizard, already open on your screen.

To get help about Help using the Answer Wizard:

1. Clear the Type your request text box and type `help me` into the box.
2. Select Search.
A listing of possibly relevant topics will appear in the Select a Topic box.
3. Double-click *Getting assistance while you work* to display a help window that identifies various parts of the Help Topics dialog box.
4. Click the various links in the help window to review ways of getting help while you're using Word.
5. Close the help window.

Exiting Word for Windows

Word for Windows 95 has a safety feature to prevent the loss of text. If you attempt to quit the program without first saving your file, Word will automatically ask if you want to save changes to your file. To see how this safety feature works, you must first type something on the screen.

To exit Word for Windows:

1. Type some text on the screen. It can be anything: your name, the name of your dog or cat, the name of your favorite rock star.
2. Choose Exit from the File menu (or click the Close box at the upper-right corner of the Word window).
Because you made changes to your document before quitting, you'll get the warning shown in Figure 0.5.

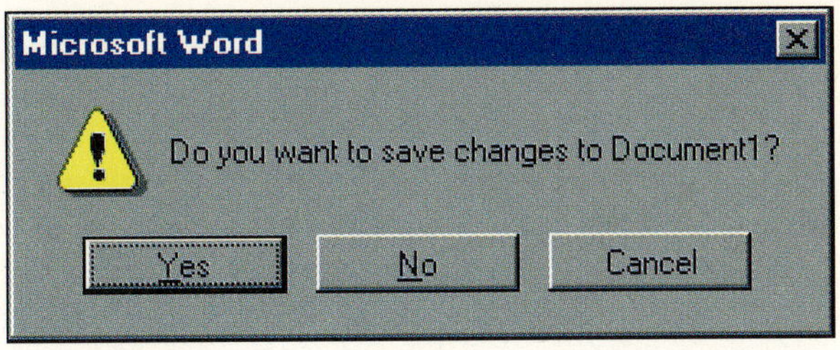

Figure 0.5

If you select Yes, the Save As dialog box will appear so that you can save your file (you'll see how to do that in the next project). If you select No, Word will quit without saving changes to the file. If you select Cancel, Word will return you to the document without quitting.

3 Select No.
This should return you to the Windows desktop.

This concludes the Overview. You can either exit Word or go on to work the Study Questions.

Summary and Exercises

Summary

- Word processing is using a computer to write, edit, format, store, and print documents.
- Word for Windows is a powerful word processing program with extensive features for creating, saving, retrieving, editing, and printing documents.
- You can modify the Word for Windows screen to suit your working habits.
- Whenever you need help with menus, commands, or concepts, you can use the Word for Windows online Help facility instead of having to page through a manual.

Key Terms and Operations

Key Terms
file
Formatting toolbar
menu bar
ruler
scroll bar
selection bar
Standard toolbar
status bar
title bar
word processing
WYSIWYG

Operations
Start Word
Get online Help
Exit Word

Study Questions

Multiple Choice

1. If you try to quit Word for Windows 95 without first saving changes to your document:
   a. The changes will be lost.
   b. Word for Windows will save the changes automatically.
   c. You will be asked if you want to save changes before quitting.
   d. You will destroy your document file.

2. To change the pointer to its Help shape (a question mark) so as to access ScreenTips:
   a. Press CTRL+H
   b. Click the Help button.
   c. Double-click the Help menu.
   d. Press and hold down the ALT and SHIFT keys.

3. What is the major reason a word processor like Word for Windows 95 saves time and effort?
   a. You don't have to retype the entire document each time you make changes or additions.
   b. You can type faster on a computer.
   c. You can format text using different typefaces and sizes.
   d. You can integrate pictures and text.

4. You can turn toolbars on and off by:
   a. pressing CTRL+T
   b. using the Tools menu.
   c. double-clicking the toolbar.
   d. clicking the toolbar using the right mouse button.

5. You normally start Word for Windows:
   a. at the DOS prompt.
   b. from the Windows Start button.
   c. from within the document you are editing.
   d. from the Windows 95 Explorer.

Short Answer

1. The __________ at the bottom of the screen gives basic information about your document or about word processing modes.

2. __________ is an acronym indicating that the screen shows your document exactly as the document will be printed.

3. Word's __________ allows you to ask for help in your own words.

4. A __________ contains a row of buttons that allow you to perform common word processing tasks with a click of the mouse.

5. To retrieve a document to edit it later, you must first save it as a __________.

For Discussion

1. How do you start Word on your system?

2. Describe three ways to access the Help system in Word for Windows 95.

3. What writing and editing functions are included in a modern word processor such as Word for Windows 95?

Project 1: Creating a Document

Objectives

After completing this project, you should be able to:

- Open a new document
- Enter text
- Display nonprinting characters
- Move around in a document
- Check spelling as you type
- Save a document
- Insert graphics
- Make backup copies of your document

In this project, you will create a new document, type text, move around in the document, make simple corrections, and save the document. You'll begin preparing a flyer for a film festival. When you finish this project, you'll know the rudiments of word processing with Word for Windows 95.

Case Study: Creating a Film Flyer

Assume that you are in charge of publicity for a film festival being organized by a campus organization. As part of the publicity effort, you and your committee have decided to produce a flyer that can be handed out to individuals and also be posted on bulletin boards.

The flyer must be bold and informative. It must attract attention at a distance, then give readers enough information to entice them to see the movies.

Designing the Solution

The festival will feature science fiction films from the 1950s that star monsters, usually either from outer space or awakened by untimely atomic explosions. Some of the movies are well made; others are decidedly "B" movie material. All are escapist, very retro, and, you hope, fun for the audience.

You want to create a flyer that captures the spirit of the festival and attracts attention. You decide to put the title of the festival at the top in bold type, then list the films below in chronological order. You'll also include information about each of the films because prospective audience members are not likely to have heard of many of them. In addition, the flyer will give dates, times, location, and admission charge for the showings.

Most writing projects are not strictly linear—that is, you rarely begin writing with the first word and write straight through to the last, ending with a final product. Instead, most of us get a few ideas down on paper, add more words, move things around, delete some words and add others, revise and reshape, change words, smooth transitions, and so on. A word processor can be a powerful tool in this evolutionary process because you can make changes without throwing any of your work away.

The festival flyer is a fairly simple document, but even it will evolve over the next four projects. You'll begin by typing the beginnings of the text. You'll add more text. You'll revise and rearrange text, as is typical in the preparation of any document produced by a committee. Then you'll polish the final product by choosing the type style and formatting the paragraph arrangement. In the end, you'll have an eye-catching flyer that will attract attention to the film festival.

Opening a New Document

Word for Windows 95 normally opens with a blank window and is ready to create a new document. If someone was using the computer before you, however, the window may already contain text. In that case, you'll need to open a blank window for your new document. (If Word for Windows isn't running already, launch it now.)

To open a blank window for a new document:

1 Choose New from the File menu.

The New dialog box will appear, as shown in Figure 1.1. This dialog box allows you to select from a variety of templates and wizards. ***Templates*** are preformatted skeleton documents ranging from memos to newsletters. A template is like a blank, formatted document that you can fill in with your own text. ***Wizards*** ask a series of questions about a document format and then use your answers to build a document for you to use. To create the flyer, you will use the default general-purpose template, named Blank Document.

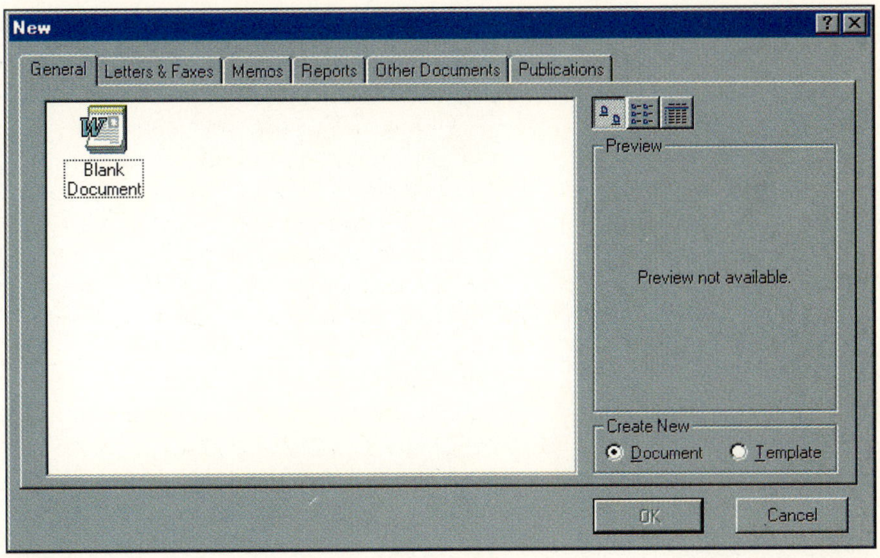

Figure 1.1

2 Select the General tab if it is not already on top.

3 Select Blank Document by double-clicking the icon, or by clicking the icon then selecting OK.

Tip You can click the New button on the Standard toolbar to open a document based on the Blank Document template.

The document area of the screen will be blank except for the blinking insertion point (|), the end mark (__), and possibly a paragraph mark (¶). The ***insertion point*** marks the position where text will be inserted or deleted when you type on the keyboard. The ***end-of-document mark*** (end mark) shows where the document ends; you cannot insert characters after the end mark. A ***paragraph mark*** indicates the end of a paragraph and forces the beginning of a new line. The paragraph mark may not show on the screen. If not, you'll see shortly how to make the paragraph mark visible.

ENTERING TEXT

In this project, you will create and edit the film flyer, the beginnings of which are shown in Figure 1.2.

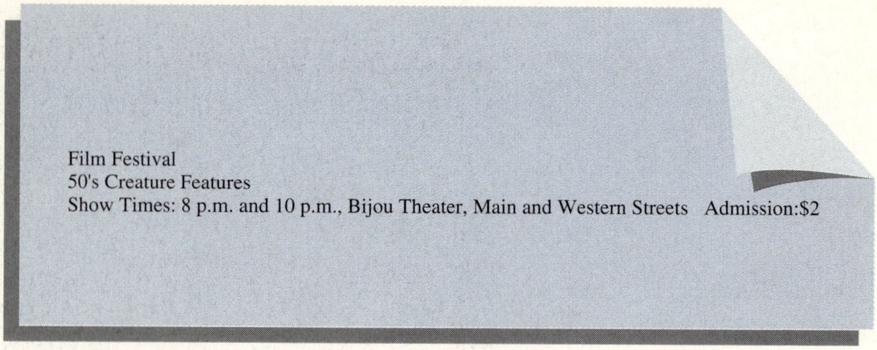

Figure 1.2

Don't worry if you make errors as you type. These errors will just give you more to practice with when you learn how to make corrections later.

To enter the first lines of the film flyer:

1 Type **`Film Festival`** and press ENTER
Notice as you type that the insertion point moves just ahead of the last character you typed. Note also that pressing ENTER forces the beginning of a new line.

2 Type **`50's Creature Features`** and press ENTER

3 Type **`Show Times: 8 p.m. and 10 p.m., Bijou Theater, Main and Western Streets`** and press TAB

4 Type **`Admission: $2`** and press ENTER

You have begun the flyer. Before continuing with it, you will learn how to display nonprinting characters and how to move the insertion point around in the document.

Displaying All Characters

Most of the characters you've just typed are printable: they will appear on the sheet of paper that eventually comes out of your printer. But some, like the spaces between words, will not be printed. ***Nonprinting characters*** include not only spaces, but also paragraph marks (inserted with ENTER) and tab characters (inserted with TAB). Often it's helpful to be able to see some or all of these characters on the screen. Word for Windows allows you to turn nonprinting characters on or off to suit yourself.

You can change the display of nonprinting characters by using the Tools menu.

To display nonprinting characters using the Tools menu:

1 Choose Options from the Tools menu.
The Options dialog box, shown in Figure 1.3, appears. You can customize Word for Windows in many ways by changing the settings in this dialog box. Right now, we're interested only in the options on the View tab.

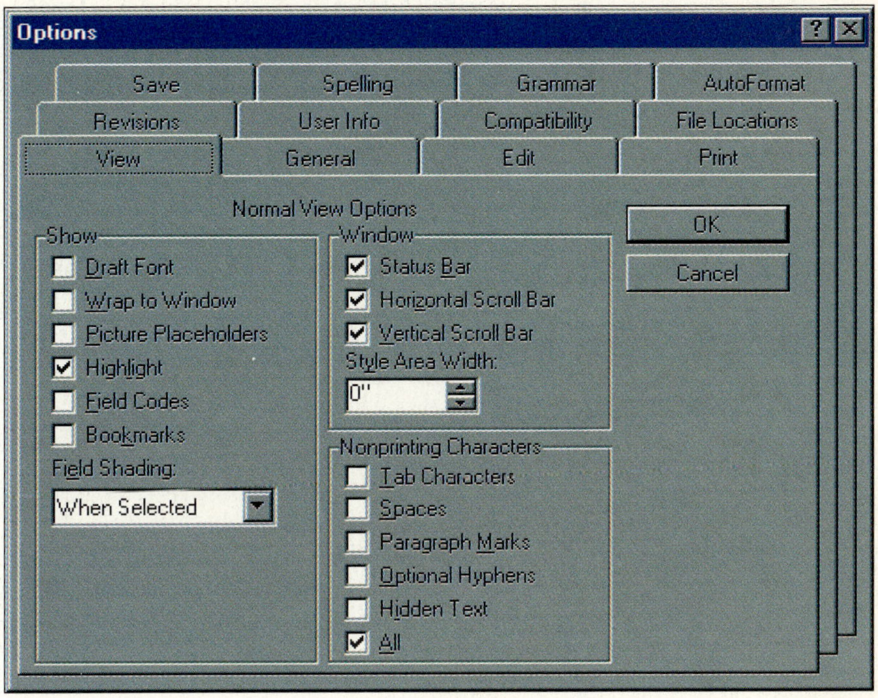

Figure 1.3

2 If it is not already visible, select the View tab, shown in Figure 1.3.

3 Select All within the Nonprinting Characters box, so a check mark appears inside the box to its left.

4 Clear all other check boxes (except All) under Nonprinting Characters.

5 Select OK.

The View tab in the Options dialog box allows you to specify precisely which nonprinting characters you want to display and which you want to stay hidden. If you just want to quickly flip back and forth between displaying and hiding nonprinting characters, however, it is much faster to use the Show/Hide ¶ button on the Standard toolbar.

To use the Show/Hide ¶ button to turn nonprinting characters on and off:

1 Make sure the Standard toolbar appears at the top of the screen. If the toolbar does not appear, choose Toolbars from the View menu and use the Toolbars dialog box to turn the toolbar on.

2 Click the Show/Hide ¶ button near the right side of the Standard toolbar.

Note that each time you click the Show/Hide ¶ button, the paragraph marks (¶) at the end of each line toggle on or off. Notice also that spaces between words, represented by a small raised dot (·), toggle on or off. And notice that the tab character, represented by an arrow (→), toggles on or off as well.

Figure 1.4 shows the screen with all nonprinting characters displayed.

Figure 1.4

Moving Around in a Document

The blinking insertion point indicates a specific location in a document: a position where some action might take place, such as changing a character or inserting and deleting text. Note that the insertion point and the mouse pointer are similar but different. The insertion point blinks and is a plain vertical line; the pointer does not blink and is shaped like an I-beam.

You can reposition the insertion point using either the mouse or the keyboard. To use the mouse, move the pointer to the new location and click once.

To position the insertion point with the mouse:

1. Position the pointer between the *e* and *a* in *Creature.*
2. Click the left mouse button.

The blinking insertion point is now positioned between the *e* and *a*.

The insertion point can only be positioned within the text of your document. The insertion point will not move into the white space at the right of the text. If you try to position it there, the insertion point will move to the end of the nearest line.

You can also use the keyboard to move the insertion point. Table 1.1 describes the actions associated with various keystrokes.

Table 1.1

Keys	Action
↑, ↓, ←, →	Moves the insertion point up or down one line, or left or right one character
HOME	Moves the insertion point to the beginning of the line
END	Moves the insertion point to the end of the line
PGUP	Moves the insertion point up one screen
PGDN	Moves the insertion point down one screen
CTRL+→ (or ←)	Moves the insertion point to the beginning of the next (or previous) word
CTRL + ↓ (or ↑)	Moves the insertion point to the beginning of the next (or previous) paragraph
CTRL+PGUP (or PGDN)	Moves the insertion point to the top (or bottom) of the screen
CTRL+HOME (or END)	Moves the insertion point to the beginning (or end) of the document

In the steps that follow, be sure that NUM LOCK is turned *off* if you are using the numeric keypad. Note as you move the insertion point how the center portion of the status bar at the bottom of the screen indicates changes in the position of the insertion point.

To move the cursor one line or one character at a time:

1. Press ↑ until the insertion point reaches the top of the screen.
2. Press ↓ until the insertion point reaches the bottom of the current document.
3. Position the insertion point somewhere in the middle of the line that begins with *Show Times.*
4. Press → until the insertion point reaches the end of the line.
5. Press ← until the insertion point reaches the beginning of the line. Practice moving with the arrow keys until you are comfortable with them.

To move the insertion point to the beginning or end of a line:

1. Position the insertion point somewhere within a line of text.
2. Press HOME to move the insertion point to the beginning of the line.
3. Press END to move the insertion point to the end of the line.

To move the insertion point from word to word:

1. Position the insertion point somewhere within a line of text.
2. Press CTRL+→ several times to move from one word to the next word in your document.
3. Press CTRL+← several times to move backward from word to word.

MAKING MINOR CORRECTIONS

One of the advantages of a word processor is that you can make corrections at any time during the document preparation process. If the ideas are flowing, you probably won't want to take the time to check the spelling of a word until later. But sometimes you'll notice a typo that you can't put out of your mind until you correct it. You can make minor corrections using the BACKSPACE or DEL key. You can also reverse previous typing or editing by using Word's Undo feature. (In Project 2, you'll learn to use even more extensive editing and correcting tools.)

Assume you want to insert *price* after *Admission* on the third line of the flyer.

To make corrections using BACKSPACE:

1. Position the insertion point between the *n* and the colon at the end of *Admission.*
2. Press SPACE and then type `price`
   After looking at it, however, you decide that *Admission* by itself is clear and decide to delete *price.*
3. Press BACKSPACE once.
   The insertion point moves one character to the left, erasing the *e* at the end of *price.*

4 Press (BACKSPACE) five more times to remove the remaining characters in *price* and restore the flyer to its original form.

Now, assume you want to remove *Streets* from the flyer.

To make corrections using (DEL):

1 Position the insertion point immediately after the *n* in *Western.*

2 Press (DEL) once.
The character to the right of the insertion point (the space) is erased.

3 Press (DEL) seven more times to remove *Streets.*

Now assume you want to see how the flyer looks with the label *Science Fiction* in front of the heading.

To make corrections using Word's Undo and Redo features:

1 Position the insertion point at the beginning of the document (in front of *Film*).

2 Type `Science Fiction` and press (SPACE)

Once you see it on the screen, however, you can tell that the label isn't really necessary and distracts from the festival title, so you decide to delete it. You can use the Undo button, shown in Figure 1.5, to reverse most word processing operations.

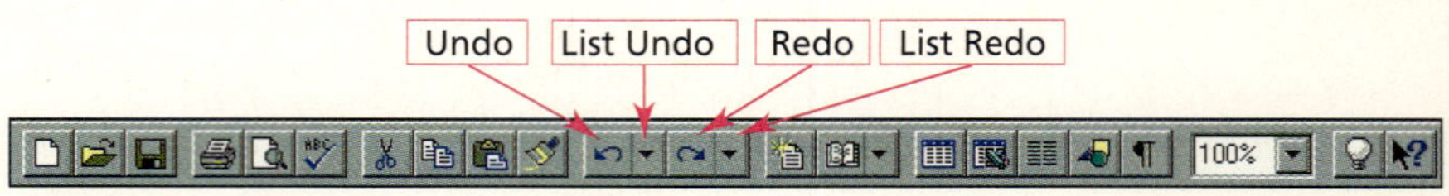

Figure 1.5

3 Select the Undo button on the Standard toolbar.
All the characters you typed are removed, and the text has been restored to its original form. Assume, however, that you're not sure about the heading and want to see it in place again.

4 Select the Redo button (see Figure 1.5) on the Standard toolbar.
This reverses the undo and restores the text. Now you decide finally that *Science Fiction* really isn't needed.

5 Select the Undo button again to remove the text.

Assume that you also decide to restore *Streets*, deleted before you added *Science Fiction* at the beginning of the flyer.

6 Select the Undo button a second time to restore Streets.

The Undo command can usually reverse any changes you have made since the last time you saved your document and does so in reverse order of the one in which you made the changes. The Undo command will reverse most (but not all) Word for Windows operations. The number of steps you can undo or redo depends on the complexity of the steps and the configuration of the computer. To see a list of operations that can be undone or redone, click the List Undo button or the List Redo button on the Standard toolbar shown in Figure 1.5.

CHECKING SPELLING AS YOU TYPE

Word monitors your input as you type and checks words against its built-in dictionary. If it can't find a word in the dictionary, it flags that word with a wavy red underline and changes the spelling icon in the lower-right corner of the screen. When Word has not detected spelling errors, the icon contains a check mark. When Word discovers what appear to be spelling errors, the icon contains a red X. To correct spelling errors, you can click the wavy underline using the right mouse button and make a selection from a list of possible corrections.

To check spelling automatically:

1 Position the insertion point on the blank line at the end of the document.

2 Type **`June 15`** and press (TAB)

3 Type **`The Blob`** and press (ENTER)

4 Type **`Paramount, USA, 1958. It's teenagers vs. ravenous Jello, as a gelatinous mass from space begins devouring small-town inhabitants.`** and press (ENTER)

If Word's AutoCorrect feature is on, the word processor will automatically capitalize *Ravenous* because it follows a period, even though the period is not at the end of a sentence.

5 Select the *R* in *ravenous* and change it to a lowercase *r*.
If Word's automatic spell checking feature is turned on, a wavy red underline will appear under *Jello.* The spelling icon in the lower-right corner of the screen will have a red X to indicate that Word has discovered what appear to be spelling errors.

6 Position the mouse pointer over *Jello,* and click the right (not left) mouse button.
A pop-up menu will appear, displaying a list of possible corrections, as shown in Figure 1.6. The correct spelling is Jell-O, a trademarked commercial name. (This spelling may look odd, but check the shelves at the grocery store next time you're shopping.)

Figure 1.6

7 Select Jell-O from the list.
The correction is made automatically. Jell-O is a proper name contained in Word's online dictionary, probably because it's an unusual word and commonly misspelled. Many proper names, however, are not in the dictionary and will be flagged as misspelled even when perfectly correct. That might include your own name, the names of people you write or refer to frequently, or the name of your town or city. If you use those words often enough, you will probably want to add them to your own personal dictionary that supplements Word's main dictionary. If you are using your own computer, Word will already be configured to store a custom dictionary where it can find and use it again, and you can skip the next set of numbered steps. However, if you are using a lab computer, you will probably need to save your custom dictionary on a floppy disk that you can take with you. The following steps show how to do that.

To save a custom dictionary on a floppy disk:

1 Select Options from the Tools menu to open the Options dialog box.

2 Select the Spelling tab if it is not already on top.

3 Select the Custom Dictionaries button.
The Custom Dictionaries dialog box will appear, as shown in Figure 1.7.

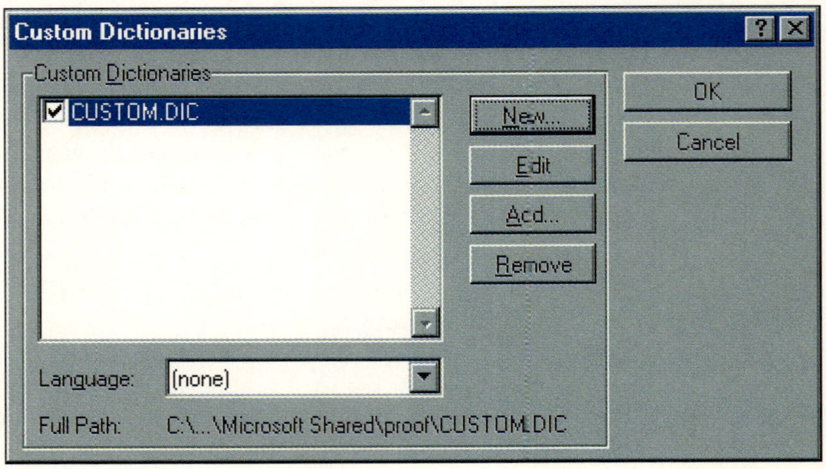

Figure 1.7

4 Select the New button.

5 Select the Save in box, and select the drive where you want to store the dictionary (probably A: or B:).

6 Select the File name box, and type in the name of your dictionary with the suffix dic, for instance, `Lee's Dictionary.dic`

7 Select Save.

8 Make sure your new dictionary is active (has a check mark to the left of it).

9 Select OK to close the Custom Dictionaries dialog box.

10 Select OK to close the Options dialog box.

When you want to use the dictionary at a subsequent word processing session, you will need to tell Word where to find your custom dictionary using the Custom Dictionaries dialog box, but selecting the Add button rather than the New button.

To add a word to the online dictionary:

1 Position the insertion point on the blank line at the end of the document.

2 Type `June 22` and press (TAB)

3 Type `Godzilla, King of the Monsters` and press (ENTER)
Godzilla is flagged as a misspelled word because it does not appear in Word's dictionary. You can add the word to the active custom dictionary so that Word will not report it as misspelled in the future.

4 Position the pointer over *Godzilla,* and click the right (not the left) mouse button to make the pop-up menu appear as before.

5 Select Add.

If you don't want red wavy lines on your screen but don't want to add a word to your custom dictionary, you can have Word ignore that word, at least during this word processing session.

To ignore a word that does not appear in the dictionary:

1 Position the insertion point on the blank line at the end of the document.

2 Type `Toho, Japan, 1954.`
Toho is the name of the Japanese film studio that produces the Godzilla movies, and because the name does not appear in Word's dictionary, it will be marked with a wavy red underline.

3 Position the pointer over *Toho,* and click the right mouse button to make the pop-up spelling menu appear.

4 Select Ignore All.
Word will now ignore all instances of the word *Toho* during the current word processing session.

COMPOSING PARAGRAPHS

Entering text in Word for Windows is a lot like typing on a typewriter—with one notable exception. You should press (ENTER), the equivalent of the carriage return on a typewriter, only at the end of a paragraph, not at the end of every line within the paragraph. Like most word processors, Word for Windows contains a feature called ***word wrap,*** which allows it to determine where line endings need to fall. Word wrap allows you to type on your keyboard without having to worry about when to break a line. If you add or delete text from a paragraph, Word for Windows will recast the lines accordingly. If you change the margins in your document so that the lines are shorter or longer, Word for Windows will again automatically revise the line endings.

As you type, text fills the line and continues to the next line automatically. Word moves the insertion point to the beginning of the next line. Further, the program moves the last word of one line to the next line if the word does not fit. At the end of a paragraph, you will press (ENTER) which inserts a paragraph mark (¶). Only the last line of each paragraph should end with a paragraph mark. To insert a blank line, you would press (ENTER) again.

Check that the beginning lines of the flyer shown in Figure 1.8 are on the screen.

Film·Festival¶
50's·Creature·Features¶
Show·Times:·8·p.m.·and·10·p.m.,·Bijou·Theater,·Main·and·Western·Streets → Admission:·$2¶
June·15→The·Blob¶
Paramount,·USA,·1958.·It's·teenagers·vs.·ravenous·Jell-O,·as·a·gelatinous·mass·from·space·begins·devouring·small-town·inhabitants.¶
June·22→Godzilla,·King·of·the·Monsters¶
Toho,·Japan,·1954.¶

Figure 1.8

To enter more of the flyer:

1 Position the insertion point after the period following *inhabitants,* on the third from the last line of the document.

2 Press (SPACE) and type **The film was one of Steve McQueen's first roles and became synonymous with bad film making despite its relative popularity, a sequel, and a remake.**

3 Move the insertion point to the very end of the document, after the period following *1954.*

4 Press (SPACE) and type the remainder of this portion of the film flyer, as shown in Figure 1.9.

At this point, information for the flyer is incomplete. Other members of your publicity committee will be giving you more information later. If you make a mistake, keep typing. You will be able to correct mistakes later when you edit the document. Press (TAB) to produce the tab character (→) shown in Figure 1.9. Remember not to press (ENTER) at the end of a line unless it is the end of a paragraph or the end of a short line or unless you want to insert a blank line.

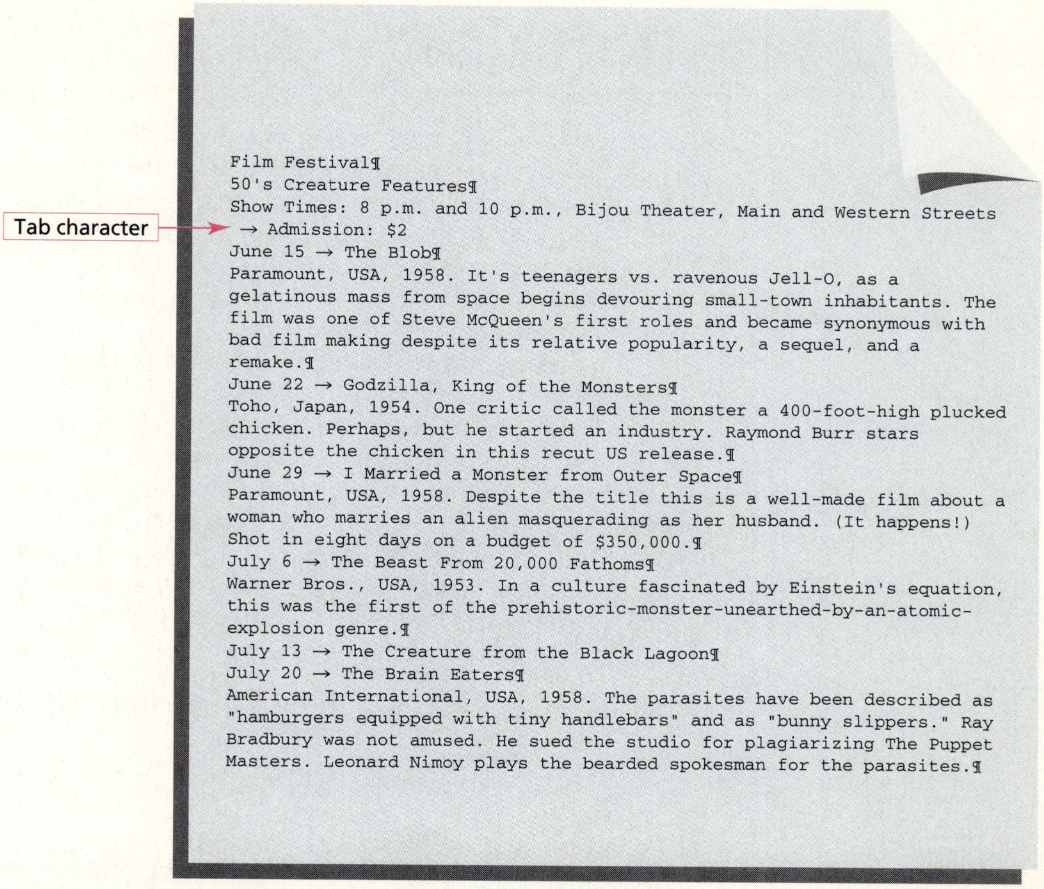

Film Festival¶
50's Creature Features¶
Show Times: 8 p.m. and 10 p.m., Bijou Theater, Main and Western Streets → Admission: $2
June 15 → The Blob¶
Paramount, USA, 1958. It's teenagers vs. ravenous Jell-O, as a gelatinous mass from space begins devouring small-town inhabitants. The film was one of Steve McQueen's first roles and became synonymous with bad film making despite its relative popularity, a sequel, and a remake.¶
June 22 → Godzilla, King of the Monsters¶
Toho, Japan, 1954. One critic called the monster a 400-foot-high plucked chicken. Perhaps, but he started an industry. Raymond Burr stars opposite the chicken in this recut US release.¶
June 29 → I Married a Monster from Outer Space¶
Paramount, USA, 1958. Despite the title this is a well-made film about a woman who marries an alien masquerading as her husband. (It happens!) Shot in eight days on a budget of $350,000.¶
July 6 → The Beast From 20,000 Fathoms¶
Warner Bros., USA, 1953. In a culture fascinated by Einstein's equation, this was the first of the prehistoric-monster-unearthed-by-an-atomic-explosion genre.¶
July 13 → The Creature from the Black Lagoon¶
July 20 → The Brain Eaters¶
American International, USA, 1958. The parasites have been described as "hamburgers equipped with tiny handlebars" and as "bunny slippers." Ray Bradbury was not amused. He sued the studio for plagiarizing The Puppet Masters. Leonard Nimoy plays the bearded spokesman for the parasites.¶

Figure 1.9

Correct any misspellings in your typing, but note that *recut* is a legitimate word and that *McQueen, Bradbury,* and *Nimoy* are all proper names, none of which appear in Word's online dictionary. You can choose to add them to your custom dictionary or simply have Word ignore them.

The content of your flyer should be the same as that of the document shown in Figure 1.9. However, the distribution of the text on each line may be different. For example, different margin settings might be in effect or a special type font (print style and number of characters per inch) may be set for the printer.

Tip If you learned to type on a typewriter, you may have picked up some habits that don't mix well with word processing. You've already seen that you should press ENTER only at the end of a paragraph, not at the end of each line as you would on a typewriter. Here are some other differences:

- The letter O and the numeral 0 are different keys—and different characters—on a computer.
- The letter l and the numeral 1 are also different.
- You should type only one space following a period.
- Don't use underlining to emphasize text except in manuscripts. Use italic instead. You'll see how to do that in Project 3.
- Use tabs, not spaces, to align text. You already know how to enter tab characters, and you'll see how to set tabs in Project 4.

Saving a New Document

Normally, you will want to save your work, with all changes, to disk. The ability to save a document is the real power of word processing or any computer program. Once a file has been saved to disk, you can call your document back to the screen, change the document, and save it again. Word for Windows provides several ways to save your document: choosing the Save or Save As options from the File menu or selecting the Save button on the Standard toolbar.

You must provide a storage location and file name for any document you wish to save. Windows 95 allows long file names. The file name plus drive designator and folder path can be up to 255 characters. The name cannot include certain special characters, such as ? or : or *. Word for Windows will automatically add the file name extension .doc to your document files. (You can also add your own file name extension, but it makes retrieving documents more awkward.) The instructions in this module assume you are saving your documents to a floppy disk in drive A:. If needed, you can modify the location specification from drive A: to the appropriate disk drive and directory as necessary for the computer system.

To save your document under the file name **Film Flyer:**

1 Select the Save button on the Standard toolbar.
The Save As dialog box should appear, as shown in Figure 1.10.

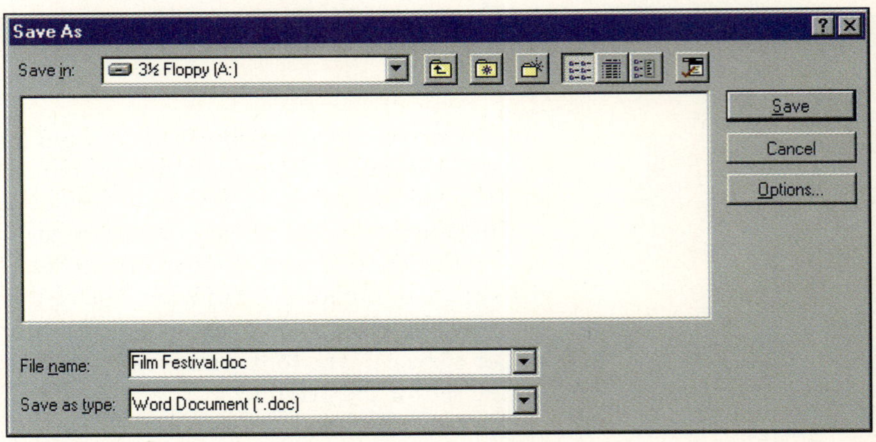

Figure 1.10

2 Type `Film Flyer` in the File name box, but do not press ENTER yet.

3 Click the Save in box to open a menu of drive choices.

4 Select the A: option.

5 Select Save.

If you get an error message, it's probably because you don't have a formatted disk in the drive you specified.

Notice that as soon as you save your file to disk, a message at the left of the status bar (at the very bottom of the screen) displays the file name, and a bar chart shows the progress of the save operation. Notice also that the title bar at the very top of the screen now indicates the new file name, with the file name extension .doc attached.

To add text to the film flyer:

1 Position the insertion point at the end of the line for the July 13 film.

2 Press (ENTER) and type the partial description of this film shown in Figure 1.11.

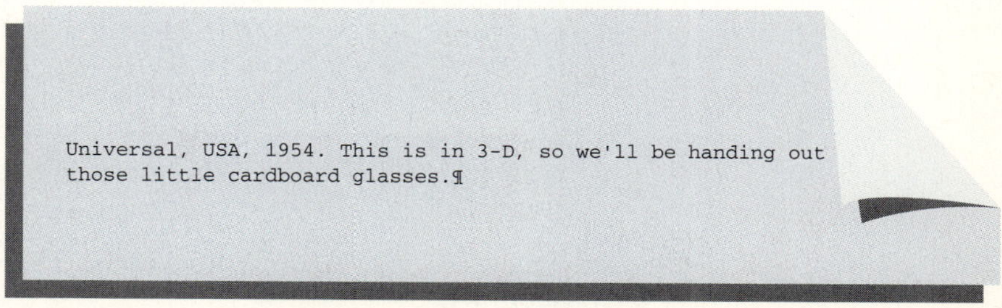

Figure 1.11

To save changes in an existing document:

1 Select the Save button on the Standard toolbar.

This time, Word for Windows 95 will not ask you the name of the file. Word assumes you want to save the file under the existing name, thus overwriting the previous version of your document. That way, you'll keep only one copy of the file and your disk won't be cluttered with different versions of the same document. In general, this is a good policy, but it's good insurance to keep one extra copy of your document on disk just in case something goes wrong, such as a scratch on the disk or a power interruption that makes the file unusable.

Word for Windows can make automatic backup copies for you so that you always have the most recent and next most recent versions of your document saved to disk. Then every time you save your document, the existing file is renamed to begin with *Backup of* and the file name extension is changed from .doc to .wbk, while the new version of the file is saved with the file name extension .doc. If something goes wrong with the original file, you can open the backup copy and work with it.

To have Word for Windows make automatic backup copies:

1 Choose Options from the Tools menu.

2 Select the Save tab if it is not already on top.

3 Select the Always Create Backup Copy box so that a check mark appears in the box to the left, as shown in Figure 1.12.

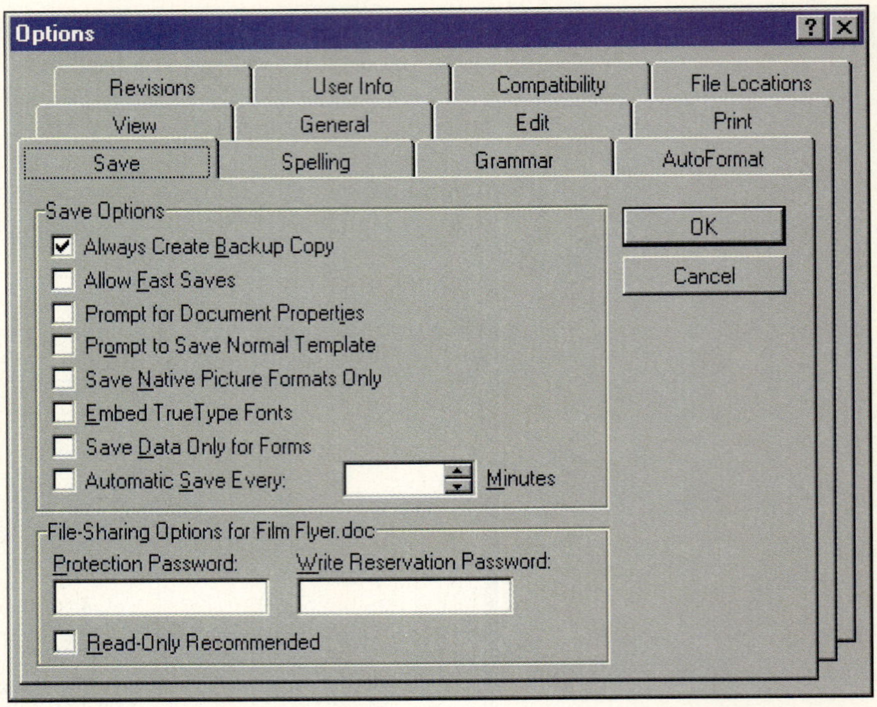

Figure 1.12

4 Select OK in the Options Save dialog box.

You can also use the Save tab of the Options dialog box to have Word save documents automatically every few minutes if you want added insurance against data loss.

Tip Be sure to save your document regularly. You're probably aware that when you turn off the computer, everything that hasn't been saved to disk is lost. You can lose hours of work in microseconds. Obviously, you should save your work every time you plan to shut off the computer. You also should save every time you take a break or every time you've typed a few paragraphs—every 10 to 15 minutes at least. You never know when a voltage spike, a power outage, or someone tripping over a power cord will unravel all those electrons that represent your efforts.

ADDING A GRAPHIC TO THE FILM FLYER

To add more visual interest to the film flyer, you will add a small picture at the top of the page. Word for Windows 95 normally includes a collection of clipart files. If those have not been installed on your computer, ask your instructor or lab assistant how to proceed.

To insert a graphic:

1 Position the insertion point at the very beginning of the flyer, in front of *Film.*

2 Select Picture from the Insert menu.

3 Select the file Film.wmf in the Insert Picture dialog box, as shown in Figure 1.13.

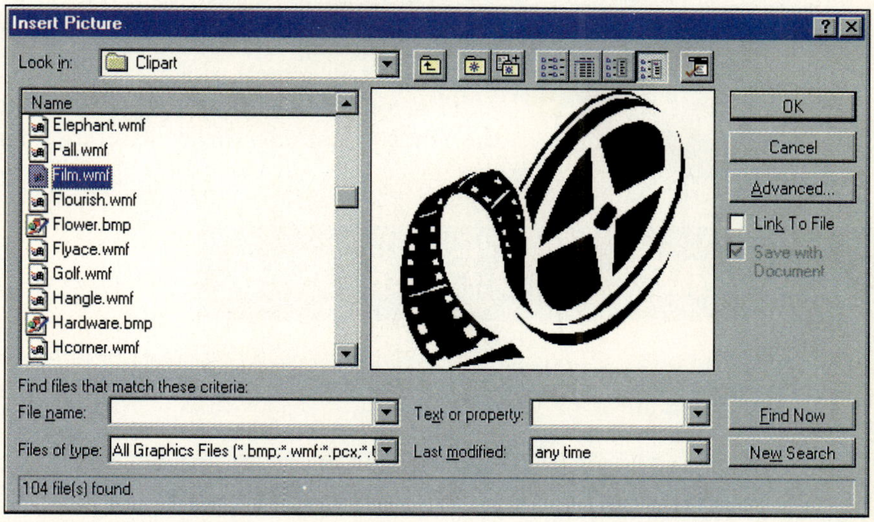

Figure 1.13

4 Select OK.

5 Save your document file.

EXITING WORD FOR WINDOWS

To quit Word for Windows and return to the Windows desktop:

1 Choose Exit from the File menu (or click the Close button, marked with an X, in the upper-right corner).
If you've made changes in your document since you last saved it, you'll get a warning message asking if you want to save changes (Yes) or discard changes (No).

2 If you get the warning message, choose Yes to save changes.
Word should return you to the Windows desktop.

THE NEXT STEP

A flyer, of course, is only one of the kinds of documents you can prepare using a word processor. The possibilities are virtually limitless. Anything that involves words can be prepared with a word processor, from simple letters or memos to complex reports or books.

All writing involves selecting that first word. The power of a word processor is that you can easily change that word, add to it, move it, delete it, save it, retrieve it, or print it. The same techniques you used to begin this flyer will also work for a news release for the film festival, for a letter, a lab report, or a term paper.

This concludes Project 1. You can either exit Word or go on to work the Study Questions, Review Exercises, and Assignments.

SUMMARY AND EXERCISES

Summary

- You can set Word to display or hide nonprinting characters such as paragraph marks (¶), spaces (·), and tabs (→).
- You can move the insertion point one or more characters at a time by using different combinations of arrow keys and command keys or by moving the pointer and clicking.
- Word allows you to undo, and subsequently redo, several previous word processing operations, including typing or deleting text.
- Word automatically spell checks your document as you work, marking any words it cannot find in its online dictionary with a wavy red line.
- In Word, text automatically "wraps" from the end of one line to the beginning of the next. You need to press ENTER (the equivalent of a carriage return on a typewriter) only at the end of a paragraph.
- To insert a blank line, press ENTER at the beginning of the line.
- When you save your document, you can choose the drive and directory where you want to store the file. Word uses the same conventions as Windows 95 does for naming files.
- You can set Word to automatically create a backup file for you each time you save a document.
- Remember to save your files frequently. You can save your document quickly by selecting the Save button on the Standard toolbar.

Key Terms and Operations

Key Terms	Operations
end-of-document mark (end mark)	Save a file
insertion point	Create a new file
nonprinting characters	Redo a command
paragraph mark	Undo a command
templates	
wizards	
word wrap	

Study Questions

Multiple Choice

1. The end of a paragraph is indicated by which of these symbols?
   a. ·
   b. |
   c. →
   d. ¶
2. Which of the following is not a nonprinting character?
   a. #
   b. ·
   c. →
   d. ¶
3. Which of the following key commands moves the insertion point to the beginning of a line?
   a. CTRL + ←
   b. ← + ←
   c. END
   d. HOME
4. When typing text in Word for Windows, you should press ENTER at the end of a:
   a. line.
   b. paragraph.
   c. page.
   d. document.
5. Word for Windows uses which of the following as a file name extension for document files?
   a. .txt
   b. .doc
   c. .wp
   d. .wbk
6. You can toggle nonprinting characters on and off by selecting:
   a. the selection bar at the left of the text.
   b. the Hide option from the View menu.
   c. the Show/Hide ¶ button on the Standard toolbar.
   d. the Print button on the Standard toolbar.
7. The Save button on the Standard toolbar looks like:
   a. a file folder.
   b. a floppy disk.
   c. two sheets of paper.
   d. an envelope.
8. The end of your document is indicated by:
   a. a ¶ mark.
   b. a → mark.
   c. a vertical bar (|).
   d. a short horizontal bar (__).
9. Which of the following key commands will take you to the end of your document?
   a. CTRL + ↓
   b. END
   c. CTRL + PGDN
   d. CTRL + END
10. To delete the character to the right of the insertion point, you would press:
    a. →
    b. BACKSPACE
    c. DEL
    d. TAB + BACKSPACE

Short Answer

1. When you type, characters appear at the spot in the text marked by the __________.
2. You can erase text using either the __________ key or the __________ key.
3. Word can keep your next-most-recent version of a document as a __________ copy.

4. __________ is a word processing feature that automatically breaks a paragraph into individual lines.
5. You can position the insertion point using either the __________ or the __________.
6. Pressing ENTER inserts a __________ mark into your document.
7. Pressing CTRL + → moves the insertion point to the __________ in your document.
8. The → symbol within your document is a nonprinting character that designates a __________.
9. The file name for your document is displayed in the __________.
10. To move immediately to the beginning of your document, press __________.

For Discussion

1. What does the Undo command do? What does the Redo command do?
2. How is a word processor different from a typewriter?
3. What are the rules for naming a file in Word?
4. What is a backup copy of a document? Why is a backup copy useful?

Review Exercises

Creating a Cover Letter

You want to have a cover letter to use when you distribute the film flyers to merchants and ask them to post the flyer or keep a small supply on hand to give out.

1. Write the cover letter shown in Figure 1.14 that will be given out to merchants.

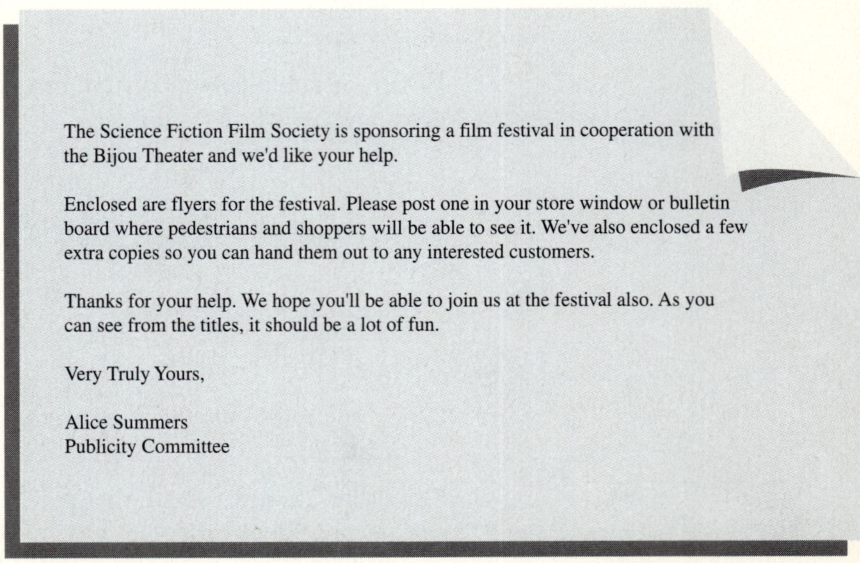

The Science Fiction Film Society is sponsoring a film festival in cooperation with the Bijou Theater and we'd like your help.

Enclosed are flyers for the festival. Please post one in your store window or bulletin board where pedestrians and shoppers will be able to see it. We've also enclosed a few extra copies so you can hand them out to any interested customers.

Thanks for your help. We hope you'll be able to join us at the festival also. As you can see from the titles, it should be a lot of fun.

Very Truly Yours,

Alice Summers
Publicity Committee

Figure 1.14

2. Add the current date to the top of the cover letter.
3. Add a salutation, *Dear Merchant:*
4. Add a sentence to the third paragraph that says to get more flyers they should call (123) 555-7890.
5. Change *Very truly yours* to *Sincerely yours.*
6. Save the cover letter under the file name *Flyer cover letter.*

Using a Wizard to Create a Letter

Word comes with a handful of preformatted and prewritten letters. All you have to do is direct the Letter Wizard to the type of letter you want, and it will do the rest. You may or may not find these letters useful, but the following process demonstrates how Word's wizards work. Wizards are not always installed. Ask your instructor or lab assistant what to do if you cannot find the wizards.

1. Select New from the File menu.
2. Select the Letters & Faxes tab.
3. Select the Letter Wizard.
4. Select the prewritten business letter option, then select Next.
5. Select Letter to Mom, then select Next.
6. Select Plain Paper, then select Next.
7. Type in your mom's name and address and your own name and address, then select Next.
8. Select Contemporary, then select Next.
9. Select Just display the letter, then select Finish.
10. Save the letter for the next time you need to write home.

Assignments

Getting Art on the Net

You will find entire galleries full of artwork on the World Wide Web. Whether you can incorporate a given piece of art into a document will depend on the graphics file format and the graphics filters installed for your copy of Word. Graphics files in the TIFF (Tagged Image File Format) format are usually safe. If you check the Benjamin/Cummings URL http://www.aw.com/is/select/word7, you will find some alternative monster movie TIFF files you can use on the film flyer. Download one and substitute it for the clipart at the top of the flyer.

Creating a Telephone List

Enter your personal list of telephone numbers for family, friends, business contacts, emergency services, and so on, using the following format:

```
Last name, first name → Telephone number
```

The list can be in any order. You will sort the list in alphabetical order and print it out in a later project. Save the file under the name *Telephone List.*

PROJECT 2: EDITING A DOCUMENT

Objectives

After completing this project, you should be able to:

- Retrieve documents
- Insert text
- Select text
- Delete text
- Move text
- Copy text
- Work with two documents at the same time
- Save documents under different names
- Preview and print documents

In this project, you will make changes in the film festival flyer you created in Project 1, save the file under a new name, and print the document. The changes will involve inserting, selecting, deleting, copying, and moving text. In the days of the typewriter, you would have made these changes with a pair of scissors in one hand and a jar of paste in the other. Then you would have had to retype the entire document, probably more than once. With Word, you'll be able to make all changes on the screen, preview the result, and print out the flyer when you're satisfied.

CASE STUDY

You created a flyer in Project 1 that should look like Figure 2.1.

Film Festival
50's Creature Features
Show Times: 8 p.m. and 10 p.m., Bijou Theater, Main and Western Streets   Admission: $2
June 15 The Blob
Paramount, USA, 1958. It's teenagers vs. ravenous Jell-O, as a gelatinous mass from space begins devouring small-town inhabitants. The film was one of Steve McQueen's first roles and became synonymous with bad film making despite its relative popularity, a sequel, and a remake.
June 22 Godzilla, King of the Monsters
Toho, Japan, 1954. One critic called the monster a 400-foot-high plucked chicken. Perhaps, but he started an industry. Raymond Burr stars opposite the chicken in this recut US release.
June 29 I Married a Monster from Outer Space
Paramount, USA, 1958. Despite the title this is a well-made film about a woman who marries an alien masquerading as her husband. (It happens!) Shot in eight days on a budget of $350,000.
July 6 The Beast From 20,000 Fathoms
Warner Bros., USA, 1953. In a culture fascinated by Einstein's equation, this was the first of the prehistoric-monster-unearthed-by-an-atomic-explosion genre.
July 13 The Creature from the Black Lagoon
Universal, USA, 1954. This is in 3-D, so we'll be handing out those little cardboard glasses.
July 20 The Brain Eaters
American International, USA, 1958. The parasites have been described as "hamburgers equipped with tiny handlebars" and as "bunny slippers." Ray Bradbury was not amused. He sued the studio for plagiarizing The Puppet Masters. Leonard Nimoy plays the bearded spokesman for the parasites.

Figure 2.1

At this point, the flyer is a first draft. As with many documents that are shaped by a committee and driven by scheduling realities, the flyer will evolve over time. Your word processor will help in this evolution by giving you something concrete to share with others and by making it easy to make alterations.

Designing the Solution

In real-life projects, things always seem to change. Schedules change. People change their minds. Opportunities arise. Challenges crop up. As the film series evolves, you will need to alter the flyer to correspond with these changes.

In this project, you'll use some of Word's editing tools to rearrange and adjust the flyer. Because you saved your file from Project 1, you'll be able to do all this with a minimum of retyping. At the end of this project, you'll preview and print out a copy of the film flyer.

Retrieving a Document

One of the major advantages of a word processing program is its ability to store documents on disk, allowing you to open documents later for revision and printing. That way you don't have to retype an entire document if you want to make changes or corrections. To open a file you've saved before, call up the Open dialog box and indicate the file you want to retrieve.

To retrieve the document Film Flyer:

1 Start Word and then choose Open from the File menu, or select the Open button on the Standard toolbar.

The Open dialog box, shown in Figure 2.2, will appear on the screen. If this dialog box looks familiar, it's because this box is very similar to the Save As dialog box you used at the end of Project 1.

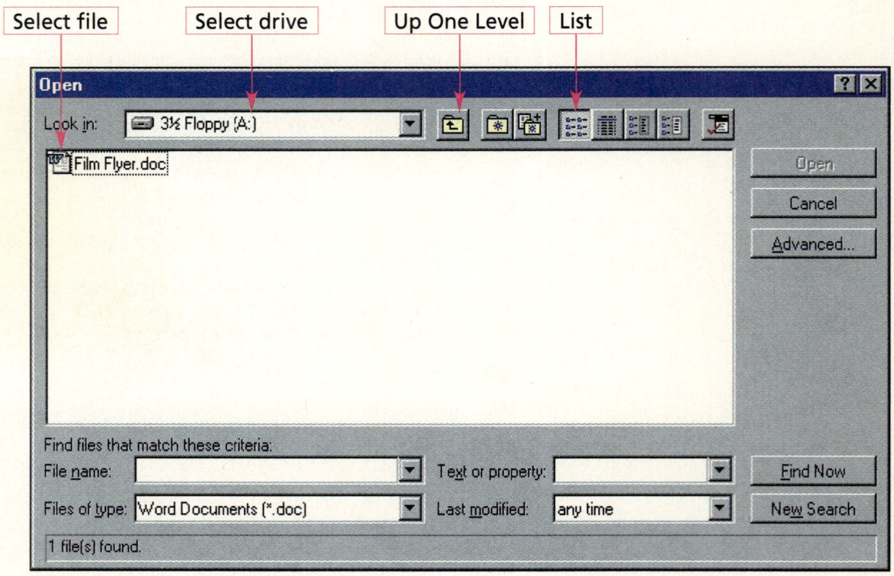

Figure 2.2

2 Select the List button.

3 If needed, change the drives shown in the Look in box to the drive where you saved the document file in Project 1.

4 In the box beneath the Look in box, select the folder containing the document file.

5 Make sure the Files of type box contains Word Documents (*.doc). If it doesn't, use the pull-down menu to change the setting so that document files will be listed.

6 Select *Film Flyer.doc* in the box beneath the Look in box.

7 Select Open.

The flyer you started in Project 1 should appear on the screen.

Tip If you want to return to exactly where you left off with a file when you were last working with it, press SHIFT + F5 before you do anything else. Word will return the insertion point to its last location.

INSERTING TEXT

Word normally operates in ***insert mode,*** which means characters you type on the keyboard are inserted into whatever text already exists in your document. You can switch to ***overtype mode,*** in which characters you type replace existing characters. If Word is in overtype mode, OVR appears darkened in the status bar at the bottom of the screen.

To toggle between insert and overtype mode:

1 Double-click OVR in the status bar at the bottom of the screen, or press INS
OVR appears darkened in the status bar, as shown in Figure 2.3. (If you're using the keyboard and OVR does not appear darkened, INS has probably been assigned another function. See the next Tip for instructions on how to reset it.)

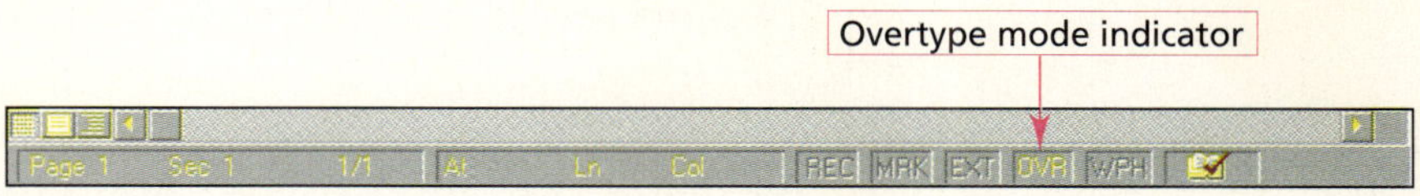

Figure 2.3

2 Double-click OVR in the status bar again, or press INS again.
Overtype mode will be cleared, and OVR will be dimmed in the status bar. Word will be in insert mode again.

> ***Tip*** The INS key can be assigned another function in Word. It can be used to paste in text that has been moved to the clipboard. You'll see how to use the clipboard later in this project, but for now you may need to change what INS is used for so that you will be able to do the preceding steps. To change the INS key assignment, first choose Options from the Tools menu. Second, select the tab labeled *Edit.* Then turn off the check mark in the box beside the line *Use the INS Key for Paste.* (You can also turn overtype mode on or off using the line just below that one, which is labeled *Overtype Mode.*) Select OK to close the Option dialog box.

Assume that your committee has just discovered that in order to break even on the film festival, it will need to charge $2.50 admission. You will have to amend the flyer accordingly. Be sure that Word is in insert mode (OVR should be dimmed in the status bar).

To insert text into your letter:

1 Position the insertion point immediately after *$2* at the end of the line in the third paragraph.

2 Type a period and **50**
Word inserts each character as you type it, moving existing text ahead to make room for the new characters. Assume your committee is given a

correction. The shooting budget for *I Married a Monster from Outer Space* was $175,000, not $350,000 as you were originally told.

To type over text in your letter:

1 Position the insertion point immediately in front of the *3* in *350,000.*

2 Switch to overtype mode so that OVR appears darkened in the status bar.

3 Type **175** to correct the cost.
The characters you type replace those already on the screen.

4 Switch back to insert mode so that OVR is again dimmed in the status bar.

Tip Although Word gives you a choice, it's usually best to work in insert mode (where OVR is dimmed). Overtyping destroys text, making it easy to accidentally wipe out valuable text or formatting information. Although using insert mode exclusively sometimes results in extra unwanted text, it's not difficult to delete such text, as you'll see shortly.

EXIT If necessary, you can save your file, exit Word now, and continue this project later.

Selecting Text

The general rule when using Word is "select, and then do." Many operations in Word involve selecting a block of text and then doing something with that selection. A selection can be a single character, a word, a sentence, a paragraph, or your entire document. Once you've selected a text block, you can move the block, copy it, delete it, or change the way it looks. As with many other operations, Word gives you several ways to select text. In the steps that follow, you will try different ways to select text although you won't do anything with the text blocks just yet. You'll see how to select text first with the mouse and then with the keyboard.

To select text by dragging:

1 If necessary, start Word, open the Film Flyer document, and position the pointer somewhere inside the word *Married* in the June 29 movie title.

2 Press the left mouse button and hold it down.

3 Without releasing the mouse button, move the pointer to a different part of the screen.
As you drag the pointer, the text you drag over appears highlighted (white letters on a black background), and your selection is anchored at the point where you initially pressed the mouse button. Notice also that you can select individual characters while you stay within the word *Married,* but that once the selection expands to include other words, Word automatically "rounds off" the selection to include whole words only (and the space that follows the word).

4 Still holding down the mouse button, position the pointer somewhere within *Space,* at the end of the line.

5 Release the mouse button to select the highlighted text. Your selection should match the block shown in Figure 2.4.

an·industry.·Raymond·Burr·stars·opposite·the·chicken·in·this·recut·US·release.¶
June·29→I·Married·a·Monster·from·Outer·Space¶
Paramount,·USA,·1958.·Despite·the·title·this·is·a·well-made·film·about·a·woman·who·marries·an·alien·masquerading·as·her·husband.·(It·happens!)·Shot·in·eight·days·on·a·budget·of·$175,000.¶
July·6 → The·Beast·From·20,000·Fathoms¶

Figure 2.4

If you want to cancel a text selection, you can simply click once or press one of the arrow keys.

To cancel a text selection:

1 Click once or press one of the arrow keys.

You can also select parts of your text using the mouse within the selection bar, the area within the document window just to the left of the text. When the pointer is in the selection bar, it changes from an I-beam shape into an arrow that points upward and to the right.

To select a line of text using the selection bar:

1 Move the pointer into the selection bar just to the left of the July 6 title line, as shown in Figure 2.5.

masquerading·as·her·husband.·(It·happens!)·Shot·in·eight·days·on·a·budget·of·$175,000.¶
July·6 → The·Beast·From·20,000·Fathoms¶
Warner·Bros.,·USA,·1953.·In·a·culture·fascinated·by·Einstein's·equation,·this·was·the·first·of·the·prehistoric-monster-unearthed-by-an-atomic-explosion·genre.¶
July·13→The·Creature·from·the·Black·Lagoon¶
Universal,·USA,·1954.·This·is·in·3-D,·so·we'll·be·handing·out·those·little·cardboard·glasses.¶

Figure 2.5

The shape of the pointer changes to an arrow.

2 Click to select one line, as shown in Figure 2.6.

masquerading·as·her·husband.·(It·happens!)·Shot·in·eight·days·on·a·budget·of·$175,000.¶
July·6 → The·Beast·From·20,000·Fathoms¶
Warner·Bros.,·USA,·1953.·In·a·culture·fascinated·by·Einstein's·equation,·this·was·the·first·of·the·prehistoric-monster-unearthed-by-an-atomic-explosion·genre.¶
July·13→The·Creature·from·the·Black·Lagoon¶
Universal,·USA,·1954.·This·is·in·3-D,·so·we'll·be·handing·out·those·little·cardboard·glasses.¶

Figure 2.6

To select several lines, click and drag the pointer up or down in the selection bar. Table 2.1 describes other ways of selecting text using the mouse.

Table 2.1

Selection	Action
Word	Double-click the word.
Sentence	Hold down CTRL and click anywhere within the sentence.
Paragraph	Double-click in the selection bar next to the paragraph, or triple-click anywhere within the paragraph.
Entire document	Hold down CTRL and click in the selection bar, or triple-click in the selection bar.

Sometimes it's faster or more convenient to select text using the keyboard. The simplest way is to use the arrow keys in combination with the SHIFT key.

To select text using SHIFT and the arrow keys:

1 Use the arrow keys to position the insertion point immediately in front of *Godzilla* on the June 22 film entry line.

2 Hold down SHIFT and press → several times.
Notice that this works like dragging. As the insertion point moves, the text is highlighted, always anchored where you began the selection. Unlike when you drag the mouse, however, Word does not round off to whole words if the selection includes more than one word.

3 With SHIFT still pressed, press ↑ several times.

4 Continuing to hold down SHIFT use the arrow keys to move the insertion point so that the selection includes the *s* in *Monsters* at the end of the line.

5 Release SHIFT to complete the selection.

6 Cancel the text selection by clicking or by pressing one of the arrow keys.

The F8 key is the Extend key. When you press F8 once, it anchors the selection and begins extend mode, signaled by the EXT indicator in the status bar at the bottom of the screen, shown in Figure 2.7. You can extend the selection using the mouse or arrow keys, or you can press F8 a second time to select a word, a third time to select a sentence, a fourth time to select a paragraph, and a fifth time to select the entire document. To cancel a selection, you must first turn off extend mode. To turn off extend mode, press ESC or double-click the EXT indicator in the status bar.

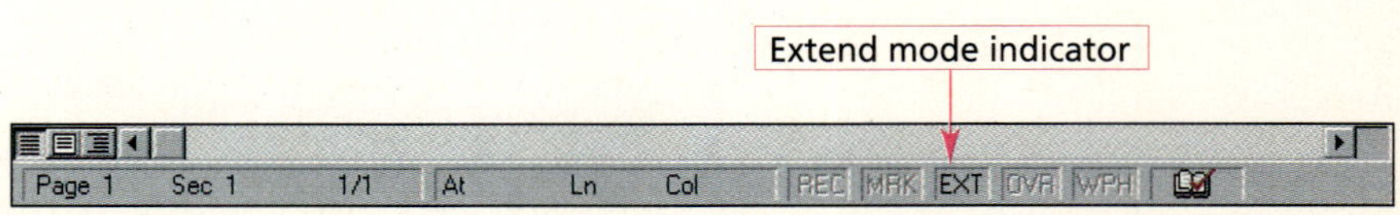

Figure 2.7

You can also extend a selection by using SHIFT in combination with keys that you might use to move the insertion point to different locations within your document, as summarized in Table 2.2.

Table 2.2

To Extend a Selection	Action
To the end of a word	CTRL+SHIFT+→
To the beginning of a word	CTRL+SHIFT+←
To the end of a line	SHIFT+END
To the beginning of a line	SHIFT+HOME
To the end of a paragraph	CTRL+SHIFT+↓
To the beginning of a paragraph	CTRL+SHIFT+↑
To the end of a document	CTRL+SHIFT+END
To the beginning of a document	CTRL+SHIFT+HOME
To the whole document	CTRL+A

DELETING TEXT

Once you've selected text, one of the things you can do with that text is delete it. You can delete text permanently, or you can remove it from your document and place it in a temporary storage location called the ***clipboard.*** Later you can retrieve that text from the clipboard and place it somewhere else in your document or in some other Windows application (such as a spreadsheet or database program).

To delete a word permanently:

1 Select the word *Streets,* as shown in Figure 2.8.

> ***Tip*** Recall that the easiest way to select a single word is to double-click the word.

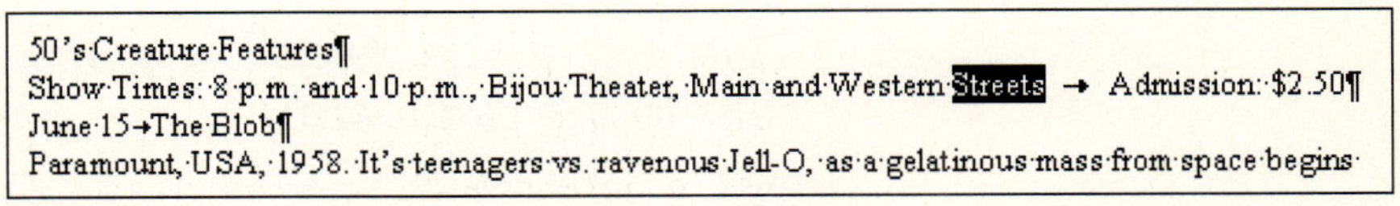
50's·Creature·Features¶
Show·Times:·8·p.m.·and·10·p.m.,·Bijou·Theater,·Main·and·Western·Streets → Admission:·$2.50¶
June·15→The·Blob¶
Paramount,·USA,·1958.·It's·teenagers·vs.·ravenous·Jell-O,·as·a·gelatinous·mass·from·space·begins·

Figure 2.8

2 Press either DEL or BACKSPACE
The word is deleted, and the remaining text closes up to fill in the space where the word used to be. If necessary, the word wrap feature resets the line endings for the entire paragraph. The word you deleted is gone forever—well, almost. You can still reverse the deletion with Word's Undo feature.

To undo a deletion:

1 Select the Undo button on the Standard toolbar.
Note that *Streets* is restored.

2 Select the Redo button to delete *Streets.*

Remember that you can undo several of the most recent operations in Word in reverse order. So even if you deleted text and went on to perform other word processing operations, you would probably still be able to retrieve that deleted text by repeating the undo operation as many times as needed.

If you have a text block selected and then begin typing on the keyboard, Word ordinarily replaces the selected text with the new text.

To replace parasites *with* bunny slippers:

1 Select *parasites* at the end of the description of the July 20 film, as shown in Figure 2.9.

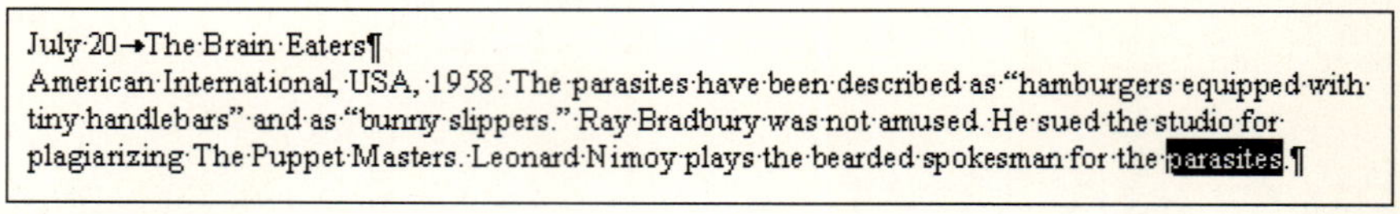
July·20→The·Brain·Eaters¶
American·International,·USA,·1958.·The·parasites·have·been·described·as·"hamburgers·equipped·with·tiny·handlebars"·and·as·"bunny·slippers."·Ray·Bradbury·was·not·amused.·He·sued·the·studio·for·plagiarizing·The·Puppet·Masters.·Leonard·Nimoy·plays·the·bearded·spokesman·for·the·parasites.¶

Figure 2.9

2 Type **b**

As soon as you type the new character, the selected text is deleted and the new text begins to replace it.

3 Finish typing *bunny slippers* to complete the replacement.

> ***Tip*** Ordinarily it's very convenient to have revised text replace selected text, but like anything that deletes text, this method can be dangerous. If you don't want Word to treat selected text this way, you can set the word processor to insert new text in front of the selection rather than replacing selected text. To do this, choose Options from the Tools menu. In the dialog box, select the Edit tab, and then set the Typing Replaces Selection box to off (clear the check mark from the box) and select OK.

To delete a text selection from a document and move the text to the clipboard:

1 Select the July 13 film entry, including the description following the movie title.

The screen should resemble Figure 2.10.

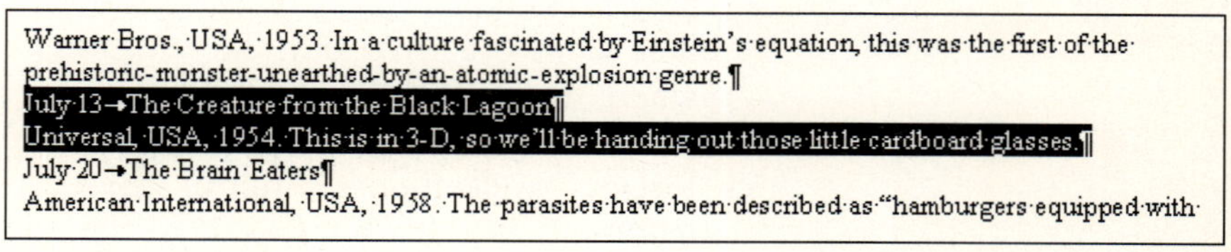
Warner·Bros.,·USA,·1953.·In·a·culture·fascinated·by·Einstein's·equation,·this·was·the·first·of·the·prehistoric-monster-unearthed-by-an-atomic-explosion·genre.¶
July·13→The·Creature·from·the·Black·Lagoon¶
Universal,·USA,·1954.·This·is·in·3-D,·so·we'll·be·handing·out·those·little·cardboard·glasses.¶
July·20→The·Brain·Eaters¶
American·International,·USA,·1958.·The·parasites·have·been·described·as·"hamburgers·equipped·with·

Figure 2.10

2 Choose Cut from the Edit menu (or select the Cut button on the Standard toolbar, or press CTRL + X).

The text has been removed from your document, but a copy of it is temporarily stored in the clipboard. The text will remain in the clipboard until you copy something else into the clipboard or until you quit Windows 95. The clipboard is part of Windows and is available to any Windows application, such as a spreadsheet or database. You can use the clipboard to transfer information back and forth between one Word document and another, or between Word and another Windows application.

Tip After you have selected the text to be cut, click the right mouse button, and then select Cut.

Moving Text

By deleting text to the clipboard in the preceding steps, you've actually performed the first half of a text-block move operation. You moved text from the document into the clipboard. All that remains is to move that text from the clipboard to some other part of your document. Assume that your publicity committee has just found that, because of a booking problem, the film you had scheduled for July 13 will be available only on July 6, so you need to change the order of the films on the flyer.

To insert text from the clipboard:

1 Position the insertion point immediately in front of *July* in July 6, as shown in Figure 2.11.

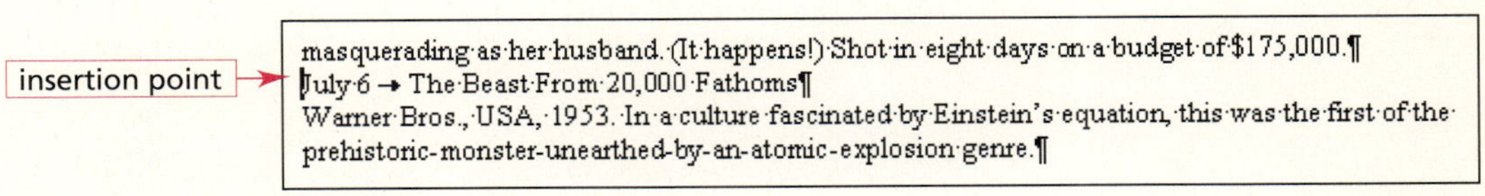

masquerading·as·her·husband.·(It·happens!)·Shot·in·eight·days·on·a·budget·of·$175,000.¶
July·6 → The·Beast·From·20,000·Fathoms¶
Warner·Bros.,·USA,·1953.·In·a·culture·fascinated·by·Einstein's·equation,·this·was·the·first·of·the·prehistoric-monster-unearthed-by-an-atomic-explosion·genre.¶

Figure 2.11

2 Choose Paste from the Edit menu (or select the Paste button on the Standard toolbar, or press CTRL + **V** or click the *right* mouse button and select Paste).

Your screen should resemble Figure 2.12. Note that the film entries have been reordered. The dates are reversed, but you will fix that shortly by moving the dates themselves.

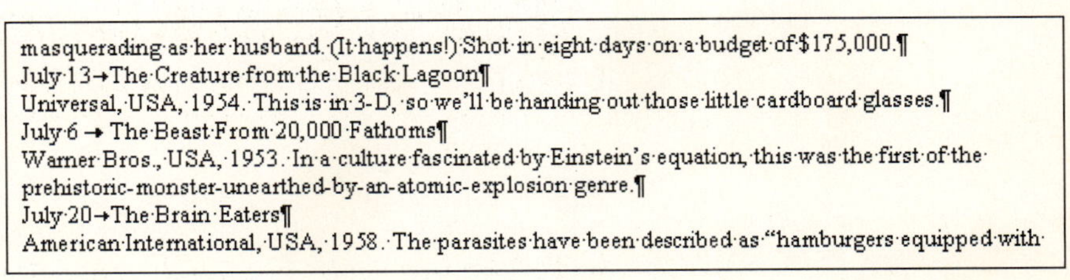
masquerading·as·her·husband.·(It·happens!)·Shot·in·eight·days·on·a·budget·of·$175,000.¶
July·13→The·Creature·from·the·Black·Lagoon¶
Universal,·USA,·1954.·This·is·in·3-D,·so·we'll·be·handing·out·those·little·cardboard·glasses.¶
July·6 → The·Beast·From·20,000·Fathoms¶
Warner·Bros.,·USA,·1953.·In·a·culture·fascinated·by·Einstein's·equation,·this·was·the·first·of·the·prehistoric-monster-unearthed-by-an-atomic-explosion·genre.¶
July·20→The·Brain·Eaters¶
American·International,·USA,·1958.·The·parasites·have·been·described·as·"hamburgers·equipped·with·

Figure 2.12

Tip The clipboard, as you know, still contains the text you just inserted, and you could insert that same text somewhere else if you wanted. If you have to repeat text, you can use this feature of the clipboard to expedite your work.

Word also allows you to move text using the (F2) key. This type of text move doesn't involve the clipboard, so whatever text is already in the clipboard won't be disturbed. To move text with (F2), you would first select the text you want to move, press (F2) to begin the move, position the insertion point where you want the text to appear, and press (ENTER) to complete the move. You will use (F2) to move the July 6 date to its correct place in the listing.

To move the July 6 date using (F2)

1 Select *July 6* but not the tab character following.
Your screen should resemble Figure 2.13.

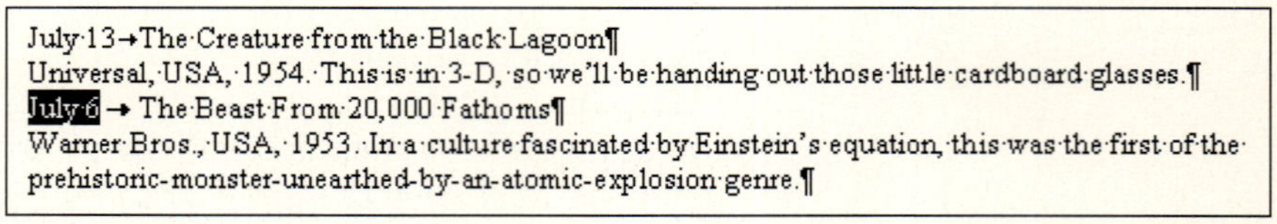
July 13→The Creature from the Black Lagoon¶
Universal, USA, 1954. This is in 3-D, so we'll be handing out those little cardboard glasses.¶
July 6→ The Beast From 20,000 Fathoms¶
Warner Bros., USA, 1953. In a culture fascinated by Einstein's equation, this was the first of the prehistoric-monster-unearthed-by-an-atomic-explosion genre.¶

Figure 2.13

2 Press (F2)
The status bar at the bottom of the screen now prompts you for the next step in the move operation, as shown in Figure 2.14.

Figure 2.14

3 Position the insertion point—now a dotted vertical line—at the destination for the move, just in front of *July 13,* as shown in Figure 2.15.

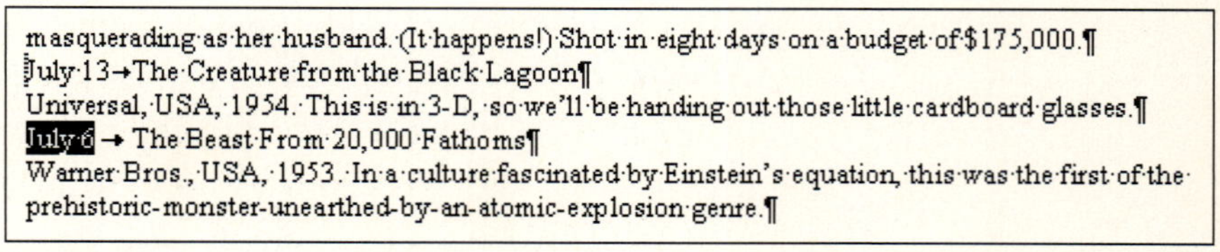
masquerading as her husband. (It happens!) Shot in eight days on a budget of $175,000.¶
July 13→The Creature from the Black Lagoon¶
Universal, USA, 1954. This is in 3-D, so we'll be handing out those little cardboard glasses.¶
July 6→ The Beast From 20,000 Fathoms¶
Warner Bros., USA, 1953. In a culture fascinated by Einstein's equation, this was the first of the prehistoric-monster-unearthed-by-an-atomic-explosion genre.¶

Figure 2.15

4 Press (ENTER)
The date *July 6* should now appear just before the *July 13* date, as shown in Figure 2.16. *The Beast From 20,000 Fathoms* movie entry is now undated.

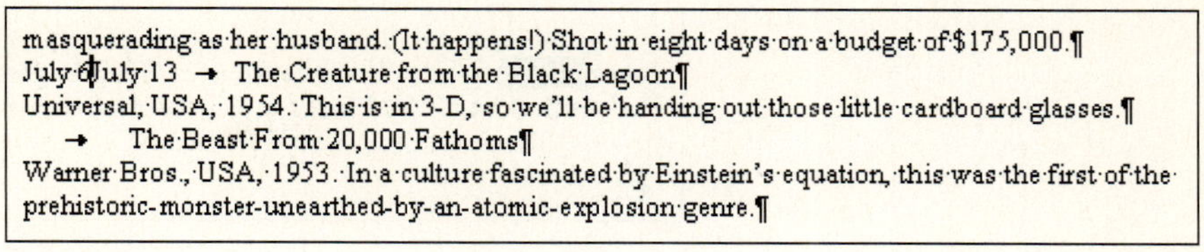

masquerading as her husband. (It happens!) Shot in eight days on a budget of $175,000.¶
July 6July 13 → The Creature from the Black Lagoon¶
Universal, USA, 1954. This is in 3-D, so we'll be handing out those little cardboard glasses.¶
→ The Beast From 20,000 Fathoms¶
Warner Bros., USA, 1953. In a culture fascinated by Einstein's equation, this was the first of the prehistoric-monster-unearthed-by-an-atomic-explosion genre.¶

Figure 2.16

Word also allows you to move selected text quickly by dragging it from one spot and dropping it in another using the mouse. This operation is called ***drag and drop***.

To move the July 13 *date using drag and drop:*

1 Select *July 13,* as shown in Figure 2.17.

> ***Tip*** Recall that you can select individual characters using (SHIFT) plus the arrow keys.

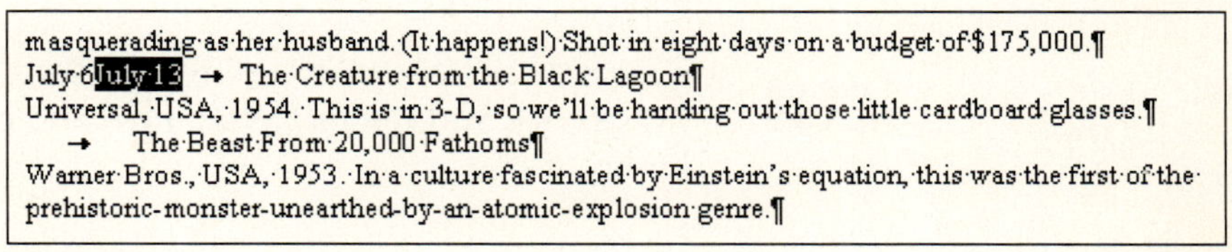

masquerading as her husband. (It happens!) Shot in eight days on a budget of $175,000.¶
July 6July 13 → The Creature from the Black Lagoon¶
Universal, USA, 1954. This is in 3-D, so we'll be handing out those little cardboard glasses.¶
→ The Beast From 20,000 Fathoms¶
Warner Bros., USA, 1953. In a culture fascinated by Einstein's equation, this was the first of the prehistoric-monster-unearthed-by-an-atomic-explosion genre.¶

Figure 2.17

2 Position the pointer somewhere within the selection to change the shape of the pointer to an arrow. Press and hold down the mouse button to "grab" the selected text block, as shown in Figure 2.18.

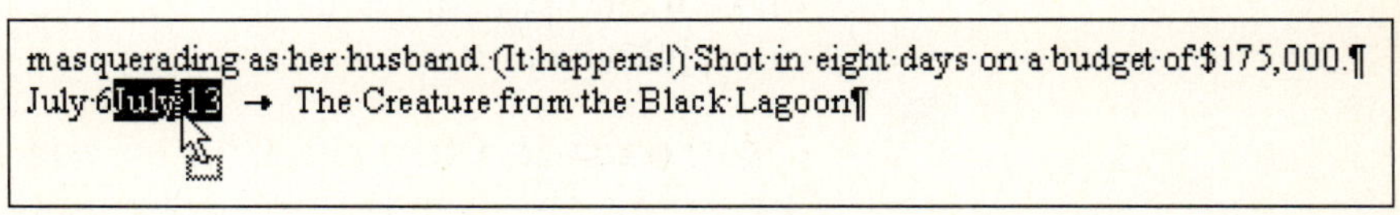

masquerading as her husband. (It happens!) Shot in eight days on a budget of $175,000.¶
July 6July 13 → The Creature from the Black Lagoon¶

Figure 2.18

Note that the pointer has a small rectangle attached to it, which signifies the block of text you are moving. Note also that you can use the pointer to move the insertion point, which has changed from an I-beam to a dotted vertical bar.

3 Continuing to hold down the mouse button, move the pointer so that the dotted insertion point is positioned just in front of the tab character preceding *The Beast From 20,000 Fathoms,* as shown in Figure 2.19.

masquerading·as·her·husband.·(It·happens!)·Shot·in·eight·days·on·a·budget·of·$175,000.¶
July·6July·13 → The·Creature·from·the·Black·Lagoon¶
Universal,·USA,·1954.·This·is·in·3-D,·so·we'll·be·handing·out·those·little·cardboard·glasses.¶
→ The·Beast·From·20,000·Fathoms¶

Figure 2.19

4 Release the mouse button.
The two dates should be correctly positioned, as shown in Figure 2.20.

July·6 → The·Creature·from·the·Black·Lagoon¶
Universal,·USA,·1954.·This·is·in·3-D,·so·we'll·be·handing·out·those·little·cardboard·glasses.¶
July·13→The·Beast·From·20,000·Fathoms¶
Warner·Bros.,·USA,·1953.·In·a·culture·fascinated·by·Einstein's·equation,·this·was·the·first·of·the·prehistoric-monster-unearthed-by-an-atomic-explosion·genre.¶

Figure 2.20

5 Save your file but do not close it.

EXIT If necessary, you can exit Word now and continue this project later.

WORKING WITH TWO DOCUMENTS AT ONCE

Assume that you've been asked to send names and descriptions of three of the movies listed in the film flyer to one of the people on your publicity committee, and you want to send the information in the form of a memo. Rather than retype all of the descriptive information, you can set up the basic memo structure and then copy the rest of the information from the film flyer document.

To create the top portion of the memo:

1 Select the New button on the Standard toolbar (do not close the film flyer document).

2 Type in the memo heading information as shown in Figure 2.21, substituting the current date for the date shown.

Reminder The arrow symbols shown on screen represent tabs.

Science·Fiction·Film·Society¶
¶
¶
MEMO¶
¶
¶
To: → Alice·Summers¶
¶
From: → Paul·Kettering¶
¶
Date: → March·14,·1999¶
¶
Subject:→Film·descriptions·as·requested¶
¶
¶
¶

Figure 2.21

3 Save the memo using the file name *Publicity Memo.*

The basic memo structure is complete. Now you need to copy the movie descriptions from the film flyer to the body of the memo. This will involve working with two documents at once, a relatively simple task with Word.

Word allows you to have several documents open at the same time and to switch from one to another easily. You can view the documents one at a time in a single document window, switching from one to another using the Window menu. Alternatively, you can have several document windows open simultaneously. You'll use both techniques as you copy information from the film flyer to the memo.

The publicity memo is now the active document—the one visible in the document window and the one you are able to edit. Both the memo and the flyer are open documents, however, and you can switch from one to the other using the Window menu.

To switch between the flyer and the memo:

1 Select *Film Flyer.doc* from the Window menu, as shown in Figure 2.22, to make the flyer the active document.

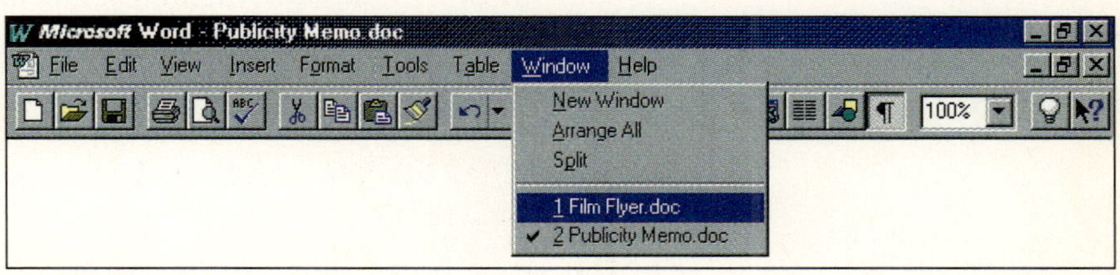

Figure 2.22

2 Select *Publicity Memo.doc* from the Window menu to make the memo the active document.

Copying Text

Copying text is very much like moving text. The difference is that the originally selected text is not deleted when a copy of it is inserted elsewhere. As with moving, you can copy by using the clipboard, by using the function keys, or by dragging and dropping. You'll try out all three methods in the following series of steps.

In completing the memo, rather than retyping the descriptions, you can pull them directly from the rough draft of the flyer and move them to the memo.

To copy text using the clipboard:

1 Make the film flyer the active document.

2 Select the title and description of the July 6 film, including the paragraph mark at the end of the description. Do not include the date or the tab character, however.
The selection should look like Figure 2.23.

```
masquerading·as·her·husband.·(It·happens!)·Shot·in·eight·days·on·a·budget·of·$175,000.¶
July·6 → The·Creature·from·the·Black·Lagoon¶
Universal,·USA,·1954.·This·is·in·3-D,·so·we'll·be·handing·out·those·little·cardboard·glasses.¶
July·13→The·Beast·From·20,000·Fathoms¶
```

Figure 2.23

3 Choose Copy from the Edit menu (or select the Copy button on the Standard toolbar, or press CTRL + C or click the right mouse button and select Copy) to copy the selection to the clipboard.
Notice that the film flyer remains unchanged.

4 Select Publicity Memo.doc from the Window menu to make the memo the active document.

5 Position the insertion point on the last (blank) line of the memo.

6 Choose Paste from the Edit menu (or select the Paste button on the Standard toolbar, or press CTRL + V or click the right mouse button and select Paste).

7 Press ENTER to leave a blank line.
Your document should resemble Figure 2.24, with the film title and description appearing in the body of the memo.

```
Science·Fiction·Film·Society¶
¶
¶
MEMO¶
¶
¶
To: → Alice·Summers¶
¶
From: → Paul·Kettering¶
¶
Date: → March·14,·1999¶
¶
Subject:→Film·descriptions·as·requested¶
¶
¶
The·Creature·from·the·Black·Lagoon¶
Universal,·USA,·1954.·This·is·in·3-D,·so·we'll·be·handing·out·those·little·cardboard·glasses.¶
¶
¶
```

Figure 2.24

To copy text using (SHIFT)+(F2)

1 Make the flyer the active document (select Film Flyer.doc from the Window menu).

2 Select the title and description of the July 13 film, including the paragraph mark following the description, but excluding the date and the tab character.

3 Press (SHIFT)+(F2)
A Copy to where? prompt appears in the status bar at the bottom of the screen.

4 Make the publicity memo the active document.

5 Click in the document and position the dotted insertion point on the blank line at the bottom of the memo.

6 Press (ENTER) to complete the copy.

7 Press (ENTER) again to leave a blank line.

You can copy text between two documents using drag and drop, but you will need to have both document windows visible on the screen at the same time.

To make two document windows:

1 Check the list of open documents using the Window menu. Close all documents except the memo and the flyer.
The Window menu should resemble Figure 2.25.

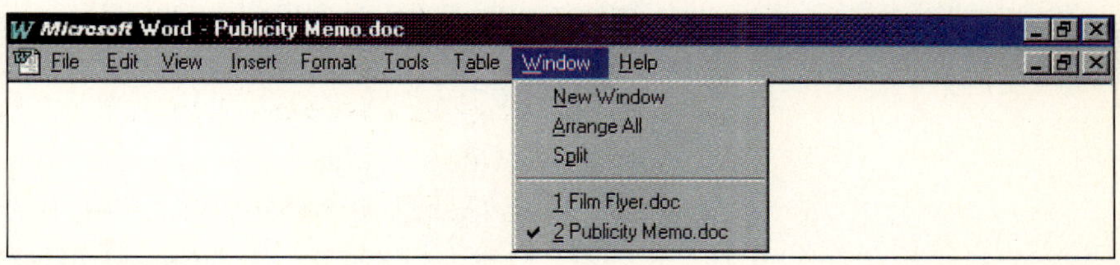

Figure 2.25

2 Select Arrange All from the Window menu.

3 Scroll each window so that you can see the film description for the June 22 movie in the film flyer window and so that you can see the bottom of the text of the memo in the publicity memo window. The screen should appear as shown in Figure 2.26.

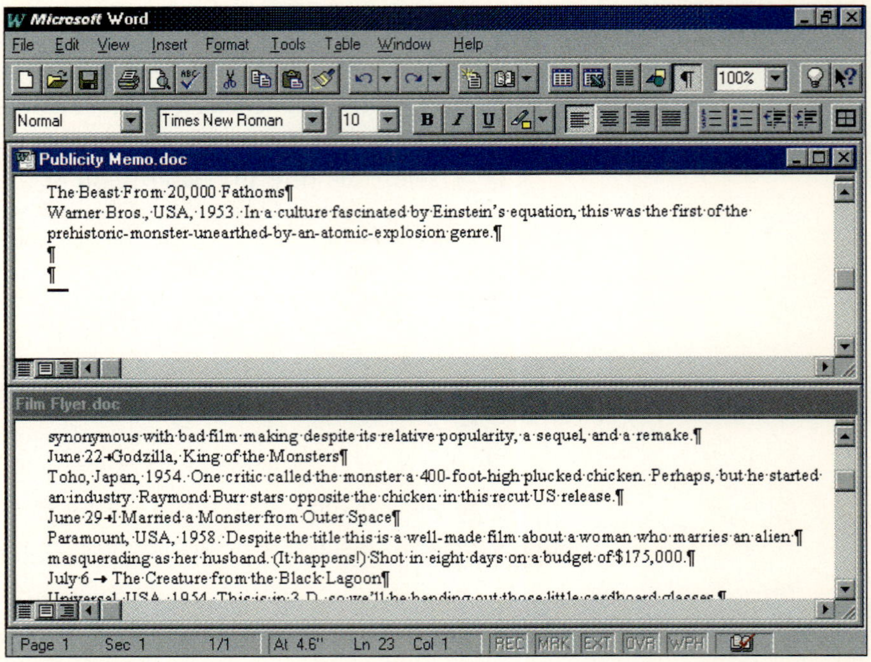

Figure 2.26

To copy text by dragging and dropping:

1 Select the title and description of the June 22 movie in the film flyer window. As before, include the paragraph mark at the end of the description, but exclude the date and tab character.

2 Move the pointer inside the selection so that the pointer turns into an arrow.

3 Hold down (CTRL) and press the mouse button. Continue to hold down both (CTRL) and the mouse button until you're ready to paste the copied text.
Note that the pointer has a small dotted rectangle attached to it and that a dotted insertion point appears beside the rectangle. The pointer includes a plus sign to indicate that this is a copy, not a move, operation.

4 Move the dotted insertion point to the last line of the memo in the other window.

5 Release both the mouse button and (CTRL) to insert the text in the memo.

6 Click the maximize button at the top of the publicity memo window to return to one document window.

Reminder Word allows great flexibility in selecting, moving, and copying text. Sometimes it might seem as if there are so many different ways to accomplish the same thing that you can't remember any of them. Recall that you can get a list of keyboard or mouse commands at any time through the Help facility. You will quickly develop your own preferences for working with text.

Saving a Document Under a Different Name

Saving a file under a new name creates a new file. The new file becomes the active file, which is the file currently being edited. The old file stored under the previous name will remain unchanged unless you deliberately open that file and alter it. You can use this feature to save intermediate drafts of a document. For instance, it is usually a good idea to save an extra copy of a document under a different name if you are about to undertake an extensive revision. That gives you a version to fall back on if you get mixed up in the middle of the revision or make a mistake and turn all of your hard work into electronic garbage.

To save an existing document under a new name:

1 Make the film flyer the active document.

2 Open the Save As dialog box by choosing Save As (*not* Save) from the File menu.

> ***Warning*** If you choose Save, Word will immediately save the file under its current name and defeat the purpose of separately saving the second draft of the film flyer.

3 In the File name box, type **`Revised Film Flyer,`** the new name for the document.

4 If needed, change the drive and directory in the Save in box.

5 Select Save.
The title bar at the top of the screen now shows the new file name.

6 Make the publicity memo the active document.

Previewing and Printing a Document

The end result of a word processing effort is usually a printed document: something you can mail, give to someone else to read, or mark up for further revision. Before you commit your document to paper, however, Word can prepare a preview on the screen. The preview shows just how the printed document will look: where page breaks will fall, where page numbers will appear, how headings and margins will look, and so on.

The Print Preview screen looks like Figure 2.27, with the Print Preview toolbar at the top just above the miniature page. You can edit your document in print-preview mode while you check margins, page breaks, heading positions, and so on, to be sure the page will look just as you want it to. The Print button prints the file immediately. The Magnifier button toggles between edit mode (with the usual I-beam pointer) and zoom mode (with a magnifying-glass pointer). When in zoom mode, you can click to switch back and forth between a full-page view and a close-up view. The One Page button displays a single page of your document, and the Multiple Pages button allows you to view several miniature pages at once. The Zoom control box allows you to set the magnification of the preview page. The View Ruler button toggles the ruler on and off. The Shrink to Fit button may be able to eliminate the last page of your document if that page contains only a few lines of text. The Full Screen button toggles to a preview display containing only your document and the Print Preview toolbar. The Close button turns off print-preview mode and returns to the display mode you were using before. The Help button can be used to obtain more information about any of these features.

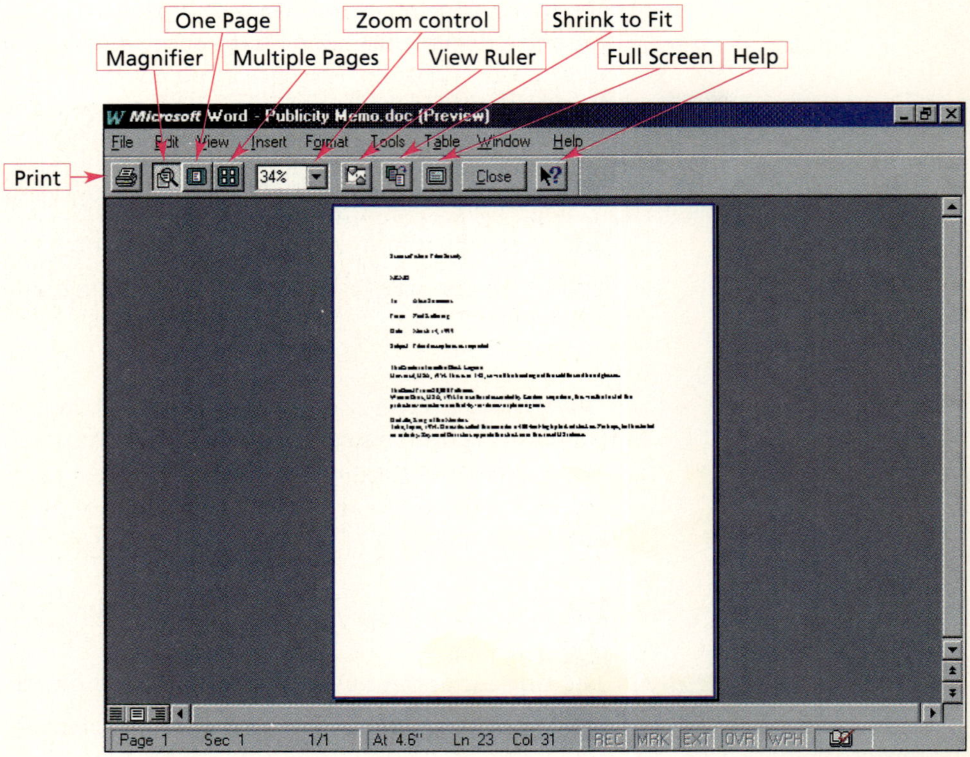

Figure 2.27

To preview and print the document:

1 Select the Print Preview button on the Standard toolbar.

2 Choose Print from the File menu (or press CTRL + **P**).

The Print dialog box will appear, as shown in Figure 2.28. The printer for the system will be listed in the Name box. The print settings default to printing one copy of your entire document. You can change the number of copies and you can set the range of pages you want if you don't need to print the entire document.

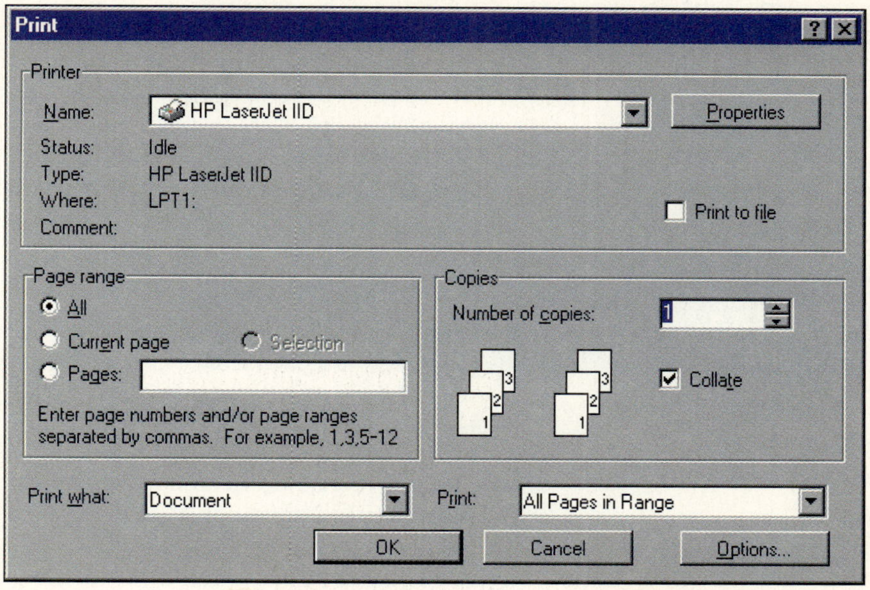

Figure 2.28

3 Select OK in the Print dialog box.
A brief message appears telling you that Word is preparing the document for printing and transmitting information to the printer.

4 Compare your printed copy to the print-preview display for your document.

5 Select the Close button on the Print Preview toolbar to exit the print-preview mode.

6 Save the memo file and close it.

If you already know that your document is formatted correctly, you can bypass the preview before printing. You can open the Print dialog box by choosing Print from the File menu, setting the defaults as needed, and then selecting OK. To really expedite printing, you can simply accept whatever defaults are in effect and print by using the Print button on the Standard toolbar. This is the approach you will use to print the revised film flyer.

To print using the Print button:

1 Make the revised film flyer the active document if it is not already.

2 Select the Print button on the Standard toolbar.

3 Close the revised film flyer.

THE NEXT STEP

The ability to move, copy, and edit text makes it relatively easy to assemble new documents from existing ones without retyping. You could take your own résumé, for example, and modify it for a specific internship or job opening, customizing the text to speak to the requirements of that particular position.

You could take a similar approach for a cover letter. By changing the name and address of the person you're writing to, and perhaps making other alterations in the text of the letter, you can quickly produce a personalized letter.

This concludes Project 2. You can either exit Word or go on to work the Study Questions, Review Exercises, and Assignments.

Summary and Exercises

Summary

- You can retrieve documents you've stored to disk by choosing Open from the File menu or by selecting the Open button on the Standard toolbar.
- You can switch between insert mode and overtype mode by pressing (INS) or by double-clicking OVR in the status bar. It is safest to work in insert mode.
- The general strategy when working in Word is "select, and then do," which means first select a block of text, and then do something with it.
- You can select blocks of text in a variety of ways: dragging with the mouse, using (SHIFT) with the arrow keys, clicking in the selection bar, or using (F8)
- You can delete text permanently by using (DEL) or (BACKSPACE) You can delete text to the clipboard by choosing Cut from the Edit menu, by pressing (CTRL)+**X** or by selecting the Cut button on the Standard toolbar.
- If you type something while a text block is selected, the typed text replaces the selected text.
- You can move text in three ways: you can delete text to the clipboard and then copy it from the clipboard back into your document; you can use (F2); and you can drag and drop text selections.
- Copying text is like moving text, except you don't delete the text from its original location. You can copy text to the clipboard, you can use (SHIFT)+(F2), or you can drag and drop using the mouse with (CTRL)
- Document templates, which are preformatted for various kinds of written materials, can be opened in the New dialog box.
- You can work with more than one open document at once in Word, switching among them using the Window menu.
- You can save separate drafts of a document by changing the file name when you save the file. To do that, select Save As from the File menu.
- Word will preview your printed document on the screen so that you can check page breaks, margins, and so on before you actually print the file.

Key Terms and Operations

Key Terms
clipboard
drag and drop
insert mode
overtype mode

Operations
Copy text
Cut text
Delete text
Paste text
Preview and print a document
Select text

Study Questions

Multiple Choice

1. When you copy a block of text, it is temporarily stored in the:
   a. buffer.
   b. clipboard.
   c. status bar.
   d. block file.

2. Which of the following will not select text?
   a. holding down SHIFT and pressing one of the arrow keys
   b. clicking in the selection bar
   c. holding down CTRL and clicking
   d. clicking at the end of a line

3. Which of the following inserts text from the clipboard?
   a. CTRL+X
   b. CTRL+C
   c. CTRL+I
   d. CTRL+V

4. If Word is in overtype mode:
   a. OVR appears in the status bar.
   b. The pointer changes to an X shape.
   c. The title bar blinks as a warning.
   d. The insertion point becomes a dotted line.

5. To select a single word:
   a. Press F8 three times.
   b. Press CTRL and click the word.
   c. Press CTRL+W
   d. Double-click the word.

6. If you delete a text block with DEL, you can retrieve the text block:
   a. by pressing CTRL+V
   b. by choosing Paste from the Edit menu.
   c. with the Undo command.
   d. by pressing F2

7. To select an entire document:
   a. Hold down CTRL and press F8
   b. Hold down CTRL and click in the selection bar.
   c. Double-click in the selection bar.
   d. Choose Entire from the Select menu.

8. The Copy button on the Standard toolbar looks like:
   a. a pair of scissors.
   b. two sheets of paper.
   c. a sheet of paper and a clipboard.
   d. a printer.

9. If you save a document under a new name:
   a. The old name and associated file are deleted.
   b. The old file gets the new name, and the old name is deleted.
   c. The file you are editing retains the old name.
   d. Both the old and the new files will be saved to disk.

10. When it is in the selection bar, the pointer:
    a. has a small rectangle attached to it.
    b. is shaped like an I-beam.
    c. is a vertical blinking line.
    d. becomes an arrow pointing up and to the right.

Short Answer

1. To toggle between insert mode and overtype mode, press ________.
2. The general rule in using Word is "________, and then do."
3. To cancel a text selection, click or press one of the ________ keys.
4. The Extend key is the ________ key.
5. The Move key is the ________ key.
6. After you copy text from the clipboard, the clipboard still contains ________.
7. To copy a text selection using the mouse, you must hold down the ________ key while dragging the selection.
8. To select text using the keyboard, you can hold down the ________ key and then press one of the arrow keys.
9. You can delete a block of text using either the ________ or ________ keys.
10. When you exit Windows, the contents of the clipboard are ________.

For Discussion

1. Why is it usually better to use insert mode than overtype mode?
2. What is the difference between deleting text using DEL or BACKSPACE and deleting text using CTRL + X?
3. Word allows you to move text blocks in several different ways, using both the mouse and the keyboard. What are the advantages and disadvantages of each?

Review Exercises

Correcting a Rough Draft

1. Type a rough draft of the memo shown in Figure 2.29 (without making the corrections yet).

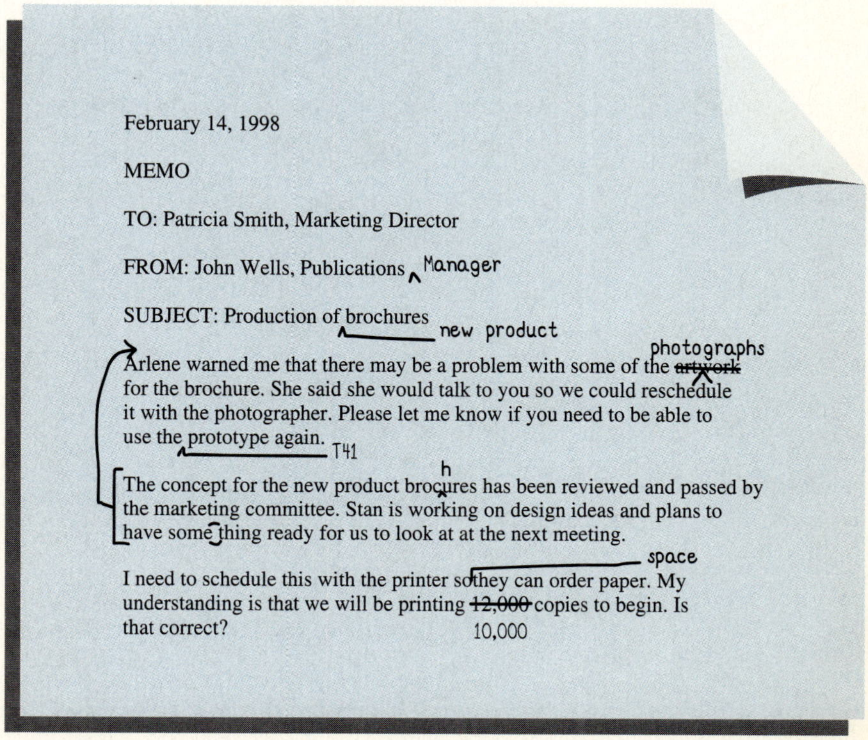
February 14, 1998

MEMO

TO: Patricia Smith, Marketing Director

FROM: John Wells, Publications

SUBJECT: Production of brochures

Arlene warned me that there may be a problem with some of the ~~artwork~~ for the brochure. She said she would talk to you so we could reschedule it with the photographer. Please let me know if you need to be able to use the prototype again.

The concept for the new product brocures has been reviewed and passed by the marketing committee. Stan is working on design ideas and plans to have some thing ready for us to look at at the next meeting.

I need to schedule this with the printer sothey can order paper. My understanding is that we will be printing ~~12,000~~ copies to begin. Is that correct?

Figure 2.29

2. Make the corrections noted.
3. Save the file under the file name *Brochure Memo,* and print the file.

Creating a Meeting Agenda

1. Type the meeting agenda items shown in Figure 2.30. Use TAB to indent the agenda items.

Agenda
Campus Service Club
Meeting of January 12, 1998

New Business
    Treasurer's report
    Big brother and big sister project
    Election of officers
        Treasurer
        Vice President
        Secretary
        President
    Other new business

Old Business

    Reading of minutes
    Continue discussion of fundraising projects

Figure 2.30

2. Substitute today's date for the date in Figure 2.30.
3. Move the *Old Business* heading and the items under it so that this section appears before the *New Business* section.
4. Move the *Election of officers* and positions listed under that heading so that this section is the first item under *New Business.*
5. Reorganize the list of officers so that it is more logical.
6. Save the revised agenda under the file name *Meeting Agenda.*
7. Print a copy of the agenda.

Assignments

Copying Web Information

In Windows 95, you can use the clipboard to move text from one application to another. Find information on the Web about a movie that interests you, and compile a set of research notes. Check the Benjamin/Cummings URL http://www.aw.com/is/select/word7 for links to movie databases on the Web. Copy information about the movie from your Web browser into a blank Word document. Find other information about the same movie, and copy it into the same document. Save your movie research notes in a file, and print a copy.

Modifying a Telephone List

Retrieve the telephone list you saved under the file name Telephone List at the end of Project 1. Reorganize the first five items on your list as follows (you'll reorganize the rest of the list using a faster method in a later project). Select what should be the first line alphabetically by clicking alongside it in the selection bar. Drag and drop that line at the top of the list. Then select what should be the second line and move it under the first. Continue until the first five lines of your list are in alphabetical order. Put a title at the top of the list if you haven't already. Save the list, and print a copy of it.

PROJECT 3: CHARACTER FORMATTING

Objectives

After completing this project, you should be able to:

- Apply character styles such as boldface, italic, and underline
- Change type styles and sizes
- Create subscripts and superscripts
- Repeat and copy character formats
- Insert special characters

In this project, you will begin to polish the appearance of the flyer using character formatting: type styles and sizes, character emphasis, and special characters. You'll begin by formatting the entire flyer so that it no longer looks like a draft. You'll add boldface headings in a different type style to set off the headings and help organize the page visually. And you'll add some special typographic characters to give the flyer a more polished and professional look. All this is a first step into desktop publishing.

CASE STUDY: POLISHING THE FLYER

Printed documents communicate not only by what they say, but also by how they look—by their form and appearance. Even though we're warned not to judge a book by its cover, most of us do exactly that. An attractive book, magazine, or brochure is more likely to be read and will probably have more credibility than one that looks sloppy, hastily put together, or unattractive. The same is true of smaller documents such as flyers, reports, and letters.

Word allows you to control the appearance of whatever document you're preparing in a variety of ways. You can select different typefaces and type sizes. You can make the type boldface or italic. You can use special characters such as foreign-language characters or mathematical symbols. With these capabilities, you can transform a rough draft into a document that looks polished and professional.

The flyer you began in the first project is complete and well organized at this point, but it lacks polish. It looks like the draft that it is. You probably wouldn't expect it to attract attention if you posted it on bulletin boards around campus. Dressing up the flyer requires the use of Word's extensive character-formatting capabilities.

Designing the Solution

A good rule of thumb in designing any document is summed up in the widely used KISS formula: keep it simple, stupid. Smart designers usually try to keep it simple by, for example:

- Using a minimum number of typefaces
- Grouping material that belongs together into blocks
- Making one element (probably an illustration or headline) stand out for emphasis
- Setting tabs and indentations so that type blocks line up and the page looks better organized

In this project, you'll format the flyer using typefaces that are professional and polished. You'll provide emphasis and clarity by making the title and headings stand out. You'll use italics and special characters to make the text conform better to common style conventions, thus raising its credibility.

At the end of this project, the flyer should look like Figure 3.1.

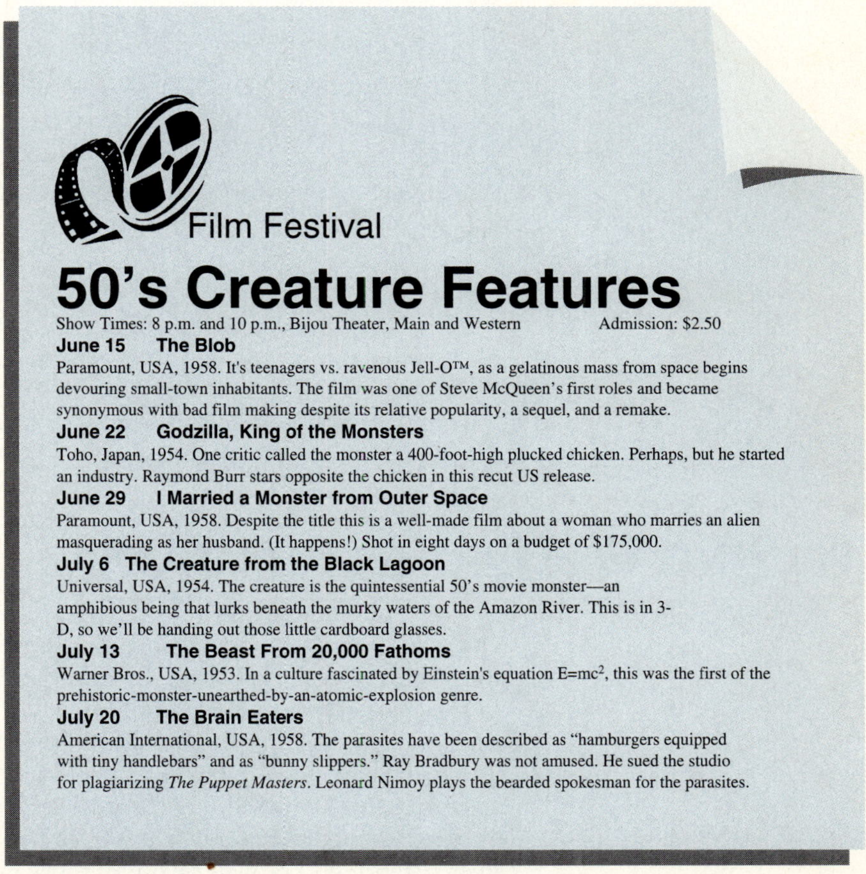
Film Festival

50's Creature Features

Show Times: 8 p.m. and 10 p.m., Bijou Theater, Main and Western Admission: $2.50

June 15 The Blob

Paramount, USA, 1958. It's teenagers vs. ravenous Jell-O™, as a gelatinous mass from space begins devouring small-town inhabitants. The film was one of Steve McQueen's first roles and became synonymous with bad film making despite its relative popularity, a sequel, and a remake.

June 22 Godzilla, King of the Monsters

Toho, Japan, 1954. One critic called the monster a 400-foot-high plucked chicken. Perhaps, but he started an industry. Raymond Burr stars opposite the chicken in this recut US release.

June 29 I Married a Monster from Outer Space

Paramount, USA, 1958. Despite the title this is a well-made film about a woman who marries an alien masquerading as her husband. (It happens!) Shot in eight days on a budget of $175,000.

July 6 The Creature from the Black Lagoon

Universal, USA, 1954. The creature is the quintessential 50's movie monster—an amphibious being that lurks beneath the murky waters of the Amazon River. This is in 3-D, so we'll be handing out those little cardboard glasses.

July 13 The Beast From 20,000 Fathoms

Warner Bros., USA, 1953. In a culture fascinated by Einstein's equation $E=mc^2$, this was the first of the prehistoric-monster-unearthed-by-an-atomic-explosion genre.

July 20 The Brain Eaters

American International, USA, 1958. The parasites have been described as "hamburgers equipped with tiny handlebars" and as "bunny slippers." Ray Bradbury was not amused. He sued the studio for plagiarizing *The Puppet Masters*. Leonard Nimoy plays the bearded spokesman for the parasites.

Figure 3.1

Characters, Paragraphs, and Sections

Word recognizes three types of building blocks that make up a document: characters, paragraphs, and sections. Each one of these building blocks has specific characteristics and can be formatted in different ways. For instance, characters can be bold or italic, paragraphs can be indented or double spaced, and sections can be page numbered or printed sideways.

As usual in Word, the general rule is "select, and then do." First you select the part of your document you want to format, and then you apply the formatting. If you want to underline text, you first select the characters you want to underline, and then you tell Word to underline them. If you want to boldface text, you select the text and then tell Word to boldface it.

Characters can have a variety of formats, as shown in Figure 3.2.

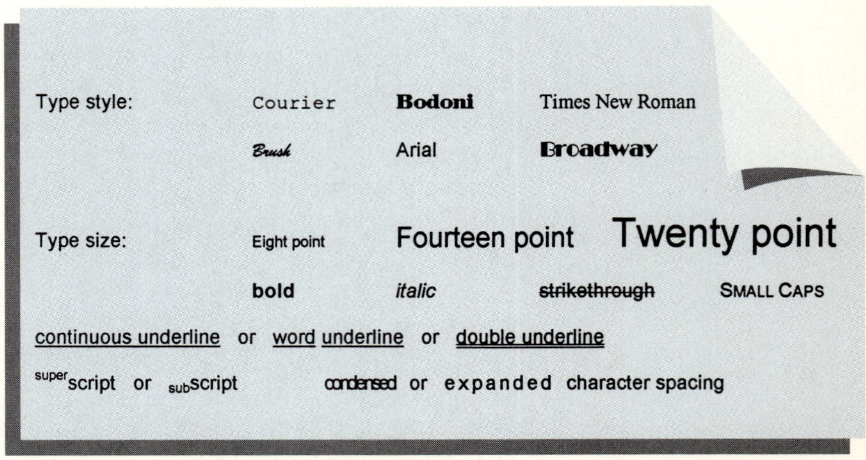

Figure 3.2

How you format your documents will affect the legibility and appearance of those documents, and probably influence the documents' credibility and attractiveness to readers. You can use character formats to establish the tone and structure of your document, to provide emphasis, and to produce special effects to gain attention.

Applying Character Formats

Once you've selected the text you want to format, you can apply character formats in any of three ways: by using the Font dialog box, the keyboard, or the Formatting toolbar. You'll learn all three in the steps that follow, working with the sample flyer from Projects 1 and 2.

The appearance of your flyer is obviously important. It must attract attention and look credible. Its precise final appearance will depend heavily on the type of printer you're using, but you can do a lot to dress up the flyer regardless. You will begin by retrieving the last version of the flyer, saved as Revised Film Flyer.doc in Project 2.

To retrieve the flyer file:

1. Start Word and click the Open button in the Standard toolbar.
2. Adjust the Look in box and box beneath as needed to locate the file.
3. Select *Revised Film Flyer.*
4. Select Open.

5 Select the Show/Hide ¶ button if needed to make nonprinting characters visible.
Your document should resemble Figure 3.3.

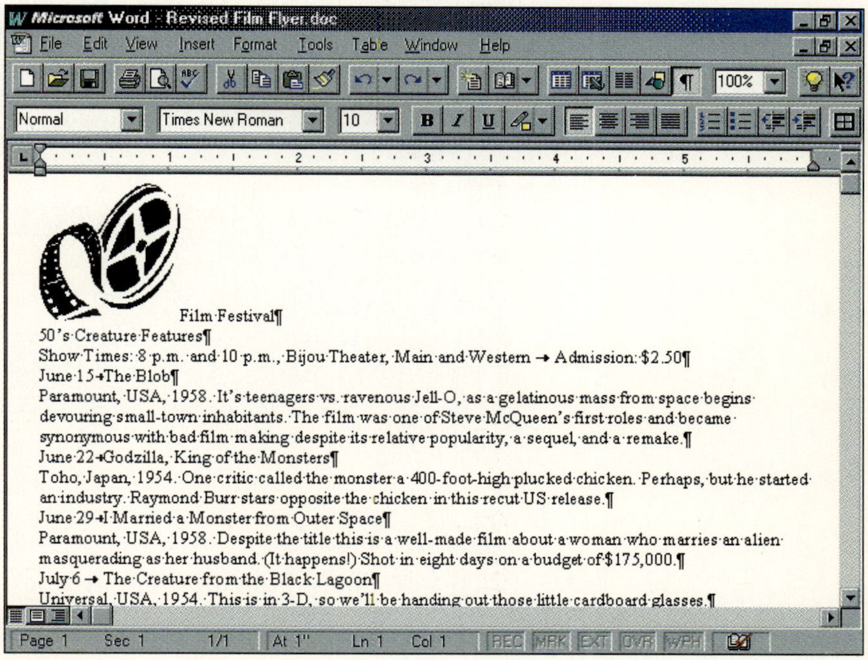

Figure 3.3

In standard style, the names of newspapers, magazines, books, and so on are normally italicized. You'll begin formatting the flyer by italicizing *The Puppet Masters,* the title of the book mentioned in the description of the July 20 film.

To italicize text using the Font dialog box:

1 Select the title of the book so that the text appears as shown in Figure 3.4.

July·20→The·Brain·Eaters¶
American·International,·USA,·1958.·The·parasites·have·been·described·as·"hamburgers·equipped·with·tiny·handlebars"·and·as·"bunny·slippers."·Ray·Bradbury·was·not·amused.·He·sued·the·studio·for·plagiarizing·The·Puppet·Masters.·Leonard·Nimoy·plays·the·bearded·spokesman·for·the·bunny·slippers.¶

Figure 3.4

2 Choose Font from the Format menu.
The Font dialog box, shown in Figure 3.5, will appear.

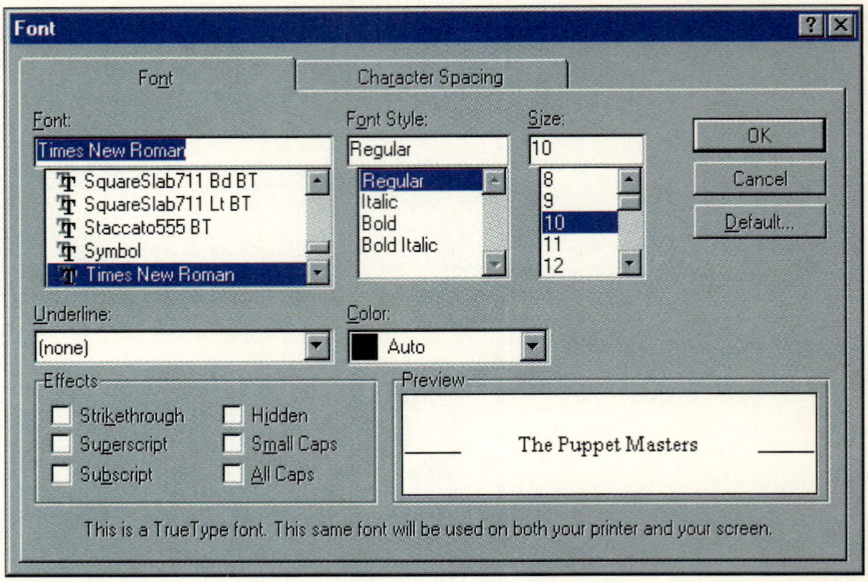

Figure 3.5

3 Select the Font tab if it is not already on top.

4 Select Italic from the Font Style box.
Note that the Preview box in the lower-right corner shows how the text will look with the italic style applied.

5 Select OK.
The title of the book now appears in italics. (Cancel the text selection if necessary to see the formatting clearly.)

To remove the italics using the Font dialog box:

1 Select the title of the book again.

2 Choose Font from the Format menu.

3 Select Regular from the Font Style box.

4 Select OK.
Normal characters have replaced the italics.

> ***Tip*** For quick access to the Font dialog box after you have selected characters to be formatted, place the pointer over the selected text, click the right mouse button, and then select Font.

The Font dialog box is the most powerful character formatting tool you have in Word. You can use it to apply or clear any character formats in any combination. But if you have frequent need for simple character formats, using the dialog box will begin to seem awkward and time consuming. Word therefore provides two shortcuts: the Formatting toolbar and keyboard formatting commands. The ***Formatting toolbar*** appears near the top of the screen and allows you to use a mouse to make quick changes in common character and paragraph formats.

To italicize text using the Formatting toolbar:

1 If the Formatting toolbar, shown in Figure 3.6, does not appear near the top of the screen, choose Toolbars from the View menu, select Formatting, and then select OK.

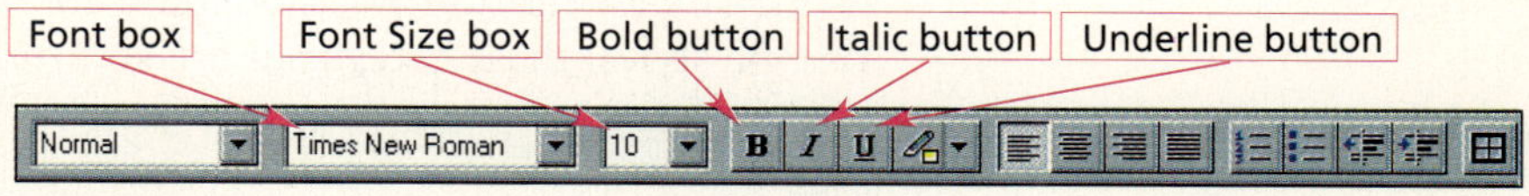

Figure 3.6

2 If necessary, select the title of the book again so that *The Puppet Masters* is highlighted once more.

3 Select the Italic button in the Formatting toolbar.

4 Select the button again to clear the italic formatting.

Each click on the button toggles back and forth between italic and nonitalic formatting. The Formatting toolbar also provides two other buttons for quick character formatting: one for boldface and one for underlining.

To italicize text using the keyboard:

1 Select the name of the book title once more so that *The Puppet Masters* is highlighted.

2 Press CTRL+**I** to apply italic.

3 Press CTRL+**I** a second time to remove the formatting.

4 Press CTRL+**I** a third time to reapply italic.

Word makes available a series of keyboard shortcuts to format characters, as shown in Table 3.1.

Table 3.1

Keyboard Shortcut	Character Style
CTRL+SHIFT+**A**	All caps
CTRL+**B**	Bold
CTRL+SHIFT+**D**	Double underline
CTRL+SHIFT+**H**	Hidden text
CTRL+**I**	Italic
CTRL+SHIFT+**K**	Small caps
CTRL+**U**	Continuous underline
CTRL+SHIFT+**W**	Word underline
CTRL+**=**	Subscript
CTRL+SHIFT+**=**	Superscript

EXIT If necessary, you can save your file, exit now, and continue this project later.

Changing Typeface and Type Size

The terminology that Word uses for type styles and sizes is the same as that used for more than two centuries by commercial printers, book publishers, and newspapers. A particular style of type is known as a ***font.*** By most classification systems, there are only a few very general categories of type styles; these categories are shown in Figure 3.7.

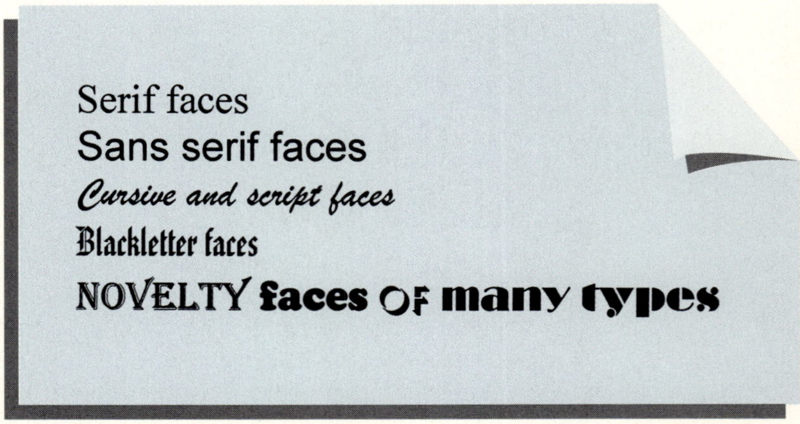

Figure 3.7

Within these general categories are thousands of type styles or fonts. Which fonts you have available in Word will depend on the printer and what fonts have been installed in Windows on the computer. A typewriter font, such as Courier New, is a ***fixed-space font,*** which means all letters have equal width and letters line up in columns. A fixed-space font is a good choice for manuscripts or other materials in draft form. Most typefaces are ***proportionally spaced,*** which means some letters are wider than others. A lowercase *i* is much thinner than an uppercase *W,* for instance, in a proportionally spaced font. ***Serif fonts*** have small crosslines, called serifs, at the end of the main letter strokes. A serif font such as Times New Roman is a good choice for ***body text***—the main reading material in reports, letters, and so on. ***Sans serif fonts,*** such as Helvetica or Arial, lack those crosslines. Sans serif fonts are slightly difficult to read for large amounts of text, but they are an excellent choice for headings, especially when bold. Cursive, blackletter, and novelty fonts should be avoided except where they are obviously appropriate, such as cursive type for a formal invitation or a particular novelty font for a poster.

Most type fonts are available in different styles, such as bold or italic. You can use styles for emphasis or to provide variation in your document. You might boldface a heading to make it stand out more clearly. Or you might italicize the title of a document to make it distinct from other information on the page.

Tip It's wonderful to have an assortment of type styles and sizes to work with in your documents. Unfortunately, it's tempting to want to use them all. Avoid the temptation because it leads to a hodgepodge of type styles that looks as though it was clipped from old magazines and pasted on paper like a ransom note.

A good rule of thumb is to avoid using more than two different typefaces in any one document. You could use a sans serif face such as Arial or Helvetica (in different styles and sizes) for the headings and a serif face such as Times New Roman (also in various styles and sizes) for body text. The result will be a cleaner, more tightly integrated document, but with enough variety that it doesn't look plain or uninteresting.

Printers measure type size in ***points.*** A point is 1/72 of an inch, so 72-point type is 1 inch high. Most books are printed using 9- to 11-point type. Most of the headings in this module are in 22-point type. Average newspaper headlines are about 30 to 40 points. Word is capable of producing type sizes from 4 to 127 points in 1/2-point increments. Whether that full range of sizes is actually available to you will depend on the font you're using and on the printer.

The steps in the pages that follow assume you have at least a few different type fonts and sizes to work with although you may not be able to match the exact fonts used in the examples. You will begin by formatting the entire flyer in 12-point Times Roman, then changing the heading lines to a sans serif font. The most common such font is Arial, which is used in the following examples. If Arial isn't available, substitute Helvetica or the closest sans serif font you have.

To change typeface and size using the Formatting toolbar:

1 Select the entire document (triple-click in the selection bar or press CTRL + **A**).

2 Click the down arrow button to the right of the Font size box in the Formatting toolbar, as shown in Figure 3.8.

Figure 3.8

3 Select 12.

Your flyer is probably already formatted as Times New Roman, the default typeface for Word's Normal template. In that case, you can skip to step 6. If it is formatted with some other typeface, steps 4 and 5 will convert it to Times New Roman.

4 Click the down arrow button to the right of the Font box in the Formatting toolbar.

5 Select Times New Roman (or some equivalent serif text face).

6 Select the text on the top line of the flyer: *Film Festival.*

7 Click the down arrow button to the right of the Font box in the Formatting toolbar.

8 Select Arial (or some equivalent sans serif face).

9. Use the Font size box to format the selected text as 24 point.

Changing fonts and point sizes with the Font dialog box works the same way as using the Formatting toolbar. The difference is that although the dialog box isn't as easily accessible, you can change other character attributes at the same time if you need to.

To change font size and character style using the Font dialog box:

1. Select the second line of the flyer: *50's Creature Features.*
2. Choose Font from the Format menu to open the Font dialog box.
3. Select the Font tab if it is not on top already.
4. Select Arial in the Font box.
5. Select Bold in the Font Style box.
6. Select 36 in the Size box.
7. Select OK.
8. Click anywhere in the text to cancel the selection.

The top of your document should resemble Figure 3.9.

Film·Festival¶

50's·Creature·Features¶

Show·Times:·8·p.m.·and·10·p.m.,·Bijou·Theater,·Main·and·Western→Admission:·$2.50¶
June·15 → The·Blob¶
Paramount,·USA,·1958.·It's·teenagers·vs.·ravenous·Jell-O,·as·a·gelatinous·mass·from·space·begins·devouring·small-town·inhabitants.·The·film·was·one·of·Steve·McQueen's·first·roles·and·became·synonymous·with·bad·film·making·despite·its·relative·popularity,·a·sequel,·and·a·remake.¶

Figure 3.9

Tip When word processors that could use various type fonts in various sizes were first developed, writing instructors noticed an interesting phenomenon. Students using the older word processors, which limited them to one set of characters, seemed to write better than students using the newer, more flexible machines. The problem, apparently, was that students using the newer word processors were being mesmerized by all the formatting options and distracted from the content of their writing. As a result, the quality of their writing suffered.

The solution, of course, is not to get rid of the formatting flexibility—the design and format of a document are part of the way the document communicates. On the other hand, it's not very wise to expect a dazzling design to cover up bad writing. In the end, it's probably best to make writing and design two distinct issues and focus on them separately. Word can help you do this with the Draft font. To use this font, you would choose Options from the Tools menu, select the View tab, and select Draft Font. Your entire document will be displayed in a single type font and size. This option makes it easier to focus on the words themselves. Then, when you are ready to address character-formatting issues, go back to the View tab in the Options dialog box and clear the Draft Font selection.

USING SUBSCRIPTS AND SUPERSCRIPTS

Subscripts and superscripts are useful for footnote references, chemical formulas, or mathematical notation. A ***subscript*** appears slightly below the normal baseline for the text (H_2O); a ***superscript*** appears slightly above the baseline ($c^2 = a^2 + b^2$). Word will automatically reduce the size of the character so that it fits as a superscript or subscript.

To format a superscript using the Font dialog box:

1 In the July 13 film description, position the insertion point between *equation* and the comma that follows.

2 Press (SPACE) then type **E=mc2**

3 Select the single character *2* in *E=mc2*.

4 Choose Font from the Format menu to open the Font dialog box.

5 Select the Font tab if it is not already on top.

6 Select Superscript in the Effects area (so that a check mark appears in the box beside it), as shown in Figure 3.10.

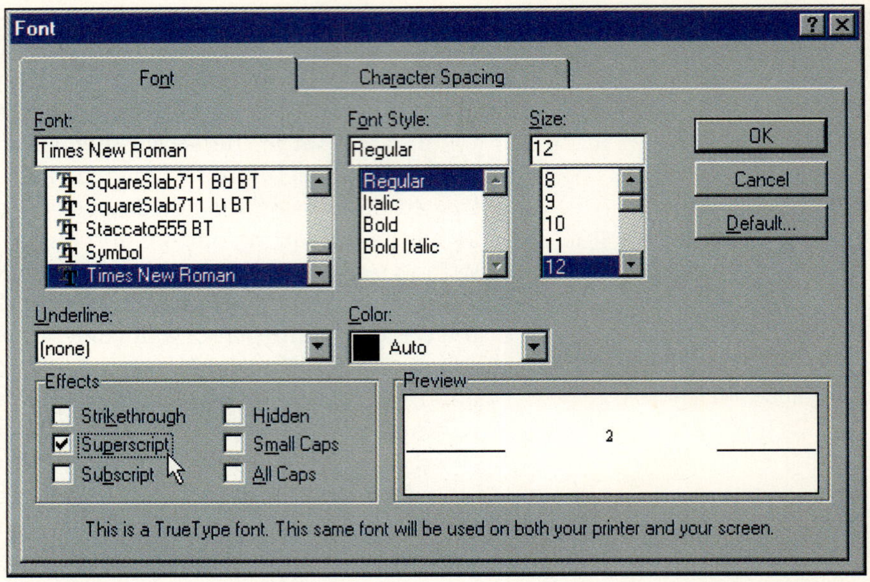

Figure 3.10

7 Select OK.
Your screen should look like Figure 3.11.

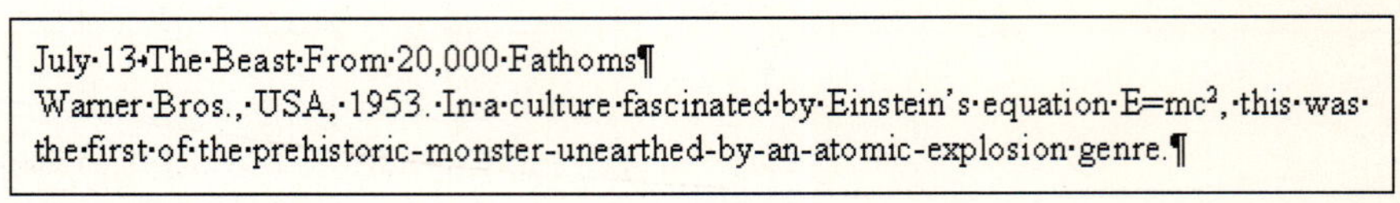

Figure 3.11

EXIT If necessary, you can save your file, exit now, and continue this project later.

REPEATING AND COPYING CHARACTER FORMATS

To polish the flyer more, it would help to have the film dates and titles appear more distinctly, in a boldface sans serif font. You could format the date and title lines by selecting each one, then applying the needed format, and then going on to the next date and title line. Obviously, the more complex the format, the longer this procedure will take. Word provides shortcuts to make this type of operation easier and faster. Repeating character formats is useful if you've just formatted one block of text and want to apply the same format to a series of other blocks. Copying character formats allows you to "borrow" the existing format information from one block of text and apply it to another block.

To repeat a character format:

1 Select the date and title line of the June 15 film. (Recall that the easiest way to select a single line is to click in the selection bar to the left of the line.)

2 Choose Font from the Format menu to open the Font dialog box.

3 Select the Font tab if it is not already on top.

4 Select the same sans serif face that you selected for the name in the top line of the document (probably Arial).

5 Select Bold in the Font Style box.

6 Select OK to complete the format choice.
Check to see that the heading is now displayed in boldface sans serif.

7 Select the date and title line for the June 22 film.

8 Choose Repeat Font Formatting from the Edit menu (or press CTRL+Y) to repeat the formatting operation.

The Repeat Font Formatting command works well as long as you do all the formatting operations at the same time. If you want to copy existing character formatting in the middle of performing other operations, however, Word allows you to borrow formatting information without copying the content itself. This is a two-step operation that uses the Format Painter button in the Standard toolbar. First you "dip the paintbrush" in the formatting that you want to copy. Then you "brush" across the text you want to format.

To copy a character format using the Format Painter button:

1 Position the insertion point somewhere within one of the two date and film title lines you've already formatted in boldface sans serif.

2 Select the Format Painter button in the Standard toolbar.
Note that the pointer now has a small paintbrush attached to it.

3 Drag the paintbrush pointer to select the date and title line for the June 29 film.
As soon as you release the mouse button to complete the text selection, the format information, but not the content, is transferred from the already formatted date and title line to the one you selected.

4 Use the same procedure to format the other three date and title lines in the flyer.

INSERTING SPECIAL CHARACTERS

A font of type normally contains many characters that don't appear on the keyboard, such as foreign-language characters, mathematical symbols, and publishing symbols. In addition, special fonts are available that consist entirely of special characters. Word allows you easy access to both through the Insert Symbol command.

Assume that one of the members of your publicity committee reminds you that Jell-O is a trademarked name and should be identified as such in the flyer by the trademark sign (™).

To insert a special publishing character:

1 Position the insertion point between *Jell-O* and the comma that follows it in the description of the June 15 film.

2 Choose Symbol from the Insert menu to open the Symbol dialog box.

3 Select the Symbols tab if it is not already on top.

4 Select *(normal text)* in the Font box if it isn't selected already.

5 Select the ™ symbol, as shown in Figure 3.12.

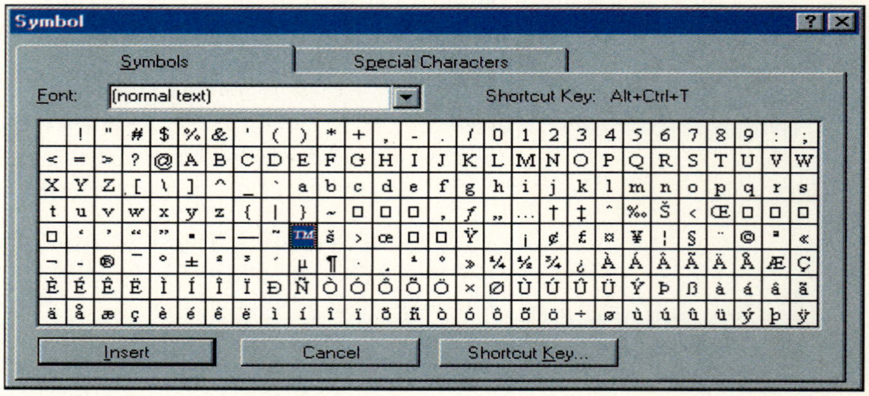

Figure 3.12

Note that the shortcut keystroke combination for this special character (ALT+CTRL+T) appears at the top of the dialog box. If you use a special symbol frequently, it would probably be faster to remember and use its keystroke combination.

6 Select Insert to insert the trademark symbol.

7 Select Close to close the Symbol dialog box.

You can also use Word's ***AutoCorrect*** feature to insert special characters, including the trademark symbol. As its name suggests, AutoCorrect is designed to automatically correct typing errors, so if you type *adn,* it will automatically substitute *and.* AutoCorrect can also substitute symbols for their typed abbreviations. If you type *(tm),* Word will substitute ™. If you type *(c),* Word will substitute ©. If you type two hyphens *(--),* Word will substitute a dash. Assume you need to add another sentence to the description of the July 6 movie.

To use AutoCorrect to create a dash character:

1 Position the insertion point immediately in front of *This* following the year of release of the July 13 movie.

2 Type **`The creature is the quintessential 50's movie monster`** (with no space following).

3 Type two hyphens, one immediately following the other and with no spaces before or after.

4 Type **`an amphibious being that lurks beneath the murky waters of the Amazon River.`**

5 Press (SPACE)
Word substitutes a single dash character for the two hyphens you typed.

To save and print your document:

1 Save your document.

2 Print a copy of the flyer.

The Next Step

Explore what other special characters are available on the computer system you are using. In addition to the special characters available in the Normal Text font, many systems have a Symbol font, containing the Greek alphabet and a variety of mathematical symbols, and a Wingdings font, containing different sorts of arrows, highlighted numbers, astrological signs, and so on.

Through these special characters and character formats, the personal computer has brought a new look to all kinds of documents, from business letters, to reports, to newsletters. The widespread availability of different typefaces in different sizes has made it straightforward and inexpensive to do what only commercial printers used to do at relatively high prices. These capabilities are part of the basis of the desktop publishing revolution.

Unfortunately, having the equipment to use typefaces doesn't teach you how to use them. Start collecting examples of documents you think are well designed, particularly documents of a type that are of special interest to you. You can adapt those design ideas to your own work. Watch also for documents you think are poorly designed, and note what it would take to transform these documents into an effective format.

Summary and Exercises

Summary

- Word distinguishes three types of building blocks in a document: characters, paragraphs, and sections. Each has its own set of formatting characteristics.
- Characters can be normal, bold, italic, underlined, or a number of other styles. They can be superscripted or subscripted. They can be different fonts or point sizes. They can have expanded or condensed character spacing.
- You can format blocks of characters by first selecting the characters and then applying the format.
- You can apply character formats by using the Font dialog box, the Formatting toolbar, or keyboard commands.
- Type styles are known as fonts. Type sizes are measured in points (1/72 of an inch).
- You can repeat formatting operations by choosing Repeat from the Edit menu (or pressing (CTRL) + **Y**).

- You can copy character formats by using the Format Painter button in the Standard toolbar.
- You can insert special characters using the Insert Symbol command and Word's AutoCorrect feature. Most systems have special fonts containing nothing but special characters and symbols.

Key Terms and Operations

Key Terms
AutoCorrect
body text
fixed-space font
font
Formatting toolbar
points
proportionally spaced font
sans serif font
serif font
subscript
superscript

Operations
Change type font and size
Copy character formats
Insert special characters

Study Questions

Multiple Choice

1. Word recognizes three types of document building blocks. Which of the following is *not* one of them?
   a. characters
   b. words
   c. paragraphs
   d. sections
2. Which of the following key combinations formats selected text as bold?
   a. SHIFT+B
   b. ALT+B
   c. CTRL+B
   d. SHIFT+CTRL+B
3. A point, the measurement system for type size, is equivalent to:
   a. 1/8 inch
   b. 1/35 inch
   c. 1/72 inch
   d. 1/100 inch
4. Which of the following type styles is generally best for large amounts of reading matter?
   a. serif
   b. sans serif
   c. cursive
   d. novelty
5. Which of the following includes a superscript?
   a. CO_2
   b. Español
   c. $A = \pi r^2$
   d. Française
6. To repeat a formatting operation, press:
   a. CTRL+R
   b. CTRL+Y
   c. CTRL+X
   d. CTRL+O
7. Which of the following is not a character attribute (a character format that can be changed in the Font dialog box)?
   a. double spacing
   b. underlining
   c. font
   d. color
8. You are most likely to find Greek characters such as π or δ in:
   a. the Times Roman font.
   b. the Wingdings font.
   c. the Helvetica font.
   d. the Symbol font.

9. Which of the following character formats is not available in the Formatting toolbar?
   a. bold
   b. font changes
   c. superscript
   d. underline

10. Foreign-language accents and other special symbols are available through which of these menus?
   a. File
   b. Edit
   c. Format
   d. Insert

Short Answer

1. To format selected text as italic, press __________.
2. To format selected text as bold, press __________.
3. The __________ allows you to set type style, type size, bold, italic, or underline with a few clicks.
4. A particular style of type is called a __________.
5. A line of 18-point type is about __________-inch tall.
6. The name of a serif typeface available on your system is __________.
7. To select a single word prior to italicizing it, place the pointer somewhere within the word and __________.
8. To remove underlining from a word, first select the word and then click __________ in the Formatting toolbar.
9. You can copy format information by using the __________ button in the Formatting toolbar.
10. If you want type that is 1 inch tall for a poster, you should select the text block and set the size to __________ points.

For Discussion

1. How can you copy character formats using the mouse?
2. How can you avoid typographical monotony if you use only two fonts in a document?
3. Take an advertisement from a magazine and classify the fonts used in it according to the following system: serif, sans serif, cursive, blackletter, and novelty.

Review Exercises

Formatting a Memo

1. Retrieve the memo you corrected at the end of Project 2, named *Brochure Memo.*
2. Format all the text in a serif face like Times New Roman.
3. Make all the characters 11 point.
4. Make the *MEMO* heading 14 point in a sans serif face (such as Arial or Helvetica).
5. Boldface the headings *To, From,* and *Subject.*
6. Save the file, and print a copy of it.

Formatting a Meeting Agenda

1. Retrieve the agenda you saved under the name *Meeting Agenda* at the end of Project 2.
2. Format all the text as 12-point Times New Roman (or a similar serif face).
3. Format the *Agenda* title line as 24-point Arial or Helvetica, in bold.
4. Format the name of the club and the date line as 14-point Arial or Helvetica.
5. Make the *Old Business* and *New Business* headings bold.
6. Save the revised memo, and print a copy of the document.

Creating a News Release

Word's templates must be installed on your system in order to work this exercise. Ask your professor if you do not find them on your system.

1. Open a new document based on the Professional Press Release template (located under the Publications tab in the New dialog box).
2. Change the name of the company to the *SciFi Film Society.*
3. Change the address and telephone information to your own. (Make up a fax number if necessary.) Change the name of the contact person to your name.
4. Change the release time to *For Immediate Release*
5. Change the main heading to *50's Creature Features Film Festival Scheduled for Summer*
6. Change the size of the main heading to 14 point so that it will all fit on one line. Delete the subheading.
7. Change the date line from San Francisco to your town. Change the date to the current date.
8. Change the body of the release to:

   Six 1950's movie monsters will invade the screen again this summer in a film festival sponsored by the SciFi Film Society and the Bijou Theater.

   ''We picked the movies to have some fun and to take a look at how movie monsters developed after King Kong was re-released in the early 1950s,'' said Paul Kettering, president of the film society.

   The festival will feature *The Beast From 20,000 Fathoms*, based on a Ray Bradbury short story, and the first of the Godzilla movies, released in the United States in 1954. Also included will be *The Blob*, one of Steve McQueen's first films and thought by some to be one of the worst films ever made.

9. Save the file as *Film Festival News Release,* and print a copy of it.

Assignments

Finding Fonts on the Web

When type was cast in metal, type foundries required complex and expensive equipment. Each type style and size required a separate set of molds to manufacture the type. As a result, relatively few type fonts were available. Computerized fonts, however, are just electronic patterns—much easier to design and manufacture. Check the B/C URL http://www.aw.com/is/select/word7 and explore the links to electronic type foundries. Some may even have samples you can download and try for yourself.

Formatting the Telephone List

Typefaces have personalities. Some are conservative, whereas others are flashy. Some are easygoing; others are forceful. Retrieve the telephone list you saved under the file name *Telephone List.* Just for fun, create a new version of the list under the file name *Silly Fone List* (you'll need to use the Save As option).

Pick a name on your list, and select the line it's on (by clicking once in the selection bar). Format that line with a typeface that matches as closely as possible the personality of the person whose name appears there. Pick a bold, conservative face if that fits, or an elegant, italic face if that fits. Repeat for each of the people on your list. Save the list and print a copy.

Now, retrieve the original version from the file *Telephone List.* Format it in a way that makes the list easy to read and use. Consider font and size. You may want to boldface names so that they stand out better. Format the heading to separate it from the names and addresses. When you're finished, save the list again under the file name *Telephone List,* and print a copy.

PROJECT 4: PARAGRAPH FORMATTING

Objectives

After completing this project, you should be able to:

- Set the alignment of lines in a paragraph
- Change paragraph shading
- Create paragraph indentations
- Set tab stops
- Set paragraph spacing
- Copy paragraph formats
- Create and apply simple styles

In this project, you will continue to polish the appearance of the film flyer using paragraph formatting. You will use paragraph indentation and tab stops to make the separate movie titles and descriptions stand out more clearly. You will use a typographic reverse (white type on a black background) to make the title more dominant. You will create your own custom indentation style and use it to create consistently formatted paragraphs within the flyer.

CASE STUDY: STRUCTURING THE FLYER

In the last project, you began to polish the flyer by using professional-looking type fonts, by adding bold and italics for emphasis, and by using special characters for precision and accuracy. The flyer still looks somewhat jumbled, however. It lacks a visible typographic structure that clearly displays its underlying organization. You can use paragraph indentations and tab stop settings to align blocks of text in a way that makes the organization of the flyer apparent at a glance.

Designing the Solution

To make the individual dates and movie titles stand out, you can indent the descriptions and put extra space between them. That will structure the flyer more like a calendar and make it much easier to comprehend. To make the main heading bolder and create typographic contrast on the flyer, you can make it white against black. To give the heading information a more interesting shape, you can move the top label to the right, center the main heading, and force the subheading to fill out the line.

When you finish, the top portion of the flyer should look like Figure 4.1.

Film Festival

50's Creature Features

Show Times: 8 p.m. and 10 p.m., Bijou Theater, Main and Western Admission: $2.50

June 15 The Blob

Paramount, USA, 1958. It's teenagers vs. ravenous Jell-O™, as a gelatinous mass from space begins devouring small-town inhabitants. The film was one of Steve McQueen's first roles and became synonymous with bad film making despite its relative popularity, a sequel, and a remake.

June 22 Godzilla, King of the Monsters

Toho, Japan, 1954. One critic called the monster a 400-foot-high plucked chicken. Perhaps, but he started an industry. Raymond Burr stars opposite the chicken in this recut US release.

Figure 4.1

Choosing Paragraph Format Options

Webster's Dictionary says a paragraph is "a distinct section or subdivision of a written or printed composition that consists of from one to many sentences, forms a rhetorical unit, and is indicated by beginning on a new, usually indented, line."

Word's operating definition is simpler and shorter: a paragraph begins after a paragraph mark (¶) and ends with the next paragraph mark. In Word, strictly speaking, paragraphs have to do with formatting, not grammar although there is often an obvious parallel.

You can format paragraphs in Word to change the alignment of lines, how lines are indented, tab stops, line spacing, spacing between paragraphs, how the paragraph will be treated at a page break, and borders and shading. It will probably come as no surprise that you format paragraphs by first selecting them and then applying the formatting. A paragraph is considered selected in Word when the insertion point is anywhere within the paragraph or when the current selection includes some part of the paragraph. If you want to format a single paragraph, you can just position the insertion point somewhere inside that paragraph. If you want to format more than one paragraph, you can create a selection block that includes at least some part of each paragraph to be formatted.

As with character styles, you can apply paragraph formatting in any of three ways: by using the Paragraph dialog box, the keyboard, or the Formatting toolbar. You can do almost all common paragraph formatting using your mouse and the Formatting toolbar.

LINE ALIGNMENT

One of the most basic paragraph formats is line alignment. Word can create four kinds of paragraph line alignment: aligned left, centered, aligned right, or justified (see Figure 4.2). For most work, ***aligned left*** is appropriate and more legible. ***Centered alignment*** works well for some headings and for small amounts of text that need a formal presentation. ***Aligned right*** formatting should be avoided except for a very few lines of text, such as a figure caption or short heading. Text with ***justified alignment*** has an even margin on both left and right sides and usually looks best with multicolumn formats such as newsletters.

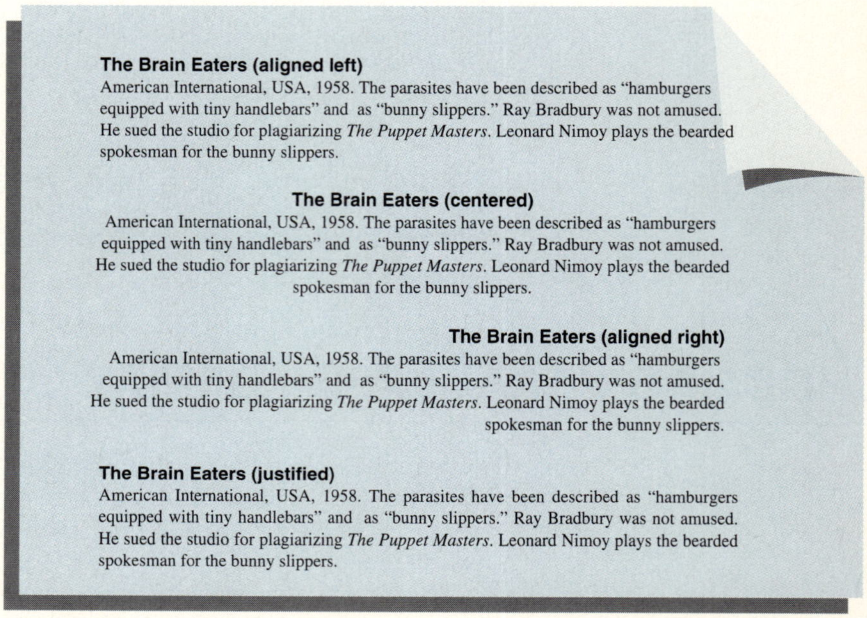

The Brain Eaters (aligned left)
American International, USA, 1958. The parasites have been described as "hamburgers equipped with tiny handlebars" and as "bunny slippers." Ray Bradbury was not amused. He sued the studio for plagiarizing *The Puppet Masters*. Leonard Nimoy plays the bearded spokesman for the bunny slippers.

The Brain Eaters (centered)
American International, USA, 1958. The parasites have been described as "hamburgers equipped with tiny handlebars" and as "bunny slippers." Ray Bradbury was not amused. He sued the studio for plagiarizing *The Puppet Masters*. Leonard Nimoy plays the bearded spokesman for the bunny slippers.

The Brain Eaters (aligned right)
American International, USA, 1958. The parasites have been described as "hamburgers equipped with tiny handlebars" and as "bunny slippers." Ray Bradbury was not amused. He sued the studio for plagiarizing *The Puppet Masters*. Leonard Nimoy plays the bearded spokesman for the bunny slippers.

The Brain Eaters (justified)
American International, USA, 1958. The parasites have been described as "hamburgers equipped with tiny handlebars" and as "bunny slippers." Ray Bradbury was not amused. He sued the studio for plagiarizing *The Puppet Masters*. Leonard Nimoy plays the bearded spokesman for the bunny slippers.

Figure 4.2

The flyer that you've begun is currently all aligned left, the default line alignment in Word. You will realign some of the heading lines to give the top of the film flyer a stronger structure.

> ***Tip*** Formatting paragraphs is easier when it's clear where they begin and end. If paragraph marks are not displayed on the screen, select the Show/Hide ¶ button in the Standard toolbar to display them.

To align the heading using the Paragraph dialog box:

1 If the flyer is not in the document window, retrieve it now. The screen should resemble Figure 4.3.

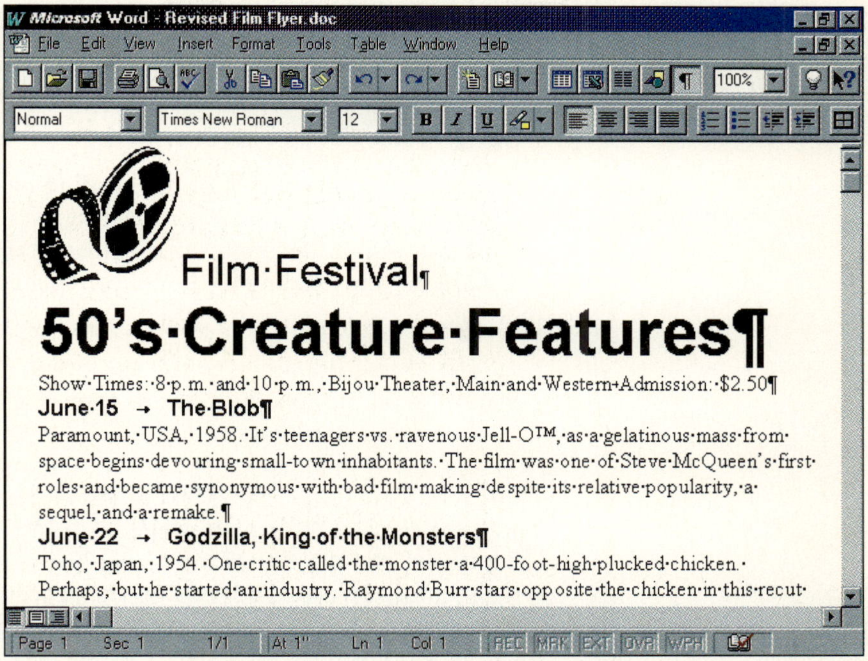

Figure 4.3

2 Position the insertion point somewhere within the title, *50's Creature Features.*

3 Choose Paragraph from the Format menu to open the Paragraph dialog box.

4 Select the Indents and Spacing tab if it is not already on top.

5 Select the Alignment pull-down list box so that the four alignment options are revealed, as shown in Figure 4.4.

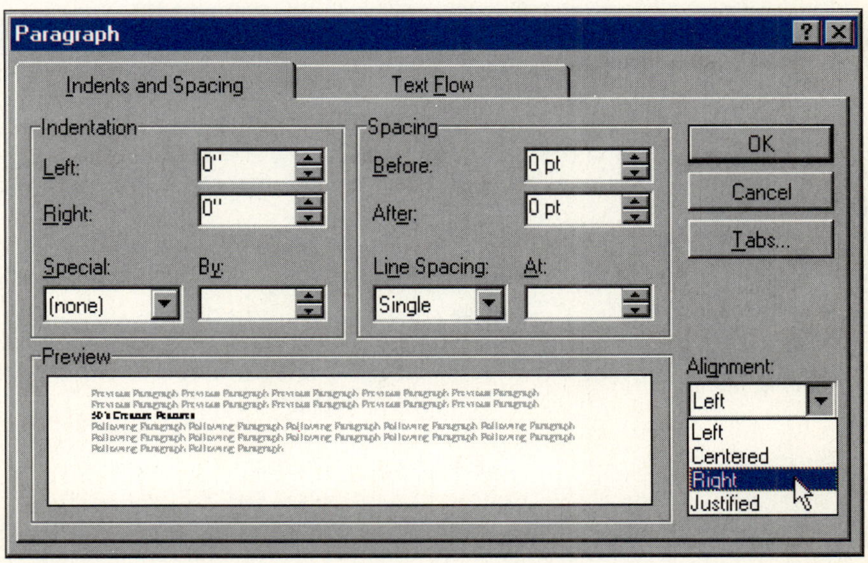

Figure 4.4

6 Select the Right option.
The bold paragraph in the Preview box changes shape to show how selected paragraphs will look after the formatting is applied.

7 Select OK to complete the formatting choice.

Note the appearance of the heading on the page. If there were many lines, or if the lines were longer, they would be very difficult to read. It's for that reason that right-aligned paragraphs are rarely used. You will be changing the heading in the following steps.

> ***Tip*** For quick access to the Paragraph dialog box, position the pointer on the paragraph you want to format, click the right mouse button, and then select Paragraph.

The Paragraph dialog box is comprehensive: it gives you access to nearly all the paragraph formats available in Word. But you'll rarely use all the formats, and the Paragraph dialog box requires several keystrokes or mouse operations to use. To speed up the process, Word allows you to use the Formatting toolbar and keyboard for the more common paragraph formatting options.

To align the heading of the flyer using the Formatting toolbar:

1 Select the heading as before (position the insertion point somewhere within *50's Creature Features*).

2 Select the Center button in the Formatting toolbar, as shown in Figure 4.5.

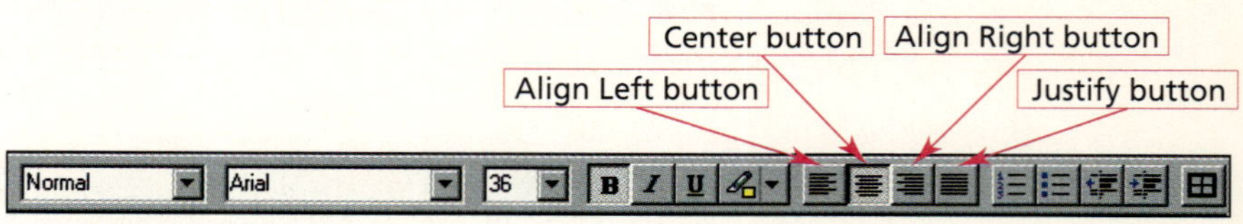

Figure 4.5

3 Select the other three alignment buttons to see how they affect the heading.
The justified alignment will look like the left alignment because the heading is only one line long.

4 Click the Align Left button to leave the heading aligned left.

Word also provides simple keyboard shortcuts for aligning paragraphs. These shortcuts are summarized in Table 4.1.

Table 4.1

Keyboard Shortcut	Paragraph Alignment
CTRL + L	Aligned left
CTRL + E	Centered
CTRL + R	Aligned right
CTRL + J	Justified

To center the heading using the keyboard:

1 Select the heading as before.

2 Press CTRL + E to center the heading.

Changing Paragraph Shading

To make the flyer more visible and commanding, it would be useful to make the title of the film series—*50's Creature Features*—more prominent. A simple way to do this is to use a typographic ***reverse,*** in which white letters appear against a black background. This type of treatment is one of the borders and shadings options available using Word's ***Borders toolbar.***

To reverse the film series title:

1 Be sure the insertion point is positioned somewhere within the film series title line: *50's Creature Features.*

2 Click the Borders button at the right end of the Formatting toolbar to make the Borders toolbar appear, shown in Figure 4.6.

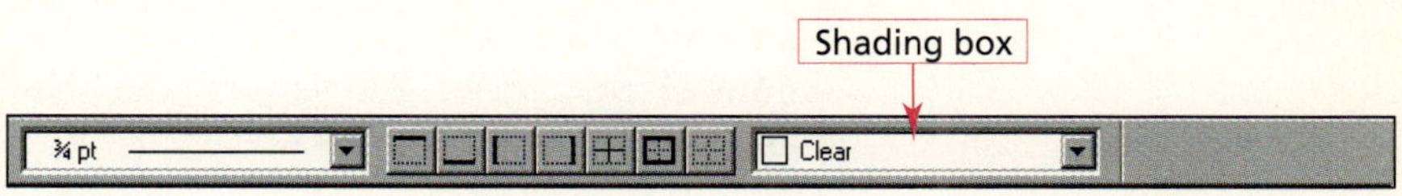

Figure 4.6

3 Click the down arrow to the right of the Shading box on the Borders toolbar.

4 Select Solid (100%) to apply the reverse.

5 Click the Borders button on the Formatting toolbar again to close the Borders toolbar.

The Borders toolbar also allows you to put gray shading or patterns behind a paragraph, to put lines above or below, or to put boxes around the paragraph. Used sparingly, these effects can be very useful in emphasizing headings or singling a paragraph out for particular emphasis.

Indenting Paragraphs

Word allows you to indent a paragraph from the left and right margins and to indent the first line independently on the left. You could, for instance, indent from both left and right margins to indicate a block of quoted material, or you could indent the first line alone to make paragraph breaks more obvious. You also could leave the first line unindented and indent only the subsequent lines in the paragraph, which is called a ***hanging indentation.***

To make the flyer easier to read and make the dates more obvious, you will format most of the paragraphs so that the movie descriptions are indented and line up with the film titles. The dates will appear to the left of each film title.

Table 4.2 shows several keyboard commands you can use to establish paragraph indentations.

Table 4.2

Keyboard Shortcut	Paragraph Indentation
CTRL + **M**	Indent to next tab
CTRL + SHIFT + **M**	Decrease indentation by one tab
CTRL + **T**	Hanging indentation to next tab
CTRL + SHIFT + **T**	Reduce hanging indentation by one tab

To establish an indentation using the keyboard:

1 Position the insertion point somewhere within the description section of the June 15 film. Do not include the date and film title line.

2 Press CTRL + **M**
The lines in the description paragraph are all indented to the first default tab stop, which is located at 1/2 inch. The date and film title line remain unindented.

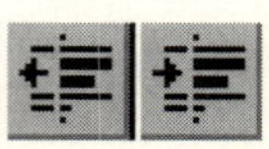

Tip You can use the Increase Indent button on the Formatting toolbar to indent selected text to the next tab stop. The Decrease Indent button will move the indentation leftward to the preceding tab stop.

You can use a mouse to set or modify indentations and tab stops on Word's ruler, which is shown in Figure 4.7. The three triangular ***indent markers*** are used to set indentations. You can "grab" each indent marker with the mouse pointer and slide the marker to the left or right to adjust the indentation. (To grab a marker, position the pointer over it and then click and hold down the mouse button; the marker will move with the pointer.) The top-left indent marker sets the amount of indentation for the first line. The bottom-left indent marker sets the amount of indentation for the remaining lines in the paragraph; this indentation determines the paragraph's left edge. The indent marker at the right sets the amount of indentation from the right edge. You'll be moving the left indent markers to increase the amount of indentation to 3/4 inch so as to leave adequate space for all the dates.

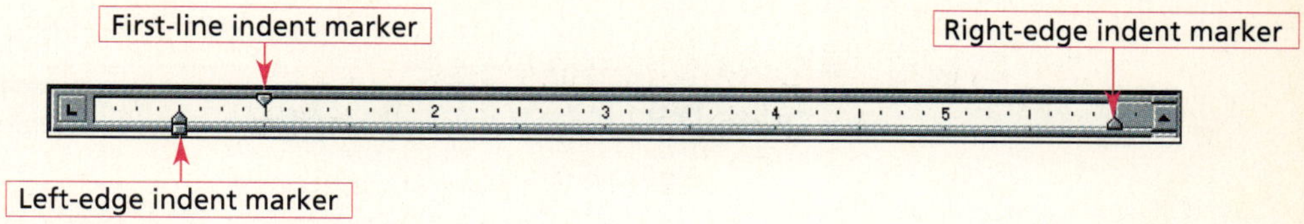

Figure 4.7

> ***Caution*** In doing the following series of numbered steps, be sure to grab the box that moves both the first-line and left-edge indent markers in tandem. If you grab only the lower triangle, which represents the left-edge indent marker, you will change only the left-edge indentation and create a hanging indent.

To set indentations with the ruler indent markers:

1 Make sure the ruler is visible on the screen. If not, choose Ruler from the View menu.

2 Make sure the insertion point is positioned somewhere inside the paragraph describing the June 15 film.

3 Position the pointer on the small box below the left-edge indent marker.

4 Press and hold down the mouse button to grab the first-line and left-edge indent markers.

5 Move the indent markers to the right so that they are positioned at the ¾-inch mark on the ruler, as shown in Figure 4.8.

6 Release the mouse button.

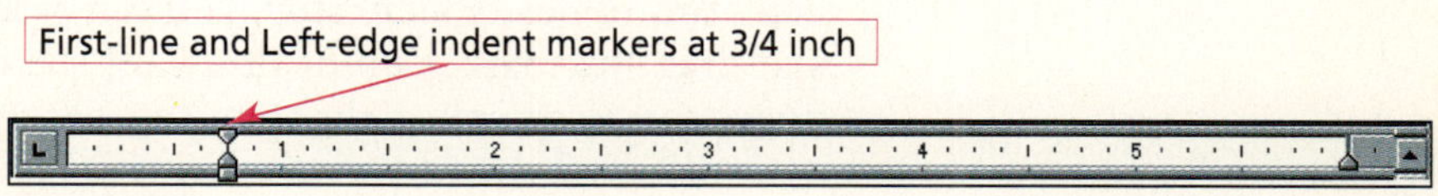

Figure 4.8

EXIT If necessary, you can save your file, exit Word now, and continue this project later.

SETTING TAB STOPS

The default tab stops in Word are normally set at ½-inch intervals. They are marked on the ruler with very small hash marks just below the ruler itself, as shown in Figure 4.9. The default settings are often satisfactory, but frequently you'll want to customize the settings to give your material optimum presentation. You can set not only the location of the tab stop, but also its style.

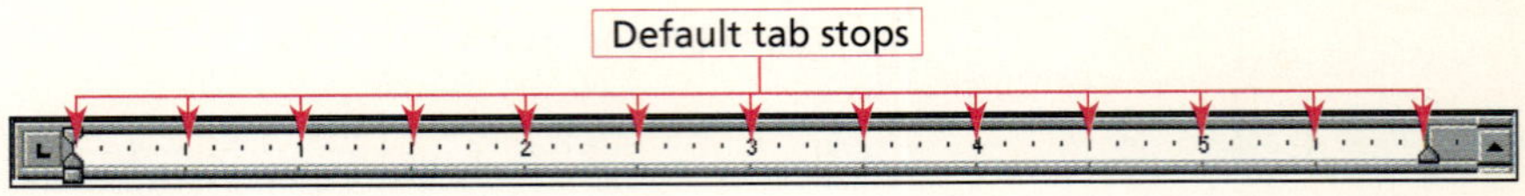

Figure 4.9

Word implements four styles of tab stops: left, center, right, and decimal. The ***left tab stop*** aligns the text on the left side under the tab stop. The ***center tab stop*** centers text on the tab stop. The ***right tab stop*** aligns text on the right side under the tab stop. The ***decimal tab stop*** aligns text (or, more commonly, numbers) on the decimal point under the tab stop. Figure 4.10 shows examples of each style of tab and the ruler line above, which indicates the tab stop settings.

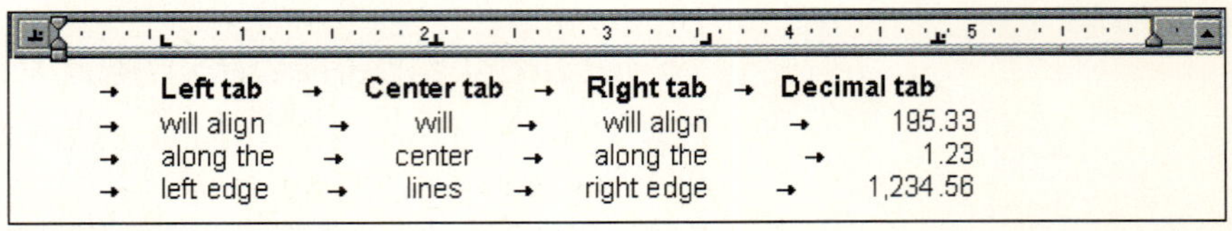

Figure 4.10

Each of the four styles of tab stops is indicated on the ruler by a different symbol and is set using the Tab Alignment button at the left edge of the ruler. You will select the Tab Alignment button until the style of tab stop you want appears. Then you will click the ruler where you want to set the tab stop. A tab stop of the style you selected will be inserted on the ruler. You can set additional tab stops by clicking at other points on the ruler. If you need to, you can grab the tab stops with the pointer and slide the markers from side to side to adjust the tab settings on the ruler. If you want to delete a tab stop, you can grab the marker with the pointer and drag the marker up or down off the ruler so that the tab marker disappears. Remember that tab stop settings are a paragraph format, so you must select all the text where you want the tab stops to be in effect before you set the tabs.

To unify the heading lines typographically, you will move the *Film Festival* heading and the admission price to the far right using tab stops. This treatment will create an overall block shape for the heading lines.

To move the Film Festival heading and admission price to the right margin:

1 Insert a tab character between the graphic and *Film Festival* in the first line of the flyer.
Be sure the insertion point is positioned somewhere within the first line.

2 Select the Tab Alignment button on the ruler until the right tab style appears, indicated by the symbol shown in Figure 4.11.

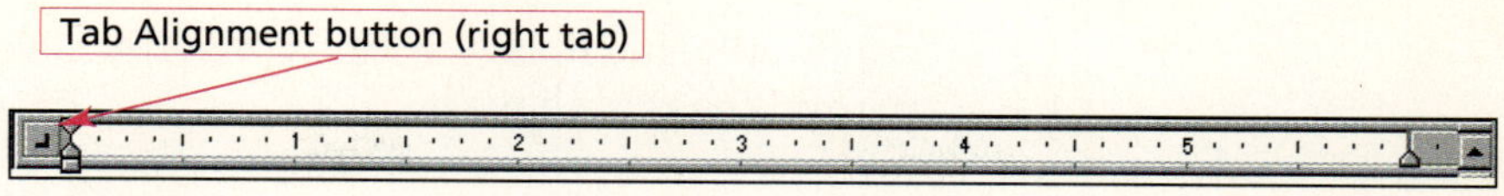

Figure 4.11

The tab actually needs to be positioned at the 6-inch mark, but Word will not allow you to set a tab stop on the margin. You can, however, set the tab stop close to the margin and then adjust it so that it is positioned correctly.

3 Click at the 5½-inch mark on the ruler to set the tab.

4 Grab the tab marker with the pointer and slide it to the right so that it is positioned at the 6-inch mark.

5 Position the insertion point somewhere on the third line of the flyer, listing the show times, theater location, and admission price.

6 Select Repeat Formatting from the Edit menu (or press CTRL + **Y**).

When you indented the description paragraph for the June 15 film earlier, you injected white space to the left of the description paragraph and helped separate one film listing from another. To make the organization neater, however, the film title should line up with the left edge of the film's description.

To set the tab stop for the film title line:

1 Position the insertion point somewhere within the date and title line for the June 15 film.

2 Select the Tab Alignment button on the ruler until the left tab style appears, indicated by the L-shaped symbol, as shown in Figure 4.12.

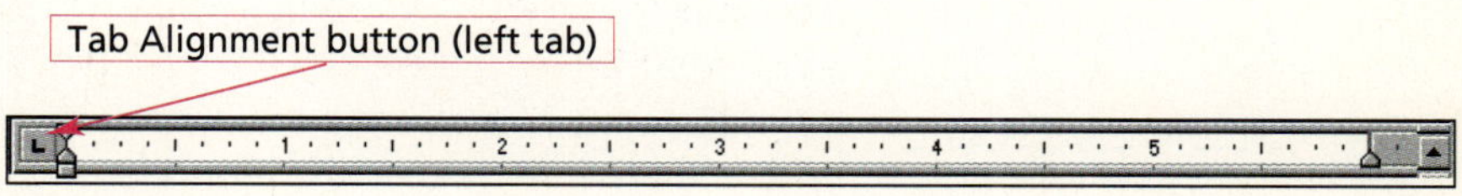

Figure 4.12

3 Click at the ¾-inch mark on the ruler to set the tab. Adjust the tab stop if needed by grabbing the marker with the pointer and sliding the marker from side to side.
The listing for the June 15 film should resemble Figure 4.13.

June 15 **The Blob**
Paramount, USA, 1958. It's teenagers vs. ravenous Jell-O™, as a gelatinous mass from space begins devouring small-town inhabitants. The film was one of Steve McQueen's first roles and became synonymous with bad film making despite its relative popularity, a sequel, and a remake.

Figure 4.13

The listing for the June 15 film is now much more clearly organized as a visual unit on the page. To complete the organization of the listing, however, it will help to add some space above the film title to separate it from the text above it.

Setting Paragraph Spacing

Paragraph spacing is a paragraph format in Word. You can set the spacing between lines in a paragraph (sometimes called ***leading*** because printers used to space lines apart using metal strips made of lead). You can also add extra space before or after a paragraph. To separate the film listing from typographic matter above it, you will add 10 points of space before the date and title paragraph.

To add space before a paragraph:

1 Using the *right* mouse button, click somewhere within the date and title line of the June 15 film.

2 Select Paragraph from the pull-down menu to open the Paragraph dialog box.

3 Type **10** in the Spacing Before box, as shown in Figure 4.14.

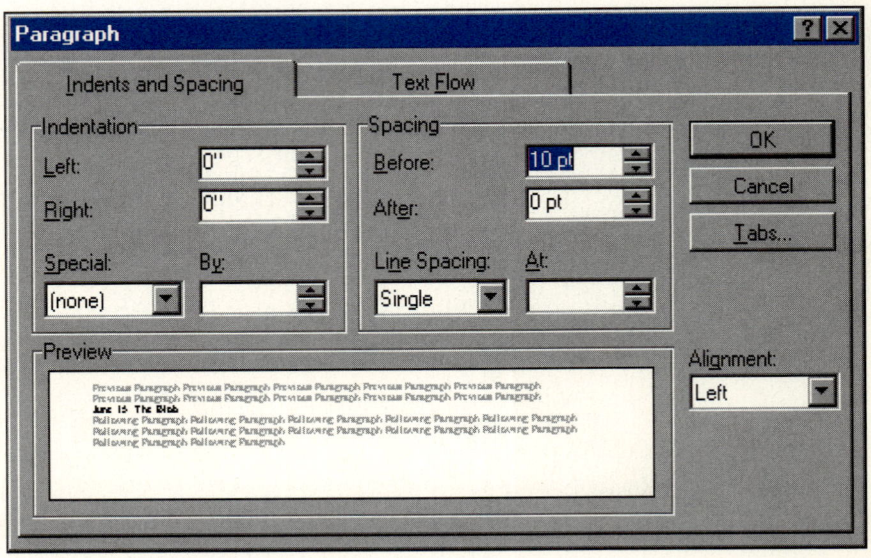

Figure 4.14

4 Select OK.

Note that 10 points of space have been inserted above the film title line, separating it from the heading information. The June 15 film listing now stands apart from the others and is much easier to read. What remains is to apply the same paragraph formatting to the other film listings so that all have the same indentation and extra spacing.

Tip If you want a quick look at font and paragraph formats, select the Help button at the right end of the Standard toolbar. The pointer will change into an arrow with a question mark attached to it. Then click anywhere in the text to get a listing of formatting information. When you are done, press (ESC) to cancel Help.

COPYING PARAGRAPH FORMATS

The formatting information for a paragraph is stored in the paragraph mark (¶) at the end of the paragraph. If you delete the paragraph mark, the formatting information for that paragraph disappears and the paragraph takes on the formatting of the paragraph it is joined with. On the other hand, if the insertion point is inside a paragraph and you press (ENTER) to begin a new paragraph, the new paragraph takes on the formatting of the previous one.

Perform the following steps to learn how Word's paragraph formatting information is copied from one paragraph to another.

To create an additional indented paragraph:

1 Be sure paragraph marks (¶) are visible to make it clear where paragraphs are located in your document.

2 Position the insertion point at the beginning of the description of the June 15 film, immediately in front of *Paramount.*

3 Press (ENTER) to start a new paragraph.
The new paragraph is indented just like the one where the insertion point was located. Anything you typed on this new line would be indented, just like the lines that follow it.

4 Press (BACKSPACE) to delete the new paragraph you just added.

To create an additional nonindented paragraph:

1 Position the insertion point at the end of the date and title line for the June 15 film, following *Blob.*

2 Press (ENTER) to start a new paragraph.
The new paragraph is not indented and has extra space before it, just like the line above it.

3 Press (BACKSPACE) to remove the new paragraph.

When you create a new paragraph from an old one, the new one receives the same formatting attributes as the old. That's helpful when you're adding text to an existing document. But it doesn't help when you want to copy formatting information from one paragraph to an already existing paragraph.

Using Styles

To complete formatting the film listings in the flyer, you need to copy formatting from one paragraph to another existing paragraph. You have formatted the June 15 film listing by indenting the description, setting tabs, and adding extra spacing above the film title line, but the other film listings are still unformatted. It's possible, of course, to format the remaining listings individually—selecting each one in turn, then applying the indent format, adjusting the indent, adding a tab stop and the extra space—but that approach would result in a lot of repetitive work and the possibility of errors and inconsistencies. Word provides an easier way: creating your own paragraph styles and then applying them to other paragraphs.

In Word, a ***style*** is a collection of formatting characteristics that is given a name and is accessible from the Style box in the Formatting toolbar. A particular style includes formatting information about the type font and size as well as about line alignment, indentations, and all other paragraph characteristics.

You have been using Word's default Normal style all along in preparing the film flyer. The style for the current selection appears in the Style box at the far left of the Formatting toolbar, as shown in Figure 4.15.

Figure 4.15

Word has a number of built-in styles such as Normal, but it also allows you to define your own styles. In the following set of steps, you will be creating two new styles, called Date & Title and Description, based on the paragraph formatting you have already applied to the listing for the June 15 film.

To create the Date & Title style:

1 Position the insertion point within the date and title line for the already formatted June 15 film.

2 Select the Style box at the left end of the Formatting toolbar.

3 Type **`Date & Title`** in the Style box.

4 Press (ENTER) to complete the style definition.

You have defined a new style named Date & Title that sets the tab stop and adds extra space above the line. Now you can apply the new style to date and title lines in the flyer.

To apply the Date & Title style to the June 22 film:

1 Position the insertion point somewhere within the date and title line for the June 22 film.

2 Select the down arrow to the right of the Style box.
The new Date & Title style will be in the list, as shown in Figure 4.16.

Figure 4.16

3 Select Date & Title to apply this style.

To apply the Date & Title style to the remainder of the flyer:

1 Position the insertion point within the date and title line for the June 29 film.

2 Select Repeat Style from the Edit menu (or press CTRL + **Y**) to apply the same styling to the selected paragraph.

3 Repeat this process with the other date and title lines.

To create and apply the Description style:

1 Position the insertion point within the description for the already formatted June 15 film.

2 Select the Style box at the left end of the Formatting toolbar.

3 Type `Description` in the Style box.

4 Press ENTER to complete the style definition.

5 Position the insertion point inside the description paragraph for the June 22 film.

6 Select Description from the Style box on the Formatting toolbar.

7 Format the description paragraphs for the other films.

At this point, the flyer is generally organized and visually structured. If you print out a copy of the flyer, or look at it with Word's Print Preview feature, you will notice that the horizontal space between the dates and the film titles is a little too tight. A slight adjustment would improve the appearance of the flyer markedly.

One of the advantages of using styles is that you can modify the style at any time, and Word will automatically apply the modifications to all paragraphs that have that style. In the steps that follow, you will increase the indent of the description paragraphs by ⅛ inch and move the tab stop in the date and title lines to the right by the same amount. But you will need to make the change in only one of the film listings and then redefine the style based on that listing.

To redefine the Date & Title style:

1 Position the insertion point somewhere within the date and title line for the June 22 film.

2 Use the mouse to grab the tab stop located at ¾ inch on the ruler and drag it to the right one mark, to ⅞ inch.

3 Select Date & Title in the Style box and press ENTER
The Reapply Style dialog box will appear. It allows you to redefine the Date & Title style so that the style will have the new ⅞-inch tab stop.

4 Press (ENTER) to redefine the style.

As soon as you redefine the style, Word reformats the other paragraphs that have the Date & Title style so that they also have a 7/8-inch tab stop.

To redefine the Description style:

1 Position the insertion point somewhere within the description paragraph for any one of the film listings.

2 Use the mouse to grab the small box on the ruler that controls the first-line and left-edge indent markers, and move it to the right, to the 7/8-inch mark.

3 Select Description in the Style box, and press (ENTER)

4 Press (ENTER) to redefine the style, which will automatically be applied to the other description paragraphs.

To save and print the flyer:

1 Save the completed flyer.

2 Print a copy of the flyer.

The Next Step

The basic character and paragraph formats you used in the film flyer can be used in almost any document to lend it credibility, emphasize its organization, and create interest. In many cases, Word can give you a head start on formatting if you use one of the many templates included in the New dialog box. You can adapt and modify any template as needed, and you can even save them to create new templates.

Summary and Exercises

Summary

- Word defines a paragraph as any amount of text that ends with a paragraph mark (¶).
- You format a paragraph by first selecting it and then applying the formatting.
- A paragraph is selected in Word when it contains the insertion point or when some portion of the paragraph is in the current selection.
- You can apply paragraph formatting using the Paragraph dialog box, the keyboard, or the Formatting toolbar. Nearly all common paragraph formatting can be accomplished using the Formatting toolbar and the ruler.
- A paragraph in Word can be formatted with different alignments (left, center, right, justified), different indentations, different tab stop settings, different line spacing, and so on.
- The paragraph mark contains the paragraph's formatting information.

When you press (ENTER) at the end of a paragraph, that paragraph's formatting information is copied into the new paragraph.

- You can use the Borders toolbar to create a typographic reverse, to put lines or boxes around paragraphs, or to put the paragraph in a shaded box.
- You can add extra space before or after a paragraph, or between the lines within the paragraph.
- You can create new paragraph styles using the Style box on the Formatting toolbar and then apply those styles to other paragraphs.
- Word uses four styles of tab stops: left, center, right, and decimal. Each paragraph can have its own settings for tab styles and positions.

Key Terms and Operations

Key Terms
aligned left
aligned right
Borders toolbar
centered alignment
center tab stop
decimal tab stop
hanging indentation
indent marker
justified alignment
leading
left tab stop
reverse
right tab stop
style

Operations
Change paragraph alignment
Copy paragraph formats
Define and use styles
Indent paragraphs
Set tab stops

Study Questions

Multiple Choice

1. To select a paragraph, you must:
   a. Select every character within the paragraph, including the paragraph mark (¶).
   b. Just be sure the paragraph mark (¶) is selected.
   c. Make sure that some part of the paragraph is selected or that the insertion point is somewhere inside the paragraph.
   d. Use the selection bar and mouse.

2. The formatting information for a paragraph is stored in:
   a. the paragraph mark (¶) at the beginning of the paragraph.
   b. the paragraph mark (¶) at the end of the paragraph.
   c. an invisible code at the beginning of the paragraph.
   d. the Formatting toolbar.

3. To create a new style based on an existing formatted paragraph:
   a. Use the Paragraph dialog box.
   b. Press (CTRL)+S
   c. Use the ruler.
   d. Use the Style box in the Formatting toolbar.

4. Which of the following is *not* one of the tab styles in Word?
   a. left
   b. center
   c. right
   d. justified

5. Which of the following keyboard commands will center a paragraph?
   a. (CTRL)+H
   b. (CTRL)+I
   c. (CTRL)+E
   d. (CTRL)+L

6. When you change tab settings or indentations on the ruler, they affect:
   a. the entire document.
   b. the paragraph at the top of the screen.
   c. the selected paragraph(s).
   d. all paragraphs after the insertion point.
7. When you press ENTER at the end of a paragraph, you create a new paragraph that has the same formatting as:
   a. a left-aligned paragraph.
   b. the paragraph below it.
   c. a Normal paragraph.
   d. the paragraph above it.
8. To establish a new tab, you should click:
   a. the selection bar.
   b. the ruler.
   c. the Formatting toolbar.
   d. the current paragraph.
9. Which of the following *cannot* be set in the Paragraph dialog box?
   a. paragraph alignment
   b. paragraph indentation
   c. extra space above or below the paragraph
   d. type font and size
10. Which of the following cannot be controlled by the indent markers on the ruler?
    a. the first line at left
    b. the right edge of all lines
    c. the left edge of all lines
    d. the right edge of the top line

Short Answer

1. To center a paragraph, select the paragraph and press ________.
2. To adjust paragraph indentations, use the ________ on the ruler.
3. You can set different styles of tab stops on the ruler by clicking first on the ________.
4. To make a paragraph aligned left, press ________.
5. The three triangular indent markers on the ruler give you independent control of the ________, ________, and ________ of a paragraph.
6. If you delete the paragraph mark between two paragraphs, the new combined paragraph will take on the formatting of the ________ paragraph.
7. The tab style that produces proper alignment in a column of figures is called a ________.
8. The paragraph alignment style that produces an even left and right edge is called ________.
9. To delete a tab stop from the ruler using the mouse, you should drag the tab marker ________.
10. You can format paragraphs in Word using the keyboard, the ruler and Formatting toolbar, or the ________.

For Discussion

1. What types of indentations can be established with Word? How is each indentation type used?
2. Describe how to set tabs so that a column of figures in an expense report would line up.
3. You can produce a table organized in columns using multiple tab settings. Would that be a workable approach to formatting the text in a multi-column document such as a newsletter? Why or why not?
4. What is a paragraph in Word?

Review Exercises

Formatting Paragraphs in a Memo

1. Retrieve the file *Brochure Memo.*
2. Select the date line at the top of the memo and format it with right paragraph alignment.
3. Select the *MEMO* heading and center it.
4. Replace the space following the colon (:) in each of the *To, From,* and *Subject* lines with a tab.
5. Select all three lines, and insert a left tab at the 1-inch mark on the ruler.
6. Select the three paragraphs that make up the body of the memo.
7. Use the mouse to adjust the first-line indent marker on the ruler so that the first line of each paragraph is indented ¼ inch.

The memo should look like Figure 4.17.

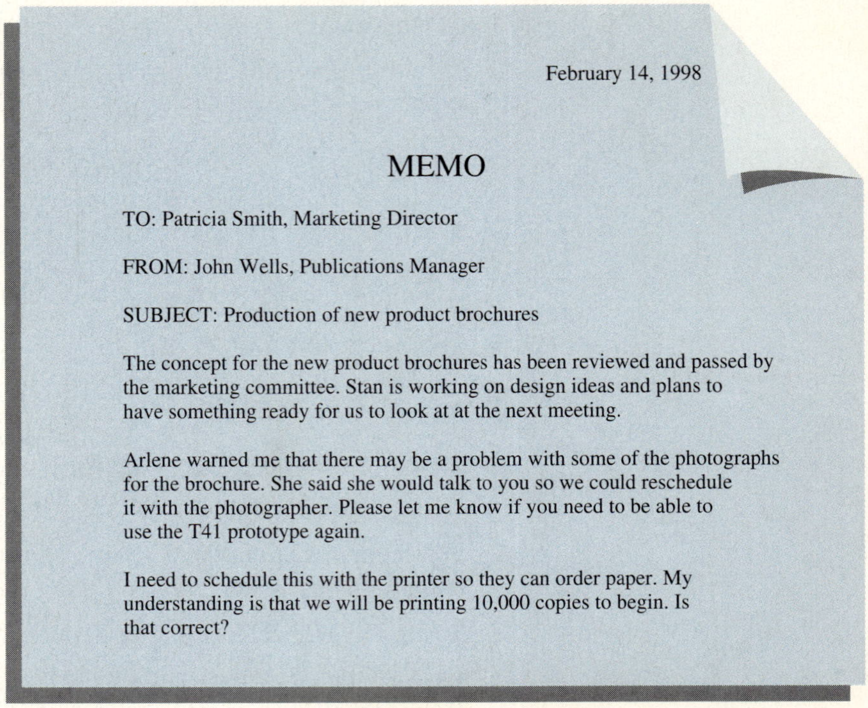

February 14, 1998

MEMO

TO: Patricia Smith, Marketing Director

FROM: John Wells, Publications Manager

SUBJECT: Production of new product brochures

The concept for the new product brochures has been reviewed and passed by the marketing committee. Stan is working on design ideas and plans to have something ready for us to look at at the next meeting.

Arlene warned me that there may be a problem with some of the photographs for the brochure. She said she would talk to you so we could reschedule it with the photographer. Please let me know if you need to be able to use the T41 prototype again.

I need to schedule this with the printer so they can order paper. My understanding is that we will be printing 10,000 copies to begin. Is that correct?

Figure 4.17

8. Save the memo, and print a copy.

Formatting Paragraphs in a Meeting Agenda

1. Retrieve the agenda you saved under the name *Meeting Agenda* at the end of Project 3.
2. Center the top three lines.
3. Delete the tab characters (→) in the document.
4. Indent all the items under the *Old Business* and *New Business* sections one level (to the first default tab stop).
5. Indent the office titles under *Election of officers* an extra heading level (to the next default tab stop).
6. Save the revised agenda, and print a copy of it.

Creating an Invoice

1. Type the information for the invoice shown in Figure 4.18. Include tabs as you think appropriate, but don't worry about alignment until steps 7 and 8.

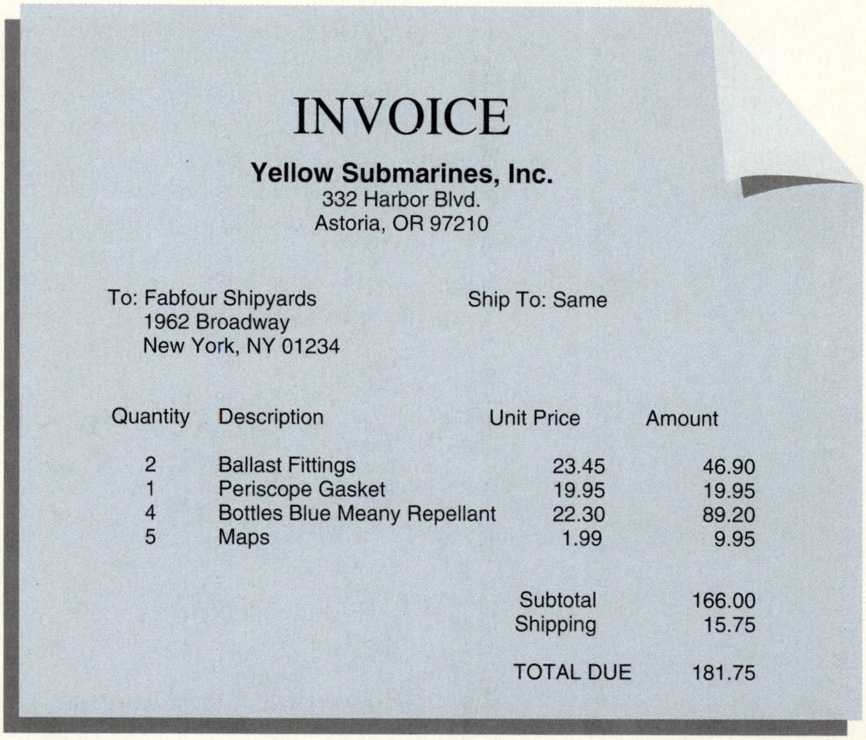

INVOICE

Yellow Submarines, Inc.
332 Harbor Blvd.
Astoria, OR 97210

To: Fabfour Shipyards
1962 Broadway
New York, NY 01234

Ship To: Same

Quantity	Description	Unit Price	Amount
2	Ballast Fittings	23.45	46.90
1	Periscope Gasket	19.95	19.95
4	Bottles Blue Meany Repellant	22.30	89.20
5	Maps	1.99	9.95
		Subtotal	166.00
		Shipping	15.75
		TOTAL DUE	181.75

Figure 4.18

2. Format the entire document in a 12-point sans serif face such as Arial or Helvetica.
3. Center the heading lines.
4. Change the *Invoice* heading to 36-point Times New Roman or a similar serif face, and boldface the heading.
5. Change the formatting of the name of the company to 18-point bold.
6. Change the formatting of the company address lines to 14-point.
7. Select the company name and address lines in the *To* and *Ship To* sections. Insert left tab stops at ⅜ inch, 3 inches, and 3¾ inches.
8. Select from the *Quantity/Description/Unit Price/Amount* heading to the bottom of the document. Insert a center tab stop at ¼ inch. Insert a left tab stop at 1 inch. Insert decimal tab stops at 4 inches and 5 inches.
9. Save your document as *Fabfour Invoice,* and print a copy of it.

Assignments

Visiting Redmond

You can use your Web browser to visit Microsoft at their URL http://www.microsoft.com. Check out the Word for Windows 95 area under Microsoft Office. You'll find free software, drivers, help files, and tips about all kinds of word processing and desktop publishing situations.

Formatting the Telephone List with Leader Tabs

Retrieve the version of your telephone list saved under the file name *Telephone List.* It should be a list of names and telephone numbers separated by tabs. Select all the lines with names and numbers on them, and use the ruler to insert a right tab at about 4 inches (adjust the location of the tab as needed to accommodate the names on your list). The names should now align on the left edge and the numbers, at the 4-inch mark on the right edge.

If the gap between the names and numbers is very wide, it makes it difficult to match numbers with names. Commercial printers use a dotted line, called a leader, to tie the parts of the line together and make the line easier to read. Word allows you to insert leader tabs.

Begin by selecting all the lines (paragraphs) you want to format. Choose Tabs from the Format menu. Select item 2 in the Leader box. As soon as you select OK, the leader will be inserted. Save the list, and print a copy of it.

PROJECT 5: SECTION FORMATTING

Objectives

After completing this project, you should be able to:

- Change paragraph line spacing
- Define and apply styles
- Change margins
- Create bulleted lists
- Add footnotes
- Create a simple table
- Add headers or footers

In this project, you will begin putting together a short research paper. Like many research papers, this will have footnotes and page numbers in a header. It will have a simple table and a bulleted list. At the end of this project, you'll be able to use basic page formatting and the features of Word that take some of the pain out of preparing reports and papers.

CASE STUDY: A RESEARCH PAPER

Assume you are a student in Sociology 415, a course in sociological research. You've been given an assignment to produce a short analytical paper dealing with a social issue and supported by data from a sample study listed in your textbook. Your paper should include relevant references, including the data you have used to support your findings.

Designing the Solution

The overall organization of almost any research paper follows this general pattern:

- Placing the study in context: introductory remarks, possibly a review of work and writings in this area, a statement of your hypothesis
- Description of your study: where your data came from
- Analysis of your study: results, discussion of results, conclusions or recommendations

We'll assume you've done your research, produced a rough draft following this overall organizational pattern, and made revisions. Now you are ready to format the paper. The standard format for a research paper is essentially the same as for a manuscript submitted for publication. The format is designed to be easy to read—and easy to edit, annotate, and revise.

The standard research paper format has been around since the days of the typewriter and is still based on the characteristics of the typewriter. Research papers are nearly always double spaced, which allows more room to mark corrections and make comments. Even with the many type fonts available with modern personal computers, the standard for a research paper remains a typewriter font such as Courier, which facilitates corrections in spelling and word choice. Margins are set wide enough to accommodate more comments, and binding if necessary. Because research papers usually run several pages, you'll want to number the pages for ease of handling. You'll frequently need to quote other people's writing in your own work and then credit these sources in a footnote reference. Some research paper characteristics, footnotes in particular, were difficult and time consuming on a typewriter, but are relatively easy to produce using Word.

You'll begin this project by typing the text for the paper or retrieving it from disk. Then you'll set up and apply the styles for the text and headings. Next you'll set margins and double-space the text. You'll create a bulleted list, add footnotes, and add an indented block quotation. You'll format the table so that it is better organized and stands apart from the text. Last, you'll add a header that prints page numbers automatically at the top of each page.

Applying and Defining Styles

The nearly complete draft of the research paper is shown in Figure 5.1. Note that a block quotation is missing from the draft. You will add that item later.

If the file *Gender Roles Paper* is available, you will not need to type the text in yourself. If you do need to type the text yourself, the lines in the document window may be longer or shorter, depending on the margin settings on the computer you are using. Don't worry about that; you'll be changing the margins shortly anyway.

Sociology 415
Professor R. Warner
December 6, 1995

Impact of Educational Level on
Views of Gender Roles
by B.J. Mitchell

I am interested in discovering if there is a relationship between educational level and views on gender roles. I believe I will find that as one's level of education increases, the likelyhood of having non-traditional views toward gender roles increases. Examples of non-traditional views include regarding the following as acceptable lifestyle choices: women working in male-dominated fields, men sharing responsibility for work in the home, and women able to hold any job solely on the basis of qualification.
I think there will be a positive connection between higher education and non-traditional views toward gender roles for a variety of reasons. Individuals with greater education are more likely to be aware of the historic and institutional discrimination against women.
[quote will go here]
In addition, persons with higher education are likely to marry others with similar educational background, making the practice of non-traditional gender roles a likely possibility in their relationships. Educated individuals are more likely than uneducated persons to work in areas of employment where women have attained some degree of success in male-dominated environments. Observing these achievements could have the effect of changing a person's views from believing women do not "belong" in the workplace to encouraging their continued success.
The Study
Data for this paper comes from mail surveys sent to probability samples of residents in metropolitan Toronto and Detroit in 1988. The response rate was 69 percent, yielding a total sample size of 1805. The data and percentage distribution of the responses are shown in the table below, along with column and row totals used in the statistical analysis.
[Insert Data Table Here]
Findings
The table shows the results of a probability sample survey. The results support my hypothesis. Specifically, while less than 20 percent of those with a high school education reported having non-traditional views toward gender roles, 42 percent of those with some college and over half of those sampled with college degrees hold non-traditional views. In addition, the data show that almost half of those with high school only and less than 15 percent of those with a college degree hold traditional views. This demonstrates that with increased education, the likelyhood of having non-traditional views also increases.
If there were no correlation between educational level and nontraditional views, the survey responses would be expected to be distributed as shown in the following table.
[Expected response table goes here]
A Chi Square analysis shows the actual data and expected results differ significantly at the 0.01 level. For this reason I must reject the null hypothesis. I conclude that as a person receives more education, the likelyhood that his or her views toward gender roles will become non-traditional increases.

Figure 5.1

The research paper is currently formatted as Normal style using Word's default set of styles. If you click the Style box on the Formatting toolbar, you will find a small collection of predefined paragraph styles usually including Normal, for normal paragraphs, and three heading styles for different heading levels. Word's Normal template actually contains many more built-in styles, but to reduce formatting confusion, they don't appear in the Style box until you begin using them. You will be using and redefining the Normal style and adding several of your own styles as you format the research paper.

Standard research paper format calls for a typewriter font like Courier and double-spaced lines, with the first line in each paragraph indented about ½ inch. You will begin by redefining Normal style to conform to this standard.

To prepare the draft and redefine Normal style:

1 Type the draft as shown, or retrieve the *Gender Roles Paper* file if it is available. (The arrows in Figure 5.1 represent tabs.)

2 Select a few words within the text of the document, and format that text as 12-point Courier New (or a similar typewriter-style face).

3 With the text still selected use the ruler to set the first-line indent to ½ inch, as shown in Figure 5.2.

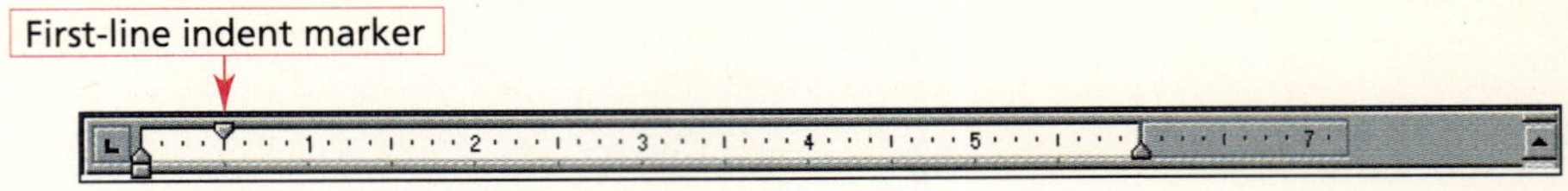

Figure 5.2

4 Press (CTRL) + **2** to double-space the text in the selected paragraph.

5 Select Normal in the Style box at the left end of the Formatting toolbar, and press (ENTER)
The Reapply Style dialog box will appear.

6 Select the top option: Redefine the style using the selection as an example?

7 Select OK to redefine the Normal style as 12-point Courier New, double-spaced and indented 1/2 inch.

All text in the research paper will change to the new style as soon as you redefine Normal style. Now you need to set up and apply different styles for the headings, titles, and table information. The section headings will be boldfaced and will not be indented.

To define and apply the Section Heading style:

1 Select the entire line for the first section heading: *The Study.* (Recall that the easiest way to select an entire line is to click in the selection bar to the left of the paragraph.)

2 Select the Bold button on the Formatting toolbar to boldface the heading.

3 Move the first-line indent marker on the ruler to the left margin to remove the first-line indent so that the heading is flush to the left margin.

4 Select Normal in the Style box at the left end of the Formatting toolbar.

5 Type in the name of the new style: **`Section Heading`**

6 Press (ENTER) to define the style.

7 Select the second heading: *Findings.*

8 Select Section Heading from the Style box to apply the style.
The title at the top of the research paper will be boldfaced, centered, and single spaced.

To define and apply the Paper Title style:

1 Select the entire first line of the title: *Impact of Educational Level on.*

2 Remove the first-line indent, as you did with the heading style.

3 Press (CTRL) + **1** to change the line spacing to single space.

4 Select the Center button on the Formatting toolbar to center the title line.

5 Select the Bold button on the Formatting toolbar to boldface the title.

6 Select the Style box on the Formatting toolbar.

7 Type in the name of the new style: **`Paper Title`**

8 Press (ENTER) to define the new style.

9 Select all three title lines as well as the blank lines above and below the title lines, and apply the new Paper Title style.
The top of the research paper should look like Figure 5.3.

```
        Sociology·415¶

        Professor·R.·Warner¶

        December·6,·1995¶

                                ¶
                 Impact·of·Educational·Level·on¶
                     Views·of·Gender·Roles¶
                       by·B.J.·Mitchell¶
                                ¶
        I·am·interested·in·discovering·if·there·is·a·

relationship·between·educational·level·and·views·on·gender·

roles.·I·believe·I·will·find·that·as·one's·level·of·
```

Figure 5.3

To define and apply the Course Number style:

1 Select the entire first line of the document, which contains the course number.

2 Remove the paragraph indent, and press CTRL + 1 to single-space the line.

3 Select the Align Right button on the Formatting toolbar to move the line to the right margin.

4 Use the Style box on the Formatting toolbar to define a new style called Course Number.

5 Apply the Course Number style to the two lines below, containing the instructor's name and the date.

Now you will format the table so that it is single spaced and has a light tint block behind it to set it off from the rest of the text of the research paper.

To define and apply the Table style:

1 Select the first line of the table *(High Some Completed).*

2 Press CTRL + 1 to single-space the text.

3 If the Borders toolbar is not open, select the Borders button on the Formatting toolbar to open it.

4 Select 10% in the Shading box on the Borders toolbar.

5 Use the Style box on the Formatting toolbar to define the Table style.

6 Select all lines in the table (but not the blank line below), and apply the new Table style.
The table will still be jumbled. You will fix that later.

7 Save your document as *Revised Gender Roles Paper.*

EXIT If necessary, you can exit Word now and continue this project later.

WORKING WITH SECTIONS AND SECTION BREAKS

A ***section*** in Word is a portion of a document that can be formatted with specific margin settings, page orientation (vertical or horizontal), page-numbering sequence, or other features affecting page layout. When you begin a new document in Word, the entire document is a single section. If necessary, you can insert section breaks to divide the document into separate sections and vary the section formatting from one section to another. For instance, you could number the first few pages of a report with small roman numerals and then switch to another section to use conventional arabic numerals for the rest of the report. Or you could include a horizontal page in a separate section to accommodate a wide table within a series of conventional vertical pages. For most simple documents, however, the entire document will be a single section. That will be the case with this research paper.

CHANGING THE MARGINS

Formatting sections in Word follows the same general rule as character and paragraph formatting: select, and then do. When formatting sections, you first select the section, and then you format it. A section is selected when any part of it is selected. If your whole document is a single section, that makes selecting it very straightforward: you just need to have the insertion point somewhere inside the document to format the whole document.

The standard margin settings for a research paper are at least 1 inch on all sides. You will set the top, bottom, left, and right margins for the paper to 1 inch exactly.

To set the margins:

1 Choose Page Setup from the File menu.
The Page Setup dialog box, shown in Figure 5.4, appears.

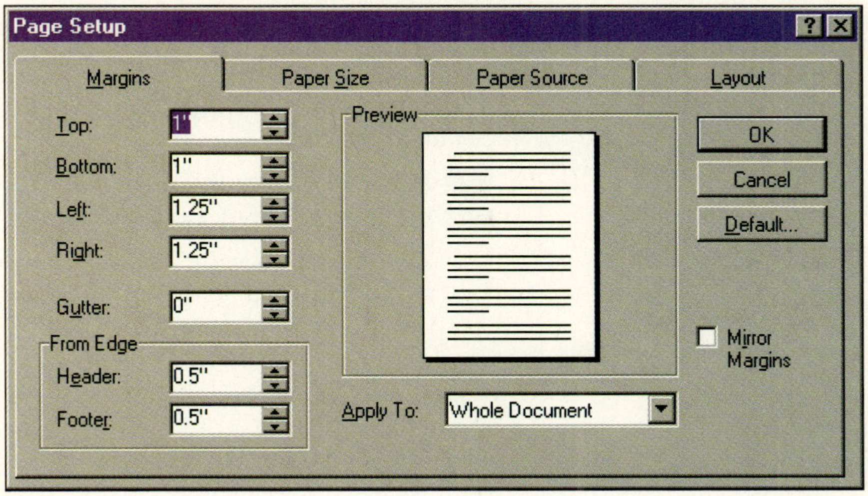

Figure 5.4

The margin settings on your screen may not exactly match those shown in Figure 5.4, but you are about to change them.

2 Select the Margins tab if it is not already on top.

3 Select the measurement within the Top box, shown in Figure 5.4, if not already selected.

4 Type **1** in the Top box.
The new measurement you type replaces the old measurement for the top margin. You can use the arrow keys, BACKSPACE, and DEL to edit the measurement in any of the boxes.

5 Select the measurement within the Bottom box, located just below the Top box.
As soon as you advance to the Bottom box, the Preview display within the dialog box is updated to indicate how the new setting for the top margin will affect general page appearance.

6 Type **1** in the Bottom box.

7 Change the measurement to **1** in the Left box.

8 Change the measurement to **1** in the Right box.

9 Select Whole Document in the Apply To box if it is not already selected.

10 Select OK.

To make the document easier to read on the screen, you can adjust the magnification of the display using the Zoom Control box at the right edge of the Standard toolbar. You can magnify your document as much as 200 percent to check intricate alignments, or as low as 10 percent to see a tiny facsimile of the page. For most of the figures in this project, the Zoom Control box is set to Page Width so that an entire line can be seen on the screen without scrolling from side to side. You will probably find it easiest to work at that magnification.

To set the screen magnification:

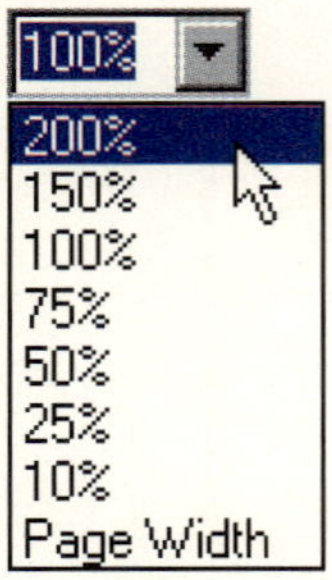

1 Select 200% from the Zoom Control box at the right end of the Standard toolbar.

2 Select 10% from the Zoom Control box.

3 Select Page Width from the Zoom Control box.

Creating a Bulleted List

To make clearer what you mean by nontraditional views of gender roles, you decide to list on separate lines each of the three example lifestyle choices mentioned in the first paragraph. To make it easier for the reader to compare these examples and understand the pattern of your thought, you will put the three examples in a bulleted list. A ***bullet*** is a typographical device, usually a large dot, that indicates separate items in a list, just as numbers do in a numbered list. Unlike numbered lists, however, bulleted lists don't suggest that items are in any particular sequence.

First you will edit the text so that each item in the list appears on a separate line and in a separate paragraph. Then you'll indent the list and add the bullets.

To create an indented list:

1 Place the insertion point just after the colon following *choices.*

2 Press ENTER to separate the list from the rest of the paragraph and establish a new paragraph.

3 Remove the first-line indentation using the top-left indent marker on the ruler.
The screen may scroll to the left when you move the marker. If necessary, you can adjust the display using the horizontal scroll bar at the bottom of the screen.

4 Edit the list so that it appears as shown in Figure 5.5. Be sure to eliminate all unneeded commas and spaces as well as the word *and* that connects the last item to the rest of the list and the period that ends the list.

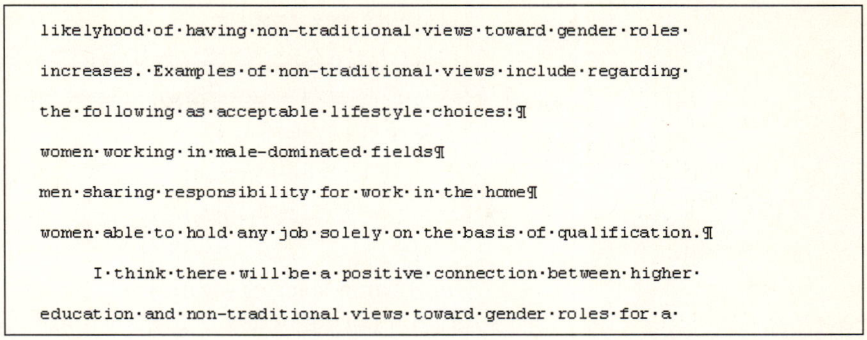

likelyhood·of·having·non-traditional·views·toward·gender·roles·
increases.·Examples·of·non-traditional·views·include·regarding·
the·following·as·acceptable·lifestyle·choices:¶
women·working·in·male-dominated·fields¶
men·sharing·responsibility·for·work·in·the·home¶
women·able·to·hold·any·job·solely·on·the·basis·of·qualification.¶
I·think·there·will·be·a·positive·connection·between·higher·
education·and·non-traditional·views·toward·gender·roles·for·a·

Figure 5.5

5 Select the three new paragraphs that compose the list.

6 Click the Increase Indent button on the Formatting toolbar to indent these lines.

The list should now look like Figure 5.6 although the way you selected the paragraphs might differ.

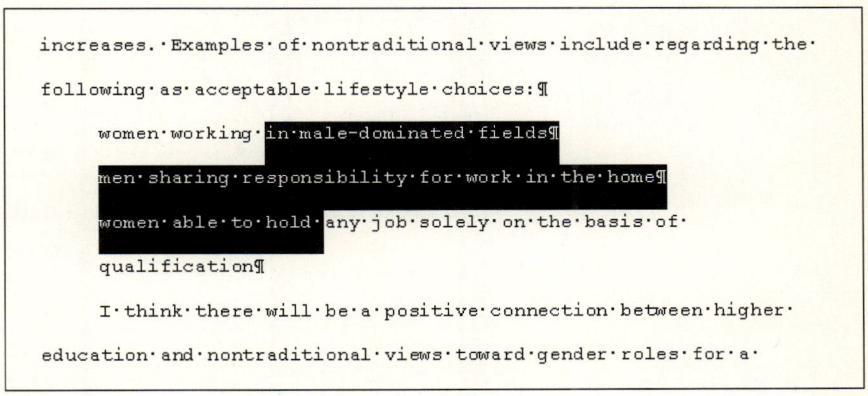

increases.·Examples·of·nontraditional·views·include·regarding·the·
following·as·acceptable·lifestyle·choices:¶
women·working·in·male-dominated·fields¶
men·sharing·responsibility·for·work·in·the·home¶
women·able·to·hold·any·job·solely·on·the·basis·of·
qualification¶
I·think·there·will·be·a·positive·connection·between·higher·
education·and·nontraditional·views·toward·gender·roles·for·a·

Figure 5.6

Tip If necessary, you can increase the size of the indentation by selecting the Increase Indent button repeatedly or by pressing CTRL + **M** Each time you increase the indentation, the text moves to the next tab, ordinarily ½ inch. To decrease the size of an indentation, you can select the Decrease Indent button or press CTRL + SHIFT + **M** You can also adjust paragraph indentation using the indent markers on the ruler, as shown in Figure 5.7.

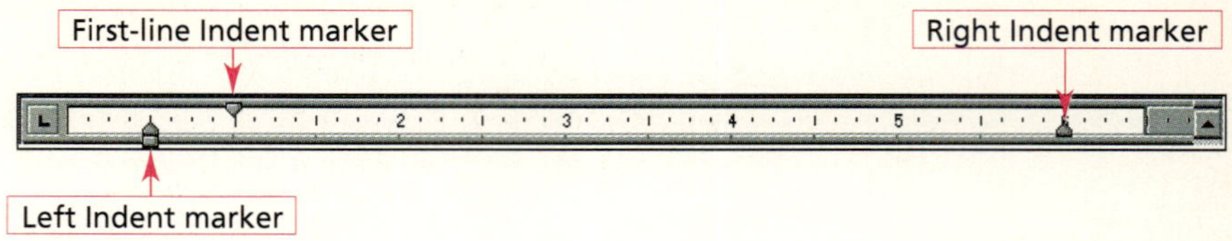

Figure 5.7

To format a series of lines as a bulleted list, you can call up the Bullets and Numbering dialog box, shown in Figure 5.8. You can use this dialog box to create both bulleted lists and numbered lists on a single level (like the one in the research paper) or on multiple levels (like an outline). You can change the character used for a bullet and customize the line spacing. For the list in the research paper, however, the default bullet style will work well. The default bullet style will have a blue border around it.

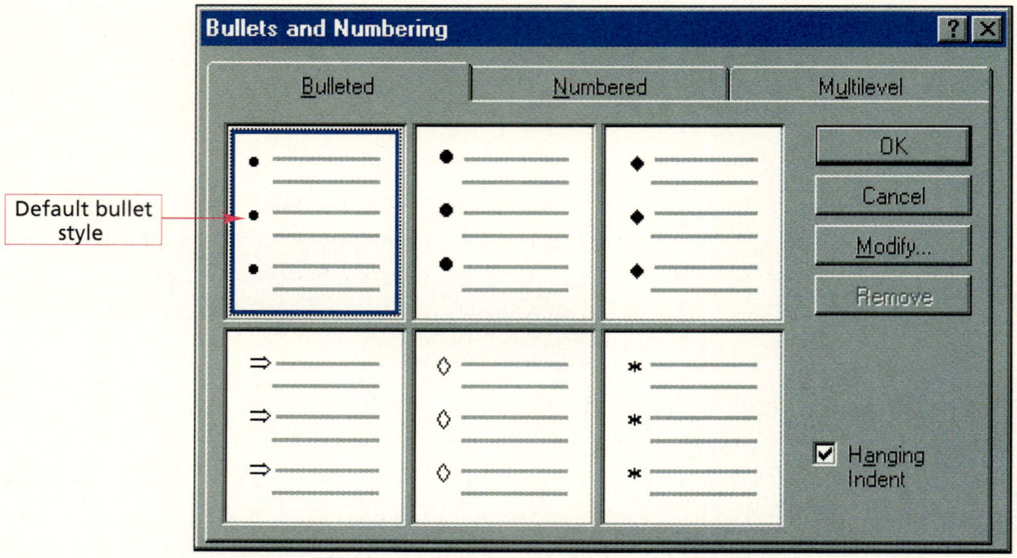

Figure 5.8

To create a bulleted list:

1. Select the three list items, as shown in Figure 5.6.
2. Choose Bullets and Numbering from the Format menu.
3. Select the Bulleted tab if it is not already on top.
4. Select OK to add bullets to the list.

The list should now look like Figure 5.9. Each item in the list stands out clearly, and the distinction between traditional and nontraditional views is made apparent.

increases.·Examples·of·nontraditional·views·include·regarding·the·
following·as·acceptable·lifestyle·choices:¶

- women·working·in·male-dominated·fields¶
- men·sharing·responsibility·for·work·in·the·home¶
- women·able·to·hold·any·job·solely·on·the·basis·of·qualification¶

I·think·there·will·be·a·positive·connection·between·higher·
education·and·nontraditional·views·toward·gender·roles·for·a·

Figure 5.9

Tip If you want to use the bullet style already selected in the Bullets and Numbering dialog box, you can produce a bulleted list quickly by selecting the list items and then selecting the Bullets button on the Formatting toolbar. The button is a toggle, so selecting it a second time will eliminate the bullets.

EXIT If necessary, you can save your file as *Revised Gender Roles Paper,* exit Word now, and continue this project later.

Adding Footnotes and a Quotation

The data for the research paper came from a study published in an academic journal. To credit those who conducted the research, you need to add a footnote citing that study. A ***footnote,*** as you are probably aware, is a brief block of text at the bottom of a page used for citing authorities or making incidental comments. Footnotes are usually numbered in sequential order.

In the days of the typewriter, footnoting was a painful operation. The typist had to type the body of the text, being careful to stop short of the bottom of the page and leave exactly enough room for the footnote. Then the typist had to switch to single spacing and type whatever footnotes belonged on that page. Word, by contrast, makes the process of footnoting relatively painless. When you insert a footnote reference in the body of a paper, Word automatically numbers and formats the footnote reference as a superscript. Word then opens a footnote window where you can enter the text of the footnote as it should appear at the bottom of the page. If you insert or delete a footnote, Word automatically renumbers all other footnotes. When you print out the paper, Word puts footnotes at the bottom of the appropriate pages, or places them at the end of the section if you select the ***endnotes*** option. Unlike footnotes, which always appear at the bottom of the page, endnotes appear at the end of the section.

To add a footnote, you use the Footnote and Endnote dialog box, shown in Figure 5.10. This dialog box allows you to customize footnotes or endnotes to suit nearly any style guide. You can click the Help button if you want more information about available options. For the research paper, however, the default—numbered footnotes—is exactly what you want.

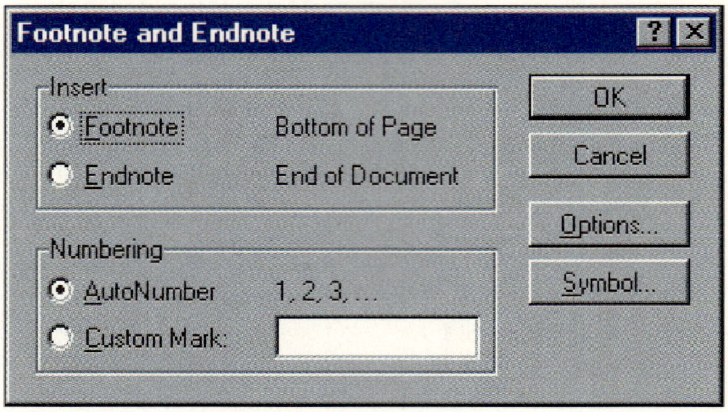

Figure 5.10

To add a footnote reference:

1 In the first paragraph after the heading *The Study,* position the insertion point immediately after the period following *Detroit in 1988,* at the end of the first sentence.

2 Choose Footnote from the Insert menu.

3 Select OK to add the footnote.

The footnote window opens at the bottom of the screen, as shown in Figure 5.11. This is a separate window, with its own vertical scroll bar, and you can switch from one window to the other by clicking inside the window or by pressing (F6) Notice that Word has inserted a superscript footnote reference mark just after *1988* in the text window and at the beginning of the footnote text in the footnote window. Now you will type the reference.

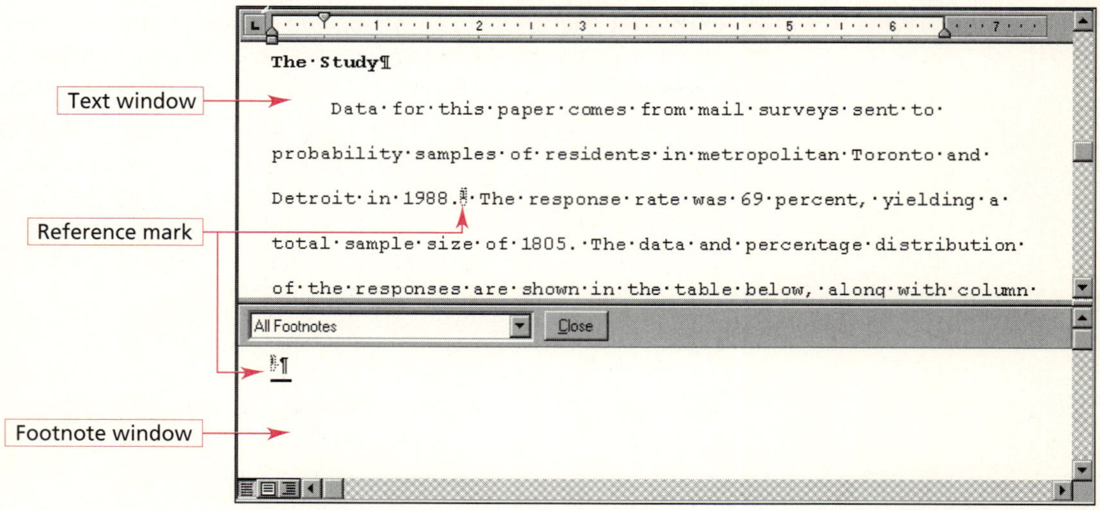

Figure 5.11

To add the footnote text and set the Footnote Text style:

1 Type the footnote text shown in Figure 5.12.

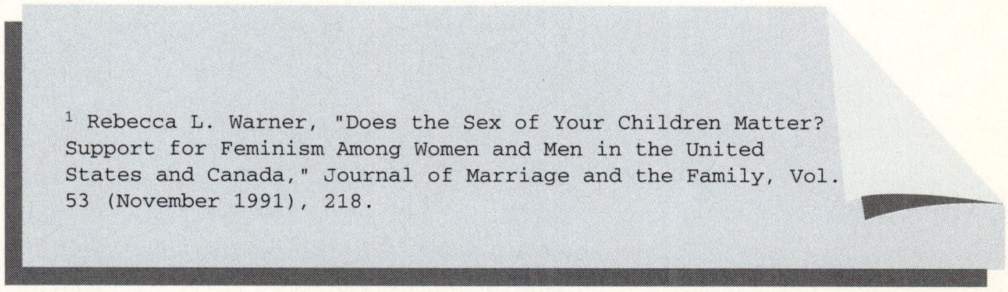
[1] Rebecca L. Warner, "Does the Sex of Your Children Matter? Support for Feminism Among Women and Men in the United States and Canada," Journal of Marriage and the Family, Vol. 53 (November 1991), 218.

Figure 5.12

2 Press (CTRL) + **1** to single-space the footnote text.

3 Select Ruler from the View menu to open the ruler in the footnote window.

4 Move the first-line indent marker on the footnote window ruler to the left margin to remove the indent from the footnote.

5 Select Ruler from the View menu to close the ruler in the footnote window.

6 Select one or two words within the footnote text and change the size to 12 point.

7 Select Footnote Text in the Style box at the left end of the Formatting toolbar, and press (ENTER)
The Reapply Style dialog box will appear.

8 If not already selected, select the top option: Redefine the style using the selection as an example?

9 Select OK to redefine the Footnote Text style as 12-point Courier New.
Any future footnotes you enter will also appear in this new Footnote Text style.

Titles of books and journals should be underlined in standard research-paper style. Recall that underlining is a character format in Word, so you will need to select the words you want to underline and then format them as underlined. You can easily select a block of words by dragging the pointer from the first word to the last. As usual, the selection will be "rounded off" to include whole words only.

To underline the journal title:

1 Select the title of the journal, as shown in Figure 5.13.

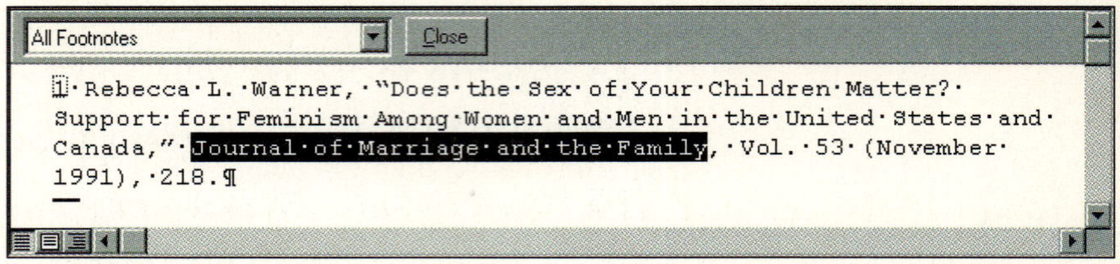

Figure 5.13

2 Click the Underline button on the Formatting toolbar to underline the title.
You will need to cancel the text selection to see the underlining.

3 Select the Close button to close the footnote window.

Next you need to add a supporting quotation and footnote it as well. Assume that in your notes for the research paper, you have a quotation that supports the argument that education influences attitudes about gender roles. The quotation will go just after the second paragraph in the body of the paper. The research paper format for longer quotations is to set them off as a separate block of single-spaced text, indented on the left side.

To add the quotation:

1 Select the line [*quote will go here*].

2 Type the quotation shown in Figure 5.14.

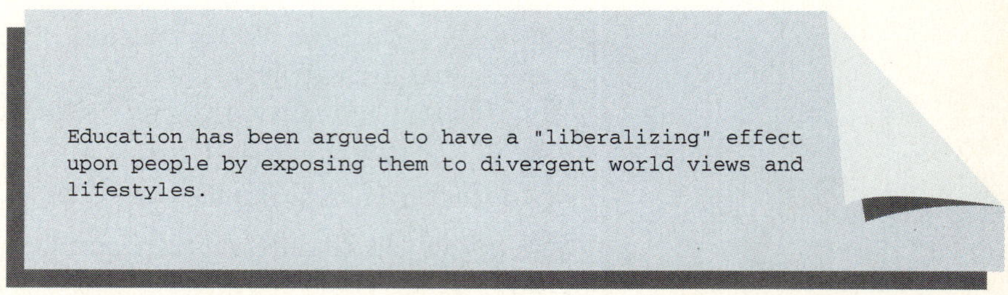

Figure 5.14

The material you type should replace the bracketed note, and it will be double spaced and indented like the other paragraphs in the body of the paper. You will need to single-space the block quotation and indent it on the left.

To single-space and indent the quotation:

1 Position the insertion point somewhere within the quotation you just added.

2 Press (CTRL) + **1** to single-space the quotation.

3 Remove the first-line indentation using the top-left indent marker on the ruler.

4 Select the Increase Indent button on the Formatting toolbar.

5 Use the *right* mouse button to click inside the new paragraph.

6 Select Paragraph from the pull-down menu to open the Paragraph dialog box.

7 Select the Indents and Spacing tab if it is not already on top.

8 Select the After box in the Spacing area.

9 Type `1 li` to set the spacing after the paragraph to one line.

10 Select OK to close the Paragraph dialog box.

If your paper were going to include more than one block quotation, you could use this paragraph to define a Block Quote style. As it is, you now need to add the footnote that gives the citation for the quotation.

To add a footnote reference for the quotation:

1 Position the insertion point just after the period at the end of the block quotation.

2 Choose Footnote from the Insert menu.

3 Select OK to add the footnote.
As before, Word inserts a footnote reference in the body of the paper and opens a footnote window for you to type the footnote text. Note that the previous footnote number 1 has already been renumbered and a new number 1 inserted for you where you can type the text for the new footnote.

To add the text for the new footnote:

1 Type the footnote text shown in Figure 5.15, underlining the name of the journal as shown.

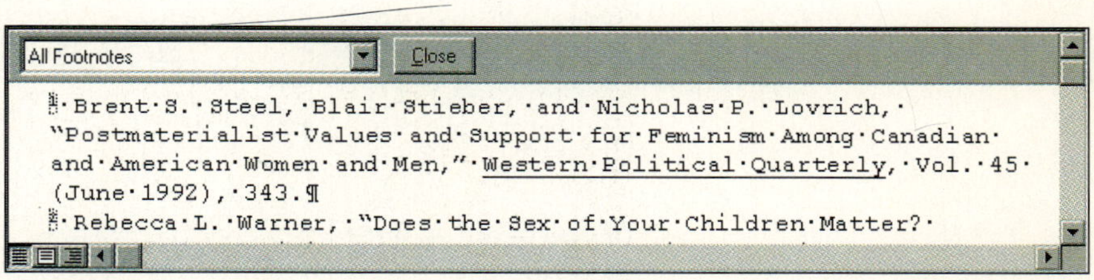

Figure 5.15

2 Position the insertion point somewhere within the second footnote.

Notice that when you move from one footnote to another in the footnote window, Word adjusts the text in the main window so that the footnote reference is displayed. This makes it easy to check the correspondence between a footnote reference and the footnote text itself.

3 Close the footnote window.

> ***Tip*** To switch quickly between footnote references and text, double-click a footnote reference to open the footnote window and view the associated footnote text. Then double-click the footnote number in the footnote window to close the footnote window and return to the document window.

EXIT If necessary, you can save your file as *Revised Gender Roles Paper,* exit Word now, and continue this project later.

Formatting the Table

The table information is currently jumbled because individual items are separated by tabs and the default tab settings create inconsistent columns. One way to make the table more orderly would be to set tab stops that created consistent columns. But Word provides an even easier way to work with tables. The Table menu contains a sophisticated set of commands for creating, manipulating, and formatting tables. You'll only begin to scratch the surface in the following set of steps.

To create a table from the table data:

1 Select all five lines of the table data.

2 Select Convert Text to Table from the Table Menu.
The Convert Text to Table dialog box will appear, shown in Figure 5.16. The dialog box correctly assumes that column items are separated by tab stops and that you want a total of four columns.

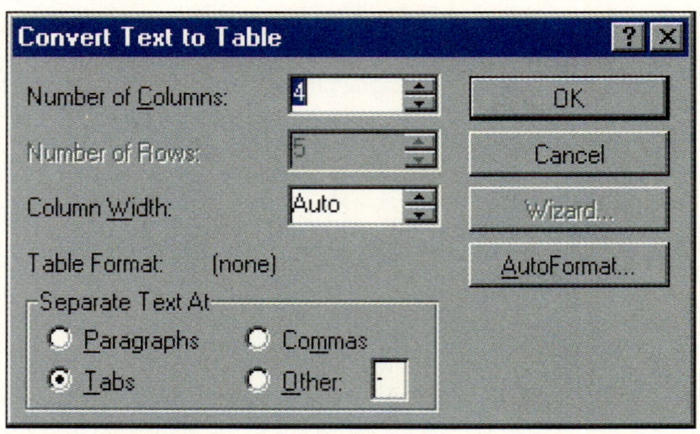

Figure 5.16

3 Select OK to create the table.

The leftmost column may be too narrow to contain the row labels without dividing single words. Adjusting the column width for better readability is a relatively simple matter using the ruler.

To adjust column width and format the table:

1 With the entire table still selected, use the pointer to grab the Column marker on the ruler for the first column, shown in Figure 5.17.
When positioned correctly, the pointer will change shape to a two-headed arrow that points left and right.

2 Drag the marker to the right, to the 2-inch mark.

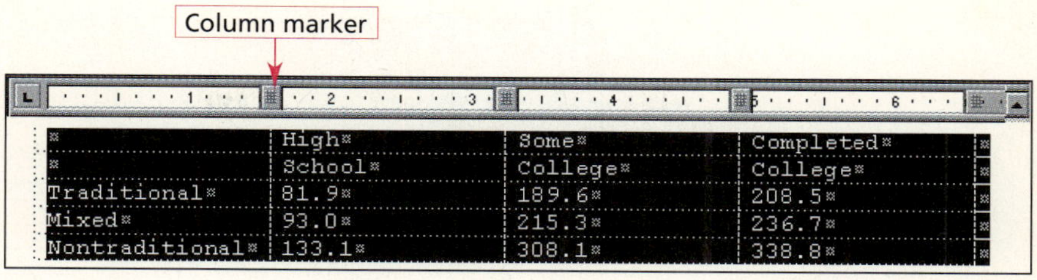

	High School	Some College	Completed College
Traditional	81.9	189.6	208.5
Mixed	93.0	215.3	236.7
Nontraditional	133.1	308.1	338.8

Figure 5.17

As you expand the width of the first column, Word automatically decreases the width of the other columns so that the overall table width remains the same.

ADDING HEADERS AND FOOTERS

You are nearly done with the basic formatting of the research paper. All that remains is to add a ***header,*** a repeating section of text at the top of each page. Word also accommodates ***footers,*** which are like headers but appear at the bottom of the page. Headers and footers often list the title of a book, the name of the chapter, or the page number. The header for the research paper will include the name of the author and the page number, a common convention for research papers.

Because the name of the author already appears on the first page, however, and because it is obvious which page that is, you won't put the header on page 1. Thus you will need to make the first page of the paper an exception in the series of headers.

To make the header for the first page different from other pages:

1 Position the insertion point anywhere within the document, but be sure no text is selected.

2 Choose Page Setup from the File menu.

3 Select the Layout tab, as shown in Figure 5.18.

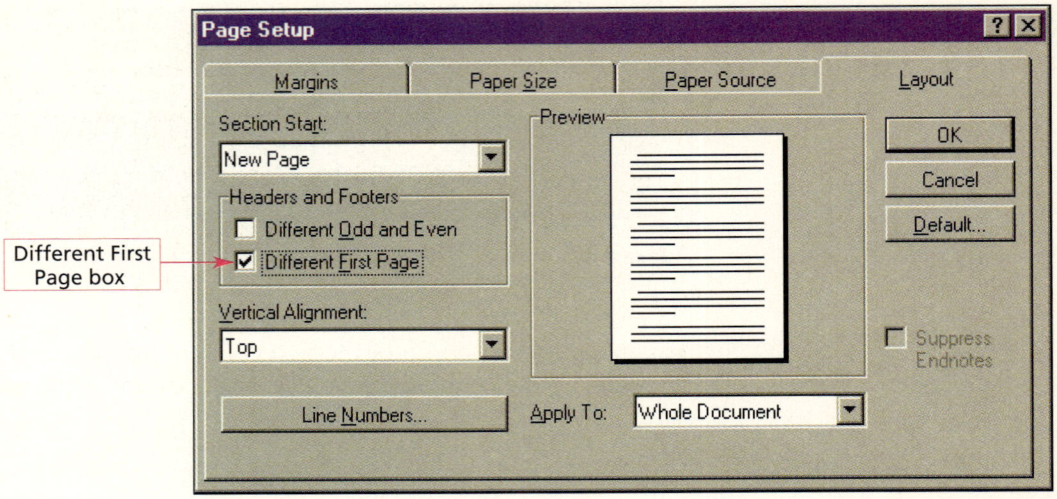

Figure 5.18

4 Select Different First Page so that a check mark appears in the box.

5 Select OK to complete the formatting choice.

You have just created two types of headers: one for the first page and one for all other pages. You will leave the first page header blank so that no header will appear on page 1, and you will use the other header to print the author name and page number on subsequent pages.

When you work with headers and footers, the display will change to Page Layout View, and a box for the header will appear at the top of the page, as shown in Figure 5.19. If the box is for page 1, it will be labeled First Page Header. Otherwise, it will simply be labeled Header. The Header and Footer toolbar will also appear, floating on the page. You can move the toolbar to other parts of the screen as needed to see what you are doing. If the magnification of the page is too small, you can change it using the Zoom Control box on the Standard toolbar near the right edge. The text of the paper itself appears dimmed because you can't edit the paper when you're working on headers and footers. You can move from page to page by selecting the Previous Page and Next Page buttons at the bottom of the vertical scroll bar. You can move between the header and footer on the page by selecting the leftmost button on the Header and Footer toolbar.

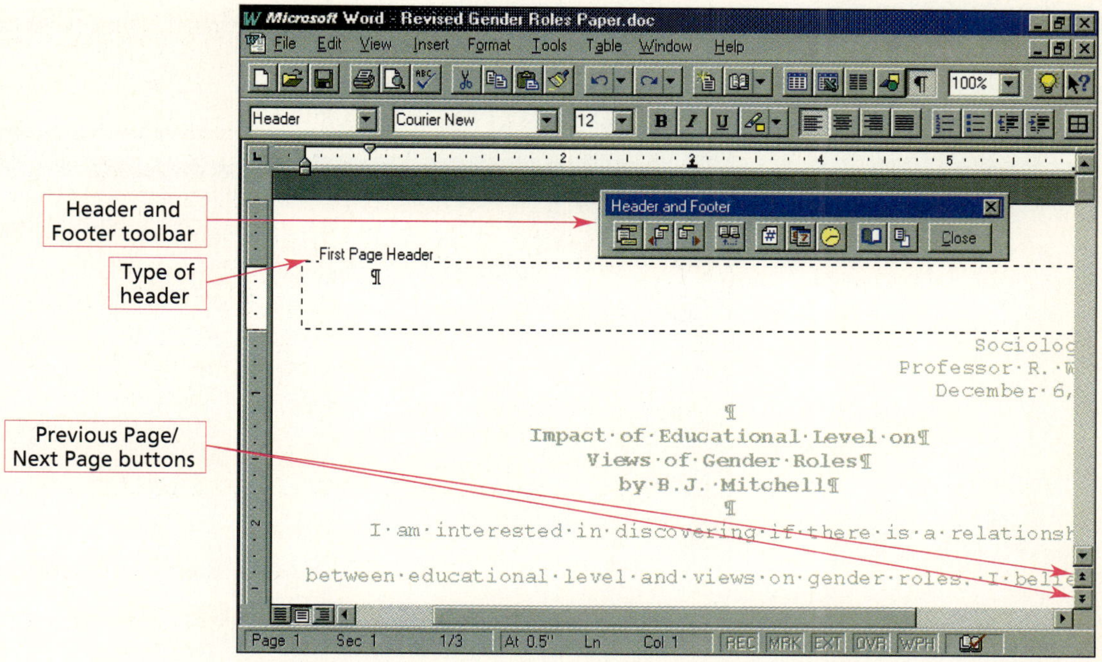

Figure 5.19

To create a header:

1 Choose Header and Footer from the View menu.

2 If you are in the first-page header, move to the next page by selecting the Next Page button on the vertical scroll bar.

3 Position the insertion point in the Header box.

4 Select Page Width in the Zoom Control box.

5 Type `Mitchell,` then a space, then a slash character (/), and then another space.

6 Click the Page Numbers button on the Header and Footer toolbar, as shown in Figure 5.20.

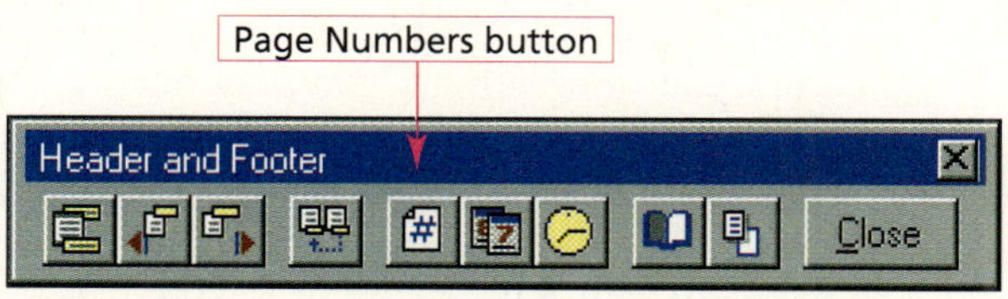

Figure 5.20

You have inserted a special code in the header that Word replaces with the appropriate page number. The code appears as a page number immediately after the header text.

To format the header:

1 Click the Align Right button on the Formatting toolbar to justify the header on the right.

The header should now look like Figure 5.21. Move from page to page to see that the page numbers do change and that the first page has a blank header.

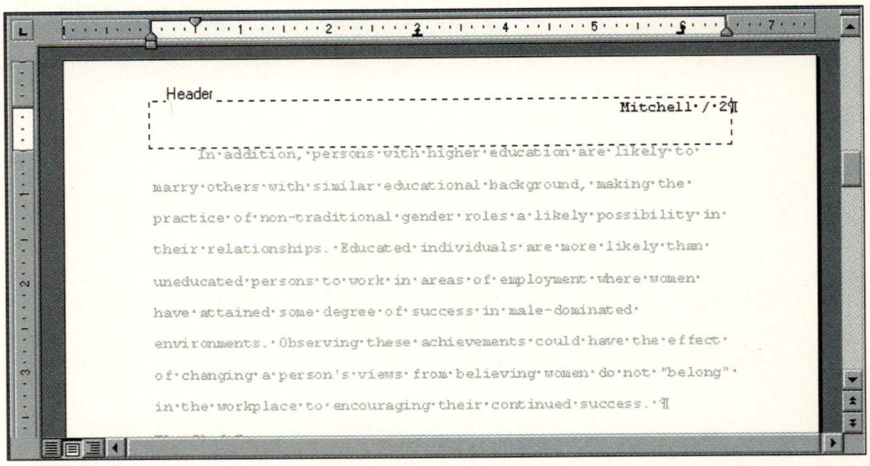

Figure 5.21

2 Select the Close button to close the Header and Footer window.

To save the paper and print a copy of it:

1 Save the paper.

2 Click the Print button on the Standard toolbar or choose Print from the File menu to print a copy of the paper.

3 Close the file.

THE NEXT STEP

When it comes to commonly used document features, Word makes many standard operations nearly automatic. You can produce standard headers, footers, footnotes, endnotes, bulleted lists, or numbered lists with a few clicks or a few keystrokes. For many documents, Word's standard formats work well. For others, you may need to modify the format. You may want to return to the Paragraph dialog box to see how you can control line spacing both within and between paragraphs on the Indents and Spacing tab. You can also switch to the Text Flow tab and format a paragraph so that it will not be split at a page break or so that a heading will be kept with the text that follows it. You may want to experiment more with the Bullets and Numbering dialog box to try other typographical devices, indentations, or even multilevel lists. You also could experiment with changing the position of headers and footers by changing the From Edge settings on the Margins tab in the Page Setup dialog box. Word can be as flexible as you need it to be, but you'll need to invest some time in learning how to accomplish what you want.

The standard research paper format used here will work for many papers you are asked to write. If you want more detail, a common authority for style and format questions is *The Chicago Manual of Style*, available in nearly any library. An adaptation of *The Chicago Manual of Style* that is especially for students is *A Manual for Writers of Term Papers, Theses, and Dissertations*, by Kate L. Turabian, also published by The University of Chicago Press. In addition, each academic field tends to have its own particular style and format. Many fields in the humanities use Modern Language Association style, many social sciences use the style of the American Psychological Association, and many life sciences use the style of the Council of Biology Editors. Your field may have its own set of conventions, and you should be relatively familiar with what those conventions are.

This concludes Project 5. You can either exit Word or go on to work the Study Questions, Review Exercises, and Assignments.

SUMMARY AND EXERCISES

Summary

- Page layout—such as margins, page orientation, page numbering, positions of headers and footers—is referred to as section formatting in Word.
- Although most simple documents are a single section, Word allows you to divide a document into many sections and change the page layout choices from section to section.
- You can set page margins in the Page Setup dialog box (choose Page Setup in the File menu).
- You can set paragraph indentation, including the first-line indentation, in the Paragraph dialog box from the Format menu or by moving the indent markers on the ruler.
- You can create a bulleted or numbered list with the Bullets and Numbering dialog box in the Format menu or by selecting either the Bullets or the Numbering button on the Formatting toolbar.
- To create a footnote, open the Footnote and Endnote dialog box from the Insert menu. Word will open a footnote window where you can type the text of the footnote.
- You can use the Table menu to convert text to a table.
- You can add headers or footers by choosing Header and Footer from the View menu.
- You can have a header and footer for the first page different from those on the other pages in a section if you specify Different First Page on the Layout tab of the Page Setup dialog box.
- Headers and footers can contain a special code that automatically inserts page numbers.

Key Terms and Operations

Key Terms	**Operations**
bullet	Change margins
endnote	Indent paragraphs
footer	Create bulleted lists
footnote	Add footnotes
header	Set up headers and footers
section	

Study Questions

Multiple Choice

1. Which of the following is *not* controlled by section formatting in Word?
   a. page numbering
   b. margins
   c. line spacing
   d. page orientation

2. Which of the following is not a paragraph format in Word?
   a. bulleted lists
   b. line spacing
   c. numbered lists
   d. line width

3. The Center button aligns:
   a. a single line of text.
   b. an entire paragraph.
   c. the characters selected.
   d. to the next tab.

4. A typographic device used to set off items in a list is called a:
   a. dingbat.
   b. logo.
   c. typo.
   d. bullet.

5. The Increase Indent button moves text to:
   a. the right ¼ inch.
   b. the next tab.
   c. align with the text above.
   d. the right margin.

6. You can double-space text by pressing:
   a. CTRL+S
   b. CTRL+2
   c. SHIFT+S
   d. CTRL+D

7. The footnote number that goes in the text of the document is called:
   a. the reference mark.
   b. the footnote text.
   c. the subscript.
   d. an asterisk.

8. Document headers or footers often contain:
   a. page numbers.
   b. copyright disclaimers.
   c. charts and graphs.
   d. footnotes.

9. You can indent the first line of a paragraph by using:
   a. the Indent dialog box.
   b. CTRL+I
   c. the Increase Indent button.
   d. the indent markers on the ruler.

10. To select a section:
    a. Triple-click in the selection bar.
    b. Select the entire document.
    c. Position the insertion point inside the section.
    d. Select all text in the section.

Short Answer

1. To change page orientation within a document from vertical to horizontal, you must establish a new ________.

2. You can change line spacing in the __________ dialog box.
3. Endnotes appear at the end of a __________.
4. To indent a paragraph from the right, you can use the __________ on the ruler.
5. Footnotes are usually used for __________ or __________.
6. Word's footnote window contains the footnote __________.
7. Most section formatting is done in the __________ dialog box.
8. The buttons for paragraph alignment (center, right, left) are on the __________ toolbar.
9. If you insert or delete a footnote, Word will __________ other footnotes.
10. If you want each chapter in a book to start numbering from page 1, you should make each chapter a separate __________.

For Discussion

1. What is a section in Word? What are sections used for?
2. Explain the general procedure for adding a footnote to a document.
3. How can you suppress a header on the first page of a section or document?

Review Exercises

Changing the Research Paper Format

Reformat the research paper you worked on in this project according to a new set of style guidelines.

1. Change the margin settings to 1 inch for the top and bottom and 1.25 inches for the sides.
2. Reorganize the header and add a footer as follows: for the header, use tabs or a table to center the date and place the course number at the right edge; for the footer, place the word *Page,* followed by the page number, at the right edge.
3. Turn the bulleted list into a numbered list beginning with number 1.
4. Add a new footnote to the research paper. Place the footnote reference at the end of the first sentence in the last paragraph, which ends *at the 0.01 level.* Add the following footnote text:

```
    That is, there is only a 1% chance that education and gender
role attitudes are not significantly related.
```

5. Save the file as *Third Gender Roles Paper,* and print it out.

Formatting the Paper in Publication Style

Reformat the research paper from the preceding exercise in a style suitable for publication as a report or journal article.

1. Set margins to 1.25 inches all around (top, bottom, and sides).
2. Delete the course number, instructor's name, and date.

3. Change the font for the entire document to 12-point Times New Roman (or a similar serif face).
4. Change the title to 18-point Times New Roman bold.
5. Change all other headings to 14-point Helvetica or Arial bold (or a similar sans serif face).
6. Single-space the entire document.
7. On the Indents and Spacing tab in the Paragraph dialog box, set extra spacing before or after paragraphs as needed to separate headings from the text above them.
8. Remove the header.
9. Format the footnotes in 10-point Times New Roman (or equivalent).
10. Insert blank lines if needed to keep the table on one page.
11. Save the file as *Publication Style Paper,* and print the result.

Assignments

Numbering with Multiple Levels

Use the Multilevel Numbering option in the Bullets and Numbering dialog box to number the agenda created at the end of Projects 2, 3, and 4. (The agenda should be in a file named *Meeting Agenda.*)

Formatting Your Own Paper

Take a term paper you've already written and saved to disk, and format that paper according to the conventions used for the research paper in this project. Word can read word processing files from many other word processors, so try this even if you didn't use Word to write your paper in the first place. You can almost always transfer text from one word processor to another if you first save the file as an ASCII, or plain text, file. The drawback is that you will lose most of your formatting information this way.

Formatting a Draft as a Finished Publication

Retrieve the file *Pasteur on Germ Theory* from the Word 7 web site (http://www.aw.com/is/word7), or ask your instructor where to get the file. This document is the presentation Louis Pasteur gave to the French Academy of Science in 1878 announcing his discoveries in germ theory. The document is formatted as a draft for publication. Your job is to turn it into a finished publication, as shown in Figure 5.22.

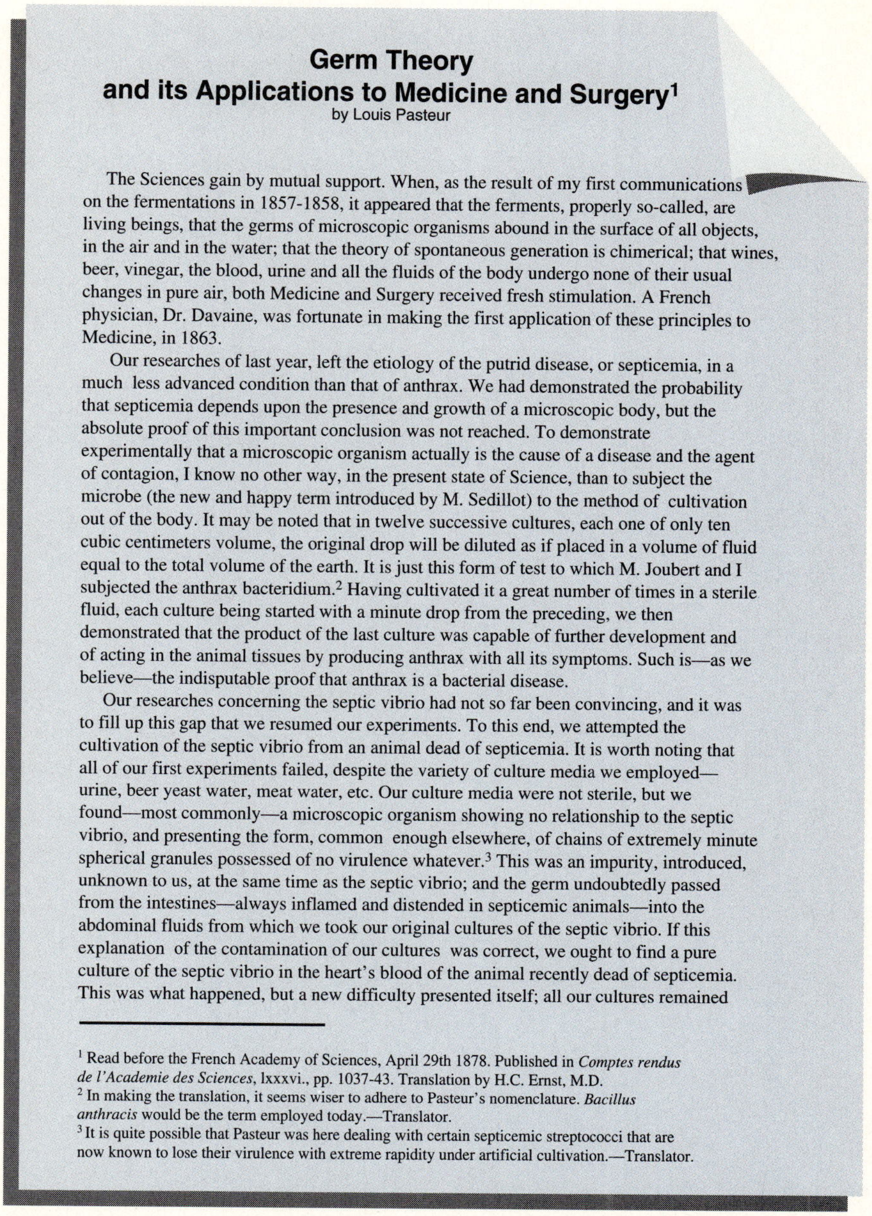

Germ Theory
and its Applications to Medicine and Surgery[1]
by Louis Pasteur

The Sciences gain by mutual support. When, as the result of my first communications on the fermentations in 1857-1858, it appeared that the ferments, properly so-called, are living beings, that the germs of microscopic organisms abound in the surface of all objects, in the air and in the water; that the theory of spontaneous generation is chimerical; that wines, beer, vinegar, the blood, urine and all the fluids of the body undergo none of their usual changes in pure air, both Medicine and Surgery received fresh stimulation. A French physician, Dr. Davaine, was fortunate in making the first application of these principles to Medicine, in 1863.

Our researches of last year, left the etiology of the putrid disease, or septicemia, in a much less advanced condition than that of anthrax. We had demonstrated the probability that septicemia depends upon the presence and growth of a microscopic body, but the absolute proof of this important conclusion was not reached. To demonstrate experimentally that a microscopic organism actually is the cause of a disease and the agent of contagion, I know no other way, in the present state of Science, than to subject the microbe (the new and happy term introduced by M. Sedillot) to the method of cultivation out of the body. It may be noted that in twelve successive cultures, each one of only ten cubic centimeters volume, the original drop will be diluted as if placed in a volume of fluid equal to the total volume of the earth. It is just this form of test to which M. Joubert and I subjected the anthrax bacteridium.[2] Having cultivated it a great number of times in a sterile fluid, each culture being started with a minute drop from the preceding, we then demonstrated that the product of the last culture was capable of further development and of acting in the animal tissues by producing anthrax with all its symptoms. Such is—as we believe—the indisputable proof that anthrax is a bacterial disease.

Our researches concerning the septic vibrio had not so far been convincing, and it was to fill up this gap that we resumed our experiments. To this end, we attempted the cultivation of the septic vibrio from an animal dead of septicemia. It is worth noting that all of our first experiments failed, despite the variety of culture media we employed—urine, beer yeast water, meat water, etc. Our culture media were not sterile, but we found—most commonly—a microscopic organism showing no relationship to the septic vibrio, and presenting the form, common enough elsewhere, of chains of extremely minute spherical granules possessed of no virulence whatever.[3] This was an impurity, introduced, unknown to us, at the same time as the septic vibrio; and the germ undoubtedly passed from the intestines—always inflamed and distended in septicemic animals—into the abdominal fluids from which we took our original cultures of the septic vibrio. If this explanation of the contamination of our cultures was correct, we ought to find a pure culture of the septic vibrio in the heart's blood of the animal recently dead of septicemia. This was what happened, but a new difficulty presented itself; all our cultures remained

---

[1] Read before the French Academy of Sciences, April 29th 1878. Published in *Comptes rendus de l'Academie des Sciences*, lxxxvi., pp. 1037-43. Translation by H.C. Ernst, M.D.
[2] In making the translation, it seems wiser to adhere to Pasteur's nomenclature. *Bacillus anthracis* would be the term employed today.—Translator.
[3] It is quite possible that Pasteur was here dealing with certain septicemic streptococci that are now known to lose their virulence with extreme rapidity under artificial cultivation.—Translator.

Figure 5.22

Here are the specifications:

- Page margins will be 1 inch top and bottom, 1½ inches at the sides.
- The main text is to be 11-point Times New Roman, single spaced, with a first-line indentation of ¼ inch.
- Underlining in the draft should be changed to italic in the final publication.
- The title of the paper should be 18-point Arial bold.
- Footnote references in the draft are given as ^ 1 for the first footnote, ^ 2 for the second, and so on. Footnote text is given in brackets with a heading such as *Footnote 1 text:* in front of the text. Change the references and text to conventional forms, like those used in the research paper in this project. All footnote text should be formatted as 10-point Times New Roman.

- All pages, including the first page, should have a footer containing the page number only. The page number should be on the right side on odd pages and on the left side on even pages. The first page should not have a header. Even pages should have headers that say *Germ Theory* on the left side of the page. Odd pages should have headers that say *by Louis Pasteur* on the right side of the page. All headers and footers should be formatted as 12-point Times New Roman bold italic.
- Save the revised document as *Revised Germ Theory,* and print it out.

PART III

Microsoft Excel 7

Overview

Objectives

After completing this overview, you should be able to:

- Start Microsoft Excel
- Navigate workbooks and worksheets
- Identify common pointer shapes
- Change the active cell
- Select cells and ranges
- Manipulate toolbars
- Access Help
- Exit Excel

Among the many far-reaching developments of the Renaissance was the widespread application, in 14th-century Tuscany, of double-entry bookkeeping. Prior to this, the accounts of bankers and merchants were kept in a haphazard, loosely organized manner. The Tuscan innovation, made possible by the importation of Arabic and Hindu numbers, was to organize accounts into tables with rows and columns, thus making them much easier to maintain.

Now double-entry bookkeeping probably doesn't rank very highly on your list of exciting things, but it contributed to the advent of the Industrial Revolution that utterly transformed the Western world.

Until about 1980, most people who created tables of numbers and text worked in much the same way as the Tuscans. Electronic calculators made the job easier, but the use of larger computers was, at the time, difficult and restricted to major projects.

Accounting tables are called ***worksheets*** or ***spreadsheets,*** and if you're creating one the traditional way, you will need some green ledger paper or a lab notebook, a pencil, and a calculator. You'll also need a big eraser because one of the worst problems with manual worksheets is revision: if one number must change, then it will probably affect dozens of other numbers. The burden of recalculating parts of a traditional worksheet makes it difficult to experiment—to perform "what-if" analysis. If you want to make a chart or graph presenting the information pictorially, you will have to get some help from a graphic artist or do your best with colored pens and a ruler.

The invention of personal computers and electronic spreadsheet programs changed this situation dramatically. An electronic spreadsheet presents the table, with its rows and columns, on a computer screen. It is much easier to make modifications because recalculation happens automatically in response to changes.

The first electronic spreadsheet programs made the basic tasks of building and modifying a worksheet much easier. Contemporary programs, such as Microsoft Excel for Windows 95, vastly extend these capabilities with such features as data analysis, charting, and typographical formatting. Erasers and green eye-visors are optional.

Designing Worksheets

An electronic spreadsheet program is a tool not only for accountants. Anyone who wants to organize information in tables can benefit from one. Financial analysts, biologists, engineers, attorneys, marketing specialists, physical scientists, managers, political analysts, health professionals, and many others routinely use electronic spreadsheets. Apart from being universally useful, spreadsheet programs are also fun because building a worksheet is like creating your own little machine—a worksheet is dynamic: it does things and responds to changes.

If you heard about a car that required you to hoist out the engine to change the oil, you would probably think the machine was poorly designed and difficult to maintain. Because, like machines, worksheets should be functional, you must pay close attention to design principles when creating them. You will want to design worksheets that are efficient, easy to use, easy to change, and easy to understand.

The projects in this module use examples that highlight many common design issues. When you finish the module, you will be able to apply your knowledge of Excel commands and worksheet design techniques to your own area of expertise.

A Note to the Student

As in other programs, there is often more than one way to perform a particular command or action in Excel. Many commands can be accessed from a regular menu bar, a toolbar button, a pop-up menu, and a keystroke shortcut. Though most mouse actions have keyboard equivalents, in general, Excel works best with a mouse. Some powerful features of the program, such as toolbars, are accessible *only* with a mouse. This module presumes that you will be using a mouse with Excel.

If you want to review how to use the mouse, windows, menus, and dialog boxes, refer to the "Introduction to Windows" section at the beginning of this module.

Starting Excel

On many systems, a menu item for Excel appears in the Programs section of the Start menu. However, depending on how your system was set up, Excel may be contained in another menu such as Microsoft Office.

To start Excel:

1. Open the Programs item in the Start menu on the Taskbar.
2. Click the Microsoft Excel menu item as shown in Figure 0.1.

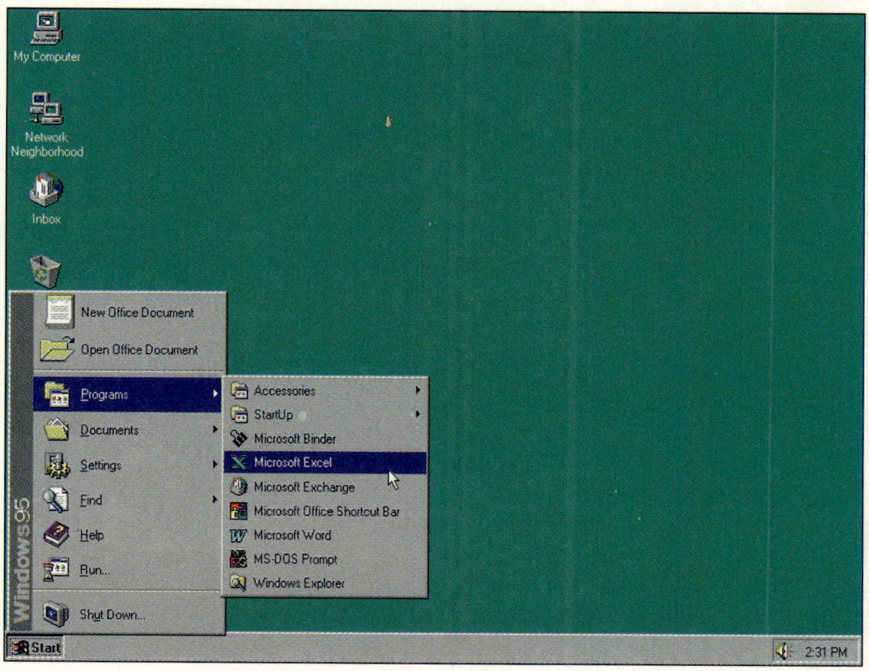

Figure 0.1

In a few moments, Excel will start, and your screen will resemble Figure 0.2.

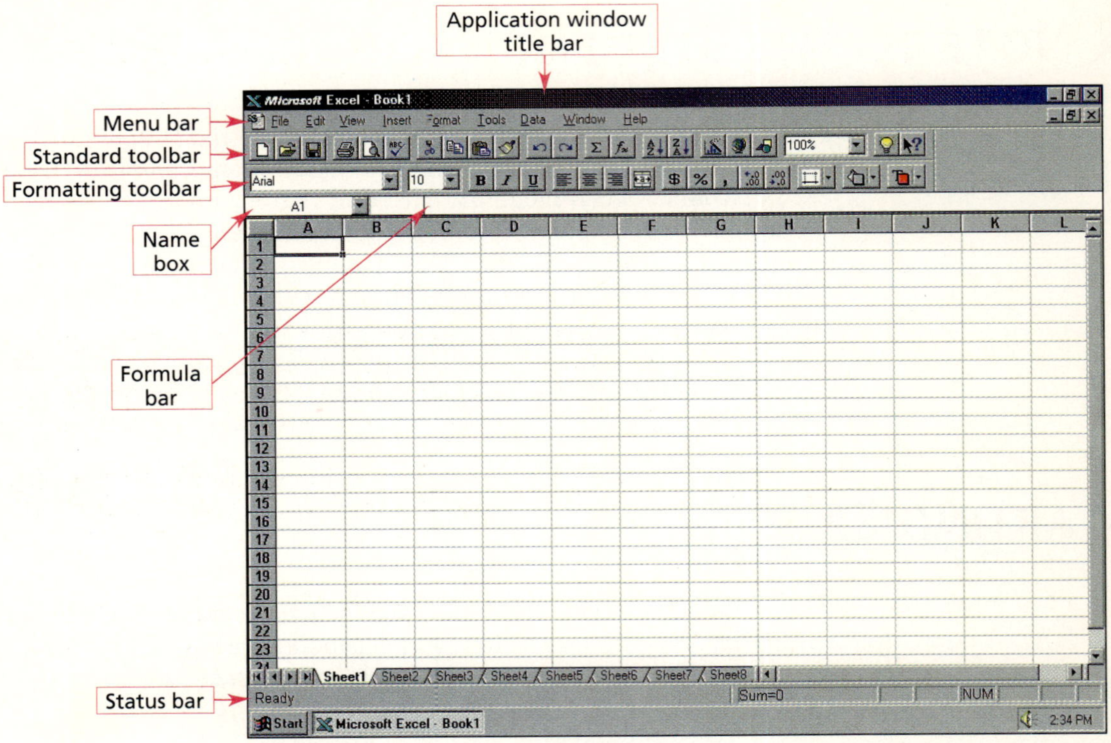

Figure 0.2

Exploring the Application Window

The two main types of windows in Excel are the ***application window,*** which you can think of as representing the Excel program itself, and ***workbook windows,*** which comprise ***sheets*** that contain things you create using Excel. The application window, whose title bar when you start Excel reads *Microsoft Excel—Book1,* frames workbook windows. The workbook window is initially maximized within the application window. Both the application window and the workbook window can have Minimize, Restore, Maximize, and Close window buttons, so it's important not to confuse the two types of windows.

To better understand the difference between these two kinds of windows, you will now reduce the size of the workbook window so that its borders are visible, and then you will minimize it to an icon.

To restore and minimize the workbook window:

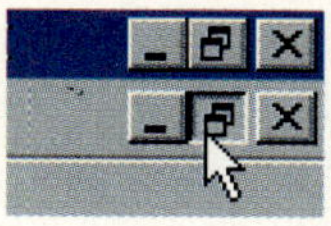

1 Click the workbook window's Restore button.
The screen should now resemble Figure 0.3. The workbook window is reduced in size so that its borders are visible. Notice that the default name for the workbook, *Book1*, appears in its title bar.

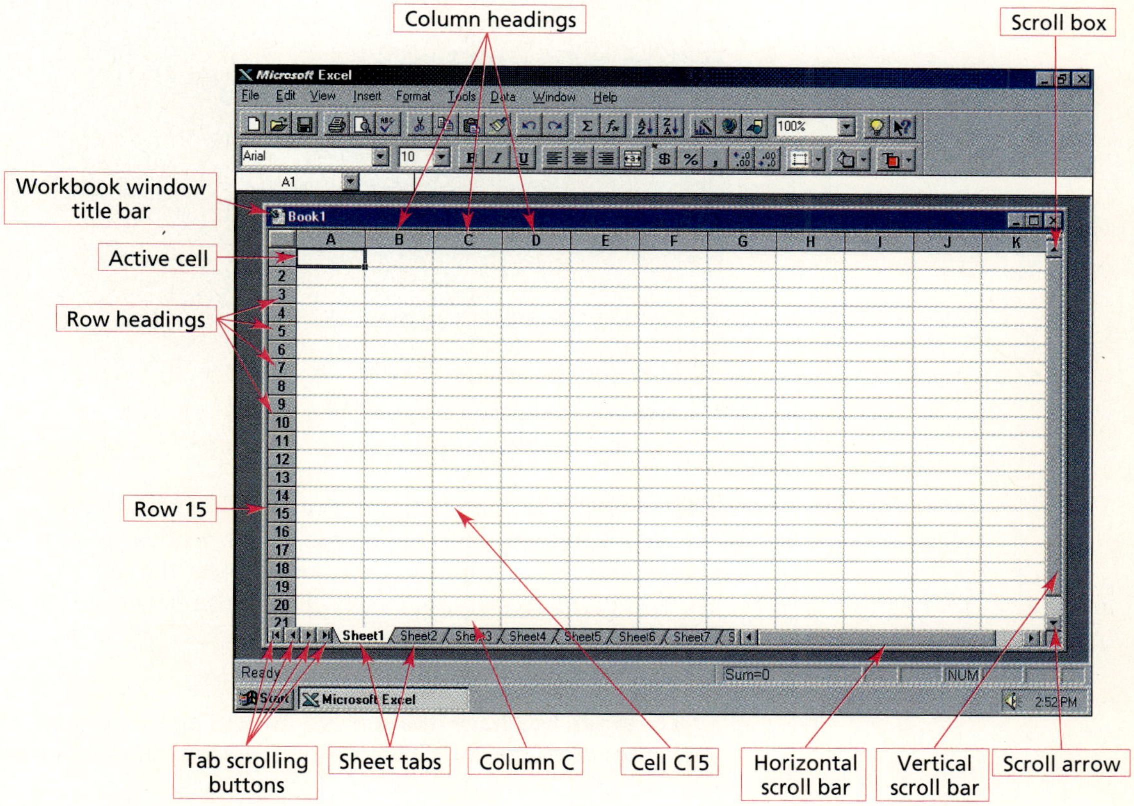

Figure 0.3

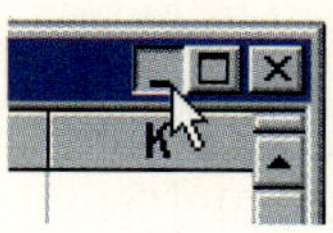

2 Click the *workbook* window's Minimize button.
The screen should now resemble Figure 0.4. The workbook window is reduced to a minimized child window icon in the lower-left corner of the application window. This icon looks like a small title bar with its own Restore, Maximize, and Close buttons.

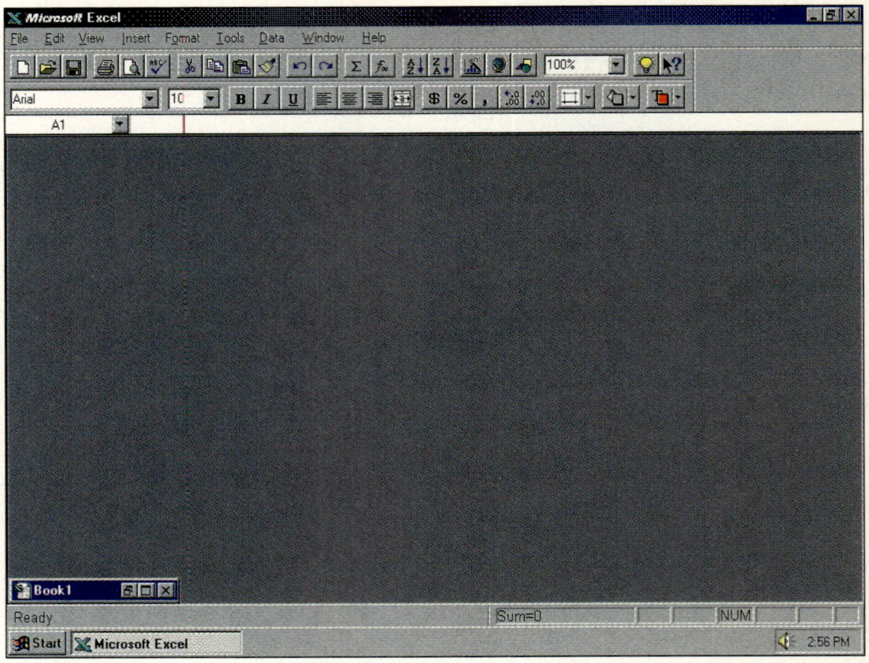

Figure 0.4

3 Click the Restore button on the child window icon.
The screen now resembles Figure 0.3; the workbook window is again visible within the application window. Repeat the minimize-and-restore procedure, if necessary, to clearly distinguish between the application and workbook windows.

> ***Tip*** When you have multiple workbooks open, examine the title bar of a window to ascertain which document you are working with.

Excel commands are grouped on the ***menu bar*** displayed across the top of the application window. You can select the options on a menu bar by clicking them with the mouse or by pressing ALT in combination with the underlined letter in the option.

Beneath the menu bar are two rows of buttons: the Standard and Formatting toolbars. A ***toolbar*** contains buttons and other controls that provide quick access to important commands and functions. Toolbars are accessible only with a mouse.

The ***name box*** and the ***formula bar*** are below the toolbars. These sections of the application window become active when you type or change information in a worksheet.

At the bottom of the application window is the ***status bar,*** which includes keyboard-status indicators and displays brief help messages when you use Excel commands.

NAVIGATING THE WORKBOOK

A ***workbook*** is composed of one or more sheets, each of which can be a worksheet, chart sheet, or module. A worksheet, designed to hold text and numbers and to perform calculations, is the most common type and is what you will spend most of your time with when using Excel. A ***chart sheet,*** a pictoral representation of data found in a worksheet, is used to hold an Excel chart. A ***module*** or macro sheet is a sheet used to hold Excel macros (programs that you create).

Changing Among Sheets

A new, blank workbook contains 16 worksheets. You can add any combination of worksheets, chart sheets, or modules to this. You can also delete any sheets.

The name of each sheet appears on its ***sheet tab*** near the bottom of the workbook window. Initially, Sheet1 is visible. You can view a sheet by clicking its tab; you can use the ***tab scrolling buttons,*** as shown in Figure 0.5, to see different tabs.

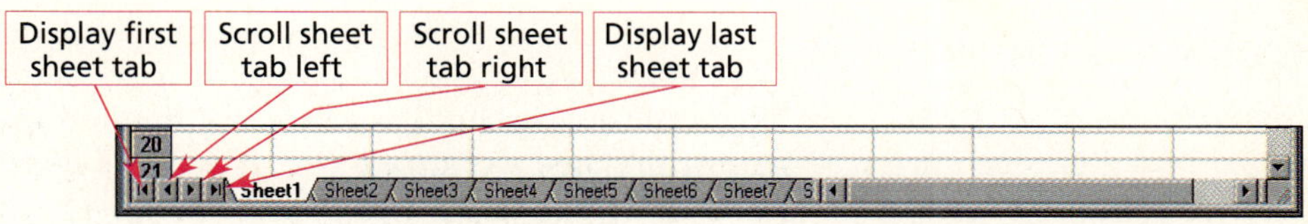

Figure 0.5

To activate a sheet:

1 Click the tab named Sheet2.
You are now viewing a different worksheet, Sheet2.

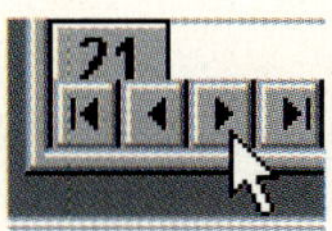

2 Click the right sheet-tab scrolling button three times so that the tab for Sheet8 is visible.
Note that though the tab for Sheet2 is not currently visible, you are still looking at the Sheet2 worksheet.

3 Click the tab scrolling button to display the last sheet tab.

4 Click the tab for Sheet16.
Sheet16 now appears.

5 Click the tab scrolling button to display the first sheet tab.

6 Click the tab for Sheet1.
The screen should once again resemble Figure 0.3.

Much of your work in this module will be done with a single worksheet.

Tip

- Scrolling the sheet tabs does not in itself change the active sheet; you must also click a sheet's tab in order to activate the sheet.
- You can use CTRL+PGDN to change to the next sheet and CTRL+PGUP to change to the previous sheet.
- If you hold down SHFT and click a sheet-tab scrolling button, you can scroll by several tabs at once.

Navigating Within a Worksheet

Each Excel worksheet is composed of ***columns*** and ***rows.*** Columns are labeled with the letters of the alphabet, starting with A and continuing through Z, followed by AA, AB, and so forth, to IV for a maximum of 256 columns. Rows are labeled with numbers from 1 to 16,384. The worksheets you will build using this module won't use nearly so large an area; the average worksheet size for this module is about 10 columns by 20 rows.

The basic building block of a worksheet, the intersection of a column and a row, is called a ***cell,*** and it is identified by its column letter and row number. For example, the ***cell reference*** C15 refers to the cell at the intersection of column C and row 15.

Scrolling a Worksheet

Think of the workbook window as a frame through which you can see only part of the total worksheet area. To view a different area, you can shift the frame using the scroll bars or arrow keys.

Because Book1 is the only workbook currently in use, you should first maximize its window to make the best use of the screen.

Tip Even if you plan primarily to use a mouse, in the steps that follow you should experiment with both the mouse and the keyboard actions.

To scroll the worksheet window:

1 Click the Maximize button of the Book1 workbook window.
The screen should appear similar to Figure 0.2.

2 Mouse: Click the down scroll arrow (at the bottom of the vertical scroll bar). Press and hold down the mouse button on a scroll arrow to repeat the scrolling action.

or Keys: Press and hold down ↓ until the window begins to move. The window will shift down row by row. You can use the other scroll arrows (and the other arrow keys, ← → ↑) to move by single columns or rows in other directions. Experiment with the other scroll arrows or arrow keys.

3 Press CTRL+HOME to return to the upper-left corner of the worksheet, cell A1.

4 Mouse: Click in the vertical scroll bar below the scroll box. Notice that the scroll box moves to the bottom of the scroll bar. You can click in the vertical scroll bar to shift the window in the opposite direction.
or Keys: Press (PGDN)
If you pressed (PGDN), the window shifts down by one window's height to show a different portion of the worksheet. Press (PGUP) to shift the window farther up; to shift the window farther down, press (PGDN) Experiment with (PGDN) and (PGUP).

5 Press (CTRL)+(HOME) to return to the upper-left corner of the worksheet, cell A1.

6 Click to the right of the horizontal scroll box to move the horizontal scroll box to the right edge of the horizontal scroll bar.
The window shifts right by one window's width to show a different portion of the worksheet.

7 Press (CTRL)+(HOME) to return to the upper-left corner of the worksheet, cell A1.

You can also scroll through the worksheet by dragging the scroll box. While you drag the box, a ScrollTip appears near the box, telling you which row or column of the worksheet you would jump to if you released the mouse button. In the following steps, you will experiment with this feature, first moving down the worksheet using keys, and then moving back up by dragging the scroll box.

To scroll using the scroll box:

1 Hold down the (PGDN) key until the worksheet has scrolled to about row 200.

2 Hold down the mouse button on the scroll box, and move the box upward.
Notice that a ScrollTip appears showing the row that the box will position to.

3 Use the scroll box to jump to row 60.

4 Press (CTRL)+(HOME) to return to the upper-left corner of the worksheet.

Positioning the Active Cell

The cell appearing with a heavy border around it indicates the ***active cell*** rectangle. The active cell (also called the selected cell, current cell, or cell pointer) is where the action will take place if you type data or perform a command. When you first activate a new, empty worksheet, A1 is the active cell.

To position the active cell:

1 Mouse: Move the pointer to cell E2, and click the mouse button.
or Keys: Use the arrow keys to move the active cell rectangle to E2.
Notice that the cell reference of the active cell is displayed in the Name box.

2 Try scrolling the window (by clicking one of the scroll arrows).

> ***Tip*** Notice that scrolling with the mouse does *not* change the active cell, whereas using the arrow keys does.

Changing Pointer Shapes

The shape of the pointer changes depending on where the pointer is positioned on the screen. In the steps that follow, you will carefully move the pointer to the locations described and observe the changes in its appearance. Notice that pointer shapes change in response to specific mouse movements and screen locations. Don't worry about memorizing the meanings of all the different pointer shapes at this time.

To change pointer shapes:

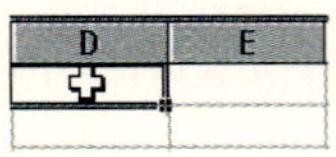

1 Position the pointer in the middle of the active cell or in any other cell.
The pointer appears as a hollow plus sign; this pointer is used to select a new active cell or a group of cells.

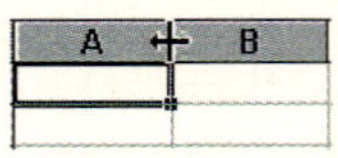

2 Position the pointer on a line separating two column letters.
The pointer appears as a double arrow, which you will use in later projects to change the width of a column.

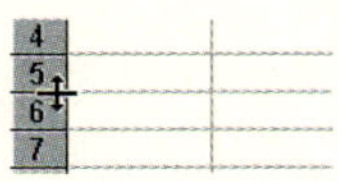

3 Position the pointer on the line separating any two row headings.
This double arrow is similar to the column-width pointer and is used to change the height of a row.

4 Position the pointer in the middle of the formula bar.
The pointer changes to an insertion symbol, called an ***I-beam;*** you will use this to edit text within the formula bar.

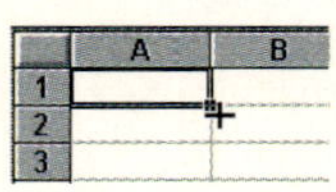

5 Position the pointer so that it just touches the lower-right corner of the active cell.
This pointer is called the ***fill handle*** and is used to copy cell contents.

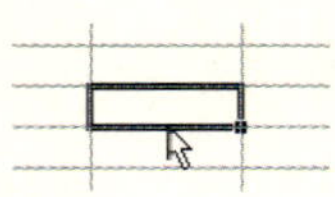

6 Position the pointer so that it just touches any of the edges of the active cell.
The pointer turns into an arrow, which you can use to move the contents of a cell to a new location.

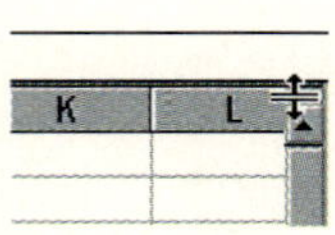

7 Position the pointer on the small rectangle at the top of the vertical scroll bar.
This area is called the ***split bar,*** and it is used to split a window into two sections. A horizontal split bar is at the right of the horizontal scroll bar.

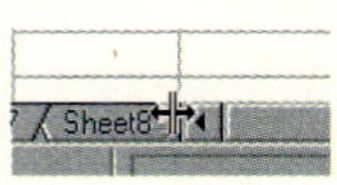

8 Position the pointer on the small rectangle just to the left of the left scroll arrow.
You can click and drag this split bar to control the relative width of the scroll bar and sheet-tab scroll areas.

9 Position the pointer on any button within a toolbar, such as the Print button. Do not click.
A small box appears, called a ***ToolTip,*** which identifies the function of the button that you position the pointer on.

MAKING SELECTIONS

As you use Excel, you will occasionally want to perform an action that affects an entire worksheet, but most of the time you will want to change only a portion of a worksheet. Before using most commands, you must first indicate your ***selection,*** the part of the worksheet you want to change. Most Excel commands operate on a selection. You can select a single cell, a *range* (a rectangular block of cells), or a group of ranges. After you make a selection, you can choose a command to affect that selection.

Selecting a Single Cell

The active cell is the currently selected cell. You can select a single cell by positioning the active-cell rectangle. You can select a cell that is not currently visible by first scrolling the window and then clicking the cell to make a selection. Suppose you want to select cell B5.

To select cell B5:

1 Mouse: Position the pointer on cell B5 and click.
or Keys: Use the arrow keys to position the active-cell rectangle on cell B5.

2 Scroll until cell J35 is visible, and then select it.

Selecting a Range of Cells

A ***range*** is a *rectangular* block of cells referred to by its upper-left and lower-right diagonal corner cells. For example, the range whose upper-left corner is cell B2 and whose lower-right corner is cell C5 would be referred to as B2:C5. A range can be as small as a single cell or as large as the entire worksheet.

To select a range, you would first select any corner cell, and then use the mouse to extend the selection to cover the entire range. Suppose you want to select the range B2:C5.

To select the range B2:C5:

1 Select cell B2 by clicking it. Be sure that the pointer forms a hollow plus sign positioned inside the active cell.

2 Hold down the mouse button and drag down to row 5 and across to column C to select the range, then release the mouse button. You could also extend the selection first to the right and then down; the order doesn't matter.

The range B2:C5 is selected, as shown in Figure 0.6.

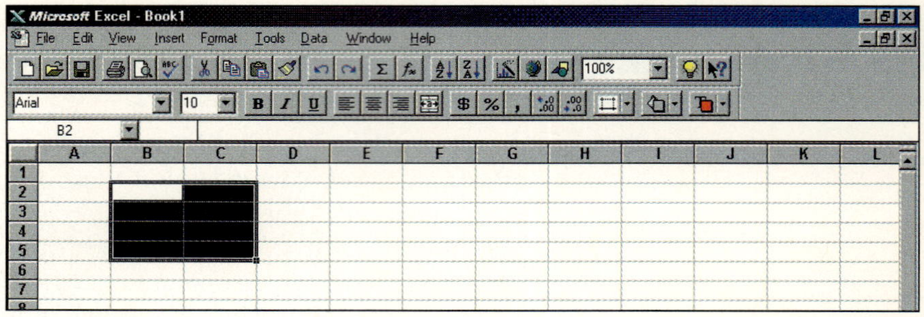

Figure 0.6

> ***Tip*** If you need to select a large range and don't want to hold down the mouse button for a long time, select a cell that is any corner of the range, use the scroll bars if necessary to shift the window, position the pointer on the cell that is the diagonally opposite corner, hold down (SHIFT) and click.

Practice selecting other ranges. Notice that when you make a new selection, the previous selection markings disappear. You will also notice that there's always one cell in the selection that is not darkened, yet is still within the thick bordered area that defines the selection.

Selecting an Entire Column or Row

A complete column or row is just a large range. Selecting an entire column or row is easy: you click the column or row heading. You must be very careful to click directly on the heading letter or number, and not a dividing line between headings (the dividing line is used to change column widths).

To select an entire column or row:

1 Click the column heading (letter) G.
This selects all of column G (the range G1:G16384).

The screen should resemble Figure 0.7.

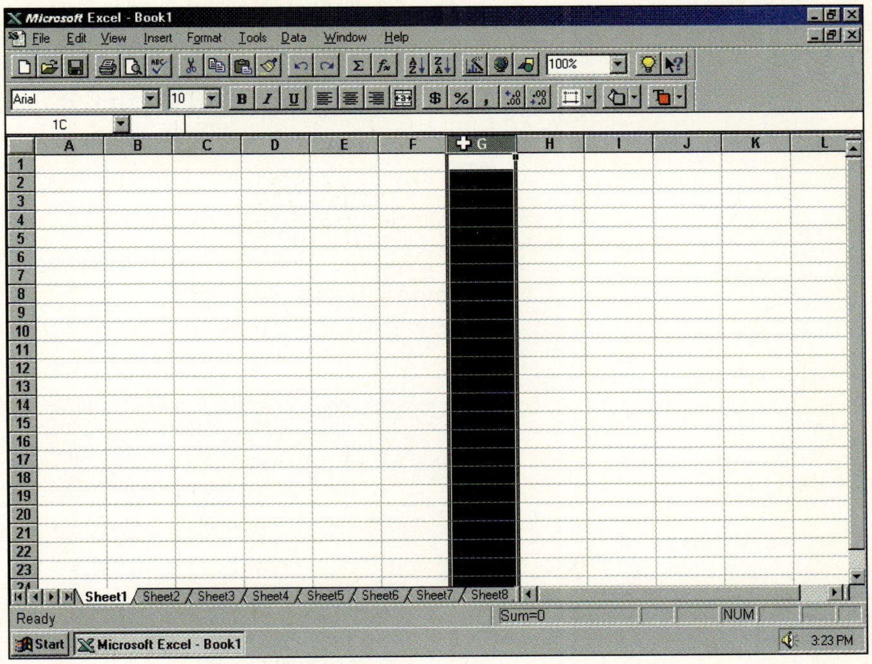

Figure 0.7

2 Click the row heading (number) 7.
This selects all of row 7 (the range A7:IV7). Practice selecting other columns and rows.

Selecting Adjacent Columns or Rows

To select a group of adjacent columns or rows, you first select one column or row and then extend the selection through the other columns or rows.

To select an adjacent group of columns or rows:

1 Select column C.

2 Hold down the mouse button, drag to column F, and then release the mouse button.
This extends the selection across column headings D, E, and F. The selected range is C1:F16384, which can be abbreviated to C:F.

3 Select row 7. (The previous selection of C:F will be canceled.)

4 Extend the selection down through row 10.
Practice with other column-and-row group selections.

Making Nonadjacent Selections

You will sometimes want to affect an area of the worksheet that is not rectangular and that cannot be selected as a single range. Excel allows you to compose a more complicated selection, called a ***nonadjacent selection,*** from a group of ranges.

You have noticed that if you move away from a selection and make another cell active, the previous selection is no longer marked. To make a composite selection out of a group of separate ranges, columns, or rows, you will hold down (CTRL) while making your selections with the mouse.

To make nonadjacent selections:

1 Select the range B3:D8. After making this selection, release the mouse button.

2 Position the mouse pointer on cell G10.

3 Hold down CTRL and then hold down the mouse button.

4 Drag the mouse to select the range G10:H15, and then release both the mouse button and CTRL

The screen should look similar to Figure 0.8.

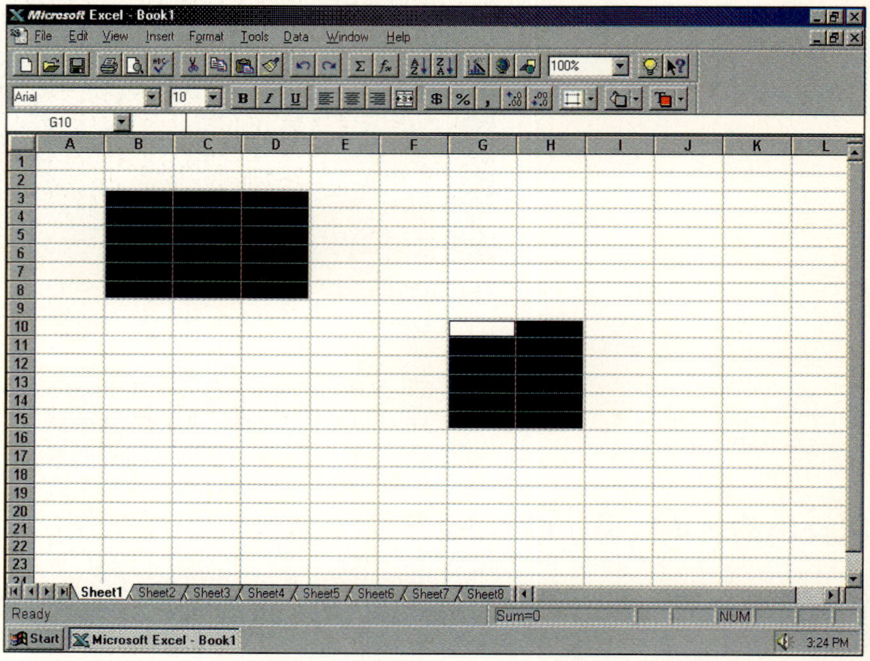

Figure 0.8

Using this method, practice making other nonadjacent selections.

Selecting an Entire Sheet

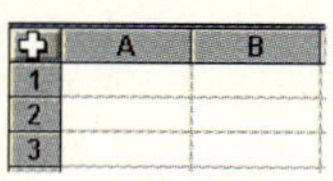

Clicking the button above the heading for row 1 and to the left of the heading for column A selects the entire worksheet.

To select the entire worksheet:

1 Click the Select All button.

The entire worksheet is selected, as shown in Figure 0.9.

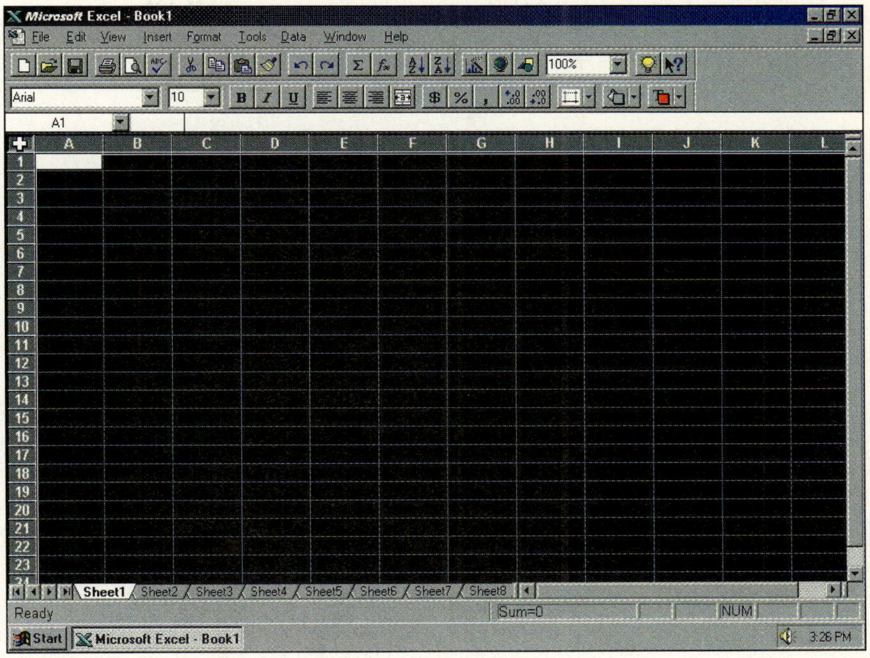

Figure 0.9

2 To cancel the selection, click any individual cell or reposition the active cell using the arrow keys.

Working with Toolbars

Though the Standard and Formatting toolbars appear by default on the screen, 11 other toolbars are available for various kinds of tasks. Any toolbar can be customized to contain tools—buttons and other controls—of your choice. You can also create new toolbars of your own design. More than 200 tools are available for placement in toolbars.

Sometimes a particular toolbar will display automatically, depending on the actions you are performing in Excel. At other times, you may want to hide, display, or rearrange toolbars as you work. You will occasionally want to hide a toolbar just to give yourself more screen space for other information.

Initially, the Standard and Formatting toolbars are ***docked*** (anchored) to the top section of the application window, but any toolbar can be made into a ***floating toolbar***—a small window that can be positioned anywhere on the screen. Any toolbar can be docked to the top or bottom of the window, and most can also be docked to the left or right side of the window.

To hide a toolbar:

1 Open the **View** menu, and then choose **Toolbars.**
The Toolbars dialog box appears.

2 Select **Formatting** to clear its check box.
The screen should now resemble Figure 0.10.

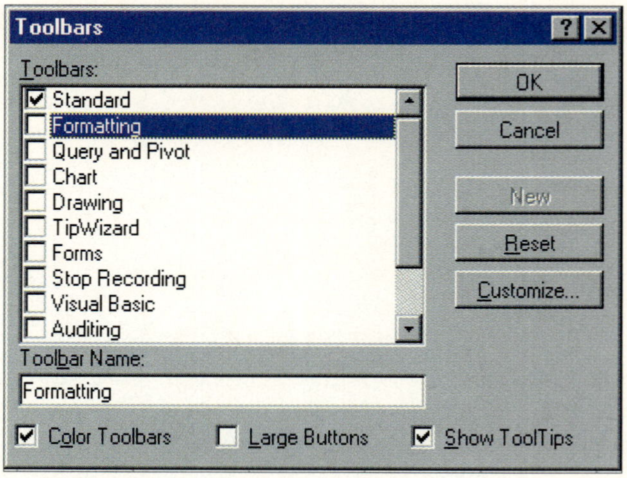

Figure 0.10

3 Select **OK.**
The Formatting toolbar no longer appears, allowing you to see a few more rows of the worksheet.

To display a floating toolbar:

1 Open the **View** menu, and then choose **Toolbars.**
The Toolbars dialog box appears.

2 Scroll down the list of toolbars (if necessary), and select **Auditing.**

3 Select **OK,** as shown in Figure 0.11.

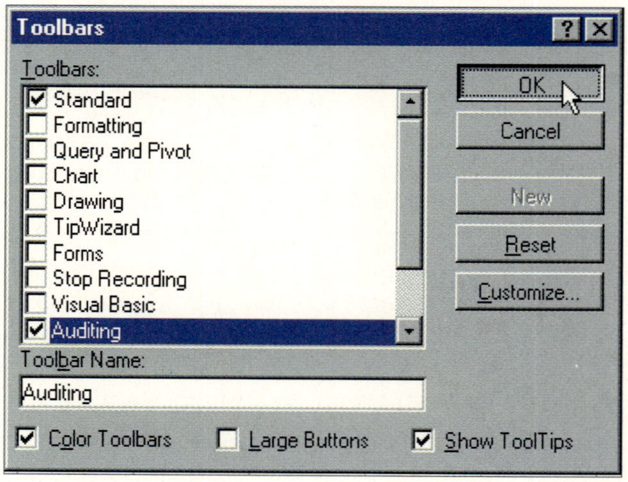

Figure 0.11

The Auditing toolbar appears in a small window of its own, "floating" on the application window. The toolbar can be moved, reproportioned, or docked against an edge.

To dock a floating toolbar:

1 Position the pointer on the Auditing toolbar's title bar.

2 Hold down the mouse button, and drag the outline image of the toolbar to the bottom center of the application window, over the status bar, as shown in Figure 0.12.

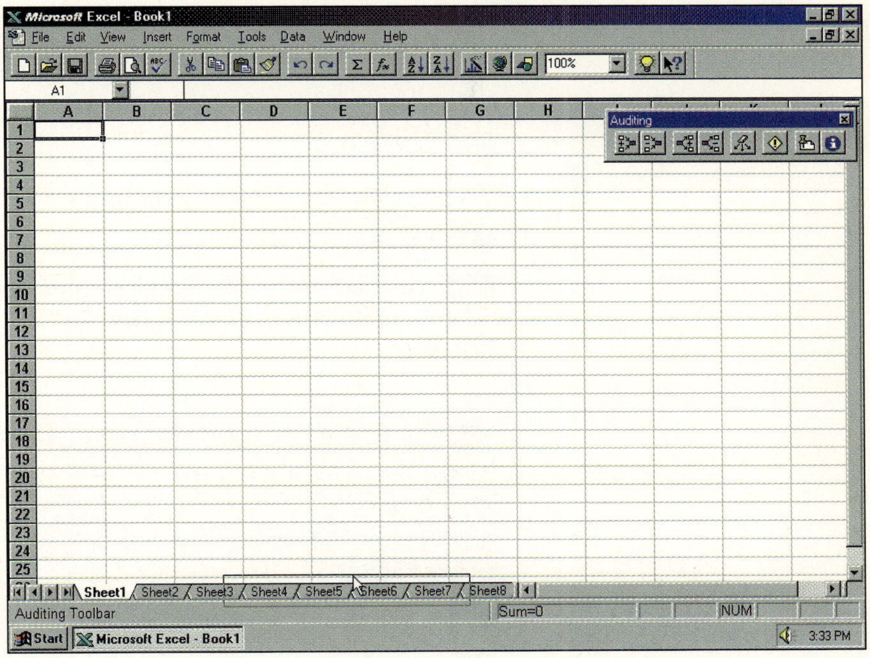

Figure 0.12

3 Release the mouse button.
The Auditing toolbar is now docked to the bottom of the application window.

Every docked toolbar has an outlined background area in which its buttons and controls are placed. If you click and drag this background, you can move the toolbar away from its docked position and make it a floating toolbar. A floating toolbar can be hidden by clicking its Close window button.

To undock and hide a docked toolbar:

1 Position the pointer within the background of the docked Auditing toolbar.

2 Click and drag the toolbar to the center of the window.
The Auditing toolbar is once again a floating toolbar.

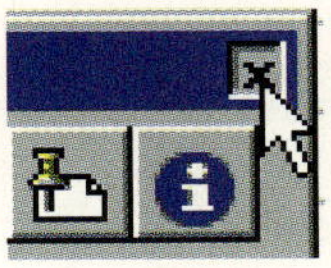

3 Click the Auditing toolbar's Close window button to hide the toolbar.

4 Open the **View** menu, choose **Toolbars,** and then display the Formatting toolbar.
The screen should once again appear as it did when you first started Excel.

> ***Tip*** Clicking the **right** mouse button in a toolbar's background displays a pop-up (shortcut) menu to provide quick access to many of the features discussed in this section.

Getting On-Screen Help

The Help system in Microsoft Excel conforms to the standard Help conventions of Windows, which may be familiar to you if you have used other Windows applications. Think of the Help system as a vast reference manual stored on disk, with convenient indexes and cross-references to help you find the information you need. In the steps that follow, you will use the Help system to get information on how to close documents.

To access the Help system:

1 Open the **Help** menu.

2 Choose **Microsoft Excel Help Topics**.
The Help Topics dialog box, shown in Figure 0.13, comprises four tabbed pages.

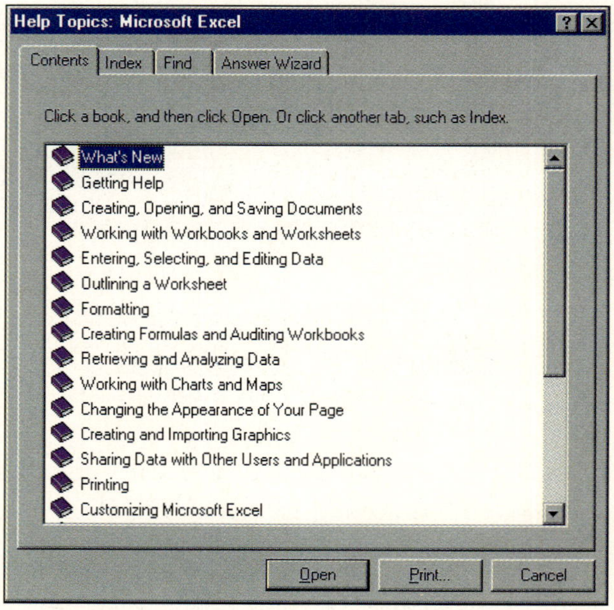

Figure 0.13

To use the Contents page:

1 Click the **Contents** tab (if not already displayed).
The Contents page displays a table of contents, similar to that found in a book. Double-clicking any of the book icons will open that topic area, displaying individual help topics and other book icons that represent topic subsections. You can also open a topic by first selecting it and then clicking the Open button at the bottom of the dialog box.

2 Double-click the **Creating, Opening, and Saving Documents** book icon.
The topic opens, revealing five subtopics.

3 Double-click the **Saving and Closing Documents** book icon.
Several individual topics display, as shown in Figure 0.14.

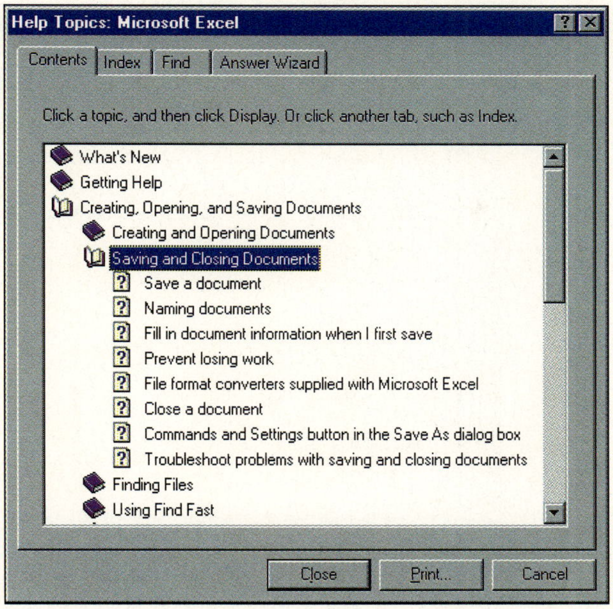

Figure 0.14

4 Double-click the **Close a document** topic.
A small Help window displays, as shown in Figure 0.15, with an explanation of how to close documents. The Help Topics dialog box disappears.

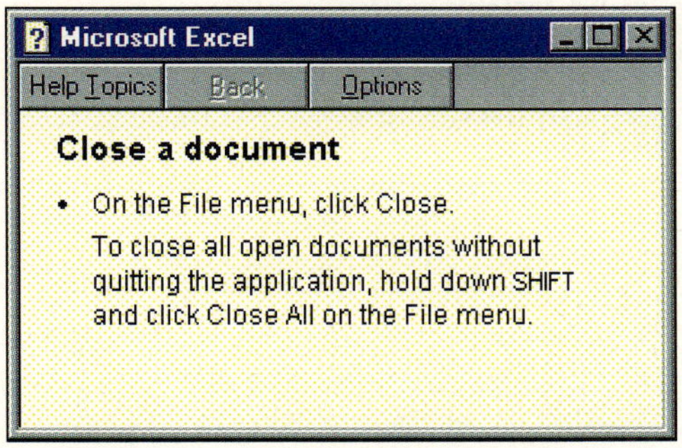

Figure 0.15

5 Click the **Help Topics** button at the top of the Help window to return to the main Help Topics dialog box.

To use the Index page:

1 Click the **Index** tab.
Like the index of a book, the Index page, shown in Figure 0.16, displays an alphabetical list of all the key words in the Excel Help system. Your list may differ slightly from the figure's.

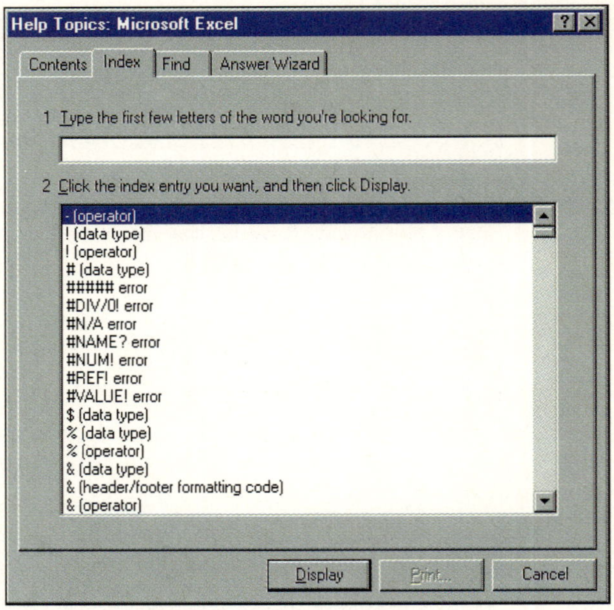

Figure 0.16

2 Type `close` in the text box to see the portion of the index that has entries beginning with this word.

3 Double-click the item **closing files.**
A Topics window appears, similar to Figure 0.17, showing various topics related to closing files.

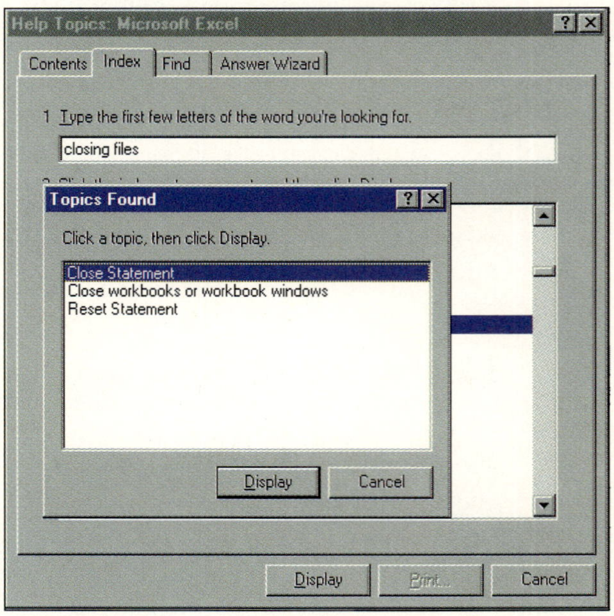

Figure 0.17

4 Double-click the **Close workbooks or workbook windows** topic.
A Help window displays with an explanation of how to close workbooks.

5 Click the **Help Topics** button at the top of the Help window to return to the main Help Topics dialog box.

To use the Find page:

1 Click the **Find** tab.

The Find page, shown in Figure 0.18, is similar to the Index page but searches a more comprehensive list of words than would be found in the index.

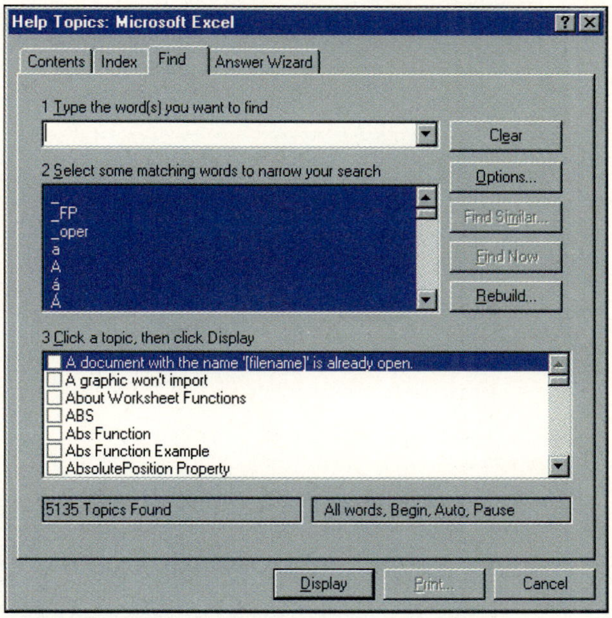

Figure 0.18

2 Type `close` in the text box.

The middle window within the dialog box shows "matching words" that can be used to narrow the focus of your search.

3 Click **close** in the middle window.

A narrowed list of topics appears in the bottom window of the dialog box.

4 Scroll the list in the bottom window, and then double-click the item **Close a document.**

A small Help window displays with an explanation of how to close documents.

5 Click the **Help Topics** button at the top of the Help window to return to the main Help Topics dialog box.

To use the Answer Wizard:

1 Click the **Answer Wizard** tab.

The Answer Wizard employs AI (artificial intelligence) technology to allow you to perform topic searches based on plain English questions that you submit. The Answer Wizard page is shown in Figure 0.19.

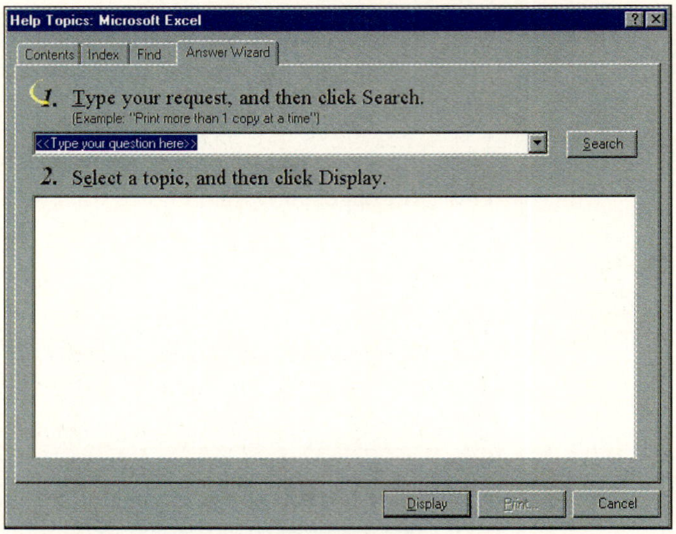

Figure 0.19

2 Type `How do I close the thing?` in the text box, and then click the **Search** button.
Various topics appear in the lower half of the window, as shown in Figure 0.20.

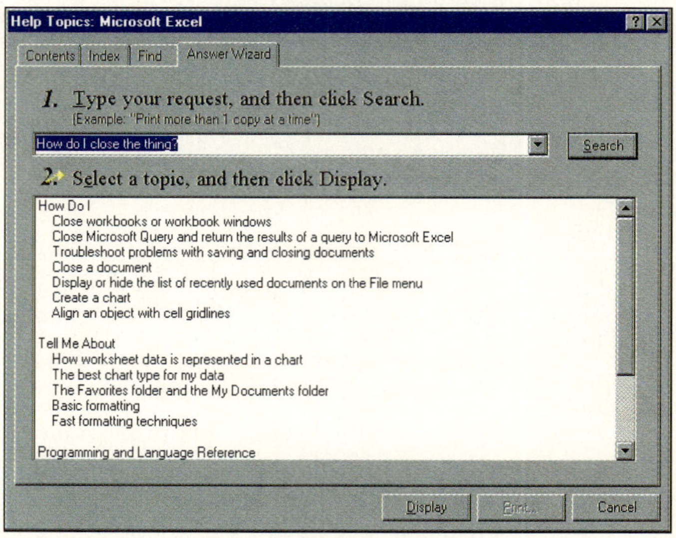

Figure 0.20

3 Double-click the topic **Close a document.**
A small Help window displays with an explanation of how to close documents.

4 Click the Close window button at the top of the Help window to end your exploration of the Help Topics system.

Using the Help Tool

The ***Help tool*** allows you to get help on a topic by pointing to a particular part of the screen containing that topic or by selecting the topic from a menu. The Help tool is available on the toolbar or by pressing SHIFT + F1

To use the Help tool:

1 Click the **Help** tool.
The pointer should now have a large question mark attached to it.

2 Open the **Format** menu, and then choose **AutoFormat.**
A Help pop-up window about AutoFormat appears. Note that because the Help tool was active, the AutoFormat command was not actually selected.

3 Close the Help window by clicking anywhere.

> ***Tip*** Using the mouse, you can also point the Help tool at a part of the screen to get help information. For example, you can activate the Help tool, point to the middle of the formula bar, and click. Help information on the formula bar then appears.

Using the TipWizard

The small button depicting a light bulb near the right edge of the Standard toolbar is called the ***TipWizard.*** This feature monitors your work in Excel and identifies possible shortcuts and alternatives to the actions you perform. When the light bulb turns yellow (or when it displays a question mark on a monochrome screen), it has a tip for you. To see the tip, you click the TipWizard tool. The text of the tip will appear in the TipWizard box. You can also view previous tips and get additional help on the currently displayed tip. To remove the tip from the screen, you click the TipWizard tool again.

To use the TipWizard:

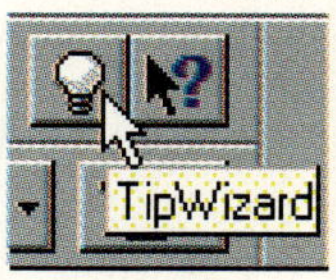

1 Click the **TipWizard** tool.
The most recent tip appears in the TipWizard box above the formula bar, as shown in Figure 0.21. The text you see may differ from the figure's.

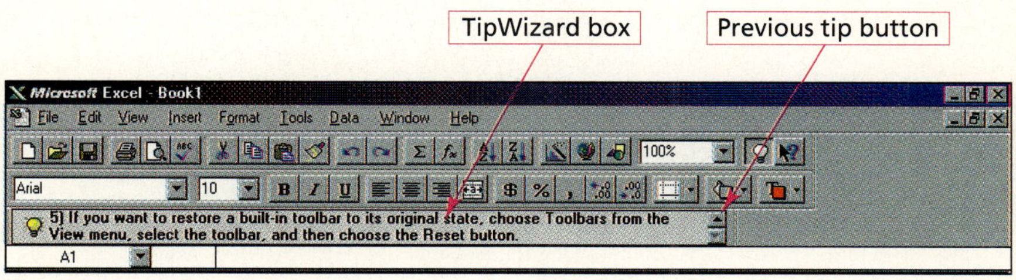

Figure 0.21

2 Click the **Previous Tip** button (the upward-pointing arrow near the right of the TipWizard box).
The text of the previous tip appears.

3 Click the **TipWizard** tool.
The TipWizard box disappears.

Exiting Excel

You will now exit the Excel program. It is not necessary to save this empty workbook (although if you happened to have made changes to it, Excel will give you the opportunity to save it before exiting). You can use either of two methods to exit Excel.

To exit Excel:

1 Open the **File** menu, and then choose **Exit.**

2 Because you do not need to save this workbook, select No in the Save Changes dialog box if it appears.

> ***Tip*** You can also exit Excel by clicking the Close window button in the upper-right corner of the Excel application window. Remember that there is also another Close window button that belongs to the current workbook window. Clicking the workbook's Close window button closes only that workbook window, not the Excel program.

Now that you've used the mouse to choose menu commands, we will state the numbered steps in a more abbreviated form. For example,

1 Open the **File** menu, and then choose **Exit**

will be represented as

2 Choose **File** and then **Exit.**

The Next Step

Now that you are acquainted with the Excel application and workbook windows, you are ready to enter information into a worksheet and to use commands to affect the information. Project 1, "Building a Small Worksheet," will illustrate many of the basic aspects of Excel worksheets.

Summary and Exercises

Summary

- Worksheets (spreadsheets) consist of tables of information presented in rows and columns. Beyond its basic ability to perform arithmetic, Excel offers powerful formatting, data analysis, and charting features.
- You can use Excel to build workbooks comprising worksheets, chart sheets, and modules.

- The top portion of the Excel application window contains the menu bar, the Standard toolbar, the Formatting toolbar, and the formula bar.
- An Excel worksheet comprises columns (labeled A, B, C, . . ., Z, AA, AB, . . ., IV) and rows (labeled 1 through 16384).
- The intersection of a row and a column is called a cell, which is the basic building block of a worksheet. You refer to a cell by its row and column (for example, the cell at the intersection of column C and row 15 is called cell C15).
- The selected cell is where the action takes place in a worksheet. The selected cell appears with a thick outline.
- The pointer can take a variety of shapes, depending on precisely where it is positioned on the screen and on what action it will perform.
- A range is a rectangular block of cells. You can select a range of cells by holding down the mouse button and dragging the pointer through the cells you want to select. You can also select whole columns, rows, and nonadjacent ranges.
- Toolbars contain controls that allow quick access to commands. You can rearrange and customize toolbars.
- A standard Windows Help system is available to explain Excel commands and features. A variety of methods can be used to search for Help topics.

Key Terms and Operations

Key Terms
active cell
application window
cell
cell reference
chart sheet
column
docked
fill handle
floating toolbar
formula bar
Help tool
I-beam
menu bar
module
name box
nonadjacent selection
range
row
selection
sheet
sheet tab
split bar
spreadsheet
status bar
tab scrolling buttons
TipWizard
toolbar
ToolTip
workbook
workbook window
worksheet

Operations
Exit Excel
Get on-screen help
Start Excel

Study Questions

Multiple Choice

1. In Excel, the intersection of a column and a row is called a:
   a. block.
   b. selection.
   c. cell.
   d. range.
   e. formula.

2. How deep (how many rows) is an Excel worksheet?
   a. 100
   b. 500
   c. 1000
   d. 1024
   e. 16,384

3. To position in the upper-left corner of the worksheet (cell A1), press:
   a. CTRL + PGUP
   b. PGUP
   c. HOME
   d. CTRL + HOME
   e. ALT + PGUP
4. A new, blank workbook contains how many worksheets?
   a. 1
   b. 2
   c. 16
   d. 100
   e. 16,384
5. A rectangular block of cells is called a:
   a. data block.
   b. paragraph.
   c. data segment.
   d. code segment.
   e. range.
6. How do you use the mouse to quickly select an entire column in Excel?
   a. Click any cell in the column.
   b. Click the column heading letter.
   c. Click the top cell and drag to the bottom cell.
   d. Click the Column Select tool on the toolbar.
   e. Click the top cell of the column and press F8.
7. What menu command gives you control over the display of toolbars?
   a. Choose View and then Toolbars.
   b. ToolTips
   c. Choose Edit and then Bars.
   d. Choose Edit and then Toolbars.
   e. Choose Tools and then View.

Short Answer

1. The intersection of column C and row 5 is referred to as what?
2. The rectangular block of cells whose upper-left corner is B3 and whose lower-right corner is E8 is referred to as what?
3. The location where the "action" takes place in the worksheet is called what?
4. How can nonadjacent selections be made using the mouse in Excel?

For Discussion

1. Who other than accountants might benefit from Excel?
2. How might you use Excel in your own work or area of expertise?
3. What were some of the problems of spreadsheets before spreadsheet computer programs were available? What distinguishes electronic spreadsheets from their manual predecessors?
4. What distinguishes Excel from the first generation of electronic spreadsheets?

PROJECT 1: BUILDING A SMALL WORKSHEET

Objectives

After completing this project, you should be able to:

- Enter text and number constants
- Change column widths
- Build simple formulas
- Recalculate a worksheet
- Use arithmetic operators
- Automatically format a worksheet
- Save, close, and open a worksheet
- Edit cell entries
- Insert and name new worksheets
- Open a new workbook

CASE STUDY: CALCULATING NET PAY

In this project, you will build a small worksheet that uses each of the three basic kinds of cell entries common to all Excel worksheets: text, numbers, and formulas. First, you will enter text to use for titles, numbers that will serve as the basic data manipulated in the worksheet, and a formula that refers to the numbers and computes a result. You will then learn how to format the worksheet to improve its appearance. Finally, you will save the workbook to disk so that the workbook can be used later.

Designing the Solution

This first worksheet will calculate a person's net pay by subtracting taxes withheld from gross pay. A rough version of the worksheet follows:

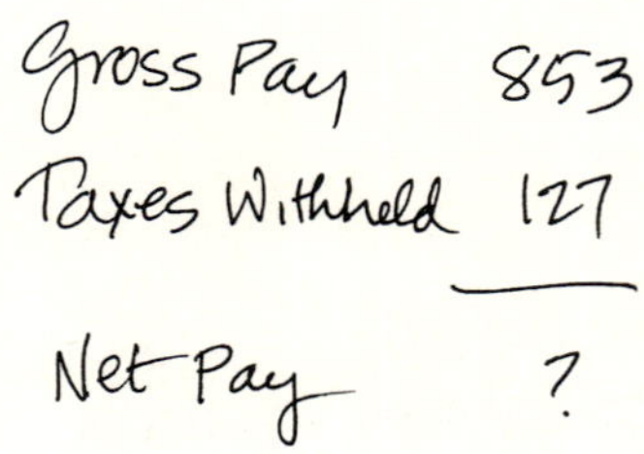

The question mark is a reminder that you will design the Excel worksheet to compute the net pay.

Entering Constants

A cell can contain three basic kinds of data: *text constants*, *number constants*, and *formulas*. Constants do not change after you type them into a cell. ***Number constants*** are numbers—mathematical values that can be used in calculations; ***text constants*** consist of words, comments, titles, and other nonmathematical information.

Formulas compute a result, usually by performing arithmetic on information obtained from other cells. The ***value*** (result) of a formula can change if any of the cells that the formula refers to change. Formulas do the work of a worksheet, and well-designed formulas are the key to building a worksheet that is flexible and powerful.

You will begin this project by entering the text constants of this worksheet. Text constants are usually words that label the different parts of a worksheet to make it easier to understand.

To enter text constants:

1 Start Excel.

2 Select cell A1 if not already selected.

3 Type **`Gross Pay`**
The screen should appear similar to Figure 1.1. Notice that the text appears in the formula bar as well as in the cell.

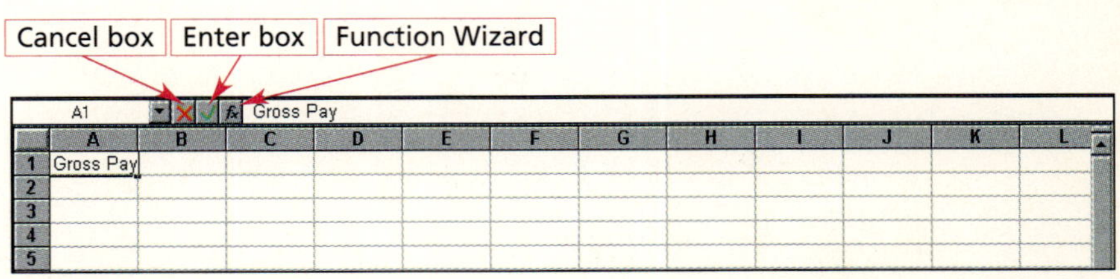

Figure 1.1

Tip To cancel an entry while you are typing it, you can select the Cancel box or press ESC

4 Select the Enter box or press ENTER or any arrow key to finish entering the text into cell A1.

Tip From now on, when you see a step that tells you to enter something in a cell, it means to type the information and then click the Enter box or press ENTER

5 Select cell A2, if necessary, and enter **`Taxes Withheld`**

6 Enter **`Net Pay`** in cell A3.

Changing the Width of a Column

The text *Taxes Withheld* in cell A2 appears to spill over into column B. However, the entire text is stored in cell A2. In this section, you will learn to manually adjust the width of a column so that it accommodates long entries.

You can adjust the width of a column by first positioning the pointer on the right edge of a column heading and then dragging the mouse, or by using the Column command in the Format menu. If, instead of dragging the mouse, you double-click the mouse button, the width will be automatically set to ***best fit*** (to accommodate the longest entry in that column).

To change the width of column A:

1 Move the pointer to the right edge of the heading for column A (to the boundary line between the headings for columns A and B).
The pointer should change to a double arrow.

2 Hold down the mouse button.
Notice that the current column width is displayed in the name box area.

3 Drag the column width so that the column is somewhat wider than the longest text entry (*Taxes Withheld*) as shown in Figure 1.2, and then release the mouse button.

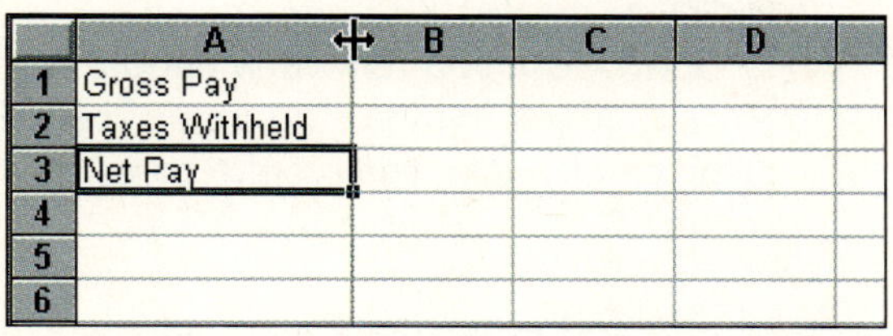

Figure 1.2

To set the column width to best fit:

1 Position the pointer on the right edge of the heading for column A (so that the pointer becomes a double arrow).

2 Double-click to set the column to best fit.

Tip Sometimes best fit will actually be too narrow, and you will need to manually increase a column's width. A column is too narrow when numeric entries appear as lines of number signs (#).

Entering Numeric Constants

In general, when you type numbers in Excel, you should leave out extra punctuation such as dollar signs and commas. Although Excel will preserve this punctuation in your entry, it is best to assign a consistent appearance to a group of cells by using Excel's extensive formatting commands.

Include a decimal point only if the number has a fractional part. If you type a percent sign after a number, the number will be divided by 100 (and assigned a percent style).

This worksheet contains two numeric constants: gross pay and taxes withheld.

To enter the numeric constants:

1 Select cell B1.

2 Enter the sample gross pay amount, **853** in cell B1.

3 Enter the sample taxes withheld amount, **127** in cell B2.
Notice that Excel aligns a number against the right edge of its cell, and text against the left edge. You will learn later how to adjust the alignment of cell contents.

Entering Formulas

There are several ways to create a formula in Excel. The simplest and least prone to error is to use ***point mode.*** In point mode, you use the mouse or arrow keys to point to the various cells that are to be included in the formula, and Excel figures out what the actual cell references are. When you use point mode, you don't have to worry about figuring out cell addresses yourself.

Riddle

Q. How can you tell when people aren't using point mode in Excel?

A. They are trying to figure out cell references by holding a ruler or piece of paper against the computer screen to line up rows and columns.

In the following steps, you will use a formula to calculate net pay. The formula will refer to the gross pay amount and subtract the taxes withheld from that amount. Note that all formulas begin with an equal sign, and you will not press ENTER until the entire formula is complete.

To enter the formula to calculate net pay:

1 Select cell B3, the cell to the right of *Net Pay.*
This cell will contain the formula to calculate net pay.

2 Type =
The screen should be similar to Figure 1.3.

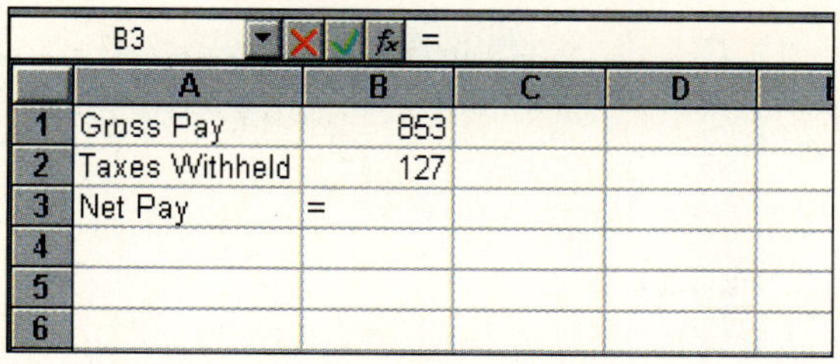

Figure 1.3

3 Point to the gross pay amount you entered in cell B1 by either clicking the cell to select it or using the arrow keys to move up to the cell.
The screen should resemble Figure 1.4. Notice that Excel is building the formula for you in the formula bar.

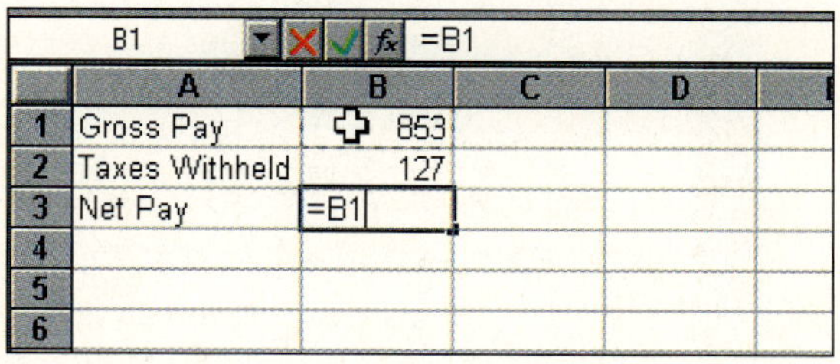

Figure 1.4

4 Type – (a minus sign) as shown in Figure 1.5.
The formula is supposed to subtract taxes withheld from the gross pay amount.

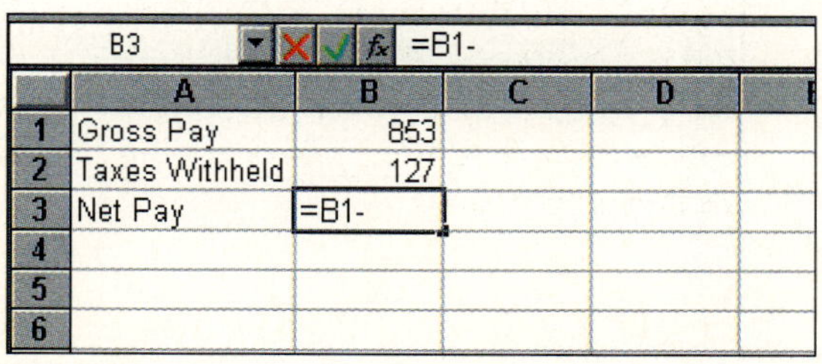

Figure 1.5

5 Point to the taxes withheld amount by either selecting cell B2 or using the arrow keys. See Figure 1.6.

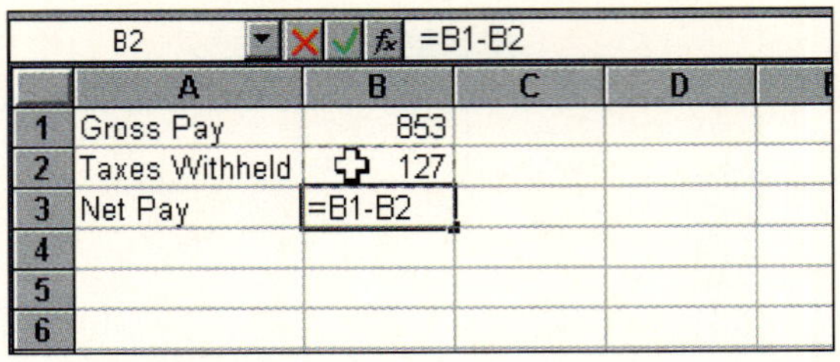

Figure 1.6

6 To finish the formula, select the Enter box or press (ENTER) (see Figure 1.7).

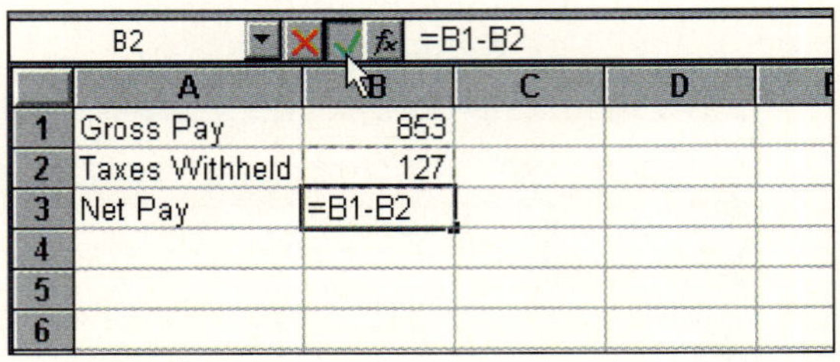

Figure 1.7

7 Select cell B3, if necessary, to examine the completed formula. Notice that Excel has built the formula =B1-B2, as shown in the formula bar of Figure 1.8. Cell B3 contains a formula whose result, currently 726, appears in the worksheet.

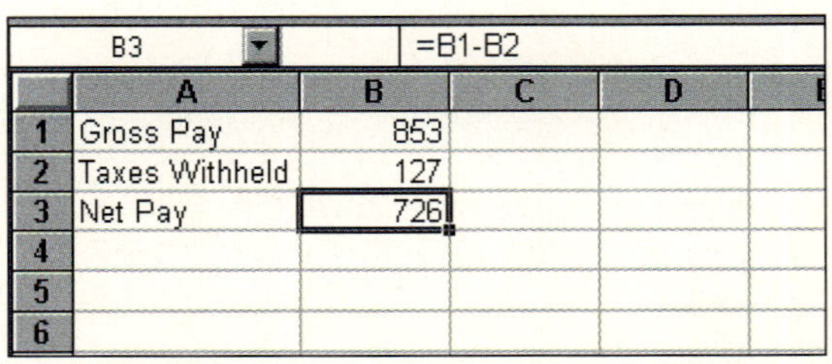

Figure 1.8

Reminders Here are some reminders about building formulas using the point method:

- All formulas start with an equal sign.
- You will use the mouse or arrow keys to select the cells that the formula refers to.
- You will press (ENTER) (or select the Enter box on the formula bar) only once when you have completed the entire formula.

Recalculating a Worksheet

The foremost advantage of an electronic spreadsheet is that its formulas can ***recalculate*** and show new results if there are changes in the cells to which the formulas refer. For example, suppose that the taxes withheld changed to 179.

To change and recalculate the worksheet:

1 Select cell B2, where you entered 127 as the taxes withheld.

2 Change the taxes withheld to 179 by typing **179** and pressing (ENTER) or clicking the Enter box.
As shown in Figure 1.9, the new entry replaces the previous one, and the result of the net pay formula adjusts automatically to 674.

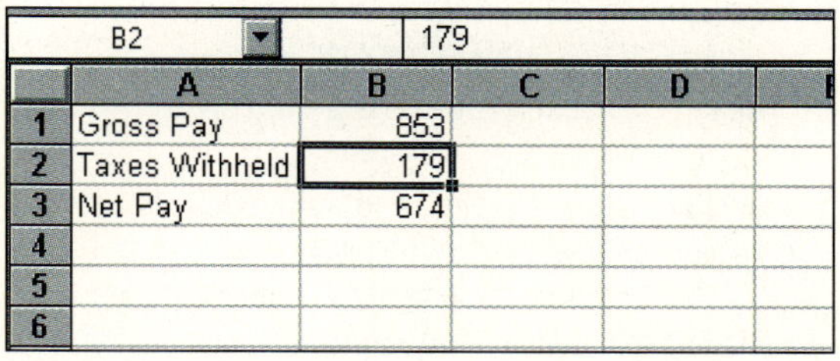

Figure 1.9

Experiment with other changes to gross pay and taxes withheld.

Arithmetic Operators

The formula you just created uses the subtraction operator. Excel has several major operators, which are listed in Table 1.1 in ***priority*** order. The priorities of the various operators in a formula determine the order in which Excel performs the operations. Higher priority operations are performed first. For example, because multiplication and division are operations of higher priority than addition and subtraction, =8-3*2 is calculated with implied parentheses: =8-(3*2), which results in 2, not 10. You can use parentheses to override the standard priorities: =(8-3)*2 is 10.

Table 1.1

Priority	Symbol	Operator	Function	Example Formula	Example Result
1	%	Percent	Divides a number by 100	=5%	0.05
2	^	Exponentiation	Raises a number to a power	=3 ^ 2	9
3	*	Multiplication	Multiplies two numbers	=4*2	8
	/	Division	Divides one number by another	=12/3	4
4	+	Addition	Adds two numbers	=3+2	5
	–	Subtraction	Subtracts one number from another	=7–4	3
5	&	Text joining	Connects two text strings	="Uh"&"Oh"	UhOh
6	=	Equal to	TRUE if a=b, FALSE otherwise	=5=3	FALSE
	<	Less than	TRUE if a<b, FALSE otherwise	=6<7	TRUE
	>	Greater than	TRUE if a>b, FALSE otherwise	=2>3	FALSE
	<=	Less than or equal to	TRUE if a<=b, FALSE otherwise	=17<=17	TRUE
	>=	Greater than or equal to	TRUE if a>=b, FALSE otherwise	=16>=17	FALSE
	<>	Not equal to	TRUE if a<>b, FALSE otherwise	=6<>7	TRUE

Tip When you need to type /, *, – , or +, use the keys on the numeric keypad at the right of the keyboard. This is often quicker than searching the main keyboard for the appropriate symbol.

FORMATTING CELLS

The ***format*** of a cell indicates how the information in the cell should appear on the screen or in a printout. The many attributes of a cell format include number punctuation (such as dollar signs and commas), alignment, borders, and font.

In the following steps, you will use the ***AutoFormat*** command to have Excel automatically assign formats to the cells in your worksheet. You will learn more about cell formats in later projects.

To format the worksheet automatically:

1 Select the range A1:B3 by selecting cell A1, holding down the left mouse button, dragging to cell B3, and then releasing the mouse button.

2 Choose **Format** and then **AutoFormat.**
The AutoFormat dialog box appears.

3 Examine samples of the AutoFormat table formats available. To see a sample, click a Table Format name in the list box.

Closing a Workbook

Closing a workbook removes it from the screen.

To close the workbook:

1 Choose **File** and then **Close,** or click the *workbook's* Close window button (which is under the Excel application window's Close window button).
If you made any changes to the workbook since you last saved it, the Save Changes dialog box will appear, asking whether you want to save the updated version of the worksheet.

2 Click **Yes,** if necessary.

Opening a Workbook

Opening the Net Pay Calculation workbook file loads a copy of the workbook from disk into memory, where you can modify the workbook. The original copy of the file remains unchanged on the disk until you save the updated workbook over the original version.

To open a workbook file:

1 Start Excel, if necessary.

2 Choose **File** and then **Open,** or select the **Open** tool on the Standard toolbar.
The Open dialog box appears, as shown in Figure 1.13.

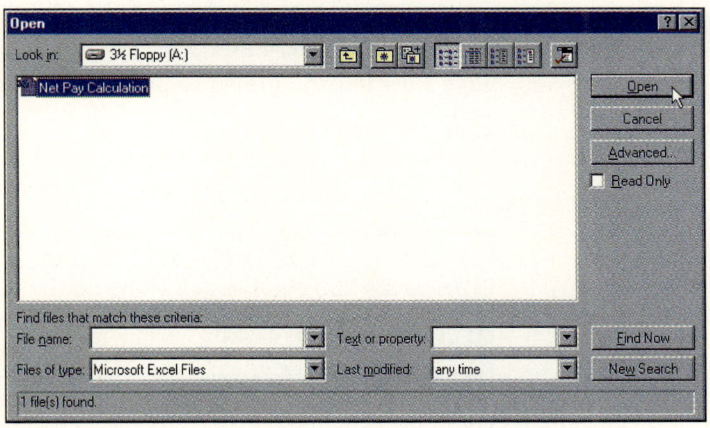

Figure 1.13

3 Change the disk drive and the folder, if necessary.

4 Select the file Net Pay Calculation from the alphabetical file list.

5 Select **Open.**

> ***Tip*** If you save your workbooks frequently, you can return to a recently saved version if you "mess up" the workbook currently on the screen. You can use the Close command in the File menu to clear the messed-up workbook from the screen (without saving) and then use the Open command to retrieve the earlier version from disk.

Editing Cell Entries

One way to change the content of a cell is to type a new entry to replace an old one, as you did when you changed the value of the taxes withheld earlier in this project. However, there will be times when you need to change just a piece of a long entry—perhaps you will need to make a small correction to a long title or formula. In such cases, editing the cell entry can save you some typing.

You can edit a cell entry by activating the cell and clicking in the formula bar. This will display an insertion point in the formula bar. You can also double-click the cell: this will allow "in-cell editing" and display the insertion point in the worksheet itself. You can position the insertion point within the text by clicking or by using the arrow keys. Pressing (BKSP) will erase characters to the left of the insertion point; pressing (DEL) will erase characters to the right.

Suppose that the title *Taxes Withheld* needed to be changed to *Tax Withheld.*

To edit a cell entry:

1 Double-click cell A2, which contains the text *Taxes Withheld.*
The insertion point appears in the cell, and the Edit indicator appears in the left side of the status bar.

2 Position the insertion point just after the *s* in *Taxes.*

3 Press (BKSP) twice.
The screen should resemble Figure 1.14.

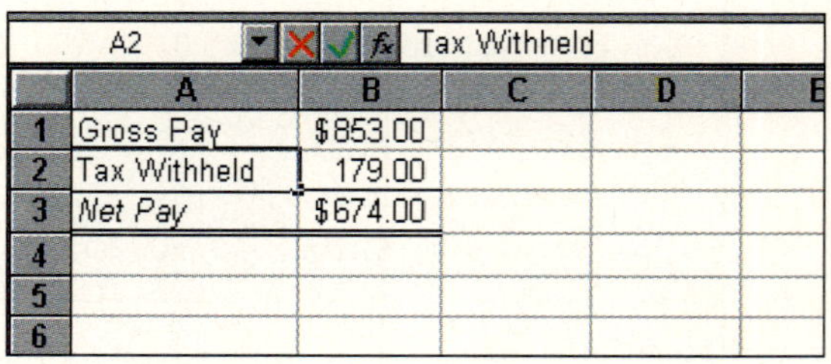

Figure 1.14

4 Select the Enter box or press (ENTER) to enter the revised text.

Creating New Worksheets and Workbooks

When you start Excel, the program presents you with a workbook containing 16 blank worksheets. A workbook, regardless of how many worksheets it contains, is stored in a single file on disk. If you "use up" the 16 worksheets initially provided, you can insert new, blank worksheets within the workbook. In general, the worksheets within a given workbook should all be concerned with the same topic or related in some way. If you need to create worksheets for some new task unrelated to an existing workbook, you should open a new workbook.

Inserting a New Worksheet

If at any time during your Excel session you want to insert a new, blank worksheet in the current workbook, you can choose the Worksheet command from the Insert menu. The new worksheet will be inserted immediately preceding the current sheet and will be automatically activated.

To insert a new worksheet:

1 Choose **Insert** and then **Worksheet.**
A new sheet, named Sheet17, is created and activated.

2 Click the **Sheet1** tab to switch back to the pay worksheet.

Naming Sheets

If you use multiple sheets in a workbook, it will be much easier to identify them if you assign names to appear on the sheet tabs. You can double-click a sheet tab to rename a sheet.

> ***Tip*** Though a sheet name can be up to 31 characters long, you should try to think of a good abbreviated name because long names in sheet tabs make it harder to see multiple tabs at once on the screen. A sheet name can contain spaces but cannot be enclosed in square brackets or contain the characters \, /, :, ?, or *. Remember that sheet names are **not** workbook (file) names.

To rename a sheet:

1 Double-click the tab for **Sheet1.**
The Rename Sheet dialog box appears.

2 Type `Payroll` and then select **OK,** as shown in Figure 1.15.

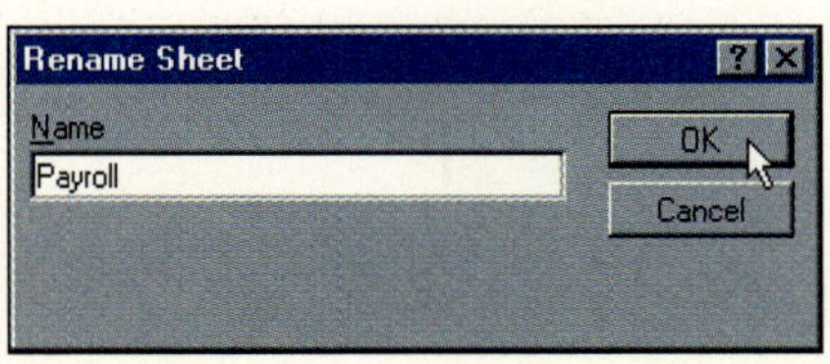

Figure 1.15

The sheet tab now shows the name Payroll.

Rearranging Sheets

By clicking and dragging a sheet tab or group of sheet tabs, you can change the order in which the sheets appear. In the following steps, you will drag the Sheet17 tab so that it appears after the Payroll tab.

To change the order of sheet tabs:

1 Click the tab for **Sheet17,** and hold down the mouse button.
A sheet icon appears, along with a small arrowhead indicating the position at which the selected sheet will be inserted, as shown in Figure 1.16.

Figure 1.16

2 Drag the sheet icon so that the arrowhead appears between the **Payroll** tab and the **Sheet2** tab, as shown in Figure 1.17.

Figure 1.17

3 Release the mouse button.
The Sheet17 tab now appears after the Payroll tab.

4 Close and save the Net Pay Calculation workbook.

Opening a New Workbook

To open a new workbook containing blank worksheets, you can choose the New command from the File menu or select the New Workbook tool on the Standard toolbar.

> ***Tip*** Remember, you can have many different workbooks open at once. If you have finished working with one workbook and want to begin a new one, you can reduce the clutter on the screen by closing the first workbook. If you need to switch between (or simultaneously view) the workbooks, you should keep them both open.

To open a new workbook:

1 Click the **New Workbook** tool on the Standard toolbar.
A new workbook window appears.

Exiting Excel

You will now exit the Excel program.

To exit Excel:

1 Choose **File** and then **Exit.**

The Next Step

Now that you have created basic cell entries common to most worksheets, you are ready to create them in a larger worksheet. In the next project, you will build more sophisticated formulas and learn how to copy and move cell contents. You will see how AutoFormat performs in a more complicated context, and you will begin to take more control over the appearance of the worksheet.

This concludes Project 1. You can either exit Excel or go on to work the Study Questions, Review Exercises, and Assignments.

Summary and Exercises

Summary

- A cell can contain a text constant, a number constant, or a formula.
- Number constants should be entered without extra punctuation.
- A formula's result is called its value.
- You can change the width of a column in a worksheet.
- Formulas do the work in a worksheet. Formulas are built most easily by using point mode.
- When a formula in one cell depends on the data in another cell, the formula will automatically recalculate if the contents of the other cell change.
- Arithmetic operators are prioritized, and this determines the order in which operations are performed in a formula.
- Workbooks should be saved frequently.
- The appearance of simple worksheets can quickly be improved by using the AutoFormat command.
- A cell entry can be edited rather than retyped.
- The Open command in the File menu is used to open a workbook that was saved to disk; the New command is used to open a new, blank workbook.
- New worksheets can be inserted into a workbook with the Worksheet command from the Insert menu.
- Worksheets can be rearranged by dragging sheet tabs.
- Worksheets can be renamed.

Key Terms and Operations

Key Terms
AutoFormat
best fit
format
formula
number constant
point mode
priority
recalculate
text constant
value

Operations
Change column width
Close a workbook
Insert a worksheet
Open a saved workbook
Rearrange sheets
Rename a sheet
Save a workbook
Start a new workbook

Study Questions

Multiple Choice

1. What determines the order in which arithmetic operations are performed in an Excel formula?
   a. The order is strictly left to right.
   b. The order is strictly right to left.
   c. The order is determined by the priority of the operators used.
   d. The order doesn't matter.
   e. The settings you specify in the Operator Precedence menu determine the order.

2. What are the two types of constants?
   a. text and number
   b. formula and value
   c. label and text
   d. relative and absolute
   e. formula and number

3. If you change a cell entry on which a formula depends (which a formula refers to), what will happen?
   a. The formula will display an error message.
   b. The formula will automatically recalculate to reflect the changed data.
   c. You will need to rebuild the formula before it will display a new result.
   d. You will need to copy the formula on itself.
   e. Nothing will happen.

4. How many times do you press (ENTER) (or select the Enter box) when building an Excel formula?
   a. once
   b. twice
   c. as many times as there are cell references in the formula
   d. as many times as there are arithmetic operators in the formula
   e. never

5. In Excel, what is the result of the formula = 3 + 25 + 4?
   a. 29
   b. 72
   c. 26
   d. 17
   e. none of the above

6. In Excel, what is the result of the formula = 3 + (4 − 2) * 3?
   a. 15
   b. 1
   c. 3
   d. 9
   e. none of the above

7. The way information appears in a cell (such as its alignment, font, or numeric punctuation) is referred to as the cell's:
   a. style.
   b. attributes.
   c. display mode.
   d. format.
   e. AutoFormat.

8. When should you save your work in Excel?
   a. when you are about to make a major modification to the worksheet
   b. every five or ten minutes
   c. when it would be time consuming to re-create the work you've done since you last saved
   d. when you are about to experiment with an unfamiliar Excel command
   e. all of the above

9. What happens when you close a workbook in Excel?
   a. The workbook is automatically saved.
   b. Excel will automatically exit.
   c. If you made changes to the workbook since you last saved, a dialog box will appear and give you the opportunity to save again.
   d. A new, empty workbook will automatically appear.
   e. You will automatically lose all changes made since you last saved the workbook.

10. How do you begin to edit a cell entry?
    a. Make the cell active, and then choose Edit from the menu bar.
    b. Make the cell active, and then select the formula bar or double-click the cell.
    c. Double-click in the formula bar.
    d. all of the above
    e. none of the above

Short Answer

1. What is the result of a formula called?
2. What kind of information is usually represented with text constants?
3. If you enter a text constant that is longer than a cell's width, what does Excel do?
4. When you enter a number constant, should you include punctuation (dollar signs, commas, and so on)? Why?
5. In general, what is the best method to use when building formulas that refer to other cells? Why?
6. What determines the order in which arithmetic operations are performed in Excel formulas?
7. What determines the way information in a cell will appear?
8. What command is used to automatically format a range?
9. What command is used to open a new, blank workbook?
10. What steps are required to edit an existing cell entry?

For Discussion

1. What aspects of a cell's appearance does the AutoFormat command affect?
2. What is the most important feature of electronic spreadsheets? Why?
3. Describe the point method for building formulas.

Review Exercises

Simple Income Statement

Build and format a worksheet based on the information shown in Figure 1.18. Income is calculated by subtracting the cost of goods sold from the sales. Pick out any one of the Accounting table formats when you use the AutoFormat command. Save the workbook as *Proj 1 Ex 1 Simple Income Statement.*

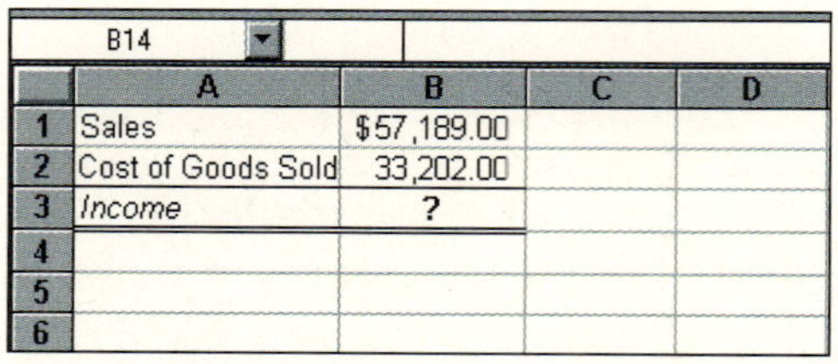
B14

	A	B	C	D
1	Sales	$57,189.00		
2	Cost of Goods Sold	33,202.00		
3	*Income*	?		
4				
5				
6				

Figure 1.18

Population Report

Build and format a worksheet similar to Figure 1.19. Use an addition formula to compute the total population of the United States, Canada, and Mexico combined. If the column containing the numbers is too narrow, Excel displays a number sign (#) or scientific notation. Once you use AutoFormat or manually widen the columns, the numbers themselves will appear. Pick out any one of the Classic or Colorful table formats. Save the workbook as *Proj 1 Ex 2 Population Report.*

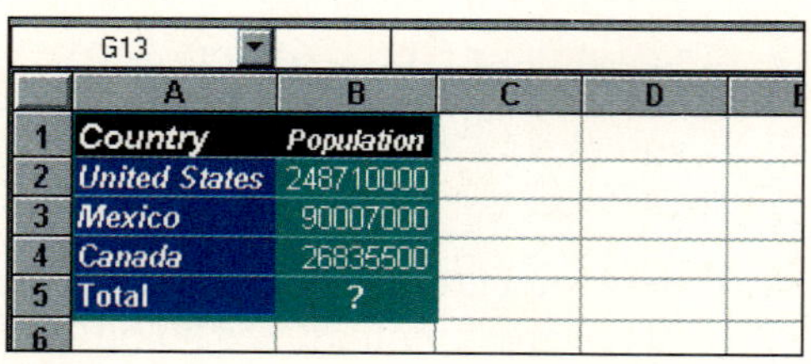
G13

	A	B	C	D	E
1	Country	Population			
2	United States	248710000			
3	Mexico	90007000			
4	Canada	26835500			
5	Total	?			
6					

Figure 1.19

Assignments

Detailed Income Statement

Build a worksheet based on Figure 1.20. Gross income is the sales minus the cost of goods sold. Net income is the gross income minus the expenses. Use AutoFormat and the Accounting 1 table format. Save the file as *Proj 1 Asn 1 Detailed Income Statement.*

	A	B	C	D
1	Sales	$ 93,126.00		
2	Cost of Goods Sold	32,117.00		
3	*Gross Income*	?		
4	*Expenses*	$ 16,909.00		
5	**Net Income**	?		
6				

Figure 1.20

Population Density

Build a worksheet based on Figure 1.21. The population density is the number of people per square mile; calculate it by dividing the population of a city by the city's area. Use AutoFormat and experiment with the various non-Accounting table formats. Notice that AutoFormat does not limit the number of digits that display to the right of the decimal point in the non-Accounting formats. Save the file as *Proj 1 Asn 2 Population Density.*

A8

	A	B	C	D
1	**City**	Population	Area (sq. mi.)	**Density**
2	**Hong Kong**	5693000	23	?
3	**Los Angeles**	10130000	1110	?
4				
5				
6				

Figure 1.21

Coffee House Income

Figure 1.22 shows cost and price information for the top-selling coffee at Clem's Coffee Clutch. Enter the data as shown in Figure 1.22. The formula that calculates income will subtract the cost from the selling price and multiply the result by the number sold. You will need to use parentheses in the formula. Adjust column widths as necessary, but do not format the worksheet; it will be used for an exercise in a later project. Save the worksheet as *Proj 1 Asn 3 Coffee House Income.*

A8

	A	B	C	D	E
1	Coffee	Cost	Selling Price	No. Sold	Income
2	House Blend	0.39	0.95	60	?
3					
4					
5					
6					

Figure 1.22

Project 2: Building a Larger Worksheet

Objectives

After completing this project, you should be able to:

- Move a cell
- Check the spelling of worksheet data
- Use preselected ranges for data entry
- Copy the contents of a cell
- Use relative cell references in formulas
- Use the SUM function and the AutoSum tool

Case Study: Historical Sales of Audio Recordings

From 1975 to 1990, the popularity of the kinds of media used for recorded music shifted dramatically. These changes are illustrated in Figure 2.1. In this project, you will build this Excel worksheet and add formulas to calculate the totals (indicated by question marks in the figure).

	A	B	C	D	E	F
1	Shipments of Audio Recordings					
2	(in millions of dollars)					
3		1975	1980	1985	1990	
4	Phonograph Records					
5	LP Albums	1485	2290.3	1280.5	86.5	
6	Singles	211.5	269.3	281	94.4	
7	Total Records	?	?	?	?	
8	Tapes					
9	8-tracks	583	526.4	25.3	0	
10	Cassettes	98.8	776.4	2411.5	3472.4	
11	Total Tapes	?	?	?	?	
12	Compact Discs					
13	Regular CDs	0	0	389.5	3451.6	
14	CD Singles	0	0	0	6	
15	Total CDs	?	?	?	?	
16	Grand Total	?	?	?	?	
17						

Figure 2.1

Designing the Solution

The formulas you will create for this worksheet will calculate totals for each year in each media category (records, tapes, and CDs) and grand totals (the totals of records, tapes, and CDs combined). You will then format the worksheet so that the information is more readable.

In the steps that follow, as important new concepts and features are introduced, you can refer to Figure 2.1 to orient yourself in the worksheet. Although you might be tempted to jump ahead and type everything in immediately, please follow the steps carefully.

Building the Skeleton of a Worksheet

When you create a worksheet, it is often easiest to enter the static (unchanging) information first. To establish an overall skeleton or shape for the worksheet, you will enter the row and column titles before you enter the number constants and formulas. In general, you should wait until the worksheet is complete and functioning correctly before doing detailed formatting.

To enter the main titles:

1 Start Excel.

2 Select cell A1 on Sheet1, and enter the text `Shipments of Audio Recordings`

3 Enter `(in millions of dollars)` in cell A2.

Moving Cells

In the following steps, you will enter the first row title, *Phonograph Records*, in the wrong cell. You will then use Excel's ***drag-and-drop*** feature to move the title to the correct cell. In Excel, to ***move*** means that you pick up an object from one location (in this case, the original contents of the cell) and place it in another location.

To move a cell:

1 Enter `Phonograph Records` in cell A3.
Notice that the sample worksheet in Figure 2.1 shows the first row title, *Phonograph Records*, in row 4, one row *below* the row containing the years. You just typed it into row 3, but rather than retyping the information you just entered in Step 1, you can move it to the correct location, cell A4.

2 Select cell A3, which should contain the text constant you just typed, *Phonograph Records*.

3 Position the pointer to touch any edge of the active-cell rectangle so that the pointer becomes an arrow (Figure 2.2).

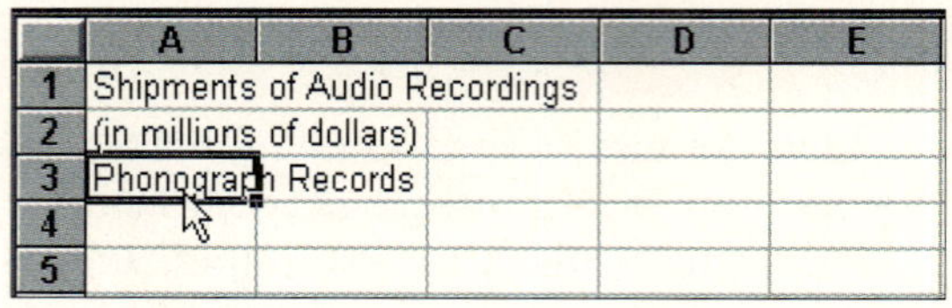

Figure 2.2

4 Hold down the mouse button and drag the dimmed image of the cell outline to cell A4, as shown in Figure 2.3. Release the mouse button. The screen should now look like Figure 2.4, with *Phonograph Records* in the new location.

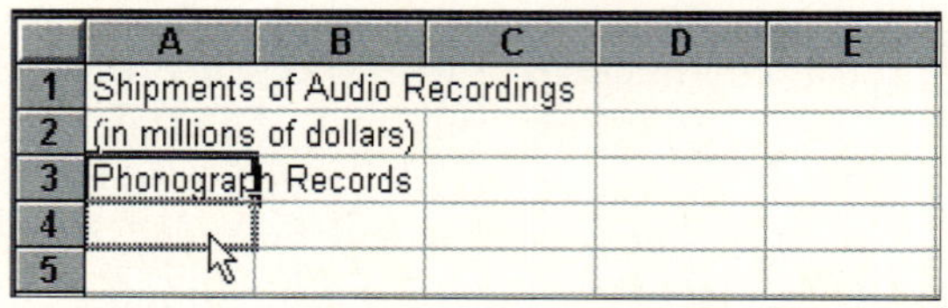

Figure 2.3

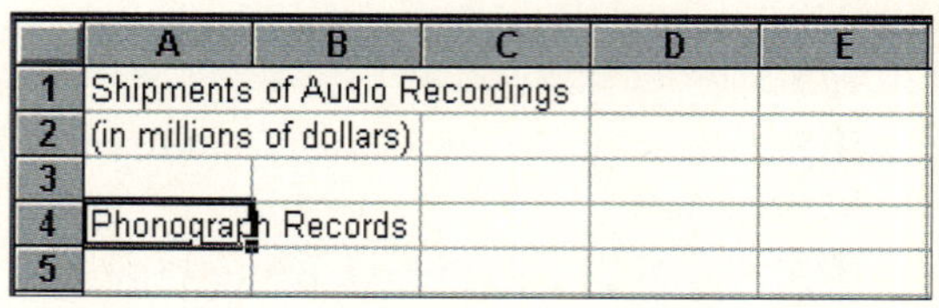

Figure 2.4

Entering Row Titles

Notice that the row subtitles in Figure 2.1 are slightly indented to create an outline format. One simple way to accomplish this in Excel is to precede each text entry with two space characters.

To enter the row titles:

1 Select cell A5.

2 Press (SPACE) twice, and then enter **`LP Albums`**

3 Select cell A6, press (SPACE) twice, and then enter **`Singles`**

4 Select cell A7, press (SPACE) twice, and then enter **`Total Records`**

5 Refer to Figure 2.1 to enter all the remaining row titles. Remember to indent where indicated in the figure.

Warning If the ***AutoComplete*** feature is activated, Excel attempts to automatically complete a cell entry for you (for example, when you begin to type *Total Tapes,* Excel will presume that you want to type *Total Records*). If you don't want the cell entry completed in this way, just keep typing what you *do* want.

Reminder If you discover that you have made an incorrect entry in a cell, you can select the cell and double-click it, or click in the formula bar. As shown in Project 1, you will then be able to type new information or use the editing keys to correct your mistake.

Checking the Spelling in a Worksheet

Once you have entered all the text constants into a worksheet, you can use Excel to check your spelling. The spelling checker will begin its check on the currently selected cell and proceed toward the lower-right corner of the worksheet. When it finishes checking the lower-right part of the worksheet, you can optionally have it check the upper-left portion. If you plan to check the spelling of the entire worksheet, it is most convenient to start at the top-left corner by making A1 the active cell.

The spelling checker will pause on any word in the worksheet that it does not find in the spelling dictionary. The Spelling dialog box will suggest replacements for the possibly misspelled word. If the original word you typed is spelled correctly, you can select Ignore All in the dialog box; the spelling checker then skips over all subsequent occurrences of that spelling. (Choosing Ignore causes only the current occurrence to be skipped.) If the spelling needs to be corrected, you can choose from the list of suggestions or type a new spelling and then select Change. As illustrated in Figure 2.5, the spelling checker paused on an incorrect spelling of the word *Phonograph*. The two suggested words are *Phonograph* and *Photograph*. Because *Phonograph* is selected in the Change To box, you would select Change. The spelling will be corrected, and the spelling checker will continue to any other words that may have been misspelled, giving you a chance to correct them.

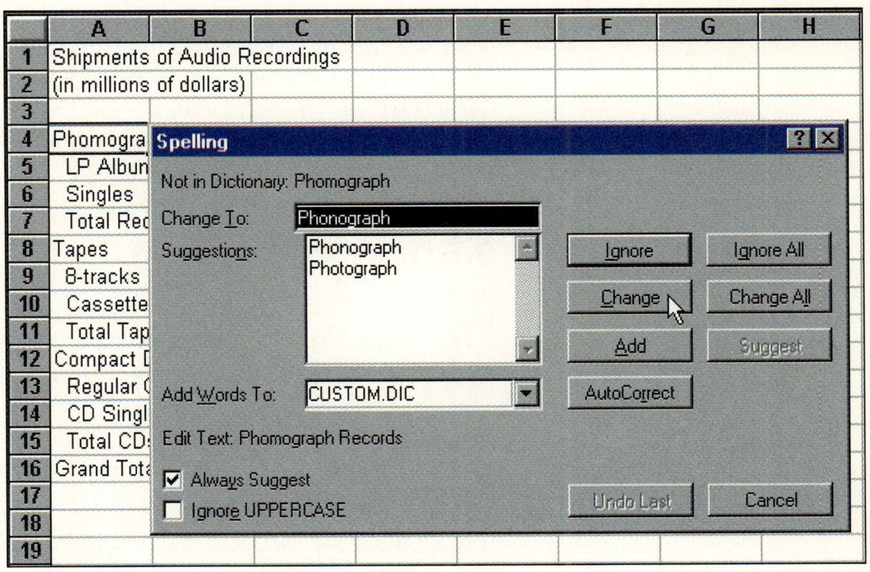

Figure 2.5

To check spelling in the worksheet:

1 Move the active cell to the top-left cell (cell A1).
A quick way to do this is by pressing CTRL + HOME

2 Choose **Tools** and then **Spelling,** or select the **Spelling** tool.

3 Correct any misspelled words that occur in your worksheet.

> ***Tip*** If ***AutoCorrect*** is activated, Excel will automatically fix common spelling errors as you type. You can control AutoCorrect's activation and features by opening the Tools menu and choosing AutoCorrect.

Entering Column Titles

The years *1975*, *1980*, *1985*, and *1990* need to be entered as column titles. In the steps that follow, you will use several methods for entering data.

To enter the column titles:

1 To make it easier to read the worksheet as you enter data, make column A slightly wider than *Phonograph Records*, the longest of the individual row titles.

2 Select cell B3, type **1975** and press ENTER
Depending on how Excel was installed on the system you are using, the active-cell rectangle may move down automatically after you press ENTER
You can change this option if you wish.

> ***Tip*** To control whether the active cell (the selection) is moved after you press ENTER, you can choose Options from the Tools menu, select the Edit tab, and select (or clear) the Move Selection after Enter check box. If the check box is cleared, the effect of pressing ENTER is the same as that of clicking the Enter button in the formula bar. If the check box is checked, the active cell will move after you press ENTER according to the direction specified in the Direction list box.

3 Select cell C3, type **1980** and press →

4 Enter the other two years **1985** and **1990** in the appropriate cells.

> ***Tip*** Pressing an arrow key after you type data will automatically enter the data and position the selection one cell in the direction of the arrow key.

Using Selection to Speed Data Entry

The various sales figures need to be entered in the main section of the worksheet. Although the sales figures could always be entered without the use of a preselected range, in the steps that follow you will learn how to make repetitive entry more convenient by preselecting a data-entry range. At the lower-right corner of a selection, pressing TAB or ENTER moves to the upper left; at the upper left of a selection, pressing SHIFT + TAB moves to the lower right. You can use these keys to change which cell is active

To save the workbook:

1 Choose **File** and then **Save,** or click the **Save** tool.
The Save As dialog box appears.

2 Navigate to the appropriate disk drive and directory.

3 Enter `Audio Sales History` for the file name, and select **Save.**

EXIT If necessary, you can quit Excel now and continue this project later.

Constructing Formulas and Functions

In the steps that follow, you will use point mode to build a formula that calculates total record sales for 1975.

To enter the formula for total record sales:

1 Select cell B7.
You will build a formula that adds the sales of LP albums and singles.

2 Type = to activate the formula bar.

3 Use the mouse or arrow keys to select cell B5, which contains sales of LP albums for 1975.

4 Type +

5 Use the mouse or arrow keys to select cell B6, which contains sales of singles for 1975.

6 Click the formula bar Enter box, or press (ENTER) to complete the formula.
Compare the screen with Figure 2.10.

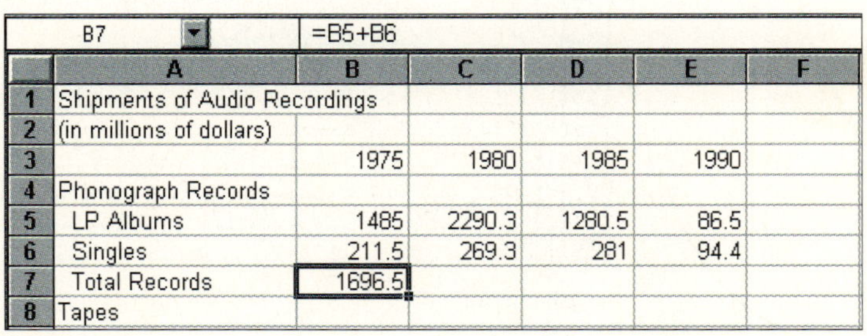

B7 =B5+B6

	A	B	C	D	E	F
1	Shipments of Audio Recordings					
2	(in millions of dollars)					
3		1975	1980	1985	1990	
4	Phonograph Records					
5	LP Albums	1485	2290.3	1280.5	86.5	
6	Singles	211.5	269.3	281	94.4	
7	Total Records	1696.5				
8	Tapes					

Figure 2.10

A formula's result is called its *value.* The value of this formula is 1696.5, which appears in cell B7. If you look in the formula bar, you will see the formula itself: =B5+B6.

Copying Formulas

In Excel, any type of cell entry—text constant, number constant, or formula—can be duplicated in other cells, but duplication of formulas is most useful. Worksheets tend to have repeating patterns. For example, total record sales for 1980, 1985, and 1990 are all calculated in a manner similar to the calculation of total record sales for 1975. Copying allows you to create a formula once and then have its operation duplicated in other cells that require the same computation.

You will now copy the formula to the cells in the range C7:E7 so that you can also calculate total record sales for 1980, 1985, and 1990.

To copy a formula using the fill handle:

1 If it is not already selected, select cell B7, which contains the total records formula for 1975.

2 Position the pointer on the lower-right corner of the active-cell rectangle.
As shown in Figure 2.11, the pointer changes to a small plus sign, which is called the *fill handle.*

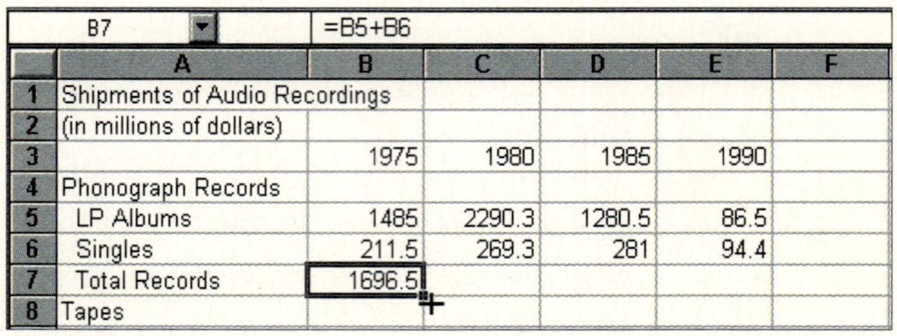

	A	B	C	D	E	F
1	Shipments of Audio Recordings					
2	(in millions of dollars)					
3		1975	1980	1985	1990	
4	Phonograph Records					
5	LP Albums	1485	2290.3	1280.5	86.5	
6	Singles	211.5	269.3	281	94.4	
7	Total Records	1696.5				
8	Tapes					

Figure 2.11

3 Press and hold down the mouse button, and drag the fill handle across the row through column E for 1990, as shown in Figure 2.12.

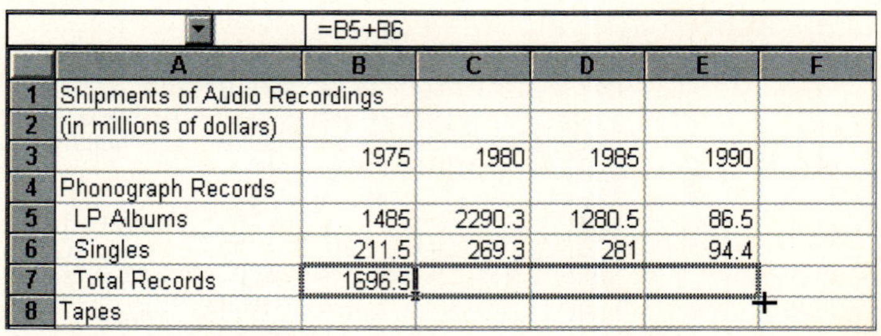

	A	B	C	D	E	F
1	Shipments of Audio Recordings					
2	(in millions of dollars)					
3		1975	1980	1985	1990	
4	Phonograph Records					
5	LP Albums	1485	2290.3	1280.5	86.5	
6	Singles	211.5	269.3	281	94.4	
7	Total Records	1696.5				
8	Tapes					

Figure 2.12

4 Release the mouse button.
Totals should now appear for the years 1980 through 1990, as shown in Figure 2.13.

B7 =B5+B6

	A	B	C	D	E	F
1	Shipments of Audio Recordings					
2	(in millions of dollars)					
3		1975	1980	1985	1990	
4	Phonograph Records					
5	LP Albums	1485	2290.3	1280.5	86.5	
6	Singles	211.5	269.3	281	94.4	
7	Total Records	1696.5	2559.6	1561.5	180.9	
8	Tapes					

Figure 2.13

The steps that follow show an alternative method of copying a cell. You will first use the Undo command, which will undo the copy performed in the previous steps. The Undo command reverses the effect of the most recent command performed and returns the worksheet to the state it was in before the command was issued.

To copy a formula using the Copy and Paste commands:

1 Choose **Edit** and then **Undo Auto Fill.**
Because Auto Fill was the most recently issued command, Excel undoes that command.

2 If not already selected, select cell B7, which contains the formula for calculating total records for 1975.

3 Choose **Edit** and then **Copy,** or select the **Copy** tool.
Notice the message at the bottom of the application window: *Select destination and press ENTER or choose Paste.*

4 Select the destination range, C7:E7.

5 Press (ENTER) to complete the copy operation.

Reminder The drag-and-drop move operation you used at the beginning of this project takes data from one location and places it in another. The Copy command *duplicates* the data—the original data remains.

Recognizing Relative Cell References

What was copied when you performed the previous steps? It wasn't the value 1696.5 because different numbers appear in each of the cells showing totals. To see what is actually in a cell, you can activate that cell and then look in the formula bar.

To examine the relative cell references:

1 Select cell B7, which contains the original formula for total record sales for 1975.

2 Examine the formula bar. The formula is =B5+B6.

3 Select cell C7, which contains the formula for 1980.
The formula in this cell is a copy of the original formula, but the formula bar shows that this formula is =C5+C6.

4 Examine the formulas for 1985 and 1990. These formulas read =D5+D6 and =E5+E6, respectively.
=B5+B6 was not literally copied. In a formula, Excel treats cell references

as being *relative* to the cell containing the formula. Although the original formula reads =B5+B6, Excel interprets the formula to mean "Take what is two cells above (the formula) and add to it what is one cell above." Unless you instruct the program otherwise, Excel will interpret cell references in formulas as being *relative* to the location of the formula; this is called a ***relative cell reference.*** When cell B7's formula is copied to cell C7, Excel shifts all the references one cell to the right, so the formula in cell C7 reads =C5+C6.

Relative cell referencing is why the duplicated formulas each read differently from the original. This adjustment of a copied formula to reflect a new location is most often what you will want Excel to do. For example, the formula that calculates total record sales for 1990 *should* read =E5+E6 and not =B5+B6.

Using Excel Functions

The total sales for tapes and compact discs also need to be calculated. You could use an addition formula identical to that used to calculate total record sales, but instead you will now try another approach: you will build a formula that contains an Excel function.

A ***function*** is an operation whose use simplifies formula building. Functions are similar to the keys on an electronic calculator that perform specialized calculations. For example, a financial calculator will have a button to calculate the periodic payment amount for a loan. Excel has more than 300 functions, including mathematical, financial, engineering, statistical, date, and text functions. Each function has an identifying name, such as SUM, AVERAGE, and PMT.

When you enter a function as part of a formula, you must follow the function name with a pair of parentheses. For most functions, you also must provide additional items of information inside the parentheses. These additional items, called ***arguments*** to the function, give the function the data it needs to complete its task and compute a ***result.*** If you are supplying multiple arguments, you should separate them with commas. Table 2.1 lists several basic Excel functions and provides examples based on Figure 2.14.

	A	B	C	D
1	Principal	$16,000.00		
2	Interest	10%	per year	
3	Term	5	years	
4				
5	**Vehicle**	**Mileage**	**Price**	
6	Velocipede	10,000	$12,000	
7	Steam Cart	20,000	$8,000	
8	Sedan Chair	30,000	$16,000	
9				

Figure 2.14

Table 2.1

Function	Syntax	Description	Example Formula	Example Result
SUM	SUM(range)	Totals a range	=SUM(C6:C8)	$36,000
AVERAGE	AVERAGE(range)	Averages a range	=AVERAGE(B6:B8)	20,000
MIN	MIN(range)	Gets smallest value in range	=MIN(C6:C8)	$8,000
MAX	MAX(range)	Gets largest value in range	=MAX(B6:B8)	30,000
COUNT	COUNT(range)	Counts values in a range	=COUNT(A5:C8)	6
IF	IF(test, result if true, result if false)	Performs test; result of function depends on whether test is true or false	=IF(B2<0.12,5,10)	5
PMT	PMT(periodic interest rate, number of periods, principal amount)	Calculates periodic payment for a loan	=PMT(B2/12, B3*12,B1)	($339.95)

The SUM function, in its basic form, is designed to total the values in a range of cells. The argument you provide to the function indicates the range it is to sum. For example, =SUM(H1:H12) totals all the values in the range H1:H12. The much longer addition formula =H1+H2+H3+H4+H5+H6+H7+H8+H9+H10+H11+H12 arrives at the same result as =SUM(H1:H12), but the SUM function is a more efficient way of creating the formula.

In the steps that follow, you will use point mode to build a SUM function formula that calculates total tape sales for 1975. As with all formulas, you will start by typing an equal sign, followed by SUM and an open parenthesis. Then, using pointing techniques, you will select the range to be summed, and finally you will end the formula with a close parenthesis.

To enter the SUM function to calculate total tape sales for 1975:

1 Select cell B11.

2 Type **=sum(**
SUM can be in uppercase or lowercase letters. The screen should resemble Figure 2.15.

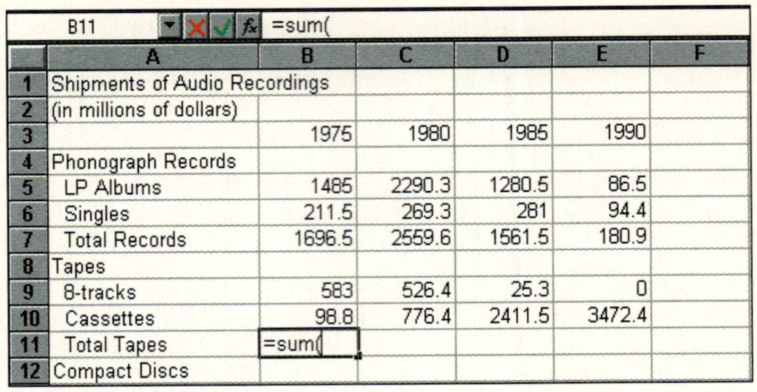

B11 =sum(

	A	B	C	D	E	F
1	Shipments of Audio Recordings					
2	(in millions of dollars)					
3		1975	1980	1985	1990	
4	Phonograph Records					
5	LP Albums	1485	2290.3	1280.5	86.5	
6	Singles	211.5	269.3	281	94.4	
7	Total Records	1696.5	2559.6	1561.5	180.9	
8	Tapes					
9	8-tracks	583	526.4	25.3	0	
10	Cassettes	98.8	776.4	2411.5	3472.4	
11	Total Tapes	=sum(				
12	Compact Discs					

Figure 2.15

3 Select cell B10, cassette sales for 1975, and drag up to cell B9, 8-track sales for 1975. Once the range B9:B10 is selected, release the mouse button. The screen should appear similar to Figure 2.16. Notice that a range selection made in point mode appears with a moving border.

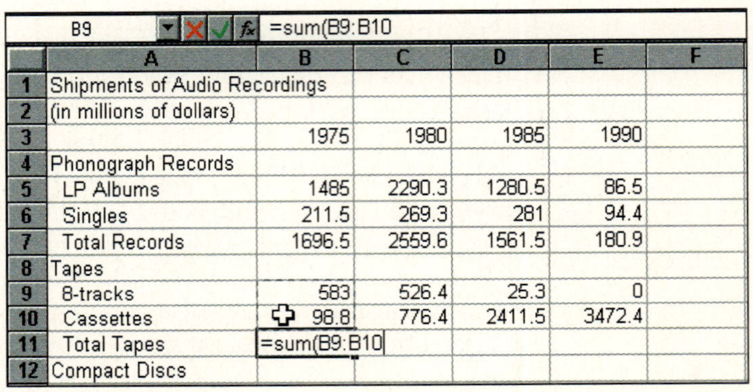

B9 =sum(B9:B10

	A	B	C	D	E	F
1	Shipments of Audio Recordings					
2	(in millions of dollars)					
3		1975	1980	1985	1990	
4	Phonograph Records					
5	LP Albums	1485	2290.3	1280.5	86.5	
6	Singles	211.5	269.3	281	94.4	
7	Total Records	1696.5	2559.6	1561.5	180.9	
8	Tapes					
9	8-tracks	583	526.4	25.3	0	
10	Cassettes	98.8	776.4	2411.5	3472.4	
11	Total Tapes	=sum(B9:B10				
12	Compact Discs					

Figure 2.16

4 Type) and press (ENTER) to complete the formula.

5 Select cell B11.

The completed formula in the formula bar reads =SUM(B9:B10), as shown in Figure 2.17.

B11 =SUM(B9:B10)

	A	B	C	D	E	F
1	Shipments of Audio Recordings					
2	(in millions of dollars)					
3		1975	1980	1985	1990	
4	Phonograph Records					
5	LP Albums	1485	2290.3	1280.5	86.5	
6	Singles	211.5	269.3	281	94.4	
7	Total Records	1696.5	2559.6	1561.5	180.9	
8	Tapes					
9	8-tracks	583	526.4	25.3	0	
10	Cassettes	98.8	776.4	2411.5	3472.4	
11	Total Tapes	681.8				
12	Compact Discs					

Figure 2.17

For totaling such a small range, the SUM function might appear to have little advantage over a regular addition formula. But functions are more flexible. For example, if you insert a new row between 8-track and cassette sales—such as a row for sales of cassette singles—the range reference in the SUM function automatically expands to include the new information. A simple addition formula would not change to include this new row.

The formula =SUM(B9:B10) uses relative cell references; the formula means "sum up the two-cell range immediately above the formula." Because it uses relative addresses, the formula will work correctly if copied. You will now learn about a shortcut method of building SUM formulas before you copy the SUM formula to other cells.

Using the AutoSum Tool

You can always write a SUM formula manually, but ***AutoSum*** is a convenient feature that writes a SUM formula for you. The AutoSum button is located on the Standard toolbar. It is labeled with a Greek capital sigma (Σ), which is traditionally used in mathematics to indicate summation.

When you choose the AutoSum command, it looks for ranges surrounding the active cell and makes a guess about what range you want to total. You have the option of accepting AutoSum's proposed range or selecting another range.

To use the AutoSum tool:

1 Select cell C11, which is to contain total tape sales for 1980.

2 Click the **AutoSum** tool.

AutoSum writes a formula for you. As shown in Figure 2.18, the formula =SUM(C9:C10) appears in the formula bar. After examining the contents of cells neighboring C11, AutoSum guesses that the range you want to sum is C9:C10, which is correct. At this point, if you wanted to select a different range to be summed, you could.

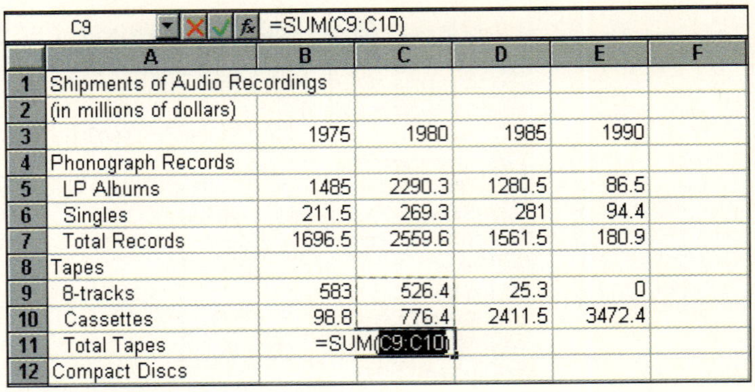

C9 =SUM(C9:C10)

	A	B	C	D	E	F
1	Shipments of Audio Recordings					
2	(in millions of dollars)					
3		1975	1980	1985	1990	
4	Phonograph Records					
5	LP Albums	1485	2290.3	1280.5	86.5	
6	Singles	211.5	269.3	281	94.4	
7	Total Records	1696.5	2559.6	1561.5	180.9	
8	Tapes					
9	8-tracks	583	526.4	25.3	0	
10	Cassettes	98.8	776.4	2411.5	3472.4	
11	Total Tapes	=SUM(C9:C10)				
12	Compact Discs					

Figure 2.18

3 Accept this formula by clicking the formula bar Enter box or by pressing ENTER

4 Copy the formula for 1980 total tape sales to the other cells designated for total tapes (for the years 1985 and 1990).

5 Select B15:E15, the range of cells that are to contain total CD sales.

6 Select the **AutoSum** tool.

A SUM formula is entered automatically in each cell of the selected range. The worksheet should now resemble Figure 2.19.

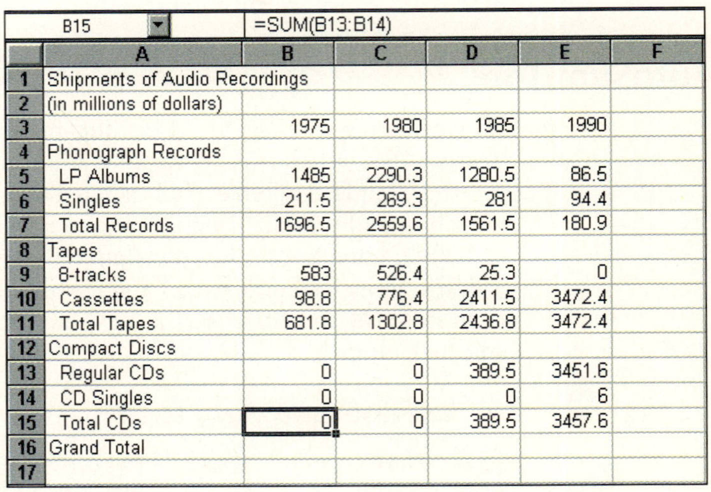

B15 =SUM(B13:B14)

	A	B	C	D	E	F
1	Shipments of Audio Recordings					
2	(in millions of dollars)					
3		1975	1980	1985	1990	
4	Phonograph Records					
5	LP Albums	1485	2290.3	1280.5	86.5	
6	Singles	211.5	269.3	281	94.4	
7	Total Records	1696.5	2559.6	1561.5	180.9	
8	Tapes					
9	8-tracks	583	526.4	25.3	0	
10	Cassettes	98.8	776.4	2411.5	3472.4	
11	Total Tapes	681.8	1302.8	2436.8	3472.4	
12	Compact Discs					
13	Regular CDs	0	0	389.5	3451.6	
14	CD Singles	0	0	0	6	
15	Total CDs	0	0	389.5	3457.6	
16	Grand Total					
17						

Figure 2.19

Calculating Grand Totals

You can compute the grand total for a year by adding total records, total tapes, and total CDs. This cannot be calculated using a SUM function of a single range because you need to add the values of three nonadjacent cells. If you were to construct the formula manually, you would make an addition formula that referred to three separate cells. For example, the grand total for 1975 would be calculated by the formula =B15+B11+B7. In the steps that follow, you will not build such an addition formula but will instead learn how AutoSum can automatically generate grand totals. If you select a range that contains subtotals and then select AutoSum, the AutoSum command will analyze the range and write grand total formulas in the first row of blank cells below the range.

To build the grand total formulas using AutoSum:

1 Select the range B5:E15, as shown in Figure 2.20.

B5 | 1485

	A	B	C	D	E	F
1	Shipments of Audio Recordings					
2	(in millions of dollars)					
3		1975	1980	1985	1990	
4	Phonograph Records					
5	LP Albums	1485	2290.3	1280.5	86.5	
6	Singles	211.5	269.3	281	94.4	
7	Total Records	1696.5	2559.6	1561.5	180.9	
8	Tapes					
9	8-tracks	583	526.4	25.3	0	
10	Cassettes	98.8	776.4	2411.5	3472.4	
11	Total Tapes	681.8	1302.8	2436.8	3472.4	
12	Compact Discs					
13	Regular CDs	0	0	389.5	3451.6	
14	CD Singles	0	0	0	6	
15	Total CDs	0	0	389.5	3457.6	
16	Grand Total					
17						

Figure 2.20

2 Select the **AutoSum** tool.
Grand total formulas appear in the grand total row, B16:E16.

3 Select cell B16.
The screen should now resemble Figure 2.21. The grand total formula for 1975, created by AutoSum, reads =SUM(B15,B11,B7).

B16 | =SUM(B15,B11,B7)

	A	B	C	D	E	F
1	Shipments of Audio Recordings					
2	(in millions of dollars)					
3		1975	1980	1985	1990	
4	Phonograph Records					
5	LP Albums	1485	2290.3	1280.5	86.5	
6	Singles	211.5	269.3	281	94.4	
7	Total Records	1696.5	2559.6	1561.5	180.9	
8	Tapes					
9	8-tracks	583	526.4	25.3	0	
10	Cassettes	98.8	776.4	2411.5	3472.4	
11	Total Tapes	681.8	1302.8	2436.8	3472.4	
12	Compact Discs					
13	Regular CDs	0	0	389.5	3451.6	
14	CD Singles	0	0	0	6	
15	Total CDs	0	0	389.5	3457.6	
16	Grand Total	2378.3	3862.4	4387.8	7110.9	
17						

Figure 2.21

4 Double-click the **Sheet1** tab, and rename the sheet `Audio Sales`

5 Save and close the file.

The Next Step

In this project, you built the functional parts of a worksheet. In the next project, your primary concern will be the appearance of the worksheet—its format. You will retrieve the worksheet, modify it, format it, print it, and learn more about several different formatting techniques.

This concludes Project 2. You can either exit Excel or go on to work the Study Questions, Review Exercises, and Assignments.

Summary and Exercises

Summary

- The first step in building a large worksheet is to enter the row and column titles, followed by any other constant information. You can then construct formulas. You should complete the worksheet before doing detailed formatting.
- A cell's contents can be moved easily with the mouse.
- Excel can check the spelling of worksheet data and can automatically correct commonly misspelled words as they are typed.
- You can use preselection of a range to speed the entry of large amounts of data.
- AutoCalculate can be used to preview summary statistics about a range of cells.
- You can copy a cell using the fill handle, the Copy tool, or the Copy command in the Edit menu. When a formula containing relative cell references is copied, those cell references will change relative to the new cell.
- A function is a built-in mathematical procedure that can be used in a formula. The SUM function, which totals a range of cells, can be typed in or entered using the AutoSum tool.

Key Terms and Operations

Key Terms
argument (to a function)
AutoCalculate
AutoComplete
AutoCorrect
AutoSum
drag-and-drop
function
move
relative cell reference
result

Operations
Copy cell contents
Move cell contents
Paste cell contents
Spell check
Undo a command

Study Questions

Multiple Choice

1. What should usually be done first when building a large worksheet?
   a. formatting
   b. entry of text and number constants
   c. entry of formulas
   d. saving
   e. column-width adjustment

2. Which of the following best describes what happens when a cell is moved?
   a. The cell's contents are duplicated in another location, and you have to erase the contents from the original.
   b. The cell's contents are removed from their original location and placed in a new location.
   c. The Move command is used to reposition the active cell in a new location.
   d. The Move command extends the current selection so that it is larger than a single cell.
   e. none of the above

3. What key can be used to move within a preselected data-entry range?
   a. ↓
   b. TAB
   c. F1
   d. →
   e. all of the above

4. What kinds of cell entries can be copied?
   a. formulas
   b. text constants
   c. number constants
   d. all of the above
   e. none of the above

5. Items of information provided to a function are called:
   a. values.
   b. formulas.
   c. variables.
   d. parameters.
   e. arguments.

6. What is a shorter way of computing =C1+C2+C3+C4+C5+C6+C7+C8?
   a. =ADD(C1..C8)
   b. =TOTAL(C1:C8)
   c. =SUM(C1:C8)
   d. =SUMMATION(C1:C8)
   e. =C1:C8

7. What tool can be used to quickly create SUM formulas?
   a. Summation
   b. =SUM
   c. AutoSum
   d. Sum-O-Matic
   e. Sum command from the Formula menu

8. To have Excel skip all occurrences of a word that it doesn't have in its dictionary, what should you select in the Spelling dialog box?
   a. Ignore
   b. Ignore All
   c. Change
   d. Change All
   e. Cancel

9. When you use the mouse to copy a cell, the pointer will change to a(n):
   a. fill handle.
   b. double arrow.
   c. hollow plus sign.
   d. insertion symbol.
   e. hollow arrow.

10. Suppose the formula =SUM(A1:A5) was entered in cell A6. What best describes the meaning of the formula?
    a. Total the cells A1 and A5.
    b. Total the five-cell range immediately above.
    c. Count the number of entries in the range A1 through A5.
    d. Total the cells A1, A2, A3, and A4.
    e. none of the above

Short Answer

1. What is a more efficient way to compute =E7+E8+E9+E10+E11+E12+E13, and what are the reasons to use it?
2. What effect does the Undo command have on a worksheet?
3. If the spelling checker pauses on a word in the worksheet, does this mean the word is misspelled? If so, what can be done?
4. What technique can be used to speed the entry of a block of data in a worksheet?
5. When a formula is copied to another cell, is it the value (result) of the formula that appears in the new cell?
6. What does the AutoSum tool do?
7. Approximately how many built-in functions does Excel have?
8. If the formula =SUM(B2:B5) were entered into cell B6, how would the formula change if copied to cell C6?
9. What is a simple way to indent text entries?
10. What menu commands can be used to copy a cell?

For Discussion

1. Describe the general steps you should follow when building a worksheet.
2. Describe how to move a cell.
3. Describe how to copy a cell.
4. Describe relative cell referencing and how this affects the way formulas are copied.
5. Describe functions and their components. Use the example of the SUM function.

Review Exercises

Municipal Waste Trends

The Environmental Protection Agency (EPA) reports the information shown in Figure 2.22 about the composition of municipal waste and how it has changed over time (the figures reflect pounds per day per person). Build a worksheet to present this data and calculate the various totals. Use the SUM function to compute the required totals. Save an unformatted version of the workbook to disk, under the name *Proj 2 Ex 1 Municipal Waste Trends*, for use in a Review Exercise at the end of Project 3. After you save the workbook, experiment with AutoFormat options, but do not save the formatted version.

	A	B	C	D	E	F
1	Municipal Waste					
2		1960	1970	1980	1990	
3	Nonfood Wastes					
4	Paper	0.91	1.19	1.32	1.6	
5	Glass	0.2	0.34	0.36	0.28	
6	Plastics	0.01	0.08	0.19	0.32	
7	Total Nonfood	?	?	?	?	
8	Other					
9	Food	0.37	0.34	0.32	0.29	
10	Yard	0.61	0.62	0.66	0.7	
11	Total Other	?	?	?	?	
12	Grand Total	?	?	?	?	
13						

Figure 2.22

Winter Olympic Medals

Figure 2.23 shows the number of medals won by selected countries during the 1992 Winter Olympic Games. Create a worksheet that presents this information and calculates the required totals. Note that both row and column totals are computed. Save an unformatted version of the workbook to disk; use the name *Proj 2 Ex 2 Winter Olympic Medals.* Experiment with AutoFormat if you wish.

	A	B	C	D	E	F
1	1992 Winter Olympiad					
2						
3	Country	Gold	Silver	Bronze	Total	
4	Germany	10	10	6	?	
5	Unified Team	9	6	8	?	
6	Austria	6	7	8	?	
7	Norway	9	6	5	?	
8	Total	?	?	?	?	
9						
10						

Figure 2.23

Assignments

Coffee House Income

Open the file Proj 1 Asn 3 Coffee House Income that you created in an assignment at the end of Project 1. Modify the worksheet, as shown in Figure 2.24, to show sales figures for other kinds of coffee. Note that the original formula for income uses relative addresses and can be copied down to compute income for the other coffee flavors. Create SUM formulas that compute totals for the number sold and income. Do not format the worksheet. Use the Save As command from the File menu to save the updated workbook under a new name, *Proj 2 Asn 1 Coffee House Income.*

	A	B	C	D	E	F
1	Coffee	Cost	Selling Price	No. Sold	Income	
2	House Blend	0.39	0.95	60	?	
3	Espresso	0.61	1.25	12	?	
4	Cappuccino	0.74	1.5	22	?	
5	Café Mocha	0.55	1.45	35	?	
6	Total			?	?	
7						

Figure 2.24

Personal Budget

Build a personal budget that describes your income and expenses for a typical month. Begin with income items such as salary, tips, and interest earned, grouped and indented under the heading *Income.* Build a formula that calculates a total of the income items. Similarly, group expense items such as food, rent, electricity, and insurance, and calculate their total. Finally, build a formula to calculate the difference between total income and total expenses. Do not format the worksheet, but save it to disk under the name *Proj 2 Asn 2 Personal Budget* for use in another project.

Space Payloads

Figure 2.25 documents the number of payloads (objects carried into space) launched by various countries for the years 1988 through 1991. Construct a worksheet to present this data and compute the totals. You can use the SUM function to calculate column totals; you can calculate the average payloads per year for each country by dividing its row total by 4 or by using the AVERAGE function. Do not format the worksheet; save it to disk under the name *Proj 2 Asn 3 Space Payloads.* You will use it in an assignment in Project 3.

	A	B	C	D	E	F	G
1	Space Payloads						
2							
3		1988	1989	1990	1991	Average	
4	USSR	107	95	96	101	?	
5	United States	15	22	31	30	?	
6	Japan	2	4	7	2	?	
7	Total	?	?	?	?	?	
8							

Figure 2.25

PROJECT 3: MODIFYING AND ENHANCING A WORKSHEET

Objectives

After completing this project, you should be able to:

- Identify and analyze formulas in a worksheet
- Insert blank cells into a worksheet
- Recognize and correct circular references
- Clear cells
- Center titles across columns
- Change row height
- Print the worksheet
- Change the standard format
- Understand and modify styles
- Use information windows
- Customize toolbars

CASE STUDY: SALES OF AUDIO RECORDINGS

In this project, you will continue to work with the audio recordings worksheet from Project 2. Sales of cassette singles, shown here, will need to be included in the worksheet. The new data will appear between the rows labeled *Cassettes* and *Total Tapes.*

	1975	1980	1985	1990
Cassette Singles	0	0	0	87.4

Once this information is added, some formulas in the worksheet will need to be adjusted to reflect the new information. In the final phase of the project, you will format the worksheet and learn about cell styles.

Designing the Solution

First you will need to make room for the new information on sales of cassette singles. You could move the lower half of the worksheet (A11:E16) down one row to create the needed space, but for this exercise you will use the Insert command. Using the Insert command is easier because it does not require that you select as large an area.

MODIFYING A WORKSHEET

When you modify a worksheet, you must consider how the change will affect other parts of the worksheet. You need to analyze carefully the way formulas depend on other cells. Usually formulas adjust automatically as you'd like them to, but in some cases, they do not. Consider the consequences of inserting a new row: the area where you want to place extra cells might be quite small, but if you choose to insert an entire row, a new blank row will extend across the entire worksheet, perhaps inserting blank space through the middle of some other portion of the worksheet that you do not want to affect. Deleting an entire row or column is even more sensitive because information is removed all the way across or down the worksheet.

Reminder You should save a workbook before performing a command that might significantly affect it. You should also consider the possible side effects of using a command. Save before you perform a command, then if the workbook is adversely affected by the command, you can close the damaged workbook without saving, return to your previously saved copy, and try again.

Tracing Precedents and Dependents

The Excel Auditing toolbar (and the Auditing option in the Tools menu) has several features that make it easier for you to understand the formulas in a worksheet. If you select a cell containing a formula and then select the Trace Precedents tool, Excel will draw ***tracer arrows*** on the screen from all the cells on which that formula directly depends. These cells are called ***direct precedents.*** Selecting the Trace Precedents tool again will draw tracer arrows from ***indirect precedents***—cells on which the direct precedent cells depend. The Trace Precedents tool can be used repeatedly to trace to the original precedents. If the precedent cells compose a range, a box is drawn around the range.

You can also use the Trace Dependents tool to draw tracer arrows to direct and indirect ***dependents***—cells that contain formulas that refer to (depend on) a particular cell. Whether you are tracing dependents or precedents, the tracer arrows have large dots on one end to show precedent cells and arrowheads on the other end to show dependent cells. The arrowheads indicate the direction of information flow.

In the following steps, you will use these tools to review how the formulas work in the audio sales worksheet.

To open and prepare the Audio Sales History workbook:

1 Choose **File** and then **Open,** and open the Audio Sales History workbook file you saved in Project 2.

2 Click the **Audio Sales** sheet tab, if necessary.

To display the Auditing toolbar:

1 Choose **View** and then **Toolbars,** and display the Auditing toolbar.

2 Dock the Auditing toolbar on the right side of the vertical scroll bar. The screen should resemble Figure 3.1.

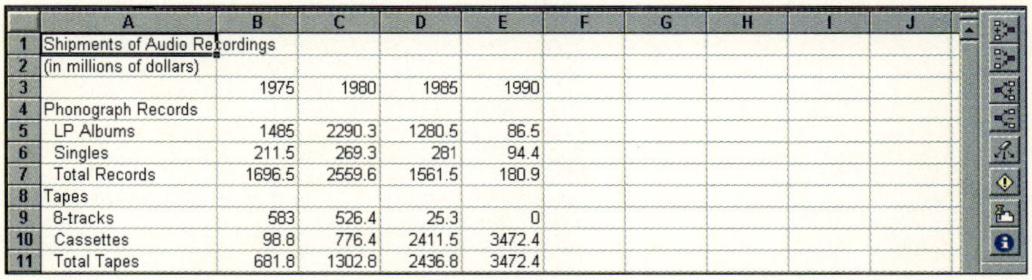

	A	B	C	D	E	F	G	H	I	J
1	Shipments of Audio Recordings									
2	(in millions of dollars)									
3		1975	1980	1985	1990					
4	Phonograph Records									
5	LP Albums	1485	2290.3	1280.5	86.5					
6	Singles	211.5	269.3	281	94.4					
7	Total Records	1696.5	2559.6	1561.5	180.9					
8	Tapes									
9	8-tracks	583	526.4	25.3	0					
10	Cassettes	98.8	776.4	2411.5	3472.4					
11	Total Tapes	681.8	1302.8	2436.8	3472.4					

Figure 3.1

To trace direct precedents:

1 Select cell B16, which contains the formula for the grand total for 1975.

2 Click the **Trace Precedents** tool.
The screen should resemble Figure 3.2. Large dots appear in cells B7, B11, and B15; these dots mark precedent cells. The arrowhead points to cell B16, indicating that the information from the marked precedent cells feeds into the formula in cell B16.

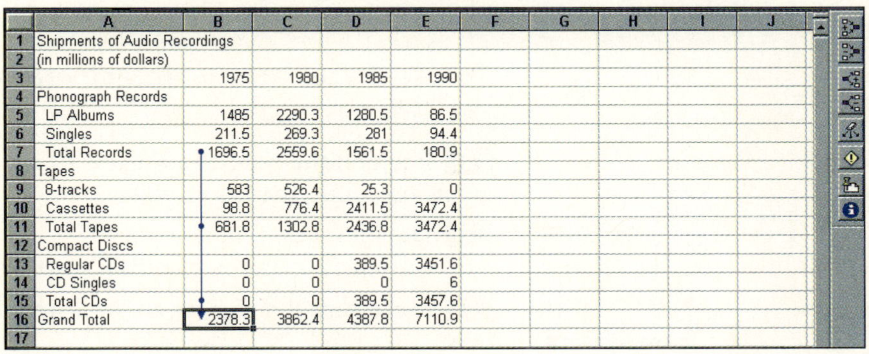

	A	B	C	D	E	F	G	H	I	J
1	Shipments of Audio Recordings									
2	(in millions of dollars)									
3		1975	1980	1985	1990					
4	Phonograph Records									
5	LP Albums	1485	2290.3	1280.5	86.5					
6	Singles	211.5	269.3	281	94.4					
7	Total Records	1696.5	2559.6	1561.5	180.9					
8	Tapes									
9	8-tracks	583	526.4	25.3	0					
10	Cassettes	98.8	776.4	2411.5	3472.4					
11	Total Tapes	681.8	1302.8	2436.8	3472.4					
12	Compact Discs									
13	Regular CDs	0	0	389.5	3451.6					
14	CD Singles	0	0	0	6					
15	Total CDs	0	0	389.5	3457.6					
16	Grand Total	2378.3	3862.4	4387.8	7110.9					
17										

Figure 3.2

The formula in cell B16 depends *directly* on the three cells marked with dots. Remember that the three cells are themselves totals; in the next steps, you will select the indirect precedents of the grand total formula.

To trace indirect precedents:

1 Click the **Trace Precedents** tool again.
The screen should now resemble Figure 3.3, which shows indirect precedents along with direct precedents. For example, cell B11 depends on the range B9:B10, so this range is outlined, a dot appears in the first cell of the range, and the connected arrow points into cell B11.

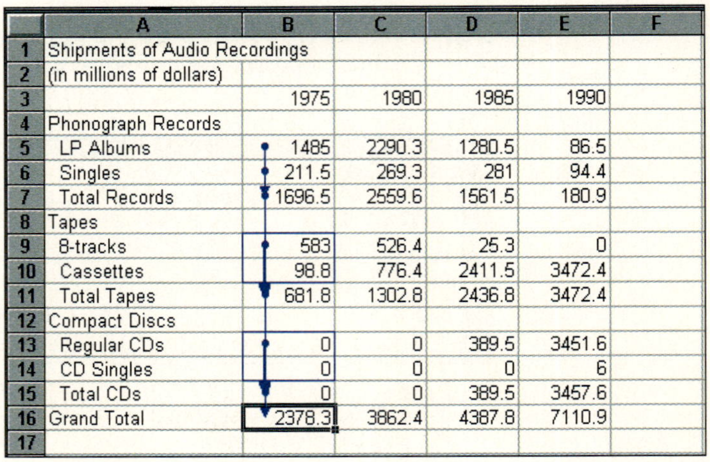

	A	B	C	D	E	F
1	Shipments of Audio Recordings					
2	(in millions of dollars)					
3		1975	1980	1985	1990	
4	Phonograph Records					
5	LP Albums	1485	2290.3	1280.5	86.5	
6	Singles	211.5	269.3	281	94.4	
7	Total Records	1696.5	2559.6	1561.5	180.9	
8	Tapes					
9	8-tracks	583	526.4	25.3	0	
10	Cassettes	98.8	776.4	2411.5	3472.4	
11	Total Tapes	681.8	1302.8	2436.8	3472.4	
12	Compact Discs					
13	Regular CDs	0	0	389.5	3451.6	
14	CD Singles	0	0	0	6	
15	Total CDs	0	0	389.5	3457.6	
16	Grand Total	2378.3	3862.4	4387.8	7110.9	
17						

Figure 3.3

2 Click the **Trace Precedents** tool again.
Excel beeps, signaling that there are no further precedents to be traced.

3 Click the **Remove Precedent Arrows** tool.
The last traced precedence arrows are cleared; the screen should once again resemble Figure 3.2.

It is sometimes useful, when analyzing a worksheet with multiple levels of precedent cells, to be able to jump quickly from a cell to its precedent. The following steps demonstrate this feature.

To use tracer arrows to activate dependent and precedent cells:

1 Position the pointer so that it forms an arrow shape, just touching anywhere along the tracer arrow.

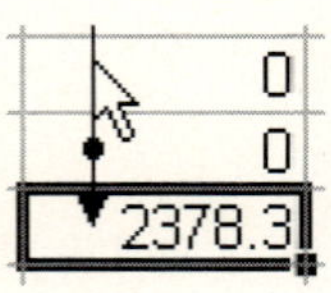

2 Double-click.
The active cell switches to cell B7, at the opposite end of the tracer arrow.

3 Make sure the pointer arrow just touches the tracer arrow, and double-click.
The active cell switches back to cell B16.

4 Click the **Remove All Arrows** tool.
No precedence arrows are visible now. The Remove Precedent Arrows tool could also have been used.

To trace dependents:

1 Select cell B5, LP album sales for 1975.

2 Click the **Trace Dependents** tool.
A tracer arrow appears, showing that cell B7, which computes total record sales for 1975, depends on the selected cell. The screen should resemble Figure 3.4.

	A	B	C
1	Shipments of Audio Recordings		
2	(in millions of dollars)		
3		1975	1980
4	Phonograph Records		
5	LP Albums	1485	2290.3
6	Singles	211.5	269.3
7	Total Records	1696.5	2559.6

Figure 3.4

3 Click the **Trace Dependents** tool again.
Another tracer arrow appears, showing that cell B16, which computes the grand total for 1975, depends indirectly on the selected cell. The screen should resemble Figure 3.5.

	A	B	C
1	Shipments of Audio Recordings		
2	(in millions of dollars)		
3		1975	1980
4	Phonograph Records		
5	LP Albums	1485	2290.3
6	Singles	211.5	269.3
7	Total Records	1696.5	2559.6
8	Tapes		
9	8-tracks	583	526.4
10	Cassettes	98.8	776.4
11	Total Tapes	681.8	1302.8
12	Compact Discs		
13	Regular CDs	0	0
14	CD Singles	0	0
15	Total CDs	0	0
16	Grand Total	2378.3	3862.4

Figure 3.5

4 Click the **Trace Dependents** tool again.
There are no further dependent cells.

5 Click the **Remove All Arrows** tool.
No tracer arrows should be visible.

Bearing in mind the modification planned for this worksheet, you will want to make sure that the data for sales of cassette singles, once entered into the worksheet, is also included in the total tape sales formula. You shouldn't have to worry about the grand total formula in this case because it depends on the total tape sales formula.

Inserting Cells in a Worksheet

A range of blank cells needs to be inserted directly above the total tapes row. Excel lets you insert either a range of cells or an entire column or row. It is often safest to insert a range because the effect doesn't stretch as far across the worksheet as it does when an entire column or row is inserted.

To insert blank cells:

1 Select cell A11, the cell containing the text *Total Tapes*, and then select the range A11:E11.

2 Choose **Insert** and then **Cells.**
The Insert dialog box appears, as shown in Figure 3.6. Because the selected range is wider than it is deep, Excel presumes that you want to shift the selected range (and everything underneath it) down, which is correct.

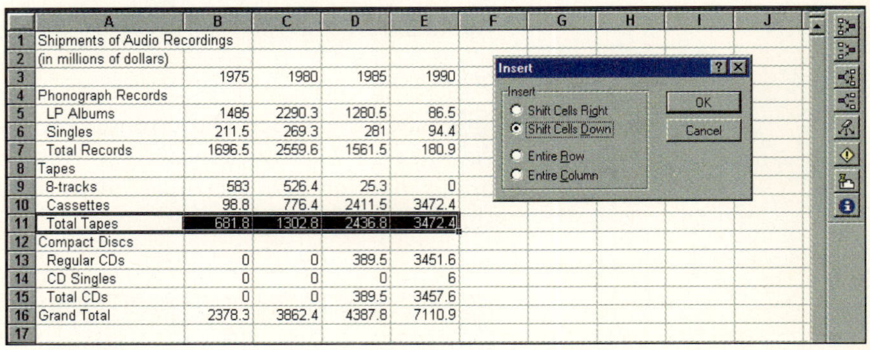

	A	B	C	D	E	F	G	H	I	J
1	Shipments of Audio Recordings									
2	(in millions of dollars)									
3		1975	1980	1985	1990					
4	Phonograph Records									
5	LP Albums	1485	2290.3	1280.5	86.5					
6	Singles	211.5	269.3	281	94.4					
7	Total Records	1696.5	2559.6	1561.5	180.9					
8	Tapes									
9	8-tracks	583	526.4	25.3	0					
10	Cassettes	98.8	776.4	2411.5	3472.4					
11	Total Tapes	681.8	1302.8	2436.8	3472.4					
12	Compact Discs									
13	Regular CDs	0	0	389.5	3451.6					
14	CD Singles	0	0	0	6					
15	Total CDs	0	0	389.5	3457.6					
16	Grand Total	2378.3	3862.4	4387.8	7110.9					
17										

Figure 3.6

3 Select **OK.**
A new range of blank cells is now available.

To enter the new information:

1 Select cell A11.

2 Press (SPACE) twice and enter `Cassette Singles`

3 Enter `0` in cells B11, C11, and D11.

4 Enter `87.4` in cell E11.
Your worksheet should now resemble Figure 3.7.

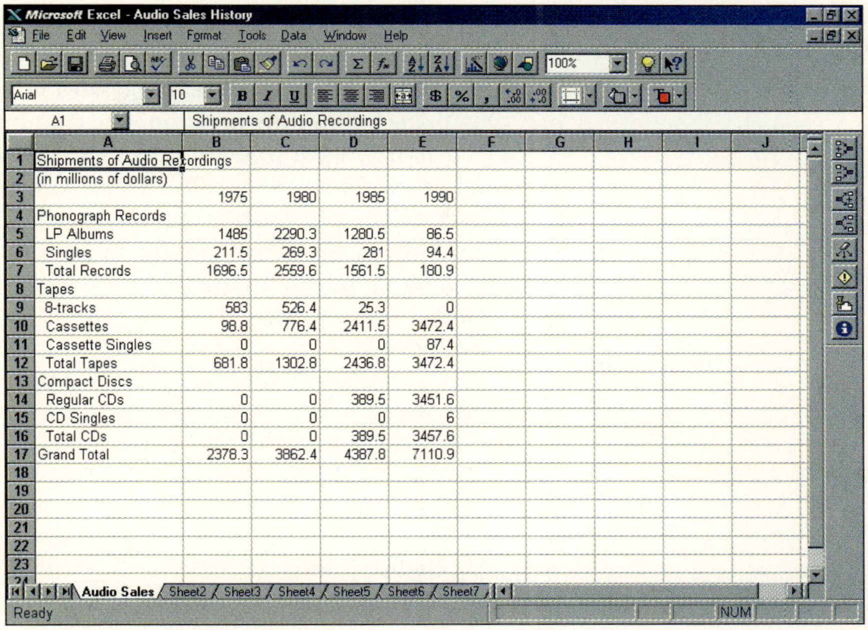

Figure 3.7

Assessing the Effects of a Command

Now that the data for sales of cassette singles is entered, you can determine whether adjustments are required to accommodate the new information. The sales of cassette singles should be included in the computation of total tapes, so you should examine the formulas in the total tapes row.

To examine the total tapes formulas:

1 Select cell E12, the total tape sales for 1990.
The formula reads =SUM(E9:E10), so the range being summed does *not* include the new information in cell E11.

2 Trace the direct precedents of cell E12.
As shown in Figure 3.8, this confirms visually that the range being totaled, B9:B10, is not correct. For the total tape sales formula to be correct, it should depend not only on the sales of 8-tracks and cassettes, but on the data in cell B11, cassette singles, as well.

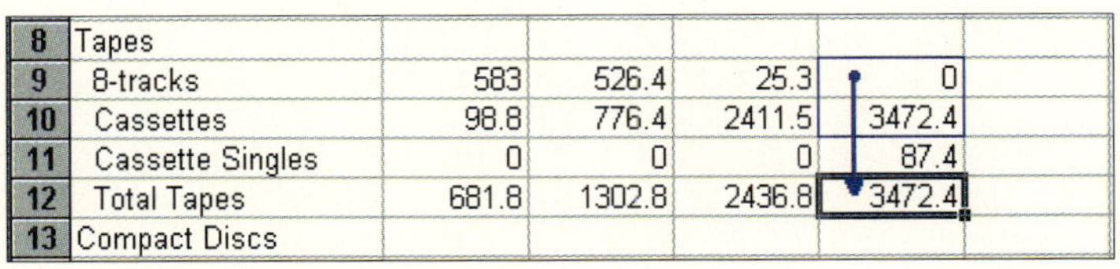

Figure 3.8

3 Remove all tracer arrows.

Because cassette singles had no sales for 1975 through 1985, you might conclude that the only formula that needs to be fixed is the one for 1990. But leaving the other total tape sales formulas unchanged would be a serious design mistake; it would create an inconsistency in the worksheet that could later prove troublesome. What if the worksheet were reused and different years' data (all with sales of cassette singles) was entered over the older data? If the incorrect tape sales formulas were still present, their results would not include the new amounts.

You may have wondered why the range referred to in the SUM function did not automatically adjust. Excel will automatically adjust a range reference within a formula if the newly inserted row is *within* the existing top and bottom rows of the range, but not if the inserted row lies outside the existing range. Had the row for cassette singles been inserted between the 8-track and cassette rows, Excel would have adjusted the range reference in the formula.

In the steps that follow, you will build a new SUM formula for total tape sales for 1975 and copy the formula to the other total tape cells. Please follow the steps carefully because the steps will purposefully instruct you to make a common mistake that you will then learn how to correct. *Do not use AutoSum for these steps.*

To build a self-referential SUM formula:

1 Select cell B12, where the formula for total tape sales for 1975 resides.

2 Type **=sum(**

3 Select cell B9, 8-track tape sales for 1975.

4 Drag the selection down through cell B12 to highlight the range B9:B12.

5 Type **)** and press ENTER
A dialog box appears with the message *Cannot resolve circular references.*

6 Select **OK** to bypass the dialog box.

7 Select cell B12.

8 Trace the direct precedents of cell B12.

9 Select another cell away from the tracer area to see the tracer arrow more clearly.
As shown in Figure 3.9, cell B12 is dependent on itself. Note that the status bar shows *Circular: B17.*

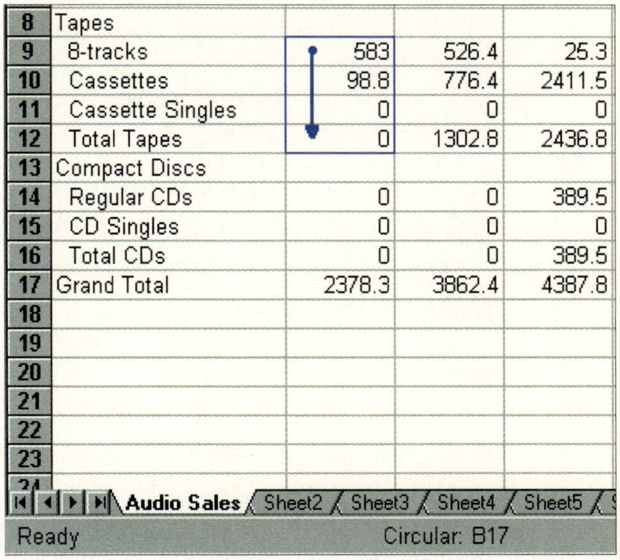

8	Tapes			
9	8-tracks	583	526.4	25.3
10	Cassettes	98.8	776.4	2411.5
11	Cassette Singles	0	0	0
12	Total Tapes	0	1302.8	2436.8
13	Compact Discs			
14	Regular CDs	0	0	389.5
15	CD Singles	0	0	0
16	Total CDs	0	0	389.5
17	Grand Total	2378.3	3862.4	4387.8
18				
19				
20				
21				
22				
23				

Figure 3.9

10 Remove all tracer arrows.

Understanding Circular References

A ***circular reference*** occurs when a formula refers, either directly or indirectly, to itself. This kind of formula usually doesn't make any sense, so it is considered an error. The erroneous formula you just entered is an example of one of the more common places where circular references can occur. When using the mouse or arrow keys to select a range within a formula, you should drag or select away from the formula: this will reduce the chance of inadvertently including the formula's own cell within the selected range.

In the following steps, you will rebuild the formula. Although it is not necessary to clear the old formulas first, you will do so to learn about the Clear command.

To clear a range of cells:

1 Select the range B12:E12, which contains the total tape formulas.

2 Choose **Edit** and then **Clear.**
The Clear submenu appears.

3 Select **Contents.**
The formulas in the range B12:E12 should now be erased. Note that if you select All from the Clear menu, both the contents and the format of the selected range will be cleared.

> ***Tip*** Another way to clear the contents of a selection is click the right mouse button to access the shortcut menu, and then choose Clear Contents. An even quicker way is to press (DEL) after making the selection.

Clearing cells is not the same as *deleting* them. When cells are cleared, their contents are erased but the cells themselves remain. Deleting cells, which you haven't done yet, removes the cells from the worksheet and shifts neighboring cells in to take up the space.

You will now create the correct formula, copy it to the total tapes cells, and save the workbook.

To build the correct total tapes formula:

1 Select the range B12:E12 (if not already selected), the cells that will contain total tape sales for each year.

2 Click the **AutoSum** tool.
SUM formulas appear in each of the selected cells.

3 Select cell B12.
The correct formula, =SUM(B9:B11), is visible in the formula bar.

4 Click the **Trace Precedents** tool, and then select another cell away from the trace area.
A tracer arrow and range outline appear, confirming that the range being totaled is correct, as shown in Figure 3.10.

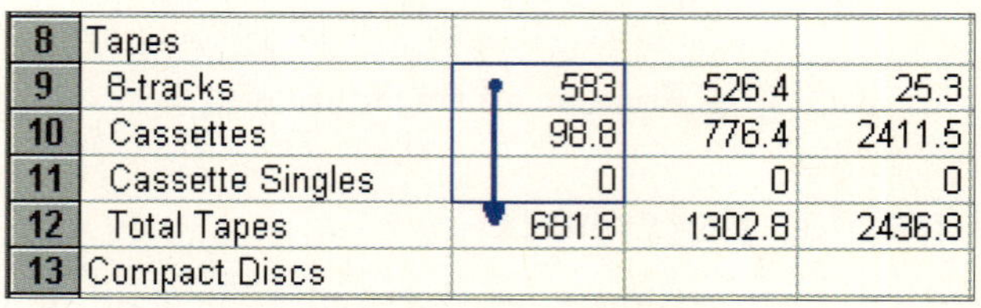

8	Tapes			
9	8-tracks	583	526.4	25.3
10	Cassettes	98.8	776.4	2411.5
11	Cassette Singles	0	0	0
12	Total Tapes	681.8	1302.8	2436.8
13	Compact Discs			

Figure 3.10

5 Click the **Remove All Arrows** tool.

6 Undock and close the Auditing toolbar.
The screen should look like Figure 3.11.

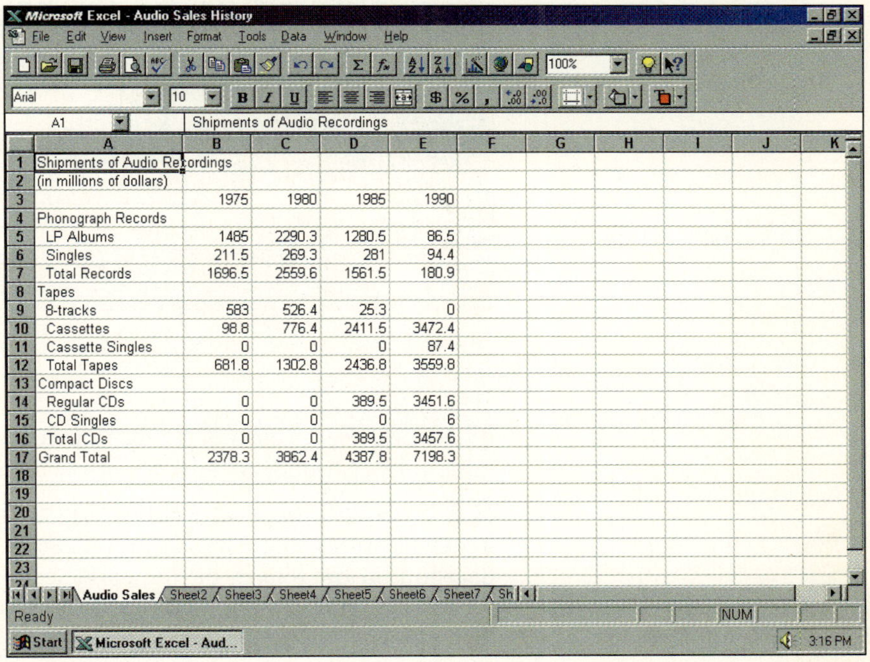

	A	B	C	D	E
1	Shipments of Audio Recordings				
2	(in millions of dollars)				
3		1975	1980	1985	1990
4	Phonograph Records				
5	LP Albums	1485	2290.3	1280.5	86.5
6	Singles	211.5	269.3	281	94.4
7	Total Records	1696.5	2559.6	1561.5	180.9
8	Tapes				
9	8-tracks	583	526.4	25.3	0
10	Cassettes	98.8	776.4	2411.5	3472.4
11	Cassette Singles	0	0	0	87.4
12	Total Tapes	681.8	1302.8	2436.8	3559.8
13	Compact Discs				
14	Regular CDs	0	0	389.5	3451.6
15	CD Singles	0	0	0	6
16	Total CDs	0	0	389.5	3457.6
17	Grand Total	2378.3	3862.4	4387.8	7198.3

Figure 3.11

7 Save the workbook using the **Save** command from the **File** menu or the **Save** button.
It is very important to save at this point because in later steps you will need to use this version of the workbook.

Enhancing the Worksheet

As in Project 1, you will use AutoFormat to format a worksheet. The AutoFormat command works best on worksheets that have a relatively simple and consistent structure. This worksheet will require several manual adjustments after you use AutoFormat.

To use AutoFormat with the worksheet:

1 Select the range A1:E17.
A quick way to do this, provided you did not type any extraneous information after the grand total for 1990, is to select cell A1 by pressing CTRL + HOME and then press CTRL + SHIFT + END (use END either on the gray keys or on the numeric keypad with NUM LOCK off).

2 Choose **Format** and then **AutoFormat.**
The AutoFormat dialog box appears.

3 Select the **Accounting 1** Table Format, and then select **OK,** as shown in Figure 3.12.

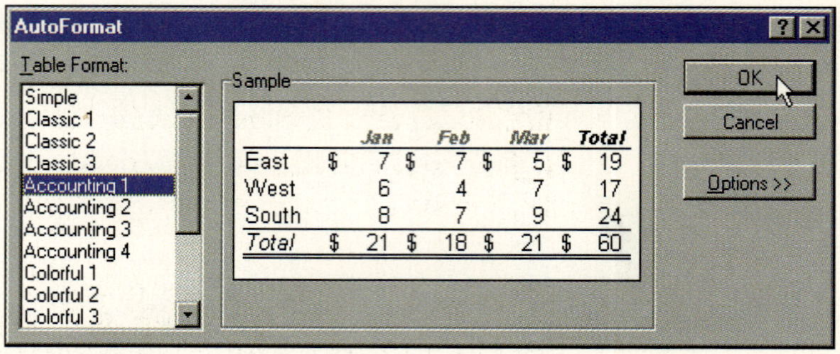

Figure 3.12

The worksheet is automatically formatted. Notice that in the Accounting 1 table format, values of zero are displayed as centered hyphens.

4 Select cell A1 to cancel the larger selected range.
You will notice that AutoFormat made column A too wide. It based its decision on the length of the worksheet's main title, *Shipments of Audio Recordings.* You will center this title across all the columns of the worksheet in the next series of steps, so column A does not need to be this wide.

5 Adjust the width of column A to about 22 so that it is slightly wider than *Phonograph Records,* as shown in Figure 3.13.

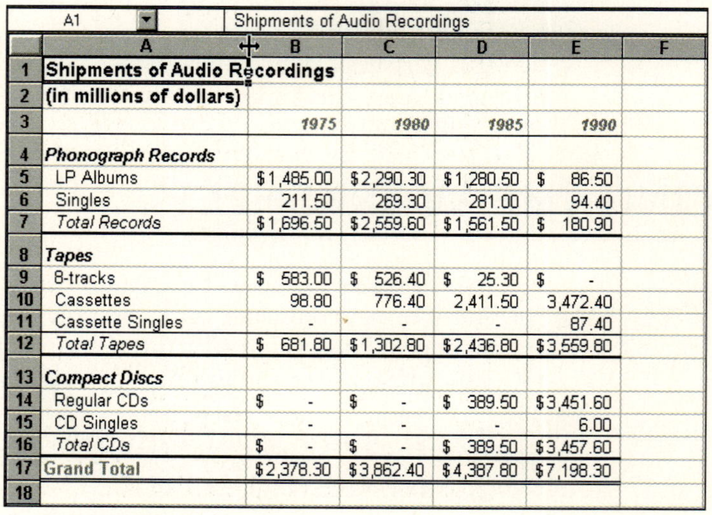

A1 | Shipments of Audio Recordings

	A	B	C	D	E	F
1	**Shipments of Audio Recordings**					
2	**(in millions of dollars)**					
3		*1975*	*1980*	*1985*	*1990*	
4	***Phonograph Records***					
5	LP Albums	$1,485.00	$2,290.30	$1,280.50	$ 86.50	
6	Singles	211.50	269.30	281.00	94.40	
7	*Total Records*	$1,696.50	$2,559.60	$1,561.50	$ 180.90	
8	***Tapes***					
9	8-tracks	$ 583.00	$ 526.40	$ 25.30	$ -	
10	Cassettes	98.80	776.40	2,411.50	3,472.40	
11	Cassette Singles	-	-	-	87.40	
12	*Total Tapes*	$ 681.80	$1,302.80	$2,436.80	$3,559.80	
13	***Compact Discs***					
14	Regular CDs	$ -	$ -	$ 389.50	$3,451.60	
15	CD Singles	-	-	-	6.00	
16	*Total CDs*	$ -	$ -	$ 389.50	$3,457.60	
17	**Grand Total**	$2,378.30	$3,862.40	$4,387.80	$7,198.30	
18						

Figure 3.13

Centering Text Across Columns

The main title, *Shipments of Audio Recordings,* and the subtitle *(in millions of dollars),* would look better centered over the worksheet. You can use the Center Across Columns tool in the Formatting toolbar to center the contents of one cell over a selected group of columns. This tool requires that you select a range whose leftmost cells contain the text you want to center; the selected range should extend across the columns that you want the text centered within.

To center text across columns:

1 Select cell A1, which contains the text *Shipments of Audio Recordings.*

2 As shown in Figure 3.14, extend the selection to include A1:E2, which includes the subtitle row (row 2) and the column for 1990 (column E).

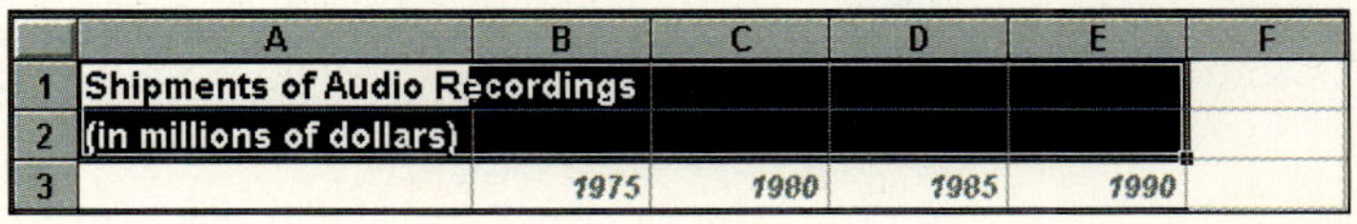

	A	B	C	D	E	F
1	Shipments of Audio Recordings					
2	(in millions of dollars)					
3		1975	1980	1985	1990	

Figure 3.14

3 Release the mouse button, and click the **Center Across Columns** tool on the Formatting toolbar.

4 Click any cell to cancel the selection.
The title and subtitle should now be centered above the worksheet, as shown in Figure 3.15. *Note that the text for these titles is still stored in cells A1 and A2.*

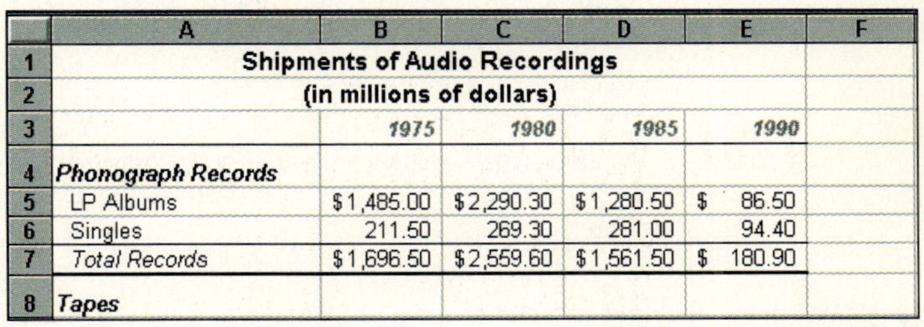

	A	B	C	D	E	F
1			Shipments of Audio Recordings			
2			(in millions of dollars)			
3		1975	1980	1985	1990	
4	*Phonograph Records*					
5	LP Albums	$1,485.00	$2,290.30	$1,280.50	$ 86.50	
6	Singles	211.50	269.30	281.00	94.40	
7	*Total Records*	$1,696.50	$2,559.60	$1,561.50	$ 180.90	
8	*Tapes*					

Figure 3.15

Changing Row Height

The worksheet might look better if there were more vertical space between the titles and the years. To create this extra space, you could insert a new row. However, you will have more precise control over the spacing if instead you change the height of the years' row. This process is very similar to that of changing the width of a column.

Whereas the width of a column is measured in characters, the height of a row is measured in ***points***, a traditional type-measurement unit employed by printers and typographers. A point, abbreviated as *pt.*, is equal to 1/72 of an inch.

To change row height:

1 Position the pointer so that it is over the *lower* edge of the heading for row 3 (on the line separating rows 3 and 4). The pointer should change to a vertical double arrow.

2 Hold down the mouse button and drag downward slightly to extend the lower edge of row 3. The reference area in the formula bar shows the height. Drag the mouse to set the height anywhere between 23 and 28 points, and then release the mouse button, as shown in Figure 3.16.

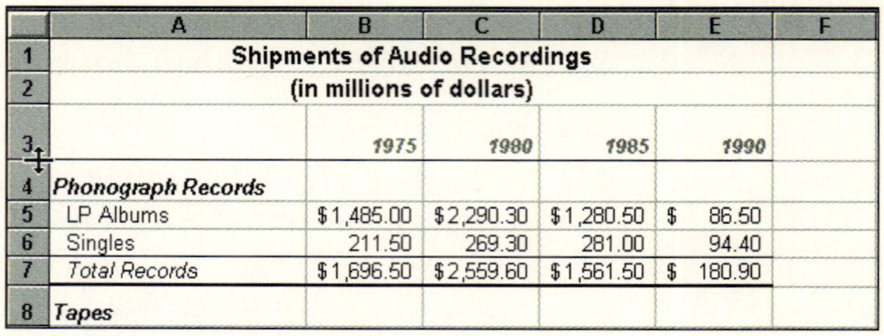

	A	B	C	D	E	F
1	Shipments of Audio Recordings					
2	(in millions of dollars)					
3		*1975*	*1980*	*1985*	*1990*	
4	***Phonograph Records***					
5	LP Albums	$1,485.00	$2,290.30	$1,280.50	$ 86.50	
6	Singles	211.50	269.30	281.00	94.40	
7	*Total Records*	$1,696.50	$2,559.60	$1,561.50	$ 180.90	
8	***Tapes***					

Figure 3.16

Saving the Worksheet Under a Different Name

The worksheet has once again changed significantly. In the steps that follow, you will save the workbook before you print it. Because you will need to work with the earlier, unformatted version of the audio worksheet in later steps, you will save this formatted workbook with a different name.

To save the workbook with a different name:

1 Choose **File** and then **Save As.**
The Save As dialog box appears.

2 Type `Formatted Audio Sales History` for the file name, and then select **Save.**

EXIT If necessary, you can quit Excel now and continue this project later.

Printing the Worksheet

Before you print a worksheet, you should check your printer to make sure it is turned on, has paper, and is online (communicating with the computer). If it is a dot-matrix printer, you should ensure that the paper is properly lined up.

To print the worksheet:

1 Make sure your printer is ready.

2 Choose **File** and then **Print.**
The Print dialog box appears.

3 Select **OK.**
You may notice dotted lines on the screen—these indicate page breaks in the worksheet. Your printout should look something like Figure 3.17.

Shipments of Audio Recordings
(in millions of dollars)

	1975	*1980*	*1985*	*1990*
Phonograph Records				
LP Albums	$ 1,485.00	$ 2,290.30	$ 1,280.50	$ 86.50
Singles	211.50	269.30	281.00	94.40
Total Records	$ 1,696.50	$ 2,559.60	$ 1,561.50	$ 180.90
Tapes				
8-tracks	$ 583.00	$ 526.40	$ 25.30	$ -
Cassettes	98.80	776.40	2,411.50	3,472.40
Cassette Singles	-	-	-	87.40
Total Tapes	$ 681.80	$ 1,302.80	$ 2,436.80	$ 3,559.80
Compact Discs				
Regular CDs	$ -	$ -	$ 389.50	$ 3,451.60
CD Singles	-	-	-	6.00
Total CDs	$ -	$ -	$ 389.50	$ 3,457.60
Grand Total	$ 2,378.30	$ 3,862.40	$ 4,387.80	$ 7,198.30

Figure 3.17

Changing the Display of Cell Gridlines

Worksheets that have been formatted with decorative border lines usually look better (and are less confusing to use) if the printout's cell gridlines are turned off, as they are by default.

To control the display of gridlines on a *printout*, you can use the Gridlines check box on the Sheet tab of the Page Setup dialog box found in the File menu. To control the display of gridlines *on the screen*, you can use the Gridlines check box on the View tab of the Options dialog box found in the Tools menu.

To remove cell gridlines from the screen:

1 Choose **Tools** and then **Options.**
The Options dialog box appears.

2 Click the **View** tab.

3 Clear the **Gridlines** check box, and then select **OK,** as shown in Figure 3.18.

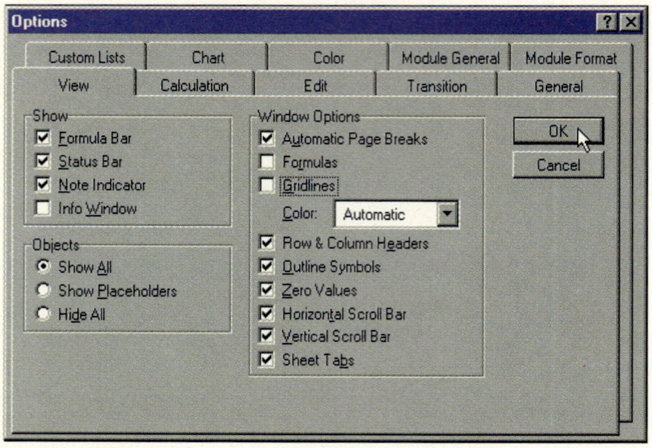

Figure 3.18

The worksheet now appears without gridlines.

4 Close (and save) the Formatted Audio Sales History workbook.

Working with Styles

In Excel, a ***style*** is a group of format settings that are collected and referred to by a name. The Normal style is used by default for all cell entries unless you specify a different style.

In the steps that follow, you will work with the original, unformatted Audio Sales History workbook. You will be changing some of the characteristics of the Normal style, but you will not be switching any cells from one style (Normal) to another (such as Comma style). Normal style is the only style used in this project.

Changing the Standard Font

With most printers, you will achieve the best printouts with the smoothest lines and clearest type if you use TrueType fonts. A ***font*** in Excel is a typeface—the form or design of letters and characters. The TrueType font technology is built directly into Windows. Several basic TrueType fonts are also provided with Windows. TrueType has the additional advantage of making the screen appear very similar to the printout. Excel's default font, called Arial, is a TrueType font.

The Style dialog box includes a brief description of the style. Six check boxes correspond to the formatting attributes that a style can include: Number, Font, Alignment, Border, Patterns, and Protection. The Normal style specifies all these. In this section, you will learn how to change the Normal style setting for a worksheet so that Courier New, another TrueType font, is used.

To change the standard font:

1 Open the Audio Sales History workbook.

2 Choose **Format** and then **Style.**
The Style dialog box appears.

The name Normal should appear in the Style Name list box. The font currently being used for the Normal style is Arial 10 (Arial, size of 10 points). You will change this to Courier New.

3 Select **Modify.**
A Format Cells dialog box appears, with tabs for each formatting attribute, as shown in Figure 3.19. You will now change the font.

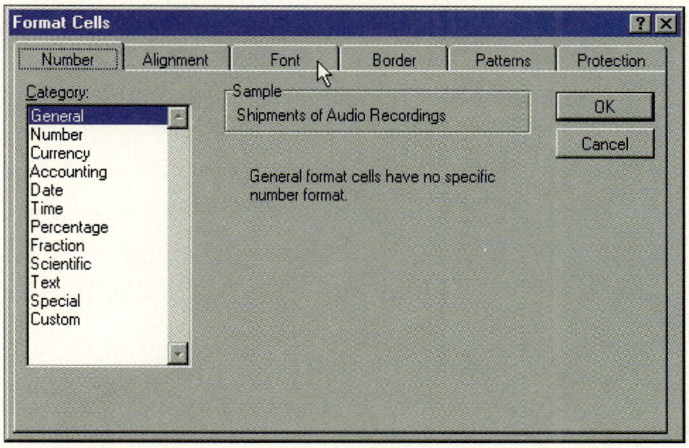

Figure 3.19

4 Click the **Font** tab.
The Font page appears. Names of TrueType fonts are preceded by a TT logo.

5 Select the TrueType **Courier New** font in the Font list box (you may need to scroll through the alphabetical list) as shown in Figure 3.20, and then select **OK.**

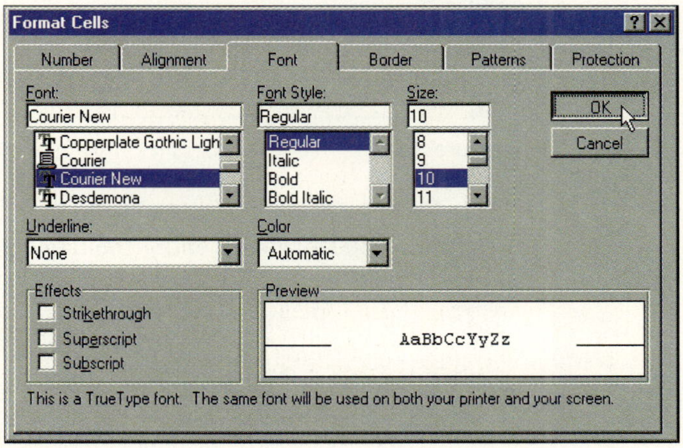

Figure 3.20

6 Select **OK** in the Style dialog box to complete the new definition of the Normal style.
All existing cell entries in this worksheet are in the Normal style and now appear in the TrueType Courier New font. The Normal style will also be

in effect if you type new cell entries, so future entries will also appear in the Courier New font.

Formatting the Worksheet

In the steps that follow, you will format and adjust the worksheet, just as you did at the beginning of this project. These steps are condensed; refer to the beginning of the project if necessary.

To format the worksheet:

1 Perform an AutoFormat on the range A1:E17 using the Accounting 1 table format.

2 Narrow column A to a width of about 20.

3 Center the main title and subtitle across columns A through E.

4 Turn off the screen display of cell gridlines by choosing **Tools** and then **Options,** clicking the **View** tab, and clearing the **Gridlines** check box.

5 Increase the height of row 3 to about 25 points.
Your worksheet should look similar to Figure 3.21.

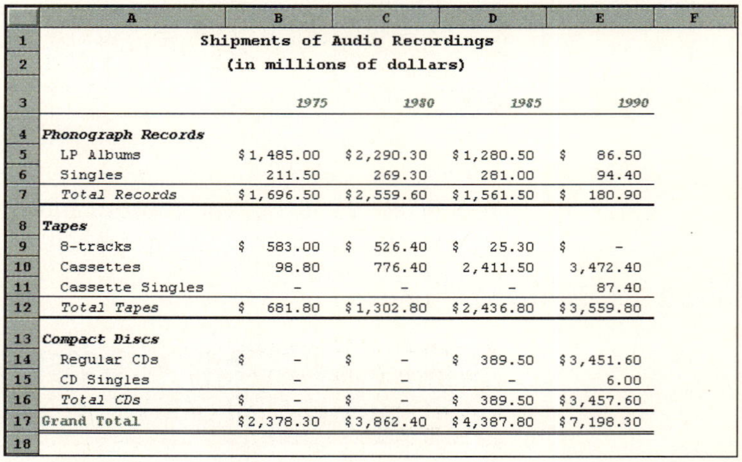

	A	B	C	D	E	F
1	Shipments of Audio Recordings					
2	(in millions of dollars)					
3		*1975*	*1980*	*1985*	*1990*	
4	***Phonograph Records***					
5	LP Albums	$1,485.00	$2,290.30	$1,280.50	$ 86.50	
6	Singles	211.50	269.30	281.00	94.40	
7	*Total Records*	$1,696.50	$2,559.60	$1,561.50	$ 180.90	
8	***Tapes***					
9	8-tracks	$ 583.00	$ 526.40	$ 25.30	$ -	
10	Cassettes	98.80	776.40	2,411.50	3,472.40	
11	Cassette Singles	-	-	-	87.40	
12	*Total Tapes*	$ 681.80	$1,302.80	$2,436.80	$3,559.80	
13	***Compact Discs***					
14	Regular CDs	$ -	$ -	$ 389.50	$3,451.60	
15	CD Singles	-	-	-	6.00	
16	*Total CDs*	$ -	$ -	$ 389.50	$3,457.60	
17	Grand Total	$2,378.30	$3,862.40	$4,387.80	$7,198.30	
18						

Figure 3.21

6 Save the workbook under the name **`Yet Another Formatted Audio Sales History`**

7 Click the **Print** tool as a shortcut to print the worksheet.
Compare your new printout with the earlier one you made. Notice that the Courier New font resembles typewriter-style characters. You may wish to experiment with the other TrueType fonts on the system you are using.

Using Information Windows

You have seen that several kinds of data can be stored in a cell and that a wide variety of formatting attributes can be applied to a cell. An ***information window*** lets you examine a cell's contents more closely. In the steps that follow, you will open an information window and then use it to find out more about the cells in your worksheet. Remember that some of these cells were extensively changed by the AutoFormat command. By studying these changes, you will better understand how to control worksheet formatting without using AutoFormat.

To activate an information window:

1 Select cell A1.

2 Choose **Tools** and then **Options.**
The Options dialog box appears.

3 Click the **View** tab.

4 Make sure the Info Window option is checked, and then select **OK.**
A new window will appear. If the workbook was maximized prior to this, the new information window will completely cover the worksheet window, as shown in Figure 3.22; otherwise, a small information window will appear on top of the worksheet window. Notice that a different menu appears on the menu bar: this is because an information window is not a worksheet, and a different set of commands applies.

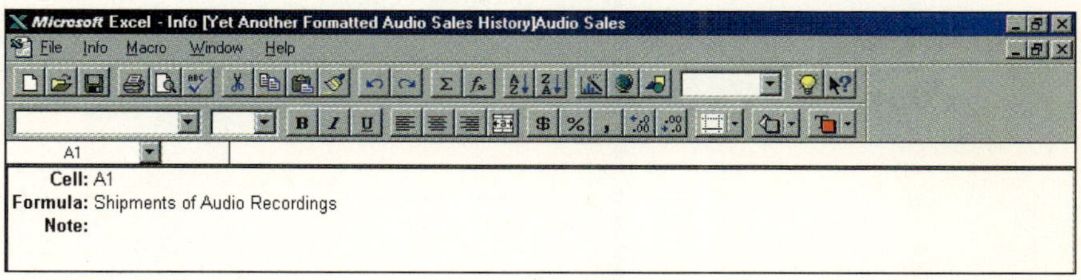

Figure 3.22

Switching Between Windows

If several windows are visible on the screen at once, you can make a particular window active by clicking anywhere in that window. The active window will appear with a darker title bar. You can also use the list in the Window menu to choose a window by name; the names of currently open windows are included in the Window menu.

To switch between windows using the Window menu:

1 Activate the audio sales workbook window by opening the **Window** menu and choosing **Yet Another Formatted Audio Sales History.** Note that the workbook name may be partly cut off in the menu.
The information window seems to disappear, but it is just underneath the workbook window.

2 To reactivate the information window, open the **Window** menu and choose **Info [Yet Another Formatted Audio Sales History].**

Arranging Multiple Windows

For you to use the information window effectively, both it and the worksheet window must be visible at the same time. One way to achieve this is to ***tile*** the windows; doing so places them side by side rather than one on top of the other. In the following steps, you will tile the two windows and then decrease the width of the information window to make more room for the worksheet window.

To arrange windows:

1 Choose **Window** and then **Arrange.**
The Arrange Windows dialog box appears.

2 Select **Tiled,** and then select **OK.**
The two windows are now tiled.

3 Select the information window by clicking it.

4 Decrease the width of the information window slightly by dragging its sizing border.

5 Select the worksheet window and increase its width, as shown in Figure 3.23.

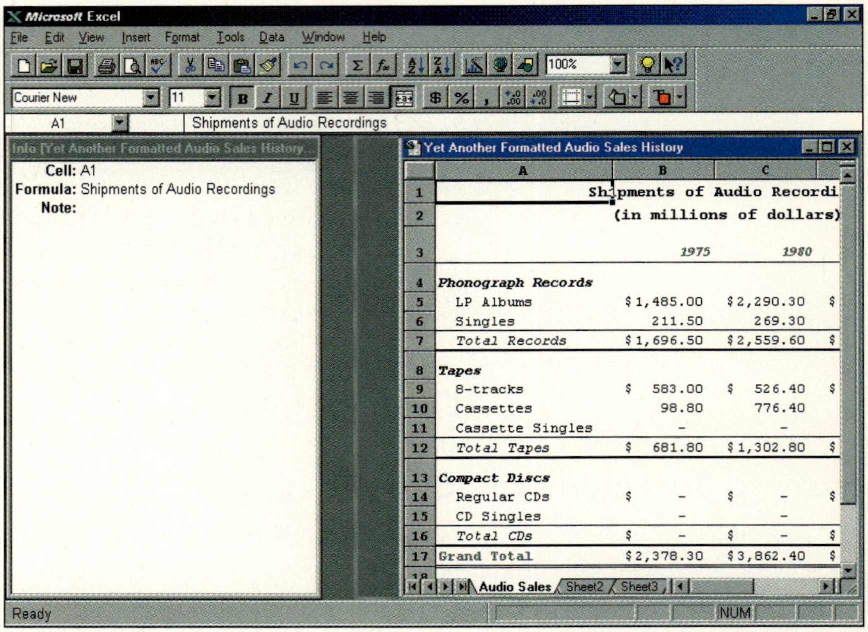

Figure 3.23

Setting Up an Information Window

The standard display of an information window is not very informative. You can control what information about a cell is shown. In the following steps, you will instruct the information window to provide more details about a cell.

To set up an information window:

1 Activate the information window.

2 Choose **Info** and then **Value.**
Notice that Cell, Formula, and Note are already checked in the menu.

3 Choose **Info** and then **Format.**
Cell, Formula, Value, Format, and Note should all be checked.

4 Select the worksheet window.

5 Select cell G1.
Observe the information window. It should appear similar to Figure 3.24.

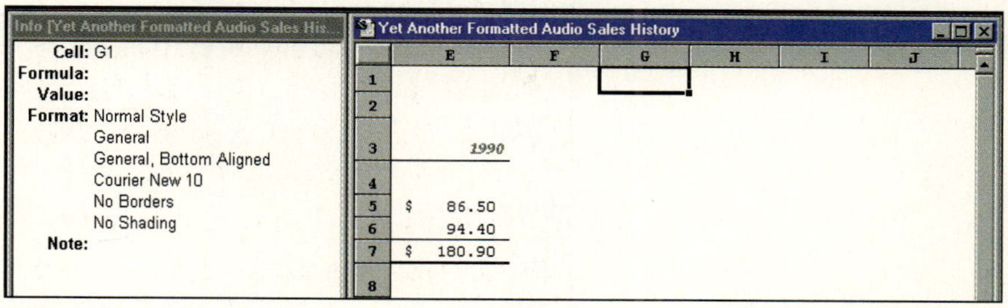

Figure 3.24

Using Information Windows to Examine Styles and Formats

The information window indicates that the active cell is G1; nothing appears next to Formula and Value because cell G1 is blank. The first line of the Format section reads *Normal Style.* This tells you that the Normal style applies to this cell. The subsequent lines provide details on what specifications of the Normal style apply. Because this cell was not included in the AutoFormat range, it has only the basic formatting attributes of the Normal style (without any additions or modifications).

General means the General Number format applies; this format does not include any special punctuation for numerical values.

General, Bottom Aligned describes the horizontal and vertical ***alignment*** of information in a cell. The horizontal alignment is *General;* this will cause numbers (and the results of formulas) to appear aligned right in their cells, and text to appear aligned left. The vertical alignment is *Bottom Aligned,* meaning that a cell's contents will appear to "sit" on the bottom edge of the cell.

Courier New 10 refers to the font—10-point Courier New. You will recall that earlier in this project you changed the font for Normal style to Courier New.

No Borders means no border lines will appear for this cell.

No Shading means no shading will be used in the cell.

To see information on cell A1:

1 Select cell A1.

2 Observe the information window; it will be similar to Figure 3.25.

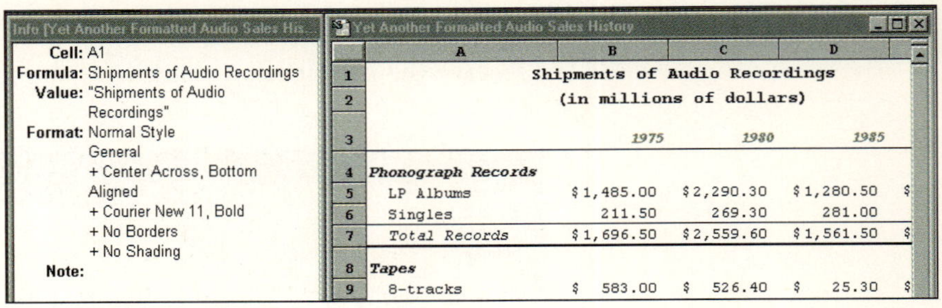

Figure 3.25

The Formula line shows what was literally typed into the cell (similar to what you would see in the formula bar); the Value line indicates, in the case of formulas, what the result of the formula is. The quotation marks around *Shipments of Audio Recordings* serve to remind you that this is a *text* entry.

The Format section indicates that the Normal style applies to this cell; certain aspects of this style still apply, but others have been overridden. The Format section of an information window will first name the style that applies to the cell, list the aspects of the style that have *not* changed (if any), and then list the formats that preempt those originally specified in the style. These overriding formats are preceded by a plus sign.

You may have noticed that some of the overriding formats (such as *No Shading*) do not differ from those in the original Normal style. These are still considered to be overriding because they were set specifically by the AutoFormat command.

The definition of the Normal style has not changed; rather, some cells in the worksheet have been given customized formats that take precedence over the formats indicated in the Normal style. If you were to change the definition of the Normal style—for example, if you changed the font specified in the style—the change would affect any cell to which the Normal style had been applied, provided that an overriding format had not been applied to the cell.

In this worksheet, if you redefined the Normal style to use the font Times New Roman 12, cell A5 would reflect the change, but not cell A4. Examine both of these cells (A4 and A5) in the information window to make sure you understand why a redefinition of the Normal style would affect cell A5 but not cell A4.

To see information on cell B7:

1 Select the cell that contains total records for 1975 (B7).
Note that the cell's literal contents are =B5+B6, as indicated on the Formula line of the information window. The *value* of the cell is the result of this formula, 1696.5. Do not be alarmed by the strange-looking number format. Examine other cells with the information window.

2 Close the information window by selecting it and then clicking its Close window button.

3 Maximize the workbook window.

CUSTOMIZING TOOLBARS

Suppose that you frequently made use of information windows and wanted to avoid having to repeatedly use the Options dialog box. You could keep the Auditing toolbar open most of the time—it contains a button, called the Show Info Window tool, that creates information windows. But if you didn't want the extra screen space used up by the entire Auditing toolbar, you could add just the Show Info Window tool to one of the toolbars already on the screen.

Excel allows you to customize toolbars—to decide which tools you want to display on any toolbar. You do this graphically by dragging the desired tool from the Customize dialog box to the toolbar you want to contain the tool. You can remove a tool from a toolbar by dragging it from the toolbar to the Customize dialog box.

The Customize dialog box groups the dozens of available tools by category. For example, the Show Info Window tool is in the Auditing category. You may need to examine several different categories before you find the particular tool you want to add to a toolbar.

In the steps that follow, you will customize the Standard toolbar by removing the Drawing button and adding the Show Info Window tool.

To customize a toolbar:

1 Choose **View** and then **Toolbars.**
The Toolbars dialog box appears.

2 Select **Customize.**
The Customize dialog box appears.

3 Click the **Drawing** tool on the Standard toolbar, drag its outline into the Customize dialog box (as shown in Figure 3.26), and then release the mouse button.
The Drawing tool is removed from the Standard toolbar.

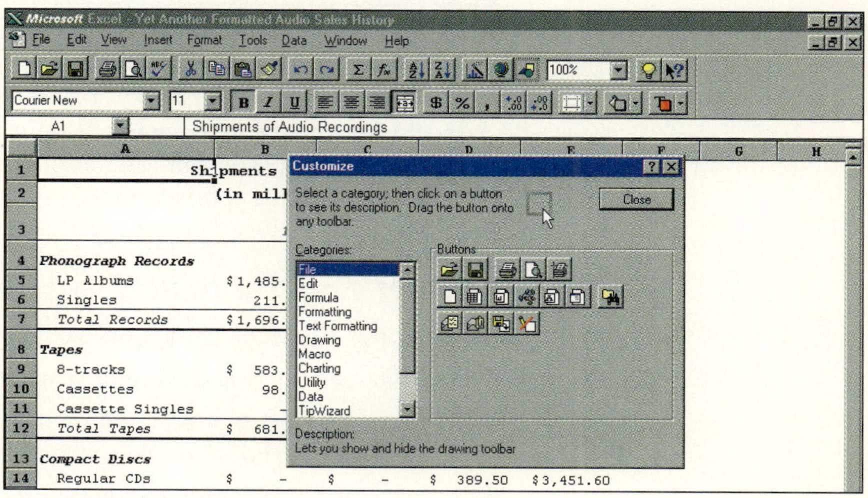

Figure 3.26

4 Scroll down the list of tool categories, and click the **Auditing** category.

This category contains the same set of buttons and tools that are on the Auditing toolbar.

5 Click the **Show Info Window** tool, as shown in Figure 3.27.
A description of the tool appears in the Customize dialog box.

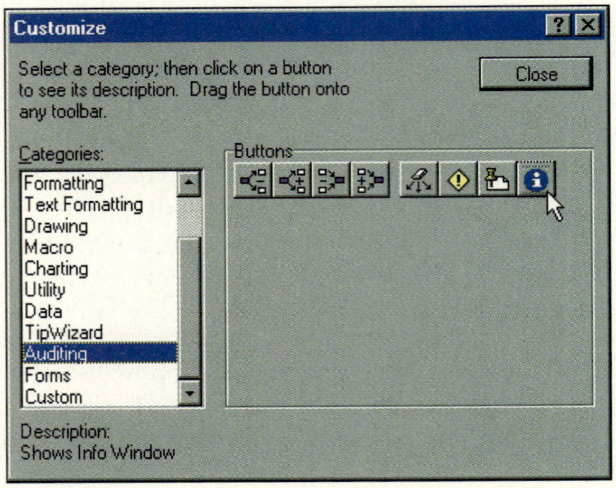

Figure 3.27

6 Drag the tool to the Standard toolbar so that it is placed where the Drawing tool used to be.

7 Select **Close.**
The Standard toolbar is now customized, as shown in Figure 3.28.

Figure 3.28

In the steps that follow, you will return the Standard toolbar to its default set of tools. You can reset a toolbar by opening the Toolbars dialog box, making sure the toolbar name is selected and checked in the list, and then selecting the Reset button.

To reset a toolbar to its default tools:

1 Choose **View** and then **Toolbars.**

2 Make sure the Standard toolbar is selected (highlighted) *and* checked.

3 Select the **Reset** button, and then select **OK.**
Notice that the Standard toolbar reverts to its default collection of tools.

4 Exit Excel, saving the workbook if necessary.

For many Excel operations, the most convenient access method is through a toolbar tool. You should feel free to customize toolbars to suit your particular needs as you work with Excel.

Tips You can create a fully customized toolbar with a name of your choice by choosing Toolbars from the View menu, double-clicking in the Toolbar Name box, typing a name, and then selecting OK. A floating toolbar will appear along with the Customize dialog box. You can then drag whatever tools you want to the new toolbar.

For Power Users Files of the form username.XLB, normally stored in the Windows subdirectory, contain the most recently saved toolbar settings for each user, including any customized toolbars the user may have created. If you want to guarantee that Excel reverts to all its original toolbar settings, you can delete your .XLB file before starting Excel. You can also rename the file (preserving the .XLB extension) and open it later, using the Open command from the File menu in Excel, to activate an .XLB file's particular toolbar settings. Placing the file in the XLSTART subdirectory will cause the file to automatically open whenever Excel is started. When browsing for .XLB files, remember that the file type is registered with Windows and the extension normally does not display (an Excel workbook icon is associated with an .XLB file).

The Next Step

You are now ready to build a larger and more powerful worksheet. With the insight you have gained about formatting, you will be able to begin taking direct control over the formatting of your worksheets because, as you have seen, AutoFormat won't always do what you want it to.

In the next project, you will build and format a worksheet on energy conservation that estimates the electricity used by a household and allows you to identify high-energy-cost appliances.

This concludes Project 3. You can either exit Excel or go on to work the Study Questions, Review Exercises, and Assignments.

Summary and Exercises

Summary

- When you make major additions or changes to a worksheet, you must consider the effect those changes might have on existing parts of the worksheet—especially formulas.
- A formula's precedents are those cells on which the formula depends; a cell's dependents are other cells containing formulas that refer to that cell.
- You can insert blank cells into a worksheet, shifting existing cells to make room. However, if you do this, formulas do not always automatically adjust the way you might want them to.
- A circular-reference error occurs when a cell either directly or indirectly refers to itself.
- Clearing a range of cells erases the contents of the cells but does not

remove the cells from the worksheet. Deleting removes both the contents and the cells.

- You can center cell entries across multiple columns; this is especially useful for worksheet titles.
- Row height can be changed in a manner similar to that for changing column width.
- You can control whether cell gridlines appear on a printout or on the screen.
- A style is a named set of format attributes that can be applied to a cell to affect the cell's appearance. The default style is called *Normal.*
- TrueType fonts are preferable in most cases because their appearance on the screen and on printouts is nearly identical, and because they produce sharper type on printouts.
- Information windows are used to find out detailed information about a cell, including its contents, value, and format.
- Customized formats applied to a cell override corresponding formats specified in the cell's style.

Key Terms and Operations

Key Terms
alignment
circular reference
dependent
direct precedent
font
indirect precedent
information window
points
style
tile
tracer arrow

Operations
Arrange windows
Clear a cell or range
Insert a cell or range
Print a worksheet
Trace Dependents
Trace Precedents

Study Questions

Multiple Choice

1. The cells that a formula either directly or indirectly refers to are called its:
   a. descendants.
   b. ancestors.
   c. lineage.
   d. dependents.
   e. precedents.

2. Cells (containing formulas) that refer either directly or indirectly to a particular cell are called that cell's:
   a. referents.
   b. dependents.
   c. terminal nodes.
   d. signs.
   e. descendants.

3. Which statement about the Insert Cells command is correct?
   a. Any information present in the insert area is automatically cleared before the inserted text is added.
   b. The command will prompt you to type the text or numeric constants to be inserted.
   c. The command works only on cells containing formulas.
   d. Existing cells in the insertion range will be shifted to accommodate the inserted, blank cells.
   e. none of the above

4. The formula =SUM(B3:E3) is stored in cell E3. What (if anything) is the problem with the formula?
   a. It contains a circular reference and should probably be =SUM(B3:D3).
   b. It should be =SUM(B3+C3+D3+E3).
   c. It contains a circular reference and should probably be =SUM(E3:B3).
   d. It should be =B3+C3+D3+E3.
   e. Nothing is wrong with the formula.

5. What font technology, built into Windows, can usually improve the printed quality of worksheets?
   a. TrueType
   b. PostScript
   c. TypeTrue
   d. Linotype
   e. monotype

6. What menu command is used to arrange multiple windows?
   a. Window Sort
   b. Sort Window
   c. Edit Arrange
   d. Window Arrange
   e. Format Windows

7. What menu command can be used to change from one window to another?
   a. Options Goto
   b. Edit Window
   c. Window
   d. File Window
   e. only mouse and keyboard shortcuts are available for this action

8. What feature can be used to get detailed information on a particular cell?
   a. an information window
   b. the reference area
   c. the formula bar
   d. the Edit menu
   e. the Format menu

9. What term is used to describe a particular typeface design in Excel?
   a. style
   b. face
   c. font
   d. format
   e. regular

10. What command should be used to save a file under a new name?
   a. New in the File menu
   b. Save in the File menu
   c. Rename in the File menu
   d. Save As in the File menu
   e. Save As in the Edit menu

Short Answer

1. The formula =A1-A2+A3 is stored in cell A2. What (if anything) is wrong with the formula?
2. What mouse action or command is used to find the direct precedents of the currently selected cell?
3. Will centering text across columns change the cells where the text is stored? Will it break up the text and distribute the pieces to be stored in various cells?
4. List the formatting settings that can be included within a style.
5. Is inserting a blank row the best way to increase the space between rows of information in a worksheet? If not, what is a better way?
6. Are cell gridlines and border lines the same thing?
7. What font technology is usually the best choice for clear printouts?
8. What menu command is used to switch among multiple windows?
9. What kinds of information can be displayed in an information window?
10. What command is used to arrange multiple windows?

For Discussion

1. Why should you be careful when making major changes to a worksheet? What things should you do before you make a change? What should you check after the change?
2. What is a circular reference? Give an example.
3. Describe what happens when a customized format is applied to a cell. How does this affect the corresponding formats specified in the cell's style?

Review Exercises

Municipal Waste Trends

In the first review exercise in Project 2, you built a workbook about municipal waste and saved it under the name Proj 2 Ex 1 Municipal Waste Trends. If you haven't already created that worksheet, refer to Project 2 to build it. Then add the new information shown in Figure 3.29 for metals in the nonfood wastes category.

	A	B	C	D	E	F
1		1960	1970	1980	1990	
2	Nonfood Wastes					
3	Paper	0.91	1.19	1.32	1.6	
4	Glass	0.2	0.34	0.36	0.28	
5	Plastics	0.01	0.08	0.19	0.32	
6	Metals	0.32	0.38	0.35	0.34	
7	Total Nonfood	1.44	1.99	2.22	2.54	
8	Other					
9	Food	0.37	0.34	0.32	0.29	
10	Yard	0.61	0.62	0.66	0.7	
11	Total Other	0.98	0.96	0.98	0.99	
12	Grand Total	2.42	2.95	3.2	3.53	
13						

Figure 3.29

Use the Insert command to create a blank row for this new information; the information should be between the rows for plastics and total nonfood. Check, adjust, and copy formulas as necessary. Format the worksheet using AutoFormat with a nonaccounting table format. Additional opportunity for numeric formatting will be possible after you complete the next project. Save the workbook under the name *Proj 3 Ex 1 Municipal Waste Trends.*

Winter Olympic Medals

In the second review exercise in Project 2, you built and saved Proj 2 Ex 2 Winter Olympic Medals, a workbook that tabulates medals won by selected countries during the 1992 Winter Olympic Games. If you haven't already created that workbook, refer to Project 2 to build it.

Use the information shown in Figure 3.30 to add Italy to the worksheet. Use the Insert command to create a blank row for this new information; Italy should be the last country in the list. Check, adjust, and copy formulas as necessary. Format the worksheet using AutoFormat with a nonfinancial table format. Additional opportunities for numeric formatting will be possible after you complete the next project. Save the workbook under the name *Proj 3 Ex 2 Winter Olympic Medals.*

	A	B	C	D	E	F
1	1992 Winter Olympiad					
2						
3	Country	Gold	Silver	Bronze	Total	
4	Germany	10	10	6	26	
5	Unified Team	9	6	8	23	
6	Austria	6	7	8	21	
7	Norway	9	6	5	20	
8	Italy	4	6	4	?	
9	Total	?	?	?	?	
10						

Figure 3.30

Assignments

Space Payloads

In the third assignment in Project 2, you built and saved Proj 2 Asn 3 Space Payloads, a workbook that tabulates rocket payloads put into space by selected countries. If you haven't already created that workbook, refer to Project 2 to build it.

Add the information for the European Space Agency (ESA) as shown in Figure 3.31. Try using the Move command rather than Insert to make space for the new information. Adjust and copy formulas as necessary, change the standard font to a TrueType font of your choice, format the worksheet using AutoFormat and a nonaccounting table format, and save the workbook under the name *Proj 3 Asn 1 Space Payloads.*

	A	B	C	D	E	F	G
1	Space Payloads						
2							
3		1988	1989	1990	1991	Average	
4	USSR	107	95	96	101	99.75	
5	United States	15	22	31	30	24.5	
6	ESA	2	2	1	4	?	
7	Japan	2	4	7	2	3.75	
8	Total	126	123	135	137	130.25	
9							

Figure 3.31

Coffee House Income

Starting with the third assignment in Project 1 and continuing in the first assignment in Project 2, you built and saved Proj 2 Asn 1 Coffee House Income, a spreadsheet that calculates the income derived from sales of various coffees at Clem's Coffee Clutch. If you haven't already created that workbook, refer to Projects 1 and 2 to build it.

Add information for Café Royale, as shown in Figure 3.32. Adjust and copy formulas as necessary, change the standard font to a TrueType font of your choice, format the worksheet using AutoFormat, and save the workbook under the name *Proj 3 Asn 2 Coffee House Income.*

	A	B	C	D	E	F
1	Coffee	Cost	Selling Price	No. Sold	Income	
2	House Blend	0.39	0.95	60	33.6	
3	Espresso	0.61	1.25	12	7.68	
4	Cappuccino	0.74	1.5	22	16.72	
5	Café Mocha	0.55	1.45	35	31.5	
6	Café Royale	0.68	1.85	55	?	
7	Total			184	89.5	
8						

Figure 3.32

Open an information window, set it to display values and formats, adjust the workbook and information windows in a tiled arrangement, and examine the format and style settings in the worksheet.

Additions to Audio Sales History

Modify the Audio Sales History worksheet to include data for 1991, as well as figures for shipments of music videos, as shown in Figure 3.33. After inserting the new information, adjust and copy formulas as necessary, reformat the worksheet, and save the workbook under the name *Proj 3 Asn 3 Audio Sales History.*

	A	B	C	D	E	F	G
1		Shipments of Audio Recordings					
2		(in millions of dollars)					
3		1975	1980	1985	1990	1991	
4	*Phonograph Records*						
5	LP Albums	$1,485.00	$2,290.30	$1,280.50	$ 86.50	$ 4.80	
6	Singles	211.50	269.30	281.00	94.40	22.00	
7	*Total Records*	$1,696.50	$2,559.60	$1,561.50	$ 180.90	$ 26.80	
8	*Tapes*						
9	8-tracks	$ 583.00	$ 526.40	$ 25.30	$ -	$ -	
10	Cassettes	98.80	776.40	2,411.50	3,472.40	360.10	
11	Cassette Singles	-	-	-	87.40	69.00	
12	*Total Tapes*	$ 681.80	$1,302.80	$2,436.80	$3,559.80	$429.10	
13	*Compact Discs*						
14	Regular CDs	$ -	$ -	$ 389.50	$3,451.60	$333.30	
15	CD Singles	-	-	-	6.00	5.70	
16	*Total CDs*	$ -	$ -	$ 389.50	$3,457.60	$339.00	
17	*Videos*						
18	*Music Videos*	$ -	$ -	$ -	$ 9.20	$ 6.10	
19	*Grand Total*	$2,378.30	$3,862.40	$4,387.80	$7,207.50	$801.00	
20							

Figure 3.33

PROJECT 4: USING FORMULAS IN A WORKSHEET

Objectives

After completing this project, you should be able to:

- Create customized numeric formats
- Magnify or reduce your view of a worksheet
- Change the alignment of cell entries
- Define and use names for constants and ranges
- Copy to nonadjacent selections
- Recognize and use absolute cell references
- Change the font style and size of a cell entry
- Apply borders to the worksheet
- Produce landscape printouts

CASE STUDY: ANALYZING HOME ENERGY USAGE

One way to decide how to save on home-electric bills—and reduce electricity consumption and related power-plant pollution—is to determine how each electrical appliance in your home or apartment contributes to your total monthly bill. Along with your personal electricity-usage patterns, many other factors, such as season, climate, and the availability of alternative energy sources, will influence the total bill. Excel is the ideal tool for making sense of these variables and simplifying the task of estimating electricity consumption.

Designing the Solution

In this project, you will build a worksheet that lists various electrical appliances and estimates their monthly consumption of electricity. The worksheet will describe a basic, all-electric home during a mild winter month in a moderate climate. Constructing this worksheet will involve calculating the monthly energy used by each appliance, a calculation based on each appliance's energy-consumption rate and the amount of time the appliance is used during a month.

There are several ways you could design a worksheet to implement this calculation. You could construct one giant formula to perform all calculations on all variables, but the worksheet will be easier to understand and modify if you break the process into smaller steps comprising a series of simpler formulas. This is the approach you will take in this project.

Figure 4.1 shows the completed worksheet. Separate columns designate each of the major variables involved in the calculation. The flexibility of this electronic worksheet will make easy experimentation and adaptation possible with variables such as different appliances and different electricity-usage habits.

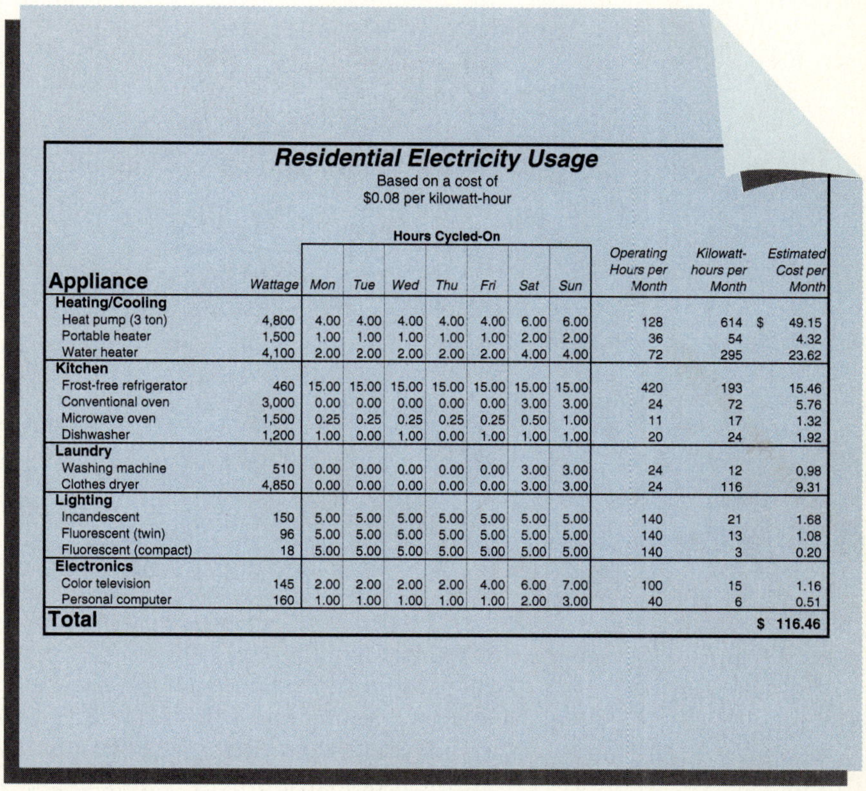

Residential Electricity Usage
Based on a cost of
$0.08 per kilowatt-hour

Appliance	Wattage	Hours Cycled-On Mon	Tue	Wed	Thu	Fri	Sat	Sun	Operating Hours per Month	Kilowatt-hours per Month	Estimated Cost per Month
Heating/Cooling											
Heat pump (3 ton)	4,800	4.00	4.00	4.00	4.00	4.00	6.00	6.00	128	614	$ 49.15
Portable heater	1,500	1.00	1.00	1.00	1.00	1.00	2.00	2.00	36	54	4.32
Water heater	4,100	2.00	2.00	2.00	2.00	2.00	4.00	4.00	72	295	23.62
Kitchen											
Frost-free refrigerator	460	15.00	15.00	15.00	15.00	15.00	15.00	15.00	420	193	15.46
Conventional oven	3,000	0.00	0.00	0.00	0.00	0.00	3.00	3.00	24	72	5.76
Microwave oven	1,500	0.25	0.25	0.25	0.25	0.25	0.50	1.00	11	17	1.32
Dishwasher	1,200	1.00	0.00	1.00	0.00	1.00	1.00	1.00	20	24	1.92
Laundry											
Washing machine	510	0.00	0.00	0.00	0.00	0.00	3.00	3.00	24	12	0.98
Clothes dryer	4,850	0.00	0.00	0.00	0.00	0.00	3.00	3.00	24	116	9.31
Lighting											
Incandescent	150	5.00	5.00	5.00	5.00	5.00	5.00	5.00	140	21	1.68
Fluorescent (twin)	96	5.00	5.00	5.00	5.00	5.00	5.00	5.00	140	13	1.08
Fluorescent (compact)	18	5.00	5.00	5.00	5.00	5.00	5.00	5.00	140	3	0.20
Electronics											
Color television	145	2.00	2.00	2.00	2.00	4.00	6.00	7.00	100	15	1.16
Personal computer	160	1.00	1.00	1.00	1.00	1.00	2.00	3.00	40	6	0.51
Total											**$ 116.46**

Figure 4.1

ENTERING THE WORKSHEET CONSTANTS

You will first enter some of the worksheet titles and number constants. You will do some formatting early so as to make subsequent data entry and formula construction easier to follow. You can refer to Figure 4.2 to see a partial, unformatted version of the worksheet. As in the previous project, the more intricate formatting steps will be completed in the final phase of worksheet construction.

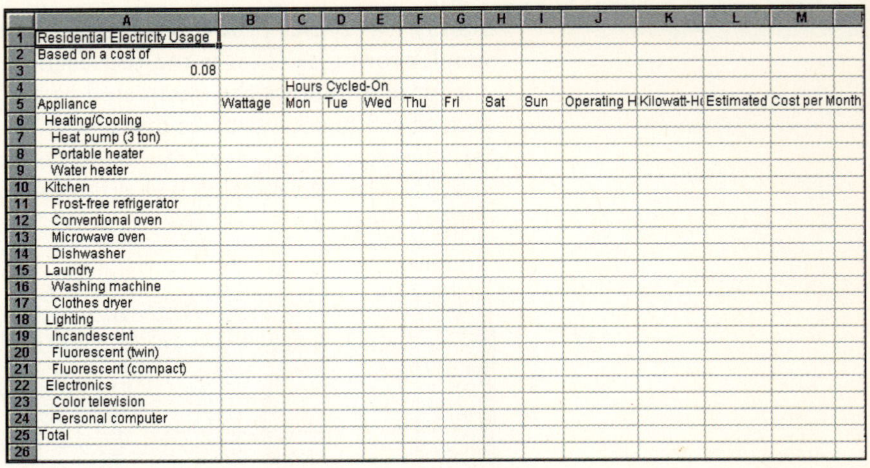

	A	B	C	D	E	F	G	H	I	J	K	L	M
1	Residential Electricity Usage												
2	Based on a cost of												
3	0.08												
4			Hours Cycled-On										
5	Appliance	Wattage	Mon	Tue	Wed	Thu	Fri	Sat	Sun	Operating H	Kilowatt-H	Estimated Cost per Month	
6	Heating/Cooling												
7	Heat pump (3 ton)												
8	Portable heater												
9	Water heater												
10	Kitchen												
11	Frost-free refrigerator												
12	Conventional oven												
13	Microwave oven												
14	Dishwasher												
15	Laundry												
16	Washing machine												
17	Clothes dryer												
18	Lighting												
19	Incandescent												
20	Fluorescent (twin)												
21	Fluorescent (compact)												
22	Electronics												
23	Color television												
24	Personal computer												
25	Total												
26													

Figure 4.2

To enter the main title and first subtitle:

1 Open a new workbook, select the **Sheet1** tab, and ensure that the font of the Normal style is Arial 10.

2 Enter **`Residential Electricity Usage`** in cell A1.

3 Enter **`Based on a cost of`** in cell A2.

Creating Customized Formats

In Figure 4.1, the second subtitle, *$0.08 per kilowatt-hour*, might appear to be a text entry. If it *were* a text entry, formulas in the worksheet could not meaningfully refer to it when calculating. In fact, it is a numeric entry, 0.08, assigned a ***customized format.*** Any time you want to have a value appear in some form other than the standard formats available, you can create your own format. For example, you might want a special date format, a format designed to represent amounts in a foreign currency, or a format that includes an abbreviation for a special unit of measurement. For this worksheet, you will create a format that will display whatever number is typed in the cell, preceded by a dollar sign and followed by the phrase *per kilowatt-hour.*

To enter and custom-format the second subtitle:

1 Enter **`0.08`** in cell A3.

2 Make sure cell A3 is still selected; choose **Format** and then **Cells.**
The Format Cells dialog box appears.

3 Select the **Number** tab, if necessary.
The Number format tab is displayed.

4 Choose the **Custom** category.

5 Click in the **Type** edit box, and delete any text that is already present.
The Type edit box is where you can enter formatting codes to specify how you want numbers to appear.

6 Type the formatting code **`$0.00 "per kilowatt-hour"`** in the **Type** box.
Note the use of quotation marks. The screen should resemble Figure 4.3. The format code instructs Excel to display a value in cell A3 with a leading

dollar sign, show a leading zero before the decimal point for numbers less than one, always show two digits to the right of the decimal, and follow the number with the phrase *per kilowatt-hour*.

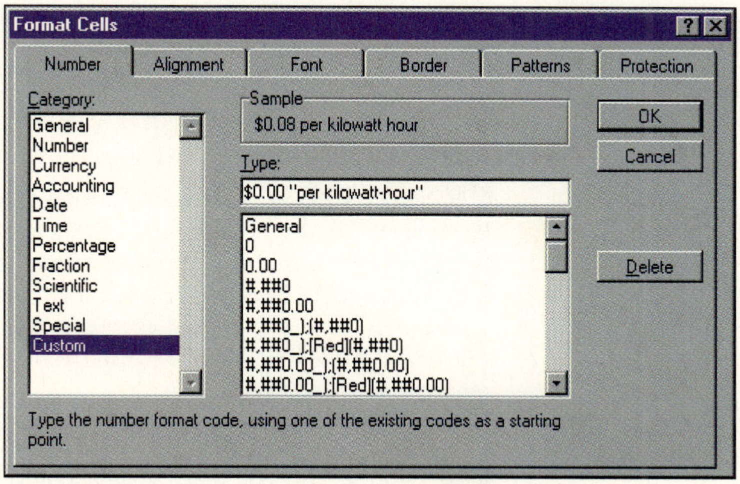

Figure 4.3

7 Select **OK** to complete the format specification.
Now you have assigned a customized format to cell A3. Number signs (#) appear in the cell, indicating that the column is too narrow to display the number 0.08 in the new format.

8 Widen column A to about 25 characters so that all three cell entries (A1, A2, and A3) are accommodated.
It is very important to recognize that for calculation purposes, cell A3 contains the *number* 0.08. Formatting affects the way a cell entry *appears* but does not change the value of the entry or its data type (text constant, number constant, or formula).

Changing the View of a Worksheet Window

At normal magnification, a worksheet is rarely visible in its entirety; the screen and the worksheet window restrict your view. Excel is capable of *zooming out* (reducing) or *zooming in* (magnifying) to let you see more or less of the worksheet.

Occasionally, you will zoom in for a closer look, but more often you will zoom out to see more of the worksheet at once. A disadvantage of zooming out is that because you see more of the worksheet in a reduced size, it is more difficult to position correctly on specific cells.

You can also change to ***full-screen view***, which temporarily removes the toolbars and status bar to allow more room for the worksheet itself. Switching to full-screen view does not in itself change the magnification of the worksheet though full-screen view can be used in conjunction with the Zoom command.

In the steps that follow, you will experiment with the Zoom and Full Screen commands.

To magnify a worksheet:

1 Open the **Zoom Control** list box on the Standard toolbar.
A list box opens, showing various magnifications.

2 Select **200%** in the **Zoom Control** list box.
Each worksheet cell appears much larger, but you can't see as many cells.

To reduce a worksheet:

1 Open the **Zoom Control** list box on the Standard toolbar.

2 Select **50%** in the **Zoom Control** list box.
You can see many more cells in the worksheet, but individual cells become more difficult to read. This is especially true when Windows is running with standard VGA video (rather than with SuperVGA).

To set a custom magnification:

1 Click the **50%,** which is currently displayed in the **Zoom Control** list box.

2 Type **85** for the magnification, and press ENTER

To return to 100% magnification:

1 Click the **Zoom Control.**

2 Select **100%** in the **Zoom Control** list box.

Tip If you want to magnify or reduce the worksheet so it accommodates a particular range of cells, select the range first, and then choose Selection from the Zoom Control list box.

The Zoom commands are also available by selecting Zoom from the View menu.

From now on, you should change your view of the worksheet whenever you want to.

To change to full-screen view:

1 Choose **View** and then **Full Screen.**
The toolbars, status bar, and Windows taskbar disappear, and more rows of the worksheet are visible. A single-tool floating toolbar also appears, called the Full Screen toolbar; if you select this tool, you can switch back to normal view. You will now close the toolbar so it does not clutter the screen.

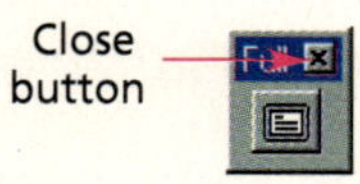

2 Click the Close window button of the floating toolbar to close the toolbar.
The toolbar disappears. You can always return to normal view by using the View menu. Excel will now remember your preference of not having the Full Screen toolbar appear in full-screen view.

3 Choose **View** and then **Full Screen.**
This "unchecks" the Full Screen option, returning the screen to normal view.

Using Series Fill

In the sections that follow, you will enter and partially format the column titles. To make it easier to see what you're typing, you will first zoom to a 75% magnification of the worksheet. As you work, you can refer to Figure 4.4.

You could manually enter the days of the week as the column headings in C5:I5, but Excel provides a shortcut called ***AutoFill*** that you can use when entering the days of the week or names of months. When you use the fill handle to copy information that represents part of a standard sequence or series, Excel automatically fills in the other members of the series. For example, if you use the fill handle to copy a cell that contains the text *Feb* and select a range three cells to the right, Excel will enter *Mar*, *Apr*, and *May*. If you don't want the series-fill effect to take place, hold down CTRL while dragging the fill handle (which will just copy the contents of the cell to all selected cells).

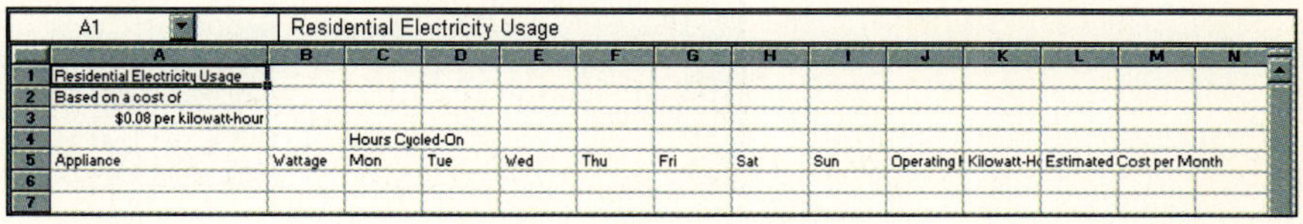

Figure 4.4

To enter the column titles:

1 Use the **Zoom Control** list box to reduce magnification of the worksheet to 75 percent.

2 Enter **`Appliance`** in cell A5.

3 Enter **`Wattage`** in cell B5.

4 Enter **`Mon`** in cell C5.

5 With cell C5 selected, position the pointer at the lower-right corner of the cell so the pointer forms the fill handle; drag the fill handle to cell I5 and release the mouse button.
The range now contains abbreviations for the days of the week, as shown in Figure 4.4.

6 In cell C4, *above* the column title *Mon*, enter **`Hours Cycled-On`**

7 In cell J5, enter **`Operating Hours per Month`**
This column is used to estimate how many hours per month an appliance is used. Do not be concerned if a column title or other cell entry appears either to spill over into a neighboring cell or to be cut off by a neighboring cell.

8 In cell K5, enter **`Kilowatt-hours per Month`**
Later you will construct a formula to calculate the number of kilowatt-hours used each month.

9 In cell L5, enter **`Estimated Cost per Month`**
This column will contain a formula that computes the electricity cost.

10 Press CTRL + HOME
The worksheet should resemble Figure 4.4.

Adjusting the Width of Multiple Columns

The columns for weekdays should be narrowed. Instead of setting each column width separately, you can adjust the width of a group of columns by selecting the group and then adjusting the width of any column in the group.

To adjust the width of a group of columns:

1 Select columns C through I by dragging across column headings C through I, and then release the mouse button.

2 Position the pointer on the *right* edge of any selected column heading. Using the width information provided in the reference area, drag the mouse to select a new width of about 5 characters, as shown in Figure 4.5.

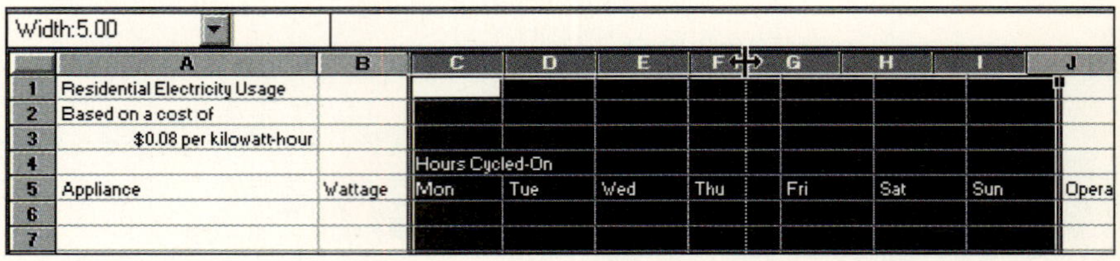

Figure 4.5

3 Release the mouse button.

Changing the Alignment of Cell Entries

A text entry is automatically aligned against the left edge of its cell, and a number entry against the right edge, but you can change this alignment. Text titles appearing above numeric entries will look better if they are aligned at the center or to the right.

Notice that Figure 4.1 shows the long column titles, such as *Operating Hours per Month*, wrapping in their cells. ***Wrapping*** means to break a long entry into separate lines.

In the steps that follow, you will align to the right the column titles *Wattage* through *Estimated Cost per Month* and specify that long entries be wrapped.

To align to the right and wrap selected column titles:

1 Select cell B5.

2 Select B5:L5, the range of text entries to be aligned.

3 Choose **Format** and then **Cells.**
The Format Cells dialog box appears.

4 Select the **Alignment** tab.
The Alignment tab appears.

5 Select the **Right** option button in the **Horizontal** group.

6 Select the **Wrap Text** check box if it is not already checked.
The screen should resemble Figure 4.6.

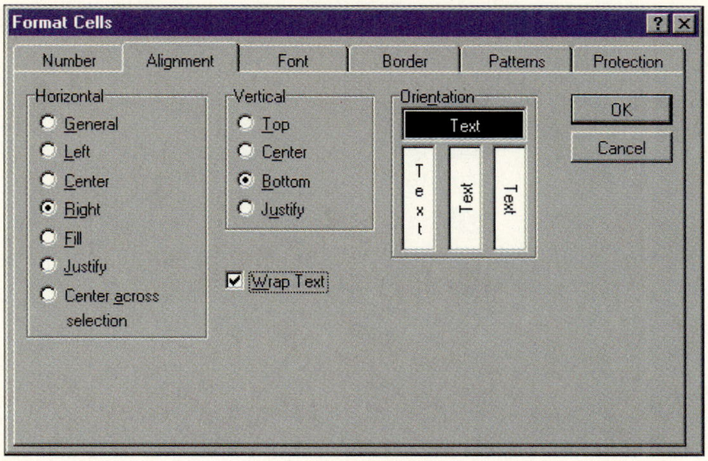

Figure 4.6

7 Select **OK** to complete the alignment.
The column headings should now be aligned to the right and, where necessary, wrap within their cells. Notice that wrapping automatically adjusted the height of row 5.

8 To make the worksheet look less cramped, increase the width of columns J, K, and L to about 10 characters.

Entering the Remaining Text Constants

In the following steps, you will enter the text constants for the row titles. Note that two levels of indentation are used for the row titles to visually outline the list of appliances. Section titles such as *Heating/Cooling* are indented two spaces, and individual appliance names, such as *Water heater*, are indented four spaces. You can use Figure 4.7 as a reference.

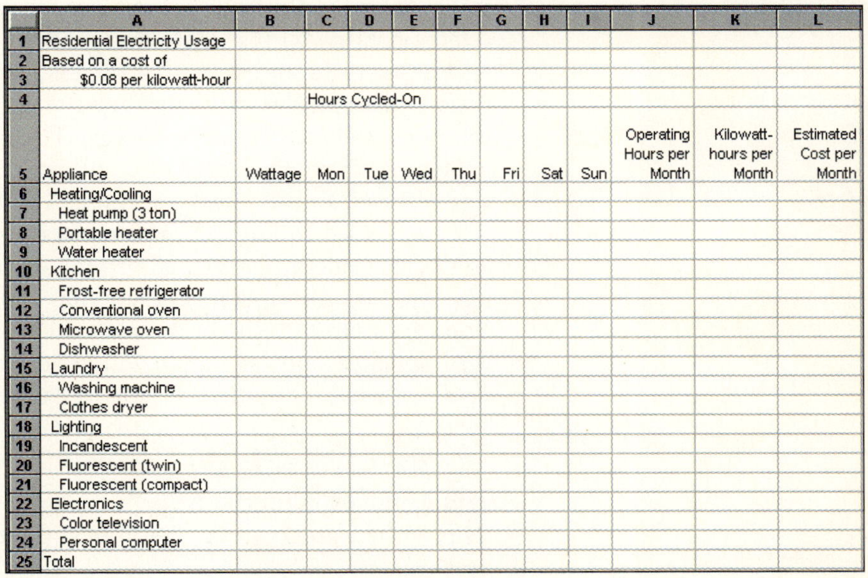

	A	B	C	D	E	F	G	H	I	J	K	L
1	Residential Electricity Usage											
2	Based on a cost of											
3	$0.08 per kilowatt-hour											
4			Hours Cycled-On									
5	Appliance	Wattage	Mon	Tue	Wed	Thu	Fri	Sat	Sun	Operating Hours per Month	Kilowatt-hours per Month	Estimated Cost per Month
6	Heating/Cooling											
7	Heat pump (3 ton)											
8	Portable heater											
9	Water heater											
10	Kitchen											
11	Frost-free refrigerator											
12	Conventional oven											
13	Microwave oven											
14	Dishwasher											
15	Laundry											
16	Washing machine											
17	Clothes dryer											
18	Lighting											
19	Incandescent											
20	Fluorescent (twin)											
21	Fluorescent (compact)											
22	Electronics											
23	Color television											
24	Personal computer											
25	Total											

Figure 4.7

To enter the row titles:

1 Select A1:L5, the entire functional area of the worksheet.

2 Click the **Zoom Control** list box, and choose **Selection** to fit the magnification to the selected range.

3 Select cell A6.

4 In cell A6, press (SPACE) twice, type **`Heating/Cooling`** and press (ENTER)

5 In cell A7, press (SPACE) four times, type **`Heat pump (3 ton)`** and press (ENTER)

6 Refer to Figure 4.7 to enter the remaining row titles.
Note that *Total* is not indented; *Kitchen*, *Laundry*, *Lighting*, and *Electronics* are indented by preceding the text with two spaces; and the remaining titles are indented four spaces.

7 Press (CTRL)+(HOME) and then choose **Tools** and then **Spelling** to check the spelling of the worksheet.

8 Save the workbook under the name **`Electricity Cost.`** The worksheet should resemble Figure 4.7.

Tip If you are building a worksheet that requires several levels of indentation, you can use separate columns for each indentation level rather than using spaces. Although this approach slightly increases the complexity of the worksheet, adjusting (via column-width changes) the amount of indentation for each level is much easier.

Entering the Number Constants

You will now enter the constants for wattage and hours cycled-on. Note that the numbers in the hours cycled-on section are ordinary decimal numbers: an hour and a half is written as 1.50, not 1:30. In the following steps, you will also learn a data-entry shortcut that allows you to fill a large selection easily with a single entry.

The first step in calculating the energy used by an appliance over the course of a month is to determine the appliance's power consumption, or the rate at which it uses up energy. The amount of electrical power an appliance consumes is measured in *watts*. A typical light bulb uses 100 watts; a typical microwave oven uses 1500 watts.

If you need to know how many watts an appliance uses, check the appliance's operating manual or look on the appliance itself. If watts are not listed on the appliance, then volts (V) and amps (A) will likely be listed. You can multiply volts by amps to calculate watts. Note that sometimes the appliance's power supply will list the maximum rated power consumption, not what the appliance actually uses under normal operating conditions.

To enter the appliance-wattage constants:

1 Enter **`4800`** in cell B7.
This is the wattage of the 3-ton heat pump.

2 Referring to Figure 4.1 or 4.8, carefully enter the remaining number constants for the wattage column *only*.

Reminder Because all punctuation is added through formatting, do not type commas in any of the numbers.

	A	B	C	D	E	F	G	H	I	J	K	L
1	Residential Electricity Usage											
2	Based on a cost of											
3	$0.08 per kilowatt-hour											
4			Hours Cycled-On									
5	Appliance	Wattage	Mon	Tue	Wed	Thu	Fri	Sat	Sun	Operating Hours per Month	Kilowatt-hours per Month	Estimated Cost per Month
6	Heating/Cooling											
7	Heat pump (3 ton)	4800	4	4	4	4	4	6	6			
8	Portable heater	1500	1	1	1	1	1	2	2			
9	Water heater	4100	2	2	2	2	2	4	4			
10	Kitchen											
11	Frost-free refrigerator	460	15	15	15	15	15	15	15			
12	Conventional oven	3000	0	0	0	0	0	3	3			
13	Microwave oven	1500	0.25	0.25	0.25	0.25	0.25	0.5	1			
14	Dishwasher	1200	1	0	1	0	1	1	1			
15	Laundry											
16	Washing machine	510	0	0	0	0	0	3	3			
17	Clothes dryer	4850	0	0	0	0	0	3	3			
18	Lighting											
19	Incandescent	150	5	5	5	5	5	5	5			
20	Fluorescent (twin)	96	5	5	5	5	5	5	5			
21	Fluorescent (compact)	18	5	5	5	5	5	5	5			
22	Electronics											
23	Color television	145	2	2	2	2	4	6	7			
24	Personal computer	160	1	1	1	1	1	2	3			
25	Total											

Figure 4.8

Your next step is to estimate how many hours per month the appliance is used. With many appliances, you can estimate how many hours the appliance runs each day of the week, total these times, and then approximate a month's worth of use by multiplying the total by four (since there are about four weeks in a month).

Notice in Figure 4.8 that all three types of lighting are estimated to run at five hours per day, every day of the week. Rather than using the Copy command or typing 5 in each of the 21 cells, you will use an alternative method for this type of repetitive entry.

To quickly enter the usage times for lighting:

1 Select C19:I21, the range encompassing hours cycled-on for each of the lighting types for all the days.

2 Type **5** and press CTRL+ENTER
The number *5* should be entered in all the cells of the selected range.

Other appliances vary in their consumption of electricity. For example, an air conditioner or oven consumes significant amounts of electricity, but only when actually in use. When calculating the hours cycled-on in your own home, you may need to refer to published approximations of typical running times for certain appliances.

To enter the remaining usage times:

1 Enter the remaining numbers for hours cycled-on. Use the various shortcut methods you've learned so far to do this quickly and easily.

2 Save the worksheet.
Your worksheet should now resemble Figure 4.8.

Electric bills are based on the number of hours each appliance runs, and the billing units are *kilowatt-hours*. A kilowatt is 1000 watts, and 1 kilowatt-hour is the energy consumed by running a 1000-watt appliance for 1 hour. If you run a 1000-watt hair dryer for 3 hours a month, you have consumed 3000 watt-hours or 3 kilowatt-hours of energy. The formula for energy consumption is generally written as (watts/1000) * hours. Remember to divide watts by 1000 when converting to kilowatts.

To estimate the monthly energy cost of an appliance, multiply the kilowatt-hours the appliance consumes by the cost per kilowatt-hour. With typical residential electric rates, electricity costs between $0.03 and $0.15 per kilowatt-hour. Check an electric bill or call your utility company to find out the rate for your area. The worksheet you build in this project will presume that electricity is billed at a flat rate.

You have already entered an electric rate of 8 cents ($0.08) per kilowatt-hour in cell A3. The monthly cost of the hair dryer mentioned earlier is 24 cents. As you can see in Figure 4.1, large appliances used for heating or cooling are the major consumers of electricity in the home.

Documenting Formulas

The total time an appliance is used in a month is calculated by multiplying a week's operating time by 4 because there are about four weeks in a month. For example, to compute the total monthly operating hours for the heat pump, the formula =SUM(C7:I7)*4 could be entered in cell J7. The SUM function computes a week's operating hours, and the result is then multiplied by 4.

It may seem that anyone examining the formula would understand that the 4 represents the four weeks in a month, but the 4 is a rather benign example of a *magic number*. Magic numbers are undocumented constants that show up in formulas. The problem with magic numbers is twofold. First, magic numbers carry little intrinsic meaning, so when people (even the worksheet's author) examine the worksheet long after it was first created, they may not understand the purpose of the number. Second, magic numbers buried within formulas make it harder to change the worksheet. For example, suppose you created and copied the formula just described and later wanted to use a more precise definition of a typical month as 4.345 weeks. You would have to first edit or rebuild the formula and then recopy it to replace the old formula.

Defining Names

One alternative to using magic numbers is to present such constants explicitly in the worksheet, in their own easily changed cells. This is an approach that you have already taken when you entered the information about the electric rate of $0.08 per kilowatt-hour. Excel offers another approach: defined names.

A ***defined name*** is a name you create that refers to other cells or to constants, such as the number of weeks per month. Each workbook has its own dictionary of defined names to which you can add or delete definitions.

In the following steps, you will define the name *WeeksPerMonth* to stand for 4. You will then use this name in the formulas for operating hours per month.

To define names for constants:

1 Choose **Insert** and then **Name.**

2 Choose **Define.**
The Define Name dialog box appears.

3 Type `WeeksPerMonth` in the **Names in Workbook** box, replacing any text that might have initially appeared in the box.
Remember to type the name with no spaces and with mixed uppercase and lowercase letters.

4 Type `4` in the box labeled **Refers to,** replacing any text that might have initially appeared in the box.

5 Select the **Add** button.
The dialog box should now resemble Figure 4.9. The newly defined name is added to the dictionary, which is listed under Names in Workbook. An equal sign is also automatically inserted.

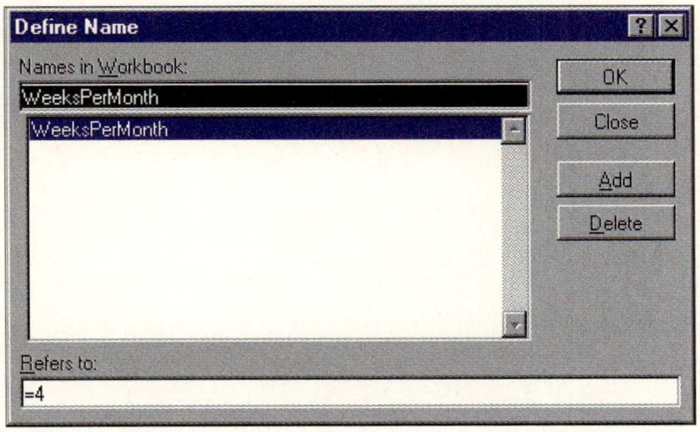

Figure 4.9

6 Select **OK** to close the dialog box.
Instead of typing the constant *4*, you can now use the name *WeeksPerMonth* in formulas within this worksheet.

Tip When you define a name, follow these guidelines:

- Make the name meaningful. Don't use names such as *X* or *N.* If a name refers to the marginal tax rate, then make the name *MarginalTaxRate,* not *X.*
- Make the name readable by mixing uppercase and lowercase letters: *MarginalTaxRate,* not *MARGINALTAXRATE.* You can also use underscores: *Marginal_Tax_Rate.*
- Use only letters, underscores, and numbers in a name; never use spaces; and don't make a name look like a cell address or formula. Excel will prevent you from creating invalid names, such as F16, B1, and Quarter-1, which are all ambiguous.

Using Names in Formulas

To use a defined name within a formula, you type the name as part of the formula. When computing the formula's result, Excel automatically refers to the dictionary and substitutes the name with its definition. In the following steps, you will build and copy a formula to compute the operating hours per month for each appliance.

To build the formula for operating hours per month:

1 Select cell J7, which will contain the operating hours per month for the heat pump.

2 Type **=sum(**

3 Using point mode, select the range to be summed, C7:I7, by selecting away from the formula (Sunday's through Monday's operating hours).

4 Type **)*WeeksPerMonth** and then press ENTER

The formula reads =SUM(C7:I7)*WeeksPerMonth, and it means "total the seven cells to the left and multiply the total by WeeksPerMonth." The formula's relative addressing will work when you copy the formula to the other cells in the column.

The result of this formula is 128. If you want to change the value of WeeksPerMonth, you can do so in the Define Name dialog box. The change would then be reflected in every formula that uses the name *WeeksPerMonth*.

Copying to Nonadjacent Selections

The formula you just completed needs to be copied to calculate operating hours per month for the other appliances. The fill handle could be used in a single step to copy the formula; however, this would leave copies in certain cells that should be blank (J10, for example). In the following steps, you will copy the formula to a nonadjacent selection—only those cells that should receive the copy.

To copy to a nonadjacent selection:

1 Select cell J7, which contains the formula to be copied.

2 Click the **Copy** tool from the Standard toolbar.

3 Hold down CTRL while dragging to select the ranges of cells that should receive the copy: J8:J9, J11:J14, J16:J17, J19:J21, and J23:J24, as shown in Figure 4.10.

	A	B	C	D	E	F	G	H	I	J	K	L
1	Residential Electricity Usage											
2	Based on a cost of											
3	$0.08 per kilowatt-hour											
4			Hours Cycled-On									
5	Appliance	Wattage	Mon	Tue	Wed	Thu	Fri	Sat	Sun	Operating Hours per Month	Kilowatt-hours per Month	Estimated Cost per Month
6	Heating/Cooling											
7	Heat pump (3 ton)	4800	4	4	4	4	4	6	6	128		
8	Portable heater	1500	1	1	1	1	1	2	2			
9	Water heater	4100	2	2	2	2	2	4	4			
10	Kitchen											
11	Frost-free refrigerator	460	15	15	15	15	15	15	15			
12	Conventional oven	3000	0	0	0	0	0	3	3			
13	Microwave oven	1500	0.25	0.25	0.25	0.25	0.25	0.5	1			
14	Dishwasher	1200	1	0	1	0	1	1	1			
15	Laundry											
16	Washing machine	510	0	0	0	0	0	3	3			
17	Clothes dryer	4850	0	0	0	0	0	3	3			
18	Lighting											
19	Incandescent	150	5	5	5	5	5	5	5			
20	Fluorescent (twin)	96	5	5	5	5	5	5	5			
21	Fluorescent (compact)	18	5	5	5	5	5	5	5			
22	Electronics											
23	Color television	145	2	2	2	2	4	6	7			
24	Personal computer	160	1	1	1	1	1	2	3			
25	Total											

Figure 4.10

4 Press (ENTER) to paste the formula into the selected cells.

Calculating Kilowatt-hours per Month

The kilowatt-hours of energy used by an appliance in a month are the number of kilowatts it consumes multiplied by the number of hours it is cycled-on.

To build the formula for kilowatt-hours per month:

1 Select cell K7, which will contain kilowatt-hours per month for the heat pump.

2 Type **=(**

3 Select the wattage for this appliance, in cell B7.

4 Type **/1000)***

5 Select the operating hours per month for this appliance, in cell J7.

6 Press (ENTER) to complete the formula.
The result of the formula is 614.4. This formula's relative addressing will work when the formula is copied to other cells. The completed formula, =(B7/1000)*J7, can be interpreted as "Take what is nine cells to the left, divide it by 1000, and multiply that result by what is one cell to the left."

7 Copy the completed formula to the cells in column K that should contain the formula.

The parentheses inserted in this formula are not required by the rules of operator priority, nor do they affect the result of the formula. They are used to help convey the logic of the computation to people who might later examine the formula.

Computing Estimated Cost per Month

The final column will compute the monthly cost of operating each appliance. This value is calculated by multiplying the cost per kilowatt-hour (currently 0.08, in cell A3) by the kilowatt-hours calculated for each appliance in column K.

Follow the next steps carefully. You will first change the view of the worksheet and then, to illustrate a common error, you will build a formula that is mathematically correct but does not work when copied to other cells. Later, you will correct the formula and copy it again.

To change the view of the worksheet:

1 Press (CTRL)+(HOME) then choose **View** and then **Full Screen.** Close the floating Full Screen toolbar if it appears.
The toolbars and status bar disappear. You will need the Standard toolbar for quick adjustment of magnification and access to the Copy tool, and you will need the Auditing toolbar to analyze formulas.

2 Choose **View** and then **Toolbars,** select the Standard and Auditing toolbars, and then select **OK.**

3 Drag the Auditing toolbar toward the upper-right corner of the worksheet window so that the toolbar is positioned above blank cells but does not cover the column headings, as shown in Figure 4.11.

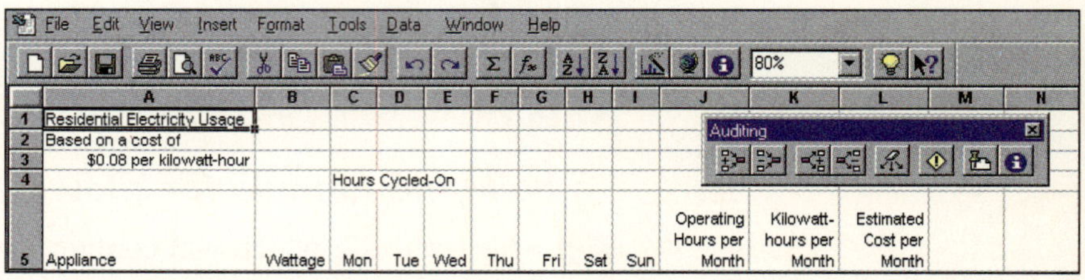

Figure 4.11

4 Choose **View** and then **Formula Bar.**
The Formula bar appears.

5 Select the range A1:L25, the entire area of the worksheet that is needed. *Make sure column L is included in the selection.*

6 Click the **Zoom Control** list box, and choose **Selection** to fit the magnification to the selected range.
The screen should resemble Figure 4.12.

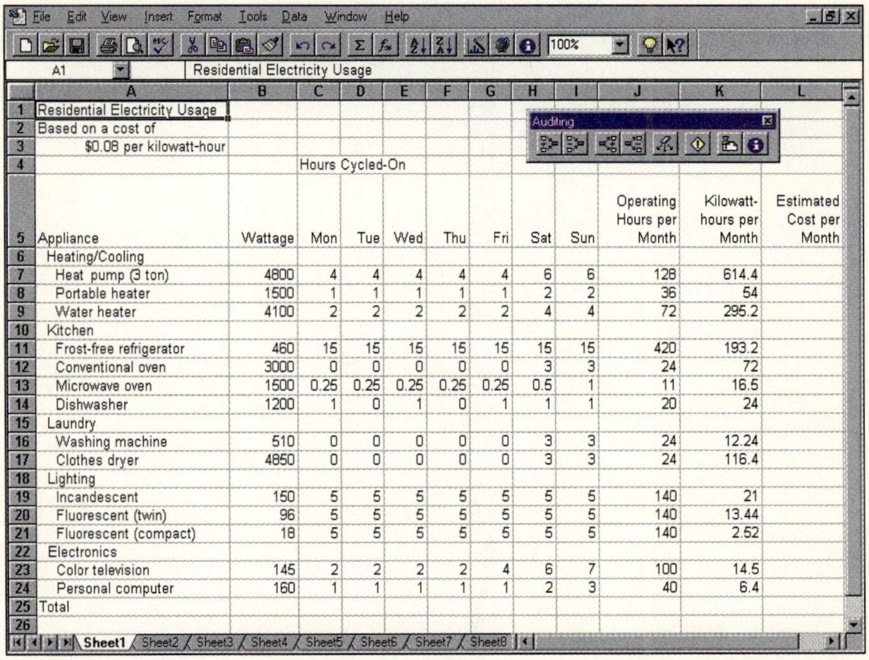

	A	B	C	D	E	F	G	H	I	J	K	L
1	Residential Electricity Usage											
2	Based on a cost of											
3	$0.08 per kilowatt-hour											
4			Hours Cycled-On									
5	Appliance	Wattage	Mon	Tue	Wed	Thu	Fri	Sat	Sun	Operating Hours per Month	Kilowatt-hours per Month	Estimated Cost per Month
6	Heating/Cooling											
7	Heat pump (3 ton)	4800	4	4	4	4	4	6	6	128	614.4	
8	Portable heater	1500	1	1	1	1	1	2	2	36	54	
9	Water heater	4100	2	2	2	2	2	4	4	72	295.2	
10	Kitchen											
11	Frost-free refrigerator	460	15	15	15	15	15	15	15	420	193.2	
12	Conventional oven	3000	0	0	0	0	0	3	3	24	72	
13	Microwave oven	1500	0.25	0.25	0.25	0.25	0.25	0.5	1	11	16.5	
14	Dishwasher	1200	1	0	1	0	1	1	1	20	24	
15	Laundry											
16	Washing machine	510	0	0	0	0	0	3	3	24	12.24	
17	Clothes dryer	4850	0	0	0	0	0	3	3	24	116.4	
18	Lighting											
19	Incandescent	150	5	5	5	5	5	5	5	140	21	
20	Fluorescent (twin)	96	5	5	5	5	5	5	5	140	13.44	
21	Fluorescent (compact)	18	5	5	5	5	5	5	5	140	2.52	
22	Electronics											
23	Color television	145	2	2	2	2	4	6	7	100	14.5	
24	Personal computer	160	1	1	1	1	1	2	3	40	6.4	
25	Total											
26												

Figure 4.12

Reminder The cost per month is the cost per kilowatt-hour multiplied by the number of kilowatt-hours used in a month.

To build the formula for estimated cost per month (first attempt):

1 Select cell L7, which will contain the estimated cost per month of the heat pump.

2 Type =

3 Select the cost per kilowatt-hour, in cell A3.

4 Type *

5 Select the number of kilowatt-hours used, in cell K7.

6 Press (ENTER)
The completed formula reads =A3*K7.

7 Using the skills you learned earlier for copying to nonadjacent selections, copy this formula to the other cells that require it in column L.
The worksheet should now resemble Figure 4.13.

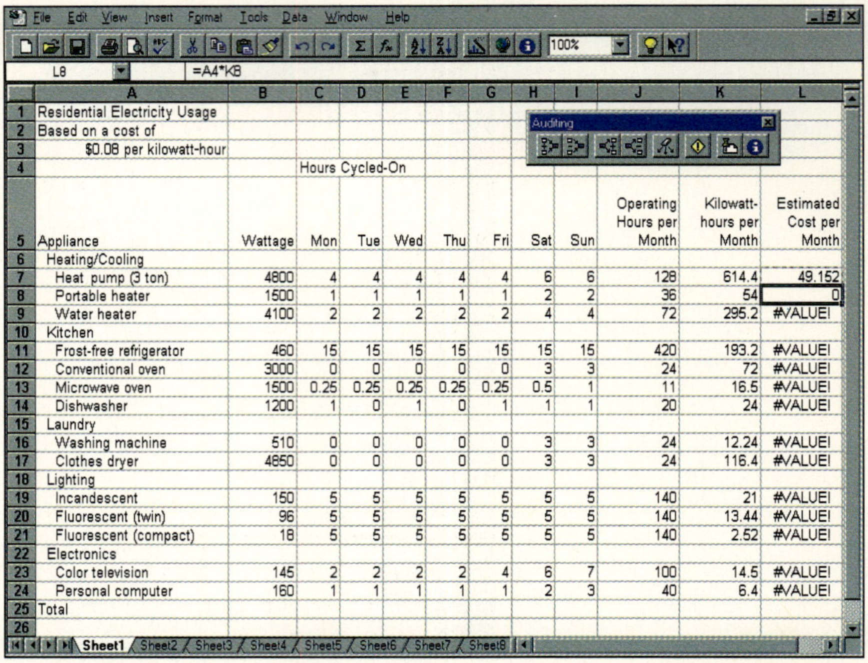

	A	B	C	D	E	F	G	H	I	J	K	L
1	Residential Electricity Usage											
2	Based on a cost of											
3	$0.08 per kilowatt-hour											
4			Hours Cycled-On									
5	Appliance	Wattage	Mon	Tue	Wed	Thu	Fri	Sat	Sun	Operating Hours per Month	Kilowatt-hours per Month	Estimated Cost per Month
6	Heating/Cooling											
7	Heat pump (3 ton)	4800	4	4	4	4	4	6	6	128	614.4	49.152
8	Portable heater	1500	1	1	1	1	1	2	2	36	54	0
9	Water heater	4100	2	2	2	2	2	4	4	72	295.2	#VALUE!
10	Kitchen											
11	Frost-free refrigerator	460	15	15	15	15	15	15	15	420	193.2	#VALUE!
12	Conventional oven	3000	0	0	0	0	0	3	3	24	72	#VALUE!
13	Microwave oven	1500	0.25	0.25	0.25	0.25	0.25	0.5	1	11	16.5	#VALUE!
14	Dishwasher	1200	1	0	1	0	1	1	1	20	24	#VALUE!
15	Laundry											
16	Washing machine	510	0	0	0	0	0	3	3	24	12.24	#VALUE!
17	Clothes dryer	4850	0	0	0	0	0	3	3	24	116.4	#VALUE!
18	Lighting											
19	Incandescent	150	5	5	5	5	5	5	5	140	21	#VALUE!
20	Fluorescent (twin)	96	5	5	5	5	5	5	5	140	13.44	#VALUE!
21	Fluorescent (compact)	18	5	5	5	5	5	5	5	140	2.52	#VALUE!
22	Electronics											
23	Color television	145	2	2	2	2	4	6	7	100	14.5	#VALUE!
24	Personal computer	160	1	1	1	1	1	2	3	40	6.4	#VALUE!
25	Total											
26												

Figure 4.13

Analyzing Problem Formulas

Obviously something is wrong with the copied formulas. The formula in cell L8 gives a result of 0, and the other cells display the error message *#VALUE!*.

Consider the original formula in cell L7. As do the other formulas you have created, =A3*K7 uses relative cell references. The formula means "Take what is 4 cells up and 11 cells to the left, and multiply that by what is 1 cell to the left." This can be visualized by tracing the precedents of the formula.

To trace the precedents of the original formula:

1 Select cell L7, the estimated cost per month for the heat pump.

2 Click the **Trace Precedents** tool.
The direct precedents are cell A3, the cost per kilowatt-hour, and cell K7, the kilowatt hours used per month for this appliance.

To trace the precedents of a copy of the formula:

1 Select cell L8, the estimated cost per month for the portable heater.

2 Click the **Trace Precedents** tool.
The screen should resemble Figure 4.14. The direct precedents are cell A4, which is blank, and cell K8, the kilowatt hours used per month for this appliance.

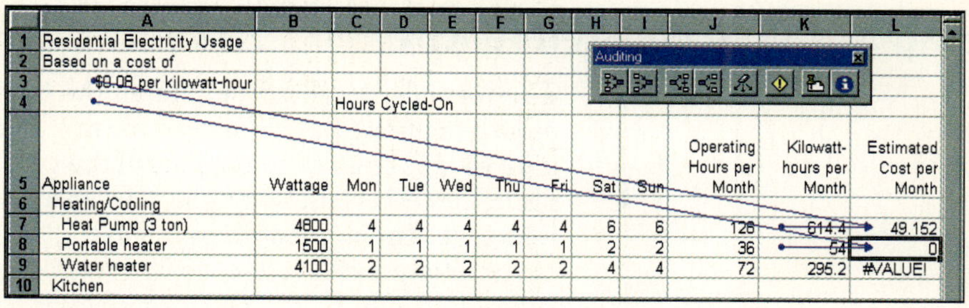

Figure 4.14

The formula in cell L8 attempts to take the contents of cell A4, which is 4 cells up and 11 cells to the left, and multiply those contents by cell K8, which is 1 cell to the left.

The K8 part is correct; the A4 reference is wrong. Cell A4 is blank, and because blank cells have a value of zero, the result of the formula is 0. The results of the other formulas give the error message *#VALUE!* because the other formulas attempt to multiply by cells that contain text, which is considered an error.

Another way of analyzing these formulas is to consider cell A3, which contains the cost per kilowatt-hour. This cell should be a direct precedent of all the formulas that compute estimated cost per month.

To trace the dependents of cell A3:

1 Click the **Remove All Arrows** tool.
All tracer arrows disappear.

2 Select cell A3, the cost per kilowatt-hour.

3 Click the **Trace Dependents** tool.
Your screen should resemble Figure 4.15. Only one cell, L7, depends on cell A3.

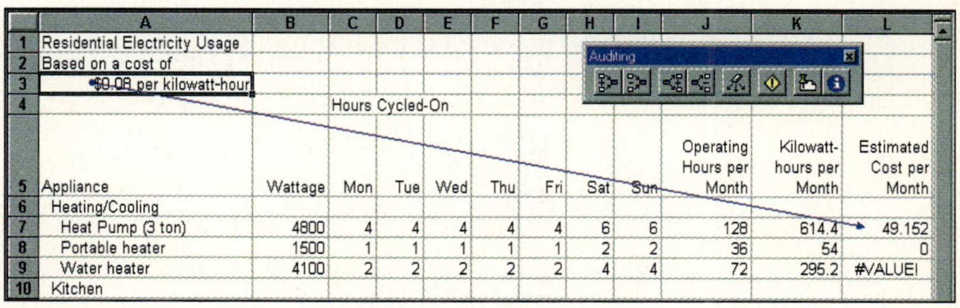

Figure 4.15

4 Click the **Remove All Arrows** tool.

Using Absolute Cell References

The formula in cell L7 (and in all the other cells in the estimated cost per month column) should instead mean "Take what is in cell A3, and multiply it by what is one cell to the left (of the cell in which this formula is located)." Using Excel terminology, the reference to cell A3 should not be a relative reference, but an ***absolute reference.***

An absolute cell reference in a formula is frozen so that the reference will not change even if the formula that contains the reference is copied. A fully absolute reference is indicated with dollar signs preceding both the column letter and the row number. For example, in $A$3, the dollar sign in front of the *A* means "Don't change the *A*," and the dollar sign in front of the *3* means "Don't change the *3*."

The most convenient way to make a reference absolute is with the Absolute function key, F4, which will work either while you are building a formula in point mode or when you are editing a formula. You can also type the dollar signs directly into a formula. In the steps that follow, you will rebuild the formula, this time making the reference to cell A3 absolute.

> ***Tip*** Any time you are pointing to a cell while building a formula, and that cell alone provides the required information for the formula and for future copies of the formula, the reference to the cell should be absolute. In short: if you're building a formula to be copied, any references to specific cells should be made absolute.

To build the formula for estimated cost per month (second attempt):

1 Select cell L7, which will contain the estimated cost per month of the heat pump.

2 Type =

3 Select the cost per kilowatt-hour, in cell A3, and press F4
Notice that the dollar signs for absolute addressing appear in the formula bar. Don't hold down F4 because it will cycle through absolute, mixed, and relative address forms. If this cycling happens, tap F4 several times to cycle back to where both the row and the column part of the address are frozen.

4 Type *

5 Select the number of kilowatt-hours used, in cell K7.

6 Press ENTER
The completed formula reads =$A$3*K7.

7 Copy this formula to the other cells that require it in column L.
The worksheet should now resemble Figure 4.16.

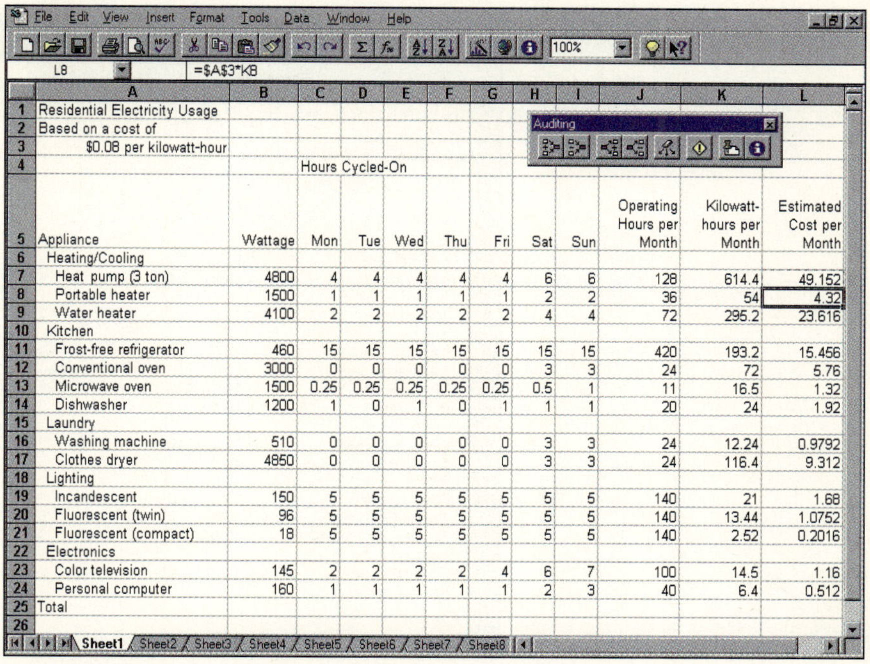

	A	B	C	D	E	F	G	H	I	J	K	L
1	Residential Electricity Usage											
2	Based on a cost of											
3	$0.08 per kilowatt-hour											
4			Hours Cycled-On									
5	Appliance	Wattage	Mon	Tue	Wed	Thu	Fri	Sat	Sun	Operating Hours per Month	Kilowatt-hours per Month	Estimated Cost per Month
6	Heating/Cooling											
7	Heat pump (3 ton)	4800	4	4	4	4	4	6	6	128	614.4	49.152
8	Portable heater	1500	1	1	1	1	1	2	2	36	54	4.32
9	Water heater	4100	2	2	2	2	2	4	4	72	295.2	23.616
10	Kitchen											
11	Frost-free refrigerator	460	15	15	15	15	15	15	15	420	193.2	15.456
12	Conventional oven	3000	0	0	0	0	0	3	3	24	72	5.76
13	Microwave oven	1500	0.25	0.25	0.25	0.25	0.25	0.5	1	11	16.5	1.32
14	Dishwasher	1200	1	0	1	0	1	1	1	20	24	1.92
15	Laundry											
16	Washing machine	510	0	0	0	0	0	3	3	24	12.24	0.9792
17	Clothes dryer	4850	0	0	0	0	0	3	3	24	116.4	9.312
18	Lighting											
19	Incandescent	150	5	5	5	5	5	5	5	140	21	1.68
20	Fluorescent (twin)	96	5	5	5	5	5	5	5	140	13.44	1.0752
21	Fluorescent (compact)	18	5	5	5	5	5	5	5	140	2.52	0.2016
22	Electronics											
23	Color television	145	2	2	2	2	4	6	7	100	14.5	1.16
24	Personal computer	160	1	1	1	1	1	2	3	40	6.4	0.512
25	Total											
26												

Figure 4.16

Once again, the formula you just created and copied means "Take what is in cell A3 and multiply it by what is one cell to the left (of the cell containing this formula)." You can use tracer arrows to confirm that all the estimated cost per month formulas now depend on cell A3.

To trace the dependents of cell A3:

1 If necessary, select the **Remove All Arrows** tool.
All tracer arrows disappear.

2 Select cell A3, the cost per kilowatt-hour.

3 Click the **Trace Dependents** tool.
The screen should resemble Figure 4.17. All the cells that calculate estimated cost per month now depend on cell A3.

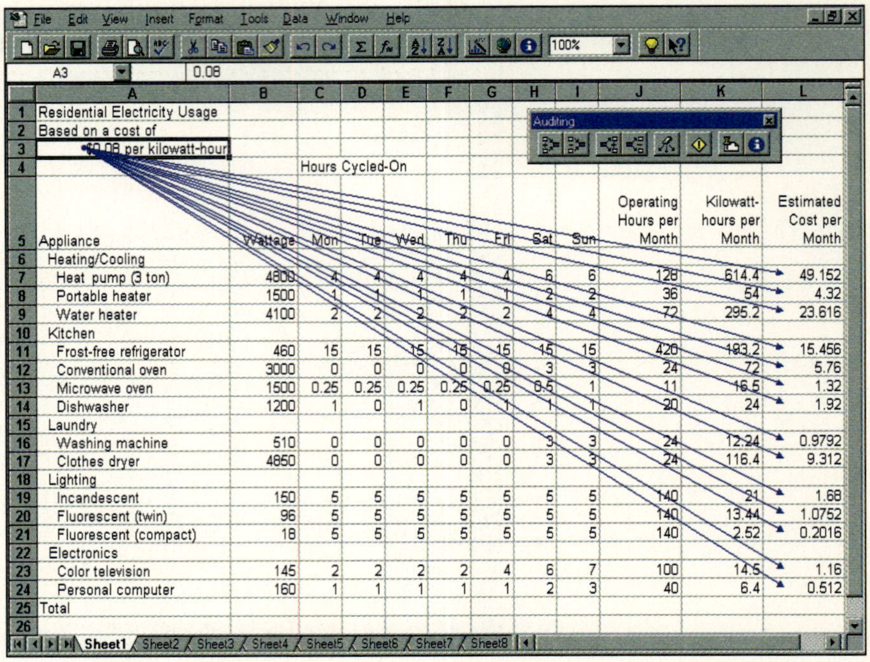

Figure 4.17

4 Click the **Remove All Arrows** tool.

> ***Tip*** Printouts will include tracer arrows unless you clear the arrows before printing.

Building the Grand Total Formula

The only remaining formula to enter on the spreadsheet is the grand total of estimated monthly electricity costs.

To build the total formula:

1 Select cell L25, which will contain the total monthly cost of all appliances.

2 Type **=sum(**

3 Select the range encompassing all the cost formulas, L7:L24.
You can select the range by moving backward, if you wish. It's okay for the range to include blank cells—they won't affect the total.

4 Type **)** and press ENTER
The completed formula reads =SUM(L7:L24). The worksheet should now resemble Figure 4.18.

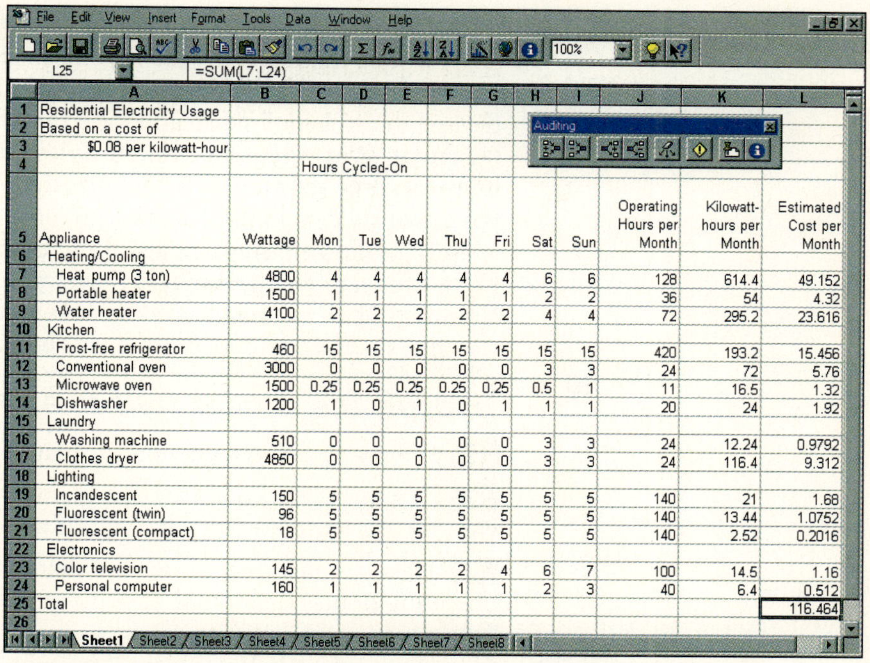

	A	B	C	D	E	F	G	H	I	J	K	L
1	Residential Electricity Usage											
2	Based on a cost of											
3	$0.08 per kilowatt-hour											
4			Hours Cycled-On									
5	Appliance	Wattage	Mon	Tue	Wed	Thu	Fri	Sat	Sun	Operating Hours per Month	Kilowatt-hours per Month	Estimated Cost per Month
6	Heating/Cooling											
7	Heat pump (3 ton)	4800	4	4	4	4	4	6	6	128	614.4	49.152
8	Portable heater	1500	1	1	1	1	1	2	2	36	54	4.32
9	Water heater	4100	2	2	2	2	2	4	4	72	295.2	23.616
10	Kitchen											
11	Frost-free refrigerator	460	15	15	15	15	15	15	15	420	193.2	15.456
12	Conventional oven	3000	0	0	0	0	0	3	3	24	72	5.76
13	Microwave oven	1500	0.25	0.25	0.25	0.25	0.25	0.5	1	11	16.5	1.32
14	Dishwasher	1200	1	0	1	0	1	1	1	20	24	1.92
15	Laundry											
16	Washing machine	510	0	0	0	0	0	3	3	24	12.24	0.9792
17	Clothes dryer	4850	0	0	0	0	0	3	3	24	116.4	9.312
18	Lighting											
19	Incandescent	150	5	5	5	5	5	5	5	140	21	1.68
20	Fluorescent (twin)	96	5	5	5	5	5	5	5	140	13.44	1.0752
21	Fluorescent (compact)	18	5	5	5	5	5	5	5	140	2.52	0.2016
22	Electronics											
23	Color television	145	2	2	2	2	4	6	7	100	14.5	1.16
24	Personal computer	160	1	1	1	1	1	2	3	40	6.4	0.512
25	Total											116.464
26												

Figure 4.18

5 Rename the Sheet1 tab **`Electricity`**

6 Close the Auditing toolbar.

7 Save the workbook.

EXIT If necessary, you can quit Excel now and continue this project later.

FORMATTING THE WORKSHEET

As you can see from Figure 4.1, the finished worksheet has several formatting features. In the remainder of this project, you will assign formats to the worksheet and arrive at a completed document very similar to Figure 4.1.

Changing Numeric Formats

Apart from the custom-formatted *0.08* in the subtitle, three kinds of numeric formats are appropriate for this worksheet:

- A comma-punctuated format with zero decimal places, used for wattage, operating hours per month, and kilowatt-hours per month.
- A format showing values two digits to the right of the decimal, used for the hours cycled-on and for most of the values in the estimated cost per month columns. Although the values in these areas are currently small numbers, in later use of the worksheet, they could become larger, so a comma-punctuated format wouldn't hurt.
- A currency or accounting format, showing two decimal places, for the first entry and grand total in the estimated cost per month column.

You can change numeric formats in a worksheet in two ways: you can apply a style that contains the desired format, or you can apply the numeric format directly. The main advantage to using styles is that you can later change the style definition and have the change take effect on all cells that have that style. The six standard styles will work for most situations; however, if no existing style includes the format you want, you can create your own style or modify an existing one.

In the following steps, you will use both approaches—styles and direct formatting—to change numeric formats. You will start by applying the Comma style to a nonadjacent selection composed of the columns for wattage, operating hours per month, and kilowatt-hours per month.

To apply the Comma style to a selection:

1 Staying in full-screen view, display the Formatting toolbar.

2 Zoom the worksheet so that you can see all the information you entered (on most systems, this will be about 90 percent magnification).

3 Make a nonadjacent selection that includes the values in the wattage, operating hours per month, and kilowatt-hours per month columns.

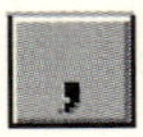

4 Click the **Comma Style** tool.
The screen should resemble Figure 4.19.

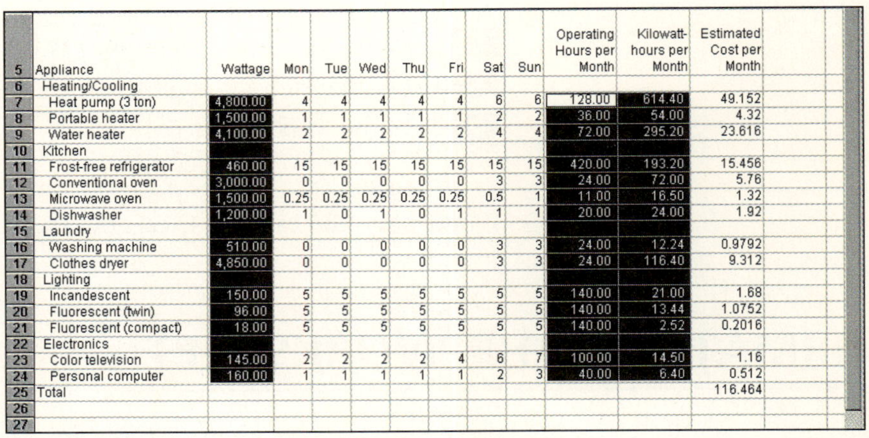

5	Appliance	Wattage	Mon	Tue	Wed	Thu	Fri	Sat	Sun	Operating Hours per Month	Kilowatt-hours per Month	Estimated Cost per Month
6	Heating/Cooling											
7	Heat pump (3 ton)	4,800.00	4	4	4	4	4	6	6	128.00	614.40	49.152
8	Portable heater	1,500.00	1	1	1	1	1	2	2	36.00	54.00	4.32
9	Water heater	4,100.00	2	2	2	2	2	4	4	72.00	295.20	23.616
10	Kitchen											
11	Frost-free refrigerator	460.00	15	15	15	15	15	15	15	420.00	193.20	15.456
12	Conventional oven	3,000.00	0	0	0	0	0	3	3	24.00	72.00	5.76
13	Microwave oven	1,500.00	0.25	0.25	0.25	0.25	0.25	0.5	1	11.00	16.50	1.32
14	Dishwasher	1,200.00	1	0	1	0	1	1	1	20.00	24.00	1.92
15	Laundry											
16	Washing machine	510.00	0	0	0	0	0	3	3	24.00	12.24	0.9792
17	Clothes dryer	4,850.00	0	0	0	0	0	3	3	24.00	116.40	9.312
18	Lighting											
19	Incandescent	150.00	5	5	5	5	5	5	5	140.00	21.00	1.68
20	Fluorescent (twin)	96.00	5	5	5	5	5	5	5	140.00	13.44	1.0752
21	Fluorescent (compact)	18.00	5	5	5	5	5	5	5	140.00	2.52	0.2016
22	Electronics											
23	Color television	145.00	2	2	2	2	4	6	7	100.00	14.50	1.16
24	Personal computer	160.00	1	1	1	1	1	2	3	40.00	6.40	0.512
25	Total											116.464
26												
27												

Figure 4.19

5 Click the **Decrease Decimal** tool twice.
The affected values will now always appear with no digits to the right of the decimal and with commas in values of 1000 and higher.

To apply a number format directly from the Format menu:

1 Select C7:I24, the range for hours cycled-on for Monday through Sunday.

2 Choose **Format** and then **Cells.**

3 Click the **Number** tab, and then choose the **Number** category.

4 Make sure the **Decimal Places** box is set to 2.
The screen should resemble Figure 4.20.

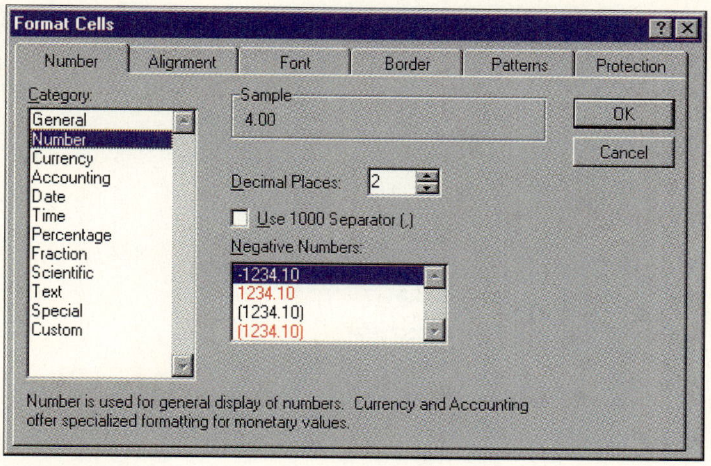

Figure 4.20

5 Select **OK** to apply the format.
The numbers for hours cycled-on now appear with two digits to the right of the decimal point.

The final numeric formatting involves the column for estimated cost per month. Because the numbers in this column are dollar amounts, they should appear with two digits to the right of the decimal. Even though all the figures in the column represent dollar amounts, preceding each by a dollar sign would make the column more difficult to read. In traditional financial-spreadsheet style, a dollar sign is used only in the first entry and the total of such a column.

The regular Comma style displays two digits to the right of the decimal; the regular Currency style is similar to Comma, except that a dollar sign precedes the displayed value.

To apply the Comma style to a selection:

1 Select L8:L24, the values for estimated cost per month (this selection *excludes* the first and last figures in the column).

2 Click the **Comma Style** tool to apply the style.

To apply the Currency style to a selection:

1 Make a nonadjacent selection of the estimated cost per month for the heat pump and the total estimated cost (in L7 and L25, respectively).

2 Click the **Currency Style** tool.
The worksheet should resemble Figure 4.21.

	A	B	C	D	E	F	G	H	I	J	K	L	M
1	Residential Electricity Usage												
2	Based on a cost of												
3	$0.08 per kilowatt-hour												
4			Hours Cycled-On										
5	Appliance	Wattage	Mon	Tue	Wed	Thu	Fri	Sat	Sun	Operating Hours per Month	Kilowatt-hours per Month	Estimated Cost per Month	
6	Heating/Cooling												
7	Heat pump (3 ton)	4,800	4.00	4.00	4.00	4.00	4.00	6.00	6.00	128	614	$ 49.15	
8	Portable heater	1,500	1.00	1.00	1.00	1.00	1.00	2.00	2.00	36	54	4.32	
9	Water heater	4,100	2.00	2.00	2.00	2.00	2.00	4.00	4.00	72	295	23.62	
10	Kitchen												
11	Frost-free refrigerator	460	15.00	15.00	15.00	15.00	15.00	15.00	15.00	420	193	15.46	
12	Conventional oven	3,000	0.00	0.00	0.00	0.00	0.00	3.00	3.00	24	72	5.76	
13	Microwave oven	1,500	0.25	0.25	0.25	0.25	0.25	0.50	1.00	11	17	1.32	
14	Dishwasher	1,200	1.00	0.00	1.00	0.00	1.00	1.00	1.00	20	24	1.92	
15	Laundry												
16	Washing machine	510	0.00	0.00	0.00	0.00	0.00	3.00	3.00	24	12	0.98	
17	Clothes dryer	4,850	0.00	0.00	0.00	0.00	0.00	3.00	3.00	24	116	9.31	
18	Lighting												
19	Incandescent	150	5.00	5.00	5.00	5.00	5.00	5.00	5.00	140	21	1.68	
20	Fluorescent (twin)	96	5.00	5.00	5.00	5.00	5.00	5.00	5.00	140	13	1.08	
21	Fluorescent (compact)	18	5.00	5.00	5.00	5.00	5.00	5.00	5.00	140	3	0.20	
22	Electronics												
23	Color television	145	2.00	2.00	2.00	2.00	4.00	6.00	7.00	100	15	1.16	
24	Personal computer	160	1.00	1.00	1.00	1.00	1.00	2.00	3.00	40	6	0.51	
25	Total											$ 116.46	
26													
27													

Figure 4.21

3 Save the worksheet.

Tip Ironically, the Currency Style tool uses an Accounting number format. If you would prefer having a format that places dollar signs immediately in front of numbers, you should use one of the Currency number formats available on the Number tab of the Format Cells dialog box. You can also redefine the Currency style to use a different number format.

If you use the Increase Decimal or Decrease Decimal tool on a cell, the tool overrides the number format specified in the cell's style. Unfortunately, this means subsequent changes to the style definition will not affect the cell (unless you reapply the style).

Changing the Font Style and Size

As you learned in a previous project, a ***font*** is a typeface design. Arial, Courier New, and Times New Roman are names of different fonts.

Along with choosing a font, you can decide whether the font should appear in a particular ***font style***. The basic font styles, which should not be confused with worksheet-cell formatting styles, are Regular, **Bold,** *Italic,* and Underline. You can also combine font styles, as in ***Bold Italic.*** The size of a font is measured in units called ***points***. One point is 1/72 of an inch; the default font size in Excel is 10 points.

As shown in Figure 4.22, the Formatting toolbar contains a group of convenient controls that can be used for the following functions: changing the font; changing the point size; turning bold formatting on or off; turning italic formatting on or off; and turning underline formatting on or off. More extensive control over fonts is available in the Font tab, accessed from the Format Cells dialog box.

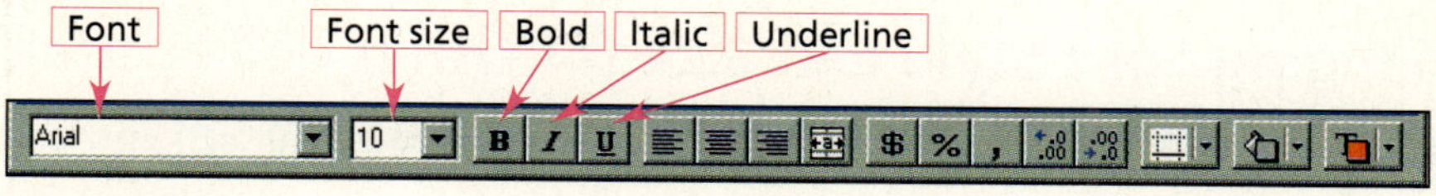

Figure 4.22

The only font used in the completed version of this worksheet is Arial although we employ a variety of point sizes and font styles. In the next series of steps, you will change the main title to appear in 18-point bold italic.

To change the font style and size for the main title:

1 Select cell A1, which contains the title *Residential Electricity Usage.*

2 Select **18** points from the **Font Size** list box.

3 Click the **Bold** tool.

4 Click the **Italic** tool.

The screen should resemble Figure 4.23.

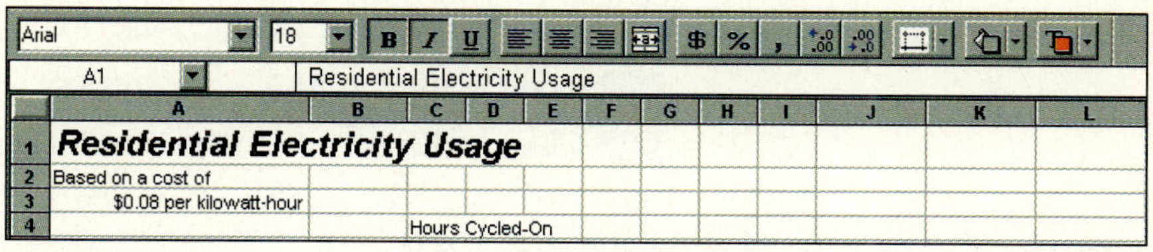

Figure 4.23

The title text should now appear in bold and italic and in a larger point size. Notice that the Bold and Italic buttons on the toolbar are highlighted; this indicates that the current selection has both the bold and the italic font styles.

The two subtitle lines each use a font size of 11 points. You can change this with the Font Size tool on the Formatting toolbar or in the Font tab of the Format Cells dialog box.

To increase the font size of the two subtitles:

1 Select A2:A3, the range containing the two subtitles.

2 Select 11 points from the **Font Size** list box.

Changing Font Style and Size for Other Cell Entries

Here's a list of the remaining cell entries whose font styles and sizes need to be changed.

- The title *Hours Cycled-On* should be 10-point bold.
- All the column titles in B5:L5 should be 10-point italic.
- The titles *Appliance* and *Total* should be 16-point bold.
- The titles *Heating/Cooling*, *Kitchen*, *Laundry*, *Lighting*, and *Electronics* should be 11-point bold.
- The formula result for total estimated cost per month in cell L25 should be 11-point bold.

To change other font attributes in the worksheet:

1 Select cell C4, which contains the text *Hours Cycled-On.*

2 Click the **Bold** tool.

3 Select the range B5:L5, which contains the column titles.

4 Click the **Italic** tool.
This changes the font style to italic. On some systems, it may be necessary to slightly adjust the width of the columns after changing the column titles to italic.

5 Select cell A5, which contains the text *Appliance.*

6 Change the font size and style to 16-point bold.

Copying Only the Format of a Cell

The title *Total* in cell A25 is supposed to have the same font style and size as *Appliance* in cell A5. Excel has the ability to copy just the format (and not the contents) of one cell to another cell.

To copy the format of cell A5 to cell A25:

1 Select cell A5, which contains *Appliance.*

2 Select the **Format Painter** tool on the Standard toolbar.
The pointer changes to a paintbrush.

3 Scroll down if necessary, and then select cell A25, which contains *Total.*

> ***Tip*** The Paste Special command from the Edit menu can also be used to copy selected attributes of a cell and to change these copies in various ways.

To complete the font settings for the worksheet:

1 Press (CTRL)+(HOME)

2 Make a nonadjacent selection to include *Heating/Cooling* (cell A6), *Kitchen* (cell A10), *Laundry* (cell A15), *Lighting* (cell A18), *Electronics* (cell A22), and the grand total formula in cell L25.

3 Set these cells to 11-point bold.

Centering Selected Titles

The titles in A1:A3 should be centered across the whole worksheet; the title *Hours Cycled-On* should be centered across the weekday columns.

To center titles across selected columns:

1 Select the range A1:L3.

2 Click the **Center Across Columns** tool, as shown in Figure 4.24. The text will now be centered within the selected range.

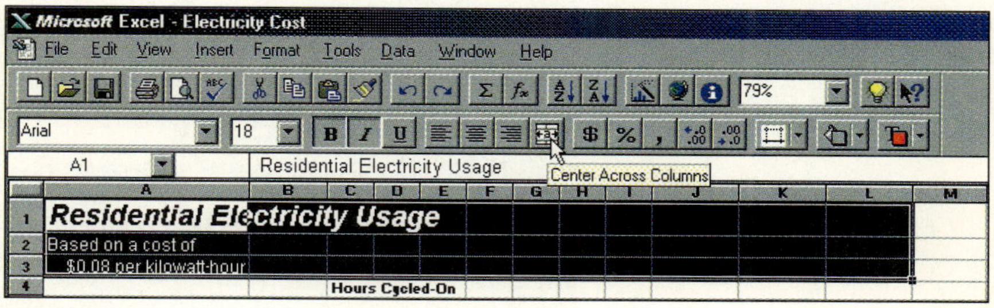

Figure 4.24

3 Change the height of row 4 to about 30 points.

4 Select the range C4:I4. This is the selection in which *Hours Cycled-On* should be centered.

5 Center *Hours Cycled-On* across the selection by clicking the **Center Across Columns tool.**

6 Save the workbook.

Adding Borders to a Worksheet

A ***border*** is a line that lends visual organization to the information in a worksheet. The completed worksheet will have several kinds of borders. You may want to turn cell gridlines off after performing a Border command because the gridlines make it harder to see the borders.

> ***Tip*** When you are applying borders, it is usually a good idea to work from within the worksheet toward the outside perimeter; that is, you should create the innermost borders first, and then proceed to the next layer, and so forth.

The innermost borders in this worksheet are those for the hours cycled-on values. Next, you will add the horizontal section borders, separating appliance categories. Finally, you will set the thick outer border.

To add borders to the hours cycled-on cells:

1 Remove the Formatting toolbar from the screen.

2 Select the range C5:I24, the hours cycled-on column headings and values.

3 Choose **Format** and then **Cells.**

4 Click the **Border** tab.
The Border page appears. Notice that in the Style section, a rectangle surrounds the currently selected line style. Figure 4.25 shows the names of the various line styles.

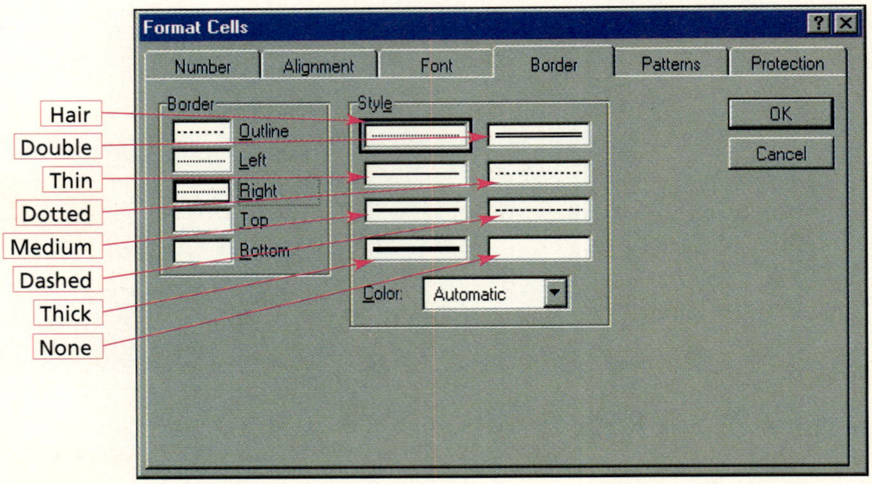

Figure 4.25

5 Select **Outline** in the **Border** group.
A thin line appears next to Outline indicating that this line style will be used to form an outline around the entire selected area.

6 Select **Left** in the **Border** group.
The left edge of each cell in the selected range will have a thin border.

7 Select the Hair line in the upper left of the **Style** group.
This selects a different line style—one that will be used for the left and right borders for each cell in the selected range. The Hair line style should appear for the Left border, and the Thin line style for the Outline, as shown in Figure 4.25.

8 Select **OK** to apply the chosen borders.

9 Choose **Tools** and then **Options,** click the **View** tab, turn off cell gridlines, and then select **OK.**
The effect of the Border command is now more apparent, as shown in Figure 4.26. Notice that outline borders override individual cell borders.

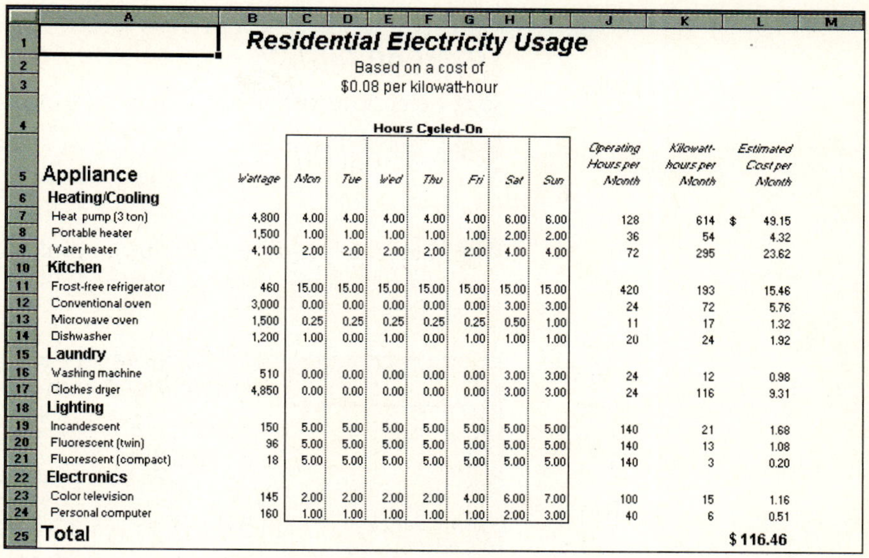

Row	Appliance	Wattage	Mon	Tue	Wed	Thu	Fri	Sat	Sun	Operating Hours per Month	Kilowatt-hours per Month	Estimated Cost per Month
1	**Residential Electricity Usage**											
2	Based on a cost of											
3	$0.08 per kilowatt-hour											
4			Hours Cycled-On									
5	Appliance	Wattage	Mon	Tue	Wed	Thu	Fri	Sat	Sun	Operating Hours per Month	Kilowatt-hours per Month	Estimated Cost per Month
6	**Heating/Cooling**											
7	Heat pump (3 ton)	4,800	4.00	4.00	4.00	4.00	4.00	6.00	6.00	128	614	$ 49.15
8	Portable heater	1,500	1.00	1.00	1.00	1.00	1.00	2.00	2.00	36	54	4.32
9	Water heater	4,100	2.00	2.00	2.00	2.00	2.00	4.00	4.00	72	295	23.62
10	**Kitchen**											
11	Frost-free refrigerator	460	15.00	15.00	15.00	15.00	15.00	15.00	15.00	420	193	15.46
12	Conventional oven	3,000	0.00	0.00	0.00	0.00	0.00	3.00	3.00	24	72	5.76
13	Microwave oven	1,500	0.25	0.25	0.25	0.25	0.25	0.50	1.00	11	17	1.32
14	Dishwasher	1,200	1.00	0.00	1.00	0.00	1.00	1.00	1.00	20	24	1.92
15	**Laundry**											
16	Washing machine	510	0.00	0.00	0.00	0.00	0.00	3.00	3.00	24	12	0.98
17	Clothes dryer	4,850	0.00	0.00	0.00	0.00	0.00	3.00	3.00	24	116	9.31
18	**Lighting**											
19	Incandescent	150	5.00	5.00	5.00	5.00	5.00	5.00	5.00	140	21	1.68
20	Fluorescent (twin)	96	5.00	5.00	5.00	5.00	5.00	5.00	5.00	140	13	1.08
21	Fluorescent (compact)	18	5.00	5.00	5.00	5.00	5.00	5.00	5.00	140	3	0.20
22	**Electronics**											
23	Color television	145	2.00	2.00	2.00	2.00	4.00	6.00	7.00	100	15	1.16
24	Personal computer	160	1.00	1.00	1.00	1.00	1.00	2.00	3.00	40	6	0.51
25	**Total**											**$ 116.46**

Figure 4.26

10 Turn gridlines back on to make it easier to position the active cell.

To set the horizontal section borders:

1 Make a nonadjacent selection to include the rows for the appliance categories and the total. The selected ranges are A6:L6, A10:L10, A15:L15, A18:L18, A22:L22, and A25:L25.

2 Choose **Format** and then **Cells,** select the **Border** tab, and specify a Thin top border, as shown in Figure 4.27.
In the dialog box, the Left and Right boxes are shaded because not all cells within the selection currently have the same setting for left and right borders.

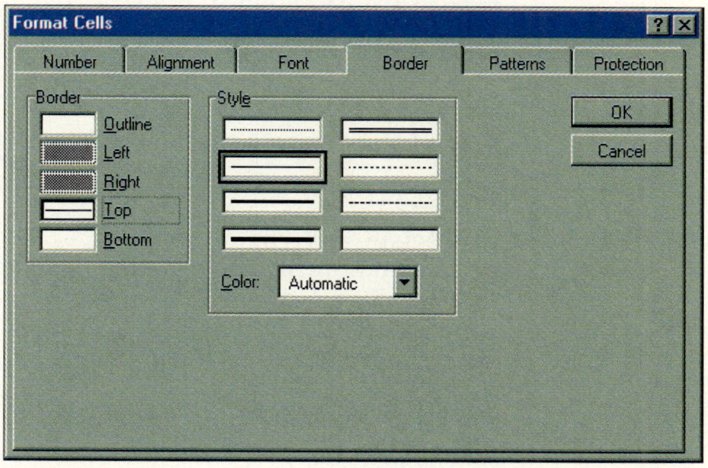

Figure 4.27

3 Select **OK** to apply the border.

To set an outline around the entire worksheet:

1 Select the entire functional area of the worksheet, A1:L25.

2 Choose **Format** and then **Cells,** select the **Border** tab, and set a Medium outline border for the worksheet. Medium is just under the Thin line style.

3 Turn cell gridlines off after completing the Border command. The worksheet should resemble Figure 4.28.

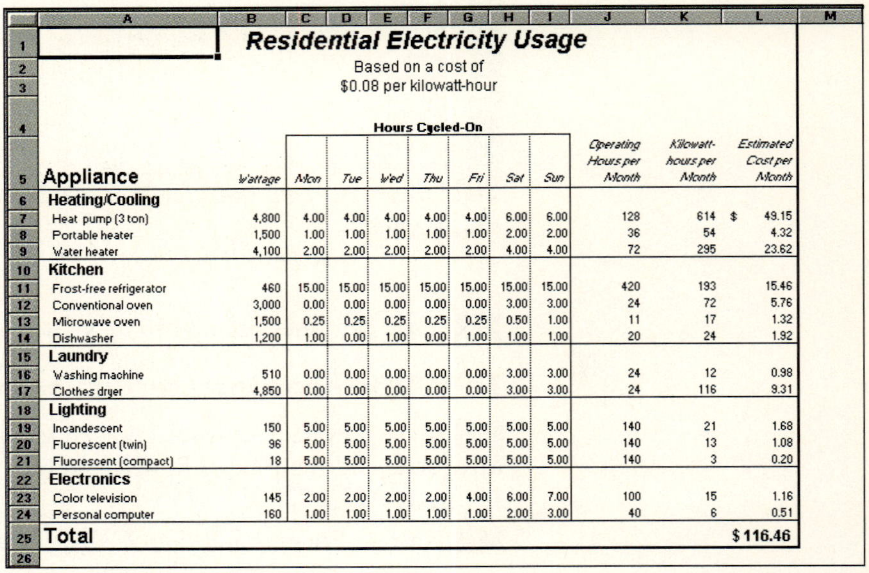

Residential Electricity Usage
Based on a cost of
$0.08 per kilowatt-hour

Appliance	Wattage	Mon	Tue	Wed	Thu	Fri	Sat	Sun	Operating Hours per Month	Kilowatt-hours per Month	Estimated Cost per Month
		Hours Cycled-On									
Heating/Cooling											
Heat pump (3 ton)	4,800	4.00	4.00	4.00	4.00	4.00	6.00	6.00	128	614	$ 49.15
Portable heater	1,500	1.00	1.00	1.00	1.00	1.00	2.00	2.00	36	54	4.32
Water heater	4,100	2.00	2.00	2.00	2.00	2.00	4.00	4.00	72	295	23.62
Kitchen											
Frost-free refrigerator	460	15.00	15.00	15.00	15.00	15.00	15.00	15.00	420	193	15.46
Conventional oven	3,000	0.00	0.00	0.00	0.00	0.00	3.00	3.00	24	72	5.76
Microwave oven	1,500	0.25	0.25	0.25	0.25	0.25	0.50	1.00	11	17	1.32
Dishwasher	1,200	1.00	0.00	1.00	0.00	1.00	1.00	1.00	20	24	1.92
Laundry											
Washing machine	510	0.00	0.00	0.00	0.00	0.00	3.00	3.00	24	12	0.98
Clothes dryer	4,850	0.00	0.00	0.00	0.00	0.00	3.00	3.00	24	116	9.31
Lighting											
Incandescent	150	5.00	5.00	5.00	5.00	5.00	5.00	5.00	140	21	1.68
Fluorescent (twin)	96	5.00	5.00	5.00	5.00	5.00	5.00	5.00	140	13	1.08
Fluorescent (compact)	18	5.00	5.00	5.00	5.00	5.00	5.00	5.00	140	3	0.20
Electronics											
Color television	145	2.00	2.00	2.00	2.00	4.00	6.00	7.00	100	15	1.16
Personal computer	160	1.00	1.00	1.00	1.00	1.00	2.00	3.00	40	6	0.51
Total											**$ 116.46**

Figure 4.28

4 Turn cell gridlines back on.

5 Switch out of full-screen view, and display the Formatting toolbar.

6 Save the workbook.

Printing and Making Final Modifications

In the steps that follow, you will print the worksheet and notice areas that require adjustments. After making these adjustments, you will then print the worksheet again.

To suppress cell gridlines on a printout:

1 Make sure the printer is powered on and is online.

2 Choose **File** and then **Print.**

3 Select **OK** in the Print dialog box.
The worksheet prints on two pages on most printers.

4 Zoom to 25 percent magnification.
If you examine the worksheet on the screen, you will see horizontal and vertical dashed lines placed by Excel at page breaks for your reference.

5 Zoom to 75 percent magnification.

Changing the Orientation of a Printout

Because the worksheet is printed on two pages, you would need to trim one of the sheets and tape the two pages together to have a single printed image of the worksheet. If you want this worksheet to fit on a single page, you can change the ***scaling*** (reducing it to fit), and you can flip the printout from ***portrait orientation*** (the default) to ***landscape orientation.*** Both the scaling and the orientation controls are in the Page tab of the Page Setup dialog box.

The text of a landscape printout reads along the long dimension of the paper. The terms *portrait* and *landscape* derive from the world of art, where portrait paintings are usually oriented with the long side on the vertical, and landscape paintings with the long side on the horizontal.

You will also notice that the days of the week might look better if they were aligned in the centers of their cells rather than aligned to the right. In the following steps, you will modify the alignment of the weekday names and instruct Excel to produce a landscape printout centered on the page.

To adjust and reprint the worksheet:

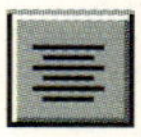

1 Select the weekday names, *Mon* through *Sun*, and select the **Center** tool on the Formatting toolbar.

> ***Reminder*** The Center tool has the same effect as choosing Center in the Alignment tab of the Format Cells dialog box. It means to center each entry within its cell; it is not the same as centering an entry across columns.

2 Save the worksheet.

3 Choose **File** and then **Page Setup.**

4 Click the **Page** tab if not already selected.
The Page tab appears.

5 Select the **Landscape** option under **Orientation.**

6 Click the **Margins** tab.
The Margins tab appears.

7 Click the check boxes to center the printout horizontally and vertically, and then select **OK.**

8 Select the **Print** tool on the Standard toolbar to print the worksheet.
The completed landscape printout should resemble Figure 4.1.

Defining Named Ranges

Earlier in this project, you saw how to define names for constants. You can also define names for cells or larger ranges on the worksheet. You can then use the name as you enter new formulas. If formulas that refer to the named range already exist in the worksheet, you must *apply* the name to those formulas before the name will show up within the formulas.

Consider the formula for estimated cost per month in cell L7. It currently reads =$A$3*K7. The same reference, $A$3, is used in every one of the estimated cost formulas. The formula would be a little more understandable if it looked like this: =CostPerKilowattHour*K7. In the following steps, you will define the name *CostPerKilowattHour* to refer to cell $A$3. You will then apply the name to the cells containing the estimated cost formulas.

A quick way to define names that refer to ranges on the worksheet is to use the Name box in the formula bar.

To define and apply a named range:

1 Select cell A3, which contains *0.08*, the cost per kilowatt-hour.

2 Click in the **Name** box in the formula bar.

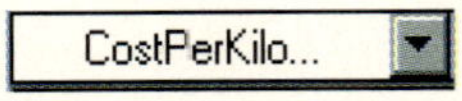

3 Type `CostPerKilowattHour` in the **Name** box and press (ENTER) Remember to type the name as a single word with mixed upper- and lowercase letters.

4 Select cell L7, the estimated cost per month for the heat pump. Notice that the formula still reads =$A$3*K7.

5 Select L7:L24, the range containing the formulas for estimated cost per month.

6 Choose **Insert, Name,** and then select **Apply.** The Apply Names dialog box appears as shown in Figure 4.29.

7 Select **OK** to apply the name *CostPerKilowattHour*.

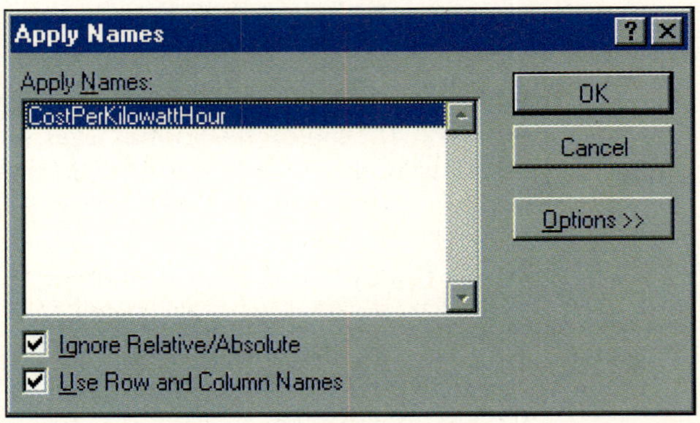

Figure 4.29

If you examine any of the formulas for estimated cost, you will discover that the name *CostPerKilowattHour* is now used instead of *$A$3*.

8 Save the workbook.

The dictionary of defined names is part of the workbook. Because the dictionary has changed, you should save the workbook.

THE NEXT STEP

Many of the commands you used in this project will help in constructing and managing larger worksheets. When the functional part of a worksheet grows to encompass thousands of cells, the increased complexity can be tamed somewhat by spending time initially on design, using named ranges, and using the Zoom Control command to view the worksheet from afar.

You have also worked with several sophisticated formatting features.

Remember that the important thing about any worksheet is its results—usually numerical values resulting from formulas. Fonts, font styles, borders, and so on enhance the legibility of the worksheet and should not in themselves become a distraction to the person who reads the worksheet.

Perhaps one of the best ways to make the results of worksheets more legible is to present the information in pictures using Excel's superb charting capability. That is the subject of the next project.

This concludes Project 4. You can either exit Excel or go on to work the Study Questions, Review Exercises, and Assignments.

SUMMARY AND EXERCISES

Summary

- Customized number formats allow you to attach special abbreviations and other text to a numeric entry.
- You can use the Zoom Control to magnify or reduce the view of the worksheet. Smaller magnifications are especially helpful for comprehending the arrangement of a large worksheet. Selecting full-screen view temporarily removes the toolbars and status bar to allow more room for the worksheet on the screen.
- You can use series fill to automatically fill a range that begins with a standard sequence or series.
- You can change the horizontal and vertical alignment of cell entries; titles above columns of numbers are usually easiest to read if they are aligned at the right or center. You can also make the text in cells wrap onto several lines.
- You can assign names to constants and to cells and ranges. Defined names make formulas more intelligible by eliminating constant numbers typed into formulas.
- You can copy to nonadjacent selections; this often saves you from using the Copy command repeatedly.
- Absolute cell references are usually necessary when you are copying a formula that contains a reference to a single cell in the worksheet.
- The font size (measured in points) and style (regular, italic, bold, underline, or bold italic) can be changed in selected cells or in a named cell style.
- Borders in a variety of thicknesses can be applied to cells and to larger selections.

Key Terms and Operations

Key Terms
absolute reference
AutoFill
border
customized format
defined name
font
font style
full-screen view
landscape orientation
points
portrait orientation
scaling
wrapping

Operations
Apply a style
Boldface text
Center across columns
Define a name
Format a cell
Italicize text
Zoom out or in

Study Questions

Multiple Choice

1. Excel displays number signs (#) in a cell when:
   a. A formatted number is too long to fit in the column.
   b. There is an error in a formula.
   c. A text entry is too long to fit in the column.
   d. An absolute cell address is required in a formula.
   e. The cell has an invalid customized format.

2. To conveniently enter a single value into a selected range, type the value in a cell within the selected range and then press:
   a. ENTER
   b. SHIFT + ENTER
   c. TAB
   d. CTRL + ENTER
   e. SHIFT + TAB

3. In the formula =SUM(G3:G12)*0.12115, *0.12115* is called a(n):
   a. defined name.
   b. number constant.
   c. absolute address.
   d. formula modifier.
   e. relative address.

4. In the formula =SUM(G3:G12)*ExpenseFactor, *ExpenseFactor* is a(n):
   a. text constant.
   b. manifest constant.
   c. hidden number.
   d. absolute address.
   e. defined name.

5. In the formula =$A$3*K7, *$A$3* is called a(n):
   a. defined constant.
   b. defined name.
   c. absolute cell address.
   d. relative cell address.
   e. manifest constant.

6. If the formula =A1+$A$2 were entered in cell A3 and then copied to cell B3, the copy in cell B3 would read:
   a. =B1+$A$2
   b. =A1+$A$2
   c. =A1+$B$2
   d. =B1+b2
   e. =B1+B2

7. Bold and Italic are examples of:
   a. font styles.
   b. patterns.
   c. alignments.
   d. font names.
   e. cell styles.

8. When adding several levels of borders to a worksheet, it is best to:
   a. Start from the innermost level and work outward.
   b. Start with the overall outline and work in.
   c. Proceed column by column.
   d. Zoom to a high magnification.
   e. Print with cell gridlines on.

9. Printing that is oriented along the long dimension of the paper is referred to as:
   a. portrait orientation.
   b. panoramic orientation.
   c. wide-angle printing.
   d. anisotopic mapping.
   e. landscape orientation.

10. Writing an incorrect formula that attempts to perform math by referring to a text entry causes Excel to display what in the formula's cell?
    a. ERROR
    b. 0
    c. #####
    d. #VALUE!
    e. !!!!!

Short Answer

1. How can you adjust the magnification of the worksheet so that the selected range occupies the entire worksheet area?
2. What term is used to describe breaking a long text entry into several lines within its cell?
3. What type of format should be used when a numeric entry, such as 45, needs to appear in a single cell with text (for example, 45 degrees)?
4. What is the easiest way to enter the month names *Jan*, *Feb*, *Mar*, and so on in a range of cells?
5. Arial and Times New Roman are examples of what?
6. What unit of measurement is used when referring to the size of characters in a font?
7. If a formula refers to a specific, single cell, and the formula will be copied to other cells, how should the reference to the single cell appear in the formula?
8. If you want a border line to appear around all four sides of a selection, what command should you use?
9. How is a text entry normally aligned when it is entered into a cell?
10. How will numbers appear if they are formatted using the Comma Style tool?

For Discussion

1. What is the difference between using a style and applying a numeric format directly? What are the advantages of using styles?

2. What is the difference between relative and absolute cell addressing? Under what circumstances should a formula contain an absolute cell reference?

3. Explain the difference between portrait and landscape orientation. When is landscape printing appropriate?

4. In general, what steps are required to suppress gridlines on a printout, yet maintain them on the screen?

Review Exercises

Projecting Coffee House Income

Follow the steps given to construct a worksheet similar to Figure 4.30. The question marks in the figure indicate cells that will contain formulas. Begin by entering all the text constants (use AutoFill to enter the month names), and then enter the numbers for cost and price, and all the values for number sold. Enter the formula for income per cup as selling price per cup minus our cost per cup. Calculate the income for January by multiplying the number sold by the income per cup. Remember, the reference to income per cup should be absolute. Copy the formula to the other months.

	A	B	C	D	E	F	G	H	I
1				Clem's Coffee Clutch					
2				*Projected Income from Cappuccino Sales*					
3	**Coffee**	**Our Cost per Cup**	**Selling Price per Cup**	**Income per Cup**					
4	Cappuccino	0.74	1.5	?					
5									
6		***Jan***	***Feb***	***Mar***	***Apr***	***May***	***Jun***	***Total***	
7	**Number Sold**	440	350	370	340	290	220	?	
8	**Income**	?	?	?	?	?	?	?	
9									

Figure 4.30

Create formulas (using the SUM function) for total number sold and total income. Style in bold and center across columns the title and subtitle. Make the title a slightly larger size than the subtitle, and make the subtitle italic. Format the column headings for Our Cost per Cup, Selling Price per Cup, and Income per Cup as bold, aligned to the right, and set to wrap. Format the month names and Total as bold, italic, and aligned to the right.

Apply the Currency style to the cost, price, and income per cup cells. Apply Currency style with no decimal places to the monthly income formulas, and Comma style with no decimal places to the values for number sold each month. Adjust column widths and row heights as necessary, turn off cell gridlines, and apply borders so that the worksheet resembles Figure 4.30. Save the workbook as *Proj 4 Ex 1 Coffee House Income*, and then print the worksheet.

Computing Coffee Brand Income as Percent of Total Income

Figure 4.31 shows an enhanced version of the Proj 3 Asn 2 Coffee House Income worksheet from Assignment 2 in Project 3. A column has been added to show the income from each flavor of coffee expressed as a percent of the total income. For a particular flavor of coffee, this value is calculated by dividing its income amount by the total income. If such a formula is to be successfully copied to all the cells in the Percent of Total Income column, the reference to the total income must be absolute. The worksheet is also formatted with various alignments, borders, cell styles, and font styles.

	A	B	C	D	E	F	G
1	**Coffee**	**Cost**	**Selling Price**	**No. Sold**	**Income**	**Percent of Total Income**	
2	House Blend	$ 0.39	$ 0.95	60.00	$ 33.60	?	
3	Espresso	0.61	1.25	12.00	7.68	?	
4	Cappuccino	0.74	1.50	22.00	16.72	?	
5	Café Mocha	0.55	1.45	35.00	31.50	?	
6	Café Royale	0.68	1.85	55.00	64.35	?	
7	***Total***			184.00	$ 153.85	?	
8							

Figure 4.31

Refer to Figure 4.31 and build a similar worksheet. Add the new column first, and then proceed with formatting and borders. Apply the Currency and Comma cell styles as indicated in the figure. Use the Percent style for the new column of formulas.

Define the name *TotalIncome* to refer to the cell containing the total income, and then apply the name to the new formulas. Save the workbook under the name *Proj 4 Ex 2 Coffee House Income.*

Assignments

Developing Your Own Electricity Worksheet

Construct a worksheet to calculate your monthly consumption of electricity. If necessary, look up energy consumption figures for the appliances in your home, apartment, or dorm room. Is there any appliance whose usage you can affect to such an extent that substantial amounts of electricity are saved? Save the workbook under the name *Proj 4 Asn 1 My Electric.*

Enhancing the Municipal Waste Worksheet

Figure 4.32 shows an enhanced version of the Proj 2 Ex 1 Municipal Waste Trends workbook from the first Review Exercise in Project 3. The formula that computes the percent of the total for a particular category takes the 1990 value and divides it by the 1990 grand total (this is similar to the second review exercise in this project). Note that the borders have been customized, titles have been added, and numeric formatting has been adjusted.

	A	B	C	D	E	F	G	H
1			**Municipal Waste Trends**					
2			*in pounds per day per person*					
3	Category	**1960**	**1970**	**1980**	**1990**	**Percent of Grand Total (for 1990)**		
4	**Nonfood Wastes**							
5	Paper	0.91	1.19	1.32	1.60	?		
6	Glass	0.20	0.34	0.36	0.28	?		
7	Plastics	0.01	0.08	0.19	0.32	?		
8	Metals	0.32	0.38	0.35	0.34	?		
9	**Total Nonfood**	1.44	1.99	2.22	2.54	?		
10	**Other**							
11	Food	0.37	0.34	0.32	0.29	?		
12	Yard	0.61	0.62	0.66	0.70	?		
13	**Total Other**	0.98	0.96	0.98	0.99	?		
14	***Grand Total***	2.42	2.95	3.20	3.53	?		
15								

Figure 4.32

Build the new formulas, and adjust the formatting as necessary to create a completed worksheet similar to Figure 4.32. Use Percent cell style for the new formulas. Save the modified workbook under the name *Proj 4 Asn 2 Municipal Waste Trends.*

Adapting to Off-Hours Discounts

Some electric utilities offer energy-savings time, a two-tier residential-electricity rate system, where customers who use electricity during off-peak hours receive a special reduced rate (for example, $0.05 per kilowatt-hour) and have to pay a premium rate (for example, $0.15 per kilowatt-hour) for electricity used during peak-demand hours. In the summer and fall, off-peak hours are usually from 9:00 p.m. to noon on weekdays and all day on weekends; in the winter and spring, off-peak hours are usually from 9:00 a.m. to 5:00 p.m. on weekdays and all day on weekends.

Adapt the electricity cost worksheet to accommodate a two-tier electricity price schedule. Save the workbook under the name *Proj 4 Asn 3 Two Tiered Electricity Cost.*

Project 5: Visualizing Information with Charts

Objectives

After completing this project, you should be able to:

- Translate a verbal description and a sketch of a chart into a completed Excel chart
- Identify the major components of a chart
- Create column charts, pie charts, and 3-D perspective column charts
- Create both embedded charts and chart sheets
- Resize, position, and customize charts
- Link chart text to the worksheet
- Print charts

Case Study: Comparing Prime-Time TV Shows

Television has reigned as the predominant communications medium in the United States since shortly after the end of the Second World War. Figure 5.1 is a worksheet that shows the popularity of various kinds of prime-time TV shows in the United States from 1950 through 1990. This information is a snapshot of mid- to late 20th-century U.S. popular culture.

The Most Popular Prime Time TV Shows
Genre by Decade (1950–1990)

Genre	1950s	1960s	1970s	1980s
Crime	8	4	13	16
Drama	10	7	8	14
Variety	20	14	2	0
Western	21	16	2	0
SitCom	23	48	61	54
Other	18	11	14	16
Total	100	100	100	100

Figure 5.1

For purposes of the worksheet, a television program is considered popular if it was among the ten most-watched *prime-time* (evening) programs each year. For each decade, there were 100 top programs. The worksheet condenses the data by considering whole decades and by classifying television shows by genre—or category—of show.

It's possible to see patterns in this table of numbers, but for most people, the best way to identify trends and interrelationships in data is to present the data visually as a ***chart,*** using lines, bars, geometric symbols, and colors.

In this project, you will construct several types of charts to display the information shown in Figure 5.1. Each type of chart emphasizes a certain aspect of the data or lends itself to a certain way of viewing or interpreting the information. Excel offers many more chart types than are needed for this project. Table 5.1 lists a few of the chart types you are likely to use for most of your charting needs.

Table 5.1

Chart Type	Description	Application
Bar	Compares individual values at a specific time. Emphasizes comparison rather than time flow	Product launch, budget
Column	Similar to bar, but emphasizes variation over time	Quarterly sales forecast
Pie	Shows relationship between portions of a whole	Sales levels in various cities
Line	Shows trends or changes over time. Emphasizes time flow and the rate of change rather than the amount of change	Price index

Designing the Solution

If you want to build a chart, first decide what it is that you want to display in the chart and the type of chart that is most appropriate for the data you will plot. You can then figure out how the various aspects of the planned chart translate into Excel commands and charting options.

Suppose you want to show how the popularity of crime and drama shows changed between 1950 and 1990, and you want your chart to resemble Figure 5.2. Crime show popularity and drama show popularity are the variables that make up the *data series* that you wish to plot as a chart. A ***data series*** is a set of related values appearing in either a column or a row. A column chart like the one in Figure 5.2 is one way to view this kind of information.

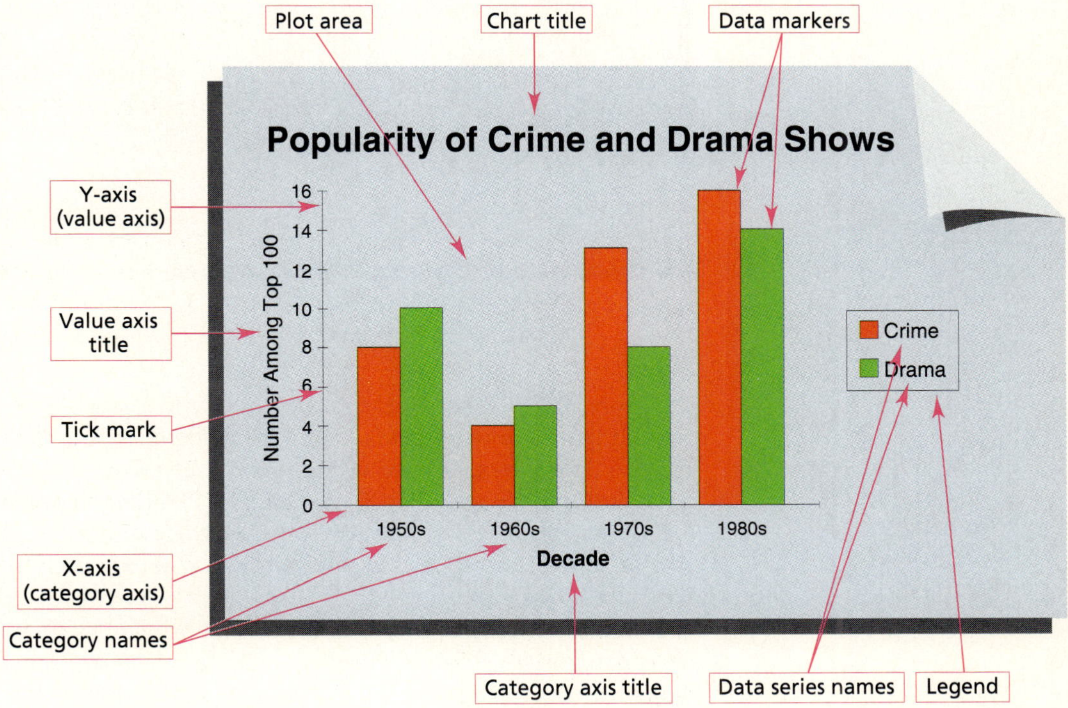

Figure 5.2

The labels along the bottom edge of the chart often correspond to worksheet column headings to tell you what the ***chart categories*** are. For example, the Drama data series has the value 7 in the 1960s category.

The graphic elements of the plot area include axes and the ***data markers*** that represent data points. Depending on the chart type, data markers can take the form of bars, lines, pictures, pie wedges, or other symbols. Each data series is graphically distinguished by the same pattern, color, or symbol. Each category, scale, or data series is marked off on the axis with a tick mark. Generally, two axes act as the major frame for plotting. The horizontal or category axis—also referred to as the ***X-axis***—plots categories of the data series. The vertical or value axis—also called the ***Y-axis***—is the ruler for plotting data values. In addition to the graphical elements of the chart, text such as titles, a legend, and labels help convey the interpretation of the data you are plotting.

In the worksheet, categories correspond to rows or columns, usually with titles that become the chart ***category names,*** used as labels along the axes. As shown in Figure 5.3, the categories for the example chart are 1950s, 1960s, 1970s, and 1980s.

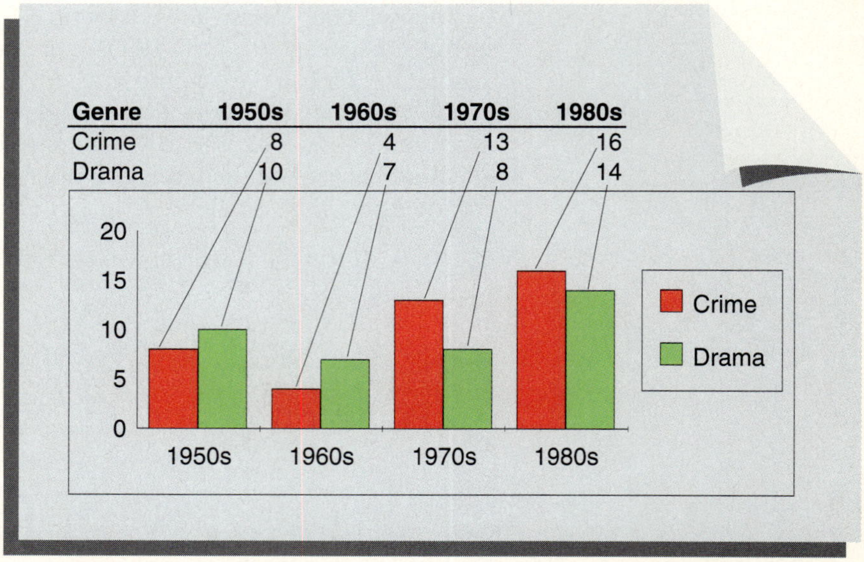

Figure 5.3

Figure 5.3 shows the relationship between a worksheet and a chart created from the worksheet. Each bar in the chart is a data marker. There are two data series: one for crime shows (represented by the red bars on the chart and the numbers 8, 4, 13, and 16 in the worksheet) and the other for drama shows (the green bars on the chart, and the numbers 10, 7, 8, and 14 in the worksheet). In a worksheet, you can often identify the data series as a group of values, in a column or a row, that *change over time.*

If a data series is a row, as is the number of shows each decade, then the chart categories of that data series—the decades—are represented in columns. Alternatively, if a data series is presented in a column, its chart categories are shown in rows. Figure 5.4 shows what the graph would look like if you switched the chart categories used in Figure 5.2 to data series, and the data series to chart categories. Whether you make the chart categories rows or columns depends entirely on the focus of the chart.

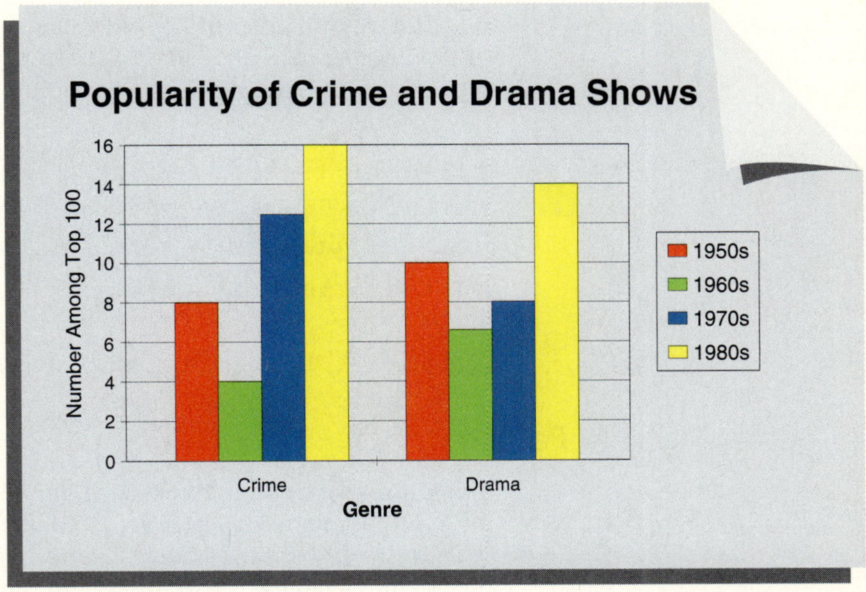

Figure 5.4

Creating the Underlying Worksheet

In this section, you will make a worksheet similar to the one shown in Figure 5.1 and use that worksheet to create charts in the remainder of this project. You can refer to Figure 5.5 (which has been zoomed to 150 percent magnification) while typing the worksheet. The worksheet contains only four formulas, which compute totals for each column; their primary purpose is to help you check that you correctly typed the number constants.

	A	B	C	D	E	F
1	***The Most Popular Prime Time TV Shows***					
2	**Genre by Decade (1950-1990)**					
3	**Genre**	**1950s**	**1960s**	**1970s**	**1980s**	
4	Crime	8	4	13	16	
5	Drama	10	7	8	14	
6	Variety	20	14	2	0	
7	Western	21	16	2	0	
8	SitCom	23	48	61	54	
9	Other	18	11	14	16	
10	**Total**	100	100	100	100	
11						

Figure 5.5

To build the basic worksheet:

1 Enter the title `The Most Popular Prime Time TV Shows` in cell A1.

2 Make the title in cell A1 11-point bold italic.

3 Enter the subtitle `Genre by Decade (1950-1990)` in cell A2, and make the subtitle bold.

4 Change the height of row 3 to about 28 points.

5 Referring to Figure 5.5, enter the column titles (*Genre* in A3 through *1980s* in E3), and make the titles bold.

6 Use the **Align Right** tool to adjust the column headings from *1950s* to *1980s*.

7 Refer to Figure 5.5 and enter the row titles (*Crime* in A4 through *Other* in A9) and the number constants (in the range B4:E9).

8 Enter `Total` in cell A10, and make the word bold.

9 Use the **AutoSum** tool to create total formulas where they are required in row 10.

10 Select A1:E2, and click the **Center Across Columns** tool.

Using the Borders Palette

The Borders tool on the Formatting toolbar contains a group or ***palette*** of buttons that represent various commonly used border styles. In the following steps, you will use the Borders palette to apply a thin bottom border to the column headings, as well as a thin top and double bottom border to the totals row.

To apply borders using the Borders palette:

1 Select the column headings in the range A3:E3.

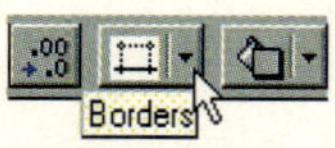

2 Open the **Borders** palette by clicking the arrowhead to its right.

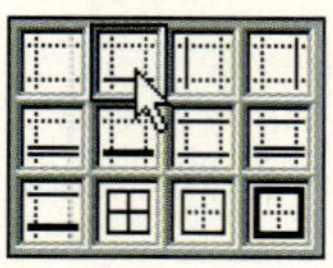

3 Click the button for a thin bottom border in the **Borders** palette.

4 Select the range A10:E10, the totals row.

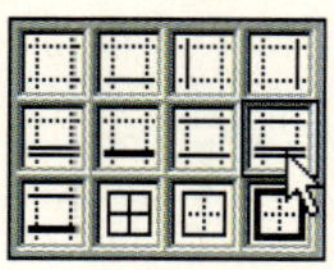

5 Open the **Borders** palette and click the button for a thin top border and double-line bottom border.

6 Rename the Sheet1 tab to `TV Data`

7 Save the workbook as `Prime Time`

Tip If you want to repeatedly apply borders from the palette, you can "tear it off" and have it appear as its own floating toolbar. To do this, open the palette and carefully position the mouse pointer on the edge of the palette. Drag the outline to the main worksheet area.

Building a Column Chart with ChartWizard

The easiest way to build basic charts is to use ***ChartWizard,*** a special command accessible only as a toolbar tool. In this section, you will build a column chart based on the plan in Figure 5.2. This first chart will be an ***embedded chart;*** that is, it will exist as an object embedded within the TV Data worksheet. Later, you will create charts as separate *chart sheets.*

When working with embedded charts, you will usually need to see a large area of the worksheet. In the steps that follow, you will change the view of the worksheet by reducing magnification to 75 percent and temporarily removing the status bar from the window.

To change the view of the worksheet:

1 Zoom the window, if necessary, so that column L is visible.

2 Remove the status bar, if it is visible, by choosing **View** and then **Status Bar.**
The status bar disappears from the window.

To specify the range to be charted:

1 Select the range A3:E5, as shown in Figure 5.6, which encompasses the data to be charted and the associated category and data series names. Excel will ignore the corner cell containing *Genre* because it is neither a data series nor a chart category.

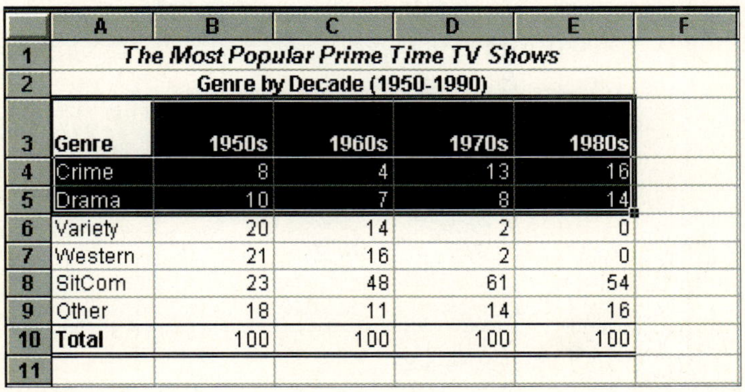

	A	B	C	D	E	F
1	The Most Popular Prime Time TV Shows					
2	Genre by Decade (1950-1990)					
3	Genre	1950s	1960s	1970s	1980s	
4	Crime	8	4	13	16	
5	Drama	10	7	8	14	
6	Variety	20	14	2	0	
7	Western	21	16	2	0	
8	SitCom	23	48	61	54	
9	Other	18	11	14	16	
10	Total	100	100	100	100	
11						

Figure 5.6

2 Click the **ChartWizard** tool.
The pointer changes to crosshairs. You can drag the mouse to select a location and size for the chart.

3 Position the crosshairs in the middle of cell G3, then hold down the mouse button and drag to the middle of cell K12, as shown in Figure 5.7, and then release the mouse button.

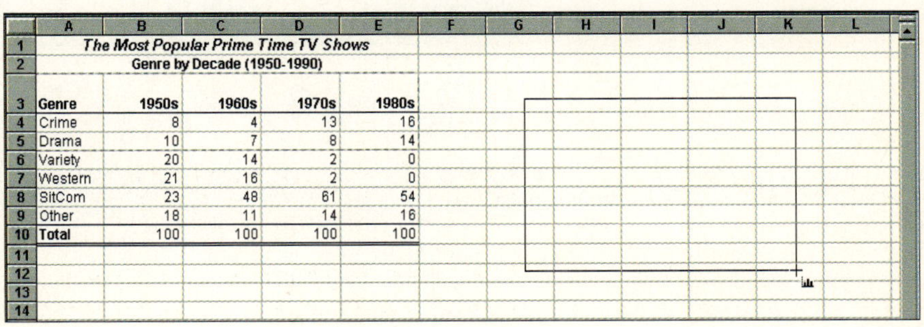

	A	B	C	D	E	F	G	H	I	J	K	L
1	The Most Popular Prime Time TV Shows											
2	Genre by Decade (1950-1990)											
3	Genre	1950s	1960s	1970s	1980s							
4	Crime	8	4	13	16							
5	Drama	10	7	8	14							
6	Variety	20	14	2	0							
7	Western	21	16	2	0							
8	SitCom	23	48	61	54							
9	Other	18	11	14	16							
10	Total	100	100	100	100							
11												
12												
13												
14												

Figure 5.7

The ChartWizard Step 1 dialog box appears. Because you have already specified the range to be charted, you do not need to change anything in this dialog box.

4 Select **Next** in the ChartWizard Step 1 dialog box.
The Step 2 dialog box appears to let you pick one of the 15 major chart types.

To set the chart type and format:

1 Select the **Column** chart type if necessary, and then select **Next,** as shown in Figure 5.8.

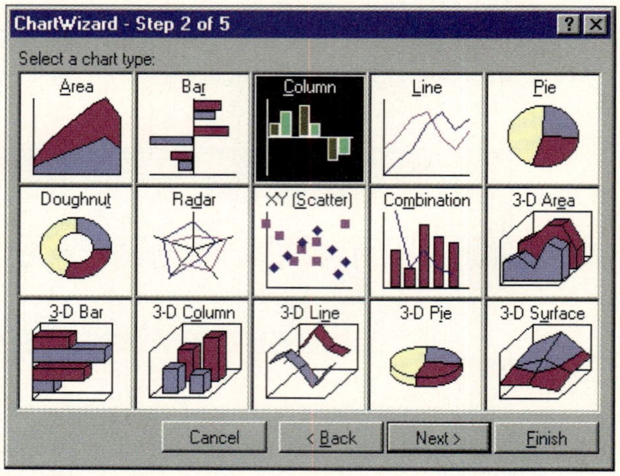

Figure 5.8

The Step 3 dialog box appears to let you pick the specific format for the chart type selected in the previous step.

2 Select chart format **1,** and then select **Next,** as shown in Figure 5.9.

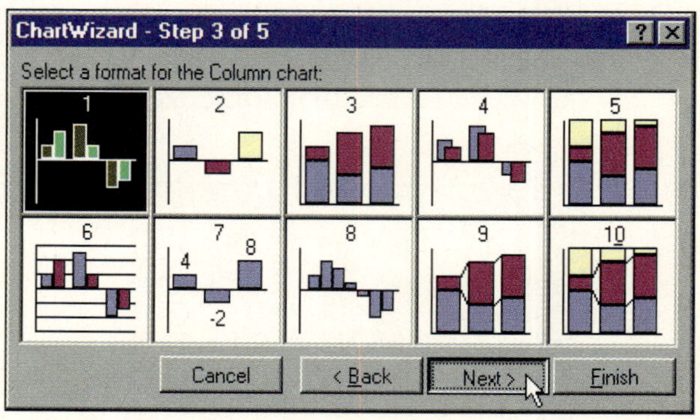

Figure 5.9

The Step 4 dialog box appears, as shown in Figure 5.10. You can use this dialog box to determine whether the data series will be in rows or columns and whether cells in the initially selected range should be used for data series and chart category names. Excel works on the assumption that you want fewer data series than chart categories, which means that for this worksheet, the data series are initially presented in rows.

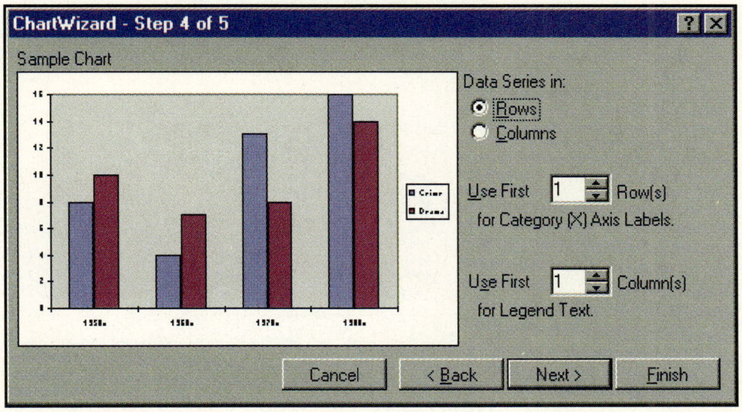

Figure 5.10

To specify data series and chart categories:

1 Click the **Columns** button in the **Data Series in** section.
The screen should now resemble Figure 5.11; you can see what the chart will look like if the data series is in columns rather than in rows. The other sections of this dialog box concern whether the first row and/or column of the range should be used for naming the chart categories and data series. These settings are currently correct because both column and row titles are part of the selected range.

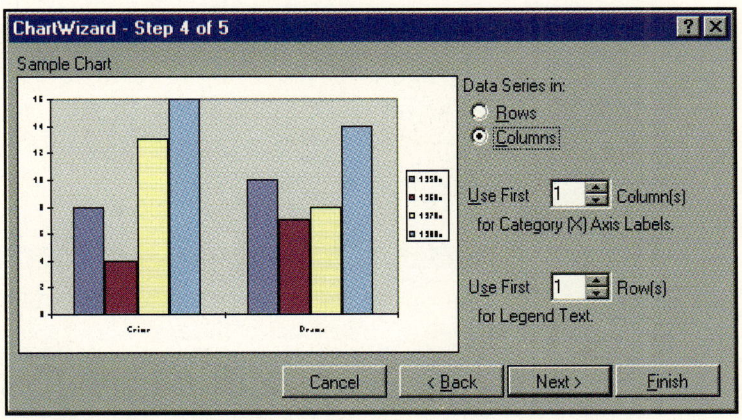

Figure 5.11

2 Click the **Rows** button.
The screen should once again resemble Figure 5.10; the data series are again set up as rows.

3 Select **Next.**
The Step 5 dialog box appears, as shown in Figure 5.12. You can use this dialog box to assign a legend and a title to the chart. A ***legend*** is a key that lists what each color or symbol stands for. The default setting includes a legend but no title.

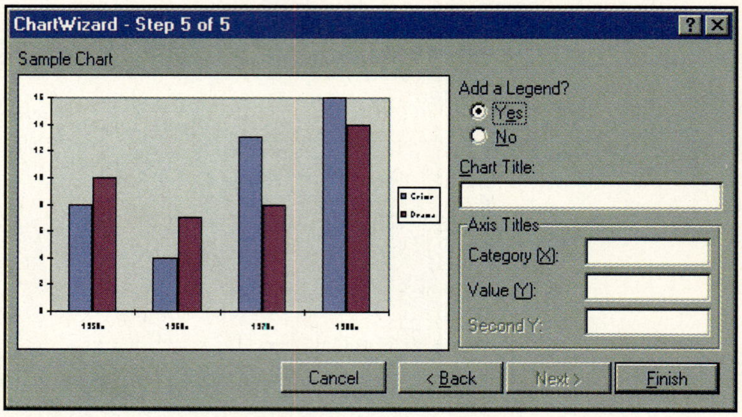

Figure 5.12

To specify a legend and titles:

1 Select **No** in the **Add a Legend** section.
Now the chart appears without a legend. Column and bar charts are difficult to use without legends.

2 Select **Yes** in the **Add a Legend** section to restore the chart legend.

3 Click in the **Chart Title** box, and type **`Popularity of Crime and Drama Shows`**

4 Click in the **Category (X)** Axis Title box, and type **`Decade`**
Although it might seem obvious that the categories along the X-axis are decades, an axis title makes it even clearer.

5 Click in the **Value (Y)** Axis Title box, and type **`Number Among Top 100`**
Titles for the Y-axis are important because they indicate what the units are—what the height of a bar stands for, for example. The screen should now resemble Figure 5.13.

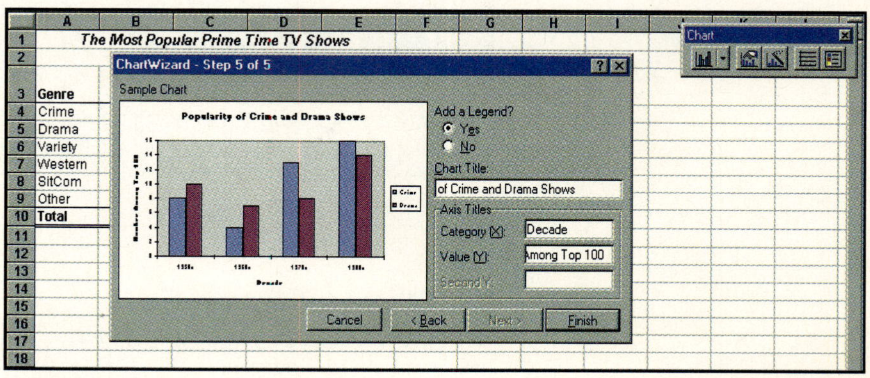

Figure 5.13

6 Select **Finish** to complete the chart.
The screen should resemble Figure 5.14. The completed chart appears, embedded in the worksheet, and a floating Chart toolbar may also appear. If necessary, you can drag the Chart toolbar so that it does not obscure the worksheet or chart.

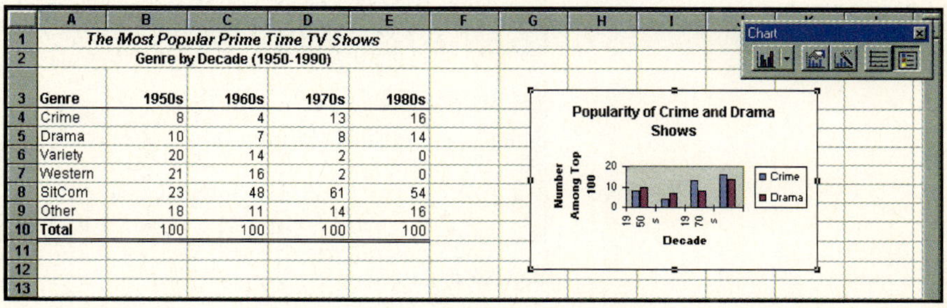

Figure 5.14

Working with Embedded Charts

The embedded chart is part of the worksheet, but it does not fill any cells, and it doesn't have a cell address. Instead, think of an embedded chart as existing in its own layer that floats on top of the worksheet cells. This means the chart can easily be moved and resized. Small black boxes, called ***handles,*** appear on the chart's corners and sides when the chart is selected. The Chart toolbar also may appear when a chart is selected. You can select a chart by clicking anywhere inside its rectangle. If you click in the chart and then drag the mouse, you can reposition the chart in the worksheet. If you click and drag one of the chart's handles, you can resize the chart window.

To reposition the embedded chart:

1 Select cell A1.
Notice that the handles on the chart rectangle disappear—the chart is no longer selected.

2 Click once anywhere inside the chart rectangle.
The handles reappear, signaling that the chart is selected.

3 With the pointer positioned inside the chart rectangle, hold down the mouse button.

4 Drag the chart's outline so that it is below the worksheet data (in rows 12 to 22), similar to Figure 5.15.

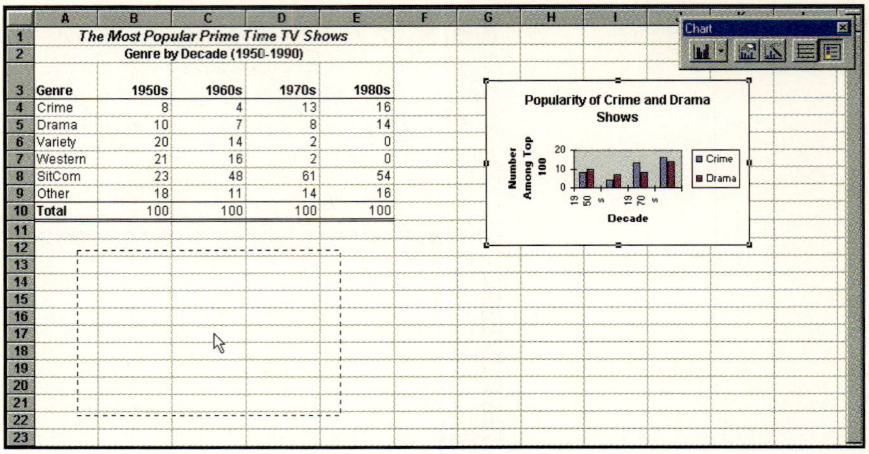

Figure 5.15

5 Release the mouse button.
The chart should now appear below the worksheet data.

The chart will be easier to read if you make it larger. You can change the width of the chart by dragging the middle handle of the left or right edge of the rectangle; change the height of the chart by dragging the middle handle at the top or bottom edge; and change both the width and the height of the chart simultaneously by dragging one of the corner handles.

It is often convenient to use the Print Preview command to see how the chart will appear on the printed page. After you use Print Preview, dotted lines will appear on the worksheet, showing you the boundaries of each printed page. You can then zoom out to 50 or even 25 percent and make adjustments to the chart location and size.

To preview the chart and worksheet printout:

1 Click the **Print Preview** tool on the Standard toolbar.
The Print Preview window appears, showing a simulated printout of the worksheet and chart. If you close the Print Preview window, you will still be able to see dotted reference lines showing page breaks.

2 Select **Close.**
The worksheet again appears, but with dotted reference lines.

3 Zoom to 25 percent magnification.
The placement of individual printout pages is more obvious if you zoom out.

To resize the embedded chart:

1 Zoom to 75 percent magnification.

2 Select the chart by clicking once in it.

3 Hold down the mouse button on the lower-right handle of the chart rectangle. The pointer becomes a cross-hair pointer.

4 Drag the right corner handle to the middle of cell G28 so that the chart is wider and taller, as shown in Figure 5.16.

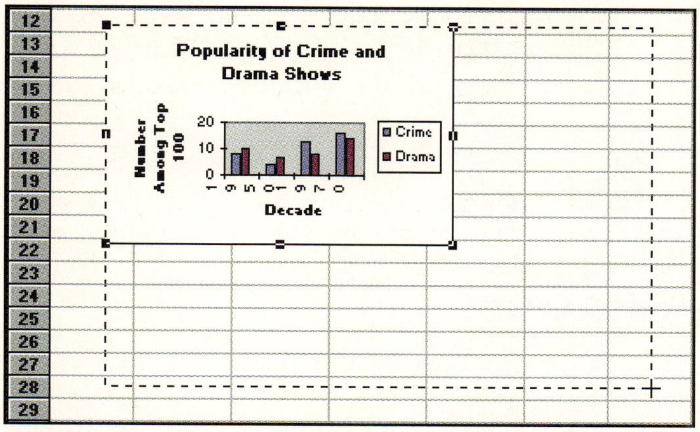

Figure 5.16

5 Release the mouse button.
The screen should now appear similar to Figure 5.17.

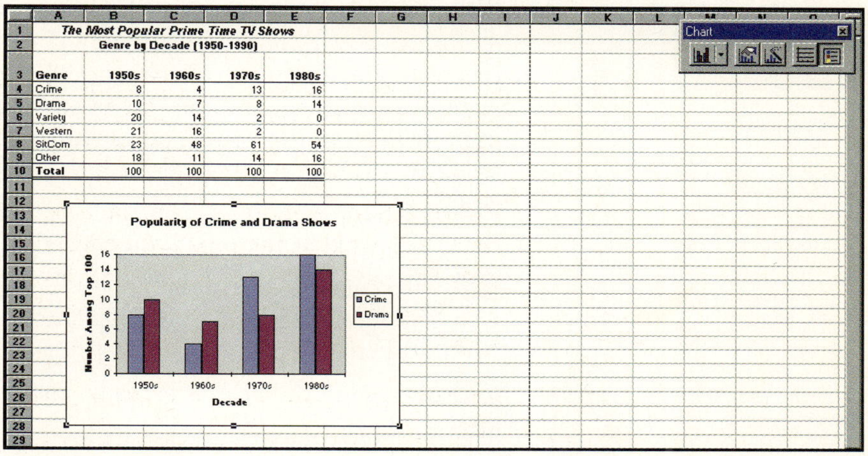

Figure 5.17

The chart you just created is ***linked*** to the worksheet: if the data on which the chart depends change, the chart will automatically update to reflect the change. In the following steps, you will change the value for crime shows in the 1960s to see the effect of this linkage. You will then use the Undo command to undo the entry and revert to the original value.

To observe the effect of linkage:

1 Select cell C4, which contains *4*, the number of crime shows popular during the 1960s.
Note the bar on the chart that corresponds to this value.

2 Type **20** and press (ENTER)
The chart changes immediately to show the change in the worksheet.

3 Click the **Undo** tool on the Standard toolbar.

4 Save the workbook.

Reminder Undo, also available from the Edit menu, reverses the effect of the most recently issued command.

EXIT If necessary, you can quit Excel now and continue this project later.

Printing Embedded Charts

An embedded chart is part of the worksheet document, and it will print with the surrounding worksheet data looking much as it does on the screen. The printing commands you have already learned will work with charts as well. In the following steps, you will use the Print Preview command to see a simulated printout on the screen; then you will print the worksheet. Print Preview is useful because it allows you to detect problems with the printout without wasting paper, ink, or time.

To print the embedded chart with its worksheet:

1 Select the **Print Preview** tool on the Standard toolbar.
A simulated printout page appears. When the pointer is positioned over this page, the pointer shape changes to a magnifying glass; if you click the page, Excel will zoom in on the printout at the point you selected. Clicking again will zoom back out. You can also access other printing commands from the Print Preview window.

2 Position the pointer over the chart and click.
Excel zooms in at the point you clicked.

3 Click again to zoom out.
Cell gridlines may appear on the printout though it might look better without them.

4 Make sure the printer is ready, and then click the **Print** button.

5 Select **OK** from the Print dialog box.

Deleting Embedded Charts

You can have many different embedded charts in a worksheet. You can delete an embedded chart by selecting the chart and pressing (DEL) or choosing Clear and then All from the Edit menu.

To delete the embedded chart:

1 Click within the chart to select it.

2 Press (DEL)

Plotting Nonadjacent Data

Suppose you wanted to make another column chart that showed the popularity of dramas and westerns for the 1950s and the 1970s only. This is *nonadjacent* information in the worksheet; that is, the ranges that contain the names and values are separated by cells that contain information that is not required for the chart.

Excel can easily make a chart from a nonadjacent selection, *provided that the pieces of the nonadjacent selection can be assembled into a rectangular range.*

When you select the various ranges that comprise the nonadjacent selection, make sure that the selections are each the same size and, if put together, that they form a rectangle. Any multicell ranges in the nonadjacent selection should be selected by dragging through the necessary cells, *not* by clicking each of the individual cells that compose the range. In the steps that follow, you will make a nonadjacent selection identical to Figure 5.18 (which is magnified for your reference), and then you will build a column chart based on that selection.

To make the nonadjacent selection:

1 Zoom to 75 percent magnification, if necessary.

2 Select cell A3, which contains *Genre*, by clicking it. Keep the pointer in the middle of cell A3.

3 Hold down the mouse button and drag to the right to extend the selection to include cell B3, which contains *1950s*, and then release the mouse button.

4 Hold down CTRL and then click cell D3, which contains *1970s*.

5 Hold down CTRL and then click and drag to select A5:B5, which contains *Drama* and *10*.

6 Hold down CTRL and then click cell D5, which contains *8*.

7 Hold down CTRL and then click and drag to select A7:B7, which contains *Western* and *21*.

8 Hold down CTRL and then click cell D7, which contains *2*. The completed nonadjacent selection should be identical to Figure 5.18. Notice that the selection includes the names that should be used on the chart and that, if assembled, the nonadjacent parts would form a rectangle. As before, the upper-left cell (containing *Genre*) will not be used in the actual chart, but it is required if the combined selection is to be rectangular.

	A	B	C	D	E	F
1	*The Most Popular Prime Time TV Shows*					
2	Genre by Decade (1950-1990)					
3	Genre	1950s	1960s	1970s	1980s	
4	Crime	8	4	13	16	
5	Drama	10	7	8	14	
6	Variety	20	14	2	0	
7	Western	21	16	2	0	
8	SitCom	23	48	61	54	
9	Other	18	11	14	16	
10	Total	100	100	100	100	
11						

Figure 5.18

To build a column chart using the nonadjacent selection:

1 Select the **ChartWizard** button on the Standard toolbar.

2 Drag to select a chart area from about cell B12 to cell H23.

3 Select **Next** from the Step 1 dialog box.

4 Select the **Column** chart type and **Next** from the Step 2 dialog box.

5 Select chart format **1** and **Next** from the Step 3 dialog box.
The Step 4 dialog box appears.

6 Select **Next.**
The Step 5 dialog box appears.

7 Select **Finish** to create the chart.
You will not bother to add titles to this chart. The completed chart should resemble Figure 5.19.

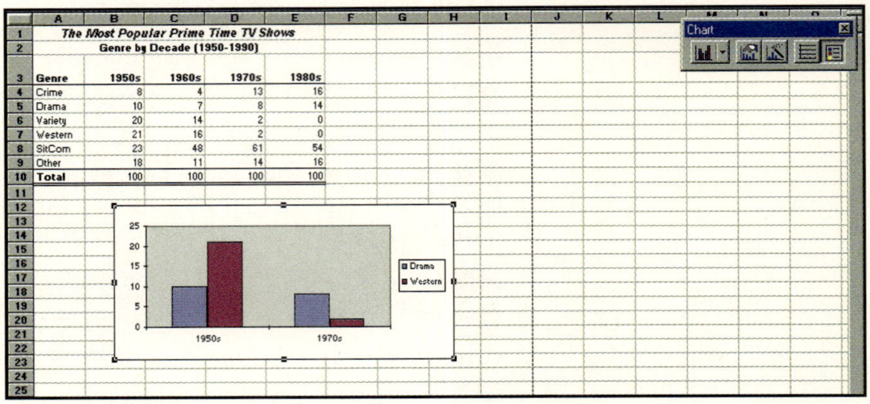

Figure 5.19

8 Delete the chart by pressing DEL once, and click any single cell to cancel the selection.

BUILDING PIE CHARTS

A pie chart is different from most of the other chart types because it shows just one data series. Pie charts are ideal for showing the relationship between a part and the whole—the relative share that each of the various categories represents.

In the following steps, you will create a pie chart showing the breakdown of different kinds of TV shows for the 1960s. This time, the data series will be in a column—the column for the 1960s—and the chart categories will be the different kinds of shows.

To build a pie chart:

1 Make a nonadjacent selection of the ranges A3:A9 and C3:C9, as shown in Figure 5.20. *Remember to drag to select multicell ranges.*

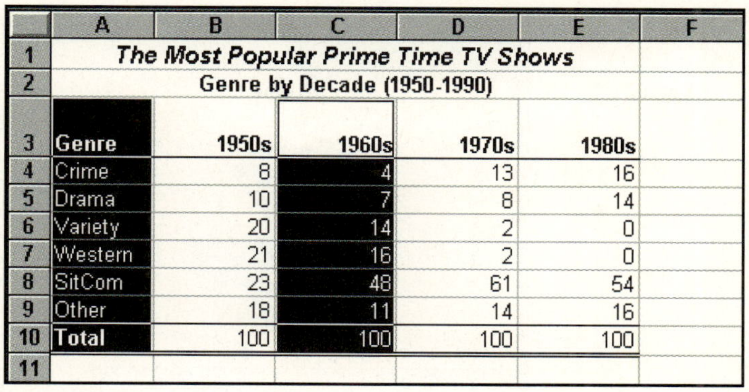

	A	B	C	D	E	F
1	*The Most Popular Prime Time TV Shows*					
2	Genre by Decade (1950-1990)					
3	Genre	1950s	1960s	1970s	1980s	
4	Crime	8	4	13	16	
5	Drama	10	7	8	14	
6	Variety	20	14	2	0	
7	Western	21	16	2	0	
8	SitCom	23	48	61	54	
9	Other	18	11	14	16	
10	Total	100	100	100	100	
11						

Figure 5.20

2 Click the **ChartWizard** button on the Standard toolbar.

3 Drag to select a chart area from about cell F2 to cell L23.

4 Select **Next** in the Step 1 dialog box.

5 Select the **Pie** chart type and then **Next** from the Step 2 dialog box.

6 Select chart format **5** and then **Next** from the Step 3 dialog box, as shown in Figure 5.21.
This pie chart format shows labels next to each slice of the pie.

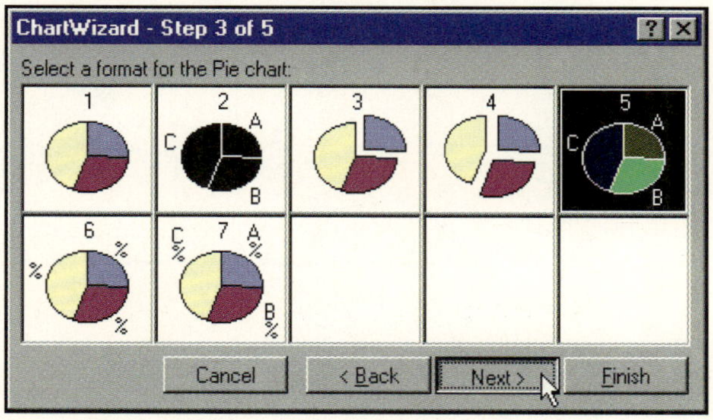

Figure 5.21

Note that the first column in the selection should be used for pie slice labels, and the first row for the chart title.

7 Select **Next** in the Step 4 dialog box, as shown in Figure 5.22.
The Step 5 dialog box appears. A legend is not really necessary for this chart because each slice is labeled.

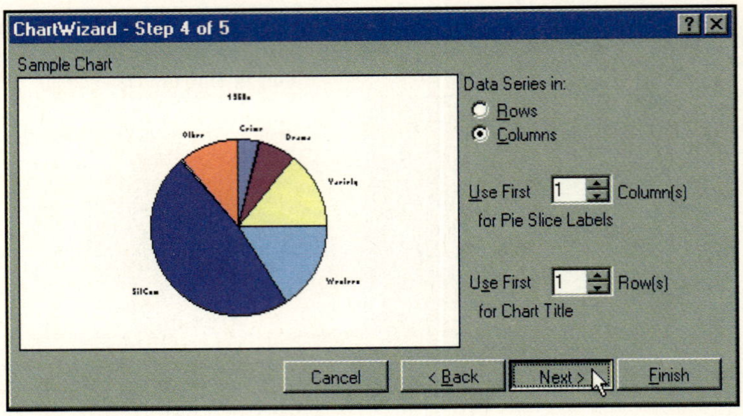

Figure 5.22

8 Select **Finish** in the Step 5 dialog box to create the chart. The screen should resemble Figure 5.23.

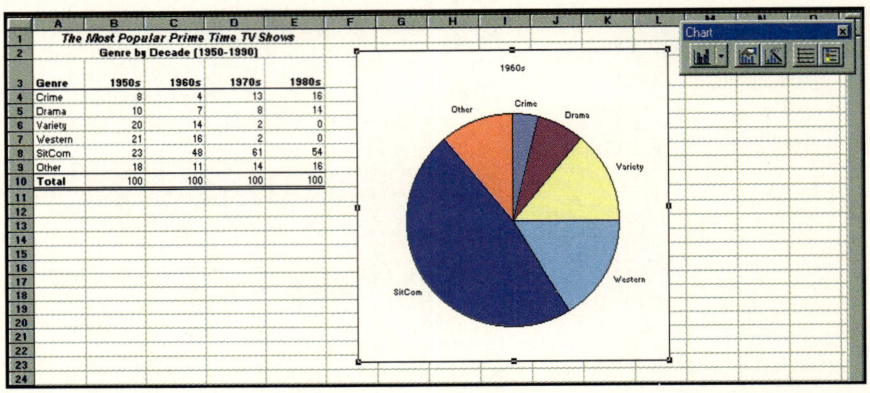

Figure 5.23

Editing an Embedded Chart

If you want to make extensive modifications to the text and graphic objects on a chart, you must first *activate* the chart for editing by *double-clicking* within the chart rectangle. In the following steps, you will activate and modify the pie chart.

Once a chart is activated, you can select an object within the chart by clicking that object. If several objects are in proximity, you must pay close attention to which object is actually selected. Selected objects appear with handles that can be used to position or resize the object.

To modify an embedded chart:

1 Double-click in the pie chart.
The pie chart should now have a thick striped border, indicating that the chart is activated. Notice that the menu bar is different from the normal worksheet menu bar—it contains commands appropriate to working with charts.

2 Click once directly on the title *1960s.*
A box with handles appears around the text, indicating that the text is selected.

3 Type **`Popular TV Shows in the 1960s`** and press (ENTER)
The text you typed is used for the chart title.

4 Use the **Font Size** and **Bold** tools to make the title text 14-point bold.

5 Click once directly on the word *Variety.*
Notice that handles appear on all the pie slice labels—the entire group of labels is selected.

6 Use the **Font Size** tool to change the size to 10 points.
All the pie slice labels are affected.

Suppose you wanted to emphasize or draw attention to the slice for the Western category. One way to do this is to ***explode***—or pull out—that slice from the pie.

To explode a pie slice:

1 Position the pointer in the middle of the slice for Western and click.
Notice that all slices are selected.

2 Click again in the middle of the slice for Western.
Now the handles appear just on that slice.

3 Hold down the mouse button on the slice for Western and drag slightly to the right, as shown in Figure 5.24.

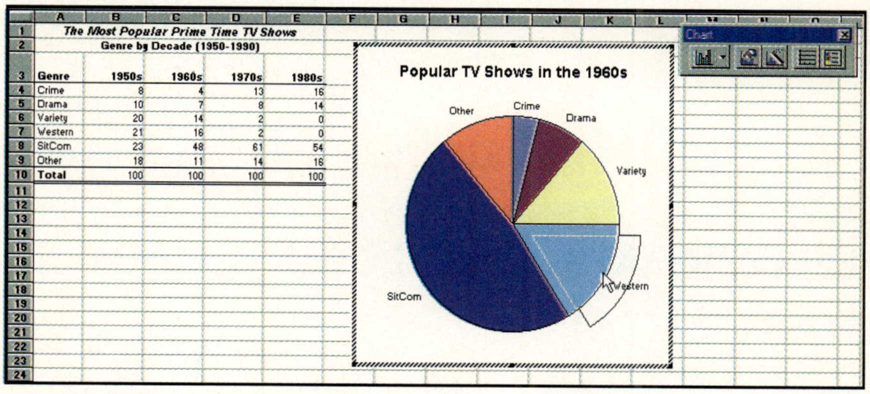

Figure 5.24

The slice for Western should now be pulled out from the pie. Once the mouse button is released, handles again appear on the slice, which means the slice is still selected within the chart. Do not be concerned if the slice label *Western* is partly cut off.

4 Clear the slice handles by pressing (ESC) once.

Changing the Chart Type

Perhaps a fancier pie chart—such as a 3-D pie chart—would look better. You can change the chart type by using the Chart toolbar or by choosing Chart Type from the Format menu.

To change the type of a chart:

1 Choose **Format** and then **Chart Type.**

2 Select **3-D** from the Chart Dimension group.

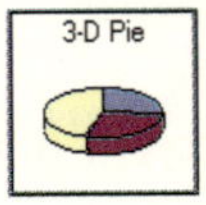

3 Select the **3-D Pie** chart type, and then select **OK.**
The chart now appears as a 3-D pie chart. The slice for Western would appear more prominent if the chart were rotated clockwise.

4 Choose **Format** and then **3-D View.**

5 Click the clockwise rotation button three times so that the chart is rotated 30 degrees clockwise, and then select **OK,** as shown in Figure 5.25.

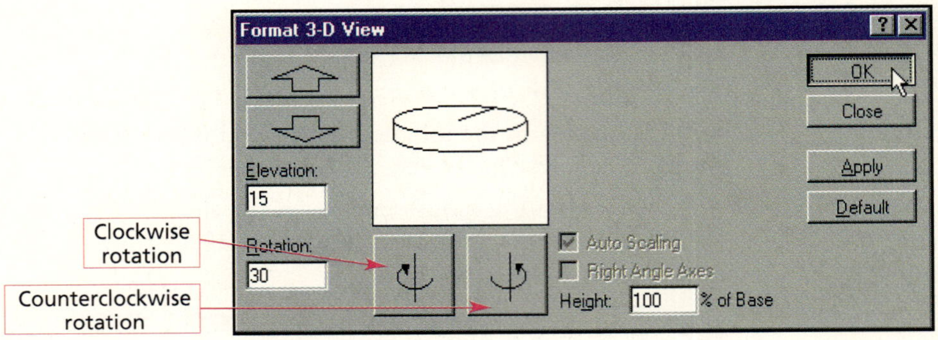

Figure 5.25

6 Click twice outside the chart to deactivate it.

Building a 3-D Column Chart on a Separate Chart Sheet

What type of chart would help you visualize the changing popularity of all the genres for the entire time span of the worksheet? A regular column chart would be cramped, as shown in Figure 5.26. A three-dimensional (3-D) column chart, which you can think of as a group of column charts seen in perspective, might be better.

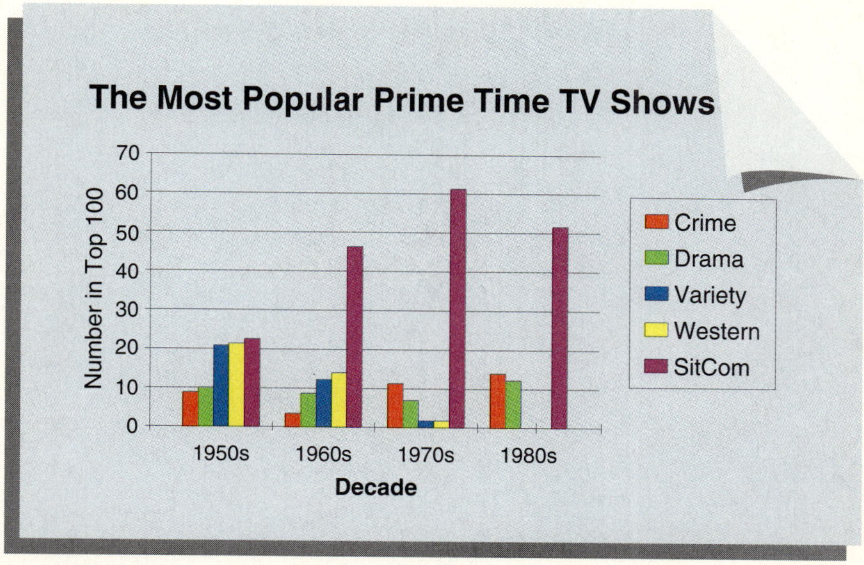

Figure 5.26

In this section, you will create a 3-D perspective column chart on a separate ***chart sheet*** within the workbook. Like embedded charts, charts in separate chart sheets are still linked to worksheet data. The primary advantage of having separate sheets for various charts is to organize your work and prevent having a single sheet cluttered with a variety of different charts.

To create a chart in a separate chart sheet:

1 Select A3:E8, as shown in Figure 5.27. *Do not include the Other or Total categories.*

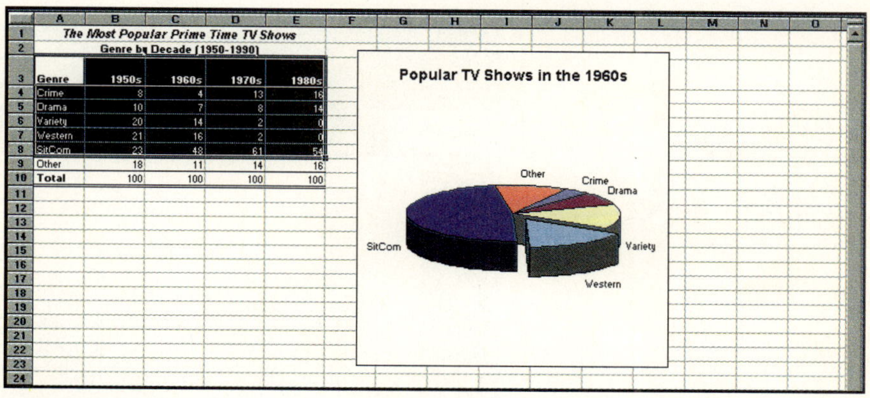

Figure 5.27

2 Choose **Insert, Chart,** and then **As New Sheet.** The ChartWizard Step 1 dialog box appears.

3 Select **Next** in the Step 1 dialog box.

4 Select the **3-D Column** chart type and then **Next** from the Step 2 dialog box.

5 Select chart format **6** and then **Next** from the Step 3 dialog box.

The Step 4 dialog box appears. It will be easier to see the various columns of the chart if the data series is in rows rather than in columns.

6 Select **Rows** from the Step 4 dialog box, and then **Next**, as shown in Figure 5.28.

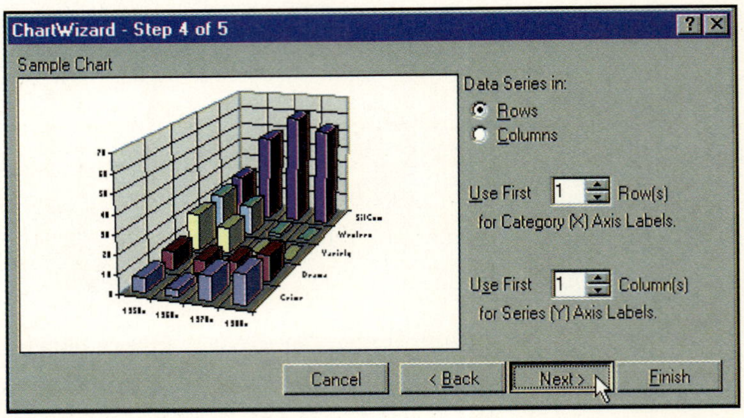

Figure 5.28

The Step 5 dialog box appears.

7 Select **Finish** to create the chart.
The chart appears in its own sheet, whose tab is named Chart1.

8 Double-click the **Chart1** sheet tab, and rename it `3-D Column`

9 Drag the 3-D Column sheet tab so that the chart sheet is layered after the TV Data worksheet.
The screen should resemble Figure 5.29.

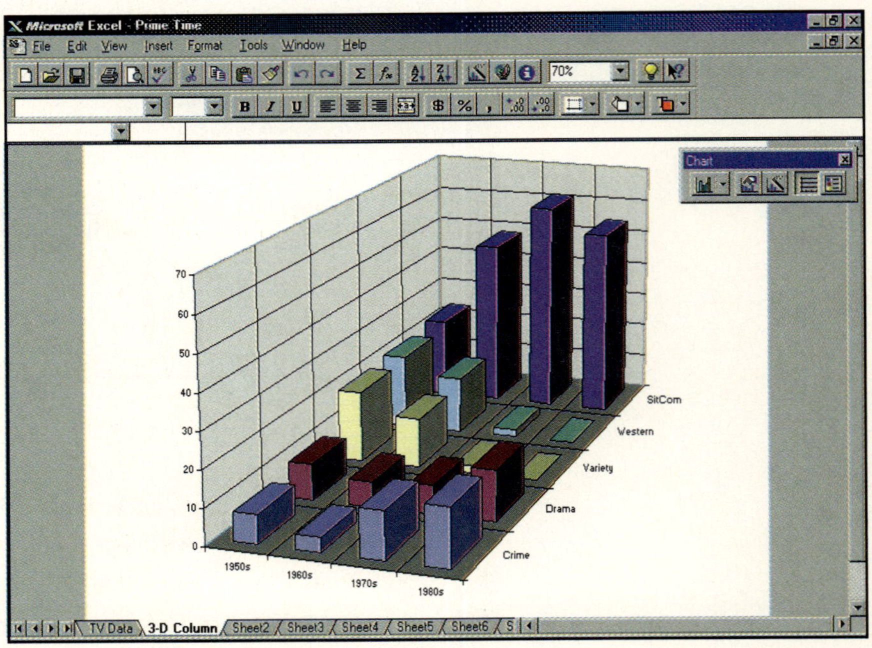

Figure 5.29

Changing the View of a 3-D Chart

The columns of the chart would be a little easier to see if the chart were viewed from a "higher" vantage point and if it were rotated clockwise slightly. It might also look better if the perspective—the three-dimensional effect—were exaggerated. The 3-D View command from the chart sheet's Format menu allows you to experiment with and set different viewing angles and perspectives.

To change the view of the 3-D chart:

1 Choose **Format** and then **3-D View.**

2 Move the pointer to the title bar of the 3-D View dialog box, and drag the dialog box to the upper-left area of the screen so that most of the chart is visible, as shown in Figure 5.30.

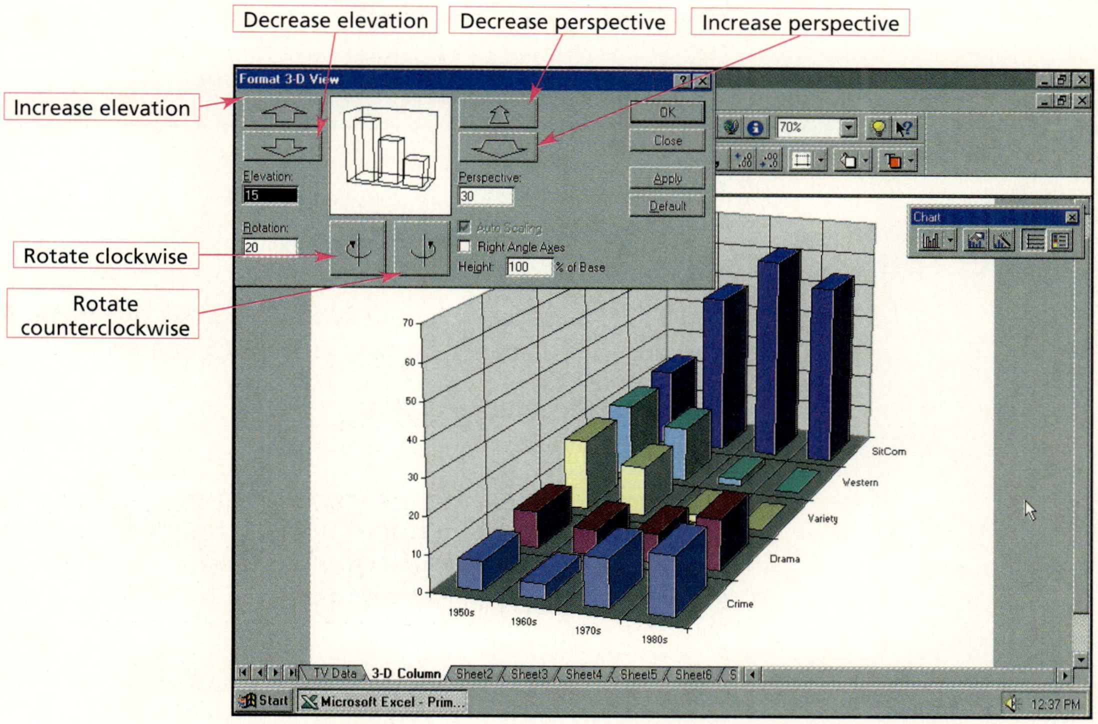

Figure 5.30

3 Use the **Increase Elevation** button to increase the degrees of elevation to 25.
Notice that the small wire-frame example chart in the dialog box changes slightly.

4 Select **Apply** to see the 3-D view settings applied to the actual chart.

5 Click the **Rotate Clockwise** button twice, until the chart is rotated to 40 degrees, and then select **Apply.**

6 Change the perspective to 40 degrees, and then select **OK,** as shown in Figure 5.31.
Selecting OK automatically applies the new 3-D view settings.

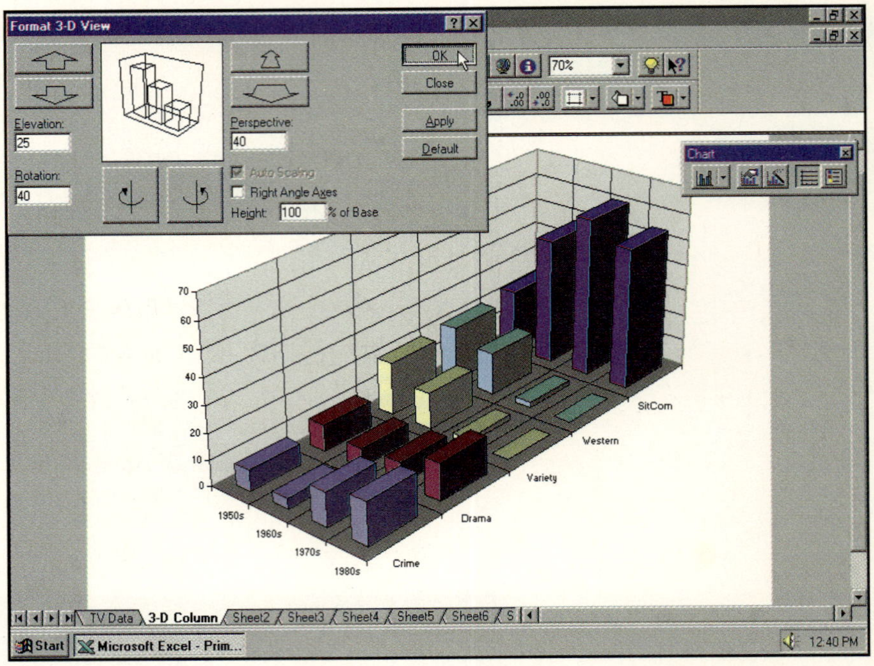

Figure 5.31

Attaching Titles to a Chart

In the following steps, you will add a main chart title that is linked to the worksheet. You will also enter titles for each of the axes.

To attach text to a chart:

1 Make sure the 3-D Column chart sheet is selected (click its tab, if necessary).

2 Zoom to 50 percent magnification; if the chart is not centered on the screen, use the scroll bars to center the chart.

3 Choose **Insert** and then **Titles.**
The Titles dialog box appears.

4 Click all the check boxes: **Chart Title, Value (Z) Axis, Category (X) Axis,** and **Series (Y) Axis.**

5 Select **OK.**
The word *Title* appears above the chart; the letters *X*, *Y*, and *Z* label their respective axes.

6 Click the word *Title* at the top of the chart.

7 Type =

8 Click the **TV Data** sheet tab, and then select cell A1 (which contains the title text), as shown in Figure 5.32.

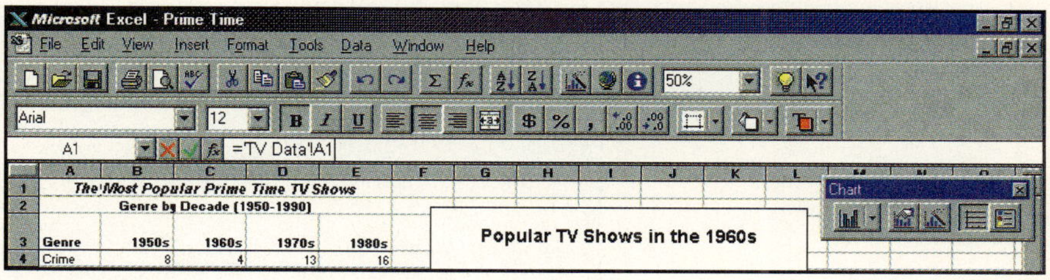

Figure 5.32

9 Press (ENTER) or click the **Enter** box on the formula bar.
The formula ='TV Data'!$A$1 means "get the contents of cell A1 from the sheet named TV Data."

10 Use the Formatting toolbar to change the main title font to Times New Roman 24-point bold italic.

To enter the other chart titles:

1 Click the label Z.
The Z-axis in a 3-D chart is marked with the measurement units of the data.

2 Type `Number in Top 100` and press (ENTER)

3 Change the font to Times New Roman 14-point bold italic.

4 Click the label *Y*.
The Y-axis comprises the data series.

5 Type `Genre` and press (ENTER)

6 Change the font to Times New Roman 14-point bold italic.

7 Click the label *X*.
The X-axis comprises the chart categories.

8 Type `Decade` and press (ENTER)

9 Change the font to Times New Roman 14-point bold italic.

To print the chart:

1 Choose **File** and then **Print Preview.**
A simulated printout appears. Notice that it includes a header and a footer—information at the top and bottom of the page. (In the next project, you will learn how to specify your own header and footer.) In this case, the header and footer are not necessary and reduce the space available for the chart itself, so they should be removed.

2 Select **Setup.**
The Page Setup dialog box appears.

3 Click the **Header/Footer** tab.

4 Scroll to the top of the **Header** list box, and select **(none).**

5 Scroll to the top of the **Footer** list box, and select **(none).**

6 Select **OK** in the Page Setup dialog box.

7 Select **Print** in the Print Preview window.
The Print dialog box appears.

8 Click **OK** to print the chart.
The printout should resemble Figure 5.33.

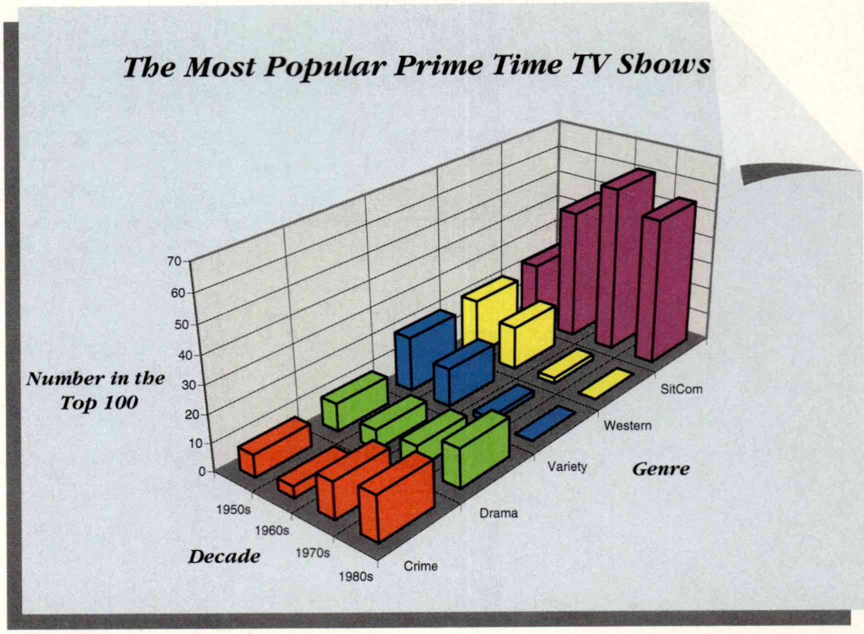

Figure 5.33

9 Save the workbook.

10 Exit Excel.

> ***Tip*** If a color or shade that Excel uses in a pie slice or bar on the printout is unacceptable (for example, too dark to show detail), double-click the specific object whose color you want to change, and select a different color and pattern from the Patterns tab of the Format Data Series dialog box.

The 3-D column chart conveys information more effectively than does the original table of numbers. If you follow a group of bars of a single color, you are tracing through time, following the changing popularity of a particular genre of TV show. If you read from lower left to upper right across the chart, you can examine the relative popularity of different kinds of shows for a particular decade.

THE NEXT STEP

Charts can help you analyze information, and they can help you convey worksheet information more effectively to other people. If you are building a worksheet to make a point—to convince or educate other people about some conclusion or decision—charting can be a powerful tool.

However, you will encounter some worksheets, such as the one in the next project, for which a chart would not be of primary value. Use charting as you would use fonts and formatting: to support the understanding of information in worksheets, and not to distract or confuse.

This concludes Project 5. You can either exit Excel or go on to work the Study Questions, Review Exercises, and Assignments.

SUMMARY AND EXERCISES

Summary

- Charting makes it easier to visualize and identify patterns in a table of numbers.
- Excel has 15 major types of charts, and many variations can be made of each type.
- The data you want to plot (display) in a chart is called a data series; each member of the data series corresponds to a chart category.
- If data series are in columns on the worksheet, their chart categories are in rows, and vice versa.
- Chart category names appear along the horizontal (X) axis of a chart. The vertical axis is called the Y-axis.
- The symbols used to plot a value—such as the columns of a column chart—are called data markers.
- Using the ChartWizard tool is the quickest way to build a basic chart. You begin by selecting the range you want to chart, including any names that you want to appear on the chart.
- An embedded chart is a chart within a worksheet; a chart sheet exists in a workbook and is accessed using a worksheet tab.
- Charts are linked to the worksheets on which they are based; if the worksheet data changes, the chart changes.
- Nonadjacent worksheet selections can be charted, provided the selections can be assembled into a rectangle.
- Embedded charts can be repositioned and resized in the worksheet and will print along with surrounding worksheet data.

Key Terms and Operations

Key Terms
category name
chart
chart category
ChartWizard
data marker
data series
embedded chart
explode
handle
legend
linked (chart)
palette
X-axis
Y-axis

Operations
Format a chart
Insert a chart
Insert titles

Study Questions

Multiple Choice

1. The labels that appear along the bottom edge of a chart are known as the chart:
   a. series.
   b. variables.
   c. categories.
   d. data markers.
   e. data points.

2. A chart that appears within a worksheet is referred to as a(n):
   a. bar chart.
   b. column chart.
   c. category chart.
   d. worksheet chart.
   e. embedded chart.

3. How many major chart types are there in Excel?
   a. 1
   b. 2
   c. 3
   d. 4
   e. 15

4. On a chart, what is used to indicate what each color or symbol stands for?
   a. the X-axis
   b. a legend
   c. a data series
   d. a category
   e. a title

5. Line charts are most appropriate for:
   a. showing trends or changes over time.
   b. comparing individual values at specific times.
   c. showing relationships among portions of a whole.
   d. all of the above.
   e. none of the above.

6. Column charts are most appropriate for:
   a. showing trends or changes over time.
   b. comparing individual values at specific times.
   c. showing relationships among portions of a whole.
   d. all of the above.
   e. none of the above.

7. Pie charts are most appropriate for:
   a. showing trends or changes over time.
   b. comparing individual values at specific times.
   c. showing relationships among portions of a whole.
   d. all of the above.
   e. none of the above.

8. A nonadjacent range to be charted should:
   a. assemble into a rectangle.
   b. contain only text.
   c. contain only values.
   d. contain more chart categories than data series.
   e. contain more data series than chart categories.

9. If you want to modify an embedded chart, you must:
   a. Double-click it.
   b. Choose Edit from the Chart menu.
   c. Choose Chart from the Edit menu.
   d. Insert the chart into a chart sheet.
   e. Link the chart to an empty cell.

10. Embedded charts are especially useful when:
    a. The chart is to be displayed or printed along with the worksheet itself.
    b. Several charts are needed, all based on the same worksheet.
    c. A chart should exist in a separate chart sheet.
    d. The worksheet contains a large number of formulas (rather than number constants).
    e. The worksheet contains a large number of number constants (rather than formulas).

Short Answer

1. What is often the best way to identify trends and interrelationships in data?
2. If the data series is horizontal (in rows) in a worksheet, how are the chart categories arranged?
3. Which axis is the X-axis? Which is the Y-axis?
4. What are chart handles used for?
5. How is a pie chart different from most of the other chart types?
6. What term is used to describe a pie slice that has been pulled out of the pie for emphasis?
7. What type of chart would be most appropriate for showing month-by-month profits for a 48-month series?
8. What type of chart would be most appropriate for showing the relative market share of various brands of automobiles?
9. How do you modify an embedded chart? How do you delete an embedded chart?
10. Can chart sheets change if the worksheets on which they were originally built change?

For Discussion

1. In what ways might a column chart provide a deceptive view of data? What about a 3-D perspective column chart? What do certain charts imply that may not really be present in the data?
2. When is a pie chart an appropriate chart type? When is a column chart appropriate?
3. What is a chart legend, and why is it usually important?

Review Exercises

Creating a Column Chart of Audio Sales for 1975–1990

Open the Formatted Audio Sales History workbook that you completed in Project 3. Using the ChartWizard tool and making nonadjacent selections, construct an embedded column chart that shows how sales of total records and total tapes changed over the period from 1975 through 1990. The data series for this chart are in rows. The chart should resemble Figure 5.34. Print the embedded chart along with the worksheet. Save the workbook.

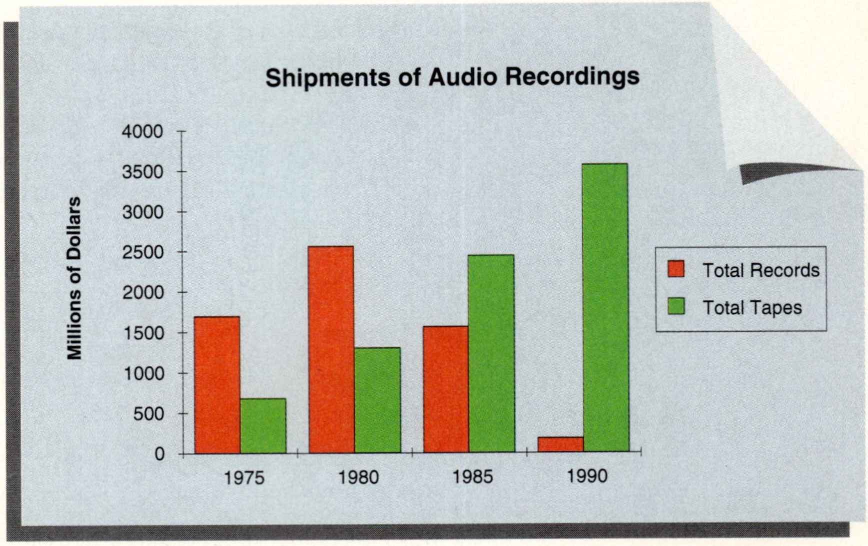

Figure 5.34

Creating a 3-D Pie Chart of Audio Sales for 1985

Open the Formatted Audio Sales History workbook that you completed in Project 3. Using the ChartWizard tool and making nonadjacent selections, construct a chart sheet that contains a 3-D pie chart that shows sales of total tapes, total records, and total CDs for 1985. Rotate the chart so that the Total CD's slice is in front. Explode the Total CD's slice. Name the sheet Audio Pie. Print the chart. Save the workbook.

Assignments

Creating a 3-D Column Chart of Audio Sales for 1975–1990

Open the Formatted Audio Sales History workbook from Project 3. In a separate chart sheet, construct a 3-D column chart showing sales of LP albums, singles, 8-tracks, cassettes, and regular CDs over the 1975 to 1990 period. Rotate the chart as needed to provide a good view of the columns. Print the chart, and save the workbook.

Creating a Pie Chart of Energy Usage of Home Appliances

Open the Electricity Cost workbook from Project 4. Construct a pie chart in a separate chart sheet, with a legend but without labels for each slice, showing the share of the total monthly energy bill for each appliance in the worksheet. Add appropriate titles to the chart. Make another pie chart that graphs only the major users of electricity. Print the charts, and save the workbook.

Creating a 3-D Column Chart of Daily Appliance Usage

Using the Electricity Cost worksheet from Project 4, construct a chart sheet containing a 3-D perspective column chart that shows, for each day of the week, the number of hours the following appliances are used: conventional oven, microwave oven, dishwasher, and clothes dryer. Rotate and format the chart as needed. Print the chart, and save the workbook.

PART IV

Integrated Project 1

Integrated Project 1: Embedding an Excel Worksheet in a Word Document

Objectives

After completing this project, you will be able to:

- Create two Office documents for reporting survey results
- Embed an object in a Word document
- Update the embedded object
- Crop the embedded object
- Move the embedded object
- Size the embedded object
- Format the embedded object

Now that you have worked with Microsoft Word and Excel separately, you will learn how to integrate information from these two software packages into one document. This means creating different document files in Word and Excel and putting them together into one file. In addition, you will create a binder to store these files and others you will create. This first project is the beginning of a large presentation project that you will create for the president of an expanding company. You will first create the body, or shell, of a report in Word and then include a worksheet as part of the document. This project will introduce you to object linking and embedding, which you will explore in greater detail as you complete your presentation throughout the other projects.

Case Study: Creating a Report

The company you work for wants to expand its business with a new product. They have hired various marketing firms to do national consumer market surveys to discover the potential sales market for two new blends of fresh-roasted coffee. Taste-test surveys are being done on college campuses to determine whether collegians prefer the taste of the traditional Colombian blend or the taste of the new European Dark Roast blend your company has created. As the survey results come in, you will record them in an Excel worksheet.

Designing the Solution

The company president, Dr. Gardener, called you this morning and asked you to keep him updated on the progress of the national taste-test surveys. He wants you to prepare a simple report that shows the survey results, which states have been reported, which have not, and so on. This report will be given to his staff every morning so they can monitor the survey's progress.

You have two options: create and print separate Excel worksheet and Word report files, or create separate files and then incorporate the Excel worksheet into the Word document. Because you have done work for Dr. Gardener in the past, you know that his simple projects usually take on a life of their own! So, to make updating and adding to the report easy, you decide to create the report in Word and include the worksheet in the Word document.

CREATING THE SURVEY RESULTS WORKSHEET AND THE DAILY REPORT DOCUMENT

Your first step is to enter the survey results into an Excel worksheet.

> ***Tip*** When you see a button or icon next to a numbered step, you can select that button or icon in place of the menu command in the numbered step, as in step 4 in the following numbered steps.

To create an Excel worksheet:

Blank Workbook

1 Select the Start a New Document button on the Shortcut Bar. Under the General tab, select the icon for a Blank Workbook. If the Shortcut Bar is not visible, use the Start button to launch Excel from within the Office program group.

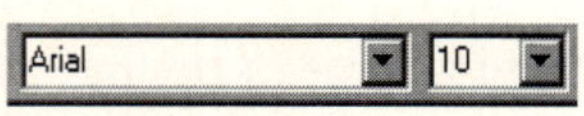

2 Select the Font button from the toolbar, and then select 10-point Arial.

3 Create the spreadsheet shown in Figure 1.1. Change the format of the title and major headings to bold. Enter the State column heading in cell A4. Use the AutoSum and AutoFill features to enter formulas in column F and row 13. Adjust column widths as necessary. Align each major heading across the selection. Use the border button to apply the borders shown.

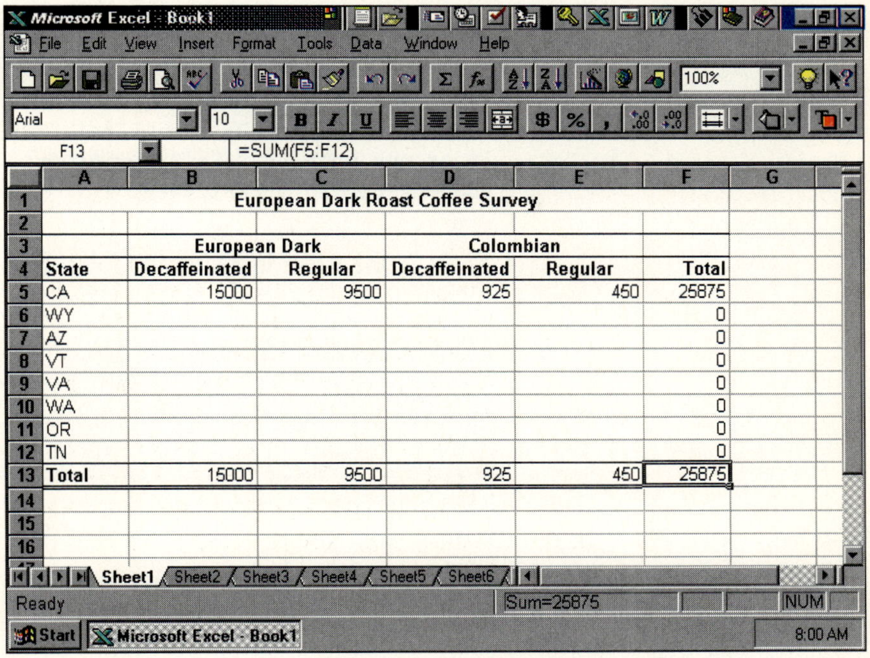

Figure 1.1

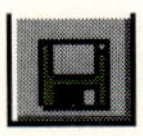

4 Choose Save from the File menu, or select the Save button.

> ***Reminder*** Office 95 supports long file names, so the file name you are about to enter is valid.

5 Type `Taste Test Results` as the file name, select drive A:, and then select OK to accept the file name and save the document.

> ***Caution*** The drive here called drive A: is the 3½-inch floppy drive on your computer. On your system, it might be called B: or by another letter, depending on your system's configuration.

6 Exit Excel.

Now that you have created the worksheet, you can write the body of the report in Word.

To create the Word document:

Blank Document

1 Select the Start a New Document button on the Shortcut Bar. Under the General tab, select the icon for a Blank Document. If the Shortcut Bar is not visible, use the Start button to launch Word from within the Office 95 program group.

2 Choose Font from the Format menu.

3 Select 14-point Arial, and then select OK to accept the font settings.

4 Type `New Product Daily Report`

5 Center and boldface the title.

6 Press (ENTER) eight times.

7 Type the following two paragraphs:

`This report is a daily update of the national research project. The listing below shows the results from the taste-test surveys as they are reported by the market researchers.`

`It is our hope that this new product will be successful in the gourmet coffee marketplace.`

8 Press (ENTER) four times.

Your Word document should look similar to the document in Figure 1.2.

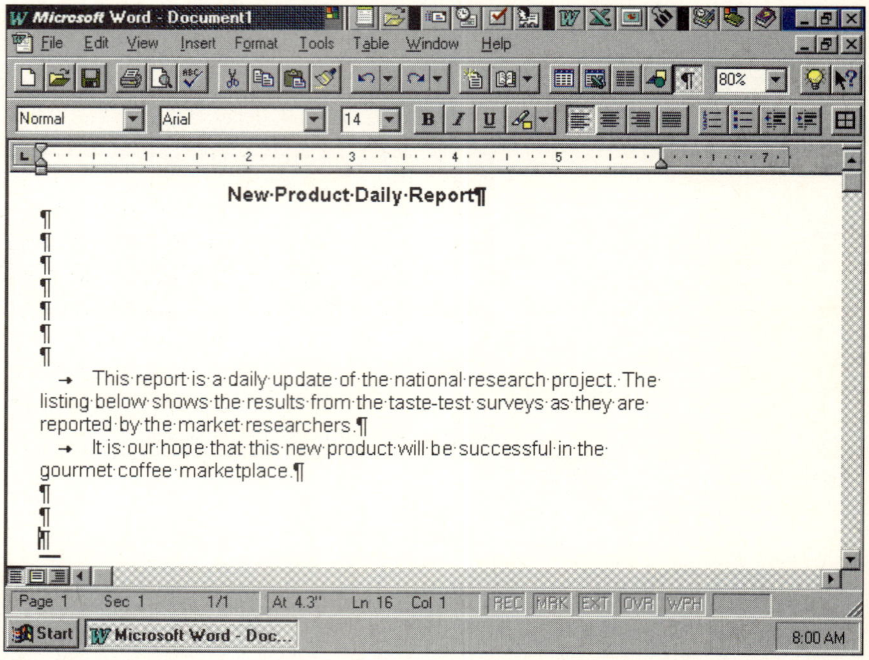

Figure 1.2

9 Choose Save from the File menu.

10 Type **`New Product Report`** as the file name, select drive A:, and then select OK to accept the file name and save the document.

EMBEDDING THE EXCEL WORKSHEET IN THE WORD DOCUMENT

You have created separate Word and Excel documents and added them to a binder for easy access, so now it's time to put them together into one document that you can update easily. There are three ways to include the worksheet in the Word document:

- Copy the object to the clipboard and paste it into the document.
- Embed the worksheet in the Word document.
- Link the worksheet to the Word document.

These three methods are summarized in Table 1.1. The first method, copying and pasting, is very limiting. This method simply pastes an image of the object, like a camera snapshot, into the document. In the same way a photographic image cannot be edited once it is printed, text that is copied from one location and pasted into another must be edited in both locations if it needs to be changed. The other two methods, embedding and linking, are part of the ***object linking and embedding (OLE)*** process. OLE (pronounced "oh-lay") is the powerful process of connecting or combining objects created in different software packages into one dynamic file. Each object's image has a ***source file*** associated with it. An object's source file can be a graphic image file, a clip art file, an equation constructed through the equation editor, or some other type of file.

When an object is ***embedded,*** the source file is inserted into an existing file called the ***target file.*** Because the source file is included as part of the target file, the object can be updated directly from the target file if its application is available on the hard drive of the computer you are using.

Linking is very similar to embedding. When an object is linked to the target file, the target file stores the location of the object but not the object's source file; it displays only an image of the object. In Office 95, linking is the best option if you want to include individual documents in an Office binder, since updating the source document automatically updates any target documents containing links to the source. In this integrated project you will learn how to use the embedding method of inserting objects. You will work with linking in the next project. In Integrated Project 3 you will learn how to share information between documents added to a binder.

Table 1.1

Method	What is stored in the target file?	Can the object in the target file be updated?	If the object is updated while in the target file, will those changes be saved in the source file?
Copy/paste method	Object's image	No	Not applicable
Embed method	Object's image and source file	Yes (if the source file's application is loaded)	No, the source file is not updated
Link method	Object's image and location of the source file	Yes (if the source file's application is loaded); the preferred method when using Office binders	Yes, since the source file is actually updated

When you embed an object, you begin by opening the target file. Next you insert the object through the Insert menu. The computer automatically opens the object's source file application on top of the target file. Either you will see a separate window that shows only the source file's application (the title bar changes to display the source file's application title) or, as shown in Figure 1.3, you will see the source file in a small secondary window displayed within the target application. The toolbar buttons and some menus change from the target file's to the source file's application toolbars and menus, but the title bar still shows the target application's title.

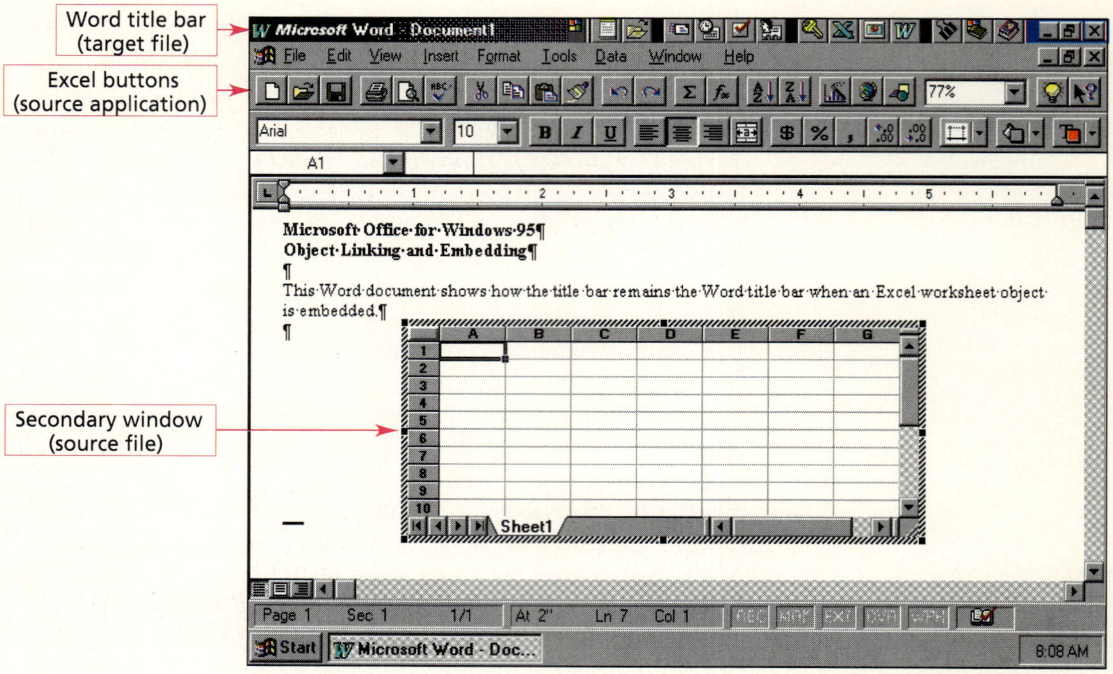

Figure 1.3

You can create an object in the source application before you embed it, or you can create an object directly from within the target application. You do not have to exit Word to create an embedded Excel worksheet if both the target and the source applications are available on the computer you are using.

Think about how you study at your desk. When you study for an exam, you probably have your textbook and class notes on your desk. You might pick up the class notes and put them on top of the textbook you were reading. It would be ridiculous to put your textbook away in a drawer every time you wanted to refer to your class notes. This concept relates to layering objects in a document. Instead of putting the word processing document away to work with the worksheet, you can open the worksheet on top of your word processing document. You can move the embedded worksheet around in the document to a different page, center the worksheet on the page, and so on, just as if you were physically moving a printed worksheet around on top of a printed word processing document. Object linking and embedding provides another method for keeping information from different source applications together.

To embed the Excel worksheet in the Word document:

1 Open the New Product Report Word document, if it is not currently open.

2 Position the insertion point at the end of the Word document, before the last paragraph mark.

3 Choose Object from the Insert menu.
A dialog box appears, offering two options for inserting an object: Create New and Create from File.

4 Select the Create from File folder tab, and click the Browse button to see the contents of the diskette in drive A:.

This option enables you to select an object file that has already been created. The screen now looks similar to Figure 1.4.

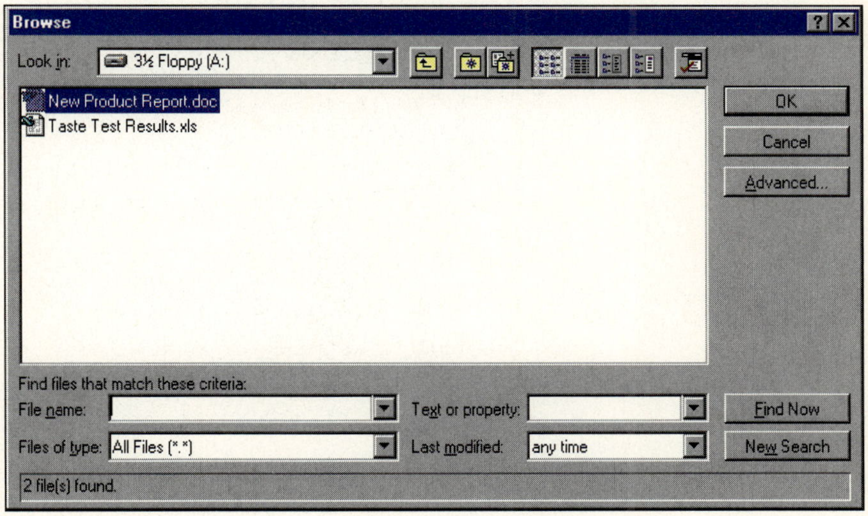

Figure 1.4

5 Select the *Taste Test Results.xls* file from drive A:, and then select OK. The screen now looks like Figure 1.5.

Tip If your computer does not display the file extensions, do the following:

1. Click the My Computer icon on the Windows 95 desktop.
2. Select Options from the View menu.
3. Deselect the Hide MS-DOS file extensions for the file types that are registered check box.
4. Click OK.

The file extensions will now be displayed whenever the Open File dialog box appears.

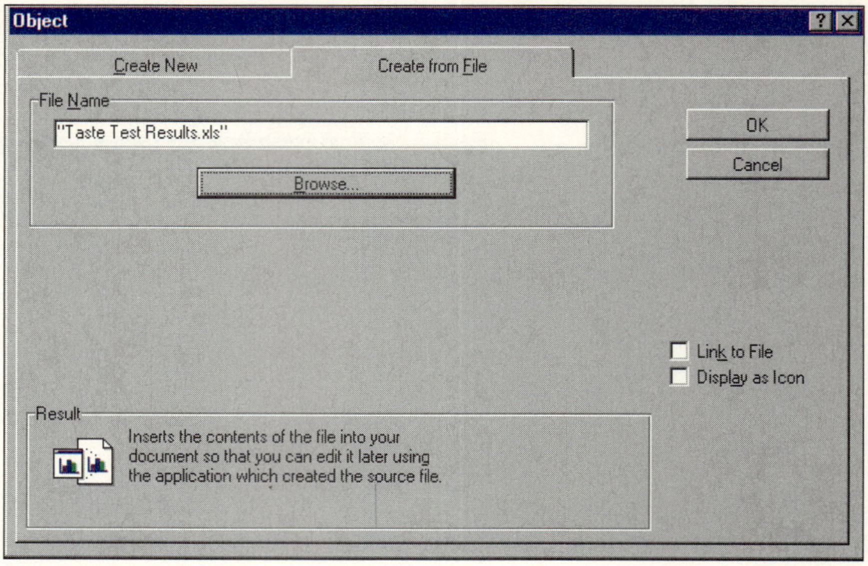

Figure 1.5

6 Select OK to embed this worksheet. The screen now looks like Figure 1.6.

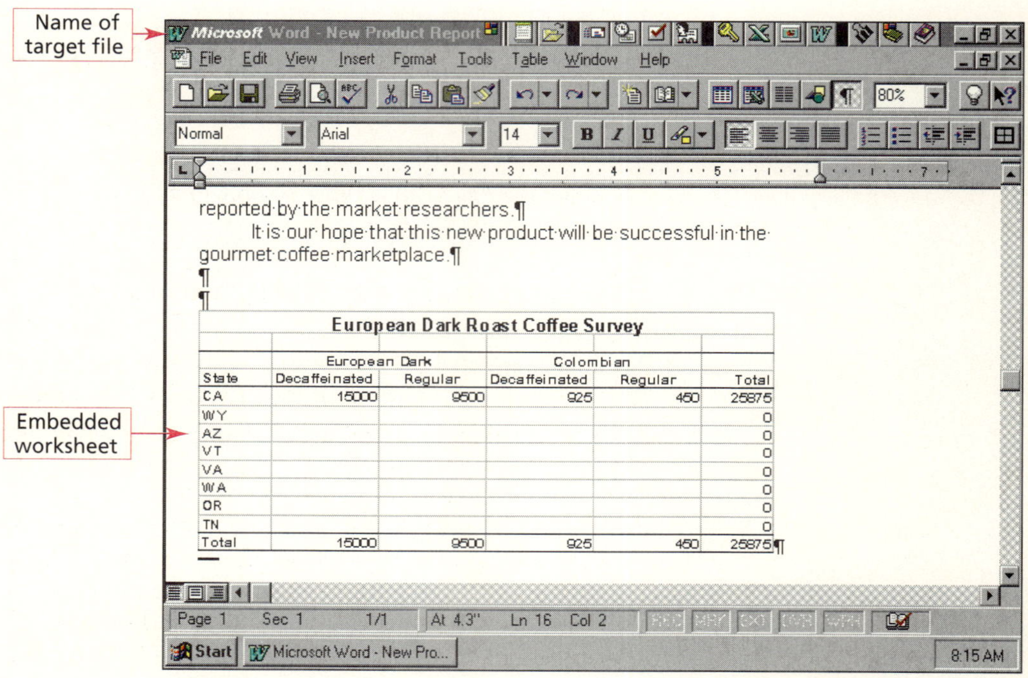

Figure 1.6

7 Wait until the hourglass icon disappears and you hear the drive activity noises stop before you try to continue.

Quick Fix If the embedded worksheet displays the actual row numbers and column labels (A, B, C . . .), and the toolbar looks like the Excel toolbar, move your mouse pointer to the top of the Word document and click once so that the insertion point is moved from the worksheet back into the Word document.

8 Select Save from the File menu to save the changes to the Word document.

When you saved your Word file, you saved the embedded worksheet as part of the Word document. The original source worksheet (Taste Test Results.xls) was not saved. When you edit the embedded object from the Word document, the changes will not be written to the Excel source file. Be careful, because the target file size will grow as you edit the embedded worksheet. Files with embedded objects can become very large and difficult to maintain on floppy disks.

Tip Embedding is a good tool when you are using a small (in bytes) object. Because the entire object resides in the target file (in this case, the Word document), the target file size can grow dramatically. You'll want to keep an eye on the target file size as you work with embedded objects.

EXIT If necessary, you can exit Word now and continue this project later.

UPDATING AN EMBEDDED OBJECT

The survey results have started to come in, and your first report is due in Dr. Gardener's office tomorrow morning. Instead of updating the worksheet in Excel and then re-embedding it in Word, you will update the embedded worksheet from within the New Product Report file. You will also *crop* and *size* the worksheet window in the Word document. Currently, the worksheet window embedded in the Word document reveals only a portion of the entire Excel worksheet. When you ***crop*** the window, you move its edges so the window reveals more or less of the object. ***Sizing,*** on the other hand, retains the boundaries of the worksheet but stretches the entire window so that the displayed worksheet is made larger or smaller.

Some source applications open a full window on top of the target file when you edit the source file. However, when you edit this worksheet, the computer will temporarily replace *some* Word menus and toolbars with *some* Excel menus and toolbars, and it will keep the Word window open.

Tip Check the title bar to confirm which type of window you are currently using. To exit from applications that change the title bar to the source application, choose Exit or Quit from the source application's File menu. When the title bar remains that of the target application, return to the target document by clicking outside of the embedded object.

To update the worksheet:

1 Start Word if necessary.

2 Open the Word document, New Product Report.doc, if necessary.

3 Double-click anywhere in the worksheet window.
The screen now looks like Figure 1.7. Notice that the document name is shortened in the Office 95 Shortcut Bar.

The Excel window is now the active window

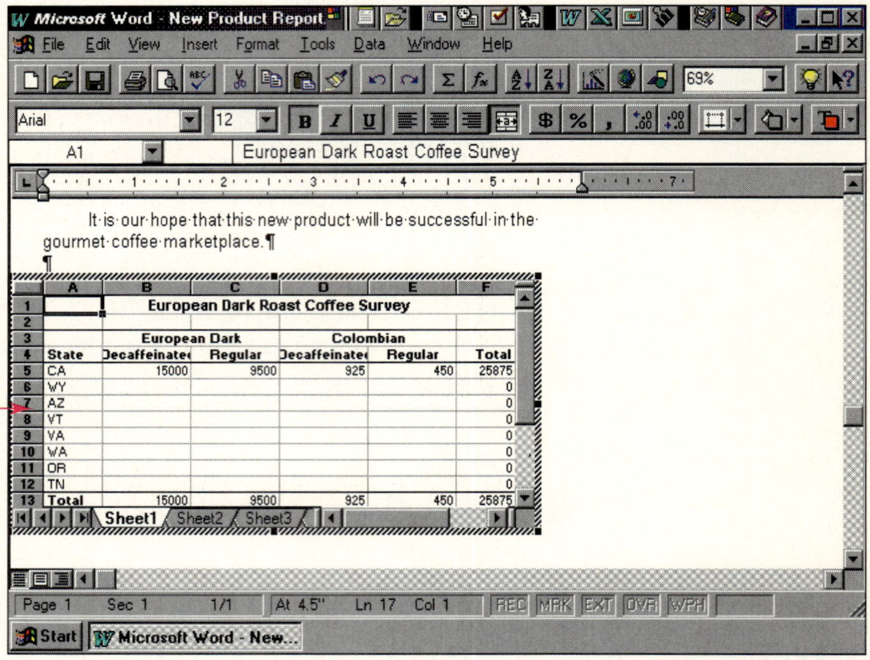

Figure 1.7

4 Enter the new survey figures for Wyoming and Arizona, as shown in Figure 1.8.

	A	B	C	D	E	F
1	European Dark Roast Coffee Survey					
2						
3		European Dark		Colombian		
4	State	Decaffeinated	Regular	Decaffeinated	Regular	Total
5	CA	15000	9500	925	450	25875
6	WY	400	500	375	200	1475
7	AZ	950	723	154	341	2168
8	VT					0
9	VA					0
10	WA					0
11	OR					0
12	TN					0
13	Total	16350	10723	1454	991	29518
14						

Figure 1.8

5 Use the handles of the window to crop the worksheet object so that the last row in the window is row 15 and the right column is column G. The worksheet window now looks like Figure 1.9.

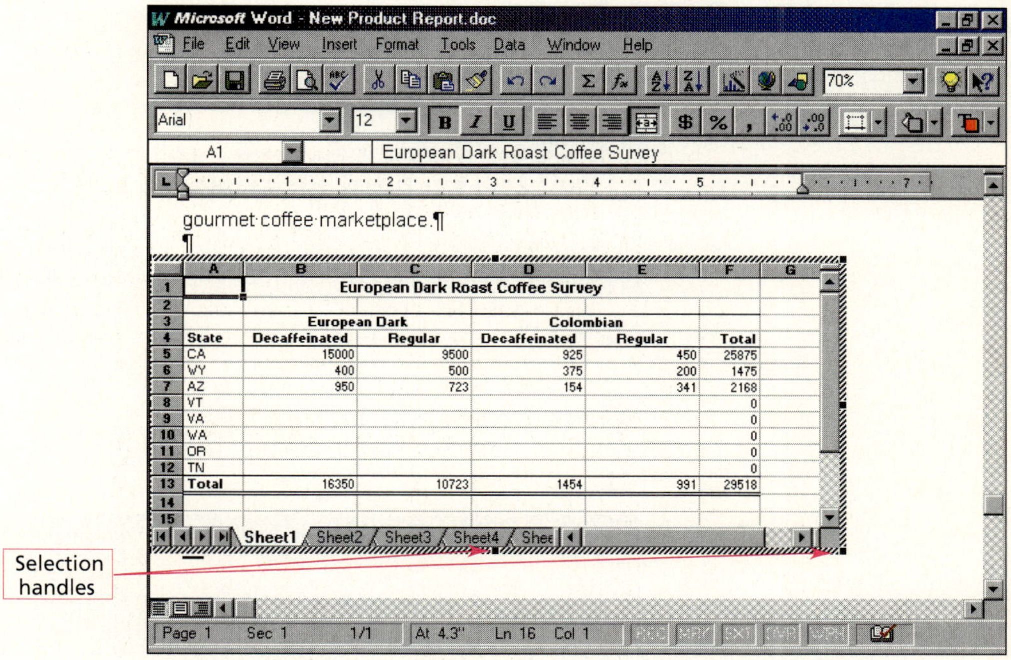

Figure 1.9

6 Click outside of the embedded object, anywhere in the Word document.

7 Save the Word document by selecting Save from the File menu. Office 95 saves the Word document with its embedded worksheet object, not the source Excel worksheet.

Moving and Sizing an Unframed Embedded Object

You can move objects that you have embedded in a document. Currently, the Excel worksheet is at the bottom of the Word document. In the following numbered steps, you will move the embedded object so it is located before the first paragraph.

To move an embedded object:

1 Select the embedded object by clicking once inside the worksheet.

2 Drag the object so that the placement icon is before the first paragraph, as shown in Figure 1.10, and then release the mouse button.

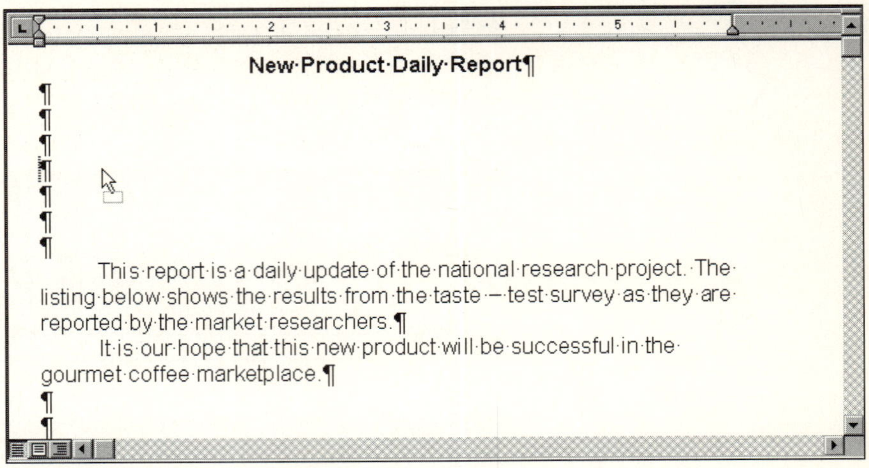

Figure 1.10

3 Click outside the embedded object.
The document now looks like Figure 1.11.

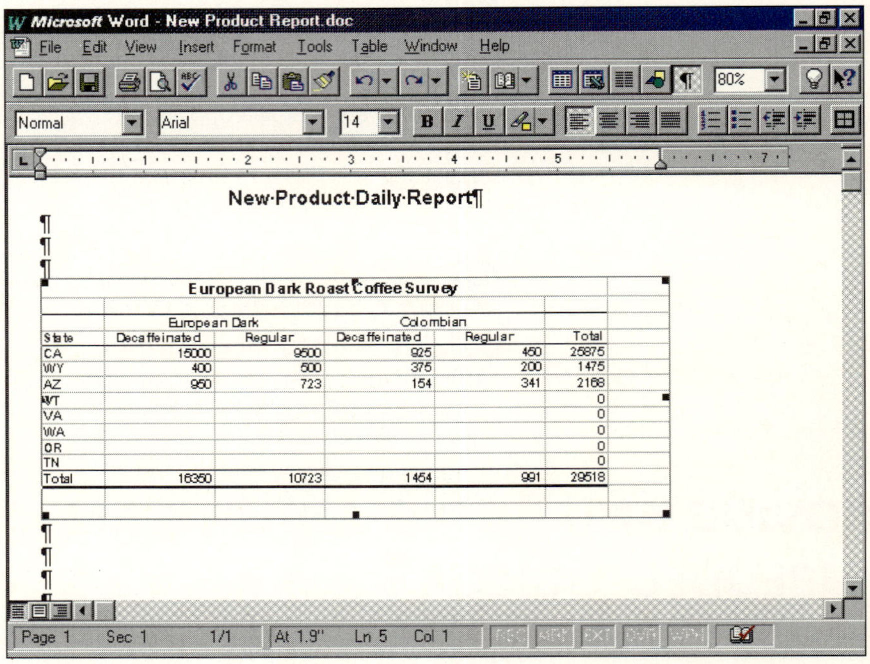

Figure 1.11

4 Save the document.
The object can also be made larger or smaller. In the steps that follow, you will make the worksheet window larger.

To size an embedded object:

1 Select the worksheet window.

2 Use the lower-right handle to increase the size of the window, and release the handle when the window meets the right side of the screen.
The new worksheet window looks like Figure 1.12.

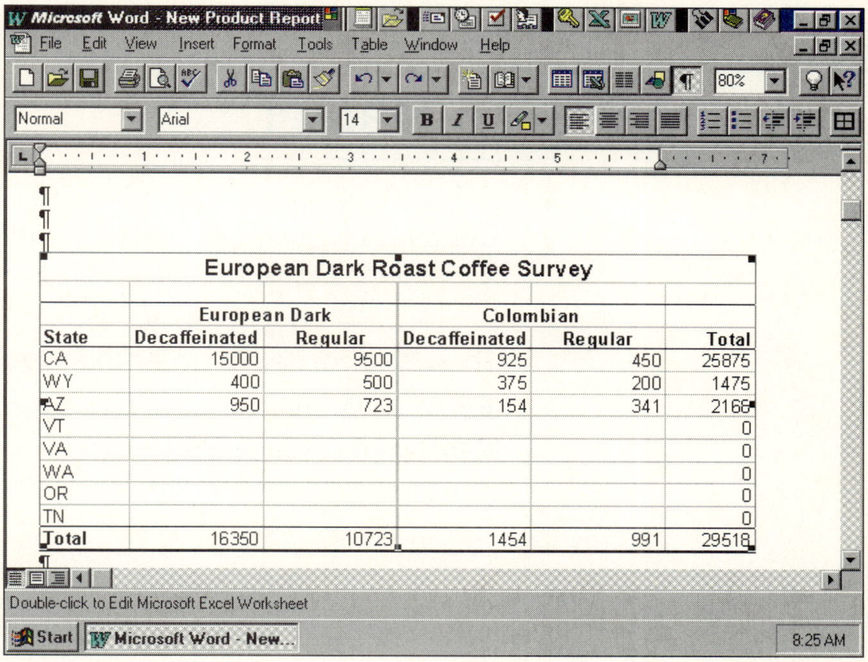

Figure 1.12

3 Decrease the window's size so that it fills approximately one half of the document width.
The worksheet window looks like Figure 1.13.

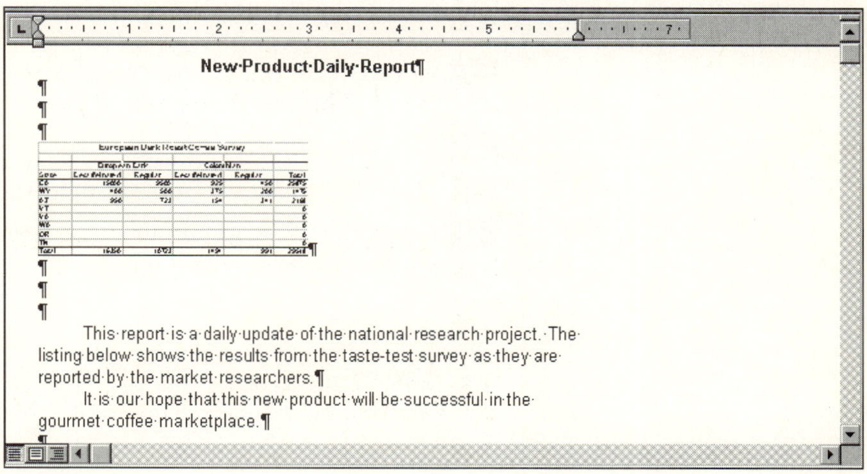

Figure 1.13

4 Resize the worksheet so its width is approximately five and one half inches.

5 While your worksheet window is selected, click on the Center button. Notice that your worksheet is now centered between the left and right margins on the page.

6 Save your document.

ADDING A BORDER AND SHADING TO AN EMBEDDED OBJECT

In Word 7, frames can be added to objects to give them greater mobility. Objects can be formatted by adding borders and shadows, and if you have a color printer, borders can be colorized to produce a sharp and professional presentation.

To add a border to an embedded object:

1 Move the insertion point over the worksheet object.

2 Click the right mouse button.
The right mouse menu shown in Figure 1.14 appears.

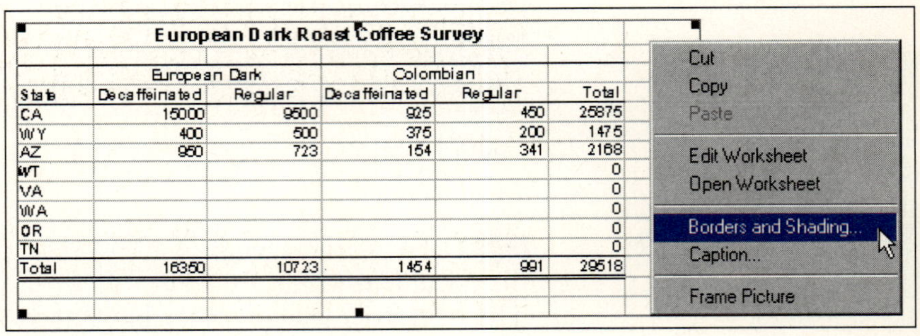

Figure 1.14

3 Choose Borders and Shading from the menu.
The Picture Borders dialog box appears.

4 Select the Borders tab.

5 Select the Shadow option in the Presets box.

6 Select the 1½-point double line from the Style column.
The screen now looks like Figure 1.15.

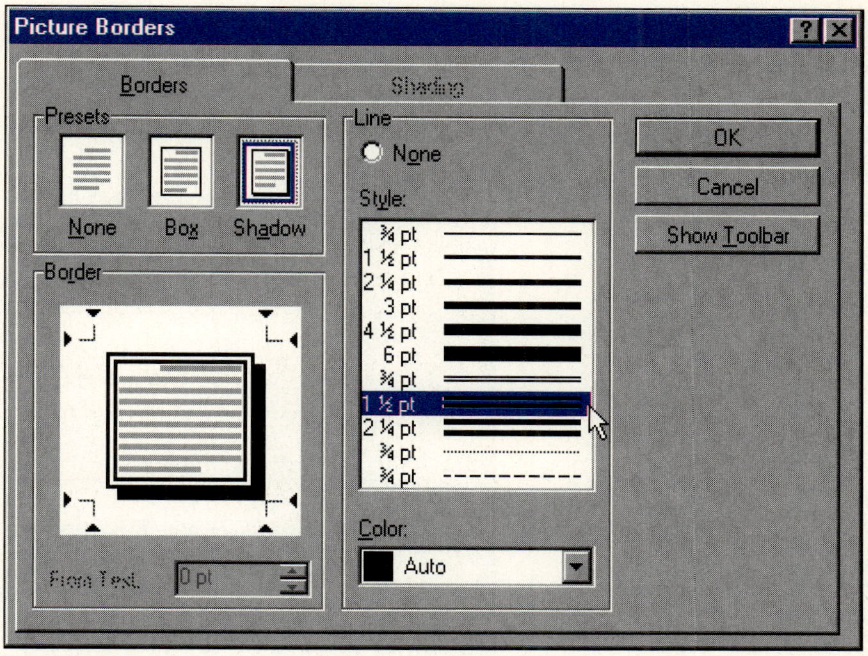

Figure 1.15

7 Select OK to accept the border options.
You are returned to the document.

8 Select the Print Preview button from the toolbar to see what your finished document will look like if you print it on a laser or inkjet printer. The document now resembles Figure 1.16.

New Product Daily Report

European Dark Roast Coffee Survey

	European Dark		Colombian		
State	**Decaffeinated**	**Regular**	**Decaffeinated**	**Regular**	**Total**
CA	15000	9500	925	450	25875
WY	400	500	375	200	1475
AZ	950	723	154	341	2168
VT					0
VA					0
WA					0
OR					0
TN					0
Total	16350	10723	1454	991	29518

This report is a daily update of the national research project. The listing below shows the results from the taste-test surveys as they are reported by the market researchers.

It is our hope that this new product will be successful in the gourmet coffee marketplace.

Figure 1.16

9 Click the Close button to return to Page Layout view.

10 Save the document.

THE NEXT STEP

This project introduced you to a new concept, embedding. You embedded a worksheet in a word processing document. There are many other types of files that you can embed, for example, database data and graphic files such as clip art and photographs. And, provided that the computer you use has both the target and source applications installed, you can easily edit and update your objects as necessary.

Spreadsheets are great for compiling rows and columns of data, but they are not the best for displaying the data to the reader in a meaningful way. Charts and graphs are much better vehicles for communication. Take another look at your spreadsheet. What information is meaningful for the president's staff? What states have the greatest sales potential for these roasts? What states have the least potential? Where should the company begin to sell its product? Should the company market those states where the response was low? These are the types of questions managers and executives ask when they are facing business decisions. These questions are more easily answered when the data is displayed in a meaningful form, such as a chart or graph. The reader can see relationships between the data quickly and easily, without having to concentrate on the rows and columns of numbers. Seeing the data displayed graphically helps the reader assimilate the data and make logical conclusions based on the data.

Remember that when you combine applications to form documents, you usually are trying to communicate some sort of message to someone. Whether it is a newsletter, a brochure, a thesis paper, or a résumé, you are communicating a message. Objects can be used to enhance the written word so that your message is reinforced and quickly assimilated by the reader.

This concludes Project 1 of the integrated projects. You can exit Word now or go on to work the Study Questions, Review Exercises, and Assignments.

SUMMARY AND EXERCISES

Summary

- Objects can be pasted, embedded, or linked to a target document.
- Objects copied from one location and pasted into another cannot be updated simultaneously; they must be edited in both locations separately.
- Object linking and embedding (OLE) is the process of combining objects from different source applications.
- An embedded object's entire source file is inserted into the target document and becomes part of the target file.
- Embedded objects can be updated within the target file.
- Only the location of the object is stored in the target file when the object is linked.
- A linked file's image is displayed in the target file.
- Objects can be created before or during the OLE process.
- An embedded object's source file is not saved after the object is embedded.
- Some applications temporarily replace the target application's toolbars and menus.
- Some applications open a separate window on top of the target window.
- Objects can be moved and sized after they are embedded.
- Objects can be enhanced with colorful borders.

Key Terms and Operations

Key Terms
crop
embed
link
object linking and embedding (OLE)
size
source file
target file

Operations
Create an object from a file
Crop an embedded object
Embed an object
Format an embedded object
Position an embedded object
Size an embedded object
Update an embedded object

Study Questions

Multiple Choice

1. An embedded object is a
   a. separate file attached to the end of a document.
   b. file inserted in a document, and the source file is no longer needed.
   c. file inserted in a document, and the source file is needed.
   d. graphics file that cannot be changed once it is embedded.
2. Cropping is a process whereby
   a. the edges of a window are manipulated to display all or part of the object.
   b. the frame is formatted to match the size of the object.
   c. you define the size of the object file.
   d. the object file size is made smaller to fit onto the disk.
3. An embedded object
   a. is always created before the target document.
   b. can never be updated without the source file.
   c. is made a part of the target document file.
   d. must always remain in the original insertion place in the document.
4. The target document
   a. will become larger (in bytes) as the embedded document is edited and expanded.
   b. must always be a word processing document.
   c. is always the first document created.
   d. must be stored on the computer's hard drive.
5. An object must always have
   a. a frame inserted around it.
   b. its application loaded on the computer in order to be updated.
   c. its application loaded on the computer in order to be visible in the target document.
   d. the source file available to update the object.
6. The target application is
   a. always a word processor.
   b. where the object is embedded.
   c. never opened.
   d. where the object is created.
7. Once an object is embedded
   a. it can never be edited.
   b. it should be edited straight from the source application.
   c. it must be saved separately from the target application.
   d. it is saved as a part of the target document.
8. Including an object when a document is saved means
   a. you must save both the target document and the object separately.
   b. you save the document and the object into the target document file.
   c. you must save the object first and then include it when you save the target document.
   d. the object cannot be saved unless it was first created outside of the target document.

9. Which of the following is true concerning embedded objects? Using a frame to format an object means that
   a. you can add borders to an object.
   b. the object cannot be sized when it contains a border.
   c. you can edit the object's border only if the border was added before the object was embedded.
   d. the object can be placed only at the top of the page.
10. Never use an object
   a. to display a graph.
   b. if you embed a scanned photograph.
   c. to include one word processing document within another.
   d. when you want to update a graphics file.

Short Answer

1. What does OLE stand for and what does it do?
2. What is the name of the file where the original object is created?
3. Which file stores the embedded object?
4. Which OLE method option puts a snapshot of the object into the file.
5. What helps make the object more mobile?
6. How do you size an object?
7. Which menu option lets you add a border to an object?
8. What verifies which toolbars and menu items are active when you are editing an object?
9. What is the term that means to shrink and enlarge the window over the object?
10. When you save a file that contains an embedded object, where is the embedded object saved?

For Discussion

1. Explain the difference between embedding, linking, and copying and pasting.
2. When would you use the copy and paste method instead of the embedding method of inserting a graph or worksheet into the document?
3. What are some important things to remember when you are saving documents with embedded objects?
4. Besides a report, what are some other practical scenarios for using embedding?

Review Exercises

Updating the Worksheet's Format

Update the president's report to include new data. The additional data includes new columns, rows, and formulas that were not part of the original worksheet.

1. Open New Product Report.doc.
2. Save this document as Updated New Product Report.doc. (You will use this file again in other integrated projects.)
3. Edit the worksheet to include new columns, rows, and formulas as shown in Figure 1.17.

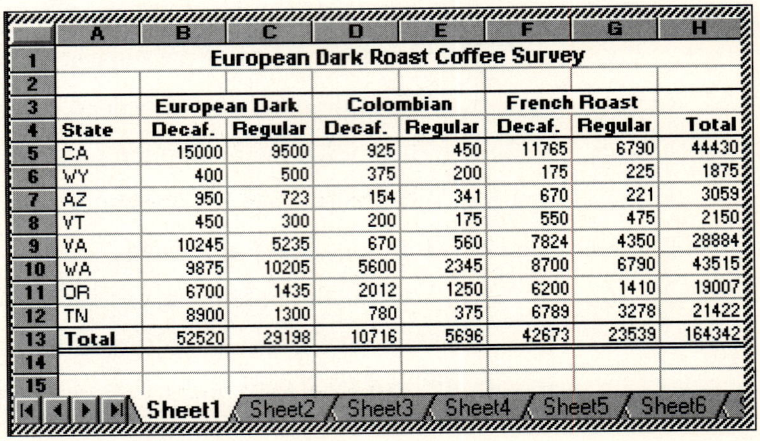

	A	B	C	D	E	F	G	H
1	European Dark Roast Coffee Survey							
2								
3		European Dark		Colombian		French Roast		
4	State	Decaf.	Regular	Decaf.	Regular	Decaf.	Regular	Total
5	CA	15000	9500	925	450	11765	6790	44430
6	WY	400	500	375	200	175	225	1875
7	AZ	950	723	154	341	670	221	3059
8	VT	450	300	200	175	550	475	2150
9	VA	10245	5235	670	560	7824	4350	28884
10	WA	9875	10205	5600	2345	8700	6790	43515
11	OR	6700	1435	2012	1250	6200	1410	19007
12	TN	8900	1300	780	375	6789	3278	21422
13	Total	52520	29198	10716	5696	42673	23539	164342
14								
15								

Sheet1 Sheet2 Sheet3 Sheet4 Sheet5 Sheet6

Figure 1.17

4. Save the document.

Moving and Formatting the Embedded Object

When you insert an object into a document, you may find that you need to move the object to another page or to another section of the document. You may also decide to change the object's border style, color, or shading. Sometimes you need to modify the way the object looks to conform to a company standard or to please a client. This exercise gives you some additional experience moving and formatting the embedded object.

1. Move the object so that the document looks like Figure 1.18.

New Product Daily Report

This report is a daily update of the national research project. The listing below shows the results from the taste-test surveys as they are reported by the market researchers.

European Dark Roast Coffee Survey

	European Dark		Colombian		French Roast		
State	Decaf.	Regular	Decaf.	Regular	Decaf.	Regular	Total
CA	15000	9500	925	450	11765	6790	44430
WY	400	500	375	200	175	225	1875
AZ	950	723	154	341	670	221	3059
VT	450	300	200	175	550	475	2150
VA	10245	5235	670	560	7824	4350	28884
WA	9875	10205	5600	2345	8700	6790	43515
OR	6700	1435	2012	1250	6200	1410	19007
TN	8900	1300	780	375	6789	3278	21422
Total	52520	29198	10716	5696	42673	23539	164342

It is our hope that this new product will be successful in the gourmet coffee marketplace.

Figure 1.18

2. Modify the borders so that there is no shadow behind the object.
3. Select a different border line and color.
4. Save the document.

Assignments

Creating a Word Document with Embedded Objects

Write a letter to your family about the classes you are taking this semester. In the letter embed an Excel worksheet that lists your classes. Rate each class on an enjoyment scale from 1 to 50, following the example in Figure 1.19. Format the object so that the box has a shadow, and experiment with colored borders. Practice putting the worksheet in the middle, beginning, and end of your letter. Save this document as My Current Classes.doc on drive A:.

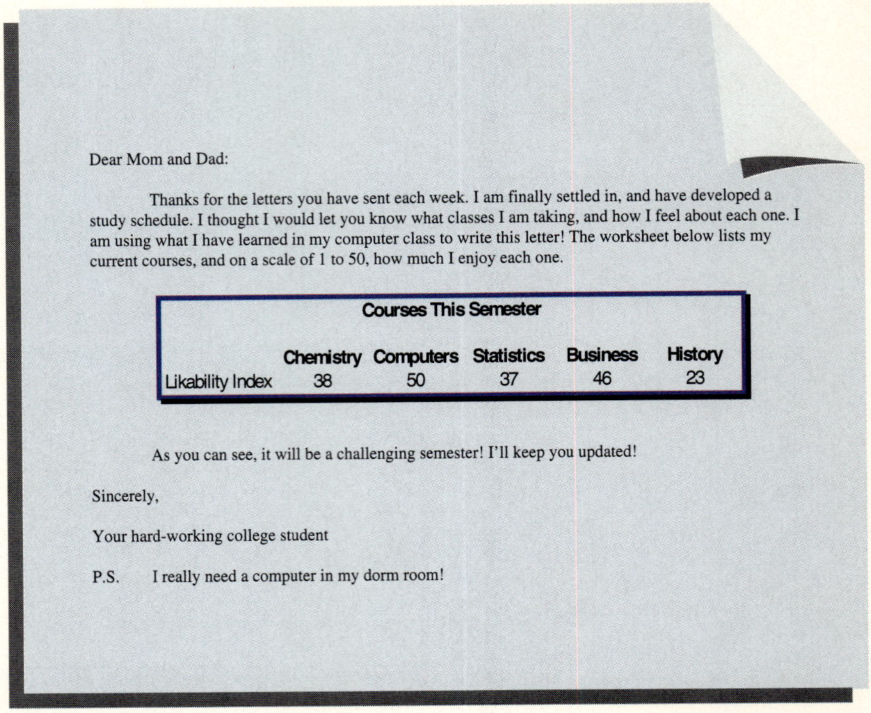

Dear Mom and Dad:

Thanks for the letters you have sent each week. I am finally settled in, and have developed a study schedule. I thought I would let you know what classes I am taking, and how I feel about each one. I am using what I have learned in my computer class to write this letter! The worksheet below lists my current courses, and on a scale of 1 to 50, how much I enjoy each one.

Courses This Semester

	Chemistry	Computers	Statistics	Business	History
Likability Index	38	50	37	46	23

As you can see, it will be a challenging semester! I'll keep you updated!

Sincerely,

Your hard-working college student

P.S. I really need a computer in my dorm room!

Figure 1.19

Embedding a Chart

Write a second letter home and call it My Favorite Courses.doc. Use the worksheet data from My Current Classes.doc to embed a 3-D bar chart into this document. This will help those reading your letter to see at a quick glance which courses are your favorites, and which courses you'd rather not be taking. Your finished document should resemble the example in Figure 1.20.

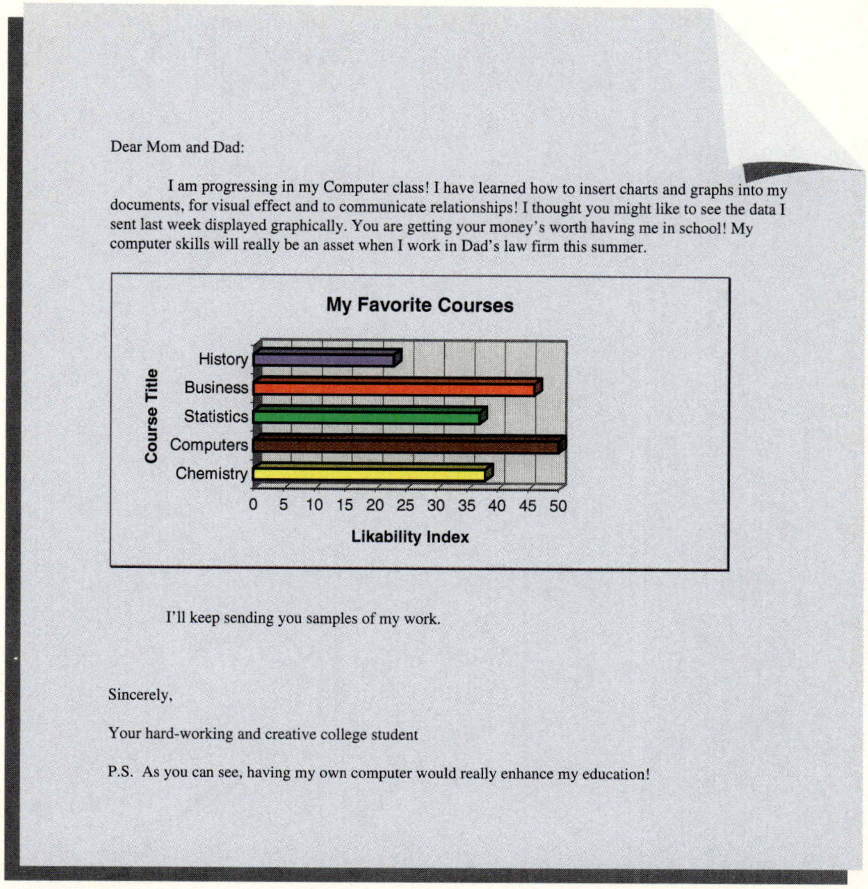
Dear Mom and Dad:

I am progressing in my Computer class! I have learned how to insert charts and graphs into my documents, for visual effect and to communicate relationships! I thought you might like to see the data I sent last week displayed graphically. You are getting your money's worth having me in school! My computer skills will really be an asset when I work in Dad's law firm this summer.

I'll keep sending you samples of my work.

Sincerely,

Your hard-working and creative college student

P.S. As you can see, having my own computer would really enhance my education!

Figure 1.20

Embedding a WordArt Document in an Excel Worksheet

Objects can be embedded in word processing documents, but they can also be embedded in other applications. From Excel, choose Object from the Insert menu. Select Microsoft WordArt 2.0 from the Create New option, and then select OK. Type your favorite activity into the text box. Use the WordArt features to shadow and shape the text, something like Figure 1.21. Save the Excel file as My Favorite Activity.xls on drive A:.

Figure 1.21

PART V

Microsoft Access 7

Do Overview project 1 & 2

Overview

Objectives

After completing this Overview, you should be able to:

- Start Access
- Describe the components of the Access screen
- Execute commands using menus and toolbars
- Navigate dialog boxes
- Access on-screen Help
- Exit Access

Imagine processing 12,000 enrollments for continuing education classes during a two-week period at a local university. Picture yourself managing registration and recording performance for 800 individuals competing in 25 track and field events. Or suppose you coordinate volunteer work on a college campus, finding students whose interests and schedules fit with an organization's needs. How do you make important decisions based on the data collected and still have time to handle all of the other responsibilities of your position? Database management software can provide the answer.

Using Database Management Software

A ***database*** is a collection of related data. A ***database management system (DBMS)*** is a system that stores data in a database and permits retrieval of selected information. For example, the entries in the yellow pages published by a phone company constitute a manual database. In that database you retrieve information by finding the category of interest, such as pizza, and viewing an alphabetized list of providers along with associated phone numbers. Folders in a file cabinet form a database, such as folders containing patient information in a physician's office. If the folders are arranged alphabetically by last name, you can easily locate and review information on one patient.

Database management software is a tool you use to manage data electronically. The essential functions of a database program are the abilities to create a database structure; add, edit, and delete data; arrange data into meaningful orders; and display or print selected information. Using a DBMS program, you can set up forms to enter and display data, queries to select and organize your data, and professional-looking reports to communicate information.

A ***relational database management system (RDBMS)*** is a system that stores data by subject and retrieves information based on predefined relationships among subjects. For example, a dealership maintains data on several subjects including vehicles available to sell and vehicles sold. The first subject includes data on make, model, features, and list price. The second subject includes data on the buyer's name, address, and phone number, the price paid, and the salesperson. Using an RDBMS, you can display or print information from several subjects, such as a daily sales report showing make, model, price paid, and salesperson. The vehicle identification number defines the relationship between the two subjects.

Using Access for Windows 95

Microsoft Access is among the best-selling relational database management systems in the world. Each database consists of one or more tables; a ***table*** is a collection of data about a particular subject organized in a row-and-column format. Figure 0.1 shows the Products table, one of several tables in the Northwind database (a sample application provided by Access). This database serves the information needs of a mail-order company, Northwind Traders, that distributes 77 food products in eight categories.

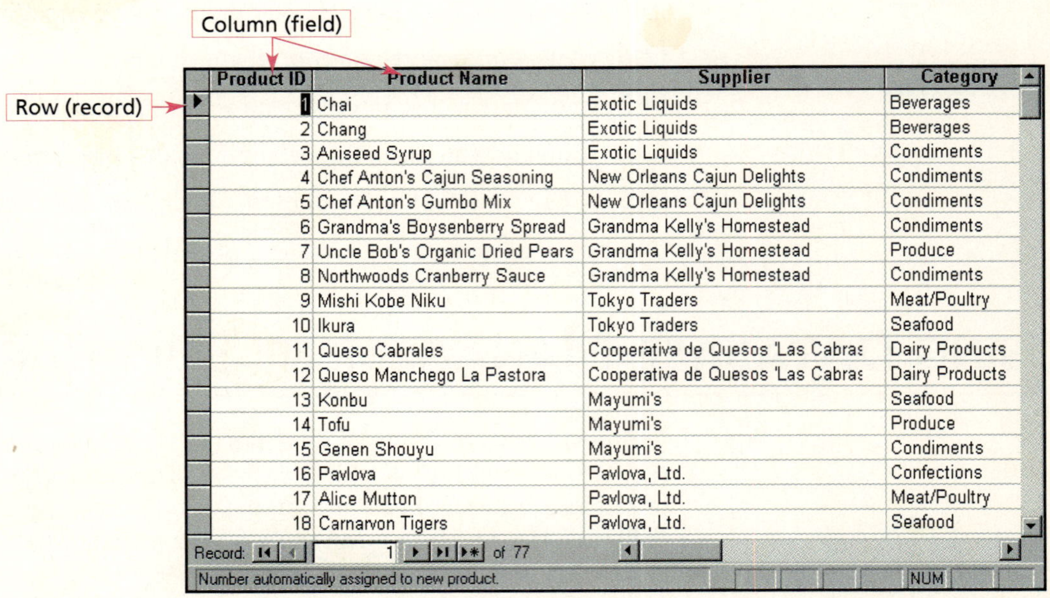

Product ID	Product Name	Supplier	Category
1	Chai	Exotic Liquids	Beverages
2	Chang	Exotic Liquids	Beverages
3	Aniseed Syrup	Exotic Liquids	Condiments
4	Chef Anton's Cajun Seasoning	New Orleans Cajun Delights	Condiments
5	Chef Anton's Gumbo Mix	New Orleans Cajun Delights	Condiments
6	Grandma's Boysenberry Spread	Grandma Kelly's Homestead	Condiments
7	Uncle Bob's Organic Dried Pears	Grandma Kelly's Homestead	Produce
8	Northwoods Cranberry Sauce	Grandma Kelly's Homestead	Condiments
9	Mishi Kobe Niku	Tokyo Traders	Meat/Poultry
10	Ikura	Tokyo Traders	Seafood
11	Queso Cabrales	Cooperativa de Quesos 'Las Cabras	Dairy Products
12	Queso Manchego La Pastora	Cooperativa de Quesos 'Las Cabras	Dairy Products
13	Konbu	Mayumi's	Seafood
14	Tofu	Mayumi's	Produce
15	Genen Shouyu	Mayumi's	Condiments
16	Pavlova	Pavlova, Ltd.	Confections
17	Alice Mutton	Pavlova, Ltd.	Meat/Poultry
18	Carnarvon Tigers	Pavlova, Ltd.	Seafood

Figure 0.1

In a table, a ***field*** is a category of information, such as Product ID or Product Name in Figure 0.1. A ***record*** is a collection of related fields, such as product 1 named Chai, a beverage supplied by Exotic Liquids, or product 10 named Ikura, a seafood item supplied by Tokyo Traders.

Using Access, you can quickly view only those records meeting your search criteria and limit display to selected fields. Figure 0.2 shows the results of a query to find the ten most expensive products. You see only the product name and unit price fields, and the records appear in descending order, with the most expensive item first.

Ten Most Expensive Products	Unit Price
Côte de Blaye	$263.50
Thüringer Rostbratwurst	$123.79
Mishi Kobe Niku	$97.00
Sir Rodney's Marmalade	$81.00
Carnarvon Tigers	$62.50
Raclette Courdavault	$55.00
Manjimup Dried Apples	$53.00
Tarte au sucre	$49.30
Ipoh Coffee	$46.00
Rössle Sauerkraut	$45.60

Figure 0.2

On-screen forms provide a convenient layout for viewing and editing data. Figure 0.3 shows the Categories form in the Northwind database. You could use this form to view the name, description, and picture representing each of the eight food categories. You could also use the scroll bar in the lower portion of the form to view or edit product data in each category.

Figure 0.3

Access also provides the tools to create complex, professional-looking reports. Figure 0.4 illustrates the top portion of a report grouping employee sales by country, and then by salesperson within each country. The report includes percentage calculations and also notes if actual sales exceeded an individual's goal.

Employee Sales by Country

Sales from 1/1/95 to 12/31/95

Country: UK

Salesperson: Buchanan, Steven *Exceeded Goal!*

Order ID:	Sale Amount:	Percent of Salesperson's Total:	Percent of Country Total:
10812	$1,693	8.60%	1.40%
10823	$2,826	14.35%	2.33%
10841	$4,581	23.26%	3.78%
10851	$2,603	13.22%	2.15%

Figure 0.4

If you're thinking that such a powerful program must be difficult to learn, you'll find that numerous *wizards* make it possible for you to create and use a sophisticated database system with little knowledge. A ***wizard*** asks you questions and builds an object such as a database, table, query, form, or report based on your answers. For example, ***Database Wizard*** builds a complete application including tables, forms, and reports. You can choose among 22 personal and business applications, including asset tracking, donations, event management, inventory, membership, and the music collection database you will create in Project 1.

A NOTE TO THE STUDENT

The projects in this module assume that your system is equipped with a mouse or trackball and that you are comfortable working in a Windows 95 environment.

Because Access allows you to customize the work area, the screen displays on your system may vary slightly from the figures in this module. For example, you can display file names with or without details such as the file size and the date and time saved.

The projects in this module present popular applications for database management. We suggest that you first read this Overview to learn about basic Access screens and the powerful Help feature. In Project 1 you will preview the power of Access by using Database Wizard to create a complete application. Your database will include tables, forms, queries, and reports concerning a music collection. As you work through Projects 2, 3, and 4 in sequence, you will develop a campus volunteer center DBMS without using Database Wizard. After you design the database, you will create tables, set field properties that control and validate data, and enter and edit data. You can then turn your attention to creating custom data entry forms, queries to retrieve data, and custom reports with help from other wizards. Let's begin!

Starting Access

An ***icon*** is an on-screen symbol that represents a program file, data file, or some other function. A ***toolbar*** contains buttons, each of which represents a command that you can execute by positioning the mouse pointer over the button and then clicking it. You can start Access by clicking its icon on the Windows 95 desktop or the Microsoft Office toolbar, as shown in Figure 0.5.

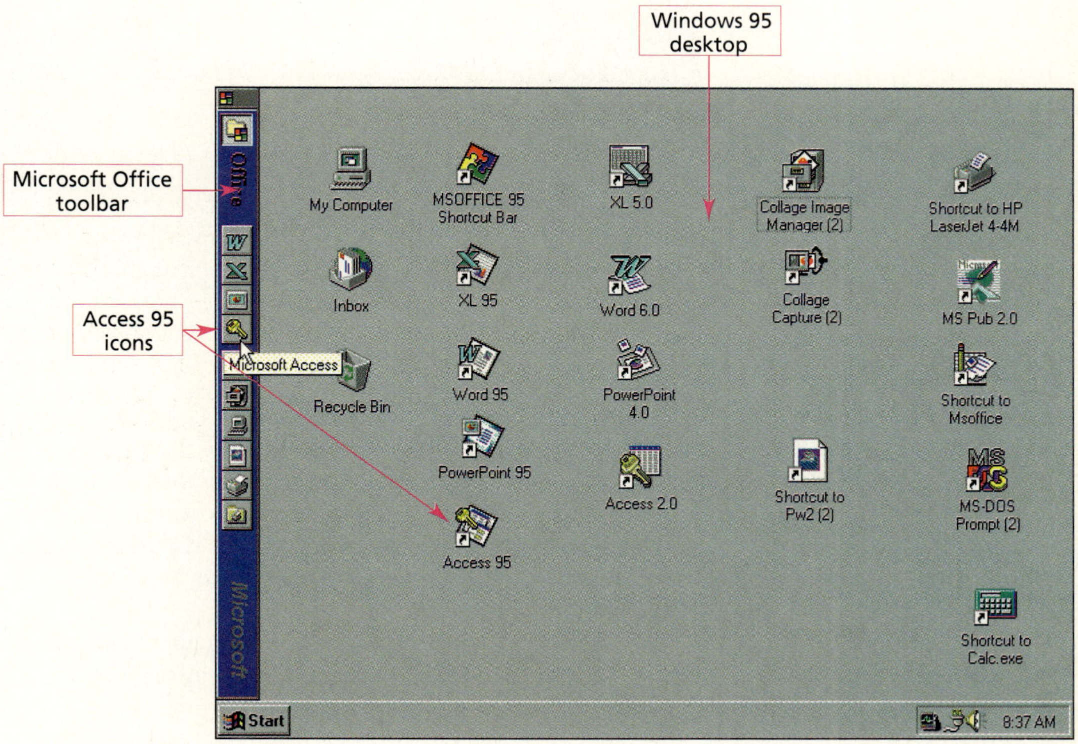

Figure 0.5

Reminder Your screen displays may vary from those shown in this module. Some of the icons on your Windows 95 desktop are likely to be different than those shown in Figure 0.5.

You can also load Access by clicking Start in the lower-left corner of the desktop, choosing Programs, and then selecting Microsoft Access. After starting Access you will see a screen similar to the one shown in Figure 0.6.

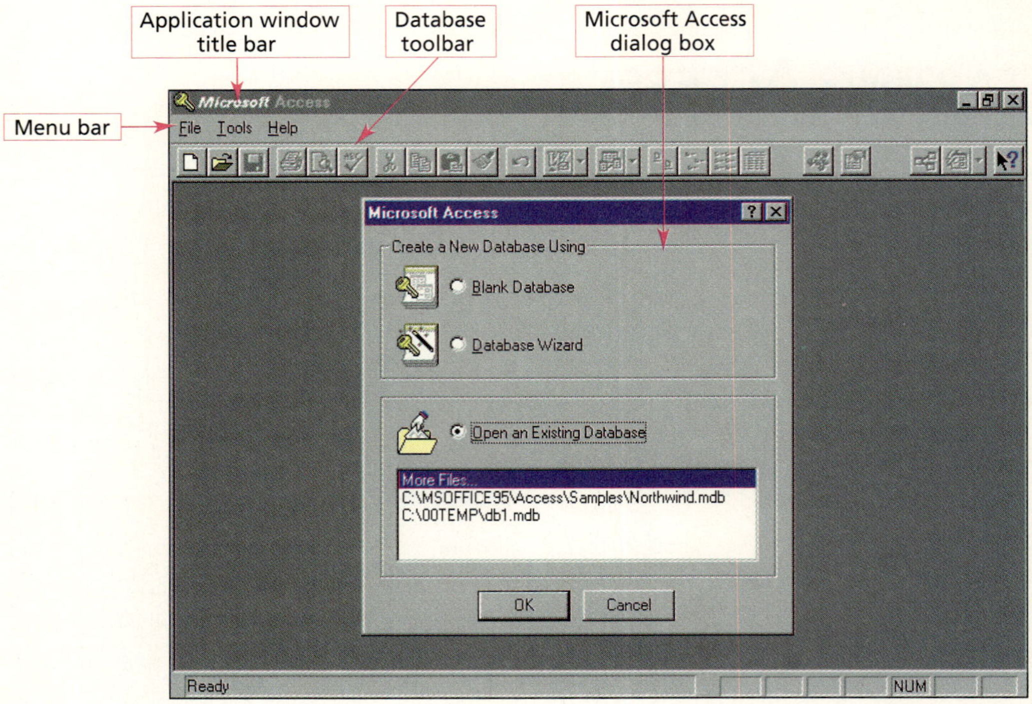

Figure 0.6

The application window title bar indicates that you are using Microsoft Access. The ***menu bar,*** located just below the title bar, is a horizontal listing of Access commands currently available. Only three commands are available if all databases are closed; seven commands are available if a database is open. Selecting an option on the menu bar causes related commands to appear in a ***pull-down menu,*** in which each new option is listed below the previous one.

In Figure 0.6, the Database toolbar appears below the menu bar. As you work, buttons that are not available will appear dim.

Tip The name of a button appears each time the mouse pointer rests on a button. If this feature is not active, you can choose Toolbars from the View menu and select Show ToolTips.

The Microsoft Access dialog box occupies most of the remainder of the screen. A ***dialog box*** appears whenever additional information is needed to complete a task. Why don't you take a look at this screen for yourself? In the steps that follow, you will start the Access relational database program.

To start Access:

1 Double-click the Access icon on your Windows 95 desktop.
After a brief display showing copyright information, the Microsoft Access dialog box shown in Figure 0.6 appears.

2 Select Cancel to close the dialog box.

Using Toolbars, Menus, and Dialog Boxes

Tip If you are already familiar with using toolbars, menus, and dialog boxes in another Windows product, you might want to skip this section and continue with the section called "Getting On-screen Help."

Access automatically displays a toolbar supporting the current operation. For example, if you are creating or changing a table design, the Table Design toolbar will appear near the top of the screen. Clicking a button on a toolbar executes the associated Access command.

When a database is open, Access includes a powerful set of commands grouped within the seven options on the menu bar, as shown in Figure 0.7. One letter of every menu option, called a mnemonic letter, is underlined. You can choose a menu bar option by using a mouse to click the option name or by pressing (ALT) in combination with the mnemonic letter. Options on a pull-down menu that appear dim, such as Save in Figure 0.7, are not currently available. Choosing an option that is followed by an arrowhead, such as Get External Data, opens a submenu. Choosing an option that is followed by an ellipsis (. . .), such as Page Setup or Print, opens a dialog box.

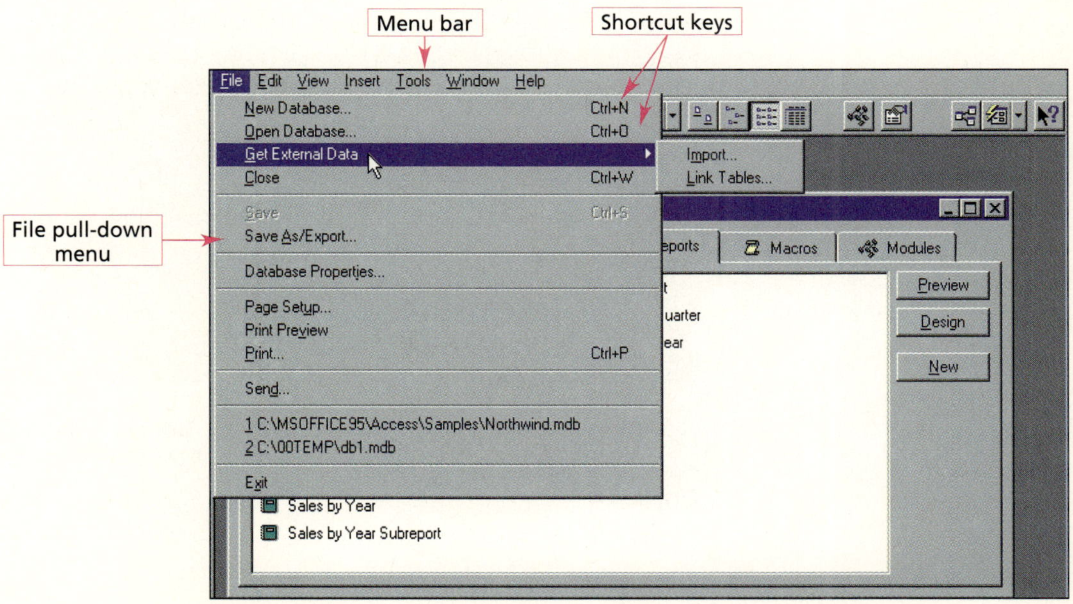

Figure 0.7

For some common command sequences, Access has assigned a key or key combination called a shortcut. Using these ***shortcut keys*** (sometimes called accelerator keys), you can bypass several menu selections. For example, five shortcut keys are available for file management tasks, such as CTRL + **O** to open a database and CTRL + **P** to print. If a shortcut key is available, it appears to the right of its associated command on a pull-down menu.

Tip If you start to choose from a menu and do not wish to continue, you can press the left mouse button after positioning the mouse pointer anywhere outside the menu, or you can press ESC one or more times.

You can select an option within a dialog box by positioning the mouse pointer and pressing the left mouse button, or by pressing TAB until the desired option is highlighted and then pressing ENTER Some options within a dialog box appear in sets called ***radio buttons.*** These options are so named because, as on a radio, you can specify only one choice from a set of items. In Figure 0.6, Open an Existing Database is selected.

Most dialog boxes contain one or more ***command buttons,*** which you can select to execute the named operations. Buttons may change as you make selections within a dialog box. If an ellipsis (. . .) appears after the name in a command button, selecting that button opens another dialog box. The Print dialog box shown in Figure 0.8 contains OK, Cancel, Setup, and Properties.

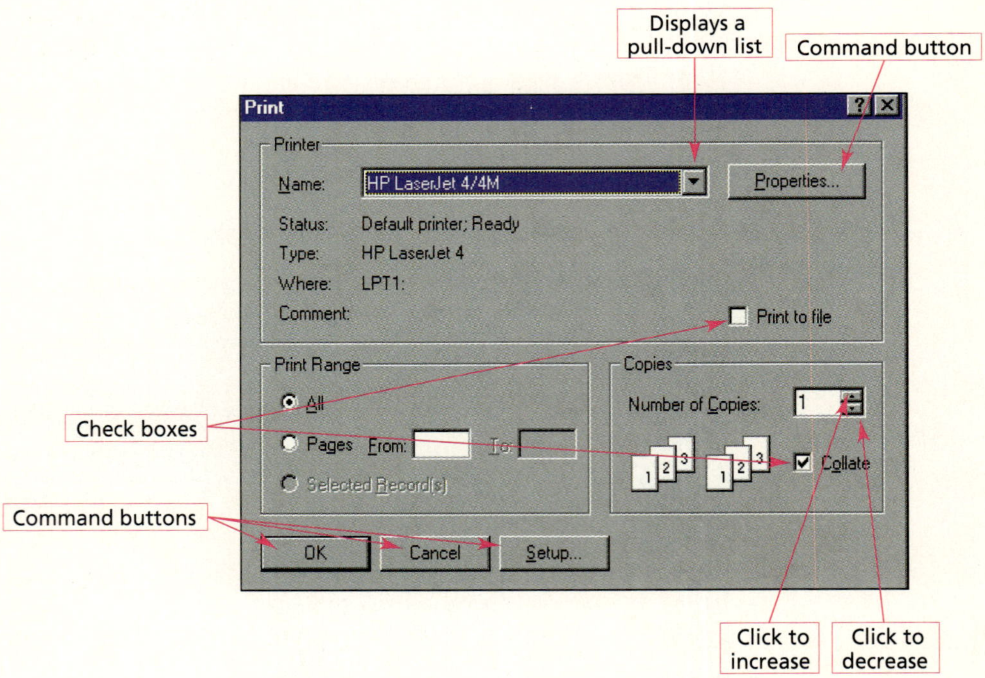

Figure 0.8

A down arrow at the right end of a box indicates the existence of a ***pull-down list,*** which shows related options. If you were to select the arrow at the right end of the Name box shown in Figure 0.8, you would see a display of printers.

You can use a ***check box*** to turn an option on or off. A checkmark (√) within the box indicates an option is on. The absence of a checkmark indicates the option is off. In Figure 0.8, for example, the Print to file option is not selected, and the Collate option is selected.

At this point you know how to specify most settings within dialog boxes and choose from toolbars and menus. For more information, you can use the powerful on-screen Help feature.

Getting On-screen Help

Access provides information about the program on the screen. This information can either be ***context-sensitive Help,*** which provides information about the operation in progress, or information of a more general nature. Help is available through options on the Help menu and a Help button, as described in the following sections.

Using Contents to Get Help

The Access Help Topics dialog box appears if you choose Help in the menu bar and then choose Microsoft Access Help Topics. You can choose among four tabs in the dialog box: Contents, Index, Find, and Answer Wizard. Instructions appear below each tab. When Contents is the current folder, as shown in Figure 0.9, you can select a topic by clicking a closed-book icon or the associated text.

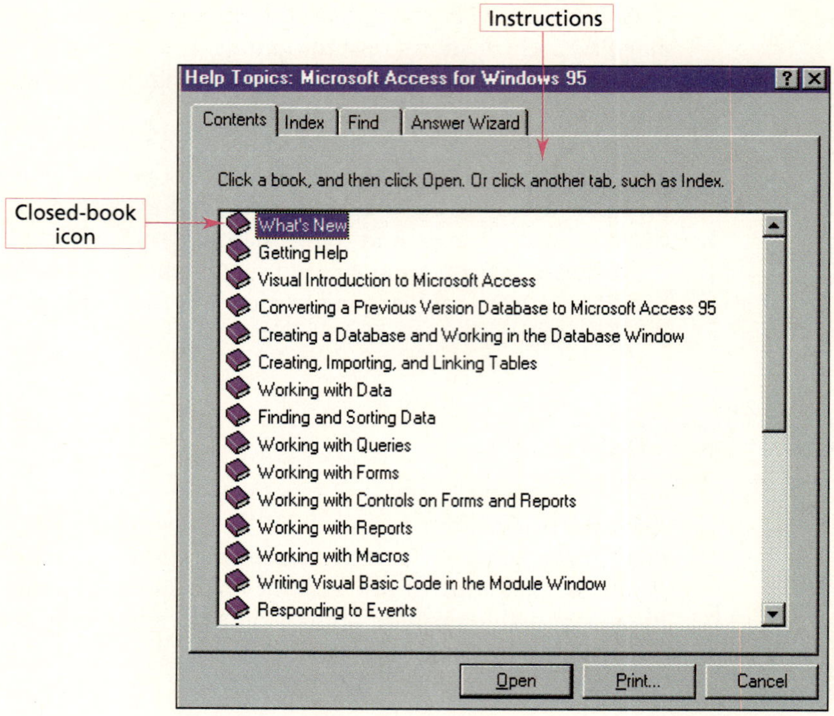

Figure 0.9

In the following steps you will view several screens accessed through the Access Help Topics dialog box. By exploring other topics on your own, you will have a better idea of the help available on-screen.

To use the Contents feature of on-screen Help:

1 Choose Help from the menu bar, and then choose Microsoft Access Help Topics.

2 Select the Contents tab, if Contents is not already the current folder. The Access Help Topics dialog box shown in Figure 0.9 appears.

3 Select *Finding and Sorting Data*, and then click Open. The icon in front of *Finding and Sorting Data* changes to an open book, and a sublist of four topics preceded by closed-book icons appears.

> ***Tip*** You can also select a topic by double-clicking its description or associated icon.

4 Select *Finding Data Using Filters*, and then click Open. A long list of related topics appears, part of which is shown in Figure 0.10. A question mark icon indicating Help precedes each topic.

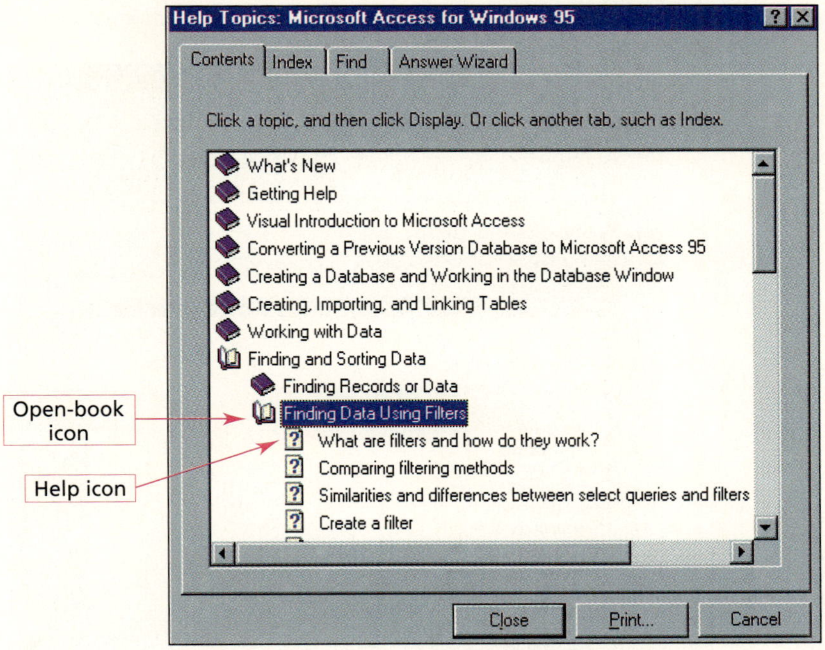

Figure 0.10

5 Select *What are filters and how do they work?*, and then select Display. Information about the selected topic appears.

6 Click each radio button at the left to view information about filters.

7 Select Close.

Using Index to Get Help

If you know the exact name of the feature about which you need help, you can look up information about the topic by selecting Index from the Help Topics dialog box. The two-part instructions to use the box appear near the top, as shown in Figure 0.11.

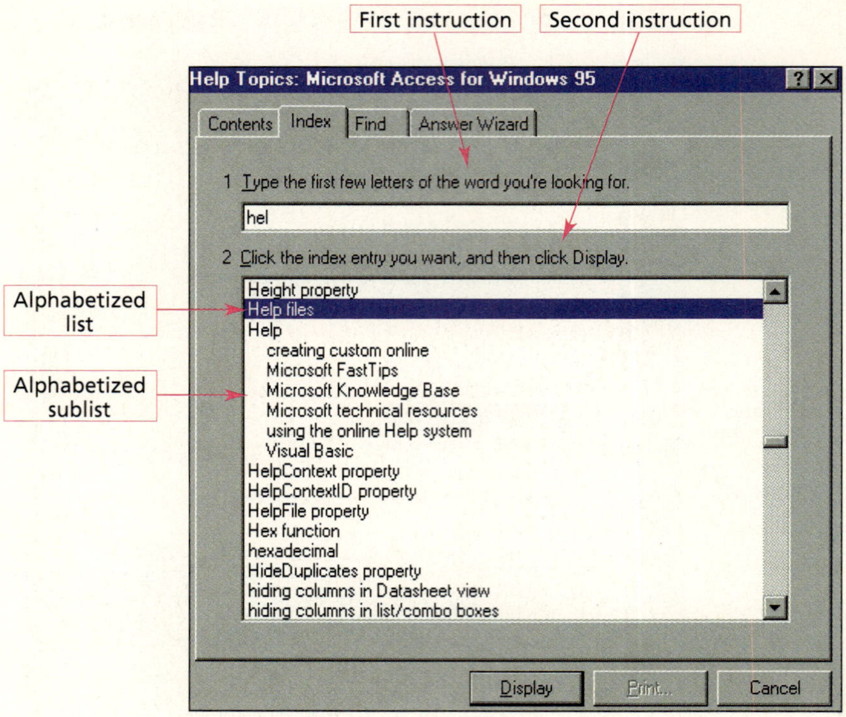

Figure 0.11

As you start to type your search word or phrase, Access displays an alphabetized list of topics that start with the same letters. Some topics, such as *Help* in Figure 0.11, display a sublist of topics. In the following steps you will use this feature to display information on using the online Help system.

To use the Index feature of on-screen Help:

1 Choose Microsoft Access Help Topics from the Help menu.

2 Select the Index tab in the Help Topics dialog box.

3 Type **hel** in the top box, as shown in Figure 0.11.

4 Select *using the online Help system*, and then select Display.
The Getting Assistance while you work screen appears.

> ***Tip*** Clicking the color bar in front of a named topic, such as *Screen Tips* or *Step-by-step Answers,* displays additional information about the associated topic.

5 View other information as desired, and then select Close.

Using Find to Get Help

You can search the Help database for any mention of a specified word or phrase by selecting Find from the Help Topics dialog box. This box contains three instructions to help you use it, as shown in Figure 0.12.

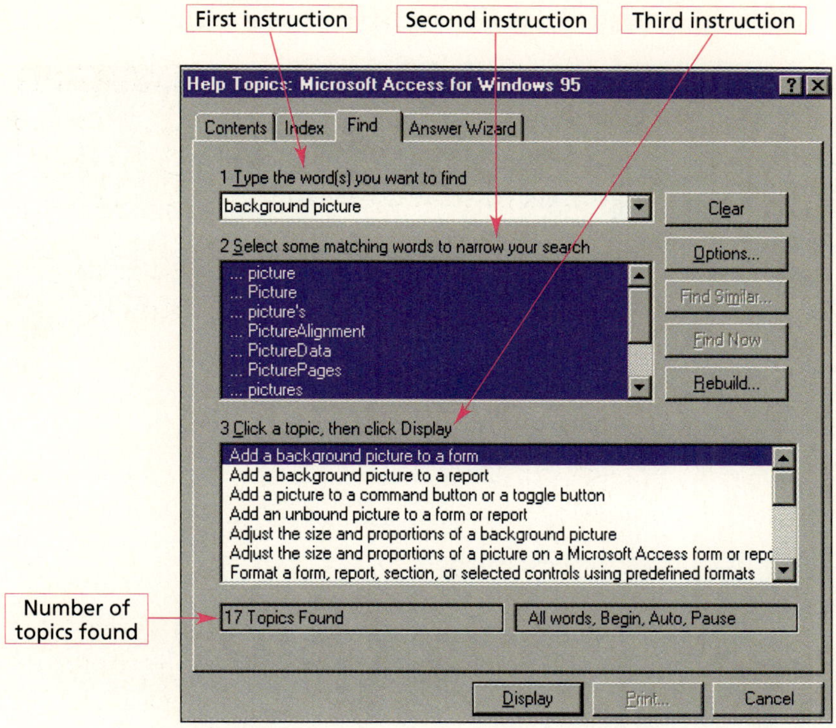

Figure 0.12

If the list of found topics is longer than the current screen display, you can use the scroll bar to view the complete list of topics. In the following steps you will use this feature to display information about shortcut keys.

To use the Find feature of on-screen Help:

1 Choose Microsoft Access Help Topics from the Help menu.

2 Select the Find tab.
The message "Loading Word List" appears briefly.

3 Type **`background picture`** in the box under the first instruction, as shown in Figure 0.12.

4 Select *Add a background picture to a report* from the list that appears under the third instruction, and then select Display.

> ***Tip*** You can select the Options button and then select Print Topic to print the information in the current Help Topics dialog box.

5 After viewing the information, select Help Topics to restore display of the Find folder.

Using Answer Wizard to Get Help

Access also provides ***Answer Wizard*** that will display a list of topics related to a search you define in your own words. There are two instructions to use the Answer Wizard dialog box, as shown in Figure 0.13.

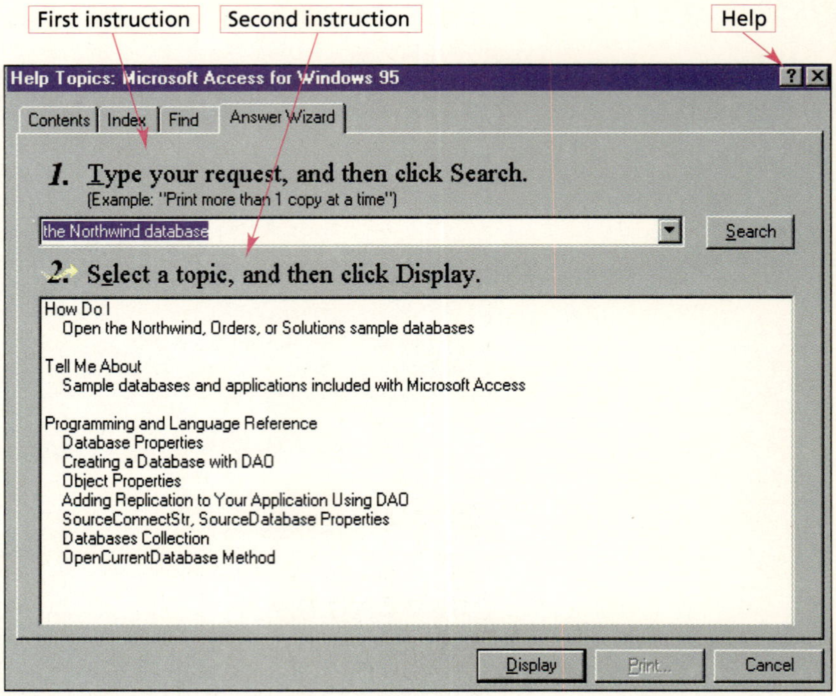

Figure 0.13

Answer Wizard will show you step-by-step instructions on how to complete a specific task if you select a topic in the *How Do I* section. Selecting a *Tell Me About* topic displays a general explanation. The *Programming and Language Reference* topics help users set up advanced applications.

In the following steps you will use Answer Wizard to learn about the Northwind sample database provided by Access.

To use the Answer Wizard feature of on-screen Help:

1 Select the Answer Wizard tab from the Help Topics dialog box.

2 Type **`the Northwind database`** as your request, and then select Search.
The list of related topics appears as shown in Figure 0.13.

3 Select *Sample databases and applications included with Microsoft Access* in the *Tell Me About* section, and then select Display.

4 Select Help Topics to restore display of the Answer Wizard folder.

5 Explore viewing other Help topics of your choice.

6 Click the Close icon in the upper-right corner of the Help Topics dialog box, or select the Cancel command button in the lower-right corner.

Using the Help Button

If you are using a mouse, you can take advantage of PowerPoint's Help button, which allows you to view information about a command or window item on the screen. You must first click the Help button on a toolbar, as shown in Figure 0.14, or the Help button within a dialog box, as shown in Figure 0.13. The pointer changes to an arrow with a question mark. You then position the pointer on the item you would like to know more about and click again. In the following steps you will use the Help button to view information about the Undo button.

To use the Help button:

1 Click the Help button at the right end of the Database toolbar.
The mouse pointer changes to an arrow with a question mark.

2 Move the pointer until it rests on the Undo button (left of center on the Database toolbar).

3 Press the left mouse button.
Information about undoing an action appears as shown in Figure 0.14.

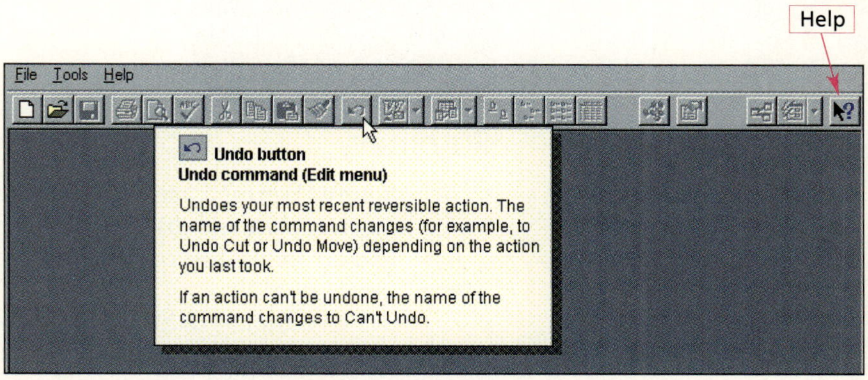

Figure 0.14

4 Click outside the information box to exit Help.

Exiting Access

When you finish working on a database, you can save or discard your changes and then continue developing another database or exit Access. You will start the process to leave the current database editing session by choosing from options (or the corresponding shortcut keys) on the File menu shown in Figure 0.7.

The Close option appears only if a database is in use. You will choose Close if you want to close the current database but continue working in Access. You will choose Exit if you want to quit working in Access. Whichever option you select, you will be prompted to save the current database if it contains any unsaved changes (saving a database is discussed in Project 1).

To exit Access:

1 Choose Exit from the File menu.

Reminder You can also exit an application by clicking the Close button in the upper-right corner of the screen.

The Next Step

At this point you have a lot of information about the Access work environment. As you complete subsequent projects, you will have many opportunities to choose from menus, select buttons, and indicate your preferences in dialog boxes. However, these step-by-step instructions do not include using on-screen Help. Starting now, get in the habit of viewing on-screen Help about each new topic you encounter.

This concludes the Overview. You can either exit Access, go on to work the Study Questions, or proceed to Project 1.

Summary and Exercises

Summary

- Access is a powerful database management system (DBMS) that allows you to enter, edit, and display data using forms; select and organize your data; and create professional-looking reports to communicate information.
- Access is a relational DBMS that stores data by subject and retrieves information based on predefined relationships among subjects.
- A database consists of one or more tables that store data in a row-and-column format. In a table, a field (column) is a category of information and a record (row) is a collection of related fields.
- Numerous wizards are available. A wizard builds an object such as a database, table, query, form, or report based on your answers to questions.
- You can execute commands using menu bars, pull-down menus, and toolbar buttons. Quite often you must also specify settings in a dialog box to complete an operation.
- Whenever you want information about some feature of Access, you can use the extensive on-screen Help feature.

Key Terms and Operations

Key Terms
Answer Wizard
check box
command button
context-sensitive Help
database
database management software
database management system (DBMS)
Database Wizard
dialog box
field
icon
menu bar
pull-down list
pull-down menu
radio button
record
relational database management system (RDBMS)
shortcut key
table
toolbar
wizard

Operations
Start Access
Get on-screen help
Exit Access

Study Questions

Multiple Choice

1. Which of the following is a method to choose a menu bar option?
   a. Use a mouse to click the name of the option.
   b. Press (CTRL) in combination with the mnemonic letter.
   c. Both a and b.
   d. None of the above.
2. Which of the following is not one of the folders in the Microsoft Access Help Topics dialog box?
   a. Find
   b. Search for Help On
   c. Index
   d. Answer Wizard
3. Which of the following is a database term for category of information?
   a. field
   b. record
   c. table
   d. database
4. Which option would you choose from the File pull-down menu to quit Access?
   a. Close
   b. Exit
   c. Quit
   d. Stop
5. Which folder in the Microsoft Access Help Topics dialog box would you select to search the Help database for any mention of a specified word or phrase?
   a. Find
   b. Contents
   c. Help button
   d. Answer Wizard

Short Answer

1. On-screen help can be general in nature or provide information about the operation in progress. What is the term used to describe help related to the operation in progress?
2. If an option on a pull-down menu is not currently available, how does that option appear relative to options that are available?
3. If you make a mistake while choosing from menus, what key can you press one or more times to restore the appropriate screen for restarting the sequence?
4. Which Access wizard creates a complete business or personal application?
5. What term describes a database management system that stores data by subject and retrieves information based on predefined relationships among subjects?

For Discussion

1. Describe the essential functions of a database program.
2. You frequently have to issue commands to perform various database management functions. Explain the various ways you can issue a command using Access. Include a description of the menu structure, toolbars, and shortcut keys in your discussion.
3. Think of a database that you might use. Give an example of a field and a record for that database.

PROJECT 1: PREVIEWING THE POWER OF ACCESS

Objectives

After completing this project, you should be able to:

- Select a database application
- Step through Database Wizard
- Enter and edit data using a form
- Preview and print a report

CASE STUDY: MANAGING YOUR MUSIC COLLECTION

Imagine that you own and manage a small business that provides DJs (disc jockeys) for special events. Your music collection—more than 1000 compact discs, tapes, and records—continues to grow, and you spend hours making selections for each booking.

Recently you purchased a computer system for the business that includes Windows 95 and Access. You plan to set up an electronic database management system that reduces the preparation time for each job and allows you to compile a variety of music lists for prospective clients.

Designing the Solution

In this situation there is very little design work to do. Using the Database Wizard, you can select a predefined Music Collection application. Access will set up the objects you need—tables, forms, and reports—and provide sample data on request. After modifying the objects as necessary, you can quickly focus your attention on using the information system.

STEPPING THROUGH THE DATABASE WIZARD

The Microsoft Access dialog box shown in Figure 1.1 appears after you load Access. At this point you can create a new database or open an existing one.

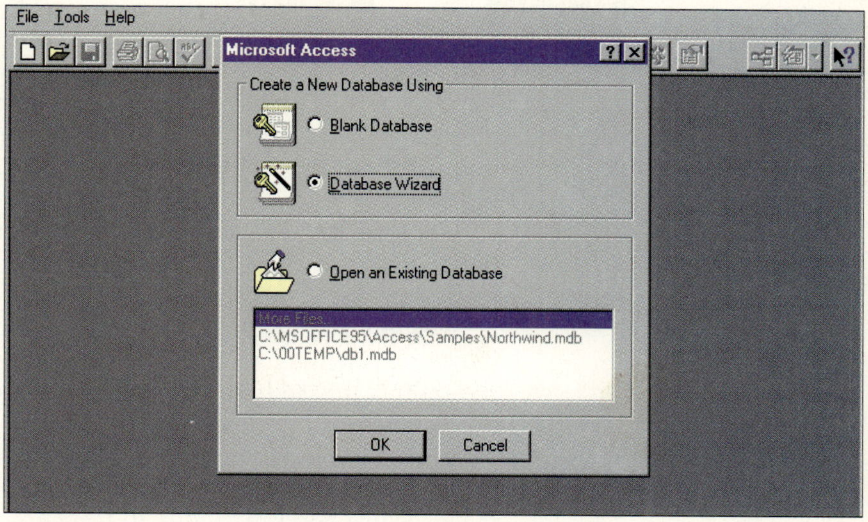

Figure 1.1

The first two options in the Microsoft Access dialog box apply to creating a new database. Database Wizard allows you to select among 22 personal and business databases listed in the Databases folder of the New dialog box, as shown in Figure 1.2.

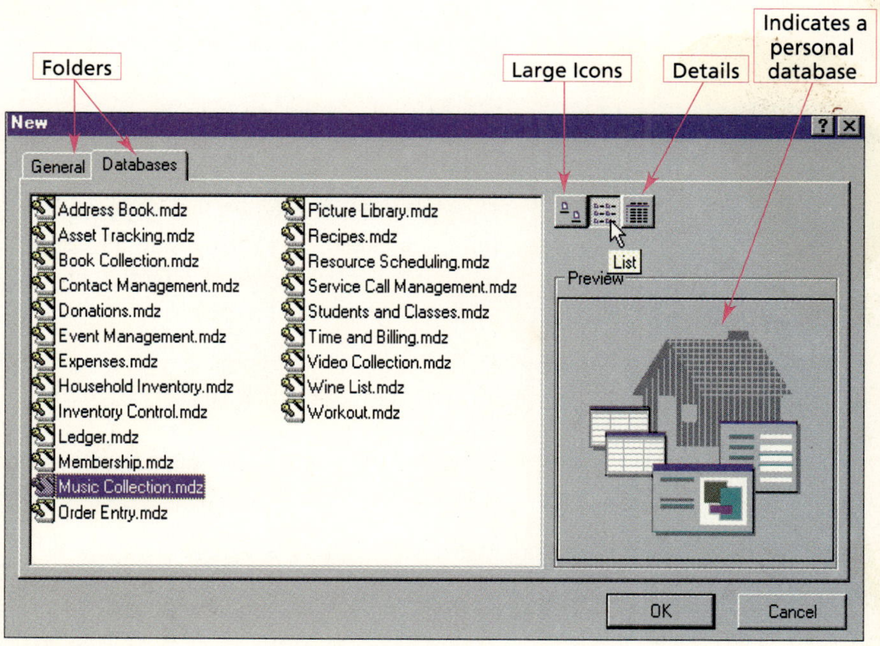

Figure 1.2

Tip If you find that Access does not provide a predefined application similar to the one you need, you can select Blank Database and create your own tables, forms, queries, and reports with the help of other wizards. You can select Blank Database from the Microsoft Access dialog box or the General folder of the New dialog box.

The three buttons above the Preview area vary the display of listed items. Selecting the List button results in a two-column display of all predefined database options.

Selecting a predefined database from the alphabetized list displays an image representing a personal or business database in the Preview area on the right. A house in the background indicates a personal database, as shown for Music Collection in Figure 1.2.

After you select, name, and save a predefined database, Access displays a series of Database Wizard dialog boxes. First you will view suggested tables, which you can modify to meet your specific needs. You'll also be able to select background color and design for screens, and add a title and print style for reports.

Tip If you tell Database Wizard to include sample data, you can immediately use the predefined forms and reports. You can then decide if revisions are necessary before entering your own data.

In the following sections you will select the predefined application Music Collection, save the database, and complete all Database Wizard dialog boxes.

Selecting and Saving a Predefined Database

Selecting a predefined database or Blank Database opens the File New Database dialog box. The entries you make in this box determine the name, type, and location of your new database. If you selected a predefined database, Access suggests a name, such as Music Collection1. You can accept that name or type a new name, as shown in Figure 1.3.

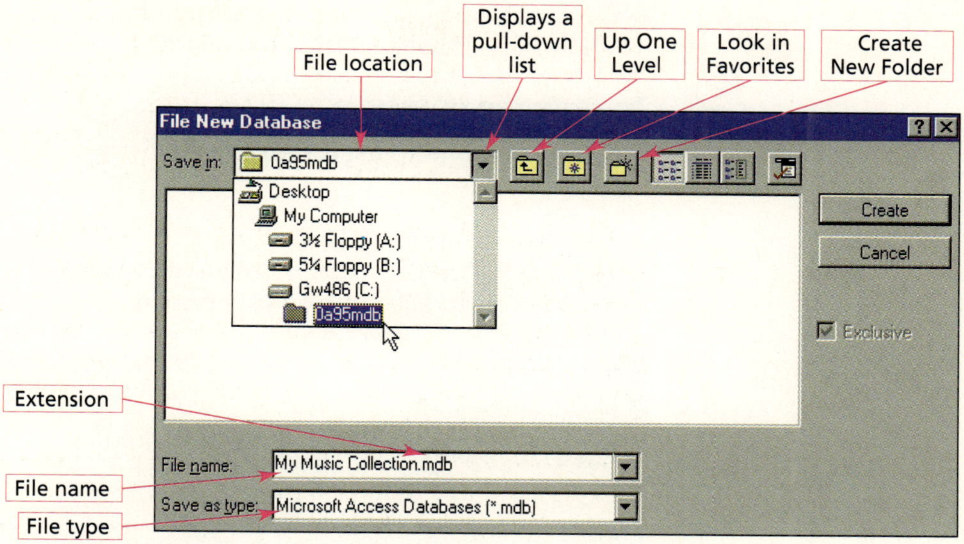

Figure 1.3

Windows 95 file names can contain up to 256 characters, including spaces. Access assigns the three-character extension .mdb, indicating a master database. It is this extension that Windows 95 uses to associate a file with the application that created it.

Tip The file name extension may be hidden. To display extensions, use My Computer or Windows Explorer to open the folder you want to look at. After choosing Options from the View menu, select the View tab and make sure the Hide MS-DOS File Extensions box is not checked.

In addition to a file name, you will specify a file location. Clicking the down arrow at the right end of the Save In box displays drives and folders for your system. You will select the drive and then select an existing folder or create a new one. In Figure 1.3 the folder 0a95mdb on drive C is selected.

Caution The predefined Music Collection database with sample data requires over 1.2 million characters of storage space, nearly the capacity of a 3-½-inch high-density disk. If you are working in a school lab environment, your instructor will tell you where to store your files.

In the following steps you will select and save the predefined Music Collection database.

To select an application:

1 Load Access.
The Microsoft Access dialog box shown in Figure 1.1 appears.

2 Select Database Wizard, and then select OK.
The New dialog box appears with two folders, General and Databases.

3 Select Databases, if that is not the current folder.

4 Select the List button to view the names of all predefined databases.

5 Select Music Collection, as shown in Figure 1.2, and then select OK. The File New Database dialog box appears.

To save the database:

1 Type or point to the name of the folder where you want to store your database.

> ***Tip*** Use the Up One Level button and Look in Favorites button to help navigate the storage areas on your system.

2 Edit the suggested file name to read `My Music Collection.mdb`

3 Select Create.
The initial Database Wizard dialog box shown in Figure 1.4 appears.

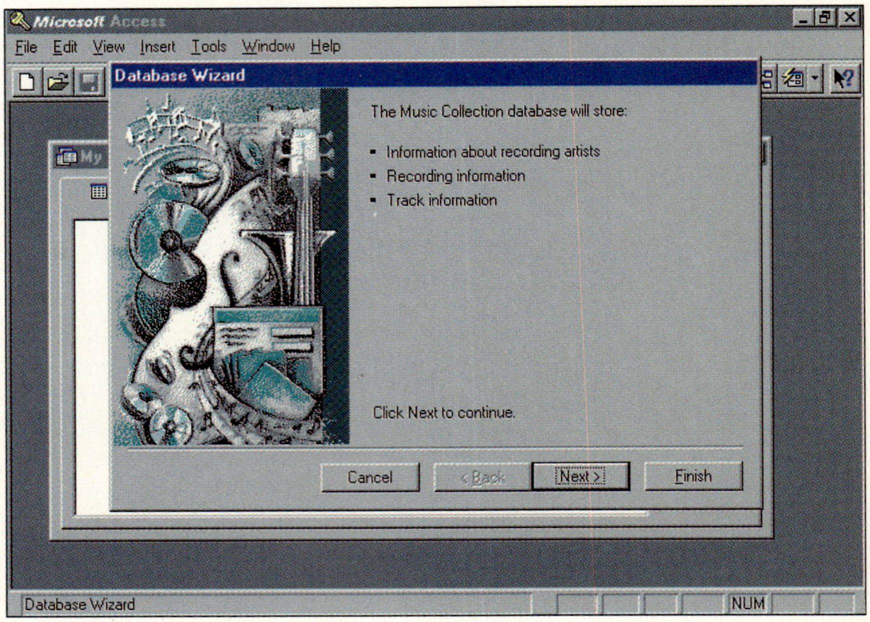

Figure 1.4

4 Select Next>.
The Database Wizard dialog box shown in Figure 1.5 appears.

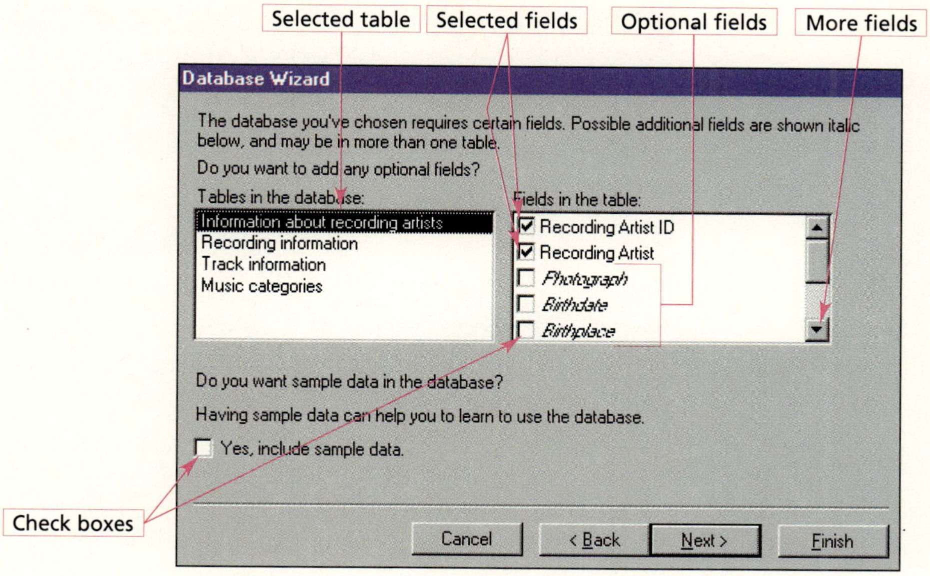

Figure 1.5

Adding Optional Fields and Sample Data

Database Wizard creates the four Music Collection tables listed at the left side of the dialog box shown in Figure 1.5. The fields in the selected table appear on the right side of the dialog box. Field names that appear in a normal typeface are required, while those in italics are optional. A checkmark indicates a selected field.

The Information about recording artists table has three required fields—Recording Artist ID, Recording Artist, and Notes. You can also add one or more of the optional fields *Photograph*, *Birthdate*, *Birthplace*, and *Date of Death*.

In the following steps you will add an optional field to two of the four tables and specify that you want sample data included for each table.

Tip You can delete sample data and add your own after you learn how to use an application.

To add an optional field to a predefined table:

1 Select the Information about recording artists table, if that table is not already highlighted.

2 Select *Birthplace* in the Fields list.
A checkmark appears in the box preceding *Birthplace,* as shown in Figure 1.6.

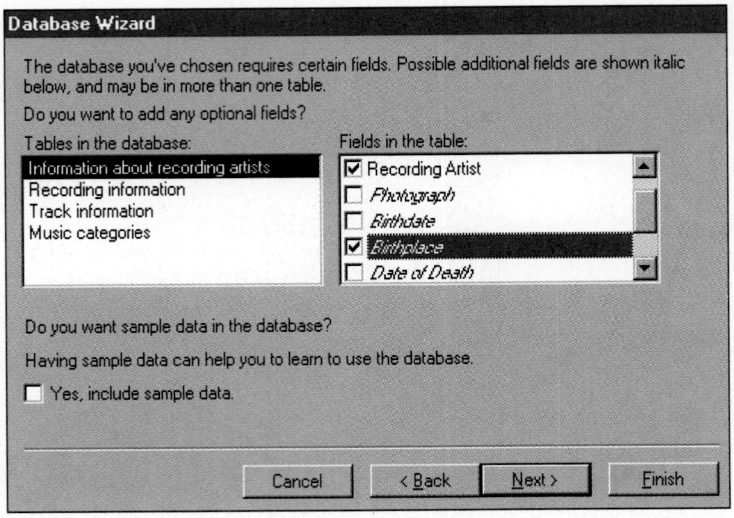

Figure 1.6

3 Select the Recording information table.

4 Scroll down the Fields in the Table list and select *Purchase Price*. A checkmark appears in the box preceding *Purchase Price*.

5 In the lower-left corner of the dialog box, select the Yes, include sample data button.
A checkmark appears in the check box, as shown in Figure 1.7.

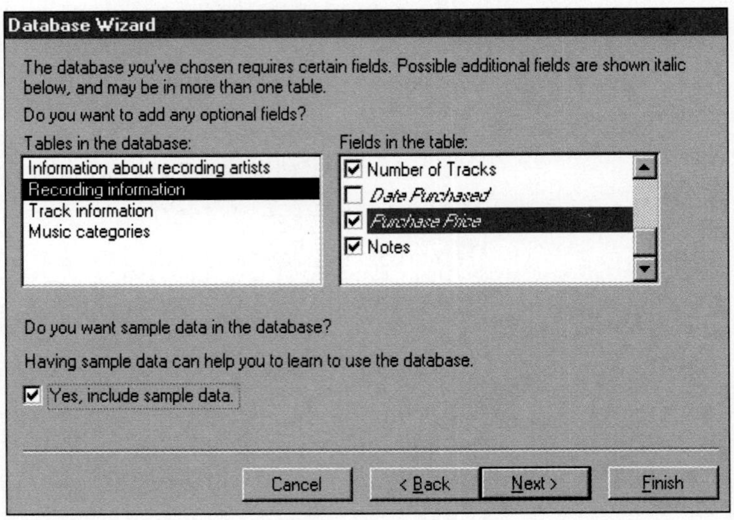

Figure 1.7

6 Select Next>.
The Database Wizard dialog box shown in Figure 1.8 appears.

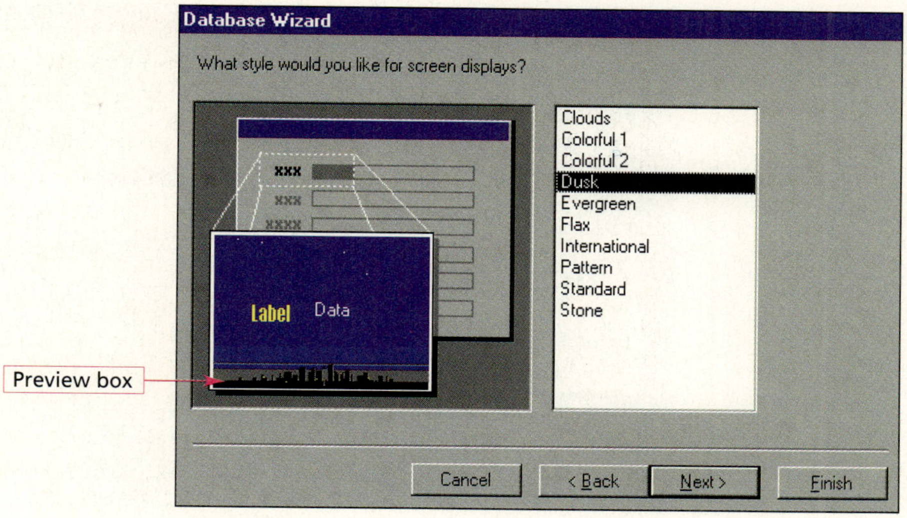

Figure 1.8

Selecting a Style for Screen Displays

Using the Database Wizard dialog box shown in Figure 1.8, you can preview and select one of ten styles to add background scenery and color to your screen displays. You will select a style from the list on the right side of the dialog box. The preview box on the left displays a sample of the selected style. In the following steps you will view several styles and then select one.

To select a style for screen displays:

1 Select *Clouds.*
The preview box displays a color background that includes clouds.

2 Select *International.*
The preview box displays a globe in the background.

3 Select your choice of other styles.

4 Select *Dusk.*
The style shown in Figure 1.8 appears.

5 Select Next>.
The Database Wizard dialog box shown in Figure 1.9 appears.

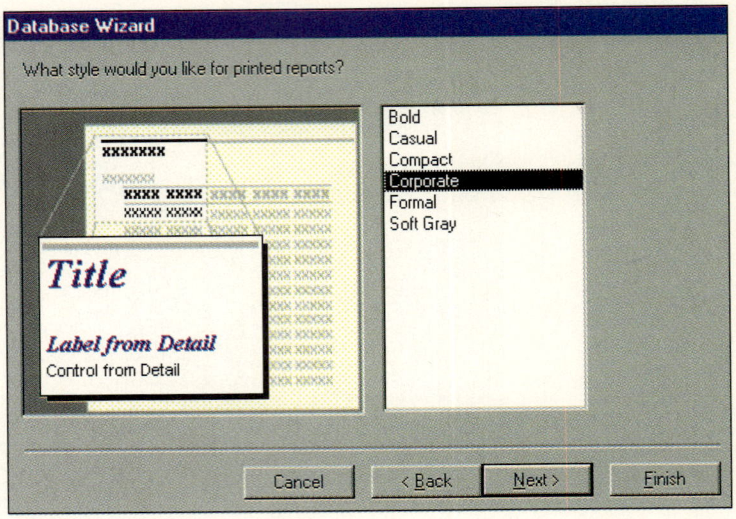

Figure 1.9

Selecting a Style for Printed Reports

Database Wizard offers six predefined combinations of type fonts and sizes that you can apply to your printed reports. You will select a style from the list on the right side of the dialog box. The preview box on the left displays a sample of the selected style.

Figure 1.9 shows a sample of the Corporate print style. In the following steps you will view several print styles and then select one.

To select a print style:

1 Select *Casual.*
The preview box displays a sample of the Casual style.

2 Select *Soft Gray.*
The display in the preview box changes to show a sample of the Soft Gray style.

3 Select your choice of other print styles.

4 Select *Corporate,* and then select Next>.
The Database Wizard dialog box shown in Figure 1.10 appears.

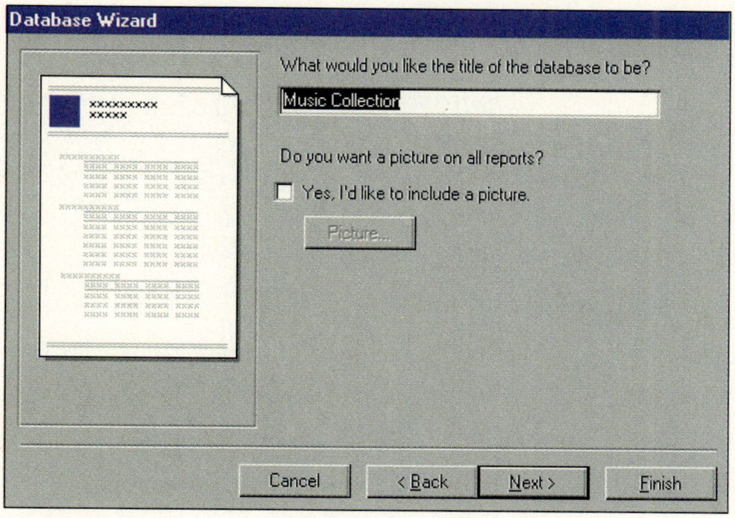

Figure 1.10

Selecting a Title and Picture

You can specify a title to appear on screen displays and printouts. Database Wizard will suggest a name, such as *Music Collection* shown in Figure 1.10. This name does not have to be the same as the one you used to save the database on disk.

You can also add a picture to reports by selecting the check box below the title. A picture is an image that has been converted (digitized) to a disk file. There are many techniques used to digitize images. Access prefers pictures created using the bitmap technique. These files end with the extension .bmp or display the file type Bitmap Image in detail view.

If you select Yes, I'd like to include a picture, the Picture command button becomes active. If you know where bitmap pictures are stored on your computer system, you can select Picture to access the Insert Picture dialog box and choose an image.

At this point you will have provided all the information needed to build your database. After Database Wizard creates the tables, forms, and reports in the Music Collection database, you will see the Main Switchboard dialog box shown in Figure 1.11.

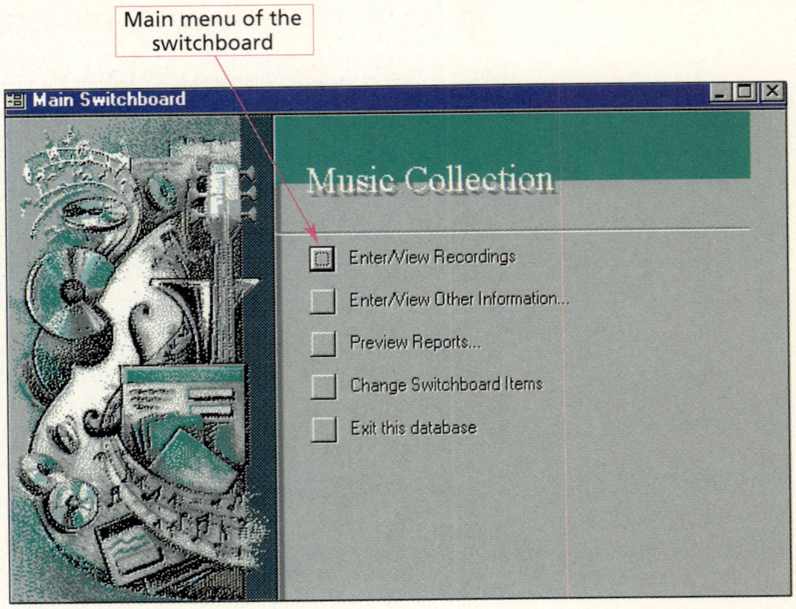

Figure 1.11

A ***switchboard*** is a menu system that helps users navigate through a database. Using the switchboard, you can update tables, view data stored in the tables, and display or print reports.

To accept the current title and picture settings and complete Database Wizard screens:

1 Select Next>.
The wizard accepts the name Music Collection and displays the final Database Wizard dialog box.

2 Check that your settings match those shown in Figure 1.12.

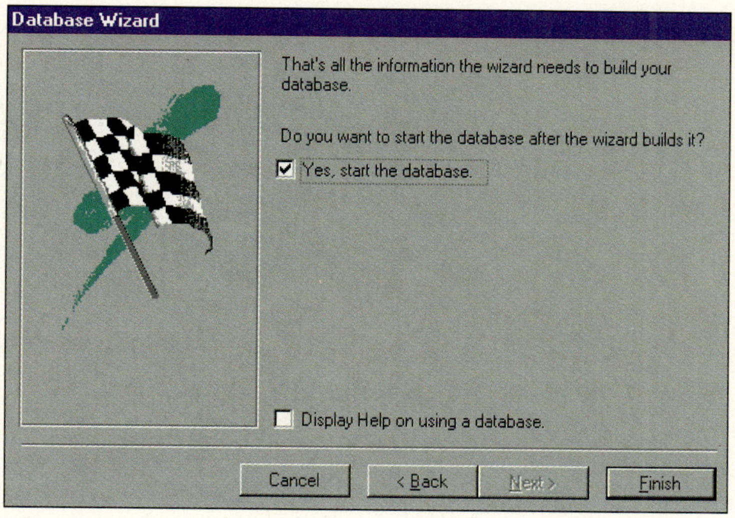

Figure 1.12

3 Select Finish.
After a brief delay while Database Wizard creates tables, forms, and reports, you will see the Music Collection switchboard shown in Figure 1.11.

EXIT If necessary, you can select the last option on the switchboard now to exit the database. You can then exit Access and continue this project later.

Entering and Editing Data in Tables

Data stored in a database has value only if it is relevant, timely, and accurate. When you design a database, you determine what data is relevant to the objectives of the database. The frequency with which you enter and edit data determines its timeliness. Two factors affect accuracy: the quality of the data collected and the precision of data entry.

To keep a database current, you will add records to tables, change data in existing records, and delete unwanted records. In the following sections you will add and edit records in your new Music Collection database.

Using a Form to Add Records

During the process to create a database system, Database Wizard sets up one or more forms on which to add, edit, and view data. Figure 1.13 shows one of the forms created for use with the Music Collection database.

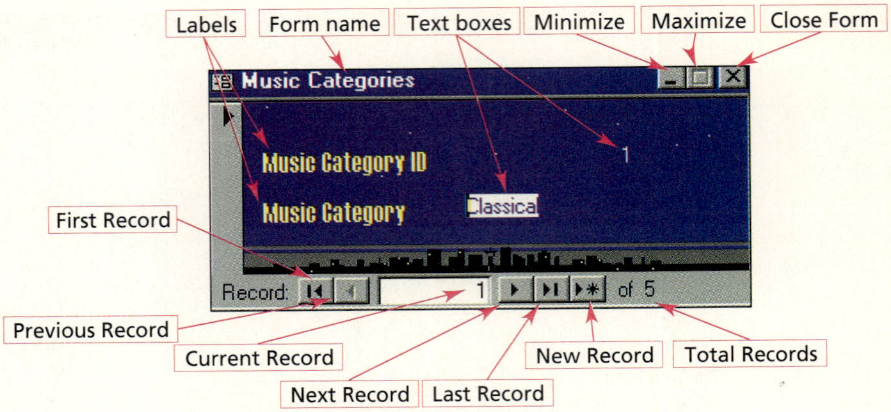

Figure 1.13

The form name and the Minimize, Maximize, and Close Form buttons appear at the top of the form. Several buttons at the bottom of the form help you navigate through the table. By clicking the appropriate button, you can display the first or last record, the previous or next record, or a blank new record. You can also see the number of the current record and the total number of records.

A form can display data from one or more tables. The form shown in Figure 1.13 is a simple one, containing only two ***text boxes*** and the corresponding ***labels.*** A text box generally displays data from a table. A ***label*** describes its associated control or some other portion of the form.

In the following steps you will use the Music Categories form to add a new record to the categories table.

To add a new record using a form:

1 If necessary, load Access and open the My Music Collection database.

2 Select Enter/View Other Information, the second option on the Music Collection Main Switchboard (see Figure 1.11).
The Forms Switchboard shown in Figure 1.14 appears.

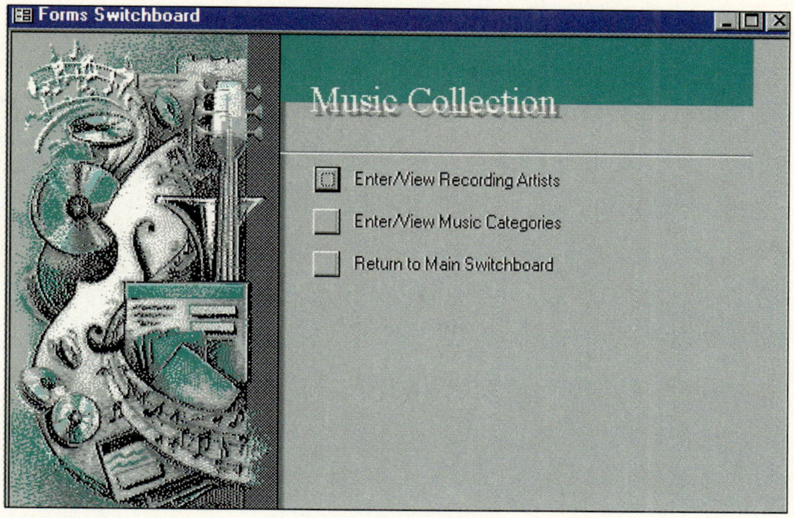

Figure 1.14

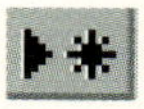

3 Select Enter/View Music Categories, the second option on the Forms Switchboard.
The form shown in Figure 1.13 appears.

4 Click New Record, the last of the buttons at the bottom of the form.
A blank record 6 appears.

5 Type `Blues` in the Music Category text box and press (ENTER)
A blank record 7 appears.

6 Close the form by clicking the Close Form button in the upper-right corner of the Music Categories form.

7 Select Return to Main Switchboard.

Using a Form to Edit Records

When data in a record is no longer valid, it must be changed. The editing process involves accessing the invalid record and changing the data field or fields that are inaccurate.

You can edit a record on a form by selecting (highlighting) the contents of a field and then typing the new data. You can also make another selection in a *combo box,* as shown in Figure 1.15. A ***combo box*** displays a list of allowable entries.

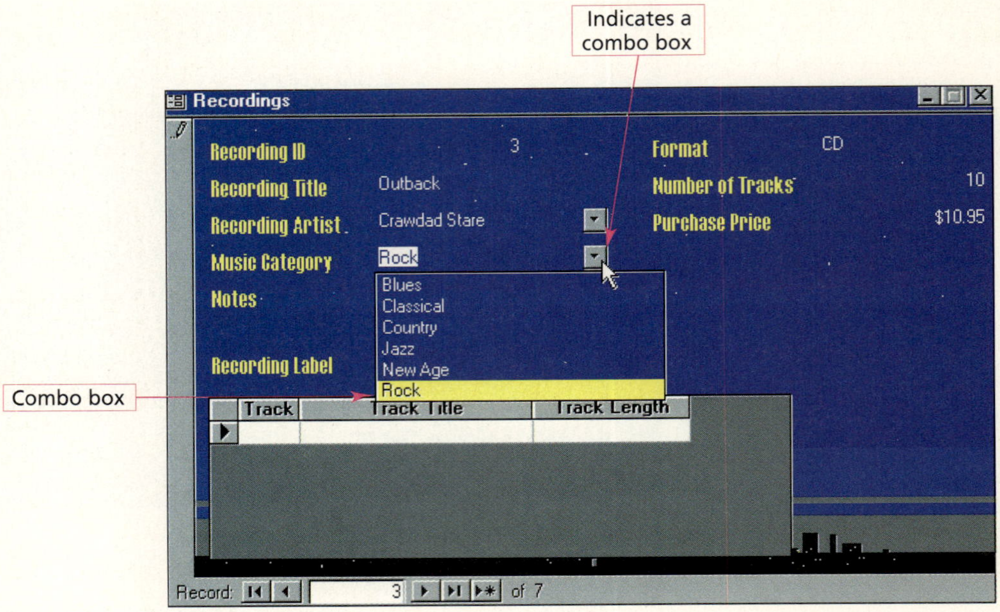

Figure 1.15

In the following steps you will display the form and record shown in Figure 1.15, type a change in purchase price, and select a different music category from choices in a combo box.

To change an existing record:

1 Select Enter/View Recordings, the first option on the Main Switchboard.

2 Display record 3.

Reminder Use the buttons at the bottom of the form to move to a different record.

3 Select 12.98 in the Purchase Price field.

4 Type **`10.95`**

5 Click the down arrow at the right end of the Music Category text box.
The combo box shown in Figure 1.15 appears.

6 Select Country.

7 Close the form.
The Main Switchboard appears on the screen.

EXIT If necessary, you can exit this database now. You can then exit Access and continue this project later.

Previewing and Printing a Report

The rows (records) and columns (fields) of a table contain data, as shown in Figure 1.16 for the Recordings table in the Music Collection database.

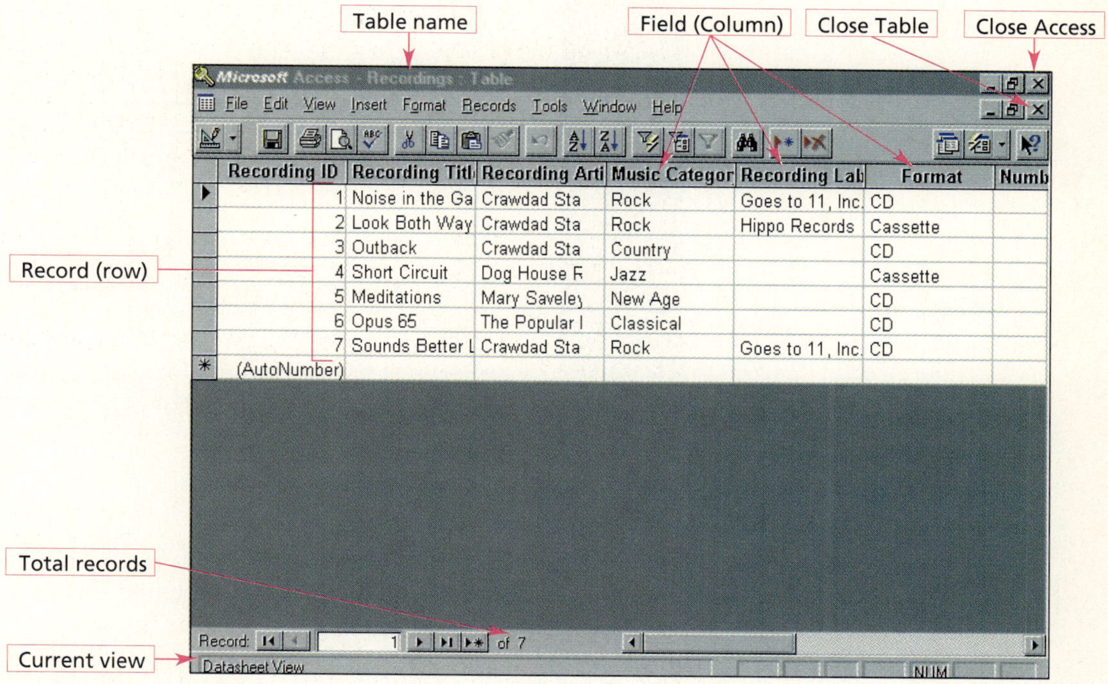

Figure 1.16

A field is a type of information, such as *Music Category, Recording Label,* or *Format.* A record is a collection of related fields, such as the record for Look Both Ways, a recording classified as rock, performed by Crawdad Stare, and distributed on cassette by Hippo Records.

Compare the datasheet (table) view in Figure 1.16 to the report shown in Figure 1.17.

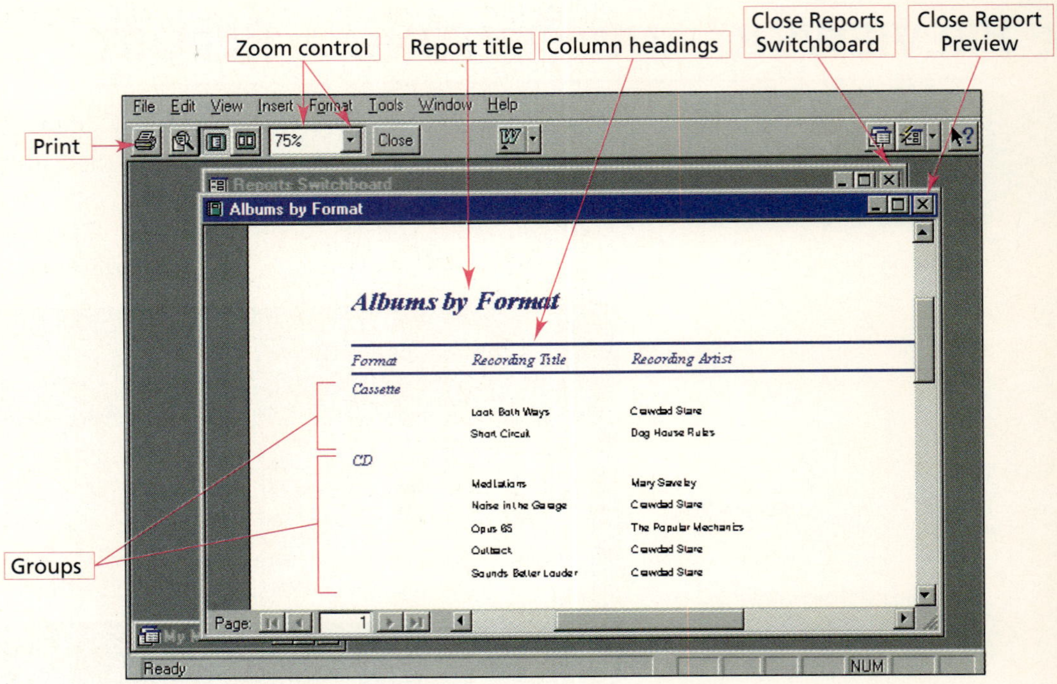

Figure 1.17

In the table, records display in the order in which they were entered, and you see only as many fields as can fit across the screen. The report groups similar records according to format (cassette or CD), limiting display to three fields. Within each group, records appear in alphabetical order by recording title. The report title, column headings, and horizontal lines add the finishing touches to professional-looking output.

Tip If you want to see more or less of a report on the screen, you can vary the magnification by changing the zoom setting. When you are satisfied with the content and format of the report, you can produce a printed report by selecting Print at the left end of the toolbar.

During the process to create a database system, Database Wizard sets up one or more reports. You can view the names of reports on the Reports Switchboard, as shown in Figure 1.18 for the Music Collection database.

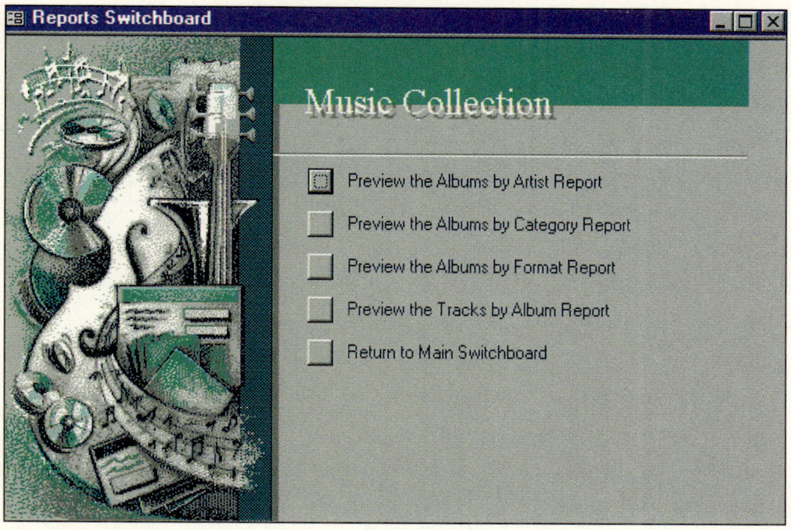

Figure 1.18

In the following steps you will view several reports created by Database Wizard for the Music Collection database. You will also print one of the reports.

To preview and print a report:

1 If necessary, load Access and open the My Music Collection database.

2 Select Preview Reports, the third option on the Music Collection Main Switchboard (see Figure 1.11).
The Reports Switchboard shown in Figure 1.18 appears.

3 Select Preview the Albums by Format Report.

4 Set zoom to 75%, and use the scroll bar to view all of the data, as shown in Figure 1.17.

5 Close the Albums by Format preview.

6 Select Preview the Albums by Artist Report, and set zoom to 50%.
Your screen displays the report shown in Figure 1.19.

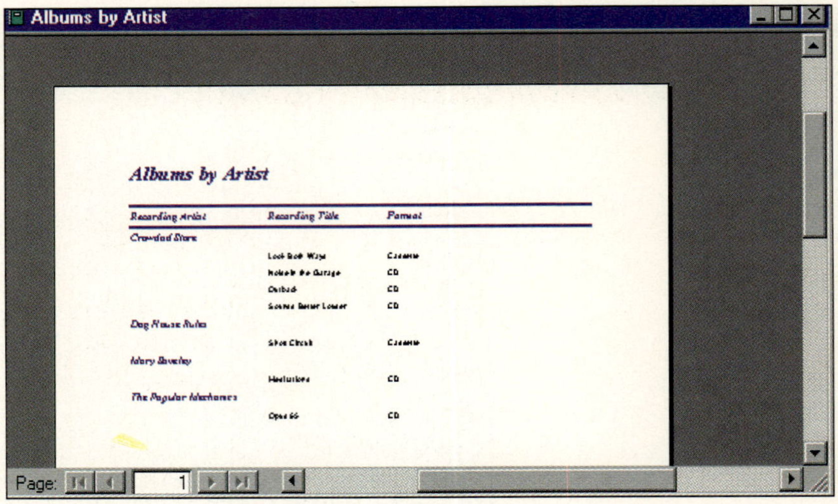

Figure 1.19

7 Select Print, the first button in the toolbar.
Your printout matches the screen display shown in Figure 1.19.

To close the switchboards and the database:

1 Close the Albums by Artist preview.
The Reports Switchboard appears.

2 Select Return to Main Switchboard.

3 Select Exit this database.

THE NEXT STEP

In this project you had a brief exposure to the power of Access. You selected a predefined Music Collection database, which put Database Wizard to work creating the required tables, forms, and reports. You performed basic data management tasks such as modifying the suggested design, entering and editing data using a form, and communicating information through reports sent to the screen or printer. On your own you might select one of the other predefined personal or business databases, include sample data, and repeat activities until you are comfortable using and closing the switchboards, forms, and reports.

This concludes Project 1. You can either exit Access or go on to work the Study Questions, Review Exercises, and Assignments.

SUMMARY AND EXERCISES

Summary

- Selecting a predefined database application causes Database Wizard to create the required tables, forms, and reports for one of 22 personal or business databases.
- The tables, forms, and reports that constitute a database are stored in a single file with an .mdb extension.
- You can modify a table suggested by Database Wizard by adding optional fields.
- Requesting sample data allows you to work with forms and reports before entering your own data.
- Database Wizard dialog boxes allow you to select a style for screen displays, a style for printed reports, and a title and picture to appear on screen displays and printouts.
- Database Wizard creates a menu system called the switchboard, which you can use to update tables, view data stored in tables, and display or print reports.
- A form displays data from one or more tables on the screen. You can add, edit, and view data using a form.
- A report sends information to the screen or printer in a professional-looking format. Report options include limiting the number of fields, grouping similar records, and presenting records in a meaningful order.

Key Terms and Operations

Key Terms
combo box
label
switchboard
text box

Operations
Create an application using Database Wizard
Enter and edit data using a form
Preview and print reports

Study Questions

Multiple Choice

1. Database Wizard sets up a predefined database application, automatically creating some features but making others optional. Which of the following is optional when Database Wizard creates the database?
   a. switchboard
   b. sample data
   c. both a and b
   d. none of the above

2. What is the three-character file name extension that indicates an Access database?
   a. .dbm
   b. .dbf
   c. .mdb
   d. none of the above

3. Using Database Wizard, you can add optional fields to a predefined table. The names of these optional fields appear
   a. italicized.
   b. in boldface.
   c. underlined.
   d. in a normal typeface.

4. Selecting a style for screen displays
   a. adds sample data to your database.
   b. adds background scenery and color to your screen displays.
   c. adds type fonts and sizes to your printed reports.
   d. All of the above.

5. How many predefined databases are available using Database Wizard?
   a. 15
   b. 20
   c. 25
   d. none of the above

Short Answer

1. Data stored in a database has value only if it is __________, __________, and __________.
2. Database Wizard provides two categories of predefined databases. What are the two categories?
3. You can add a picture to reports. What file type does Access prefer for this picture?
4. What is the name of the menu system that helps users navigate through a database?
5. On a form, a(n) __________ displays a list of allowable entries.

For Discussion

1. What is Database Wizard? What determines whether or not you would use this feature of the Access program?
2. Database Wizard creates one or more forms for a predefined database application. Describe the purpose and layout (text boxes and labels) of a form.
3. Database Wizard creates one or more reports for a predefined database application. Describe the enhancements you can view in a report that are not available when viewing the same data in a table.

Review Exercises

Creating a Personal Address Book

1. Load Access and select Database Wizard.
2. Select and save the Address Book database.
3. Add fields for nicknames and mobile phone numbers (do not add sample data).

4. Select a style for screen displays and printed reports.
5. Provide an appropriate title to appear on screen displays and printouts (do not include a picture).
6. Use a form(s) to enter ten records.
7. View predefined reports (also print if instructed to do so).
8. Close the database.

Creating an Inventory of Personal Property

1. Load Access and select Database Wizard.
2. Select and save the Household Inventory database.
3. Add fields for manufacturer's name and photograph, and add sample data.
4. Select a style for screen displays and printed reports.
5. Provide an appropriate title to appear on screen displays and printouts (do not include a picture).
6. Use a form(s) to edit two records.
7. View predefined reports (also print if instructed to do so).
8. Close the database.

Assignments

Using Contents in On-screen Help

Using Contents in on-screen Help, view the Visual Introduction to Microsoft Access. Read the three sections titled *What is a database*, *Tables: What they are and how they work*, and *Customizing a table*. Write a brief summary of what you learned about databases, tables, and how they are related.

Using Index in On-screen Help

Use Index to learn about creating a database using Database Wizard. Write a brief summary explaining the steps necessary to create a database using Database Wizard.

Cataloging Your Video Tape Collection

Use Database Wizard to create a database that will track your collection of video tapes. Use a form(s) to add data. Print one or more reports providing information about your collection.

Tracking Your Workout

Use Database Wizard to create a database that will track your exercise program. Use a form(s) to add data. Print one or more reports providing information about your workouts and performance.

Project 2: Designing and Creating a Database

Objectives

After completing this project, you should be able to:

- Design a database management system
- Create a table with Table Wizard
- Create a table on your own

Case Study: Coordinating Volunteer Activities

Assume that you are a summer intern at your campus volunteer center. Recently the center acquired Access for Windows 95 software, and the director has asked you to create an Access database management system to provide information about student volunteers and agencies in need of help.

Designing the Solution

No formal design process is necessary when you create and maintain a small information system for your own use, such as the music collection database you created with Database Wizard in Project 1. When you design a larger system for use by others, however, there is a lot of work to do! You must first talk with users of the new system so that you understand the database objectives and desired outputs. With that information you are prepared to develop a ***data dictionary,*** which shows the tables, fields, and relationships you feel are needed to accomplish the goals of the database. After users review and approve your design as detailed in the data dictionary, you can load Access and use a variety of wizards to set up the tables, queries, forms, and reports that constitute the information system.

> ***Tip*** Working through such a formal process to design a multiuser database can be tedious and time-consuming, often taking weeks before output is available. Taking time to interact with users at the design stage, however, makes it far less likely that you'll have major revisions to table structures, queries, forms, and reports later on.

This project focuses on the initial steps in the database design process: understanding the database objectives and desired outputs, developing a data dictionary, and creating the necessary tables. In subsequent projects you will enter and edit data as well as output information.

DETERMINING OBJECTIVES AND OUTPUTS

Setting up interviews with users is an excellent way to start the database design process. You will use these meetings to gain a clear understanding of problems with the current information system and users' expectations concerning the new database. As soon as possible after each interview, you should write down your conclusions regarding objectives and desired outputs.

Tip You may need to interview an individual more than once to have the necessary depth of information. Do not rely on recall of verbal comments as the basis for your written analysis. If the person being interviewed agrees, tape the conversation. You might also prepare a list of questions, with space for comments on the responses you receive.

To give you a glimpse of the interview process, imagine that you are the intern in the following dialogue with the director of the campus volunteer center.

Intern	*You told me earlier that your current system provides information in two areas: students interested in volunteering and organizations that have volunteer opportunities. Let's focus on students for a moment. How do you collect and store data on those individuals interested in volunteering?*
Director	The campus newspaper and radio station donate space and time for us to promote opportunities for volunteer service. We also post flyers in every building. Any student interested in volunteering is invited to phone or stop by the center. One of my two assistants writes the student's name, local address, and local phone number on an index card, and also notes whether the student can provide transportation. Preferences for type of volunteer activity are written on the back of the card, as are days and times available to work. The cards are filed in alphabetical order by last name.
Intern	*Does this system provide the information you need in a timely manner?*

Director The card system meets my objectives of knowing which students are interested in volunteering and being able to contact a specific student. However, using the card file to find students for a specific volunteer opportunity just doesn't work. For example, this morning I had a phone call from an organization looking for two students to work with teens at a gym on Saturday mornings. To process that request using our current system, a staff member has to read the notes on the backs of the student cards, and then phone potential volunteers. All too often we find out that a student's interests and availability have changed, and the search for a match starts again. I'm in favor of dropping data on interests and availability, which is so hard to keep current, and collecting e-mail (electronic mail) names instead. Hours of staff time could be saved by sending a single e-mail message about a volunteer opportunity and inviting interested parties to respond.

Intern *I've noted your desire to exclude data on student interests and availability but retain local phone numbers and add e-mail names. Do you want to include local addresses?*

Director Not for students. However, we do need to communicate by mail and fax with organizations needing volunteers.

Intern *I'm confident that I understand what's needed to contact students interested in volunteering. With a computerized database, however, you can output information in ways that weren't possible with a manual system. What student-related information would you like to have that's not available now?*

Director Let me toss a couple of ideas your way, and we can both be thinking about the details before meeting again tomorrow at noon. My top priority is to provide some recognition for outstanding service each month, but until now I've not had the resources to record volunteer hours, much less total them. The dean of students would like a summary of student volunteer activity by college or major each term. Once in awhile an organization will request a report showing all volunteer activity provided to that organization by our students within a specified time frame. I'd like to send a similar report to each organization every month. Students often ask me to write letters of recommendation. It would be very helpful if I could refer to a list showing volunteer activity of a single student, with information clustered by term or agency. How's that for a preliminary "wish list?"

Intern *Using Access, those wishes can come true! If you will make sketches of the reports you'd like to have, we should be able to finish the student part of our design discussion over lunch tomorrow. Afterward I'll meet with your assistant who works directly with the volunteer organizations.*

As soon as possible after each interview, you should write your conclusions regarding database objectives and desired outputs. You should refer to these notes when you compose a ***database objective statement,*** which is a one-paragraph explanation of the goal of the complete system, and develop a list of desired outputs.

Tip You may also find it helpful to mention your perceptions of information that won't be available with the new system. For example, users should clearly understand they will not be able to search the volunteer center database for the names of students whose interests and availability fit the needs of an organization needing volunteers.

Be sure to circulate among users the database objective statement, a list of desired outputs, and sketches of suggested reports. After users review, revise, and approve these preliminary design documents, you can start work on a data dictionary.

Creating a Data Dictionary

Once users clearly specify what they want for output, it's time to think about the data needed to produce the output. A good first step is looking over the sketches of desired reports and listing the data items that appear in each report. The next steps in the design process, considered by many to be the most difficult, involve separating the data items into some logical arrangement and planning enough tables to avoid entering data more than once.

Tip The formal procedure by which data items are grouped into tables and tables are grouped into databases is called *normalization*. In-depth information about the normalizing process can be found in texts on database design.

The data dictionary serves as a worksheet that defines the tables and field specifications in a database. You will use this worksheet when you actually create the database on the computer. Later the data dictionary can be used as a reference document to keep near the computer.

Figure 2.1 illustrates a data dictionary for the Volunteer Center database, with field names listed in the fourth column. Although you can specify up to 64 characters in a field name, including spaces, each name should be just long enough to describe the field.

Tip If you type an uppercase letter within a field name, Access automatically inserts a space before that letter whenever the field name appears on-screen or in printed output. For example, ContactFirstName will display as Contact First Name.

Table/Data Cross Reference			Field Specifications - Volunteer Center Database			
Organizations Table	Volunteers Table	Time Cards Table	Field Name	Field Size	Data Type	Comments
x		x	OrganizationID		Text	User supplied. Contains letter code such as HH (Habitat for Humanity) or MOW (Meals on Wheels). Primary key in organizations table: required in both tables
x			OrganizationName	30	Text	Full name of the organization such as Meals on Wheels
x			ContactFirstName	12	Text	Full name of contact such as Michelle
x			ContactLastName	15	Text	Last name of contact such as Fox, Smith-Jones, or Van Horn
x			Address	35	Text	Street address or post office box
x			City	20	Text	City such as Greenwood or Indianapolis
x			State	2	Text	2-digit state code; default value IN (for Indiana) may be edited
x			ZipCode	10	Text	Zip code such as 46299 or 46299-9999; controlled by an input mask
x			WorkPhone	14	Text	Phone number such as (317)111-1111; controlled by an input mask
x			FaxNumber	14	Text	Fax number such as (317)111-1112; controlled by an input mask
	x	x	Volunteer ID	12	Text	Social security number. Primary key in Volunteers table; required in both tables
	x		FirstName	12	Text	First name of student volunteer such as Eric
	x		LastName	15	Text	Last name of student volunteer such as Fox or Smith-Jones
	x		College	18	Text	Chose one:Arts & Sciences, Business, Education, Fine Arts, Pharmacy
	x		Major	30	Text	Major such as Marketing, Secondary Education, or Biology
	x		EmailName	20	Text	E-mail name/address in the form name@school.edu
	x		LocalPhone	9	Text	Phone while at school; controlled by an input mask
	x		Birthdate		Date/Time	Date of birth; controlled by input mask mm/dd/yy
	x		HasCar		Yes/No	√ = can provide transportation
		x	DateWorked		Date/Time	Date of volunteer service; controlled by input mask mm/dd/yy
		x	HoursWorked		Number	Total hours to nearest quarter hour such as 1.5, 3.25, 6, or 4.75

Figure 2.1

22 7

The three columns on the left constitute a table/data cross-reference that shows the planned distribution of fields among three tables named Organizations, Volunteers, and Time Cards. Each *x* represents a field in the associated table. For example, the four fields named OrganizationID, VolunteerID, DateWorked, and HoursWorked make up the Time Cards table. The remaining columns in the data dictionary provide information about field specifications.

Tip You can create an electronic data dictionary using spreadsheet or word processing software. The data dictionary shown in Figure 2.1 was developed using the table feature in Microsoft Word for Windows 95.

In this project the critical task of developing the data dictionary has been done for you. However, before you create the tables identified in the data dictionary, let's look at the thought processes underlying table selection and field specifications suggested for the Volunteer Center database.

Caution Avoid skipping over or merely skimming through the next six sections so that you can "get to the good part" of working with the Access software. If you do not thoroughly understand the terms and design concepts involved, you will find it very hard to design a relational database on your own.

Organizing Data in Tables

Opinions may vary on the number of tables to set up for a given database. You should, however, follow some general guidelines to organize data in tables. To start with, look for data items that relate to the same subject and separate them from data items dealing with another subject. For example, analyzing interview notes and sketches of desired outputs from volunteer center staff reveals that some data items relate to organizations, while others describe students and their volunteer efforts. In this situation you should plan for at least one table for organization-specific data and at least one table for student-specific data.

You should then check that the tables you have in mind eliminate unnecessary duplication of data, sometimes referred to as ***redundant data.*** Setting up *organization*-related items in one table will not result in duplicate data. The name, contact person, address, phone number, and fax number for each organization will only be entered once. However, putting all *student*-related data items in one table would result in duplicate data. Some sample records illustrate the problem.

Imagine that a pharmacy student named Anna Weist volunteered 4 hours every other Friday during November for Meals on Wheels and 10 hours the Saturday before Thanksgiving on a Habitat for Humanity project. Consider how a table might look if you mix data describing a student (first name, last name, e-mail name, and college) with data describing that student's volunteer efforts (the volunteer organization, the date worked, and the hours involved).

First Name	Last Name	E-mail Name	College	Organization	Date Worked	Hours Worked
Anna	Weist	AWEIST	Pharmacy	Meals on Wheels	11/1/96	4
Anna	Weist	AWEIST	Pharmacy	Meals on Wheels	11/15/96	4
Anna	Weist	AWEIST	Pharmacy	Habitat for Humanity	11/23/96	10
Anna	Weist	AWEIST	Pharmacy	Meals on Wheels	11/29/96	4

The First Name, Last Name, E-mail Name, and College fields in the sample table contain redundant data. These details about a specific student should appear only once in the database. However, repeating the identity of an organization such as Meals on Wheels is necessary because this student or any other student can work for one organization many times.

Creating two student-related tables instead of one in the Volunteer Center database will eliminate unnecessary duplication of data. Look again at Figure 2.1. The fields in the Volunteers table will store data describing students, one record only for each student interested in volunteer work. A separate Time Cards table will store details of actual volunteer efforts, with one record per activity and multiple records possible for one volunteer.

Tip Plan to use coded data where possible. For example, being able to enter a code such as MOW instead of the full name Meals on Wheels would speed data entry in the Time Cards table where multiple entries are possible. Accuracy would likely improve as well because there are fewer characters to type.

Deciding on Primary Keys

A table's ***primary key,*** which can be one field or a combination of fields, makes each record unique. When you add new records to a table that has a primary key, Access checks for duplicate data and won't let you repeat data in the primary key field(s). Access won't let you leave a primary key field blank either, which helps ensure that you'll have only valid records in your table.

In the Volunteer Center database, you will designate OrganizationID (containing a unique code such as MOW for Meals on Wheels) as the primary key in the Organizations table, and VolunteerID (containing a student's social security number) as the primary key in the Volunteers table. You will not designate any field as a primary key in the Time Cards table because the same organization code, student ID, date worked, or hours worked can appear more than once.

Planning Links Between Tables

What if the director of the volunteer center were to ask for a list of volunteer activity in the last month showing student names, the dates and number of hours worked, and the organizations receiving help? Generating this information requires first and last name data from the Volunteers table, date and number of hours data from the Time Cards table, and name data from the Organizations table.

You can output data from more than one table at a time if a common field provides a link between tables. According to the data dictionary in Figure 2.1, the Organizations and Time Cards tables have the OrganizationID field in common. The VolunteerID field provides the link between the Volunteers and Time Cards tables.

Tip When linking tables, you should link the primary key field from one table to a field in the other table that has the same data type (see the next section) and field size. However, the name of the common field does not have to be the same in both tables.

Assigning an Appropriate Data Type

As part of the data dictionary, you must decide which type of data each field will hold. Access data types include Currency, Date/Time, Number, Text, and Yes/No as well as several others that will not be specified in the Volunteer Center database. Figure 2.1 shows that the data type for most of the fields will be Text, which can store letters, numbers, spaces, or special characters. You will select Currency as the field type to display monetary data and Number as the field type to display most other numeric values. The Volunteer Center database will contain only one number field, the one storing hours worked in the Time Cards table.

Tip You should specify Text as the field type if a field will contain only numbers that will never be used in calculations, such as social security numbers, zip codes, and phone numbers.

You should specify Yes/No as the data type if the entry in the field indicates Yes, No, True, or False. For example, Yes/No is the appropriate field type for the HasCar field in the Volunteers table, because the contents will indicate Yes, the student can provide transportation or No, the student cannot provide transportation.

If you will store dates or times in a table, you should select Date/Time as the data type. Doing so will allow you to vary display of the data. For example, you could display the 12th day of January in 1997 several ways including 1/12/97, 12-Jan-97, or January 12, 1997. As shown in Figure 2.1, you will assign this field type to the Birthdate field in the Volunteers table and the DateWorked field in the Time Cards table.

Estimating Field Size

Field size refers to the maximum space Access reserves for data. For all field types except Text and Number, Access determines a maximum size automatically according to the data type. For example, the size of a Yes/No field is 1. If the data type is Text, you can specify a field size from 1 to 255 or let Access assign the default size, initially set at 50.

Tip You should assign a realistic field size but one that is as small as possible. For example, a maximum field size of 20 for a City field is more realistic than the default size of 50. Smaller field sizes require less memory and can result in faster processing.

If you specify Number as the data type, you will choose among predefined settings such as Integer or Single instead of specifying a maximum field size. The setting you select defines the smallest and largest numbers the field can hold as well as the maximum number of decimal places.

Adding Comments

A data dictionary should serve as a planning document, a worksheet guiding the creation of a database, and a reference for those who use the database. Therefore, remarks concerning field setup and contents should be an integral part of a data dictionary, as shown for the Volunteer Center database in Figure 2.1.

The time and effort you spend to organize data in tables, decide on primary keys, plan links between tables, assign appropriate data types, estimate field sizes, and provide comments will give you a clear picture of the database that you can present to users for approval. After users approve the data dictionary, you can see how much help Access wizards provide in converting design to reality.

CREATING THE ORGANIZATIONS TABLE USING TABLE WIZARD

Before you start to set up tables and fields, you should check to see if Database Wizard includes a predefined application that closely resembles the overall database design reflected in the data dictionary. Recall that you can make your selection from the 22 personal and business databases shown in Figure 1.2. A good match exists if the application you choose provides the tables you want and requires only a few field modifications.

If using Database Wizard to create a predefined application would produce tables, forms, and reports requiring a lot of revision, you can set up each object one at a time yourself, with or without the help of other wizards. Let's focus for the moment on creating a table using ***Table Wizard,*** which asks you questions and builds a table based on your answers.

You can work with Business or Personal sample tables in the Table Wizard dialog box. When you select Business in the lower-left corner of the dialog box, you will see names of business-related sample tables, as shown in Figure 2.2. You can choose among 25 business tables, including Contacts, Customers, Employees, Payments, Projects, Reservations, and Time Billed. If you select Personal in the lower-left corner of the dialog box, you can choose among 20 personal tables, including Household Inventory, Exercise Log, Rolls of Film, Service Records, and Video Collection.

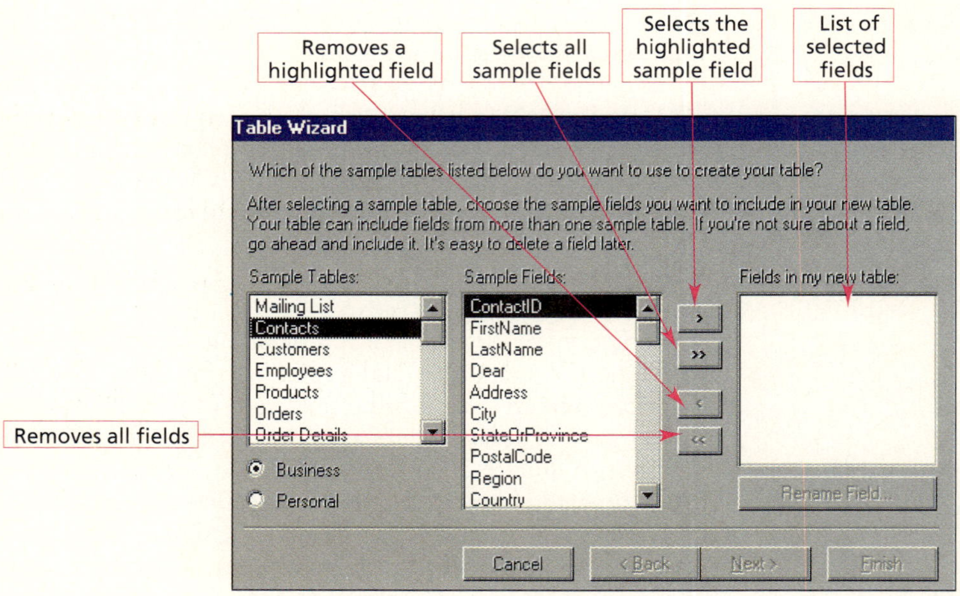

Figure 2.2

In the Table Wizard dialog box, the names of sample tables will appear in the Sample Tables list box on the left, the names of fields available for the selected table will appear in the Sample Fields list box in the middle, and the fields you select for your new table will appear in the list box on the right. General instructions appear above those three boxes. You will be looking for sample tables that resemble those specified in the data dictionary. A good match exists if a sample table you choose provides a number of the fields you need.

You will add or remove fields by double-clicking the name of a field or by using the four buttons between the Sample Fields and Fields in my new table boxes. The arrow on a button indicates the direction of movement. Selecting the button with a single arrow pointing to the right will copy the highlighted sample field name from the middle box to the box on the right. Selecting the button with two arrows pointing to the right will copy all sample fields. You will use the other two buttons to remove previously selected field names, either one at a time (using the button with a single arrow pointing to the left) or all at once (using the button with two arrows pointing to the left).

Tip If you will need only a few fields from a list of sample fields, select each field one at a time. If you need most of the sample fields, select all of them at once and then remove the ones you don't want to keep.

If you were to browse through the sample tables, you would find that the predefined Contacts table provides all the fields you need for the Organizations table in your Volunteer Center database. In the following sections you will use Table Wizard to create that table.

To create the Volunteer Center database:

1 Start Access.
The Microsoft Access dialog box appears.

Tip If Access is already active, close all open databases, choose New Database from the File pull-down menu, and select General if that is not the current folder in the New dialog box.

2 Select Blank Database, and then select OK.
The File New Database dialog box opens.

3 Type or point in the Save in list box the name of the folder where you want to store your database.

4 Type `Volunteer Center` in the File name list box, as shown in Figure 2.3 (Access automatically provides the .mdb extension).

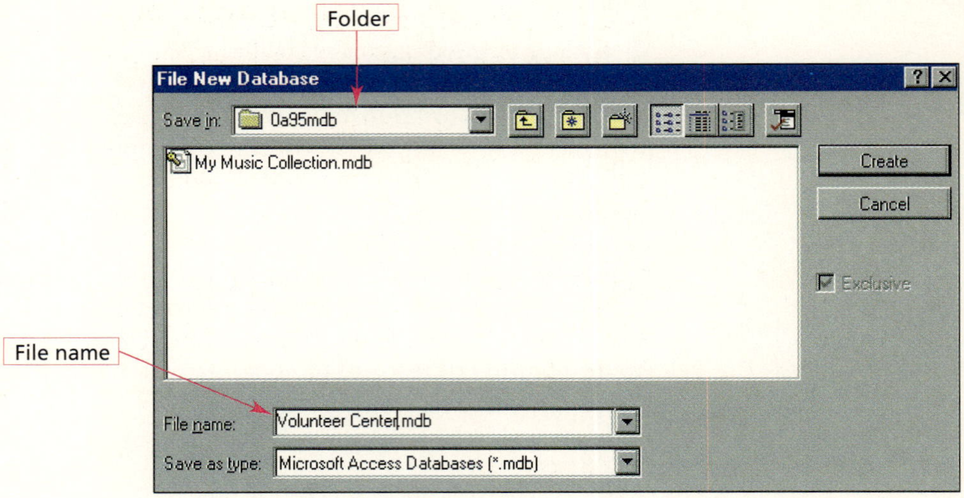

Figure 2.3

5 Select Create.
The Volunteer Center database dialog box appears on the screen with the Tables tab selected, as shown in Figure 2.4.

Figure 2.4

To create the Organizations table using Table Wizard:

1 Select New.
The New Table dialog box appears as shown in Figure 2.5.

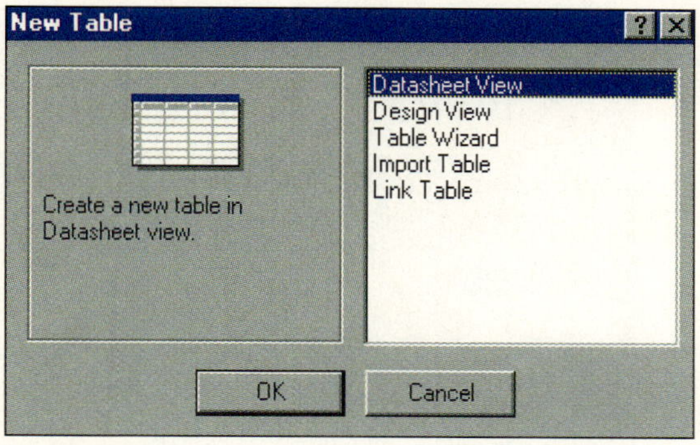

Figure 2.5

2 Select Table Wizard, and then select OK.
The Table Wizard dialog box appears.

3 Select Business in the lower-left corner, and then select Contacts in the Sample Tables list box.
The three list boxes within the dialog box should match those shown in Figure 2.2.

4 Select the sample field ContactID and press the > button.
Access copies the selected field name from the Sample Fields list box to the Fields in my new table list box.

5 Copy the following field names from the Sample Fields list box to the Fields in My New Table list box in the order given: CompanyName, FirstName, LastName, Address, City, StateOrProvince, PostalCode, WorkPhone, and FaxNumber.

> ***Tip*** Using a two-step process, you can insert the name of a sample field between two fields already listed for a new table. First select the field in the Fields in my new table list box that you want to precede the inserted field, and then double-click the desired field in the Sample Fields list box. For example, suppose you missed selecting the WorkPhone field in the previous step. To correct this omission, you would select the PostalCode field in the list box on the right and then double-click the WorkPhone field in the middle list box.

At this point you have selected the fields you want in a new table. Do not move to the next screen, however, until you change field names to match those in the data dictionary.

Renaming a Field

You can easily change the name given a sample field by selecting the field you want to rename, selecting the Rename Field command button, and then entering the new name in the Rename Field dialog box shown in Figure 2.6.

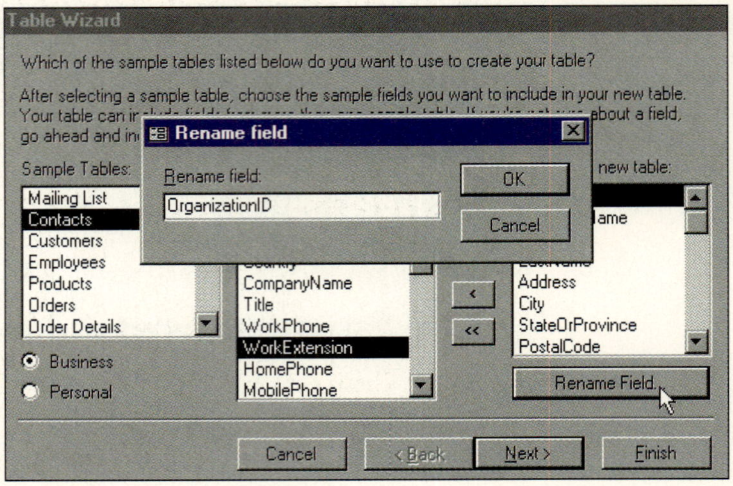

Figure 2.6

In the following steps you will change the names of selected fields to match those listed for the Organizations table in the Volunteer Center data dictionary.

To rename selected fields:

1 Select ContactID in the Fields in my new table list box.

2 Select Rename Field.

3 Type **`OrganizationID`** in the Rename Field dialog box, as shown in Figure 2.6.

4 Select OK.

5 Repeat steps 1 through 4 five times, renaming as follows:
Change CompanyName to **`OrganizationName`**
Change FirstName to **`ContactFirstName`**
Change LastName to **`ContactLastName`**
Change StateOrProvince to **`State`**
Change PostalCode to **`ZipCode`**

6 Scroll to the top of the list of selected field names and check that your renamed fields match those shown in Figure 2.7. Make corrections as necessary.

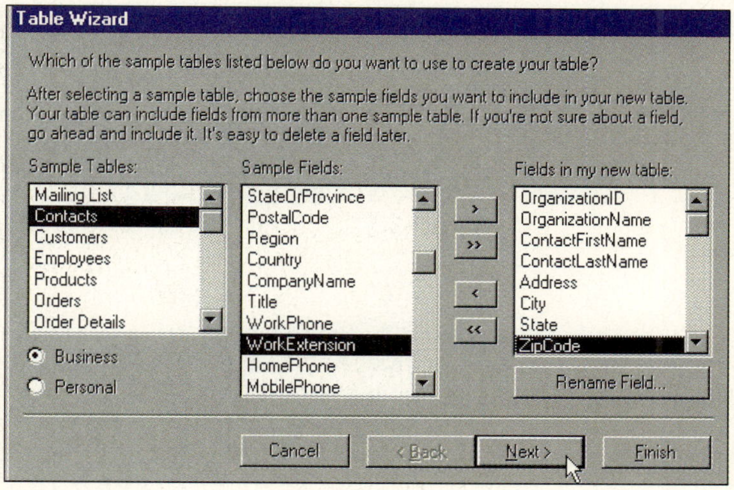

Figure 2.7

Now that you have selected fields for a table and renamed fields to match those shown in the data dictionary, Table Wizard wants to know the table's name and whether or not you will set a primary key.

Specifying a Primary Key

Recall that a primary key, which can be one field or a combination of fields, makes each record in a table unique. Table Wizard will set the key for you or you can specify your own. In the following steps you will name the new table and specify that the unique part of each record will be an organization code.

To name the table, set the primary key, and view the design:

1 Select Next>.

2 Type **`Organizations`** in the What do you want to name your table? box.

3 Select No, I'll set the primary key.
The settings in your Table Wizard dialog box should match those shown in Figure 2.8. Make corrections as necessary.

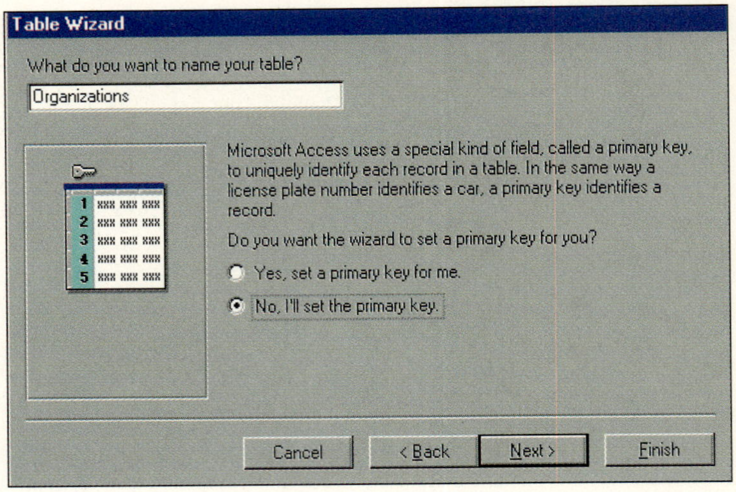

Figure 2.8

4 Select Next>.

5 Enter the specifications for field and type of data shown in Figure 2.9.

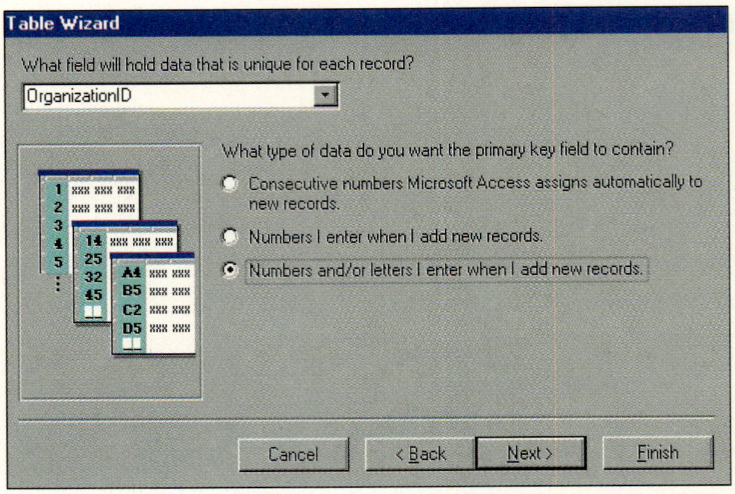

Figure 2.9

6 Select Next>.

Table Wizard indicates that you have supplied all the information necessary to create the Organizations table and asks you what you want to do.

7 Select Modify the table design, as shown in Figure 2.10.

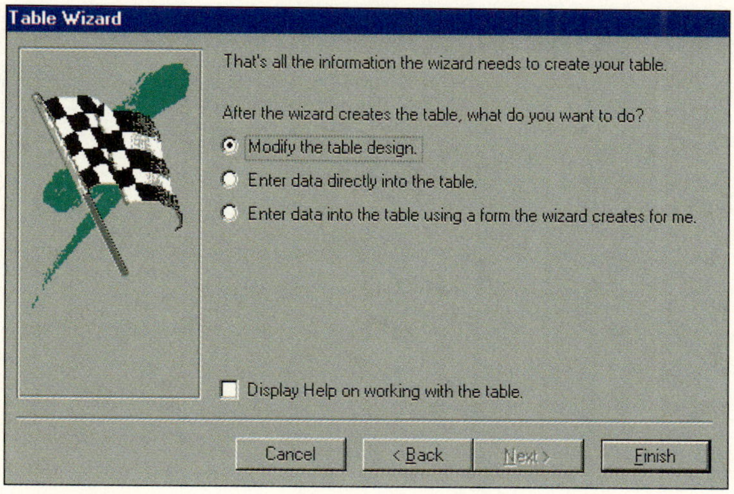

Figure 2.10

8 Select Finish.
Information about the Organizations table appears as shown in Figure 2.11. The key symbol to the left of the first field name indicates that OrganizationID is the primary key. You will work with field properties and enter data in Project 3.

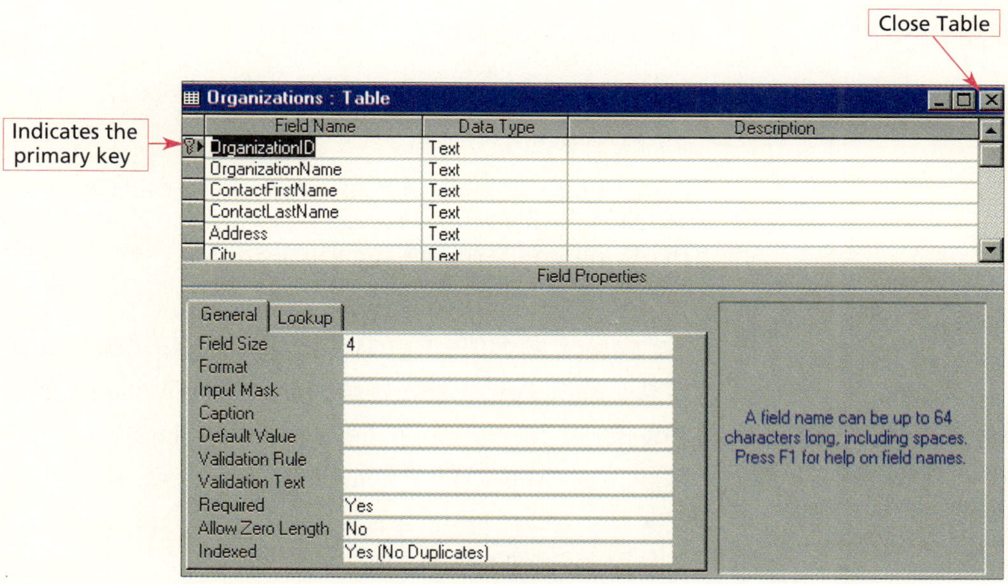

Figure 2.11

9 Close the table.
The Database dialog box appears as shown in Figure 2.12. At this time, the Organizations table is the only object in the Volunteer Center database.

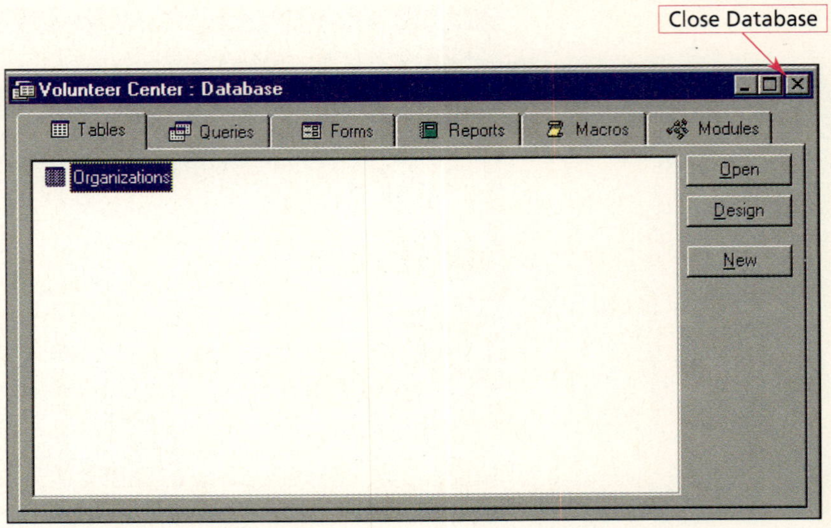

Figure 2.12

EXIT If necessary, you can close the database now. You can then exit Access and continue this project later.

Creating the Volunteers Table Using Table Wizard

The Volunteers table will contain personal data about each volunteer. Table Wizard's Employees table can provide most of the fields you need. In the following sections you will use Table Wizard to create the Volunteers table and add a few fields on your own.

To select sample fields for the Volunteers table:

1. If necessary, start Access and open the Volunteer Center database.
2. Select New from the Database dialog box shown in Figure 2.12.
3. Select Table Wizard, and then select OK.
4. Check that Business is selected as the type of sample table, and then select Employees.
5. Copy the following field names from the Sample Fields list box to the Fields in my new table list box: SocialSecurityNumber, FirstName, LastName, EmailName, HomePhone, and Birthdate.
6. Change the name of the SocialSecurityNumber field to VolunteerID, and change the name of the HomePhone field to LocalPhone.
The fields in your new table should match those shown in Figure 2.13.

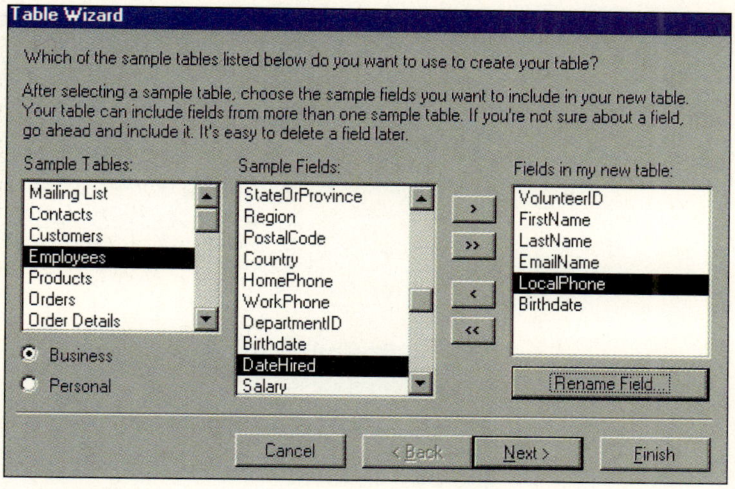

Figure 2.13

7 Select Next>.

To name the table and specify a primary key:

1 Type **`Volunteers`** in the What do you want to name your table? box, and then select No, I'll set the primary key.

2 Select Next>.

3 Check that the settings in your dialog box match those shown in Figure 2.14.

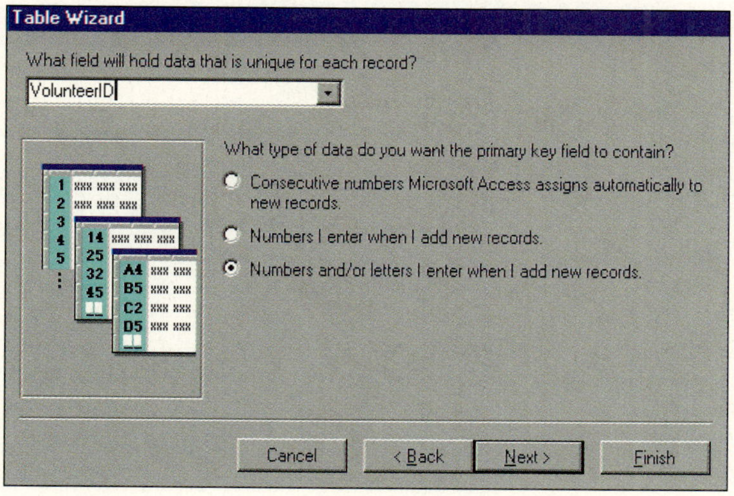

Figure 2.14

4 Select Next>.
A new Table Wizard screen appears, asking if this new table is related to any other table in the database, as shown in Figure 2.15. Access tells you that the new Volunteers table is not related to the Organizations table.

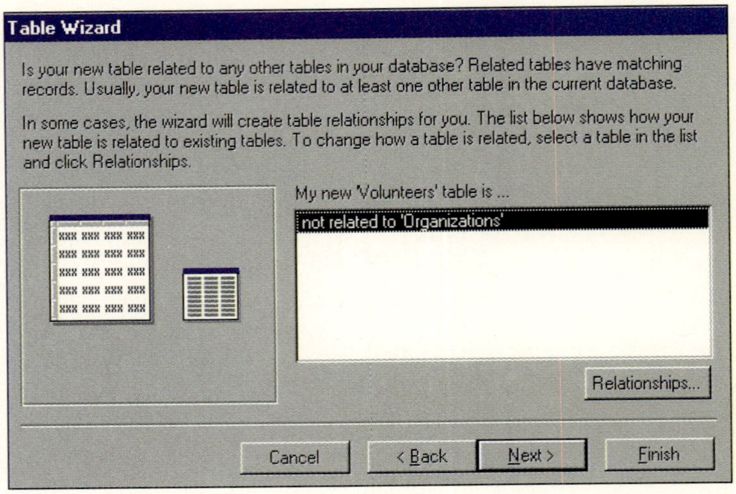

Figure 2.15

5 Select Next> to exit the current Table Wizard dialog box without defining a relationship.
Table Wizard indicates that you have supplied all the information necessary to create the Volunteers table and asks you what you want to do.

6 Select Modify the table design, and then select Finish.
Information about the Volunteers table appears as shown in Figure 2.16. The key symbol to the left of the first field name indicates that VolunteerID is the primary key.

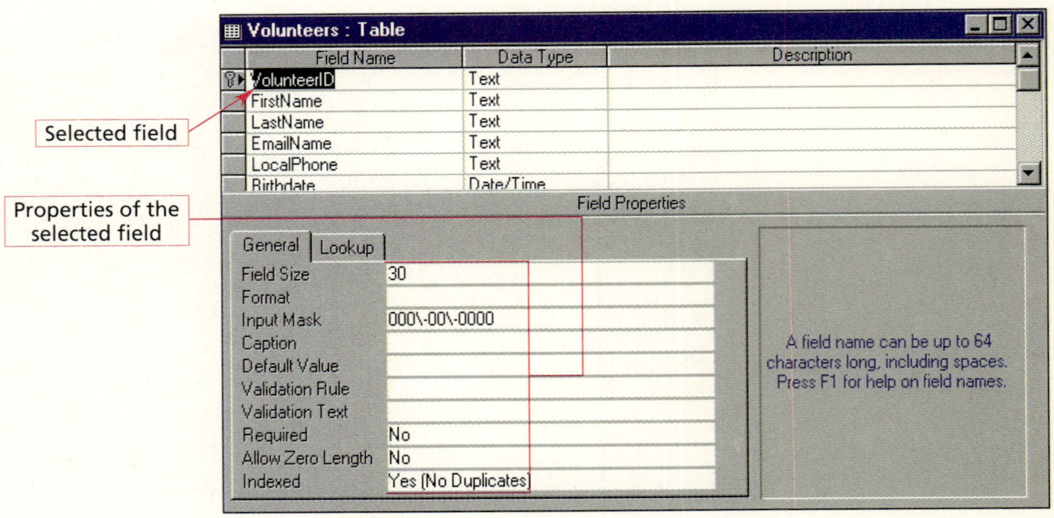

Figure 2.16

The Volunteer Center data dictionary indicates that nine fields are needed in the Volunteers table, as shown in Figure 2.1. You created six of those fields using Table Wizard. In the following sections you will insert the remaining fields.

Adding Fields

Figure 2.16 displays the Table dialog box in ***design view,*** in which you can create and modify the structure of a table. You can also display a table in ***datasheet view,*** in which you can view and modify data. You will switch between the two views to enter data in Project 3.

The design view of a table shows information about fields. Names and associated data types appear in the upper portion of the display, one field per row. Descriptions are not required but may help a user to understand the purpose and content of each field if the data dictionary does not already provide that information. The lower portion of the screen displays settings related to the selected field, such as its size and whether or not an entry is required in the field.

To add a field, you will type the new field name below the last field in the list. To insert a field, you can select Insert Row on the toolbar or choose Field from the Insert menu. Access will create a blank row above the current row. For example, Figure 2.17 shows the results of selecting Insert Row on the toolbar after positioning the pointer in the row containing EmailName.

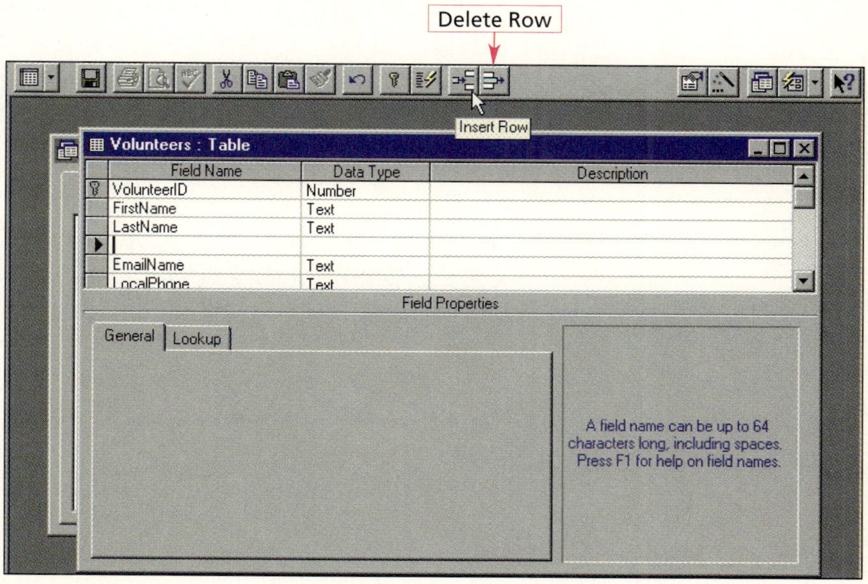

Figure 2.17

In the following steps you will modify the Volunteers table by inserting a text field between existing fields and then adding a Yes/No field.

> ***Quick Fix*** If you insert a new field in the wrong place, you can eliminate it by positioning the pointer on the row you want to remove and selecting Delete Row in the toolbar.

To insert a field in a table:

1. Click within the field name EmailName.
2. Select Insert Row in the toolbar.

Access creates a blank row, as shown in Figure 2.17.

3 Type **Major** as the field name.

4 Click within the blank Data Type area to the right of the field name Major.
Text appears automatically as the data type.

5 Change Field Size to 30 as shown in Figure 2.18.

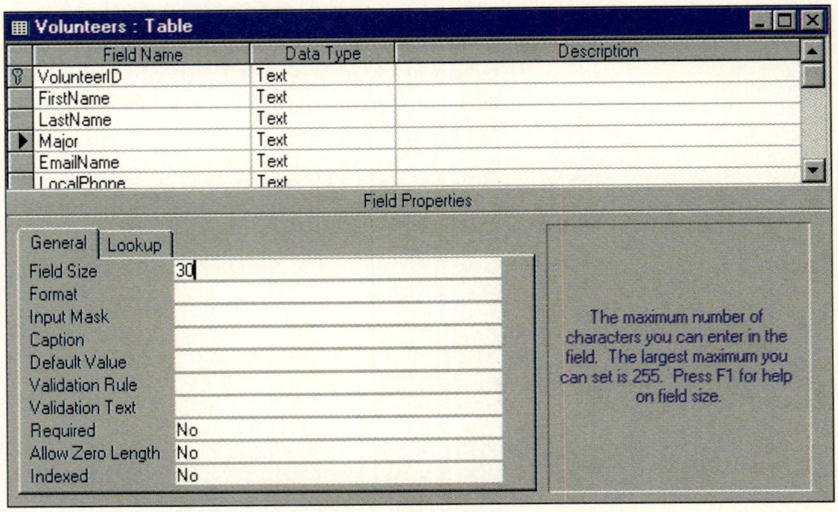

Figure 2.18

To add a field at the end of the table:

1 Scroll to the bottom of the Field Name list.

2 Type **HasCar** as the new field name in the first blank row after Birthdate.

3 Click within the blank Data Type area to the right of the field name HasCar.

4 Click the arrow to display the Data Type list box shown in Figure 2.19.

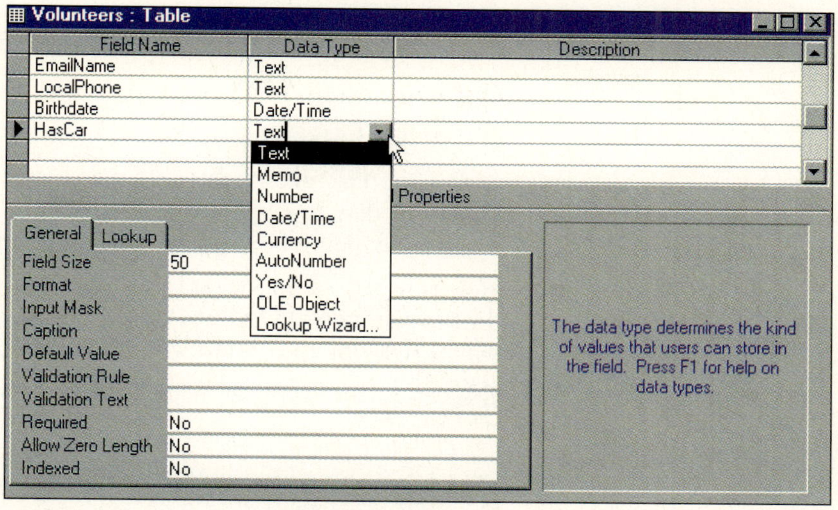

Figure 2.19

5 Select Yes/No as the data type.

6 Scroll to the top of the Field Name list.

Using Lookup Wizard

Access includes Lookup Wizard in the Data Type list box, as shown in Figure 2.20. ***Lookup Wizard*** creates a lookup column that allows you to choose a value from a list of values. Choosing a value instead of typing it saves time and eliminates typing errors.

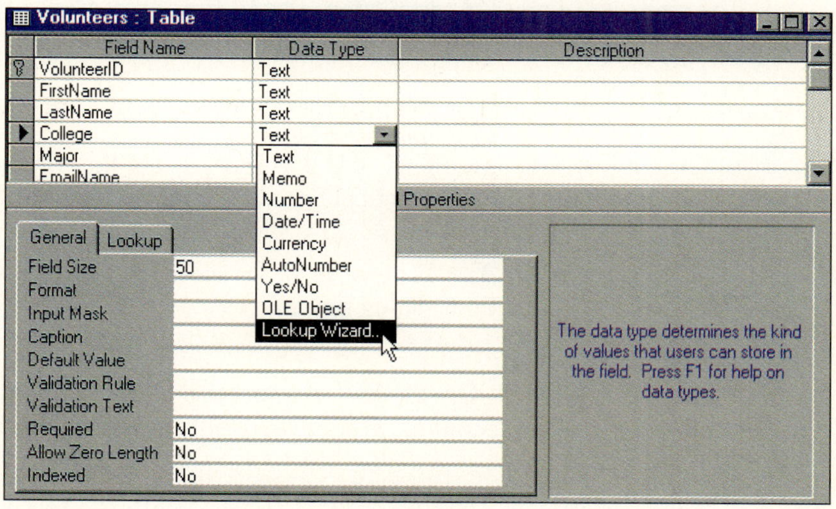

Figure 2.20

You can type the values that you want or tell Access to look up the values in a table. In the following steps you will insert a College field before the Major field in the Volunteers table, select Lookup Wizard, and type the college choices in a single column.

To create a lookup column using Lookup Wizard:

1 Click within the field name Major.

2 Select Insert Row in the toolbar.

3 Type `College` as the field name, move to the next column, and display the list of data types.
Your table dialog box should match the one shown in Figure 2.20.

4 Select Lookup Wizard.
The initial Lookup Wizard dialog box appears, in which you will specify where the lookup column will get its values.

5 Select *I will type in the values that I want,* as shown in Figure 2.21.

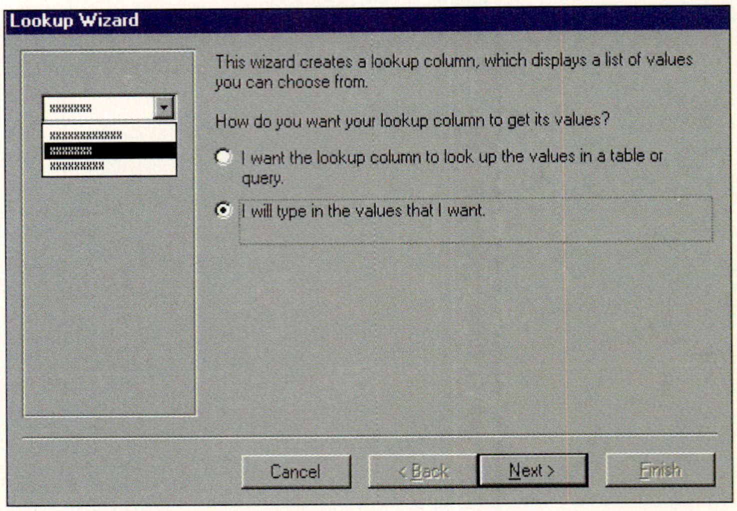

Figure 2.21

6 Select Next>.
Another Lookup Wizard dialog box appears. Instructions to specify the number of columns and change the width of a column appear at the top of the box.

7 Type `Arts & Sciences` for the first value.
Your dialog box should match the one shown in Figure 2.22.

Quick Fix If another dialog box appears requesting a name for the column, you pressed ENTER after typing the first value, which caused the next dialog box to appear. Select Back to restore the display shown in Figure 2.22.

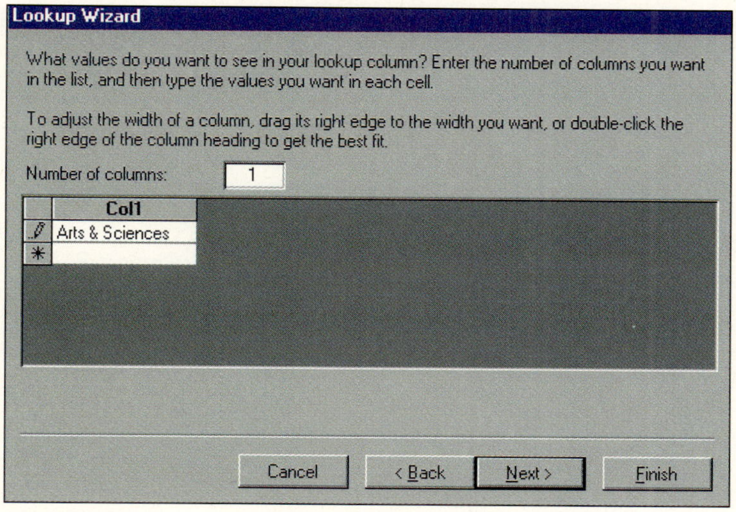

Figure 2.22

8 After clicking in the next blank box, type each of the other values shown in Figure 2.23.

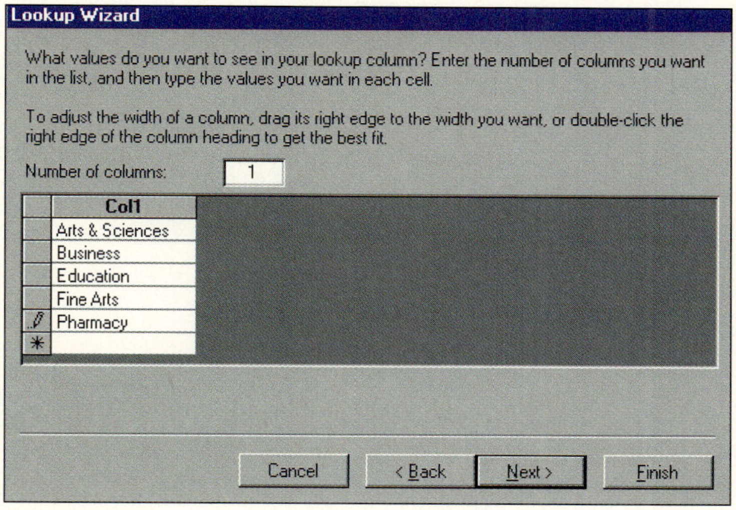

Figure 2.23

9 Select Next>.
The field name College appears automatically as the label for the lookup column.

10 Select Finish to exit Lookup Wizard without changing the suggested label.

11 Close the table, and select Yes when prompted to save the design changes.
Two tables appear in the Tables folder of the Database dialog box, as shown in Figure 2.24.

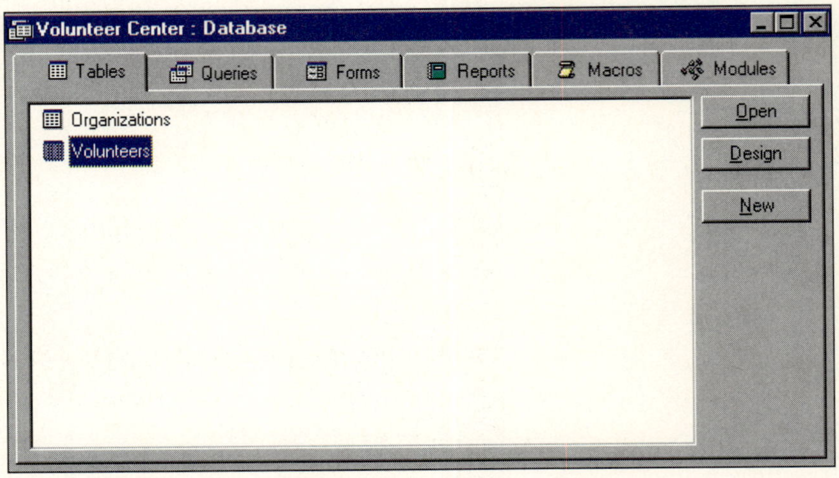

Figure 2.24

CREATING THE TIME CARDS TABLE

According to the data dictionary, the Time Cards table will contain only four fields. In this case you can create a new table on your own in less time than it would take using Table Wizard.

To specify field names, data types, and field sizes in the Time Cards table:

1 Check that Tables is the active folder in the Volunteer Center Database dialog box, as shown in Figure 2.24.

2 Select New, select Design View, and then select OK.

3 Enter the field name, data type, and field size for the first field, as shown in Figure 2.25.

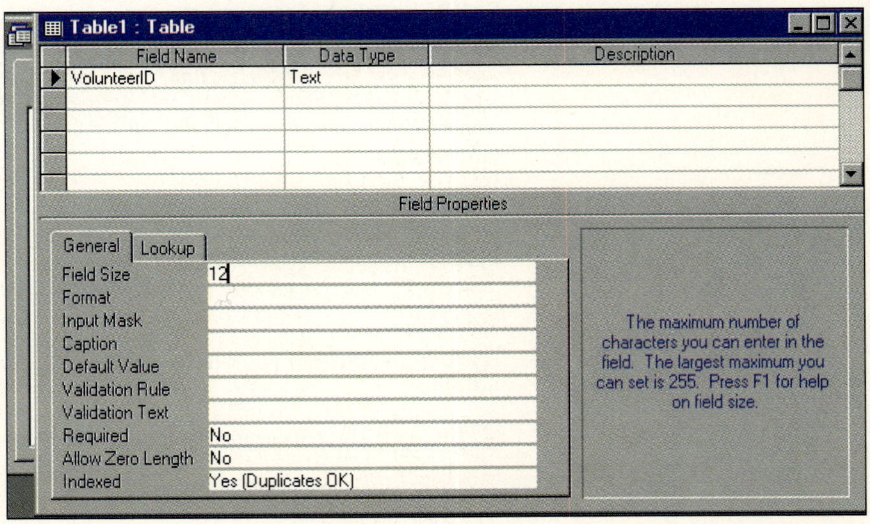

Figure 2.25

4 Type **`OrganizationID`** as the second field name, select Text as the field type, and change the field size to 5.

5 Type **`DateWorked`** as the third field name, and select Date/Time as the field type.

6 Type **`HoursWorked`** as the fourth field name, and select Number as the field type.

7 Select Field Size in the Field Properties area, and then click the arrow to display the predefined options shown in Figure 2.26.

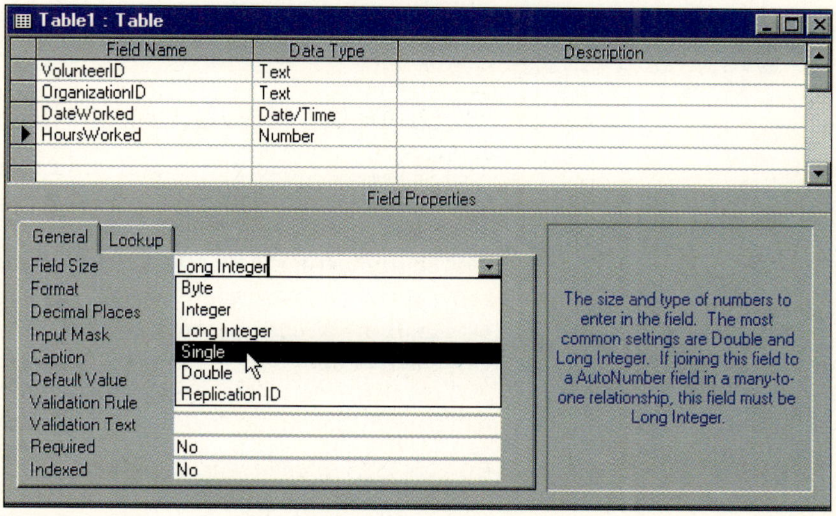

Figure 2.26

8 Select Single.

9 Change Decimal Places to 2.

Your field specifications should match those shown in Figure 2.27. Make corrections as necessary.

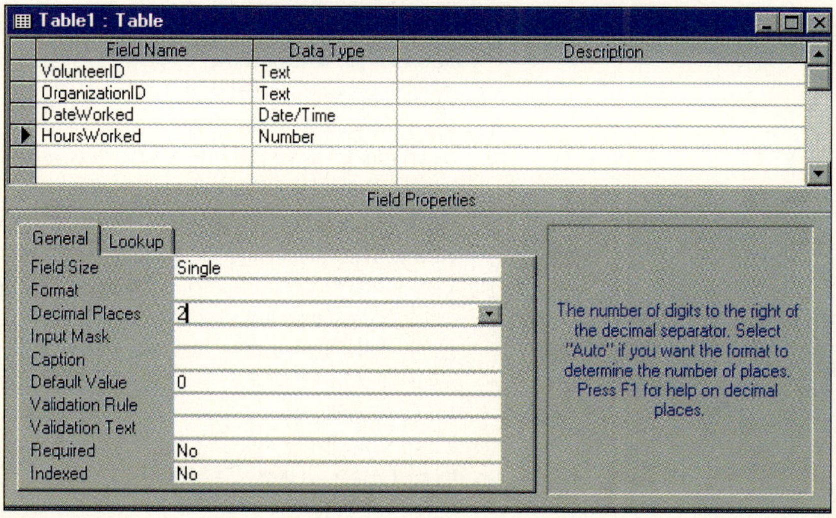

Figure 2.27

To close and save the table and then close the database:

1. Close the table.
2. Select Yes when prompted to save changes to the design of Table 1.
3. Type `Time Cards` in the Save As dialog box, and then select OK.
4. Select No when prompted to create a primary key.

Three tables appear in alphabetical order in the Tables folder of the Database dialog box: Organizations, Time Cards, and Volunteers.

5. Close the database.

THE NEXT STEP

You're beginning to get an idea of just how much work is involved to create a database on your own. In this project you learned that the design work you do before starting Access determines how effective the system will be in meeting your information needs. As a next step, find out all you can about database design. A good reference book on Access, with detailed explanations of design considerations for a sample company, can be a valuable resource.

You also created the basic table structure for the Volunteer Center database by specifying field names, data types, and field sizes. You can expand your knowledge by using on-screen Help to learn about other data types and find out what happens if you change the field size.

This concludes Project 2. You can either exit Access or go on to work the Study Questions, Review Exercises, and Assignments.

SUMMARY AND EXERCISES

Summary

- Designing a multiuser database generally involves stating database objectives, identifying desired outputs, and developing a data dictionary that shows the tables, fields, and relationships needed to accomplish the goals of the database.
- A properly designed database has sufficient tables set up to avoid unnecessary duplication of data, sometimes referred to as redundant data.
- A primary key makes each record in a table unique. Access won't let you repeat data in the primary key field or leave the field blank.
- You can output data from more than one table at a time if a common field provides a link between tables.
- Each field in a table holds a specific type of data. Access data types include Currency, Date/Time, Number, Text, and Yes/No as well as several others.
- Field size refers to the maximum space Access reserves for data. For all field types except Text and Number, Access determines a maximum size automatically, according to the data type.

- Access includes Table Wizard, which asks you questions and builds a business or personal table based on your answers.
- You can create and modify the structure of a table when the Table dialog box appears in design view.
- Lookup Wizard creates a lookup column that allows you to choose a value from a list of values. Choosing a value instead of typing it saves time and eliminates typing errors.

Key Terms and Operations

Key Terms
database objective statement
data dictionary
datasheet view
design view
field size
Lookup Wizard
normalization
primary key
redundant data
Table Wizard

Operations
Add or insert a field
Change field size
Create a table using Table Wizard
Rename a field
Select a data type
Set a primary key

Study Questions

Multiple Choice

1. Which of the following is an excellent way to start designing a multiuser database?
   a. Set up interviews with individuals who will use the system.
   b. Interview the people who designed the previous system.
   c. Design a sample system and see if the user likes it.
   d. Create a data dictionary.
2. Which is not a true statement related to following a formal process to design a multiuser database?
   a. The process can be tedious and time consuming.
   b. Output is generally available within a week.
   c. The process lessens the likelihood of major revisions.
   d. Approval of users should be obtained at several points.
3. Which action should you take with respect to interviewing a user?
   a. Write down your conclusions immediately following an interview.
   b. Tape the interview if the user agrees.
   c. Prepare a list of questions to help guide the interview.
   d. All of the above.
4. Which of the following is a one-paragraph explanation of the goal of a complete system?
   a. data dictionary
   b. database objective statement
   c. mission statement
   d. none of the above

5. What is the term describing a formal process in which data items are grouped into tables and tables are grouped into databases?
   a. data distribution
   b. normalization
   c. rationalization
   d. cross-referencing
6. Which of the following is a guideline for organizing data in tables?
   a. Group items that relate to the same subject.
   b. Group items in such a way as to eliminate unnecessary duplication of data.
   c. Group items so that they appear in alphabetic order.
   d. Both a and b.
7. Which is not a true statement about data types?
   a. Access data types include Currency, Date/Time, Number, Text, and Yes/No.
   b. If you do not specify a data type, Access assigns Number as the data type.
   c. Text fields can store letters, numbers, spaces, and special characters.
   d. If a field will contain only numbers, and the numbers will not be used for calculations, you should specify Text as the data type.
8. Which is not a true statement about the Table Wizard?
   a. Table Wizard asks you questions and builds a table based on your answers.
   b. Table Wizard contains business and personal sample tables.
   c. If you need most, but not all, of the sample fields suggested by Table Wizard, you can select all of them at once and then remove the ones you don't want.
   d. Table Wizard will create the forms necessary to enter data in the new table.
9. If you are entering data in a table, and social security number (SSN) is the primary key in the table, you can
   a. leave the SSN field blank in a record.
   b. enter the same SSN more than once.
   c. both a and b.
   d. None of the above.
10. Which of the following is an advantage of using coded data?
    a. improves data accuracy
    b. speeds data entry
    c. both a and b
    d. None of the above

Short Answer

1. What data type should you select for a field if you want to enter monetary data such as $5.50?
2. What is the next step in a formal design process after determining the objective of the database?
3. Name the design product that contains a list of fields with cross-reference to tables that you will refer to when you create a database.
4. Which wizard provides sample tables you can use to copy data fields into your own table definitions?

5. What field property sets the amount of space for data in a table?
6. Which wizard creates a lookup column that allows you to choose a value from a list of values?
7. If you select a field from a sample table but prefer a different name for the field, what action can you take?
8. Name the setting that makes each record unique in a table.
9. Which view mode shows information about fields?
10. What data type should you select for a field if you want to enter a zip code such as 43250?

For Discussion

1. Describe the major steps in the database design process. Include in your answer an explanation of why the design process focuses on outputs before inputs.
2. Explain the purpose and content of a data dictionary.
3. Discuss the purpose of organizing data into tables within a relational database.
4. Discuss the role of wizards such as Table Wizard. Include in your discussion how wizards can be of benefit even if they do not create the exact result that you need.
5. In this project you created a lookup column for college data in the Volunteer Center database. Explain the advantages of using the lookup feature, and give another example of how this feature might be used in the Volunteer Center database.

Review Exercises

The data dictionary shown in Figure 2.28 describes the design of the Job Search database, a multitable information system tracking job search efforts and results. Complete the following exercises to set up the three tables. In the Project 3 Review Exercises you will make a few more design changes and enter data in these tables.

Table/Data Cross Reference			Field Specifications - Job Search Database			
Companies Table	Applications Table	Interviews Table	Field Name	Field Size	Data Type	Comments
x	x	x	CompanyID	10	Text	User supplied. Contains letter code such as ABTECH. Primary key in Companies table; required in all three tables.
x			CompanyName	30	Text	Full name of the organization such as ABC Technologies, Inc.
	x		FirstName	12	Text	First name of person to contact such as Michelle
	x		LastName	15	Text	Last name of person to contact such as Fox, Smith-Jones, or van Horn
	x		Title	25	Text	Position of person to contact such as Human Resources Director
	x		Note: The applications table would not be complete without Address, City State and Zip Code Fields. However, you will omit these fields in the review exercise to reduce setup and data entry time.			
	x		SendDate		Date/Time	Date sent an application letter with attached resume
	x		OpenPosition	25	Text	Title of the open position such as Staff Accountant
	x		RatePerHour		Currency	Rate per hour up to two decimal places, such as $11.25 or $10.00
	x		InfoSource	20	Text	Lookup column: Placement Office Networking, Newspaper Ad
	x		ResponseDate		Date/Time	Blank field unless response received; enter date on response letter
	x		InterviewInvite		Yes/No	√ = invited to interview
		x	FirstName	12	Text	First name of interviewer
		x	LastName	15	Text	Last name of interviewer
		x	Title	25	Text	Position of interviewer such as Vice President of Marketing
		x	InterviewDate		Date/Time	Date of the interview
		x	StartTime		Date/Time	Start time of the interview
		x	Notes		Memo	Personal comments about the interview

Figure 2.28

Creating the Companies Table

1. Start Access, select Blank Database, specify where you want to store the new database, and name the database Job Search.
2. From the Tables folder of the Job Search Database window, create a new table using Table Wizard. Select Categories from the Business sample tables, and select both sample fields for the new table.
3. Change the name of CategoryID, to CompanyID, and change the name of CategoryName to CompanyName.
4. Type **`Companies`** as the name of the table, and specify that you want Access to set the primary key.
5. Specify that you want to modify the table design, and then change the data type of CompanyID to Text.
6. Change the size of Text fields to match those shown in the data dictionary.
7. Check your results against Figure 2.28, make changes as necessary, and close the table, saving your changes.

Creating the Applications Table

1. From the Tables folder of the Job Search Database window, create a new table using Design View.

2. Enter the field name, data type, and field size for each of the eleven fields in the Applications table as shown in the data dictionary in Figure 2.28.

Hints Be sure to start with the CompanyID field. Set two decimal places for the currency field RatePerHour. Use Lookup Wizard and type the values for the InfoSource field.

3. Close the table, save it using the name Applications, and select No when prompted to create a primary key.

Creating the Interviews Table

1. From the Tables folder of the Job Search Database window, create a new table using Design View.
2. Enter the field name, data type, and field size for each of the seven fields in the Interviews table as shown in the data dictionary in Figure 2.28.
3. Close the table, save it using the name Interviews, and select No when prompted to create a primary key.

Assignments

Viewing On-screen Help on Table Wizard

Use Answer Wizard to look up *What is Table Wizard?* When the list of topics appears, read *Create a table.*

Using Help's Answer Wizard to Learn More About Other Data Types

Use Answer Wizard to read about Memo, AutoNumber, Currency, OLE Object, and Lookup Wizard fields. Write a brief description of each data type, including a description of the data type, and give an example of how it might be used.

Using Help's Answer Wizard to Learn About Changing Field Sizes

Use Help to look up information about field sizes. Write a brief description about changing numeric and text field sizes. Include in your discussion how to change the field size and the potential problems that can occur when you change the Field Size property.

Putting on a Fund-Raiser

Assume that your school, club, dorm, fraternity, or sorority is sponsoring a fund raiser. There will be contests such as darts, pitch and putt golf, and a walk-a-thon. There will be a picnic in the afternoon and a dance in the evening. Sponsors have agreed to contribute money for points earned for each event or mile walked. Naturally a database system will make your job managing the fund raiser easier. Using the skills you learned in this project, design a database system that will track events, sponsors, and participants. After you have completed the design process, use the data dictionary to create the database and its associated tables.

PROJECT 3: ENTERING AND EDITING DATA

Objectives

After completing this project, you should be able to:

- Designate a field as required
- Specify an input mask
- Set a default value
- Assign a validation rule and associated text
- Define relationships among tables
- Create a form
- Enter and edit data in datasheet view and a form

CASE STUDY: COORDINATING VOLUNTEER ACTIVITIES II

Developing and using a database management system generally involves three phases: designing and creating the database, entering and editing data, and converting data into information. In your job as a summer intern for your campus volunteer center, you have nearly finished the first phase, which involved working with end users on design matters and creating three tables. Now you are ready to work on data entry concerns, taking advantage of built-in editing features and on-screen data entry forms.

Designing the Solution

The acronym GIGO (garbage in, garbage out) applies to database management. You cannot rely on information provided in reports if data are wrong or missing. Access allows you to customize fields in a table to help ensure that data are complete, accurate, and presented in a consistent manner. Figure 3.1 shows a Help screen displaying five customizing techniques you can apply to a field.

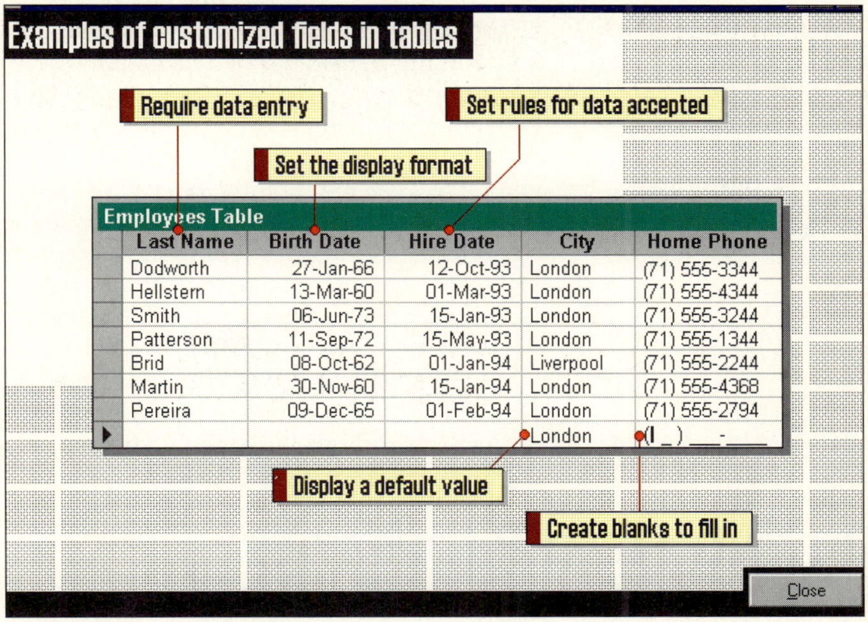

Figure 3.1

Other built-in editing features relate to common fields. For example, you can tell Access that a ***one-to-many relationship*** exists between two tables that share a common field. In a one-to-many relationship, data restricted to one entry in one table can be duplicated in its related table. Figure 3.2 shows the one-to-many relationships you should specify in the Volunteer Center database.

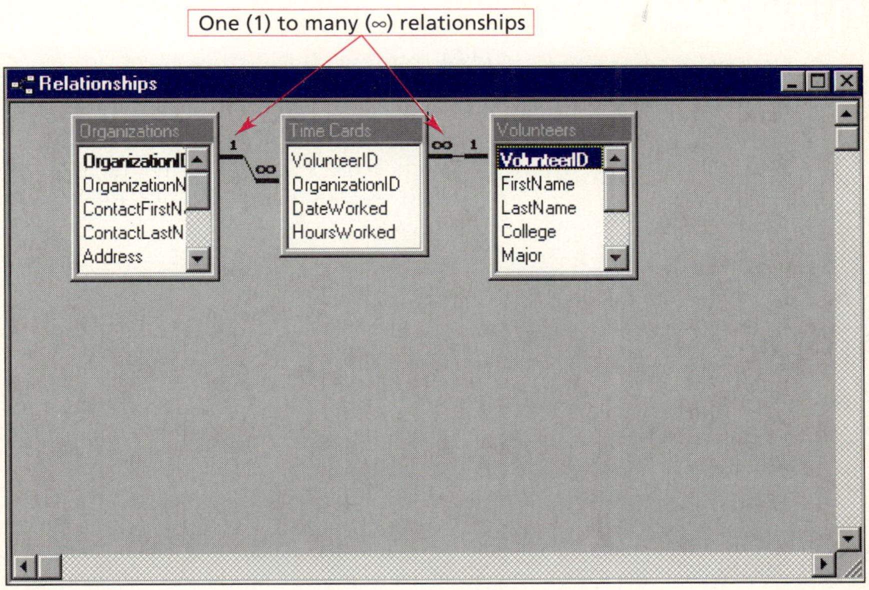

Figure 3.2

In the Volunteer Center database, you will set up one-to-many relationships among its tables. You will then be able to enter an identification code such as HH only once in the Organizations table, but that code will appear in the Time Cards table each time you add a record for a volunteer working at Habitat for Humanity. You will also be able to enter the social security number of a student only once in the Volunteers table, but that number will appear in the Time Cards table each time you record another volunteer activity for that student.

You can also enforce ***referential integrity,*** a set of rules that make sure relationships between records in related tables are valid. For example, if referential integrity is in force between the Organizations and Time Cards tables, you will not be able to enter an organization code in the Time Cards table unless that code has already been entered in the Organizations table.

You will enter data after you establish the field properties controlling data entry and define the appropriate relationships. You can enter data with or without the use of a form.

Setting Field Properties

On-screen Help includes many topics related to field properties. Using Answer Wizard, you can gain a general understanding of five ways to customize fields in tables. You will then have most of the information you need to make changes in your tables.

To view on-screen Help about customized fields:

1 Start Access, and then select Cancel to close the Microsoft Access dialog box.

2 Choose Answer Wizard from the Help menu.

3 Type `field properties` in the Type your request box, and then select Search.

4 In the Tell Me About section, select *Examples of customized fields in tables,* and then select Display.
The Help screen shown in Figure 3.1 appears.

5 Click the vertical bar at the left end of *Require data entry,* and then read the explanation shown in Figure 3.3.

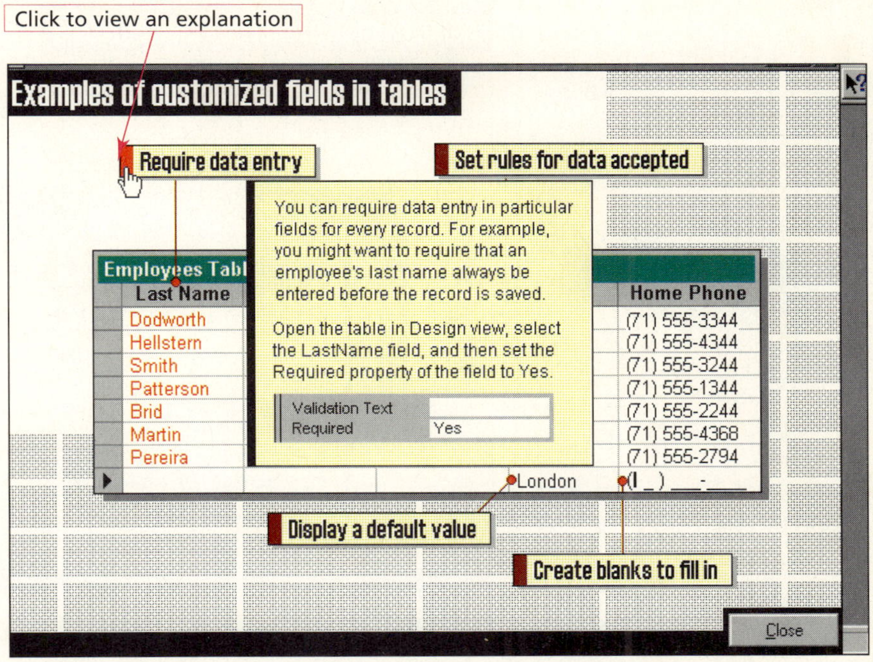

Figure 3.3

6 Click outside the explanation box.

7 Click the vertical bar at the left end of *Set the display format,* and then read the explanation shown in Figure 3.4.

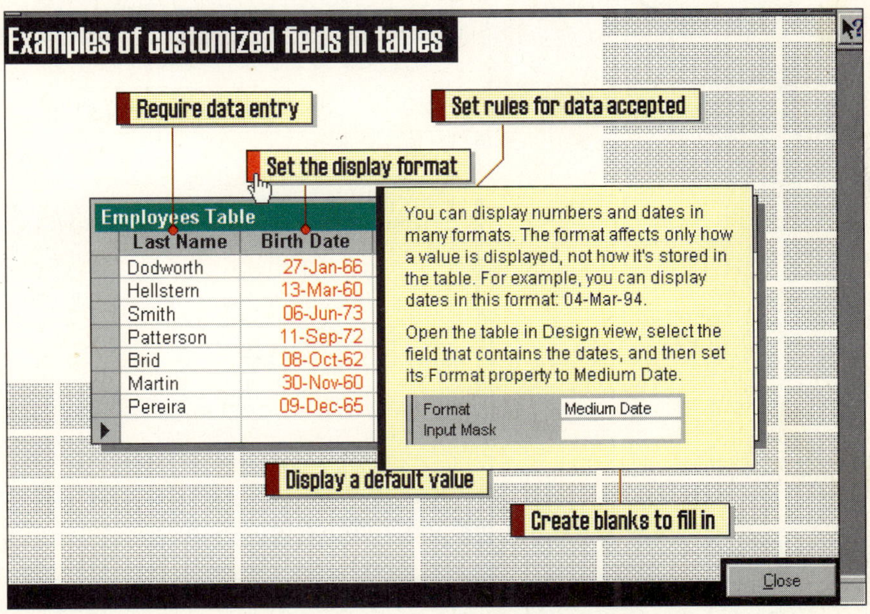

Figure 3.4

8 Click the vertical bar at the left end of *Create blanks to fill in,* and then read the explanation shown in Figure 3.5.

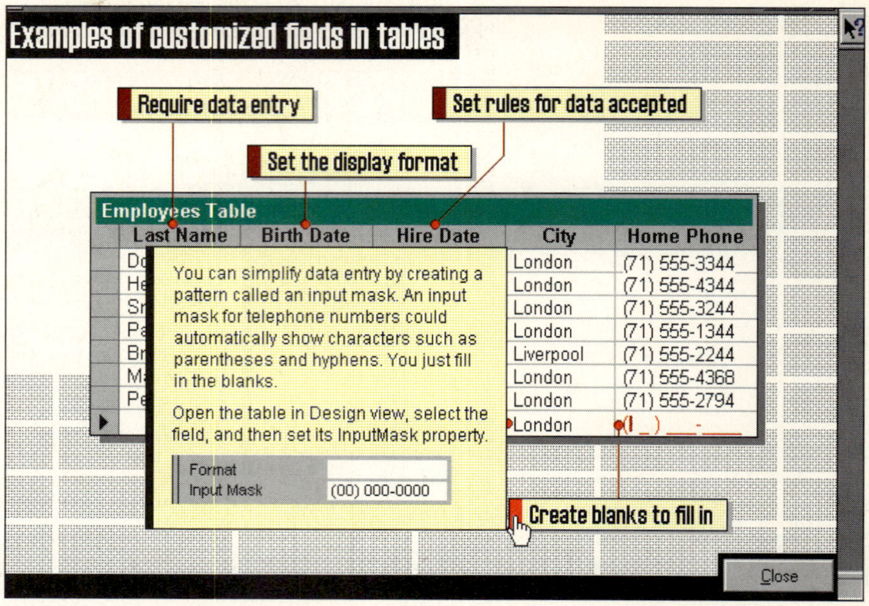

Figure 3.5

9 Click outside the explanation box.

10 Click the vertical bar at the left end of *Display a default value,* and then read the explanation shown in Figure 3.6.

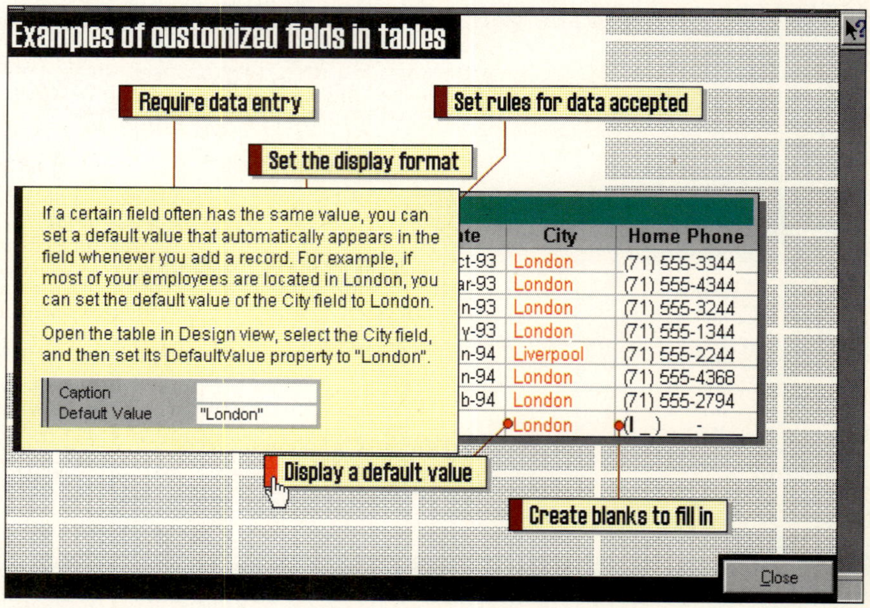

Figure 3.6

11 Click the vertical bar at the left end of *Set rules for data accepted,* and then read the explanation shown in Figure 3.7.

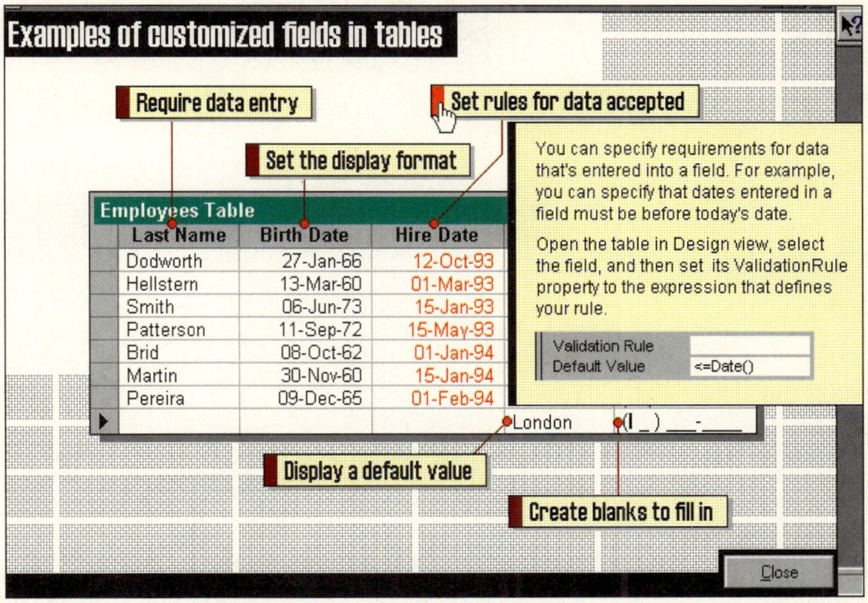

Figure 3.7

12 Select Close to exit on-screen Help.

In the following sections you will work in design view to set field properties in each table within the Volunteer Center database.

Designating Fields as Required

Every table has one or more essential fields, such as VolunteerID, FirstName, and LastName in the Volunteers table. Such a field should be set up as a ***required field,*** which means that Access will not save a new record in a table unless the associated data are present.

> ***Tip*** Other data you think are essential for desired outputs, such as e-mail name or birth date, may not be available when you want to enter a record in a table. If you do not designate the associated field(s) as required, you can enter the data you have and edit the record later.

You will set the Required property in the Field Properties section of a table in design view, as shown in Figure 3.8. Clicking the arrow at the right end of the Required box displays the two options Yes and No.

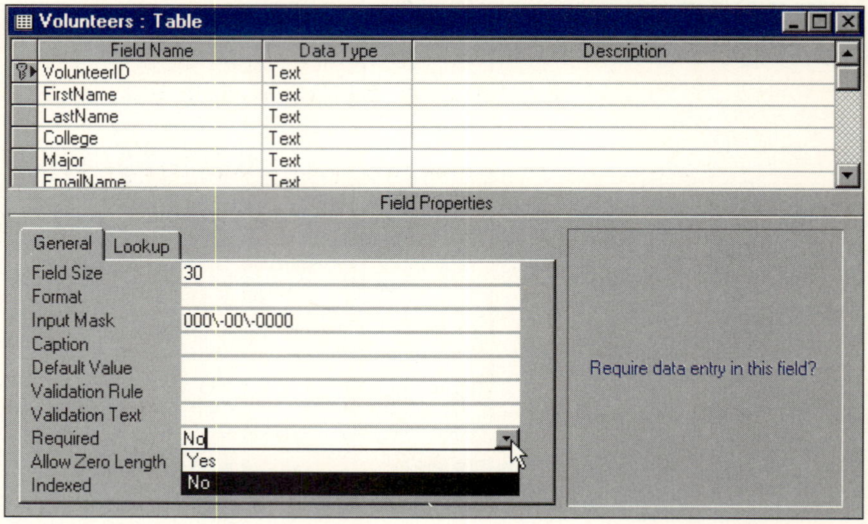

Figure 3.8

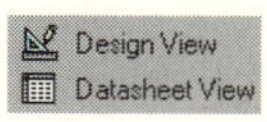

Tip Selecting Design in the Database dialog box displays the current table in design view, which allows you to edit field specifications. Selecting Open in the Database dialog box displays the current table in datasheet view, which allows you to add or edit data. To switch views, select the View icon that appears at the left end of the toolbar.

In the following steps you will specify as required only the most essential fields in the three tables of your Volunteer Center database.

To specify required fields:

1 Open the Volunteer Center database, and then open the Volunteers table in design view.
The first field VolunteerID is automatically selected.

2 Click in the Required box in the Field Properties section, and then click the arrow to display your options, as shown in Figure 3.8.

3 Select Yes to make VolunteerID a required field.

4 Set Required to Yes for the FirstName and LastName fields.

5 Close the table and save your changes.

6 Open the Organizations table in design view, and then set OrganizationName as a required field.

7 Close the table and save your changes.

8 Open the Time Cards table in design view, and then set all four fields as required fields.

9 Close the table and save your changes.

Specifying Formats and Input Masks

Access provides two field properties that produce similar results: Format and Input Mask. A ***format*** determines how a value is displayed, not how it is entered or stored in a table. You can apply a format to fields with AutoNumber, Number, Currency, Date/Time, Text, or Yes/No data types.

For example, Figure 3.4 shows the results of applying the Medium Date format to the Birth Date field. Figure 3.9 shows other predefined formats available for Date/Time fields.

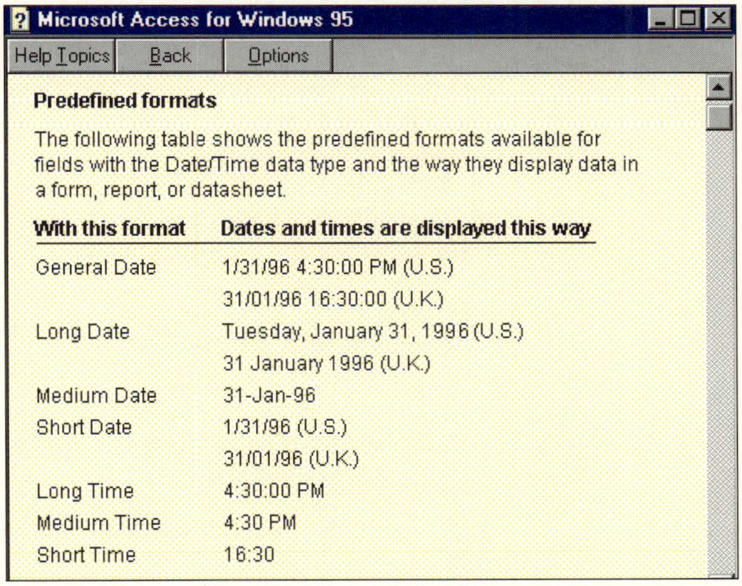

Predefined formats

The following table shows the predefined formats available for fields with the Date/Time data type and the way they display data in a form, report, or datasheet.

With this format	Dates and times are displayed this way
General Date	1/31/96 4:30:00 PM (U.S.)
	31/01/96 16:30:00 (U.K.)
Long Date	Tuesday, January 31, 1996 (U.S.)
	31 January 1996 (U.K.)
Medium Date	31-Jan-96
Short Date	1/31/96 (U.S.)
	31/01/96 (U.K.)
Long Time	4:30:00 PM
Medium Time	4:30 PM
Short Time	16:30

Figure 3.9

An ***input mask*** is a pattern controlling data entry, usually applied to text and date/time fields. The pattern may contain characters that separate data, such as parentheses and dashes, and characters that represent allowable data entry. For example, if you set up the input mask (000)000-0000 for a phone number field, Access will display the parentheses and dash, leaving blank spaces for you to enter a digit from 0 to 9 for each number in the area code and phone number. Figure 3.10 shows a Help screen that explains most of the input mask characters.

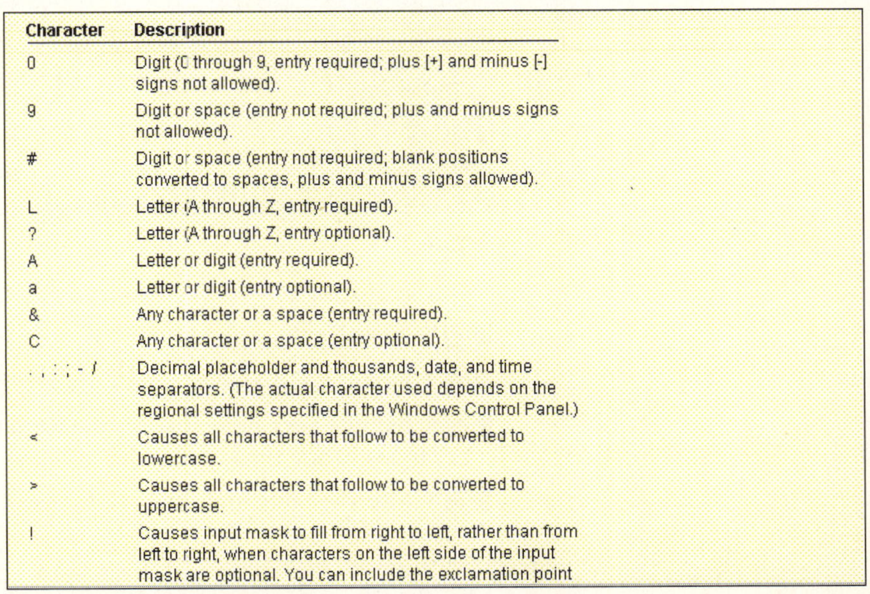

Character	Description
0	Digit (0 through 9, entry required; plus [+] and minus [-] signs not allowed).
9	Digit or space (entry not required; plus and minus signs not allowed).
#	Digit or space (entry not required; blank positions converted to spaces, plus and minus signs allowed).
L	Letter (A through Z, entry required).
?	Letter (A through Z, entry optional).
A	Letter or digit (entry required).
a	Letter or digit (entry optional).
&	Any character or a space (entry required).
C	Any character or a space (entry optional).
. , : ; - /	Decimal placeholder and thousands, date, and time separators. (The actual character used depends on the regional settings specified in the Windows Control Panel.)
<	Causes all characters that follow to be converted to lowercase.
>	Causes all characters that follow to be converted to uppercase.
!	Causes input mask to fill from right to left, rather than from left to right, when characters on the left side of the input mask are optional. You can include the exclamation point

Figure 3.10

Note that a zero in an input mask indicates required entry of a single digit, a 9 means that entry of a digit from 0 to 9 is optional, and an exclamation point causes an input mask to fill from the right as you enter data. Knowing these rules, you could change an input mask for a phone number to !(999)000-0000 if you anticipate that an area code will not be needed or available for some records.

You will set input masks in the Field Properties section of a table in design view. You can type your own data entry pattern or select among predefined patterns using ***Input Mask Wizard.*** In the following steps you will look at the Format and Input Mask properties set up by Table Wizard in the Volunteer Center database. You will also establish additional input masks in all three tables and adjust remaining Text field sizes to match those shown in the data dictionary.

> ***Tip*** Make sure that common fields have the same Field Size and Input Mask properties in both tables.

To edit field size and input mask properties in the Organizations table:

1 Open the Organizations table in design view.

2 Change the field size of OrganizationID to 5.

3 Type **>CCCCC** in the Input Mask box, as shown in Figure 3.11.

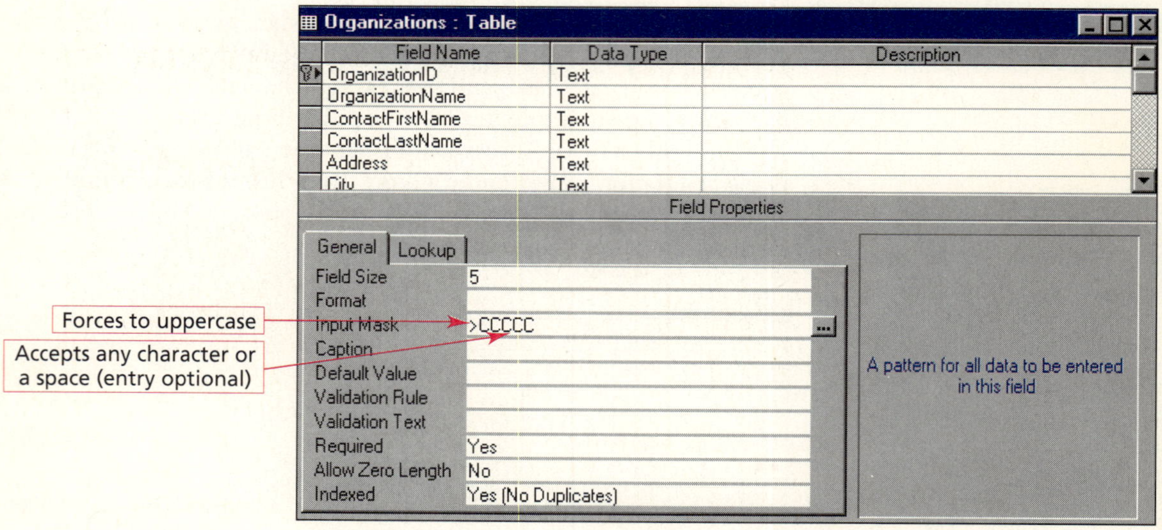

Figure 3.11

4 Select the State field.

5 Change Field Size to 2, and then type **>CC** in the Input Mask box.

6 Change other field sizes in the Organizations table to match those for Text fields in the data dictionary, as shown in Figure 2.1.

7 Close the table and save your changes.

To edit predefined properties for one field in the Volunteers table:

1 Open the Volunteers table in design view.

2 Change the field size of VolunteerID to 12.

3 Click within the Input Mask box in the Field Properties section.
A flashing cursor appears at the left end of the Input Mask box, and the Build button appears at the right end.

4 Click the Build button at the right end of the Input Mask box.

5 Select Yes if prompted to save the table.
A dialog box appears that asks you which input mask matches how you want data to look.

6 Select Social Security Number, as shown in Figure 3.12.

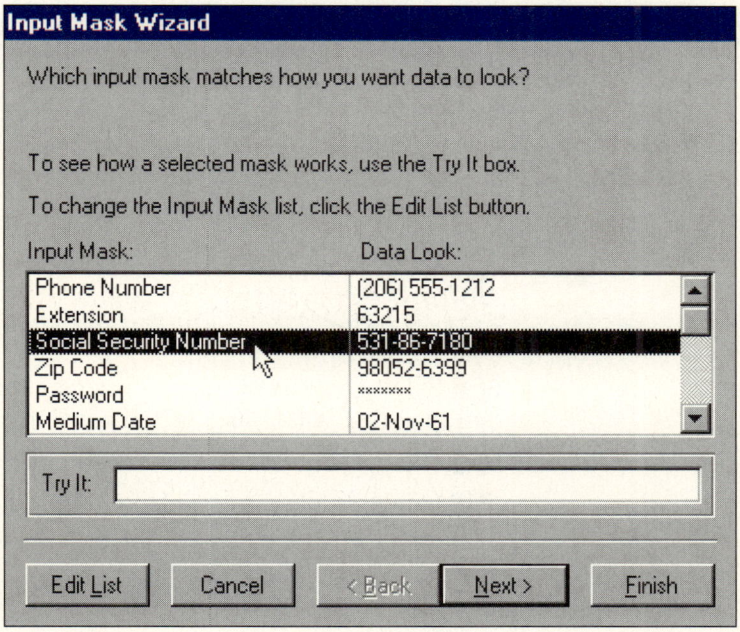

Figure 3.12

7 Select Next>.
A dialog box appears that asks if you want to change the input mask and set the placeholder character.

8 Select Next>.
A dialog box appears that asks how you want to store the data.

9 Select Without the symbols in the mask, as shown in Figure 3.13.

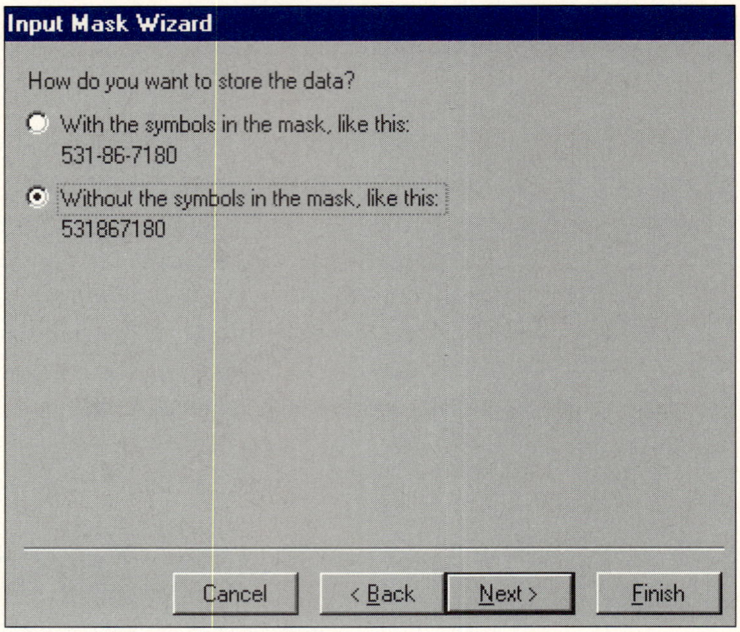

Figure 3.13

10 Select Next>, and then select Finish.

To view and edit other field properties in the Volunteers table:

1 Select the LocalPhone field.

2 Select the current input mask containing placeholders for area code, and then type **`000\-0000`** as the new input mask.

3 Change the field size of LocalPhone to 9.

4 Select the Birthdate field and note the Short Date format set by Table Wizard.

5 Select the HasCar field and note the Yes/No format set by Table Wizard.

6 Change other field sizes in the Volunteers table to match those for Text fields in the data dictionary, as shown in Figure 2.1.

7 Close the table and save your changes.

To edit field properties in the Time Cards table:

1 Open the Time Cards table in design view.

2 Select the VolunteerID field, click within the Input Mask box, and then select the Build button.

3 Select Yes if prompted to save the table.

4 Select Social Security Number as shown in Figure 3.12, and then select Next>.
A dialog box appears that asks if you want to change the input mask and set the placeholder character.

5 Select Next>, and then select Without the symbols in the mask, as shown in Figure 3.13.

6 Select Next>, and then select Finish.

7 Select the OrganizationID field, and then type **>CCCCC** in the Input Mask box.

8 Select the DateWorked field, and then select the Input Mask box.

9 Select the Build button, and then select Yes if prompted to save the table.

10 Select the predefined input mask Short Date, select Next>, and then select Finish.

11 Close the table and save your changes.

Setting Default Values

A ***default value*** appears automatically in a field when you add a new record. You can accept this value in the record or type a new one over it.

Setting default values will eliminate typing errors and save data entry time if the specified value is the one usually entered in the field. For example, the Organizations table of the Volunteer Center database includes City and State fields. Assume that most of the organizations served by the center are located in the city of Indianapolis and all of them are located in the state of Indiana. Setting Indianapolis and IN (the code for Indiana) as defaults will eliminate the need to enter those values in each new record. For the few times when the city is not Indianapolis, you can type the new name over the default.

A text default value must be enclosed in quotation marks, as shown for the State field in Figure 3.14. You will set several default values in the following steps.

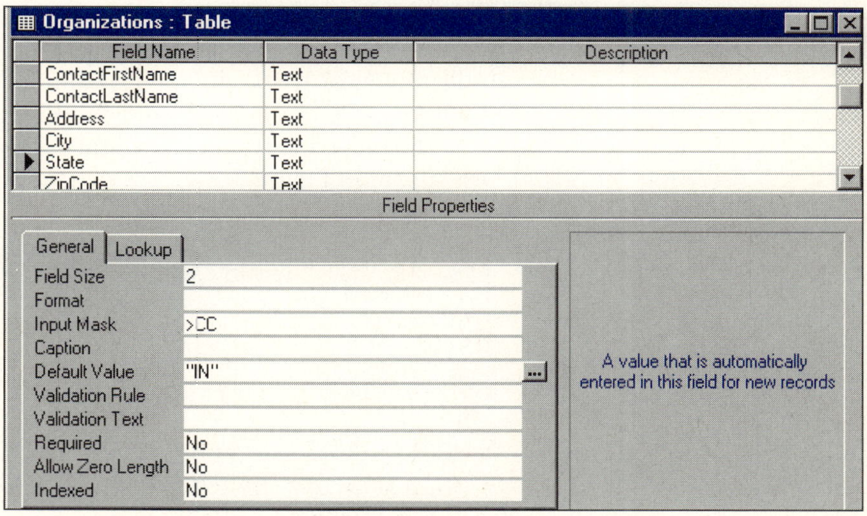

Figure 3.14

To set a default value:

1 Open the Organizations table in design view.

2 Select the City field.

3 Type **"Indianapolis"** in the Default Value box (be sure to include the quotation marks).

4 Select the State field.

5 Type **"IN"** in the Default Value box, as shown in Figure 3.14.

6 Close the table and save your changes.

Now every time you add a record in the Organizations table, the City and State fields will already contain data. However, if you want to enter different data in either field, you can type over the default value.

Assigning Validation Rules and Text

Access provides some validation of data based on data type. For example, you cannot enter text in a number field or an invalid date in a date field. Access will halt data entry and display an error message if you enter a number other than 1 through 12 to represent a month, or you enter an invalid day such as 31 for the month of April.

You can also set your own validation rules in the Field Properties section of a table in design view. A ***validation rule*** determines whether or not data being entered in a field should be rejected. For example, a validation rule might specify that hours worked on a specific date cannot exceed 24. If you try to enter a number higher than 24, Access will not allow the data entry.

> ***Tip*** Although a validation rule is set up to reject data, you should write the rule in terms of what data are acceptable. For example, a validation rule concerning maximum hours in a day should be written as <=24, which means that acceptable hours are less than or equal to 24.

Validation text appears on the screen if attempted data entry violates a validation rule. If you do not specify validation text when you set up a validation rule, Access will supply a general error message.

In the following steps you will specify the validation rule and its associated text shown in Figure 3.15.

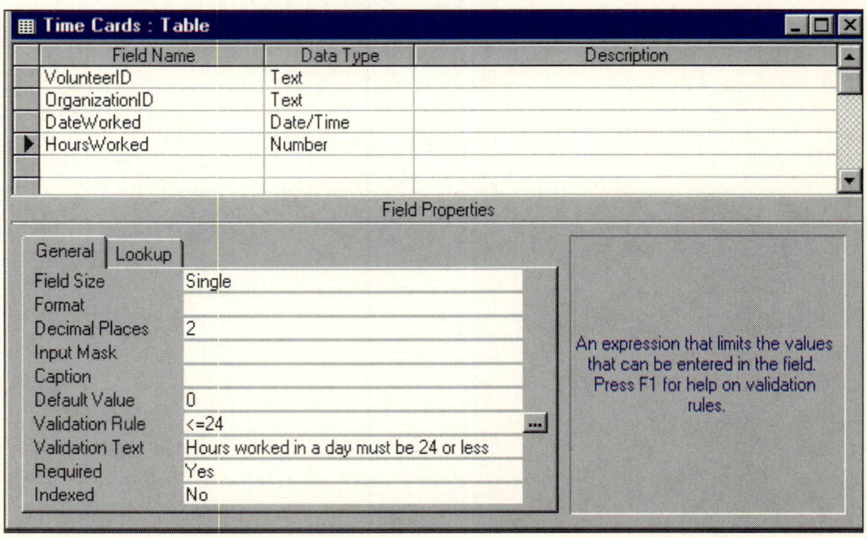

Figure 3.15

To work with validation settings in Field Properties:

1 Open the Time Cards table in design view.

2 Select the HoursWorked field.

3 Type `<=24` in the Validation Rule box.

4 Type **`Hours worked in a day must be 24 or less`** in the Validation Text box.

5 Check that your validation rule and text match those shown in Figure 3.15, and make corrections as necessary.

6 Close the Time Cards table and save your changes.

All essential field properties are now set. As soon as you specify relationships among the tables, you'll be ready to enter data.

EXIT If necessary, you can close this database now. You can then exit Access and continue this project later.

DEFINING RELATIONSHIPS AMONG TABLES

You can specify relationships among tables by using the Relationships dialog box, accessed through the Relationships button on the toolbar. First you will add the tables you want to relate to the Relationships dialog box and then drag the key field from one table and drop it on the equivalent field in the other table. Figure 3.16 illustrates the process for establishing a relationship between the Organizations and Time Cards tables in the Volunteer Center database based on the common field OrganizationID.

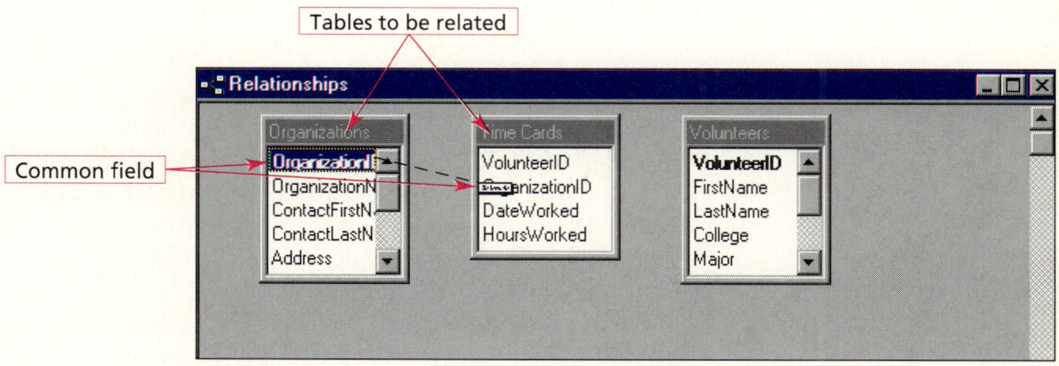

Figure 3.16

As soon as you release the mouse button from the drag-and-drop operation, Access will display the field and tables in the relationship and the relationship type. If the common field is a primary key in one table but not in the other table, the relationship type will be One-To-Many, as shown in Figure 3.17.

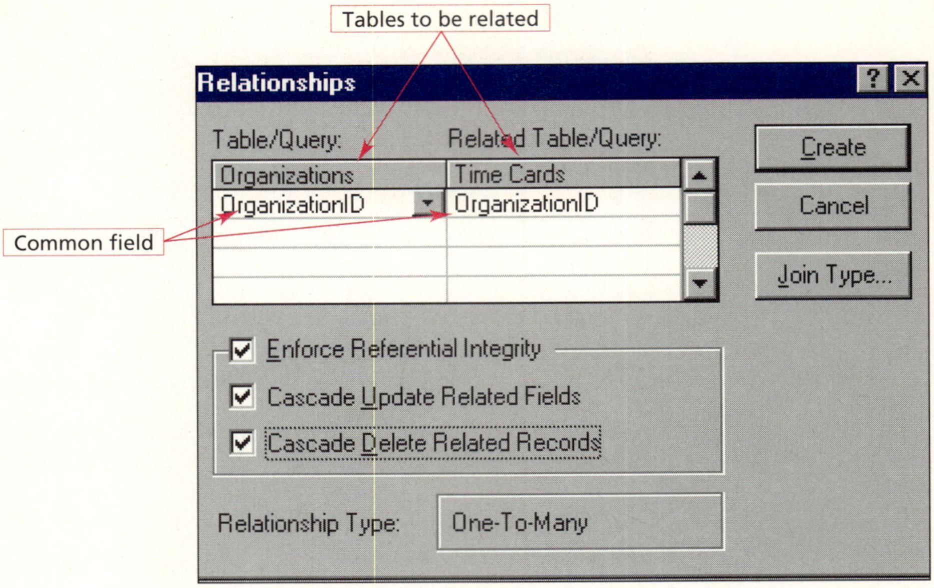

Figure 3.17

If you select Enforce Referential Integrity in the Relationships dialog box, Access applies a set of rules that makes sure relationships between records in related tables are valid. For example, if referential integrity is in force between the Organizations and Time Cards tables, you cannot enter a value for the organization code (OrganizationID) in the Time Cards table unless that value exists in the Organizations table. You also cannot change or delete an organization code in the Organizations table if there are records containing that code in the Time Cards table.

Checking the Enforce Referential Integrity box also gives you the option of updating related fields and deleting related records, actions that would normally be prevented by referential integrity rules. If you select Cascade Update Related Fields, Access will automatically update related records if you change a primary key. For example, if you were to change OrganizationID from MOW (Meals on Wheels) to MEALS in the Organizations table of the Volunteer Center database, Access would also change MOW to MEALS in each record of the Time Cards table. If you select Cascade Delete Related Records, Access will automatically delete related records if you delete a record in the primary table. For example, if you were to delete the record containing MOW in the Organizations table, Access would automatically delete all records containing MOW in the Time Cards table.

When you create a one-to-many relationship, Access displays a connecting line with two symbols, as shown in Figure 3.18. The 1 indicates that specific data can appear only once, while the ∞ symbol indicates the same data can appear many times. For example, you will enter the OrganizationID MOW only once in the Organizations table, but that same code can appear many times in the Time Cards table.

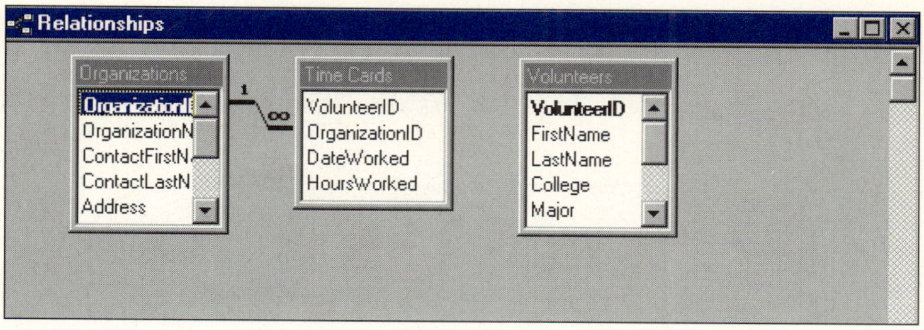

Figure 3.18

Figure 3.2 shows the relationships among tables in the Volunteer Center database. In the following steps you will create those relationships.

To add tables to the Relationships dialog box:

1 If necessary, start Access and open the Volunteer Center database.

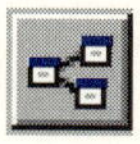

2 Select Relationships in the toolbar (or select Relationships from the Tools menu).
A blank Relationships dialog box appears in the background, and you see the Show Table dialog box shown in Figure 3.19.

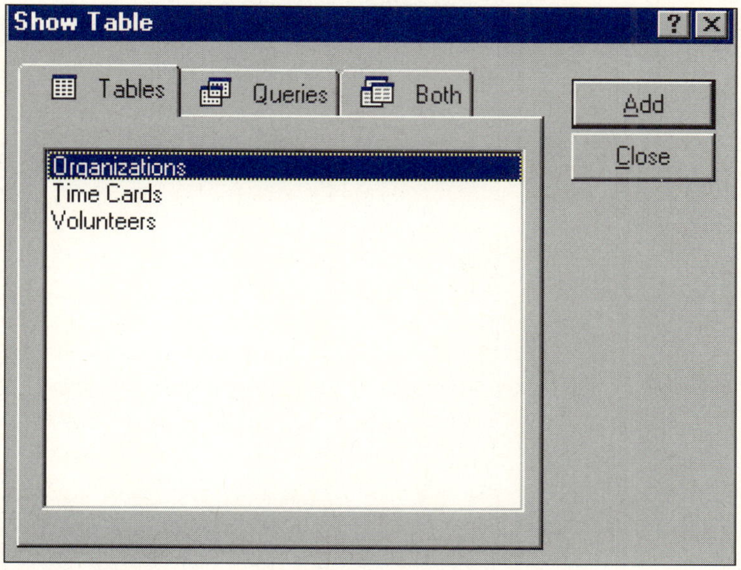

Figure 3.19

3 Select Add.
Access adds the Organizations table to the Relationships dialog box. You can see part of the field list in the background.

4 Select Time Cards, and then select Add.

5 Select Volunteers, and then select Add.

6 Select Close.
Three tables appear in the Relationships dialog box, as shown in Figure 3.20.

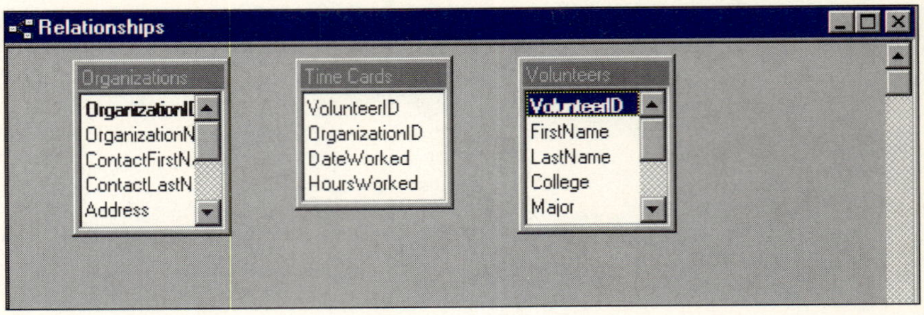

Figure 3.20

Tip You can also select a table by double-clicking its name. To select several tables at once, you can press and hold down CTRL click each table name you need, and then select Add.

To set relationships among tables:

1 Position the pointer on OrganizationID in the Organizations table, press and hold down the mouse button, and move the pointer to OrganizationID in the Time Cards table.
A small horizontal bar should appear on OrganizationID in the Time Cards table.

2 Release the mouse button.
The Relationships dialog box shown in Figure 3.21 appears.

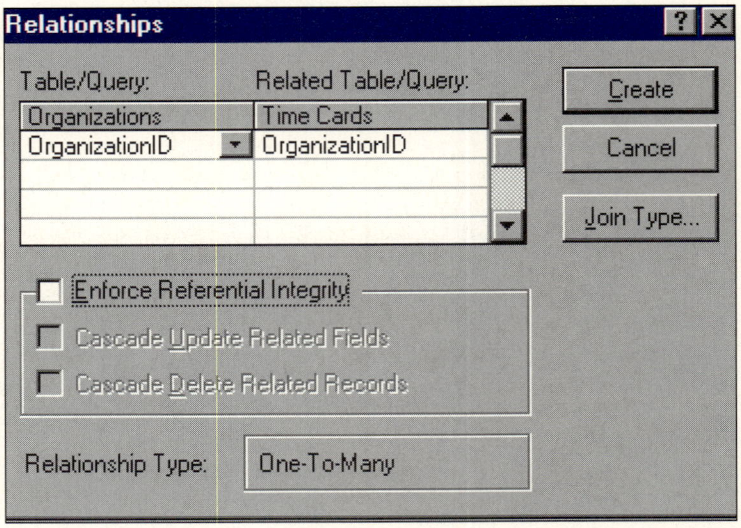

Figure 3.21

3 Select Enforce Referential Integrity.

4 Select Cascade Update Related Fields.

5 Select Cascade Delete Related Records.

Reminder Selected options appear with checkmarks.

6 Select Create.
Access creates a one-to-many relationship between the Organizations table and the Time Cards table based on the OrganizationID field, as shown in Figure 3.18.

Tip You can remove a relationship by clicking its connecting line in the Relationships dialog box and then pressing (DEL) If necessary, you can then specify another relationship.

7 Repeat the process described in steps 1 and 2 to connect the VolunteerID fields in the Time Cards and Volunteers tables.

Tip You can drag the VolunteerID field from the Volunteers table to the Time Cards table, or you can drag the field in the opposite direction. Access knows that VolunteerID is a primary key in the Volunteers table (primary keys appear boldface) and will set the one-to-many relationship in the proper direction.

8 Select the settings shown in Figure 3.22.

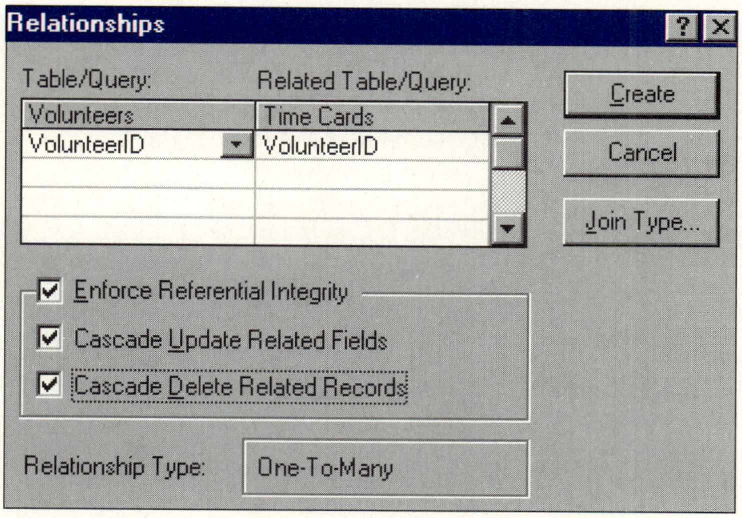

Figure 3.22

9 Select Create.
Access sets another one-to-many relationship, as shown in Figure 3.23.

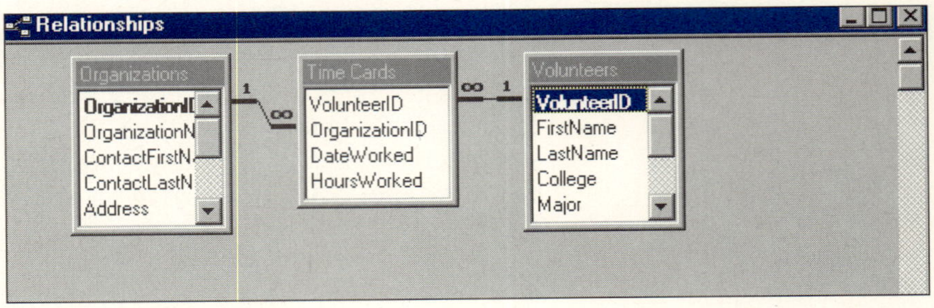

Figure 3.23

10 Close the Relationships dialog box and save your changes.

Entering and Editing Data in Datasheet View

In datasheet view, data are displayed in rows and columns. Each row is a complete record, and each column holds data for a field. Figure 3.24 shows the initial portions of three records in datasheet view. Moving the horizontal scroll bar allows you to see other fields.

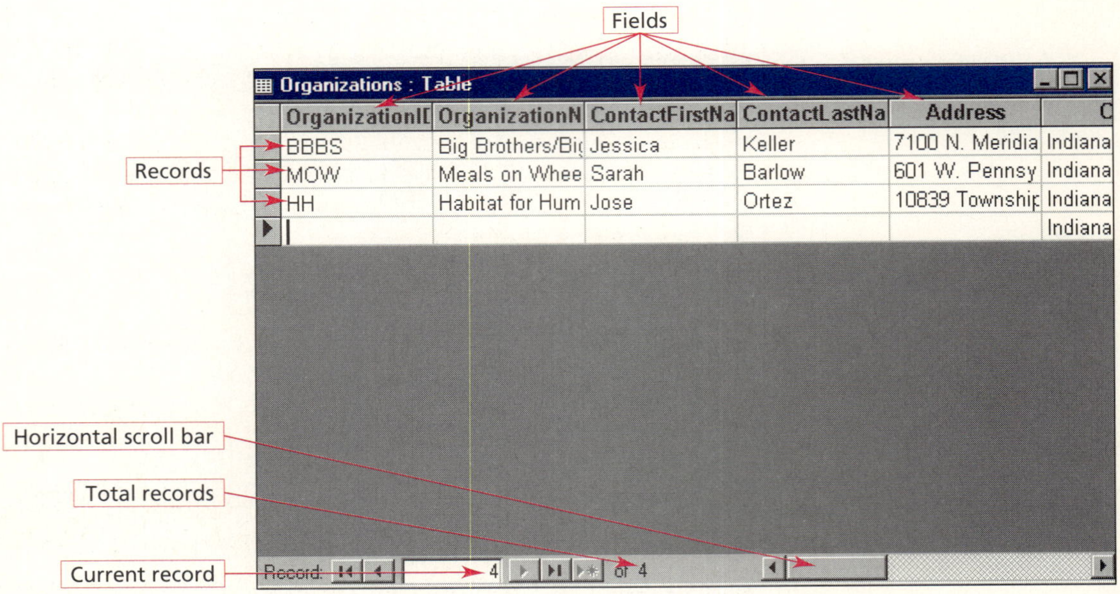

Figure 3.24

To enter data, you will click within the desired field and row and then start typing. You can press TAB or ENTER to move to the next field in the row. Generally, the data you enter in a table can be found on a ***source document,*** which is a standard paper form with spaces to enter details that vary from one record to the next. The Organizations Table Data Entry Form shown in Figure 3.25 is an example of a source document, in which data that you will enter in the Organizations table appear in italics.

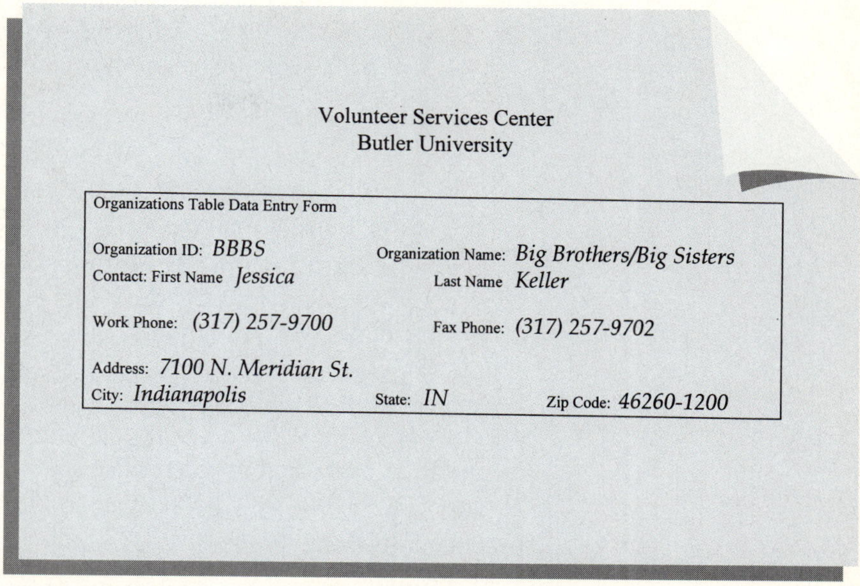
Volunteer Services Center
Butler University

Organizations Table Data Entry Form

Organization ID: *BBBS* Organization Name: *Big Brothers/Big Sisters*
Contact: First Name *Jessica* Last Name *Keller*

Work Phone: *(317) 257-9700* Fax Phone: *(317) 257-9702*

Address: *7100 N. Meridian St.*
City: *Indianapolis* State: *IN* Zip Code: *46260-1200*

Figure 3.25

If you enforced referential integrity in one or more relationships, be sure to enter records in each table containing a primary key before you attempt to enter duplicate data in the related tables. In the Volunteer Center database, for example, you must enter records in the Organizations and Volunteers tables before you can enter social security numbers and organization codes in the Time Cards table.

In the following steps you will enter data for three records in the Organizations table of the Volunteer Center database. Data entry may seem a bit awkward because fields in the datasheet view are not in the same order as those in the source document.

To enter records in datasheet view:

1 Select the Organizations table in the Volunteer Center database, and then select Open.
An incomplete record 1 appears in datasheet view, as shown in Figure 3.26.

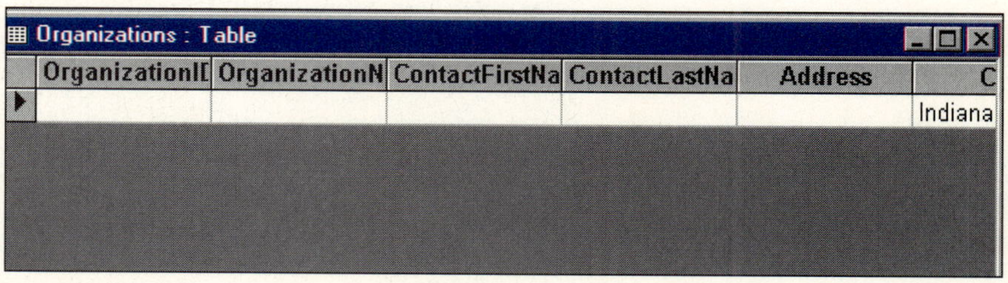

Figure 3.26

2 Type **bbbs** in the OrganizationID field, and then press TAB
The letters in the OrganizationID field automatically appear uppercase due to the input mask controlling the field.

3 Type **Big Brothers/Big Sisters** in the OrganizationName field, and then press TAB

Currently, the column is too narrow to display the entire entry; the contents scroll within the column as you type.

4 Type **Jessica** in the ContactFirstName field, and then press (TAB)

5 Type **Keller** in the ContactLastName field, and then press (TAB)

6 Type **7100 N. Meridian St.** in the Address field, and then press (TAB) three times to bypass the default entries in the City and State fields.

7 Type **462601200** in the ZipCode field, and then press (TAB)
Access automatically inserts the dash between the first five digits and the last four digits, as specified in the field's input mask.

8 Type **3172579700** in the WorkPhone field, and then press (TAB)
Access automatically inserts the parentheses around the area code and the dash between the first three digits and the last four digits of the phone number, as specified in the field's input mask.

9 Type **3172579702** in the FaxNumber field and press (TAB)
A blank record 2 appears.

10 Enter record 2 using Meals on Wheels data in the first of two source documents in Figure 3.27.

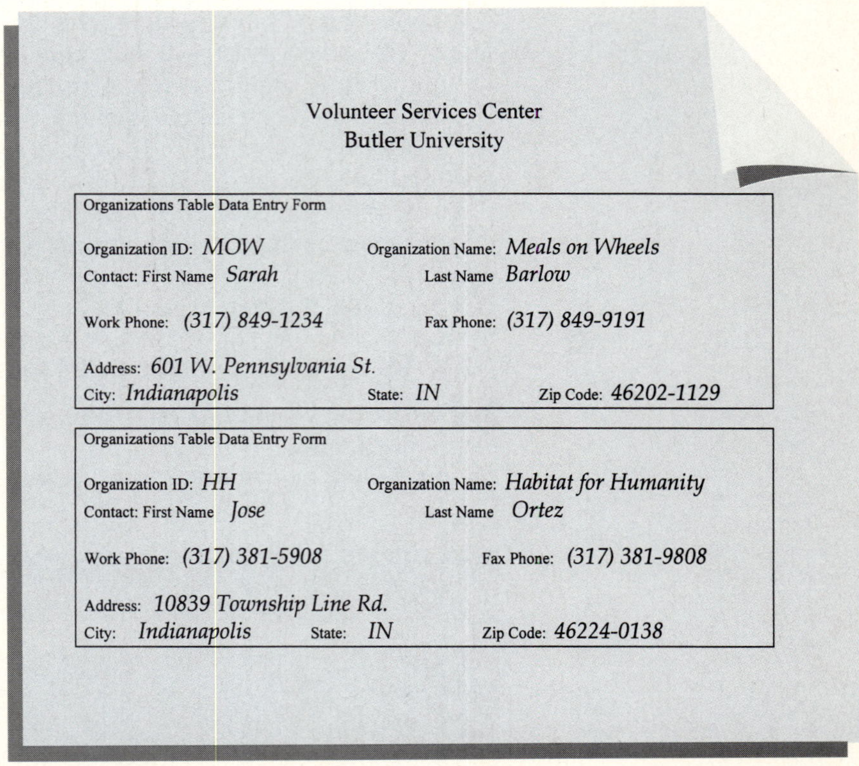

Volunteer Services Center
Butler University

Organizations Table Data Entry Form

Organization ID: *MOW* Organization Name: *Meals on Wheels*
Contact: First Name *Sarah* Last Name *Barlow*
Work Phone: *(317) 849-1234* Fax Phone: *(317) 849-9191*
Address: *601 W. Pennsylvania St.*
City: *Indianapolis* State: *IN* Zip Code: *46202-1129*

Organizations Table Data Entry Form

Organization ID: *HH* Organization Name: *Habitat for Humanity*
Contact: First Name *Jose* Last Name *Ortez*
Work Phone: *(317) 381-5908* Fax Phone: *(317) 381-9808*
Address: *10839 Township Line Rd.*
City: *Indianapolis* State: *IN* Zip Code: *46224-0138*

Figure 3.27

11 Enter record 3 using Habitat for Humanity data in the second source document in Figure 3.27.
The initial portions of three records appear as shown in Figure 3.24.

12 Close the Organizations table.

EXIT If necessary, you can close this database now. You can then exit Access and continue this project later.

ENTERING AND EDITING DATA IN A FORM

The datasheet view of records is not easy to read if you cannot see all of the fields on one screen, as shown in Figure 3.24. A table may contain more fields than you want to work with during a routine editing session. The order of fields in datasheet view may not match the order of fields in the source document, thus slowing data entry.

You can improve the environment in which you add, edit, and view data by creating and using a form. Figure 3.28 illustrates a form displaying all fields for one record.

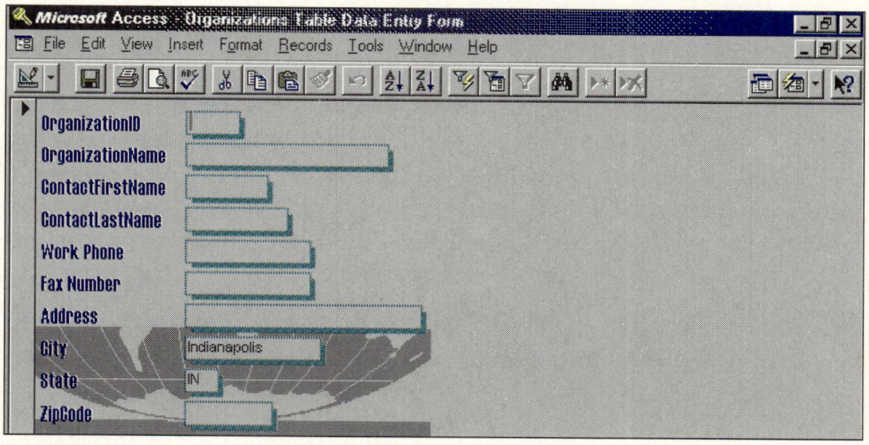

Figure 3.28

In Project 1 you entered data in one of the Music Collection forms you created by using Database Wizard. In this project you will create a form using Form Wizard, modify the form, and use the form to add more records to the Organizations table in the Volunteer Center database.

Creating a Form with Form Wizard

Form Wizard works much like Table Wizard, which you used in Project 2. You will start Form Wizard from the Forms tab in the Database window. First you will select each table or query containing the fields you need in the form (you will work with queries in Project 4). Then you will transfer the fields you want to include from the Available Fields box to the Selected Fields box, as shown in Figure 3.29. The order in which you transfer fields to the Selected Fields box is the order in which they will appear on the form.

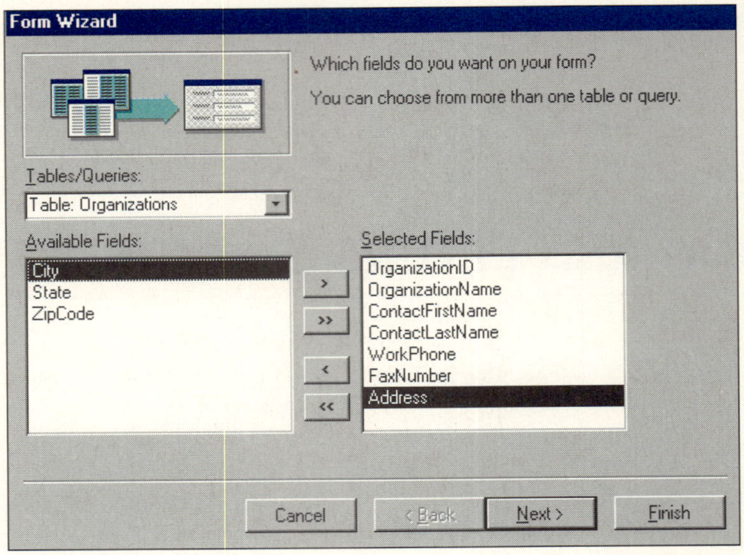

Figure 3.29

After selecting fields for the form, you will select among the following layouts: Columnar, Tabular, and Datasheet. If you want to view multiple records, one per row, you will select Tabular or Datasheet. If you want to view all fields for one record, you will select Columnar. In this view, fields display from top to bottom in a column, with additional columns added as necessary.

In the following steps you will use Form Wizard to create a columnar form to display data from the Organizations table in the Volunteer Center database. You will select the fields one at a time, so that the order of fields matches that shown in the Organizations Table Data Entry Form. Finally, you will add one record using this form.

To create a columnar form:

1 If necessary, start Access and open the Volunteer Center database.

2 Select the Forms tab, and then select New.

The New Form dialog box appears.

3 Select Form Wizard from the list at the right side of the box.

4 Click the arrow shown in Figure 3.30.

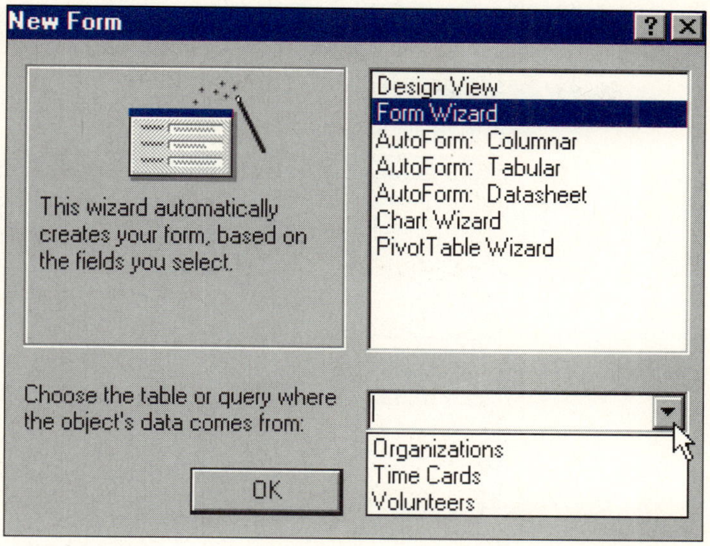

Figure 3.30

5 Select Organizations from the pull-down list, and then select OK. The initial Form Wizard dialog box appears as shown in Figure 3.31.

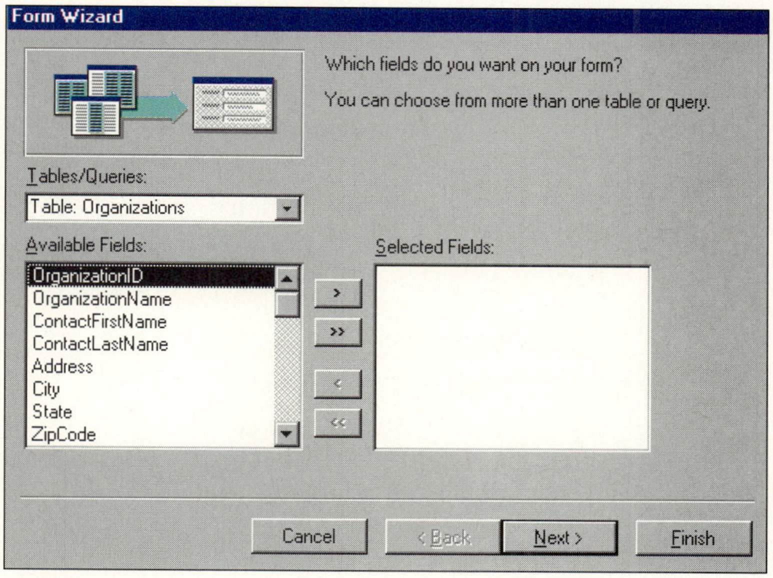

Figure 3.31

6 Select the following fields from the Available Fields box in the order given: OrganizationID, OrganizationName, ContactFirstName, ContactLastName, WorkPhone, FaxNumber, Address, City, State, and ZipCode.

Reminder To select a field, double-click its name in the Available Fields box, or highlight the field name and click the Next> button. To remove a field, double-click its name in the Selected Fields box, or highlight the field name and click the <Back button.

7 Check that your Selected Fields box includes the appropriate fields in the proper order as shown in Figure 3.32. Make changes as necessary.

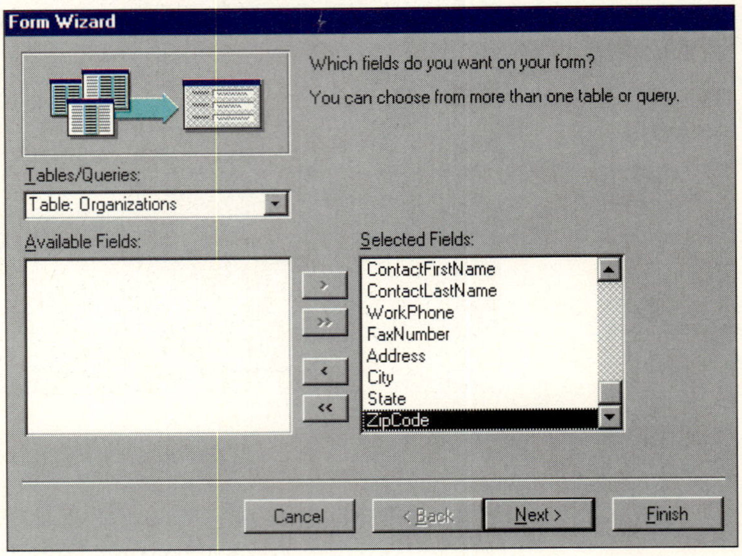

Figure 3.32

8 Select Next>.
Form Wizard displays a dialog box for selecting a layout.

9 Select Columnar, and then select Next>.
Form Wizard displays a dialog box for selecting a background style.

10 Select International, and then select Next>.
Form Wizard displays a dialog box for naming the form.

11 Enter the title and setting shown in Figure 3.33.

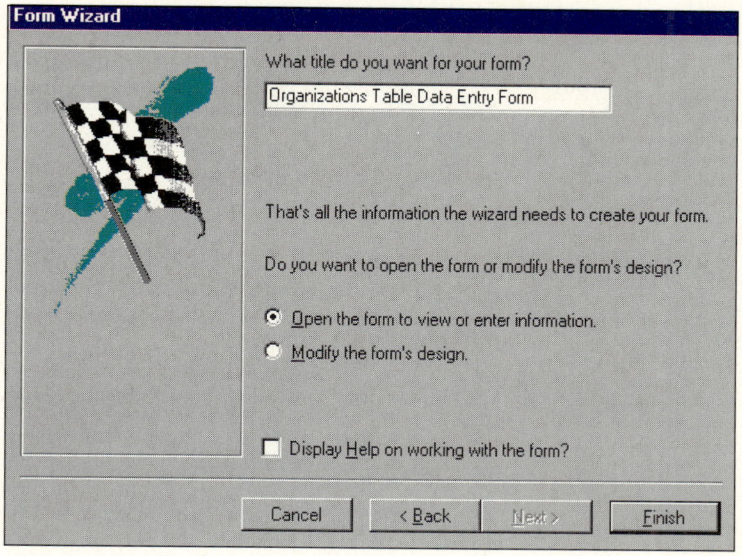

Figure 3.33

12 Select Finish.
Access displays the first record in the Organizations table in columnar form, as shown in Figure 3.34.

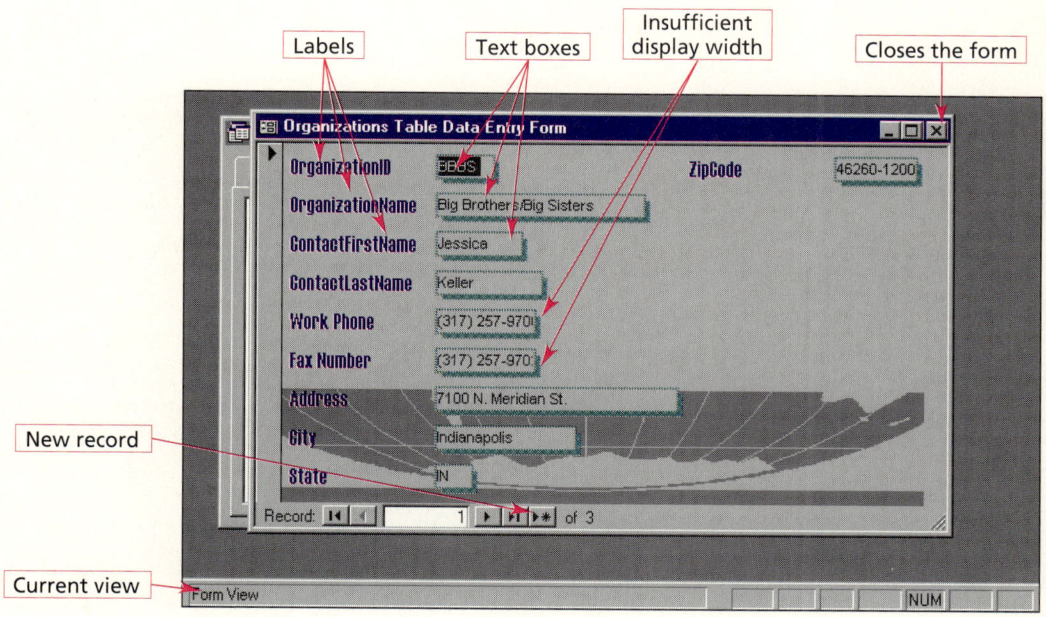

Figure 3.34

The contents of each field appear in text boxes down a column in the order selected. Descriptive labels appear to the left of the text boxes. Although the Work Phone and Fax Number text boxes on the form are not wide enough to display all the data, the field widths defined in the table structure are sufficient to store the data you enter.

To enter a record in the columnar form:

1 Click New Record, the last of the buttons at the bottom of the form.

2 Enter the data shown in Figure 3.35, pressing (TAB) or (ENTER) to advance to the next field.

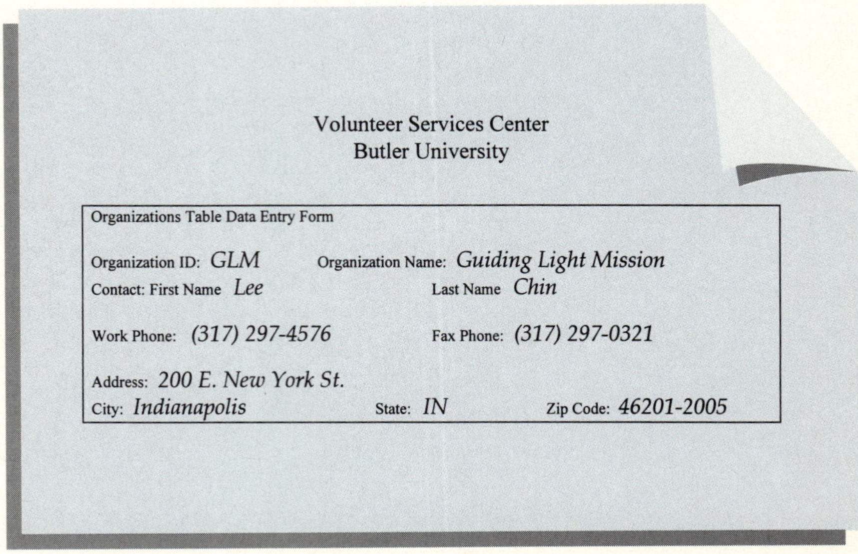

Figure 3.35

3 Close the form by clicking the X button in the upper-right corner of the dialog box, as shown in Figure 3.34.
The name Organizations Table Data Entry Form appears on the Forms tab in the Database window.

Modifying a Form

You may want to make changes to a form created by Form Wizard, such as adding or deleting a field, moving one or more fields to make the form match a source document, or increasing the display width of a field. Perhaps you'd like to change a label describing a text box, add a background picture, or vary font style and size. You can make such changes to a form in design view.

Figure 3.36 shows the Organizations Table Data Entry Form in design view with the WorkPhone field selected for sizing. In the following steps you will slightly widen the display of the WorkPhone and FaxNumber fields so that all data are in view.

> ***Tip*** If the Toolbox blocks part of the design work area, you can click its title and drag it to another location.

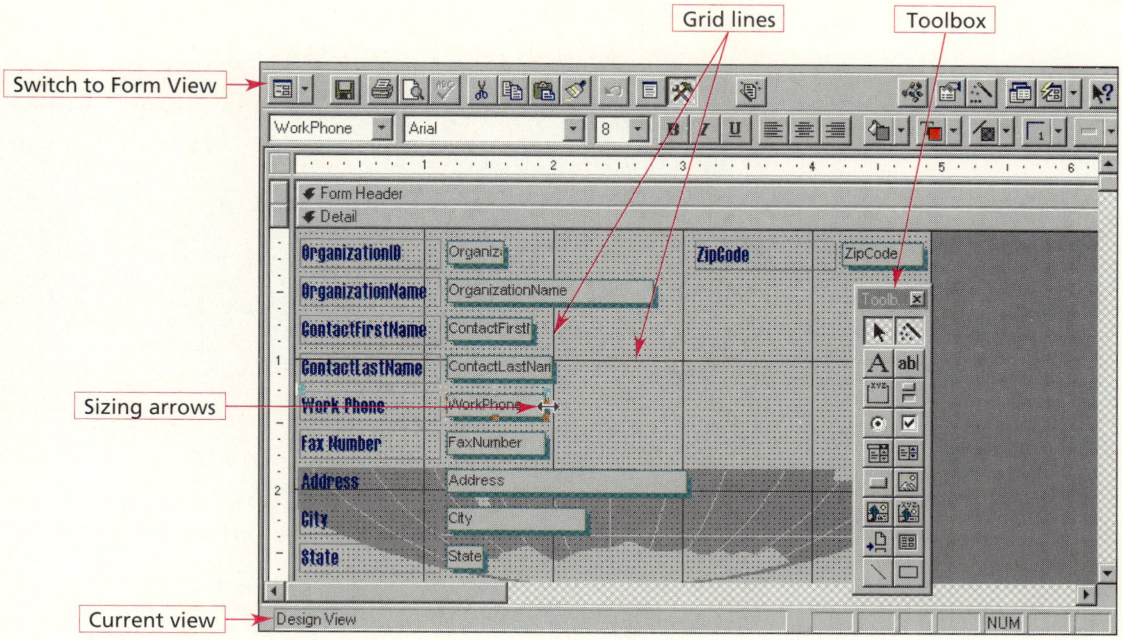

Figure 3.36

To size a text box on a form:

1 Open the Organizations Table Data Entry Form in design view.

2 Click Maximize in the upper-right corner to enlarge the work surface.

3 Click within the Work Phone text box to select it, and then move the pointer to the right border of the text box.
The sizing arrows appear as shown in Figure 3.36.

4 Drag the right side of the text box several spaces past the grid line on the right, and then release the mouse button.

5 Repeat steps 3 and 4 to increase the size of the Fax Number text box.

6 Click outside the Fax Number text box to deselect it.

7 Check that your Work Phone and Fax Number text boxes display widths similar to those shown in Figure 3.37, and resize if necessary.

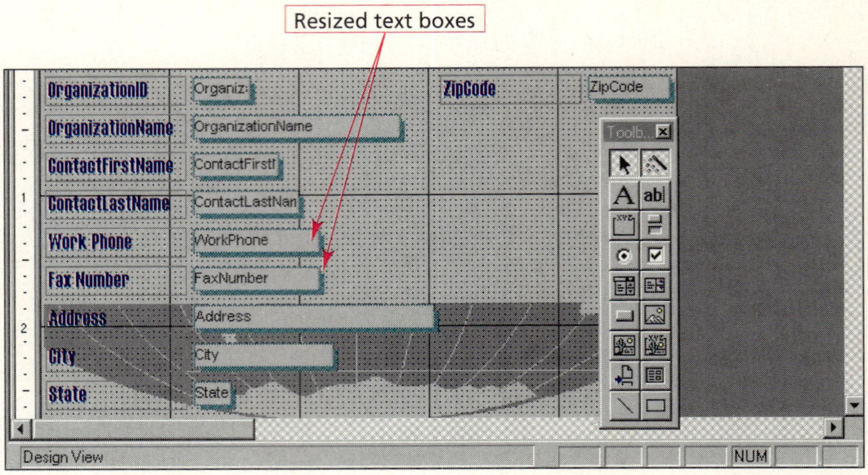

Figure 3.37

8 Switch to form view, click New Record, and then enter the record shown in Figure 3.38.

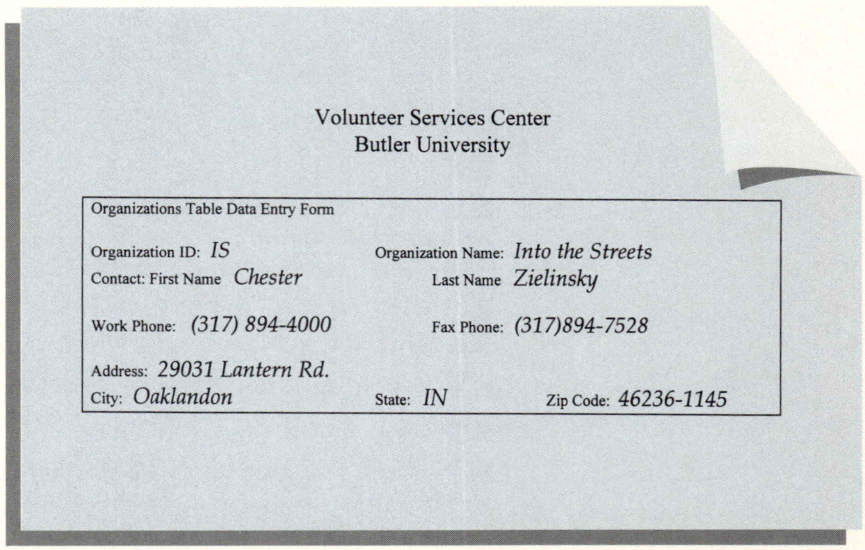

Volunteer Services Center
Butler University

Organizations Table Data Entry Form

Organization ID: *IS* Organization Name: *Into the Streets*
Contact: First Name *Chester* Last Name *Zielinsky*

Work Phone: *(317) 894-4000* Fax Phone: *(317)894-7528*

Address: *29031 Lantern Rd.*
City: *Oaklandon* State: *IN* Zip Code: *46236-1145*

Figure 3.38

9 Close the form and save your design changes.
Data entry in the Organizations table is complete. In the final section of this project, you will create and use data entry forms for the other two tables in the Volunteer Center database.

Completing Data Entry

Generally, you can start data entry with actual data if a table has a primary key based on a single field and if that table has a small number of records in comparison to other tables. The Organizations table in the Volunteer Center database fits this description, and you can assume that it contains actual data.

If a table could have hundreds or thousands of records, such as the Volunteers or Time Cards table, respectively, you should start data entry with data that will test output. For example, suppose that student volunteers are enrolled in one of five colleges, and you want to group records by college in a report. To test grouping, it is sufficient to enter test data for just two colleges, with several volunteer records for each of those two colleges. You can then design and test the desired report to make sure that changes do not have to be made to the structure of the table. With careful planning, you can generally check for output problems with fewer than 50 test records. You can then delete the test records and enter actual data.

Tip You should also include data that will test the data entry process. For example, try to leave a required field blank or attempt to enter duplicate data in a primary key field.

With minimal instruction in the following steps, you will create a data entry form for the Volunteers table and use the form to enter test data in 5 records. You will then enter test data in the Time Cards table, adding 25 records in datasheet view. Refer to instructions in prior sections if you cannot remember how to do a specific task.

To create the Volunteers Table Data Entry Form:

1 Select the Forms tab, and then select New.

2 Make the wizard and table selections shown in Figure 3.39.

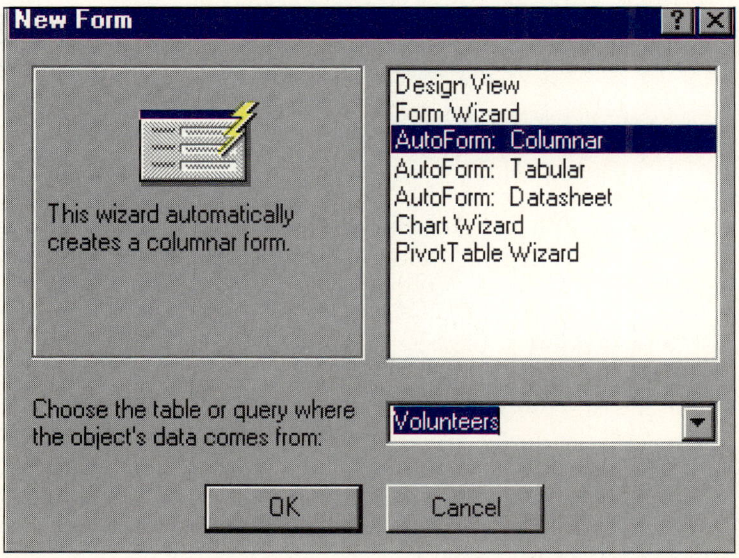

Figure 3.39

3 Select OK.
AutoForm Wizard automatically creates a form and displays the first record, as shown in Figure 3.40. The form displays all fields in the table in the same order as found in datasheet view, except the fields display down a column instead of across a row.

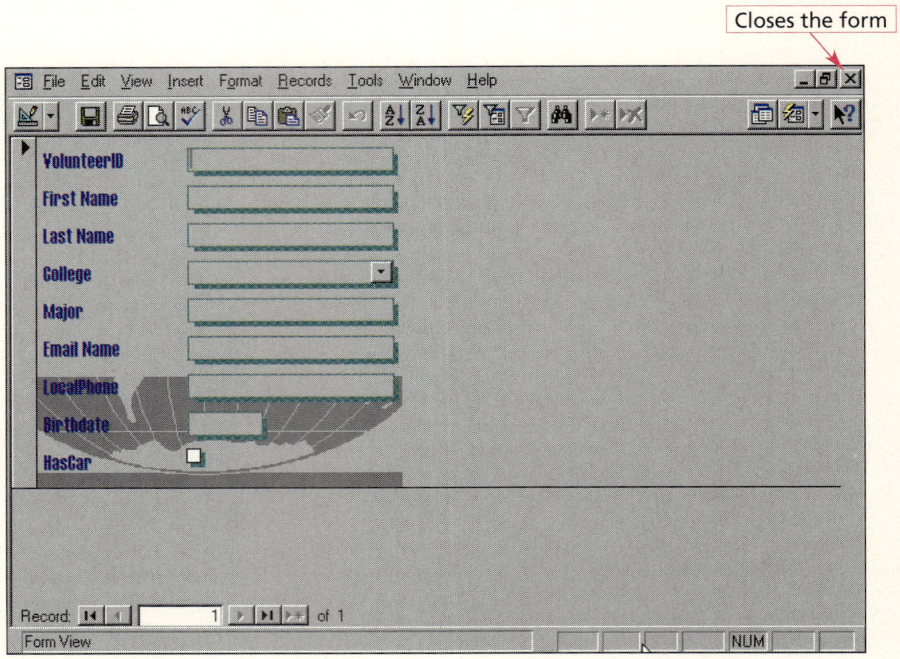

Figure 3.40

To enter records and save the form:

1 Enter the VolunteerID, First Name, and Last Name data shown in Figure 3.41.

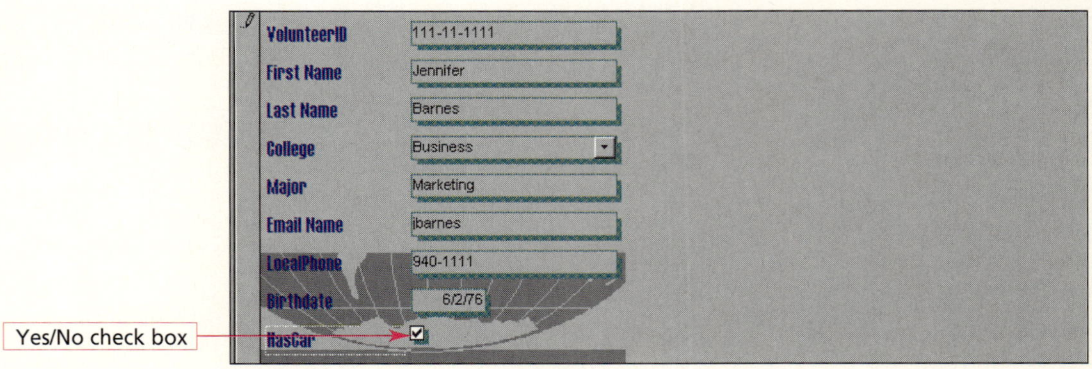

Figure 3.41

2 Click the arrow at the right end of the College text box, and select Business from the pull-down list.

3 Enter the Major, Email Name, LocalPhone, and Birthdate data shown in Figure 3.41.

Reminder Enter leading zeros in dates. When you enter 060276, Access displays 6/2/76.

4 Click the HasCar check box to indicate Yes.
A checkmark appears in the box.

5 Enter the four additional records shown in Table 3.1.

Field	Record 2	Record 3	Record 4	Record 5
VolunteerID	222-22-2222	333-33-3333	444-44-4444	555-55-5555
FirstName	Tonya	Tom	Michael	Nathan
LastName	Wilson	Long	Barnes	Smith
College	Business	Arts & Sciences	Arts & Sciences	Business
Major	Accounting	Psychology	Biology	Marketing
EmailName	twilson	tlong	mbarnes	nsmith
LocalPhone	940-2222	940-3333	940-4444	940-5555
Birthdate	12/12/77	5/13/77	10/17/78	11/20/76
HasCar	Yes	No	Yes	No

Table 3.1

6 Click the X button in the upper-right corner of the form window to close the Volunteers form, and then select Yes when prompted to save changes to the design of the form.

7 Type `Volunteers Table Data Entry Form` in the Save As dialog box, and then select OK.
The names of two forms appear on the Forms tab of the Database window.

To enter records in the Time Cards table:

1 Select the Tables tab in the Database window, select the Time Cards table, and then select Open.

2 Enter the records shown in Table 3.2.

Record	VolunteerID	OrganizationID	Date Worked	Hours Worked
1	111-11-1111	BBBS	1/3/96	2.5
2	111-11-1111	MOW	1/5/96	4
3	111-11-1111	HH	1/15/96	10
4	111-11-1111	BBBS	1/17/96	4
5	222-22-2222	MOW	1/10/96	3
6	222-22-2222	HH	1/15/96	12
7	222-22-2222	BBBS	1/17/96	3
8	222-22-2222	HH	1/22/96	8
9	222-22-2222	IS	2/25/96	4
10	222-22-2222	BBBS	2/28/96	4
11	333-33-3333	MOW	2/6/96	3
12	333-33-3333	MOW	2/13/96	3.5
13	333-33-3333	MOW	2/20/96	3
14	333-33-3333	IS	2/25/96	8
15	333-33-3333	MOW	2/27/96	3.5
16	444-44-4444	GLM	1/13/96	6
17	444-44-4444	GLM	1/20/96	5
18	444-44-4444	GLM	1/27/96	8
19	444-44-4444	IS	2/25/96	5
20	555-55-5555	GLM	1/6/96	4
21	555-55-5555	GLM	1/13/96	10
22	555-55-5555	HH	1/15/96	6
23	555-55-5555	GLM	1/20/96	5.5
24	555-55-5555	HH	1/22/96	6
25	555-55-5555	IS	1/25/96	8

Table 3.2

Quick Fix If you get an error message that referential integrity rules require a matching record in a table, check that field sizes and input masks for the common fields are identical.

3 Close the table, and then close the database.

The Next Step

In this project you learned how to set most of the field properties in a table and set a one-to-many relationship between tables. As a next step, use on-screen Help to find out all you can about the Caption, Allow Zero Length, and Indexed field properties as well as the one-to-one and many-to-many relationships.

You also created columnar forms using Form Wizard and AutoForm Wizard. Try using the same techniques to create tabular forms. If you also take a look at datasheet forms, you'll have a better idea of your options to enter and edit data.

This concludes Project 3. You can either exit Access or go on to work the Study Questions, Review Exercises, and Assignments.

Summary and Exercises

Summary

- By setting field properties, you can help ensure that data are complete, accurate, and presented in a consistent manner.
- If you specify Required as a field property, Access will not save a record that does not contain the required data.
- The Format field property determines how a value is displayed, not how it is entered or stored in a table.
- The Input Mask property controls data entry through a pattern for allowable characters, such as (999)000-0000 for an optional area code with a dash automatically separating the first three and last four digits of a phone number.
- If you set Default Value as a field property, the value you specify appears automatically in a field when you add a new record.
- You can set Validation Rule and Validation Text field properties. A validation rule determines whether or not data being entered in a field should be rejected. Validation text appears on the screen if attempted data entry violates a validation rule.
- Tables are related if the same data can be entered in both tables. A one-to-many relationship exists if data restricted to one entry in one table can appear many times in its related table.
- Referential integrity refers to a set of rules that make sure relationships among records in related tables are valid.
- You can enter and edit data in datasheet view or a form. A form contains only the fields you specify in the order selected.
- Using Form Wizard, you can create a columnar, tabular, or datasheet form. You can modify a form in design view.

Key Terms and Operations

Key Terms
default value
format
input mask
Input Mask Wizard
one-to-many relationship
referential integrity
required field
source document
validation rule
validation text

Operations
Designate a field as required
Specify an input mask on your own
Select a predefined input mask
Set a default value
Specify a validation rule and associated text
Define a one-to-many relationship between tables
Enforce referential integrity
Enter data in datasheet view
Create columnar forms using Form Wizard and AutoForm Wizard
Modify a form by resizing a text box
Enter test data

Study Questions

Multiple Choice

1. Which is not a phase in developing and using a database management system?
   a. designing and creating the database
   b. entering and editing data
   c. selecting the font used to display data
   d. converting data into information

2. GIGO means
   a. garbage in, garbage out.
   b. general input, general output.
   c. that you cannot rely on information in reports if the data are wrong or missing.
   d. Both a and c.

3. Which is not an action that controls data entry?
   a. set the display format
   b. set rules for data accepted
   c. create blanks to fill in
   d. display a default value

4. Which is a true statement about required fields?
   a. Access will not save a record unless data in required fields are present.
   b. The Required property is set in the design view of a table.
   c. Data in a Required field cannot be edited later.
   d. Both a and b.

5. The Format property serves what purpose?
   a. determines how a value displays
   b. controls data entry
   c. is used with date/time fields only
   d. All of the above.

6. Which is not a true statement about default values?
   a. Default values appear automatically in a field when you add a record.
   b. A default value cannot be typed over.
   c. Setting a default value will save data entry time.
   d. Default values reduce typing errors.

7. Access validates data
   a. based on data type.
   b. based on validation rules you specify as field properties.
   c. by rejecting data and displaying an error message on the screen.
   d. All of the above.

8. If you select Enforce Referential Integrity,
   a. Access checks the integrity of the data entered in each data field.
   b. Access applies a set of rules that make sure relationships between records in related tables are valid.
   c. Access automatically spell checks data as it is entered.
   d. Both a and b.

9. When you enter and edit data in datasheet view,
   a. data display in rows and columns.
   b. data in each column represent a complete record.
   c. each row holds data for a field.
   d. Both b and c.

10. Which is not a layout offered by AutoForm Wizard?
    a. Columnar
    b. Tabular
    c. Object Linking and Embedding
    d. Datasheet

Short Answer

1. __________ integrity refers to a set of rules that make sure relationships between records in related tables are valid.
2. What field property would you set to prevent saving a new record in a table unless the associated data were present?
3. What field property, other than Input Mask, determines how data are displayed?
4. Which two data types are most associated with input masks?
5. Although a validation rule is set up to reject data, how should you write the rule?
6. How do you set a relationship between two tables?
7. How do you remove a relationship between two tables?
8. What two views allow you to enter data in a table?
9. What two benefits do default values provide?
10. You can use two methods to select a field name from the Available Fields box. Highlighting the field and clicking the Next> button is one method. What is the other method?

For Discussion

Answer the following discussion questions in the context of a new situation. Assume that you provide lawn care services during the summer. Your business is expanding, so you plan to set up a two-table Access database named Lawn Care to keep track of it. One table named Customers will contain one record per customer, with fields showing customer number, name, address, and phone number data. The other table named Services will track the type of service performed, date performed, time involved, and fee charged.

1. Discuss the purpose of the Required field property. What fields in the Customers and Services tables would likely be set as required fields?
2. What is an input mask? What input masks might you specify in the Lawn Care database?
3. What is a one-to-many relationship? Assume that such a relationship exists between the two tables in the Lawn Care database, based on the contents of a customer number field. Explain which table would be the "one" portion of the relationship and which table would be the "many" portion of the relationship.

4. Explain referential integrity. Give an example of data entry that would not be allowed if referential integrity were enforced in the Lawn Care database.
5. Describe two ways that you could enter a record in the Customers table.

Review Exercises

Project 2 review exercises involved creating three tables in the Job Search database, a multitable information system tracking job search efforts and results. In these review exercises you will modify several field properties, set relationships, create forms, and enter data.

Modifying Field Properties

1. Start Access and open the Job Search database.
2. Open the Companies table in design view, type **>CCCCCCCCCC** as the input mask for the CompanyID field, and specify that CompanyID is a required field.
3. Close the table, saving your changes.
4. Open the Applications table in design view, type **>CCCCCCCCCC** as the input mask for the CompanyID field, and specify that CompanyID is a required field.
5. Set a Short Date input mask for the SendDate and ResponseDate fields, and then close the table and save your changes.
6. Open the Interviews table in design view, type **>CCCCCCCCCC** as the input mask for the CompanyID field, and specify that CompanyID is a required field.
7. Set a Short Date input mask for the InterviewDate field and a Medium Time input mask for the StartTime field.
8. Close the table and save your changes.

Setting Relationships

1. Specify the relationships shown in Figure 3.42.

Tip If one or more tables do not appear when you select Relationships in the toolbar, you can select Show Table from the Relationships menu, and then add any missing tables before specifying the relationships.

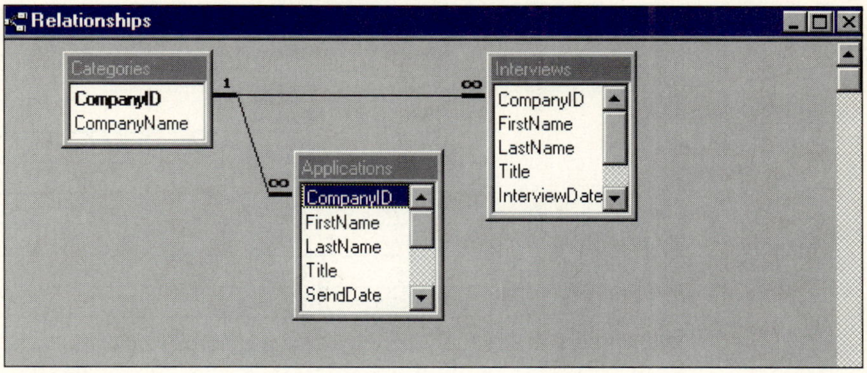

Figure 3.42

2. Close the Relationships dialog box and save your changes.

Creating Forms

1. Select the Forms tab, select New, and then select AutoForm: Columnar and the Companies table.
2. Adjust display widths of fields as needed, close the form, and save your changes using the name Enter company codes and names.
3. Repeat steps 1 and 2 to create a form based on the Applications table. Name the form Enter initial contacts and responses.
4. Repeat steps 1 and 2 to create a form based on the Interviews table. Name the form Enter interviews and results.

Using Forms to Enter Data

1. Open the Enter company codes and names form, enter the data shown in Table 3.3, and then close the form.

Record	Company ID	Company Name
1	ABCTECH	ABC Technologies, Inc.
2	SUN	Sun Landscaping
3	A1FLAG	A1 Flag Specialties, Inc.
4	KELLY	Kelly Personnel Services
5	ADP	ADP Processing, Inc.
6	SNELL	Snell & Snell Associates
7	WALKER	Walker Research

Table 3.3

2. Open the Enter initial contacts and responses form, enter the data shown in Tables 3.4 and 3.5, and then close the form.

Field	Record 1	Record 2	Record 3	Record 4
CompanyID	ABCTECH	SUN	A1FLAG	KELLY
FirstName	Sandra	Tom	Jeffrey	Karel
LastName	Bennett	King	Orris	Sander
Title	Personnel Manager	HR Director	HR Director	Office Manager
SendDate	04/21/97	04/21/97	04/21/97	04/21/97
OpenPosition	Data Entry	Lawn Care	Telemarketing	Data Entry
RatePerHour	8.75	10	9.50	9.25
InfoSource	Newspaper Ad	Networking	Newspaper Ad	Placement Office
ResponseDate	04/25/97	04/24/97	04/25/97	04/28/97
InterviewInvite	Yes	Yes	Yes	No

Table 3.4

Field	Record 5	Record 6	Record 7	Record 8
CompanyID	ADP	SNELL	WALKER	KELLY
FirstName	Peter	Susan	Lee	Karel
LastName	Osland	Rieber	Fountain	Sander
Title	Personnel Manager	HR Director	HR Director	Office Manager
SendDate	04/21/97	04/21/97	04/28/97	04/28/97
OpenPosition	Data Entry	Data Entry	Data Entry	Telemarketing
RatePerHour	9.50	11.25	11.00	8.25
InfoSource	Placement Office	Networking	Newspaper Ad	Newspaper Ad
ResponseDate	04/25/97	04/28/97		05/2/97
InterviewInvite	Yes	No		Yes

Table 3.5

3. Open the Enter interviews and results form, enter the data shown in Table 3.6, and then close the form.

Field	Record 1	Record 2	Record 3	Record 4
CompanyID	SUN	ABCTECH	ABCTECH	A1FLAG
FirstName	Tom	Jordan	Sandra	Sarah
LastName	Betts	Fields	Bennett	Fox
Title	Field Manager	Director of Research	Personnel Manager	Sales Director
InterviewDate	04/25/97	04/28/97	04/28/97	04/29/97
StartTime	9:30 AM	10:00 AM	1:30 PM	3:30 PM
Notes	Job offer made. I have one week to respond.	30 minute interview followed by tests. Second interview at 1:30.		

Table 3.6

Assignments

Writing Validation Rules

Using on-screen Help, find out how to write a validation rule for each of the following independent situations: a date must be in 1997, an entry must be a nonzero value, and a value must be three characters beginning with the letter *S*.

Viewing On-screen Help on Relationships

Use Answer Wizard to look up information about relationships. Select *Determining the relationships for your database* in the Tell Me About section, and read the multiscreen display. Explain the examples used to illustrate a one-to-many relationship, a many-to-many relationship, and a one-to-one relationship.

Viewing On-screen Help on Forms

In this project you created a data entry form. Explain two other types of forms, as described in the Tell Me About section of Answer Wizard's Help on forms.

Putting on a Fund-Raiser II

Continue to develop the database for tracking fund-raising activities that you designed and created in Project 2. Set field properties and relationships as appropriate. Create a data entry form for each table. Enter a sufficient number of records to test desired outputs.

Project 4: Converting Data into Information

Objectives

After completing this project, you should be able to:

- Find records matching a search condition
- Filter records by selection and form
- Create a select query using Simple Query Wizard
- Resize, hide, and unhide columns
- Sort records on one or more fields
- Print results
- Create reports using Report Wizard

Case Study: Coordinating Volunteer Activities III

Recall that developing and using a database management system generally involves three phases: designing and creating the database, entering and editing data, and converting data into information. In your job as a summer intern, you have completed the second phase by entering enough sample data to test output. Now you are ready to produce the information requested by volunteer center personnel during database design interviews.

Designing the Solution

The terms *data* and *information* are often used interchangeably, but in the context of database management they have different meanings. *Data* are the raw facts or assumptions stored in a database. *Information* is data presented in a usable form.

Creating information from data requires four steps: selecting, organizing, formatting, and displaying data stored in the database. First you will *select* the data you need from one or more tables. For example, to list volunteers and their phone numbers, you will work with only the Volunteers table in the Volunteer Center database. However, to report volunteer activity including the names of volunteers, the hours they worked, and the organizations involved, you will use the Volunteers, Time Cards, and Organizations tables. As part of the selection process, you can limit output to the fields and records you specify.

When you *organize* output you arrange records based on the contents of one or more fields. For example, if you were to list the names and dates worked of students who volunteered during the last month, you could arrange output in order by last name or by date worked.

In the context of converting data into information, *format* refers to arranging fields in a useful layout, with descriptive text to explain each element. For example, a telephone list will be easy to read if you display each name and number on one line, with the name preceding the phone number.

When you *display* information, you send output to the screen or a printer. Sometimes you can view the field contents on-screen to get the information you need, such as a student's e-mail address or a list of volunteer activities available at an organization. At other times you will need to print information, such as reports you have prepared for distribution outside the volunteer center.

The options on the toolbar shown in Figure 4.1 can help you convert data to information quickly. With little more than a click of a button, you can rearrange the order of records, *filter* records by specifying a condition for record selection, and find each record containing the data you specify.

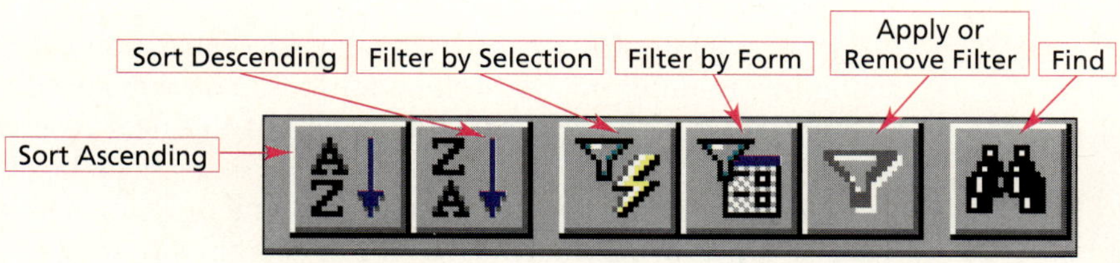

Figure 4.1

If your information needs are relatively complex or you want to save output specifications for reuse later, you can create queries and reports. A *query* allows you to display and analyze data in different ways, for example, to show fields from more than one table. A *report* provides an effective way to print professional-looking output based on a table or query. The names of queries and reports appear on their respective tabs in the Database window; the Reports tab is shown in Figure 4.2.

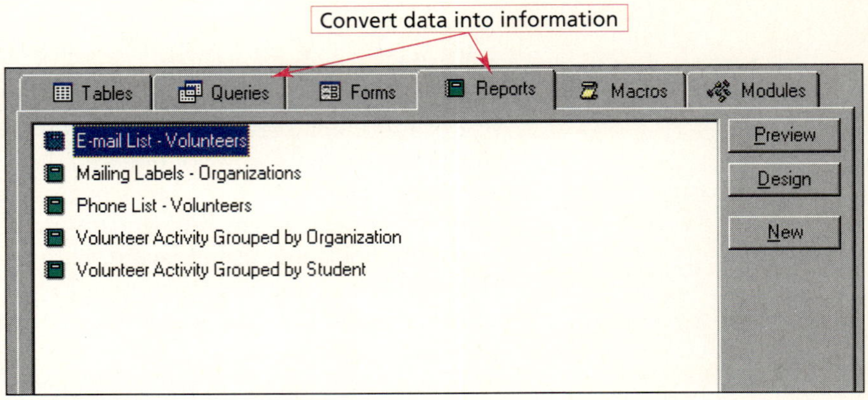

Figure 4.2

In this project you will first use toolbar buttons to vary the content and format of information displayed on the screen. You will also create simple queries and reports with the aid of wizards.

FINDING A MATCH

If you are looking for a particular value in a table, you can use the Find dialog box to enter your search conditions. You will specify what you want to find, where to search, and how much of the field to match in text boxes, as shown in Figure 4.3. You can also use check boxes to further restrict the search; for example, you can look only for data that matches the case typed in the Find What box or search only the current field. Access can search a single field much faster than it can search an entire table.

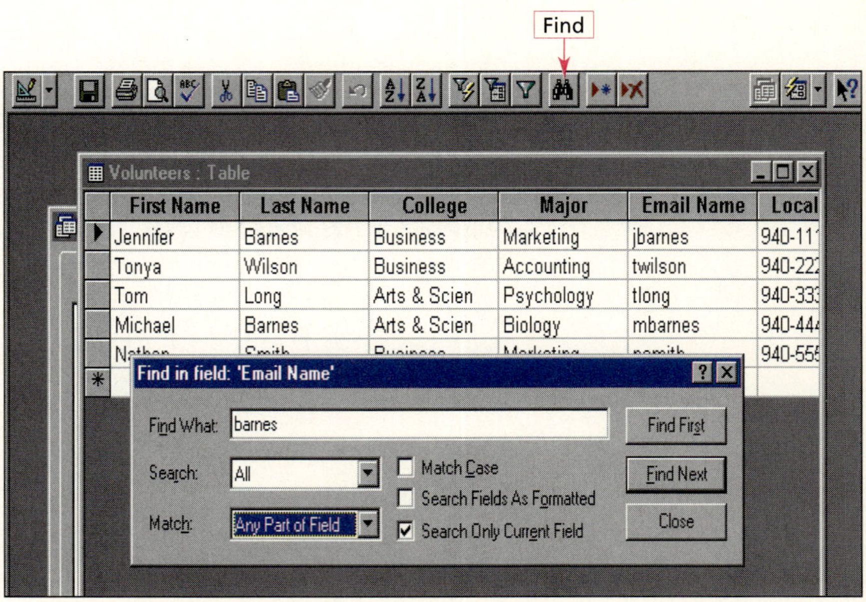

Figure 4.3

Tip If you don't know the exact value you want to find, you can use wildcard characters in the Find What box. You can use an asterisk (*) at the beginning or end of your search text to represent any number of characters. A question mark (?) represents any single alphabetic character. A number sign (#) represents any single numeric character.

In the following steps you will locate specific records using the Find dialog box. You will also move a column to a different location in the table so that the results of a find operation are more meaningful.

To find a match to any part of a field:

1 Start Access and open the Volunteer Center database.

2 Open the Volunteers table in datasheet view.

3 Click within the Email Name column.

4 Select Find in the toolbar.
The Find in field dialog box opens.

5 Type **barnes** in the Find What box.

6 Select Any Part of Field from the Match pull-down list.

7 Change other settings as necessary to match those shown in Figure 4.3.

8 Select Find First.
Access highlights *barnes* in the Email Name field of the first record found (*jbarnes* for *Jennifer Barnes*).

9 Select Find Next.
Access highlights *barnes* in the Email Name field of the second record found (*mbarnes* for *Michael Barnes*).

10 Select Find Next.
Access tells you the search is over.

11 Select OK, and then select Close.

To find a match at the start of a field:

1 Click within the Birthdate column, and then select Find in the toolbar.

2 Type **10** in the Find What box, and then select Start of Field from the Match pull-down list.

3 Select Find First.
Access highlights 10/17/78 in the first record containing 10 at the start of the Birthdate field, as shown in Figure 4.4. The name of the volunteer with this October birthday is not visible.

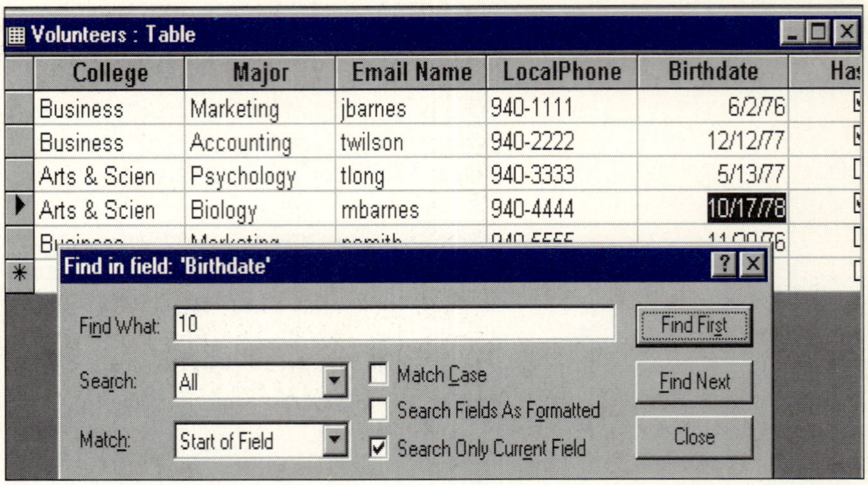

Figure 4.4

4 Select Find Next, select OK, and then select Close.

To move a column and repeat a find operation:

1 Click within the column heading Birthdate, and then press and hold down the mouse button.

A small rectangle at the bottom of the pointer indicates a move operation, as shown in Figure 4.5.

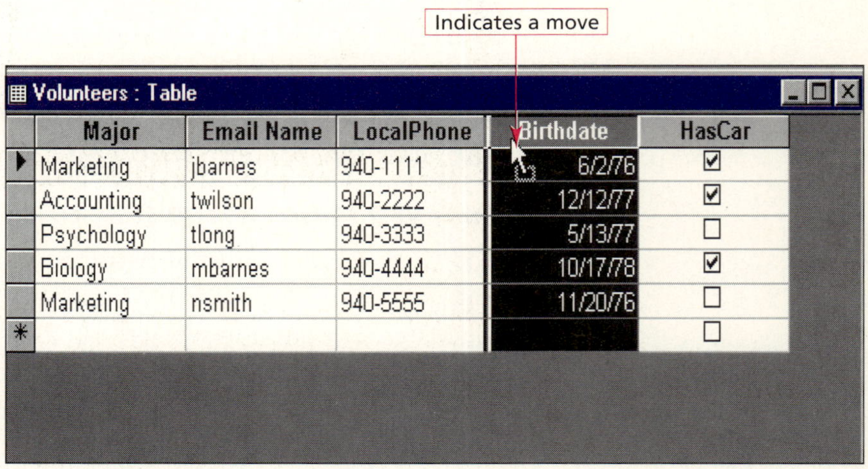

Figure 4.5

2 Drag the pointer to the left until the thick vertical bar appears between the Last Name and College columns, as shown in Figure 4.6.

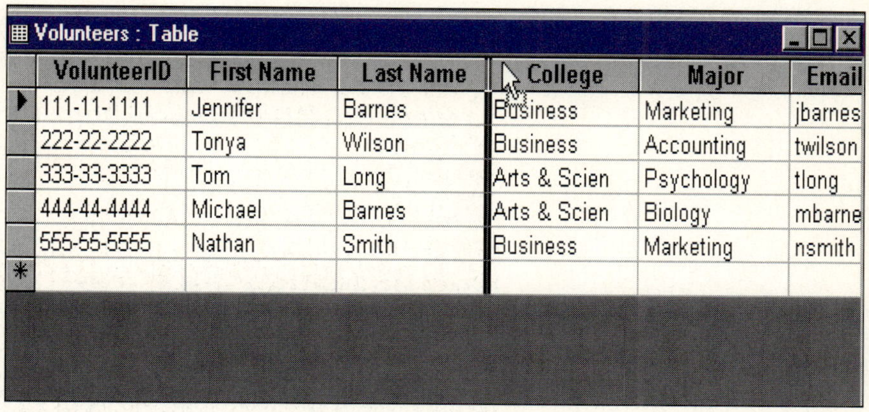

Volunteers : Table

VolunteerID	First Name	Last Name	College	Major	Email
111-11-1111	Jennifer	Barnes	Business	Marketing	jbarnes
222-22-2222	Tonya	Wilson	Business	Accounting	twilson
333-33-3333	Tom	Long	Arts & Scien	Psychology	tlong
444-44-4444	Michael	Barnes	Arts & Scien	Biology	mbarne
555-55-5555	Nathan	Smith	Business	Marketing	nsmith

Figure 4.6

3 Release the mouse button.
Access inserts the Birthdate column between the Last Name and College columns, as shown in Figure 4.7.

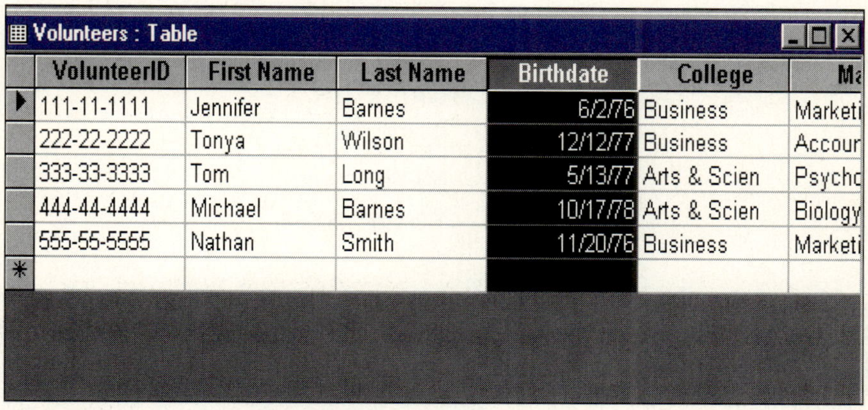

Volunteers : Table

VolunteerID	First Name	Last Name	Birthdate	College	Ma
111-11-1111	Jennifer	Barnes	6/2/76	Business	Marketi
222-22-2222	Tonya	Wilson	12/12/77	Business	Accour
333-33-3333	Tom	Long	5/13/77	Arts & Scien	Psycho
444-44-4444	Michael	Barnes	10/17/78	Arts & Scien	Biology
555-55-5555	Nathan	Smith	11/20/76	Business	Marketi

Figure 4.7

4 Select Find in the toolbar, and then select Find First.
Access again highlights 10/17/78, which you can now see is the birthdate of Michael Barnes.

5 Close the dialog box.

6 Close the table without saving your changes.

Using Filters to Select Records

Rarely do you want to view or print every record in a database table. In fact, most database tables become so large that it is not practical to view or print every record. The term ***filter*** is used for both the means and the process of limiting the records that are selected to those that meet specific criteria.

Access provides three ways to filter records: Filter By Selection, Filter

By Form, and the Advanced Filter/Sort window. In the following steps you will view general information about each method.

To view on-screen Help about filters:

1 Choose Answer Wizard from the Help menu.

2 Type `filters` in the Type your request box, and then select Search.

3 In the Tell Me About section, select *What are filters and how do they work?*, and then select Display.
The Help screen shown in Figure 4.8 appears.

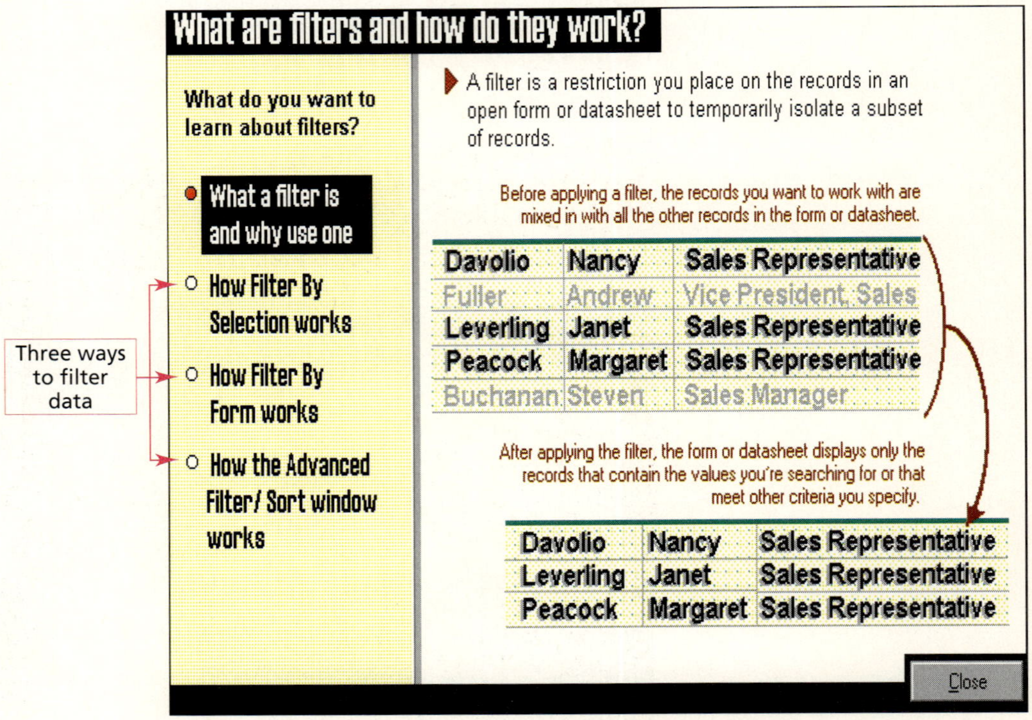

Figure 4.8

4 Read the definition of a filter and study the example of filtered records.

5 Select How Filter By Selection works, and study the example.

6 Select How Filter By Form works, and study the example.

7 Select How the Advanced Filter/Sort window works, and study the example.

8 Select Close.

Filter By Selection and Filter By Form are the easiest ways to filter records. You will work with both of these methods in the following sections.

Filtering by Selection

Using Filter By Selection, you can limit display to those records that meet one search condition at a time. To use this method, you must be able to find and select an example of the value you want the filtered records to contain.

> ***Tip*** Once you display a set of records that meet your first search condition, you can select another value from within that set. For example, if you filtered records in the Volunteers table to show individuals enrolled in the College of Business, you could then filter those records to show marketing majors within the college.

You can specify your search condition in form or datasheet view. In the following steps you will filter records by selecting a value in datasheet view.

To filter by selection:

1 Open the Time Cards table in datasheet view.

2 Select BBBS in any cell of the OrganizationID field, as shown in Figure 4.9.

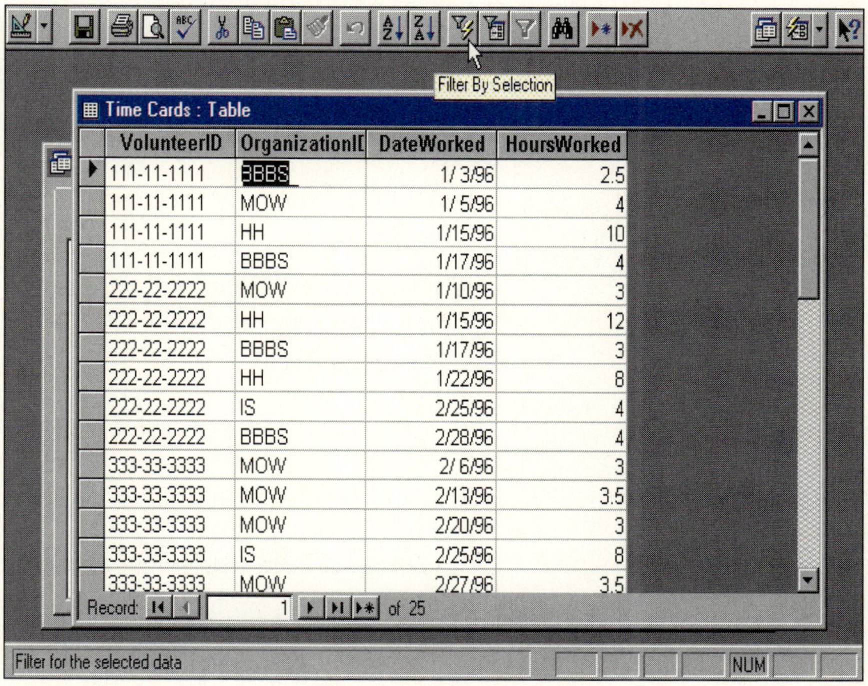

Figure 4.9

3 Select Filter By Selection in the toolbar.
Only the four records containing BBBS in the OrganizationID field appear on the screen, as shown in Figure 4.10.

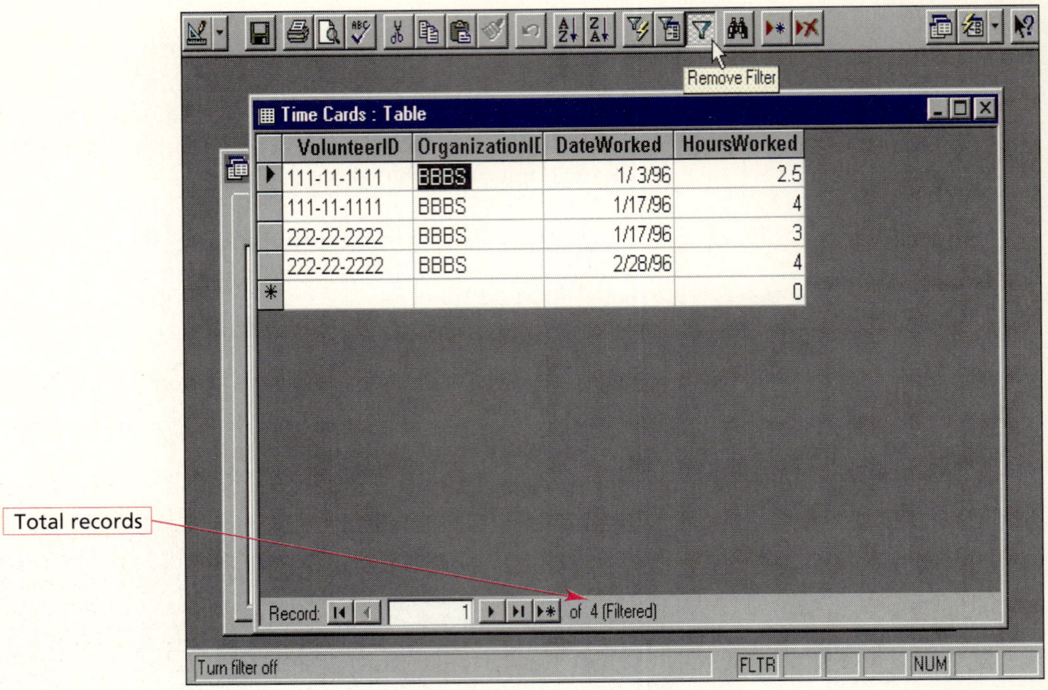

Figure 4.10

4 Select Remove Filter in the toolbar.
Access removes the filter. The record counter shows 25 records again.

5 Select HH in any cell of the OrganizationID field, and then select Filter By Selection.
Only the five records containing HH in the OrganizationID field appear on the screen.

6 Select 1/15/96 in any cell of the DateWorked field, and then select Filter By Selection.
Of the original five records containing HH in the OrganizationID field, only three records remain that display 1/15/96 as the date worked.

7 Select Remove Filter in the toolbar.

8 Close the table without saving your changes.

Filtering by Form

Using Filter By Form, you can limit display to those records that meet one or more search conditions. You can specify multiple conditions as ***And criteria,*** which means that all conditions must be met for a record to be selected. For example, you might restrict records to those showing volunteer activities for a specific organization on a specific date. Both the organization and date conditions must be met before a record will be selected. You can also specify multiple conditions as *Or criteria,* which means that a record will be selected if any one of the conditions is met, such as working for one organization or another.

When you use the Filter By Form feature, your search criteria are not limited to matching values found in a form or table. You can also use an ***expression,*** which is a combination of symbols and values that produces a result. For example, you might use the expression >=8 to select records showing hours worked greater than or equal to 8.

Selecting Filter By Form from the toolbar opens a window displaying a blank view of your form or datasheet. Clicking any field and then clicking the arrow at the right end of that field displays a list of values stored in the field. In Figure 4.11, for example, you see the unique entries in the Last Name field of the Volunteers table. You will specify your criteria by selecting from a field list or by typing a value or expression in the blank space below a field name.

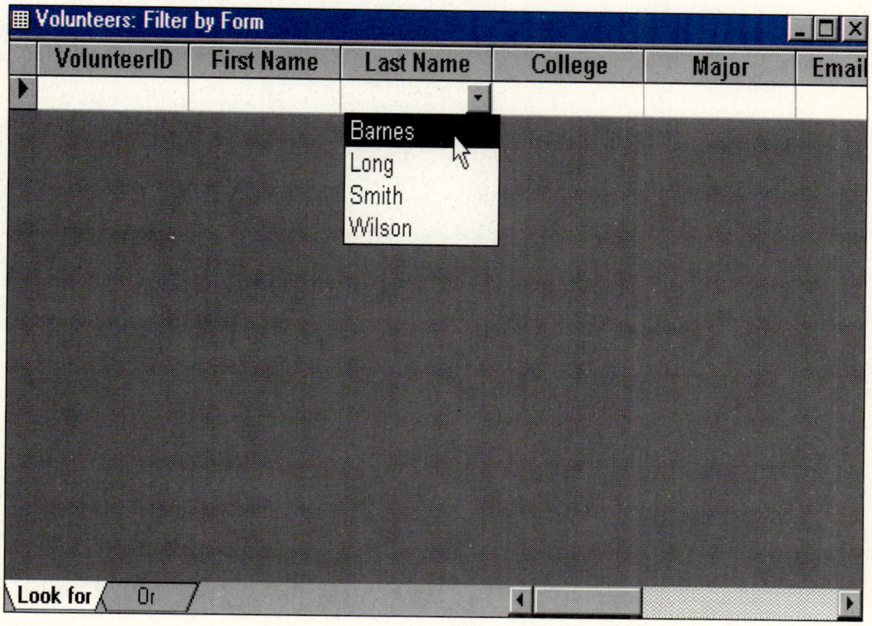

Figure 4.11

If you do not select Or in the lower-left corner of the Filter By Form window, Access will select only those records meeting all search conditions. If you select Or, Access will select a record if any condition is met. In the following steps you will open a Filter By Form window from datasheet view and work with various combinations of search criteria.

> ***Tip*** When setting a filter, be sure to delete unwanted search criteria that carry over from prior specifications by selecting (highlighting) each search condition and pressing DEL

To filter by form with a single exact-match search condition:

1 Open the Volunteers table in datasheet view.

Five records appear as shown in Figure 4.12.

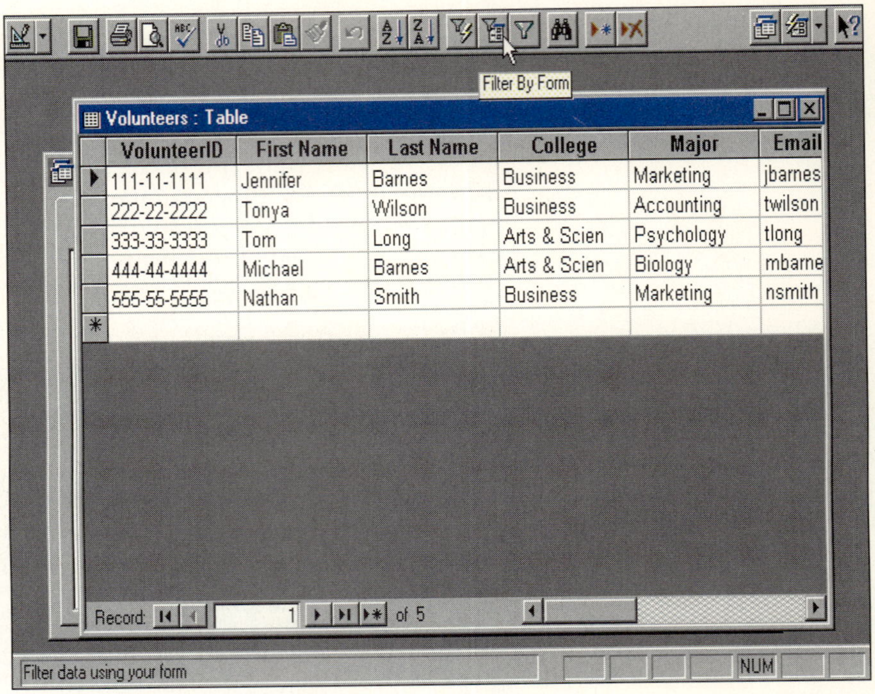

Figure 4.12

2 Select Filter By Form in the toolbar.
The Filter by Form window appears.

3 Click within the Last Name field, and then click the arrow at the right end of the field.
The unique last names appear in a pull-down list, as shown in Figure 4.11.

4 Select Barnes.
Access displays a text search condition encased in quotation marks, as shown in Figure 4.13.

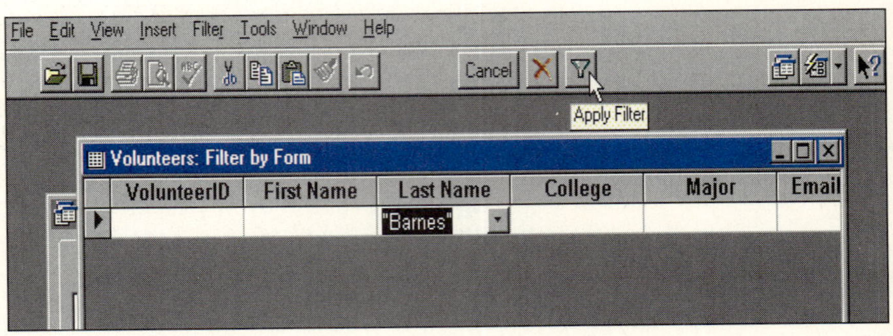

Figure 4.13

5 Select Apply Filter in the toolbar.
Two records display with last name Barnes.

You could have executed this exact-match search on one field more quickly by using Filter By Selection. The remaining examples, however, require a more advanced filtering process.

To filter by form with two exact-match search conditions, both of which must be met:

1 Select Filter By Form.

2 Click within the Major field, and then select Marketing from the pull-down list.
Your search criteria should match those shown in Figure 4.14.

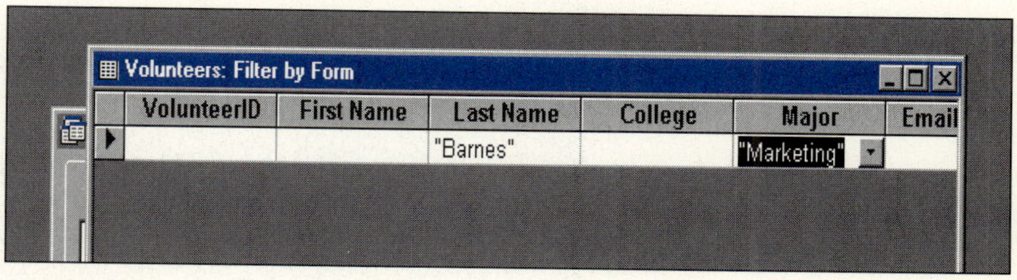

Figure 4.14

3 Select Apply Filter.
One record meeting both criteria is displayed.

4 Close the table without saving the changes.

To filter by form with an expression:

1 Open the Time Cards table in datasheet view.
The record counter indicates 25 records.

2 Select Filter By Form.

3 Type **>=8** beneath the HoursWorked field name, as shown in Figure 4.15.

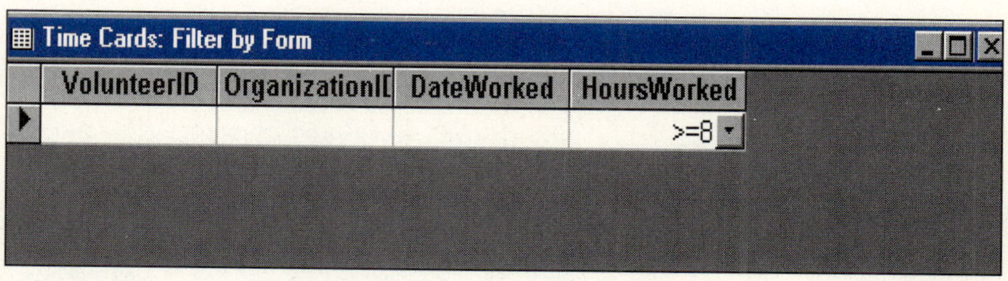

Figure 4.15

4 Select Apply Filter.
The seven records meeting the search condition are displayed as shown in Figure 4.16.

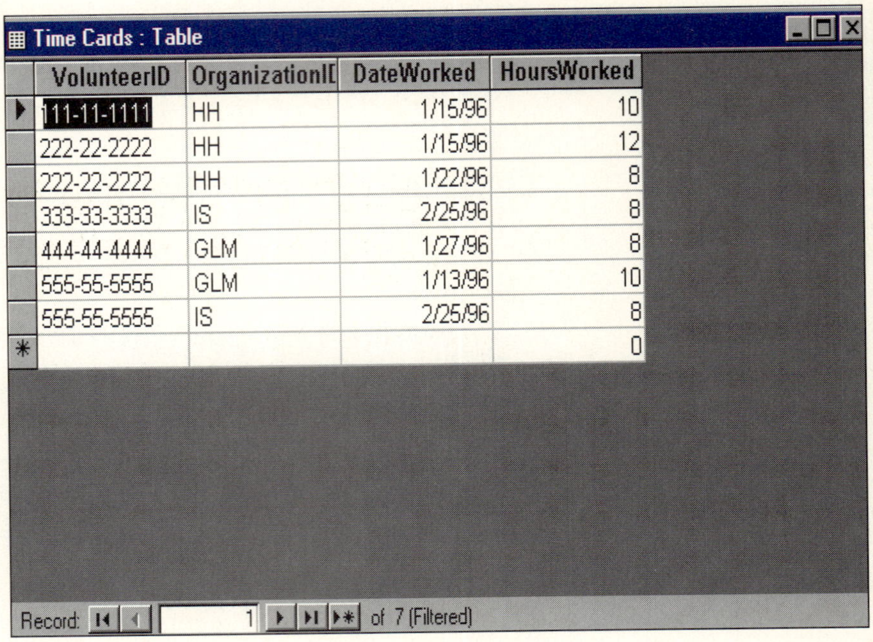
Time Cards : Table

	VolunteerID	OrganizationID	DateWorked	HoursWorked
▶	111-11-1111	HH	1/15/96	10
	222-22-2222	HH	1/15/96	12
	222-22-2222	HH	1/22/96	8
	333-33-3333	IS	2/25/96	8
	444-44-4444	GLM	1/27/96	8
	555-55-5555	GLM	1/13/96	10
	555-55-5555	IS	2/25/96	8
*				0

Record: 1 of 7 (Filtered)

Figure 4.16

To filter by form with two exact-match search conditions, either one of which causes a record to be selected:

1. Select Filter By Form.
2. Delete the search condition >=8 from the HoursWorked field.
3. Select HH from the OrganizationID pull-down list.
4. Click Or in the bottom-left corner of the window.
5. Select MOW from the OrganizationID pull-down list.

The screen now looks like Figure 4.17.

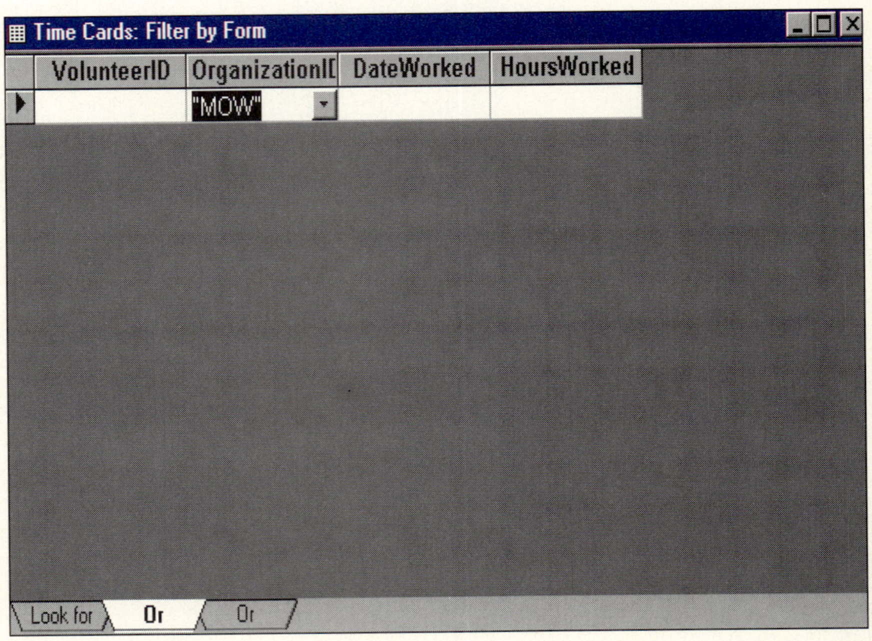

Figure 4.17

6 Select Apply Filter.
The 11 records meeting either search condition are displayed as shown in Figure 4.18.

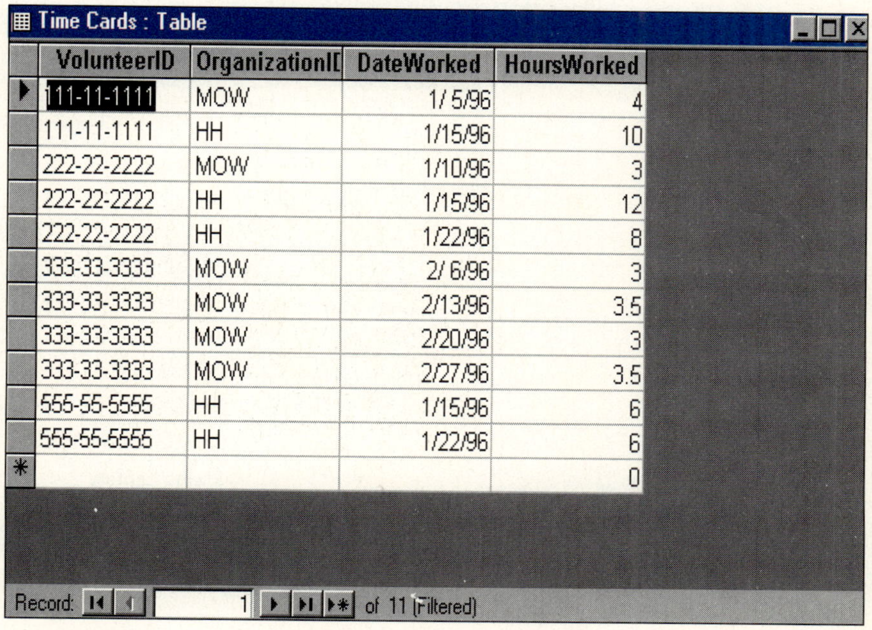

Time Cards : Table

	VolunteerID	OrganizationID	DateWorked	HoursWorked
▶	111-11-1111	MOW	1/ 5/96	4
	111-11-1111	HH	1/15/96	10
	222-22-2222	MOW	1/10/96	3
	222-22-2222	HH	1/15/96	12
	222-22-2222	HH	1/22/96	8
	333-33-3333	MOW	2/ 6/96	3
	333-33-3333	MOW	2/13/96	3.5
	333-33-3333	MOW	2/20/96	3
	333-33-3333	MOW	2/27/96	3.5
	555-55-5555	HH	1/15/96	6
	555-55-5555	HH	1/22/96	6
*				0

Record: 1 of 11 (Filtered)

Figure 4.18

7 Close the table without saving your changes.

EXIT If necessary, you can close this database now. You can then exit Access and continue this project later.

USING QUERIES TO SELECT AND ORGANIZE DATA

Filters allow you to restrict display of records in a single table. What if you want to view and print specified fields instead of entire records? What if those fields are not all in the same table? You can meet these information needs using queries, as explained in on-screen Help.

To view on-screen Help about queries:

1 If necessary, start Access and open the Volunteer Center database.

2 Choose Answer Wizard from the Help menu.

3 Type `queries` in the Type your request box, and then select Search.

4 In the Tell Me About section, select *Queries: What they are and how they work,* and then select Display.
The Help screen shown in Figure 4.19 appears.

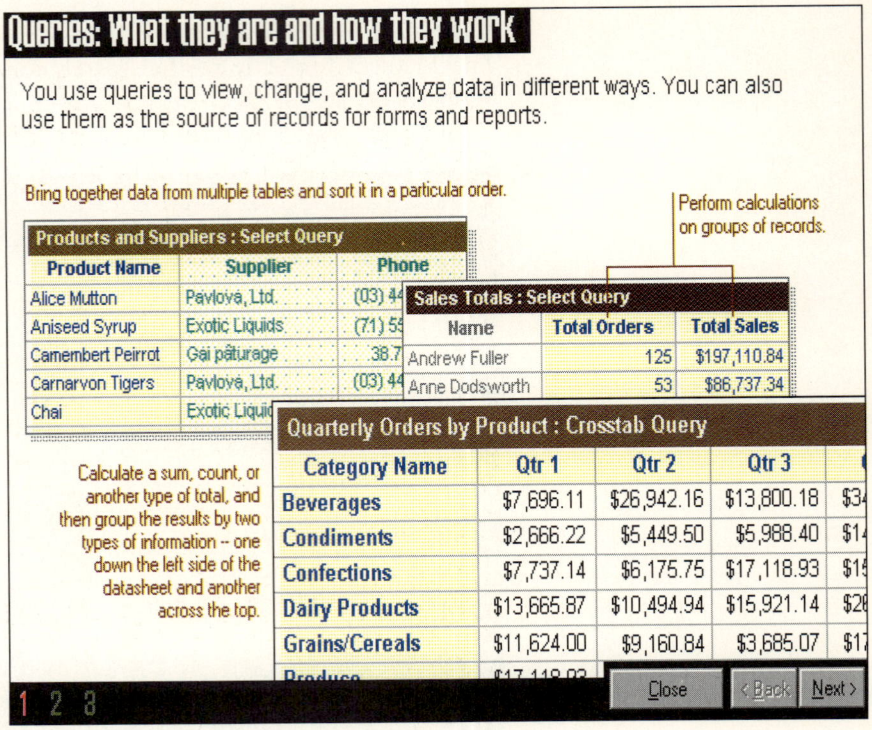

Figure 4.19

5 Read the general introduction to queries, and then select Next> in the lower-right corner or 2 in the lower-left corner.
The second of three screens appears.

6 Study the diagram showing how a query can pull data from more than one table and display information in the order you specify.

7 Select Next> or 3 to view the final Help screen, and then select Close.

As explained in on-screen Help, a ***select query*** retrieves data from one or more tables. Figure 4.20 shows a select query in datasheet view that displays information from the three tables in the Volunteer Center database.

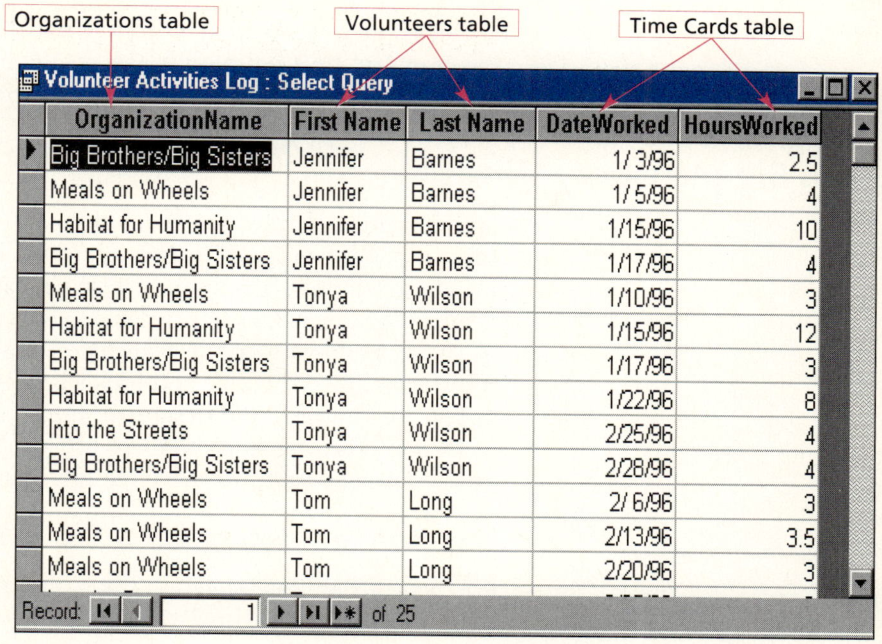

OrganizationName	First Name	Last Name	DateWorked	HoursWorked
Big Brothers/Big Sisters	Jennifer	Barnes	1/ 3/96	2.5
Meals on Wheels	Jennifer	Barnes	1/ 5/96	4
Habitat for Humanity	Jennifer	Barnes	1/15/96	10
Big Brothers/Big Sisters	Jennifer	Barnes	1/17/96	4
Meals on Wheels	Tonya	Wilson	1/10/96	3
Habitat for Humanity	Tonya	Wilson	1/15/96	12
Big Brothers/Big Sisters	Tonya	Wilson	1/17/96	3
Habitat for Humanity	Tonya	Wilson	1/22/96	8
Into the Streets	Tonya	Wilson	2/25/96	4
Big Brothers/Big Sisters	Tonya	Wilson	2/28/96	4
Meals on Wheels	Tom	Long	2/ 6/96	3
Meals on Wheels	Tom	Long	2/13/96	3.5
Meals on Wheels	Tom	Long	2/20/96	3

Figure 4.20

You can switch between the datasheet and design views of a query. Design view shows tables and relationships in the top half of the screen and a columnar display of fields and related tables in the bottom half, as shown in Figure 4.21. The Sort, Show, and Criteria rows allow you to sort records in the query, hide or unhide columns, and limit the view to records meeting search criteria.

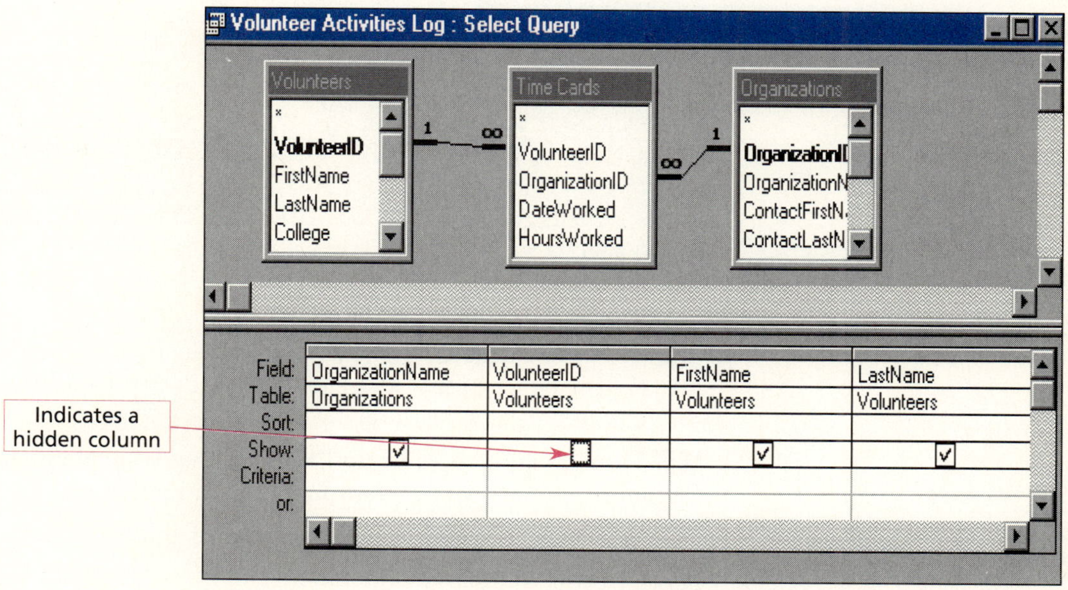

Figure 4.21

Access provides ***Simple Query Wizard*** to guide you as you create a select query. You can modify the results by hiding one or more fields, changing column width, changing the order of fields, and sorting records.

Using Simple Query Wizard

Simple Query Wizard works much like Form Wizard, which you used in Project 3. You will start Simple Query Wizard from the Queries tab in the Database window. Then you will select each table containing fields you need in the query and transfer the fields you want to include from the Available Fields box to the Selected Fields box. The order in which you transfer fields to the Selected Fields box is the order in which they will appear in datasheet and design views.

In the following steps you will use Simple Query Wizard to create a query pulling data from the three tables in the Volunteer Center database.

To create a select query using Simple Query Wizard:

1 Select the Queries tab in the Volunteer Center Database window, and then select New.

2 Select Simple Query Wizard, as shown in Figure 4.22, and then select OK.

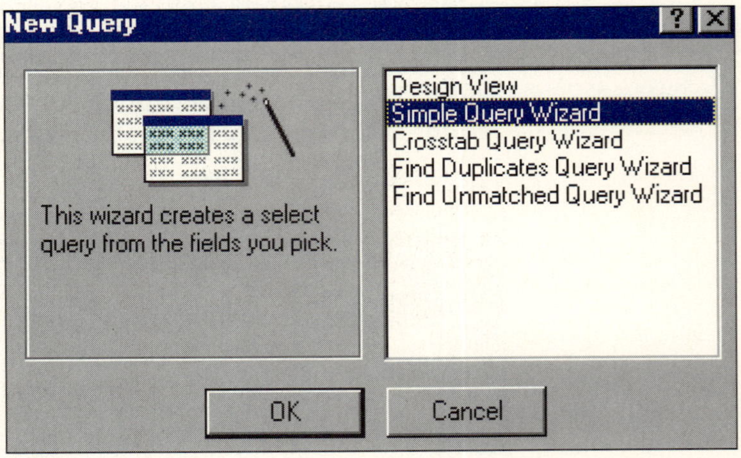

Figure 4.22

3 Select the Organizations table from the Tables/Queries pull-down list if that table name does not already appear in the Tables/Queries box in the Simple Query Wizard dialog box.

4 Double-click OrganizationName in the Available Fields box. OrganizationName appears in the Selected Fields box.

5 Select the Volunteers table from the Tables/Queries pull-down list.

6 Select VolunteerID, FirstName, and LastName from the Available Fields box.
The specifications on the screen should match those shown in Figure 4.23.

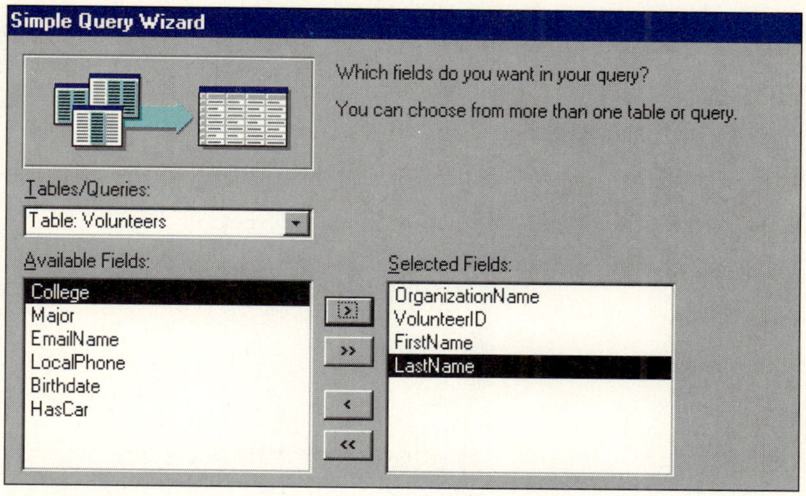

Figure 4.23

7 Select the Time Cards table from the Tables/Queries pull-down list.

8 Select DateWorked and HoursWorked from the Available Fields box. The specifications on the screen should match those shown in Figure 4.24.

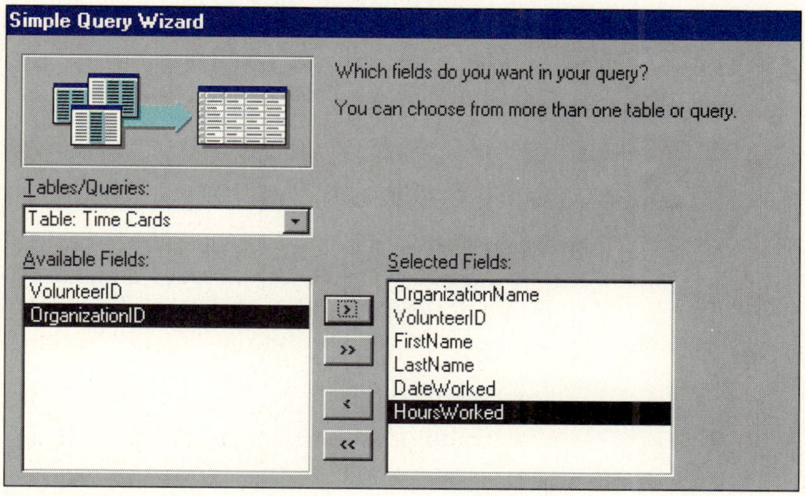

Figure 4.24

9 Select Next>.
Simple Query Wizard prompts you to specify a detail or summary query.

10 Select Detail, and then select Next>.

11 Type `Volunteer Activities Log` in the What title do you want for your query box.

12 Select the Open the query to view information button, and then select Finish.
Access displays a datasheet showing data pulled from three tables as shown in Figure 4.25.

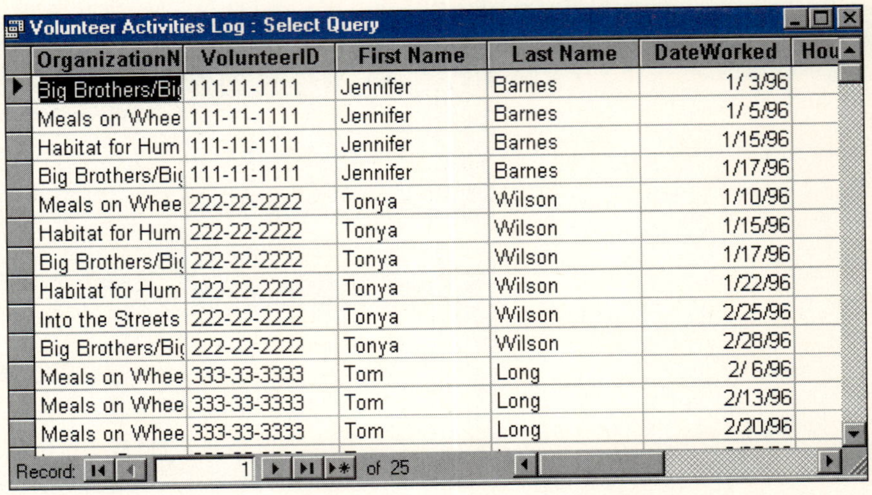

Figure 4.25

Resizing and Hiding Columns

You can adjust the size of columns to take up more or less space in datasheet view. In Figure 4.25, for example, the first column could be widened to show the full names of the organizations. Reducing the width of the other columns would allow more information to be displayed.

You will resize a column in datasheet view by dragging the right edge of its column heading in either direction until the column is the desired width. If you double-click the right edge of a column heading, Access automatically sizes the column to fit its data or column heading, whichever is larger. Choosing Column Width from the Format menu and then selecting Best Fit serves the same purpose.

Tip To avoid excess space created by a long column title, such as HoursWorked, you can select the field's Caption box in design view and type a smaller description, such as Hrs.

Figure 4.26 shows you where to position the pointer to change the width of the first column in the Volunteer Activities Log query.

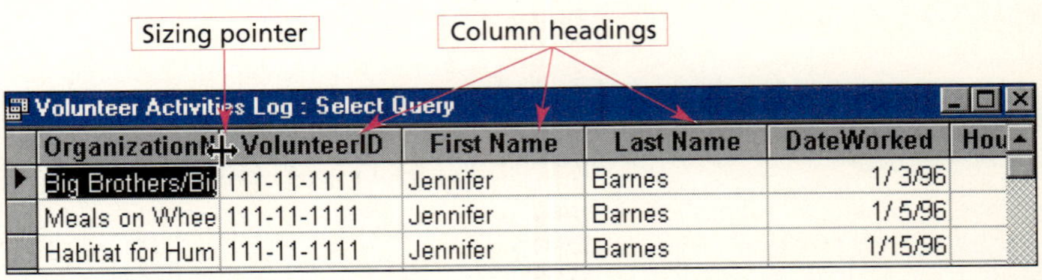

Figure 4.26

Tip You cannot use Undo to restore original column widths. To undo column width changes, you must close the datasheet without saving layout changes.

Some data should be kept confidential, such as social security numbers and pay rates. You can store such data in a table or query and hide or unhide columns displaying the data as necessary. You will find commands to hide and unhide columns on the Format menu. You can also hide a column by deselecting its Show box in design view, as shown for the VolunteerID field in Figure 4.21.

Caution When you save changes to a query, Access deletes hidden columns from the query. To avoid deletion, choose Unhide Columns from the Format menu, and check the boxes in front of the fields you want to keep. You can also select the appropriate Show boxes in design view.

In the following steps you will widen the first column in the Volunteer Activities Log query and narrow the other columns. You will also hide the VolunteerID column showing social security numbers.

To adjust the widths of columns in datasheet view:

1 Position the pointer on the right edge of the OrganizationName column heading, as shown in Figure 4.26.

2 Double-click the mouse.
The OrganizationName column automatically widens to display the longest organization name.

3 Position the pointer on the right edge of the First Name column heading.

4 Drag the pointer to the left to reduce column size, as shown in Figure 4.27.

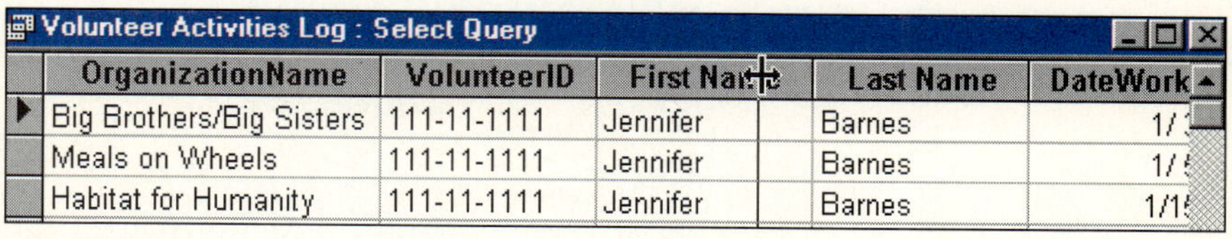

Figure 4.27

5 Release the mouse button.

6 Repeat steps 3 through 5 to reduce the size of the Last Name column.

To hide a column in datasheet view and save your changes:

1 Click within the VolunteerID field.

2 Choose Hide Columns from the Format menu.
The VolunteerID column disappears, as shown in Figure 4.20.

3 Close the query, and select Yes when prompted to save your changes.

Sorting on One or More Fields

It is often necessary to view records in a sequence different from that in which they were entered and stored in the database. Reordering of records is based on the contents of a field, which you can arrange in ascending or descending order. For example, you might organize records by last name in ascending order or by date in descending order.

The Sort Ascending and Sort Descending buttons on the toolbar shown in Figure 4.1 allow you to reorder records based on the contents of a single field. To sort on more than one field, you will use the query design view shown in Figure 4.21.

Fields controlling a multiple sort do not have to be adjacent to each other, but their columns must be in order of importance from left to right. For example, to sort records in the Volunteer Activities Log query by date worked and then by last name within each date worked, you would have to position the DateWorked field to the left of the LastName field.

In the following steps you will use both the query design view and a sort button to sort records in the Volunteer Activities Log query based on the contents of a single field. You will then rearrange columns and sort on two fields.

To sort on one field in query design view:

1 Open the Volunteer Activities Log query in design view.

> ***Tip*** The tables and the relationships among tables appear in the top half of the Select Query window. Your tables may appear in a different order that makes it harder to view the relationships. You can change the order by dragging a table by its title to a new location.

2 Click the arrow at the right end of the Sort box in the OrganizationName column to display the Sort pull-down list, as shown in Figure 4.28.

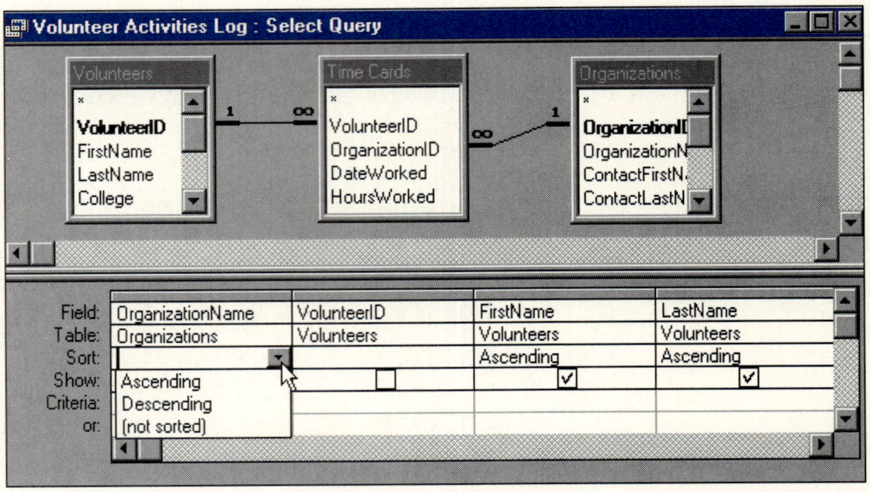

Figure 4.28

3 Select Ascending.

4 Switch to datasheet view to see the records listed in alphabetical order by organization name, as shown in Figure 4.29.

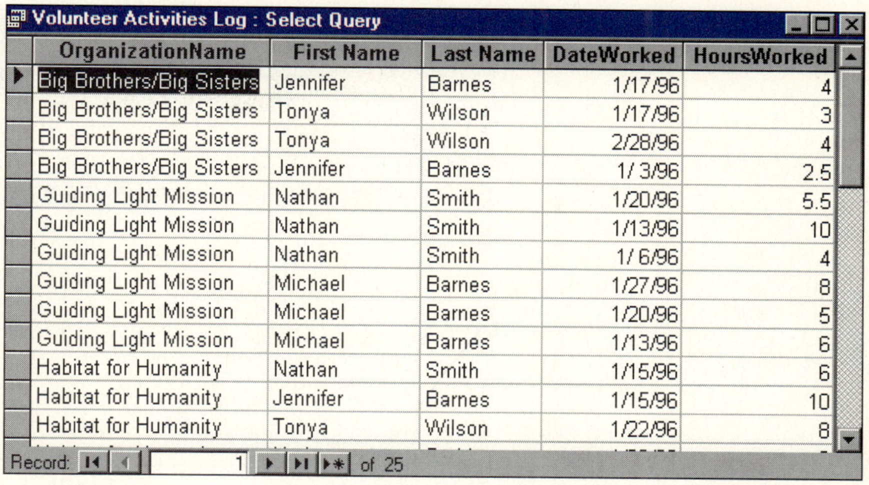

Volunteer Activities Log : Select Query

OrganizationName	First Name	Last Name	DateWorked	HoursWorked
Big Brothers/Big Sisters	Jennifer	Barnes	1/17/96	4
Big Brothers/Big Sisters	Tonya	Wilson	1/17/96	3
Big Brothers/Big Sisters	Tonya	Wilson	2/28/96	4
Big Brothers/Big Sisters	Jennifer	Barnes	1/ 3/96	2.5
Guiding Light Mission	Nathan	Smith	1/20/96	5.5
Guiding Light Mission	Nathan	Smith	1/13/96	10
Guiding Light Mission	Nathan	Smith	1/ 6/96	4
Guiding Light Mission	Michael	Barnes	1/27/96	8
Guiding Light Mission	Michael	Barnes	1/20/96	5
Guiding Light Mission	Michael	Barnes	1/13/96	6
Habitat for Humanity	Nathan	Smith	1/15/96	6
Habitat for Humanity	Jennifer	Barnes	1/15/96	10
Habitat for Humanity	Tonya	Wilson	1/22/96	8

Record: 1 of 25

Figure 4.29

To sort on one field using a Sort button:

1 Select the DateWorked column.

2 Select Sort Ascending in the toolbar.
Records appear in order by date, starting with the earliest date.

To sort on more than one field:

1 Switch to query design view.

2 Display the Sort pull-down list in the OrganizationName column, and select (not sorted).

3 Select the LastName column by clicking LastName at the top of the column.
Access highlights the entire column.

4 Position the pointer on the narrow bar above LastName, as shown in Figure 4.30.

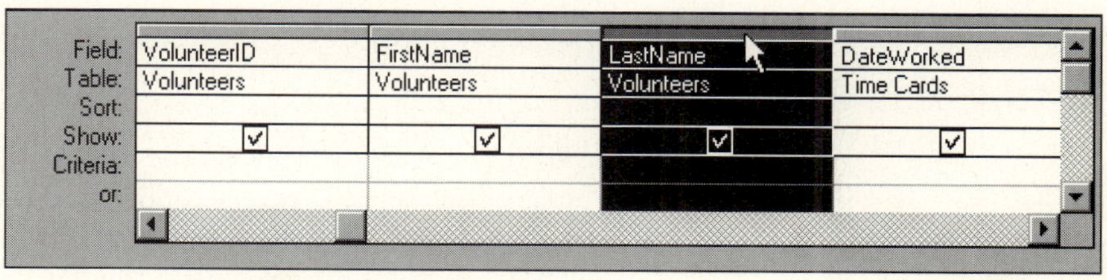

Figure 4.30

5 Drag and drop the column to the left of the FirstName column.

6 Select the Sort settings for LastName, FirstName, and DateWorked shown in Figure 4.31.

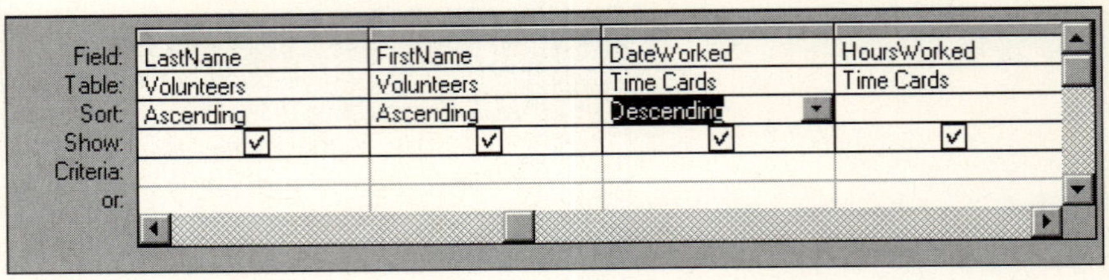

Figure 4.31

7 Switch to datasheet view to see the sorted records, as shown in Figure 4.32.

Records appear in order by last name (*Barnes* before *Long*), and then by first name within last name (*Jennifer Barnes* before *Michael Barnes*). For each student, the records then appear in order of date worked, with the most recent first.

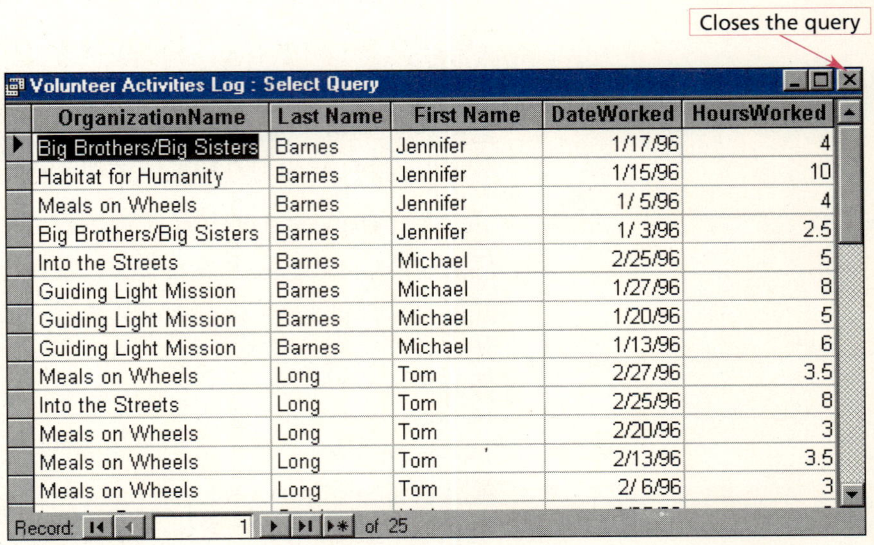

OrganizationName	Last Name	First Name	DateWorked	HoursWorked
Big Brothers/Big Sisters	Barnes	Jennifer	1/17/96	4
Habitat for Humanity	Barnes	Jennifer	1/15/96	10
Meals on Wheels	Barnes	Jennifer	1/ 5/96	4
Big Brothers/Big Sisters	Barnes	Jennifer	1/ 3/96	2.5
Into the Streets	Barnes	Michael	2/25/96	5
Guiding Light Mission	Barnes	Michael	1/27/96	8
Guiding Light Mission	Barnes	Michael	1/20/96	5
Guiding Light Mission	Barnes	Michael	1/13/96	6
Meals on Wheels	Long	Tom	2/27/96	3.5
Into the Streets	Long	Tom	2/25/96	8
Meals on Wheels	Long	Tom	2/20/96	3
Meals on Wheels	Long	Tom	2/13/96	3.5
Meals on Wheels	Long	Tom	2/ 6/96	3

Figure 4.32

Printing Results

Up to this point you viewed the results of find, filter, and query operations in a window on the screen. You can also print any of these results immediately by selecting Print in the toolbar, or you can open Page Setup and Print dialog boxes through the File menu to change settings before you print.

Figure 4.33 shows the Page Setup dialog box. You can select the Margins tab to change the top, bottom, left, and right margins. On the Page tab you can make changes to the orientation, paper, and printer.

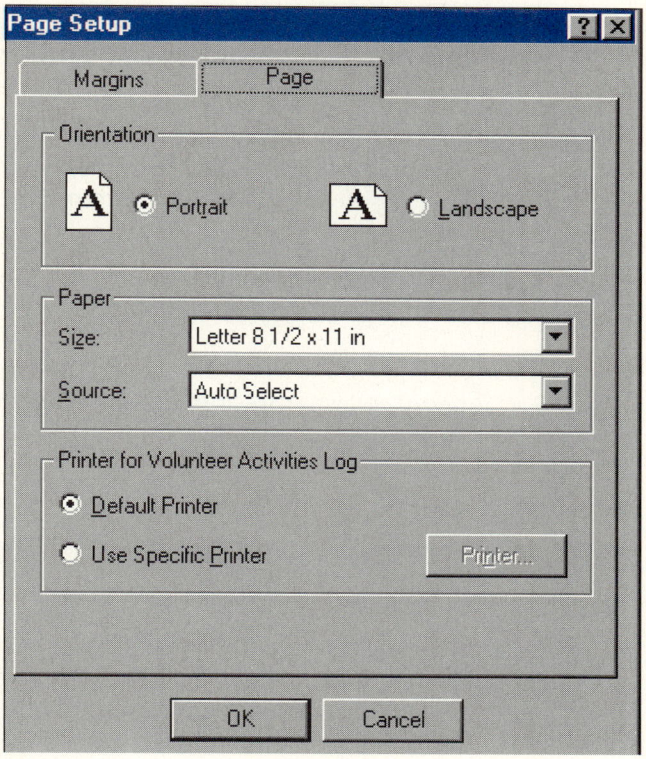

Figure 4.33

Figure 4.34 shows the Print dialog box. After you make changes as needed to the print range and the number of copies, you will select OK to begin printing.

In the following steps you will print all the records in the Volunteer Activities Log query at default settings.

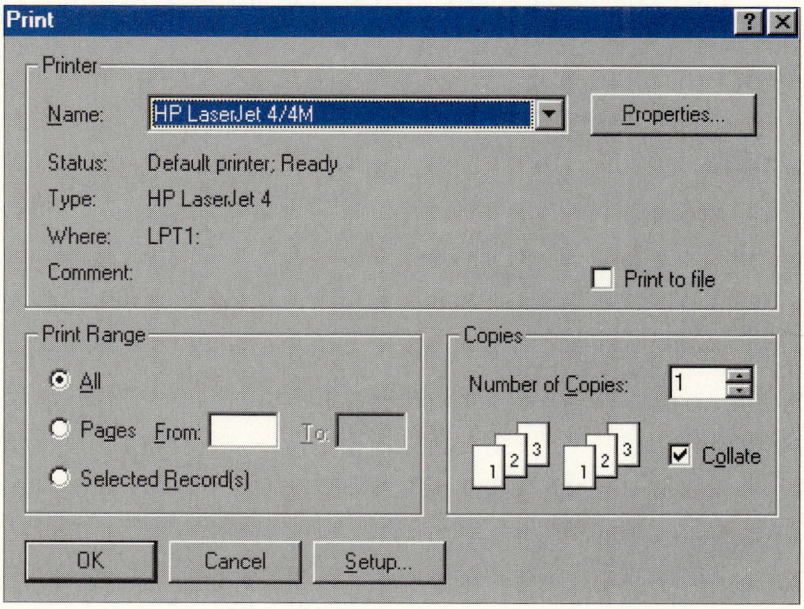

Figure 4.34

To print the current query results and close the query:

1 Select Print in the toolbar.
The records appear in a datasheet layout on paper. Access adds the name of the query as a title, places the current date in the upper-right corner, and places the page number bottom center.

2 Close the query by clicking the X button in the upper-right corner of the Select Query window, as shown in Figure 4.32, and select Yes when prompted to save your changes.

EXIT

If necessary, you can close this database now. You can then exit Access and continue this project later.

Creating Reports with Report Wizard

Filters and queries both produce lists of records, one record per row, with field names as column headings. You may, however, prefer to present data in a more formal manner. You can, for example, create output containing several title lines and header or footer information that appears at the top or bottom of each page in a multiple-page printout. You can also group similar records, create new fields based on data in existing fields, calculate subtotals as well as grand totals of numeric fields, generate mailing labels, and present data in a graph. These features are available in reports, as explained through on-screen Help.

To view on-screen Help about reports:

1 If necessary, start Access and open the Volunteer Center database.

2 Choose Answer Wizard from the Help menu.

3 Type `reports` in the Type your request box, and then select Search.

4 In the Tell Me About section, select *Reports: What they are and how they work,* and then select Display.
The Help screen shown in Figure 4.35 appears.

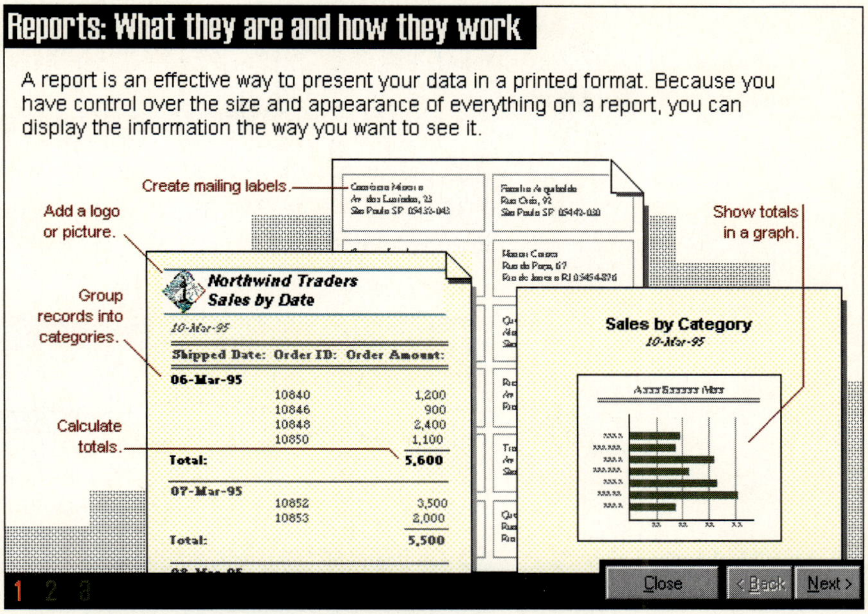

Figure 4.35

5 Read the general introduction to reports, and then select Next>.

6 Study the sample report showing which parts are stored in the report's design and which parts pull data from the database.

7 Select Next> to view the third of three Help screens, which shows a sample report in design view.

8 Select Close.

Access is a powerful database management product that allows you to design your own reports as well as take advantage of predefined features available through Report Wizard. This wizard presents a series of screens for selecting the content and appearance of a report. After you select the table or query containing the data you need, you will select fields in the order you want them to appear and specify the sort order of records. You can then select vertical or tabular layout, portrait or landscape orientation, and tell Access to adjust field widths so all fields fit on a page. You will finish your report specifications by choosing among predefined styles and naming the report.

Tip If the report you have in mind will contain all fields in order from a table or query, you can select AutoReport: Columnar or AutoReport: Tabular to create a report without responding to screen prompts.

In the following sections you will use Report Wizard to create three reports of increasing complexity for the Volunteer Center database.

Creating a List

During the database design process, users identified desired outputs, one of which was a list showing how to contact volunteers. Creating a four-column report that pulls last name, first name, local phone number, and e-mail name data from the Volunteers table will meet this information need.

To select fields and the sort order using Report Wizard:

1 Select the Reports tab, and then select New.

2 Select Report Wizard, and then select the Volunteers table, as shown in Figure 4.36.

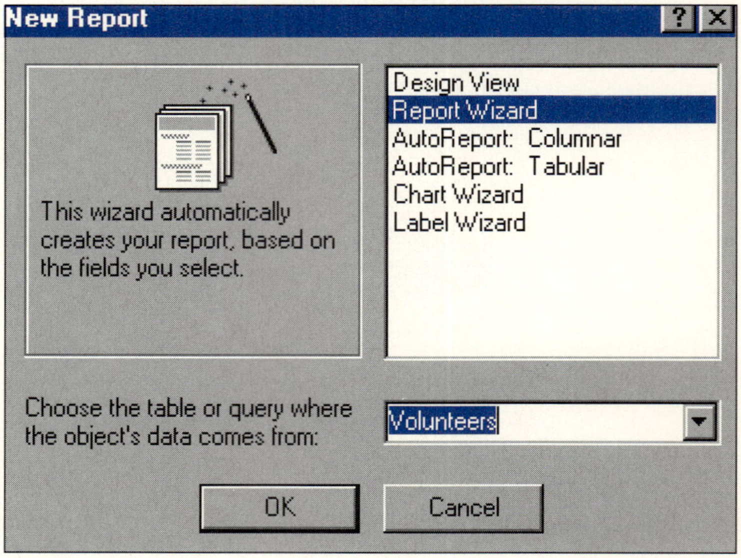

Figure 4.36

3 Select OK.

4 Select LastName, FirstName, LocalPhone, and EmailName from the Available Fields box, and then select Next>.

> ***Reminder*** You can select a field by double-clicking its name or by highlighting its name and clicking the > button.

A Report Wizard screen appears, asking if you want to add grouping levels.

5 Select Next>.

6 Click the arrow at the right end of the first sort field to display a pull-down list, as shown in Figure 4.37.

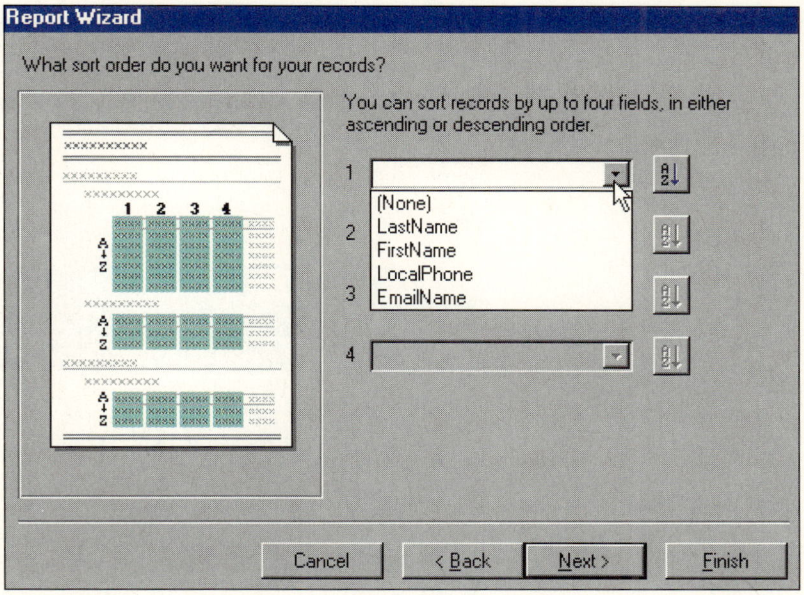

Figure 4.37

7 Select LastName.

8 Display the second sort field pull-down list, and then select FirstName.

9 Select Next>.

To complete the specifications and print the report:

1 Check that your settings match those shown in Figure 4.38, and then select Next>.

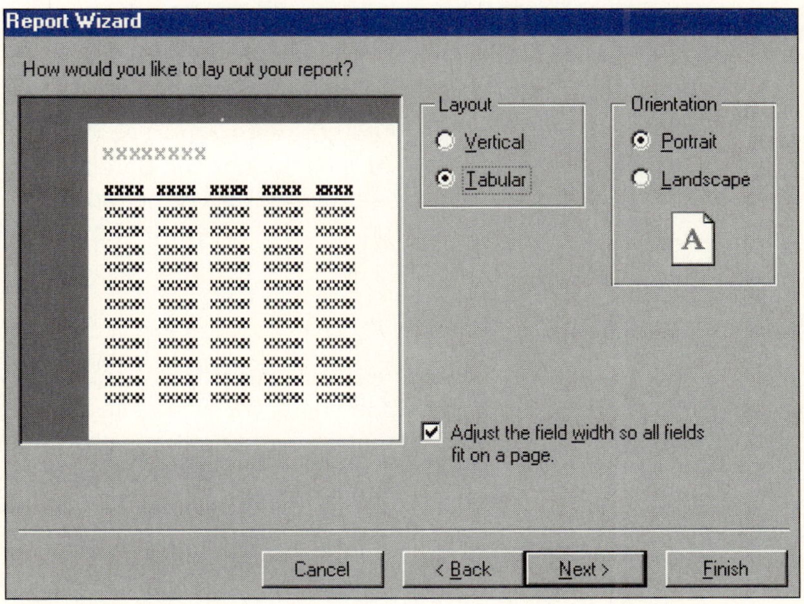

Figure 4.38

2 Select Formal as the style, and then select Next>.

3 Type **`Volunteer Contact List`** as the title of the report.

4 Select Preview the report, and then select Finish.
Report Wizard creates the report and displays it on the screen as shown in Figure 4.39.

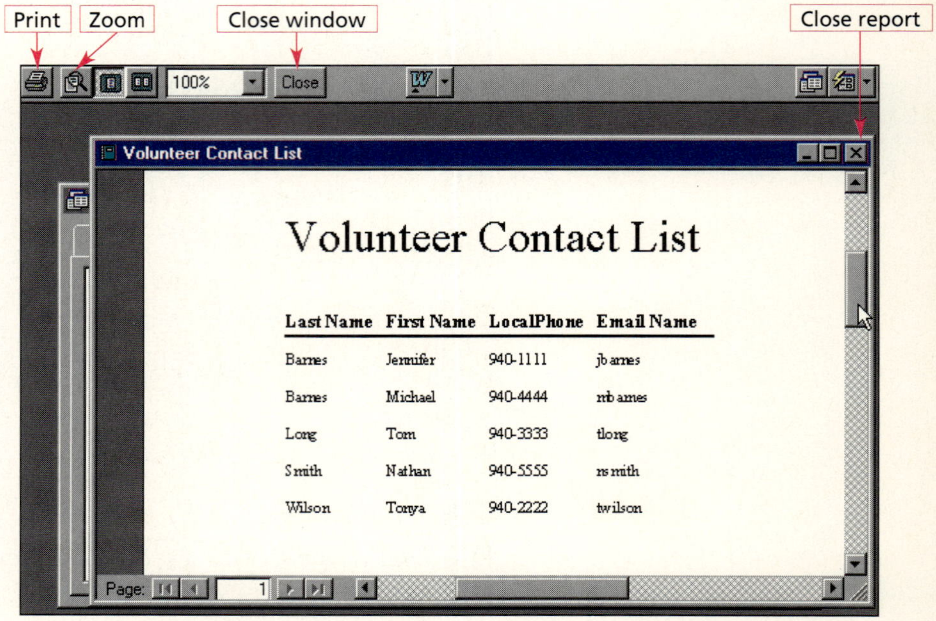

Figure 4.39

5 Select Print in the toolbar.

6 Close the report.
The report named Volunteer Contact List appears under the Reports tab in the Database window.

> ***Tip*** If you close the report by clicking the X button in the upper-right corner of the window, the Database window reappears. Selecting Close from the toolbar displays the report in design view, so you will need to close that window to return to the Database window.

Summarizing Information

Sometimes listing records row after row without a break produces all the information you need, such as an alphabetized list of volunteers and their phone numbers. Other outputs provide more information if similar records are grouped. Figure 4.40, for example, shows part of a two-page report in which records appear grouped by volunteer.

Volunteer Time Card Summary Report

First Name	Last Name	DateWorked	HoursWorked
Jennifer	Barnes		
		1/ 3/96	2.5
		1/ 5/96	4
		1/15/96	10
		1/17/96	4
Summary for 'VolunteerID' = 111111111 (4 detail records)			
Sum			20.5
Tonya	Wilson		
		1/10/96	3
		1/15/96	12
		1/17/96	3
		1/22/96	8
		2/25/96	4
		2/28/96	4
Summary for 'VolunteerID' = 222222222 (6 detail records)			
Sum			34
Tom	Long		
		2/ 6/96	3
		2/13/96	3.5
		2/20/96	3
		2/25/96	8
		2/27/96	3.5
Summary for 'VolunteerID' = 333333333 (5 detail records)			
Sum			21

Figure 4.40

On your own or by using Report Wizard, you can provide summary information based on the contents of a field, such as the total number of hours worked by each volunteer shown in Figure 4.40. You can also display the minimum and maximum values in a field, the average of all numbers in a field, and a percent of the total for each group.

In the following steps you will use Report Wizard to create the report shown in Figure 4.40. This report pulls data from two tables.

To select fields from two tables:

1 Select the Reports tab, and then select New.

2 Select Report Wizard, select the Volunteers table, and then select OK.

3 Select FirstName and LastName from the Available Fields box.

4 Display the Tables/Queries pull-down list, and then select the Time Cards table.

5 Select DateWorked and HoursWorked from the Available Fields box. Your field selections should match those shown in Figure 4.41.

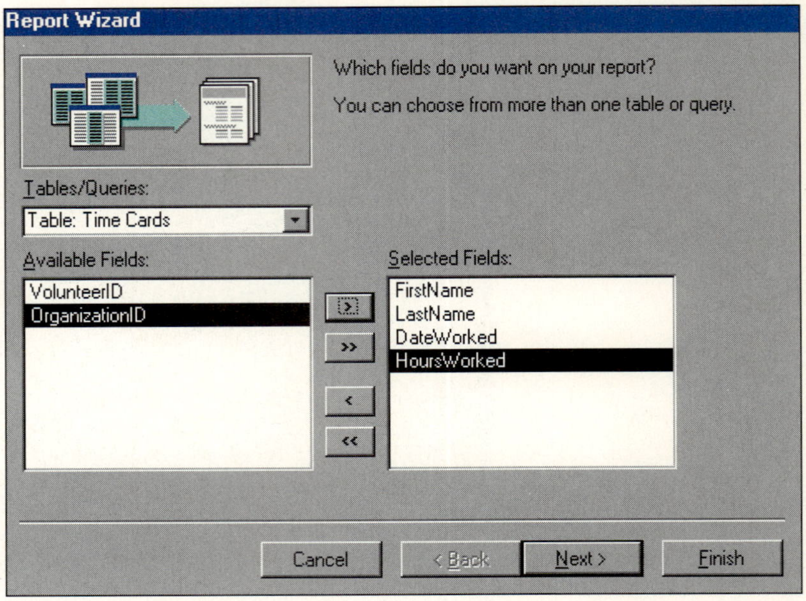

Figure 4.41

6 Select Next>.
Report Wizard asks how you want to view your data.

7 Select Next> to accept viewing your data by volunteers.
Report Wizard asks if you want to add any grouping levels.

8 Select Next> to accept grouping on volunteer name.

To specify the sort order and complete the report specifications:

1 Display the first sort box pull-down list and select DateWorked.
Your setting for sort order of detail records should match that shown in Figure 4.42.

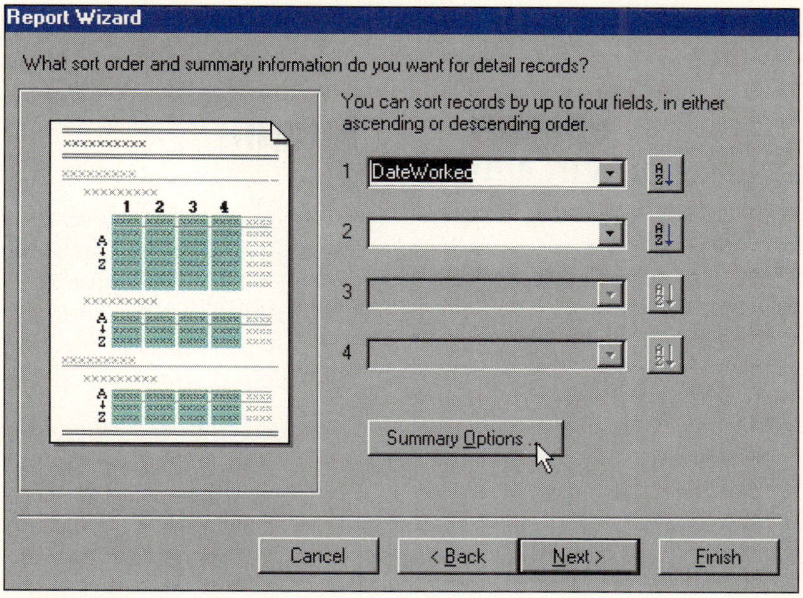

Figure 4.42

2 Select Summary Options.

3 Select the settings shown in Figure 4.43, and then select OK.

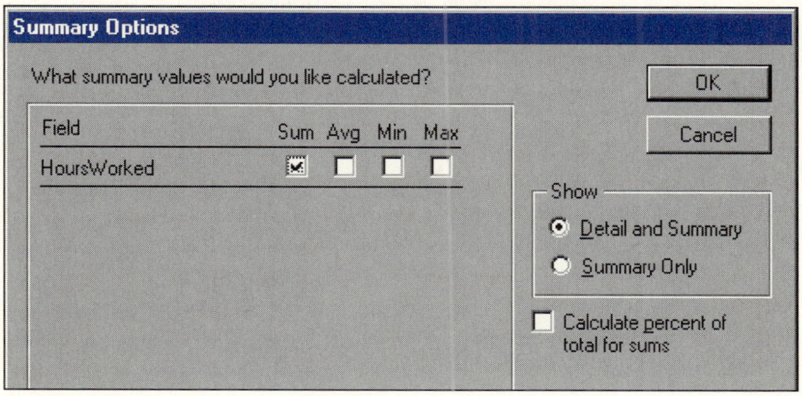

Figure 4.43

4 Select Next>.

5 Select Stepped layout, Portrait orientation, and Adjusts the field width so all fields fit on a page.

6 Select Next>.

7 Select Formal style, and then select Next>.

8 Type `Volunteer Time Card Summary Report` as the title of the report.

9 Select Preview the report, and then select Finish.
Report Wizard creates the report and displays it on the screen.

10 Use vertical and horizontal scroll bars to view the report.

11 Select Print in the toolbar.
Access prints the report, part of which is shown in Figure 4.40.

12 Close the report.
Volunteer Time Card Summary Report appears under the Reports tab in the Database window.

Using Subgroups in a Report

Occasionally you may want to group records within a group. In the previous report a group consisted of the dates and hours worked by one volunteer. Suppose you want to know the number of hours each student worked for a specific organization, as well as the total hours overall. You can display this information by grouping on the contents of the last name and first name fields and then subgrouping on the contents of the organization field name.

In the following steps you will use Report Wizard to create a report with subgroups. This report pulls data from three tables.

> ***Tip*** You could copy the previous report and then modify it in design view to include subgroupings, but using Report Wizard to create a new report is easier. On-screen Help provides information about saving a database object.

To select fields from three tables:

1 Select the Reports tab, and then select New.

2 Select Report Wizard, select the Volunteers table, and then select OK.

3 Select FirstName and LastName from the Available Fields box.

4 Display the Tables/Queries pull-down list, and then select the Organizations table.

5 Select OrganizationName from the Available Fields box.

6 Display the Tables/Queries pull-down list, and then select the Time Cards table.

7 Select DateWorked and HoursWorked from the Available Fields box.
Your field selections should match those shown in Figure 4.44.

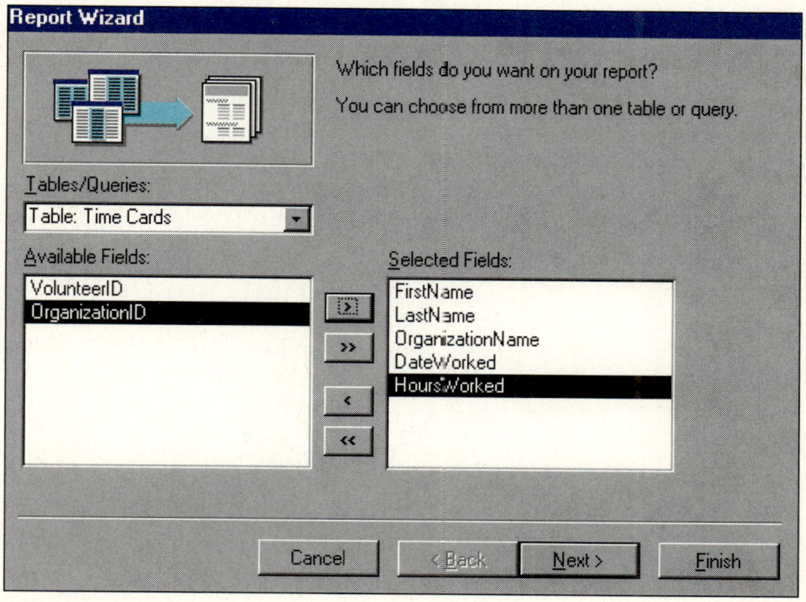

Figure 4.44

8 Select Next>.
Report Wizard asks how you want to view your data.

9 Select Next> to accept viewing your data by volunteers.
Report Wizard asks if you want to add any grouping levels.

10 Double-click OrganizationName to select it.
Your grouping levels should match those shown in Figure 4.45.

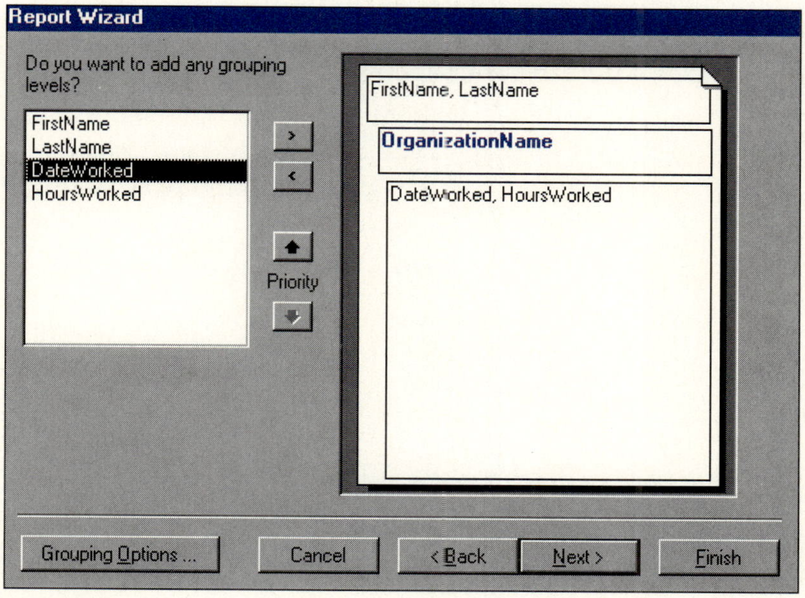

Figure 4.45

11 Select Next>.

To specify sort order and complete the report specifications:

1 Display the first sort box pull-down list and select DateWorked.

2 Select Summary Options, check Sum, and then select OK.

3 Select Next>.
Database Wizard displays layout and orientation options.

4 Select Next> to accept the current layout and orientation settings.

5 Select Next> to accept the current style setting.

6 Type **`Volunteer Time Report by Organization`** as the title of the report.

7 Select Preview the report, and then select Finish.
Report Wizard creates the report and displays it on the screen.

8 Use vertical and horizontal scroll bars to view the report.

9 Select Print in the toolbar.
Access prints the report, part of which is shown in Figure 4.46.

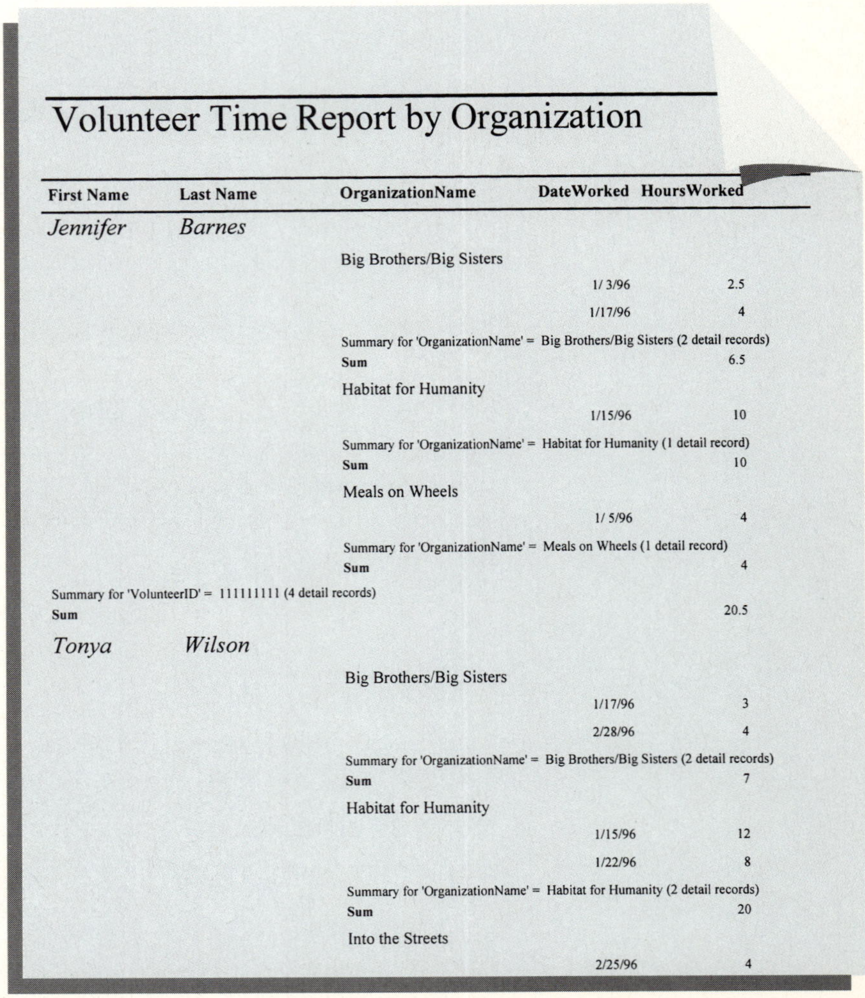

Volunteer Time Report by Organization

First Name	Last Name	OrganizationName	DateWorked	HoursWorked
Jennifer	*Barnes*			
		Big Brothers/Big Sisters		
			1/ 3/96	2.5
			1/17/96	4
		Summary for 'OrganizationName' = Big Brothers/Big Sisters (2 detail records)		
		Sum		6.5
		Habitat for Humanity		
			1/15/96	10
		Summary for 'OrganizationName' = Habitat for Humanity (1 detail record)		
		Sum		10
		Meals on Wheels		
			1/ 5/96	4
		Summary for 'OrganizationName' = Meals on Wheels (1 detail record)		
		Sum		4
Summary for 'VolunteerID' = 111111111 (4 detail records)				
Sum				20.5
Tonya	*Wilson*			
		Big Brothers/Big Sisters		
			1/17/96	3
			2/28/96	4
		Summary for 'OrganizationName' = Big Brothers/Big Sisters (2 detail records)		
		Sum		7
		Habitat for Humanity		
			1/15/96	12
			1/22/96	8
		Summary for 'OrganizationName' = Habitat for Humanity (2 detail records)		
		Sum		20
		Into the Streets		
			2/25/96	4

Figure 4.46

10 Close the report.
Volunteer Time Report by Organization appears under the Reports tab in the Database window.

11 Close the database.

THE NEXT STEP

In this project you created filters, queries, and reports to convert data into information. In the process you also sorted output based on the contents of one or more fields and printed results.

As a next step, you might look into other features in each area. For example, learn how to set up complex select and sort criteria using the Advanced Filter/Sort window. Discover the purpose of a cross-tab query. Make changes to the layout of a report in design view, such as rearranging fields and adding a picture or logo. Determine the results you can achieve using Chart Wizard and Label Wizard. You can also set up your own switchboard system to execute common tasks.

This concludes Project 4. You can either exit Access or go on to work the Study Questions, Review Exercises, and Assignments.

SUMMARY AND EXERCISES

Summary

- Data are the raw facts or assumptions stored in a database. Information is data presented in a usable form.
- You can create information using techniques to select, organize, format, and display data.
- Find operations and filters allow you to focus on records in one table that meet specified criteria. A find operation moves the cursor to the next record meeting the search condition. A filter hides records that do not meet search criteria.
- You can filter by selection or filter by form, or you can specify both sort and filter conditions in the Advanced Filter/Sort window.
- Use a query instead of a filter if you want to restrict display of fields as well as records. A select query can retrieve data from more than one table.
- Sort Ascending and Sort Descending buttons on the toolbar allow you to reorder records based on the contents of a single field. You can sort on more than one field using query design view.
- Access provides a variety of wizards to help you create queries and reports, including Simple Query Wizard and Report Wizard.
- Reports present data in a more formal way than queries or filters. Report features include title lines, header or footer information, groups of similar information, subtotals and grand totals of numeric fields, and new fields based on data in existing fields.

Key Terms and Operations

Key Terms
And criteria
data
expression
filter
information
Or criteria
query
report
select query
Simple Query Wizard

Operations
Find a match
Filter by selection
Filter by form
Create a select query
Resize a column
Hide a column
Sort on one or more fields
Print results
Create a list
Summarize information
Use subgroups in a report

Study Questions

Multiple Choice

1. Which feature would you use to locate each occurrence of a particular value?
   a. Search
   b. Find
   c. Replace
   d. Locate
2. If you do not know the exact value you are looking for in a table, which of the following symbols can you use to substitute for more than one character in your search condition?
   a. #
   b. $
   c. ?
   d. None of the above.
3. You can limit screen display to those records that meet one or more search conditions at a time by using Filter By
   a. Query
   b. Form
   c. Selection
   d. Sort
4. Which of the following is true about resizing or hiding columns?
   a. To avoid excess space created by a long column title, you can use a smaller title in the field's Caption property.
   b. When you save changes to a query, Access removes hidden columns from a query.
   c. To avoid removal of hidden columns, unhide the columns before saving changes to a query.
   d. All of the above.
5. Fields controlling a multiple-field sort
   a. must be adjacent to each other.
   b. must be in order of importance from left to right in the table.
   c. must contain the same data type.
   d. All of the above.

6. Which of the following is true about sorting data?
   a. You often need to view records in a sequence different from that in which they were entered and stored in the database.
   b. Reordering of records is based on the contents of a field.
   c. You can arrange records in ascending or descending order.
   d. All of the above.

7. Which of the following is not one of four actions concerning the conversion of data into information as described in this project?
   a. selecting
   b. saving
   c. formatting
   d. displaying

8. Which of the following would be valid search criteria in a table containing city and state fields?
   a. filtering for city Indianapolis and state Indiana
   b. filtering for city Indianapolis and city Cincinnati
   c. Both a and b.
   d. Neither a nor b.

9. Which Wizard can you use to create a select query?
   a. Select Query Wizard
   b. Simple Query Wizard
   c. Cross-tab Query Wizard
   d. None of the above.

10. Which is a true statement about using Report Wizard to create output?
   a. You can create a simple list of data.
   b. You can group and summarize data on a common field of data.
   c. You can subgroup but not summarize data within an existing group.
   d. Both a and b.

Short Answer

1. What term describes data presented in a usable form?
2. In this project you read about four actions to convert data into information. Which of the four actions refers to arranging data based on the contents of one or more fields?
3. What options do you have to display fields from more than one table?
4. What wildcard character in a search condition accepts any single number?
5. After you display a set of records that meet your first search condition, you can select another value from within that set. Give an example other than the one provided in the text.
6. When using Filter By Form, you can enter a search condition as an expression. What expression would tell Access to select only those records in which a value was less than or equal to 50?
7. What wizard would you use to create formal displays of your data, complete with titles, headers, and footers?
8. Use a __________ to specify a condition for record selection, and find each record containing the data you specify.

9. A ________ provides an effective way to print professional-looking output based on a table or query.
10. Sorting data in reverse order (z to a) or from the largest to the smallest (9 to 0) is called ________ order.

For Discussion

Answer the following discussion questions assuming that you have created a two-table Access database named Lawn Care. One table named Customers contains one record per customer, with fields showing customer number, name, address, and phone number data. The other table named Services tracks the type of service performed, date performed, time involved, and fee charged.

1. Assume that your Customers table has over 200 records, including 3 customers with the last name Smith. Describe how you could quickly look up the phone number of Joseph Smith.
2. What steps would you take to produce a list of customers and their phone numbers, arranged in order by customer last name and then by first name within duplicate last names?
3. You can filter records based on two exact-match search conditions, either one of which would cause a record to be selected and you can filter records based on two exact-match search conditions, both of which must be met before a record is selected. Give an example of each related to the Lawn Care database.
4. A query can retrieve data from more than one table. Describe a query you might create involving both tables of the Lawn Care database. Explain also how to print query results.
5. You can group and sort records using Report Wizard. Describe a report you might create exhibiting grouped and sorted records. Explain also the steps involved in using Report Wizard to create the report.

Review Exercises

In Project 3 review exercises you modified field properties, set relationships, created forms, and entered data in the Job Search database. In these review exercises you will convert data into information by finding matches, setting filters, and creating queries and reports.

Finding Matches

1. Start Access, open the Job Search database, and open the Applications table in datasheet view.
2. Click within the OpenPosition column, select Find in the toolbar, and specify Data Entry as the search condition.
3. Find each occurrence of Data Entry.
4. Find each occurrence of News at the beginning of the InfoSource field.

Filtering by Selection

1. Display the Applications table in datasheet view, select (highlight) Data Entry in one of the OpenPosition fields, and then select Filter By Selection in the toolbar.

2. Within the records limited to Data Entry positions, select Newspaper Ad in one of the InfoSource fields, and then select Filter By Selection again.
3. Remove the filter.

Filtering by Form

1. Display the Applications table in datasheet view, and select Filter By Form in the toolbar.
2. Specify Data Entry or Lawn Care as the open position, and then select Apply Filter.
3. Check that only records containing Data Entry or Lawn Care in the OpenPosition field appear on the screen, and then remove the filter.
4. Use Filter By Form to display only those records for which the rate per hour is greater than or equal to $10, and then remove the filter.
5. Close the table without saving your changes.

Creating a Query

1. Start Simple Query Wizard and select the CompanyName field from the Companies table.
2. Select the OpenPosition, SendDate, and ResponseDate fields from the Applications table.
3. Name the detail query Applications Log, and then view the results.
4. Sort on company name, adjust column widths as necessary, and then print the results.
5. Close the table without saving your changes.

Creating a Report

1. Start Report Wizard, select the Companies table, and then select the CompanyName field.
2. Select the Applications table, and then select the OpenPosition, RatePerHour, ResponseDate, and InterviewInvite fields.
3. View data by Companies, and set up grouping on OpenPosition and sort in descending order on RatePerHour.
4. Select Stepped layout, Portrait orientation, and Adjust the field width so all fields fit on a page.
5. Select the style of your choice, and then name the report Responses Grouped by Job Type.
6. Preview, print, and close the report.

Assignments

Exploring Other Wizards

You now have experience using Answer, Database, Table, Lookup, Simple Query, Form, and Report Wizards. Use on-screen Help to learn about four other wizards, including Chart Wizard and Label Wizard. Write a few sentences describing the purpose of each of the four wizards.

Comparing Select Queries and Filters

Select queries and filters both restrict display of records to those meeting specified criteria. Display Answer Wizard, enter select queries as the search condition, and then select *Similarities and differences between select queries and filters* in the Tell Me About section. Summarize your findings.

Learning About Action Queries

In this project you used Simple Query Wizard to create a select query. Now use on-screen Help to learn about action queries. Write a paragraph summarizing your findings.

Putting On a Fund-Raiser III

Using the fund-raising database you created in prior assignments, convert data into information. Find and filter records in one table at a time. Create and save one or more queries that pull data from multiple tables. Preview, print, and save a variety of reports consistent with desired outputs identified in the database design phase.

PART VI

Integrated Project 2

Integrated Project 2: Linking an Access Database File to a Word Document

Objectives

After completing this project, you will be able to:

- Link a Word document to an Access database object
- Display the linked object as a data field in the Word document
- Display the linked object as a table in the Word document
- Update the linked object in the Word document
- Link a query to the Word document
- Format the linked object

The first integrated project introduced you to OLE (object linking and embedding). In that project you embedded an Excel worksheet by inserting the source file into a Word document. You then updated the object by updating the Word document. In this project you will also insert an object, an Access database. Instead of embedding the source file, however, you will create a link between the Word document and the source file

A linked object is treated differently than an embedded object. When you link an object, you do not actually insert the object into the target file. The target file stores only the location of the source file. This means that each time an object is updated, the source file must be available. The source file must have the same name and location as it did when it was first linked; otherwise, Word won't be able to find the source file.

Linking displays an image of the source file in the target file. When the object is an Access database, the image displayed is a Word table. You can also display the link itself, which is displayed as a ***field code.*** The field code contains only the location of the source file and not the contents of the source file. Because the source file is not included in the target file, you do not have the same file size concerns you have when you embed a file. The contents of the source file remain separate from the target file, so the size of the target file doesn't grow as large as it can when you embed an object.

CASE STUDY: CREATING A LINK

The report you created in the first integrated project collected survey results from a national taste-test. Respondents tasted a variety of coffee roasts. The results were tallied by state and entered into an Excel worksheet. You created a Word document to present the data and embedded the Excel worksheet into the report. Company president, Dr. Gardener, and his staff are so excited about tracking the survey on a daily basis that they have asked you to expand the contents of the report. They want to see the results from another survey the marketing department is taking. This survey queries food stores and gourmet coffee shops to see if they will sell the new European blend. The president's staff wants to know which stores have been contacted and which stores have agreed to carry the new blend.

Designing the Solution

You could create another worksheet and embed it in your Word document, just like you did in the first integrated project. The challenge, however, is that this data will be collected by the marketing department. They have their own computers, which are connected to the network, and they have control over the database in their department. This data will constantly change as the marketing department collects new data and modifies the database to meet the needs of the president and his staff. It is impractical to reproduce the data from the marketing database every day for the daily report. The best option is to create a link to the marketing database. Then each morning you can update the Word document with the new data from the database and print the report.

CREATING THE ACCESS DATABASE

Even though this database will be maintained by the marketing department, your boss asked you to create it for them.

To create an Access database:

1 Select the Access button in the Shortcut Bar.

Tip If the Shortcut Bar does not start automatically when Windows 95 is loaded, use the Start button on the Windows 95 Taskbar to select the Shortcut Bar icon from the appropriate cascading menu. Once the Shortcut Bar is displayed, select Access.

2 Choose Blank Database in the Create a New Database Using portion of the Microsoft Access dialog box, or select New from the File menu and then select the Blank Database icon.
The File New Database dialog box appears.

3 Select drive A: from the Save in list box.

4 Type **`Potential Marketing Channels`** in the File name text box.
The screen now looks like Figure 2.1.

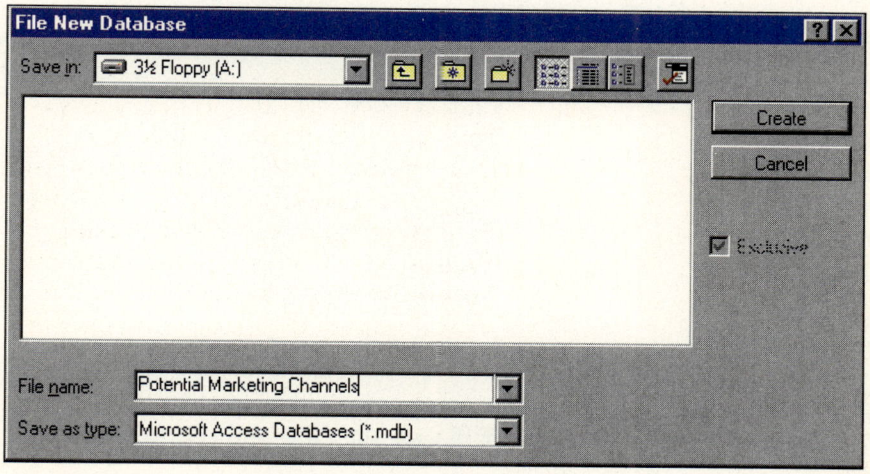

Figure 2.1

5 Select Create to close the dialog box and create the database.

6 Create a Microsoft Access table using the skills and steps you learned in the Microsoft Access projects.
Table 2.1 shows the database structure.

Table 2.1

Field Name	Data Type	Field Size
ID Number	AutoNumber (primary key)	Long Integer
Business Name	Text	35
Survey Response	Text	50

7 Save the table as Market Survey Results.

8 Open the database table and enter the data as shown in Figure 2.2.

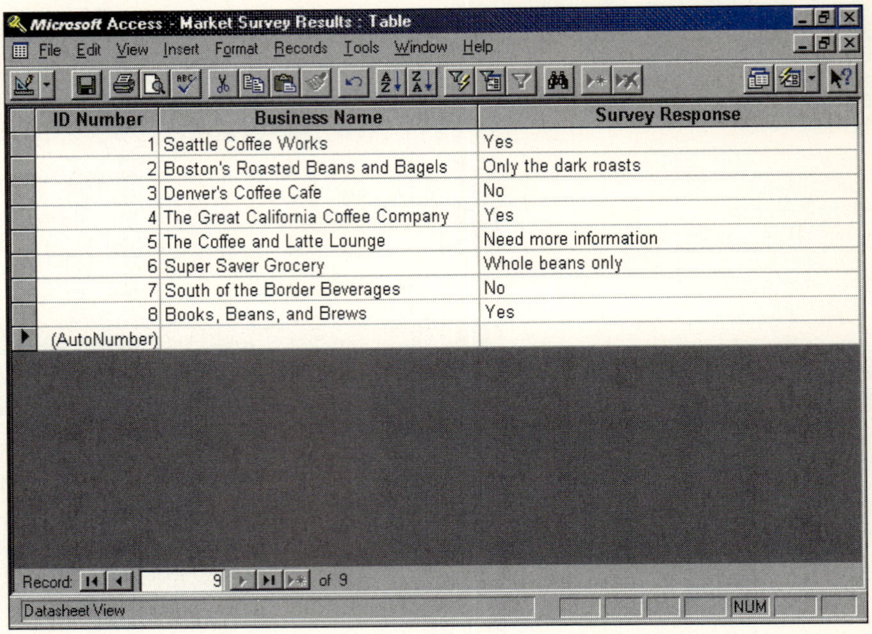

ID Number	Business Name	Survey Response
1	Seattle Coffee Works	Yes
2	Boston's Roasted Beans and Bagels	Only the dark roasts
3	Denver's Coffee Cafe	No
4	The Great California Coffee Company	Yes
5	The Coffee and Latte Lounge	Need more information
6	Super Saver Grocery	Whole beans only
7	South of the Border Beverages	No
8	Books, Beans, and Brews	Yes
(AutoNumber)		

Figure 2.2

9 Save the table and exit Access.

UPDATING THE WORD DOCUMENT

Now it's time to get your report ready to receive the new database. In the steps that follow, you will open the Word document you created in the first integrated project and revise it slightly.

To update the Word document:

1 Open Word and the Updated New Product Report.doc file.

> ***Tip*** If you did not complete the review exercises at the end of Integrated Project 1, ask your instructor for the file Integrated Project 1.doc.

2 Modify the font setting so that all text in the Word document is 12-point Arial.

3 Position the insertion point at the end of the document, and type the following paragraph:

`As a result of the positive feedback from the taste-test surveys, we are petitioning gourmet coffee shops and grocery stores to see if they will carry our new product. The database below shows the stores we have contacted and their responses to carrying the new coffee blends we offer.`

4 Press (ENTER) three times.

5 Save the file as My Updated Project.

The document now looks like Figure 2.3.

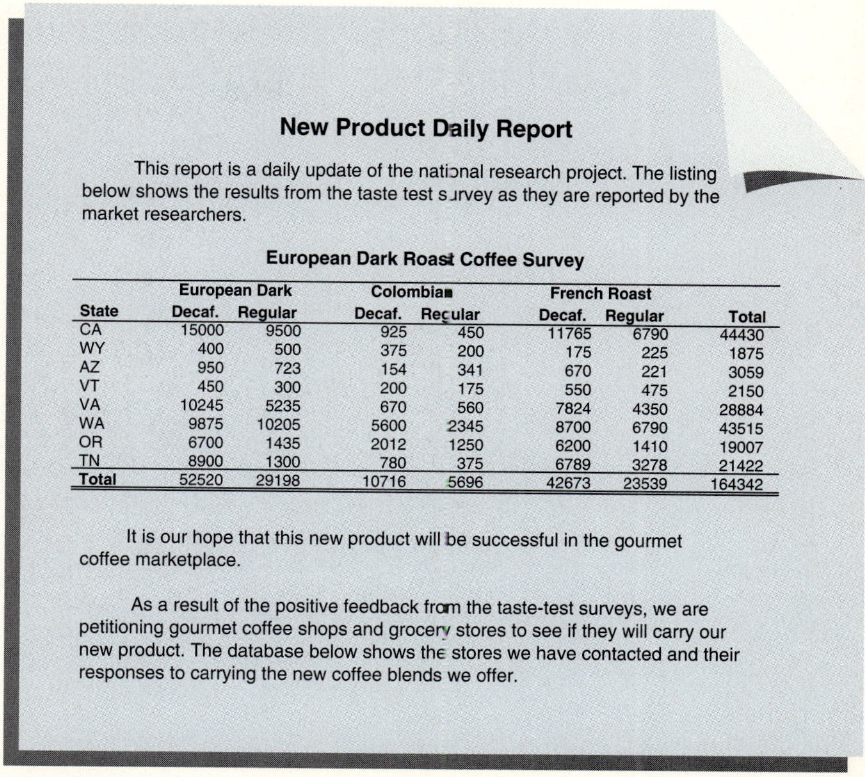

New Product Daily Report

This report is a daily update of the national research project. The listing below shows the results from the taste test survey as they are reported by the market researchers.

European Dark Roast Coffee Survey

	European Dark		Colombian		French Roast		
State	**Decaf.**	**Regular**	**Decaf.**	**Regular**	**Decaf.**	**Regular**	**Total**
CA	15000	9500	925	450	11765	6790	44430
WY	400	500	375	200	175	225	1875
AZ	950	723	154	341	670	221	3059
VT	450	300	200	175	550	475	2150
VA	10245	5235	670	560	7824	4350	28884
WA	9875	10205	5600	2345	8700	6790	43515
OR	6700	1435	2012	1250	6200	1410	19007
TN	8900	1300	780	375	6789	3278	21422
Total	52520	29198	10716	5696	42673	23539	164342

It is our hope that this new product will be successful in the gourmet coffee marketplace.

As a result of the positive feedback from the taste-test surveys, we are petitioning gourmet coffee shops and grocery stores to see if they will carry our new product. The database below shows the stores we have contacted and their responses to carrying the new coffee blends we offer.

Figure 2.3

Linking the Database

With your descriptive paragraph in place, you can now link to the Market Survey Results table. Your first step will be to activate field codes so the linked data will be displayed as a code.

To activate field codes:

1 Choose Options from the Tools menu.

2 Select the View tab, and then select the Field Codes option so it is checked, as shown in Figure 2.4.

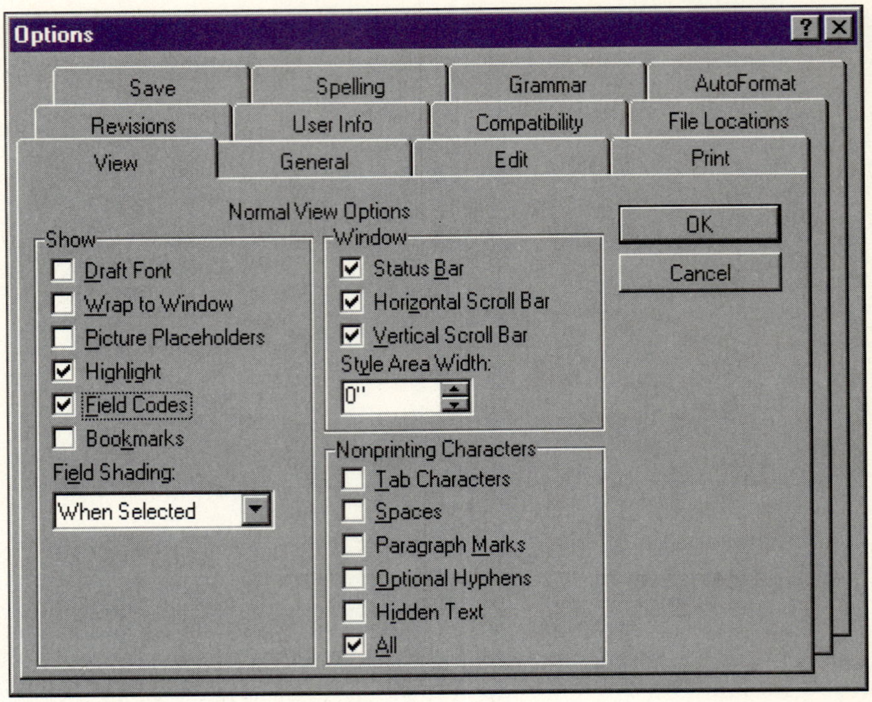

Figure 2.4

If a checkmark already appears next to the Field Codes option, do not select the option.

3 Select OK to close the dialog box.
Now you can create the link between the two documents.

> ***Tip*** You will notice that the embedded worksheet is no longer visible in the Word document, but has been replaced with a field code indicating the name of the embedded worksheet object. You may view the embedded worksheet at any time by deselecting the Field Codes option in the View tab of the Options dialog box.

To link the Access table:

1 Choose Database from the Insert menu.
The Database dialog box appears as shown in Figure 2.5.

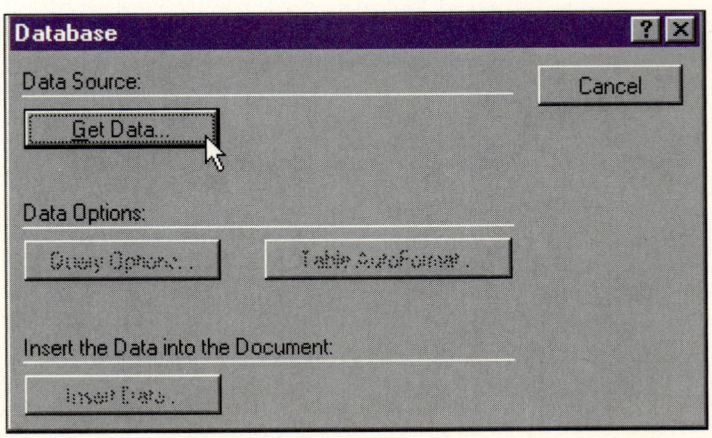

Figure 2.5

2 Select Get Data.
The Open Data Source dialog box appears.

3 Select *MS Access Databases (*.mdb)* from the Files of type text box, as shown in Figure 2.6.

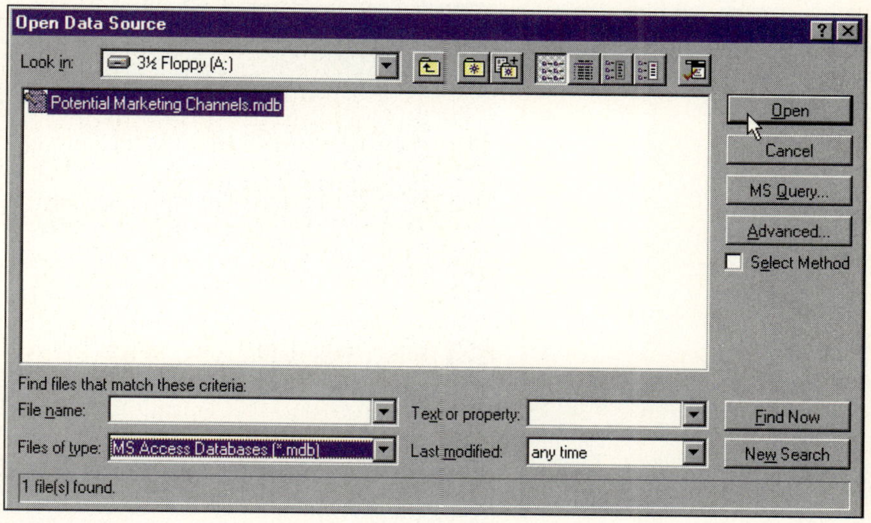

Figure 2.6

4 Select drive A, select *Potential Marketing Channels.mdb,* and then select Open.
The Microsoft Access dialog box appears as shown in Figure 2.7.

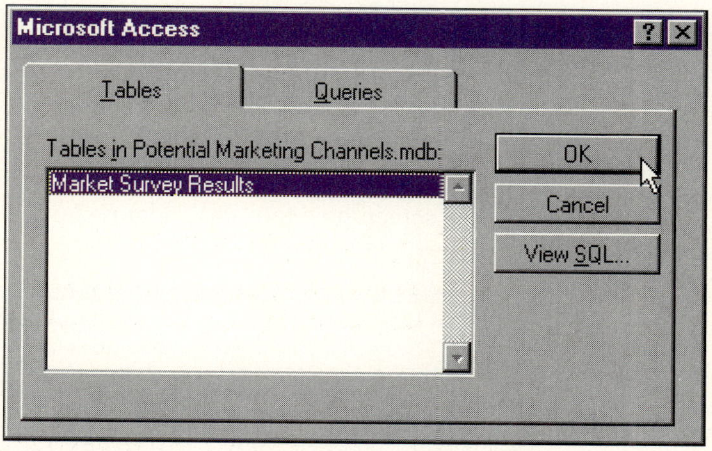

Figure 2.7

5 Select the Tables tab and the Market Survey Results table, and then select OK.
The Database dialog box appears as shown in Figure 2.8.

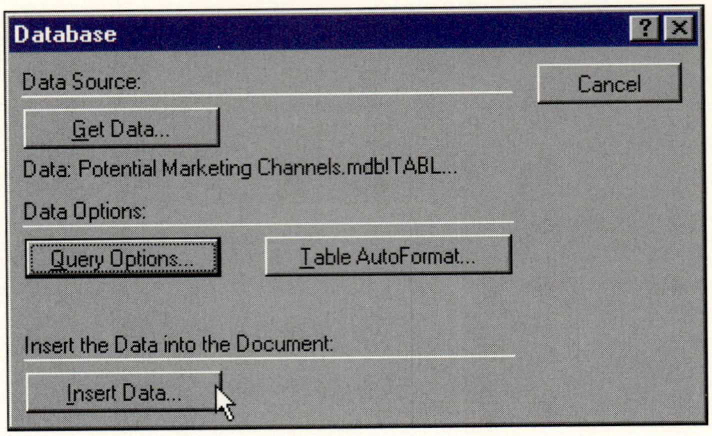

Figure 2.8

6 Select Insert Data.
The Insert Data dialog box appears as shown in Figure 2.9.

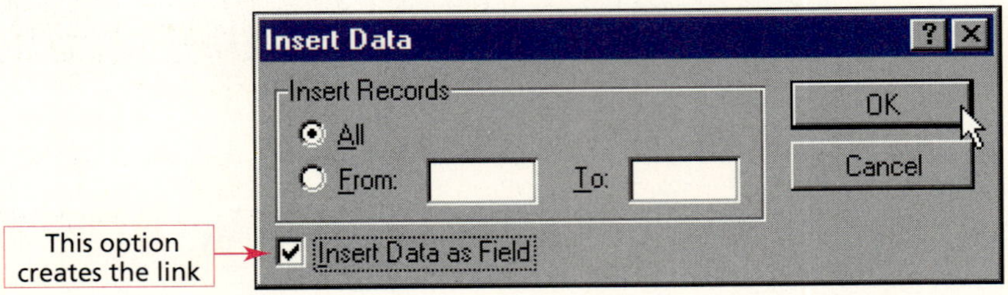

Figure 2.9

7 Select the Insert Data as Field check box.
Selecting this option ensures that the database will be a linked object and cannot be updated in Word. If this option is not selected, the data will be inserted as a Word table.

8 Select OK.
The screen now looks like Figure 2.10.

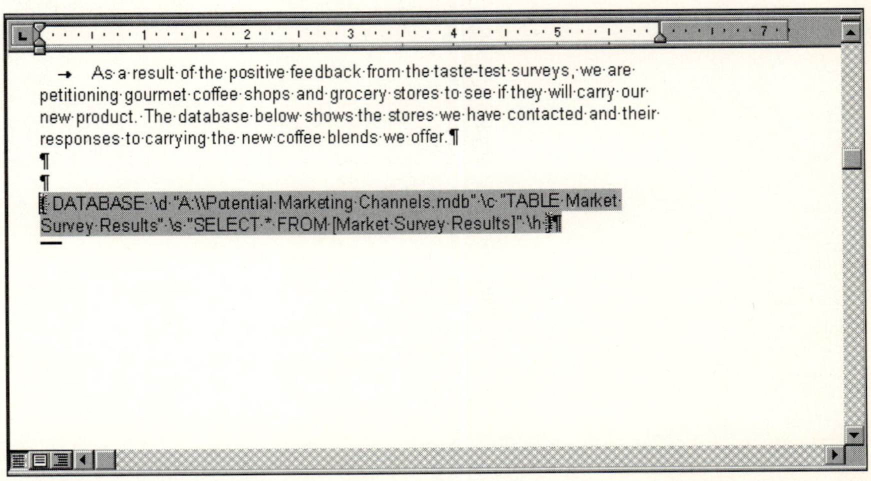

Figure 2.10

Quick Fix If your data looks like a Word table and not the field code shown in Figure 2.10, you probably did not select the View options properly. Choose Options from the Tools menu. Select the View tab, and then select the Field Codes option. If this option is already selected (a check mark appears next to it), select the table in your document and press (DELETE) Go back to step 1 and insert the database again, being sure to select the Insert Data as Field option from the Insert Data dialog box.

To save and view the linked document:

1 Select the Save button from the toolbar to save My Updated Project.doc.

2 Select the Print Preview button to view the document.
Notice that even though the database field code was displayed in the document, the actual data is displayed in the Print Preview window just as it will be printed, as shown in Figure 2.11.

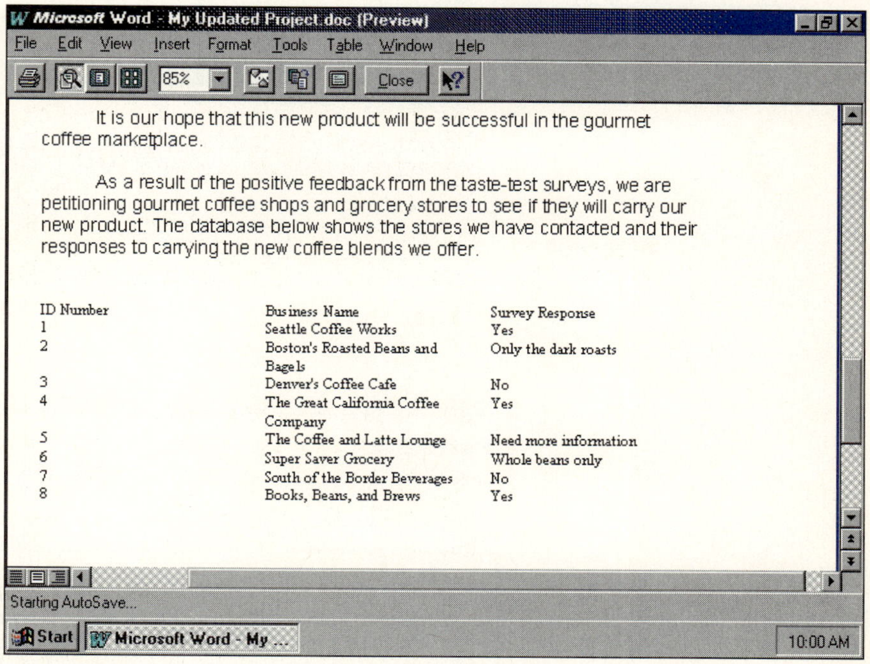

Figure 2.11

3 Close the Print Preview window.

VIEWING THE LINKED OBJECT IN THE WORD DOCUMENT

When you created the linked object, you selected the Insert Data as Field option. This option actually establishes the link by inserting a field code in the document that stores the location of the database. You then used Print Preview to see the image of the data. You can, however, display the object's image in the Word document without having to activate Print Preview. This is done through the Options choice on the Tools menu. As you turn the Field Codes option on and off, the linked database is displayed as either a field code, as shown in Figure 2.12, or as a Word table, as shown in Figure 2.13. (The table in Figure 2.13 is shaded to help you see that it is not an ordinary Word table.)

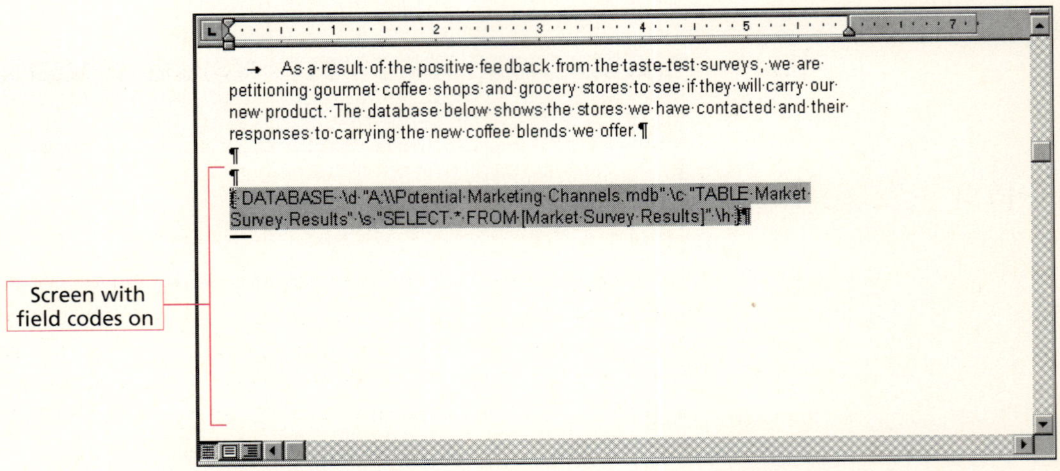

Figure 2.12

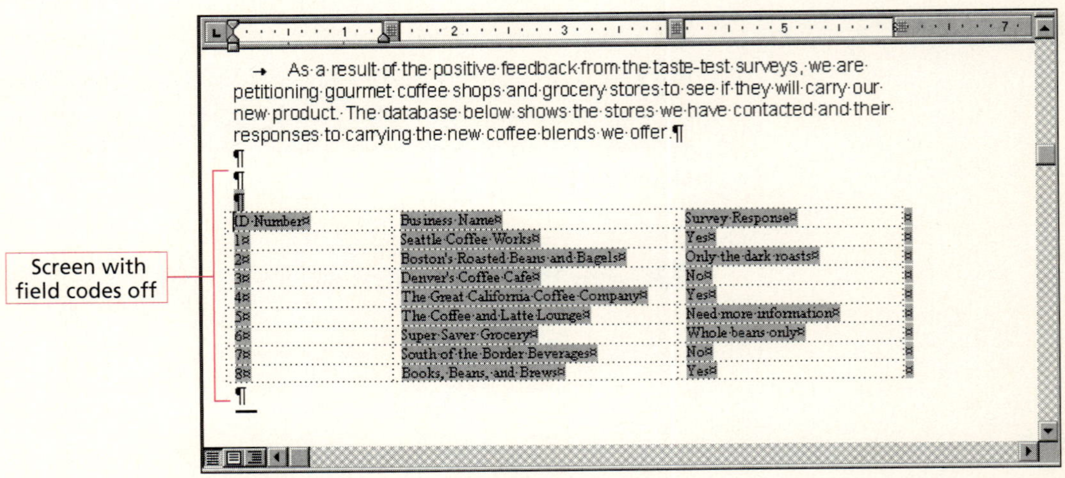

Figure 2.13

Tip Notice that the data displayed in Figure 2.13 differs from Figure 2.11. The column width of the leftmost column in the data table was adjusted in Figure 2.13 so each cell of the table occupies only one line.

To view the linked data image:

1. Choose Options from the Tools menu.
2. In the View tab select the Field Codes option so that it is not checked and click OK.
3. Adjust the ID Number Column so that each record occupies only one line.
4. Scroll through My Updated Project.doc and see the object's image. It should look like Figure 2.13.
5. Select the Save button.

EXIT If necessary, you can exit Word now and continue this project later.

Updating the Linked Data

As the marketing department updates this database, you will be able to update the data in your document with only two keystrokes. What you see in your document is actually an image of the real data located in another file. Since the Word document stores only the location of the database and displays only an image of the data, the image must be updated to reflect any changes that have been made to the database.

To update the linked data in the Word document:

1. Start Word and open My Updated Project.doc, if necessary.
2. Start Access, and open the Potential Marketing Channels.mdb database.
3. Add records 9 through 12 to the Market Survey Results table, as shown in Figure 2.14.

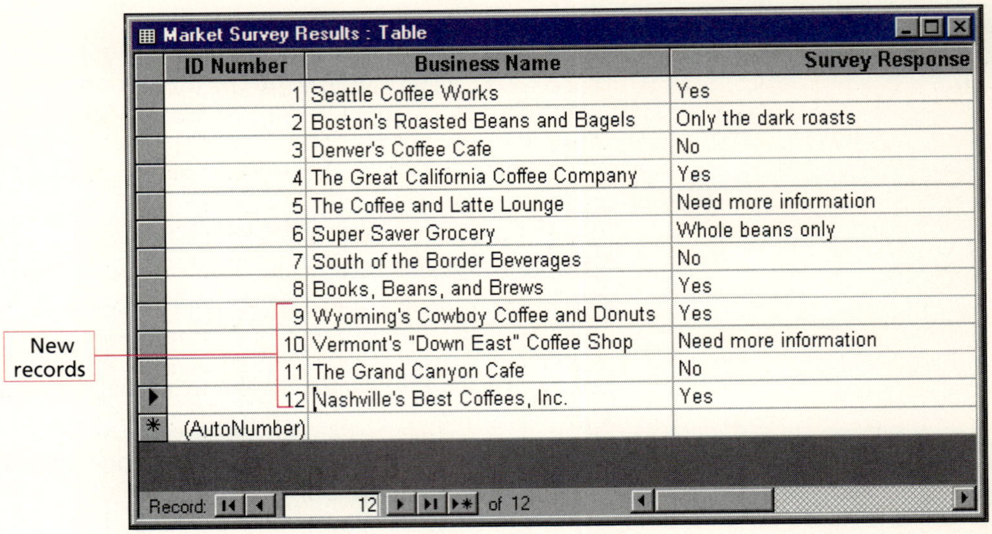

ID Number	Business Name	Survey Response
1	Seattle Coffee Works	Yes
2	Boston's Roasted Beans and Bagels	Only the dark roasts
3	Denver's Coffee Cafe	No
4	The Great California Coffee Company	Yes
5	The Coffee and Latte Lounge	Need more information
6	Super Saver Grocery	Whole beans only
7	South of the Border Beverages	No
8	Books, Beans, and Brews	Yes
9	Wyoming's Cowboy Coffee and Donuts	Yes
10	Vermont's "Down East" Coffee Shop	Need more information
11	The Grand Canyon Cafe	No
12	Nashville's Best Coffees, Inc.	Yes

Figure 2.14

4 Save the table, and exit Access.

5 Make sure the object is displayed in the Word document as a table. If the object is displayed as a field code, choose Options from the Tools menu and then turn off Field Codes so you can see the object in a Word table format.

6 Position the insertion point anywhere in the displayed table, and click once.

7 Press F9 to complete the updating process.
The newly added records are displayed in the object's updated image, as shown in Figure 2.15.

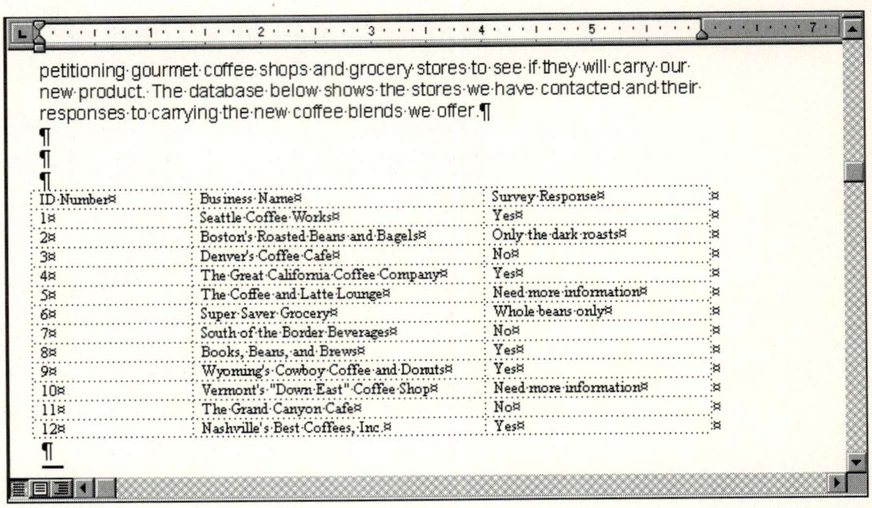

ID Number	Business Name	Survey Response
1	Seattle Coffee Works	Yes
2	Boston's Roasted Beans and Bagels	Only the dark roasts
3	Denver's Coffee Cafe	No
4	The Great California Coffee Company	Yes
5	The Coffee and Latte Lounge	Need more information
6	Super Saver Grocery	Whole beans only
7	South of the Border Beverages	No
8	Books, Beans, and Brews	Yes
9	Wyoming's Cowboy Coffee and Donuts	Yes
10	Vermont's "Down East" Coffee Shop	Need more information
11	The Grand Canyon Cafe	No
12	Nashville's Best Coffees, Inc.	Yes

Figure 2.15

QUERYING THE LINKED DATABASE

The report you have created displays all of the data in the database. But what if you wanted to include only the stores answering yes to the survey question? You can do this by inserting a database ***query*** into the report. A query, as you learned in the Access 7 projects, lets you ask the database simple or complex questions. When you insert a query object, you can insert either a query made from within Access or a new query created through the Query Options dialog box. You can also sort the data into a meaningful order through a query. When you link to a query, Word remembers the query questions you answered in the Query Options dialog box. Each time you press F9 to update the object, Word repeats the query instructions behind the scenes and inserts the updated data from the source file.

You will use the Query Options dialog box to establish ***selection rules*** for the query. Selection rules allow you to extract or display certain records from the database. To set up a selection rule, you will follow three basic steps:

- Identify field names in the database.
- Select a comparison phrase, such as *Greater Than or Equal To.*
- Enter numbers or characters (text) that will be compared to the data in the database field.

You can create up to six selection rules in a query and connect them by using AND or OR. For example, if you wanted to select all store names that begin with *A* through *F,* you would enter the selection rules shown in Figure 2.16.

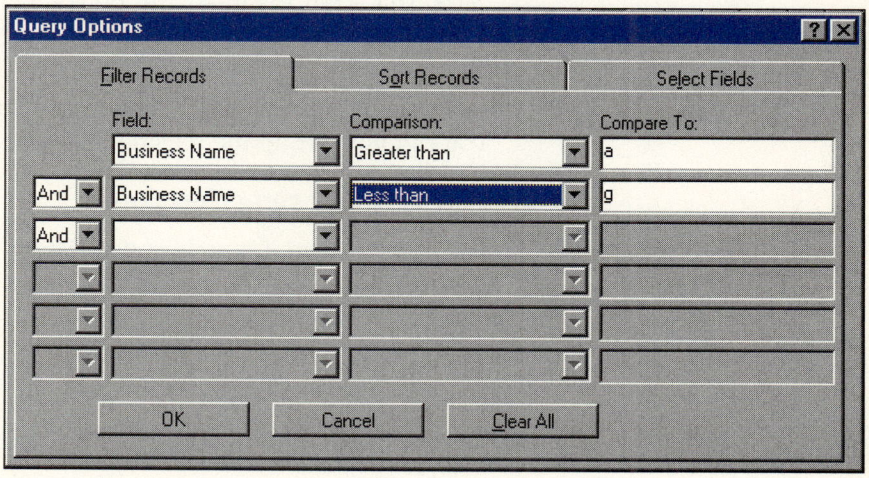

Figure 2.16

Tip Fields containing text and numbers are sorted and compared differently. Word uses the ANSI (American National Standards Institute) sorting order, which means that *Colombian* is "less than" *European Dark Roast* because *Colombian* comes before *European Dark Roast* alphabetically.

To begin the query process, you will enter text into the Word document and prepare a place to insert the new table that will result from the query.

To prepare the Word document for the query:

1 Insert a page break at the end of the document, after the linked object.

2 Type the following paragraph:
`The following stores have agreed to carry our product without reservation. The marketing team will contact production and arrange for the first shipment of European Dark Roast coffee beans to arrive next month.`

3 Press (ENTER) three times.

4 Save My Updated Project.doc.

Now you are ready to designate the database that will be the source of the data.

To establish a data source for the query:

1 Choose Database from the Insert menu.

2 Select Get Data from the Database dialog box.

3 Select *MS Access Databases (*.mdb)* from the Files of type box.

4 Select drive A: from the Look in list box.

5 Select Potential Marketing Channels.mdb in the File name box.

6 Select Open to accept the data source.

> **Caution** Do not select MS Query from the Open Data Source dialog box. This is not the query option you will use in this project.

7 Select the Tables tab from the Microsoft Access dialog box.

8 Select Market Survey Results as the table, and then select OK.
You can now set up the selection rules for the query.

To establish selection rules:

1 Select Query Options under Data Options in the Database dialog box.
The screen now looks like Figure 2.17.

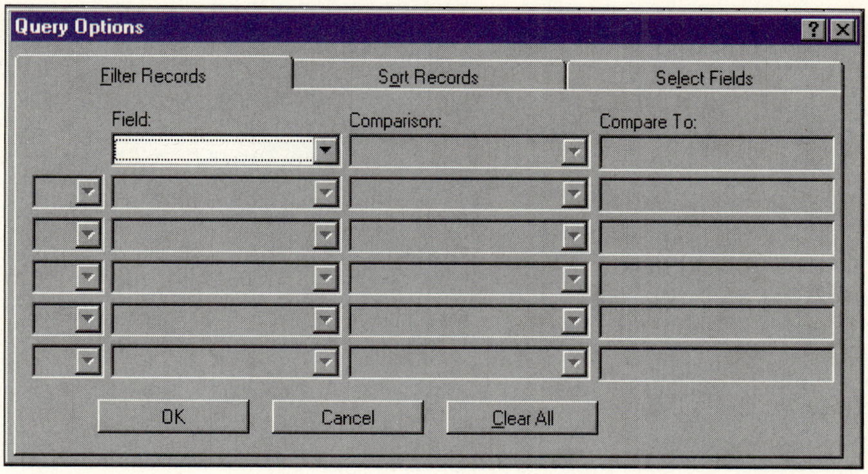

Figure 2.17

2 Select the Filter Records tab.

3 Select the field Survey Response from the Field list box.
The Comparison list box displays *Equal to.*

4 Type **yes** in the first row of the column labeled Compare To.
The screen now looks like Figure 2.18. Notice that the query is not case-sensitive, so you can enter upper- or lowercase letters.

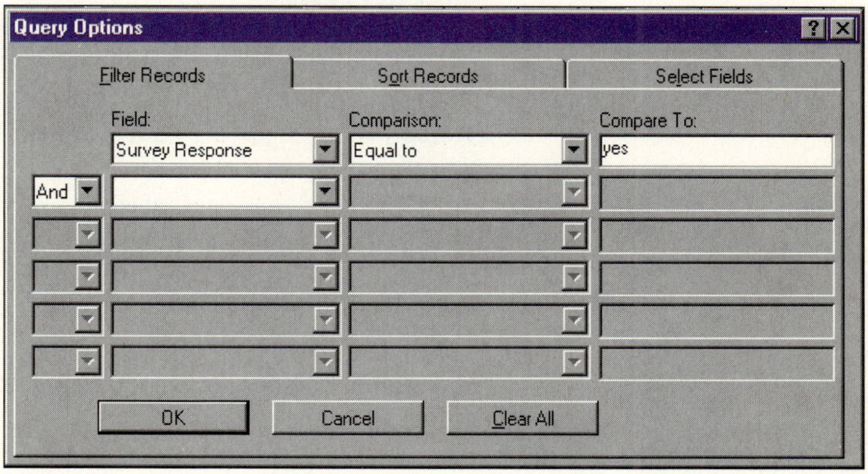

Figure 2.18

In the following steps you will complete the query by designating how you want the object displayed. You will then insert the object in the report.

To sort and delete records from the database:

1 Select the Sort Records tab.

2 Select Business Name from the Sort By list box.
The screen now looks like Figure 2.19.

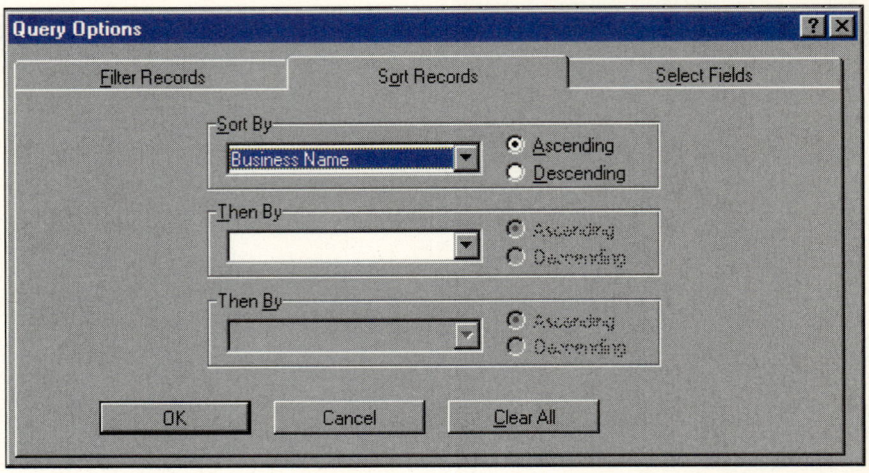

Figure 2.19

3 Select the Select Fields tab.

4 Select the ID Number field in the Field in Data Source box, and then select Remove to delete the ID field from the object's displayed image. The screen now looks like Figure 2.20.

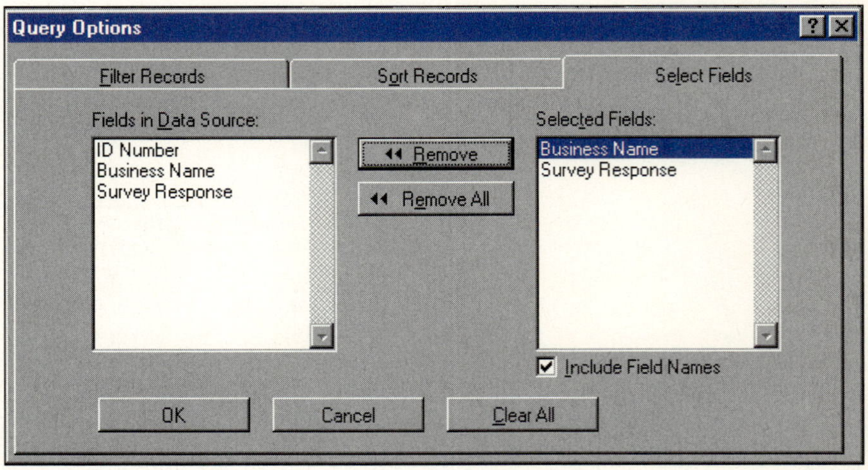

Figure 2.20

5 Select OK to accept the query.

To insert the query object:

1 Select Insert Data from the Database dialog box.

2 Select Insert Data as Field from the Insert Data dialog box, and then select OK.

3 Save My Updated Project.doc.
Word displays only the data that matches the query you created: the five stores with Yes in the Answer field, as shown in Figure 2.21.

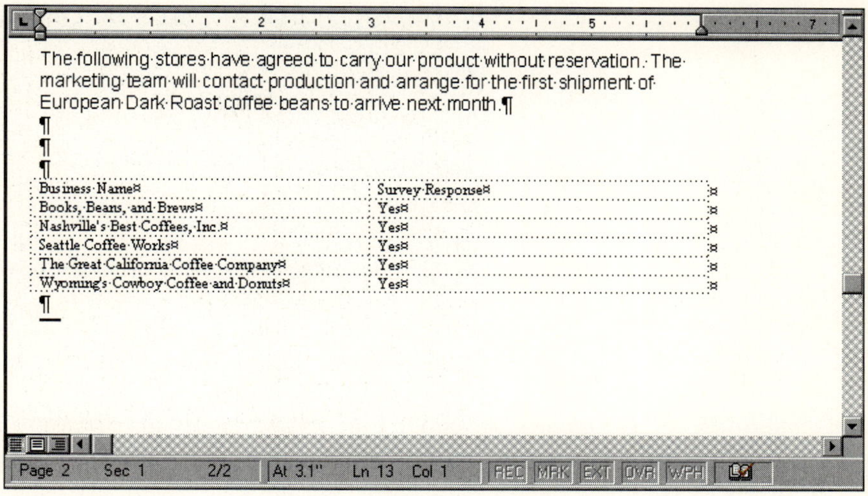

Figure 2.21

FORMATTING THE LINKED OBJECT

The linked object looks like a Word table, and you can format it as you would a Word table. You can add grid lines, create a border, and add shading to the object's image. However, any formatting, such as sizing the table columns, modifying or adding borders, and adding colors or shading, is lost each time you use (F9) to update the data. To help you maintain the formatting when you update your linked object, you will format the data with one of the Access ***templates,*** or patterns, provided in the Table AutoFormat feature.

To format a linked object:

1 Click once anywhere in the first complete database object on page 1, not the query object.

2 Choose Database from the Insert menu.

3 Select Get Data from the Database dialog box.

4 Select MS Access Databases (*.mdb) from the Files of type list box in the Open Data Source dialog box.

5 Select drive A: and *Potential Marketing Channels.mdb,* and then select Open.

6 Select the Tables tab from the Microsoft Access dialog box.

7 Select Market Survey Results as the table, and then select OK.

8 From the Database dialog box, select Table AutoFormat, as shown in Figure 2.22.

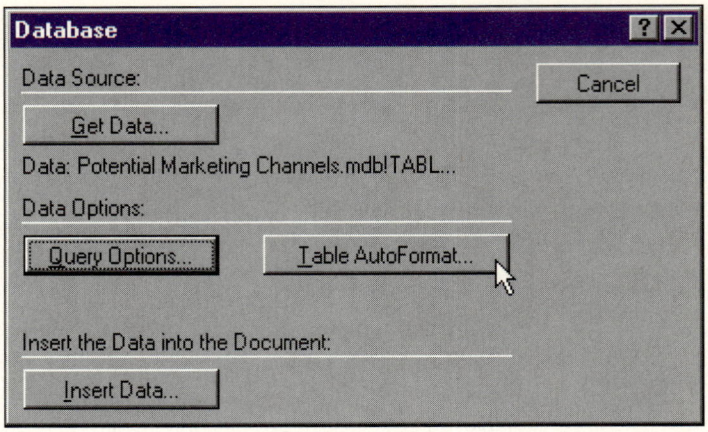

Figure 2.22

The Table AutoFormat dialog box appears.

9 Select Grid 8 from the Formats list box to designate the template.

10 Make sure the other dialog box settings are the same as those shown in Figure 2.23, and then select OK.

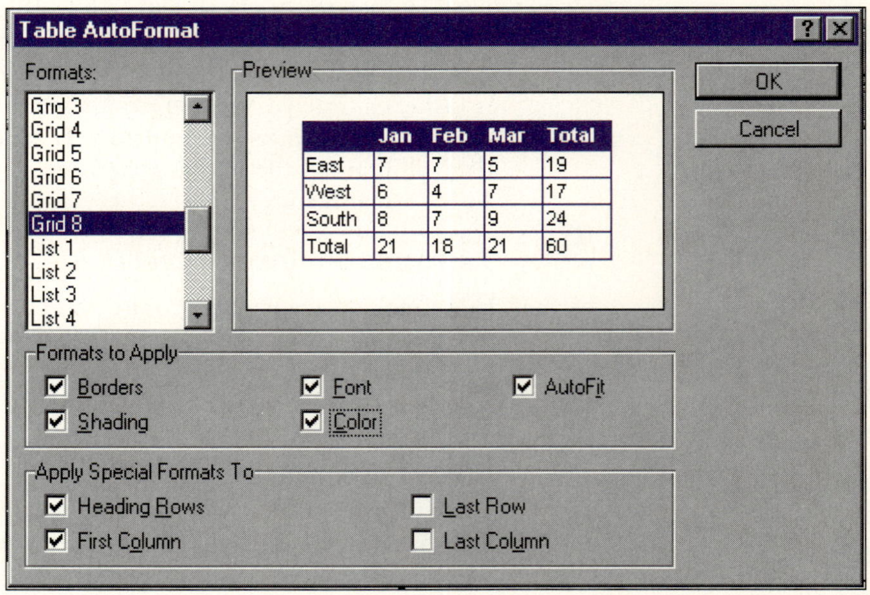

Figure 2.23

Now you can replace the unformatted object currently in the document with the newly formatted object.

To insert the formatted object:

1 Select Insert Data from the Database dialog box.

2 Select Insert Data as Field from the Insert Data dialog box, and then select OK.

The message box shown in Figure 2.24 appears, warning you that if you continue you will replace the existing linked object with a new linked object.

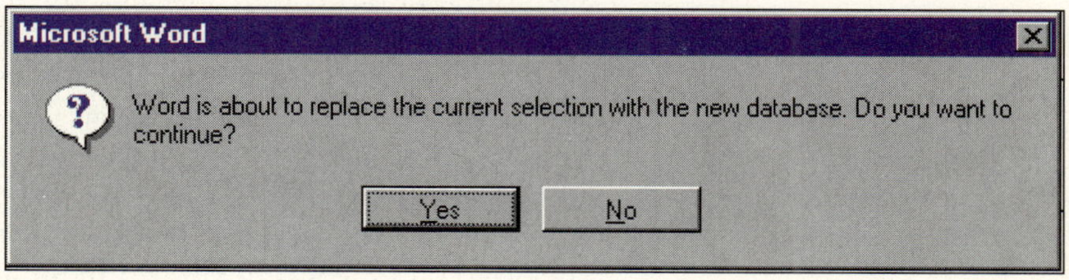

Figure 2.24

3 Select Yes to continue the link process.

4 Save My Updated Project.doc.
The database object now looks like Figure 2.25.

ID·Numbers	Business·Name	Survey·Response	
1¤	Seattle·Coffee·Works¤	Yes¤	¤
2¤	Boston's·Roasted·Beans·and·Bagles¤	Only·the·dark·roast¤	¤
3¤	Denver's·Coffee·Cafe¤	No¤	¤
4¤	The·Great·California·Coffee·Company¤	Yes¤	¤
5¤	The·Coffee·and·Latte·Longue¤	Need·more·information¤	¤
6¤	Super·Saver·Grocery¤	Whole·beans·only¤	¤
7¤	South·of·the·Border·Beverages¤	No¤	¤
8¤	Books,·Beans,·and·Brews¤	Yes¤	¤
9¤	Wyoming's·Cowboy·Coffee·and·Donuts¤	Yes¤	¤
10¤	Vermont's·"Down·East·Coffee·Shop"¤	Need·more·information¤	¤
11¤	The·Grand·Canyon·Cafe¤	No¤	¤
12¤	Nashville's·Best·Coffees,·Inc.¤	Yes¤	¤

Figure 2.25

5 Use Print Preview to see what the formatted object will look like when it is printed.

The Next Step

What if the president's staff wants the contents of the marketing database to change? Marketing may expand the contents of the database to include the suggested retail price of the European Dark Roast blend, the date the store wants delivery of the coffee, and the number of pounds sold during the first month. As the requirements for the report grow and change, you can use linking and querying to change the type of data reported and to modify how the data looks. You can sort it in a different order, include other fields, and keep it up to date.

If the database you are querying has hundreds or thousands of records, you should query only a small portion of the data. A sample of 50 to 100 records is a good test to verify that your query will really produce the data you want to see. Always test the query before you put it in your final report. Another important point to remember when you are creating an advanced query is AND and OR are not necessarily interpreted by the computer the same way you interpret the words when speaking. Suppose the president said, "Give me a report of all the stores and gourmet coffee shops answering yes and all the stores in Ohio." Should the report show all stores in Ohio, regardless of their answer and all stores answering yes regardless of their state or should the report contain all Ohio stores answering yes? You must clarify exactly what has been requested, because what the requester says is not necessarily what he or she really wants!

This concludes Project 2 of the integrated projects. You can exit Word now or go on to work the Study Questions, Review Exercises, and Assignments.

SUMMARY AND EXERCISES

Summary

- The target file stores the location of the linked source file, not the contents.
- The source file must be available every time the linked object is updated.
- Linking displays an image of the source file in the target file.
- When the target file contains a linked object, it does not grow as large as it does when it contains an embedded object.
- A linked database's image is displayed as a Word table.
- A linked object can be displayed as a field code, which contains the link—the location of the object.
- The Insert Data as Field option in the Insert Data dialog box is the option that establishes the link.
- Field codes can be turned on and off by choosing Options from the Tools menu. Turning on Field Codes displays the database as a field code. Turning off Field Codes displays the database as a Word table.
- To update the linked database, you click anywhere in the displayed table and press F9
- A linked database object can be formatted using Table AutoFormat.
- You can link to a database query.
- A query can have up to six selection rules and can be sorted.
- Always test a query on a sample of records to verify the accuracy of the query instructions.

Key Terms and Operations

Key Terms
field code
query
selection rule
template

Operations
Create a query
Format a linked object
Get a data source
Insert data as a field
Link a database
Sort records in a query
Turn on field code display
Update a linked object's data

Study Questions

Multiple Choice

1. The main difference between a linked object and an embedded object is
   a. a linked object can never be updated in the target file.
   b. embedded objects must always have the source file available.
   c. the linked object's source file's location is stored in the target file.
   d. All of the above.
2. The linked object is displayed in the target file as
   a. an image of the source file.
   b. an icon representing the source file.
   c. a framed empty box.
   d. an image of the target file.
3. The field code contains
   a. the list of fields in the database object.
   b. the database data in encrypted form.
   c. a password needed to access the linked object.
   d. the location of the database source file.
4. You should link an object when
   a. you don't need the source file to update the object.
   b. you want the target file's byte size to remain as small as possible.
   c. the source file is not on a network.
   d. the target file is on a network.
5. To insert an Access database as a linked object you
   a. use the copy and paste method to create the link.
   b. choose Object from the Insert menu.
   c. choose Database from the Insert menu.
   d. always use the embed method.
6. If you want to insert an Access database as a linked object you must
   a. select Insert Data as Field from the Insert Data dialog box.
   b. never select Insert Data as Field from the Insert Data dialog box.
   c. always choose Options from the Tools menu to turn Field Codes on.
   d. first create a Word table to hold the database data.
7. To view the linked object's data you must
   a. use Print Preview to see how the data will look when it prints.
   b. insert the database as a Picture from the Insert menu.
   c. use the Zoom feature of Word to magnify the field code.
   d. turn the field code display off by choosing Options from the Tools menu.
8. To update a linked database object, you will
   a. re-establish the link by deleting the old object and inserting the database again.
   b. select AutoUpdate from the Database dialog box.
   c. double-click the insertion point in the linked database object to make the changes.
   d. position the insertion point in the database object and press F9

9. A query
   a. must be made in Access before the linked object is created.
   b. must be repeated manually every time you update the database object.
   c. can be created through the Query Options dialog box.
   d. can be created through MS Query if Access is not available.

10. To sort a query, Word uses
    a. the ASCII standard rules of sorting.
    b. the ANSI standard rules of sorting.
    c. the Excel sort feature.
    d. the ACQV standard rules of alphabetizing.

Short Answer

1. When a database is linked to a target file, what does the target file actually store?
2. What is the field code?
3. When should you use link to create instead of embed an object?
4. How does linking affect the size of the target file?
5. What Word option changes the way the image of the database is displayed in the document?
6. How do you update the database object after it has been linked to the document?
7. What option do you use to format the database object with colors and borders?
8. What is the purpose of a query?
9. What are the three steps involved in creating a selection rule?
10. How many selection rules can you use when you create a query?

For Discussion

1. Explain what happens when an object is linked to a target file.
2. What is a field code? Why is it important?
3. Explain which Word option actually creates the link. How does this relate to turning field codes on and off?
4. Explain what a query is. Why is it important to test your queries with sample data? What would happen in this integrated project if the president's staff saw incorrect data in the report? How would that affect their business decisions?
5. What do you need to remember when someone asks you to build an advanced query?

Review Exercises

Linking a Query

Save My Updated Project.doc as My Additional Query.doc, and create another linked database object at the end of My Additional Query.doc. This time, insert a query to display all stores that answered no to the survey question. Display the image as a table, not a field code. Add an opening paragraph to identify this new table in the report. Your new query object and text should resemble Figure 2.26. Update your document.

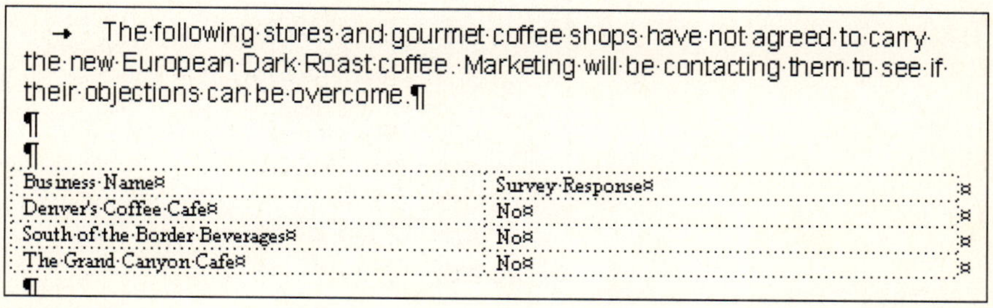
→ The·following·stores·and·gourmet·coffee·shops·have·not·agreed·to·carry·the·new·European·Dark·Roast·coffee.·Marketing·will·be·contacting·them·to·see·if·their·objections·can·be·overcome.¶

¶

¶

Business·Name¤	Survey·Response¤
Denver's·Coffee·Cafe¤	No¤
South·of·the·Border·Beverages¤	No¤
The·Grand·Canyon·Cafe¤	No¤

¶

Figure 2.26

Formatting a Linked Database Object

Create another linked database and format it using the AutoFormat feature. The query should display all stores that answered anything other than *yes* or *no* to the survey. Do not display the store's ID in the object. Choose one of the format templates available, and display the table in color. Save your updated document as My Additional Linked Query.doc. Use Print Preview to see what the object will look like when it prints.

Assignments

Creating an Advanced Query

In Access, add new fields to the Market Survey Results table in the Potential Marketing Channels database, as shown in Table 2.2.

Table 2.2

Field Name	Data Type	Description	Field Size
Region	Text	Region of US	10
Years	Number	Length of time in business	Double
Zip Code	Number	Postal code	Double

Update the data in the Market Survey Results table as shown in Figure 2.27. Use the AutoFormat feature to create a pleasing color effect.

ID N	Business Name	Survey Response	Region	Years	Zip Code
1	Seattle Coffee Works	Yes	Western	10	94021
2	Boston's Roasted Beans and Bagels	Only the dark roasts	Eastern	6	10134
3	Denver's Coffee Cafe	No	Western	7	80250
4	The Great California Coffee Company	Yes	Western	6	90221
5	The Coffee and Latte Lounge	Need more information	South	3	47689
6	Super Saver Grocery	Whole beans only	South	6	32178
7	South of the Border Beverages	No	South	2	23211
8	Books, Beans, and Brews	Yes	North	3	70661
9	Wyoming's Cowboy Coffee and Donuts	Yes	Western	18	85660
10	Vermont's "Down East" Coffee Shop	Need more information	Eastern	9	32118
11	The Grand Canyon Cafe	No	Western	4	90005
12	Nashville's Best Coffees, Inc.	Yes	South	4	67880

Figure 2.27

Suppose the president called you and said, "Create a report showing all stores that said yes, they would carry the new product, but only display them if they are in states in the western region of the country. And, if a store has been in business less than 5 years, I don't want it on the report." This requires an advanced query. Create a new Word document named Advance Decision.doc, and link to the president's new query. Sort the records by store name in descending order. Do not display the store ID. Your report should resemble Figure 2.28.

European Dark Roast Survey Report

At the request of the president, this report queries the Market Survey Results data table kept by Marketing. This report includes records that meet the following criteria:

- All stores or gourmet coffee shops agree to carry the new product
- All stores or shops are located in the Western region
- No store or shop has been in business for less than 5 years

	Survey Response	*Region*	*Years*	*Zip Code*
Seattle Coffee Works	Yes	Western	10	94021
The Great California Coffee Company	Yes	Western	6	90221
Wyoming's Cowboy Coffee and Donuts	Yes	Western	18	85660

Figure 2.28

Querying a Range of Values

The president wants one last query. Save Advance Decision.doc as Eliminated Zip Codes.doc. Modify the report, and create a query that will eliminate all stores with zip codes of 20000 through 80000. Sort the query by zip code. Your report should resemble Figure 2.29.

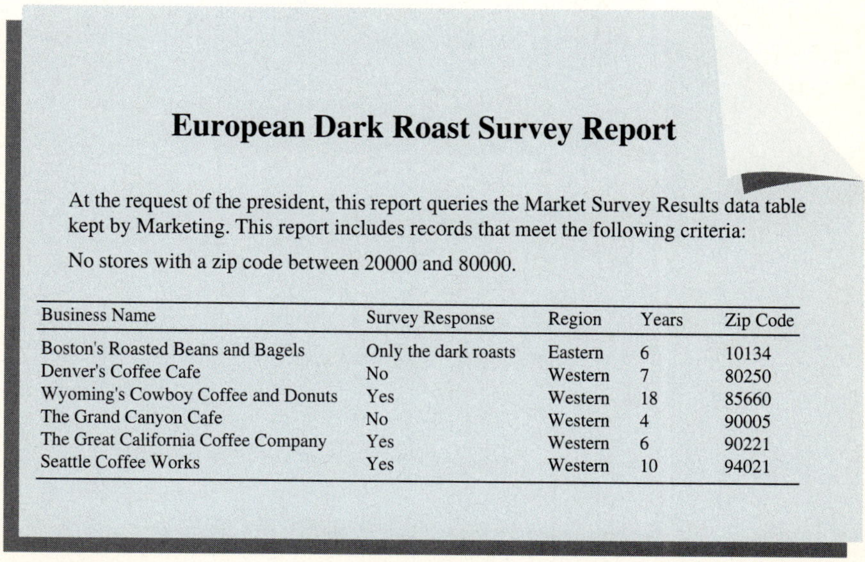

European Dark Roast Survey Report

At the request of the president, this report queries the Market Survey Results data table kept by Marketing. This report includes records that meet the following criteria:

No stores with a zip code between 20000 and 80000.

Business Name	Survey Response	Region	Years	Zip Code
Boston's Roasted Beans and Bagels	Only the dark roasts	Eastern	6	10134
Denver's Coffee Cafe	No	Western	7	80250
Wyoming's Cowboy Coffee and Donuts	Yes	Western	18	85660
The Grand Canyon Cafe	No	Western	4	90005
The Great California Coffee Company	Yes	Western	6	90221
Seattle Coffee Works	Yes	Western	10	94021

Figure 2.29

PART VII

Microsoft PowerPoint 7

Overview

Objectives

After completing this Overview, you should be able to:

- Start PowerPoint
- Describe the components of the PowerPoint screen
- Execute commands using menus and toolbars
- Navigate through dialog boxes
- Access on-screen Help
- Exit PowerPoint

In the past an articulate and substantive presentation, delivered from a podium with the help of notes, was sufficient to capture and hold the attention of an audience. Today's listeners, however, have grown accustomed to speakers conveying their key points by highly visual means, such as professional graphics, animated slide shows, and coordinated handouts.

The technology is now available for you to develop computer-generated and computer-controlled presentations. A powerful microcomputer, a color monitor, and a projection device are all the equipment you need to create on-screen presentations. Letter-quality printers allow you to produce overheads when a projection system is unavailable. Add an easy-to-use presentation graphics program, and you can quickly develop professional, eye-catching presentations.

Using a Presentation Graphics Program

A ***presentation graphics program*** is a software tool you use to develop professional-looking presentations in the form of paper copies, overhead transparencies, 35mm slides, and automated slide shows. To help you develop the content of your presentation, a presentation graphics program offers many features, such as outlining, word processing, drawing, charting, and spell-checking. You can polish your final product by adding background designs, color, and animation. Within seconds you can also generate an outline of your presentation and audience handouts that duplicate several slides on each page.

Using PowerPoint for Windows 95

Microsoft PowerPoint for Windows 95 is among the best-selling presentation graphics programs in the world. Using this program you can quickly and easily create slides that display text in bulleted lists as well as art, tables, or business graphs. PowerPoint includes the ***AutoContent Wizard,*** which helps you set up a basic theme for the presentation and guides you through the steps to create all the slides. This wizard provides suggested outlines for common types of presentations, such as sales reports, training programs, and news bulletins, and enables you to adapt these outlines to reflect your ideas. Figure 0.1 illustrates several slides created using AutoContent Wizard.

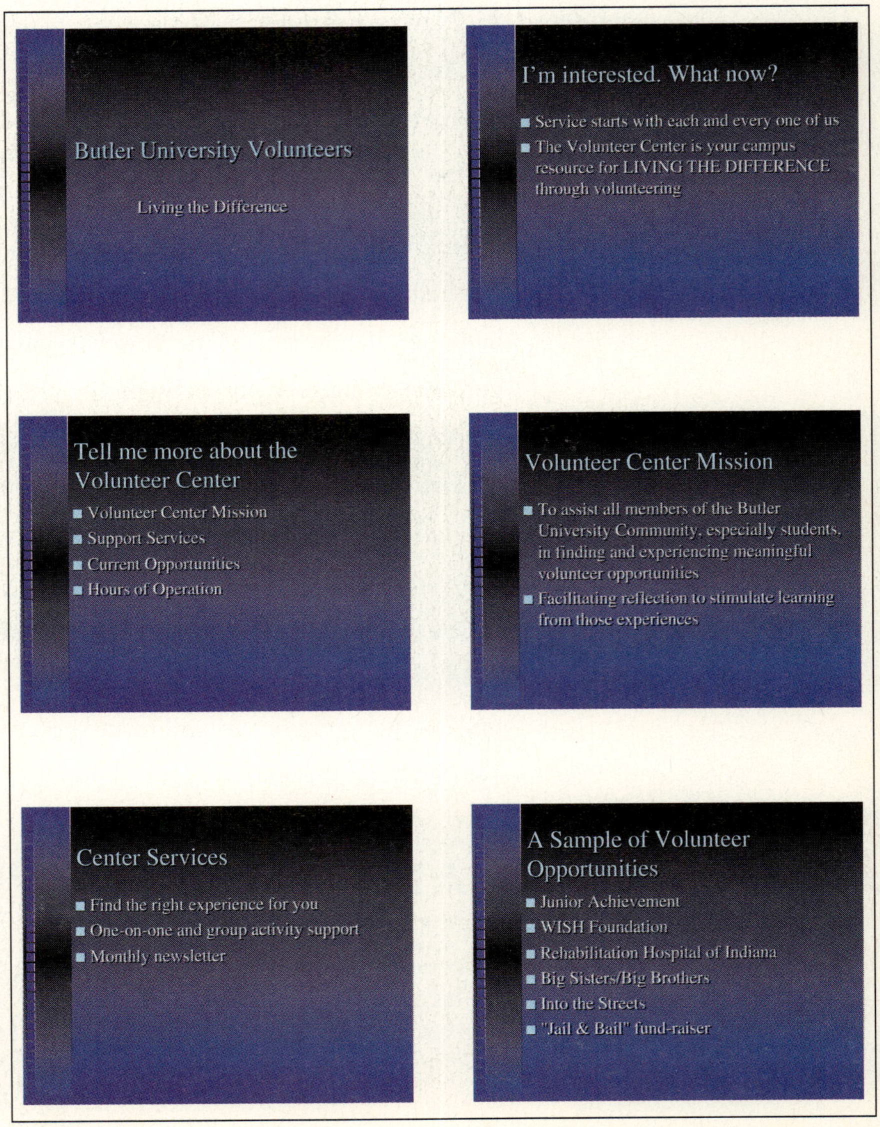

Figure 0.1

Whether you use AutoContent Wizard or not, you can choose among predefined visual styles; determine the type of output, such as 35mm slides or an on-screen presentation; and specify types of printouts, including speaker's notes and audience handout pages. Your slides can include words, images, and special effects, as shown in Figure 0.2.

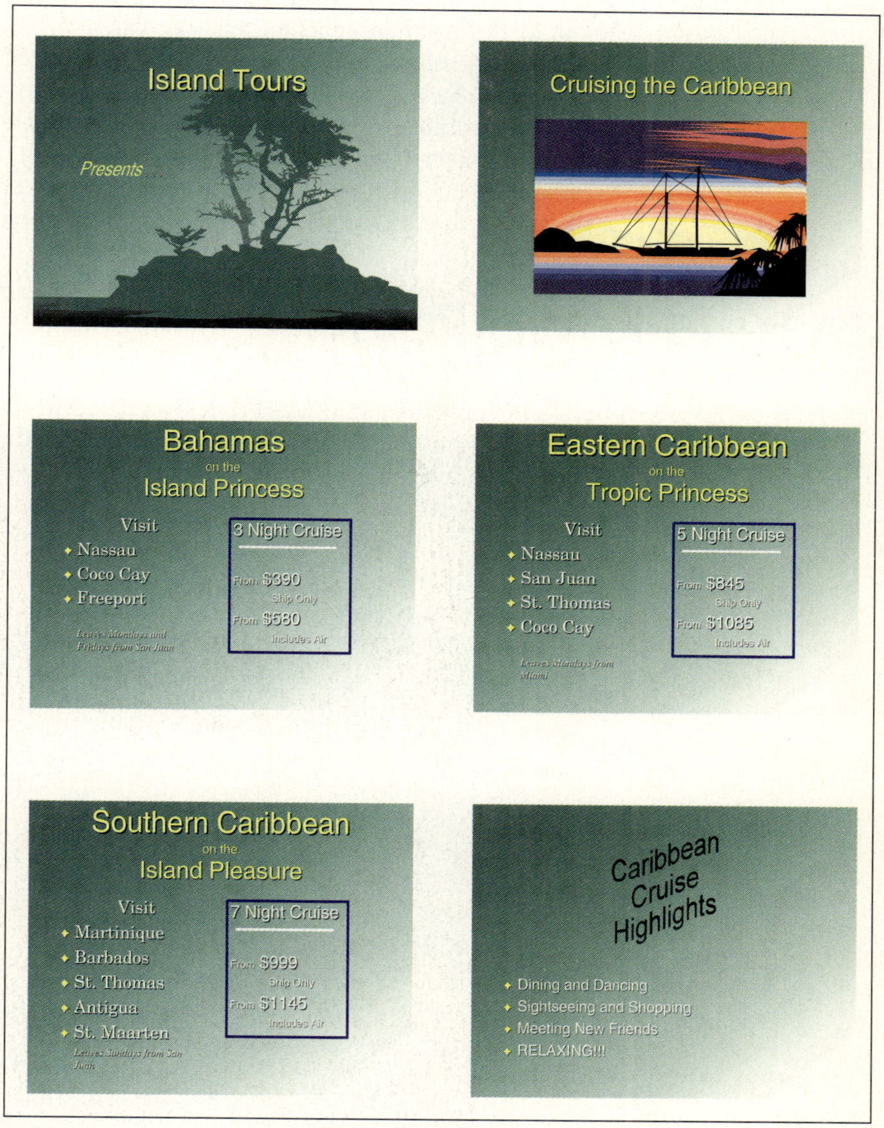

Figure 0.2

A Note to the Student

The projects in this module assume that your system is equipped with a mouse and that you are comfortable working in a Windows 95 environment. Because PowerPoint allows you to customize the work area, your system's on-screen displays may vary slightly from the figures in this module. For example, PowerPoint allows you to display one or more *toolbars* on your screen. A ***toolbar*** contains buttons representing PowerPoint commands, as discussed later in the Overview. Figures in the module usually show only the Standard, Formatting, and Drawing toolbars provided by PowerPoint, but your system may display a different combination of toolbars.

The projects in this module present several popular applications for presentation graphics. We suggest that you first read this Overview to learn about basic PowerPoint screens and PowerPoint's powerful Help feature. Then, as you work through Projects 1 and 2 in sequence, you will use the AutoContent Wizard to create a presentation on volunteerism. In the process you will learn to enter and edit text as well as save and print your slides. You can then turn your attention to creating a presentation promoting Caribbean cruises: In Project 3 you will learn to position text, and in Project 4 you will add shapes, draw lines, insert images, and create special effects. You might then proceed to Project 5 so that you know how to present an on-screen slide show. Let's begin!

Starting PowerPoint

You can start PowerPoint from the Microsoft PowerPoint folder or the Microsoft Office folder, one of which should appear on the Programs menu after you start Windows 95. For example, you can choose Microsoft PowerPoint, as shown in Figure 0.3.

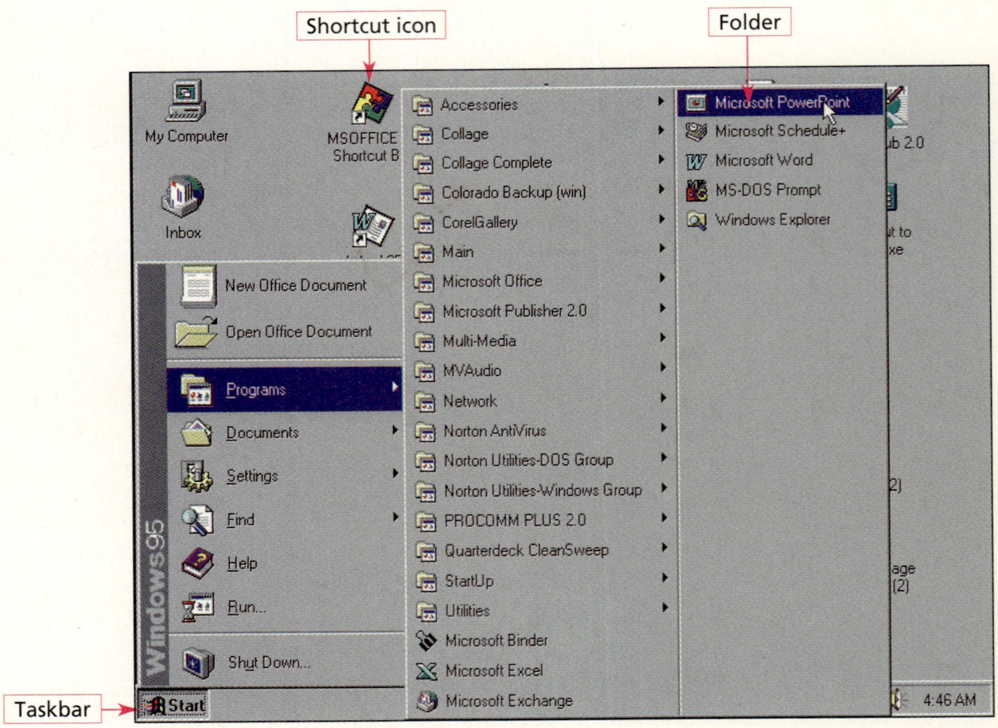

Figure 0.3

Tip If a shortcut *icon* for Microsoft Office or PowerPoint appears on your desktop, you can double-click the icon to start the program. An ***icon*** is an on-screen symbol that represents a program file, data file, or some other function.

After loading PowerPoint you will see a Tip of the Day dialog box, unless this feature has been turned off. You can read the information and view additional tips if you choose, and then you can select OK to see the initial PowerPoint screen shown in Figure 0.4.

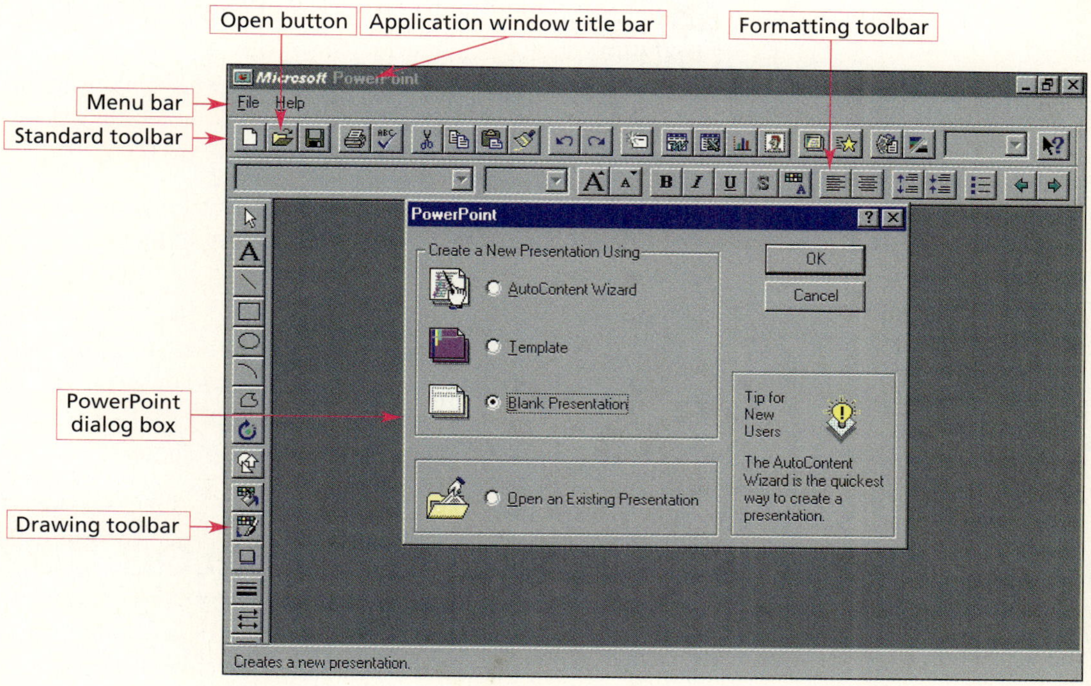

Figure 0.4

The application window title bar indicates you are using Microsoft PowerPoint. When you save a presentation to disk or open an existing presentation, the name of the presentation file also appears in the title bar.

The ***menu bar,*** located just below the title bar, is a horizontal list of PowerPoint commands. When you select an option on the menu bar, a ***pull-down menu*** appears vertically listing related commands.

When you start PowerPoint for the first time, several toolbars appear on-screen, as shown in Figure 0.4. A toolbar contains buttons representing commands. Selecting a button on a toolbar executes the associated PowerPoint command. You can decide which toolbars you want to display and where they will appear on-screen, as described later in the Overview.

Tip PowerPoint's ToolTips displays the name of a button each time you position the pointer over the button. If this feature is not active, you can choose Toolbars from the View menu and select Show ToolTips.

The PowerPoint dialog box occupies most of the remainder of the screen. A ***dialog box*** appears whenever additional information is needed to complete a task. In the steps that follow, you will start the PowerPoint program and take a look at the PowerPoint dialog box.

To start PowerPoint:

1 Select Start at the left end of the Windows 95 taskbar, and then select Programs.

2 Position the pointer on Microsoft PowerPoint, as shown in Figure 0.3, and then click.

Reminder If a PowerPoint icon appears on your desktop, you can double-click the icon to start the program in place of steps 1 and 2 above.

After a brief display showing copyright information, the Microsoft PowerPoint dialog box shown in Figure 0.4 appears. If a Tip of the Day dialog box appears instead, select OK to remove it.

3 Select Cancel to close the PowerPoint dialog box.

Using Toolbars, Menus, and Dialog Boxes

Tip If you are already familiar with using toolbars, menus, and dialog boxes in another Windows product, you might want to skip this section and continue with the section called "Getting On-Screen Help."

The three toolbars shown in Figure 0.4 provide quick access to the most commonly used PowerPoint commands. Other toolbars are available including Drawing+, Microsoft, AutoShapes, Outlining and Animation Effects.

Some buttons replace two or more menu selections. For example, clicking the Open File Folder button (the second button on the Standard toolbar) can substitute for choosing Open from the File menu. When you have such a choice in this module, you will see a picture of the button in the left margin next to the step that describes the associated menu sequence. A button will only be shown the first time you can use it in these projects.

Other commands, like the ones on the AutoShapes toolbar, can be applied only by using a toolbar. When you first start PowerPoint and open a presentation, the Standard and Formatting toolbars are displayed just below the menu bar, and the Drawing toolbar is displayed vertically on the left side of the window, as shown in Figure 0.4. You can, however, display any or all toolbars on your screen, as well as drag them to different locations.

When you exit the program, PowerPoint remembers which toolbars were active and displays the same arrangement when you access PowerPoint again.

PowerPoint includes a powerful set of commands grouped within the nine options in the menu bar shown in Figure 0.5. Choosing an option on a menu bar displays a pull-down menu in which more options are arranged vertically.

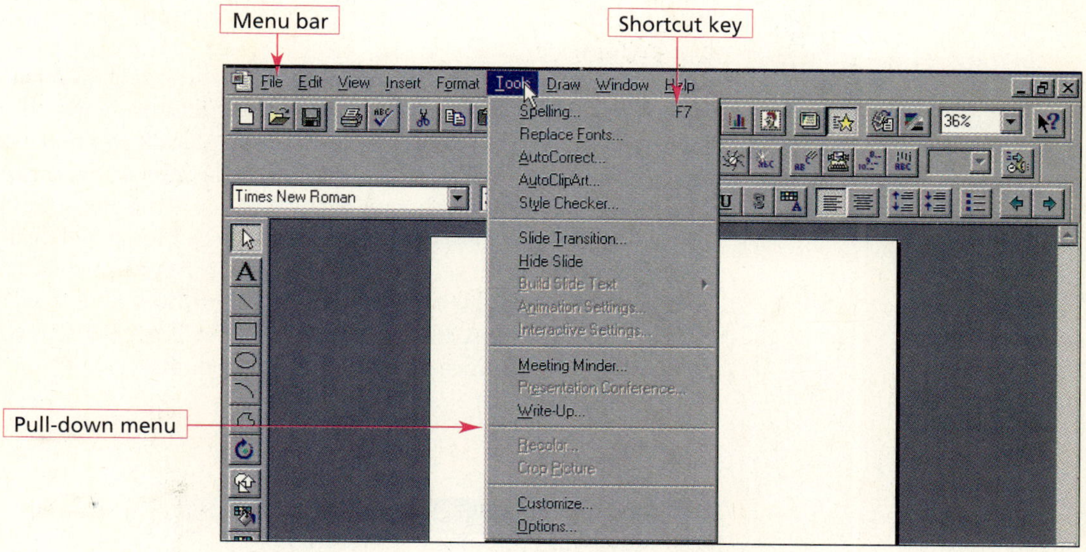

Figure 0.5

Pull-down menu options that appear dimmed, such as Build Slide Text and Animation Settings on the Tools menu shown in Figure 0.5, are not currently available. Choosing an option followed by ellipsis (...) opens a dialog box. Choosing an option followed by a right arrowhead opens another menu.

You can choose a menu bar option by using a mouse to click the option name, by pressing ALT in combination with the mnemonic letter (the underlined letter in each menu name), or by pressing F10 and then pointing to the selection from the keyboard (pressing arrow keys to select the desired option and then pressing ENTER). You can choose a pull-down menu option by using the mouse to click the option name, by typing the mnemonic letter, or by pointing to the selection from the keyboard.

For some common command sequences, PowerPoint has assigned a key or key combination. Using these ***shortcut keys*** (sometimes called accelerator keys), you can bypass several menu selections. For example, four shortcut keys are available for file management tasks, such as CTRL + **O** to open a file and CTRL + **P** to print. If a shortcut key is available, it appears to the right of its associated command in a pull-down menu, as shown in Figure 0.5.

Tip If you start working with menus but then decide not to continue, you can click anywhere outside the set of menus to close all of them at once, or you can press (ESC) one or more times to close one menu at a time.

Choosing a command that opens a dialog box gives you the opportunity to provide additional information for completing a task. You can select a dialog box option by positioning the pointer and clicking the left mouse button or by pressing (TAB) until the desired option is highlighted and then pressing (ENTER)

Some options within a dialog box appear in sets called ***radio buttons.*** These options are so named because, as on a radio, you can specify only one choice from a set of items. For example, look again at the PowerPoint dialog box shown in Figure 0.4 and note the four options preceded by circles. You can select only one of the options at a time, such as AutoContent Wizard or Open an Existing Presentation. In Figure 0.4 you can see that Blank Presentation is selected because a black dot appears in the preceding circle and a box appears around the name of the button.

Some dialog boxes, like the one shown in Figure 0.6, display more information and require you to make several choices.

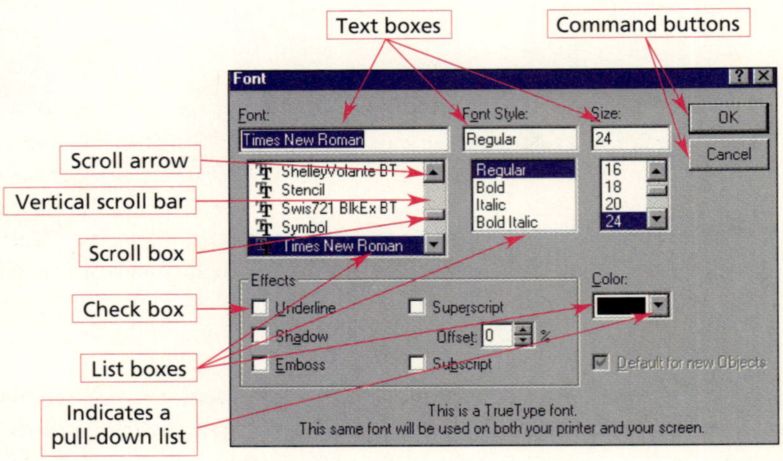

Figure 0.6

In the upper-right corner of most dialog boxes are one or more ***command buttons,*** which you can select to execute the named operation. The Font dialog box in Figure 0.6 has the OK and Cancel command buttons. Choosing OK accepts all the settings you make and closes the dialog box. Choosing Cancel closes the dialog box without changing any settings. If a command button name has an ellipsis (...) after it, then another dialog box will open when you select that button.

Two other common features of a dialog box are *text boxes* and *list boxes.*

You can use a ***text box*** to type information or view a current setting. In Figure 0.6 the text boxes display the current settings for font, font style, and font size. ***Font*** refers to the shape (typeface) of characters. To change the setting displayed in a text box, you can type the desired setting directly into the text box. If a ***list box*** appears below a text box, you can select one of the choices shown in the list box, and your selection will be displayed in the text box as the current setting. Figure 0.6 shows three types of list boxes. The list boxes displayed under the Font and Size text boxes have ***scroll bars,*** which contain ***scroll boxes*** and ***scroll arrows.*** To select an option from such a list box, you can move the scroll box within the scroll box until the option you want is displayed, or you can click the scroll arrows to move up or down the list one option at a time. The list box under the Font Style text box has all of its small number of options displayed; no scroll box is required. If a list box has a down arrow at its right end, you can click the arrow to display a ***pull-down list,*** which provides related options. If you were to select the arrow at the right end of the Color list box shown in Figure 0.6, you would see a display of available colors.

You can use a ***check box*** to turn an option on or off. A checkmark within the box indicates an option is on; the absence of a checkmark indicates an option is off. In Figure 0.6 the Underline effect is not selected, and the dimmed option Default for new Objects is selected.

GETTING ON-SCREEN HELP

PowerPoint provides on-screen information about the program to help you use its various features. This information can either be ***context-sensitive Help,*** which gives details on the operation in progress, or information of a more general nature. Help is available through options on the Help menu and a Help button, as described in the following sections.

Using Contents to Get Help

When you choose Microsoft PowerPoint Help Topics from the Help menu, the Help Topics dialog box is displayed, offering you a choice of four tabs: Contents, Index, Find, and Answer Wizard. When Contents is the current view, as shown in Figure 0.7, you can select a topic by clicking either the text of the topic or the closed book icon that appears to the left of text.

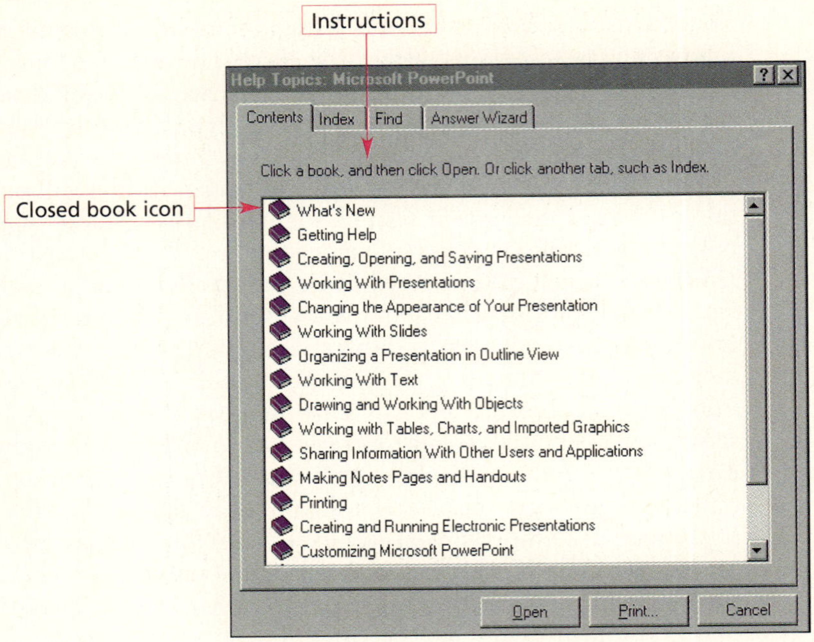

Figure 0.7

In the following steps you will view several screens accessed through the Help Topics dialog box. By exploring other topics on your own, you will have a better idea of the help available on-screen.

To use the Contents feature of on-screen Help:

1 Choose Help from the menu bar, and then choose Microsoft PowerPoint Help Topics.
The Help Topics dialog box appears.

2 Select the Contents tab, if Contents is not already the current folder.
The Help Topics dialog box should look like Figure 0.7.

3 Select *Creating and Running Electronic Presentations,* and then select the Open button.
Another list of five topics preceded by closed book icons appears.

> ***Tip*** You can also select a topic by double-clicking its description or associated icon.

4 Select *Adding Sound and Movies to Your Slides,* and then select the Open button.

5 Select *Using music and sound,* as shown in Figure 0.8.

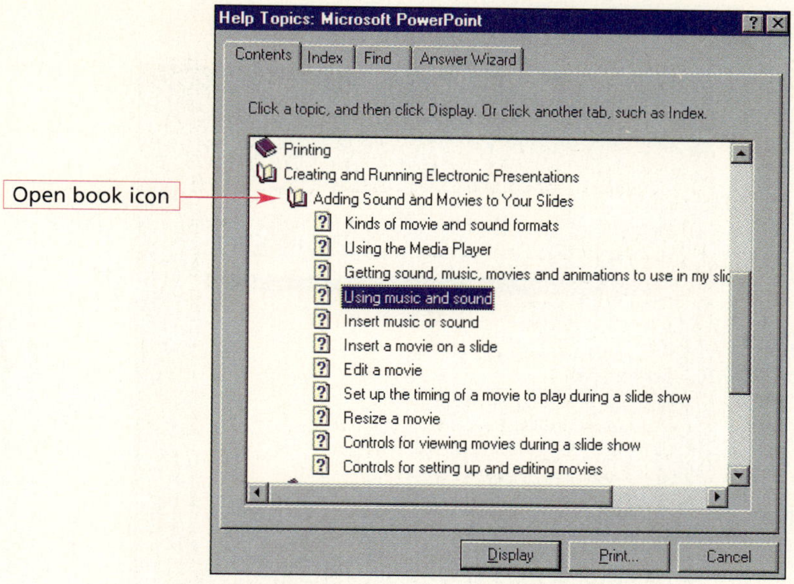

Figure 0.8

6 Select the Display button.
Information about the selected topic appears.

> ***Tip*** You can choose Print Topic from the Options menu to print the information in the current Help box.

7 Select Help Topics to redisplay the Contents folder.

8 Double-click the open book icon in front of *Creating and Running Electronic Presentations* to close the open Help books.

Using Index to Get Help

If you know the exact name of the feature about which you need help, you can look up information about the topic by selecting Index from the Help Topics dialog box. The two-part instructions to use the box appear near the top, as shown in Figure 0.9.

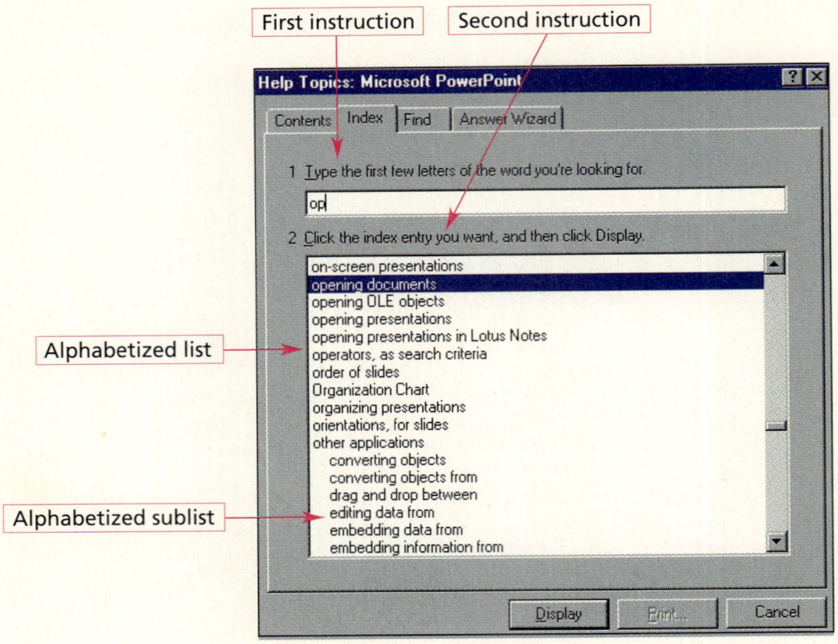

Figure 0.9

As you type the word or phrase you are looking for, PowerPoint displays an alphabetized list of topics that start with the same letters. Some topics, such as *other applications* shown in Figure 0.9, display a sublist of topics. In the following steps you will use this feature to display information about opening presentations.

To use the Index feature of on-screen Help:

1 Select the Index tab from the Help Topics dialog box.

2 Select the top text box and type **op**, as shown in Figure 0.9.

> ***Tip*** You can select a box by clicking anywhere in it or by pressing TAB until the flashing cursor appears within the box.

3 Select *opening presentations*, and then select the Display button. A Topics Found dialog box opens, which lists topics related to opening a presentation.

4 Select *Open an existing presentation*, and then select the Display button. PowerPoint displays information about the Open button in the Standard toolbar.

5 Click outside the information area to close on-screen Help.

Using Find to Get Help

You can search the Help database for any mention of a specified word or phrase by selecting Find from the Help Topics dialog box. There are three instructions to use the box, as shown in Figure 0.10.

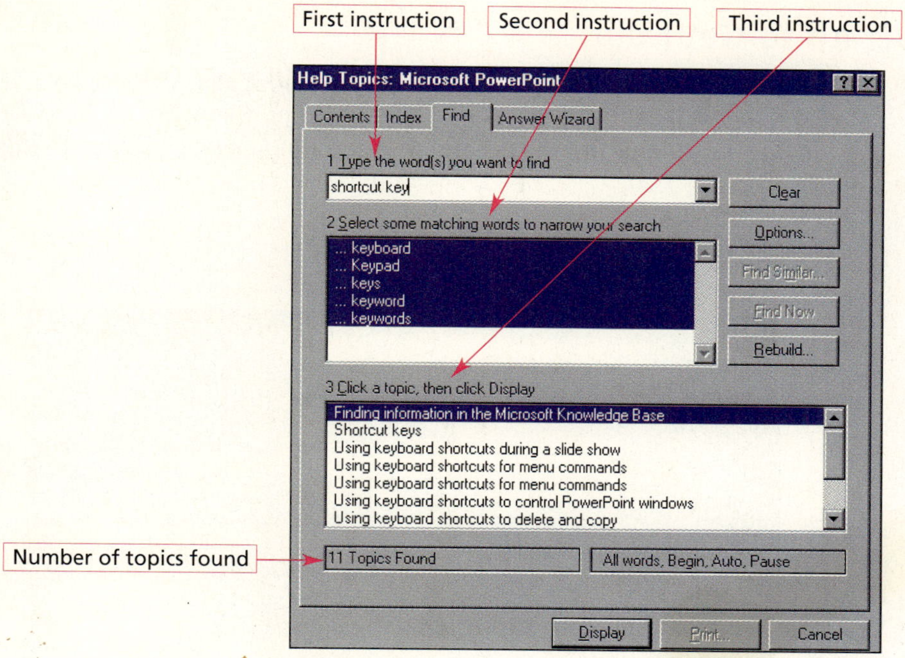

Figure 0.10

If the list of found topics is longer than the current screen display, you can use the scroll bar to view the complete list of topics. In the following steps you will use this feature to display information about shortcut keys.

To use the Find feature of on-screen Help:

1 Choose Microsoft PowerPoint Help Topics from the Help menu.

2 Select the Find tab.

3 Type **`shortcut key`** in the top text box, as shown in Figure 0.10.

4 Select *Shortcut keys* from the list of found topics, and then select the Display button.
A Shortcut Keys dialog box opens, displaying a list of topics specifically related to the use of shortcut keys.

5 Select *Using keyboard shortcuts to move around in text.*
A two-column display appears showing the key or key combinations for moving around in text.

6 Select the Back button.

7 Select *Using keyboard shortcuts for menu commands.*
A two-column display organized by menu option appears, showing keys or key combinations that produce the described actions.

8 Select Help Topics to redisplay the Find folder.

Using Answer Wizard to Get Help

PowerPoint also provides an ***Answer Wizard,*** that will display a list of topics related to a search you define in your own words. There are two instructions to use the Answer Wizard dialog box, as shown in Figure 0.11.

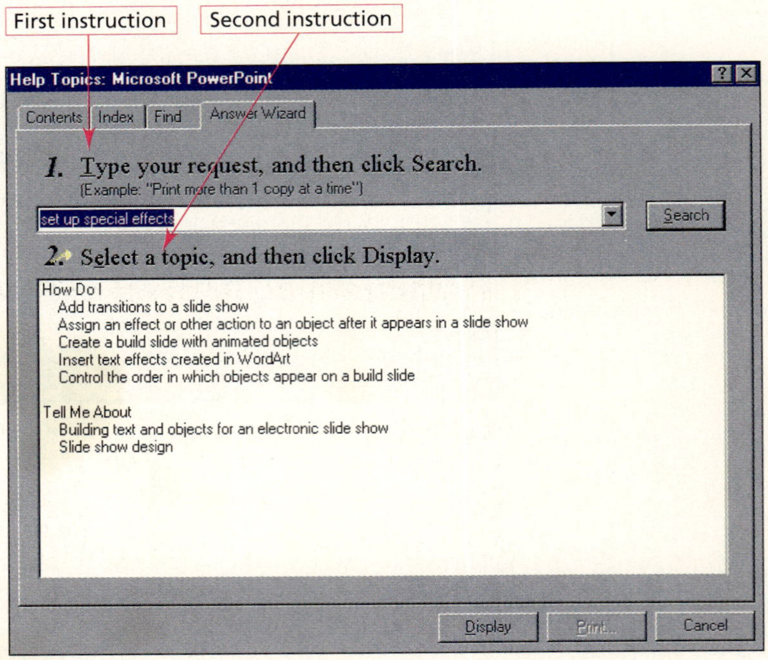

Figure 0.11

Answer Wizard will show you step-by-step instructions on how to complete a specific task if you select a topic in the How Do I section. Selecting a Tell Me About topic displays general information. For example, selecting *Slide show design* from the Answer Wizard screen shown in Figure 0.11 opens the dialog box shown in Figure 0.12. You would then click the color bar in front of a named topic, such as *Animated Builds* or *Slide annotations* shown in Figure 0.12, to display additional information about that topic. In the following steps you will use Answer Wizard to learn about slide show design and slide annotations.

To use the Answer Wizard feature of on-screen Help:

1 Select the Answer Wizard tab from the Help Topics dialog box.

2 Type `set up special effects` in the text box, and then select the Search button.
A list of related topics appears as shown in Figure 0.11.

3 Select *Slide show design* in the Tell Me About section, and then select the Display button.

4 Select the color bar in front of *Slide annotations,* as shown in Figure 0.12, and read how to annotate a slide.

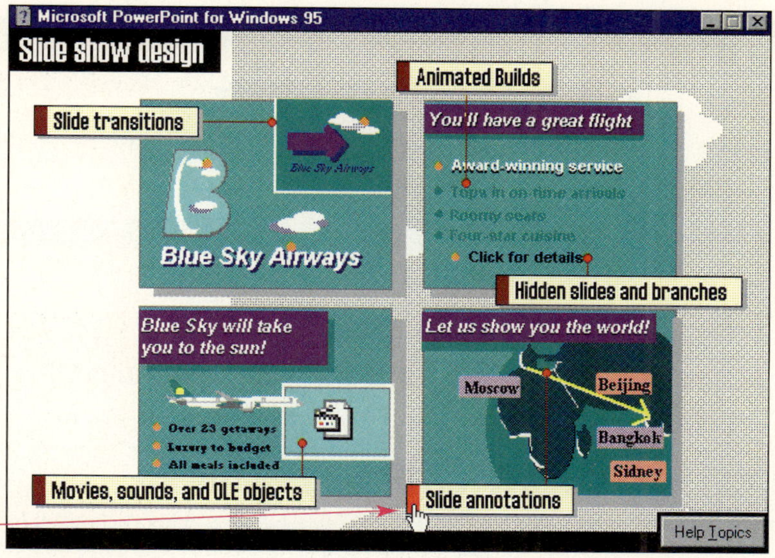

Selects the named topic

Figure 0.12

5 Select the color bar in front of *Hidden slides and branches,* and read how to hide slides and include other presentations in the current one.

6 Select Help Topics to redisplay the Answer Wizard folder.

7 Explore viewing other Help topics of your choice.

8 Click the Close button in the upper-right corner of the Help Topics dialog box.

Using the Help Button

If you are using a mouse, you can click the Help button to view information about a command or window item on the screen. When you click the Help button at the right end of the Standard toolbar, the pointer changes to an arrow with a question mark. You then position the pointer on the item you would like to know more about and click again. In the following steps you will use the Help button to view information about the Insert New Slide button.

To use the Help button:

1 Select the Help button at the right end of the Standard toolbar. The pointer changes to an arrow with a question mark.

2 Place the pointer on the Insert New Slide button (near the middle of the Standard toolbar).

3 Press the left mouse button.
Information about inserting a new slide appears as shown in Figure 0.13.

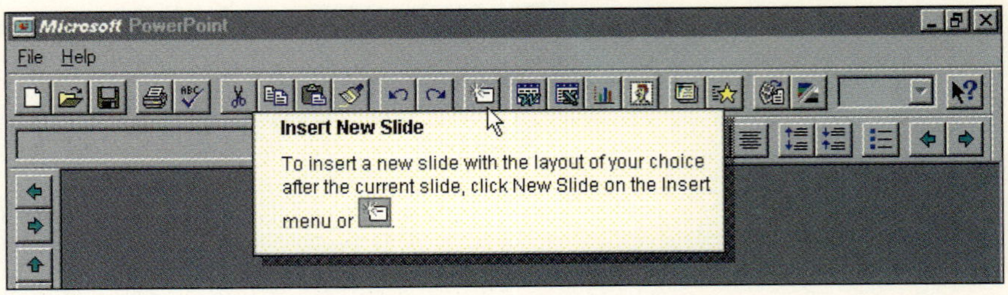

Figure 0.13

4 Click outside the information box to exit Help.

Exiting PowerPoint

When you finish working on a presentation, you can save or discard your changes and then continue developing another presentation or exit PowerPoint. You will start the process to leave the current presentation by choosing one of several options (or the corresponding shortcut keys) on the File menu.

You will choose Close if you want to close the current presentation but continue working in PowerPoint. You will choose Exit if you want to quit working in PowerPoint. Whichever option you select, you will be prompted to save a presentation if it contains any unsaved changes (saving a presentation is discussed in Project 1).

To exit PowerPoint:

1 Choose Exit from the File menu.

The Next Step

At this point you have a lot of information about the PowerPoint work environment. As you complete subsequent projects, you will have many opportunities to choose from menus, select buttons, and indicate your preferences in dialog boxes. However, these step-by-step instructions do not include using on-screen Help. Starting now, get in the habit of viewing on-screen Help about each new topic you encounter.

This concludes the Overview. You can either exit PowerPoint, go on to work the Study Questions, or proceed to Project 1.

Summary and Exercises

Summary

- PowerPoint is an outstanding presentation graphics program you can use to develop professional-looking presentations in the form of paper copies, overhead transparencies, 35mm slides, and automated slide shows.

- PowerPoint includes AutoContent Wizard, which guides you through the steps to create multiple slides around a common theme. You can also choose background settings and output forms.
- You can execute commands using menu bars, pull-down menus, and toolbar buttons. Often you must also specify settings in a dialog box to complete an operation.
- Whenever you want information about some feature of PowerPoint, you can use the extensive on-screen Help feature.

Key Terms and Operations

Key Terms

Answer Wizard
AutoContent Wizard
check box
command button
context-sensitive Help
dialog box
font
icon
list box
menu bar
presentation graphics program
pull-down list
pull-down menu
radio button
shortcut key
text box
toolbar

Operations

Start PowerPoint
Exit PowerPoint
Get on-screen Help

Study Questions

Multiple Choice

1. Which of the following is not a method to choose a menu bar option?
   a. Using a mouse to click the name of the option.
   b. Pressing CTRL in combination with the mnemonic letter.
   c. Pressing F10 and then pointing to the selection from the keyboard.
   d. All of the above are methods to choose a menu bar option.

2. Which of the following is not a true statement about toolbars?
   a. A toolbar can be positioned vertically or horizontally on the screen.
   b. A toolbar can be moved and sized.
   c. You can select a button on a toolbar using a mouse or the keyboard.
   d. All of the above.

3. Which type of box will you use to turn an option on or off?
   a. text box
   b. check box
   c. list box
   d. pull-down box

4. Which of the following is not a PowerPoint toolbar?
   a. Standard
   b. Formatting
   c. Drawshapes
   d. All of the above are PowerPoint toolbars.

5. Which tab in the Help Topics dialog box should you select if you know the exact name of the feature about which you need help?
   a. Index
   b. Answer Wizard
   c. Find
   d. Contents

Short Answer

1. On-screen Help can be general in nature or provide information about the operation in progress. What is the term used to describe help related to the operation in progress?
2. If an option on a pull-down menu is not currently available, how does that option appear relative to options that are available?
3. If you make a mistake while choosing from menus, what key can you press one or more times to restart the sequence?
4. Which PowerPoint wizard allows you to pick a theme for a presentation and guides you through the steps to create all the slides?
5. What type of program would you use to develop a professional-looking presentation in the form of paper copies, overhead transparencies, 35mm slides, and automated slide shows?

For Discussion

1. PowerPoint provides many buttons on seven toolbars. If you do not know the purpose of one of the buttons, what action(s) might you take to find out?
2. Describe features generally found in presentation graphics programs. In addition to features related to appearance, discuss the types of output and features that help you develop the content of a presentation.
3. You frequently have to issue commands to perform various presentation graphics functions. Explain the various ways you can issue a command using PowerPoint. Include a description of the menu structure, toolbars, and shortcut keys in your discussion.

PROJECT 1: CREATING A PRESENTATION

Objectives

After completing this project, you should be able to:

- Create a presentation using AutoContent Wizard
- Save a presentation
- Open an existing presentation
- Enter and edit text in Outline view
- Switch among alternative views of a presentation

CASE STUDY: PROMOTING VOLUNTEERISM

Assume that you are a student actively involved with the volunteer center on your campus. You are working with the staff to increase student awareness and participation in volunteer activities coordinated by the center. Just recently the center acquired PowerPoint for Windows 95 software, and you see an opportunity to develop a series of slides that you or other center representatives can present during classes and meetings of student organizations.

Designing the Solution

Before you begin to develop the content of your slides, you need to decide on the length of the presentation. For example, you might allocate 15 minutes or so to make your comments and provide additional time for questions. You must also know what equipment will be available, such as an overhead projector for black-and-white transparencies or a computer with color projection capabilities for an on-screen slide show.

Next you need to plan what you want to say and how you can best use slides for visual support during your presentation. For increased readability, the slides should generally show key points in short phrases preceded by bullets. A ***bullet*** is a symbol, such as a solid square block or open circle, that you use to set off an item in a list. You can add detail as you speak.

To create a new presentation, you can work with AutoContent Wizard, which will help you set up the content and appearance of your slides. You can also start with a blank presentation. In this project you will use the wizard approach to create the volunteerism presentation.

Using AutoContent Wizard

When you access PowerPoint, the dialog box shown in Figure 1.1 appears automatically. The Tip for New Users box in the lower-right corner tells you that AutoContent Wizard is the quickest way to create a presentation.

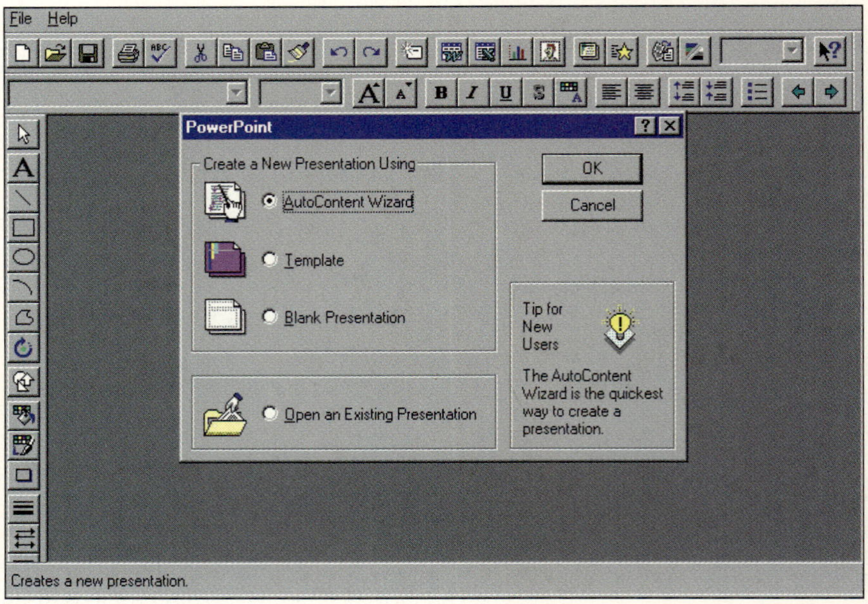

Figure 1.1

Selecting AutoContent Wizard starts a process in which you create a title slide and then choose one of 19 predefined presentation outlines: Recommending a Strategy; Selling a Product, Service, or Idea; Training; Reporting Progress; Communicating Bad News; General; and 13 others. Each predefined presentation includes a ***design template,*** which tells PowerPoint how the various parts of your presentation should appear. For example, the design template controls the background pattern and colors assigned to a slide.

AutoContent Wizard allows you to select one of three predefined visual styles, specify whether the presentation will be more or less than 30 minutes, and designate the type of slide you want and whether you will print handouts. If an overhead projector is the only equipment you will be able to use during a presentation, you should select ***Color Overheads*** (color printer only) or ***Black and White Overheads*** as the type of slide. Some printers, such as laser printers, allow you to print directly on plastic transparencies. Otherwise, you can print paper copies of your slides and have transparencies made at a copy center. If you have computer projection equipment, which allows you to display the current monitor image on a screen, you should select ***On-screen Presentation*** as the type of slide. PowerPoint provides one other slide output form, ***35mm Slides,*** which you can select if you have a desktop film recorder or you plan to send the file to a service bureau that will make the slides for you.

Tip You will usually print overheads, outlines, audience handouts, and speaker's notes using ***portrait orientation,*** in which the image is longer than it is wide. Presentations projected from a computer monitor or 35mm slides should be set up with ***Landscape orientation,*** in which the image is wider than it is long.

In this project you will use the General outline in AutoContent Wizard to create slides containing text shown in bulleted lists. You will edit the outline, adding or deleting bulleted items and adding or deleting slides.

To start AutoContent Wizard:

1 Start PowerPoint.
After a brief display showing copyright information, the PowerPoint dialog box shown in Figure 1.1 appears. If a Tip of the Day dialog box appears instead, select OK to remove it.

2 Select the AutoContent Wizard radio button if a black circle does not already appear in that button.

3 Select OK.
The initial AutoContent Wizard screen shown in Figure 1.2 appears.

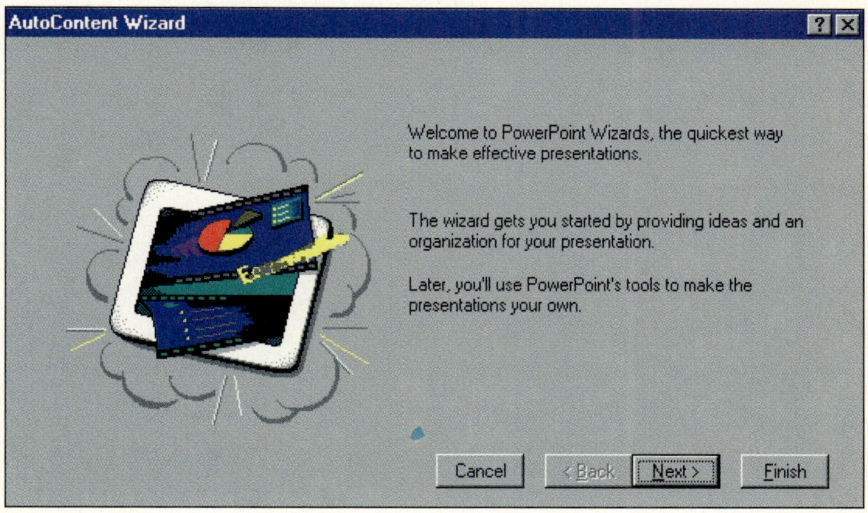

Figure 1.2

4 Select Next > or press (ENTER)
The second AutoContent Wizard screen appears as shown in Figure 1.3. One or more of the text boxes may already contain information provided by the registered owner of the program. You can change this text as described later in the project.

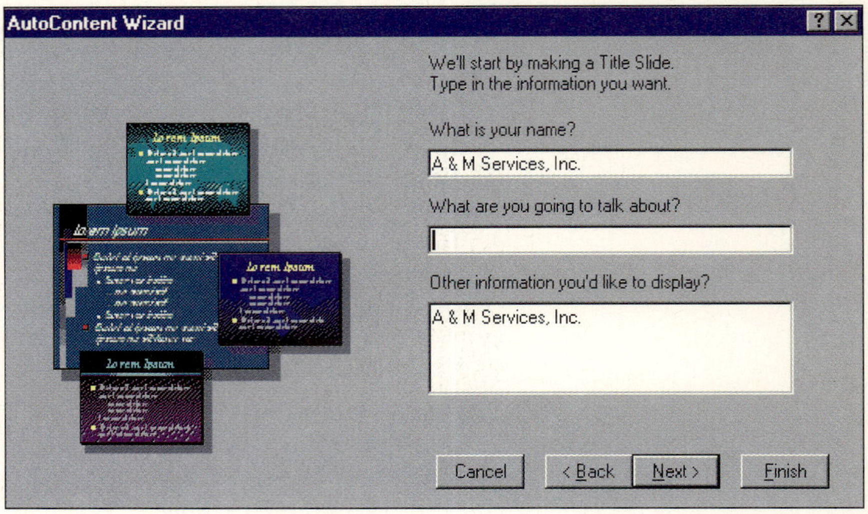

Figure 1.3

To create a title slide:

1 Select the What are you going to talk about? text box, if the flashing cursor doesn't already appear there.

2 Type **`Butler University Volunteers`** (do not press ENTER)

> ***Quick Fix*** If you accidentally press ENTER and the next AutoContent Wizard screen appears, select Back to return to the preceding screen.

3 Select the What is your name? text box.

4 Press DEL or BKSP until existing characters in the text box disappear.

5 Type **`Living the Difference`**

> ***Tip*** The text you enter in this box appears as the second line in the slide. You do not necessarily have to enter a person's name here. In these steps, for example, you do not enter a name because the slides will be used by more than one presenter.

6 Select the Other information you'd like to display? text box.

7 Press DEL or BKSP until existing characters in the text box disappear. The text for your title slide should appear as shown in Figure 1.4. If necessary, select a text box and make changes.

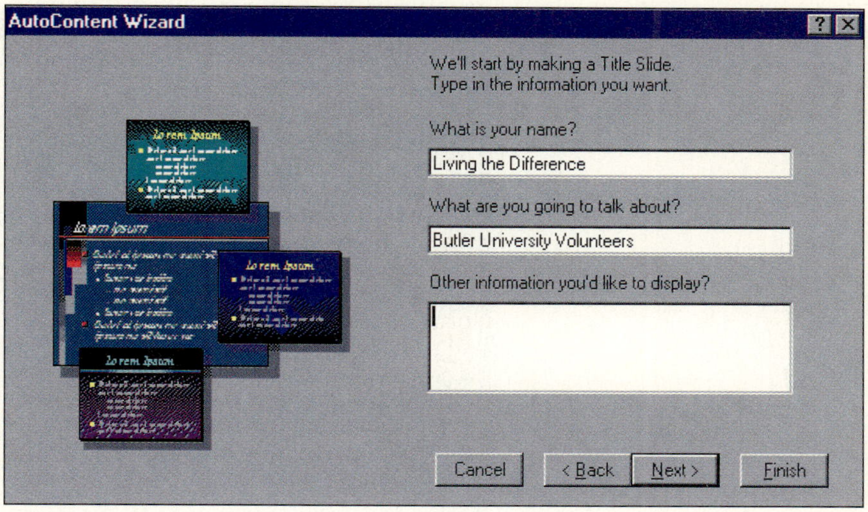

Figure 1.4

8 Select Next >.
The AutoContent Wizard screen shown in Figure 1.5 appears.

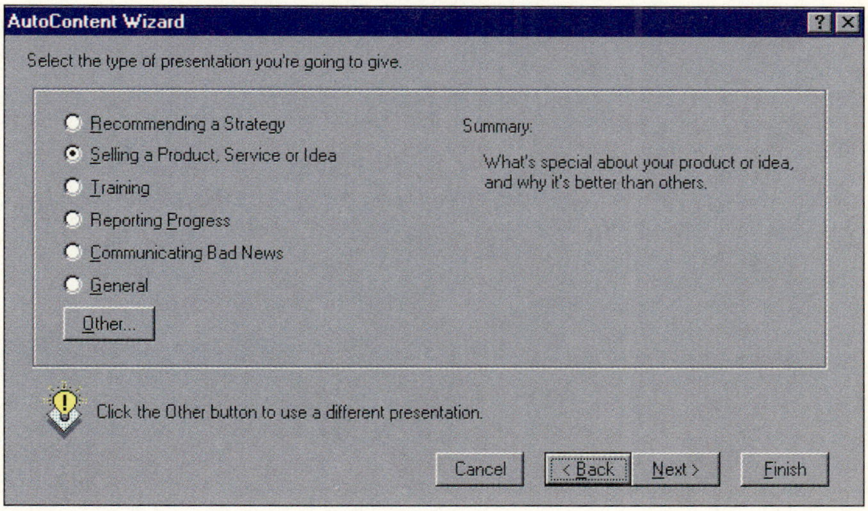

Figure 1.5

To view explanations of predefined presentation types and then select one:

1 Select any radio button.
The Summary area displays a brief explanation of the selected presentation type.

2 After viewing explanations of the initial six presentation types, select the Other command button.
The Select Presentation Template dialog box appears as shown in Figure 1.6. The title slide for the selected template (Business Plan in Figure 1.6) appears in a window to the right of the named presentation templates.

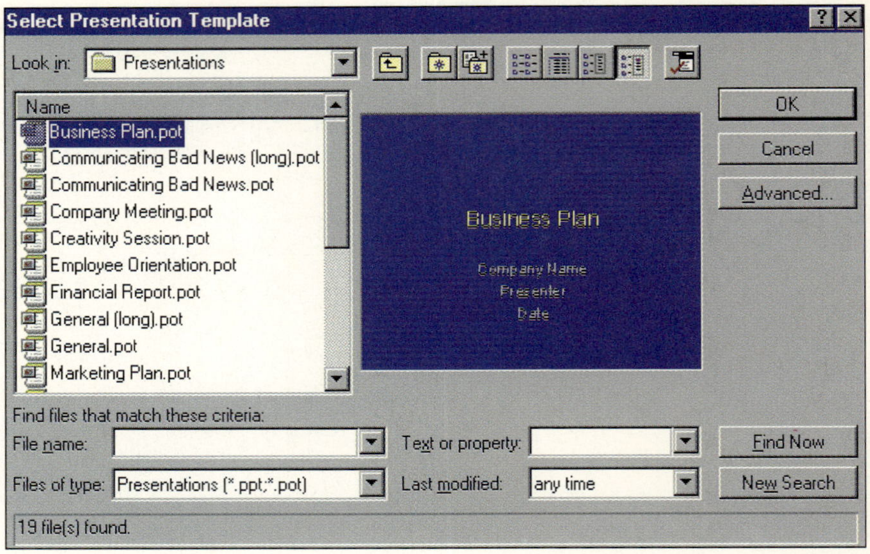

Figure 1.6

3 Select another presentation type, such as Marketing Plan.
The background color and design change to reflect the selected template.

4 After viewing other templates of your choice, select Cancel.
The AutoContent Wizard screen shown in Figure 1.5 reappears.

5 Select General as the presentation type, and then select Next >.

To complete the remaining AutoContent Wizard screens:

1 Select Default as the visual style and 30 Minutes or Less as the time to present.
The screen shown look like Figure 1.7.

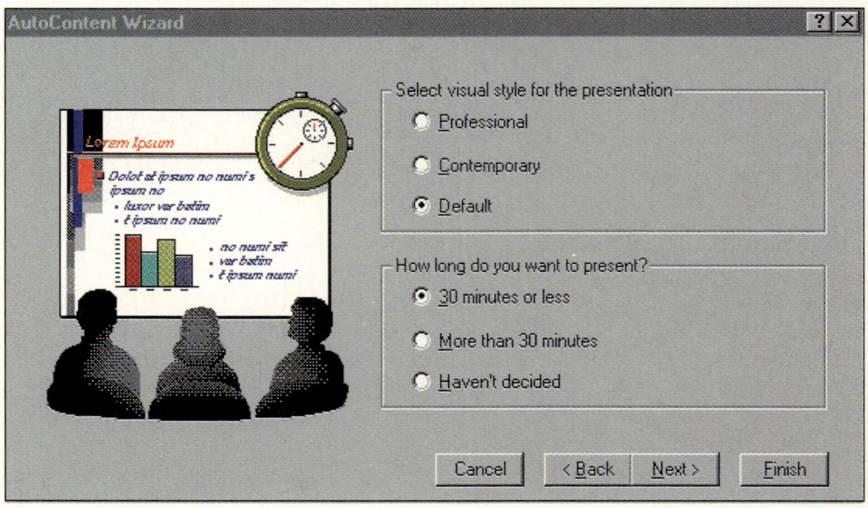

Figure 1.7

2 Select Next >.
The AutoContent Wizard screen shown in Figure 1.8 appears.

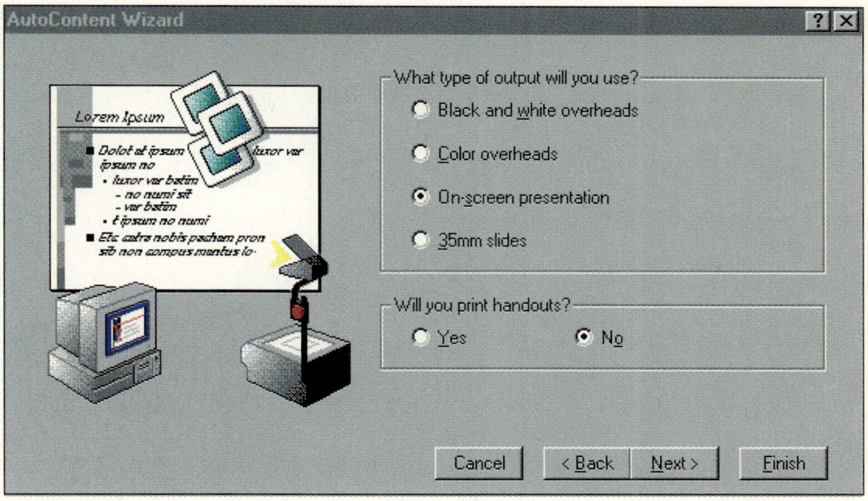

Figure 1.8

3 Change settings, if necessary, to match those shown in Figure 1.8.

4 Select Next >.

The AutoContent Wizard screen shown in Figure 1.9 appears.

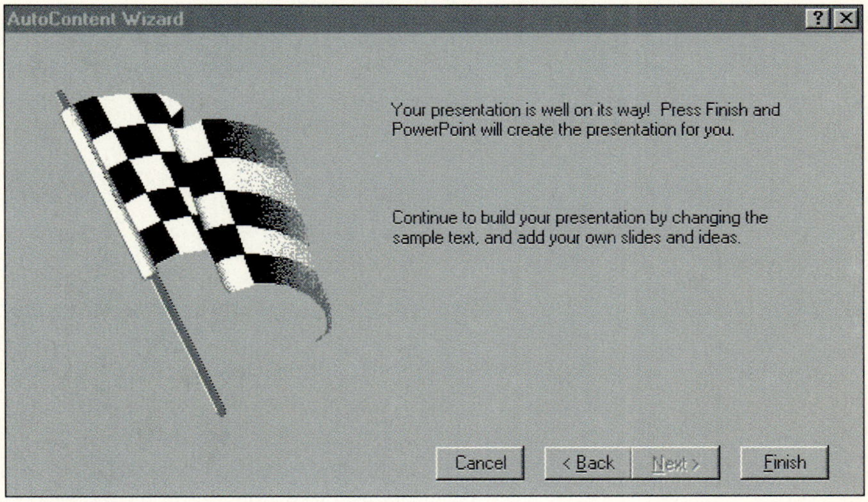

Figure 1.9

5 Select Finish.

The title slide appears as shown in Figure 1.10. PowerPoint creates eight slides in addition to the title slide.

Caution Before you begin to edit the suggested slides in a General presentation, you should save the work you have done up to this point.

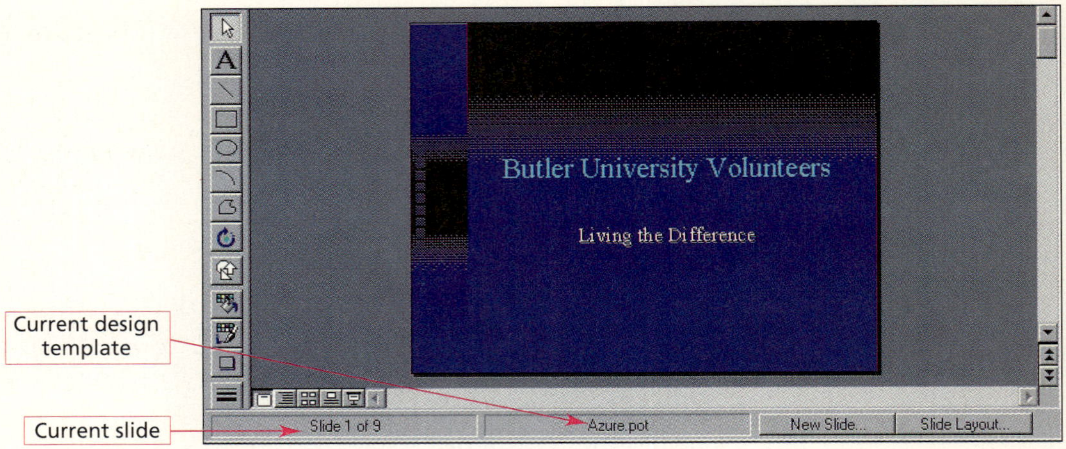

Figure 1.10

Tip The design template controls the background pattern and colors assigned to slides. If you don't like the look assigned by PowerPoint, you can choose Apply Design Template from the Format menu and select another one.

Caution Once you have finished using AutoContent Wizard, the outline that results can only be changed by editing. To select a different outline, start a new presentation using AutoContent Wizard.

Saving a Presentation

Your ability to save a presentation to disk is one major advantage of using a presentation graphics program. Once saved to disk the presentation may be called back onto the screen, changed, and saved again. Frequently saving your presentation can save you substantial retyping time should a power outage occur during a work session.

When you save a file, you must specify both its name and location on disk. You will supply the file name; the program supplies the three-character extension .ppt, identifying a PowerPoint presentation.

Tip Because most school computer labs do not allow you to save files to the hard disk or network, the illustrations in this module assume that you are saving your files to a disk in drive A:. To save a presentation in a different location, in the following steps you can replace any drive A: designation with the drive you prefer.

If you want to save a presentation to disk and continue to work on the presentation, you can select the Save button, or you can choose the Save or Save As command on the File menu. Choosing Save will replace the copy of a presentation on disk with the version of the presentation on the screen. Choosing Save As allows you to change the name or storage location on disk of a previously saved presentation.

Caution If you select the Save button or choose the Save command on the File menu, the presentation on-screen is automatically saved under its current name. You do not have an opportunity to verify the file name.

A new presentation is named presentation until you save it. Thereafter, the name of the presentation displays in the title bar at the top of the screen. In the following steps, you will save the initial outline for the presentation on promoting volunteerism.

Reminder A button or icon next to a numbered step shows the button or icon on your screen you can select to execute the instructions in the step.

To save a presentation and close the file:

1 Choose Save from the File menu.
The File Save dialog box appears.

2 Click the down arrow at the right end of the Save In text box.
A pull-down list of the drives attached to your computer appears, similar to the one shown in Figure 1.11.

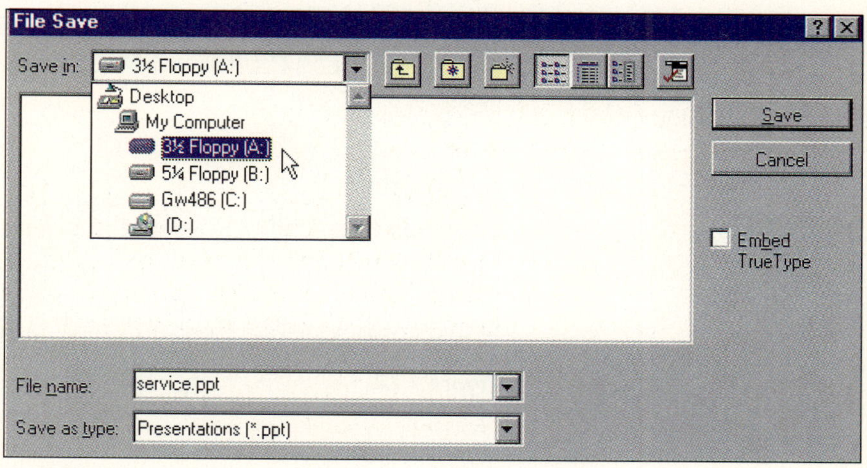

Figure 1.11

3 Select Floppy [A:].
The pull-down list disappears, and the drive A: specification appears in the Save In text box.

Reminder Substitute the appropriate drive if you are saving your presentation in another location.

4 Type `service` in the File Name text box.

5 Select Save.
After a brief delay the Properties dialog box appears.

> ***Tip*** If the Properties dialog box does not appear automatically when you save a presentation for the first time, choose Options from the Tools menu, select the General tab, select the Prompt for File Properties check box, select OK, and then save your changes. If you do not have the ability to change options or do not want the Properties dialog box displayed, skip to step 9.

6 Click the Summary tab, if Summary is not the current folder.

7 Add and delete text as necessary to display the information shown in Figure 1.12.

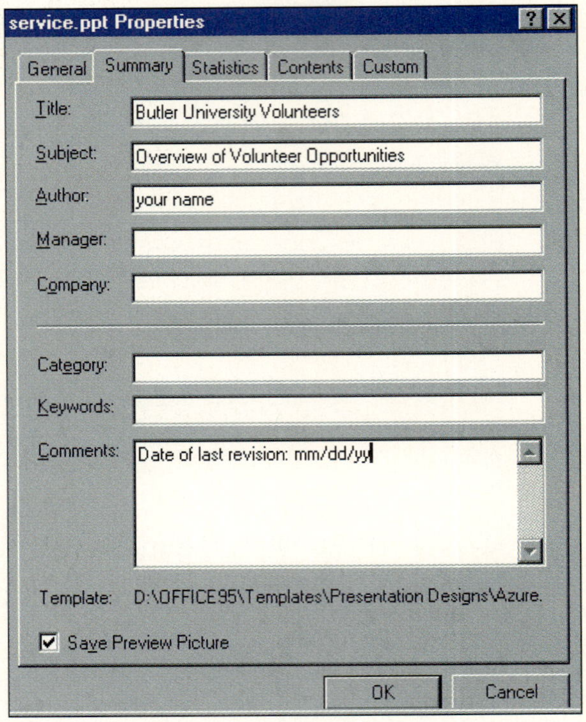

Figure 1.12

8 Select OK to complete saving the file and to restore the display of the title slide.
Your presentation should now be saved on the drive you specified. PowerPoint displays the file name in the title bar at the top of the screen.

9 Choose Close from the File menu to close the presentation.

EXIT If necessary, you can exit PowerPoint now and continue this project later.

Opening a Presentation

To open a previously stored presentation, you can select the Open button from the Standard toolbar, choose Open from the File menu, or select Open an Existing Presentation from the PowerPoint dialog box. After any of these selections the File Open dialog box opens and should look similar to Figure 1.13.

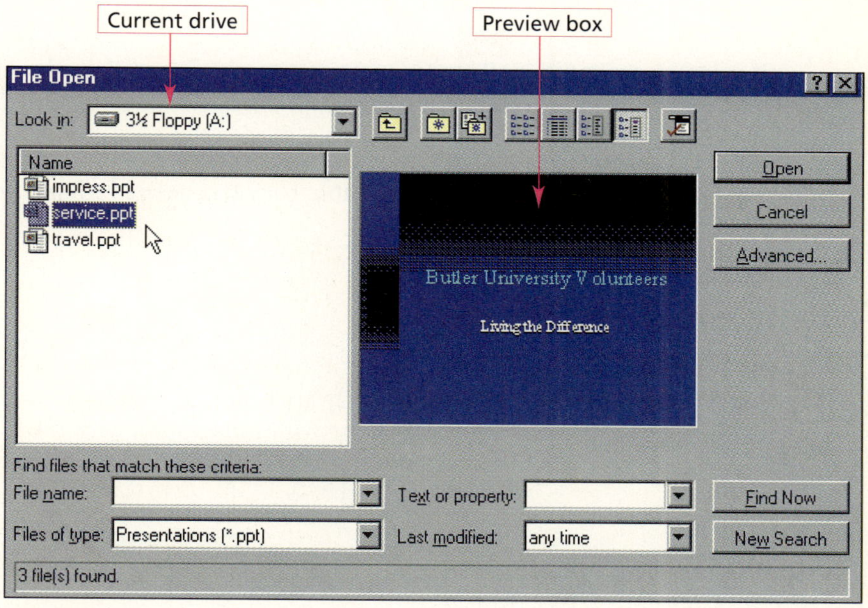

Figure 1.13

Recall that you must specify a location and file name in a dialog box in order to *save* a file. You will make the same specifications to *open* a file. After you select a presentation in the Name box, the first slide appears in the Preview box (see Figure 1.13), allowing you to verify that this is the file you want. If you have many files stored on disk, you can limit the display to those files matching criteria you specify.

Tip Files created in other programs can be used in PowerPoint. For example, if you typed an outline using Microsoft Word, you can open the file in PowerPoint. Each heading becomes a slide, and subtopics under each heading appear in bulleted lists.

You can open several presentations at a time. The one you are currently working on, called the ***active presentation,*** appears in the top window. To see a list of open presentations, you can choose Window from the menu bar.

In the following steps you will open the service.ppt presentation, which you set up using AutoContent Wizard earlier in the project. Remember to substitute the correct location if you did not store this file on the disk in drive A:.

To open an existing presentation:

1 Start PowerPoint if necessary.

2 Select Open on the Standard toolbar.
The File Open dialog box appears.

3 Select the drive on which you are storing your PowerPoint files.

4 Select *service* in the list of file names at the left side of the dialog box.
After a brief delay the title slide of the selected presentation appears in the Preview box, as shown in Figure 1.13.

5 Select Open.
The selected presentation appears as shown in Figure 1.10.

> ***Tip*** If you are sure of the name of the presentation you want to open, you can double-click the desired file name in place of steps 4 and 5.

Switching Views

A ***view*** is a way to look at the slides in a PowerPoint presentation. PowerPoint provides five views within which you can see the results of your work and make changes. You will switch views using the View toolbar shown in Figure 1.14.

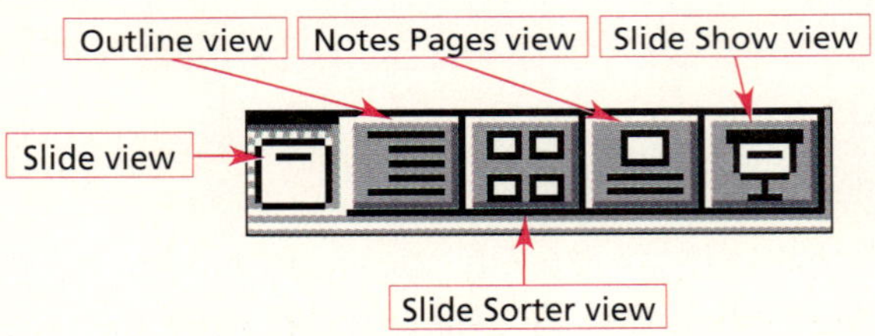

Figure 1.14

You see one slide at a time in ***Slide view,*** and on this work surface you can add graphics, draw shapes, and change the slide layout as well as edit text. ***Outline view*** displays the entire presentation in outline form, the preferred work surface on which to make major text changes. In ***Notes Pages view*** you also see one slide at a time, but a slide occupies only the top half of the work surface. In the bottom half you can add speaker's notes.

Slide Sorter view displays reduced images (text and graphics) of all slides on a single screen. In this view you can change the order of slides as well as set timing between slides for an on-screen presentation. After making changes in this view, you can see the complete electronic presentation in ***Slide Show view,*** in which each slide fills the screen.

In the following steps you will switch the view of the volunteerism presentation to Outline view.

To look at a presentation in Outline view:

1 Select Outline View from the View toolbar.
The selected presentation appears in outline form, as shown in Figure 1.15.

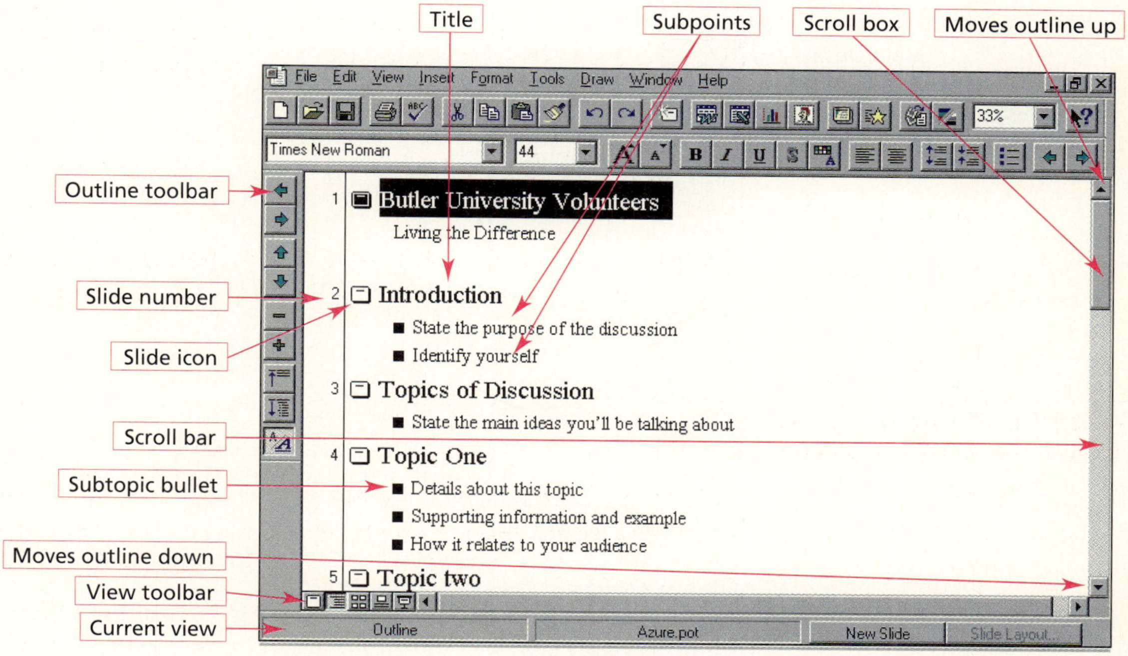

Figure 1.15

WORKING IN OUTLINE VIEW

In Outline view, you work with slide titles and main text. The title and subpoints of each slide are listed in order, as shown in Figure 1.15. A slide icon appears to the left of each slide's title, and subtopic bullets precede key points. You will use Outline view when you want to see the organization of your presentation, edit text, add and delete bulleted items, add and delete slides, and change the order of slides.

Using the Outlining Toolbar

The Outlining toolbar includes the nine buttons shown in Figure 1.16. The first four buttons help you change the arrangement of text, and the next four buttons control the level of detail shown. You can use the last button to switch between a display of ***formatted text***, which shows variations in font and type size, and unformatted text.

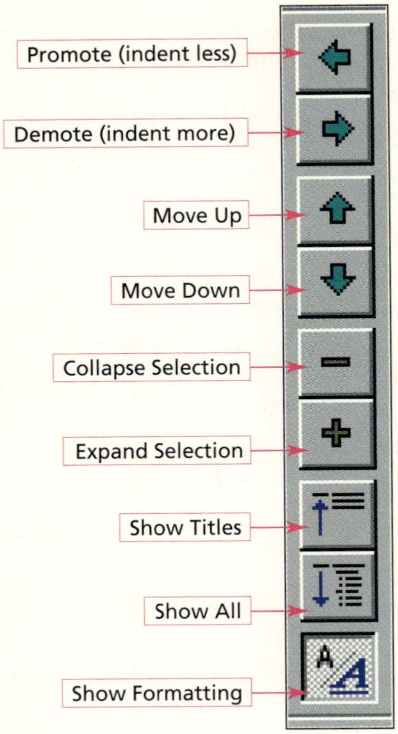

Figure 1.16

Before selecting one of the first four buttons, position the *insertion point* within the paragraph you want to move. The ***insertion point*** is a blinking vertical bar that marks the position where text will be inserted or deleted when you type on the keyboard. If you ***promote*** a topic, the selected text shifts left one level in the outline, and the bullet character changes to match other bullets at that level. If you ***demote*** a topic, the selected text shifts right one level in the outline, and the bullet character changes to match other bullets at that level. (Promoting and demoting slide topics is discussed further in Project 2.) The Move Up and Move Down buttons move the paragraph containing the insertion point above the preceding item and below the next item, respectively.

Use the Collapse Selection button to display only the title of the slide containing the insertion point. A line appears below the title, indicating the text is collapsed. The Expand Selection button expands text that has been collapsed in one slide. The next two buttons collapse all levels of text for all slides (Show Titles) and expand the outline so all levels of text for all slides appear (Show All).

In the following steps you will change the view from formatted text to unformatted text, switch to a collapsed view of the outline, and then restore the expanded display.

To display unformatted text in Outline view and then restore formatted text:

1 Check that the volunteerism presentation (service.ppt) appears on-screen in Outline view, as shown in Figure 1.15.

2 Press CTRL + HOME if the insertion point is not at the top of the outline.

3 Select Show Formatting on the Outlining toolbar until formatting (boldface and larger type size) disappears from the outline.
The smaller type size in the unformatted display allows you to see more of the outline.

4 Select Show Formatting on the Outlining toolbar to restore formatting.

To collapse and expand the outline:

1 Select Show Titles on the Outlining toolbar.
Only slide titles appear in the outline. The line beneath a title indicates that slide is collapsed.

2 Select Show All on the Outlining toolbar to expand the outline.

Editing Text in Outline View

Whether you use one of the predefined presentation types available through AutoContent Wizard or develop a presentation from scratch, you will find that Outline view provides an easy-to-use work surface on which to make text changes. You will edit text in Outline view in much the same way as you edit text in your favorite word processor. For example, you can delete the character preceding the insertion point by pressing (BKSP) and remove the character at the insertion point by pressing (DEL) To add text, you will move the insertion point to the location where you want new characters to appear and start typing.

If you want to replace an entire phrase, however, you do not have to delete the unwanted text in a separate step. Instead, you will select the block of text to replace and then start typing. The highlighted text disappears automatically as the first new character appears. You can select text using a mouse by positioning the mouse pointer at the beginning of the phrase, pressing and holding down the left mouse button, dragging the mouse pointer until the rest of the phrase is highlighted, and releasing the mouse button. In PowerPoint's Outline view you can also select all text in a subpoint by clicking its bullet or select the contents of an entire slide by clicking the slide icon (see Figure 1.15).

In the following steps you will work in Outline view to edit the presentation on promoting volunteerism that you created using AutoContent Wizard. The title slide changes are done, but the remaining topics still show AutoContent Wizard's suggested organization and hints for developing the content. For example, the General presentation form shown in Figure 1.15 suggests that after you explain the purpose of the discussion and identify yourself (slide 2), you provide an overview of the key points you intend to address (slide 3). You will now replace this outline with your own speaking points, which are shown in Figure 1.17. Remember to save your work frequently.

1 Butler University Volunteers
   Living the Difference
2 I'm interested. What now?
   - Service starts with each and every one of us
   - Volunteer Center - your campuse resource for LIVING THE DIFFERENCE through volunteering
3 More about the Volunteer Center
   - Volunteer Center Mission
   - Support Services
   - Current Opportunities
4 Volunteer Center Mission
   - Assisting Butler University members, especially students, in finding and experiencing meaningful volunteer opportunities
   - Facilitating reflection to stimulate learning from those experiences
5 Volunteer Center Support Services
   - Finding the right activity
   - Monthly Newsletter
   - One on and group activity support
6 A Sample of Volunteer Opportunities
   - Junior Achievement
   - WISH Foundation
   - Rehabilitation Hospital of Indiana
   - Big Sisters/Big Brothers
   - Into the streets
   - "Jail & Bail" fund-raiser
7 Making a Difference
   - What: Dyslexia Institute of Indiana
   - What: Give tours in a beautiful $1 million dollar draem home
   - When: September 3 - September 18 (2-hr shifts everyday except Thurdays; 5-hr shift Thursday)
   - Where: Admirals Point model home
8 Rewards of Volunteerism
   - Making a difference in someone's life
   - Developing as a future leader in your discipline and your community
9 Live the Difference
   - Take some time to stop by the Volunteer Center
   - Make a commitment that is meaningful
   - Reflect on your volunteer experience

Figure 1.17

> ***Caution*** Pressing ENTER at the end of an outline item will insert a blank new item. If this is not the effect you want, position the insertion point to the right of the new bullet and press BKSP to remove the bullet.

To edit the second slide:

1 Locate slide 2 and select the title.
The title of slide 2 appears highlighted, as shown in Figure 1.18.

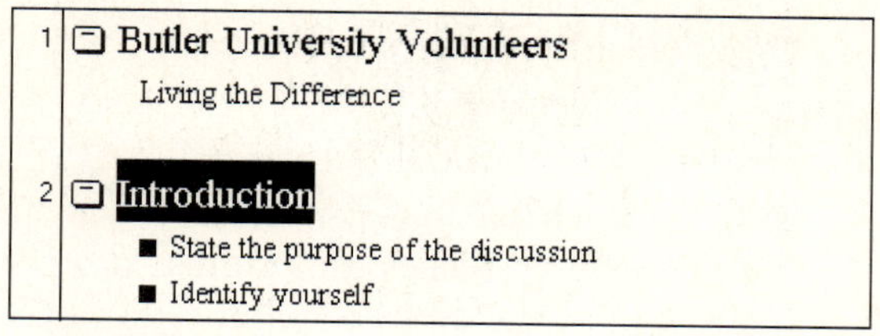

Figure 1.18

2 Type **`I'm interested. What now?`** (Do *not* press (ENTER)).
The highlighted text disappears, replaced by the text you typed.

> ***Quick Fix*** Pressing (ENTER) at the end of a slide's title will insert a new slide. If this happens, press (BKSP) to delete the slide and move the insertion point to the previous title.

3 Select the first bulleted subtopic in slide 2.
The subtopic *State the purpose of the discussion* appears highlighted on the screen.

> ***Reminder*** Clicking the bullet preceding a subtopic automatically selects the associated text on that line. This technique cannot be used to highlight only a title line, because clicking the icon preceding a slide's title selects all text on the slide.

4 Type **`Service starts with each and every one of us`** (do *not* press (ENTER)).

5 Select the second bulleted subtopic in slide 2.
The subtopic *Identify yourself* appears highlighted on the screen.

6 Type (including any spelling errors) **`Volunteer Center-your campuse resource for LIVING THE DIFFERENCE through volunteering`** (do *not* press (ENTER)).
Check that slide 2 of your outline view matches the text shown in Figure 1.19. Make changes if necessary.

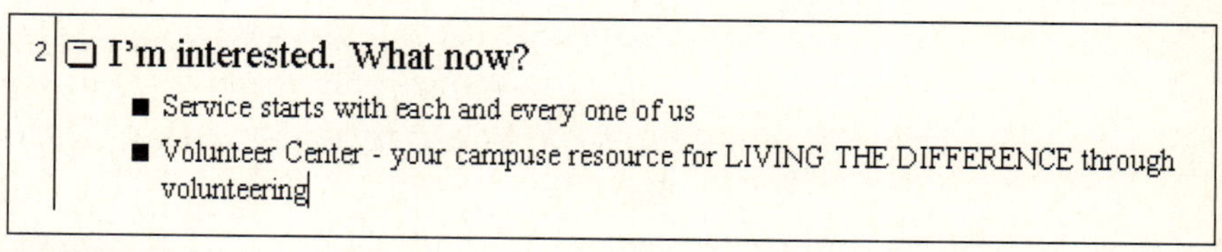

Figure 1.19

To edit the remaining slides:

1 Locate slide 3 and select the title.
The original slide title *Topics of Discussion* appears highlighted on the screen.

2 Type **`More about the Volunteer Center`** (do *not* press (ENTER)).
The new text replaces the original title.

3 Select the bulleted subtopic.
The subtopic *State the main ideas you'll be talking about* appears highlighted on the screen.

4 Type **`Volunteer Center Mission`** and press (ENTER)
The new text replaces the original subtopic, and PowerPoint inserts a new blank line preceded by a bullet.

5 Type **`Support Services`** and press (ENTER)

6 Type **`Current Opportunities`** (do *not* press (ENTER)).
Check that the text on your slide 3 matches that shown for slide 3 in Figure 1.17. Make changes as necessary.

7 Edit the title and first two topics in slide 4 to match the text shown in Figure 1.17.

8 Select the third subtopic.
The screen should look like Figure 1.20.

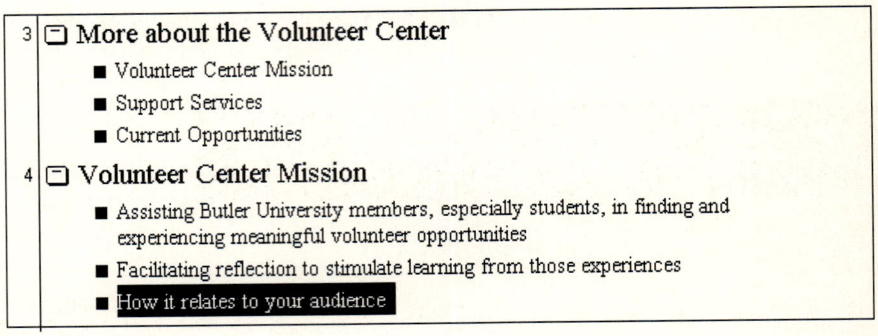

Figure 1.20

9 Press (DEL) to delete the original third topic.

10 Edit the remaining slides 5 through 9 to match those shown in Figure 1.17 (be sure to include the spelling errors in slide 7).

11 Save the file.

> ***Caution*** Be sure to save your work frequently during any long editing process.

To look at a presentation in Slide Show view and then close the file:

1 Select Slide Show View from the View toolbar.
The Windows operating environment disappears, and the first slide fills the entire screen.

2 Press the left mouse button to see the next slide.

> ***Tip*** You can also view the next slide by typing **N**, pressing (SPACE), or pressing (PGDN) To view a previous slide in a slide show, you can type **P**, press (PGUP) or press the right mouse button and then select Previous.

3 Press (SPACE) or (PGDN) until you have viewed all slides.
At the end of the slide show, the most recent view appears on the screen (in this case, Outline).

4 Close the file.

The Next Step

In this project you worked in Outline view to modify a General type multislide presentation suggested by AutoContent Wizard and then looked at the slides in Slide Show view. You will work within the various views throughout subsequent projects, but you will not have a guided tour using another predefined presentation type. On your own you might select one of the other types, such as Selling a Product, Service or Idea, and then modify the suggested organization and hints for content to suit your needs.

This concludes Project 1. You can either exit PowerPoint or go on to work the Study Questions, Review Exercises, and Assignments.

Summary and Exercises

Summary

- Before you begin using PowerPoint to develop a graphics presentation, you should decide on the length of the presentation, find out what type of equipment will be available, and plan what you want to say.
- PowerPoint's AutoContent Wizard helps you set up one of 19 basic outlines for a presentation and guides you through the steps to create all the slides.
- When you save a presentation, you must specify both its name and its location on disk. PowerPoint applies a .PPT extension.
- PowerPoint provides two options to save a presentation: Save and Save As. Choose Save to replace the copy of a presentation on disk with the version of the document on the screen. Choose Save As to save a presentation for the first time or to change the name or location of a previously saved document.
- To open a presentation, you must specify both its name and location on disk. You can open several presentations at a time.
- A view is a way to look at the slides in a PowerPoint presentation. You can work with a presentation in any one of five views: Slide, Outline, Slide Sorter, Notes Pages, and Slide Show.
- Outline view provides an easy-to-use work surface on which to make text changes. You edit text in Outline view in much the same way as you edit text in your favorite word processor.

Key Terms and Operations

Key Terms
35mm Slides
active presentation
Black and White Overheads
bullet
Color Overheads
demote
formatted text
insertion point
landscape orientation
Notes Pages view
On-screen Presentation
Outline view
portrait orientation
promote
Slide view
Slide Show view
Slide Sorter view
template
view

Operations
Create a presentation using AutoContent Wizard
Edit text in Outline view
Open a presentation
Save a presentation
Switch from one view to another

Study Questions

Multiple Choice

1. Which of the following PowerPoint views shows more than one slide per screen?
   a. Slide
   b. Slide Sorter
   c. Slide Show
   d. Notes Pages

2. Which of the following is a false statement about PowerPoint?
   a. Files created in other programs cannot be used in PowerPoint.
   b. You can open several presentations at a time.
   c. When you save a presentation for the first time, PowerPoint automatically displays the File Save dialog box.
   d. When you access PowerPoint, the PowerPoint dialog box appears automatically.

3. To save an existing presentation under a different name, use the PowerPoint command:
   a. Save
   b. Save As
   c. Rename
   d. Replace

4. Which of the following buttons on the Outlining toolbar would you select to show only the title of the slide containing the insertion point?
   a. Collapse Selection
   b. Show Titles
   c. Demote
   d. None of the above.

5. While working in Outline view, which key could you press at the end of a slide's title to insert a new slide?
   a. ↓
   b. PGDN
   c. ENTER
   d. None of the above.

6. Which of the following is a false statement about AutoContent Wizard?
   a. Once you have finished using AutoContent Wizard, you can change the outline that results only by editing.
   b. To select a different outline, start a new presentation using AutoContent Wizard.
   c. You can choose among eight predefined outlines.
   d. AutoContent Wizard is one of the options in the PowerPoint dialog box that you can use to create a new presentation.

7. To view the previous slide during a slide show,
   a. press PGUP
   b. press the right mouse button, and then select Previous.
   c. Both a and b.
   d. None of the above.

8. In which of the following PowerPoint views does a slide occupy the entire screen?
   a. Slide
   b. Slide Sorter
   c. Slide Show
   d. Notes Pages

9. Which of the following is not a valid type of slide presentation?
   a. Color Overheads
   b. On-screen Presentation
   c. Landscape
   d. 35mm Slides

10. Which of the following is not one of the basic outlines you can select using AutoContent Wizard?
    a. Recommending a Strategy
    b. Communicating Good News
    c. Training
    d. Selling a Product, Service, or Idea

Short Answer

1. What is the term describing the flashing vertical bar that marks the position where text will be inserted or deleted when you type on the keyboard?
2. Which dialog box would you use to document the title, subject, and author of a presentation? (This information would not appear on any slide in the presentation.)
3. What is the term for a symbol such as a solid square block or open circle used to set off an item in a list?
4. In some software a three-character extension identifies the type of file. What is the extension that identifies a PowerPoint presentation?
5. Which button on the Outlining toolbar would you select to expand a collapsed outline so that all levels of text for all slides appear?
6. What key can you press to delete a character to the left of the insertion point?
7. What term describes shifting selected text left one level in an outline?
8. Which button on the Outlining toolbar would you select to switch between showing plain text and showing text with changes in print style and size?
9. In which PowerPoint view can you set up speaker's notes?
10. What key can you press at the end of an outline item to insert a blank new item below?

For Discussion

1. Describe some of the actions you should take to plan a presentation before you start creating it using the PowerPoint software.
2. Selecting AutoContent Wizard starts a multistep process. Describe the actions you must take during the process and the results you achieve.
3. You can work with a PowerPoint presentation in any one of five views. Briefly describe the primary reason(s) to use each view.
4. Describe how you would insert, delete, and replace text while working in Outline view.
5. When you are working in Outline view, you can hide some of the text. Explain what text can be hidden and how you know from looking at an outline that some text is not in view.

Review Exercises

Promoting a Service

1. Start PowerPoint and select AutoContent Wizard.

> ***Tip*** If PowerPoint is already running, you can find AutoContent Wizard by choosing New from the File menu and selecting the Presentations tab in the New Presentation dialog box.

2. On AutoContent Wizard's title slide screen, enter **`First Impressions`** in the What are you going to talk about? text box.
3. Enter **`For students, by students`** in the What is your name? text box. Also delete text, if any, in the Other information you'd like to display? text box.
4. On AutoContent Wizard's presentation type screen, select Selling a Product, Service, or Idea.
5. Set Contemporary as the visual style and 30 minutes or less as the time estimate for the presentation.
6. Set the type of output as On-screen Presentation (and do not print handouts).
7. Switch to Outline view, and edit the suggested outline to match the text shown in Figure 1.21. Include the spelling errors in slides 6 and 7.

1	❑ *First Impressions* For students, by students
2	❑ *The Problem: Presenting a Professional Image* ◆ A full line of paper products supporting a job search ◆ Ability to update information
3	❑ *The Solution: Using Campus Resources* ◆ All products developed by members of the Entrepreneurship Club ◆ Guidance provided by faculty in the Communications department
4	❑ *First Impressions Product Line* ◆ Resumes ◆ Letterhead stationery ◆ Matching envelopes ◆ Business cards
5	*Cost Analysis* ◆ Prices at or below those of commercial printers ◆ Volume discounts
6	*Our Strengths* ◆ Three year record of doing quality work ◆ Wide veriety of colors and print styles ◆ On-campus location
7	❑ *Key Benefits* ◆ Quality products at resonable prices ◆ Quik turnaround
8	❑ *For more information* ◆ Call campus extension 9876 ◆ E-mail ENCLUB ◆ Pick up a brochure in the Student Activities Office

Figure 1.21

8. Save your work using the name impress.ppt (you will use this file in the Project 2 review exercises.)

Buying a Computer

1. Start PowerPoint and select AutoContent Wizard.

> ***Tip*** If PowerPoint is already running, you can find AutoContent Wizard by choosing New from the File menu and selecting the Presentations tab in the New Presentation dialog box.

2. On AutoContent Wizard's title slide screen, type `Buying a Computer` in the What are you going to talk about? text box.
3. Type your name in the What is your name? text box. Also delete text, if any, in the Other information you'd like to display? text box.
4. On AutoContent Wizard's presentation type screen, select General.

5. Set Professional as the visual style and 30 minutes or less as the time estimate for the presentation.
6. Set the type of output as On-screen Presentation (and do not print handouts).
7. Switch to Outline view, and edit the suggested outline to match the text shown in Figure 1.22.

1 ❑ BUYING A COMPUTER
   Your Name Here

2 ❑ Introduction
   - Buying the right computer for you
   - Who can you trust?

3 ❑ Strategy for Buying a Computer
   - Deciding what you need
   - Choosing the right software and hardware
   - Shopping for your computer
   - Taking the first step

4 ❑ Deciding What You Need
   - Be an informed buyer
   - Make a list - what do you need?
   - Decide what you can afford

5 ❑ Selecting Software and Hardware
   - Selecting hardware first
   - Selecting software second
   - Make a shopping list

6 ❑ Shopping for Your Computer
   - Get three price quotes
   - Compare warranties and services
   - Experience the difference - check with friends

7 ❑ Taking the First Step
   - Become computer literate

Figure 1.22

8. Save your work using the name computer.ppt (you will use this file in the Project 2 review exercises).

Assignments

Getting Help on Finding a File

Use the Answer Wizard in on-screen Help to look up information about finding a file. Write a brief summary of what you learned.

Reporting on Progress

Create a new presentation using AutoContent Wizard. Select Communicating Bad News as the presentation type. Modify the suggested organization and content to communicate to members of a class, team, or club that goals have not been met for participation in a school, sport, or charity event. Save the file using the name update.ppt.

Presenting Your Plan

Create a new presentation using AutoContent Wizard. Select Marketing Plan as the presentation type. Modify the suggested organization and content to communicate your ideas for promoting a service (such as personal shopping, child care, lawn and landscape, home health, hot-air ballooning or sky-diving). Save the file using the name myplan.ppt.

PROJECT 2: POLISHING A PRESENTATION

Objectives

After completing this project, you should be able to:

- Proofread a presentation
- Move and copy text
- Promote and demote topics
- Add, delete, and duplicate slides
- Create speaker's notes
- Spell-check a presentation
- Print a presentation

CASE STUDY: PROMOTING VOLUNTEERISM II

Very few individuals can produce a perfectly worded, well-organized, and complete presentation on the first attempt. For example, in Project 1 you edited an outline suggested by PowerPoint's AutoContent Wizard. In this project you will examine this first draft with a critical eye toward improving organization, completeness, and grammar. After you are satisfied that the slides convey your message and have no misspelled words, you can concentrate on techniques to improve delivery.

Designing the Solution

You must check every presentation you create for accuracy, completeness, organization, proper grammar, and correct spelling. The wrong date for a volunteer activity would indicate a problem with accuracy. If you suggested that viewers contact the Volunteer Center and failed to include a phone number, the presentation would not be complete. When you check organization, you might ask yourself if the words flow easily and if there are logical transitions between slides. You might notice that an apostrophe is missing or several words run together. Using PowerPoint, you can easily retrieve the initial draft of a presentation and make revisions. It is up to you, however, to review your work carefully and decide what revisions you need to make.

In the following sections you will continue editing the service.ppt presentation you created in Project 1. The changes you will make include correcting grammar, inserting a new slide, duplicating a slide, adding and demoting bulleted subtopics, moving text to another location, and correcting spelling errors. After adding speaker's notes, you will print the slides.

Proofreading a Presentation

When you ***proofread*** a presentation, you read the text on each slide, noting omissions as well as corrections to be made in content and organization. After making the desired changes, you should always proofread the revised presentation. Several editing sessions may be required before you are satisfied with the quality of the slides.

If you are comfortable proofreading text on the screen, you can display the presentation in Outline view, which shows the title and bulleted subtopics from all slides. You can also print an Outline view of the presentation and mark your revisions on paper. Figure 2.1 shows handwritten annotations to the initial draft of the volunteerism presentation.

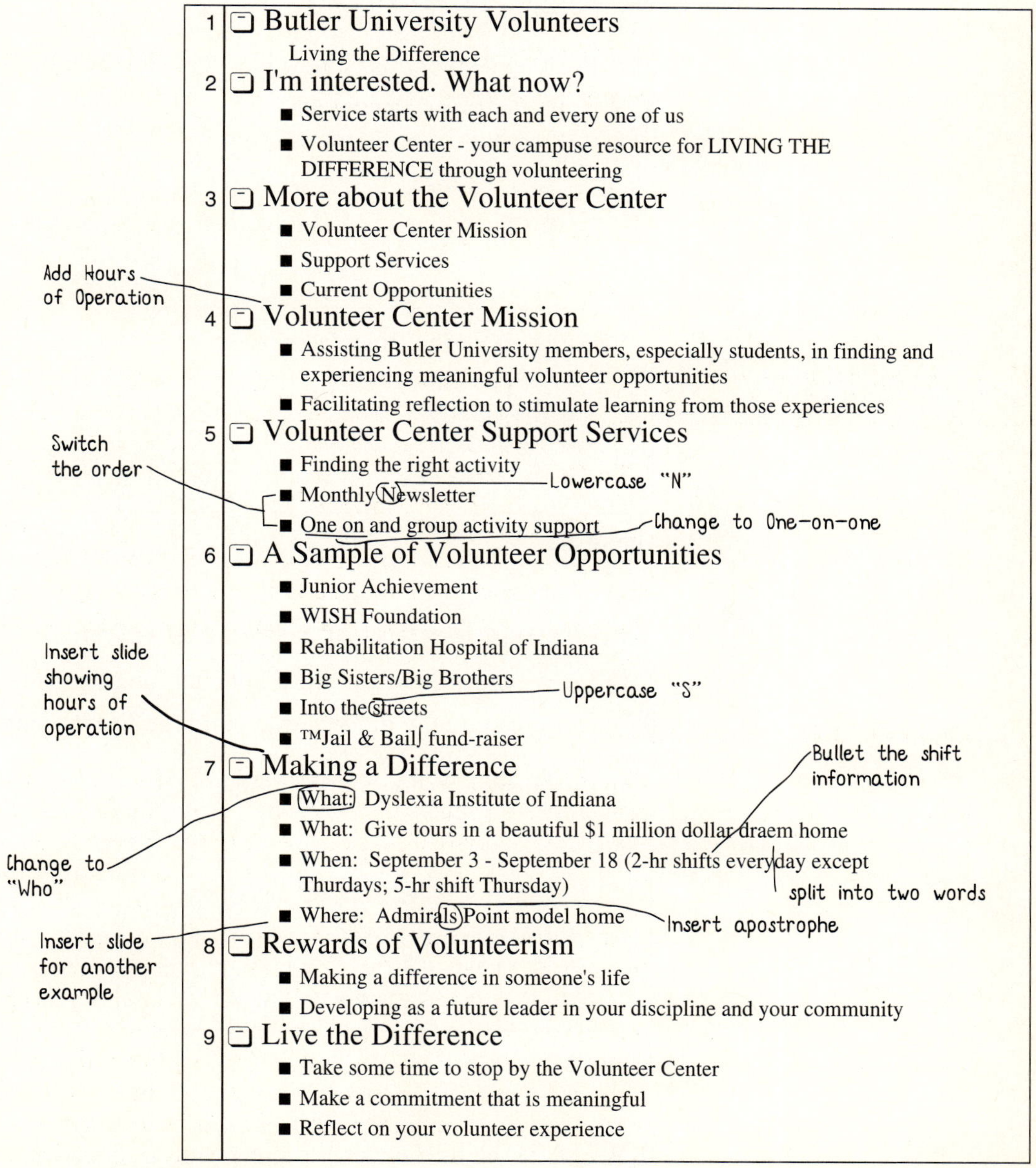

Figure 2.1

In the following sets of numbered steps, you will make the changes shown in Figure 2.1. You will begin by inserting and deleting text in existing slides.

To open an existing presentation:

1 Start PowerPoint, and open the service.ppt presentation.
The initial nine-slide volunteerism presentation you created in Project 1 appears.

2 Make sure the presentation is in Outline view.

3 Check the formatting mode to make sure the presentation looks like Figure 2.1.

To insert a new bulleted topic:

1 Position the insertion point at the end of the last bulleted topic in slide 3.

2 Press (ENTER) to insert a new line preceded by a bullet.

3 Type `Hours of Operation`
The text in slide 3 should match Figure 2.2.

> ***Reminder*** You may need to correct spacing around edited text.

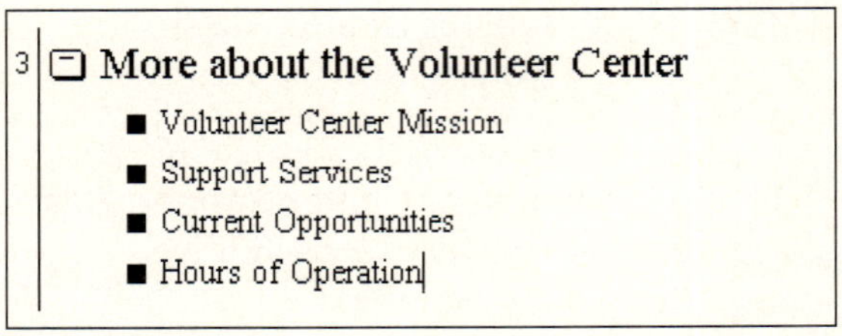

Figure 2.2

To edit existing text and save the revisions:

1 Locate the second and third bulleted topics in slide 5.

2 Lowercase the *N* in *Newsletter* and type `One-on-one` in place of *One on*.
The text in slide 5 should match Figure 2.3.

Figure 2.3

3 Locate the fifth bulleted topic in slide 6, and capitalize the *s* in *streets.*

4 Locate slide 7.

5 Revise the first bulleted topic by typing **Who** in place of *What*.

6 Revise the third bulleted topic by inserting a space to separate *everyday* into the words *every* and *day*.

7 Revise the fourth bulleted topic by inserting an apostrophe before the *s* in *Admirals*.
The text in slide 7 should match Figure 2.4.

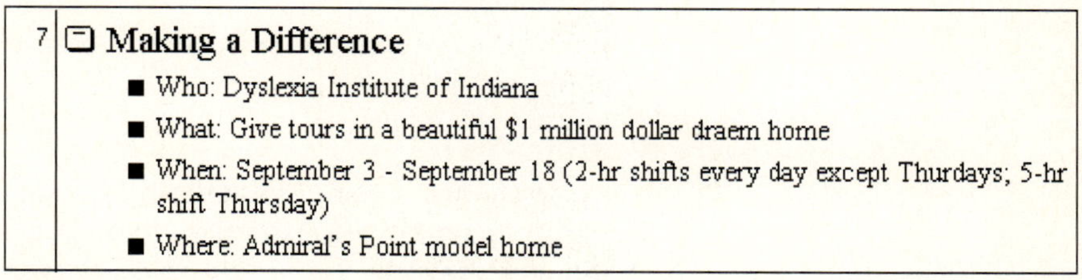

Figure 2.4

8 Locate the third bulleted topic in slide 9 and type **on** between *Reflect* and *your*.
The text in slide 9 should match Figure 2.5.

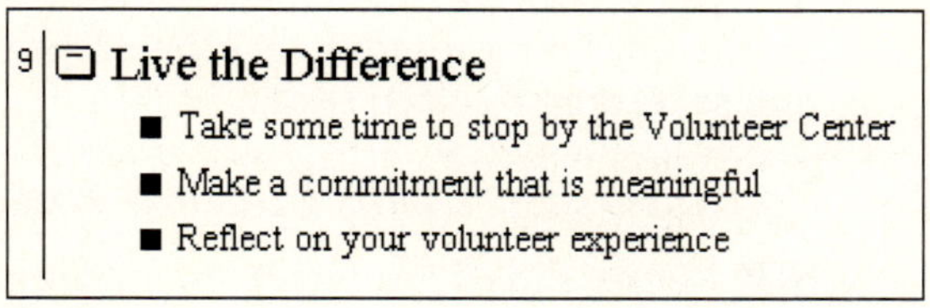

Figure 2.5

9 Save the file.

Moving and Copying Text

As you make changes to the initial draft of a presentation, you may want to move text from one position to another. To move selected text, you can choose the Cut command to cut (remove) the block from its current position, and then choose the Paste command to paste (insert) the block in a new location. You can also use a mouse to select a block of text and drag it to a new location.

Tip In Outline view you can use the Move Up or Move Down button on the Outlining toolbar to switch a selected topic with one that precedes or follows it.

You can avoid typing the same text twice by copying the block of text you want repeated. You can choose the Copy command to duplicate the selected text and then choose the Paste command to insert the block. Although the new location can be in the current set of slides, you are more likely to copy selected text to another presentation or a blank presentation window.

Tip You can also copy a block of text you have selected by holding down CTRL while you drag the highlighted text to a second location.

When you first cut or copy a block of text, the text is stored on the ***clipboard,*** a temporary storage area located in the computer's memory. Each time you cut or copy a new block, the previous contents of the clipboard are erased.

Quick Fix Using PowerPoint's Undo feature, you can reverse an editing action. For example, if you cut or copy the wrong block of text, you can reverse the action if you choose Undo from the Edit menu. By repeatedly clicking Undo, you can undo up to your last 20 actions. You can find out how to set a different limit on the number of undo operations by selecting the *Multiple undo* topic from the What's New book listed on the Contents tab of the Help Topics dialog box.

In the following steps you will switch the second and third bulleted topics in slide 5 using the Cut and Paste buttons on the Standard toolbar, restore the moved text to its original position using the Move Up button on the Outlining toolbar, and then repeat the move process using the mouse to drag selected text.

To move text using Cut and Paste:

1 Locate slide 5, and click the bullet next to *Monthly newsletter*.
PowerPoint automatically selects (highlights) all text in the bulleted topic, as shown in Figure 2.6.

Figure 2.6

2 Select Cut on the Standard toolbar.
The selected text disappears, and two bulleted topics remain in slide 5.

3 Position the insertion point at the end of the second bulleted topic.

4 Select Paste on the Standard toolbar.
Monthly newsletter becomes the third bulleted topic, and the highlighting disappears, as shown in Figure 2.7.

Figure 2.7

To move text using the Outline toolbar:

1 Click the bullet next to *Monthly newsletter* in slide 5.

2 Select Move Up on the Outlining toolbar.
The selected text moves up one bulleted topic to its original position. The text remains selected (highlighted).

To move text using a mouse and then save the change:

1 Position the pointer on the selected text.

2 Press and hold down the left mouse button.

3 Drag the pointer to the end of the third bulleted topic.
The hollow square at the bottom of the pointer indicates that you are dragging text.

4 Release the mouse button.
Monthly newsletter becomes the third bulleted topic, as shown in Figure 2.7. The highlighting remains.

5 Click unselected text or white space to remove highlighting on the block of text.

6 Save the file.
The change in topic order on slide 5 is saved to disk. The outline of the presentation remains on-screen.

Promoting and Demoting Topics

In Outline view an item's position indicates its importance in relation to other items. For example, slide 7 has three text levels, as shown in Figure 2.8. If you set the display to show formatting, a different bullet character will precede each level, such as a square for level 2 and a diamond for level 3.

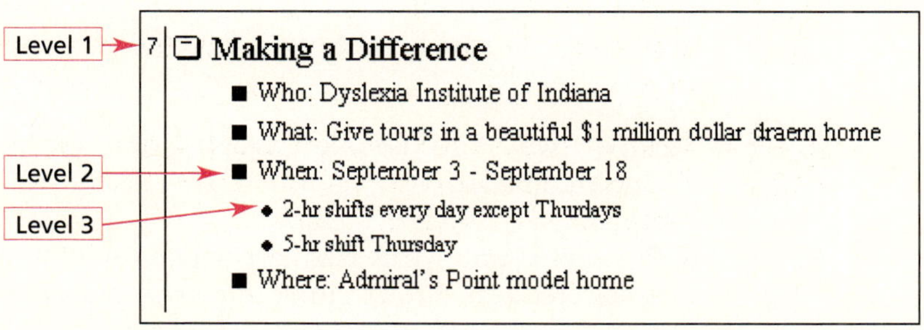

Figure 2.8

The title of a slide displays at level 1. Each major topic within a slide appears at level 2. Each subtopic supporting a major topic occupies a level-3 position.

If you demote a topic, it shifts to the right, forming a subtopic at the next level in the outline. The bullet character changes to match other bullets at that level. You will use the Demote (right-arrow) button on the Outlining toolbar for this change. If you promote a topic, it shifts to the left, forming a topic at the previous level in the outline. The bullet character changes to match other bullets at that level. The Promote (left-arrow) button on the Outlining toolbar executes this action.

In the following steps you will edit slide 7 to show shift information in level-3 subpoints, as shown in Figure 2.8. You will start by placing shift-related text on two separate level-2 lines. To complete the process, you will demote the two phrases to level 3.

To demote topics and save the changes:

1 Locate slide 7 in Outline view, and position the insertion point immediately after *September 18* in the third bulleted topic.

2 Press ENTER to shift the remaining text to a new bulleted topic.

3 Delete the extra space and parenthesis preceding the text.

4 Position the insertion point before the semicolon at the end of the text describing two-hour shifts.
The insertion point should be just after the *s* in *Thurdays*.

5 Press ENTER to create another bulleted topic.

6 Delete the semicolon and the extra spaces preceding the text, and the parenthesis at the end.
The shift information appears as shown in Figure 2.9.

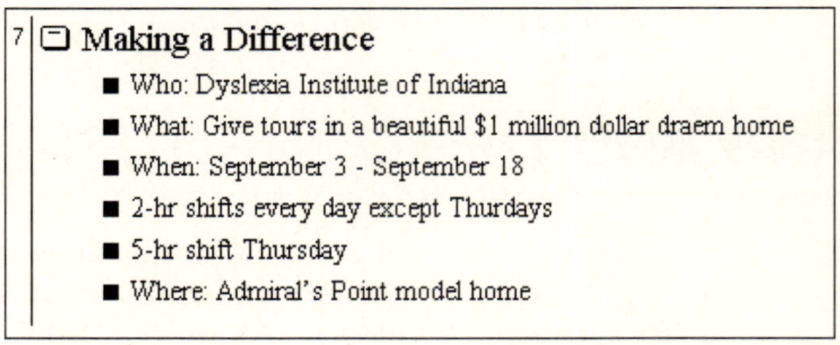

Figure 2.9

7 Select the text that begins *2-hr shifts*.

> ***Reminder*** You can select a level-2 or lower topic by clicking the associated bullet.

8 Select Demote (the right arrow) on the Outlining toolbar.
The selected text shifts to the right to form a subtopic under the range of dates.

9 Select the text that begins *5-hr shift*.

10 Select Demote.

The selected text shifts to the right to form a subtopic under the range of dates.

11 Click text or white space to unselect the highlighted block of text. Your changes to slide 7 should match those shown in Figure 2.8.

12 Save the file.

EXIT If necessary, you can exit PowerPoint now and continue this project later.

Adding and Deleting Slides

As you revise a presentation, you may need to add or delete a slide. Adding a slide involves a two-step process: positioning the insertion point anywhere within the slide that will precede the new slide and then choosing New Slide from the Insert menu or selecting the New Slide button near the lower-right corner of the screen.

Deleting a slide requires a similar two-step process: selecting the slide to remove and then executing the delete operation. In Outline view you can select the slide by clicking the icon to the left of the slide's title. You can then press DEL or choose Delete Slide from the Edit menu.

You can add or delete slides while you work in any view. In the following steps you will work in Outline view, inserting a new slide after the current slide 6. The new slide will show the hours of operation for the Volunteer Center.

To add a slide:

1 If necessary, start PowerPoint and open the service.ppt presentation in Outline view.

2 Position the insertion point on any text within slide 6.

3 Select New Slide at the bottom of the screen.

A new slide appears as shown in Figure 2.10. Subsequent slides are renumbered automatically.

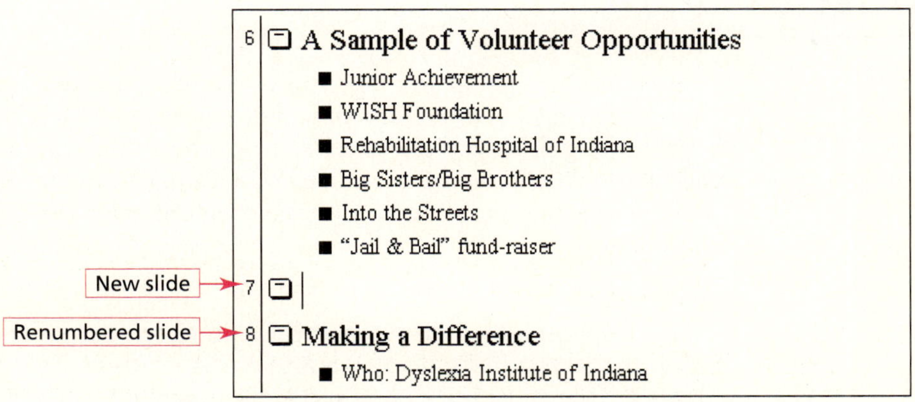

Figure 2.10

To add text to the new slide and save your changes:

1 Check that the insertion point appears to the right of the slide 7 symbol.

2 Type **Hours of Operation** and press (ENTER)

Reminder Pressing (ENTER) while in Outline view inserts a line at the same level. In this case pressing (ENTER) has created an unwanted new slide.

3 Select Demote on the Outlining toolbar.
The slide 8 symbol changes to a level-2 bullet under slide 7.

4 Type **Monday 8:00 a.m. - 8:00 p.m.** and press (ENTER)

5 Type **Tuesday 9:00 a.m. - 5:00 p.m.** and press (ENTER)

6 Type **Wednesday 8:00 a.m. - 5:00 p.m.** and press (ENTER)

7 Type **Thursday 10:00 a.m. - 8:00 p.m.** and press (ENTER)

8 Type **Friday 8:00 a.m. - 3:00 p.m.**
The text in the new slide 7 should match Figure 2.11.

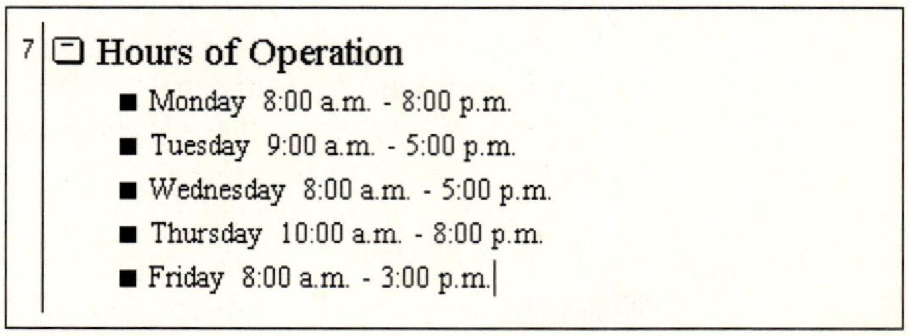

Figure 2.11

9 Save the file.

Duplicating a Slide

In the previous section you typed all of the text on a new slide. If the content you have in mind for a new slide corresponds closely to the content of an existing slide, you can save keystrokes by duplicating the existing slide and then editing the new slide. Duplicating a slide involves a two-step process: selecting the slide to copy and then choosing Duplicate from the Edit menu.

Tip Duplicating a slide automatically inserts the copy immediately after the current slide. If you want to make a copy of a slide at another location, you must use a Copy and Paste command sequence.

In the following steps you will duplicate slide 8, which shows an example of a volunteer activity. You will then edit the new slide 9 to illustrate a second volunteer opportunity, as shown in Figure 2.12.

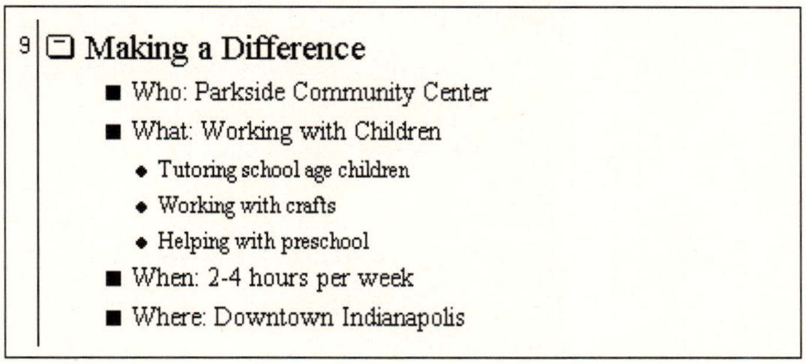

Figure 2.12

To duplicate a slide:

1 Select slide 8 titled *Making a Difference.*

2 Choose Duplicate from the Edit menu.
The new slide 9 appears with the same text as slide 8.

> ***Quick Fix*** If you were not able to complete step 2 because the Duplicate option was dimmed, you may not have selected slide 8 properly. Check that you clicked the slide icon next to the slide title, and then repeat step 2.

To modify the duplicate slide:

1 Select *Dyslexia Institute of Indiana* in slide 9 (do not include *Who:*).

2 Type **`Parkside Community Center`**
The text you just typed replaces the original who information.

3 Select *Give tours in a beautiful $1 million dollar draem home*, type **`Working with Children`** and press (ENTER)
The text you just typed replaces the original what information, and PowerPoint inserts a blank bulleted topic.

4 Click Demote on the Outlining toolbar to insert the first of three subtopics.

5 Type **`Tutoring school age children`** and press (ENTER)

6 Type **`Working with crafts`** and press (ENTER)

7 Type **`Helping with preschool`**

> ***Quick Fix*** If a new subtopic bullet appears, you accidentally pressed (ENTER) again. Delete the unwanted blank subtopic by clicking its bullet and pressing (DEL) or by pressing (BKSP)

8 Select *September 3–September 18*, and type **`2-4 hours per week`**
The text you just typed replaces the original when information.

9 Click the bullet in front of *2-hr shifts*, and press (DEL)

10 Click the bullet in front of *5-hr shift*, and press DEL

11 Select *Admiral's Point model home* and type **`Downtown Indianapolis`**
The text you just typed replaces the original where information.

12 Compare your edited slide 9 to Figure 2.12, and make changes as necessary.
Do not, however, change spelling errors. You will use a feature to check all spelling later in the project.

13 Save the file.

EXIT If necessary, you can exit PowerPoint now and continue this project later.

ADDING SPEAKER'S NOTES

Slides generally show only key points in short phrases. Many speakers use printed notes in addition to their presentation slides to help them deliver a talk. You can easily develop speaker's notes in PowerPoint's Notes Pages view. As shown in Figure 2.13, Notes Pages view displays an image of the current slide at the top of the page and a box for your notes at the bottom of the page.

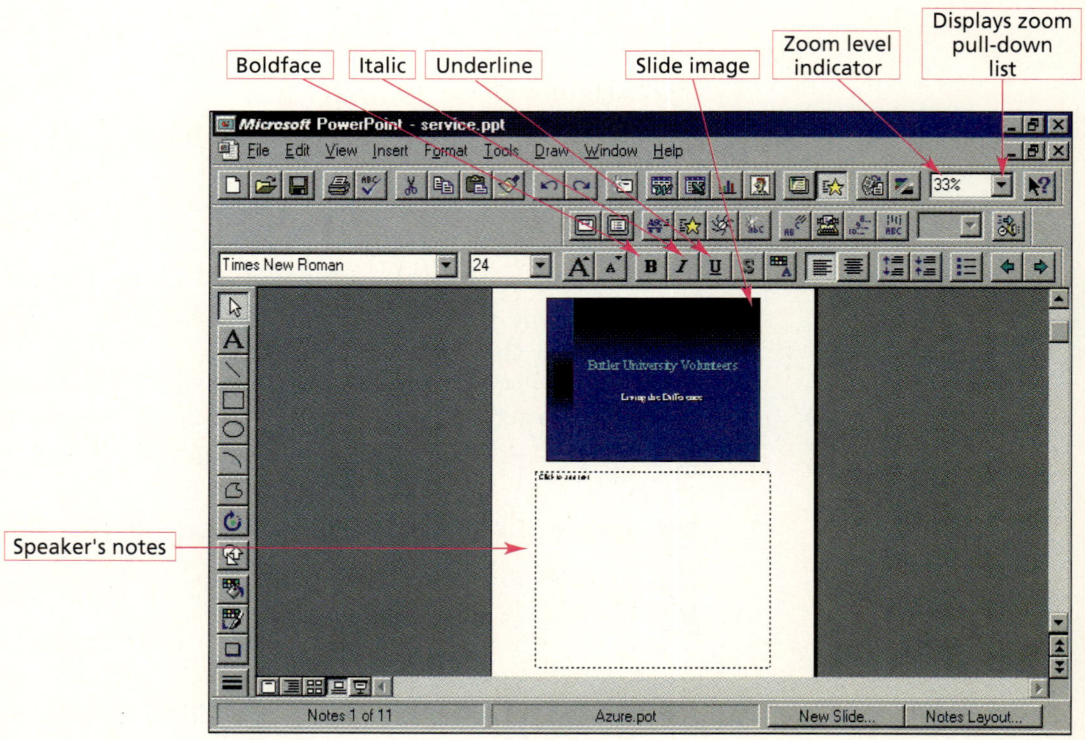

Figure 2.13

Many word processing features are available as you type your notes. For example, you can move and copy text as well as boldface, italicize, and underline selected text using buttons on the Standard toolbar.

PowerPoint's Zoom feature allows you to increase and decrease the size of the image on your screen in relation to the printed output (100%). The current Zoom level appears in the Standard toolbar, such as 33% in Figure 2.13. You can easily change this setting by clicking the down arrow to the right of the Zoom level indicator and selecting one of the predetermined settings from a pull-down list.

> ***Tip*** You can add and edit speaker's notes at any time during the process of developing a presentation. Rather than waiting until you have created all the slides, however, you might add notes while your thoughts about a specific slide are fresh in your mind.

In the following steps you will add speaker's notes to the first slide in the service.ppt presentation on volunteerism. You will also boldface key words and phrases in your notes so that you can tell at a glance what point you should be making next.

To change the view to Notes Pages:

1 If necessary, start PowerPoint and open the service.ppt presentation in Outline view.

2 Position the insertion point anywhere in slide 1.

3 Select Notes Pages in the View toolbar.
Your screen displays an image of slide 1 above an empty speaker's notes box with a narrow dotted border, as shown in Figure 2.13. The relative size of the display will vary if 33% is not the current Zoom setting.

To change the Zoom setting:

1 Click the down arrow to the right of the Zoom level indicator.

2 Choose 50% from the pull-down list.

3 Click the down arrow to the right of the Zoom level indicator.

4 Choose 100% from the pull-down list.

5 View the slide at other Zoom settings, and then restore a 100% view.

To enter speaker's notes:

1 Click within the notes box containing the phrase *Click to add text.*
The border of the box changes to a wider pattern formed by a series of forward slashes.

2 Type **`Welcome participants to the presentation`** and press (ENTER) twice.

3 Type **`Tell listeners who I am`** and press (ENTER) twice.

4 Type **`Get show of hands from audience-# students, faculty, staff`** and press (ENTER) twice.

5 Type **`Explain format and timing (a few slides, question/answer period)`**

6 Check that your notes for slide 1 match the text shown in Figure 2.14, except for the boldfacing. You will add the boldfacing in the next set of numbered steps.

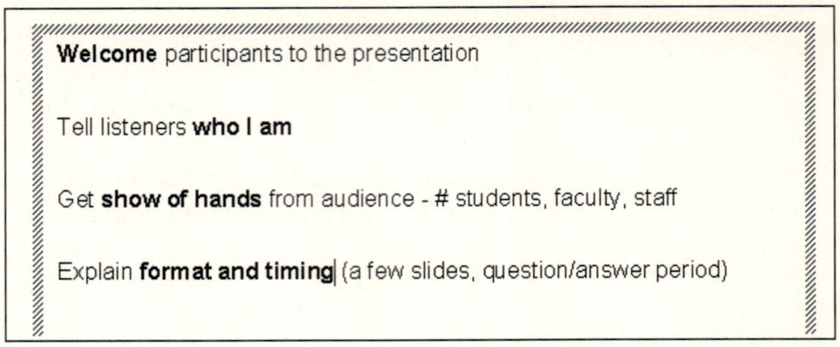

Figure 2.14

To boldface selected text and save the changes to your presentation:

B

1 Select *Welcome* in the first note, and then select Boldface in the Standard toolbar.

2 Select *who I am* in the second note, and then select Boldface.

3 Select *show of hands* in the third note, and then select Boldface.

4 Select *format and timing* in the fourth note, and then select Boldface. The notes display selected words and phrases in boldface type, as shown in Figure 2.14.

5 Click unselected text or white space to remove highlighting on the block of text.

6 Save the file.

Spell-Checking a Presentation

Nothing ruins your credibility as a presenter faster than displaying a spelling error on a slide. PowerPoint uses the same powerful spell-checking feature used in other Microsoft programs to find and correct spelling errors in all slides, notes pages, and handout pages.

Spell-checking begins at the location of the insertion point. PowerPoint "looks up" each word in its dictionary. If a word is either misspelled or not found in the dictionary, the Spelling dialog box shown in Figure 2.15 appears, with the problem word displayed in the Not in Dictionary text box. A suggested spelling appears in the Change To text box. Other suggested spellings may appear in the Suggestions list box.

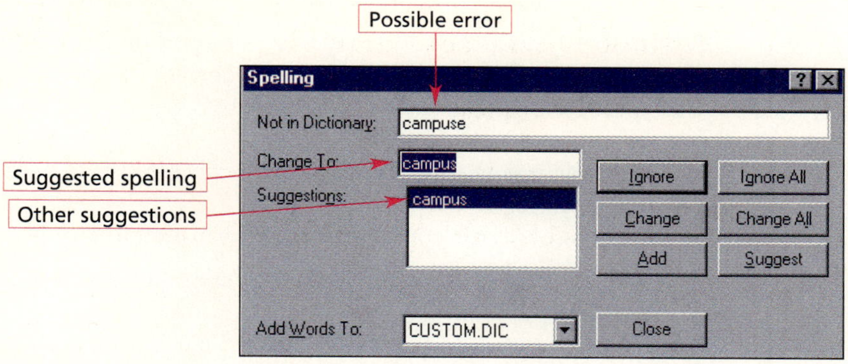

Figure 2.15

You may recognize one of the suggestions as the correct spelling. Selecting that word places it in the Change To box. If you know the correct spelling, you can also edit the word in the Change To box. You can then replace that particular instance of the misspelled word with the correct one by selecting Change. To replace all possible instances of the misspelled word throughout the presentation, you can select Change All.

Some suggested misspellings are not errors. For example, many proper names (such as Parkside), acronyms, abbreviations, slang words, and specialized terms are not in the dictionary. You can choose to ignore the suggested error one time only by selecting Ignore, or for the rest of the presentation by selecting Ignore All.

Tip If a word you will be using frequently shows as misspelled, you can add the word to the dictionary. Exercise caution, however, because you cannot remove a word from the dictionary once you have added it.

In the following steps you will check the spelling in the volunteerism presentation. The steps assume that you have typed the document exactly as directed, including spelling errors. If you corrected one or more given misspelled words as you typed, you will need to skip one or more steps below. If you misspelled other words, you should correct those errors on your own.

Tip Spell checking can be done from any view mode. However, it is easier to start with Outline view, which is the one that displays the most text on one screen.

To check spelling, replacing misspelled words and ignoring some suggested changes:

1 Choose Outline from the View menu.

2 Press CTRL + HOME to position the cursor at the beginning of slide 1.

3 Choose Spelling from the Tools menu.
The first possible error, *campuse*, appears at the top of the Spelling dialog box, followed by the most likely correction, *campus*, as shown in Figure 2.15.

Reminder Spell-checking may have stopped on another word if you made an unintentional spelling error earlier or you corrected *campuse* as you typed.

4 Select Change to replace the spelling error, *campuse*, with the suggested correction, *campus*.
The next possible error appears in the Not in Dictionary box.

5 Select Ignore All to bypass making changes to *a.m.* and again to bypass making changes to *p.m.*

6 Select Change to replace *draem* with *dream* and *Thurdays* with *Thursdays*.

7 Select Ignore to bypass the suggested spelling *Paradise* for *Parkside*.

8 Select OK to end spell-checking.

9 Click unselected text or white space to remove the highlighting on the last word found in spell-checking.

10 Save the file.

Printing a Presentation

Whenever you want to output your presentation on paper, you can activate a number of PowerPoint features that control the printer. In this section you will execute a Print command from the Print dialog box, which is shown in Figure 2.16 (your dialog box may show a different printer). By default, PowerPoint will print slides. You can also print notes pages, handouts (two, three, or six slides per page), or an outline of your presentation by using the Print What pull-down list box located in the lower-left corner of the Print dialog box.

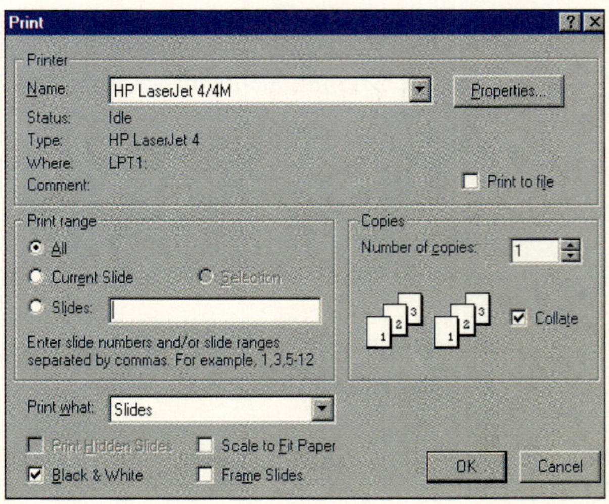

Figure 2.16

The Copies option in the Print dialog box lets you specify the number of copies you want to print. The Collate check box relates to printing multiple copies. When this feature is active (that is, when a checkmark appears in the box), a complete set of slides will print before the next set of slides.

Select Black & White to print a presentation on a noncolor printer; otherwise, time and toner will be wasted. You can print your slide show directly onto overhead transparencies if you have a laser printer.

Caution Use only transparencies designed for laser printers. Others may melt inside your printer. The box of transparencies will be labeled *Laser Printer Transparencies.* If you are not sure, do not use them.

In the following steps you will select the outline form of output and then print the volunteerism presentation without changing the other default settings.

Tip If your printer does not support color, you do not have to specify black and white when printing an outline, which contains only text. However, any other output form shows slides with background designs, and you should select the Black & White setting before printing.

Caution Do not use the Print button in the Standard toolbar in place of the two menu selections in the following step 1. If you do, printing will begin immediately using the default settings, and PowerPoint will print slides instead of the outline.

To print a presentation outline and close the file:

1 Choose Print from the File menu.
The Print dialog box opens.

2 Click the down arrow to the right of the Print What list box.
The pull-down list appears.

3 Select Outline View.
The pull-down list disappears, and Outline View appears in the Print What list box.

4 Select OK to begin printing one copy of the presentation outline shown in Figure 2.17.

1 ❑ Butler University Volunteers
Living the Difference

2 ❑ I'm interested. What now?
- Service starts with each and every one of us
- Volunteer Center - your campus resource for LIVING THE DIFFERENCE through volunteering

3 ❑ More about the Volunteer Center
- Volunteer Center Mission
- Support Services
- Current Opportunities
- Hours of Operation

4 ❑ Volunteer Center Mission
- Assisting Butler University members, especially students, in finding and experiencing meaningful volunteer opportunities
- Facilitating reflection to stimulate learning from those experiences

5 ❑ Volunteer Center Support Services
- Finding the right activity
- One-on-one and group activity support
- Monthly newsletter

6 ❑ A Sample of Volunteer Opportunities
- Junior Achievement
- WISH Foundation
- Rehabilitation Hospital of Indiana
- Big Sisters/Big Brothers
- Into the Streets
- "Jail & Bail" fund-raiser

7 ❑ Hours of Operation
- Monday 8:00 a.m. - 8:00 p.m.
- Tuesday 9:00 a.m. - 5:00 p.m.
- Wednesday 8:00 a.m. - 5:00 p.m.
- Thursday 10:00 a.m. - 8:00 p.m.
- Friday 8:00 a.m. - 3:00 p.m.

8 ❑ Making a Difference
- Who: Dyslexia Institute of Indiana
- What: Give tours in a beautiful $1 million dollar dream home
- When: September 3 - September 18
  - 2-hr shifts every day except Thursdays
  - 5-hr shift Thursday
- Where: Admiral's Point model home

9 ❑ Making a Difference
- Who: Parkside Community Center
- What: Working with children
  - Tutoring school age children
  - Working with crafts
  - Helping with preschool
- When: 2 - 4 hours per week
- Where: Downtown Indianapolis

10 ❑ Rewards of Volunteerism
- Making a difference in someone's life
- Developing as a future leader in your discipline and your community

11 ❑ Live the Difference
- Take some time to stop by the Volunteer Center
- Make a commitment that is meaningful
- Reflect on your volunteer experience

Figure 2.17

5 Choose Close from the File menu.

THE NEXT STEP

In this project you added the finishing touches to your first PowerPoint presentation. After proofreading your work, you moved text, corrected grammar, added two slides, added speaker's notes, and checked spelling. Actions such as these allow you to turn an initial draft into a polished presentation.

To go beyond the material in this project, look for opportunities to experiment with activities that were described but not worked through. For example, you experienced moving text within a slide. Now try copying selected text in another presentation of your own. Add another slide to a presentation and then see if you can delete it. You added boldface. Use on-screen Help to find out how to remove that enhancement. Exploring can be fun!

This concludes Project 2. You can either exit PowerPoint or go on to work the Study Questions, Review Exercises, and Assignments.

SUMMARY AND EXERCISES

Summary

- As you proofread a presentation, you should check the set of slides for accuracy, completeness, organization, proper grammar, and correct spelling.
- Editing activities include moving and copying text, demoting and promoting topics, adding and deleting a slide, and duplicating a slide.
- Many speakers use printed notes in addition to slides to help them deliver a presentation. Using PowerPoint, you can develop speaker's notes in Notes Pages view.
- PowerPoint includes a powerful spell-checking feature to find and correct spelling errors in all slides, notes pages, and handout pages.
- You can print a presentation in several forms: slides, notes pages, handouts, and an outline.

Key Terms and Operations

Key Terms
clipboard
proofread

Operations
Add a slide
Add speaker's notes
Boldface text
Demote a topic
Duplicate a slide
Move text
Print the outline of a presentation
Proofread a presentation
Spell-check a presentation

Study Questions

Multiple Choice

1. Which of the following is not an option for printing handout pages?
   a. Two slides per page
   b. Three slides per page
   c. Four slides per page
   d. Six slides per page

2. As you drag selected text to a new location, which key do you press and hold down to copy instead of move?
   a. ALT
   b. CTRL
   c. SHFT
   d. None of the above.

3. Which of the following is not a true statement about developing speaker's notes?
   a. In Notes Pages view you see a box for your notes at the top of the page and an image of the current slide at the bottom of the page.
   b. You can boldface, italicize, and underline text in notes pages.
   c. You can add and edit speaker's notes at any time during the process of developing a presentation.
   d. All of the above.

4. If you do not have a color printer, you should always specify Black & White as a print setting unless the selected output form is
   a. Slides.
   b. Notes Pages.
   c. Handouts.
   d. Outline View.

5. To delete a selected slide, you choose
   a. Remove from the Edit menu.
   b. Delete from the Layout menu.
   c. Delete from the Tools menu.
   d. None of the above.

Short Answer

1. What is the temporary storage area located in the computer's memory that holds text cut from a presentation?

2. If you demote a topic in an outline, in which direction does the selected text shift?

3. Explain the menu sequence you can choose to reverse the most recent editing action.

4. What command button do you select in the Spelling dialog box to replace the word in error with the suggested word throughout the remainder of the presentation?

5. What single action begins printing immediately, without giving you the opportunity to change default print settings?

For Discussion

1. What tasks are involved in proofreading a presentation?

2. Describe the process of spell-checking a presentation.

3. You can add a slide to a presentation by inserting a new blank slide or by duplicating an existing slide and editing the copy. Briefly explain why you might choose one method over the other, and then describe the steps to take for each process.

Review Exercises

Promoting a Service (Part 2)

1. Open the impress.ppt presentation you created in the Project 1 review exercises (see Figure 1.21).
2. Locate slide 3 (The Solution), and uppercase the *d* in *department.*
3. Locate slide 4 (Product Line), and insert another bulleted item, *Cover letters,* after *Resumes.*
4. Locate slide 5 (Cost Analysis), and move the two bulleted topics to subtopics under *Quality products at resonable prices* in slide 7.
5. Delete slide 5.
6. Create a notes page for slide 4. Include two notes: one to tell the audience about a free sample available after the presentation, and the other to direct attendees to an exhibit of products in the hall outside the meeting room.
7. Spell-check the presentation.
8. Save your changes, print the revised presentation in outline form, and then close the file.

Buying a Computer (Part 2)

1. Open the computer.ppt presentation you created in the Project 1 review exercises (see Figure 1.22).
2. Make the handwritten changes for slides 5 and 7 as shown in Figure 2.18.

1 ❑ BUYING A COMPUTER

Your Name Here

2 ❑ Introduction

- Buying the right computer for you
- Who can you trust?

3 ❑ Strategy for Buying a Computer

- Deciding what you need
- Choosing the right software and hardware
- Shopping for your computer
- Taking the first step

4 ❑ Deciding What You Need

- Be an informed buyer
- Make a list - what do you need?
- Decide what you can afford

5 ❑ Selecting Software and Hardware

- Selecting hardware first
- Selecting software second
- Make a shopping list

6 ❑ Shopping for Your Computer

- Get three price quotes
- Compare warranties and services
- Experience the difference - check with friends

7 ❑ Taking the First Step

- Become computer literate

Figure 2.18

3. In slide 4 add two subtopics under *Be an informed buyer* that suggest ways to become an informed buyer (read computer magazines, talk to other users, and so on).
4. Spell-check your presentation.
5. Save your changes, print the revised presentation in outline form, and then close the file.

Assignments

Getting Help on Undo

Using Index in on-screen Help, look up additional information about undoing PowerPoint operations (select *U* as the first letter of the word you want to look up). Write a brief summary of what you learned, and include a sketch of the Undo button.

Getting Help on Boldface and Italics

Using Answer Wizard in on-screen Help, find out if you can apply both boldface and italics to text. Also determine how to restore plain text. Write a brief summary of what you learned.

Getting Help on Hidden Slides

One of the options in the Print dialog box is Print Hidden Slides. Using Answer Wizard in on-screen Help, find out what hidden slides are. Write a brief summary of what you learned. Include a sketch of the Hide Slide button.

Duplicating a Slide

Open the service.ppt presentation. Insert a duplicate of slide 9 (entitled Making a Difference and about the Parkside Community Center) immediately after slide 9. Revise text on the new slide 10 to give one more example of a volunteer activity of your choice. Save your changes, print the new slide (optional), and then close the file.

Project 3: Working with Text Objects

Objectives

After completing this project, you should be able to:

- Use AutoLayout to design a slide
- Select a design template
- Create, edit, move, and size a text box
- Change text font and size
- Enhance text with special effects and color
- Set up two-column text and a bulleted list
- Center text

Case Study: Cruising the Caribbean

Assume that you are a summer intern at the Island Tours travel agency. Recently the agency acquired PowerPoint for Windows software, and your supervisor has asked you to create a slide presentation explaining some of the firm's cruise packages.

Designing the Solution

You are well on your way to developing a well-received presentation because you have an interesting subject. Your objective now should be to develop slides that will grab and hold the attention of an audience.

Some presentations do not lend themselves to the text-only suggested outlines provided by AutoContent Wizard. You have an opportunity to include pictures as well as words on your cruise-related slides and to arrange those items in creative ways. Figure 3.1 illustrates ideas for an eight-slide presentation combining text and pictures: a lead-in slide showing the firm's name; a title slide for the cruise-related presentation; three slides describing specific cruises (Bahamas, Eastern Caribbean, and Southern Caribbean); a sixth slide showing cruise highlights; a slide explaining how to plan the vacation through your agency; and a final slide repeating the firm's name.

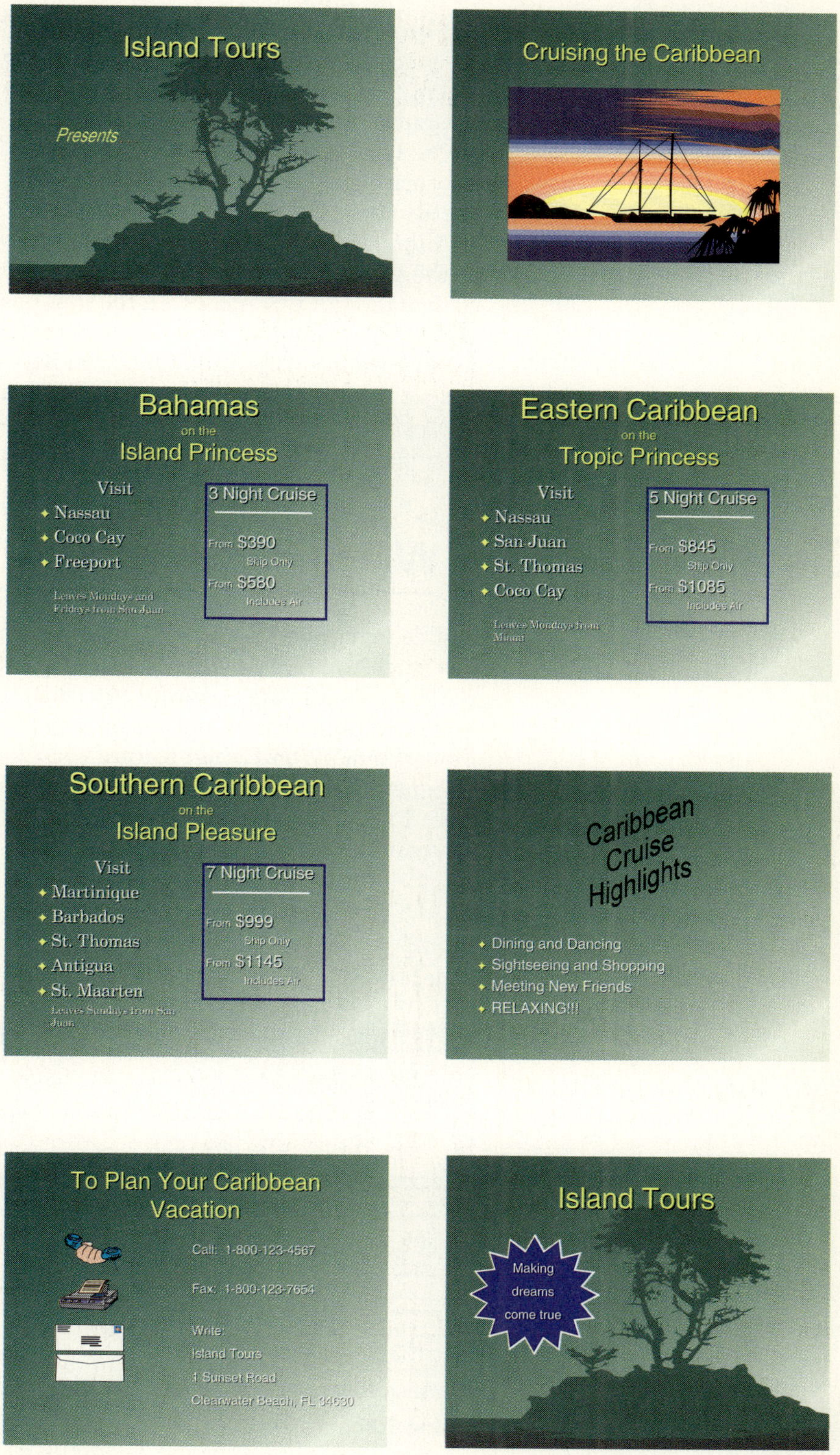
Island Tours
Presents
Cruising the Caribbean
Bahamas
on the
Island Princess
Visit
Nassau
Coco Cay
Freeport
Leaves Mondays and Fridays from San Juan
3 Night Cruise
From $390
Ship Only
From $580
Includes Air
Eastern Caribbean
on the
Tropic Princess
Visit
Nassau
San Juan
St. Thomas
Coco Cay
Leaves Mondays from Miami
5 Night Cruise
From $845
Ship Only
From $1085
Includes Air
Southern Caribbean
on the
Island Pleasure
Visit
Martinique
Barbados
St. Thomas
Antigua
St. Maarten
Leaves Sundays from San Juan
7 Night Cruise
From $999
Ship Only
From $1145
Includes Air
Caribbean Cruise Highlights
Dining and Dancing
Sightseeing and Shopping
Meeting New Friends
RELAXING!!!
To Plan Your Caribbean Vacation
Call: 1-800-123-4567
Fax: 1-800-123-7654
Write:
Island Tours
1 Sunset Road
Clearwater Beach, FL 34630
Island Tours
Making dreams come true

Figure 3.1

The suggested slides shown in Figure 3.1 contain text, art, lines, and other special effects. The image of a sail boat appears in slide 2. In slides 3, 4, and 5, a solid line forms a box. Within each box a horizontal line separates information about the length of the cruise from the associated prices. Changing the print style for selected text, such as italicizing departure information (slides 3, 4, and 5) and adding shapes containing text (slide 8), can also help to focus a viewer's attention.

Although you can create each complete slide before turning your attention to the next one, you might find it easier to build a text and graphics presentation in two phases. In the first phase you select a layout for each slide, add text to the slides, and format the text; these are the tasks you will accomplish in this project. Once you have the content established, you can add art work, lines, and other features that will transform the presentation to an effective, professional-looking product; you will do this phase of creating the presentation in Project 4.

Creating Slides with AutoLayout

A slide may contain one or more *objects*. In PowerPoint, an ***object*** can be text (such as a title or bulleted list), clip art, a table, a graph, an organization chart, or a *media clip*. A ***media clip*** adds video, music, or sound to a slide.

The arrangement of objects on a slide is called the ***slide layout.*** With PowerPoint's ***AutoLayout*** feature you can select among 24 professionally designed layouts. You will select an AutoLayout using the New Slide or Slide Layout dialog box. Figure 3.2 shows the first 12 designs. A thick surrounding border indicates the current selection.

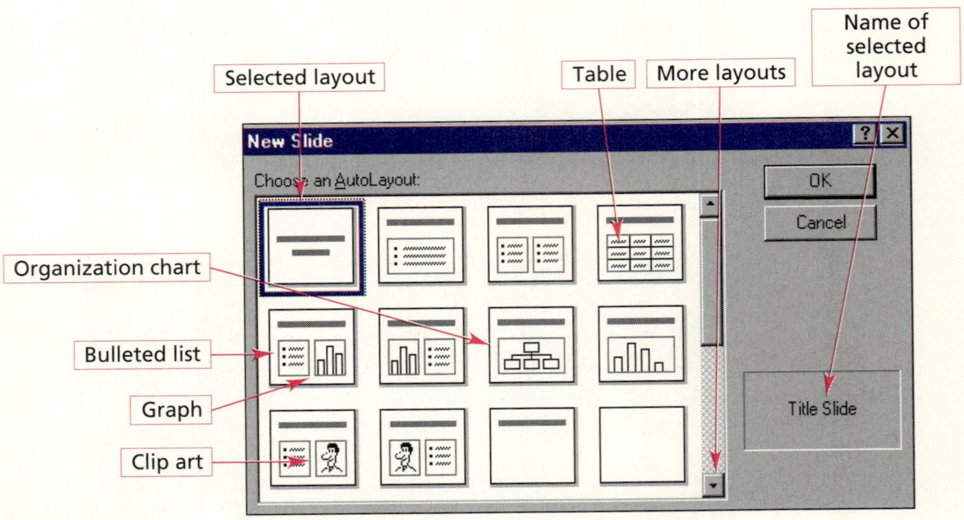

Figure 3.2

The first layout shown in the upper-left corner of Figure 3.2 sets *placeholders* for two objects, one a title text box and the other a subtitle text box. A ***placeholder*** is a rectangular box containing a ***text prompt,*** which tells you how to use the placeholder. For example, if you were to select the

Title Slide layout, you would see the placeholders and text prompts shown in Figure 3.3.

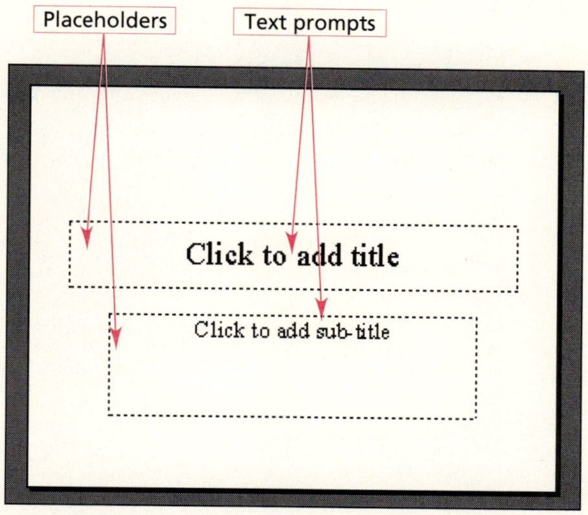

Figure 3.3

The other layouts shown in Figure 3.2 set up two or three objects. For example, the slide design in the lower-left corner includes a title text box above a bulleted list on the left and a clip art image on the right.

In the following steps you will load PowerPoint, start a blank presentation, and then select a Title Slide layout for the first slide in your cruises presentation.

To start a blank presentation and select an AutoLayout:

Tip If PowerPoint is already loaded, you can click New at the left end of the Standard toolbar in place of steps 1 and 2 below.

1 Load PowerPoint.
The PowerPoint dialog box appears. If a Tip of the Day box appears instead, select OK to remove it.

2 Select Blank Presentation if a black circle does not already appear in front of that option, and then select OK.
The New Slide dialog box appears as shown in Figure 3.2. The selected layout is Title Slide.

3 Select OK to apply the Title Slide layout.
PowerPoint designs a title slide with the placeholders shown in Figure 3.3.

SELECTING A DESIGN TEMPLATE

PowerPoint allows you to select a predefined ***design template,*** which controls the background pattern and colors assigned to slides. This is an effective way to put together a presentation on a tight schedule because you can select among more than two dozen professionally designed templates. Figure 3.4 shows the initial choices in an alphabetized list of design templates. A sample of the selected design template appears in the preview box.

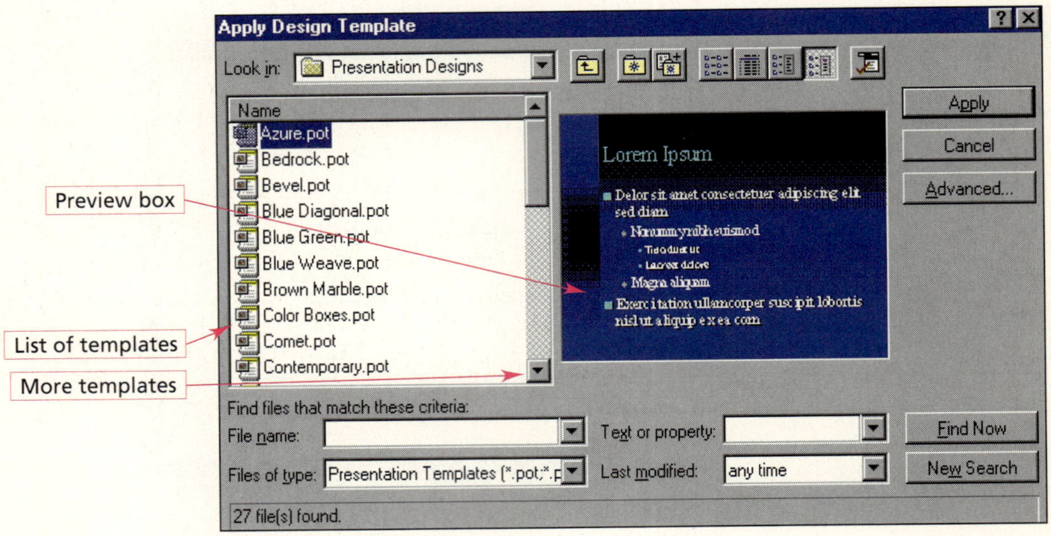

Figure 3.4

If you use AutoContent Wizard to create a presentation, PowerPoint automatically assigns a design template to the suggested slides. If you start with a blank presentation, you can select a design template right away or wait until you are finished entering text and other objects on the slides. You can apply or change a design template at any time by selecting the Apply Design Template button on the Standard toolbar or by choosing Apply Design Template from the Format menu. In this project you will establish the look first and then add slide content.

To apply a design template:

1 Select Apply Design Template on the Standard toolbar. The Apply Design Template dialog box appears as shown in Figure 3.4.

2 Display the Presentation Designs folder, scroll through the list of template names, and then select Tropical.pot as shown in Figure 3.5.

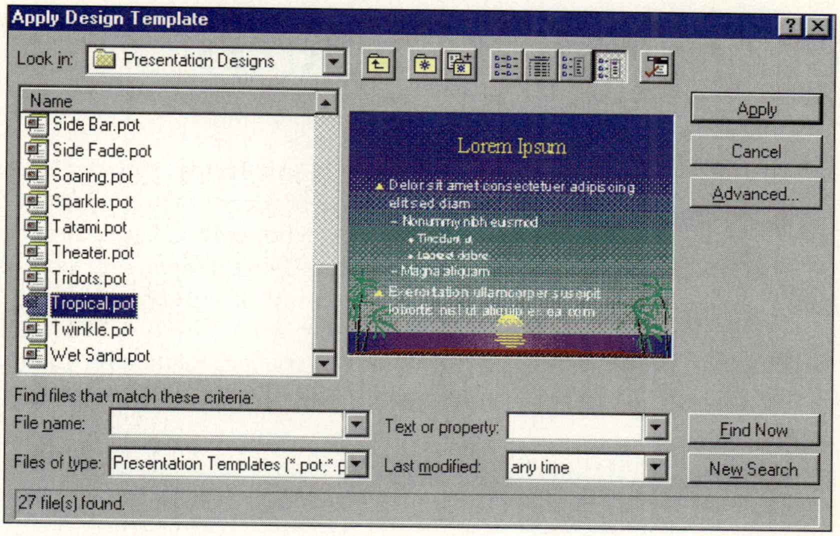

Figure 3.5

3 Select Apply.
PowerPoint applies the selected design template to the title slide as shown in Figure 3.6.

Figure 3.6

4 Save the new presentation using the name Cruises.ppt. (You may not have to type in .ppt.)

> ***Tip*** If necessary, refer to the detailed instructions for saving a new PowerPoint presentation provided in Project 1.

Working with Text Boxes

Think of a slide as a work surface on which you can set up placeholders for one or more objects. If a placeholder marks the position for text, you can click within the borders of the associated box and type the words you want to display. PowerPoint also supports a variety of features associated with word processing. For example, you can center text, alter line spacing, and change the style and size of characters.

Your ability to work with text boxes is not limited to content, however. Using a mouse, you can easily alter the dimensions of a box as well as move it to another position on the slide.

Creating and Editing a Text Box

PowerPoint's AutoLayout will create one or more predefined text boxes of your choice. You can also place a text box on the current slide by clicking the Text Tool button on the Drawing toolbar, positioning the mouse pointer where you want the upper-left corner of the box to appear, and then dragging the mouse down and to the right to form the boundaries of the box.

> ***Tip*** Text that you type in title and main text placeholders will appear in Outline view. Text that you type with the Text Tool does not appear in Outline view.

To enter text in a blank box, click within the box borders and begin typing. To edit existing contents, click anywhere on the text. The object becomes a ***selection box,*** which you can recognize by the border of forward slashes shown in Figure 3.7. After you select a box, you can make corrections as you would on any word-processed document.

Figure 3.7

In the following steps you will turn on the Drawing toolbar. You will also add text in three places on slide 1: your firm's name in the title placeholder, the word *Presents* in the subtitle placeholder, and additional text in a newly drawn box.

To turn on the Drawing toolbar:

1 Choose Toolbars from the View menu.

2 Select the Drawing toolbar, if it is not already selected.
A ✔ appears in the box to the left of the Drawing toolbar name. Standard and Formatting toolbars should already be selected.

3 Select OK.

Tip If necessary, review information about using toolbars provided in the Overview.

To enter text in an existing box:

1 Click within the borders of the title placeholder at the top of the slide.
The box border changes, and the message "Click to add title" disappears.

2 Type **`Island Tours`**

3 Click anywhere outside the box to cancel editing.
The new title appears centered near the top of the slide. PowerPoint automatically assigns a large print size.

4 Click within the borders of the subtitle placeholder.

5 Type **`Presents . . .`**

6 Click outside the box to cancel editing.

To draw a box and enter text:

1 Select Text Tool on the Drawing toolbar.

2 Position the mouse pointer below and to the left of the word *Presents.*

3 Click and drag the mouse pointer down about 1 inch and to the right about 3 inches, forming a box on the screen.
While you are drawing the box, the mouse pointer changes from an arrow to a thin square cross at the lower-right corner of the box.

4 Release the mouse button.
A blank selection box appears.

5 Type **`Your place in the sun!`**
The newly created box resembles the one shown in Figure 3.7.

6 Click anywhere outside the box.
The slide resembles the first slide in Figure 3.1 except for the position of the most recent text entry. In the next section you will move that text.

Moving and Sizing a Text Box

Moving an object requires a two-step process: displaying the moving-and-sizing border shown in Figure 3.8 and then dragging the box to its new location.

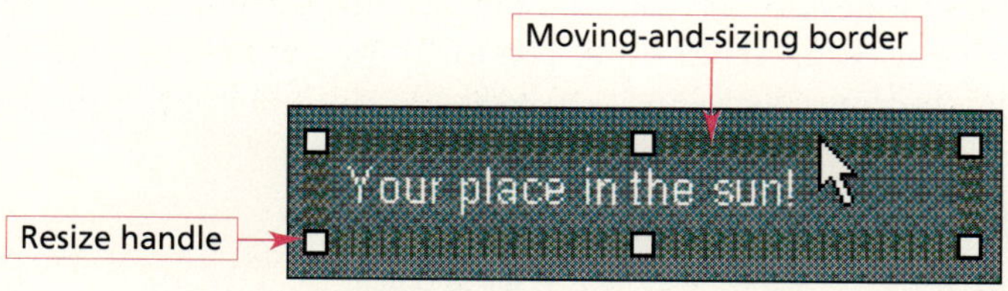

Figure 3.8

Clicking a border of the object's selection box will display the moving-and-sizing border. To ***drag*** the box, position the mouse pointer on a border (see Figure 3.8), click and hold down the left mouse button, move the box to its new position, and release the mouse button.

The square at each corner and midpoint of the moving-and-sizing border is a ***resize handle.*** With one exception, dragging a resize handle resizes the object. If you added text to an object you've drawn on the screen, the text won't resize. (You will learn to change the style and size of text later in this project.)

Tip To delete an object drawn with PowerPoint's drawing tools, display the moving-and-sizing border and then press DEL

In the following steps you will move the text box to the lower-left corner of the slide.

To move a text box and save your changes:

1 Position the mouse pointer on *Your place in the sun!* and click.
A selection box appears as shown in Figure 3.7.

2 Click anywhere on the selection box border.
The moving-and-sizing border displays as shown in Figure 3.8.

3 Click the moving-and-sizing border (not a resize handle) and drag the box to the left side of the slide just above the water line.
The text *Your place in the sun!* should appear as shown in Figure 3.1.

4 Click outside the box.

5 Save the file.

EXIT If necessary, you can exit PowerPoint now and continue this project later.

Enhancing Text

Anytime you develop slides, you should think about how to focus a reader's attention on key points. For example, you might increase the size of selected text, ***bold*** a phrase, which displays it darker than the surrounding text, or use various colors. Effective use of such text enhancements is an art that you will develop as you examine techniques used by others and experiment on your own. Avoid using too many text enhancements, or the viewer may become distracted.

Changing Font Style and Size

Font refers to the style (typeface) of characters. Size is expressed in terms of ***points,*** such as 12-point or 18-point. Each point equals 1/72 inch. You can change fonts and points using the Formatting toolbar or the Font dialog box, both of which are shown in Figure 3.9. Changes apply to selected text within a box.

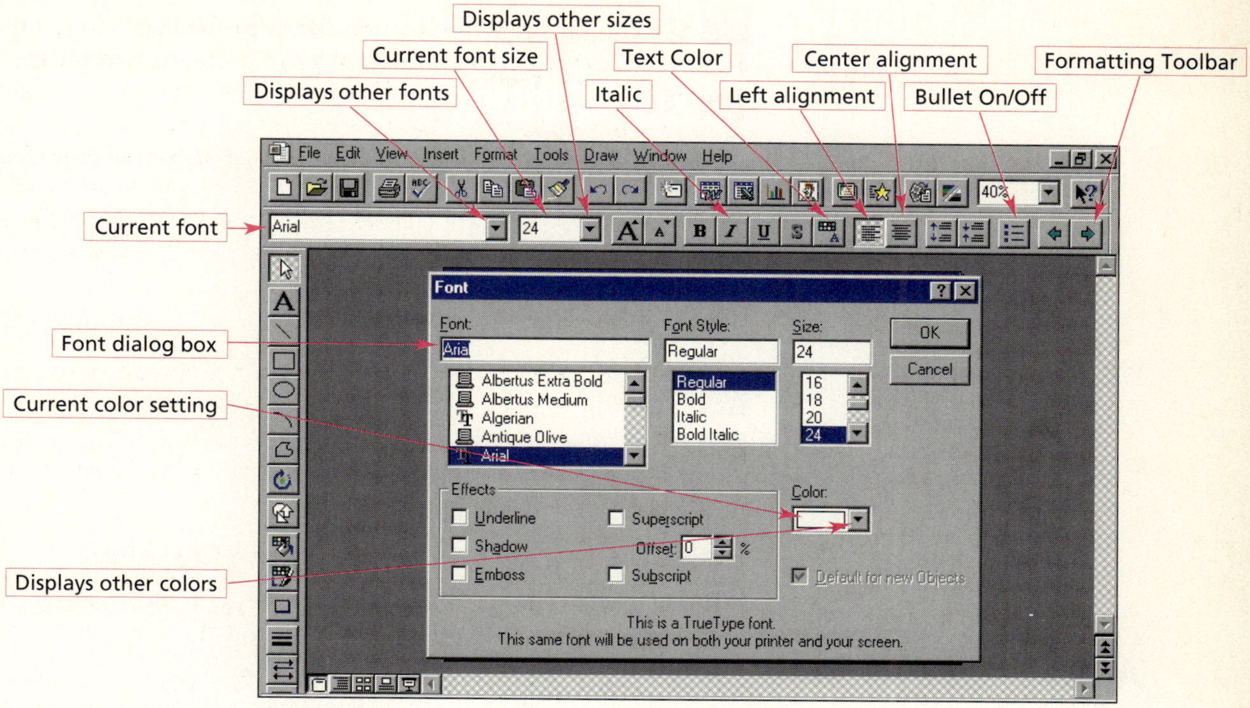

Figure 3.9

> ***Tip*** Do not mix too many fonts in a presentation. You should also standardize fonts as much as possible, such as using the same font for all slide titles.

In the following steps you will alter the font and increase the text size on the current slide. First you will use the Formatting toolbar to make those changes to the slide title. You will then use the Font dialog box to make similar changes in the remaining text.

To change font size using the Formatting toolbar:

1 If necessary, load PowerPoint and open the Cruises.ppt presentation.

2 Select the slide title.

A selection box appears, surrounding the words *Island Tours.*

3 Select both words in the title.

> ***Caution*** If you omit this step, PowerPoint will change only the word at the current insertion point position.

4 Click the down arrow to the right of the current font size in the Formatting toolbar.

> ***Caution*** Do not click the down arrow to the left of the current font size, or you will view the font *style* options instead of the font *size* options.

5 Select 54 from the pull-down list of point sizes.
54 displays as the current font size in the Formatting toolbar.

6 Click outside the selection box.

To change font and font size using the Font dialog box:

1 Select the *Presents* text box.

2 Choose Font from the Format menu.

3 Select Arial Narrow in the Font list box.
If Arial Narrow is not available on your system, substitute another font such as Times New Roman or Century Gothic.

4 Select 36 in the Size list box.

5 Turn off active features in the Effects section of the dialog box by clicking in any checked boxes.

6 Select OK to apply the font changes.
Text within the selection box appears in a larger size.

7 Click outside the selection box.

Adding Special Effects

Several changes can be made to the appearance of characters. For example, you can bold, italicize, and underline text. When you ***shadow*** text you add a drop shadow of the text behind the selected text. If you want text to take on the same color as the background and appear slightly raised, you can ***emboss*** it. Once in awhile you may want to change the position of a character, altering its location on a line in relation to other characters on the line. For example, you can position a ***superscript*** character slightly above characters on the same line or a ***subscript*** character slightly below characters on the same line.

In the following steps you will use the Italic tool on the Formatting toolbar to italicize a phrase.

To italicize selected text:

1 Select the *Presents* text box.

2 Select Italic on the Formatting toolbar.
The selected text appears italicized.

> ***Tip*** Choosing Font from the Format menu and selecting Italic in the Font Style dialog box produces the same result.

3 Click outside the selection box.

Applying Color

If you will be giving an on-screen presentation or using color slides, color can be a powerful tool for emphasizing text. Research has shown that "hot" colors such as red and yellow tend to excite or antagonize, while "cool" colors such as green and blue tend to relax or pacify.

You can change the background color of slides, the background color of objects on a slide, and text color. For example, you can use the Custom

Background dialog box shown in Figure 3.10 to change the background color of the current slide or all slides.

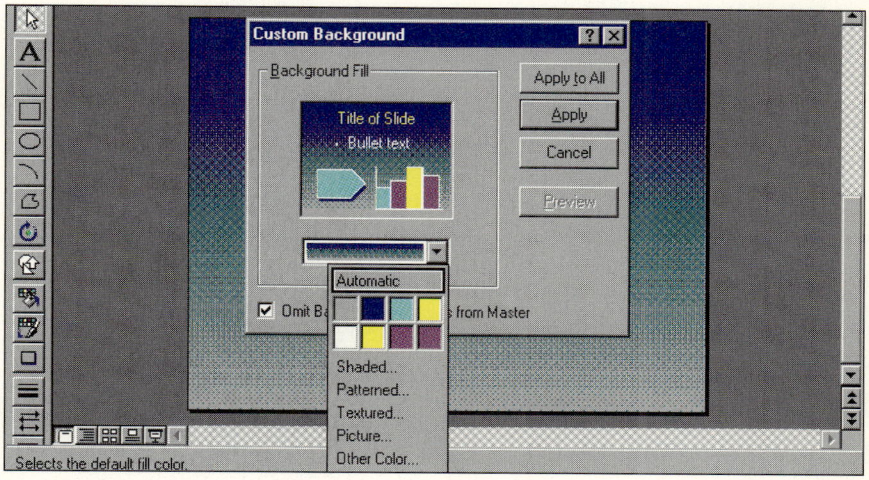

Figure 3.10

PowerPoint also provides predefined color schemes that you can apply to the current slide or all slides. You can pick one of the standard schemes or create a custom combination using the Color Scheme dialog box shown in Figure 3.11. You will find the Custom Background and Slide Color Scheme options on the Format menu.

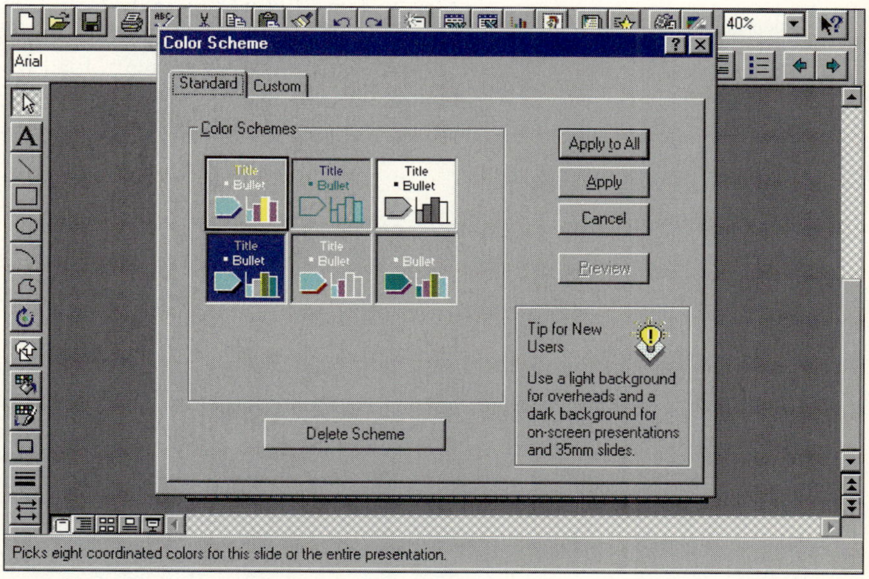

Figure 3.11

Clicking the Text Color button on the Formatting toolbar, or selecting the Color pull-down list in the Font dialog box, displays an initial 8-color palette. If the color you want for selected text does not appear in the initial color set, you can select Other Color to view a standard color palette with over 120 colors.

Caution Be careful not to use too many color variations, which can be distracting to a viewer.

In the following steps you will change the standard color of selected text.

To apply color and save your changes:

1. Select the *Presents* text box.
2. Select Text Color on the Formatting toolbar.
3. Select yellow from the color palette.
4. Click outside the selection box.
5. Save the file.

EXIT If necessary, you can exit PowerPoint now and continue this project later.

Completing Text Entry

Throughout the remainder of this project, you will set up the *text* portions of slides 2 and 3 as shown in Figure 3.1 (you will add lines and clip art in Project 4). In the process you will work with variations of earlier activities, such as selecting a different AutoLayout design, and a few new features, such as centering text.

You will be instructed to save your changes at the end of each section. If necessary, you can exit PowerPoint after saving your work and complete the project later. To begin again, load PowerPoint, open the Cruises.ppt presentation, and display the last slide you were editing.

Using Object AutoLayout

You want slide 2 to display a title above a picture of a sail boat (see Figure 3.1). To create this slide, you will select the AutoLayout named Object and add the title *Cruising the Caribbean,* as shown in Figure 3.12.

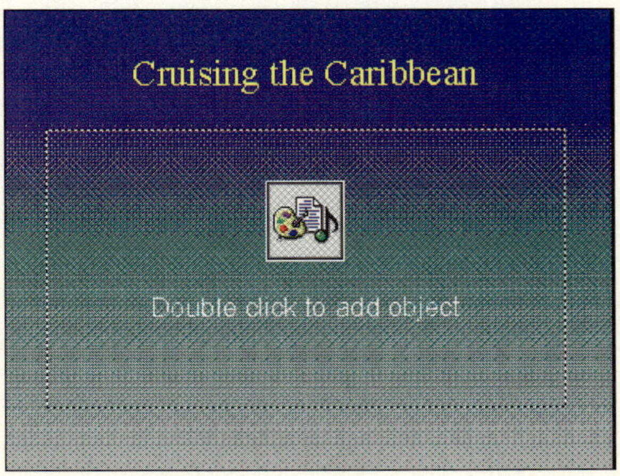

Figure 3.12

To create slide two:

1 If necessary, load PowerPoint and open the Cruises.ppt presentation.

2 Select New Slide near the lower-right corner of the screen.
The New Slide dialog box appears.

3 Display additional layouts using the scroll bar, and then select the Object layout.

4 Select OK to create the slide.
Two placeholders appear, one for a title and the other for an object (you will add the sail boat art in Project 4).

5 Choose Custom Background from the Format menu.

6 If a ✓ does not appear in the Omit Background Graphics from Master check box, click the check box so that a check appears.
The setting that controls display of background objects is turned off.

7 Select Apply.
The tropical background disappears.

8 Select the title text box.

9 Type `Cruising the Caribbean` and then click outside either box.
Check that your slide matches Figure 3.12.

10 Save the file.

Using 2 Column Text AutoLayout

Slides 3, 4, and 5 have a more complex layout than the first two slides (see Figure 3.1). Each title occupies three lines. Other text displays in two columns, one of which contains a bulleted list.

You could create each slide from scratch. However, once you set up the two-column text design on slide 3 using AutoLayout and then enter text, you can duplicate that slide twice to form slides 4 and 5 (which you will do in Project 4). It's a relatively simple task to then edit the two new slides to reflect different cruise packages.

In the following steps you will use AutoLayout to select a basic design for slide 3, remove the slide background, enter a three-line title, vary the font size in the title, and move the lower two boxes to add space below the title. Remember to save your work frequently during a long editing session.

To select the layout for slide 3 and remove the background:

1 Select New Slide.

2 Select 2 Column Text layout (the third layout in the top row), and then select OK.
Three boxes appear: one for the title and two other text boxes side by side. The bullet in the upper-left corner of each text box indicates the box is a placeholder for a bulleted list.

3 Remove the tropical background from the slide.
If you do not remember how to complete this task, review steps 5 through 7 in the previous numbered steps.

Caution The Omit Background Graphics from Master check box must be checked.

To specify the title for slide 3 and vary font size:

1 Select the title box at the top of the slide.

2 Type **Bahamas** and press ENTER

3 Type **on the** and press ENTER

4 Type **Island Princess** (do not press ENTER)

5 Select *Bahamas* and apply a 54-point Arial font.

Reminder If a font you are instructed to use does not appear on your font list, select another font.

6 Select *on the* and apply a 24-point Arial font.

7 Select *Island Princess* and apply a 44-point Arial font.

8 Click outside the slide to clear the text box outline.

To move the boxes and save your changes:

1 Select the left box below the title.

2 Drag the box downward by its border to add space below the title, as shown in Figure 3.13.

Figure 3.13

3 Select the right box below the title.

4 Drag the box downward the same distance as the left box.

5 Save the file.

Aligning Text

By default, text aligns at the left edge of a box. The Formatting toolbar contains Left Alignment and Center Alignment buttons. You can also choose Alignment from the Format menu to left-align, center, or right-align text. In the following steps you will finish entering the text for slide 3. You will also change fonts and alignment.

To apply a font to a blank text box:

1 Click within the left box below the title.

2 Apply a 32-point Century Schoolbook font to the box.
This font will apply to all text typed in the box unless you specify otherwise.

To center text:

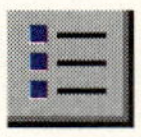

1 Select Bullet On/Off on the Formatting toolbar.
The bullet in the text box disappears.

2 Type **`Visit`**

3 Select Center Alignment on the Formatting toolbar.
Text is now centered on the current line.

4 Press (ENTER) to position the insertion point on the next line.

5 Select Left Alignment on the Formatting toolbar.

6 Select Bullet On/Off.
A bullet appears on the slide. The Bullet On/Off button appears slightly depressed and lighter in color compared to other buttons in the Formatting toolbar, which tells you that the feature is active.

To complete the bulleted list:

1 Type **`Nassau`** and press (ENTER)

2 Type **`Coco Cay`** and press (ENTER)

3 Type **`Freeport`** and press (ENTER)

4 Select Bullet On/Off to turn bullets off.

5 Apply a 20-point Century Schoolbook font.

6 Press (ENTER) and then press (TAB)

7 Type **`Leaves Mondays and Fridays from San Juan`**
Text that won't fit on one line automatically wraps to the next line.

8 Select the text typed in the previous step, and then click Italic in the Formatting toolbar.

9 Click outside the box to deselect it.
The text on your slide should match that shown in Figure 3.14. Positioning may vary if you chose different font styles or sizes.

10 Save the file.

Figure 3.14

To change fonts and enter text in the right text box:

1 Select the text box on the right side of the slide.

2 Apply a 32-point Century Schoolbook font to the box.

3 Select Bullet On/Off to remove the bullet.

4 Type **3 Night Cruise** and press ENTER twice.

5 Type **From $390** and press ENTER

6 Press TAB twice, type **Ship Only** and then press ENTER

7 Type **From $580** and then press ENTER

8 Press TAB twice, and then type **Includes Air**

9 Apply a 20-point Century Schoolbook font to four words and phrases: the word *From* preceding $390, the phrase *Ship Only,* the word *From* preceding $580, and the phrase *Includes Air.*

10 Click outside the box.

11 Check that the text on your slide matches that shown in Figure 3.15. Make changes as necessary.

Figure 3.15

12 Save the file.

You have created the text portion of slide 3. After adding lines in the next project, you will use this slide to create two similar slides.

THE NEXT STEP

Think of all the PowerPoint features presented in this project! Several AutoLayout designs provided the starting points for new slides. You selected a design template and worked extensively with text boxes, entering and editing text as well as moving and sizing the boxes. Of course, you also enhanced text by varying font and size, changing color, and applying special effects.

To build on your skills, plan your own presentation combining text with other objects. Up to this point the decisions as to layout, font, text to type, and so forth were made for you. Now prepare to make your own decisions. Take a look at the available design templates. View other AutoLayout slide designs, and imagine a slide in which you might use each layout. Try out options you read about but didn't work through, such as shadowing or embossing text. Type some words in a new presentation, and apply different fonts, font sizes, and special effects. By experimenting with the program on your own, you'll quickly gain confidence.

This concludes Project 3. You can either exit PowerPoint or go on to work the Study Questions, Review Exercises, and Assignments.

SUMMARY AND EXERCISES

Summary

- A slide may contain one or more objects. In PowerPoint an object can be text (such as a title or bulleted list), art, a table, a graph, an organization chart, or a media clip.
- The arrangement of objects on a slide is called the slide layout. PowerPoint provides the AutoLayout feature, through which you can select among 24 professionally designed layouts.
- A design template controls how the various parts of your presentation should appear, including background patterns and colors.
- You work with objects in boxes on a slide. You can create, edit, move, and size a box.
- Font refers to the style (typeface) of characters, and font size refers to height. You can make changes to font and font size as well as display text in color and with special effects.
- Text can appear left-aligned (the default), centered, and right-aligned.

Key Terms and Operations

Key Terms
AutoLayout
bold
design template
drag
emboss
font
media clip
object
placeholder
point
resize handle
selection box
shadow
slide layout
subscript
superscript
text prompt

Operations
Apply color to text
Center text
Change font and font size
Create and edit a text box
Create placeholders with AutoLayout
Italicize text
Move a text box
Select a design template

Study Questions

Multiple Choice

1. Which of the following is not associated with a media clip?
   a. video
   b. graph
   c. music
   d. sound

2. Which of the following refers to the arrangement of objects on a slide?
   a. slide layout
   b. resize handle
   c. AutoLayout
   d. AutoContent Wizard

3. Which of the following can be controlled by a design template?
   a. background pattern
   b. colors
   c. repeating text such as a company name or the date
   d. All of the above.

4. What is the feature that provides 24 professionally designed arrangements of objects on a slide?
   a. Pick a Look
   b. AutoLayout
   c. object orientation
   d. None of the above.

5. What are the objects on a slide that reserve space and are filled in later?
   a. placeholders
   b. text boxes
   c. clip art boxes
   d. Both b and c are true.

6. The border of forward slashes that appears around the text box when you click the text indicates
   a. adjustment handles.
   b. sizing handles.
   c. a selection box.
   d. a border box.

7. What term refers to moving a box using a mouse?
   a. click
   b. move
   c. cut and paste
   d. drag

8. The term *points* refers to
   a. typeface.
   b. font size.
   c. italics.
   d. shadow effect.

9. Which is not a true statement about slide layouts?
   a. You can design your own layout.
   b. You can select a layout using AutoLayout.
   c. You can change the size of an object on the slide.
   d. All previous statements are true.
10. Which is not a true statement about aligning text?
   a. The default alignment is along the left edge of a box.
   b. You can center and right-align text by choosing Alignment from the Format menu.
   c. You can center and right-align text using the Formatting toolbar.
   d. All previous statements are true.

Short Answer

1. What is the term that refers to graphics images stored on disk?
2. What controls how the various parts of your presentation should appear, including background patterns and colors?
3. How do you eliminate background objects that are on design templates?
4. What is the name of the AutoLayout displaying side-by-side text boxes below a title box?
5. When you click anywhere inside a text box, what kind of box does the object become?
6. When you click on a text box, what are the squares at each corner and the midpoints called?
7. What is the style (typeface) of characters called?
8. Name three font styles or special effects.
9. What term refers to arranging text along the left edge of a text box?
10. What options, accessed from the Format menu, let you adjust a slide's shading and color intensity?

For Discussion

1. What is an object in PowerPoint? Provide examples.
2. Describe the process for dragging a text box to a different location.
3. Explain the options for aligning text in a box.
4. Why is it important to enhance the appearance of text? What are some of your options to make some characters look different than others?
5. Which of the 24 predefined layouts provide placeholders for text?

Review Exercises

Buying a Car

Create a six-slide presentation showing the steps to buying a car. Figure 3.16 shows the plan for the completed presentation, which includes clip art, word art, lines, borders, and color fills.

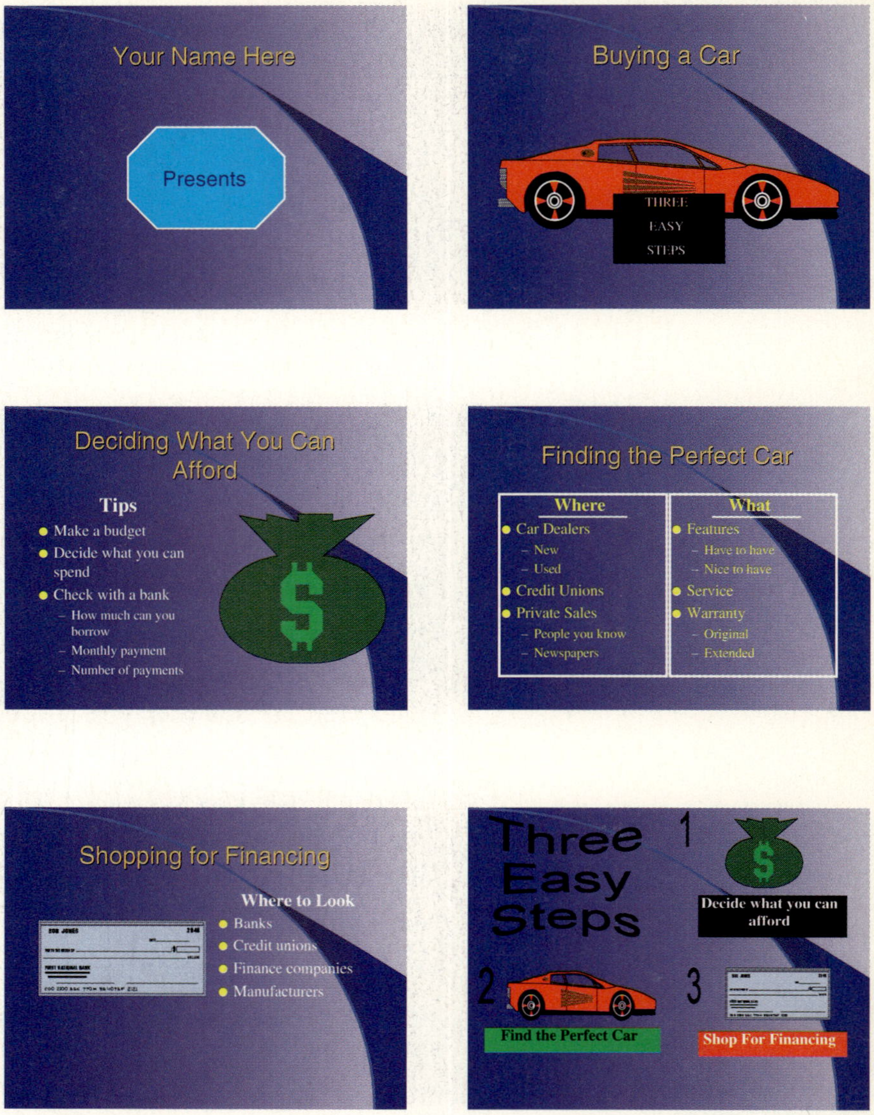

Figure 3.16

In this review exercise you will create each slide from AutoLayout and then add text (the other enhancements are part of the review exercises in Project 4). When you finish the following instructions, your presentation will include the layouts and text shown in Figure 3.17. Refer to this figure as you complete the following steps. Save your work after each new slide (use the name Buycar.ppt).

Figure 3.17

> ***Tip*** Your background colors may be different, depending on the type of resolution your computer uses.

1. Load PowerPoint and select Blank Presentation. (If you are already in PowerPoint, choose New from the File menu.)
2. Create slide 1. Select the Title Only layout, and type your name in the Title text box.
3. Select Apply Design Template from the Format menu and select Soaring.pot from the list of file names in the Apply Design Template dialog box (template files are stored in the Presentation Designs folder).
4. Create slide 2. Select the Title Only layout, and add the title shown in Figure 3.17.

5. Create slide 3. Select the Text & Clip Art layout, and enter the title and tips shown in Figure 3.17.
6. Create slide 4. Select the 2 Column Text layout, and enter the title as well as the *Where* and *What* information shown in Figure 3.17.
7. Create slide 5. Select the Clip Art & Text layout, and enter the title and Where to Look information.
8. Create slide 6. Select the Blank layout. (You will add the text summarizing the three steps after adding word art and clip art in the Project 4 review exercises.)
9. Review your Buycar presentation, make changes as necessary and save it.

Getting Involved in Campus Life

Create a six-slide presentation showing some of the ways that students can get involved in campus life. Figure 3.18 shows the plan for the completed presentation, which includes special text effects and clip art.

Figure 3.18

In this review exercise you will create each slide from AutoLayout and add text (the other enhancements are part of the Project 4 Review Exercises). When you finish the following instructions, your presentation will include the layouts and text shown in Figure 3.19. Refer to this figure as you complete the following steps. Save your work after each new slide (use the name Getalife.ppt).

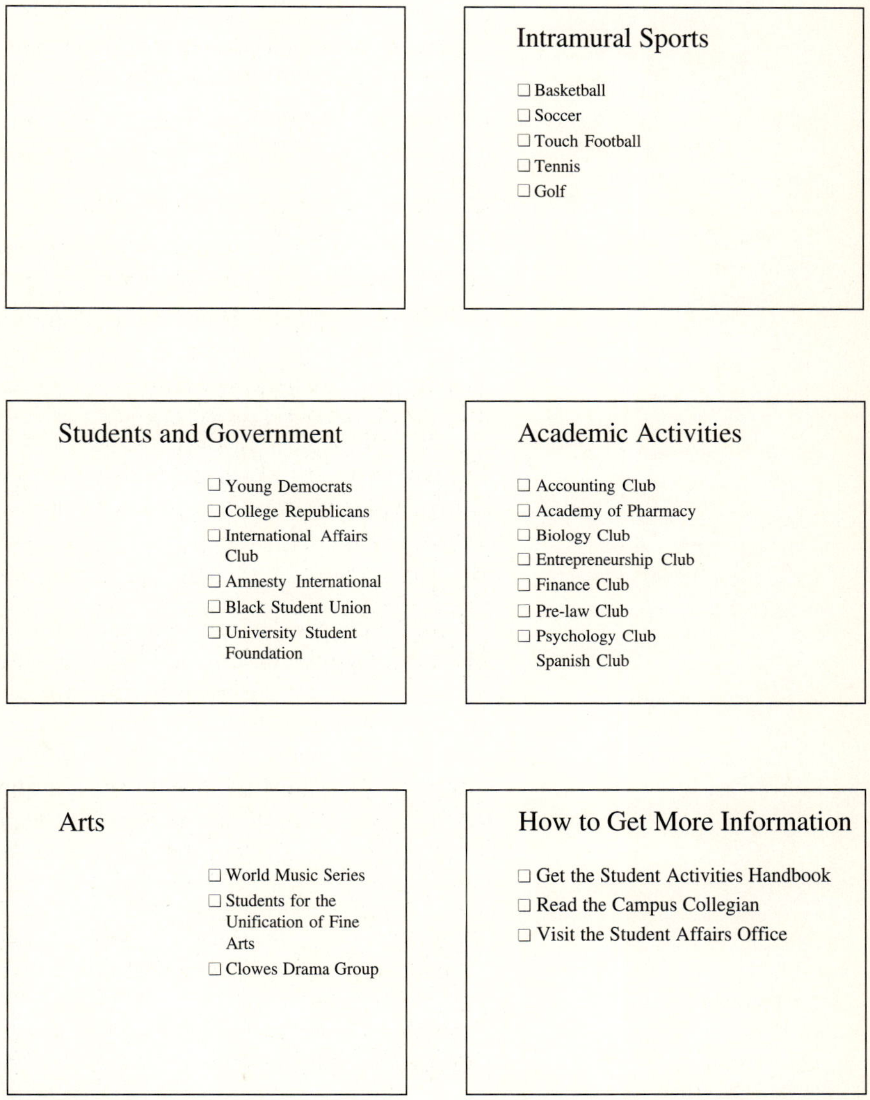

Figure 3.19

1. Load PowerPoint and select Blank Presentation. (If you are already in PowerPoint, choose New from the File menu.)
2. Create slide 1. Select the Blank layout. Leave the slide blank until Project 4.
3. Create slide 2. Select the Text & Clip Art layout, and then add the *Intramural Sports* title and text in a bulleted list, as shown in Figure 3.19.

4. Create slide 3. Select the Clip Art & Text layout, and then add the *Students and Government* title and text in a bulleted list, as shown in Figure 3.19.
5. Create slide 4. Select the Text & Clip Art layout, and then add the *Academic Activities* title and text in a bulleted list, as shown in Figure 3.19.
6. Create slide 5. Select the Clip Art & Text layout, and then add the *Arts* title and text in a bulleted list, as shown in Figure 3.19.
7. Create slide 6. Select the Bulleted List layout, and then add the *How to Get More Information* title and text in a bulleted list, as shown in Figure 3.19.
8. Review your Getalife presentation, and make changes as necessary.

Assignments

Getting Help on Typing Text

Use Microsoft PowerPoint Help Topics in on-screen Help to look up information about terms that apply to typing text. Write a brief summary of what you learned.

Getting Help on Moving Text

Use Microsoft PowerPoint Help Topics in on-screen Help to look up information about moving text with a mouse. Write a brief summary of what you learned.

Combining Text and Clip Art

Create a new presentation. Select among the following topics (or substitute another of your choice): selling a product, organizing a social event, registering for classes, or repairing a broken item. The presentation should instruct viewers to follow at least a three-step process. First provide a sketch of the text and art you have in mind for each slide (try to include at least four variations in slide layout). Then look through the clip art gallery to find appropriate graphics. Create the slides but enter only the text. Save your work using a name that helps you remember the presentation topic.

Project 4: Combining Text and Art

Objectives

After completing this project, you should be able to:

- Select and insert clip art
- Add lines and borders
- Duplicate slides in Slide Sorter view
- Use Word Art to enhance text
- Arrange multiple objects effectively
- Display AutoShapes containing text

Case Study: Cruising the Caribbean II

Think back to times you have walked down a hall past a bulletin board, thumbed through the telephone yellow pages, or watched billboards as you traveled on an interstate highway. What did you see that caused you to take a second look? In many cases you would say it was an image that first caught your attention. Viewing a combination of art and text on slide presentations can have a similar attention-grabbing effect.

In Project 3 you entered most of the text for an eight-slide presentation about Caribbean cruises. In this project you will add art, borders, lines, shapes, and color to emphasize your message.

Designing the Solution

Most of the design work is already done. Before you created the first cruise-related slide, you had an overall layout in mind (see Figure 3.1):

- An introductory slide showing your company's name, with a background of an island sunset
- A second slide announcing the subject of the presentation *(Cruising the Caribbean)* with a picture of a sailing vessel occupying most of the slide
- Three slides promoting different cruise packages, with bulleted lists of destinations along with departure and rate information set apart from other text
- A slide summarizing cruise highlights
- A slide letting viewers know how to get more information (you'd like pictures of a phone, a fax machine, and an envelope placed next to associated numbers and address)
- A final slide showing your firm's name, along with a promotional message within an eye-catching shape

The remaining design work is very hands-on in nature. In this project you will receive instructions on which art to select, the shape in which to type text, exactly where to draw a line, and so forth. For your own presentations, however, this phase will involve looking through a lot of art, moving and sizing selected objects, and experimenting with color and other visual effects until you are satisfied that the slides will capture the attention of an audience.

Adding Clip Art

Clip art refers to a graphics image stored on disk. Clip art pictures are created by computer drawing programs, digital cameras, and scanners that turn images into computer files stored on disk. Examples of this process can be found in retail outlets that place your image on t-shirts, calendars, and cakes. Some public and school libraries have scanners that you can use to digitize pictures as easily as duplicating pages on a copy machine.

Caution U.S. copyright laws apply to photographs and art as well as written material. They apply to images digitized from hard copy or downloaded from a network such as the Internet. Be aware that you may have to get permission to use an image, such as a Disney character.

PowerPoint provides an extensive gallery of more than 1000 clip art images organized into many categories, such as Academic, Banners, Business & Finance, Cartoons, Energy, Technology, and Transportation. Choosing the Clip Art option from the Insert menu displays the initial Microsoft ClipArt Gallery dialog box shown in Figure 4.1.

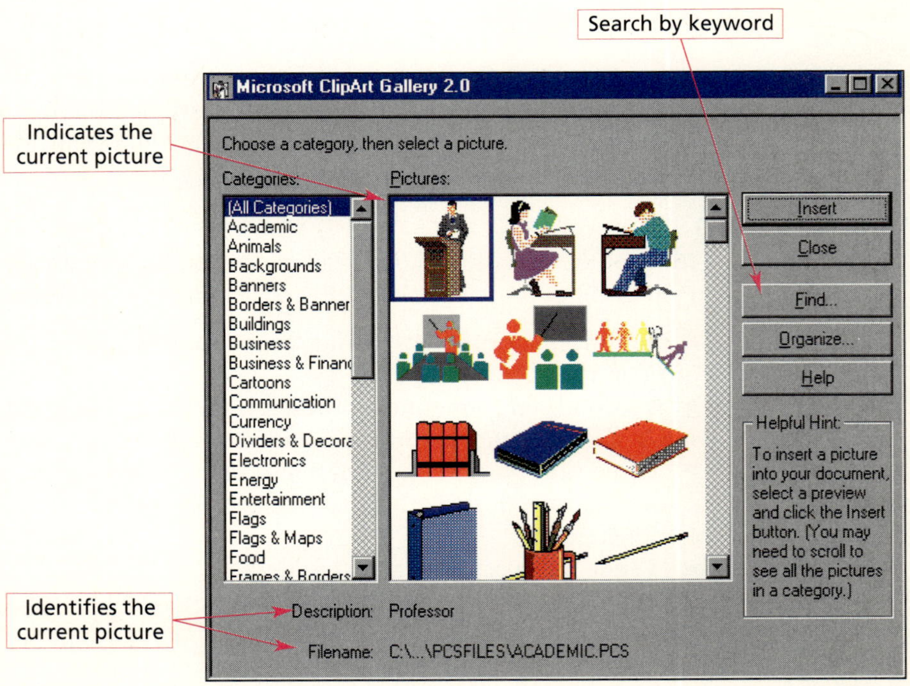

Figure 4.1

Directions to select a picture appear in a Helpful Hint box in the lower-right corner of the dialog box. A thick surrounding border indicates the current picture; its description and file name are displayed at the bottom. You can select among other sets of pictures using the Categories list box. The Find option helps you locate a specific picture or type of picture quickly. For example, you can display all clip art in a specified category or with names containing a certain word or phrase, such as *sailing*.

In the following steps you will add a sailing clip art figure to the object box in slide 2. (You will also add clip art to slide 7 near the end of the project.)

Tip The full set of PowerPoint clip art may not be installed on your system. Therefore, one or more of the clip art pictures specified in this project may not be available. If you should encounter a message stating that a matching picture could not be found, select an appropriate substitute.

To add clip art to an existing object box:

1 Load PowerPoint and open the Cruises.ppt presentation.
The opening slide appears, showing the title and background sunset.

2 Display slide 2.

3 Double-click the icon within the object box.
The Insert Object dialog box appears on the screen.

4 Select Microsoft ClipArt Gallery in the Object Type list box.

5 Select OK.
The Microsoft ClipArt Gallery appears as shown in Figure 4.1.

6 Select Find.
The Find ClipArt dialog box appears.

7 Select the Description list box.

8 Type `sailing` and then select Find Now.
One or more pictures with a sailing theme appear, such as those shown in Figure 4.2. The selected figure (the first one) is the one you want.

Reminder If the specified clip art is not available, select an appropriate substitute. You might, for example, look in the Transportation or Travel categories.

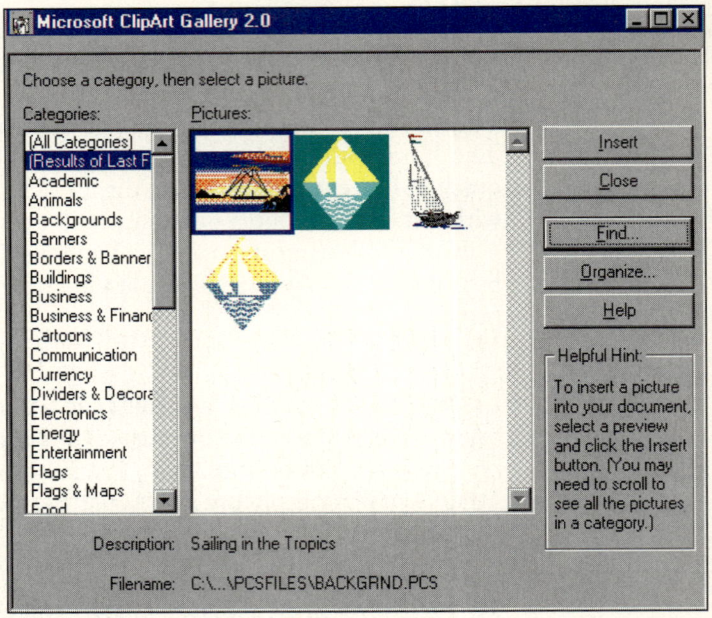

Figure 4.2

9 Select Insert to place the current clip art object into the slide.

10 Click outside the object box to deselect it.

The completed slide 2 is shown in Figure 4.3.

Figure 4.3

11 Save the file.

Tip PowerPoint can suggest appropriate clip art based on the text in your presentation. When you select AutoClipArt from the Tools menu, PowerPoint will search your computer for clip art that may match words in your titles. You can then view the clip art in the Microsoft ClipArt Gallery and insert it into your slide.

ADDING LINES AND BORDERS

You can create interesting visual effects by using horizontal lines, vertical lines, and borders to separate sections of a slide, as shown in Figure 4.4. A border is a line drawn around the edge of an object.

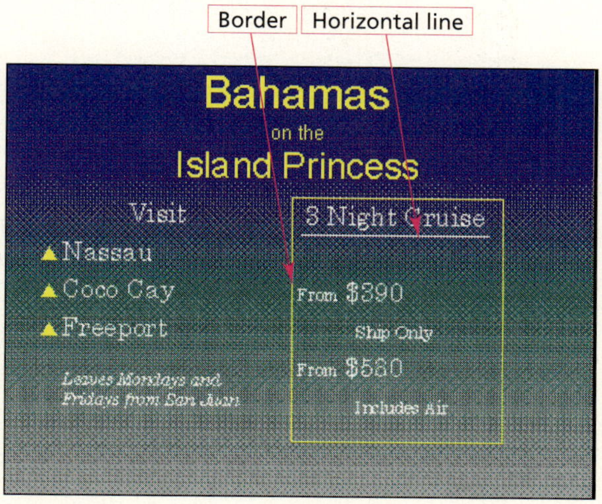

Figure 4.4

To draw a line, you will first select the Line Tool button on the Drawing toolbar. Next you will move the pointer to the location where you want the line to start (the arrow pointer changes to a cross-hair pointer when you cross the boundary of the slide, as shown in Figure 4.5). You will then drag the pointer to the ending point.

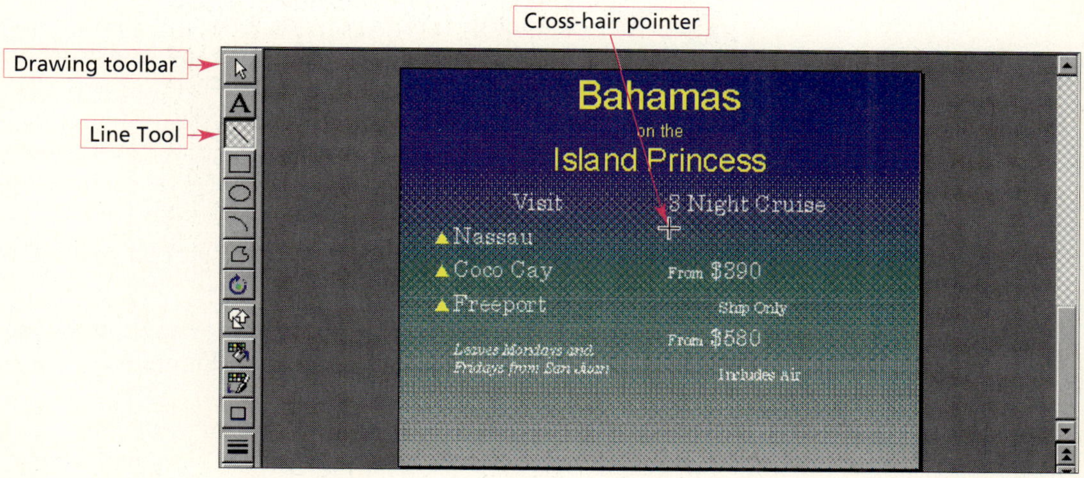

Figure 4.5

To create a border, you will select the object you want to surround with a line and then open the Colors and Lines dialog box shown in Figure 4.6. You can select among solid and dashed line styles and select color from one of the Line pull-down lists. You can also select a pattern from the Fill pull-down list.

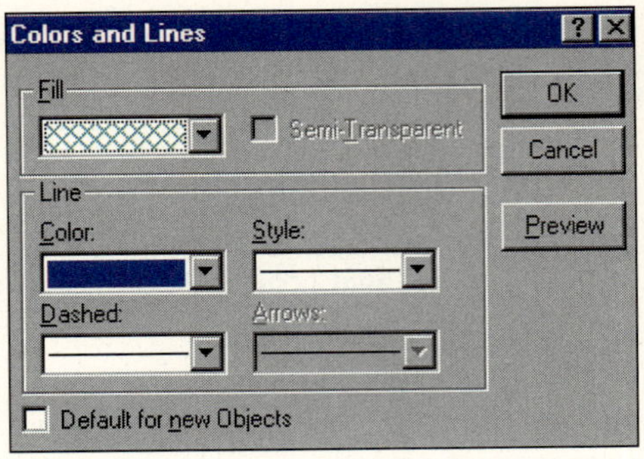

Figure 4.6

> ***Tip*** To remove a line drawn with Line Tool, click the line to display the moving and sizing handles, and then press DEL
> To remove a border, select the box displaying the border, choose Colors and Lines from the Format menu, and then select No Line from the Color pull-down list.

In the following steps you will enhance slide 3 by adding a horizontal line to separate the length of a cruise from the prices that follow. You will also add a colored border.

To display the Drawing toolbar (skip these steps if the Drawing toolbar is already displayed):

1 Choose Toolbars from the View menu.

2 Click the box to the left of Drawing until a check (√) appears in the box.

3 Select OK.

> ***Tip*** Subsequent instructions will not contain the level of detail shown in steps 1 through 3. Instead, you will see a single instruction to turn on the Drawing (or some other) toolbar.

To add a horizontal line:

1 Display slide 3.

2 Select Line Tool on the Drawing toolbar, and position the cross-hair pointer beneath the *3* in *3 Night Cruise*.

3 Hold down the left mouse button and draw a line by moving the cross-hair pointer to the right, as shown in Figure 4.7.

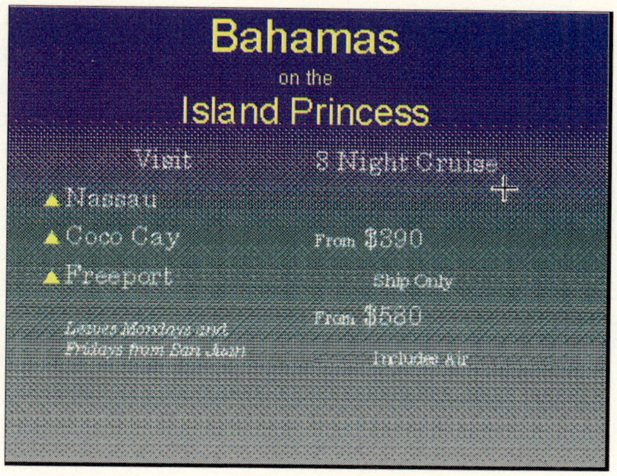

Figure 4.7

4 Release the left mouse button.

5 Click outside the line to deselect Line Tool.
A horizontal separator line appears as shown in Figure 4.4.

To add a border:

1 Select the text box on the right side of slide 3 that contains price information.

2 Choose Colors and Lines from the Format menu.
The Colors and Lines dialog box appears.

3 Select the Style pull-down list, and then select the first line style (a thin solid line).

4 Select the Color pull-down list.
The default list of eight color boxes appears.

5 Select Yellow.

6 Select OK to close the dialog box.
A yellow border appears around the text box.

7 Move and size the box, if needed, until its location and size matches that shown in Figure 4.4.

8 Click outside the box to deselect it.

9 Save the file.

EXIT If necessary, you can exit PowerPoint now and continue this project later.

Duplicating Slides in Slide Sorter View

Look again at Figure 3.1. Slides 4 and 5 have the same text arrangements, fonts, font sizes, lines, and borders as slide 3. Duplicating slide 3 twice will save you time in developing the next two slides.

You can duplicate slides in Slide Sorter view or Outline view by choosing Duplicate from the Edit menu. PowerPoint automatically inserts the duplicate slide immediately after the original slide.

Tip To duplicate a slide in a nonadjacent position, use the Copy and Paste commands on the Edit menu. For example, later in this project you will use copy and paste techniques to duplicate the contents of slide 1 on a new slide 8.

In the following steps you will duplicate a slide twice in Slide Sorter view. You will then edit the text in the new slides to display information about two other cruises.

To duplicate a slide in Slide Sorter view:

1 If necessary, load PowerPoint and open the Cruises.ppt presentation.

2 Select Slide Sorter view.

3 Select slide 3.
A thick black border appears around slide 3.

4 Choose Duplicate from the Edit menu to create slide 4.

5 Choose Duplicate from the Edit menu to create slide 5.
Slides 3, 4, and 5 are identical for the moment. You will edit slides 4 and 5 in the following sets of numbered steps.

To change the title in slide 4:

1 Select slide 4.

2 Select Slide view.

Caution Slides 3, 4, and 5 are identical until you change them. Be sure you have accessed the correct slide by checking the slide number in the lower-left corner of the screen.

3 Click within the title text box.

4 Select *Bahamas* and type `Eastern Caribbean`
The new text replaces the selected text.

5 Select *Island* and type `Tropic`
Tropic Princess appears in place of *Island Princess.*

To edit text in the left text box on slide 4:

1 Click within the left text box.

2 Select *Coco Cay* and type `San Juan`

3 Select *Freeport* and type `St. Thomas`

4 Press (ENTER) to insert a blank bulleted line.

5 Type `Coco Cay`

6 Edit the departure information by typing `Leaves Mondays from Miami` to replace *Leaves Mondays and Fridays from San Juan.*

7 Check that the text in your left text box matches that shown on slide 4 in Figure 3.1. Make changes as necessary.

To edit text in the right text box on slide 4:

1 Click within the right text box.

2 Select the *3* in *3 Night Cruise* and type `5`

3 Select *$390* and type **$845**

4 Select *$580* and type **$1085**

5 Click anywhere outside the box to clear the text box outline.

6 Check that your slide 4 matches Figure 4.8. Make changes as necessary.

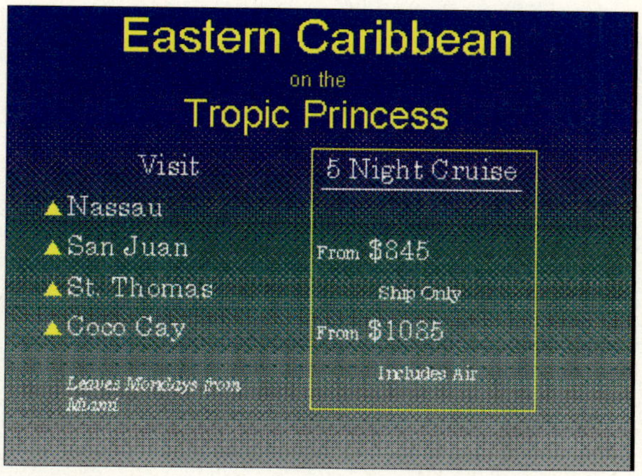

Figure 4.8

7 Save the file.

To change the title in slide 5:

1 Select slide 5.
Be sure that slide 5 is selected by checking the current slide number in the lower-left corner of the screen.

2 Click within the title text box.

3 Select *Bahamas* and type **Southern Caribbean**

4 Select *Princess* and type **Pleasure**

To edit text in the left text box on slide 5:

1 Click within the left text box.

2 Select *Nassau* and type **Martinique**

3 Select *Coco Cay* and type **Barbados**

4 Select *Freeport* and type **St. Thomas**

5 Press (ENTER) to insert a blank bulleted line.

6 Type **Antigua** and press (ENTER) to insert another blank bulleted line.

7 Type **St. Maarten**

8 Delete the blank line after St. Maarten.

9 Edit the departure information by typing **Leaves Sundays from San Juan** to replace *Leaves Mondays and Fridays from San Juan.*

10 Click anywhere outside the box.

11 Check that the text in your left text box matches that shown on slide 5 in Figure 3.1. Make changes as necessary.

12 Save the file.

To edit text in the right text box on slide 5:

1. Click within the right text box.
2. Select the *3* in *3 Night Cruise* and type **7**
3. Select *$390* and type **$999**
4. Select *$580* and type **$1145**
5. Click anywhere outside the box to clear the text box outline.
6. Check that your slide 5 matches Figure 4.9. Make changes as necessary.

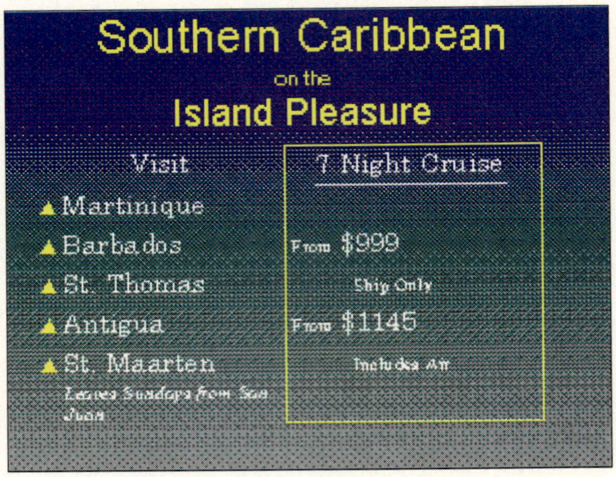

Figure 4.9

7. Save the file.

EXIT If necessary, you can exit PowerPoint now and continue this project later.

Adding Word Art

Word art refers to the special text effects created by slanting, curving, or otherwise manipulating text to form an eye-catching design. The phrase *Caribbean Cruise Highlights* above the bulleted list in Figure 4.10 is an example of word art.

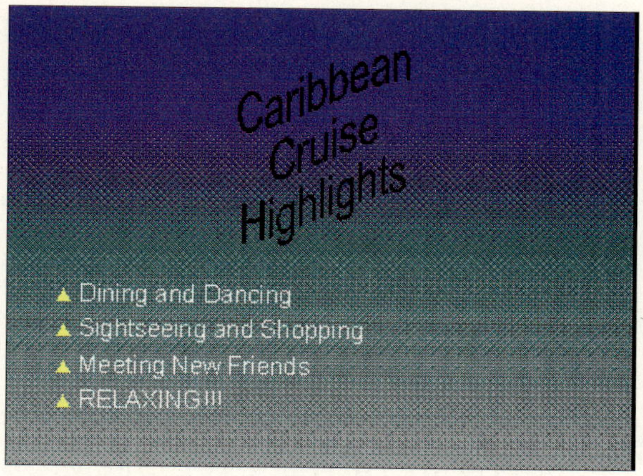

Figure 4.10

PowerPoint includes the Microsoft WordArt application, which lets you select among predefined special effects after typing your text. The choices are displayed in the special text effects gallery such as those shown in Figure 4.11.

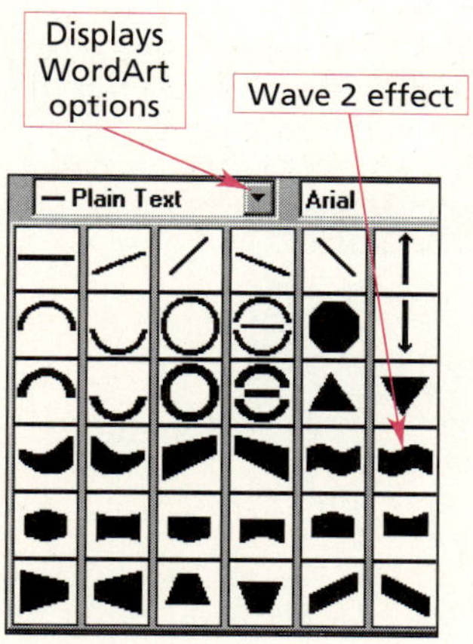

Figure 4.11

Tip For best results, use this feature on only one or two words or a short phrase.

In the sets of numbered steps that follow, you will add a blank slide 6 and create the word art and bulleted list shown in Figure 4.10.

To create a new slide without a background:

1 If necessary, load PowerPoint and open the Cruises.ppt presentation.

2 Display slide 5, and then select New Slide.

3 Select the Object over Text layout, and then select OK.

A new slide 6 appears with placeholders for a title, an object, and a bulleted list. A seaside sunset and island trees appear in the background automatically because you selected the Tropical.pot template.

4 Choose Custom Background from the Format menu.

5 Click the Omit Background Graphics from Master check box until the box has a check.

6 Select Apply.
The setting that controls the display of background objects is turned off.

To remove the unwanted title text box:

1 Click the border of the title text box at the top of the slide.
The resize handles appear.

2 Press DEL to remove the selected box.

To create curved text using Microsoft WordArt:

1 Double-click within the object box.
The Insert Object dialog box appears.

2 Select Microsoft WordArt 2.0, and then select OK.
The Enter Your Text Here dialog box appears.

3 Type **`Caribbean`** and press ENTER

4 Type **`Cruise`** and press ENTER

5 Type **`Highlights`**
The word *Caribbean* scrolls out of view, but the other two words are displayed in the Enter Your Text Here dialog box, as shown in Figure 4.12.

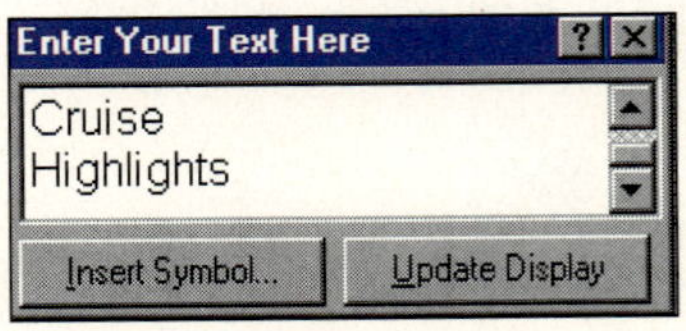

Figure 4.12

6 Click the down arrow to the right of the Plain Text box in the upper-left corner of the screen.
A gallery of 36 special effects appears as shown in Figure 4.11.

7 Select the last option in the fourth row of the special text effects gallery (Wave 2).
Check that your screen matches the one shown in Figure 4.13.

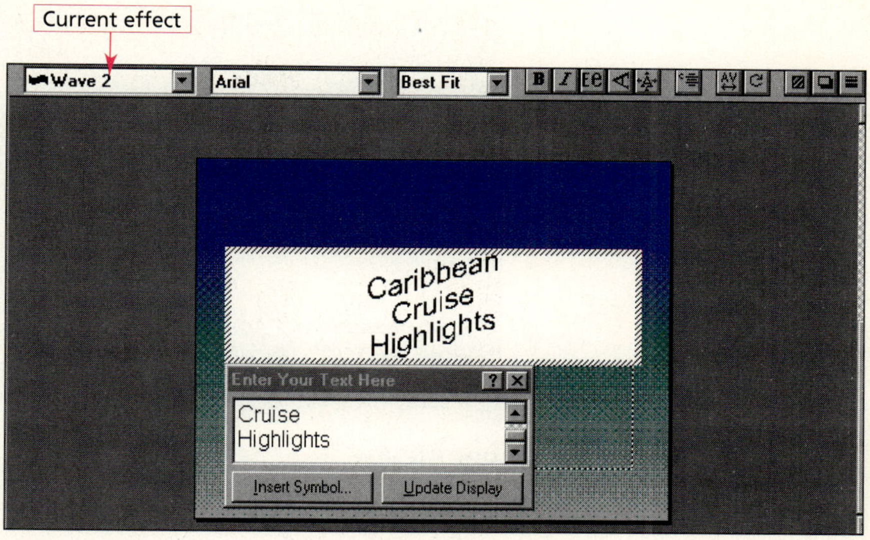

Figure 4.13

8 Click outside the slide area to exit Microsoft WordArt. The selected text effect with resize handles appears on the screen.

To move and size the word art and text to the bulleted list:

1 Position the pointer within the word art object and drag it to the top of the slide.

2 Drag one or more resize handles until the word art occupies the space shown in Figure 4.10.

3 Click within the bulleted list box.

4 Enter the four lines of text shown in Figure 4.10.

5 Move and size the text box as necessary.

6 Save the file.

EXIT If necessary, you can exit PowerPoint now and continue this project later.

WORKING WITH MULTIPLE OBJECTS

You'll want viewers to pay attention to, rather than be distracted by, your slide layouts. Providing balance among objects can help to achieve the effect you want. In this section you will create slide 7 (see Figure 4.14), which combines text and pictures to let viewers know how to get more information.

Figure 4.14

The design includes a title box across the top, three clip art boxes down the left side, and three associated text boxes down the right side.

Most of the tasks involved in creating slide 7—inserting clip art and creating text boxes—have already been described in detail in other sections of this project and Project 3. For those steps, only limited instructions will be provided. However, you will be adding clip art and text boxes without placeholders marking the locations (PowerPoint doesn't provide a predefined layout for three clip art boxes on the left and three text boxes on the right). Therefore it will be necessary to size and move each box.

Reminder Substitute similar clip art if a specified figure is not available on your system. If you can't find three suitable figures, limit the clip art to one or two.

To select a layout and turn off the background:

1 If necessary, load PowerPoint and open the Cruises.ppt presentation.

2 Display slide 6 in Slide view, and then select New Slide.

3 Select Title Only as the layout, and then select OK.
A blank slide 7 with a tropical background appears.

4 Choose Custom Background from the Format menu, and turn off the display of the background on the current slide.

To add a slide title and three clip art figures (use Figure 4.14 as a guide, and save your work frequently):

1 Click the title box and enter the title `To Plan Your Caribbean Vacation.`

2 Click Insert Clip Art on the Standard toolbar.
The Microsoft ClipArt Gallery appears.

3 Select Find.
The Find ClipArt dialog box appears.

4 Select the Description list box.

5 Type **hand** and select Find Now.

6 Select the clip art of a hand holding a telephone receiver, and then select Insert.
The selected clip art fills the center of the slide, as shown in Figure 4.15.

Figure 4.15

7 Move and size the clip art until its location and size resembles that shown in Figure 4.16.

Figure 4.16

Reminder Save your work frequently—in this case, after every step.

8 Repeat steps 2 through 7 and create the fax clip art object (use the word *fax* to find the desired clip art).

9 Repeat steps 2 through 7 and create the envelope clip art object (use the word *envelope* to find the desired clip art).

10 Save the file.

Now you will use Figure 4.14 as a guide to create the text boxes to the right of the clip art. Be sure to save your work frequently.

To create the three associated text boxes:

1 Select Text Tool on the Drawing toolbar, and create a text box to the right of the hand-holding-phone clip art.

2 Type `Call: 1-800-123-4567` in the text box.

3 Move and size the box until its location and size resemble that shown in Figure 4.14.

4 Click outside the slide to deselect the box.

5 Repeat steps 1 through 4 to create the fax information to the right of the fax clip art.

6 Repeat steps 1 through 4 to create the write information to the right of the envelope clip art (enter all four lines of text in one box).

7 Check that your final slide displays the content and layout shown in Figure 4.14. Make changes as necessary.

8 Save the file.

EXIT If necessary, you can exit PowerPoint now and continue this project later.

Adding AutoShapes with Text

An ***AutoShape*** is one of 24 complex predefined shapes, such as the thick arrow shown in Figure 4.17. These shapes can be stretched over the top of a text box, or you can place one on the screen, fill it with color, and add text to it.

Figure 4.17

Drawing a predefined shape requires steps similar to those for drawing a text box or line. You begin by clicking the desired shape on the AutoShapes toolbar shown in Figure 4.18. Next you will move the mouse pointer to the location where you want the shape to start and then drag the pointer to the ending point. You can move an AutoShape by dragging on a border of its selection box, and you can change its size by dragging one of the eight resize handles.

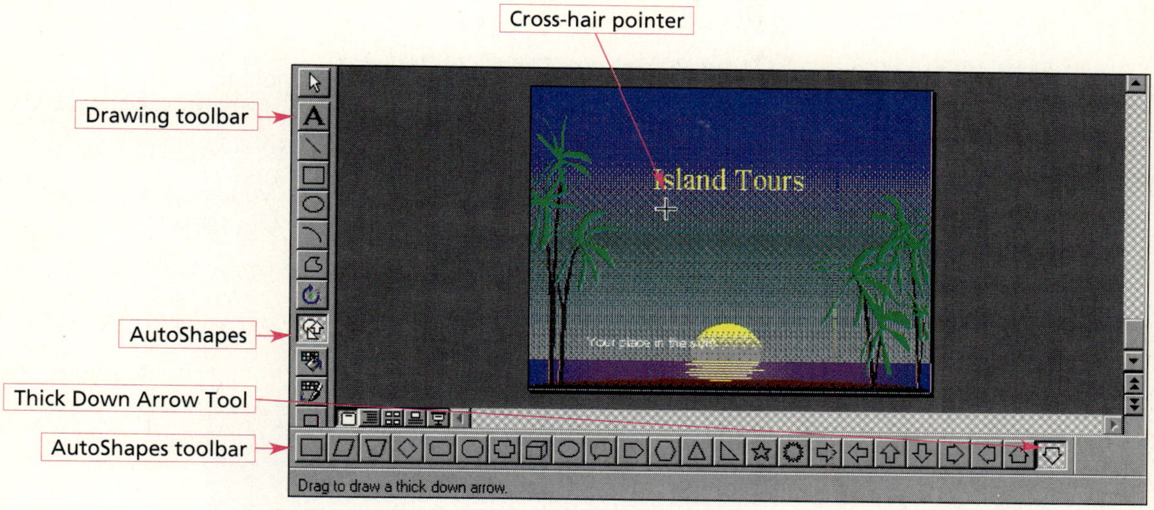

Figure 4.18

> ***Tip*** If you intend to manipulate text inside a shape, you add the shape to the screen first and then add text. You can then manipulate both objects as one.

In the following steps you will use the Copy and Paste commands to create the final slide 8 from slide 1. You will then modify slide 8 by deleting text below the title and substituting the arrow and text shown in Figure 4.17.

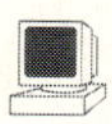

To copy a slide:

1. If necessary, load PowerPoint and open the Cruises.ppt presentation.
2. Select Slide Sorter view.
3. Select slide 1.

4. Select Copy on the Standard toolbar (or choose Copy from the Edit menu).
5. Select slide 7.

6. Select Paste on the Standard toolbar (or choose Paste from the Edit menu).
   PowerPoint duplicates slide 1, automatically inserting it as a new slide 8 after slide 7.
7. Select Slide view.
   The label Slide 8 of 8 appears in the lower-left corner of the screen.

To edit a slide and insert an AutoShape:

1 Click *Presents*, click the selection box around *Presents*, and then press (DEL) twice.
The text box below the title disappears.

2 Select AutoShapes on the Drawing toolbar.
The AutoShapes toolbar appears as shown in Figure 4.18.

3 Select Thick Down Arrow Tool on the AutoShapes toolbar.

4 Position the cross-hair pointer where you want the upper-left corner of the shape to appear (use Figure 4.18 as a guide).

5 Click and drag the pointer down and to the right to create the thick down arrow.
The thick down arrow appears as shown in Figure 4.19.

Figure 4.19

> ***Tip*** If you are not satisfied with the selected shape, you can remove the shape by pressing (DEL) while the selection box is on. You can also move and size the shape until it is acceptable.

6 Choose Colors and Lines from the Format menu.

7 Select Purple from the Fill pull-down list, and then select OK.

8 Click outside the AutoShape to deselect it.

9 Save the file.

To add a text box to an AutoShape:

1 Select Text Tool on the Drawing toolbar.

2 Position the cross-hair pointer just outside the upper-left corner of the thick down arrow.

3 Click and drag the pointer down and to the right to create the box across the thick down arrow.

4 Select Center Alignment on the Formatting toolbar.

5 Type the text on three lines, as shown in Figure 4.20.

Figure 4.20

6 Click outside the selection box.

7 Move and size the arrow shape and text box as necessary to resemble Figure 4.17.

> ***Tip*** Click in the center of the arrow to select the text box. Click in the point of the arrow to select the AutoShape instead of the text box.

8 Save the file.

To view the complete presentation in Slide Show view:

1 Display slide 1.

2 Select Slide Show in the View toolbar.
The first slide appears, filling the screen.

3 Press (PGDN) or (SPACE) to view the next slide.

4 Repeat step 3 until you have viewed all slides and exited Slide Show.

5 Choose Close from the File menu.

The Next Step

In this project you completed a second PowerPoint presentation. You used AutoLayout to select a predefined layout for each slide and then worked with many features designed to capture the attention of an audience—clip art, shapes, word art, colors, borders, and more. The next step involves putting those features to work in your own presentations, leaving behind the step-by-step guidance on choice of layout, content, special effects, and so forth. Combine imagination with experimentation!

This concludes Project 4. You can either exit PowerPoint or go on to work the Study Questions, Review Exercises, and Assignments.

Summary and Exercises

Summary

- Clip art pictures are images stored on disk. PowerPoint provides a gallery of more than 1000 clip art images organized into many categories.
- You can create interesting visual effects by using borders, horizontal lines, and vertical lines to separate sections of a slide.
- PowerPoint includes the Microsoft WordArt application, which lets you choose among 36 predefined effects including slanted and curved text.
- PowerPoint provides 24 complex predefined shapes, such as a star or arrow, that you can create using the AutoShapes toolbar.

Key Terms and Operations

Key Terms	**Operations**
AutoShape	Add AutoShapes
border	Add borders
clip art	Add clip art
word art	Add lines
	Add word art
	Combine shapes and text

Study Questions

Multiple Choice

1. What is the term used to describe digitized pictures stored on disk?
   a. word art　　c. borders
   b. clip art　　d. AutoShapes
2. What command could you use to locate an image in PowerPoint's large clip art gallery?
   a. Locate　　c. Load
   b. Find　　d. Get
3. What is the term used to describe text displayed with special effects?
   a. word art　　c. borders
   b. clip art　　d. AutoShapes
4. Which key do you press to delete a selected object?
   a. ENTER　　c. SHIFT
   b. CTRL　　d. DEL
5. What is the term used to describe lines placed around text boxes?
   a. word art　　c. borders
   b. clip art　　d. AutoShapes

Short Answer

1. Computer drawing programs, digital cameras, and scanners are used to produce what type of graphics?
2. What toolbar is used to access the predefined shapes PowerPoint offers?
3. What type of pointer appears on the screen when you select Line Tool?
4. What do you call a line around the edge of an object?
5. Name the feature that allows you to slant or curve text.

For Discussion

1. Describe the process of adding PowerPoint's clip art to slides.
2. What are AutoShapes? Explain the process to draw an AutoShape.
3. What is word art? When would it be appropriate to use word art?

Review Exercises

Buying a Car (Part Two)

In a review exercise in Project 3 you created the text objects in a six-slide presentation on buying a car. In this exercise you will complete the presentation Buycar.ppt by adding clip art and other enhancements shown in Figure 4.21.

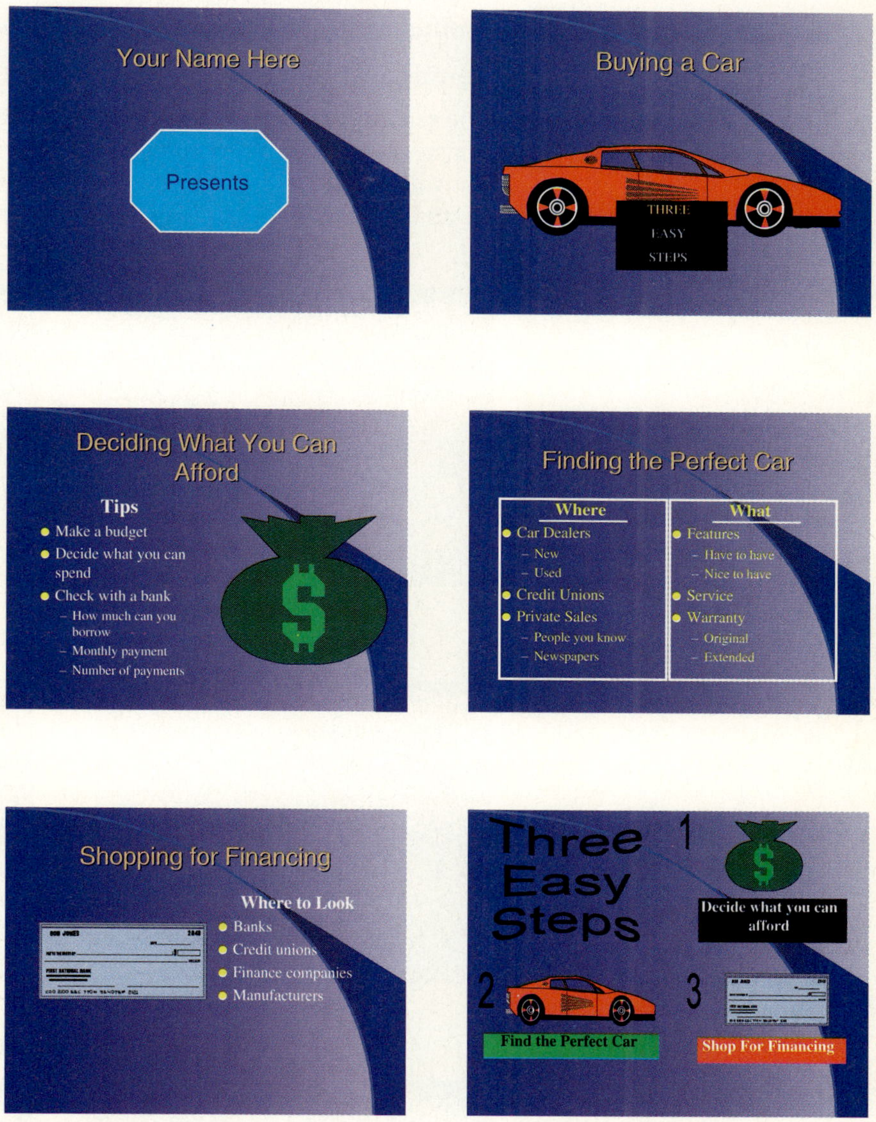

Figure 4.21

Refer to Figure 4.21 as you complete the following steps and move or size boxes as necessary. Save your work after revising each slide.

1. Open the Buycar.ppt presentation in Slide view.
2. Display slide 1. Add the octagon AutoShape with the text *PRESENTS,* and fill the AutoShape with a light blue color.
3. Display slide 2. Add the Red Sports Car clip art (Transportation category) and the *THREE EASY STEPS* text box, and then fill the text box with black. Apply a 44-pt Braggadocio font to the slide title.

4. Display slide 3 and add the Bag of Money clip art (Currency category).
5. Display slide 4 and add the borders and lines.
6. Display slide 5 and add the Check clip art (Business category).
7. Display slide 6 and add the *Three Easy Steps* word art in the upper-left corner of the slide. Also add the money bag, car, and check clip art.
8. On slide 6, add the three text boxes *Decide What You Can Afford, Find the Perfect Car,* and *Shop for Financing*. Fill the text boxes with black, green, and red, respectively.
9. After saving your changes, run a slide show of the presentation.

Getting Involved in Campus Life (Part Two)

The second review exercise in Project 3 involved creating the text objects in a six-slide presentation on getting involved in campus life. In this exercise you will complete that presentation named Getalife.ppt by adding the clip art and other enhancements shown in Figure 4.22.

Figure 4.22

Refer to Figure 4.22 as you complete the following steps. Save your work after revising each slide.

1. Open the Getalife.ppt presentation in Slide view.
2. Display slide 1 and add the word art shown in Figure 4.22 (apply the Deflate (Bottom) effect).
3. Display slide 2 and add the Hand Holding Torch clip art (Sports & Leisure category).
4. Display slide 3 and add the Courthouse clip art (Buildings category).
5. Display slide 4 and add the Lecture clip art (Academic category).
6. Display slide 5 and add the Artist at easel clip art (People category).
7. Apply the Embossed.pot template (you can choose Apply Design Template from the Format menu).
8. After saving your changes, run a slide show of the presentation.

Assignments

Getting Help on Clip Art and Word Art

Use on-screen Help to look up information about inserting clip art, word art, and other pictures tips, which you will find under the *Clip Art* topic.

Getting Help on AutoShapes

Use on-screen Help to look up information about hints for working with shapes, which you will find under the *AutoShape* topic. Also, review other topics about using AutoShapes.

Combining Text and Clip Art (Part Two)

Directions to begin your own presentation combining text and art were provided in the Assignments section at the end of Project 3. Open the presentation you started, and add clip art, word art, AutoShapes, borders, colors, and fills of your choice to complete the presentation.

Project 5: Presenting a Slide Show

Objectives

After completing this project, you should be able to:

- Change the order of slides in Slide Sorter view
- Print black-and-white handouts
- Set transitions among slides
- Add builds and other animation
- Rehearse a presentation

Case Study: Cruising the Caribbean III

In Project 4 you completed the eight-slide Caribbean cruise presentation you began developing in Project 3. If your presentation medium will be overhead transparencies or 35mm slides, you will print the results of your efforts and rehearse delivery on your own. Projecting slides from computer to screen, however, provides several opportunities for turning your slide show into a truly professional production.

Designing the Solution

Some PowerPoint features apply only to on-screen presentations. For example, you can select a ***transition*** between slides, which controls how each slide appears and disappears. You can also set up a ***build,*** which makes text fly onto the screen from the left, right, top, or bottom—one character, word, or paragraph at a time. To capture a viewer's attention, you can apply predefined ***animation effects*** that display text in unusual ways and incorporate ***multimedia,*** including sounds, music, photos, and film clips. You can also set up ***hidden slides,*** which you can activate as necessary during an on-screen presentation. ***Slide Navigator*** lets you jump to slides out of sequence, and ***Slide Meter*** lets you monitor how your presentation is proceeding compared to timings you set up during rehearsal.

> ***Tip*** Be sure to rehearse the delivery of your presentation. For a professional presentation, your accompanying remarks must be as polished as your slides.

In this project you will add the finishing touches to an on-screen presentation of the cruise slides. You will begin by using Slide Sorter view to make a final adjustment in the order of the slides and then print black-and-white handouts.

ORGANIZING SLIDES WITH SLIDE SORTER

The arrangement of slides should be well established by the time you finish developing a presentation. However, as you rehearse delivering your presentation, you may want to make a last-minute change to the order of your slides. In Project 4 you used Slide Sorter view to duplicate slides. You can also use this view to change the arrangement of slides by dragging and dropping a slide into a new location.

When you begin to drag a slide, the pointer changes to a small arrow with a slide attached. A vertical line shows where PowerPoint will place the slide.

In the following steps you will reposition the information about the least costly Bahamas cruise (currently slide 3) after the more expensive Eastern Caribbean and Southern Caribbean cruises (slides 4 and 5).

To change the order of slides:

1 Load PowerPoint and open the Cruises.ppt presentation.

2 Select Slide Sorter on the View toolbar.

3 Click slide 3 and hold down the mouse button.

4 Move the pointer between slides 5 and 6.
The pointer changes to a small arrow with a slide attached. A vertical line appears between slides 5 and 6, showing where PowerPoint will place the slide.

5 Release the mouse button.
The slides appear in the revised order shown in Figure 5.1.

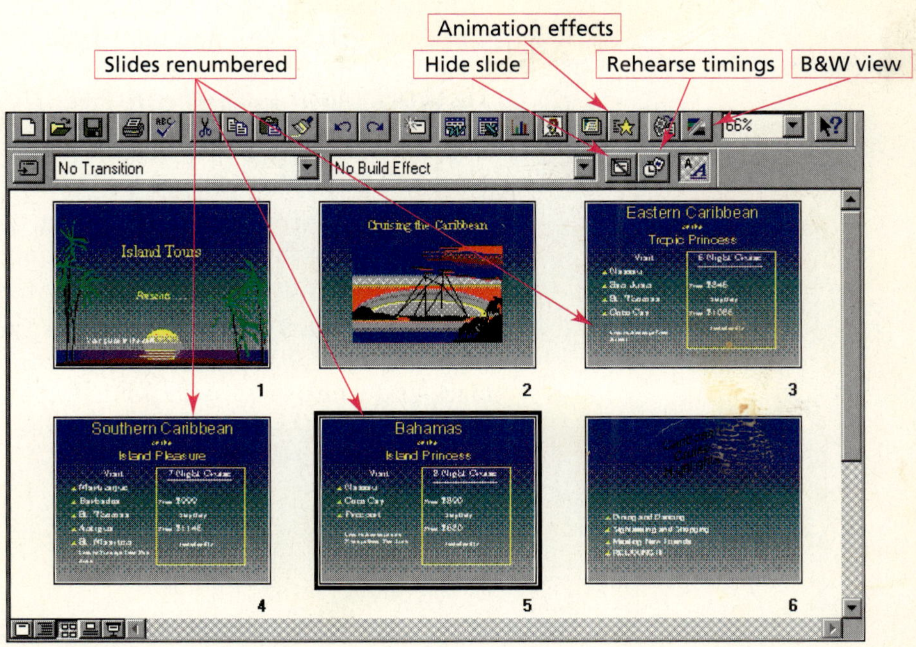

Figure 5.1

Printing Black-and-White Handouts

The slides in a colorful on-screen presentation may not print well on a noncolor printer. PowerPoint displays a grayscale preview of how your slides will print when you select B&W View on the Standard toolbar; selecting B&W View a second time restores color. You can change how a slide will look when printed by clicking the right mouse button, pointing to Black and White, and selecting one of the options shown in Figure 5.2. The changes you make in Black and White view do not change the colors in your on-screen presentation.

Figure 5.2

In the following steps you will switch to Black and White view, apply a Black and White option to one of the slides, and print six slides to a page.

To work with a Black-and-White view:

1 Select B&W View on the Standard toolbar.
Shades of gray appear on the slides instead of color.

2 Move the scroll bar to view other slides, including slide 8.
The text within the thick down arrow object on slide 8 doesn't appear as clear as other text on the slide.

3 Select slide 8, and then switch to Slide view.
PowerPoint displays a small window containing a color view of the current black-and-white slide, as shown in Figure 5.3.

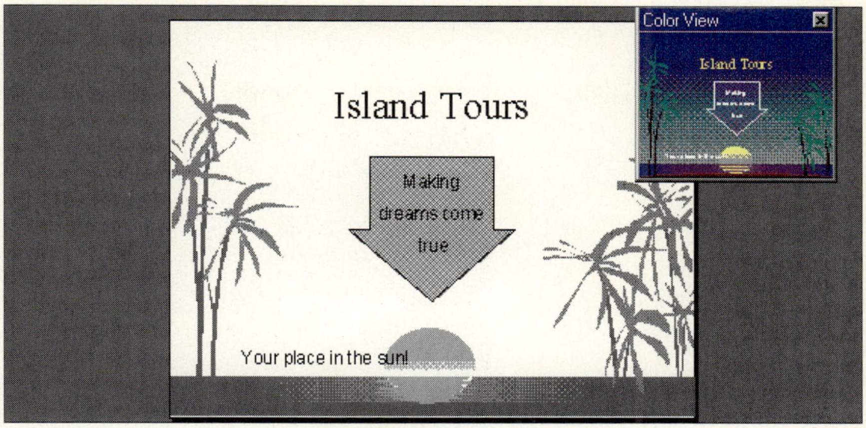

Figure 5.3

4 Position the pointer within the thick down arrow near its point, and then click to select the object.
Sizing handles appear at the corners and midpoints of the arrow.

5 Without moving the mouse, click its right button, and then move the pointer to Black and White.
A list with ten options appears as shown in Figure 5.2.

6 Select Black with White Fill, and then click outside the arrow to deselect it.
The background of the arrow changes from gray to white, making the text easier to read. The color view of the slide does not change.

7 Save the file.

To print black-and-white slides, six to a page:

> **Caution** Do not select Print on the Standard toolbar in place of step 1 below. If you do, PowerPoint will automatically print one slide per page, which would not be suitable for audience handouts.

1 Select Print from the File menu.
The Print dialog box appears.

2 Select Handouts (6 slides per page) from the Print what pull-down list shown in Figure 5.4.

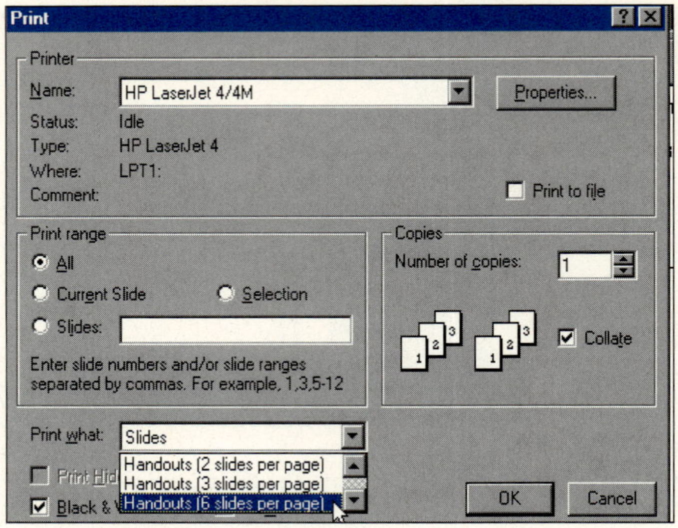

Figure 5.4

3 Select OK (or select Cancel if you do not want to print at this time).

4 Select B&W View on the Standard toolbar to restore color.

5 Switch to Slide Sorter view.

Adding Transitions

Transitions are special effects controlling how slides appear and disappear. You can select among 45 transitions, including Blinds Horizontal or Vertical, Box In or Out, Checkerboard Across or Down, and Dissolve. You can also select Random Transition to let PowerPoint automatically select a variety of effects.

Although transitions can be applied in any view, you can see the results more easily in Slide Sorter view. A pull-down list of transition effects will appear when you click a down arrow in one of two locations: at the right end of the Slide Transition Effect box on the Slide Sorter toolbar, or at the right end of the Effect box in the Slide Transition dialog box shown in Figure 5.5.

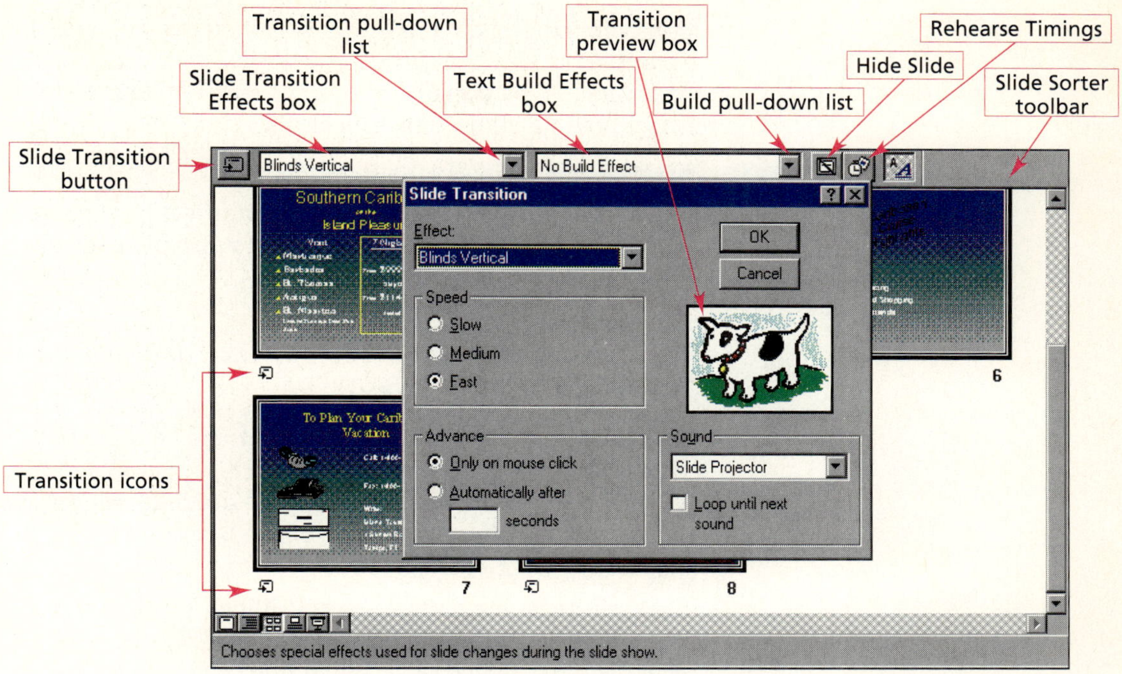

Figure 5.5

If you use the Slide Transition dialog box to select an effect, you can also select three other settings: Speed, Advance, and Sound. Speed controls the quickness of the transition (slow, medium, or fast). Advance lets you set an automatic or mouse-activated movement to the next slide. Sound lets you select a predefined sound or other sound file. You can display the Slide Transition dialog box by clicking the Slide Transition button at the left end of the Slide Sorter toolbar or by choosing Slide Transition from the Tools menu.

Transitions can be applied to the current slide or to multiple slides. You can select multiple slides by holding down (SHFT) while you click the mouse on the desired slides. Choosing Select All from the Edit menu selects all slides.

> ***Tip*** For consistency in a presentation, you will generally apply transitions to all slides. You will hear the sounds if your equipment includes a sound card and speakers.

When you select an effect, the Transition preview box demonstrates that setting. In Slide Sorter view a Transition icon appears below the lower-left corner of a slide if a transition has been set. Clicking the icon lets you preview the effect.

In the following steps you will select all slides, view several transition effects, and save your final choice.

To select slides and display the Slide Transition dialog box:

1 Make sure slides are displayed in Slide Sorter view.

2 Choose Select All from the Edit menu.

A thick border appears around all slides.

3 Select the Slide Transition button at the left end of the Slide Sorter toolbar.
The Slide Transition dialog box appears. No Transition appears in the Effect box. All slides remain selected.

Reminder If you want a transition effect to apply to all slides, as you do in the next two sets of numbered steps, be sure to select all slides first.

To select transition effect, speed, and sound using the Slide Transition dialog box:

1 Click the down arrow at the right end of the Effect box in the Slide Transition dialog box.
A list of effects appears in alphabetical order except for No Transition at the top and Random Transition at the bottom.

2 Select Blinds Vertical.
The pull-down list disappears, and Blinds Vertical appears in the Effect box.

3 Select Fast in the Speed box if Slow or Medium is the current setting.

4 Select Slide Projector from the Sound pull-down list.

5 Select OK to close the dialog box.

6 Click the Transition icon under slide 1 to see and hear the selected effects.

7 Click the Transition icon under several other slides in succession to continue previewing and hearing the selected effects.

To select other transition effects using the Slide Sorter toolbar and then save your final choice:

1 With all slides selected, click the down arrow at the right end of the Slide Transition Effects box on the Slide Sorter toolbar.

2 Select Box Out from the Transition Effect pull-down list.

3 Click the Transition icon under slide 1 to preview the selected effect.

4 Click the Transition icon under several other slides in succession to continue previewing the selected effect.

5 Repeat steps 1 through 4, except select Checkerboard Across in step 2.

6 Repeat steps 1 through 4, except select Dissolve in step 2.

7 Repeat steps 1 through 4, except select Wipe Right in step 2.

8 Select other transition effects of your choice, and then specify Box Out as the transition setting for all slides.

9 Click anywhere between slides to deselect all slides.

10 Save the file.

EXIT If necessary, you can exit PowerPoint now and continue this project later.

ADDING BUILDS AND OTHER ANIMATION

You may have attended a presentation in which the speaker uncovered one line of text at a time on an overhead transparency. This technique focuses an audience's attention on the current point under discussion, rather than allowing the audience to read ahead.

You can produce this special effect during an on-screen PowerPoint presentation by specifying a build, sometimes called a ***progressive disclosure list.*** When you first show a slide containing a build, bulleted items are hidden. Each time you press (ENTER) or click the left mouse button, the next line in the bulleted list appears.

You can select from more than 30 builds, including Fly from Left (also Fly from Bottom, Top, or Right), Blinds Horizontal or Vertical, Box In or Out, and Checkerboard Across or Down. You can also select Random Effects to let PowerPoint automatically select among a variety of effects.

Tip If a slide contains one or more objects other than the bulleted list, select a build that displays text from the closest side. For example, if a bulleted list appears in the lower-left corner of the slide, select a build such as Fly from Left or Fly from Bottom. If you were to select Fly from Right or Top, the text would first have to cross other information, which could be distracting to viewers.

A pull-down list of build effects will appear when you click the down arrow at the right end of the Build Effects box on the Slide Sorter toolbar. You can also select one or more slides, choose Build Slide Text from the Tools menu, and then select Other from the cascading menu to specify build effects in the Animation Settings dialog box, as shown in Figure 5.6.

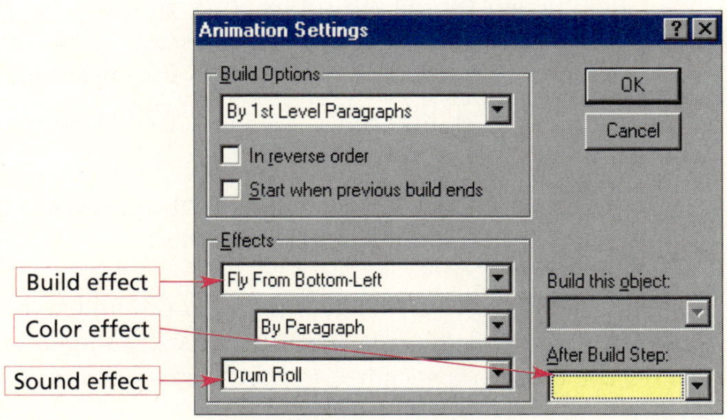

Figure 5.6

Builds can be applied to the current slide or to multiple slides. You can select multiple slides by holding down (SHIFT) while you click the mouse on the desired slides.

You can select among a variety of predefined settings including build-and-sound combinations using the Animation Effects toolbar shown in Figure 5.7.

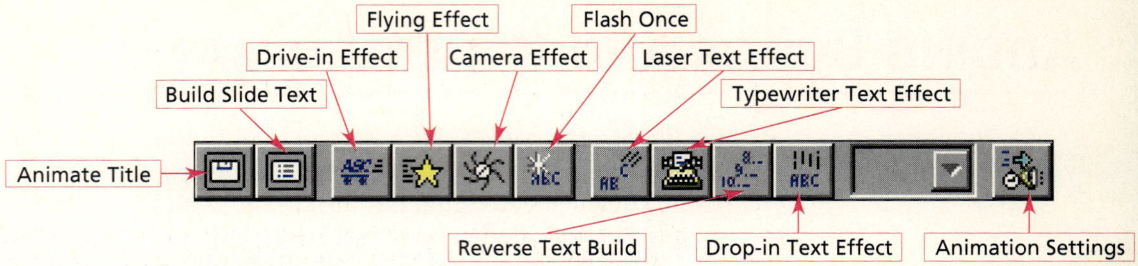

Figure 5.7

In the following steps you will select a build using the Animation Settings dialog box, specify several animation effects, and view the results in Slide Show view.

To select a build using the Animation Settings dialog box:

1 If necessary, load PowerPoint, open the Cruises.ppt presentation, and display slides in Slide Sorter view.

2 Select slide 6.

3 Choose Build Slide Text from the Tools menu.

4 Select Other.

5 Specify the settings shown in Figure 5.6.

6 Select OK to apply the selected settings to slide 6.

To view and hear the animation settings:

1 If necessary, select slide 6.

2 Select Slide Show view.
The Caribbean Cruise Highlights slide appears without its bulleted list.

3 Click the left mouse button or press ENTER to see the first line in the hidden bulleted list.
The first line (*Dining and Dancing*) moves into position from the lower-left corner of the slide to the sound of a drum roll.

> ***Reminder*** You will not hear the drum roll sound unless your system is equipped with a sound card and speakers.

4 Press ENTER to see the second line in the bulleted list.
The new text appears white. Text in the first bulleted item changes to yellow, the color you specified in the Animation Settings dialog box.

5 Press ENTER until slide 7 appears on the screen.

6 Press ESC to end the slide show and restore Slide Sorter view.

To apply effects using the Animation Settings toolbar:

1 Choose Toolbars from the View menu.

2 Select Animation Effects, and then select OK.
You will see the Animation Effects toolbar shown in Figure 5.7 or the Animation Effects window shown in Figure 5.8, depending on how this feature appeared the last time it was used.

3 Switch to Slide view, and then select slide 7.

4 Select *Call: 1-800-123-4567,* as shown in Figure 5.8.

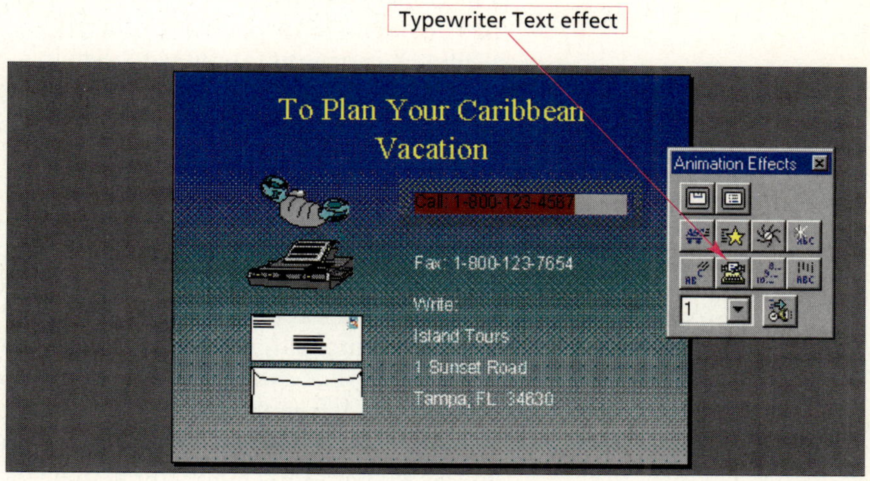

Figure 5.8

5 Select Typewriter Text as the animation effect.

6 Select *Fax: 1-800-123-7654.*

7 Select Typewriter Text as the animation effect.

8 Click in a corner of the slide to deselect the Fax text box.

9 Save the file.

To view and hear animation settings:

1 Select Slide Show view.
The phone and fax information do not appear on the slide.

2 Press (ENTER) to display the phone number one character at a time to the sound of a typewriter.

3 Repeat step 2 to display the fax number.

4 Press (ESC) to exit the slide show.

5 Close the Animation Effects window/toolbar.

> ***Tip*** You can apply an animation effect to objects other than a text box by clicking to select the object, such as clip art, and then selecting the animation effect.

EXIT If necessary, you can exit PowerPoint now and continue this project later.

Rehearsing the Presentation

The amount of rehearsal needed for a slide show depends on the presentation environment. No practice is needed if your slides stand alone as part of an exhibit. You can set the show to play in a ***continuous loop,*** which means that PowerPoint automatically starts over with slide 1 after reaching the end of the set of slides. To set this display mode, choose Slide Show from the View menu and then select the Loop Continuously Until 'Esc' check box.

It is more likely that you will be giving a live presentation, in which slides provide a framework for your personal comments. In this case it is essential that you practice your delivery. The content of your remarks is up to you. PowerPoint assists in the mechanics of delivery by providing manual or automatic shifts to the next slide.

During a slide show, you can manually advance to the next slide by pressing the left mouse button, ENTER, or SPACE In other words, you manually set the ***timing,*** which determines the amount of time a slide stays on the screen. PowerPoint also allows you to advance slides automatically by setting slide timings.

Tip You can use a combination of manual and automatic advances. For example, you can set the first few introductory slides to advance automatically after a few seconds and then use a manual advance after more complex slides.

You can set slide timings in the Slide Transition dialog box by typing the desired number of seconds in the Advance section. You can also adjust the timing as you cycle through slides while you rehearse a presentation. To use the latter method, you will choose Slide Show from the View menu and then select Rehearse New Timings. PowerPoint notes the length of time each slide is displayed and sets the time intervals for you.

Tip To remove one or more automatic advances, select the desired slides in Slide Sorter view, choose Transition from the Tools menu, and then select Only on Mouse Click.

In the following steps you will set timing for the first two slides in the cruise presentation.

To set an automatic advance using the Transition dialog box:

1. If necessary, load PowerPoint, open the Cruises.ppt presentation, and display slides in Slide Sorter view.
2. Select slides 1 and 2.
3. Select the Slide Transition button on the Slide Sorter toolbar.
4. Select Automatically After in the Advance section.
5. In the Seconds text box type **5** as the number of seconds.

6 Select OK to apply the time intervals and close the dialog box.
The notation :05 appears below slides 1 and 2, indicating the automatic slide timing.

7 Click anywhere between slides.

To view automatic advances:

1 Select slide 1.

2 Choose Slide Show from the View menu.
The Slide Show dialog box appears.

3 Select Use Slide Timings, and then select Show.
Slide 1 appears for five seconds, slide 2 appears for five seconds, and then slide 3 appears but does not advance.

> ***Tip*** At this point you would begin rehearsing your presentation, manually advancing to the next slide after practicing the comments associated with the current slide.

4 Press (ESC) to end the slide show and restore Slide Sorter view.

5 Save and close the file.

> ***Tip*** PowerPoint's Slide Meter can help you rehearse your presentation. After you have timed your slides, start your slide show in manual advance mode. Then on slide 1, click the right mouse button and select Slide Meter. Rehearse your presentation while the meter times you, and see how you compare with the timing you set in Slide Sorter view. You can even have the Slide Meter display on your PC while others watch the slide show on their PC's on a network—and they won't see the meter.

The Next Step

While Projects 3 and 4 focused on the creation of an eye-catching cruise presentation, this project focused on giving a well-rehearsed presentation. Prior to rehearsing, you added builds, sounds, and transitions that produced special effects within and between slides during an on-screen slide show. You also learned a few techniques to polish the presentation, including advancing slides automatically and printing audience handouts.

As a next step, learn how to use ***PowerPoint Viewer,*** a special application that allows you to run a PowerPoint presentation on a computer that does not have PowerPoint installed. This application is also useful if you want to send your presentation to someone who does not have PowerPoint. You cannot legally give someone a copy of PowerPoint, but it is legal to provide a copy of PowerPoint Viewer. You will find information through on-screen Help if you use Answer Wizard to look up PowerPoint Viewer.

Try adding other sounds and video clips to your slides. Windows 95 includes a Media Player that you can use in PowerPoint to insert a video or audio clip. If you acquired Office 95 on CD-ROM, you have access to a wide variety of sound and film files.

Learn how to develop interactive slide shows. PowerPoint allows you to branch to other slide presentations or even other applications. Insert one or more hidden slides in a presentation, which you can display or not as needed. On-screen Help can get you started with unfamiliar features.

This concludes Project 5. You can either exit PowerPoint or go on to work the Study Questions, Review Exercises, and Assignments.

SUMMARY AND EXERCISES

Summary

- In Slide Sorter view, you can change the order of slides by using a mouse to drag a slide to its new location.
- Color slides may not print well on a black-and-white printer unless you select Black and White view and change background shading.
- Some PowerPoint features, such as transitions, builds, slide timings, and animation effects, apply only to on-screen presentations.
- A transition controls how each slide appears and disappears. Using PowerPoint you can select among 45 transitions, set the speed of a transition at Slow, Medium, or Fast, and specify a sound to play during transitions.
- A build causes text to fly onto the screen one character, word, or paragraph at a time. Using PowerPoint, you can select among 37 builds and specify a sound to play during builds.
- During a slide show, you can manually advance to the next slide by pressing the left mouse button, (ENTER) or (SPACE) You can also advance slides automatically by setting slide timings.

Key Terms and Operations

Key Terms
animation effects
build
continuous loop
hidden slides
multimedia
PowerPoint Viewer
progressive disclosure list
Slide Meter
Slide Navigator
timing
transition

Operations
Add animation effects
Advance slides automatically
Change the order of slides
Change the speed of transitions
Rehearse an on-screen presentation
Set builds
Set slide timings
Set transitions

Study Questions

Multiple Choice

1. In Slide Sorter view, you can
   a. duplicate slides.
   b. rearrange the order of slides.
   c. Both a and b.
   d. None of the above.
2. During an on-screen presentation, what special effect relates to the appearance and disappearance of entire slides?
   a. build
   b. progressive disclosure
   c. transition
   d. 3-D advance
3. During an on-screen presentation, what special effect displays one line at a time from a bulleted list?
   a. 3-D advance
   b. build
   c. transition
   d. None of the above.
4. Which of the following is not a true statement about transitions?
   a. Transitions can be applied in any view mode.
   b. Although PowerPoint provides 45 transition effects, only one transition style may be used in a presentation.
   c. Transition styles appear in a pull-down list in alphabetical order (except for the No Transition and Random Transition options).
   d. If you prefer, you can select a transition for only one slide or a few slides—instead of all slides—in an on-screen presentation.
5. Using the Animation Effects toolbar, you can select predefined
   a. builds
   b. sounds
   c. Both a and b
   d. None of the above

Short Answer

1. What is the phrase that describes automatically playing a slide show over and over?
2. What is an alternate term for the word *build?*
3. What settings are available for transition speed?
4. What actions advance a slide manually?
5. What key should you press and hold down prior to selecting multiple slides in Slide Sorter view?

For Discussion

1. What is a build? What purpose does it serve? Explain how you would establish builds in an on-screen presentation.
2. What is a transition? What purpose does it serve? Explain how you would establish transitions in an on-screen presentation.
3. Describe some of the animation effects you can select.

Review Exercises

Changing the Cruises Slide Show

1. Open Cruises.ppt and save it to disk as Showsail.ppt.
2. Change the slide timings for slides 1 and 2 from 5 seconds to 10 seconds.
3. Apply a different animation effect to the phone and fax numbers in slide 7.

4. Select all slides and change the transition to Random Transition.
5. Rehearse the slide show.
6. Save your changes and close the Showsail.ppt file.

Presenting the Getalife Slide Show

1. Open Getalife.ppt and save it as Showlife.ppt (instructions to create this presentation were provided in Review Exercise 2 in Projects 3 and 4).
2. Access Slide Sorter view, and change the order of slides 2 through 5 to Academic Activities, Arts, Intramural Sports, and Students and Government.
3. Set the build effects for all slides to Random Effects.
4. Change the transition to each slide so that they alternate between Blinds Vertical and Blinds Horizontal.
5. Apply animation effects of your choosing to text and/or objects in slides 2 through 6.
6. Rehearse the slide show.
7. Save your changes and close the Showlife.ppt presentation.

Assignments

Getting Help on Slide Timings

Use on-screen Help to look up information about setting slide timings while rehearsing (see the *Moving from slide to slide during a slide show* topic).

Getting Help on Slide Shows

Use Help topics in on-screen Help to review general information about slide shows (see the *Slide show design* topic).

Adding Builds and Transitions to Service.ppt

Open the Service.ppt presentation you created by working Projects 1 and 2. Immediately save the file to disk as Showservice.ppt. Add appropriate builds, transitions, and animation effects to slides, and save your changes. Rehearse the presentation.

Adding Other Builds and Transitions

If you created another presentation as directed in end-of-project assignments for Projects 3 and 4, open that presentation. Immediately save the presentation under another name. Add appropriate builds, transitions, and animation effects to all slides, and save your changes. Rehearse the presentation.

PART VIII

Integrated Project 3

Integrated Project 3: Linking Word, Excel, Access, and PowerPoint in an Office Binder

Objectives

After completing this project, you should be able to:

- Work in multiple applications concurrently
- Link to PowerPoint an object previously embedded into Word
- Link to PowerPoint an object previously linked to Word
- Create an Office binder
- Add the Word and PowerPoint documents to the binder
- Change the format of the linked objects in PowerPoint from within the binder
- Update an Access database and display the changes in PowerPoint from within the binder

You have learned how to embed and link objects from Word, Excel, and Access into one updatable document. PowerPoint, a member of the Microsoft Office 95 suite, can also be used to link and embed objects. In this project you will learn how to create a slide in PowerPoint and embed that slide into a Word document. You will also learn how to create a multiapplication presentation by embedding and linking Word documents, Excel worksheets, and Access databases in a PowerPoint slide. Finally, you will learn how to create an Office binder to organize all the documents related to your report.

Case Study: Creating a Multiapplication Presentation

The reports you have created and sent to the president's staff have caused quite a lot of excitement. Not only is the staff excited about the data in the reports, but also they are very impressed with the way you presented the reports. They are even more impressed that you were able to give them all of the data they wanted to see at a moment's notice. You have done such a great job that you have been promoted! You are now the new Director of Information Resources, and your first task is to produce a report for the stockholders' meeting at the end of the week. The president wants you to explain the progress of the European Dark Roast coffee blend versus the Colombian blend taste-test surveys using a computer-generated slide presentation.

Designing the Solution

You know that you could display the Word reports you created for the daily staff meeting, but you really want to impress the stockholders with something exciting. You decide to use PowerPoint to create the presentation. You know that the PowerPoint AutoContent Wizard will help you create an appealing background, and you won't need to retype all of the data from the Word reports. PowerPoint will let you create the presentation today and then update the statistics, if they change, right before the presentation.

Once you've created the PowerPoint presentation, you can add the slide show and the Word document to an Office binder to help organize these resources and assist you in making last minute changes as the database is updated. Like a traditional three-ring binder, an Office binder makes it easy to work with completed documents that need only minor changes.

CREATING THE PRESENTATION

Your first step in creating your PowerPoint presentation is to set up the type of presentation you want. You will then enter the text for each slide in your presentation.

To set up the PowerPoint presentation:

1 Select the PowerPoint button from the Shortcut Bar or, if the Shortcut Bar does not start automatically when Windows 95 loads, select the PowerPoint icon using the Windows 95 Start button.

2 If your system displays the Tip of the Day, select OK to close the dialog box.
The PowerPoint dialog box appears as shown in Figure 3.1.

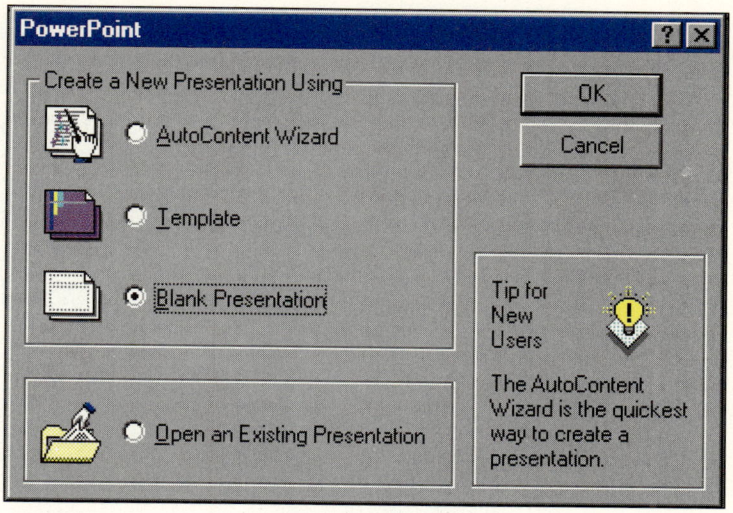

Figure 3.1

3 Select AutoContent Wizard from the PowerPoint dialog box and then select OK.

The first AutoContent Wizard dialog box appears as shown in Figure 3.2.

Figure 3.2

4 Select Next> to continue.

The dialog box that appears allows you to enter information about your presentation.

5 Enter your name in the What is your name? text box, and type ***European Dark Roast Taste Test Survey*** in the What are you going to talk about? text box, as shown in Figure 3.3.

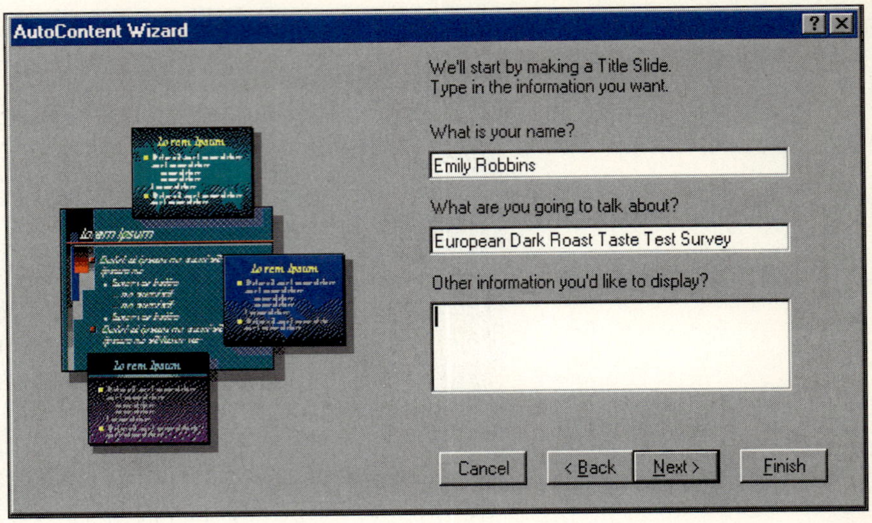

Figure 3.3

6 Select Next> to continue.
A dialog box allowing you to specify your type of presentation appears.

7 Select the Reporting Progress button, as shown in Figure 3.4.

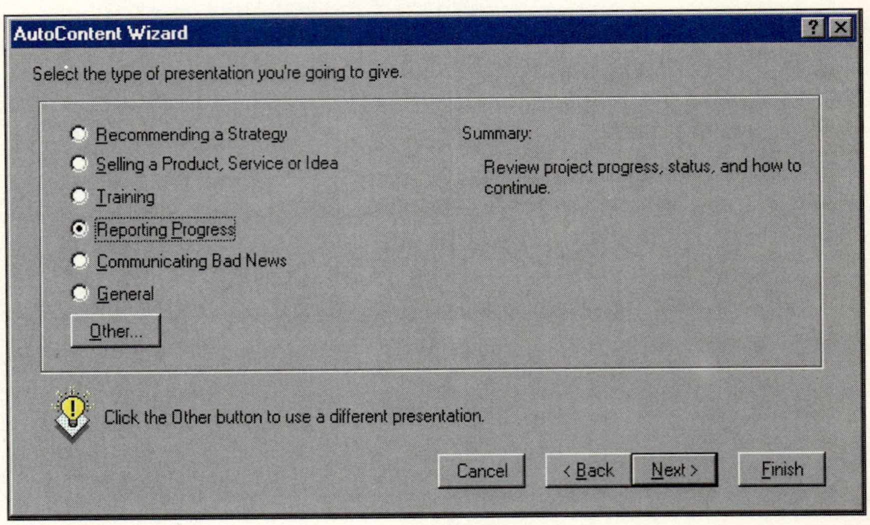

Figure 3.4

8 Select Next>.
The AutoContent Wizard now allows you to enter a default style for your presentation and specify the approximate length of your presentation in minutes.

9 Select Professional as a style and 30 minutes or less as an approximate length, as shown in Figure 3.5.

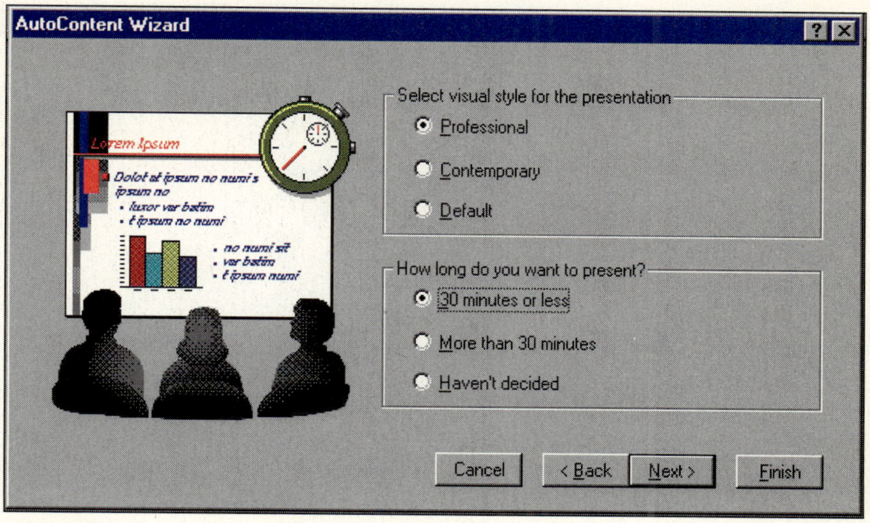

Figure 3.5

> ***Tip*** When you select 30 minutes or less, PowerPoint creates nine slides by default. You may add or delete slides from your final presentation, as necessary.

10 Select Next>.

The AutoContent Wizard now allows you to specify your presentation output.

11 Select the On-screen presentation option for the type of output and No for printing handouts, as shown in Figure 3.6.

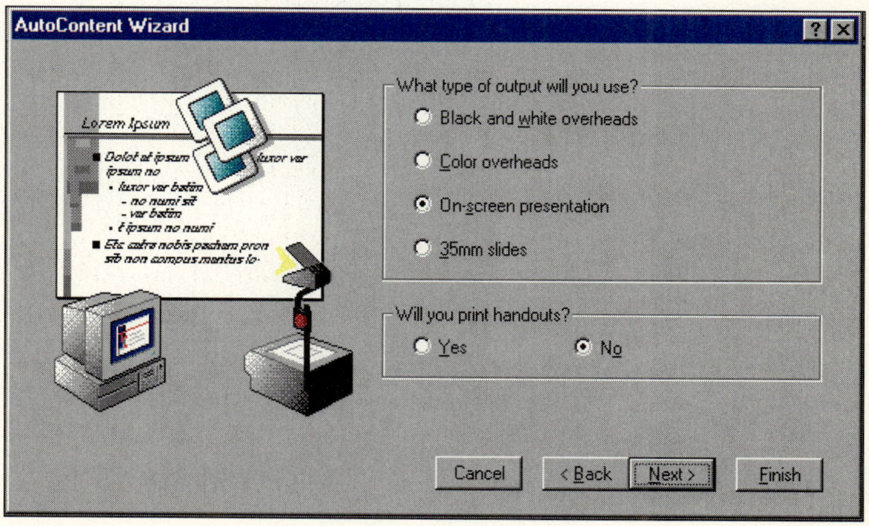

Figure 3.6

12 Select Next>.

The screen shown in Figure 3.7 appears.

13 Click Finish to have PowerPoint design your presentation for you.

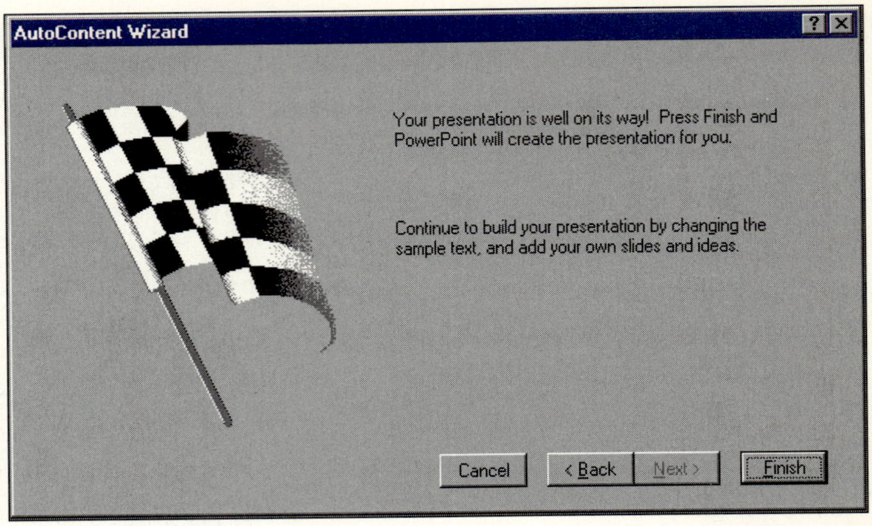

Figure 3.7

The title slide of your presentation is displayed, as shown in Figure 3.8. You are now ready to enter additional content for your presentation, but you should first save your presentation before you continue.

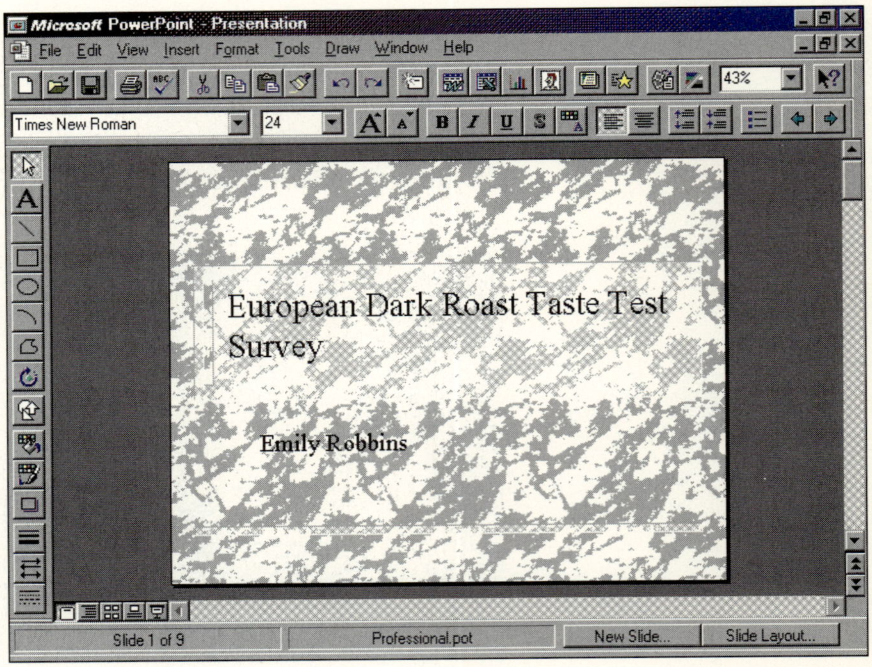

Figure 3.8

14 Save your PowerPoint presentation on drive A: (your 3½″ floppy drive) under the name European Dark Roast.

You can now enter the text you want to appear in your presentation slides. Since PowerPoint created nine default slides, creating your presentation is a matter of changing the text currently in each default slide.

Reminder Save your PowerPoint presentation often.

To edit the default slides:

1 Position the pointer over the vertical scroll bar on the right side of the screen, hold down the left mouse button, and pull the scroll bar down to move to the next slide, as shown in Figure 3.9.

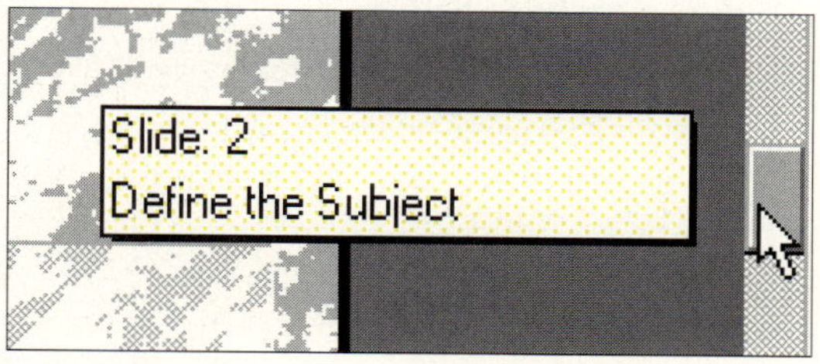

Figure 3.9

When you release the mouse button, the second slide in the presentation, *Define the Subject,* is displayed.

2 Enter the text shown in Figure 3.10.

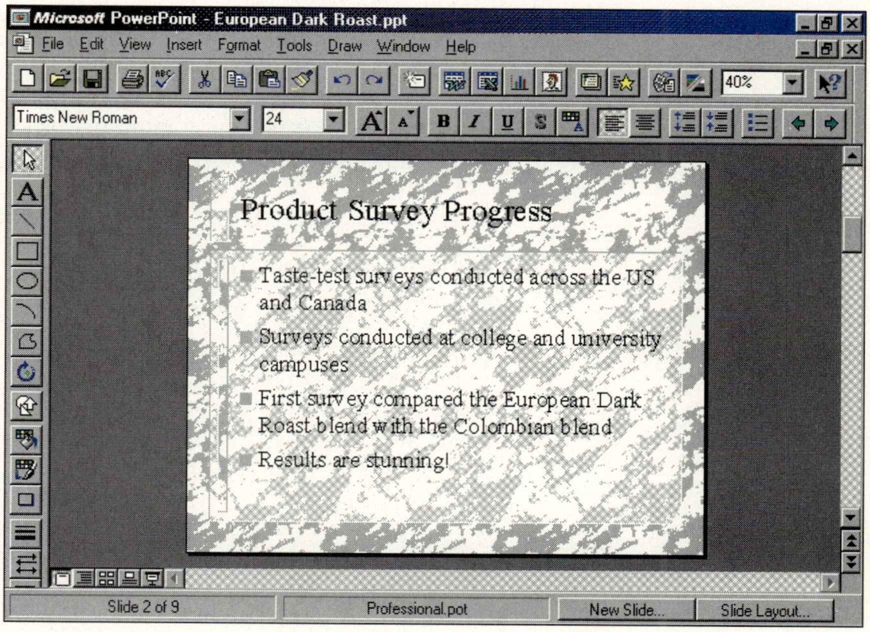

Figure 3.10

3 Use the vertical scroll bar to move to the next default slide, *Overall Status.*

4 Type `Survey Results` in the top text box, and enter the subpoints shown in Figure 3.11 in the lower text box.

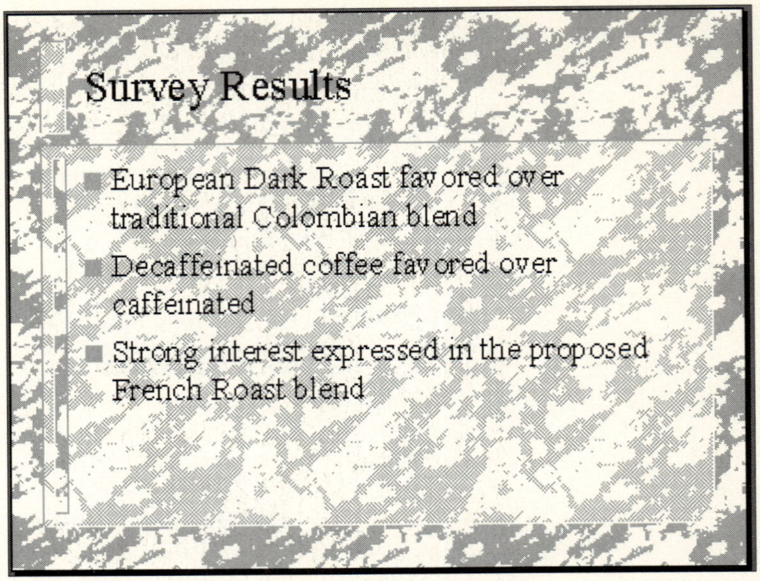

Figure 3.11

5 Move to the next default slide, named *Component One: Background.* Highlight the slide title in the upper box, and type `State-by-State Results`

6 Delete the text in the lower text box of the current slide.

7 Move to the next slide. Highlight the slide title, and type `Feedback from the Marketplace`

8 Highlight and delete the text in the lower box of the current slide. You will now delete the remainder of the default slides. The easiest way to delete multiple slides is by using Outline view.

To switch to Outline view and delete the remaining slides:

1 Select Outline from the View menu.

2 Highlight slides 6 through 9, as shown in Figure 3.12.

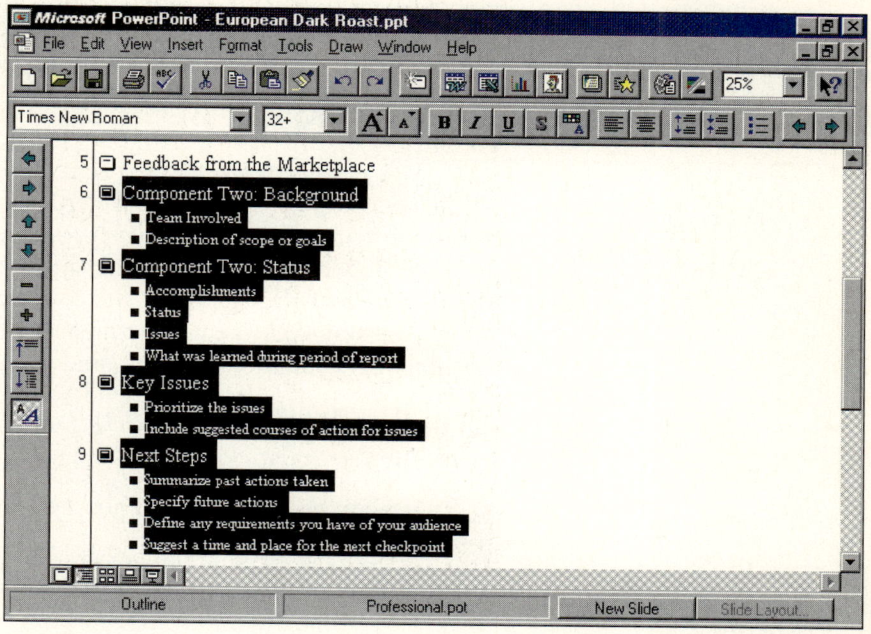

Figure 3.12

3 Select Cut from the Edit menu.

The presentation outline now contains five slides, as shown in Figure 3.13.

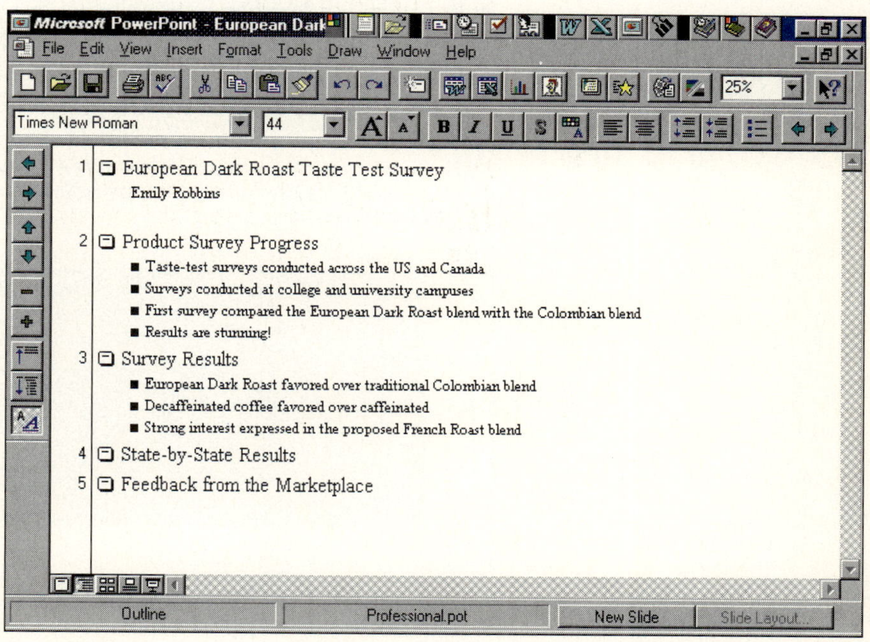

Figure 3.13

4 Select Slides from the View menu to return to Slide view.

5 Save your presentation.

EMBEDDING THE EXCEL WORKSHEET INTO THE PRESENTATION

You have completed the basic skeleton of your presentation. The first section of data you will display is the Excel worksheet from Updated New Product Report.doc. You will link this embedded object from Word into the PowerPoint slide by using the copy and paste special method. This will allow you to update the worksheet easily from within Word, once this document is added to an Office binder document later in this project.

To embed Word's embedded worksheet into the PowerPoint presentation:

1 Display the fourth slide, *State-by-State Results.*

2 Start Word using either the Windows 95 Start button or the Microsoft Word button on the Shortcut Bar.

> ***Tip*** If you did not complete Integrated Project 2, please ask your instructor for the file Integrated Project 2.doc. Save this as My Updated Project.doc and use this file to continue this project.

3 Open the word file called My Updated Project.doc.

4 Select the worksheet by anchoring the mouse in the paragraph symbol before the worksheet and dragging the mouse over the worksheet. The screen now looks like Figure 3.14.

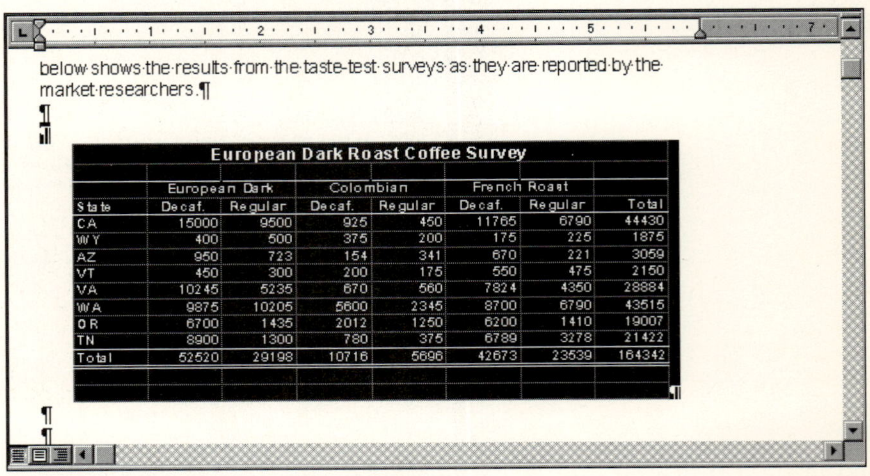

European Dark Roast Coffee Survey							
	European Dark		Colombian		French Roast		
State	Decaf.	Regular	Decaf.	Regular	Decaf.	Regular	Total
CA	15000	9500	925	450	11765	6790	44430
WY	400	500	375	200	175	225	1875
AZ	950	723	154	341	670	221	3059
VT	450	300	200	175	550	475	2150
VA	10245	5235	670	560	7824	4350	28884
WA	9875	10205	5600	2345	8700	6790	43515
OR	6700	1435	2012	1250	6200	1410	19007
TN	8900	1300	780	375	6789	3278	21422
Total	52520	29198	10716	5696	42673	23539	164342

Figure 3.14

5 Select Copy from the Edit menu.

6 Switch to the PowerPoint document.

7 Select Paste from the Edit menu.
The embedded worksheet appears on the slide, as shown in Figure 3.15.

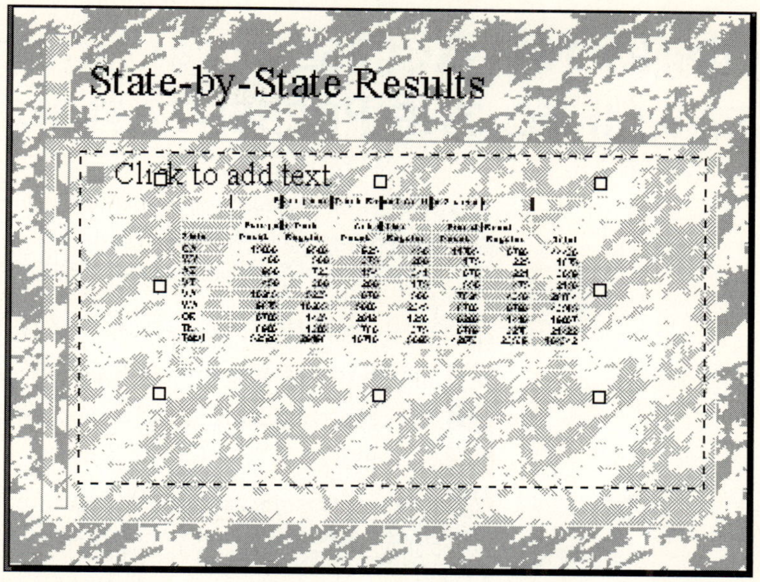

Figure 3.15

8 Use the selection handles on the embedded object to resize and move it, as shown in Figure 3.16.

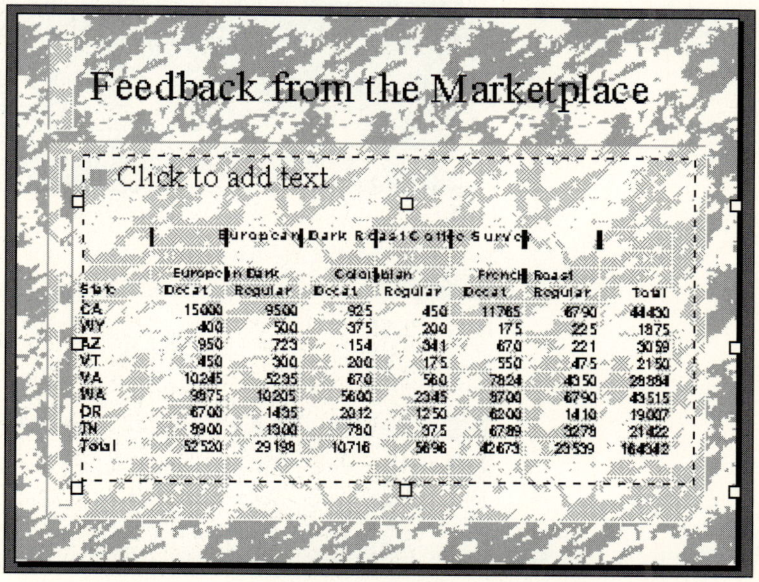

Figure 3.16

9 Save your presentation.

EXIT If necessary, you can exit PowerPoint now and continue this project later.

EMBEDDING THE ACCESS DATABASE INTO THE PRESENTATION

The fifth slide in your presentation will display the database data. You will move back into Word, select the linked database, and then use the copy and paste special method to create a link on the slide.

To embed the linked Access database in the presentation:

1 Start PowerPoint and open European Dark Roast.ppt, if necessary.

2 Move to the fifth slide in the presentation.

3 Switch to the Word document My Updated Project.doc.

4 Using the same technique as you did when you copied the embedded worksheet, select the first database table on page 1, as shown in Figure 3.17, and select copy.

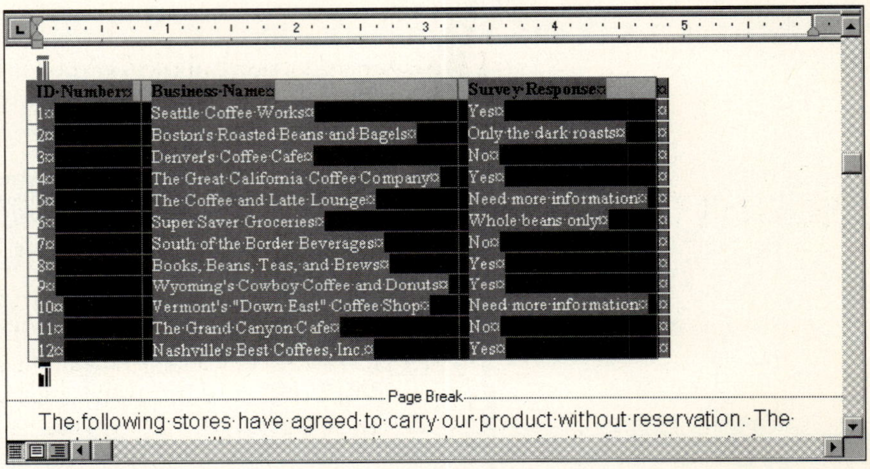

Figure 3.17

5 Return to the PowerPoint presentation.

6 Select Paste Special, then select the Paste Link option. The screen now looks like Figure 3.18.

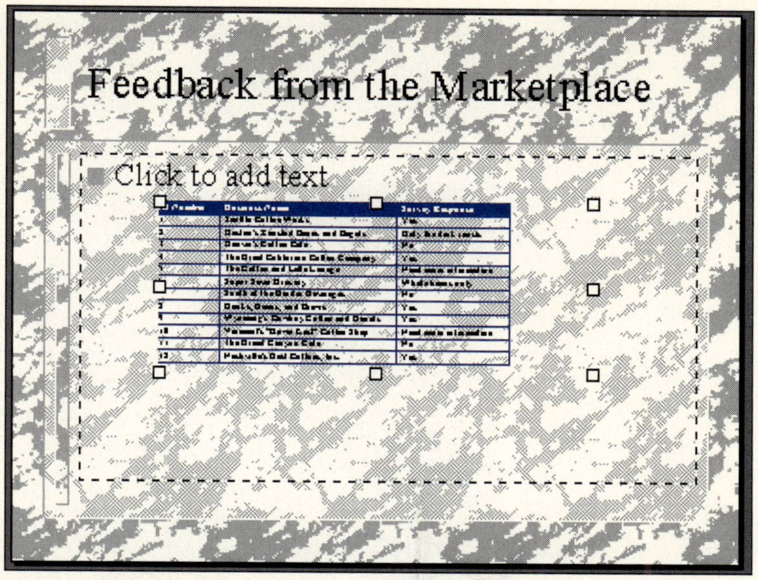

Figure 3.18

7 Move and resize the linked object as necessary.

8 Save your presentation.

FORMATTING THE SLIDE PRESENTATION

Your data is now in the presentation, but the gridlines in the embedded worksheet make it difficult to read the data. To make the presentation more effective, you will change the gridlines setting of the embedded Excel object in Word and then update the link between Word and PowerPoint to apply the changes to the PowerPoint presentation.

To change the gridlines setting in the embedded worksheet:

1 Double-click inside the embedded worksheet object to make its source application active.

2 When the embedded worksheet in Word appears, double-click inside the worksheet to activate Excel, its source application.

3 Select Options from the Tools menu.

4 Deselect the Gridlines option, as shown in Figure 3.19.

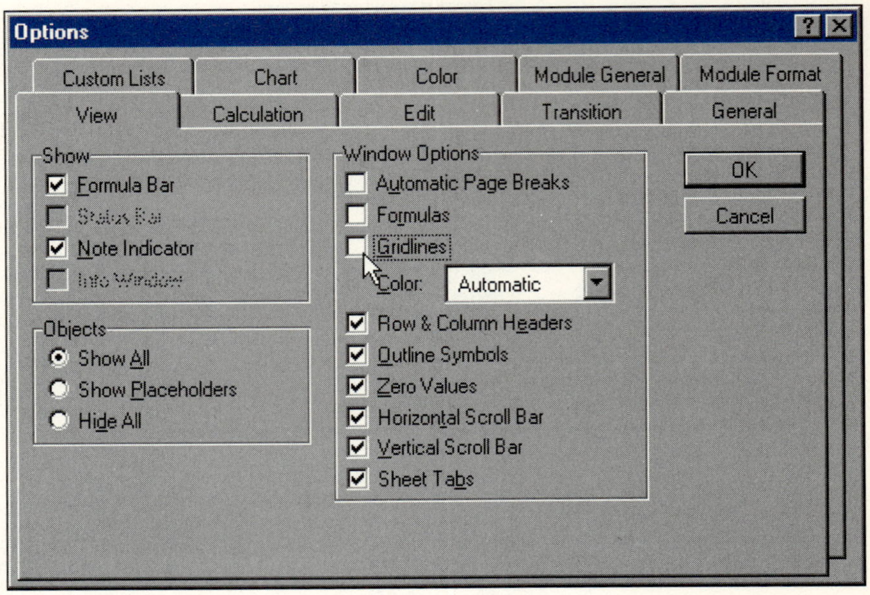

Figure 3.19

5 Select OK to accept the change.
The gridlines are no longer displayed, as shown in Figure 3.20.

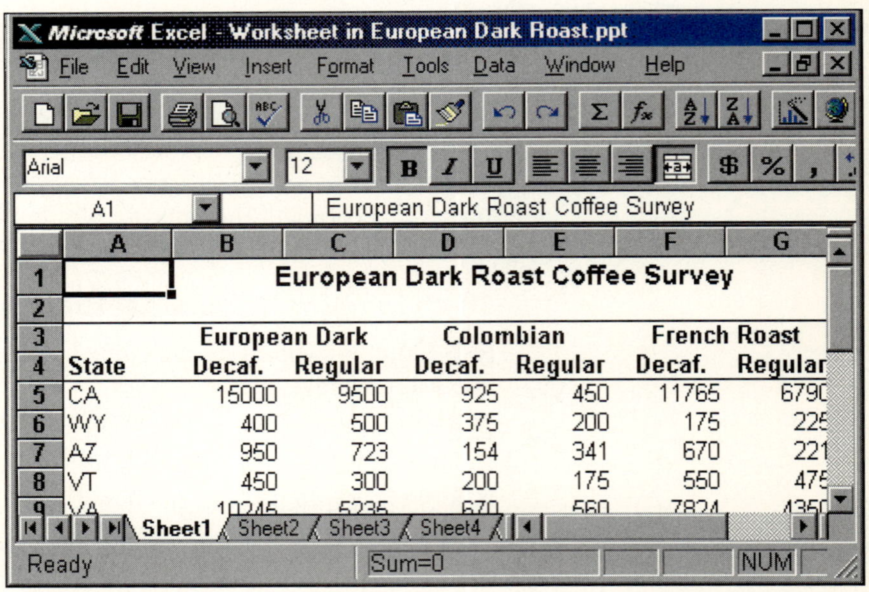

Figure 3.20

6 Click outside the Excel window to deselect it. When the Word window appears, click outside of it to deactivate it also.
The screen now resembles Figure 3.21.

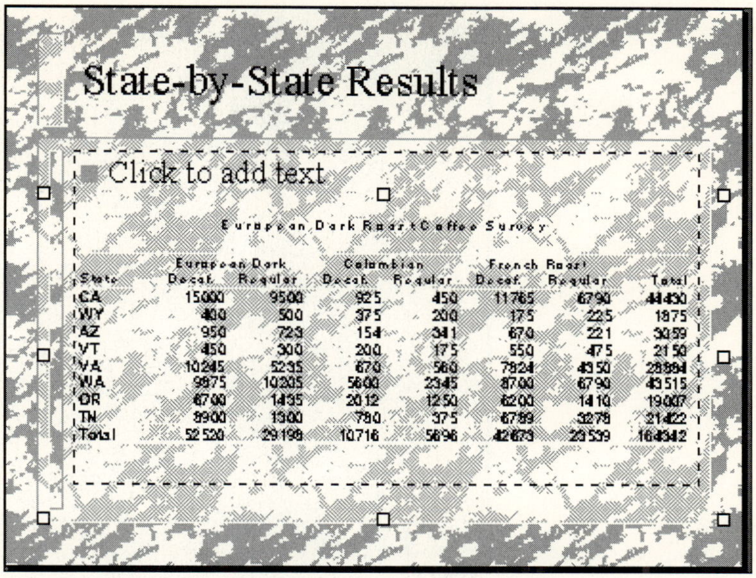

Figure 3.21

7 Save your presentation and exit PowerPoint.

Creating an Office Binder

Since you are almost ready to give your presentation to the company president, you decide to create a binder to organize the Office 95 documents related to this project. Using the analogy of a traditional three-ring binder, an Office binder is an electronic resource for managing and distributing documents. A binder will allow you to make final updates as new data comes in from the field, all from within the binder document.

To create a binder and add two documents:

1 Customize the Shortcut Bar so the Binder button is displayed.

2 Select the Binder button to create a blank binder.

3 Select Add from File from the Section menu, as shown in Figure 3.22.

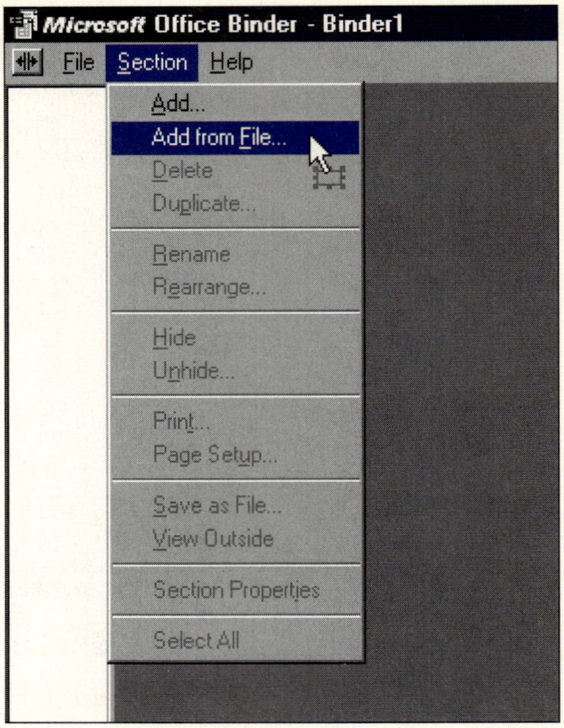

Figure 3.22

4 Select drive A: in the Look in list box.

5 Hold down the CTRL key and select two files, as shown in Figure 3.23.

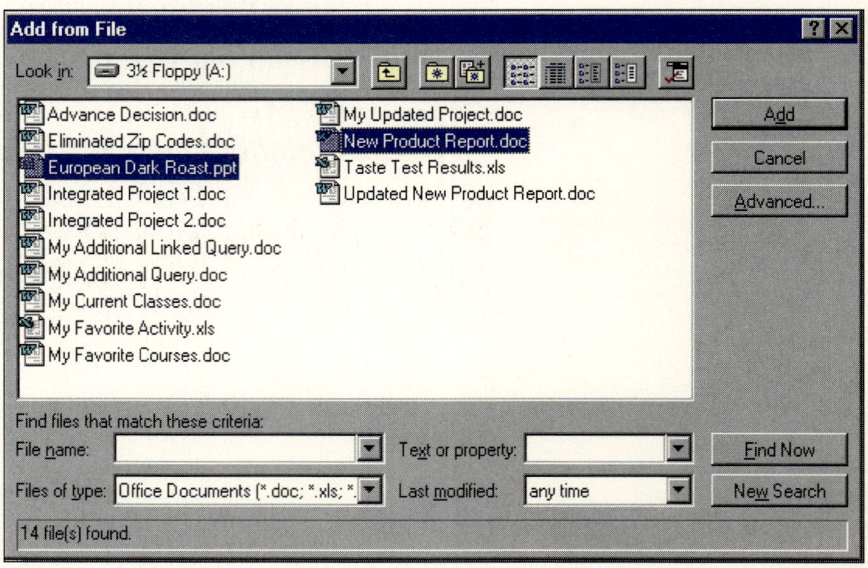

Figure 3.23

6 Select the Add button.

The documents are added to the binder, and the PowerPoint presentation is displayed in the right pane of the Binder window, as shown in Figure 3.24.

Figure 3.24

A binder is like any other Office 95 document, so you will need to save the binder to use its contents later. By default, binders have the file extension *.OBD.

To save the Office binder:

1 Select Save Binder from the File menu.

2 When the Save Binder As dialog box appears, select drive A: from the Save in list box.

3 Type **`Taste Test Presentation`** in the File name text box, as shown in Figure 3.25.

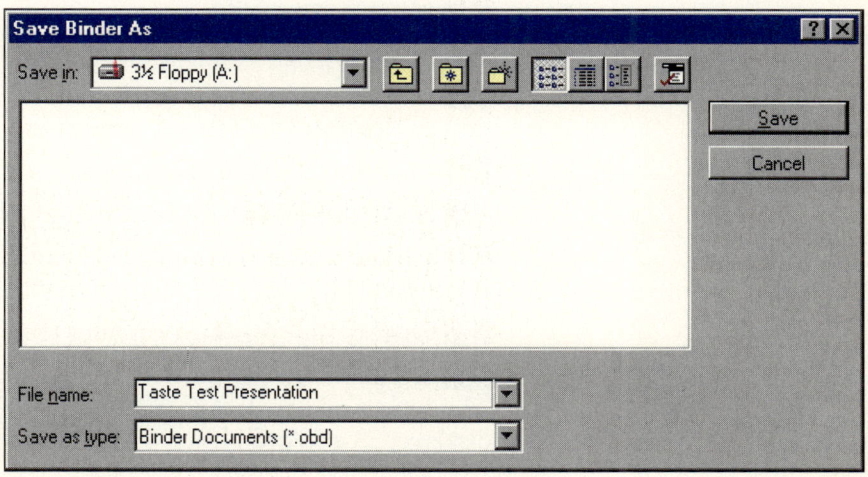

Figure 3.25

4 Select the Save button.

Your binder, containing two documents, is now saved to disk.

UPDATING THE SLIDE PRESENTATION'S DATA

Today is the big day. The president has reviewed your slide show and is very pleased with the way it looks. The staff and stockholders are gathered in the lecture room, and the presentation will begin in about one hour.

Your phone just rang. The president called to tell you that the marketing department had convinced all of the stores to carry the new product. He wants to know if you can modify your presentation so that slide 5 shows all of the stores as answering yes to the survey. You assure the president that the changes can easily be made.

Since marketing has been so busy meeting with store managers, they haven't had time to update the database. You must update the database in Access before you update your presentation.

The objects you copied from Word into PowerPoint are now ***multi-application objects*** in PowerPoint. This term describes an object that has been embedded or linked through a ***primary source application*** and a ***secondary source application.*** In this project Excel and Access are the primary source applications, because these are the applications where the objects were first created. Word takes on the role of the secondary application for the objects embedded in your presentation. What is actually embedded in PowerPoint is the secondary application's image of the data. If you double-click the worksheet or the database, the toolbars will change to reflect the secondary application's features. Any changes you make to the objects are restricted to the changes you would make if you were in Word when you selected the object. Once you have activated Word as the secondary source application and you double-click the Excel worksheet object, the primary source application opens so that you can change the worksheet data. Since the Access database is a linked object in the Word document, you cannot double-click the database to change the data. Instead, the data must be changed through Access. Then you can activate the secondary source application, Word, by double-clicking the object, locating the insertion point in the database, and pressing F9 to update the data.

To modify the embedded and linked data:

1. Open Access.
2. Open *Potential Marketing Channels.mdb* from drive A:.
3. Open the Market Survey Results table, and change the contents of the Survey Response field for all records to Yes.
4. Save the table and exit Access.
5. Make the Taste Test Presentation.obd binder active.
6. Click the icon for the PowerPoint file entitled European Dark Roast.ppt.
7. Display slide 5, which contains the embedded database object.
8. Double-click any portion of the embedded Access data table.

The screen now looks like Figure 3.26. Notice that the database is being displayed as a Word object, with the Word ruler.

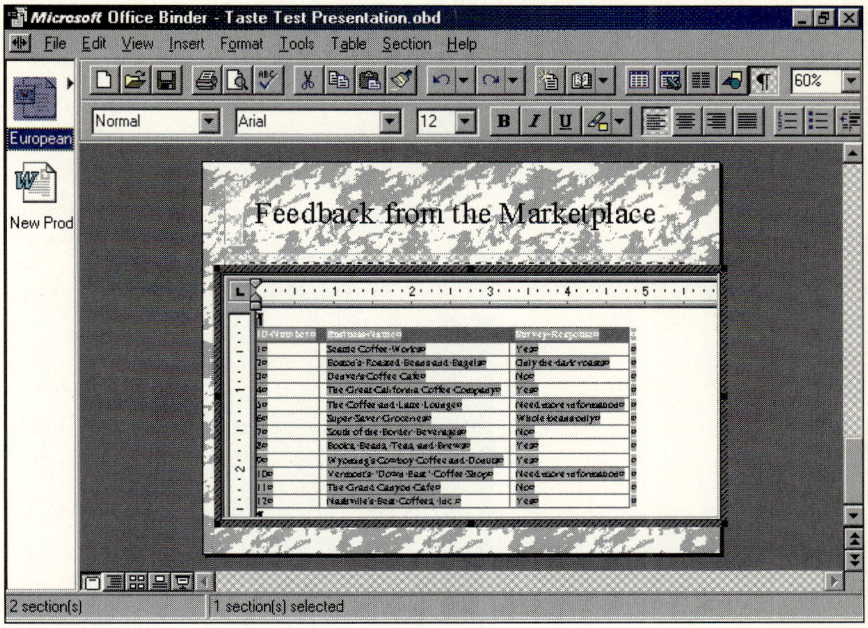

Figure 3.26

9 Click anywhere in the displayed database object in Word.

10 Press (F9) to update the data.

The screen now looks like Figure 3.27.

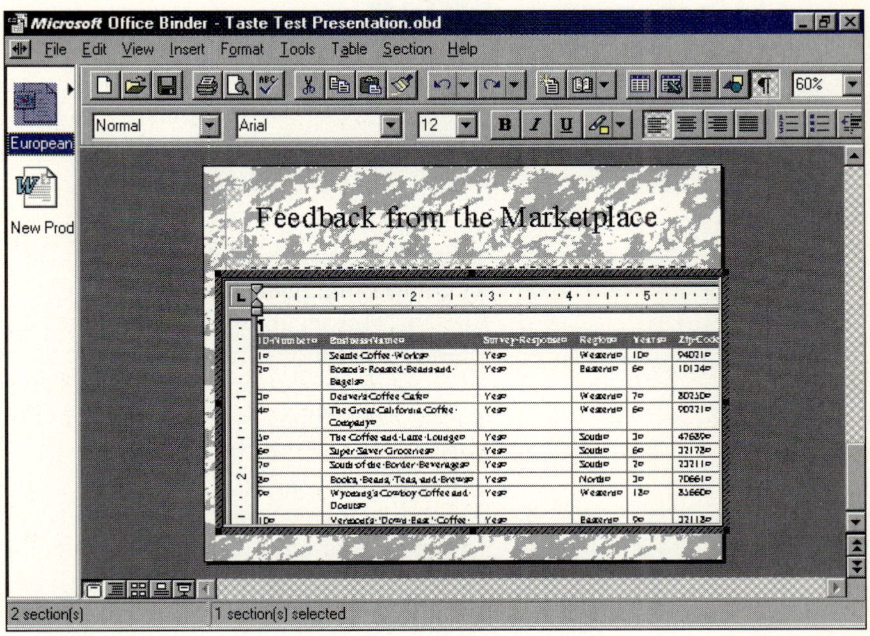

Figure 3.27

11 Crop, size, and move the Access database object so that only the first three columns are displayed and it is centered on the slide.

12 Apply additional Word table formats to the embedded object to enhance its appearance.

13 Deselect the object.
The slide, in Slide Show view, now resembles Figure 3.28.

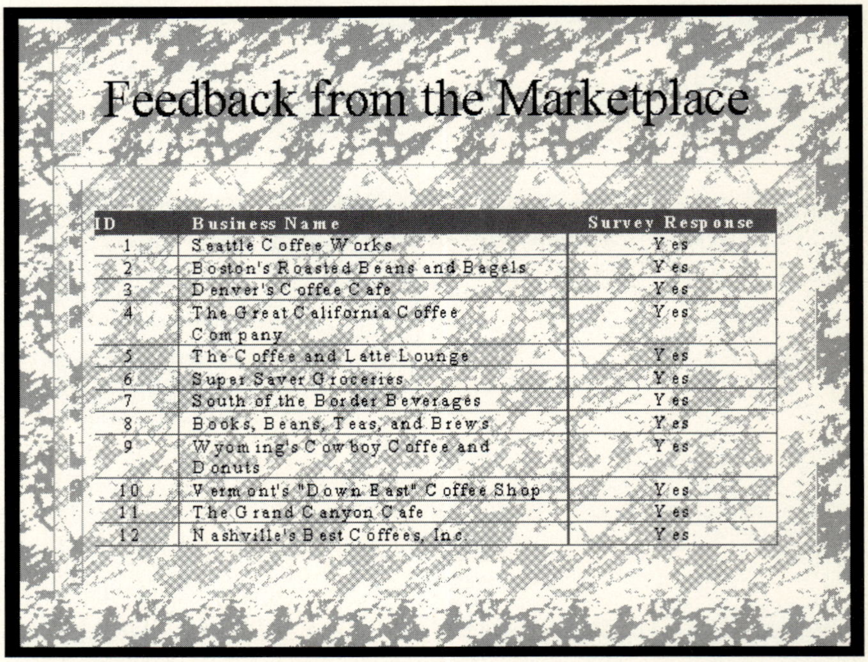

Figure 3.28

THE NEXT STEP

As you can see, the power of OLE is very great. The problem of redundant construction of data has been solved. In the ever-increasing traffic on the information superhighway, data exchange needs to be fast, efficient, and accurate. Linking and embedding helps to ensure that sharing data *is* fast, efficient, and accurate. Individual files included in a project can be added to an Office binder and then treated as one file.

Throughout the integrated projects you have seen several ways to connect objects from different applications. In PowerPoint you can insert an Excel worksheet or graph through the Insert menu, and you can follow the same steps to embed the worksheet into the presentation as you did with the Word document. You cannot, however, insert a database object into either PowerPoint or an Office binder. There is no facility in either tool to do this, except by including the database as an embedded object in Word or Excel.

You also saw that you can have as many applications open as your computer system can handle. Different systems have different amounts of RAM and hard disk space, so sometimes there are limitations. But the Office 95 suite was designed so that you can move from one application to another with just the click of a button.

Think about ways you can use OLE to create the types of linked files you might use. What about creating a résumé with your photograph embedded in it? If you apply to graduate school, you can include a summary sheet on the classes you are currently involved in, including your GPA. Keep your grade statistics in a worksheet or database, and then embed and link them into a graduate school application, a letter home, or other documents you may create. You can even embed movies into your PowerPoint presentations. Wouldn't it be fun to send a friend a video of your class activity, embedded in a slide presentation?

This concludes Project 3 of the integrated projects. You can exit PowerPoint now or go on to work the Study Questions, Review Exercises, and Assignments.

SUMMARY AND EXERCISES

Summary

- You can use OLE to create a multiapplication presentation.
- You can copy and paste objects embedded in Word into PowerPoint.
- The copied embedded object can be updated from PowerPoint.
- You can copy and paste objects linked in Word into PowerPoint.
- The copied linked object can be updated from PowerPoint.
- The color scheme of the objects can be changed in PowerPoint.
- Individual documents can be organized in an Office Binder.
- Objects can pass through multiple applications.

Key Terms and Operations

Key Terms
multiapplication object
primary source application
secondary source application

Operations
Create a presentation in PowerPoint
Copy and paste objects into a presentation
Format a presentation
Update embedded and linked data in a presentation

Study Questions

Multiple Choice

1. A multiapplication presentation is
   a. a presentation made up of separate application files; that is, a Word file, a PowerPoint file, an Excel file, and an Access file, printed and bound into one document.
   b. a PowerPoint slide show.
   c. a presentation in one file with objects created in different applications.
   d. a Word document that is more than one page in length.

2. Once an object is embedded in Word and is then embedded in PowerPoint,
   a. it can no longer be updated.
   b. it can no longer be formatted.
   c. it can be updated from PowerPoint.
   d. it cannot be moved.

3. Objects in PowerPoint
   a. must be formatted and sized in Word first.
   b. cannot have primary source files.
   c. must have secondary source files.
   d. can be movies, Word documents, clip art, or other types of files.
4. The primary source application
   a. is always Word.
   b. is where the object is first created.
   c. is where the object will be placed.
   d. is never Word.
5. The secondary source application
   a. is where the object is first created.
   b. is where an embedded or linked object was first inserted.
   c. doesn't allow the object to be updated.
   d. None of the above.
6. An embedded object in PowerPoint
   a. cannot be edited if it was inserted through the copy and paste method.
   b. must always be edited in the primary application.
   c. can be edited if it was inserted through the copy and paste method.
   d. must never be edited in the primary application.
7. The difference between an embedded file and a linked file is that
   a. the embedded file's source file is a part of the target file, and the linked file's source file is not.
   b. the linked file can be updated, but the embedded file cannot.
   c. the linked file's source file is a part of the target file, and the embedded file's source file is not.
   d. an embedded file cannot be copied into another application like PowerPoint, but a linked file can be copied.
8. PowerPoint can
   a. only accept embedded objects from other applications.
   b. only accept an Access database as an object if a secondary source application exists.
   c. accept an Access database as an object without a secondary source application.
   d. only accept linked objects from other applications.
9. OLE is a tool that
   a. is very limiting in its capacity and scope.
   b. is very powerful if used well.
   c. cannot be used if you have more than one application open at a time.
   d. can only connect objects created in the Office 95 suite.
10. Copy and paste is a method that
    a. usually disallows updating of the copied object.
    b. lets you embed a linked Access database in Word to a PowerPoint slide.
    c. is a part of the OLE process.
    d. All of the above.

Short Answer

1. What is a primary source application file? When is it created?
2. What is a secondary source application file?
3. What is the difference between embedding and linking?
4. How do you embed an Access database file in PowerPoint?
5. What happens when you double-click on the Excel worksheet in PowerPoint?
6. What happens when you double-click on the Excel worksheet two times in a row in PowerPoint?
7. How do you update the Access database data in PowerPoint?
8. How many applications can you open at the same time?
9. What dictates how many applications can be open at the same time on a computer system?
10. What are some ways you can use OLE now? What about in the future?

For Discussion

1. What are the three OLE methods and how do they differ? How are they similar?
2. What are the advantages of using the embed method to create objects?
3. What are the advantages of using the link method?
4. Explain the concept of passing objects through multiple applications. Why is this a good tool?
5. How can you use an Office binder to organize related files? How can you update linked and embedded documents that are added to a binder?

Review Exercises

A Presentation to the Employees

1. Design a six-slide (or longer) PowerPoint presentation to include the worksheet showing the entire taste-test survey results, and include the database queries you created in Integrated Project 2.
2. Include some text to explain to the employees why the company has been so preoccupied lately.
3. Use a different Wizard, or come up with your own master slide background and color scheme.
4. Save this presentation as Employee Presentation.ppt.

Update the Excel Data

1. Edit the Excel worksheet in Employee Presentation.ppt. Add five rows of states and their responses to the taste-test survey. Make up the states you add and their responses.
2. Crop and size the edited worksheet so that it fits nicely on the PowerPoint slide.

Assignments

Presenting a Pie Chart

Create a PowerPoint presentation to present the bar chart you embedded in the first integrated project's assignment document, My Favorite Courses.doc. Use PowerPoint features to border the bar chart, and put some sharp colors in the slide. Save this presentation as Classes.ppt.

Creating a Hobby Poster

In Word write a two-paragraph description of your favorite hobby. Save the document as My Favorite Hobby.doc. Then create a PowerPoint slide. Insert a clip art file that best represents your hobby. Choose Object from the Insert menu and select the My Favorite Hobby.doc file. Size the two objects so that they create a poster of your favorite hobby.

PART IX

Introduction to the Internet

Introduction to the Internet

Objectives

After completing this project, you will be able to:

- Describe the Internet
- Describe the major tools and resources of the Internet and how to use them
- Compose, send, and receive electronic mail
- Access newsgroups by using Usenet
- Navigate the Net by using Gophers
- Access Telnet to log in to other Internet hosts
- Download files by using the File Transfer Protocol
- Create your own home page using Microsoft's Internet Assistant

Describing the Internet

The ***Internet,*** also called simply the ***Net,*** is a network of thousands of computers spanning the globe. It emerged out of ARPANET, the Department of Defense's Advanced Research Projects Agency network created 30 years ago to facilitate and protect military communications in the event of nuclear attack. This network was designed so that different computers using different hardware and software could communicate easily. In the 1970s and 1980s, universities and researchers, looking for a way to communicate and share data such as literature, photographs, research results, and computer programs, began connecting their computer systems to other computer systems through ARPANET, thus informally establishing the Internet network of computers.

Today the Internet consists of millions of computers that transfer information through a common set of communication rules called the ***Internet protocol.*** Much information on the Internet is text, but other forms of information, such as images, animations, video, and sound, are also available.

Accessing the Internet

To use the Internet, you must have access to a ***host*** computer. It is called a host because the computer is letting you enter its system and use its resources. Most colleges and universities have host computers that provide Internet access for students and faculty. If your computer is equipped with a modem, you can purchase Internet access from a commercial provider. Commercial providers of the Net usually charge monthly fees and/or assess an hourly or minute-by-minute charge for their services. Most commercial providers support a variety of Internet resources, such as

- *Electronic mail (e-mail),* which allows you to send messages to or receive messages from one or more users of the Internet
- *World Wide Web (WWW, or the Web),* which provides you with access to almost unlimited sources of information
- *Newsgroups,* which allow you to subscribe to electronic discussion groups on a variety of topics
- *File Transfer Protocol (FTP),* which allows you to copy files from one computer to another
- *Telnet,* which provides you with remote login capabilities
- *Gophers,* which allow you to conduct information searches

All of these Internet resources will be discussed in more depth later in this introduction. Table 1 lists a few popular commercial providers and the numbers to call to get information or to sign up.

Table 1 Commercial Internet Service Providers

Provider	Phone number
America Online	800-827-6364
CompuServe	800-848-8990
Delphi Internet Services	800-695-4005
MCI Mail	800-444-6245
NetCom Online Communication Services	800-501-8649
Prodigy	800-776-3449

A host computer provides the means to access Internet resources, a process known as ***navigation.*** A software program for navigating the Internet provides an ***interface,*** which determines the kind of resources you can access and how they are displayed on your computer screen. When it was first established, the Internet's interface was *text-based.* When a person accesses the Net through a ***text-based*** (or ***character-based***) ***interface,*** the computer presents a screen of words and numbers only. Lynx is a commonly used text-based application for viewing content on the World Wide Web. The screen shown in Figure 1 displays one of the Benjamin/Cummings World Wide Web resources as it appears using the Lynx text browser.

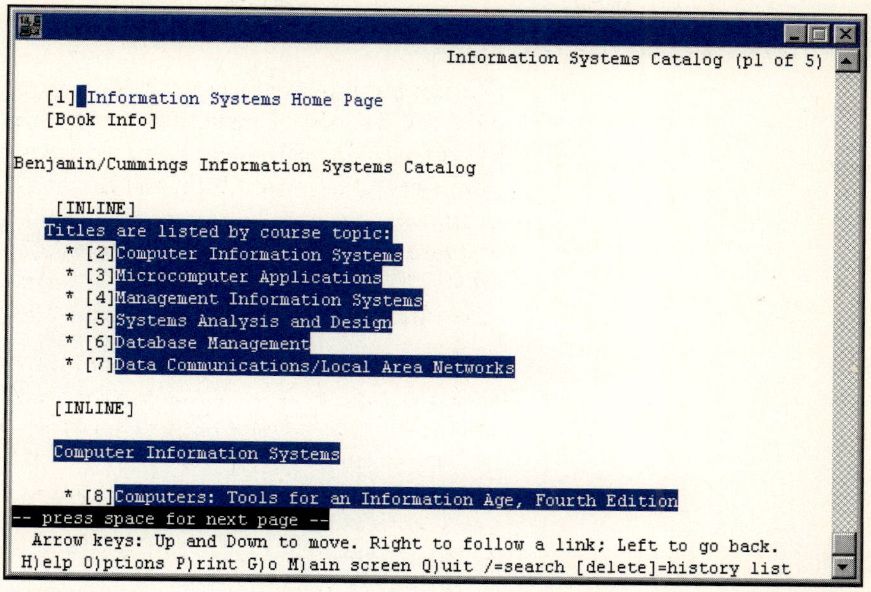

Figure 1

To interact with this screen, the user would type a series of letters (words) and/or numbers at a command prompt. Colleges and universities using VAX or Unix Internet servers often provide text-based interfaces. Many Gopher servers, Telnet resources, and anonymous FTP sites also use text-based interfaces.

Text-based interfaces are relatively crude compared with today's most common interface standard, the ***graphical user interface,*** or ***GUI*** (pronounced "gooey"). With this new interface standard, you can use a mouse to make selections from menus and icons. You see graphical displays and photographs on the screen rather than plain characters. Graphical ***browsers,*** such as NetScape and Mosaic, have become the standard means of navigating the World Wide Web. A graphical browser is a software application that allows users to access information on the Web by browsing, or following the links that are used to move from one Web resource to another. The Netscape Web browser is shown in Figure 2.

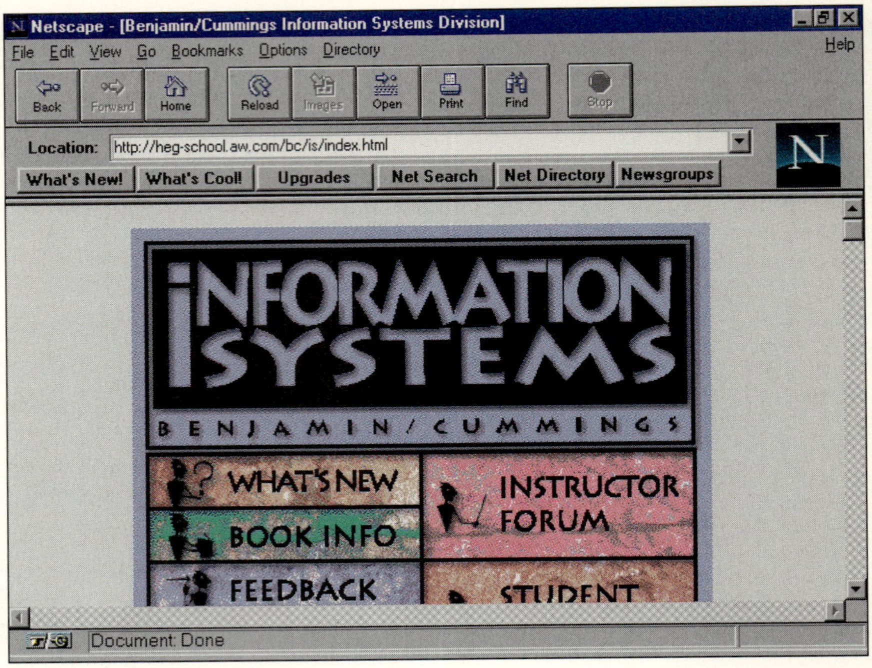

Figure 2

Identifying Internet Resources

Usually an Internet resource, or ***site,*** is identified by a ***domain name,*** which specifies the host computer's physical location, or domain, on the Internet. A domain name represents the ***Internet protocol address*** for a site, and each element of the domain name indicates a hierarchy of groups that are responsible for the computer networks underneath that site. For example, to access the Benjamin/Cummings FTP you type in the domain name bc.aw.com. The letters *bc* refer to The Benjamin/Cummings Publishing Company, *aw* refers to its parent company, Addison-Wesley, and *com* identifies Benjamin/Cummings as a commercial organization. Another element that appears at the end of some domain names is called the ***top-level domain.*** It usually specifies either the site's country, if it is not in the United States, or the type of institution or organization responsible for the site. Table 2 lists several top-level domains. The elements of a domain name are separated by periods, which in computer-speak are called ***dots.***

Table 2 Common Internet Top-level Domains

Domain	Domain type or location
au	Australia
ca	Canada
com	Commercial organization
edu	Educational institution
gov	Government agency
mil	Military installation
org	Nonprofit organization
uk	United Kingdom

USING INTERNET RESOURCES AND TOOLS

You can exchange and use information in many different ways across the Net. You can send and receive messages from other people to share ideas and exchange thoughts among groups of people, or transfer files from one computer to another. You can access libraries through the Net for research purposes, and many organizations and institutions offer information on the Net that you can use for commercial purposes or as informational resources.

Communicating on the Net Using E-mail

On a day-to-day basis, ***electronic mail (e-mail)*** is probably the most valuable resource available to Internet users. E-mail is both a product and a process. The product is a letter, memo, or message created on a computer. The process is transmitting this message to the recipient. You can attach computer files, such as worksheets, clip art files, or graphic files, to an e-mail message you send. The process is similar to sending a letter through the postal service, except e-mail is all done electronically.

You can use electronic mail to communicate just about anything that you usually communicate verbally or in written form. For example, members of a business project team can use e-mail to exchange ideas on the project, relay work that each member has done to other team members, and keep the momentum of the project going. With e-mail you can work closely with others on a daily basis and yet be geographically separated by tens or thousands of miles. Electronic mail also helps you communicate quickly and inexpensively, without relying on long distance phone calls or expensive overnight mail costs.

Another e-mail benefit is that it can help you become more productive. If you are working on a tight deadline for a project and you suddenly remember you need to tell someone something, you can quickly send an e-mail and return to your work with a minimal amount of interruption. With e-mail you can communicate important concepts or ideas without getting stuck on the phone with someone who loves to talk.

Sending and Receiving E-mail

If you want to send or receive mail electronically, you must have an ***e-mail address.*** This address uniquely identifies you, so that only you can receive the messages addressed to you. An e-mail address has two basic identifiers separated by the @ sign. To the left of the @ sign is a username that you choose or is assigned to you; it can be your first or last name, a portion of your name, a nickname, or even a set of numbers. To the right of the @ sign is a computer domain name. The domain name itself can have several identifiers that specify the host computer. The exact number of characters that form your e-mail address will vary depending upon your Internet host. Figure 3 shows you an example of a fictitious e-mail address.

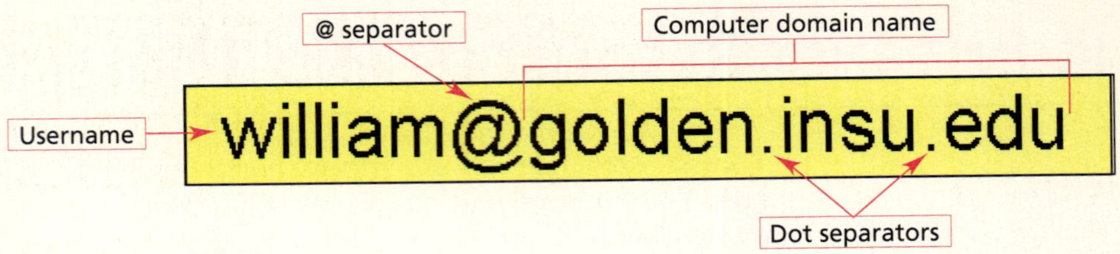

Figure 3

Part of the domain name included in an e-mail address identifies the ***mail server.*** The mail server is a computer that acts much like a local post office, with an address that identifies it on the Internet. E-mail sent to you is routed to the mail server, which holds the mail until you want to retrieve it from your mailbox. Likewise, when you send e-mail to someone, it goes to the recipient's mail server and then into his or her mailbox. This is much like a local post office that holds mail until the recipients can come to open their mailboxes with their keys. A password is required to access the e-mail account.

Composing an E-mail Message

How you compose and send e-mail messages will depend on the configuration of your personal computer or Internet host. In addition to an e-mail address, you need a ***mail editor*** to send and receive e-mail. A mail editor is an application that allows you to compose and send messages to others and to display, save, and print the messages that you receive. In addition, most mail editors allow you to keep a list of e-mail addresses, similar to a telephone book, to use when composing messages.

If your computer or network uses Microsoft Exchange in Windows 95, you can compose and send an e-mail message from within Microsoft Word. If you access the Internet through a commercial provider, an e-mail editor is usually available. Regardless of which e-mail editor you use, the process of composing and sending messages is similar.

Composing and sending an e-mail message using Microsoft Exchange:

1 Click the Microsoft Exchange icon on the Windows 95 desktop to launch Microsoft Exchange.
The Inbox-Microsoft Exchange dialog box appears as shown in Figure 4.

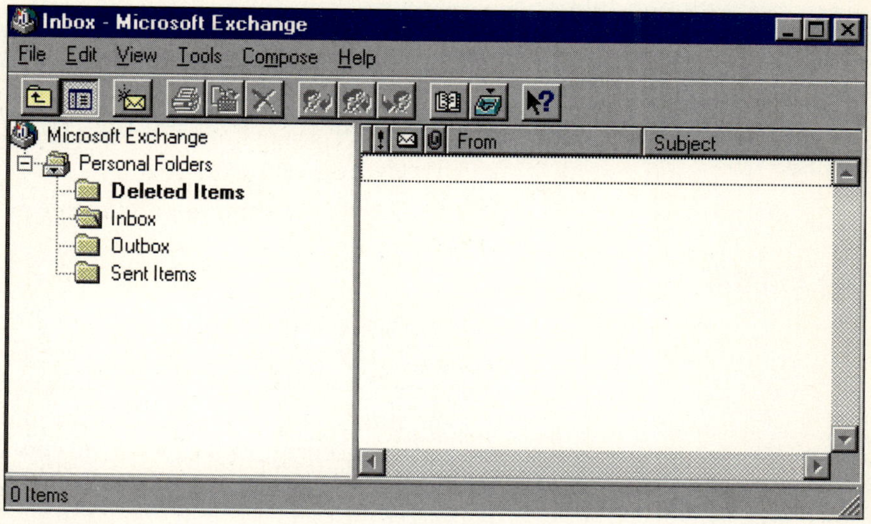

Figure 4

2 Choose New Message from the Compose menu.

3 Enter the recipient's e-mail address, and type your message. A sample message is shown in Figure 5.

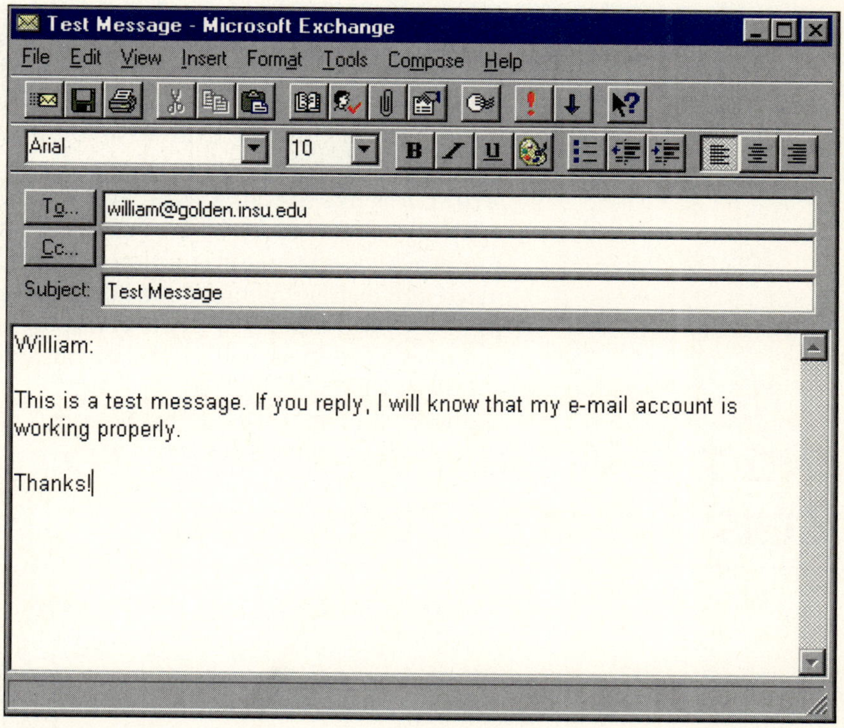

Figure 5

4 Choose Send from the File menu, or click the Send button, to send the message.
The message is sent, and a copy of the message is saved in the Sent Items folder in Microsoft Exchange.

Depending on your system's configuration, your message may appear in the Out box instead of the Sent Items folder after you've completed this step.

5 You can compose and send additional messages or view messages you have received.

6 Choose Close from the File menu to close Microsoft Exchange.

Using E-mail

Commercial companies often use e-mail to keep in touch with their clients or people who purchase their products. For example, a television newsmagazine show, "Dateline NBC," uses e-mail to gather viewer responses to a question or topic presented at the end of each show. This gives the show's producers an idea of what viewers think about each show's topics and helps them to plan future programs. Their e-mail address is dateline@nbc.com.

Many celebrities, sports figures, and politicians have e-mail addresses. You can even e-mail the president of the United States at president@whitehouse.gov.

Surviving on the Net

Just as there are rules of etiquette in our society, the Net has its own rules of social behavior, referred to as ***netiquette.*** There are no Net police to enforce these standards; the Net is self-monitored by the user community. Anytime you send messages across the Net, you must remember you are communicating with people who have feelings and emotions that must be respected. These people cannot see your facial expressions or hear the intonations of your voice; they can only read your words, so you need to choose your words carefully. If you use all capital letters in a message or article, it is like SHOUTING VERY LOUDLY at someone. A casual joke or wisecrack can easily be misunderstood or taken seriously. There are some cute ***emoticons,*** or emotion icons, that have evolved to help communicate the feelings behind your words. Character strings such as **:>)** (smiling face), **:<(** (sad face), or **;-)** (wink) display certain feelings when viewed sideways. Often you will see emoticons in e-mail postings.

USING THE WORLD WIDE WEB TO ACCESS INTERNET RESOURCES

The ***World Wide Web, WWW,*** or ***Web,*** is the fastest growing and most popular Internet resource. The increasing popularity of the Web is evidenced by the number of businesses and organizations that have sites on the Web, and by the fact that most Internet providers now offer graphical browsers such as Netscape, Mosiac, or a proprietary browser for accessing Web resources. Many providers also allow subscribers to create their own Web sites.

Originally developed in 1989 by the European Particle Physics Laboratory (CERN) in Switzerland, the Web was created to provide a consistent and seamless way of linking information presented as text, graphics, video, and sound. The Web uses ***hypertext*** technology to give you the ability to randomly "jump" from one Web site to another. Hypertext is a technology for storing information in small units that are linked to other related units of information. Using a graphical browser such as Netscape, you can easily follow links established between Web sites.

Each Web site has a ***home page.*** A home page is a file containing text, images, and links to other Web sites that are displayed graphically on the screen. Each home page consists of a text document written using ***hypertext markup language (HTML).*** HTML documents contain a series of ASCII characters, called ***tags,*** that specify how the various elements included on the home page will appear or list the names of other linked Web resources stored on remote ***Web servers,*** host computers that store Web resources. Thus, the Web is a distributed system that is sometimes referred to as a global hypertext. Since accessing nontextual information on the Web using a graphical browser is now a common practice, the Web may be more accurately described as a global hypermedia system. New languages such as ***Virtual Reality Modeling Language (VRML)*** from Silicon Graphics, Inc., and Sun Microsystems' ***JAVA*** represent new aspects of the World Wide Web.

Web resources consist of individual files that are posted to a Web server, which uses the ***Hypertext Transport Protocol (HTTP)*** to deliver files. Every file on the Web is identified by its ***uniform resource locator (URL),*** which is the domain name for Web resources. The URL provides a universal, consistent method for finding and accessing information. A Web browser such as Netscape uses URLs to display home pages. To access information on the Web, you will first type http://, which tells the browser to use the Hypertext Transport Protocol to display the specified Web resource. In addition, the URL for most Web resources also contains the letters *www,* indicating that the resource is found on a Web server. For example, the URL http://www.aw.com/bc/home.html will display the Benjamin/Cummings home page shown in Figure 6.

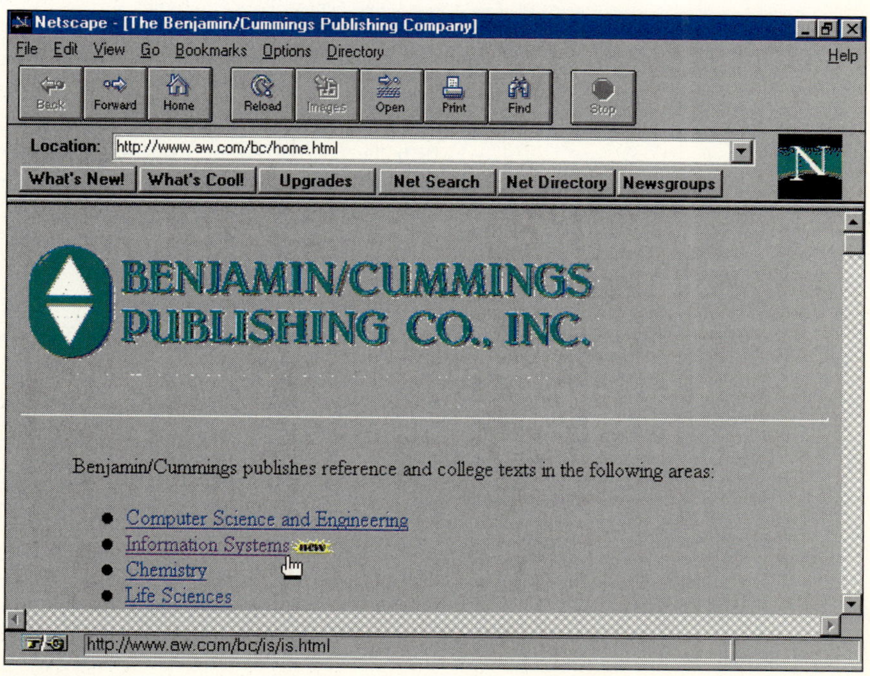

Figure 6

Most home pages contain ***links*** to other Web resources, which may reside on the same server or a server anywhere on the Web. Links are usually identified by a graphic or by text that appears in blue and is underlined. Most browsers display the URL for the current resource, or the URL of the destination resource specified in a link. Notice that the pointer in Figure 6 is over the link to the Information Systems resource. The URL for the Information Systems link, http://www.aw.com/bc/is/is.html, is displayed in the lower portion of Figure 6. This link appears in purple, indicating that it has been visited before by the current user. Selecting the link to this resource will display the page shown in Figure 7.

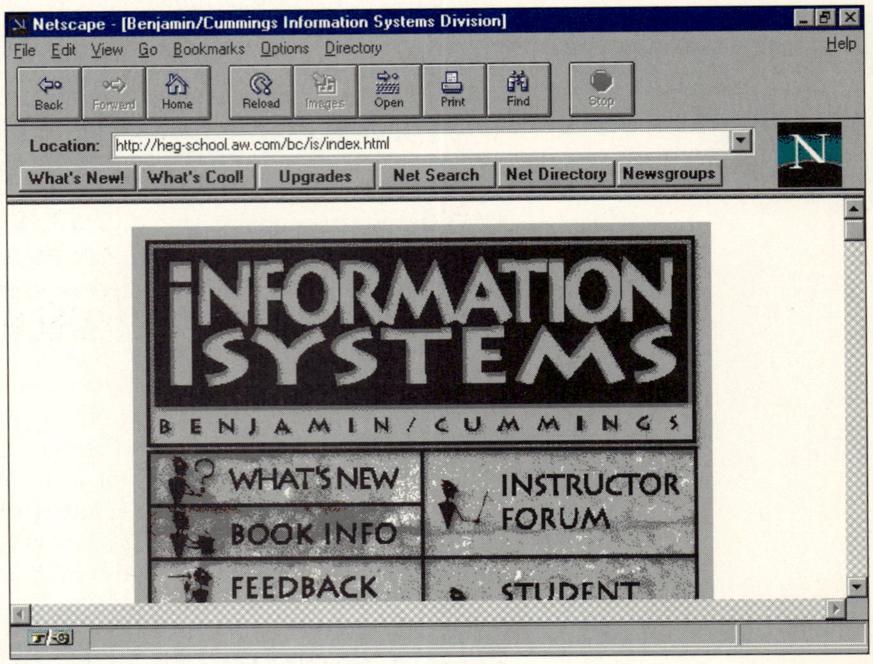

Figure 7

When using a browser such as Netscape, you can link to another Web resource by entering its URL in the Location text box. For example, entering http://www.microsoft.com as the location will display Microsoft's home page, which will look similar to Figure 8.

> ***Tip*** When you replace the current text in the Location text box, the box label will change to Go To.

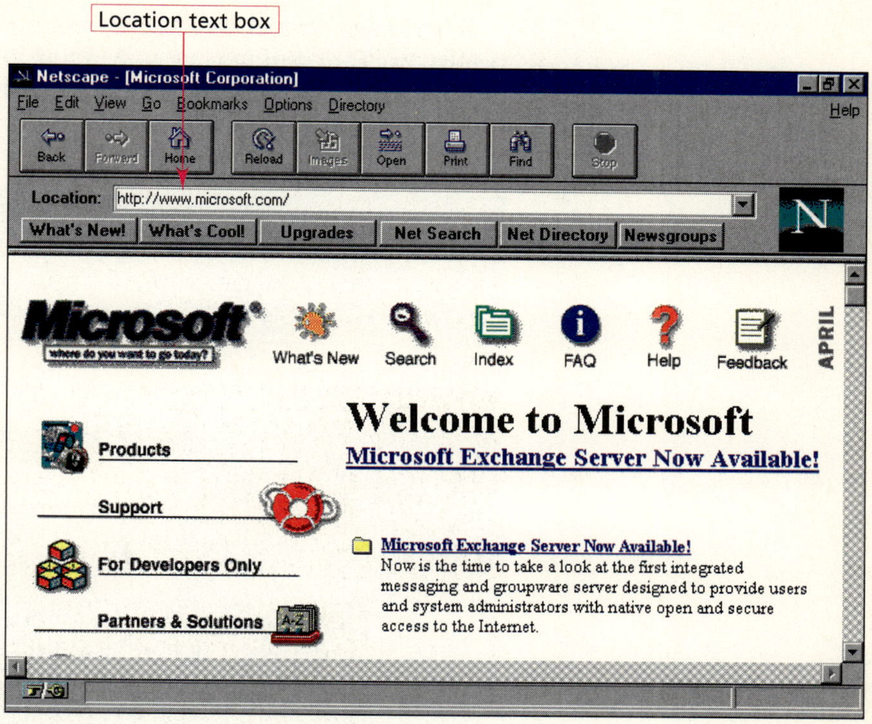

Figure 8

Tip If you get an error message when accessing a known Web site, it may be that the site is not accessible because the host's computer is down for maintenance. Try again later.

Most Web browsers provide a way to keep track of the Web sites you have visited. A bookmark file is a list of ***bookmarks,*** which consist of the titles and URLs of pages you want to visit again easily. By clicking the appropriate button or selecting the appropriate menu item, you can add the currently displayed Web page to a personal bookmark file. Figure 9 shows a bookmark list stored in Netscape.

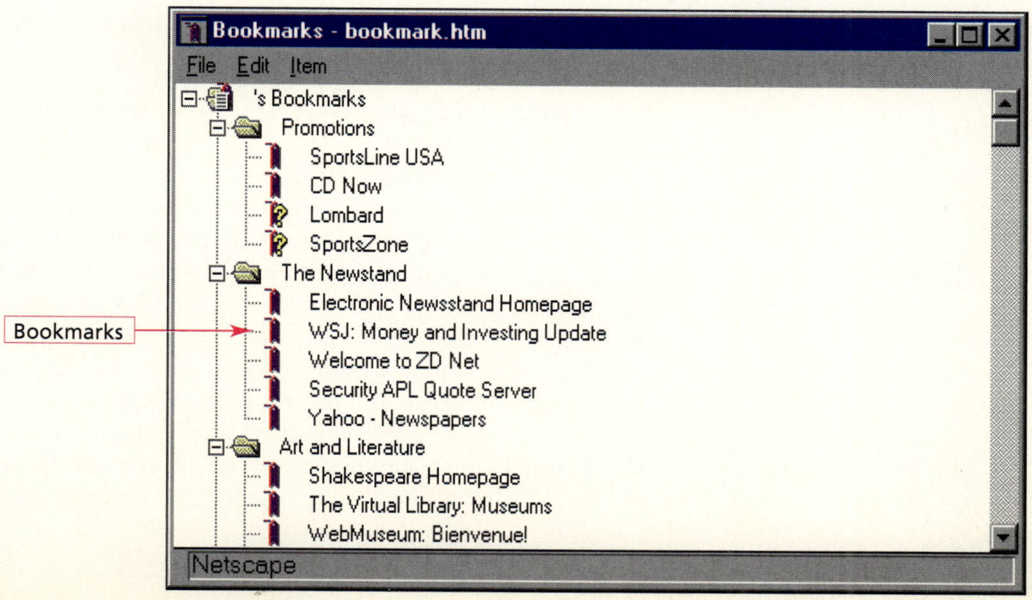

Figure 9

In a similar manner most browsers keep a running ***history*** of the sites you have visited during your current session. Figure 10 shows a history list in Netscape. Clicking any of the titles in this list will cause that resource to be displayed.

Figure 10

The more you navigate the Web, the more you will realize that it is a constantly changing, dynamic resource. New sites will appear, and existing sites will change location or cease to exist. To survive on the Web, you must be able to adapt to a powerful but fluid resource.

In addition to browsing information contained on Web sites, a Web browser can be used to retrieve information from other Internet resources including newsgroups, Gopher sites, Telnet hosts, and FTP sites.

EXIT If necessary, you can quit now and continue this project later.

Accessing Newsgroups Through Usenet

Through the Internet resource called Usenet, you can access thousands of ***newsgroups,*** which provide forums for the exchange of ideas and information. Newsgroups are formed around a specialized topic of interest: computer programming, bungee jumping, parenting, classical music, cycling, the theater—if there's a topic of interest, there's a newsgroup. If the group doesn't exist, you can create it. People write articles and post, or display, the articles to the members of the group. You can join, or subscribe, to any newsgroup and read any posted article or post your own. You can also personally respond to writers of articles by e-mail.

Newsgroups are broken down into categories and have names that look much like e-mail addresses. The first level of a newsgroup name identifies the type of group it is. There are specific first-level group types for Canada, Japan, and the United States, as well as for regions of the United States. Some alternative newsgroups have rather bizarre group types. There are also semicommercial and education groups; groups relating to recreation and sports, computer topics, science fields, social cultures; and a miscellaneous group for newsgroups that don't really fit anywhere else. After the first-level group type, the other parts of the name identify the group topic. As you read the name from left to right, the sections and subsections are separated by periods. Each name to the right of the period is a subset of the name to the left. It's much like the system of directories and subdirectories on a computer disk. For instance, the group alt.dcom.telecom for discussions of data communications has a subgroup, alt.dcom.telecom.ip that deals specifically with Internet protocol questions. A group called clari.sports.baseball has a subset group called clari.sports.baseball.games. Figure 11 shows an actual newsgroup posting from the rec.bicycles.tech group.

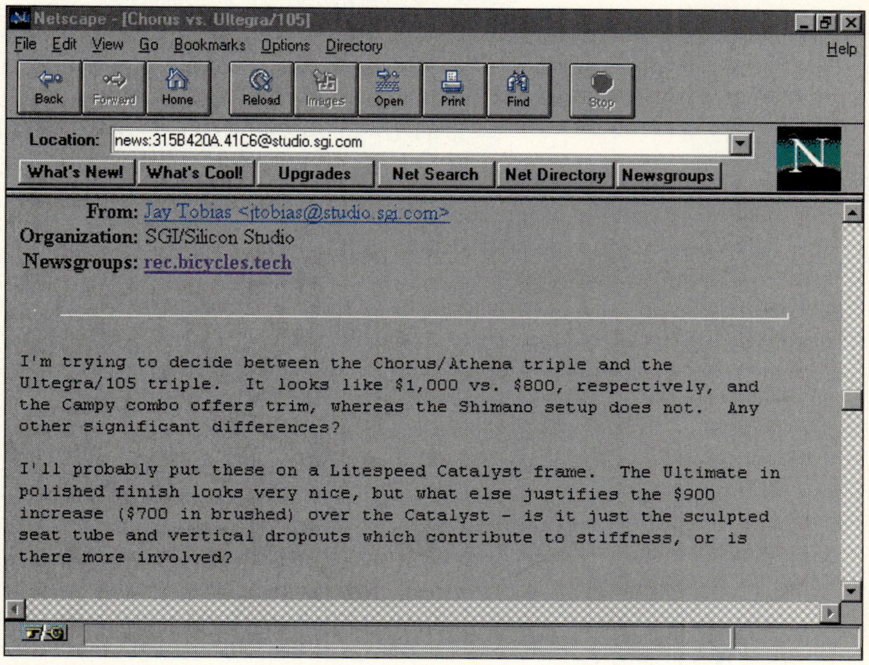

Figure 11

To access the rec.bicycles.tech newsgroup using Netscape:

1 Type **`news:rec.bicycles.tech`** in the Location text field. Note that the title of the text field changes from *Location* to *Go to* as you enter text. The rec.bicycles.tech newsgroup is added to the list of current newsgroups, as shown in Figure 12.

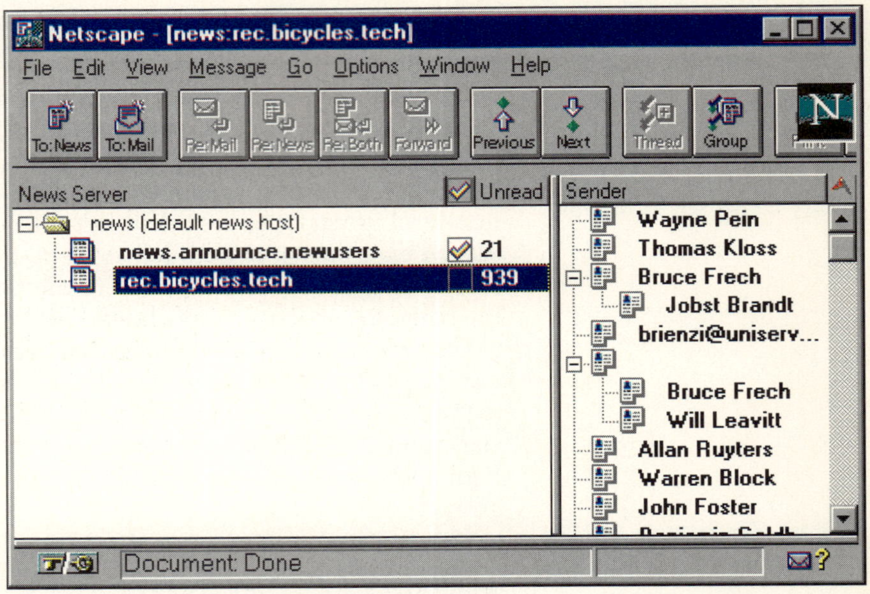

Figure 12

2 Select an article to read from the list of articles appearing in the sender list in the News Server dialog box.

Navigating the Net with Gophers

The Internet ***Gopher*** is a distributed document search and retrieval system. The Web and Gopher have a similar goal in that both resources make accessing information on the Net a simple and straightforward task. They differ, however, in how they are structured. In contrast to Web sites that support links, Gopher sites use a hierarchical menu system to locate Net resources. Gophers began at the University of Minnesota and have quickly spread throughout the worldwide Internet community. You can find information in files that are organized in a Gopher's hierarchical menu system. First you will choose the Internet resource you want, and then you can browse through file offerings and retrieve, or ***download,*** files that interest you. Downloading is the process of copying files from one computer to another through a modem. When you access a Gopher menu, you will generally see two types of data: another menu and a data file. The data file can be text, graphics, or sound. Figure 13 shows a submenu from the University of Minnesota Gopher. The list includes items such as 2 through 7 that, when selected, open other menus (indicated by the slashes), and downloadable text and graphic files. The bracketed text at the end of items 13 through 16 describes what you will get when you download those files—movies and pictures.

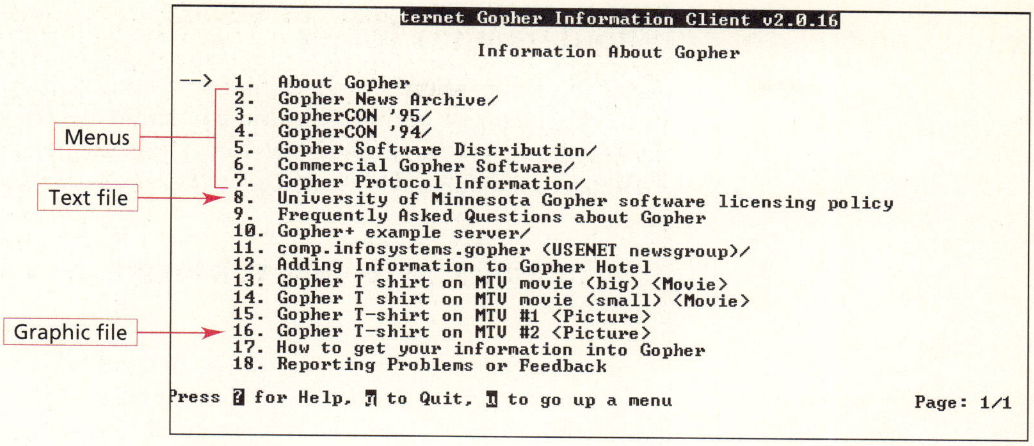

Figure 13

If you have access to the Internet, you can usually access a Gopher site if you know the Gopher server domain name. For example, the Gopher submenu from the University of Minnesota shown in Figure 13 was accessed by typing gopher://gopher.tc.umn.edu in the Netscape Location Go to text box and then selecting the first Gopher menu option. The first term, *gopher://*, runs the Gopher client software needed to access Gopher sites. The phrase *gopher.tc.umn.edu* is the domain name for the University of Minnesota Gopher.

Most commercial providers also provide Gopher access. Figure 14 displays the same Gopher listing, viewed using the Netscape graphical browser. Notice that an icon appears next to each Gopher item, indicating the item's content.

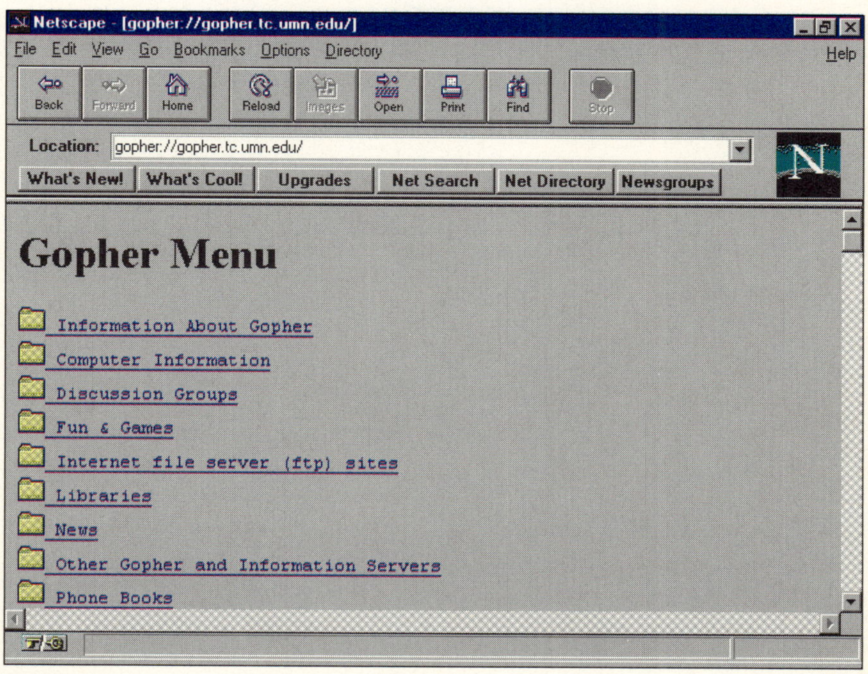

Figure 14

Connecting to Other Computers with Telnet

Accessing and connecting to a computer, whether you are one block away or on the other side of the world, is the function of ***Telnet.*** Many universities and government sites offer Telnet access. For example, the Library of Congress maintains a Telnet site, offering access to an online catalog.

Tip Telnet may not be available, depending upon your system's configuration.

As with other Internet resources, you need to know the domain name for Telnet resources. In addition, you must either have an account on the remote host or use a host that offers a guest (public) account. The opening screen for the Library of Congress online catalog is shown in Figure 15. This site was accessed by entering telnet://locis.loc.gov in the Location text box in Netscape. Typing *telnet* loads the software needed to access remote Telnet sites.

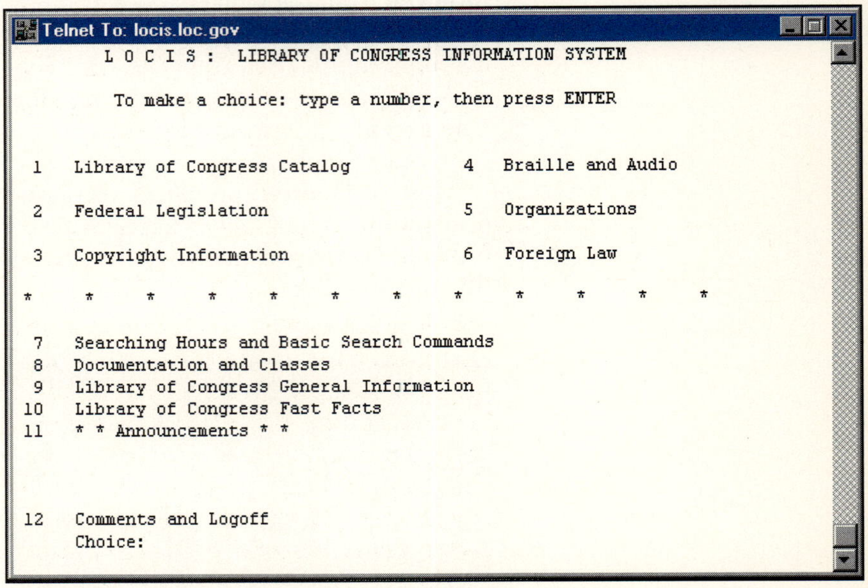

Figure 15

Reminder Notice the top-level designation in this domain name, indicating that this site is maintained by the government.

Once you are connected to a Telnet site, you are an online user and can access anything the computer system will allow you to access. Usually the menus are lines of text. You will respond by moving the arrow key, or typing a one-word response and pressing ENTER and then following any instructions provided on the screen.

Sharing Information Through File Transfer Protocol

One of the exciting uses of the Internet is sharing information. You can access files on computers all over the world and download them to your computer system at home. You can download antivirus software, gather data files to support a term paper, collect photos of interest—the possibilities are endless. ***File Transfer Protocol (FTP),*** is the tool that systems use across the Internet to send files. Many sites, which are computers you can access on the Internet, allow FTP access. FTP servers often include executable program files (files which you can download and launch on your computer). In contrast to Gopher, which is a file resource locator, FTP sites are libraries of downloadable files. When you access a site through FTP, you begin by entering a username and password to connect to the site's host computer. Many sites accept the username anonymous if you enter your Internet address as the password. Once you are connected to the host computer, you can browse through its offerings and download any files that interest you. Later in this chapter you will download a file from Microsoft's anonymous FTP site.

USING THE INTERNET ASSISTANT

While browsing the Web, you may get the impression that designing a home page is a complicated task, since Web sites can contain many links and provide capabilities for e-mail and file downloads. Actually, a home page document is a text file containing HTML tags specifying exactly how the page should be displayed and what should occur in response to actions by the user, such as clicking the text for a link.

Internet Assistant is a flexible tool for Web access and home page construction. Although you can create HTML documents using a text editor and adding the markup tags manually, the Internet Assistant provides a series of tools available on the Formatting toolbar for adding HTML tags to selected text.

The Internet Assistant is a flexible tool for Web access and home page construction. Although you can create HTML documents using a text editor and adding the markup tags manually, the Internet Assistant provides a series of tools available on the Formatting toolbar for adding HTML tags to selected text.

Figure 16 displays the text and HTML markup tags for the Benjamin/ Cummings home page.

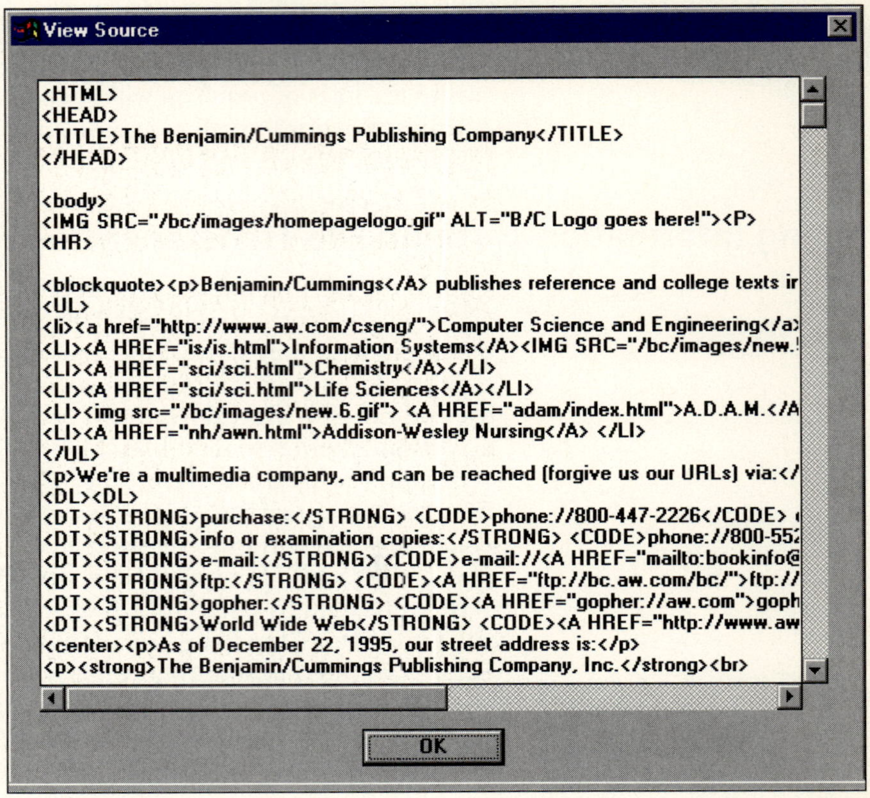

Figure 16

Caution If you are accessing the Internet from a network, check with your information systems director before completing this project. Installing the Internet Assistant will change the configuration of Microsoft Word.

Downloading the Internet Assistant

Before you can use the Internet Assistant, you must acquire it. This add-on is available free of charge from Microsoft. In the following steps you will download the Internet Assistant from Microsoft's FTP site.

To download Microsoft's Internet Assistant

1. Launch Netscape using your computer or network workstation.
2. Type **ftp://ftp.microsoft.com** in the Go to text box, as shown in Figure 17.

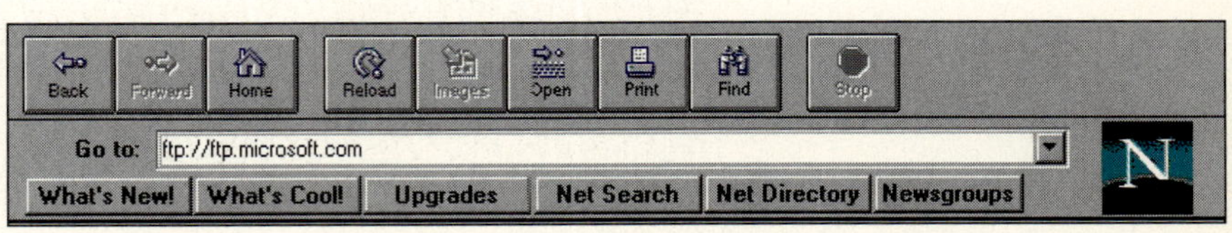

Figure 17

3 Press ENTER

The screen now looks similar to Figure 18.

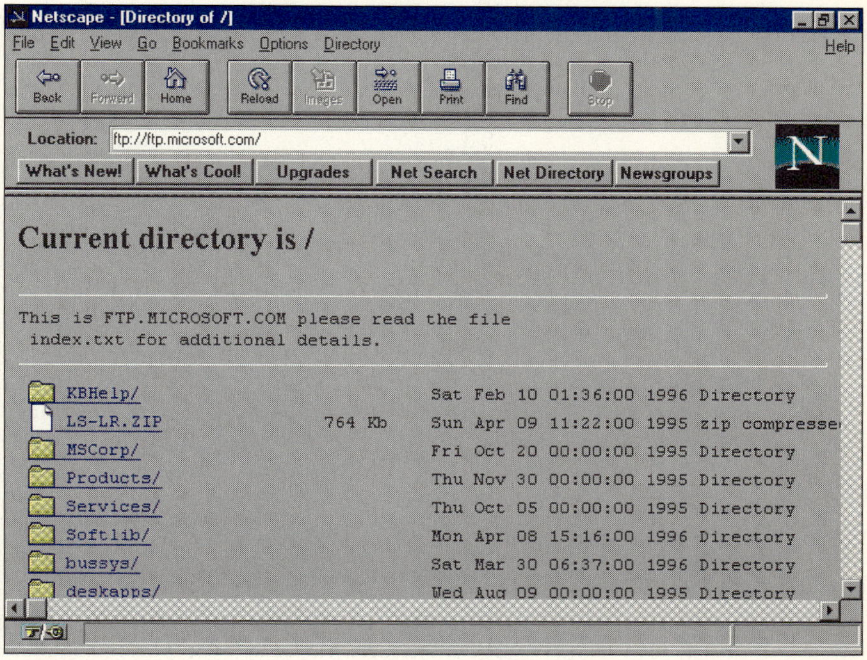

Figure 18

4 Click the Softlib folder.

The Softlib directory similar to the one shown in Figure 19 appears.

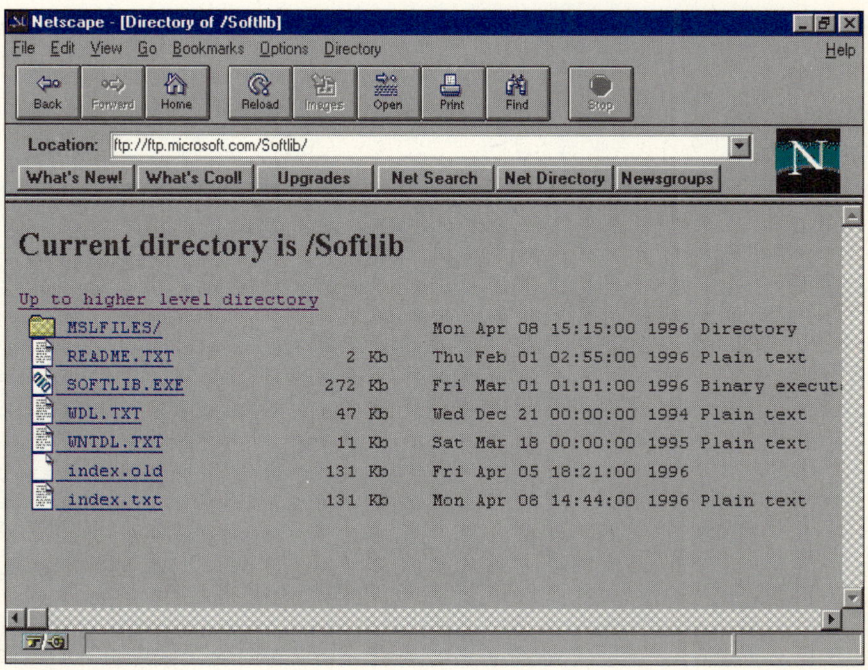

Figure 19

5 Select the MSLFILES subdirectory.
After a few minutes the file list shown in Figure 20 appears.

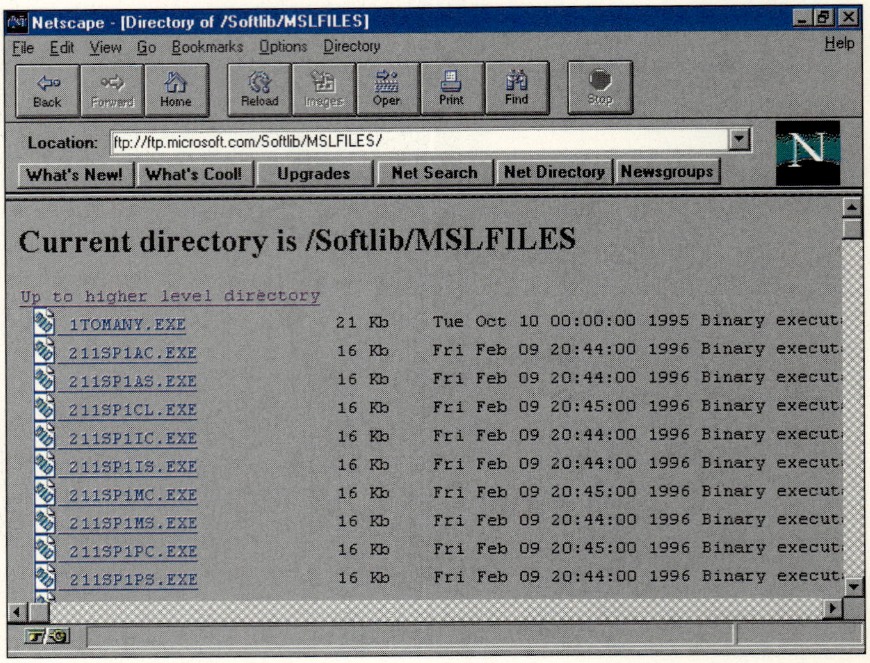

Figure 20

Tip If you are using a text-based interface, remember that some commands are case-sensitive. You may need to type cd\MSLFILES to switch to this subdirectory.

6 Move the vertical scroll bar until the file WORDIA2B.EXE appears, as shown in Figure 21.

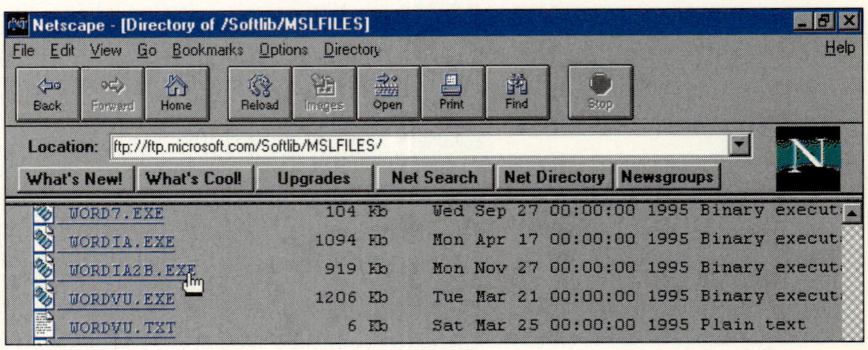

Figure 21

7 Click the filename to download this file.
Depending upon your Netscape version, the dialog box shown in Figure 22 may appear.

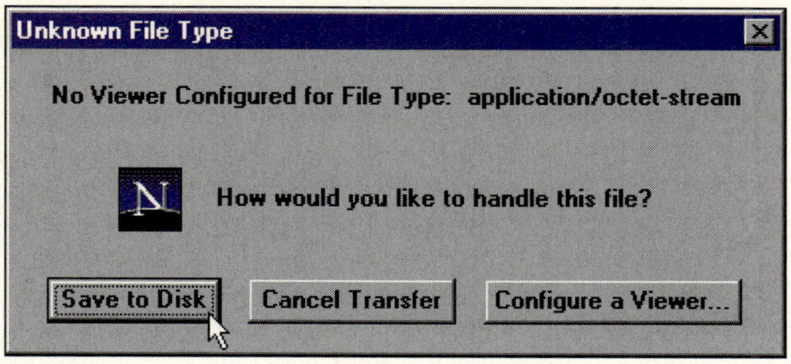

Figure 22

8 Select Save to Disk (if this dialog box appears). The Save As dialog box shown in Figure 23 appears.

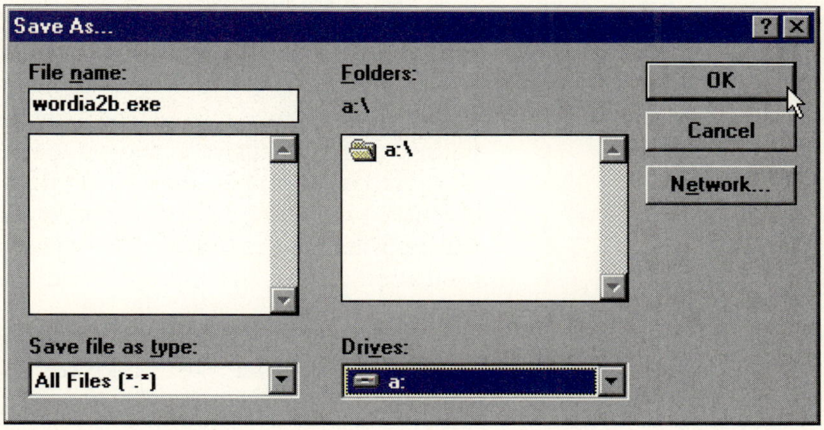

Figure 23

9 Select an appropriate location for saving the file, and click OK. The Saving Location message box shown in Figure 24 appears.

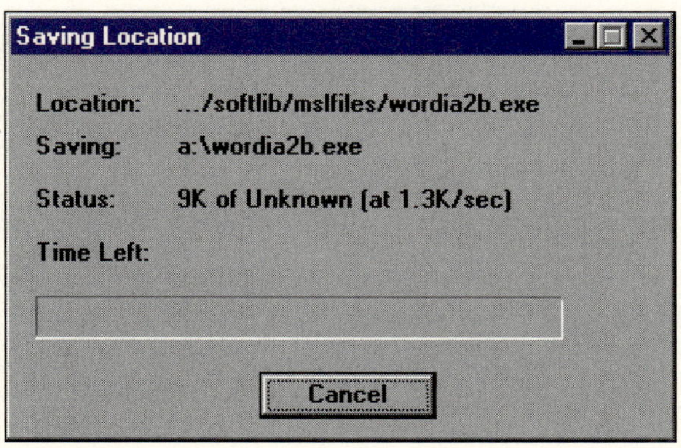

Figure 24

Tip When downloading program (executable) files using a text-based interface, you will need to specify a binary, not ASCII, transfer mode.

Depending on how your computer or network is configured, it can take just a few minutes, 30 minutes, or more to complete the download. The status of the download will be displayed on the screen. When the download is finished, you can quit the FTP session.

Tip If you are using a text-based interface, type **`quit`** at the Unix prompt to end your FTP session. When you return to your local host, close the current communication session.

EXIT If necessary, you can quit now and continue this project later.

Installing the Internet Assistant

If you are using your own personal computer, you will be able to install the Internet Assistant as an add-on for Microsoft Word. If you are using a network computer, you most likely do not have the access privileges necessary to load the Internet Assistant. The steps that follow assume that you are installing the Internet Assistant on your own computer. For network installation contact the appropriate information systems technician at your institution.

To install the Internet Assistant:

1 Locate the subdirectory on your computer that contains Microsoft Word.
If your program files are installed on drive C: and the default directories were used during installation, the Word program files should be in the WINWORD subdirectory.

Caution Microsoft recommends that you do not copy the Internet Assistant executable file into either the WINWORD or the INTERNET subdirectories. If you do, the Internet Assistant will not install properly.

2 Create a subdirectory named IA one level below the WINWORD subdirectory.

3 Copy the file wordia2b.exe into the IA subdirectory.

4 Using the Windows 95 Explorer, locate the WORDIA2B.EXE file.

5 Double-click the WORDIA2B.EXE icon.
The dialog box shown in Figure 25 appears.

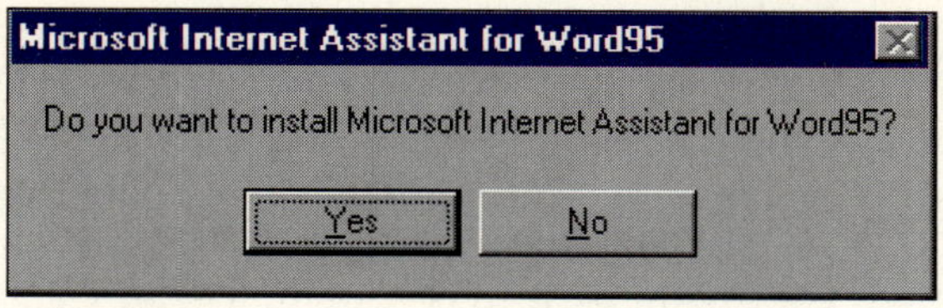

Figure 25

6 Select Yes.

7 Follow the directions for installation as they appear on the screen. When the Internet Assistant installation is successfully completed, the dialog box shown in Figure 26 appears. This dialog box allows you to launch the Internet Assistant or exit the setup program.

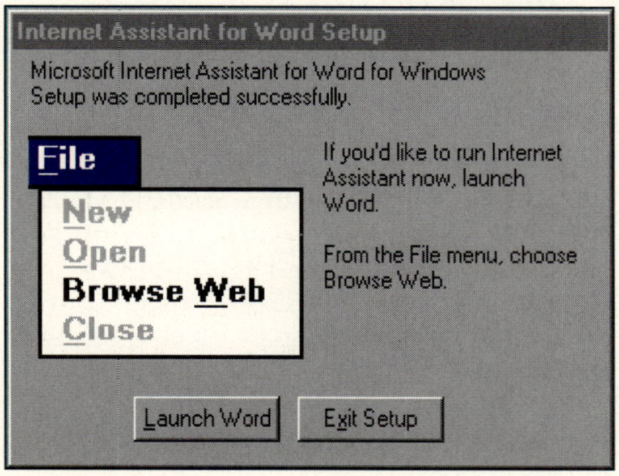

Figure 26

Creating a Home Page Using the Internet Assistant

In this section you will use the Internet Assistant and learn how to construct an HTML document containing three links to other Web documents.

To post a home page on the WWW, you must have access to a Web server. Many organizations and educational institutions have the capability of posting resources on the Web. The four documents you will create here are simple in that they contain only text and therefore will not occupy much space on a Web server.

The first document you create will act as a menu for accessing information about some of the Microsoft Office applications. This document will be named index.htm and will contain links to the other three documents. The second, third, and fourth documents will each contain information about Microsoft Word, Excel, and PowerPoint, and will have the names word.htm, excel.htm, and powerppt.htm, respectively. When you post these four documents to the same location on a Web server, you can access them using either a text-based or a graphical browser by typing the appropriate URL for the index.htm file.

Creating the index.htm Document

You will follow a three-step process for creating Web documents. First you will enter the text. Then you will format the text. Finally, you will add links to other Web resources.

The index.htm document will contain a heading explaining the purpose and contents of your home page. Below this explanation you will enter three links to other documents. Your completed document will look like the one shown in Figure 27.

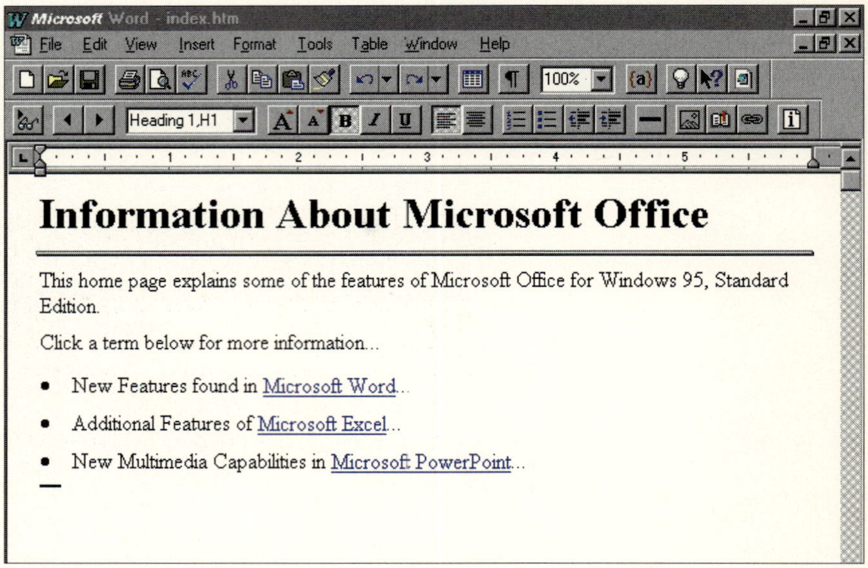

Figure 27

To enter the text for the index.htm document:

1 Start Microsoft Word, if it isn't currently running.

2 Choose New from the File menu.

The New dialog box shown in Figure 28 appears. The General tab should be active. Note the icons for HTMLVIEW and WEBVIEW documents.

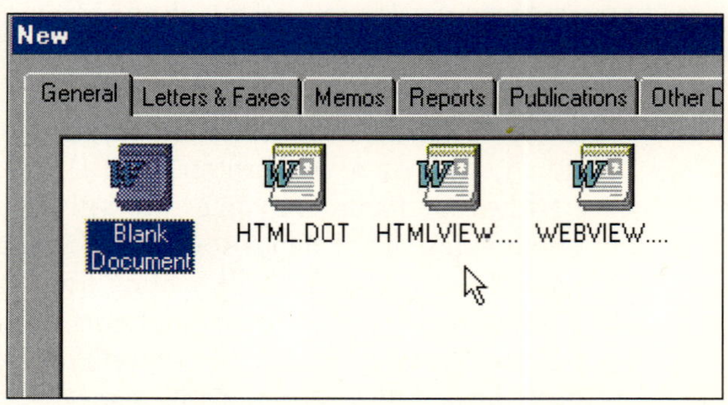

Figure 28

3 Select the WEBVIEW icon, and then select OK.
A blank Word HTML document window appears.

4 Type **`Information About Microsoft Office`** and press ENTER

5 Type **`This home page explains some of the features of Microsoft Office for Windows 95, Standard Edition.`** and press ENTER twice.

6 Type **`Click a term below for more information...`** and press ENTER twice.

7 Type **`New Features found in Microsoft Word...`** and press ENTER twice

8 Type **`Additional Features of Microsoft Excel...`** and press ENTER twice.

9 Type **`New Multimedia Capabilities in Microsoft PowerPoint...`**
The screen should look like Figure 29.

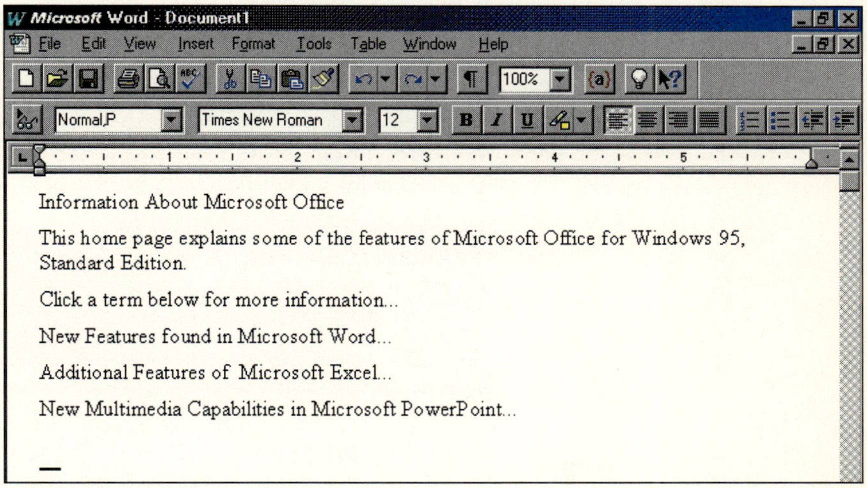

Figure 29

Next you will add formatting tags, or HTML codes, that specify how the text should look when displayed on a text-based or graphical browser.

To format the title and list of options:

1 Highlight the first line of text you entered.

2 Select Heading 1,H1 from the style list in the Formatting toolbar, as shown in Figure 30.

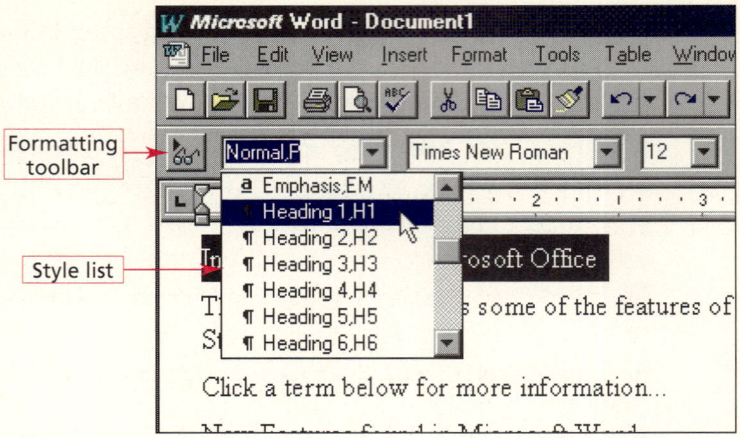

Figure 30

3 Place the insertion point in front of the word *This* in the second line.

4 Click the horizontal rule button on the Formatting toolbar.

5 Select the last three lines.

6 Select the Listbullets style from the style list in the Formatting toolbar. Your document should now look like Figure 31.

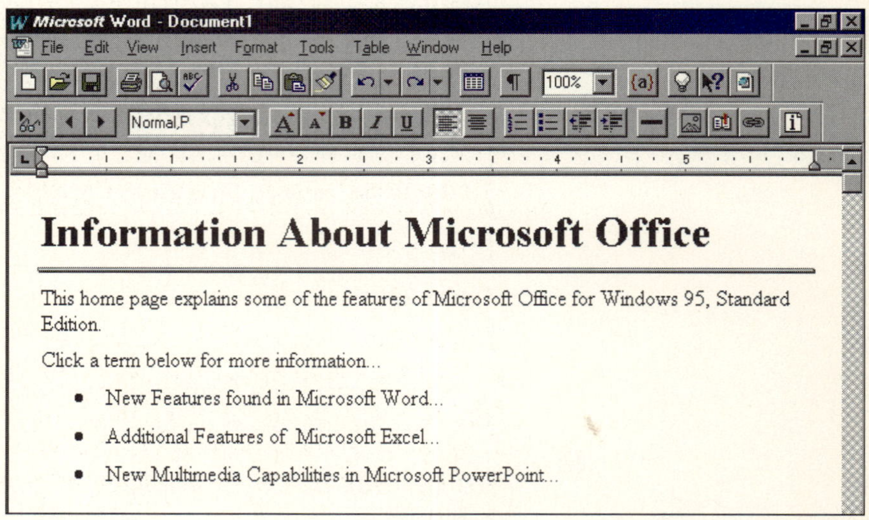

Figure 31

7 Select Save from the File menu.
Since you began this document as an HTMLVIEW document, the default name is HTML document for the World Wide Web.htm.

8 Type `index` in the File name text box.

9 Make sure the file type is set to HTML Document, and then select OK.

> ***Tip*** Microsoft Windows 95 supports file names of up to 255 characters. However, since many Web documents are posted on Unix-based servers, it is best to name the file with eight or fewer characters.

To complete the index.htm document, you need to add tags that specify the documents that will be linked to this file. Links are defined by ***anchors,*** which are HTML tags that reference information at a different location in the current document, information in a separate document on the current server, or information in a document on a server half way around the world. Anchors are what give Web documents their hypermedia capabilities.

Although you have not created the other documents yet, in this section you will add anchors specifying the documents that you will create in the next section.

To add anchors to the index.htm document:

1 Highlight the phrase *Microsoft Word* in the index.htm document.

2 Select the Anchor button on the Formatting toolbar.
The Hyperlink dialog box appears.

3 Type **`word.htm`** as the file name, as shown in Figure 32.

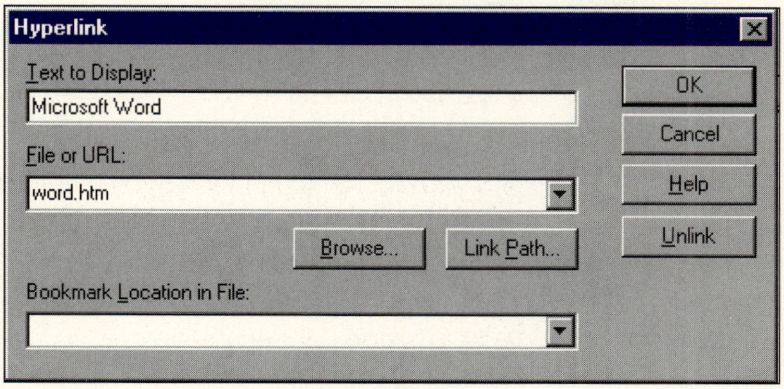

Figure 32

4 Repeat these steps for the phrases *Microsoft Excel* and *Microsoft PowerPoint,* naming the links excel.htm and powerppt.htm respectively.

5 Select the Save button on the Formatting toolbar to save these changes. Each of the links should appear as blue text that is underlined, indicating that each phrase is now a hot spot that can be used to access linked Web resources.

EXIT If necessary, you can quit now and continue this project later.

Creating Three Additional HTML Documents

Before you post the index.htm document to a Web server, the documents linked to this one must be created. Each document will consist of a title, horizontal rule, and text. At the bottom of each document will be an anchor to return to the index.htm document.

To create the word.htm document:

1 Choose New from the File menu. With the General tab active, select the icon for an HTMLVIEW document.

2 Type **`New Features of Microsoft Word`** and press ENTER twice.

3 Type the following paragraph, and press ENTER twice when you are finished:

`Microsoft Word 7.0 has features that make it even easier to create sophisticated documents than with previous versions of Word. For example, Word now contains tools for automatic borders and numbered or bulleted lists. Autocorrect now flags misspelled words by underlining them in red for easy detection. Finally, Word can now be used as an e-mail editor by taking advantage of Microsoft Exchange.`

4 Type **`Click here to Return to Information About Microsoft Office...`**

5 Choose Save from the File menu, and type **`word.htm`** as the file name. Make sure you save the document as an HTML file.

> ***Tip*** You must save the file as an HTML document before adding an anchor tag.

6 Highlight the entire line that begins with *Click here to Return.*

7 Click the Anchor button on the Formatting toolbar.

8 Type **`index.htm`** as the file name in the Hyperlink dialog box.

9 Highlight the first line of the document, and set the style to Heading2,H2.

10 Choose Save from the File menu to save your most recent changes. The completed document should look like Figure 33.

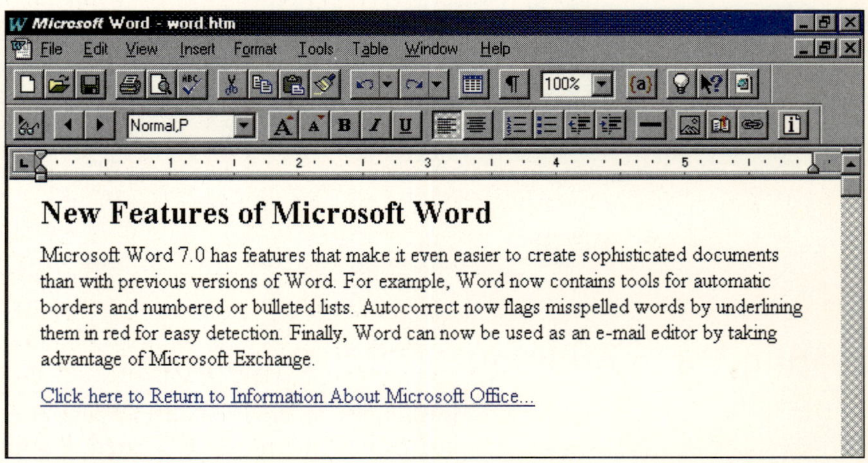

Figure 33

To create the excel.htm and powerppt.htm documents:

1 Choose New from the file menu. With the General tab active, select the icon for an HTML document.

2 Type **`Additional Features of Microsoft Excel`** as the document heading, and apply the Heading 2,H2 style.

3 Type the following paragraph as the document text:
`Microsoft Excel is also new and improved. AutoCalculate, AutoComplete, and AutoCorrect monitor the development of your worksheet application. Numbers are now easier to format. Finally, Excels' Automap feature allows you to create stunning geographical maps based upon your demographic data.`

4 Save this document with the file name excel.htm.

5 Add the same line of text with the anchor tag to return to the index.htm document that you added to word.htm.

6 Save the document again.

> ***Tip*** If the word.htm document is still open, you can use copy and paste to copy this anchor from word.htm to excel.htm.

7 Repeat step 1 to create a final document named powerppt.htm. Type **`New Multimedia Capabilities in Microsoft PowerPoint...`** as the heading, and apply the Heading 2,H2 style.

8 Type the following paragraph as the document text:
`Microsoft PowerPoint now has new multimedia capabilities to enhance the effectiveness of your presentations. You may add sounds, music, textures, photos, and media clips to your presentations. In addition, you can use the Slide Navigator during a presentation to jump to any slide out of sequence.`

9 Save this document with the file name powerppt.htm.

10 Apply the same anchor to this document that you applied to the word.htm and excel.htm documents, and then save your changes.

You are finished creating your HTML documents! Close each document so they can be posted to your Web server.

Posting HTML Documents to a Web Server

To add HTML documents to the World Wide Web, you must have copied them to the same location on a Web server. This step is necessary because the links specified in each document are relative, which means that only the file name of the linked document and not its Web location is specified. You may need to contact your information systems director or network manager for assistance in posting your HTML documents to a Web server.

Once your documents are posted, you may use any Web browser to view them. Figure 34 shows how the index.htm document appears using Netcom's Netscape browser.

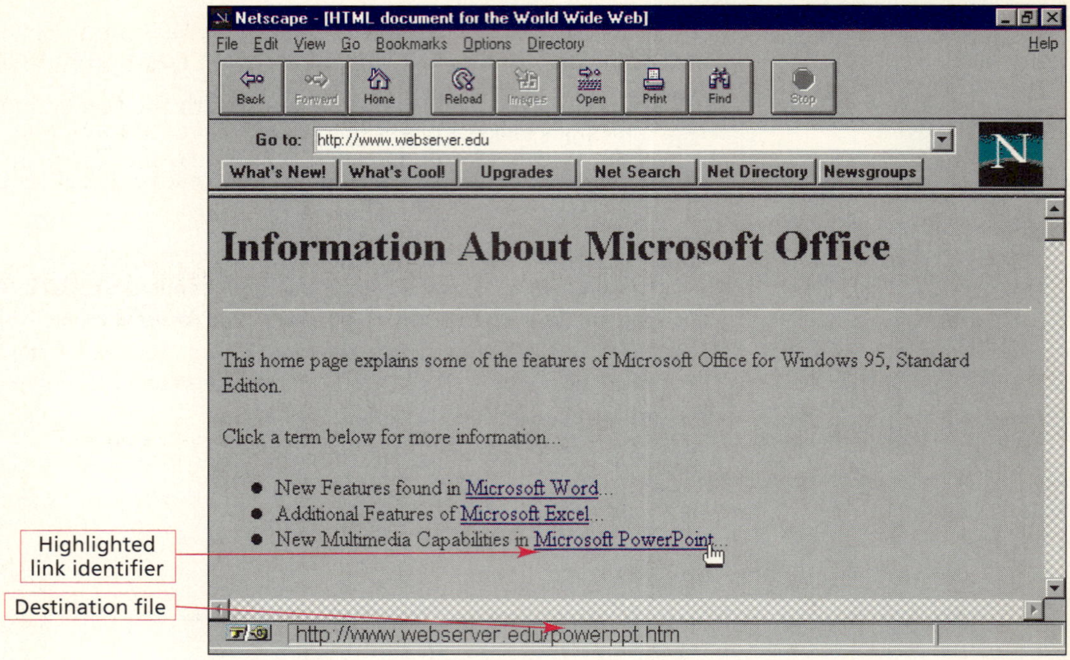

Figure 34

Notice that the pointer in Figure 34 is directly over the link for information about Microsoft PowerPoint. In the lower-left corner, the file name powerppt.htm appears. This specifies the document that will be displayed when you select the link. Clicking this link will cause the powerppt.htm document to be displayed, as shown in Figure 35.

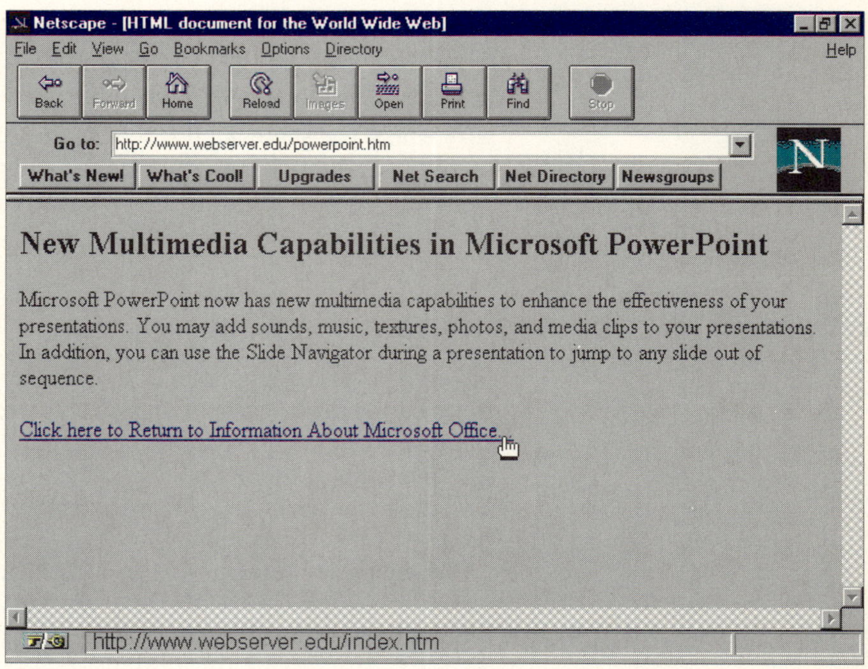

Figure 35

Although you used Microsoft's Internet Assistant to create your HTML documents, you can use any text editor to enter text and HTML tags. You can add images, sound, and media clips to HTML documents by specifying the appropriate file names for these resources in the tags specifying where they are to appear in the document. Figure 36 shows the source text for the index.htm document.

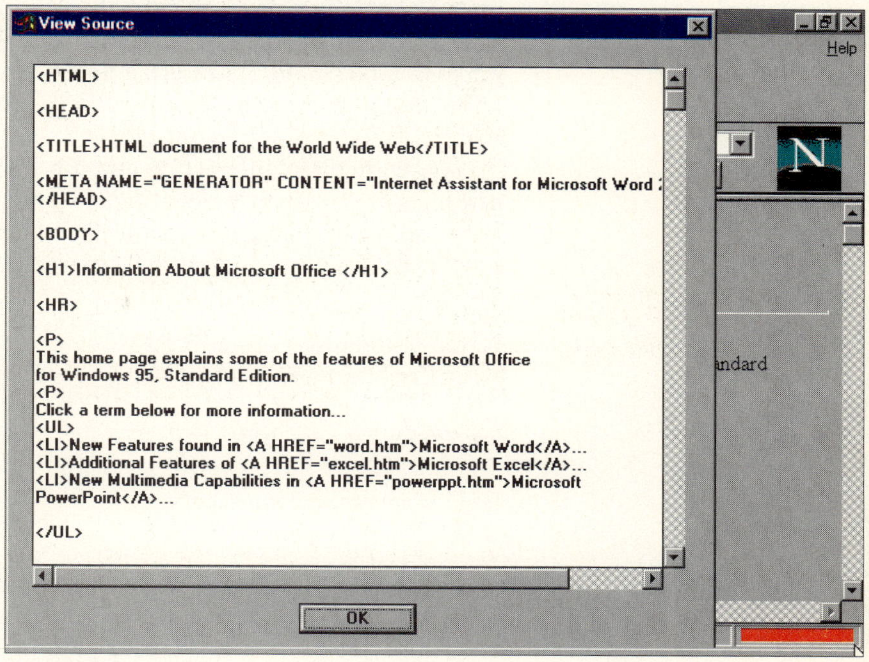

Figure 36

All HTML tags are enclosed within the greater-than and less-than characters (< and >). Table 3 explains the HTML codes displayed in Figure 36.

Table 3 HTML Codes

HTML Tag	Purpose
<HTML>	A structure tag specifying this as an HTML document
<HEAD>	A structure tag enclosing the heading of the document
<TITLE><?TITLE>	Indicates the title of the document
<META>	Indicates meta-information about the document
<BODY>	Encloses the body (text and tags) of the document
<H1></H1>	Encloses text to be displayed as a level-1 heading
<HR>	Indicates a horizontal rule line
<P>	Specifies a plain paragraph
<UL></UL>	Specifies an unordered (bulleted) list
<LI>	A list of items enclosed within the list
<A></A>	With HREF specifies a link to another document
HREF	The URL of a linked document

The Next Step

In this introduction you learned how to use basic Internet resources such as e-mail, newsgroups, IRC, Gopher, Telnet, and the World Wide Web. You also experienced creating HTML documents, which introduced you to how information is accessed on the Web. There are other tools you can use to find your way around the Internet. Spend some time researching the Archie (via FTP) and Veronica (via Gopher) tools. Go to your library and find some books on the Internet and read about European sites. Did you know that you can actually download pictures of paintings at the Louvre in Paris?

There are many interesting and fun FTP and Web sites available. The offerings are constantly changing, so don't be surprised if a site you accessed last month has changed dramatically or is no longer available. Here are a few Web sites you may want to experience at your leisure:

Uniform Resource Locator (URL)	Description
http://www.yahoo.com	One of the best indexes of Web sites
http://www.microsoft.com	Microsoft's Web site, which includes download capabilities
http://white.nosc.mil/sandiego.html	The city of San Diego has a beautiful home page with lots of interesting photos
http://www.stones.com	Home page of the Rolling Stones
http://www.cba.uh.edu/ylowpges/yc.html	A listing of other Web sites, a "yellow pages" for the Web

The electronic capabilities are mind boggling. Electronic mail, coupled with the power of the Internet, can actually make our planet smaller as we travel the globe and communicate with people all over the world—all without leaving the comfort of home.

Summary and Exercises

Summary

- The Internet is a system of networked computers from all over the world that began out of ARPANET about 30 years ago.
- You can access the Internet through a school or business that has access or through a commercial provider, bulletin board service, or an independent network offering the service.
- The Internet uses both text-based interfaces and graphical user interfaces.
- Electronic mail is a product as well as the process of sending and receiving messages electronically.
- Electronic mail can be sent to anyone with an e-mail or an Internet address.
- An e-mail address is made up of two components: your name and a computer name.

- E-mail address components are separated by the @ sign, and the computer name identifiers are separated by dots.
- When communicating on the Net, you need to keep netiquette rules of social behavior.
- Emoticons are symbols that you can type to help you express your true feelings when you communicate with others on the Net.
- Newsgroups are forums for the exchange of ideas and information.
- Gophers are computers that allow you to search and retrieve documents.
- Telnet allows you to connect to remote computers throughout the world, provided you have a valid username and password.
- Data can be downloaded from computers on the Internet onto your computer.
- File Transfer Protocol lets you download files from the Internet onto your home computer.
- The World Wide Web is a global hypermedia system providing access to text, image, sound, and video resources.
- The Internet Assistant can be used to create HTML documents.

Key Terms and Operations

Key Terms
anchor
bookmark
browser
domain name
dot
download
electronic mail (e-mail)
e-mail address
emoticon
File Transfer Protocol (FTP)
Gopher
graphical user interface (GUI)
history
home page
host
hypertext
hypertext markup language (HTML)
Hypertext Transport Protocol (HTTP)
interface
Internet (Net)
Internet protocol
Internet protocol address
JAVA
link
mail editor
mail server
navigate
netiquette
newsgroup
site
tag
Telnet
text-based (character-based) interface
top-level domain
uniform resource locator (URL)
Virtual Reality Modeling Language (VRML)
Web server
World Wide Web (WWW, Web)

Study Questions

Multiple Choice

1. The Internet is
   a. a network of thousands of computers spanning the globe.
   b. the term used to describe a network of computers residing in the same building.
   c. accessible only to government and education employees.
   d. a network of e-mail servers providing e-mail delivery to members of the Internet Association.

2. The Internet Assistant is a
   a. toll-free number for getting advice on using the Internet.
   b. commercial Internet service provider.
   c. Microsoft add-in for Microsoft Word.
   d. MIS person responsible for maintaining a school's host computers.
3. A link on a home page is most often used to
   a. conduct Gopher searches.
   b. read articles posted to a newsgroup.
   c. connect to another Web resource.
   d. Telnet to another Internet host.
4. A graphical user interface will
   a. always be needed to access the Internet.
   b. display data screens with icons and pictures that can be activated by clicking a mouse.
   c. never work on an IBM PC.
   d. display text and numbers so that the user doesn't need a mouse.
5. Electronic mail is
   a. used extensively around the world as a means of communication.
   b. limited to communication between users on the same local area network.
   c. only used when people cannot send mail through the postal service.
   d. always confidential; only the recipient can read it.
6. File Transfer Protocol is
   a. a network of computers that can be accessed and looked at.
   b. a software tool that allows files to be downloaded from an FTP site to your computer.
   c. a way of sending attachments to your e-mail messages.
   d. another way of sending electronic mail.
7. If you have a computer, communications software, and a modem, you can
   a. access the Internet directly.
   b. access the Internet only during the netiquette prime-time hours.
   c. access the Internet through your school, business, bulletin board, or a commercial provider.
   d. send e-mail through the Internet without a special e-mail address.
8. A mail server is
   a. an icon on the screen that looks like a waiter in a restaurant and is used to access the Internet.
   b. a computer that receives e-mail messages for users and holds them until the user picks up the e-mail.
   c. not available through a text-based interface.
   d. never used after midnight, according to netiquette rules.

9. The Internet is
   a. a complex network of computers run by the International Network Association.
   b. an informal organization designed to regulate standards of international networking hardware and software.
   c. a global network of computers that evolved from the United States Department of Defense Advanced Research Projects Agency network.
   d. an internal network organization in the United States for use by educational institutions only.
10. The difference between a graphical user interface and a character-based interface is that
    a. a graphical user interface requires use of a Macintosh computer to interpret the graphical images, and a character-based interface requires a DOS-based PC.
    b. the character-based interface was written in the BASIC programming language, and the graphical user interface was written in Visual BASIC.
    c. the graphical user interface relies on a complex, high-speed modem to process the images, and the character-based interface does not need a modem at all.
    d. a character-based interface presents a screen of words and numbers, and a graphical user interface uses the mouse to make selections from menus and icons, and displays graphic images and photographs on the screen.

Short Answer

1. How did the Internet come into existence?
2. What are some of the uses of the Internet?
3. What does Telnet do and how does it work?
4. What are newsgroups?
5. How are the newsgroups used to communicate?
6. What is FTP?
7. Explain netiquette and why it is important.
8. What are Gophers and what is their function?
9. What is a home page?
10. What is HTML and when is it used?

For Discussion

1. Why is the Internet a valuable tool?
2. Why is netiquette so important?
3. Would you or do you use the Internet? Explain why you use it or why you would not choose to use it.
4. Describe the World Wide Web. Why is the Web so popular?
5. What is HTML? How is HTML used to create a home page?

Review Exercise

Download a File from Microsoft ftp Server

1. Use ftp to connect to the Microsoft ftp site.
2. Locate the Softlib subdirectory ftp://microsoft.com/softlib and go to MSL file subdirectory.
3. Download a file of your choice.

Assignment

Create a Home Page

Use the Internet Assistant to create a home page on your favorite vacation destination(s). Consider including the following:

- a heading
- a brief introduction
- a related graphic or photo of your destination
- a bulleted list of tips on what to see and do
- suggestions for places to stay and where to eat
- an e-mail link to your e-mail address
- text links to other related travel sights

Operations Reference

FILE

Button	Menu Option	Keys	Description	Word	Excel	Access	PowerPoint	Binder
	New	CTRL+N	Creates a new table, query form, report, macro, or module.			•		
	New (Database) (Binder)	CTRL+N	Creates a new document, worksheet or presentation file. Creates a new database.	•	•	•	•	•
	Open (Database) (Binder)	CTRL+O	Opens an existing document, workbook, presentation, or database.	•	•	•	•	•
	Get External Data					•		
	Close (Database)	CTRL+F4	Closes a document, database, worksheet, or presentation file.	•	•	•	•	
	Rename		Renames a selected object.			•		
	Save	CTRL+S	Saves the current document.	•	•	•	•	•
	Save As		Saves the current document under a new name.	•	•		•	•
	Save As/Export		Save the current action or object under a new name		•	•	•	
 (No button option for Binder)	Properties (Database) (Binder)		View and change document properties		•	•	•	•
	Pack And Go		Packages your presentation for delivery to another computer.				•	

Button	Menu Option	Keys	Description	Word	Excel	Access	PowerPoint
	Send to Genigraphics		Sends your presentation to Genigraphics for overnight imaging to 35mm slides, posters, etc.				•
	Send		Sends the active presentation through electronic mail.				•
	Add Routing Slip		Adds or changes the electronic mail routing slip of the active document.		•		•
	Find File		Searches a disk by a specific file name or other attributes.	•	•		
	Summary Info		Displays or modifies information about the open document.	•	•		
	Slide Setup		Modifies the size and orientation of a slide or slides.				•
	Page Setup		Sets page layout: margins, orientation, paper size, treatment of headers and footers, and so on.	•	•	•	
	Print Area		Allows setting or clearing the print area.		•		
	Print Preview		Previews printer output on-screen.	•	•	•	
	Print	CTRL + P	Prints the current document, worksheet, or presentation.	•	•	•	•
	Send		Sends output from current object to electronic mail.		•	•	
	Exit		Closes application and exits to Windows.	•	•	•	•
	Save All		Saves all open documents and components.	•			
	Template		Lists templates.	•			

SECTION

Button	Menu Option	Keys	Description	Word	Excel	Access	PowerPoint	Binder
	Add		Adds a new section to a Binder document.					•
	Add from File		Adds a new section from an existing file to a Binder document					•

EDIT

Button	Menu Option	Keys	Description	Word	Excel	Access	PowerPoint
	Undo	CTRL + Z	Undoes the last operation.	•	•	•	•
	Repeat	CTRL + Y	Repeats the last operation.	•	•		•
	Cut	CTRL + X	Cuts selected text to clipboard.	•	•	•	•
	Copy	CTRL + C	Copies selected text to clipboard.	•	•	•	•
	Paste	CTRL + V	Pastes clipboard text segment into document.	•	•	•	•
	Create Shortcut		Places a shortcut to the selected object on the Windows 95 desktop.			•	
	Paste Special		Pastes or embeds formats, values, or other attributes of information from the clipboard to a selection.	•	•		•
	Clear	DEL	Erases contents and/or formats from a selection.	•	•		•
	Delete	DEL (Access)	Deletes a marked block or object at the cursor.		•	•	
	Delete Sheet		Removes an entire sheet from the workbook.		•		

Button	Menu Option	Keys	Description	Word	Excel	Access	PowerPoint
	Move or Copy Sheet		Changes order of sheets in workbook or duplicates sheets in workbook.		•		
	Select All	CTRL+A	Selects entire document.	•			•
	Duplicate	CTRL+D	Duplicates the selected slide or object.				•
	Delete Slide		Removes the selected slide from the presentation.				•
	Find	CTRL+F	Finds specified text.	•	•		•
	Delete Slide		Removes the selected slide from the presentation.				•
	Find	CTRL+F	Finds specified text.	•	•		•
	Replace	CTRL+H	Replaces one text string with another.	•	•		•
	Go To Property		Displays properties.				•
	Go To	CTRL+G	Goes to certain page (or other marker).	•	•		
	Links		Connects an object in the active file with a file on disk.	•	•		•
	Object		Switches the selected object into the edit mode.	•	•		•
	Bookmark		Creates for selected text, graphics or other elements.	•			
	AutoText		Creates an AutoText entry from selected text or frequently used graphics. Inserts AutoText entry into a document.	•			

View

Button	Menu Option	Keys	Description	Word	Excel	Access	PowerPoint
	Normal		Displays in normal editing view.	•			
	Slides		Selects the single Slide view mode.				•
	Outline		Displays in Outline view.	•			•
	Page Layout		Displays in Page Layout view.	•			
	Formula Bar		Displays/hides formula bar.		•		
	Status Bar		Displays/hides status bar.		•		
	Full screen		Displays file contents only (no menus, toolbars, etc.).	•	•		
	Slide Sorter		Selects the Slide Sorter view mode.				•
	Notes Pages		Selects the Notes Pages view mode.				•
	Slide Show		Selects the Slide Show view mode.				•
	Master		Accesses the Master slide menu.				•
	Black and White		Displays the presentation in black and white (toggle).				•
	Slide Miniature		Shows or hides the slide preview window (toggle).				•
	Toolbars		Displays or hides toolbars.	•	•	•	•
	Ruler		Displays or hides ruler(s).	•			•
	Guides		Turns on/off vertical and horizontal guides on the screen.				•
	Header and Footer		Shows headers and footers.	•			•
	Footnotes		Opens Footnote window.	•			
	Zoom		Increases/decreases document magnification.	•	•		•
	Master Document		Displays master document as an outline.	•			
	Annotations		Displays annotations from the document.	•			

Insert

Button	Menu Option	Keys	Description	Word	Excel	Access	PowerPoint
	Break		Inserts page, column, or section break.	•			
	Symbol		Inserts special symbol.	•			
	Footnote		Inserts footnote reference.	•			
	File		Inserts another file into document.	•			
	Frame		Inserts selected text or object into frame.	•			
	Object		Inserts object, such as WordArt object, equation, graph, and so on.	•	•		•
	Database		Inserts a database into the document.	•			
	Cells		Inserts a range of cells, shifting worksheet contents to make room.		•		
	Rows		Inserts row(s) into worksheet, shifting other information down.		•		
	Columns		Inserts column(s) into worksheet, shifting other information right.		•		
	Worksheet		Inserts a new worksheet before current worksheet in workbook.		•		
	Chart		Creates a chart (as new sheet or as embedded chart).		•		
	Macro		Inserts a macro module sheet, a dialog sheet, or an Excel macro.		•		

Button	Menu Option	Keys	Description	Word	Excel	Access	PowerPoint
	Page Break		Forces a printout page break at the current cell location.		•		
	Function		Uses Function Wizard to step through building a function.		•		
	Name		Creates named range or names constant.		•		
	Note		Creates cell note.		•		
New Slide...	New Slide	CTRL+M	Inserts a new slide following the current slide.				•
	Tab		Inserts a tab stop character when editing text.				•
	Page Number		Inserts page numbering on a master slide.	•			
	Slide Number		Adds slide numbers.				•
	Slides from File		Inserts slides from a disk file in the active presentation.				•
	Slides from Outline		Creates slides from a text outline on disk.				•
	Clip Art		Adds an image from the clip art library to the current slide.	•	•		•
	Picture		Adds a graphic file to the current slide.	•	•		•
	Movie		Adds a movie to the slide.				•
	Sound		Adds sound to the slide.				•
	Map		Allows inserting one of several maps into the worksheet.		•		
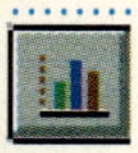	Microsoft Graph		Adds a Microsoft graph to the current Slide.				•
	Microsoft Word Table		Adds a Microsoft Word table to the current slide.				•
	Annotation		Inserts an annotation mark.	•			
	Date and Time		Inserts the date or time.	•			•
	Field		Inserts a field.	•			
	Form Field		Inserts a text check box or a drop-down form field.	•			

Button	Menu Option	Keys	Description	Word	Excel	Access	PowerPoint
	Caption		Inserts captions to document items.	•			
	Cross-reference		Inserts a cross-reference to an item in a document.	•			
	Index and Tables		Creates indexes, Tables of Contents, figure tables and tables of authorities.	•			
	Table		Inserts a new table in the current database			•	
	Query		Inserts a new query in the current database			•	
	Form		Inserts a new form in the current database			•	
	Report		Inserts a new report in the current database			•	
	Macro		Inserts a new macro in the current database.			•	
	Module		Inserts a new module in the current database.			•	
	AutoForm		Inserts a new form in the current database			•	
	AutoReport		Inserts a new report in the current database.			•	

FORMAT

Button	Menu Option	Keys	Description	Word	Excel	Access	PowerPoint
 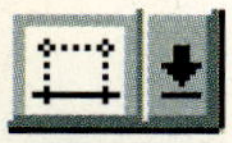 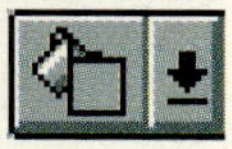	Alignment Protection Borders Patterns Cells		Controls the appearance, alignment, font characteristics, and so on, of cell contents.		•		
	Font		Sets character formats.	•			•
	Paragraph		Sets paragraph formats.	•			
	Tabs		Sets, changes, and clears tabs.	•			
	Borders and Shading		Formats paragraphs and tables with borders and shading.	•			
	Row		Controls height of row and whether row is hidden.		•		
	Column		Sets width and number of columns in Word, controls height and whether column is hidden in Excel.	•	•		
	Sheet		Sets name of sheet on tab, hides/displays sheet.		•		
	AutoFormat		Applies combinations of formats automatically.	•	•		
	Change Case	SHFT + F3	Switches from capital to lowercase letters or vice versa.	•			•
	Bullets and Numbering		Establishes bulleted or numbered lists. In PowerPoint, changes bullet character for selected text.	•			•
	Style		Defines, edits, and applies styles.	•			
	Placement		Changes the display of overlapping objects.		•		

Button	Menu Option	Keys	Description	Word	Excel	Access	PowerPoint
	Frame		Adjusts size and position of frame.	•			
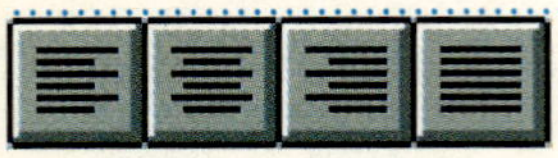	Alignment		Aligns selected text left, right, or centered between margins.				•
	Line Spacing		Sets line spacing for selected text.				•
	Text Anchor		Adjusts the shape of a text object within a graphic object.				•
	Colors and Lines		Changes lines and fill colors.				•
	Shadow		Adjusts the shadow around an object.				•
	Pick Up Object Style		Picks up the text and object attributes of the selection.				•
	Apply Object Style		Applies the previously picked up text and object attributes to the selection.				•
	Slide Layout		Displays available AutoLayouts.				•
	Custom Background		Changes background color or shading.				•
	Slide Color Scheme		Changes color of one or more elements in a slide.				•
	Apply Design Template		Applies the format from an existing presentation to the active presentation.				•
	Drop Cap		Formats paragraph with a drop cap.	•			
	Heading numbering		Creates a numbered list from a series of styled headings.	•			
	Style Gallery		Applies the style from a selected template to the active document.	•			
	Picture		Inserts a graphic from another application.	•			
	Drawing Object		Changes formatting elements of drawing objects.	•			

TOOLS

Button	Menu Option	Keys	Description	Word	Excel	Access	PowerPoint
	Spelling	F7	Checks spelling.	•	•	•	•
	Thesaurus	SHFT + F7	Suggests alternative word choices.	•			
	Word Count		Counts words, characters, paragraphs, lines, or pages.	•			
	AutoCorrect		Lists errors to be automatically corrected.	•	•	•	•
	AutoClipArt		Recommends ClipArt for your presentation.				•
	Style Checker		Checks for inconsistencies in the active presentation.				•
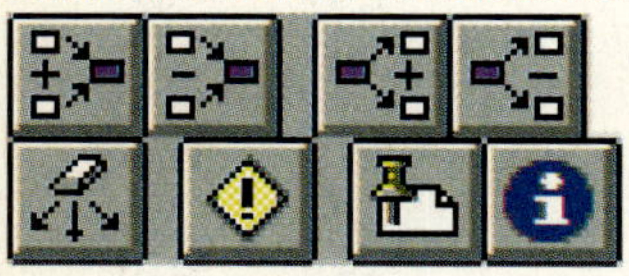	Auditing		Traces cell precedents, dependents, and errors; displays cell notes.		•		
	Look Up Reference		Searches external reference material for key words or phrases.		•		
	Protection		Activates/deactivates sheet and workbook protection.		•		
	Macro		Allows macros to be run or edited.	•	•		
	Record Macro		Records commands into a macro.		•		
	Replace Fonts		Replaces one typeface with another throughout the active presentation.				•
	Slide Transition		Applies a special effect during a change from one slide to the next slide.				•
	Hide Slide		Skips a slide during a slide show.				•
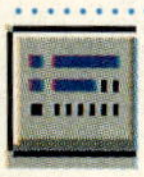	Build Slide Text		Causes items in a list to appear one at a time during a slide show.				•

Button	Menu Option	Keys	Description	Word	Excel	Access	PowerPoint
	Animation Settings		Chooses how objects appear on screen during a slide show.				•
	Interactive Settings		Chooses how Objects react when clicked during a slide show.				•
	Meeting Minder		Displays Notes pages, meeting minutes, and action items.				•
	Presentation Conference		Puts on a presentation over a network.				•
	Write-Up		Creates handouts in Word for the active presentation.				•
	Recolor		Recolors the selected picture, graph, or slide.				•
	Crop Picture		Hides portions of the selected picture.				•
	Customize		Edits menus and toolbars.	•			•
	Options		Changes various options.	•	•		•
	Grammar		Checks document for grammar errors and displays suggested corrections.	•			
	Hyphenation		Inserts proper hyphens.	•			
	Language		Designates selected text's language.	•			
	Mail Merge		Merges main document with data source.	•			
	Envelopes and Labels		Prints envelopes and labels.	•			
	Protect Document		Protects documents from alterations.	•			
	Revisions		Traces revisions made to a document.	•			
	OfficeLinks		Exports data to other office applications.			•	
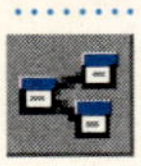	Relationships		Set up or modify relationships between tables.			•	

Button	Menu Option	Keys	Description	Word	Excel	Access	PowerPoint
	Analyze		Analyze table structure and performance, and display documentation about a table.			•	
	Security		Set and change passwords and levels of access permission for the current database.			•	
	Replication		Replicates the current database at a designated location.			•	
	Startup		Control and customize various database startup properties and actions.			•	
	Custom Controls		Register and unregister custom controls in the Window registration database.			•	
	Add-Ins		Installs and uninstalls add-ins.			•	

Table

Button	Menu Option	Keys	Description	Word	Excel	Access	PowerPoint
	Insert		Inserts table, row, or column.	•			
	Delete		Deletes row or column.	•			
	Merge		Merges several cells into one.	•			
	Select Table	ALT + 5	Selects an entire table.	•			
	Table AutoFormat		Applies format options to a table.	•			
	Cell Height and Width		Changes height or width of rows or columns.	•			
	Convert Text to Table		Changes text into a table or a table into text.	•			
	Sort		Sorts text or rows in a table.	•			
	Gridlines		Turns table gridlines on or off.	•			
	Split Cells		Splits a cell horizontally.	•			
	Select Row		Selects row containing insertion point.	•			
	Select Table	ALT + 5	Selects table containing insertion point.	•			
	Select Column		Selects column containing insertion point.	•			
	Headings		Automatically repeats table headings for tables spanning more than one page.	•			
	Formula		Performs mathematical calculations.	•			
	Split Table		Divides a table.	•			

DATA

Button	Menu Option	Keys	Description	Word	Excel	Access	PowerPoint
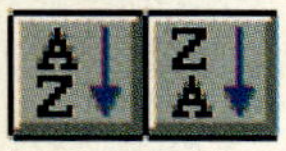	Sort		Sorts information in database or other selection.		•		
	Filter		Activates/deactivates database AutoFilter mode (to allow criteria to be used for controlling record display).		•		
	Form		Activates database data entry form.		•		
	Subtotals		Automatically creates subtotals for number tables.		•		

Draw

Button	Menu Option	Keys	Description	Word	Excel	Access	PowerPoint
	Group		Combines selected objects into a group so they function as a single object.				•
	Ungroup		Breaks a group into its components.				•
	Regroup		Reapplies grouping to previously grouped items.				•
	Bring to Front		Moves an object in front of all other objects that may be covering it.				•
	Send to Back		Moves an object behind all other objects on the slide.				•
	Bring Forward		Moves a slide forward one layer at a time.				•
	Send Backward		Moves a slide backward one layer at a time.				•
	Align		Changes the alignment of selected objects in relation to each other.				•
	Snap to Grid		Attaches objects to an invisible grid.				•
	Rotate/Flip		Rotates an object to an exact position (Free Rotate) or 90 degrees to the left or right.				•
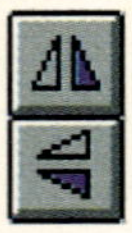			Flips an object 180 degrees horizontally or vertically.				
	Scale		Resizes selection by a precise percentage.				•
	Change AutoShape		Changes a selected AutoShape to another shape.				•

WINDOW

Button	Menu Option	Keys	Description	Word	Excel	Access	PowerPoint
	New Window		Opens new window into active document.	•	•		•
	Tile Horizontally		Arranges windows in Microsoft Access as nonoverlapping horizontal planes.			•	
	Tile Vertically		Arranges windows in Microsoft Access as nonoverlapping vertical panes.			•	
	Fit to Page		Fits active window to slide size.				•
	Cascade		Cascades currently open windows.			•	•
	Arrange Icons		Arranges current icons into neat rows.			•	•
	Hide		Hides current window.		•	•	
	Unhide		Unhides hidden window.		•	•	
	Arrange		Arranges open windows.		•		
	Freeze Panes		Freezes portion of worksheet so that portion is always visible.		•		
	Split		Splits the worksheet, allowing scrolling of one region of the worksheet.		•		

Help

Button	Menu Option	Keys	Description	Word	Excel	Access	PowerPoint
		F1	Displays contents for Help.	•	•	•	•
			Searches Help by clicking on-screen elements..	•	•	•	
	About Microsoft		Displays information about the open software application and your computer system; can also be used to run another application.	•	•	•	•
	Microsoft Help Topics		Provides several entry points to Help.	•	•	•	•
	Answer Wizard		Provides help topics based on written questions.	•	•	•	•
	The Microsoft Network		Provides help about The Microsoft Network.	•	•	•	•
	About Microsoft Word, Excel, Access, PowerPoint		Provides information about Windows 95 applications and the operating system installed on your computer.	•	•	•	•

Glossary

35mm Slides An output medium in which slides are displayed using a slide projector.

386 enhanced mode A Windows operating mode that provides access to the advanced memory management features of the Intel 80386 processor, including virtual memory capabilities and the ability to run non-Windows applications in sizable windows.

A protocol allowing file transfer between computers on the Internet. Many Internet host computers provide anonymous FTP sites where users can download a variety of files.

absolute cell reference A cell reference that does not change, even when the formula containing the reference is copied. Either the row, the column, or both the row and the column may be absolute. Examples: A$1, $A1, $A$1. Also called absolute address. Contrast with relative cell reference.

active Describes the application or window that is currently in use.

active cell The current, selected cell, as outlined by the thick border of the selection rectangle. The active cell is where the next action or command will take place. Its address is displayed in the reference area.

active presentation The presentation being viewed or edited when more than one presentation is open.

active table is the table in which the record pointer moves down one record when you press ⇩ and up one record when you press ⇧

address A phrase which identifies an individual on the Internet network. Electronic mail is sent to a person's address. The computer user then accesses his or her mailbox and retrieves the mail. An address example: earthplanet@galaxy.com

aligned left Paragraph format in which lines are aligned along the left edge. Used for most text. Select the paragraph and then select the Align Left button on the Formatting toolbar, or press CTRL + **L**

aligned right Paragraph format in which lines are aligned along the right edge. Difficult to read, but can be used for small amounts of text such as a figure caption or a short heading. To align text to the right, select the paragraph and then select the Align RIght button on the Formatting toolbar, or press CTRL + **R**

alignment How information (text or value) is oriented within a cell or range. Numerical values are usually right aligned, and text is either center or left aligned, though any choice of left, center, or right is possible. You can also wrap long text entries within a cell and cener a title across a rango of cells.

Anchor A word or phrase appearing in a Web document that links to other information on the World Wide Web.

And criteria Multiple criteria in which all conditions must be met in order for a record to be selected.

animation effects Display slide text in unusual ways.

Answer Wizard Displays a list of Help topics related to a search you define in your own words.

application A program designed to accomplish a particular task. Word processor programs and electronic spreadsheets are applications. Often used interchangeably with program.

application Control-menu boxes are the buttons at the left end of the application title bar.

application icon A Windows icon that represents a minimized program.

application title bars are the bars across the top of the main screen window.

application window A window that contains a running application in Windows.

argument A piece of information provided to a function. Some functions, such as =NOW( ), require no arguments; others require one or several. Multiple arguments are separated by commas, as in =IF(A3>5,1,0).

ascending order is A-Z order for text type fields, oldest to newest for date fields, and smallest to largest for number fields.

AutoContent Wizard Provides suggested outlines for common types of presentations such as sales, training, and communicating news which you can adapt to reflect your ideas.

AutoLayout Provides twenty-one predefined slide layouts including placeholders for titles, text, clip art, tables, graphs, and organization charts.

AutoShape One of twenty-four complex predefined shapes that can be added to a slide.

band-oriented report generators allow you to design a report by dividing it into bands. (See also report header, report footer, page header, page footer, groupings.)

best fit A way to accommodate the longest entry in a column by double-clicking the mouse button. The width is adjusted automatically.

binder In Office, keeps electronic files created with different applications together in one visual workspace for easy access and editing.

black and white overhead An output medium in which slides are printed on a black and white printer and displayed using an overhead projector.

body text The main text of a report, letter, or other document, as contrasted with headings or headlines.

bold Emphasizes text by making it appear darker than the surrounding text.

Bookmark An reference to a site that has been visited on the Web. A bookmark is usually kept in a bookmark list, and most Web browsers allow users to create personalized bookmark lists.

border A line drawn around the edge of an object.

Borders toolbar Toolbar with buttons showing border and shading options.

Browser An application used to access information on the World Wide Web. A browser (client) retrieves information from a Web server. Lynx is a popular text-based browser; Mosaic and Netscape are common graphical browsers.

build A special effect that displays items in a bulleted list, one at a time. The list is called a progressive disclosure list.

bullet A symbol, such as a solid square block or open circle, that precedes an item in a list. A small typographical device, usually a large dot, that indicates separate items in a list. Used to create bulleted lists.

Calculator A Windows utility program, or accessory, that operates as a typical calculator.

Calendar A Windows utility program, or accessory, that serves as an electronic appointment calendar.

Cardfile A Windows utility program, or accessory, that serves as an electronic set of index cards.

cascade menus are menu selections that open another menu.

cascading A method of arranging windows in which all windows are placed in an overlapping pattern with their title bars showing.

category In charting, a category describes a certain circumstance for a variable, which means that a variable has a particular value under a certain category. The categories appear along the bottom edge (X-axis) of a chart. Each category is labeled with a category name.

cell reference A cell's address, usually expressed in terms of the cell's column and row on the worksheet. For example, the cell at the intersection of column C and row 15 has the reference C15.

cell The basic building block of an electronic spreadsheet; the intersection of a column and a row. Cells are referred to by indicating their column and row. A cell is a holding place where you can store information.

center tab Centers text under a tab. You can choose from various tab options by selecting the Tab Alignment button at the left edge of the ruler.

centered alignment Paragraph format in which lines are centered between margins or column edges. Often used with headings or small amounts of text that require a formal presentation. To center text, select the paragraph and then select the Center button on the Formatting toolbar, or press (CTRL)+**E**

channel A place on the Internet where two or more people hold an online conversation. Channels have names, like #chat or #friendly, and can be joined at any time. Channels are used by the Internet Relay Chat to provide a place for users to talk about the channel's current topic.

character-based See text-based.

chart A graph that displays quantitative information visually rather than using text and figures.

chart sheet A document or sheet type in Excel, designed to hold a chart; can be linked to worksheets.

chart type The kind of graph or chart. Excel has 14 major chart types, such as pie, line, and column charts.

check box Indicates an option in a dialog box that can be on or off. A checkmark in the box indicates the feature is active. The absence of a checkmark indicates the feature is not active.

check box Indicates an option in a dialog box that can be on or off. An "X" indicates the feature is active; the absence of an "X" indicates the feature is not active.

checkmark A mark next to a command name that indicates an active command.

child tables are those whose record pointers are controlled by parent tables. (See also related tables.)

circular reference A formula which directly or indirectly refers to itself. Circular references are almost always mistakes. Example: the formula =0.08*C15 if contained in cell C15 would be a circular reference.

click To press and quickly release the left mouse button after positioning the pointer on a character or object.

clip art Graphic images stored on disk.

clipboard A temporary storage location in the computer's memory used for transferring data from one document to another.

Clock A Windows utility program, or accessory, that displays the current time.

color overhead Output medium in which slides are printed on a color printer and displayed using an overhead projector.

column The vertical subdivision of a worksheet; columns are labeled with letters of the alphabet.

combo box Displays a list of allowable entries in a field.

command button A button in a dialog box which you can select to execute the named operation.

constant A number or text entry which does not change; information typed in literally rather than a formula.

context-sensitive Help Takes you directly to Help information about a feature you have selected or are using without having to search through a list of Help topics.

continuous loop A function whereby PowerPoint automatically replays a presentation after reaching the end of the set of slides.

Control menu box The box in the upper left corner of all windows from which the Control menu pulls down.

Control menu The pull-down menu from the Control menu box used to control a window.

controls contain pieces of information in screen forms and reports. For example, when a field is placed on a form, it's called a control.

copy To duplicate some or all of the contents of a cell or range.

crop The process of shrinking or enlarging an object's window. The object's size under the window remains the same while the borders of the window are moved to reveal more or less of the underlying object.

cross reference tables contain a key value from the original parent and a key from the child.

cue card Provides detailed instructions to complete a task.

customized number format A user-defined cell format designed to display specialized number entries in a particular form. Common examples include formats for serial numbers, telephone numbers, Social Security numbers, zip codes, and part numbers.

data Raw facts or assumptions stored in a database.

data dictionary a list of all fields, queries, forms, reports, relationships, formatting instructions, and validations in the database.

data marker The graphic symbol used to plot information on a chart. Data markers include lines, bars, and other symbols.

data series Set of related data values or observations used in constructing charts. The gross national product for each year from 1970 to 1990 is an example of a data series.

data types are the kinds of data that can be stored in a table. Access data types include text, memo, number, date/time, currency, counter, yes/no, and OLE object.

database A collection of related data.

database management software A tool you can use to manage data electronically.

database management system (DBMS) A system that stores data in a database and permits retrieval of selected information.

database objective statement A design document that states the goal of the complete system in a brief paragraph.
Database Wizard Builds a complete application including tables, forms, and reports. You can choose from 22 personal and business applications including asset tracking, donations, event management, inventory, membership, and a music collection.
datasheet view A view of a table in which data appear in rows (records) and columns (data fields).
decimal tab Aligns textor, more commonly, numberson the decimal point under the tab. You can choose from various tab options by selecting the Tab Alignment button at the left edge of the ruler.
default value A value that appears automatically in a field when you add a new record.
defined name A user-created name that refers to a constant, a cell, or a range of cells. Defined names can make formulas and macros easier to read and understand. Also called range names.
delimiters are characters used in pairs to surround some data.
demote Shifts selected text right one level in the outline and changes the bullet character to match other bullets at that level.
dependent cell Cell (containing a formula) that depends on a particular cell for information.
descending order is Z-A order for text type fields, newest to oldest for date fields and largest to smallest for number fields.
design template Controls the background pattern and colors assigned to slides.
design view A view in which you can create or modify the structure of a table, form, or report.
desktop The background screen of a graphical operating environment, which serves as a graphics-based work area.
Detail bands will be printed between the page header and page footer (unless the report includes groups).
dialog box A box that appears on the screen prompting the user to enter additional information.
dialog box A box that appears on the screen to prompt the user to enter more information; also displays information, warnings, and error messages.
dimmed commands Command names in menus appearing in a lighter shade to indicate that a command is not available at the current time.
directory Groups related files on a disk.
directory icon Icons that look like small folders and represent directories on the current disk.
directory path In the title bar of a directory window, a label that displays the current drive letter and directory.
directory window In the File Manager, a split window where the left half displays the directory structure of the current drive and the right half displays the contents of the current directory.
disk A floppy disk is a removable data storage medium either 3 1/2″ or 5 ¼″ in size. A hard disk is a rigid data storage medium, either inside or connected to a computer, usually rated in MB (millions of bytes) of storage.
disk drive Writes data to and reads data from a disk. A letter designates a specific disk drive, such as disk drive A:.
document A file created by an application program.
document window A window that contains a document.
domain name The portion of an Internet address that uniquely identifies specifies e host computer's physical location on the Internet.
Dot The periods that separate the elements of a domain name.
double-click To press and quickly release the left mouse button twice in rapid succession.
Download The process of copying a file from one computer to another.
download To copy or move a file electronically from one computer to another.
drag-and-drop An operation that allows you to move selected text quickly by dragging it from one spot and dropping it in another using the mouse.
drag Moving an object using the mouse pointer.
drive icon In a directory window, an icon that represents floppy and hard disk drives, optical drives, or other storage devices.
e-mail address The unique identifier for an individual electronic mail account. An e-mail address usually includes a portion of the user's name, the @ symbol, and the computer domain name where the e-mail account resides.
e-mail The abbreviated form of electronic mail.
electronic mail Messages that are sent from one computer user to another via the Internet. Each user must have a valid e-mail account, which is uniquely identified with an address.
ellipsis A series of three dots (...) following a command indicating that a dialog box with more information will appear before the command can be completed.
embed Part of the OLE process of inserting a source file created in one software program into a target file created in a different software program. The embedded file becomes part of the target file, and can be updated and edited. Once embedded and edited
embedded chart A chart contained within a worksheet. Contrast with chart sheet.
emboss Emphasizes text by making letters appear slightly raised.
emoticon "Emotion icons" are a series of symbols people send to add emotive content to their e-mail messages.
end-of-document mark (end mark) A short horizontal line that marks the end of a document. You cannot insert characters after the end-of-document mark.
endnote Like a footnote, a brief block of text used for citing authorities or making incidental comments. An endnote appears at the end of a section rather than at the bottom of a page.
execute To run a program or macro; to cause the program or macro to perform the instructions that comprise it.
explode In pie charts, to emphasize a particular pie slice by pulling it out from the pie.
expression A combination of symbols and values used in a filter or query to create a search condition. >=8 is an example of an expression that would select a record if the value in the specified field was greater than or equal to 8.
field A category of data in a table, such as last name or zip code.
field code This code represents the location of a linked object. The code can be displayed in the target file, or an image of the object can be displayed in the target file by turning field codes on and off through the Options choice on the Tools menu.

field size The maximum number of characters you can enter in a field.
field width is the maximum length entry that will be allowed in a field.
file A block of storage on disk that contains the text and formatting information for a document.
file icon In the directory window, the icon next to a file name. Different icons represent different types of documents and programs.
File Manager The Windows program that is used to manage files and directories.
file name The name assigned to a file stored on disk.
File Transfer Protocol (FTP)
filter Restricts display of records to those meeting specified criteria.
fixed-space font A type style, such as Courier New, in which all characters are allotted the same width regardless of the letterform.
flamed A strong rebuke on the Internet because of incorrect behavior on the Net. Harsh articles are posted to newsgroups, often containing foul language, when someone commits a major faux pas on the Net. Flames can be avoided if you read the FAQs carefully and follow their instructions.
font Refers to the shape (typeface) of characters; a kind of letterform. Each font has a name (such as Arial), a size (such as 12 point), and a style (such as italic).
footer A repeating block of text at the bottom of each page in a section. Might contain a chapter heading, page number, or similar information. Word allows different footers for even and odd pages.
footnote A brief block of text at the bottom of a page that is used for citing authorities or making incidental comments.
Form Footers are the part of the form shown after a screenful of records has been displayed.
format The appearance of information within a section of a document. Font, alignment, and number format are among the more important aspects of formatting.
formatted text Shows variations in font and text size.
Formatting toolbar Contains information, menus, and buttons related to formatting a document.
formula A kind of cell entry that performs a calculation. All formulas begin with an equal sign. Normally, the result of the formula (as opposed to the formula itself) appears within the worksheet. Formulas can automatically change their result if there are changes in the cells upon which they depend, and formulas are the main reason that spreadsheets are so useful.
Freehand Annotation A PowerPoint feature that allows you to use a mouse to draw on a slide during a slide show.
Frequently Asked Questions (FAQs) Documents that contain the answers to the most frequently asked questions about using the Internet. These documents can be found by using the FTP tool, on the Web, and in newsgroups.
function A built-in mathematical operation in Excel. There are hundreds of functions with many uses. Perhaps the most common function is SUM, which totals the values in a range of cells. Example: =SUM(A3:A7) sums the range of cells from A3 to A7.
Gopher A system that helps you find information in files throughout the Internet. You can browse and retrieve documents that reside on many different computers throughout the world.
graphical query by example allows you to drag fields into the view and use standard Windows techniques to set up your view.
Graphical user interface (GUI) A common interface standard used with personal computers that emphasizes the display of textual and graphic information in windows that are accessed with a mouse via pull-down menus and icons.
group icon In the Program Manager, an icon that represents a group of programs.
group window A window that displays the items in a group within the Program Manager.
groupings cluster records that are similar in some respect.
GUI Graphical user interface.
hanging indentation Paragraph format in which the first line is not indented but subsequent lines are indented. The fastest way to create a hanging indentation is to press CTRL+T.
header A repeating block of text at the top of each page in a section. Might contain a chapter heading, page number, or similar information. Word allows different headers for even and odd pages.
Help button The button at the right end of the toolbar used to obtain online help.
hidden slides Slides that do not appear in your presentation unless activated by you as needed.
history A list of Internet sites visited by a user during an Internet session. Most on-line help systems and any multimedia applications also include a history feature.
home page On the Internet's World Wide Web, the home page is a file which lets people visit the organization sponsoring the home page. When you access a home page, the Web is actually displaying a file on your computer. Home pages usually contain some type of graphics, a photograph, or logo, and some text to explain the creator's ideas, services, or products
host A computer on the Internet that allows a user to access various Internet resources.
hypertext markup language (HTML) A text file stored on a Web server containing a series of ASCII characters, called tags, that specify how the various elements included on the home page will appear, or including the names of other linked Web resources s
Hypertext Transfer Protocol (HTTP) A file transfer protocol specifying how documents residing on Web servers exchange information.
icon A graphical representation of a Windows element, such as a program file, data file, or some other function.
indentation marker Triangular markers on the ruler. The marker at the top left controls the first-line indentation. The marker at the bottom left controls the left edge indentation. The marker at the right side of the ruler controls the right indentation.
information Data presented in a usable form.
information window A special window designed to provide additional information about the active cell in a worksheet. Information windows can be used to monitor such things as cell formats, protection, dependents, and precedents.
inner joins select only records that have matching values in both tables.
input mask A pattern, usually applied to text and date/time fields, that controls data entry.

Input Mask Wizard Allows you to select a predefined pattern such as one that controls entry of social security numbers or phone numbers.

insert mode In insert mode, characters that you type on the keyboard are inserted into whatever text already exists in the document. Select the Overtype indicator (OVR) in the status bar to switch between insert mode and overtype mode.

insertion point A blinking vertical bar that marks the position where text will be inserted or deleted when you type on the keyboard.

integrates software An integrated software program is several programs in one product. The separate programs cannot be purchased alone. Most integrated packages have a word processor, a spreadsheet, a database and some type of communications software.

interface A term referring to how information is presented to a user on the computer's screen. The newest interface standard is the GUI.

Internet A system of computers informally connected together throughout the world.

Internet Protocol the protocol used to assign an Internet Protocol Address.

Internet Protocol Address the distinctive address for a node on the Internet.

Internet Relay Chat (IRC) A system of channels on which two or more people can hold online, live conversations. An IRC channel is not totally private; conversations can be heard by systems administrators as they pass through their computer systems.

JAVA An object-oriented language based on C++ used for creating applets, which are small programs used by the HotJava browser.

join To link two tables to form a view.

jump In a Help screen, a reference to related definitions or Help topics. A jump is displayed in a contrasting color. Select a jump to see that definition or related topic.

justified alignment Paragraph format in which lines are aligned along both left and right edges. Often used with text that appears in multiple columns on a page. To justify text, select the paragraph and then select the Justify button on the Formatting toolbar, or press CTRL+J

label Describes its associated text box or some other portion of a form or report.

labels are text in a screen form or report that describes something about the form itself or one of the controls the form contains.

landscape orientation A print option producing a slide that is wider than it is tall.

leading The spacing between lines in a paragraph.

left tab Aligns text on the left side under the tab. You can choose from various tab options by selecting the Tab Alignment button at the left edge of the ruler.

legend On a chart, a legend shows how different colors and data markers correspond to the data series used to make the chart.

link A connection between two nodes or sources of information. Links on the World Wide Web are used to connect and access Web resources. Also, to insert the location of an object file in another file.

linked text On a chart sheet, linked text is derived from a worksheet cell. If the original text changes in the worksheet, the linked text in the chart changes as well.

linking key fields are fields used to relate tables.

list box Displays an alphabetized list of choices in a dialog box.

local area network A system of computers connected together. Usually the computers all occupy the same building and are connected with cabling.

Lookup Wizard Creates a lookup column that allows you to enter data by choosing a value from a list of values.

mail editor A program used to compose, send, and read electronic mail messages.

mail server A host computer that routes electronic mail messages sent across the Internet.

mail server A computer which receives incoming electronic mail and manages the outgoing electronic mail from the users.

many-to-many relationships have several parent records with matching keys in the child and several child records with matching keys in the parent.

maximize button The small box on the right corner of the title bar containing an up arrow. Used to enlarge a window to its maximum size.

maximize To fill the entire screen with one window.

media clip Adds video, music, or sound to a PowerPoint slide.

menu A list of available commands in an application window.

menu bar A horizontal listing of commands located near the top of the screen. Selecting an option on a menu bar displays the associated pull-down menu.

minimize button The small box on the right corner of the title bar containing a down arrow. Used to reduce a window to an icon.

minimize To shrink a window to an icon.

mouse A palm-sized input device equipped with two or three control buttons. Movement causes movement of a mouse pointer in the same direction on the screen.

mouse pointer Indicates the area on the screen that the next action affects.

move To remove information from one location and place it in another. Unlike copying, moving "picks up" the contents of a cell or range and places them elsewhere.

multi-application object An object which has passed through more than one application before being linked or embedded in the final document file.

multimedia Sounds, music, photos, and film clips that can be incorporated in to your slide layout and presentation.

multitasking The capability of running multiple programs simultaneously.

navigate to move from one document to another by way of links.

netiquette informal rules of etiquette governing electronic correspondence.

newsgroups An electronic forum on the Internet for the exchange of ideas and information. Newsgroups are formed around a specialized topic of interest.

non-Windows applications Programs not specifically designed to run under Windows and that cannot take advantage of many Windows' features, such as a consistent user interface.

nonadjacent selection A compound selection of multiple ranges. A nonadjacent selection need not form a rectangle or be composed of a single selected area.

nonprinting characters Characters that can be displayed on the screen but will not be printed. Include spaces, paragraph marks, and tabs. You can toggle screen display of nonprinting characters on and off by selecting the Show/Hide button on the Standard toolbar.

normalization The process of eliminating unnecessary duplication of data by separating related data into tables.

Notepad A Windows utility program that serves as an electronic note pad.

Notes Pages view Displays a slide with speaker's notes, if any, below the slide.

number (number constant) Numbers are constant numeric values (such as 3 or -1.9) and are a basic kind of cell entry.

object Text, clip art, a table, a graph, or an organization chart attached to a slide.

OLE Object Linking and Embedding is the process of connecting or inserting files created in one software package into a file created in another software package so that the OLE files can be updated and modified.

on-screen presentation An output medium in which slides are viewed on a computer monitor or displayed on a screen using a computer projection device.

one-to-many relationship have more than one child for each parent record.

one-to-one relationships have exactly one child record for each parent record.

operating environment A graphics-based work area allowing easy access to multiple programs.

operating system Software required for use on a computer to manage the computer's resources.

option buttons In a dialog box, round buttons that appear in small groups of related options from which you can select only one item.

Or criteria Multiple criteria in which a record will be selected if any search condition is met.

Originally established at the University of Minnesota, the Internet Gopher is a hierarchical system for organizing and locating information on the Internet.

orphan records are records in a child table that have no matching key in the parent table.

outer joins display all records from each table regardless of whether or not there is a matching record in the other table.

Outline view Displays slide titles and main text in outline format.

overtype mode In overtype mode, characters you type replace existing characters. Select the Overtype indicator (OVR) on the status bar to switch between overtype mode and insert mode.

Page Footer bands will be printed at the bottom of each page of the report.

Page Header bands will be printed at the top of each page of the report.

Paintbrush A Windows utility program used for creating drawings.

paragraph mark Marks the end of a paragraph in Word. Inserted with the ENTER key. Shows on-screen as a symbol.

parent tables are used as the main tables in a relationship. (See also primary tables.)

path Describes the route an application must follow to locate a document on disk.

Pick a Look Wizard Provides 57 pre-defined background settings and prompts the user to select one or more types of output.

placeholder An empty box or other shape that you can fill later.

point (point mode) A method of building formulas that reduces the need to keep track of literal cell references and instead allows you to use the mouse or arrow keys to "point" to the cells or ranges that will be referred to in the formula.

point A measure of the type size of characters. A point equals 1/72 inch, thus 72-point type is 1 inch high. Text matter is usually from 8 to 12 points. Headings are usually 14 points or larger.

pointer The arrow-shaped cursor that follows the movement of a pointing device to indicate which area will be affected when you press the mouse button. May change shape in different applications.

portrait orientation A print option producing a slide that is taller than it is wide.

PowerPoint Viewer A special application that allows you to run a PowerPoint presentation on a computer that does not have PowerPoint installed.

precedent cell Cell upon which formulas in other cells depend. A change in a precedent cell can cause the result of a dependent formula to change.

presentation graphics program A software tool for developing professional-looking presentations.

primary key A single field or a combination of fields that makes each record unique.

primary key fields are used to permanently link one table with another in the database. The records in a table will be in the order of its primary key. The primary key must be unique; that is, no duplicate values will be allowed unless it is sorted on another expression.

primary source application The application used to create an object's source file. An Access database object's primary source file is Access.

primary tables are used as the main tables in a relationship. (See also parent table.)

priority The relative "binding strength" of an Excel arithmetic operator. The priority of operators in a formula determines the order in which operations are performed. For example, because multiplication has higher priority than addition, the formula =2+2*10 has the result 22, not 40.

Program Manager An integral part of Windows that enables the user to easily start applications and logically organize programs.

program-item icon An icon chosen to start a program.

progressive disclosure list See build.

project To pick fields from one or more tables.

promote Shifts selected text left one level in the outline and changes the bullet character to match other bullets at that level.

proofread Read the text on each slide, noting omissions and corrections to be made in content and organization.

proportionally spaced font A type style, such as Arial or Times New Roman, in which the width of a letter depends on the letterform. For example, the letter i is thinner than the letter M.

pull-down list A list of related items that appears after selecting a down arrow at the right end of a box.

pull-down menu A list of options that appears after choosing an item on the menu bar.

query Lets you ask the database simple or complex questions.
radio buttons Allow you to select only one choice from a set of options.
range A rectangular block of cells, identified by any two of its diagonal corner cells. A range can be as small as one cell or as large as the entire worksheet. Example: the rectangle of cells whose upper-left corner is A3 and whose lower-right corner is D5 is called A3:D5.
record A collection of related fields.
record pointer keeps track of which record is currently available for editing, copying, and other activities.
Redo command Restores editing or typing that has been reversed with the Undo feature.
redundant data The unnecessary duplication of data within one or more tables.
referential integrity A set of rules that make sure relationships between records in related tables are valid.
related tables are those whose record pointers are controlled by parent tables. (See also child tables.)
relational database management system (RDBMS) A system that stores data by subject and retrieves information based on predefined relationships among subjects.
relationships are permanent links between tables.
relative cell reference Within a formula, a cell reference that can change if the formula is copied. This is the default (standard) kind of cell reference in Excel formulas and is most often what will work best when a formula is copied. Contrast with absolute cell reference.
report An effective way to print professional-looking output based on a table or query.
Report Footer bands will be printed at the bottom of the last page of the report.
Report Header bands will be printed at the top of the first page of the report.
required field A field property that prevents saving a new record if data are missing from the field.
resize handle A point on the border of a selected object. Dragging a resize handle changes the size of the object.
restore button The small box on the right edge of the title bar containing up and down arrows. Used to restore a maximized window.
restore To return an icon or maximized window back to its former size.
retrieving data means finding groups of entries that meet certain criteria and copying them to another location.
right tab Aligns text on the right side under the tab. You can choose from various tab options by selecting the Tab Alignment button at the left edge of the ruler.
row The horizontal subdivision of a worksheet. Rows are labeled with numbers.
ruler Displays and allows you to control margins, indentation, tab settings, and column widths. Page Layout view shows a vertical as well as a horizontal ruler.
sans serif font Typefaces that lack serifs, or small crosslines at the end of the main letter strokes. Arial is a sans serif font.
screen forms are used to display, enter, and edit data on the screen.
scroll arrow The arrow at either end of a scroll bar that enables the user to shift the screen display in the direction of the arrow.
scroll bar The bar at the right side and bottom edge of a window that enables the user to scroll through text and graphics that do not fit within a window's boundaries.
scroll box Within the scroll bar, the box that is dragged to scroll through a window.
search To look for an entry or entries that meet certain criteria.
secondary keys are index keys used to speed up searches.
secondary source application The application used to create the secondary source file in a multiapplication object. In the case of an Access database object linked to a Word document embedded in a third application, the secondary source application is Word.
section A portion of a document that can be formatted with specific margin settings, page orientation (portrait or landscape), page numbering sequence, multiple columns, or other features affecting page layout.
select To pick records from one or more tables based on specified criteria.
select query Displays data from specified fields in one or more tables based if field contents match search criteria.
selection A group of cells that have been marked to be affected by a command or other action. Selection is usually done by dragging with the mouse, though several other methods are available.
selection bar Allows you to select part of a document using a mouse.
selection box A box selected for editing. A selection box is surrounded by a border of forward slashes.
selection rule Selection rules are set up by identifying field names, selecting comparison phrases, and stating numbers or characters which are compared to the data in the database. You can extract or display certain records from the database based upon the selection rule.
sequentially searching a table means searching the data table by reading each consecutive entry.
serif font Typefaces that have small crosslines, called serifs, at the end of the main letter strokes. Times New Roman is a serif font.
shadow Emphasizes text by adding a drop shadow behind it.
shortcut In Windows 95, a selectable icon that directs you to an object such as an application program, folder, or individual document.
shortcut keys Keystrokes or combinations of keystrokes that let you bypass several menu selections.
Simple Query Wizard Guides the creation of a select query based on your answers to a series of questions.
site A term used to describe an Internet resource.
size Changing the size of an object's window. The object will grow or shrink proportionately as the window is sized. Use the mouse to grab one of the object's handles and drag the window edge to make the window larger or smaller.
sizing buttons The small boxes on the right edge of the title bar containing arrows. Used to quickly change the dimensions of the window.
slide layout The arrangement of objects on a slide.
Slide meter Lets you monitor how your presentation is proceeding compared to timings you set during rehearsal.
Slide navigator Lets you jump to slides in your presentation out of sequence.

Slide Show view Displays a presentation one slide at a time. Each slide fills the screen.

Slide Sorter view Displays reduced images (text and graphics) of all slides in order on the screen, three to a row.

Slide view Displays a presentation one slide at a time for edit. You can add graphics, draw shapes, and change the slide layout in addition to editing text.

software applications Software programs which perform specific functions like word processing, database, spreadsheet, drawing and painting, communications. Each individual program type is a software application.

software suite A set of programs which work together, especially in support of OLE. Microsoft Office is a software suite because the programs, while fully operational and available separately, work together as if they were one software program.

sort To present data in a sequence different than the way it's stored in the database.

source application The software application or package being used to create an object file. This object file will be either linked or embedded into a target file.

source document A standard paper form with spaces to enter details that vary from one record to the next.

source file The actual object which was created in the source application. This object will be linked or embedded into a target file.

spelling checker Word's spelling checker will compare every word in a document with an online dictionary. If a word is not in the dictionary, Word reports the word as a possible misspelling.

standard mode Windows' basic operating mode. A non-Windows application runs in a full-screen window that cannot be sized into a smaller window.

Standard toolbar Contains buttons that allow you to perform many tasks with a click of a mouse.

status bar Gives basic information about a document or about word processing modes.

strikeover mode Characters are typed on the screen at the location of the cursor, and existing characters are replaced by the new characters.

style A collection of formatting characteristics that is given a name and is accessible from the Style box in the Formatting toolbar. In Excel, several predefined but modifiable cell styles are available; you can also create your own cell styles.

subscript A character slightly below characters on the same line.

summary fields summarize some aspect of another field in the table.

superscript A character slightly above characters on the same line.

switchboard An Access menu system that helps users navigate through a database.

table A collection of data about a specific topic.

table structures are lists of fields in tables.

Table Wizard Builds a table based on your answers to a series of questions.

tag An HTML code inserted into a text document that is transferred using HTTP.

target application The software application or package being used to create a file which will contain embedded or linked objects.

target file The actual file created to contain an embedded or a linked object. The source file will be inserted into the target file.

task A term that is sometimes used to refer to a program.

Task List A Windows utility program that enables the user to manage multiple running programs.

Telnet A resource used to access remote Internet hosts.

template A template is a formatting blueprint. Colors, lines, shadows, and other formatting settings are established in the template. This blueprint is used to format a new object or file when it is created.

text (text constant) Data, usually consisting of words, that serves to identify parts of the worksheet or to store non-numeric information.

text box Used to type information, such as a file name, in a dialog box.

text prompt Sample text in a placeholder box in an Auto-Layout template which tells you how to use the placeholder.

text-based (character-based) interface An interface that appears as text (ASCII) characters on the computer screen.

text-based An interface made up of displaying numbers and characters only. This interface requires the computer user to respond to the screen by typing numbers and letters. A mouse is not used in a text-based interface.

thesaurus Word's built-in thesaurus can look up a word and provide a list of synonyms, or words with similar meanings.

tiling A method of arranging windows in which all windows are visible but are reduced in size so that they fit like tiles side-by-side on the screen.

timing The amount of time a slide stays on the screen.

title bar Bar at the top of all windows containing the title of the application and that of the current document file.

toggle To alternately turn commands or options on and off.

toolbar A set of buttons representing commands that can be executed by positioning the mouse pointer and clicking the button.

top-level domain An element of an Internet address that specifies the site's country, if it is not in the United States, or the type of institution or organization responsible for the site.

track ball A pointing device with a ball exposed on the top. Moving the ball with your fingers correspondingly moves a pointer on the screen.

transient links are temporary links between two tables.

transition A special effect that controls how each entire slide appears and disappears from the screen.

Undo Reverses a previous editing or typing step. You can usually undo several word processing steps in reverse order.

uniform resource locator (URL) the domain name for Web resources.

validation rule A field property that determines whether attempted data entry should be rejected.

validation text A message that appears on-screen if attempted data entry violates a validation rule.

validations are restrictions on the data that can be entered in a field.

value A number constant or a formula that produces a numeric result. Values can participate in arithmetic calculations.

Virtual Reality Modeling Language (VRML) A language used to describe three-dimensional, multi-user worlds contained on the World Wide Web.

volume label A name for a disk. Usually assigned when a disk is formatted.

Web server An Internet host that houses Web documents.

window A well-defined rectangular area on the desktop. Contains applications and documents.

window border Defines the outside edge of a window.

Windows application A program that is specially designed to take full advantage of all the powerful features of Windows.

Wizards are sequences of windows and dialog boxes that ask a series of questions about a document format and use your answers to lead you through the process of building a document, table, query, screen form, or report.

Word art A special text effect, such as slanting or curving.

word processing Using a computer to write, edit, format, store, and print documents.

word wrap A word processing feature that determines where line breaks need to fall and automatically begins a new line where necessary. You should press ENTER only to start a new paragraph.

workbook The basic file type in Excel. Workbooks can contain sheets of various kinds: worksheets, chart sheets, and modules (module sheets).

worksheet (spreadsheet) A table consisting of rows and columns of information, ideal for setting up calculations for a wide variety of applications. Originally implemented on green columnar paper, worksheets can now be manipulated with programs such as Ex

World Wide Web (WWW) A cross-platform Internet graphical hypertext information system for storing and accessing a variety of resources.

wrap To break a long line of text into two or more lines.

Write A Windows word processing program used for creating small documents.

WYSIWYG An acronym for "What You See Is What You Get," which refers to the fact that the screen shows the document formatted as it will be printed.

X-axis The horizontal axis (usually the bottom edge) of a chart. The X-axis is often broken into the various chart categories.

Y-axis The vertical axis (usually the left edge) of a chart. The Y-axis is often a numerical scale.

zoom To magnify or reduce the view of a worksheet or chart.

Index